James Thurber

James Thurber

HIS LIFE AND TIMES

Harrison Kinney

HENRY HOLT AND COMPANY
NEW YORK

Henry Holt and Company, Inc.
Publishers since 1866
115 West 18th Street
New York, New York 10011

Henry Holt® is a registered
trademark of Henry Holt and Company, Inc.

Library of Congress Cataloging-in-Publication Data
Kinney, Harrison.
James Thurber: his life and times / by Harrison Kinney. — 1st
ed.
p.   cm.
Includes bibliographical references and index.
1. Thurber, James, 1894–1961—Biography.   2. Humorists,
American—20th century—Biography.   3. Cartoonists—United States—
Biography.   I. Title.
PS3569.H94Z75   1995
818'.5209—dc20   95-9989
[B]   CIP
ISBN 0-8050-3966-X

Henry Holt books are available for special
promotions and premiums. For details contact:
Director, Special Markets.

First Edition—1995

Designed by Paula R. Szafranski

Printed in the United States of America
All first editions are printed on acid-free paper. ∞

1   3   5   7   9   10   8   6   4   2

For Susan Edith, Barbara Lee, Joanne Leslie,
and John Harrison, with love

Contents

II. Those Years with Ross

Preface

What I like best is a book that's at least funny once in a while. . . .
What really knocks me out is a book that, when you're all done
reading it, you wish the author that wrote it was a terrific friend of
yours and you could call him up on the phone whenever you felt like
it. That doesn't happen often, though.

—Holden Caulfield, in *Catcher in the Rye*

Though he didn't know it at the time, James Thurber became a terrific friend
of mine when I was in the seventh grade in Houlton, Maine, a town of seven
thousand people on the Canadian border. At the time, the Great Depression
had Houlton's single economy—potato farming—in a paralyzing hammer-
lock, and the Cary Library, free to the public, had become for me a blessed
refuge. The library's fortlike granite walls sheltered literary treasures always
ready to team up with the imagination for temporary escape from the social
discouragements outside.

Earlier friends—Leacock, Wodehouse, Cobb, Benchley, Lardner, Ford,
Marquis, and others—lived in the rear of the stacks, on shelves labeled "Humor," next to a window overlooking the small town park. Their comic
grudges, cheerful self-exposures of ineptitude, hilarious narratives, clever nonsense, and, always, courageous commitment to circumstances in which they
could only lose, seemed both redeeming and lovable. They appeared to prevail over life's entrapments by wisecracking about them. I loved them all.

A new name, Thurber, took up residence with the others at Christmastime
of 1933. Clearly a master of the genre, he was late getting there, and I
wondered where he had been. (Thurber's first book, *Is Sex Necessary?*, written
with E. B. White, had been purchased by the library four years before, I've
learned; a borrower lost it and paid for it, but it was never replaced. The
library's strained budget could not accommodate his next two books, *The Owl
in the Attic* and *The Seal in the Bedroom.)* Houlton was a *Reader's Digest* and

Saturday Evening Post community. Almost all of Thurber's writing and drawings were appearing in the *New Yorker*, whose readers were then mostly a cosmopolitan élite. Now here he was, positioned by the Dewey decimal system just ahead of Twain, perhaps a prophetic arrangement.

His new ticket of admission was his fourth book, My *Life and Hard Times*, long since elected to the ranks of classics in American literature by three generations of readers, critics, and college faculties. I remember it as a work that had seemed to seek me out. This slender book of improbable characters living an improbable family life in the years before World War I, and illustrated by Thurber's improbable figures, was to make the city of Columbus, Ohio, forever his trademark and Thurber a beloved name. The funny but fatalistic world-weary tone both of the book's "Preface to a Life" and "A Note at the End," while not fully meant, does manage to suggest that in some way he is taking the rap for the rest of us; that his role as humorist was predetermined, to be played by the rules of a literary caste system from which there is no deliverance; that he is sentenced forever to the hard life and times of comic confession, below the reach of serious critical recognition and reward. Writers of light pieces, he observes, "sit on the edge of the chair of Literature. In the house of Life they have the feeling that they have never taken off their overcoats."

Though Thurber was rarely less funny than he meant to be, there is something engagingly serious about his humor. The other literary comedians are like party friends whose antics and jokes are difficult to remember the next morning. Thurber's perfectly structured short pieces linger on, and one yearns for more at the end of each book of collected prose and drawings. Other humorists obligingly take pratfalls, laugh along with you, and get up again. Thurber stays down. One worries for him. P. G. Wodehouse describes one of his own characters looking as if he had drained the cup of life only to find a dead mouse at the bottom. Thurber's self-representations lead one to suspect that he actually has.

So it was love at first sight. My fondness for Thurber and his work was instantly personal and proprietary. Somehow I owed him something. I became a Thurber watcher. Now and then, in the years following, another Thurber volume would appear in the library stacks, or the ubiquitous *Reader's Digest* would reprint a Thurber item from one of his books. In college, I could, at last, track his production regularly in the *New Yorker* at the campus library. During World War II, I found Thurber paperback books (Armed Services Edition) at Army installations "stateside" and overseas. Like that special friend, he kept turning up when I needed him.

A chance to make a down payment on my debt to Thurber offered itself when I was to choose a postgraduate thesis subject. It wasn't that easy. Proposing a writer of humor as a subject for satisfying the requirements of a master's degree in literature—at least at postwar Columbia University—to judge from the reaction, was comparable to suggesting an artistic assessment of Renaissance Italy through a study of a Medici court jester. Mark Twain, of course, was the exception; a humorist could be sneaked past the guardians of literary scholarship if he survived a half-century's wear and tear of historical judgment, and if the humor was embedded in the novel form. Twain seemed to be the only qualifier.

My faculty adviser was William York Tindall, a gifted scholar and entertaining lecturer whose popularity regularly filled a classroom amphitheater. He taught a semester-long course on James Joyce's *Ulysses*, which kept him in a relentless and protracted game of hide-and-seek with Joyce's possible multiple meanings and symbolisms, and he urged Joycean targets of study on his seminar students. I held out for Thurber.

The war seemed to have put American literature in deep freeze for the duration. The academic fashions in the fiction and poetry of the last half of the 1940s seemed only to be taking up where those of the 1930s left off. At Columbia, such creative-writing courses as Martha Foley's were jammed with service veterans who felt the war had equipped them all to write like Hemingway. The GI bill beneficiaries were a no-nonsense crowd, determined to make up for lost time and presumably to build a new world. But their interest in American writing still focused on such social-protest novelists as Steinbeck, Dos Passos, Farrell, and Dreiser. Among the heady trends in deciphering Joyce, chasing Hemingway, and fostering social and political reform in that ideological presidential-election year of 1948, my advancement of Thurber as a thesis candidate was regarded by my classmates as an irrelevancy and met with an initial skepticism by my faculty adviser.

More than forty years later—three decades after Thurber's death in 1961 —one might wonder what the fuss was about. A dozen books about Thurber and his work have been published, a number by college professors, and though, according to Thurber, mine was the first graduate dissertation on his work, so many followed that he was obliged to get up a standard résumé of his career to mail, along with a form letter that in effect told the supplicants the task was theirs, not his. In the 1950s he received honorary degrees from three top-notch colleges, was featured on the covers of the two principal weekly news magazines, and garnered several prestigious honors from literary societies. After his death, his widow, Helen, was besieged by college faculty members armed with fellowship grants and sabbaticals, wanting to write about Thurber or to edit his letters. "I have professors in my life," she wrote me, paraphrasing her husband, "the way other people have mice."

There were similarities between Thurber and Joyce that Tindall, a patient, pipe-smoking listener, conceded and eventually yielded to: their fondness for wordplay and the infinite possibilities of language; and their impaired eyesight, which had left both men especially vulnerable to dreams and fancies and the sounds of words—and to the shenanigans of the subconscious, a favorite area of Tindall's when critiquing literature. As for Thurber's art, the hand he drew with had always seemed under remote control by inner selves over whom he apparently had little sway. The afflictions that erased most of his sight in his mid-forties had sharpened his other powers of observation and had turned him inward to roam an altered landscape of memory and mind. All these things made Thurber as much of a scholar's happy hunting ground as Joyce.

Tindall's tentative consent was contingent on my boning up on Freud and combing Thurber's text and art for the hidden meanings that lurked there, with or without Thurber's intention. This troubled me, for I planned to enlist the master personally in my effort, and was aware from such writings as those in his book *Let Your Mind Alone!* of how Thurber probably felt about behavioral scientists. I needn't have worried.

October 30, 1948

Dear Mr. Kinney:

I took a crack at answering your letter but to do a proper job of opinion on the Freudian approach to anything would use up a month of mine. I will be in New York next Thursday and Friday and could arrange to see you in the afternoon on either day at The New Yorker offices. Maybe I could answer your questions in person better. . . .

Sincerely yours,
James Thurber

And so the dreamed-of happened; I would meet my terrific friend of fifteen years at last.

Pictures of him rarely prepared one for Thurber in person. He was tall, reedy, with an exploded head of hair, and wearing what must have been the thickest glasses known to optometry. Even while seated in the *New Yorker*'s gloomy art-meeting room, he seemed in full motion, his clothes atwitch with nervous shiftings of arm and leg, his head jerking toward his interviewer as he asked a question or made a point. The quaver in his voice gradually took on a melodious rise and fall; his hand, holding one cigarette after another, shook slightly as he talked. His gaze, directed at my voice, disavowed the fact that he could only tell light from dark. Dimly profiled by a murky window that looked out on a gray day, he seemed only partly revealed. In that room of halftones, it was easy to think I had imagined him—that this restless god of literature and high comedy had condescended to take spectral form briefly to reward a kindred spirit and would be gone if the lights went on.

Much of what he told me in that and other meetings I would read again and again in newspaper and magazine accounts in later years, but it was all exhilaratingly new to me then. My completed thesis pleased him, of course, for it ceded him a number of points over Mark Twain in the perennial struggle for top honors in the field of American literary humor. By the time I joined the *New Yorker* as a reporter the next year, I was planning his biography—a project he viewed doubtfully. His faded vision had practically ended his ability to draw, and most of the prose he would be best remembered for was already written. Still, he felt a book about him could only be premature —that it would even suggest an obituary.

Fortunately for my ends, Thurber remained forever curious about himself. Like so many social extroverts, he was a shy man, uncertain as to just who he was, which led him to make "Thurber" the subject that interested him more than anything else. This enabled me to manage several subsequent interviews with him and a number of letter exchanges. Once when we planned to meet, I wrote Thurber that I might be hard to find because my office at the *New Yorker* was isolated on the fifteenth floor, between Exide Battery and The Trinity Bag & Paper Company, and that William Shawn, then the managing editor for "facts," had seemed surprised to see me get off the elevator there, apparently not realizing that the magazine had offices on a floor so far below the core of editorial operations. Thurber replied:

Dear Harrison:

I'm glad to hear you have become connected with the Trinity Bag and Paper Company, an excellent firm, and a starting place for young men who want to work into the box and carton game. Ross and Shawn are embarrassed and confused with anybody in an elevator, and think I am with WINS [a radio station also in the building] when they see me there. I will drop into the paper company to see you.

In expansive moments, he invited his friend Peter De Vries to join us during one meeting, and included me in a cocktail date with another of my heroes, E. B. White—both occasions a heady brew for a young staff novitiate. After Thurber's death, De Vries and White were among those skeptical about anyone's attempting a biography of him. For though Thurber's work endeared him to legions of strangers, those who knew him as other than a literary personality were aware that he harbored a dozen different Thurbers, some unpredictable and no one of which easily explained the others. The weather of his moods could range from sunny benevolence to the wildest of tempests in a second. His record contains testimonials both to his incomparable kindnesses and to a hurtful behavior that was usually the consequence of boozy evenings. He could be easy to know and difficult to understand. As John O'Hara wrote me, "He was as complicated as only a simple man can be."

The riddle of a Thurber both simple and complicated has occupied much of my spare time over forty years. When I first contracted to write a Thurber biography, the year after Thurber's death, E. B. (Andy) White warned: "You better hitch your belt up. He is not a simple subject. . . . It will take you at least 125 years." Perhaps moved to pity, he added: "I think there are two ways I can, and will, help you in your project. One, I can give you a list of people to question. Two, I can read what you write and tell you where I think you are off and where I think you are on."

Both White and his wife, Katharine, did provide a list of people to question, and in interviews in New York and at their home in North Brooklin, Maine, contributed candid comment about Thurber's work, life, and times. Additional friendly and discouraging advice came from De Vries, whose long association with the *New Yorker* began largely through Thurber's patronage. "You're taking on something I wouldn't stick my big toe in," he said.

Well, it is nearly ninety years short of White's estimated date for the book's completion, which offers the comforting delusion that it's way ahead of schedule. And certainly I have committed more than my big toe to the project. Since it was begun, my four children have grown up, attended college, and scattered. The family joke used to be that when I finally finished the book I should call it *The Years with Thurber*. I considered it.

This leisurely but dogged pursuit of the many aspects of Thurber, the personality and the artist, has meant bothering an inordinate number of people, either those acquainted with Thurber and his times, or custodians of his heritage. Others provided writing refuges, leaves-of-absence, research and typing assistance. Whenever I thought of giving up the seemingly endless chase, the debt I had accrued to so many interested people helped persuade me to go on.

Most of Thurber's generation, of course, have passed beyond the reach of my gratitude, but their willing assistance and cheerful encouragement still live throughout these pages. I offer their names at the back of the book as an acknowledgment they perhaps would not have sought but are entitled to. Meanwhile, I continue as a thankful debtor to the many surviving participants in this effort. I sincerely hope they find the results of their cooperation faithfully represented here, and worth the wait.

Introduction

James Grover Thurber (1894–1961) is considered the preeminent American humorist of the twentieth century by those who keep score in grand matters of this kind. Mark Twain, who had previously worn the crown, lived ten years into that century, but he had stopped being funny by the mid-1890s. Both men contributed a perennial classic to literature. Twain's *The Adventures of Huckleberry Finn* gave intelligent humor a significant and respectable place in fiction and demonstrated the power of narration expressed in simple declarative sentences. Thurber's *My Life and Hard Times* raised the bar of comic literary reminiscence to a height that no other practitioner of the genre has come close to clearing.

But Thurber's name evokes much that Twain's does not. There are scores of those outlandish drawings—unerasable from the mind—of the uncontrollable women, beleaguered men, and comforting dogs who populated Thurber's highly productive passage through the 1930s, before blindness gradually put an end to them. Frequently and soberly compared to the work of Matisse and other postimpressionist artists, the drawings seem to leave Thurber one up on Twain.

Most of the better drawings flowed directly onto paper from his subconscious. He rarely knew when he began a drawing exactly what would emerge. The ludicrous, sexless, nude woman he had meant to be crouching at the top of the stairs would find herself inexplicably atop a bookcase. A seal, flopped on what Thurber had begun as a rock, would end fantastically perched on the headboard of somebody's bed. To these bewildering situations he would append captions that startled and amused but did nothing to explain. Thurber declared himself the founder and sole member of the "pre-intentionalist" school of art. His drawings, as he put it, "sometimes seem to have reached completion by some other route than the common one of intent."

The critic Wilfrid Sheed points out that "the stories plus the drawings give us the extra angle that reveals a genius," and adds: "Like Disney and later Walt Kelly and Charles Schulz, [Thurber] produced universal archetypes fit for a T-shirt. But fine as Pogo and Snoopy are, they do not wake you with palms sweating the way Thurber's people do."

Thurber paraphrased Wordsworth in defining humor as "emotional chaos told about calmly and quietly in retrospect," but his restless and inventive mind had no trouble generating the chaos on the spot and dealing with it artistically in one sitting. In a rare confession of professional envy, his *New Yorker* colleague Wolcott Gibbs, who had just read Thurber's "A Final Note on Chanda Bell," wrote him that he wished to god he had Thurber's "sure grasp of confusion."

Thurber's art and prose live on as superb entertainment, but often as not they were born of his private defeats—frequently at the hands of women who fell short of his ideal, a hopelessly impractical one modeled on the protected, mannered, and unworldly Victorian heroines of Henry James's novels.

Twain could bring down the house as an after-dinner speaker, and though Thurber could entertain a crowd, too, he wasn't comfortable with a live audience larger than a dozen people. Quite miraculously, toward the end of his life he made it to the Broadway stage, appearing in a "revue" of his own work. It was the fulfillment of a Walter Mitty dream, according to his wife, Helen, for since his college days he had longed to act professionally.

Thurber's work has attracted so much serious critical attention over the years that it seems almost mischievous to suggest that although he frequently drew his material from the well of despair, the best of what he wrote and illustrated results largely from his highly refined sense of fun. In his professional prime, he enjoyed more than anything else getting a laugh out of the sophisticated, hard-to-please crowd he consorted and competed with.

Salient among Thurber's contributions to humor and literature are those he made to the editorial format, tone, and maturing of the *New Yorker*. "He was simply one of its founding fathers," says former editor William Shawn, who, upon Thurber's death, wrote:

> In a lifelong act of generosity, he poured out his hundreds upon hundreds of drawings, stories, fables, memoirs, and essays—many of them among the funniest any writer or artist has ever produced—and turned them over to us in the warranted expectation that they would make us laugh, instruct us, shake us up, and keep us going. His work was largely unclassifiable (it was simply Thurber), and by the end it gave him a place in history as one of the great comic artists and one of the great American humorists. . . . His tremendously original point of view, his literary style, his peculiar kind of vigor and restlessness all

went into the magazine and became a part of its tradition. . . . Certainly there will never be an issue of *The New Yorker* of which Thurber is not a part.

Those who knew Thurber as colleague and friend were frequent beneficiaries of his more private talents: The personal letters of his mature years could be masterpieces of wit, good writing, and intellectual stimulation. On social occasions, he could be far more comical than any paid stand-up comedian. His skill at mimicry enabled him to create havoc in the lives of others with a telephone call, which he took wicked delight in doing.

His life was beset by the childhood loss of an eye, a frustrating first marriage, disappointments in love, medical problems, and the blindness that not only ended his drawing but necessitated an irritating dependency on others. The experiences and emotions he processed into art were sometimes so painful they seem to have been cut out of his hide, but they emerge as human commentary that readers find easy to apply to themselves or people they know. Whether through text or graphics, Thurber makes the connection between himself and the reader so direct a one as to invite intimacy and a tender concern for him as man and artist.

A body of work assures its place in literary history by its continued life. Thurber's professional heritage is gathered into thirty books, most still available in frequent reprintings or readily accessible in any library worth its salt. Thirty-four years after his death, they continue to offer new generations of readers a rich selection unmatched in originality, mastery of language, perceptive satire, and hilarious entertainment.

His work has been translated into many languages and appeared in many forms: as ballet, opera, radio drama, a half-dozen feature-length movies, short films, musical revues, and a long-running television series. *The Male Animal*, the play Thurber coauthored with Elliott Nugent, is standard fare for summer stock and amateur theater groups. Each year brings more Thurber—previously uncollected pieces published in book form, new anthologies containing Thurber stories, and reissues of his old classics, both for children and adults.

Though 1994 was celebrated as Thurber's centennial year, complete with a U.S. Postal commemorative stamp bearing his self-portrait, he was born on December 8, 1894. This, according to his daughter, Rosemary, makes 1995 the truer year of Thurber's centennial, and the author is proud to present this volume as part of the extended celebration.

One who remembers how, in 1948, a fifty-three-year-old Thurber expressed genuine surprise that he was to be the subject of a graduate student's dissertation, wonders how he would view all this latter-day evidence of his literary immortality.

Note: Letter excerpts are reproduced as originally written, except where the biographer's carelessness would be suspected. (Thurber's impatience with the typewriter's shift key, for example, bequeaths a plethora of "cant" and "dont.")

PART I

That Life and Hard Times

At forty my faculties may have closed up like flowers at evening, leaving me unable to write my memoirs with a fitting and discreet inaccuracy or, having written them, unable to carry them to the publisher's. A writer verging into the middle years lives in dread of losing his way to the publishing house and wandering down to the Bowery or the Battery, there to disappear like Ambrose Bierce. He has sometimes also the kindred dread of turning a sudden corner and meeting himself sauntering along in the opposite direction. I have known writers at this dangerous and tricky age to phone their homes from their offices, or their offices from their homes, ask for themselves in a low tone, and then, having fortunately discovered that they were "out," to collapse in hard-breathing relief. This is particularly true of writers of light pieces running from a thousand to two thousand words.

—from "Preface to a Life,"
in My *Life and Hard Times*

1

Those Clocks of Columbus

In the early years of the nineteenth century, Columbus won out, as state capital, by only one vote over Lancaster, and ever since then has had the hallucination that it is being followed, a curious municipal state of mind which affects, in some way or other, all those who live there. Columbus is a town in which almost anything is likely to happen and in which almost everything has.

—from "More Alarms at Night"

In the period of McCarthyism, America's political nightmare of the 1950s, Donald Ogden Stewart, actor, playwright, screenplay writer, and satirist, found himself being chased through the ideological badlands by congressional posses in hot pursuit of un-American Americans. His career and livelihood in danger of being lynched at home, he moved abroad. He was from Columbus, Ohio, and writes: "When I first came to live in London, I was amazed at the number of Englishmen who said, 'Oh, yes, Columbus, of course. I know it very well, from Thurber's books, you know.' "

Stewart's observation is seconded by a *Columbus Citizen-Journal* radio-television editor who once interviewed the English actor Charles Laughton over long distance telephone: "So you're plugged in from Columbus, eh?"

Laughton remarked. "The home of James Thurber. He is a good friend of mine and the greatest living master of the English language."

Irrepressibly disposed as he was to autobiography both playful and serious, Thurber would have made any small city of early twentieth-century America seem meant for him and he for it. But Columbus, Ohio, it was. And although over the decades the state capital has nurtured other durable authors and artists, as well as memorable sports figures, war heroes, and American presidents, it is Thurber's name that is most prominently associated with Columbus. He knew the city as child, student, and newspaperman. He began his first marriage there. His most popular and admired book, *My Life and Hard Times*, was about Columbus and life there with his family.

To the end, he remained uncertain of his feelings toward the city and its university, but by making them his literary playground he immortalized both. He was slow to develop his intellectual and political opposition to the conservative culture of his hometown, its newspapers, politics, and university, and when he did he was too sentimental to hold grudges. He refused an honorary degree from Ohio State University at a time when he felt that it was knuckling under to McCarthyism (it had imposed a ban on lecturers suspected of Marxist leanings from speaking on campus). But he forgave, accepting all other local honors paid him, and would undoubtedly have had a change of heart about the degree had his "reformed" alma mater offered it to him a second time.

In 1959, he wrote: "Such readers as I have collected through the years are all aware of where I was born and brought up, and they know that half of my books could not have been written if it had not been for the city of my birth."

The occasion for Thurber's extravagance here was Columbus's selection as "All-America City" by the National Municipal League, an award cosponsored by *Look* magazine as a promotion stunt by that financially troubled publication. Thurber was not being taken in; the city had made an official and giddy response of approval to the designation, and asked Thurber to contribute to the event. He not only enjoyed publicizing parts of his life, he had caused some resentment in Columbus and saw this as a chance to make a peace offering.

The testimonial is imprecise Thurber. Of his thirty books, only two deal directly with his life in Columbus, with a small percentage of Columbus-related pieces scattered throughout a few of his others. If the statement suggests—as perhaps it should—that the very wellsprings of his creativity were significantly flavored by the nearly thirty years he lived in Columbus, then he has shortchanged the city of his birth by 50 percent.

Some consider the environment of Thurber's origins to be every bit as unlikely as that of Mark Twain. And like the hometown of anyone who spent an undistinguished youth there and left to achieve fame elsewhere, Columbus only gradually grasped Thurber's importance to it. It knew from the start, however, that it was being written about. Unlike the towns of Thomas Wolfe, William Faulkner, and Sinclair Lewis, Columbus is called by its true name throughout its bard's writing. If Thurber was granted instant forgiveness for satirizing his hometown, and Wolfe, Faulkner, and Lewis were not, it was because Thurber's truth was softened with a rich comedy too enjoyable to offend. He could always go home again—and to a red-carpet treatment, at that.

In another sense, he never left home. In "A Note at the End" of *My Life and Hard Times,* he says he has been moved to thoughts

> of spending the rest of my days wandering aimlessly around the South Seas, like a character out of Conrad, silent and inscrutable. But the necessity for frequent visits to my oculist and dentist has prevented this. . . . And a wanderer who isn't inscrutable might just as well be back at Broad and High Streets in Columbus sitting in the Baltimore Dairy Lunch. Nobody from Columbus has ever made a first-rate wanderer in the Conradean tradition. Some of them have been fairly good at disappearing for a few days to turn up in a hotel in Louisville with a bad headache and no recollection of how they got there, but they always scurry back.

Some of Thurber's finer literary moments are those tailored to special occasions or friends in Columbus. In 1953, when the Ohioana Sesquicentennial Medal was awarded him by the Martha Kinney Cooper Ohioana Library Association, Thurber thanked Columbus all over again, in a speech read for him in his absence by George Smallsreed, the editor of the *Columbus Dispatch:* "I am never very far away from Ohio in my thoughts, and . . . the clocks that strike in my dreams are often the clocks of Columbus. They have never struck, and never will strike, a finer hour for me than this one."

Columbus continues to repay Thurber for his role in bringing it to the world's attention. An uptown street near the Ohio State University campus has been named Thurber Drive. A ten-story apartment building is called Thurber Towers. There are Thurber Club Apartments and Thurber Square Apartments. In 1962, Helen Thurber traveled to Columbus to unveil a bronze memorial plaque at the opening of the Thurber Village Shopping Center. Helen, who knew how to play the public-relations game as well as anyone, had got the consent of Thurber's brothers, Robert and William, and she accepted the proffered honor with: "It is especially good that his name is connected with something that's growing—that is what he would appreciate more than anything else." But later, having toured the mall, which contained the Thurber Village Barber Shop, the Thurber Village Cleaning Center, and the Thurber Village Pharmacy, she sighed and remarked to Robert, "I hope it's what he would have wanted."

Nobody could be certain where Thurber wished to be buried; he collapsed from a blood clot on the brain in October 1961, in New York, remained nearly comatose for a month after an operation, and died without regaining full consciousness. Helen carried his cremated remains back to Columbus, where they were buried in the Fisher family area of Green Lawn Cemetery, near his parents and maternal grandparents. ("His family was so angry with me for having him cremated that I didn't dare do anything else with the ashes," Helen says.)

His Columbus associations were unique to Thurber, and Helen, even after twenty-six years of marriage, never felt a part of them. When Helen died in 1986, Rosemary, Thurber's daughter (by his first wife) and his only child, inherited the Thurber estate, including Helen's ashes. Says Rosemary: "The only instruction Helen ever gave me was '*not* in Columbus.' There are those, I am sure, who think I should have buried her [there], but I honored Helen's [request] as best I could."

Biographers sifting the soil of their subjects' beginnings are never fully certain whether to attribute the marvels of a creative personality to childhood environment, genetic inheritance, the mysterious coincidences of serendipity, or the whimsy of the gods. Thurber's *New Yorker* colleague, E. B. White, felt that one factor too frequently overlooked in explaining success and fame is luck. "Every man should be lucky," he once said when asked how he accounted for his own literary achievements.

It was clearly good luck that Thurber, still unknown at age thirty-two, happened to connect with the founding editor, Harold Ross, and White at the *New Yorker*, a magazine whose unrealized potential at the time summoned forth the inspired best of each. But his luck began before that—in being born and raised in Columbus.

2

That Thurber Album

Jacob Fisher, born in a log cabin when Jefferson was President, was twenty-one when Andrew Jackson took office. "Your great-grandpa's prime that the fella speaks of," said Uncle Mahlon, "began about then and lasted up to Cleveland's first term. He couldn't go through another Democratic administration, and so he died."

—from "Adam's Anvil"

In 1799, Thurber's mother's great-grandfather, Michael Fisher, left Virginia for Ohio to claim land being offered free, or with affordable conditions, to citizens who had supported the American Revolution. The land he chose to farm on the Scioto River was just south of what became Columbus. One of Michael's children, Jacob, was Thurber's great-grandfather.

Thurber's interest in his ancestry began in the late 1930s, when he came upon Jacob Fisher's 1885 obituary, clipped from a Columbus newspaper and pasted into a Fisher family scrapbook. It reported that "Jake" was "the strongest man for many miles below the city." An intrigued Thurber consulted a step-great-uncle on his mother's side, Mahlon Taylor, who knew the Fisher story. Taylor's accounts forever made Jake Fisher, by then dead for fifty years, Thurber's favorite ancestor.

Jake once lifted and threw a locomotive wheel thirty-four inches farther than the runner-up, and never lost a fight. He fought men for cursing, saying, "There's too goddam much blasphemin' goes on," a quotation remarkably similar to those Thurber would later, in another book, attribute to Harold

Ross. Jake, a devoted Whig, hated Andrew Jackson and once ascended a speaker's platform to knock down a lecturer who had happened to praise Jackson and was unaware that a man of Jake's partisan passions, prone to direct action, was in the audience.

It was a day of roads built by private contractors. Travelers passed through a turnpike after paying the gate-keeper a toll. The builder of the Chillicothe turnpike was allowed to use gravel from Jake's land, on condition that Jake would never have to pay to use the road. The agreement wasn't in writing, and Jake had to beat up successive gate-keepers and threaten to do the same to the road's owners before he was given unchallenged access to the highway. As a blacksmith who sometimes lifted a horse into position for shoeing, Jake once put a challenger to flight by carrying the man's horse out of the way to make room for the fight.

Was the Thurber penchant for exaggerated storytelling at work here? Clifford Fisher, Thurber's cousin and another great-grandson of Jake's, says, "No. Jim's grandfather and mine, William Fisher, Jake's son, always admired his father, and talked about him a lot, so what Jim wrote about Jake was well known to us all.

"Jake was always fighting with somebody. Sometimes he'd beat a guy up and then take him home so he could nurse him back to health. After that he'd let the fellow go his own way with a warning not to do again whatever it was he'd done to cause the fight. There was usually a good reason for Jake's fights. That toll road, for example. Jake had to use it to get to his farm, and when the toll keeper wouldn't let him through Jake felt he had no choice but to beat him up.

"But Jake, you might say, was a doctor of sorts, too, helping people out. He had an herb garden and he'd make concoctions to cure the ailments of liver, stomach, fevers and such. He called it his 'physic' business. He felt people ought to go to church, and if somebody didn't have a good reason for not going, or if someone beat his wife and Jake heard about it, he'd beat the guy up. If he thought it ought to be done, he'd just do it whether it was legal or not."

Thurber's and Clifford's grandfather, William Fisher, took his cue from the vigilante father he admired. "My grandfather did a lot of fighting, too," Clifford says. "There were a lot of Sicilian [immigrants] in town when he was a young man, and street fighting was a way of life here, a bit like the old West."

Traits of both Great-Grandfather Jake and Grandfather William seem detectable in the fictitious "grandfather" in My Life and Hard Times. At the start of the Civil War, Jake, fifty-three, was told he was too old for the army, though he had demonstrated his fitness by pulling a thick oak door from its hinges in front of the recruiting officers. He was fiercely pro-Union, and would beat up Copperheads or anyone else who questioned Lincoln's policies or evidenced fear of the Rebels. In "The Night the Ghost Got In," investigating policemen climb into the Thurber attic, where grandfather sleeps. The old man, who lives periodically in the past, fires a pistol at them in the belief that they are all "cowardly dogs" who deserted Meade's army, and slightly wounds one of them. (" 'Of all things!' said mother. " 'He was such a nice-looking young man.' ")

As the public's curiosity about Thurber grew with his popularity, Thurber's curiosity about himself and his family roots grew along with it. Following five devastating and unsuccessful eye operations in 1940 and 1941, Thurber began to reflect again on his heritage. In 1942, the *New Yorker* ran his "A Good Man," an early portrait of Jake, his maternal great-grandfather. Six years later, Thurber enlisted his brother Robert and others in a further search for his parents' antecedents.

Harold Ross agreed that Thurber fans might be interested in "straight" accounts of Thurber's family, after all the stretched facts published about his relatives. In addition to "A Good Man," most of what became *The Thurber Album* began in the *New Yorker* in December 1950, as a series called "Photograph Album." The book that resulted, fattened with previously unpublished material, provides the best record of the Fisher, or maternal, side of Thurber's family. His paternal side remains conjectural.

3

That Man with a Rose

William M. Fisher, of Columbus, Ohio, was a man of average height and build . . . but he managed a visibility all his own, since he had a compelling urge to stand out among men. He had had all his teeth capped with gold when he was still a young man, and their gleam was not only set off by a black beard but vividly accented by a red rose, whose stem he clamped between his teeth like a cigar.

—from "Man with a Rose"

Thurber's grandfather looked for toughness in his children and grandchildren, attributing all evidence of it to Fisher blood and lack of it to the families the Fishers married into. "Show your Fisher!" he would shout at a weeping grandchild.

Born in 1840, he married Katherine (Kate) Matheny when she was sixteen and he was twenty-one. He farmed for his father until he was twenty-seven, and clerked in a grocery store before taking over a forty-acre farm Jake deeded to him. The next year, he sold the farm and started a grocery store in partnership with another man.

In 1870, when he was thirty, he bought out his partner and began a fruit-and-vegetable wholesale business; it prospered, eventually enabling him to build the large Fisher house in the then-fashionable East Side of Columbus, on Bryden Road. A dozen years after its start, the business was moved into a larger building, the site of the William M. Fisher & Sons Co. that Thurber remembers.

"He thought of himself as a fighter up to the year he died," Thurber writes of his grandfather, "and was usually unable to argue with a man without letting go a right swing." (Thurber in later years, when in his cups, could show his Fisher in an equally pugnacious manner, sometimes throwing drinks or furniture when an argument frustrated or angered him.) Young James, with his glass eye and propensity for horseplay, used to irritate Grandfather Fisher, who on some occasions, according to Robert, would twist the youngster's arm until it hurt, ordering him to "stop the foolery!" or to "stop acting the fool!"

Thurber may have settled scores with Grandfather Fisher later, though ordinarily, when he wrote of traceable people, he was gentlemanly and careful to spare feelings. In his "Album" memoirs, a bullying newspaper editor, a fascist-minded professor, an ineffectual father, a flighty mother—and in the 1935 story "Doc Marlowe" a patent-medicine charlatan—all receive charitable tributes from a sentimental Thurber. Even his book about the *New Yorker* and its founder, *The Years with Ross*, considered mischievously inaccurate by some of his colleagues and other Ross admirers, may reflect nothing more sinister than Thurber's trying to fit a revised version of himself into a patch of history others had shared and saw from their own proprietary perspectives. Thurber's loyalty to good storytelling frequently led him to choose to misunderstand his subject, usually a harmless and artistically compelling technique.

With children of Grandfather Fisher—including Thurber's mother—still alive when *The Thurber Album* appeared, Thurber presents the old man as only a laughable eccentric, with nothing said about his small cruelties to young James when the Thurbers were visiting or living with the Fishers. In "Man with a Rose," Thurber writes that William Fisher "had a passion for having his picture taken." One photograph showed him

> wearing his derby and overcoat and carrying a satchel. The picture's enlargement was placed under glass by Grandfather Fisher along with a telegram that read, "Urgent. Do not go to Catawba tonight. Details follow." . . . He had been about to leave his hotel in Port Clinton, Ohio, where he had gone one summer in the eighteen-eighties to buy peaches, when the telegram arrived from his store. If it had come ten minutes later, he said, he would have been aboard a small excursion steamer sailing for Catawba Island that sank with the loss of everyone aboard. . . . Any other man, learning of . . . his close escape, would have gone to a bar for a stiff drink. My grandfather hunted up the nearest photographer.

Thurber seems to have got even with the old blusterer earlier, in a 1934 *New Yorker* piece called "The Luck of Jad Peters," in which he fictionalizes the episode and makes Grandfather Fisher (alias Jad Peters) the victim of wishful negative thinking:

> [Jad Peters] is remembered in his later years as a garrulous, boring old fellow whose business slowly went to pieces because of his lack of industry . . . and [who] barely scraped out an existence. He took to drinking in his sixties, and . . . made Aunt Emma's life miserable. . . . Some . . . said . . . it would be a blessing if Jad died in one of his frequent fits of nausea. . . . Aunt Emma had never liked him very much—she married him . . . because there had been nobody else she cared about; she stayed married to him on account of the children.

Thurber finally has Jad killed accidentally when the survival instinct, which the tiresome old man bragged about incessantly, fails him.

Thurber takes not only his own revenge here but that of his grandmother, Kate Fisher, a sweet, husband-dominated soul whom he liked and felt sorry for. Grandfather Fisher, of course, continued as a prosperous businessman, a pillar of Columbus's business community, and a domestic tyrant until his death in 1918, at age seventy-eight. Kate's final seven years after that seem to have been her happiest. She outlived three of her children, and with her death in 1925 the Fisher home on Bryden Road was closed up.

Not that William M. Fisher lacked cause for his cantankerousness. Building the ornate, seven-bedroom house on Bryden Road was an implied invitation to relatives to freeload. Besides offering an occasional haven for the Thurbers, for years the place housed intermittently other members of the Fisher clan, including, among the six Fisher children, able-bodied men seemingly indisposed to self-support. The eldest child, Mary Agnes (she was "Mary" to her father, "Mamie" or "Mame" to everyone else), who became Thurber's mother, was once so impatient with the middle-aged indolence of her brother William that she threw dishes at him—another way of punctuating debate which her son James would sometimes adopt in later years. William Jr.—Uncle Willie—sank into a deepening lethargy over the years, seeming inclined finally to do little else than keep the clocks in the house wound and sun himself in the backyard.

Another son, Grant S. Fisher, was named for Ulysses S. Grant, a hero of Grandfather Fisher's. "Grandpa always kept a lot of pictures of General Grant around," says Clifford Fisher. "Uncle Grant died in Albuquerque, New Mexico"—at forty-eight, of a "knee disease," if a Thurber letter intended more to amuse than inform can be believed.

Kirt Bride Fisher, the youngest son, was another who hung out at the Bryden Road house for years before he married. "I don't know as you'd call Uncle Kirt a live wire," says Clifford. "He did a lot of traveling for the [Fisher produce] company. In those days you had to send people out to make contacts and buy produce. That's what Uncle Kirt did." Kirt, proud to be regarded as the family black sheep, also died in young middle age, from, according to Thurber, "unprecedented complications" of several varieties of venereal disease. The Fisher girls were less of a nuisance to their father. Mame's two sisters quietly removed themselves from the Bryden Road scene through respectable and successful marriages.

Thurber may also have chosen to spare Grandfather Fisher's progeny from reminders of the old man's lapses into senility in his last days. Joel Sayre, another *New Yorker* writer and Columbus native, remembers that during World War I, the old gentleman, with his gold teeth and gray beard, would frequently buy a ticket to the vaudeville show at the B. F. Keith theater and pace up and down the aisles. These wartime performances often featured patriotic skits, which inevitably closed with the waving of the American flag, usually the only guarantee of a standing ovation. Given Grandfather Fisher's respectable position in Columbus business society, the management tolerated him, warning the actors in advance not to let his pacing disconcert them. One afternoon, however, Grandfather glanced up at the actors just as the man playing President Lincoln was being roughed up in a cabinet meeting. Having been a fierce Union supporter, he angrily climbed onto the stage and flailed away at the culprit, until the cast subdued him.

With this audition, William Fisher was given a role in Thurber's *My Life and Hard Times* as "grandfather," the imaginary part-time resident of the Thurber household who usually emerges from the attic to misunderstand the situation and conclude that whatever mishap is afoot is somehow tied to the Civil War. In "Draft Board Nights" Thurber writes that "grandfather" volunteered to join up during World War I.

> He applied several times and each time he took off his coat and threat-ened to whip the men who said he was too old. The disappointment of not getting to Germany (he saw no sense in everybody going to France) and the strain of running around town seeing influential officials finally got him down in bed. . . . One reason we didn't want grandfather to roam around at night was that he had said something once or twice about going over to Lancaster, his old home town, and putting his prob-lem up to "Cump"—that is, General William Tecumseh Sherman, also an old Lancaster boy. We knew that his inability to find Sherman would be bad for him.

By 1940, Thurber, in a column for the newspaper *PM*, had drafted a fictitious brother of Grandfather Fisher's to play the part. Noting the new draft law just passed by Congress that year, he reflects that "in 1917, the draft boards seemed to have had access only to old Sears, Roebuck mailing lists, early nineteenth-century phone books, and the master rolls of Civil War regiments." There is a rumor that General Sherman, dead twenty-five years, has been called up, and that the Columbus draft board has also summoned Grandfather Fisher's brother, "Milt," "who showed up, raring to go, wearing the uniform which he had worn under Scott in Mexico and carrying an old muzzle-loading squirrel gun. Several draft board officials took a pretty bad tossing around before they could get him back home, shouting and swearing and demanding to see Grant in person."

Grandfather Fisher had served Thurber's literary purposes so well by 1950 that Thurber may have decided that anything more than a light roasting of the old curmudgeon in *The Thurber Album* would be overkill.

4

That Lavender with a Difference

In 1884, when Mamie Fisher got out of high school, she wanted to go on the stage, but her unladylike and godless urge was discouraged by her family. . . . Deprived of a larger audience, the frustrated comedienne performed for whoever would listen, and once distressed a couple of stately guests in her father's home by descending the front stairs in her dressing gown, her hair tumbling and her eyes staring, to announce that she had escaped from the attic, where she was kept because of her ardent and hapless love for Mr. Briscoe, the postman.

—from "Lavender with a Difference"

Soliciting information about his family in 1949, Thurber wrote his cousin Clifford that their grandfather, William Fisher, was "the greatest ham actor in the family," a characteristic he "passed on to my mother and me." A decade later, Thurber was still crediting Mame for much of his view that life offered infinite comic possibilities, and for endowing him with her love of make-believe: "I've been acting since I was five, along with my mother—in private and public," he told an interviewer.

Kate Fisher's sister, Aunt Melissa Matheny, "who knew the Bible by heart and was convinced that Man's day was done," helped try to persuade her young niece to give up thoughts of acting professionally. Appearing to be listening to the warnings against the immoral life led by theater people,

Mame was memorizing the way Aunt Melissa talked. Like her son, she became a convincing mimic. In the summer, at family get-togethers, young
Mame, dressed in her mother's skirt and a shawl, would deliver monologs for
the relatives' amusement. "It was the closest I ever got to being an actress,"
she said, "and I wrote those skits myself."

In school, she was the clown of her class—"the livest wire of the old Rich
Street and Mound Street schools," a classmate recalls. She was active in
school plays, usually getting the leading parts and helping the teachers coach
the others. One teacher suggested to Mame's parents that they send their
daughter to a dramatic school. Both William and Kate, stern Methodists,
were horrified.

In those days of vaudeville, a well-known group of actors, the Joseph
Jefferson Troupe, traveled the theater circuit. Jefferson, a tragedian, was associated with Shakespearean roles and the classic stage character Rip Van Win-
kle. As a teenager, Mame saw the Jefferson Troupe in a Columbus theater and
decided on a career for herself, "I always planned for a life on the wicked
stage," she said years later. "Being a comedienne was the life, was the way I
looked at it. I don't know if I was any funnier than the next guy, but I
couldn't see myself swooning and dying onstage. I put off getting married,
hoping to get on the stage, and once I had all my clothes packed. Ray Brown,
a schoolmate of mine, was going to run away with me to study dramatics—he
finally did become an actor—but my folks caught me and made sure I stayed
home after that. I was born too soon."

Why Mame grew up needing to "play the fool," in her father's words, is a
puzzle. It may have been a reaction to the forbidding and disciplined Fisher
household; it may simply have been competition for attention with her sister
Katherine, described by Clifford Fisher, her nephew, as "one of the most
beautiful girls in Columbus." In his opinion, Aunt Mamie, a little sparrow of
a woman, was "far from beautiful."

Mame never did relinquish her fondness for center stage. The curtain was
always up, and as she grew into a nonstop talker at home and on the telephone, some found her too exhausting to take for long. There are those who
wonder if Charles Thurber would have been routinely described as quiet and
retired had he been married to a woman who let him get a word in.

There were times when a weary Charles arrived home from work to learn
that his absent wife was somewhere executing an elaborate joke on a neighbor. Once, she hid from their sons when they got home from school; she
climbed onto the roof and concealed herself behind the chimney. The Thurber males would worry about Mame's absences the way, in other households,
mothers worried about tardy husbands or children. Spontaneous or planned,

her stand-up performances ranged from the outrageous practical joke to the embellishment of truth in the interest of good theater, and from telephone mimicry to other aspects of that relentless kidding that makes its successful practitioners the wary fascination of friend and neighbor.

Mame remained a dynamo of a woman to the end, regarded as a neighborhood character always good for laughs. In 1951, when she was eighty-five, she met an old schoolmate named Mollie Harmon in Lazarus's department store, in downtown Columbus. When Mrs. Harmon introduced the legendary Mary Thurber to her two granddaughters, they hopped about excitedly and cried, "Oh, Grandma, make her do something!"

Mame did plenty, right into her twilight years. Just before her eightieth birthday, she brought a cardboard egg container into a ladies' club meeting, announced that she had always wanted to break a dozen eggs at once, and threw the closed but empty carton at the wall, sending a clutch of aging, screaming ladies scrambling to get out of the way.

She delighted in shocking the conservative women members of the several social clubs she belonged to. Her nephew Earl Fisher remembers Mame on a downtown shopping trip with friends. A pitchman atop a makeshift stage in one store was talking up a sure cure for corns. Mame at once removed her shoe and stocking and asked him to apply his product to her corn. She then replaced her shoe and stocking, excitedly told the gathering crowd how wonderful her foot felt, and danced a jig on the stage. Only the few in the crowd who didn't know Mame Thurber thought she was a shill for the pitchman.

On one of her visits to New York in the 1930s, Thurber took her to a party at the Algonquin Hotel. Mame didn't drink or smoke, but she pretended to be a little drunk and asked a guest for a cigarette and a light. Each time a match was lit for her, she blew through the cigarette and put out the flame. This went on for some time before the guest caught on.

Her endless chatter and wild antics flourished without noticeable abatement until the bedridden years before her death in 1955 at age eighty-nine. Thurber commemorated it all, in writing and interviews. He recognized and appreciated their common heritage: the fondness for playing tricks and for mental telepathy—they often tried to read one another's mind—and their instinctive bent for creating uproar for their personal amusement.

Thurber's "sure grasp of confusion," which Wolcott Gibbs confessed to admire most in his writing, was given early direction by Mame, who is remembered as talking all the time—to visitors, to the dogs, to her family, store clerks, strangers on the street, and on the telephone. She made exaggerated storytelling second nature for her son. "She was a famous hand at ornamenting a tale," Thurber, guilty of the same charge, writes innocently.

When a member of one of Mame's clubs married after many years, only to throw her husband out of the house a few weeks later, nobody dared to ask her what happened except Mame Thurber, who reported that the disappointed bride had told her, "Why, he said things to me my own brother wouldn't say!" Mame's friends suspected that she had made up this answer; like her son, if the fact wasn't sufficiently entertaining, she felt it was fair game to invent one.

"My first wife used to invite a group of lady friends to our house," says Clifford Fisher. "Once, she included Mame, who held the floor telling funny and outlandish stories. All the women said they had never had so much fun or laughed so hard. Aunt Mamie would tell the stories as if they were the gospel truth, and you couldn't budge her from that stand. For years she had her boys believing a lot of things that were funny but just not true. She could read palms and tea leaves and the bumps on your head—phrenology—and anything else she thought would entertain. She would keep the straightest face, but I had a feeling she was always laughing to herself."

Mrs. Ruth Taylor Davis, of Punxsutawney, Pennsylvania, knew the Thurbers prior to marrying and leaving Columbus in 1911. Mame, she writes, "was a rare individual, and could wring humor out of any situation. She didn't object to embellishing the truth, but never at the expense of anyone but herself." The same could be said for her second son, despite occasional arguments to the contrary. And to those who heard the floor-hogging monologs of both, the similarities were a revelation.

In "The Night the Ghost Got In," Thurber has his mother throwing a shoe through the neighbors' window to alert them to the presence of burglars in the Thurber house. Asked about it, Robert Thurber said: "A couple of times when we thought there were burglars in the house, and nobody was looking, Mother would throw her shoes down the hall in the dark, or down the stairs, just to add to the confusion. Maybe Jim got the idea from that."

Both Thurber and his mother took delight in confounding friends and strangers alike. In her sixties, Mame traveled to Washington, D.C., to meet a friend she hadn't seen in decades. Mame had said she could be recognized by a rose she would pin to her coat. At Union Station, she pinned the rose on the coat of an elderly lady asleep on a bench and watched while the old acquaintance endured embarrassment and the risk of an assault charge by shaking the stranger awake and trying to embrace her.

Mame was interested in the occult and in any theory, simple or elaborate, that might explain or improve life. She invited to her home the famous French psychotherapist and lecturer Professor Émile Coué, who recommended that his audiences seek self-improvement by repeating the words

"Every day in every way I am getting better and better." She kept up a lively correspondence with Evangeline Adams, whose 1926 book *The Bowl of Heaven* was the manual of astrology buffs. She detected "bad vibrations" in certain houses and rooms, and once had her husband return their car's license plates because the numbers comprised an ominous combination in numerology. In *The Years with Ross*, Thurber credits her with having predicted the nature of Ross's death through her astrological prowess.

She insisted on knowing the day and hour that physicians were born before accepting treatment from them. When Thurber was scheduled for his second eye operation, in October 1940, Mame, then seventy-five, wrote two touching letters to Dr. Gordon Bruce, the surgeon, expressing her concern and asking him to take the fullest astrological advantage of the hour and planetary positions when he operated. The date, October 22, she wrote to Bruce, was "a perfect time," and "after 1:30—Eastern Standard Time—would be ideal." Any time before that hour, "according to [Thurber's] planets would not give such good results." In case the surgeon had scheduled another time, she hoped he could change it

> if convenient to you—[and] if only to please the *mother*. . . .
> When I was in hospital in N.Y. last June—my operation day and time was set by my Astrologer and I came out fine in every way—and at my age—74—and only weighing 85 lbs it didn't look very encouraging. . . .
> James knows I am interested in Astrology—but he wouldn't want me to interfere with your plans—if [an] exact time [has been] set.

And on October 12, she wrote again:

> In case Jim's operation wouldn't be a success or [he] should get worse afterwards—wouldn't it be possible to graft an eye so that he could be able to see . . . in case it would not come out as you expect it to . . . ? With the time set and your skill and [with the] confidence of Jim and all the rest of us in you he is bound to come out with flying colors [but] I am perfectly willing and would gladly give him one of my eyes—I have really very good eyes—my age and all—I only wear glasses for very fine print. . . . I write all my letters without glasses—my father and mother were past 80

when they died and neither one ever wore glasses [except for] reading fine print as I do—so Jim has a good inheritance you see. . . . I do feel a little concerned—he is such a darling boy and he accomplished so much and needs his eye to continue his work, and I feel God will give him even better sight than before.

Excuse me for taking up so much of your time.

Sincerely yours,
Mary A. Thurber

But astrological strategy, surgical skill, and the willingness of Thurber's mother to sacrifice one of her eyes to the cause were all for naught.

Mame's addiction to fads, seances, numerology, and astrology (Thurber was "Sagittarius with the moon in Aries") provided Thurber with ideas both for fictional and illustrated situations. Mame-inspired Thurber cartoon captions include: (angry wife to husband) "I'd like to get my hands on the astrologer who told you that!"; and (seance practitioner) "I can't get in touch with your uncle, but there's a horse here that wants to say hello"; and the courtroom scene below.

Social scientists might well believe that Mame's manic behavior had a

"I'm Virgo with the moon in Aries, if that will help you any."

disorienting effect on her middle son, who witnessed it from infancy—and so Thurber suggests. As a toddler, he watched her transform herself from mother to witch to play a joke on her neighbor, and says he experienced "a mixture of wonder and worry that lingered in my memory for years." Thurber was assigned a role in that particular charade, and years later wrote, "I feel that this twisted or marked the occupation of my mind by a sense of confusion that has never left it." But these assertions are not fully meant. He was always delighted with his mother's shenanigans and proud to be part of them. If Grandfather Fisher was dismayed at the way young James "acted the fool," Mame encouraged it. In Lazarus's department store, where the Thurbers opened an account in 1910, Thurber and his mother would sometimes pretend to be shoplifters, soon gaining recognition among the floorwalkers as habitual but harmless pranksters.

Joel Sayre, six years younger than Thurber, grew up in Columbus and later became a novelist, a reporter for the *New Yorker*, and a screenwriter. As an admirer of Robert Thurber, the captain and star pitcher of the East High baseball team, Sayre would wander over to the Thurbers' house to be near his hero. "When I used to visit the Thurber home as a kid," Sayre recalls, "there was a three-ring circus in progress all the time. Their mother had them all competing to be the funniest. Years later, when Jim began to ring the bell with his *New Yorker* pieces about his family life in Columbus, I'd think, Who couldn't be a successful comic writer with that kind of mother and family? He just had to write it straight."

Mame's uncanny ability to absorb and recollect the minutiae of daily life in unerring fashion was every bit as good as that of "Jamie," according to a variety of sources. Both Thurber and his mother could support their claims to near-total recall ("It isn't often that my memory outdoes my mother's," writes Thurber modestly). She could remember a mountain of names, dates, and numbers. Her family rarely consulted the Columbus telephone directory; they had only to ask Mame. "My father had an outstanding memory," says Robert, "but not the equal of my mother's. We all got our ability to recall names and dates from both, but more so from her."

Thurber became the apple of his mother's eye as he attained success. He was the weak chick that overcame great handicaps and grew to become an eagle. Given his achievements at the *New Yorker*, she didn't doubt it when a friend reported rumors that Thurber had bought the magazine. Mame promptly wrote to him and scolded him for not hiring his brothers. (She wrote to him and Helen every week for years. "She loved Helen like the daughter she never had," a family friend says.) Once, in New York after an operation that Thurber had paid for, Mame was being wheeled across the floor of Grand Central Terminal when a man bumped into her. "Don't do that," she told him with a smile. "I'm James Thurber's mother."

And there on another occasion, when she was buying a train ticket back to Columbus, the jovial clerk said, "Columbus, eh? James Thurber's hometown." "Yes, I'm his mother," Mame proudly replied. The clerk studied the diminutive elderly Mame, asked her to wait a moment, and alerted his supervisor that an unchaperoned lady of unreliable age with delusions of grandeur was about to board the train for Columbus. A message was sent to the conductor to keep a close eye on her.

She found a few of her son's cartoons hard to fathom, and some of Thurber's short pieces didn't make sense to her, but her son was still her favorite author and cartoonist. She once told Thurber how much she liked William Steig's "Small Fry" cartoon series in the *New Yorker*, and Thurber from then on insisted that Steig was his mother's favorite artist. Asked about this by a reporter from *Time*, she said, "I couldn't even remember what a Steig cartoon looked like until Robert showed me one. Jamie always did exaggerate. You mustn't believe a thing he says." But Thurber, who tended to denigrate his own drawing, continued to tell people that his mother preferred Steig.

In her seventies, Mame announced that she was writing a play. The news worried Thurber, who had been struggling for years to complete one of his own. He was concerned on two counts: that his mother would finish hers and suffer a rejection she would find hard to take, or worse, that she would come up with one that would beat his to Broadway.

"She was a gay and happy and witty person," says Millicent Easter, who lived at the Southern Hotel, a residential hotel in Columbus where Mame and her sons Robert and William resided for a number of years. "A very attractive lady, with white hair and black eyebrows that never turned white. Her sons would take both of us for rides in the country. They'd stop along the road and whistle to imitate birds. Mame could imitate birds better than either of them. She loved birds, lace, and flowers. When she was past eighty, she could laugh like she was sixteen years old. When she was eighty-five, Emerson Burkhart, a well-known Columbus artist, painted her picture. She was sick and weak, but she smiled and joked all the time, and the portrait shows her laughing eyes and those beautiful, arched, rich black eyebrows."

Even in her eighties, Mame refused to wear black. "It's for old ladies," she explained.

In Mame's later years, there were worrisome tendencies to fall down or get sick. Robert, her youngest son, never married, and lived with her in Columbus until her death. Both of them were largely financially supported by Thurber in the last two decades of his mother's life. In exchange, Robert served as companion and nurse to Mame, sparing Thurber the expense, guilt, and sorrow of having to consign her to a nursing home.

In 1952, a *Columbus Dispatch* feature writer, Beverly Smith, visited Mame, then eighty-six, at her residential-hotel apartment in Columbus, and recorded this high-spirited delivery:

"I've been inactive the last few months with high blood pressure. Now look at me. Stuck here in this room. I even have to get up to look at my clothes and hats in the closet; I miss them, you know. Robert gets in a tizzy if I try to get up alone. I suppose he's right; I can't stand up long by myself. He went down to the lobby not long ago and told me, 'I'll be gone just four-and-a-half minutes. When I come back I don't want to find you sprawled in the middle of the floor.' Well, I felt pretty good, so as soon as he shut the door I started for the closet but didn't make it. When he came back he yelled, 'You see? Just what I said!' I yelled right back, 'Didn't disappoint you, then, did I?' I probably looked pretty startling at first glance. I hit my eye on the first step going up to the bath. It was swollen. I've been confined temporarily. It isn't lonely. My two sons [Robert and William] keep me company, and old friends."

Interviewed in her later years, she was undiplomatically asked by a young reporter if she had personally known several people who had figured in Ohio's early history, well before Mame was born. She didn't bat an eye. "No, but I was a friend of Thomas Jefferson's," she said.

Robert's letters to Thurber reporting problems concerning Mame increased with her advancing years, often interrupting Thurber's work schedule or travel plans. It was never Mame who complained, though she was too weak to be far from her bed the last five years of her life. "She didn't want to be a bother," Robert says. "She kept saying 'Everything is fine,' right up till her stroke." She suffered a stroke in November 1955, and died a month later, twenty-five days short of her ninetieth birthday.

Robert's and Mame's stubborn objections to what Thurber wrote about the family—his father in particular—in the *New Yorker* "Photograph Album" series exasperated Thurber and Helen. But Thurber took the time to explain, to argue, and finally to revise his text—all in the hope of resolving their complaints and always out of concern for their feelings. Mame, who had been a good sport over the years about Thurber's literary handling of his family, was apparently persuaded by Robert this time that her late husband was not being portrayed fairly.

Robert's explosive criticism of the "Photograph Album" piece on Charles Thurber aroused Thurber's anger in turn. The result was a residue of hard feelings on both sides; Robert never overcame his, and blamed his inability to do so on what he said was Thurber's unforgiving manner toward his mother. In 1975, fourteen years after his brother's death, Robert wrote in a letter:

> I still can't erase from my mind the way James treated my mother when he had just finished [the "Album" series]. He talked cross to her over the phone and actually hung up on her on one occasion. It wasn't long after that (about September, 1951) that my mother became ill and bed-ridden and passed away some four years later.
>
> And it was over three years . . . after she took ill that he finally came to see her. But he never embraced her, or even held her hand as I recall. Practically ignored her. He had absolutely no sympathy for her. Not easy to forget things like that. During that stay he was mean, critical and sarcastic.

Nevertheless, Thurber's devotion to his mother seems convincing. On Mame's visits to New York over two decades—her last was in 1947, when she was eighty-two—he proudly showed her off to *New Yorker* colleagues and other friends. A dozen had stories of the delight Thurber took in sharing his mother with them. It pleased him that Harold Ross was always amused by Mame when Thurber brought her to Ross's office. An outsider searches *The Thurber Album* in vain for any reason for the angry protests of Thurber's mother and brother at its publication. The Thurber family, the outsider would conclude, could not have been shown to greater advantage if the writer had been its hired press agent. Never in private or public interviews was Thurber anything but respectful of his father, or admiring and almost worshipful of his mother. In his 1953 speech accepting the Ohioana award, he says, "My only . . . regret is that my [ailing] mother couldn't attend this meeting, for without her I never would have been able to write what I have managed to write. One of my friends who heard my mother tell stories one evening a few years ago when she visited me in Connecticut, said, 'Your humor is only a pale reflection of your mother's, but if you keep at it you might be almost as good as she is some day.' This fond and wistful hope . . . is one of the things that keeps me going and will keep me going."

Even when accusing Thurber of a loss of affection for his mother, Robert felt compelled to offer balancing evidence: "James was very generous and unselfish about money," he wrote. "He was always ready to help financially (and did), especially when anyone was ill—he would always insist on the best of care and an outstanding doctor or specialist to take over." Thurber saw to it, when Robert could no longer drive, that a chauffeured limousine was available to him and Mame.

As to Thurber's literary treatment of his father in this instance, it remains unclear what he could have done to placate Robert. He made concessions in the *Album* portraits of both his parents, to the point of sounding maudlin.

5

That Gentleman from Indiana

Everybody's father is a great, good man, someone has said, and mine was no exception. There was never, I truly believe, a purely selfish day in his life. He was sorrowfully aware, from twilight to twilight, that most men, and all children, are continuously caught in one predicament or another, and his shoulder was always ready to help lift a man's cross, or a child's, when it became too heavy to be carried alone.

—from "Gentleman from Indiana"

Thurber's review of his father's side of the family in *The Thurber Album* is based on the little that Charles Thurber had been told by his mother, and padded with a few graceful, space-filling observations by Thurber, which, he privately admitted, he didn't believe himself. In the chapter entitled "Gentleman from Indiana," he writes:

My father's father [Leander Thurber] is a dim figure in the annals of the family, a gentleman of retiring nature and private thought, who was thrown from a horse on a lonely ride and killed in the year 1867, when his only child was a few months old, leaving his widow to teach school for a living until frailty condemned her to a life of rocking chair contemplation. Her son began by selling morning newspapers in Indianapolis. . . . He had no other relatives to turn to. The Thurbers of his father's generation had originated in Boston and Providence, but most of them set out for the West when they were young, ending up in a dozen different states. My grandfather, on his way to hunt for gold in California, had fallen in love with Indiana and settled there.

"All we were told about Leander," writes Robert, "is that he was killed, thrown from a horse, according to my father, whose word I would never doubt. It happened before my father was born, in '66 or '67, since he was born in March 1867."

In 1951, absorbed in ancestry research, Thurber was put in touch with Charles H. Thurber, Sr. (no known relation), a self-appointed, determined family genealogist from Rhode Island, born in 1887. This dogged climber of the Thurber family tree substantiated, through courthouse documents, tombstone readings, and state historical records, that the first Thurbers had arrived from England in 1667. He had found grave markers of the early Thurbers in Rehoboth and Swansea, Massachusetts, and in neighboring Warren, Rhode Island. (The Thurber name is still found in abundance today in the Providence area—a Providence street is named Thurbers Avenue.)

Through the genealogist's twelve hundred pages of Thurber lineage, the trail of Leander, Thurber's paternal grandfather, is too faint to follow. There is no record of his marriage to Thurber's grandmother, Sarah Emeline Hull. Thurber settled for the anemic account above and dropped the matter; the persistent Charles H. Thurber, Sr., did not. In 1961, at age seventy-five, he was back in touch with Helen Thurber, who turned him over to Robert. With the help of a professional genealogist and the Rhode Island Historical Society, fresh clues had turned up.

Thurber's great-grandmother was Sarah Ann Thurber, one of ten children of Ruth and John Thurber III, of Warren, Rhode Island. Born in 1802, Sarah Ann married a Burrisville, Rhode Island, carpenter, Peleg Hull, in 1824. They had eleven children. Their eighth, Sarah Emeline, was Thurber's grandmother, born November 2, 1842.

Burrisville was a small mill town near North Providence, where, according to the 1850 national census records, a seventeen-year-old Leander Thurber was living with the family of Owen and Penelope Metcalf. Seven years later, a vague reference places a Leander Thurber in California, perhaps married and the father of two daughters. He may have left his family there to return East right after the end of the Civil War.

Because Sarah's mother's maiden name was Thurber, it is likely that Sarah Hull and Leander Thurber, living near one another, were cousins of one degree or another. Had he persuaded her to leave Providence with him for the Midwest? Was she already in Indianapolis when, on his way back from California, he looked her up? When a possible love affair had gone too far, had he told her he was already married? Despite the absence of records, had they married and divorced? Had he abandoned her upon her pregnancy?

Thurber's father, Charles Leander, born March 19, 1867, in Indianapolis, was named in part for a father he never knew. He had no sentimental reservations about giving up the "Leander" for "Lincoln" when his wife made fun of his middle name. Either Charles had been told little or nothing about Leander by his mother or had decided to keep secret what he had been told. None of the Columbus Thurbers seems to have known where Leander was buried, and though Charles took his children to visit Indianapolis on occasion, there was no visit to a grave or mention of one. What Leander did for a living is equally mysterious. And so is what sort of person he was.

All we know officially of Grandmother Sarah Emeline is a record showing that she married one Tunis Dangler of New Jersey on October 22, 1871, in Atlanta, Illinois, Logan County. That would be more than four years after her son, Charles—Thurber's father—was born. However, the Illinois court entry, made several years after the marriage to Dangler was over, reads: "Lives in Indiana, divorced, no children." (Writes the librarian of the Rhode Island Historical Society: "This seems very confusing, but of course there is the possibility that she was married to a Thurber previously.")

But who was Tunis Dangler, and what happened to him?

When Charles was eleven, he was sent to Columbus by his mother in Indianapolis to stay for a school term with "Aunt" Margery Dangler Albright, as she was known to the Thurbers. Destined for fond commemoration by Thurber in his "Daguerreotype of a Lady," Aunt Margery used to tell how the Danglers had traveled by covered wagon from Long Branch, New Jersey, to Kokomo, Indiana, in the late 1830s. An arguable guess is that she was a sister of Tunis, and thus a sister-in-law of Sarah's; young Charles Thurber would come to call her "Aunt." Not only did Charles never know his father, but Tunis, the stepfather he may have known at age four, was soon gone as well.

Thurber adds to the mystery with his mention of Aunt Margery's dog, Tuney, "named after her brother, Tunis, who was later killed at Shiloh by a ramrod fired from a nervous Southern farmboy's musket." Yet Tunis—no more common a name than Leander, surely—is recorded as marrying Sarah Emeline Hull nine years after Shiloh and divorcing her four years later. Apparently a duty-bound Margery Albright, who all her life lived in the service of others, had gone to the rescue of a twice-abandoned sister-in-law by helping with young Charles.

Though Aunt Margery's husband, a farmer named John Albright, died in 1865, leaving her with a daughter to support, she helped rear Charles, whom she learned to cherish. As late as 1905, when Charles, age thirty-eight, was taken deathly ill, it was Aunt Margery who hurried to the Fisher home to nurse him back to health. "It was the first time she had been out of her own dooryard in several years," Thurber writes, "but she didn't enjoy the April drive [to the Fisher house]. My father was her favorite person in the world, and they had told her he was dying."

Thurber never makes clear the connection between Aunt Margery and his father, or why Charles was her favorite person in the world, nor does he mention that as a boy Charles had lived with her in Columbus for a time. But a close stepaunt-stepnephew relationship would help explain Aunt Margery's ongoing willingness to take in Charles's sons whenever circumstance required.

Grandmother Sarah Hull Dangler remained a peripheral memory for the Thurber boys. In an 1884 letter to Mame, seventeen-year-old Charles mentions that his mother has left for a visit to Providence to spend Thanksgiving with "Grandma," Sarah's mother. Robert believes that by the time Charles moved to Columbus and married Mame Fisher in 1892, Sarah had long since left Indianapolis to live with relatives in Providence. The Thurber boys first met her when she returned from the Northeast in 1905 to live with Margery Albright. She told William she would have preferred to remain in Providence had there been someone able to take care of her there. Robert writes, "By then she was in rather feeble health with failing vision." In the fall of 1906, she was moved from Aunt Margery's to a local hospital, where she died on November 3, at age sixty-four. She is buried in Green Lawn Cemetery, in a grave some distance from the Fisher/Thurber plots.

Thurber was nearly twelve at his paternal grandmother's death, but whatever thoughts he had of her he chose to keep out of his memoirs. In July 1951, during his "Album" research, he wrote to his mother:

> I keep wondering why none of us has ever know[n] about Leander. He was never mentioned by Belle [Margery Albright's daughter], or Mrs. Albright, or my father's mother, whom I knew for several years. She looked exactly like Papa. Also there are no photographs, letters, records, or anecdotes. . . . Maybe he was a rascal who got the hell out, leaving his wife stuck with an infant son. I never believed he was thrown from a horse. He may have gone to Texas where there is a town named Thur-

ber. I'm not going to write anything about him, but I'm interested in finding out and astonished that we never showed any curiosity before. It is rare, indeed, when three male adults know nothing whatever about their grandfather. Maybe he didn't even marry Sarah. This would account for the clamming up of everybody. He seems to be the only one of his siblings without any record.

Charles grew up to fit the description Thurber applies to the mysterious Leander: a man of "retiring nature and private thought." His two younger sons, James and Robert, inherited his long face and aquiline nose (he faintly resembled the actor Alec Guinness), though in their later pictures, through some evolving metamorphosis, the two boys partly came to resemble Mame as well. Charles was not quite six feet tall; Robert and James reached nearly six feet, two inches. William's rounder face and shorter physique favored the Fisher family.

Mame and Charles met in 1878, when Charles was eleven and living with Aunt Margery, who, with her daughter, Belle, occupied the north half of a run-down two-family house at South Fifth Street and Walnut Alley. Mother and daughter took in sewing and washing and ironing, and rented out the upstairs front room to help pay the ten-dollars-a-month rent. The Fishers, whose Bryden Road mansion would not be built until 1884, lived on the same street, but in a respectable two-story house with an upstairs porch. If it wasn't the best part of town, it meant an easy walk for Grandfather Fisher to his wholesale produce business.

Mame and Charles attended the same elementary school; she was fourteen months older than Charles and a grade ahead of him, but she fell in love with him "the first day I laid eyes on him," she told *Time*'s Richard Oulahan in 1950. "He came to live across the street from us, with an aunt. I never cared for anybody else. I had beaux galore later on, but I guess it really was a love match."

Illness forced Sarah to quit teaching, and Charles had to drop out of school and return to Indianapolis to work full time to support them. "It was quite a blow to him not to attend high school, let alone college," says Robert, who remained forever devoted to his father's memory. "He was an exceptional student and ambitious to continue his education. His diction, English, and general knowledge was above [the] average plane of a college graduate. He worked for a bakery for a while, and [for] a firm of patent attorneys in Indianapolis." Evenings, Charles took courses in stenography and became proficient at typing and shorthand.

His courtship of Mame began in earnest in 1884, upon her graduation from high school. It was conducted mostly by mail, though Charles found reasons to visit Aunt Margery in Columbus and to see the only girl he ever loved. The directions of his Walter Mitty daydreams were now set by infatuation with the bubbling adolescent in Columbus. She, in turn, was pleased by his ornate handwriting and cherished and kept all his love letters to her, styled as they were in a worshipful Victorian courtliness. They exchanged pictures, and in a shy 1884 letter that Henry James would find faintly familiar, Charles thanks her for her photograph, adding that though it "looks just like the charming miss it represents, if you will permit me it," it *misrepresents*, he adds, "the little miss in not being quite so—(well I'm so far away it will be safe to say it—and 'honor bright' too)—*pretty."* His letters grew longer and bolder. "I feel so sure that you and I will be married," he was writing her, only months later.

Like Columbus, Indianapolis was a state capital, whose residents were surrounded by political talk and thought. In 1884, at seventeen, Charles paraded most of one night for the Republican candidate for president, James G. Blaine. He wrote to Mame predicting Blaine's election, which seemed a safe bet; the Republicans had held the White House ever since Lincoln's first inauguration, twenty-four years before. But the political game was destined always to trick Charlie Thurber. Blaine lost to Grover Cleveland.

In the election year of 1888, twenty-one-year-old Charles was riding a winning horse at last. He was made secretary of a civic club organized to promote the Republican presidential candidacy of Benjamin Harrison. This time Cleveland was defeated, the local ticket did well, too, and Charles was rewarded with a clerical job in the office of Indiana's secretary of state from 1889 to 1891. The new position emboldened Charles, after his five-year courtship, to propose to Mame. She accepted. He spent the Christmas holidays of 1889 with her and her family, during which a business friend and neighbor of the Fishers named Poe kidded Charles a great deal about his shyness. Back in Indianapolis, Charles wrote Mame his letter of thanks, beginning:

My Dear Mame,

    My joy, my hope my pride, and *mine only.* Wonder how Mr. Poe would like [that] for a beginning. . . . Of course the genial good-natured auditor has doubtless had more experience in this line than I, but I *seriously* doubt whether he ever crowded more happiness in five days consecutively than did I from December 25th to 29th, 1889. Tell him that time will gradually obliterate my bashfulness but that it can never remove my happiness, though my love for you will accumulate with the days.

Your pictures arrived yesterday. I wish you had not stipulated the return of either for I would like to keep them both. It's Hoosier, you know, to want everything in sight, and sigh for the unseen. But, of course, you are always to have your way. . . . It affords me great pleasure to sincerely thank you for the kind invitation to dinner—and—lunch. I will be pleased to accept for next Sunday should circumstances permit. I hope to be in Columbus.

He was handling his busy days in a Benjamin Franklin manner, making them longer by getting up earlier, he said. He has heard of a lecture given on "The Model Wife"—one he sees pointless to attend, because "I'll have a model wife of my own some of these days." Knowing Mame's penchant for humor, he tries his best:

Like you I fancy a 72 hour day *might* be a good idea. Still, as the burglar said, 'we must take things as we find them.'

I am almost counting the hours until 7:15 next Saturday evening when I hope and expect to board the train bound for Columbus to again see and kiss and hug, of course, the dearest and sweetest girl in all the universe to me. Wonder how Mr. Poe would like to read the above and hear me assure you that I am

Yours, regardless of death and taxes.
Charlie.

Charles was by now fascinated with the possibilities of state politics in Indiana, as he would be later by Ohio politics. He followed civic events eagerly in the daily newspapers all his life. He had high hopes to "better himself" professionally and culturally, and in the course of it please his beloved fiancée. His letters to her represent himself as interested in the theater, as she is. He waits three hours outside the stage door of an Indianapolis theater, he tells her, to see Joe Jefferson, whose troupe Mame had come close to leaving home to join. In an amateur dramatic group, he is playing Mark Tapley, "one of my favorite characters," and is reading Dickens's *Martin Chuzzlewit* in preparation for it. He is reading Shakespeare, as well. In his sixties, he would put down "reading good books" and "bowling" as his hobbies.

He had fallen under the spell of the Hoosier Poet, James Whitcomb Riley, at an early age, and could recite much of his poetry from memory years later. Riley, Charles felt, had put Indianapolis on the literary map, and to see the famous poet in the flesh from time to time was always news of high priority to report to Mame. He doubtless identified with Riley's Horatio Alger ideology, which championed the impoverished man of integrity and saw greater merit and virtue in the industrious poor than in the idle rich. Charles, a lifelong teetotaler, regretted only the Hoosier Poet's rumored fondness for drink. "Poor James Whitcomb Riley!" he writes Mame. "He is, it seems, on the down track. It is a pitiful thing for so bright and lovable a man as he to become such a slave to drink. This is his home, you know, and he is loved here by everyone. He is our Hoosier Burns. I hope he will brace up and be a man yet."

He had dreamed of becoming an actor, of going to law school, of entering politics. The lack of confidence that poverty can inflict, his devotion to duty, his dedication to his employers, and his willingness to do whatever was asked of him all worked against him in a government bureaucracy. He was seen as somebody too useful and easy to get along with to lose through job promotions, too unaggressive to do much about it, and too naively honest for the rough-and-tumble dealings and compromises of political office. Chiefs abound; able Indians content to follow are hard to find and keep. Charles was too competent in his work to succeed.

During his two years with the Indianapolis government (1890–1891), he persuaded himself that he belonged in politics, that unholy relative to the theater he would have Mame believe he had also aspired to. And perhaps he had. In his later public service, he was delighted to represent his superiors as a dinner speaker, an extroverted trait that his shy, nervous son James was slow to develop.

It was an age, too, when long engagements were common, during which time the betrothed male—and often the female—worked and saved toward the day when they could afford a home and a life independent of their families. From the start, Charles was given to understand that marriage to Mame meant living in Columbus, not Indianapolis. Through the recommendations and influence of his colleagues and friends in the office of Indiana's secretary of state, Charles finally got what he wanted—a similar position with the Ohio secretary of state. A marriage date was set.

Charles Thurber was not the husband William Fisher would have chosen for his daughter. Charles was of good character but not a businessman with financial prospects. Columbus was a clannish town in those days. According to Ben Williamson, a former Columbus newspaperman: "Social levels were determined by wealth. Grandpa Fisher was in the second echelon from the top; the top level were members of the elite Columbus Club, whose wealth came from coal mines to the south in the Hocking Valley, from early railroading, the making and vending of agricultural supplies; from heavy, steel-based industries such as railroad-car works and mining-machinery manufacture. Not being in the *top* echelon of wealth, Grandpa Fisher was probably twice as sensitive to social status. Thurber's impoverished father didn't stand a chance with him, and there was little that happened to Charlie to change his father-in-law's mind."

But Mame was twenty-six ("very old for those days," she said); her family had waited for fourteen years for her single-minded devotion to Charles to die out. Furthermore, twenty-six *was* old for those days, and her parents still lived in dread over what wild misadventure their headstrong daughter would get into if she didn't settle down.

Mary Agnes and Charles were married on a Tuesday evening, July 12, 1892, in the Fisher home, by James L. Grover, the Methodist minister and city librarian. The bridal party descended the stairs to the Mendelssohn wedding march, played on the piano by Mame's sister Martha. Mame wore a silk gown, legitimately, virtuously white, and carried carnations. One of her bridesmaids was Laura Poe, daughter of Charles's tormentor.

There was no honeymoon. The newlyweds took an apartment on South Grant Avenue while awaiting the completion of the dowry house Mame's father was having built for them. In the spring of 1893, Mame announced that she was pregnant. All three sons, William (October 1893), James (December 8, 1894) and Robert (December 15, 1896), were born in the new, narrow, brick two-story house at 251 Parsons Avenue, a short distance from the Fisher home. Aunt Margery Albright, skilled in midwifery, was on hand to deliver all three of the Thurber boys.

At age twenty-five, Charles was a daydreamer, but not on the scale his second son would be. His visions rarely rose above the pragmatic challenges of politics. He believed, like James Whitcomb Riley, that success was the inevitable reward of hard work, loyalty, and commitment to ideals. Disappointments were part of the game. Year after year, public recognition and material rewards of any substance eluded him, and though this turned him into a worried and nervous person, it seems not to have lastingly discouraged him. Like most practiced daydreamers, he knew how to wall out reality when he had to. As late as 1934, at sixty-seven, he was running again for the Ohio legislature. And losing.

After marrying, Charles worked briefly at the Fisher produce market. Mame blames her brother William for getting Charles fired. "Willie put your father out of the store and treated him like a dog," she writes Thurber in 1950. "We neither one spoke to Willie for years. . . . Grant and Kirt were fine to Charlie. Willie was crazy even then—and you know he lost his mind *finally*. And if your father had remained in [the] store things would be different. My father loved Charlie but for peace sake had to let him go. I should have shot Willie."

Charles clerked at the office of Ohio's secretary of state until 1895, when he was appointed a clerk in Ohio governor Asa Bushnell's office. He was described by his associates in one report as "amiable and quiet, but willing to help." That was what the newspaper correspondents covering the state legislature wanted to hear; they hired him as their secretary. For two years he served as their liaison with the legislators and the governor's office, keeping the journalists informed of the status of pending legislation, taking notes for them in legislative sessions, and making their access to sources in state government easier. He passed on to them all the information they were entitled to, and scrupulously declined to comment on what he had been told was confidential. He transcribed his stenographic notes so faithfully that the reporters at times didn't bother to attend a meeting being covered by Charlie Thurber. As a reward they made him an honorary member of the Ohio Legislative Correspondents Association, one of the few nonjournalists ever so honored.

In 1899, Charles sought the Republican nomination for Franklin County clerk of the court, and the Thurbers had to move from Parsons Avenue to establish his residence in the proper political district. The move was to South Champion Avenue, on the outskirts of East Columbus. ("I think my Grandfather Fisher bought the house for us," says William. "It was the only house we ever owned.") Too modest to boast personally about his qualifications for office, Charles enlisted his more influential friends and colleagues to hand out a promotional flyer that read: "I am a friend of Charles L. Thurber and wish you would vote for him for County Clerk at the Republican Primaries, Friday, July 21, 1899."

He lost.

In 1900, President William McKinley, a native Buckeye, again defeated his Democratic challenger, William Jennings Bryan, to win a second term. But Governor Bushnell was retired from office in the same election. Displaced by the new governor's staff, Charles was forced to freelance his stenographic skills for a time, and he also sold Underwood typewriters. His son James, going on age six, had begun first grade in the fall of 1900 at the Ohio

Avenue School and later said he learned at that time to type on the Underwood machine at home—the hunt-and-peck method he would use until his blindness put an end to typing.

In 1901, McKinley appointed his fellow Ohioan, Congressman David K. Watson, to head a Justice Department commission to revise and codify the nation's criminal and penal laws. Watson selected Charles Thurber as the commission's stenographer, at a salary of a hundred dollars a month. In April 1902, Charles took William and James out of school and moved the family from Columbus into a rented brownstone on "I" Street in Washington. When Mame complained of Washington's humid summer heat, Charles, ever solicitous of his wife, rented a house across the Potomac in Falls Church, Virginia, for the month of August.

That house, rented by the Thurbers for only a month, became the subject of newspaper and magazine articles in 1958, when a lively housewife from Falls Church, Elizabeth Cleland Acosta, like hundreds of readers before her, decided to write Thurber a fan letter:

> Because I feel that I know you so well . . . through your work, the houses in which you lived, your brothers, your parents, your maids and dogs—I feel that I may make bold and tell you that I love you.

Mrs. Acosta later explained her reason for writing: "It was November, bleak and cold. [My] twelve-year-old girl was learning to smoke; the ten-year-old boy was failing math; the six-year-old boy was a problem to his teacher; the four-year-old girl had an ear infection, and the baby had just given up his morning nap. My husband traveled a great deal, and who can blame him?" While in her doldrums, she had read Thurber's 1957 collection of short pieces and drawings, *Alarms and Diversions*, and discovered that she could still laugh. "I feel that I am in your debt," she added in her letter to Thurber, "and if there is anything I can do for you, you have but to ask. (I frankly cannot imagine what this might be, but I live quite near Washington and perhaps I could do away with someone for you.)" Her return address was Maple Avenue, Falls Church, Virginia.

It was a level of humor he appreciated, and the delighted Thurber replied, "I don't think you know about all the houses I've lived in, because one of them was a house on Maple Avenue in Falls Church, Virginia. This was . . . in the summer of 1901 [actually 1902] when my father had a job in Washington. . . . We had a big backyard and an apple orchard and there were some Seckel pear trees."

The ecstatic Mrs. Acosta tracked down the house with the help of—at times, in spite of—ancient Falls Church citizens and of a snapshot Robert forwarded from Columbus at Thurber's request. The house, she learned, had been built in 1895 by a man named Ogg at the start of his married life; Ogg had soon died, a man named Loving bought it, and it was he who had rented it to Charles Thurber. Though the house had been remodeled drastically, Mrs. Acosta's research proved it to be the one next door to hers.

She celebrated the local Thurber connection by publicizing the exchange of letters in the *Washington Star* (with Thurber's permission). Four years later, the Ogg and Acosta houses were demolished to make way for a housing development. Mrs. Acosta, with the aid of neighbors (a few of whom had never until then heard of James Thurber) persuaded the Falls Church City Council to name the new street—a cul-de-sac—James Thurber Court, which also became the new street address for Mrs. Acosta.

Though only seven that summer of 1902, Thurber collected a basketful of memories of the Falls Church house at 319 Maple Avenue: his father turning the corner at the end of the block on his way home from work, swinging a malacca cane, a common accessory in Washington at the time; the little lead soldiers the Thurber boys played with on the porch; the maid who served dinner in bare feet and who deliberately burned a finger in the kettle steam to try out a salve that a patent-medicine huckster had sold to her as an instant cure for burns.

"I remember that Negro maid," Mame recalled in 1950. "She was so good to Jamie after the accident. She was born on July 6, but I just can't think of her name."

It was during that fateful August in Falls Church, on a Sunday afternoon, that the only real tragedy of Thurber's life occurred: the sickening accident that would eventually blind him. Eight-year-old William, armed with a toy bow and arrow, told his younger brother to stand facing the yard fence while he tried to hit him in the back with the blunt-nosed arrow. "I wouldn't shoot anyone in the back," Thurber says he replied, but he obligingly faced the fence and waited. William, naturally slow of thought and action, took so long fitting arrow to bow and aiming it that Thurber turned to see what was happening—in time for the arrow to smash into his left eye. William said his brother cried from pain and fright, then the pain lessened and the eye didn't appear to bother him. Charles had gone fishing for the day. Mame took the boy to a general practitioner, who dressed the eye. After a few days, the eye began hurting. This time his parents took him to a Washington eye specialist, Dr. Swann Burnett, who told them the eye would have to come out. Thurber's repeated declaration over the years that its instant removal would have saved the good eye is a hypothesis some ophthalmologists feel is difficult to prove, but it became gospel to Thurber, a cause of latter-day lapses into tearful self-pity and a growing anger with his mother and father over their handling of the ghastly event.

His worried parents kept Thurber at home at the "I" Street house in Washington that school year of 1902–03, while his brothers attended Grant Elementary School nearby. "My mother had a Christian Science reader visit us," says Thurber. Charles spent as much time with his injured son as he could. Thurber remembers his father taking him to hear Ohio's Senator Albert Beveridge speak on the floor of the Senate, introducing him to Admiral Robert Peary, the Arctic explorer, in the elevator of the House Office Building, and, after watching the Washington Senators play ball—Thurber's first major-league game—arranging for the boy to visit the players' locker room.

In June 1903, the Thurbers moved back to Columbus, to 625 Oak Street. That fall, the boys attended Sullivant School, a quarter of a mile away, which Thurber would immortalize in his 1935 New Yorker casual "I Went to Sullivant." James was now two grades behind William and only one ahead of Robert.

"I don't remember why Charlie wanted to move so much," Mame said when she was in her eighties. For, between 1892 and 1918, the Thurbers moved fourteen times, nearly always within the same square mile in Columbus. "We moved around so much," says Robert, "that all of us boys were always being told at school that we were in the wrong school district." He was as much at a loss to explain his father's many moves as his mother was. He remembered, in one instance, that there had been the need for a bigger yard for the growing boys and their dogs. "A couple of moves were made to be in different voting districts," he writes. "[The] move we made from 227 S. 17th Street was because of the high cost of heating by steam. . . . I guess our parents were just restless by nature . . . and loved changes of residence." According to Thurber, his father "never made more than fifty dollars a week in his life," but the family was never evicted, Robert says. "My father never had a big salary but he was never behind in the rent, though it was a struggle to keep making ends meet." They frequently had to take in roomers.

With the end of his job in Washington, Charles went back to freelancing his stenographic skills. In the spring of 1905, he was stricken with a near-fatal illness that William describes as "a brain disease." Grandmother Fisher persuaded her husband to take the entire financially destitute Thurber family into their home. The illness and its aftereffects lasted throughout the year. Recovered, Charles moved the family into an apartment in the Norwich Hotel in 1906 and for part of 1907, while he resumed working at temporary clerical jobs. Times were still lean, and the family may have moved back to

Grandfather Fisher's house for a while; twelve-year-old James gave the Bryden Road address as his own when, on April 9, 1907, he signed for his library card at the new Columbus Public Library, the day after it opened.

By 1908, Charles was clerking in the office of the Ohio state dairy and food commissioner, and during the next two years was a clerk again with the state legislature. From 1910 to 1912, he was freelancing his office and organizational skills in local, state, and national Republican campaigns, and once more served as secretary to the chairman of the Republican State Committee. "I sincerely doubt," Robert says, "whether my father could [himself] recall accurately all the positions and temporary jobs he filled from, let's say, 1895 to 1916."

In September 1901, while Charles was still in Washington, President McKinley was assassinated at Buffalo, New York. Charles was devastated by the news. McKinley had been an Ohio congressman for twelve years, and was governor when Charles clerked at the state house. Charles had worked for his election as president. But his despair over McKinley's death was ameliorated by a growing admiration for Theodore Roosevelt, who, as McKinley's vice president, succeeded him and went on to win the 1904 presidential election.

In 1908, declining to run again, Roosevelt arranged the nomination of his secretary of war, William Howard Taft, who was, like McKinley, an Ohioan. But Roosevelt missed the power he had forfeited and became impatient with Taft, whose conservative administration was out of step with the new Republican progressive wing Roosevelt favored. In 1912, at the Republican National Convention in Chicago, after Taft was again nominated, Roosevelt formed the Progressive, or Bull Moose, Party, and ran against both Taft and the Democratic candidate, Woodrow Wilson.

Charles Thurber, until then an unswervingly loyal member of the Buckeye Republican Club and a supporter of regular Republican tickets, became secretary of the Progressive State Campaign Committee in Ohio, eagerly working for Teddy Roosevelt's election. The Progressive campaign split the Republican vote and allowed Wilson to win. When it was over, Thurber writes, "the state organizer of the Bull Moose Party [Charles] got six dozen yellow Mongol pencils, a few typewriter ribbons, and several boxes of stationery."

It wasn't quite over. In 1913, asked to give his father's occupation upon enrolling at Ohio State University, Thurber, perhaps in some embarrassment, put down "Secretary of the Progressive State Committee." Charles stayed with the ever-hopeful Progressives through the 1914 election year, campaigning for James Garfield, a Cleveland lawyer and son of the former president. Garfield ran on the fading Republican Progressive ticket for governor of Ohio. He lost. Charles was also keeping a candle in the window in case his hero, Teddy Roosevelt, decided to run again. After two years of defeat at both the national and state level, the committee had no money to pay Charles for his services. The months following Wilson's victory found Charles "doing occasional political work, while not employed regularly," according to Robert.

In 1916, Charles was appointed cashier of the municipal court, a job he kept until 1923, when Mayor James J. Thomas, looking for a secretary who knew the local press, hired him. Thomas had offered the job to young James, who was covering Capitol Square for the *Columbus Evening Dispatch*, as it was then called. But by then Thurber was happily writing a Sunday column, and he politely but quickly refused the mayor's offer. Lunching in a restaurant across the street from City Hall, the mayor found himself sharing a table with Charles, whom he had never met. Charles introduced himself. The mayor asked his relationship, if any, to Thurber of the *Dispatch*, and told Charles he had just offered his son the job of secretary but had been refused. That evening, Charles telephoned James, who was by then married and living in an apartment nearby, and told him that he would be interested in the job himself. Thurber agreed to talk to the mayor the next day, but the mayor, impressed by Charles and having consulted friends who knew him, had already made up his mind to offer the elder Thurber the job. That, at least, is the story Thurber permitted to circulate. Perhaps he pleaded his father's case to the mayor and didn't want his newspaper associates to know.

With Mayor Thomas running successfully on a stand-pat ticket throughout the prosperous twenties, Charles held the job until the end of 1931. By then the Depression had soured voters on Republicans, and Thomas lost to a Democrat, taking Charles out the door with him.

His nine years as secretary to the mayor were the happiest of Charles's life. After seven years in an anonymous role in the municipal court, he now had to be reckoned with as a principal guardian and interpreter of the mayor's office. In ceremonial matters, he frequently was designated acting mayor when Thomas was out of town. He welcomed visiting dignitaries in the name of Columbus, and was called upon to give after-dinner speeches. According to a 1927 local newspaper feature about Charles, "anyone desiring an interview with the mayor . . . will first meet Mr. Thurber, and may not get to 'hizzoner' unless that meeting is considered absolutely necessary."

Charles was on the job less than four months when he lost another favorite president and Ohioan whom he had known personally: Warren G. Harding died of apoplexy in San Francisco, in August 1923. Charles had been employed by the state legislature when Harding was first elected to the Ohio Senate in 1900, and, later, worked for the state ticket on which Harding was elected lieutenant governor. In 1910, Charles contributed his services to Harding's campaign for governor of Ohio. Harding lost.

One cause of Harding's death is thought to have been his anguish after reading a confidential report that several of his cabinet officers had been caught in larcenous and criminal activities. The scandals had not been publicized when Charles, acting for Mayor Thomas, innocently honored the late president in a mayoral proclamation he may have hoped would top Walt Whitman's eulogy to Lincoln: "Our beloved President is dead," Charles wrote. "The chief has fallen. Columbus, which knew him so well and loved him as a friend and neighbor, mourns with the nation. . . . He was peculiarly and eminently the one man for these unsettled times. . . . Let us all, then, rededicate ourselves as citizens of the republic and resolve to profit by the lesson of citizenship so well taught us by the captain who has gone."

He followed this with a telegram to Washington asking that Harding's body be allowed to lie in state in the Ohio capitol before its burial in Marion, Ohio. So it was.

Besides having worked for Harding's election, Charles may have felt a kinship because of Harding's fondness for baseball. Charles and his sons were all obsessed followers of the game, and among Harding's last words were "How did the Cincinnati Reds come out yesterday?" One aches for the ever-honest and idealistic Charles, imagining his shocked Victorian reaction to revelations that exposed Harding's administration as the most corrupt since that of U. S. Grant—or the pained disillusion he must have felt when Harding's dalliance with a married woman in Marion surfaced; or when Nan Britton, Harding's New York mistress, who had a child by him, told all in a book published in 1926.

Reporters covering City Hall frequently made mention of the likable Charles Thurber in their stories. He is pictured buying the first poppy for a Memorial Day celebration. He greets Betty Fox, a champion flagpole sitter—a popular fad of the period—and makes her an honorary city official. A news photo features Charles showing Miss Fox a sheaf of blueprints prior to her sitting atop the flagpole of the Chittenden Hotel. ("She evinced much interest in the Civic Center plans which were explained to her by Secretary Thurber," the caption reads.) In a 1930 newspaper feature, Charles is shown shaking hands with young Fred Waring, who was in Columbus with his glee club of Pennsylvanians for a concert. And what to do about mail in foreign languages received by the mayor's office? another article asked. "His official position demands that Mr. Thurber act as a matrimonial agent, information bureau, lost and found department, and a buffer for Mayor Thomas, but nothing was said when he accepted the position that he had to be a linguist."

Charles, having the time of his life, collected all such items and turned them over to Robert, who had begun his family scrapbooks in 1922. In turn, Charles kept the press buttered up. "What success has been mine," he said in a press release, "has been due largely to my close association with members of the newspaper profession in whom I have the utmost confidence. I have always been for them and I have endeavored to work with them in all my political connections."

When in Washington, Charles had made friends with George Hugh Marvin, a Cleveland newspaper political reporter assigned to the Washington press corps. A hopeless practical joker, Marvin and Mame Thurber became unholy collaborators. Marvin was, Thurber recalls in *The Thurber Album*, "a superior wag, with a round mobile face, a trick of protruding his large eyeballs that entranced the Thurber boys, and a gift of confusion that matched my mother's." Together, Mame and Marvin tormented the shopkeepers of the District of Columbia, ordering one dish of ice cream with two spoons, or one glove for the left hand, or one shoe. Upon the inevitable refusal, the two would leave in pretended outrage, with Marvin shouting, "Senator Beveridge will hear about this!"

Later, when Marvin was in Columbus covering the state government, he and Mame teamed up again. During a meeting held by a woman faith healer at Memorial Hall, Marvin wheeled a bundled-up Mame down the aisle of the auditorium in a purloined wheelchair. The lecturer's high-pitched theme was an offer from the Lord—belief in Him in exchange for being able to do once again whatever you had come to believe you could do no longer. During a pregnant pause in the sermon, Mame leaped from the wheelchair and announced that she could walk again, thanks to the inspiring message she had just heard. The surprised and grateful evangelist shouted, "Hallelujah, sister!" Then Marvin faced the audience, bulged out his eyes, dropped a twisted jaw, and announced that he, too, found that what he had not done for some time he was doing now—losing his mind. The wheelchair was recognized by its owner, and in the following confusion the terrible two made their escape.

Charles, portrayed by Thurber as uncomfortable and unhappy with Mame's antics, may actually have appreciated many of them. He and Mame belonged to the Frioleras, a social club Mame had joined as a single woman (its members had attended her wedding). The group staged dramatic skits and harmless practical jokes, activities to which Charles was a willing and able contributor. And Charles had his own fun with his friend Marvin. General Dan Sickles, who lost his leg during the battle of Gettysburg, was on the same speakers' platform with Marvin once in Columbus. All the speakers made moving reference to the General's leg having been sacrificed in the Union cause. When Charles, the master of ceremonies, introduced Marvin, he ended his remarks by saying, "Let me now introduce you to George Hugh Marvin, who lost his *head* at the battle of Gettysburg." It wasn't a joke Thurber would have coveted, but it got picked up as an anecdote in the *Reader's Digest.*

"All the Thurbers were funny," Joel Sayre recalls. "Their father was quiet, but he could be funny, too, in a dry, sweet way. He accepted the circus with good humor. His humor was different from Mame's. She went for practical jokes, which require props. Charlie Thurber was a practitioner of the better kind of humor. You might have to wait for it but sooner or later it came out in a droll remark."

The writer John McNulty became acquainted with Thurber when both were Columbus newspapermen, and, before Thurber was married, McNulty sometimes visited him at the Thurber house at 330 Gay Street. Having listened to the muttered, patient asides Charles would make in the midst of the endless domestic uproar that Mame and the boys normally maintained, McNulty told Sayre years later that he found Charles unquestionably the funniest member of the family. He was also, McNulty commented upon news of Charles's death in 1939, "a good-minded man."

There is ample evidence that, as Thurber remarks in "Gentleman from Indiana," "Charley Thurber was the most beloved man in city hall." Unlike so many petty bureaucrats with surrogate power, Charles never took advantage of his position to act arrogantly, show favor, flaunt his delegated authority, or behave dishonestly or unethically. After his retirement from the mayor's office, a Sunday newspaper in 1932 noted: "In spite of [his] long and varied public and party service, [Charles] Thurber retains the energy and enthusiasm of his youthful days. His recent nine years in the mayor's office . . . was a supreme test of difficult, long-sustained service. He is still the same old efficient, cheerful and courteous 'Charlie' Thurber that he was at the beginning of his career."

Jake Meckstroth, a reporter who covered City Hall and eventually became editor of the *Columbus Citizen-Journal,* assesses Charles and his work in this way: "He was a good man, though not brilliant. Charlie was a hard worker and what you'd call a propaganda writer. That is, he'd write campaign literature for the candidates. He wasn't a bad idea man. He knew the issues inside out and would make appropriate suggestions to the candidates on what to use in their speeches. He was able to tell them, and pretty accurately, what points certain newspaper reporters were bound to pick up and use."

Deprived of his childhood, Charles did his best to make sure his sons had one, and often shared it with them. He took their questions seriously, participated in their games, and did his best to indulge them. Children are flattered by nonpatronizing adult attention, and their playmates regarded the Thurber boys as lucky to have a father like Charles, who was fond of memory games, riddles, and puzzles. Earl Fisher remembered often visiting the Thurber home and envying his cousins its permissive atmosphere. "Uncle Charlie would sit there with all of us kids and play a game or two," he said.

"The neighborhood kids liked to play at our house," Robert adds. "They knew they could run wild there. Other homes might have signs on the lawn keeping them off the grass. Like all youngsters, we lost our tempers and had fights, but our father was very patient, had a nice way with children, and the kids all liked him."

It was Charles's fascination with baseball that made fans of his sons. Across Parsons Avenue from the Thurbers' first house was a large lake of green lawn, enclosed by an iron-spiked fence, that reached to the back of Grandfather Fisher's property on Bryden Road. It was the grounds of the Ohio State School for the Blind, which fielded a baseball team that rarely lost at home, thanks to a topography the school's players knew well and took advantage of. There was, for example, a tree between first and second base to confound the opposing team.

Thurber was not encouraged by his parents to play baseball. He wore glasses over an artificial eye, and, following his eye surgery and convalescence, Charles and Mame had been warned by the doctor to keep him from the running, jumping, racing, and roughhouse activities of growing boys. His playmates regarded his thick spectacles and passiveness as disqualifiers when they chose up sides. Impressed by his parents' continued concern, Thurber became more of an observer of games than a participant, and none fascinated him more than those played on the field of "the Blinkies." The allure of their Saturday games, practically in his grandfather's backyard, also included the relief they provided Thurber from the restrictive life within the Fisher home when the Thurbers stayed there.

Thurber pays tribute to "the Blinkies" in "The Tree on the Diamond," faithfully mimicking the accent and shouts of the team's colorful manager, Frank James. But according to Robert, it was Charles who first became a fascinated follower of the school's ball team. Robert remembers his father's running discussions of the games that were played on the cramped diamond behind the school, and believes that it was Charles's interest that aroused Thurber's.

The Thurber males were enthusiastic followers of the Columbus Senators, the city's professional ball team, which was organized in 1902 and played on the newly constructed Neil Park field. The team took the league pennant in

1905, 1906, and 1907, beating out its chief rival, the Toledo Mud Hens. In 1909, Charles took Robert on the train to Toledo for the Fourth of July game between the two teams. Robert remembers it as one of the most exciting days in both their lives. Columbus won in the eighteenth inning. "Probably I was taken to baseball games more often than my brothers, being such an intense lover of the game," Robert writes, "but they also went along on numerous occasions and were always welcome." (One can speculate with probable accuracy about what Thurber would have said years later, when the successor to the Columbus team became the premier farm club of the New York Yankees, whom Thurber detested.)

Charles also taught his sons bowling, at which he was expert, and was exhilarated at being asked by the Ohio governor to represent him at the official opening of the state bowling tournament in Columbus. Thurber writes of his father: "He was addicted to contests . . . of any kind. . . . He would estimate the number of beans in an enormous jar, write essays, make up slogans, find the hidden figures in trick drawings, write the last line of an unfinished jingle or limerick, praise a product in twenty-five words or fewer, get thousands of words out of a trade name. . . . But it was on proverb contests and book- and play-title contests, run by newspapers, that he worked hardest."

Robert's family scrapbooks have pages of newspaper clippings noting Charles's contest triumphs. "My father often had sidelines to supplement his income while he held public offices," Robert writes. "[Besides] working on . . . picture and puzzle contests conducted by newspapers and magazines, he did quite a bit of typing for individuals in his spare time. . . . He engaged in these activities also while waiting for a . . . regular job, or at the end of a [political] campaign."

In December 1933, no longer employed regularly and recently defeated for the state legislature, sixty-six-year-old Charles drove to upstate New York with Robert to visit newspaper offices, trying to sell their ideas for contests, puzzles, and pamphlets of quotations or historical facts as circulation promotions. At that low point of the Great Depression, no enterprise was considered too gimmicky or undignified if it might bring in a dollar.

They then drove to New York City without calling Thurber in advance, and decided to drop in on him at the *New Yorker*. Directed to the editorial floor by the elevator operator, they began wandering the halls. Thurber hadn't arrived as yet, and Katharine White found the two tall, lean, bewildered strangers outside her office door. Katharine, at age forty-one, had earned the right to a proprietary attitude toward the magazine, its people, and its editorial operations. Almost from the start, she had been the principal counselor to the editor, Harold Ross, helping him to know what he wanted for his periodical and how to publish it literately and attractively. She saw herself as housemother to the contributors, staff writers, and editors. In a sharp, authoritative manner honed by eight years of dealing with professional associates chronically disposed to emotional collapse and organizational chaos, she asked Charles and Robert who they were and what they wanted.

"We felt as if we'd been caught robbing the place," Robert said. "My father explained we were Jim's brother and dad. The *New Yorker* had just been publishing Jim's pieces about his family that came out as *My Life and Hard Times*, and Mrs. White was as nice to us as could be. It occurred to me later maybe she thought we'd sneaked in to blow up the place for revenge, and was trying to humor us until she could find Jim. We did see him, but not for long. We couldn't stay. We didn't have the money."

The conclusion among biographers that Charles was a born loser, of only glancing importance to the Thurber story, has been the conventional wisdom for so long that it may seem quixotic to re-examine it. St. Clair McKelway, the managing editor of the *New Yorker* in the 1930s, was among those who cheerfully paid the price of Thurber's companionship by listening to his occasional evening-long confessional diatribes. McKelway believed that it was easy to be misled by Thurber's airy and ambivalent literary treatment of his father. "You can't really find in what Thurber wrote about his father what he really thought about him," McKelway says. "It wasn't all that clear to himself. No one who loved his mother as Thurber did finds it easy to make peace with his father, however real or fancied the reasons. What Thurber really felt toward his father would have put most writers out of business, or kept them from becoming one."

Nobody could consider Charles Thurber the best of family providers. Even Robert, who all his life lovingly regarded both parents as his best friends, writes: "I always thought that my father was just a little too self-effacing for his own good; he was always helping someone else get a position he desired, but was possibly just not aggressive enough so far as *his* . . . future [was] concerned."

Yet, from the several "what success has been mine" references in Charles's public comments, it seems likely that if his accomplishments didn't fit others' conceptions of success, they often fitted his own. While his positions on the economic and social charts of the day may have ranked low, Charles could have been measuring his progress by how far he had come, which was from well behind the starting line for most of those he worked with.

Fatherless, in all likelihood an unwanted, illegitimate child, sent to board in a strange city by an ailing mother, selling newspapers in the morning darkness to help support her, forced to forfeit a high-school education to work in a bakery while learning stenography and typing at night, Charles Thurber still managed to realize a number of the Walter Mitty fantasies all young men nourish. Few marry their first and only love, the girl of their dreams, as did Charles, and one from a comparatively affluent and locally prestigious family at that. Fewer can claim a relationship of mutual devotion over forty-seven years, which all three Thurber boys agree characterized that of their parents. If Charles was by nature nervous, reticent, thoughtful, and worried, and Mame was outgoing and self-assured in a slightly scatterbrained way, it resulted in a compatible synergism, perhaps comparable to that of Jack Spratt and his wife, of nursery-rhyme fame.

It has been suggested that Mame's antics were antidotes to the boredom of living with a dull husband, but Robert points out that Mame lived at the same manic high long before marriage. Nor was Charles all that subservient to her. "Each respected the other's feelings and as a rule raised no objection to [one another's] desires or decisions," he writes. "My mother was more aggressive while my father was more retiring, but there was no conflict. A wonderfully devoted couple."

In later years, if Charles wasn't always up to the bedlam that had become his family's lifestyle, he accepted most of it in good temper and learned how to avoid it when it became too much. "My father frequently slept in the attic to get away from any possible uproar or undue noise," Robert writes. "He required a great deal of rest and sleep and consequently selected a quiet spot."

At work, favors were few in coming, as were the political victories necessary for the rewards of patronage. Presenting a cheerful front was part of Charles's personal code, and when bad luck continued to dog his career he kept his festering anxieties to himself, a practice thought to have helped bring on the prolonged illness in 1905 that nearly took his life. Today's employee benefits were nonexistent in Charles's time. He worked ten- and twelve-hour days, with no job security, no compensation in the several instances when he was laid off, no unemployment doles from the government, no employee health insurance or pension plan. The union movement was gaining strength by the turn of the century but would not benefit government employees for years to come.

Most of his contemporaries saw Charlie Thurber as a successful person on a number of counts. He had a consistently pleasant life at home, one that probably eluded most of his more prominent colleagues. "Pop," or "Pa," or "Papa," as they called him, was a friend and hero to his boys through their formative years. His wife and his eldest and youngest sons loved him and defended his memory until their deaths. A worshipful William says: "When [my father] worked on state presidential-election committees, there were Harvard graduates on them who were both surprised and impressed with the effective and well-written speeches my father wrote."

Robert speaks for William and Mame, too, when he writes:

> I admired my father for his many wonderful qualities and never gave a thought to his lack of material gains. [He] seldom became real angry at anyone, although at times he was obviously upset and extremely annoyed. He was a very friendly, gentle, unselfish and tolerant person. It was often said that anyone who could not get along with my father could not get along with anyone. . . . Naturally at times the three of us [boys] would do something that made him nervous and he would admonish us firmly, but not harshly. I recall on occasion when disturbed over someone's remark or behavior he would raise his voice and . . . say, "You would try the patience of a saint!"

It is unlikely that Thurber recognized many of his father's influences on him, concealed as they were in the ordinariness of family routine. Charles augmented his education with countless hours of reading at the public libraries of Indianapolis and Columbus. The librarian of the Columbus Public Library was asked years later, by a reporter looking into the background of the city's famous son, if she remembered seeing Thurber in the reading room there a great deal of the time. She certainly did, she replied, and added that she saw his father there just as often. If Charles didn't actively encourage Thurber to read, he provided a parental example. Grandfather Fisher is credited with naming Thurber after his friend the Methodist pastor James Grover, but Grover was also the city's first librarian, and Charles, with his love of books, would have sponsored the choice of names with equal enthusiasm.

Literature professors at Ohio State University would later open Thurber's mind to what the best writers are capable of, and the early successes of his college soul mate, the playwright and actor Elliott Nugent, would stay a shining reminder to Thurber that a career in the arts was not so wild a dream. But the prospect of writing for a living may have seeded itself in his mind long before. In his later years, Thurber would say that he knew he was going to be a writer from age seven, though his friend Joel Sayre commented that this might only have been Thurber's Friday night position, to be superseded by a different autobiographical declaration on Monday. Still, as a handicapped, bookish youngster, he was open to suggestions, overt or subliminal. Charles may have inadvertently provided one or two.

Charles's work compelled him to keep up with all the city and state newspapers. It was in those he brought home that Thurber came to know the comic strips of the day—said to have helped condition the doodling that evolved into his art—and the columns of the *Ohio State Journal*'s editor, Robert Ryder, which Thurber would claim as one of his everlasting models of light, subjective writing. Thurber also gained an early and practical appreciation of typewriters, thanks to watching his father at work on his Underwood. And through his father Thurber was introduced to many of the local journalists he admired as a young man, including Ryder. Charles helped in more direct ways, as well. During World War I, Thurber was turned down by the military because of his eyesight and sought civil service. Charles asked press acquaintances in Washington to assist in getting Thurber his job as a code clerk with the State Department, and accompanied his son to Washington to make the introductions and ensure that there would be no hitches.

In a June 1918 letter to Elliott Nugent, Thurber expresses wonder that his father, a well-known Ohio Republican, has been able to pull strings to help get him a job in a Democratic administration. "We had newspaper influence for the most part on this thing," he writes. "I have been surprised and pleased to find out that political pull under the present regime here is not the *sine qua non* it was wont to be." And he sounds a note of apprehension at being left by his father: "Dad goes back tomorrow and I will be like a painted ship upon a painted ocean. . . . Papa asks me to add his best regards and luck."

Thurber had taken with him to Washington a classic case of girl problem. He had nurtured a seventh-grade infatuation with a classmate, Eva Prout, who, shortly afterward, had become a child actress in silent films. Now, in 1918, her mother had recently returned with Eva to nearby Zanesville, and, miracle of miracles, Eva was answering his letters. Then there was Minnette Fritts, a popular Ohio State coed he had dated and sometimes brought home to visit with the family on Gay Street. Which one should he ask to be "his girl"?

Unsure of his Washington address before he left home, Thurber had told both young women to write to him in care of his family. Mame forwarded their letters and asked Thurber about them. Mame and Charles knew and liked Minnie Fritts, but Charles, especially, had his puritanical doubts about Eva, who had lived the suspect life of an actress. Perhaps, too, after twenty-six years of marriage to Mame, he hoped to save his middle son from a life with any woman who showed an instinct for theatrics. He pointedly sent Thurber a newspaper clipping reporting that Minnette was leaving Columbus for Red Cross training.

"My folks are very strong for her," Thurber continues to Nugent. "Indeed I received some weeks ago a very remarkable letter from my father full of mellow advice . . . that I do or say nothing to jeopardize my relations with Minnette and be not too sure of the felicity of things Eva. . . . The folks of course remember very clearly my terrible schooldays case on Eva."

Years later, on the eve of his marriage to Helen, his second wife, a confused and uncertain Thurber wrote Eva that he was about to visit his family and wished to stop by Zanesville to see her. Was she still married? Eva, fearful that he would not get her warm and welcoming reply in time, enclosed it in a letter to his parents. Worried for their son and hopeful that his upcoming marriage would save him from his chaotic, self-destructive single life, Mame and Charles kept Eva's note a secret. Thurber managed to see Eva briefly, anyway. And though contentedly married to Helen, when he learned of the withheld note, he decided that it had been an unforgivable interference with his life, one he blamed mostly on his father, probably with cause.

Despite all the distractions Thurber found in Paris from October 1918 to February 1920, he dutifully sandwiched in letters to his family—addressed primarily to Robert—between those to Nugent and other former classmates. The Thurbers tried to reply as frequently, and in one of his letters to his son, Charles apologizes for not writing more often. Thurber solicitously replies in his next letter home, "I realize how busy papa is, and tell him not to feel at all that I do not understand it. . . . I know he would like to write more, but Lord knows he has enough other things to keep him busy."

It seems natural and necessary for children to outgrow their parents, to see them more objectively from the vantage point of adulthood. Thurber continued to revere his mother long after declaring his emancipation from her and the family. His impression of his father steadily faded from that of boyhood idol to one of the lesser mortals. Robert (and William to a lesser extent) seems never to have acquired the self-reliance needed to free him from a lifelong emotional dependency on both parents. But Thurber was eagerly committed to self-inquiry and soon matching himself and his family against his new friends in the university and abroad. After his return from Europe in 1920, the Thurber home became for him little more than a congenial and inexpensive place to live while he got on with his career.

This was remembered and resented by Robert when he reviewed Thurber's relations with Charles. "My father and Jim got along fine," he writes. "He never got angry at [Jim] that I can recall. [But] Jim kept to himself a lot after he got back from Paris. . . . He was seldom in the open about his plans or activities. He did not like arguments and avoided scenes whenever possible in those days. . . . He didn't confide in us much anymore. . . . We didn't know he was engaged to Althea until we read it in the papers."

Robert never forgave Althea Adams, who married Thurber in 1922, for what he saw as her superior attitude toward Thurber's family. And because her disdain seemed evident from the first introduction, Robert wondered whether her negative feelings toward his family had been conditioned by Thurber's.

Thurber has left no recorded indication of disrespect for his father, not even when Charles eagerly took the job in the mayor's office which Thurber had turned down. In his weekly Credos and Curios column for the *Dispatch*, he composed what he called "Dad Dialogs," in which Thurber argues the contemporary state of mores and literature with a mythical father, a contrivance that might have been suggested by a book-reading Charles—though by then Thurber would have found few of his father's cultural biases worthy of challenge.

By the early thirties, in New York, Thurber was writing funny letters about his family to his perennial love, Ann Honeycutt, and to others. In speakeasies or apartments around town, he could also be counted upon for dramatic monologs, skillfully crafted and acted out, which pictured him and his Columbus family in one ridiculous predicament after another. His audiences urged him to write them down.

A few literary humorists, most notably Robert Benchley and Clarence Day, were making their families subject material, but their gently whimsical references to relatives elicit affable chuckles, not belly laughs. Thurber set no such constraints on himself when he finally decided to write out what he had been verbalizing and pantomiming for months. The short pieces, engagingly supported by his ludicrous illustrations, immediately made literary history when they were published as *My Life and Hard Times*, the book for which Thurber is universally remembered.

Some believe that Thurber had qualms about offering the stories for publication, for he seems to have released them in one dollop, in what may have been an "Oh, what the hell!" decision. Others say that Harold Ross hesitated to begin any series by a writer until a sufficient number of the pieces were in hand, ensuring a fast-paced continuity. They appeared in the *New Yorker* in one glorious starburst—eight flawless "casuals" (short, personal pieces, in the magazine's parlance) in thirteen weeks, July 8 to September 30, 1933. ("The

Dog that Bit People" was included in *My Life and Hard Times*, but never printed in the *New Yorker*.)

Everybody in the family, including the dogs, contributes to elaborate mis-understandings that sustain magnificent confusions somehow constructed to defy rational resolution. "Mamma" does plenty of outlandish things but somehow remains a respected figure in control of her situations. "Father," on the other hand, is as much a hapless victim of circumstance as Charlie Chaplin's tramp. He not only doesn't understand his wife and sons, but he is afraid of them, and the humor springs from his doomed efforts to assume the tradi-tional roles of father and husband.

In "The Night the Bed Fell," Charles is sleeping in the attic, "to be away where he could think." Mamma is worried that the ancient bed in the attic will collapse and Charles will be killed by the heavy bedstead falling on him. Thurber's Army cot accidentally overturns in the night, setting off hysterical misapprehensions by everyone on the second floor. "Let's go to your poor father!" Mamma shouts, believing her fears have been realized and pounding on the attic door, which is stuck. Charles, awakened, thinks the house is on fire and catches cold prowling around in his bare feet, asking, "What in the name of God is going on here?"

In "The Car We Had to Push," Thurber writes: "My father used to get sick at his stomach pushing the car, and very often was unable to go to work." Thurber's brother "Roy," given to playing jokes on his father, gathers kitchen articles in a square of canvas and attaches this under the family Reo, the utensils and tins ready to fall on the road at the twitch of a string. "This was a little scheme of Roy's to frighten father, who had always expected the car might explode. It worked perfectly." Charles, the innocent passenger, is prop-erly startled by the clatter of the released metal objects. " 'Stop the *car!*' shouted father. 'I can't,' Roy said. 'The engine fell out.' 'God Almighty!' said father. . . . We finally had to drive back and pick up the stuff and even father knew the difference between the works of an automobile and the equipment of a pantry."

In "More Alarms at Night," Roy pretends to be delirious, goes to his father's room, shakes Charles awake, and tells him, "Buck, your time has come!"

"My father's name," Thurber writes, "was not Buck but Charles, nor had he ever been called Buck. He was a tall, mildly nervous, peaceable gen-tleman, given to quiet pleasures, and eager that everything should run smoothly. . . . My father leaped out of bed, on the side away from his son, rushed from the room, locked the door behind him, and shouted us all up."

Roy then pretends to be asleep, and denies that he had awakened his father, a story his mother accepts. "You had a dream," Mamma tells her husband. "My father," adds Thurber, "*had* been known to have nightmares, usually about Lillian Russell and President Cleveland, who chased him."

On another night it is Thurber, unable to sleep while trying to recall the name "Perth Amboy," who awakens his father, demanding, "Name some towns in New Jersey quick!"

It must have been around three in the morning. Father got up, keeping the bed between him and me, and started to pull his trousers on. "Don't bother about dressing," I said. "Just name some towns in New Jersey." While he hastily pulled on his clothes . . . father began to name, in a shaky voice, various New Jersey cities. I can still see him reaching for his coat without taking his eyes off me. "Newark," he said, "Jersey City, Atlantic City, Elizabeth, Paterson, Passaic, Trenton, Jersey City, Trenton, Paterson—" "It has two names," I snapped. "Elizabeth and Paterson," he said. "No, no!" I told him, irritably. "This is one town with one name, but there are two words in it, like helter-skelter." "Helter-skelter," said my father, moving slowly toward the bedroom door and smiling in a faint, strained way which . . . was meant to humor me. When he was within a few paces of the door, he fairly leaped for it and ran out into the hall, his coat-tails and shoelaces flying. . . . "Mary! Roy! Herman!" he shouted. . . .

"*Now*, what?" demanded my mother. . . . She was capable, fortunately, of handling any two of us and she never in her life was alarmed by the words or actions of any one of us. . . .

"Get to bed, both of you," she said. "I don't want to hear any more out of you tonight. Dressing and tearing up and down the hall at this hour in the morning!"

Though in theory the master of the house, Charles is frequently cast as the vulnerable victim of the Thurber servants. Mrs. Doody "went berserk while doing the dishes," writes Thurber, "and, under the impression that father was the Antichrist, pursued him several times up the backstairs and down the front. He had been sitting quietly over his coffee in the living room when she burst in from the kitchen waving a bread knife. . . . Mother . . . appearing on the scene in the midst of it all, got the quick and mistaken impression that father was chasing Mrs. Doody." ("I don't think any servant chased my father with a knife," Robert volunteers, in a needless effort to put the record straight. However, Mrs. Robertson, who did the Thurbers' washing for a time, would sometimes stare at Charles and suddenly tell him, "Look out!" and *"Dey ain't no way!"* ("It upset him for days," writes Thurber.) Another maid fires a revolver at her lover in her room in the Thurber house, and the man escapes into Charles's bedroom, shouting at him to get out of the house before he's killed.

Thurber enjoyed an appreciative audience above all else, and when he found that certain material worked he stayed with it. He needed one rational and sober character for comic contrast to those given to zany or hysterical behavior, and Charles drew the role of fall guy. It was some time before the family began to realize and resent the fact that Thurber's fiction failed to disguise his father adequately. As the put-upon victim, Charles was simply not all that different from reality.

Thurber would have vehemently denied that hostility toward any of his family ever showed up in his art. Though his obvious exaggerations signaled the fictitious nature of My *Life and Hard Times,* once his mother and brothers had overcome their surprise at its success and their mixed feelings about their literary participation in it, they began to wonder whether a subtle, vengeful attitude was behind Thurber's playful put-downs of Charles, and if, perhaps, in some degree it extended to *them.*

The dedication of My *Life and Hard Times* reads "For Mary A. Thurber"; none of Thurber's other books similarly acknowledged his father, though Charles lived to see six of them published. E. B. White was to say that when Thurber repeated a story that stretched truth beyond recognition, Thurber himself came to believe the invented version. It's possible that Thurber's portrayals of Charles, as much more of a dull, hapless, wife-dominated, laughable, and ineffectual husband and father than anyone remembers his having been, turned gradually into Thurber's personal perception of him. "Jim wasn't as close to his father in later years as he had been, and I'm sure my father sensed it," Robert writes.

> It did seem to me that there was a resentment of some kind building up over the years. Several times when I was in New York . . . I recall several remarks of Jim's that surprised me. "Pop was never a big man." "We boys just grew up like Topsy" [inferring neglect]. Jim never went out of his way to praise my father [but] would mildly belittle [him] (not to my father but to me) such as the way my father threw a baseball, or attempted to repair something around the house, or give his version of some current problem or situation. As far as any mechanical ability in

the family . . . I might add that we boys were little more adept than he was.

But that may be the point, for clearly Thurber saw, and came to resent, much in his father that he saw in himself. "He had never liked the machine," Thurber writes of his father in "The Car We Had to Push," "sharing my ignorance and suspicion of all automobiles of twenty years ago and longer."

This was a rare concession for Thurber, who seldom admitted, in either public or private expression, that his self-deprecating humor usually drew upon the jittery apprehensions, absentmindedness, and inadequacies he felt had been handed down to him by his father. The more acceptable features of his lineage, he always believed, were from his mother. Charles had an encyclopedic capacity for names, dates, and events, which made him an expert solver of newspaper contests and puzzles. Yet Thurber credits his own remarkable memory to Mame alone.

Caught up in a belated process of self-discovery in his twenties, Thurber had come to fear his biological makeup on his father's side. At age twenty-five, he was writing to Elliott Nugent that he had decided "never to bring any children into this old vale to inherit the Thurber nervousness which is sure constitutional if anything ever was."

Much of what Thurber sees as frustrating and handicapping his father seems indigenous to them both, but only once or twice does he redeem the elder Thurber by a sympathetic acknowledgment of their common plight; more often, he distances himself from Charles in his writing, with a patronizing attitude and a cream pie in the face. He may have made his own social and mechanical inadequacies his stock in trade as a humorist (thereby beating others to the laugh), but privately those are never laughing matters to a man battling an inferiority complex. To call writers of comic pieces "humorists," he writes in "Preface to a Life," "is to miss the nature of their dilemma and the dilemma of their nature. The little wheels of their invention are set in motion by the damp hand of melancholy."

Though Thurber had the genius to create a world of his own in which he safely prevailed, Charles did not, and Thurber shows little mercy. Charles's record as a parent was increasingly subject to his son's recall and negative revision. In a letter to Elizabeth Acosta in 1957, Thurber reviews the afternoon his eye was injured: "My father was on a fishing trip, of course, when I got hurt," he writes.

Why "of course"? Charles was no outdoorsman frequently absent from home. Was Mame less responsible? What Robert and William saw as the behavior of a kindly, gentle, permissive parent Thurber saw as neglect and impotence, fostering an environment in which it was all too easy to grow up in the same image—that of a "pussycat," a label Thurber dreaded and would always fear he merited.

In 1949, when he had begun reviewing his past in preparation for *The Thurber Album*, he wrote "Teacher's Pet," a short story that startled Thurber followers, who had come to expect his special brand of humorous self-exposure, word games, and satirical comment. This piece seemed spawned by some childhood defeat Thurber had finally decided to deal with decades later:

> It set in train, as all Kelby's moments of weakness did, discomforting thoughts that took him back as far as his youth. It carried him relentlessly, against his will, to the awful day before the First World War when Zeke Leonard had faced him down, with a crowd of eager kids looking on and expecting a fight. Kelby marvelled that at fifty he still could not get that day out of his consciousness for very long. . . .
>
> . . . Leonard . . . had . . . started teasing him after school (they were in the eighth grade) by calling him "Willber, dear!" in a shrill falsetto. . . . His teacher . . . had called him "Willber, dear" one afternoon in the hearing of Zeke and several other kids. . . . Zeke Leonard . . . had hated Willber from the time they were seven for his intelligence, his name, his frail body, and his inability, according to Zeke, to do anything except study.
>
> . . . The grinning Zeke had pushed him, slapped him, bumped him, and kicked him around, holding one arm behind his back and calling attention to this handicap. Kelby had flailed his shorter arms a few times with ludicrous ineffectiveness, and then he had merely tried to cover his face against Zeke's pummelling. Finally, he had started to cry. The other boys had laughed and hooted and whistled.

Kelby, thirty-seven years later, encounters a similar situation in which one schoolboy is bullying the other. Kelby intervenes, harshly sending the bully on his way and then turns on the victim, Elbert, a bright, studious, intellectual boy, as Kelby had been at that age:

> [Elbert] was sniffling and whimpering. "Shut up!" shouted Kelby. "Shut up!" But the boy kept on. Kelby looked at his quivering lower lip and at the convulsion of his stomach [and] was suddenly upon him. He grabbed him tightly by the shoulders and shook him until his head bobbed back and forth. He let go of the boy's left shoulder and slapped

him on the cheek. "You little crybaby!" sobbed Kelby. "You goddam little coward!"

Thurber's later compulsions to argue, antagonize, and brawl when he was drinking may have had their roots in some childhood, schoolyard humiliation he frequently relived, needing to prove again and again that he was no sniveling crybaby.

Whatever else Thurber thought of Grandfather Fisher's arrogance, the old man had never been a pussycat. For a time, however, Thurber had wondered about Grandfather's manliness, too: he hadn't fought in the Civil War. Then he learned that the old man had been one of the home guard "squirrel hunters," with a military-reservist role to play, saving that side of the family's honor at least. And Mame showed her Fisher too often to be suspect.

There were father-son similarities Thurber couldn't ignore. His handwriting had been formed in the graceful Palmer method taught by women schoolteachers of the period, and eventually approached Charles's neat and almost effeminate Spencerian script. Both men were shy, high-strung, wary of what each day would bring, and given to daydreaming. Worse, Thurber saw in his father every dreaded promise that he, too, would be unable to avoid domination by women.

Some Thurber followers long assumed that the harried, henpecked little man in the cartoons illustrated only Thurber's conceptions of himself in his wretched relationship with Althea, his first wife, or with other strong-minded women in his life who rarely, if ever, granted him his way. But in several instances the cartoon character is more likely to represent Thurber's view of a spineless father as husband.

The Thurber Man of his drawings often wears a derby, as did Charles;

Thurber rarely wore a hat at all, for no sooner had he bought one than he would lose it. Charles's derby seems to have acquired symbolic status for Thurber, as if the hat revealed the man. In "Gentleman from Indiana," he dwells on it:

> He began wearing one . . . when he was only twenty, and he didn't give up the comic, unequal struggle . . . until the middle nineteen-twenties, when he was in his fifties.
>
> At least three times, in my fascinated view, sudden impish winds at the corner of Broad and High blew the derby off his head and sent it bock-flopping across the busy and noisy intersection, my father pursuing it slowly, partly crouched, his arms spread out as if he were shooing a flock of mischievous and unpredictable chicks. . . .
>
> A photograph . . . shows him sitting on a bench in a park, surrounded by his wife and infant sons, looking haunted and harassed in a derby with an unusually large and blocky crown. In this study he somehow suggests Sherlock Holmes trying to disguise himself as a cabman and being instantly recognized by the far from astute Dr. Watson, rounding a corner and crying, "Great heavens, Holmes, you've muffed it, old fellow! You look precisely like yourself in an enormous bowler."

In the *Album*, Thurber lashes out at those who took advantage of his father:

> He missed nine or ten other answers, and failed to get even one of the $5 or $10 consolation prizes. He had labored over the contest nights and Sundays for several months, and at the same time, in addition to his regular work he managed to type voluminous pages of stuff from ponderous ledgers on behalf of the private vanity of some Ohio Senator. . . . As the result of his over-work, my father was stricken with what the doctors called brain fever, and almost died.

He attacks the 1912 Progressive vice-presidential candidate, Hiram Johnson ("the Lord's candidate"), for being an irritable bully with Charles, the overworked committee secretary of that campaign. As a seventeen-year-old high-school student, Thurber had spent time in his father's office at the Ohio Progressive Party headquarters and witnessed with shame and anger the way his hardworking father was often treated as a lackey by those he served so eagerly. "I know [Jim] felt pretty strongly about the failure of some of the politicians who employed my father to [give] him a better salary or appointment . . . in return for the fine work he did for them," says Robert.

But the real target of Thurber's resentment would have been a father who needed defending, a child among men, a pussycat lacking the will to stand up to his tormentors.

On January 1, 1932, Mayor Thomas having been defeated in the November elections, Charles cleaned out his desk at City Hall, his glory days ended after nine years. He and Mrs. Charlotte Pennington, the city's dance-hall inspector, who occupied the suite of offices with him, exchanged notes of appreciation and sadness at leaving, and Charles, too bashful to deliver his message in person, wrote a farewell letter to the departing mayor:

> You have been so darned good and kind that I just don't know how to thank you. White-haired and ever immaculate of dress who is loved by every person in the City Hall.
>
> You ought to keep this letter for the grandchildren, for if a man has the good-will of his secretary after so long an association, he must be some man. I want to tell you how very much I think of you as Mayor, as an employer—or rather, an associate—for you never have treated me as an employee, and which means so very much more, how I prize you as a real friend.

Charles felt strongly enough about his sentiments to release this missive to the press. Reading the newspaper clipping of the letter, which Robert mailed to him, Thurber doubtless cringed inwardly at his father's public display of gush. It may have reminded him uncomfortably of juvenile and sentimental self-revelations of his own—for example, the elegies to Rex and Scottie, the Thurber and Fisher dogs, which he had written at age eighteen for his high-school publication. But by 1932, the year of the letter, the sixty-five-year-old Charles would have sounded to Thurber like a house servant expressing hand-licking gratitude for years of underpay and overwork.

Whatever the distance Thurber's later attitudes put between him and his family, Charles took pride in his son's success, even when it was hard for him to explain it. In 1930, after *Is Sex Necessary?*—the popular Thurber and White lampooning of self-help books—was published, Thurber returned to Columbus, where Charles, then the mayor's secretary, proudly posed with his son for press photographers. Thurber had sent his parents an early copy with an affectionate salutation on the flyleaf. Asked what he thought of the book, Charles played the straight man: "In my opinion it's a darned good book," he told a reporter. "That name sort of bothered me at first. I spent plenty of time dodging the young woman [librarian] every time I visited the public library. Imagine having to carry on a conversation with a girl on the question, Is Sex Necessary?" Yes, his wife had been put off by the title, too, but "she read it and everything was lovely."

And two years later, after Thurber's cartoon book *The Seal in the Bedroom* had been published, a woman reporter for the *Ohio State Journal* came upon Charles standing "tall, slender, pleasant" in front of McClelland's bookstore, on High Street, staring with a bemused smile at a large display of the book in the window. "Fern," he said to her, "can you imagine, he gets paid for drawings like that? Paid big money!" (Besides his salary, the *New Yorker* was then paying Thurber twenty-five dollars per cartoon, by itself a fair weekly salary in that period of the Great Depression.) Apparently, Charles was certain that Thurber's public and employer were being duped and would find him out sooner or later. Meanwhile, as an inveterate politician and self-publicist, still running for office, he was more than happy to be known locally as the father of James Thurber.

Charles was a good sport about having to play the father in the wild family fantasies of *My Life and Hard Times*. Identified by his own name, without previous permission or warning, he is shown throughout as being terrorized by his sons, misunderstood by his wife, and harassed by crazy domestics. It is nearly all delicious fiction, but Thurber never disguises his parents, as he does his brothers. To Mame, her son was performing for the reading public, as she had always wished to perform onstage. ("Jamie and I are both comedians," she once said somewhat wistfully, "but it's all coming out in him.")

Charles, who had no such explanation, could only put his best diplomatic foot forward. Asked by a *Columbus Citizen* feature writer about some of the incidents involving him in the book, Charles grinned and said, "I remember there was some talk about that bed falling on me. But pshaw! Jamie is a great hand to enlarge on those little things that used to happen when he was a kid."

In 1937, Charles developed prostate problems. Thurber paid his train fare to New York to be certain that he got the best medical opinions. Robert writes:

> Jim arranged for [his father] to see a specialist. He was told that his condition called for surgery, but he seemed to fear the knife and refused to be operated on. His condition worsened from then until his death in 1939. It is quite possible an operation could have prolonged his life, but as this condition had weakened his system for many years, no one can say for sure.

Thurber and Helen drove Charles to their home in Litchfield, Connecticut, after the medical tests in New York. Thurber was busy writing for much of the short time his father was there, leaving Charles to make friends with local policemen and firemen. Helen seems to have found the physically failing Charles something of a nuisance during his stay with them, though, she says, it was evident that "he was proud of his son."

Back in Columbus, Charles died on Easter morning, 1939. Mame writes Minnette Fritts:

> He was ill about 3 months with prostate gland trouble but uremic poisoning set [in]. . . . He was in the hospital about 4 weeks. . . . Poor Jim was on the phone 4 times a week at least. . . . Jim came on about March 20 and staid [sic] 10 days to visit his Dad. Helen didn't come with him that time. . . . His father enjoyed having him here too & they had many nice talks together—but the dear soul had to leave us April 9. . . .

> Robert and his father were in bookstore business together for the last four years & they were *pals* too and it has surely crushed him and not being well anyway—has made it so much worse.

> Of course Jamie & Helen came on immediately and remained a week. . . . Rob and I went to N.Y. on to Woodbury, Conn. where they were living then . . . & staid with them until about 1st or 2nd of May. We just felt we must get away—and too Jamie wanted us to see the wonderful home he had . . . & a beautiful country home it was—they had a fine cook—and Helen is a marvellous housewife—fine manager & very sweet & stylish—and *boy* how she *dresses*.

During the weeks of Charles's failing health, Thurber wrote his classic "The Secret Life of Walter Mitty," in Connecticut. It was published on March 18, 1939, shortly before his father's death. There are those who find similarities to Charles in the inept, wife-dominated, daydreaming Mitty, and one or two who think it may be Thurber's personal obituary of his father. This is far-fetched. The middle-aged loser fleeing the insurmountable realities of life in fantasy had been a stock figure in Thurber's work for more than a decade. In prose and drawing, Mitty is how Thurber frequently chose to cast himself. He would have found Charles's inner life artistically uninteresting, as well as embarrassing to contemplate. Mitty's original, he wrote, a few months before his own death, "is every other man I have ever known. . . . No writer can ever put his finger on the exact inspiration of any character in

fiction. . . . Even those commonly supposed to be taken from real characters rarely show much similarity in the end."

In his correspondence, little if any mention of his father's death can be
found. One wonders about his thoughts on the occasion of the crowded
Methodist funeral service and at the wake, at which a throng of prominent
city officials, judges, business and newspaper acquaintances, and friends from
the neighborhood all lined up to tell the family what the beloved Charlie
Thurber had meant to them.

6

That Unique Hermit

I called my family in Columbus Saturday and my brother Robert
answered the phone and began to bawl hell out of me for the piece on
my father. He was so nasty that I hung up on him. It turned out that a
letter from him was at the Algonquin desk and we got it and read it. It
is a savage and relentless attack on almost everything I said and he
seems to have persuaded my mother to react in the same way, except
not violently. He says the piece should have been called "Hoosier Half-
wit," claims I must have had a deep resentment of my father, and
categorically denounces almost every paragraph. . . . It is a rather
shocking situation.

—Thurber letter to E. B. White, June 1951

In all likelihood, Thurber would have preferred to leave Charles out of the
collection of reminiscences that became *The Thurber Album*, but the omission would have been too conspicuous to explain away. And since he had to

deal with the subject, he would approach it through the humorous and anecdotal perspective he felt most comfortable with. He saw no potential problems with his family over the matter; they had been hesitant but finally acquiescent when featured as nutty characters in *My Life and Hard Times*, eighteen years before; now, their comic masks removed, they would be offered for public consideration as just plain, lovable folks, in a *fin-de-siècle* setting. What he never for a moment suspected was his younger brother's gradually acquired conviction that Thurber had cared little for their father and had no right to use Charles's memory for further self-serving literary purposes. It is doubtful that anything Thurber wrote about his father would have assuaged the defensive and suspicious Robert, who didn't understand in the first place why Thurber wanted to write the family into the limelight all over again.

Thurber's cavalier approach to the subject didn't help. On October 26, 1950, he put Robert on guard against what might be in the offing, writing:

> Be sure to send a copy of those letters of my father's, and also I could use anything interesting and amusing from my mother's diary. I have five pieces done, including the one on William Fisher, and I will send you a proof soon. . . .
>
> You will have to take the truth about the family, since I am telling the flaws as well as the perfections, but everybody comes out of it in completely good shape.

That December, galley proofs of "Man with a Rose," the first in the *New Yorker*'s "Photograph Album" series, arrived in Columbus, and Thurber was at once struggling to explain to mother and brother his literary version of Mame's father:

> I sent the proof without permission of Ross, for we have found out that people involved in a story have so many objections it takes weeks to iron them out. Subjects of Profiles used to see proofs, but we had to stop it, and "My Life and Hard Times" would have lost the incident of the mice if Mama had got her hands on it. Now nobody in the world believes that I didn't make it up . . .
>
> Making a man perfect, as those old vanity books did, is to make him colorless and unreal, and readers are suspicious of glossing over a character, as witness [Columbus newspaper columnist] Hayes's observation that I saw Columbus people through clear, but "slightly rose-tinted lenses." The danger my book runs is in this direction and not the other. I will

emphasize Grandpa's essential work as a farmer during the Civil War and the fact that sending substitutes was common in such cases, but I want to make him tick and to present him in the round, and the perceptive reader, familiar with psychology, would realize that something interesting and actual lay behind his exaggerated love of U. S. Grant and his constant tendency to "make a pass." These are manifestations of one of the simplest of human impulses, known as over-compensation, and in the New Yorker I am writing for a sharp audience. Satisfied by my analysis they would forget about it, but if I left it out they would pick at me. These considerations are the natural result of thirty years in the writing game as writer and editor. The editors and others who have read the piece here, lacking your intimacy, look upon the piece as a tribute to an interesting and living character. . . .

I think you can trust me completely in dealing with Mama and the others, but I am not going to concern you unnecessarily over a period of months by sending out proofs, which are hard to read, and, as we found out long ago, falsely magnify both length and dull spots. Incidentally you would be surprised how little the story of a man in any war, even the last one, affects youngsters in this war.

By this time the floundering Thurber realized the pickle he was in, adding in a postscripted sulk to Robert:

After reading your letter I have decided to eliminate one of Mama's wittiest remarks—her "Why, Mrs. Miller, it's the business [contraceptives] to go into." If I wrote it, the editors and other admirers of Mame Thurber would refuse to leave it out, but I want to stay away from any disturbing factor. Joe Sayre is doing the TIME piece on me, and writes, "It is not easy to get you down on paper without kicking you in the crotch." This is sound, right, and deserved, although you wouldn't guess it—and I have insisted that he do a well-rounded portrait, complete with my yelling at people.

Though the usual Christmas gifts were exchanged between West Cornwall, Connecticut, and Columbus that month, there were tension and apprehension along with them, on both sides. In March, Thurber and Helen sailed to Bermuda, where he wrote Robert and Mame a chatty note, mentioning, in an "Oh, by the way" paragraph, that "the New Yorker will send you a proof or a carbon of the piece on Mary Thurber called 'Lavender with a Difference.' The next piece coming out is about Belle and Mrs. Allbright [sic] and I have finished the one on Charles Thurber. . . . I will send you some of the letters I have got about the piece on William M. Fisher."

A rough, first typescript of "Gentleman from Indiana" in the Thurber archives bears deletions and changes that mark the struggle Thurber was having to avoid fictionalizing his father and their relationship. This passage, which refers to Charles's political work, was cut before he submitted the piece to the *New Yorker:* "I couldn't comprehend, as a boy, what he got out of such a dull and patternless commotion, but I later understood that it was a combination of the love of contest and a curious hope and belief that out of it all would emerge, in the end, an honorable race of selfless men, sincerely dedicated to the ideal and practice of good government."

On reflection Thurber must have realized that though his father did enjoy political hassles as a work environment, his motivation was primarily that of making a living, one that by itself was hardly ennobling. Also deleted: "When he found out that I wanted to become a writer, and had no lust for campaign and contest, he was sympathetic and encouraging. He always listened quietly to argument and explanation, giving the closest attention."

In deleting this passage, Thurber withdraws Charles from the spurious role of the father whose wise counsel is routinely sought by his sons. Robert is probably correct in his assertion that the family seldom knew what Thurber was thinking or doing. Thurber rarely confided in them, and it would hardly have mattered to him what Charles thought of his intention to become a writer. Like several others in the "Album" series, Charles emerges only partly delineated—photographed in shadow, too quickly summoned into anecdote, and retired before his nature, his personality, or his thoughts can be made out.

Thurber and Helen had just returned from Bermuda when "Gentleman from Indiana" appeared in the *New Yorker* (June 9, 1951). Robert read nearly all of it as mean-spirited score settling with a father unable to defend himself. In the very first line, Charles Thurber takes a header off a bicycle when the contraption disintegrates under him in downtown Columbus. Doorknobs freeze in his hand, lines foul, doors stick, the mechanical confounds him, the adjustable frustrates him. He gets trapped in the rabbit hutch he is building for his sons, cannot prevent his derby from causing him humiliations time and again, and, though Thurber credits him with the ability to bowl and win newspaper contests, "he never could kick a football or catch the swift pitch of a baseball." (Neither, of course, could Thurber.)

Thurber was handling a touchy subject in the light manner most comfortable for him, and in his more sincere-sounding references to Charles he seemed to be trying his best to suspend any lingering poor feelings toward his father for the sake of the project. But Robert viewed even Thurber's warm tributes to Charles as strained and unmeant. The anecdotes about his father, he thought, constituted a put-down—especially because they were all true. Yes, Robert could confirm years later, his father's bike (a Columbia) *had* collapsed under him on the street; yes, Charles *had* trapped himself in a rabbit hutch for quite a while, until somebody noticed he was missing and went to look for him; yes, their father had been unfairly used and inadequately re-warded throughout his life. But why harp on all that? Charles had been a hero to Robert, a man he looked up to, and if the hero was made a laughing-stock, a squashed icon, what did that do to Robert's self-respect?

In his piece, Thurber had also maligned the Ohio Republican politicians Charles had given much of his life to—proof in Robert's mind that his brother, corrupted by those un-American New York communist fellow trav-elers, was out to cut the last piece of ground from under their father's contri-butions to American Midwestern values. Until his death, Robert fully shared the conservative views of the Ohio Republicans of his father's day: their distrust of the Eastern establishment, their geopolitical isolationism, their disdain for Franklin Roosevelt. That his brother did not was a further sign of Thurber's contempt for his father's beliefs and another explanation for his growing resentment of Charles over the years. ("Robert once started a schoolyard fistfight," Mame told a reporter, "by calling another boy a Demo-crat.")

Robert could well have been going through a midlife crisis, the causes of his resentment well beyond the reach of his self-comprehension. The youn-gest of the three children, he seemed ill-equipped for a life that he found threaded by personal disappointments. He had been the captain of his high-school baseball team and a pitcher of professional potential, until physical ailments began to plague him, beginning with a broken arm he sustained while trying to crank the family Reo. He was forced to drop out of his freshman year at Ohio State University in March 1915 for a goiter operation, followed by an emergency appendectomy. His Army enlistment in World War I ended in a medical discharge after five months. By 1919, he had contracted pulmonary tuberculosis, which confined him to bed under a doc-tor's care all spring and summer. But though he remained sickly and frail, he outlived most of his generation—as do so many who find self-justification in hypochondria ("Robert is always talking about his bowels," Thurber com-plained)—dying in 1988 at the age of ninety-two.

Like the father he adored—and like Thurber, when he was able to rise above the corruptions of success, booze, disappointments in love, and his rage at being blind—Robert was of a gentle, kindly nature. Inclined to be more considerate of others than of themselves, both Robert and his father settled for the leftovers of the contemporary social order. Though Thurber tried a couple of times to set up Robert in a rare-book business, it didn't succeed. Nothing seemed to work for Robert. Always aware of the comparisons being made with his illustrious older brother, he became steadily more defensive and subject to illnesses whose pain was certainly real, however much they may have been self-induced.

Until the "Album" donnybrook, the two brothers had been on the best of terms over the years. From the time he first left Columbus in 1918, Thurber's letters home were directed principally to Robert. They shared a love of sports, popular songs, and local gossip. Robert faithfully acted as the family historian; he kept newspaper clippings about his brother's achievements all of Thurber's professional life, as well as the family letters. Though some items were lost in a fire in the Thurbers' Columbus apartment in 1934, much of what we know about Thurber's early years is thanks to Robert's scrapbooks, which cover more than forty years of the Thurber family, and which he sold to the Ohio State University Thurber Collection in the 1960s.

In the twenties and thirties, Thurber invited Robert for lengthy visits to New York during a couple of Thurber's loneliest periods, and Robert in turn kept his older brother informed of the Columbus scene, in which Thurber was always interested. A gaggle of biographers who sought out Robert for information after Thurber's death rarely heard anything negative from him about his brother. But the case against Thurber had been building in Robert's mind, beginning with his and Mame's dependence on Thurber and the suspicion that Thurber might be regarding it as a form of charity. In actuality, Robert was providing housekeeping services, nursing care, and affectionate companionship for their mother, who would otherwise have been consigned to a nursing home. And that role was destined to be lived out in lackluster residential hotels in downtown Columbus. He was surely aware that a life of any real significance had passed him by, and was ready to believe that a past he remembered fondly was being publicly revealed by his brother, piece by piece, as something for people to snicker at.

Furthermore, Thurber had written about dogs that his brothers, not he, had owned; and about the family car that Robert had cranked, driven, and taught his brothers to drive. He had appropriated family anecdotes they had all contributed to and drew upon for the enjoyment of one another, friends, and guests. Somehow, "Jamie" had made off with it all, without properly paying for it with credits or recognition.

Robert's furious remarks by telephone and letter both angered and shattered Thurber, who described the sorry situation in a letter to E. B. (Andy)
White. White, who rarely wrote about his own family, preferring to discuss
the idiosyncrasies of the sheep, geese, and chickens in his Maine barnyard,
read Thurber's reminiscence of his father in the *New Yorker* and dutifully
offered the reassurance Thurber sought:

> I don't think you need have any qualms about the . . . piece, as there
> isn't a word in it that isn't affectionately written, and even if Robert
> queried every line, you still have every right to paint a portrait as it
> appears to your eye. Probably it is natural that members of a family
> should get lathered up when one of them sets out to explain an ancestor,
> and there is a kind of jealousy involved in it, and that, too, is natural.
> But as you say, it is distressing.

For years, Thurber had asked White to serve as chaplain in the war-torn
province of his literary soul. Five years younger than Thurber, White seemed
to have most things settled with himself, rarely sought counsel from others,
and somehow appears to have avoided most of the writer's emotional pitfalls
that Thurber kept falling into. Though it was a relief to Thurber that White
found the portrait of Charles innocent of malice, his qualms remained—
mostly over whether what he had written was honest, especially those fawning tributes to Charles.

Robert believed they were not, but spoiled his case by resting it on the
superficial, the silly, the biased, and a nearly total ignorance of what Thurber
was trying to overcome. His protests: (1) if Thurber could write an article
glorifying Grandfather Fisher, who never liked Thurber, why couldn't he do
the same for his own father? (Robert completely failed to detect Thurber's
subtle skewering of that testy, hard-to-please martinet in "Man with a
Rose"); (2) what of Papa's elegant and distinguished handwriting, admired by
so many? (3) Why place Charles and Kenesaw Mountain Landis as young
men on the Indiana governor's staff, and then show Landis, "an ambitious
man," going on to become the national commissioner of baseball, leaving
Charles looking like a failure by comparison? Charles couldn't afford a law
education, Landis could; (4) the attack on the Ohio politicians was evidence
of Thurber's subversion by the snobbish intellectuals he consorted with; (5)
the article betrayed Thurber's downright annoyance with Charles's skill in
puzzles and contests; (6) Thurber hadn't emphasized the ways in which
Charles had helped so many people; (7) by quoting Charles's letter to Mame

about James Whitcomb Riley's drinking, and then disclaiming any personal knowledge of Riley's problem, Thurber had left their father looking like a libelous gossip; (8) it wasn't true, as Thurber had told him, that other writers' families had not objected to being used in this manner—Clarence Day's parents had. Finally (9), Thurber had been so determined to malign his father that he had not had proofs of the article sent to them before it was published, intentionally evading the changes he knew his family would have wanted made.

Helen Thurber agreed with Andy White that Robert should be told to go climb a tree. But it was the first real falling-out Thurber had had with Robert and Mame, its severity had taken him completely by surprise, and, in the end, was so seriously upsetting as to dampen the entire "Album" project for him. Worse, he couldn't overcome the suspicion that his family might have a point or two. The irony was that Thurber had never quarreled with Charles; in death, his father had become a source of trouble that he never was when he was alive.

William, who lived his own bachelor existence apart from Robert and Mame—sometimes occupying a room nearby in their hotel, sometimes elsewhere—seems not to have taken a recognizable stand in the conflict. He worked for one of the city agencies and was much less dependent on Thurber for money. Then, too, he dreamed of acting in the play Thurber was writing, in which Thurber had promised him a part written especially for him.

Robert didn't respond to any of Thurber's calls or letters for nearly seven months. Thurber remained fitful and distressed. Not only was the earlier public image he had created of an eccentric but likable Columbus family at stake, but so was his own, as the congenial and madcap member of that family his readership assumed him to be.

The personal hurt was real, as well. His fondness for Robert was genuine. He was occasionally amused or bored by William, for the most part feeling indifference toward him, but "Jamie" and "Bob" had enjoyed a natural camaraderie since boyhood. Now, after some fifty years, that relationship was over. For though Mame eventually chose to forget the quarrel—she had never felt as strongly about the matter as had Robert—and the two men resumed speaking terms, neither ever forgave the other.

Meanwhile, Thurber couldn't drop the subject. He had written White that he had forwarded to Columbus praise of "Gentleman from Indiana" from "six or eight people." There were actually three: Elliott Nugent, Ann Honeycutt, and Tim Costello—the owner of Costello's, one of Thurber's favorite pubs and a hangout for several other regular imbibers from the *New Yorker*. He followed that the next day with a letter of firm reasonableness, meant for Robert:

> Dear Thurbers:
> . . . I have been over your letter for the third time and there are several points I want to clear up. . . . I have the greatest love and admiration of Papa's great ability at contests, and everybody else thought I brought that out. I showed no annoyance whatever. . . .
>
> I will be glad to add a paragraph or two for the book, incorporating some of the things you mention about his helping people and the like. To do this in the New Yorker would have made me self-conscious and . . . disturbed the editors. The whole implication of the piece is that he was just such a man as you describe. In the long months I worked on it, I did have a section about his penmanship, but it simply did not stand up. Few other people would share your belief that penmanship is something special. The French refer to it as "the art of the donkey," and I was aware . . . of the present day feeling about Spencerian handwriting and other fancy penmanship, so popular forty years ago, but not held in great esteem today.

As to Robert's objections to Thurber's remarks about Ohio politics:

> I was a newspaper reporter in Columbus for four years, covered the State House and City Hall, and developed my own convictions about Ohio politics. I am a writer who puts down his own convictions, changing them to fit nobody else's opinion and omitting nothing under pressure if I think it is right. Your judgment of the two Roosevelts is your own and you obviously feel deeply enough about it to use obscenity in a letter Helen had to read aloud [the last thing that would have bothered the tough-minded, worldly Helen]. Every man is entitled to his own political opinions. You say, "I don't understand why you don't see it this way," as if everybody must naturally feel the same as you about your critical judgments, which are surely not your strongest virtue.

Though Robert had stopped communicating with him, Thurber couldn't let it go. Three days later, he was writing again:

Dear Thurbers:

I knew you would be interested in the two enclosed letters. . . . Don't overlook what Raynolds says . . . showing that he shares my viewpoint about Ohio politics of the old days and does not think I ran the boys into the ground. . . . It indicates that others would [like that section] too.

In my files I have a carbon I could send you of a letter I wrote to Lobrano [Gus Lobrano, then the fiction editor of the *New Yorker*], perhaps six weeks ago or longer, asking him to be sure and send you the proofs on "Gentleman From Indiana." . . . Since several other editors were ill at the time, he was overwhelmed by work and overlooked my letter. There was no desire on anybody's part to delay the sending of the proofs, but these things happen. I would not have known what to do if you had read the piece on Papa a month before it was published. I will, of course, correct all misstatements of fact and I will build up that commission, if you insist. I always felt he hated that work, but if you are sure he didn't, I will say so.

The New Yorker has a checking department consisting of experts who try to verify everything. The books about Reilly [James Whitcomb Riley] and every biographical article on him were carefully checked and not a single reference to his drinking was found, but one biographer quoted Reilly's opposition to "taking too much wine." All this being true, I was forced to say, in fairness, that I didn't really know about his drinking. I feel sure that my father did and was correct, but he was pretty young then and I have no record or memory of his citing actual facts that could be substantiated at this late date. His opposition to Reilly's drinking shows that he was a sound and sympathetic man, and a true admirer of Reilly's talent.

It now transpires that [the] Days [Clarence Day's parents] did not do more than object to being put on the stage in characterizations of them when they were from six to seventeen years old and any stronger statement, if it got out, would be libelous. Clarence Day, of course, was dead and had nothing whatever to do with the play [*Life with Father*], but it remains a great and fond American comedy.

I have gone over the piece on Mamma for the twentieth time and can't see anything to object to. In writing any story, however, it is necessary to make up a few things, and I hope you won't be too literal about minor facts. Because we have all been so upset, out there and here, I will engage to make any and all reasonable omissions or changes, but if we disagree, I wonder if you would pick two persons and I will pick two and let them decide. If they voted two to two they could select a fifth person and take his opinion.

. . . This thing has been as much of a shock to me as to you for, in thirty years of writing, no one has ever attacked a piece of mine with such vehemence, or questioned my integrity, honor and decency. My publisher just phoned this morning to say, "I wish I had known your father. The piece is wonderful." I will let you see the changes and additions when I make them.

I don't know what you mean by a "final, summarizing sentence." Everybody loved the ending of the piece, and I simply would not know how to do it your way. No one has told me how to do anything in writing for a great many years and our behavior patterns are well established in our fifties. I can never understand why you thought the piece was humorless, and I wish you would some day mention one of mine that you think is humorous.

"He and I had some sharp exchanges over the phone and by letter," Robert says. "It was tough on me. To try and argue with him at that time was like trying to push over a concrete fence. When I pointed out that he had misspelled Riley's name, he went wild. He couldn't stand criticism of any kind. At least not from me."

A fortnight later, Thurber was writing about it to John O'Hara: "My brother Robert took a Freudian . . . dive off the high board after reading my piece on my father and I have had to quiet him down with common sense which he won't accept. . . . My family kept looking for the laugh all the time, didn't find the ones that were there and—but this happens to everybody, I guess."

In preparing Mame for his piece about her, he had further alarmed her and Robert with his remark that "in writing any story . . . it is necessary to make up a few things." They knew he had done so throughout My Life and Hard Times, but the "Album" accounts were intended as literal. Nor were they comforted when, a week later, he was expressing concern over how the three Columbus Thurbers would react to the upcoming Time cover story on him, written by Joel Sayre. In that letter, he preached to them the merits of positive thinking:

June and July 1951 will be remembered by you as a trying period, but you will have to get through it the best you can, calling on your patience, tolerance, and restraint. As you know, "Gentleman from Indiana" has been widely hailed as a good piece about a good man and I will fix up the piece for the book. . . . Your biggest hurdle, however, will probably be the cover story about me in TIME. I don't know whether you will like it or not, and I haven't seen it, but a great many pieces have been written about me and I never worry about them. I expect TIME to do a realistic piece and not a blurb or puff, but the piece will no doubt mention my family and I hope it does not upset you.

Helen and Thurber both feared that the impulsive Mame and the hot-tempered Robert might write a wild letter to the editors of *Time* after reading the article—either not understanding that unlike the *New Yorker* (which had never had a letters-to-the-editor page) *Time* would dutifully print it, or worse, understanding exactly that. Thurber sought to head off the possibility:

Remember that a letter to a magazine is privileged, that is, it can be reprinted in whole or in part. I strongly urge you not to write any letters about it, or to show them to someone before you mail them. . . . The TIME piece is the result of last year's research and was set up in proof a couple of months ago. I had no control over it. I anticipate that it will be a sound and friendly piece, but I cannot anticipate your reactions to it. Take it as calmly as you can, remembering that the piece on Mama, to appear three weeks later [in the *New Yorker*] will be what is remembered.

He again offers himself as an object lesson to Robert on how to behave when one or one's family is written about:

A book called "Ross of the New Yorker [sic]," to be published this fall [by Dale Kramer], says that I was a failure before I got on the New Yorker, and I did not object to this. About seven years ago, a book you didn't see, called "Horse Sense in American Humor" and written by a Chicago University professor, batted me around quite a bit and said I had spent a life of drudgery on newspapers, which was partly true. Far from getting mad and writing the guy, I wrote a piece for the New Yorker called "Memoirs of a Drudge" and openly quoted the man's cracks. "Drudgery stole marches for me, when Lee's brilliance was asleep," wrote U. S. Grant. I should have sent you this book and some other critical pieces, which would have prepared you for the ordeal of 1951. The pieces were soundly thought out and I have never had the desire to be pictured differently from what I am.

But that was exactly the point of Robert's protest: that Thurber was picturing his father as different from what he had been, in Robert's opinion. And what corrective course was Thurber advocating for Robert—that if he didn't like what he read about his father he should write his own version and sell it to the *New Yorker*? Though none of the Thurbers were responding, Thurber couldn't stop lecturing them on the troubling issue:

All in all, the Thurbers will come out better rather than worse, and you must try not to get agonized by criticism or interpretation, and to see the good as well as the unfavorable. Remember that articles do not stick long in anybody's mind, because they are soon outdated and people have too much to think about. The individual concerned in a story magnifies what is said because of his personal interest, but tests have shown that only two percent of people can quote accurately from a piece, even two weeks after it comes out.

Mama has told me that my father finished second or third in one race for the legislature, and I hope you can get the facts for me. I am glad, of course, that he did not become a "state politico" and have tried to explain why. A man who does not get on the primary slate, but, independently, heads all the other candidates, is my idea of a success. The attainment of a goal can sometimes constitute failure. Harry Arnold was elected Lt. Governor because his name was first on the ballot, and this man Addison probably won for the same reason. Thurber comes down pretty far in any list alphabetically. . . . The good state legislator is either lost among the fools and cheap politicians, or tainted by association. I covered the legislature and know.

Through it all, Thurber had his eye on posterity and his place in it, adding: "I will return Robert's letter which should be destroyed, I think, along with mine, since this is not an exchange worthy of preserving." And, in another slap at Robert: "I would like to know William's address in Columbus since I always send him a check for his vacation. He has always been able to laugh at himself, and this helps a man get through life more easily than most men."

Mame had forwarded comments by others, also protesting his piece on Charles. Thurber replied:

Mrs. Pennington, Maud, and Katherine were talking about . . . what *they* would have written about [my father] rather than about the piece I wrote about him. I suggest that you all try to write about him and let me see the result. I think that an outside opinion is always the best, and these people were [too] close to him personally or related to him. I covered City Hall when Mrs. Pennington was dance inspector and she used to embarrass the newspapermen by her breathtaking reports on the immorality of some dance halls. The true story of Mrs. Pennington would be interesting, but I couldn't write it. I couldn't write about Maud and Katherine either. Could you? Love and kisses.

The long-awaited issue of *Time* was published in early July. Omitting the sullen Robert from the salutation, Thurber writes in both hope and apprehension:

Dear Mama:

Well, TIME got the stories about you wrong, but they will be cleared up in [my] piece coming out in a little over two weeks and, as I told you, the ones in my story will be remembered. I may put in a phrase saying that you have passed into legend, because when [one has,] stories are always exaggerated. All kinds have been printed about me, including one saying I have a case of glass eyes, each with a different shade of inflammation, which I change during the evening, ending up with one that has a flag for an iris. Everybody seemed to like the TIME piece and I'm glad they didn't send it to me before publication, because if I had corrected the anecdote about you, the New Yorker might not have wanted to print my piece. As we say, the edge would have been taken off, but now my piece can run without changes.

Through Mame, he had been able to enlist the help of cousins-in-law in straightening out his Grandmother Fisher's ancestry for another "Album" piece. Beall Matheny Smith, a descendant of Grandmother Fisher's stepfather, John Matheny, had contributed to the cause, once visiting the Thurbers in West Cornwall. But upon reading the *Time* story, she wrote to Mame and Robert, unknowingly reinforcing their resentment of Thurber's article about his father, "For [*Time*] to call our dear Charles Thurber an unsuccessful politician who kept running for offices until he was 65 and was never elected to any, made me almost have a brainstorm. He *was* a success in his work and was loved by everyone who knew him."

Mame's principal objection to the *Time* piece seems to have been a family picture accompanying it; William and Robert had been cropped out. Thurber explained:

> Dear Mama [Robert was still boycotted]:
> We just got your letter and are glad you like the piece. Joe Sayre had no more to do with the pictures or layout than Eva Prout. . . . The brothers were blocked out to focus attention on three of the principle [sic] figures. This is up to the make-up man and the editor. They wanted photos of me and Nugent, and me and White. Miss Terry [Daise Terry, office manager] spent three hours finding one of White and me, but it wasn't used. About forty others were thrown out, too.

Meanwhile, Thurber had forwarded to Robert, still fiddling with his rare-book business, excerpts from letters Andy and Katharine White had written Thurber from Maine, knowing the family trouble he was in and praising "Gentleman from Indiana." Thurber acknowledged their letters on July 10, a few days after the *Time* cover story was on the stands, bringing it to their attention and thanking them for their help in his struggle with Robert:

> Your wonderful and generous letters helped me and the situation a lot. . . . Nothing much can be done about [my brother], I'm afraid, since he has become a unique hermit in the past forty years, out of touch with everybody and everything, except his mother. He has no sense of English or of writing, actually thought "Daguerreotype of a Lady" [Thurber's piece about Margery Albright] was purely funny, and never reads any books. The life of a specialist in first editions and those made valuable by errata and failure is distorting. To him Sinclair Lewis's "Our Mr. Wrenn" is the most important Lewis book, because of errors in the first run-off. The early failures of established writers are worth more than their successes. Failure, mistakes, and scarcity make up a strange criterion of value. He never reads any of his prize items.

In late August, Thurber learned from William that Mame was in the hospital. Normally he would have called Robert, but wrote Mame a solicitous and caring letter instead:

Dear Mama:

William called up yesterday and told us you are in the hospital, but he said we were not to worry because you are coming along fine. Otherwise, of course, we would have come out, but we didn't want to alarm you. And what you need is fewer people, not more. You have been doing too much and writing too many letters, and there was bound to be a strain with all those pieces being printed at the same time. . . .

We want you to . . . stay there as long as you have to. I hope you have a good room, but you could be moved to a better one if you want to. We know that Dr. Kissane is a fine doctor and that you have great confidence in him. You will have got some flowers from us and from the New Yorker. Ross was in the office yesterday for the first time in three months, and he and Miss Terry and the others were sorry to hear you weren't feeling well and they all send their love. . . .

Rosie [Rosemary, Thurber's twenty-year-old daughter by Althea] had a walk-on part in one play and a small speaking part in another. She was very proud of the piece about you, the first actress in the family. . . . Let me know what I can do for you or send you.

Nine days later, he wrote his mother again, sending money and assurances that he would cover all her medical expenses, and hoping she was home and back on her feet, though "we both wanted you to stay in the hospital as long as the doctors suggested. I got one good letter from William and I know he would have phoned me collect if you were not doing all right. . . . You must try to relax and not write more letters, for William can handle the correspondence all right. I'll write again soon and telephone William tonight."

The letter crossed with one to him signed by both William and Robert. Worried that Robert would think he was ignoring what might be a gesture at reconciliation, Thurber replied at once: "I wrote my last letter before I got the one signed by William and Robert and after I found out that Main 6761 had been temporarily disconnected, so I thought old Bill was doing the communication. . . . I know Robert has a lot to do trying to keep people from staying too long. There is nothing more tiring than a two-hour visitor."

Hopefully, he tried the old "Dear Thurbers" salutation in a chatty letter later that month, to see if he could get a response from Robert. Both men loved listening to baseball games on the radio and Thurber threw in an item that could only have been a friendly gesture to his brother: "I'm glad the Yankees are through with Cleveland and up against the White Sox and Boston. Cleveland doesn't get the breaks at the Stadium, but ought to win the pennant. I wouldn't bet against the Yankees again, as I did last year."

No reply. And though his next letter was to "Dear Mama," he set out more bait in hopes that the intransigent Robert would answer in kind: "I hated to see Cleveland lose three in Detroit, and I don't know how to stop the Yankees." But Robert only forwarded Mame's medical bills to Thurber without a line, which finally led Thurber to complain: "Dear folks, we got back from New York . . . to find an envelope [with a doctor's bill] from Robert, but no note, and we wonder who Dr. Vance is. . . . A few scribbled lines explaining such things would reassure us, but I can only figure that there was nothing serious. We want you to get all possible medical attention, but we want to keep in touch." To which Helen added: "William called last night and we were glad to get some direct news about you, Mame, for all we had heard for a long time was indirectly [given us]."

Perhaps to underscore his unwillingness to communicate with the Connecticut Thurbers, Robert had not had an outside telephone line reinstalled in the apartment he and Mame shared at the Southern Hotel, and Thurber expressed his annoyance at that: "I tried to call you through the Southern switchboard," he wrote to "Dear Thurbers," "but there was no answer and I didn't want to make Mama get up. . . . When you want calls you will probably put 6761 back, and I will wait, as I told you before, for that." But there was additional balm for Robert:

> I have been working very hard on the book which will be called "The Thurber Album." I have rewritten "Gentleman From Indiana," cutting out many things you didn't like, including the line about his "finishing at the top of the losers." I said he was beaten by a narrow margin. I put in the name of the commission to recodify federal statutes and said he was its secretary, as he was. I said he was a good rider and first president of the Columbus Bicycle Club, and that governors and others depended on his writing of effective speeches and tactful letters, and handling difficult men. . . .
>
> I hope you are all getting along well. William called me on Sunday and it might be a good idea to have him do that every Sunday for awhile.

Still no response. Thurber persisted, asking ten days before Christmas that the usual presents from Columbus not be sent them, given Mame's condition, and adding: " 'Gentleman from Indiana' will satisfy everybody. It was forgotten in the magazine, but will be in permanent form in the book."

Worried that the family dispute would erupt again, and in public, when the *Album* book was published, Thurber seemed a blackmail victim of Robert's continued anger. Furthermore, "Jamie couldn't stand being estranged," Helen says. At Christmas, Thurber telephoned Robert. It was a difficult moment for them both. Thurber suggested they forget their quarrel. Robert mumbled a grudging agreement. Thurber paid him to look up the old newspaper columns of Robert Ryder, former editor and paragrapher of the *Ohio State Journal* and a literary hero of Thurber's, to be featured in the *Album*. Robert resumed their correspondence, but things were never the same between them.

The *Thurber Album* was published four months later, in April 1952. In the chapter on Charles, a harried Thurber begins with: "Everybody's father is a great, good man, someone has said, and mine was no exception." The anonymous "someone" who authored this flimsy generality is Thurber. In the *New Yorker*, he had written flippantly of Charles: "He had wanted to study law, and although he never made it, he had some kind of job, turning twenty, in an Indianapolis firm." In the *Album*, "he never made it" is dropped and the face-saving explanation that "he didn't have the time or the money to go to law school" is inserted. "He had some kind of job" vanishes, and Charles's appointment at age twenty to the staff of the Indiana governor appears. In the magazine, Charles "also finished sixth several times as a candidate for the state legislature. Out of about twenty candidates in the primaries, five to be elected, he was invariably at the top of the losers." At Robert's insistence that that was factually incorrect, the book version explains that "although he wasn't an organization candidate, he was defeated each time by only a narrow margin."

Thurber's fear of being publicly rejected by his family over the matter led him to give them the whiphand, and in the end he substitutes greeting-card sentimentality for those personal feelings regarding his father that he either was unsure of or couldn't admit. For all the certitude in his lectures to the family, he was the one who compromised, as the mild, peace-loving "pussycat" Charles would have done.

Mame took to her bed in September 1951; Robert later blamed her illness on what Thurber's "Album" series had put her through. Mame's condition became both Robert's and William's excuse for declining an invitation to Rosemary's wedding, in Philadelphia, in February 1953. But Robert was steadily accumulating grievances against Thurber. He had heard about Thurber's refusal to accept an honorary degree from Ohio State on grounds that McCarthyism had scared the university trustees and administration into screening campus speakers for viewpoints that could be considered treasonable. Robert, and probably William and Mame, went along with many Columbusites in the belief that Senator McCarthy had done well to alert the nation to the threat of a domestic political conspiracy to sell out the country to the Soviets, and Thurber's slighting of the university for leftist reasons was simply another embarrassment he had exposed them to.

Thurber seems to have been buoyed by Rosemary's recent marriage to Frederick Sauers; his letters to nearly everyone in 1953 seem filled with merriment, and those to his family contain jokes, baseball comments, and a genuine concern for Mame's health and her living conditions, which he made certain were adequate, occasionally writing to the management of her residential hotel, asking third parties to look into such problems as an unexplained increase in rent.

It was a little over two years after Mame became bedridden before Thurber visited her, with Helen, over the Christmas holidays of 1953. Robert found Thurber unloving and ungracious toward Mame, but Thurber had not blamed her for the "Album" controversy as he had Robert, and he was not usually a bearer of grudges for any length of time. It was the trip itself that subdued Thurber; he was downcast at how many of his old friends and acquaintances were in the hospital or had gone from it to the grave. He especially missed his close friend of many years, Herman Miller, an O.S.U. professor who had died a few years before. He was also tired and nervous, having been worn out as the city's leading celebrity by endless interviews and his own nonstop monologs.

He and Helen were back two years later for his mother's death and burial, too late to be recognized by the comatose Mame. Thurber read into Robert's grief and loneliness his end as a functioning human being, writing to William:

> I didn't want to be rough on Robert and I know he cannot work, but I was afraid he was sinking into hopelessness. Probably he does go to the library and read the papers and have other activities. Inactivity to me is death or worse; he never writes about his routine and I was alarmed when he said he 'Rested more and wrote less'. He had some good research for me on the Ryder stuff in 1952, and I had some hope of something else like that. An hour a week or every two weeks, but I take it back.

Robert lived on, beset by the hypochondria and ailments that had conditioned nearly all of his life, and survived Thurber by twenty-seven years. The family scrapbooks of clippings, pictures, and letters he had conscientiously maintained were bought by the Thurber Collection in the Ohio State University library for ten thousand dollars, which he shared with William, and this gave Robert a new lease on life. Out from under the shadow of his older brother, he took seriously his role as a primary Thurber source—a role that steadily expanded as more and more writers of doctoral dissertations and books on Thurber consulted him. Though arthritis crippled his fingers, he wrote dozens of pages of letters in longhand to scholars, journalists, and authors, offering what he felt to be the conclusive word on many questions, and seeming at last to be receiving the recognition previously denied him.

He could even make allowances for what he still considered to be the shabby treatment of his mother and himself at Thurber's hands, writing in 1974: "I can't help but think that the brain clot he had for so long might easily have been the contributing factor for a lot of his behavior." And, a year later: "Who knows how one would have acted had one been in the shoes of my brother? He had some very serious troubles and probably just was not his normal self many times during his years of complete darkness." In summary, he seems finally to have put things into proper perspective: "I firmly believe most people will always remember James for his great contribution to literature rather than for any controversies or tempestuous episodes which occurred in his later years."

The Thurber Album contained Thurber's final public comment on the "Gentleman from Indiana." Though a few years later he makes several fond references to Mame in *The Years with Ross*, including the fact that Ross approved of her, Charles is never mentioned, for all that his life overlapped the first twelve of those years. His selections from his previous work, collected in *Alarms and Diversions* in 1957, include his affectionate tributes to his mother and to Aunt Margery Albright but not the chapter on his father.

When *The Thurber Album* was published, in April 1952, a weary Thurber wrote Andy White: "I am going to write about imaginary people from now on since real ones take too much out of me." The pledge held up for four years, and then he took on the subject of his years with Ross and others at the *New Yorker* and found himself back in a soup of another kind.

7

That Secret Life of
James Thurber

James Thurber was born on a night of wild portent and high wind in the year 1894, at 147 Parsons Avenue. [His] boyhood (1900–1913) was pretty well devoid of significance. I see no reason why it should take up much of our time. There is no clearly traceable figure or pattern in this phase of his life. If he knew where he was going, it is not apparent from this distance. He fell down a great deal during this period, because of a trick he had of walking into himself. His gold-rimmed glasses forever needed straightening, which gave him the appearance of a person who hears somebody calling but can't make out where the sound is coming from. Because of his badly focussed lenses, he saw, not two of everything, but one and a half.

—Thurber, from "My Fifty Years with James Thurber"

Pictures of Thurber as infant and preschooler in no way hint at the tall, skinny boy he would become; even with curled lip and shrewd eye, he appears as winningly plump as a toy stuffed animal. At age three, he poses with his brothers, all in navy-blue coats. James sits at a low table with a surprised look on his face. By his teens, group photographs confirm Thurber's personal assessment of his appearance as that of the ugly duckling. In family and school pictures, he appears at the extreme right, most often in the last row, his head turned slightly to his left to keep the glass eye as hidden as possible from the camera. He is usually wearing the look of a beaten dog. Later family portraits show William's development as the best-looking of the boys, with Robert next.

As Thurber grew older, he looked more and more like a young Ichabod Crane, thin wrists dangling from his sleeves, his hair unnaturally brushed and parted in preparation for the picture. Even when he passed his father in height, he remained of slight build, and his lack of physical confidence kept him awkward in looks and movement throughout adolescence and early manhood.

He began wearing glasses at age eight, partly because his parents wished to protect him from further eye injury, and because, denied the roughhouse life of his brothers, he had become a constant reader, bothered occasionally by slight shifts of vision in his good eye. Blanche C. Roberts, who retired in 1947 after fifty-three years with the Columbus Public Library, remembers that as a child Thurber never missed the library's story hours.

The Thurbers' first house, at 251 Parsons Avenue (he deliberately used wrong street numbers in his memoirs), is not included in Thurber's personal reminiscences; he was only four when the family left it for the big house on the eastern edge of town, at 921 South Champion Avenue. The Parsons Avenue house, of red brick, stood in a rank of almost identical homes crowded onto twenty-five-foot-wide plots, their proximity darkening the days for their inhabitants. The brickwork displayed the demanding, decorative masonry of late nineteenth-century America, found even in modestly priced houses. The heavy front door held a rectangle of thick bevelled glass, which lit the front hall by day. The windows were large, those upstairs catching the morning sun and a view of the broad campus of the Ohio State School for the Blind, across the street. The big living-room windows were bayed, crowding into even stingier dimensions the tiny front porch, where the Thurber boys rode a rocking horse.

Thurber's memories of his Columbus family life seem to begin with the house on South Champion Avenue. It was a fine big place of brick, with bay windows on one side, cut-glass panes in those in front, a silver maple on the lawn, and a small flower garden in a side yard.

It was also a remote, lonely place, lit at night only by kerosene lamps, hidden by woods that continued unbroken to the east and south; it was the last house on a street that turned into a dirt road beyond. Charles's departure for Washington in 1901 accentuated the house's isolation, which relatives and servants never failed to comment upon. "We had a terrible time getting help out there," Mame recalls. The live-in cook she did hire came armed with a .38-caliber revolver. Once, after midnight, she aroused the household by firing the gun out her bedroom window, insisting she had seen a skulking figure in the backyard.

"All three boys were on the bottle at the same time when we moved there," Mame says. "William was six before he'd quit. I took him out in the country one day, showed him a cow and told him that was where milk came from. After that he wouldn't touch milk."

Fires plagued the Thurbers throughout their lives. In the Champion Avenue house, four-year-old Robert ignited the mattress, and Mame frantically pushed it out the window onto the porch roof. In that house on another occasion, Mame splashed the outside of a kerosene lamp bowl with oil, which blazed up when she tried to light the wick. She hurried the three youngsters outside, announcing that the lamp was about to explode. William—and perhaps Mame—was disappointed when it didn't.

It was also on Champion Avenue that Mame coaxed a dozen neighborhood dogs into the cellar and kept them there until Great Aunt Mary York, who hated dogs, innocently opened the cellar door and was knocked over by the whole yelping pack. ("Great God Almighty, it's a dog factory!")

William and Robert were both athletic and enjoyed a carefree childhood, which the handicapped Thurber must have found discouraging. William had a fondness for horses—Mame said he rode a hobbyhorse longer than the other boys. He would run in front of oncoming horses as a child, and he and Robert would duck under their bellies on a dare.

Thurber could be no such physical exhibitionist. He left the rougher yard play and street games to his brothers. In a pathetic underscoring of that fact, he would brag throughout his life of his prowess at such activities as tossing cards into a hat, throwing rocks at bottles, or winning prizes by throwing softballs in carnival booths. In 1939, asked to be a guest on NBC radio's "Information Please," he wrote a third-person résumé for the network's house organ, volunteering, "He has never been defeated at singles in Crochinole. At Buckeye Lake, Ohio in 1923 he won a canary bird throwing baseballs at bells."

In 1954, George Smallsreed, the *Columbus Dispatch* editor, wrote Thurber that he had just heard from John McNulty, their mutual friend and former Columbus newspaper colleague, who remembered Thurber's wishing to be called "Iron Man" in the old days. Thurber replied:

John is wrong. . . . I wanted to be called "Slugger." Around 1910 my brothers and cousins and I invented a ball game with a broom handle for a bat and a ball made by stuffing a Bull Durham [tobacco] sack tightly full of rags. Boy, the curves you could get on that sack! Two guys could play the game and the diamond was in Walnut Alley. I remember beating Earl Fisher one to nothing. He got careless in the last of the ninth and threw me a sack that didn't curve more than a foot or a foot and a half, and I hit it for a home run.

By then an inveterate self-publicist, he invited Smallsreed to show the letter "to the boys on the sports desk, who might want to make an item out of it, unless the facts are known to them already."

But the "baccy ball" incident must have been a rare one, thinks Earl Fisher, who recalls that his cousin James was no good at the game, getting only a lucky hit now and then.

Home, on the other hand, sometimes held more physical hazards for young Thurber than did the schoolyard and street. Mame wasn't all that attentive, talking incessantly on the telephone, or to roomers and visitors, or to the dogs. Thurber's brothers competed for her attention with constant high-decibel squabbles, complaints, and shoving matches. Robert confesses to a hot temper that led to fistfights with William and other boys. He was the principal disturber of the domestic peace, he said, "due to my temper flare-ups."

"Oh, they were a lively group," Mame recalled. "Always throwing rocks and making a lot of noise. I remember one day when we were living at the Norwich Hotel, Robert threw a rock at Jamie. Jamie ducked. The rock smashed into a window of the hotel. Robert got mad at Jamie and said it was his fault because he ducked. I remember sometimes I'd get off the streetcar and you could hear them fighting three squares [blocks] away. And their dog in it, too. Jamie was the peacemaker. By the time he was a teenager, he could laugh the boys out of their fights by imitating how they looked, acted, and talked while fighting." Mame had her own defense against the boys' fights: she would pretend to go crazy.

William, as "Herman," completes the cast of family characters in *My Life and Hard Times* and deserves his own playbill mention. He never overcame his wonder at how his quiet, handicapped younger brother, a product of the same childhood, environment, and genetic heritage, was able to parlay stories about what was familiar to all of them into fame and fortune.

For years the Thurbers protected William from any guilt over the eye accident. It happened "during a childhood game," they said; the arrow was fired by "a playmate." But as his brother acquired public renown, William found the family tie a valuable social property, and eventually his part in the tragedy became a personal distinction he was always willing to discuss. In interview after interview, he offered the embarrassing and idiotic view that it had all been for the best. His words seemed issued by rote: "If people are curious about me, it's mostly because of that incident. So in one way it has been hell being Jim's brother. And it was an awful thing. But accidents do happen. And they say if a person loses one of his senses, like his eyesight, other things develop to compensate for it. I look at all Jamie got done and figure maybe it was a blessing in disguise." (The writer William Maxwell, a veteran editor at the *New Yorker*, offers the obvious, humane rebuttal, "But Thurber would have been a much happier man.")

Thurber never resented William for his part in the Falls Church accident. "We were taking turns with the bow and arrow that day," Thurber told an interviewer. "I could have shot out *his* eye by mistake." If he was never close to William, it was because he recognized early that there was little about his older brother that would ever interest him. When both were working in New York in the late twenties, they rarely saw one another. For one thing, William's get-rich-quick schemes, which sometimes cost Thurber money, were to be avoided, though Thurber remained amused by them all his life.

In 1927, on a business trip to New York, William stayed at the Shelton Hotel, which was located near a mental institution whose patients were sometimes caught trespassing by the hotel's detectives. William made the mistake of telling Thurber, who visited him there one day and found the room empty while his brother was taking a bath in the bathroom down the hall. Thurber stole into the room and locked William out. Disguising his voice, Thurber told William over the transom that he had escaped from the asylum and couldn't return until he had killed someone. When he heard Thurber unlocking the door, William fled in robe and slippers.

In January 1946, the press was invited to Mame's huge eightieth birthday party, held at the Deshler-Wallick Hotel in Columbus and sponsored by Thurber. Introducing William to reporters, Mame said: "Here's my son, Bill. He's crazier than Jamie but he just doesn't know how to write it down." Years later, William, reminded of the statement, called it one of his mother's "nifties," meaning an exaggeration not to be believed. "I could put it down if I wanted to," he told Lewis Branscomb, a professor of Thurber studies at Ohio State, "because I used to write letters to my friends and they looked forward to my wit and humor."

In his way, William Fisher Thurber was a Walter Mitty dreamer who went public with his fantasies and demanded recognition on their basis alone. In all that he volunteered about himself, there is only one recorded instance indicating that he might for one insightful moment have understood his chronic propensity for self-delusion: asked shortly before his death about "The Secret Life of Walter Mitty," William commented that it was popular because "we all want to be something we're not."

William had a somewhat slow and pedestrian mind that held reality at bay much of the time. It was reflected in his habits. When he got out of an automobile, he was apt to walk away in a fog, leaving the car door open. Once when he and Thurber, as boys, were having lunch at the home of Uncle Kirt and Aunt Bessie Fisher, William unthinkingly put butter in his coffee. ("For God's sake, Bessie, hide the eggs," Uncle Kirt said.) Though William believed that "Bobby" was his mother's favorite, and Mame was genuinely convinced that William was mildly insane, she loved him as she did all her boys, becoming nearly hysterical when, in his mid-forties, he underwent surgery to stop the spread of cancer.

William dropped out of his third year in high school because of a thyrotoxic goiter—thyroid ailments plagued all three of the brothers—and was unable to work for several years. But he later claimed that he had gone to night school, received tutoring, and "done a lot of reading" to make up for it. "I could hold my own with most of these college graduates," he told Branscomb. He had wanted to act professionally, he went on, but his illness had spoiled that plan.

William's "night school" had been an evening course in agriculture at the university. He had trouble sticking to one thing for long, being, in Robert's words, "a little restless and changeable." He did learn to swim in his late twenties, at the local YMCA, in order to qualify as a counselor in a boys' camp in Maine, where he worked for two summers. He helped his father get out an information booklet for newspaper-contest participants, worked for a stockbroker, for a dealer in drafting supplies, and for the Waterman Pen Company, selling out of New York on a sales quota in the late twenties. The Waterman job was the one he was proudest of, though he lost it soon enough and was frequently unemployed during the Depression years.

In the early thirties, Mame wrote Thurber a letter saying she was very worried about William, who was unemployed, stayed in bed a great deal, laughed insanely through much of the night, and had recently threatened to kill them all with a tommy gun. Thurber, who was delighted with accounts of William's "spells," quotes Mame in a letter to Ann Honeycutt.

> "William has no job and simply worries the life out of us
> because he hasn't—it has almost finished us the way he gets his
> spells and wants to run a 'machine gun' on all of us and relieve us

of our 'misery'—then end his own life. Last Sat.—week ago—he got one of his mean insane spells and tore around here raising his voice—and with no excuse for it—Just goes nite after nite without sleep and isn't really responsible for his actions—My heart aches for that boy who has so many fine qualities and when he is *making* money he is so good to us and everybody and happy, but even *then* is never well—has these awful thots constantly running thru his mind, as he puts it, and worst feature about it all is the way he *laughs* to himself all nite. . . . I have slipped in and listened and he laughs so loud—it startled me—just like one would do in seeing a funny picture of Charlie Chaplin. It is not a case for a physician but a psycho analyst something must be got out of his subconscious mind. Well, any way—not . . . to worry you but I feel you should know something of what is going on here in Thurber family—so I must tell you what happened last Friday Aug. 19th about ten o'clock in the A.M. William sleeps in front room, gets up about 9:30. . . . He had a bad night worrying about all of our lives and inheritances way *back* as he puts it—in family—always begins about what our ancestors handed down to my two afflicted sons—whatever he means God only knows."

(Ed. note [Thurber to Honeycutt]: the "two afflicted sons" is not supposed to include Jamie.)

"Well of course your father asked him to keep still, that he himself was worried to death also—that he wasn't well either etc. —Then the big fight was on—Wm. raised his voice and *raved* and declared he'd get a 'machine gun' and put us *all* out of our misery —one word brot on another of course and I turning to quiet the bunch on acct of the neighbors here—and Robert getting so mad at Wm's actions told him to 'shut up.' Then Wm had a good chance to lay Robt out—told him he was worse of[f] physically than [Robt] was and that [Robt] should get out and work.

"By this time the 'fighting squad' had gotten into the narrow hall near the bathroom—not much room to fist fight, so I drove them best I could back into dining room—more space—[the fistfight] kept up until your father fell to the floor in sort of a faint afraid Wm would kill Bob. . . . Bob and I thot he was dead he did look so white—I ran for Mr. [Kimmey]—landlord—he came in and helped us get your father on sofa in the front room. And we got all remedies we could and finally got him to himself—Robt sure was frightened about his father and is so cool-headed at such a time—got pillows for under his head, rubbed his head and all while I was heating milk to get up a circulation—Then when Wm saw what he had caused he came to himself and begged for a doctor and how he cried and was sorry. But we had to have it quiet so Mr. [Kimmey] kept him back. Then Wm said to me 'Mamma, let me help my poor father' and I wanted to frighten him for his crazy actions. So in a very *dramatic* way" (Ed. note: You'd have to see this to know what Mrs. T. is like when she's very dramatic) "I told Wm. it was 'TOO LATE NOW.' Then the unearthly yell he gave. Then Mr. [Kimmey] told him his father would be okay. The woman below heard it all and ran across the street. It was the worst, Jamie, I ever knew in my life" (Ed. note: This is exaggerated—she has known worse.) "and I am so ashamed and mortified I dont know what to do for everyone seemed to think we were the '*cream*' of the building as I class them here as *trashy*—'Bootleggers' one tenant—and Elevator Man—other Blacksmith and one a shoemaker and other one a 'Huckster' but good kind folks but now I feel we are the '*alley trash.*' "

You will remember, Miss [Honeycutt], that I told you I hadn't been doing anything but laugh. . . . The Thurber laughing has come on me. It can't be long now, I'm sure. Robt hasn't got the laughs yet but he is younger than me. . . . I've heard Wm laugh the night out—sometimes he sings, too.

Of course I have to make the family believe that I'm the normal one, so don't let on. Also destroy this letter and keep its contents to yourself. . . .

Ha ha ha ha ha ha ha ha ha ha ha ha ha ha ha ha ha ha ha ha ha haha h ha ha ha ha ha ha ha ha ha ha ha ha ha ha ahha hahhahhahhahhahh . . . HA HA HA HA HA HA HA HA HA HA HA . . .

this is terrible . . .

Jamie

"We were all three great mimics," William bragged to Branscomb. "We inherited our humor from our mother. We could mimic anyone." But earlier he had conceded Thurber's superiority in the art through an anecdote he liked to tell: Arriving in Columbus unannounced once in 1934, Thurber called William on the telephone and, in a heavy accent, pretended to be a foreign-born Jewish tailor in downtown Columbus:

"Mista T'ubber, on the eighteenth of January I took from you the measurements of a suit." The suit, the "tailor" went on, was still on the premises months later, unpaid for. A confused William swore he had ordered no suit. Thurber, as tailor, then got excited and threatened legal action. That got William angry, and he shouted that he would never order anything from the likes of such a person (William held the usual provincial anti-Semitic biases of the day, another later embarrassment for Thurber), and that the tailor was obviously a crook trying to blackmail him. "Ha," Thurber shouted back, "for you it is blackmail; for me with your suit I am being stuck!" Mame wrested the telephone from the near-apoplectic William and took up the argument. Finally deciding there must be mistaken identity involved, she asked Thurber to describe William. "Ha!" Thurber exclaimed. "A fine mudder what don't know her own son!"

When the joke was out, William was delighted. Proud of his own talent for mimicry, he tried the same stunt, telephoning a friend. "But somehow it didn't work," William told Richard Oulahan of *Time*. "I did it just like Jamie, and the guy got sore. Jamie could get away with those things. But when you try his stunts yourself, they always go sour. Now this guy I tried the Jewish tailor act on, he just got as mad as a wet hen. He hasn't spoken to me since, and it's been sixteen years."

In 1935, William was hired as a sealer in Columbus's Division of Weights and Measures, in the Department of Safety. The next summer, when Thurber and Helen were vacationing, they allowed William to stay in their New York apartment. Typically, he lost the key and tried to climb through a window. He was seen by the lady in the next apartment, who called the police. "I told them I was James Thurber's brother," William says. "The policeman said, Sure, he was Jimmy Walker's cousin."

Thurber structured even his most fanciful tales too skillfully to forfeit all credibility, but William could not. He was still trying at nearly age eighty, when he told Branscomb how Thurber used to drive his Grandfather Fisher dotty by singing over and over, "Yes, We Have No Bananas." "My grandfather, who was getting a bit senile," said William, "would finally telephone the commissary and say, 'We have plenty of bananas, don't we, Josie? What the hell are they talking about?' " But that song wasn't around until 1923, five years after old man Fisher died. Thurber would have known or researched the fact.

William never understood that Thurber had the rare magician's touch at mixing fact successfully with the stuff of dreams in what he wrote. Impressed by the apparent ease with which his younger brother "cashed in" on stories about their family, William gradually came to believe that, had he thought of them first, he could have done the same. Nothing so bothered him as Thurber's making off with Rex, in the 1935 *New Yorker* casual "Snapshot of a Dog:"

> I ran across a dim photograph of him the other day. . . . He's been dead twenty-five years. His name was Rex (my two brothers and I named him when we were in our early teens) and he was a bull terrier. "An American bull terrier," we used to say, proudly; none of your English bulls. . . . He never lost his dignity even when trying to accomplish the extravagant tasks my brothers and myself used to set for him. . . .
>
> Late one afternoon he wandered home, too slowly and too uncertainly to be the Rex that had trotted briskly homeward up our avenue for ten years. I think we all knew when he came through the gate that he was dying. He had apparently taken a terrible beating, probably from the owner of some dog that he had got into a fight with. . . . He licked at our hands and, staggering, fell, but got up again. We could see that he was looking for someone. One of his three masters [William] was not home. He did not get home for an hour. During that hour the bull terrier fought against death as he had fought against the cold, strong current of Alum Creek, as he had fought to climb twelve-foot walls. When the person he was waiting for did come through the gate, whistling, ceasing to whistle, Rex walked a few wabbly paces toward him, touched his hand with his muzzle, and fell down again. This time he didn't get up.

William had been the first to get after-school and summer jobs and so was able to buy Rex through an ad in a Columbus newspaper. Rex was *his*. They had all felt bad about Rex's death, but only William's grief could be considered legitimate, he thought, which led him to try to elaborate on Thurber's classic account: "Rex had markings on him that looked like an Eton jacket," William added. "He could climb up a tree about twelve feet before he lost momentum and footing and came down. He'd crouch for a signal and go after a deflated football we threw for him. We think he was poisoned and then beaten."

What was all this about the three boys naming Rex, or his having three masters, William asked? The *Reader's Digest* reprinted "Snapshot of a Dog" a year after its *New Yorker* appearance, prompting William to collaborate with a local acquaintance on a piece that tells of how William bought the dog and trained it, and largely repeats Thurber's accounts of Rex's ability to scale walls and drag home heavy objects. William mailed the article to the *Digest*. Not only was the clumsy, repetitive piece returned, innocent insult to injury was added by an enclosed ebullient note to William from an editor saying how much the *Digest* admired the writings of his brother.

William knew further frustrations. In July 1933, "The Night the Bed Fell" kicked off Thurber's *My Life and Hard Times* series in the *New Yorker*. As has been noted in it, father decides to sleep in the attic one night, "to be away where he could think." Thurber shares his own room with his cousin, "Briggs Beall, who believed that he was likely to cease breathing when he was asleep . . . if he were not awakened every hour." Thurber is sleeping on an Army cot, which tips over in the night with a crash. This awakens Mame, who believes the large wooden bed in the attic has fallen on Charles. Her shouts of "Let's go to your poor father!" awaken and frighten Herman [William], who begins to yell, "You're all right, Mama!" Briggs believes the shouting is a collective effort to revive him from near-suffocation; he douses himself with spirits of camphor and breaks a window for air. Thurber, under the overturned cot, wakes in the nightmarish belief that he is entombed in a mine, and begins calling, "Get me out of here!" Rex the dog attacks Briggs, whom he never liked, and has to be wrestled to the floor by Roy [Robert]. The door to the attic is stuck, and Mame's pounding arouses Charles, who comes down the stairs in the belief that the house is on fire.

But it had been William who fell out of the Army cot. He had let out an Indian whoop that aroused Mame, who indeed thought the bed in the attic had collapsed on Charles, as it had once before. The Thurbers frequently rented out rooms to help ends meet, William adds, and a woman roomer at the time worried constantly about burglars. Aroused by the crash of William's cot and Mame's shouts, the roomer decided that there was a burglar in the darkened room with her, promptly threw her shoe through the glass transom above the door, and called for help. James hadn't figured in it at all, and as far as William was concerned he had again made off with a story that was properly William's. Furthermore, he said, if he did sing in his sleep, as Herman did in "The Night the Bed Fell," it wouldn't have been "Marching Through Georgia," or "Onward, Christian Soldiers."

If William influenced Thurber at all, it may have been in two respects:

"My oldest brother was supposed to be the family artist," Thurber told Alistair Cooke in 1956, "and nobody paid any attention to what they called my scrawls. William would copy very carefully with pen and ink the pen-and-ink drawings of Charles Dana Gibson. I think my mother and father thought at first that these were originals that they saw around the house."

From age ten, William did show a knack for sketching accurate reproductions of photographs and pictures, and even careful and literal representations of real people and objects. William's first sketch, one he kept all his life, was of a little girl telling an old man, "You're going on a long journey." Robert thinks William's drawing habits at home may have given Thurber the idea, though Thurber's loose and careless lines seem more of a doodling nature, inspired by, if anything, newspaper comic strips. His parents remained convinced that it was "Bill" who had the true artistic potential, even after Thurber became one of the most popular professional cartoonists in the business. William's disciplined drawing was never liberated by a creative bent; he could only watch in bafflement as his younger brother went on to glory with a strange form of art William couldn't have understood or emulated if he had wanted to.

A more likely influence on Thurber were William's dime novels and pulp adventure literature of the day, which he read and Thurber picked up. Thur-

An early drawing.

ber's avid following of Captain Dick Slater and Lieutenant Bob Eastbrook in the series called *The Liberty Boys of '76* led to his first story, written at age ten, "Horse Sandusky and the Intrepid Scout," which, to Thurber's relief in later years, was lost to posterity.

On those rare occasions when William would get in touch with Thurber after the latter left Columbus, it was usually to ask a favor. In reply to one such request, for money to invest in a business venture in Puerto Rico, Thurber observed, "You think of more remarkable things than Walter Mitty. I'd love to hear you match your nervous Ohio accent with a West Indian's broken English. Why not try selling wood-burning sets to the Eskimos, or Adler elevator shoes to the Pygmies?"

When the Thurber/Nugent play, *The Male Animal,* was revived, William telephoned Thurber in Williamsburg, Virginia, to ask for complimentary tickets to the road show, then playing in Columbus. "I told him to buy the seats he wanted and I would reimburse him," Thurber wrote Mame and Robert. "I said I would do this in the case of [your] nurse, too, if you still wanted to get her some. Authors haven't got passes for years, but people don't realize this, and we paid more than $40 for tickets the night the play opened in New York in 1940."

William knew a brief moment of local glory in 1958, when the house at 625 Oak Street was torn down. The Thurbers had lived there for less than a year, but it turns up in Thurber's hilarious classic "File and Forget." Following misaddressed shipments of books he never ordered and letters to him filled with misspelled names, a frustrated Thurber invites additional confusion by sarcastically writing the publisher: "It would not come as a surprise to me if your firm . . . wrote me in care of my mother at 568 [actually 625] Oak Street, Columbus, Ohio. I was thirteen years old when we lived there, back in 1908 [actually 1903]." Three dozen copies of "Grandma Was a Nudist" were, of course, sent promptly to 568 Oak Street, to the consternation of a fictional Mrs. Edwards at that address.

Even this slight brushstroke on the city map by a famous local son made it a newspaper feature when the church that owned the property decided to tear it down for more parking space. The *Columbus Citizen* posed William atop a pile of rubble at the location and quoted him as saying he could remember only that the house had always been very damp.

Over the last fifteen years of his life, Thurber worked away at a play about the *New Yorker*. On July 27, 1948, he outlined a version of it for Elliott Nugent:

The play opens on a Tuesday just as the weekly art meeting is about to start. Tim [Thurber] has worked at the office all night instead of going back to his home in Ludlow, Connecticut. I am using real names with the exception of Ross and one or two others. Managing editor No. 33 is just quitting and No. 34 starting in. At the end of the play we see the advent of No. 35. Ross—Walter Bruce—has many problems this day including the descent of Tim's mother and brother Willard from Illinois. Willard is my brother William who thinks he is "shelled," who has never been able to work, and who thinks he could have been better at anything than anybody. I have always wanted to put William on the stage, since he would make wonderful comedy and now fits into my plot.

By the time he was calling the play *Make My Bed*, Thurber had taken the precaution of telling William of his plans to write him into the plot and assured him he would be compensated for it. It would, he told Robert, turn "Bill into a character never to be forgotten." What kind of character and why it would never be forgotten he didn't say, but in all likelihood William was fortunate in being denied this dubious immortality. The play was never finished.

Still, Thurber remained more amused by his older brother than disdainful of him. After William's retirement in 1960, he visited Thurber in New York. "We had a memory game about the Columbus of 55 years ago and longer," Thurber writes the family. "Turned out we could both name all the players on the Columbus Senators in 1904 and 1905 and all members of the Empire Stock Company of about the same time."

William stayed with the family intermittently during the 1930s, when the Thurbers lived on Gay Street. After Charles's death in 1939, Robert and his mother moved into the two-bedroom apartment in the Southern Hotel, where William, ever the loner, had a room of his own for at least six of the fourteen years his mother and brother lived there. Unlike Robert, who had never felt well enough to court women, William occasionally escorted ladies —always of respectable repute and proper standing, and usually known to Mame and Robert personally—to a restaurant or the theater.

He retired with a pension in 1960, after twenty-five years with the city government. In September 1962, he moved to Clemson, South Carolina, in pursuit of warmer weather and a lower cost of living, and still full of his get-rich-quick dreams. "My brother has a business connection [in real estate, in Greensboro, North Carolina]," Robert wrote. "He will give it a good try for a couple of months. If it works out o.k., he will probably be there indefinitely.

. . . This makes me the last of the clan in Ohio and it is not exactly an uplifting feeling."

Robert was stunned when his older brother finally translated a daydream into reality by marrying in 1963 at age seventy, and into a Clemson family of some apparent local distinction. Thurber had been warning William away from marriage since 1927, when, during a falling-out with Althea, he wrote to William: "It's for life. All the tinsel and the glamour and the glory, and soon it all becomes one smelly substance." William may have kept this in mind for the next thirty-six years, but less than two years after Thurber's death he gave in.

Robert didn't make it to the wedding, but he was invited to live with the newlyweds. He visited them briefly, and then William lured him from Columbus to Greensboro. The bait, which Robert readily took, was that Greensboro was the hometown of William Sydney Porter, better known by his pseudonym, O. Henry, and one of Robert's favorite authors. But Robert missed Columbus, and two months later he was back there, again living alone in a residential hotel.

William appeared to possess many of his father's kind and gentle manners, but his chronic forgetfulness and thoughtlessness frustrated Robert to the end. "Although I write my brother frequently, he seldom bothers to communicate or reply or even to acknowledge receipt of letters, cards, clippings, magazines, etc.," Robert wrote sadly in 1969.

William died at age eighty, in November 1973, and was buried in South Carolina at his wife's request. It may have been inevitable that he be the one Thurber not to lie in the family plot in Green Lawn Cemetery. Frequently out of touch with himself, he had chosen to live on the periphery of his family circle. He survived much of his solitary life on Mitty illusions, and seems to have ended happily on the greatest one of all: that as a product of the same circumstances and environment as Jamie, he had to have been as talented as his brother. It was enough, finally, that he, William Fisher Thurber, understood that—even if nobody else did.

8

That Daguerreotype of a Lady

The old house was a fire trap, menaced by burning coal and by lighted lamps carried by ladies of dimming vision, but these perils . . . are lost upon the very young. I spent a lot of time there as a child, and I thought it was a wonderful place, different from the dull formality of the ordinary home and in every difference enchanting. The floors were uneven . . . and the lower sash of one of the windows in the sitting room was flush with the floor—a perfect place to sit and watch the lightning or the snow."

—from "Daguerreotype of a Lady"

By 1940, when his sight was fading, recovering, blurring, and playing other maddening tricks on him, Thurber was scheduled for an eye operation, with no guarantee that his sight would be better. The gods of fortune had permitted him his limited vision longer than medical science could explain, the doctor said, and Thurber knew that this borrowed time was running out.

One night at Robert Benchley's apartment at the Royalton Hotel, a depressed Thurber drank himself into a noisy state of self-pity. Enraged by his bad luck, he threw his glass and then smashed a wooden desk chair. Benchley calmed him and, putting a soothing hand on his back, said, "Please go home, Jim. You're not having a good time and you're spoiling the evening for everyone else."

Thurber dissolved in tears, citing all the unfair obstacles he'd had to overcome in his life. He had never had the kind of support from his father that Elliott Nugent had had from his. He'd been put out to board as a kid by his family. He was about to go through more hell with his eye because his parents hadn't had the sense to obtain the proper treatment promptly after the accident. There were also laments over unrequited love, and, finally, the general damnation of all women to hell. Then he lay down on a bed and fell asleep.

In such lubricated entreaties for love, sympathy, and understanding, Thurber regularly drew upon this master list of complaints, which included the relevant, the irrelevant, and the ambivalent. Among the last was that of parental neglect, which centered on being "put out to board as a kid." For the woman who boarded him was Aunt Margery Dangler Albright, whom he would commemorate with affection and elegance in his *Album* and elsewhere.

Though good art is frequently alive with the germ of inner conflict, and though Thurber seems uncertain about how he finally felt about a number of his subjects in *The Thurber Album*, the surest and best of that effort is "Daguerreotype of a Lady." His recollections of life with Aunt Margery Albright inspired a written gem too genuine to harbor anything but the purer elements of sincerity. Unluckily, in qualifying himself as a victim of family rejection, he left others to assume that boarding with Margery Albright, her daughter Belle, and their transient roomers amounted to bitter involuntary exile. But Thurber's splendid literary canonization of Aunt Margery is no exercise in guilt. And if he really ever had hard feelings about his days with the Albrights, he wrote his way out of them; one who lives much of his life by illusion finds it an easy matter to forgive through it. Though Thurber sets the written record straight, Thurber scholars have preferred the darker versions he talked about over the preceding years, comments usually carelessly tossed off in a restless quest for pity and an instinct for good theater.

Ann Honeycutt, an agreeable and regular pub-crawling companion of Thurber's during the seven years before his marriage to Helen, had never met Mrs. Albright and totally accepted Thurber's comments to her that his childhood included periods of living "with that awful old woman," in Honeycutt's words. Thurber's agent and close friend John (Jap) Gude was also led to believe that Thurber was an unwilling boarder at the Albrights.

In the mid-seventies, Charles H. Cooke, a former *New Yorker* reporter who had worked closely with Thurber in the 1930s and idolized him, wrote to Katharine White to express dismay over two books that had just been published containing depressing summaries of Thurber. Katharine replied that if the Thurber story was "somber and tragic . . . so was Jim's life." She was, she added, "astounded at the full report of his really dreadful childhood."

Katharine had edited many a Thurber piece in her time and was well aware of Thurber's readiness to remake himself to suit the moment and the audience. Knowing of my own plans to decipher some Thurber complexities through biography, she reminded me, "You are dealing with an exaggerator." Either she failed to consider that the principal origin of that "full report" of a "dreadful childhood," garnered from Thurber's friends and colleagues, could only have been the old exaggerator himself, or, ever a lady of gracious instinct, she welcomed a deprived-childhood theory as partial explanation for Thurber's rudeness to her over the years.

Certainly Thurber's boyhood was cruelly conditioned by the loss of his eye; it left him introverted, a frequent object of scorn to himself, and a perpetual seeker of personal recognition and acceptance, even if that meant "playing the fool." By the time he joined the boisterous, literary/journalism segment of New York life in the 1920s, psychoanalytical theory had for some time made it fashionable to lay one's inadequacies of personality on one's parents. The role of "victim of circumstance" diminished the need for personal accounting of one's behavior, and offered friend and lover the opportunity to forgive, sympathize, and even to "make it all up" in some way. It was a popular avenue of romantic pursuit for a man to offer himself as deserving of love now because he had been denied it in his early, defenseless years.

In the dramatic games he played with Honeycutt, the actress Paula Trueman, and other women, Thurber never interfered with their impressions that his flights of professional achievement were the more remarkable given the burden of an unhappy marriage, doomed eyesight, and a neglected childhood. His case had its valid points; much of his humor masked private and persistent terrors. It is simply difficult to square his indictment of family banishment with the record, including his own.

In 1964, a Thurber biographer wrote that for a number of years "Thurber did not even live at home"—that, not being his mother's favorite, he was sent by her to live with Mrs. Albright (adding, correctly, "whom he adored"). The biography doesn't have Thurber living with his family again until he is attending college. In response, Robert writes:

> Jim wasn't put out to board with the Albrights for a number of years, but in his grade school days particularly he spent much time there for various reasons: When we had to stay with the Fishers because of my father's serious illness [and] crowded conditions, Jim spent a lot of time [at the Albrights] for . . . two or three weeks at a time. It posed no hardship for him as they were especially fond of him and he enjoyed being there. It was a relief, too, due to Fisher family flare-ups. . . .

Young as we boys were [in 1905], we sensed a resentment [at the Fishers] which was all too apparent at times. Our grandfather, although quite hospitable and generous, on some of his bad days seemed to take things out on us. He imbibed too freely at certain times which no doubt accounted for it. Actually it was not a pleasant situation for any of us, but we had to go through with it. . . . For years after that Jim was a frequent visitor at the Albrights, but not for years or months [at a time] as [has been written].

The house rule was that when Grandfather Fisher entered a room, its occupants would fall silent until he spoke to them. If he liked Jamie, the one-eyed ugly duckling, least of his Thurber grandsons, it may be because he was often at the center of household commotion. A young cousin remembers a visit to the Fishers at which Thurber purposely frightened her by offering to remove his glass eye and give it to her. She fled in horror.

Grandfather Fisher did resent the situation. He had built his business to a satisfying point of local economic influence. Success was the proper measurement of a breadwinner. It annoyed him that his daughter's husband not only failed to meet the measurement but could so mismanage his affairs that at the first serious family illness the entire Thurber family had to be sheltered for a number of months, at Grandma Fisher's insistence.

To ease matters for both Jamie and the Fisher household, Mame sent Jamie, the one Grandfather found the most unsettling and disruptive, to board with the Albrights. She had been warned by doctors to keep Jamie from roughhousing with his energetic and physically disposed brothers or with other playmates, his poor eyesight affecting his coordination and leaving him vulnerable to further injury. She saw the Albrights as a reliable and agreeable sanctuary for him. There is no recorded suggestion that he was anything but warmly welcomed and glad to be there. Aunt Margery had delivered him at birth and was fondly protective of ten-year-old James.

William and Robert, in their life with Grandfather, frequently had reason to envy their brother. They, as well as their mother, felt that James gave every indication of enjoying the peaceful stays at the Albrights, where he liked to read, observe a constantly changing assortment of roomers, and listen to Aunt Margery's outlandish stories of maintaining the health of friend, neighbor, and relative with her homemade concoctions. These ranged from slippery-elm bark to a broth of sheep droppings. (It is said that her husband, who died in 1865, finally chose death to his wife's proposed preventions of it.)

The Albrights—widow and daughter—were considered "family" by Charles Thurber, who, as a schoolboy, had also been cared for by Aunt Margery. In "Gentleman from Indiana," Thurber recalls that "a great aunt of mine once told me that in 1884 Charley had marched most of the night . . . on behalf of James G. Blaine." The only "great-aunt" in a position to know this would have been Margery Albright. Charles's inevitable reference to her as "Aunt Margery" was adopted by the three Thurber boys.

All the Thurbers were frequent visitors at the Albrights. William remembers Aunt Margery as "a truly remarkable woman" who "had a great influence on my father, and all three of his boys. . . . She was our nurse from early childhood, and left an indelible benign imprint on all of us." Cousin Earl Fisher says that Aunt Margery occasionally cared for members of his own family at times of sickness. As the eye tragedy drove Thurber in on himself, Aunt Margery's became not only a good place to avoid the mishaps of home life but to develop a few independent resources that would help him prevail over a childhood in which he was "different" from the others—perhaps, to his own mind, even a freak. When he dropped out of college in his sophomore year, he spent his time in libraries or visiting the Albrights.

Helen Thurber, as stern a pragmatist in her own way as Mrs. Albright, believes that her husband didn't really enjoy the closeness to Aunt Margery —or even to his mother—that his writing portrays; that he described his relationships with them to suit his creative purposes. But Thurber could hardly have kept airborne his long flights of affectionate adulation of Aunt Margery—or of his mother, for that matter—unless they were largely powered by honest conviction. If the Albright home was an exile, it seems to have been a pleasant and beneficial one for Thurber. In the mid-seventies, having read the reviews of the book that presumably reported Helen's position on the subject, Robert writes:

> Evidently Helen believed all those things that my brother told her about his early life. You would think [my parents] were abusive . . . to read the [book's] reviews, when in fact they were kinder, more unselfish and considerate than probably 90 percent of any parents. . . . They would have been puzzled over statements about mistreatment or abuse. My brother for some reason saw fit to give this impression. He was never very close to my parents for reasons of his own. . . . If he was ever discontented he never mentioned it . . . so it was a great surprise [to] read he was abused and unhappy at home. It is extremely hard for me to believe that he [said such things].

New Yorker fiction editor William Maxwell believes that some of Thurber's lines in "Daguerreotype of a Lady" are among the best the magazine had run until then, and hardly the product of an angry and resentful mind:

> She had fractured her right kneecap in a fall on the ice when she was in her late teens, and the leg remained twisted, so that when she was standing, she bent over as if she were about to lean down and tie her shoelace, and her torso swayed from side to side when she walked, like the slow pendulum of an ancient clock, arousing sympathy in the old and wonder in the young. . . . In her moments of repose, which were rare enough in a long and arduous lifetime, the gentleness of her face, enhanced by white hair smoothly parted in the middle, belied the energy of her body and the strength of her spirit, but her mouth grew firm, her eyes turned serious or severe, and her will overcame her handicap when she felt called upon, as she often did, to take up some burden too heavy for the shoulders of lesser women, or too formidable for mere menfolks to cope with.

"The clocks that strike in my dreams are often the clocks of Columbus," Thurber wrote in 1953, a sentence that E. B. White, in his *New Yorker* obituary of Thurber, immortalized by ordaining it one of Thurber's loveliest thoughts. Though the university's Orton Hall clock tolled the class hours during Thurber's years of attendance, the clock tower Thurber had in mind was that of the church across from where Margery Dangler Albright lived from the late 1870s to 1918, with her daughter, Belle. As Thurber writes: "On the opposite side of the street, the deep-toned clock in the steeple of Holy Cross Church marked, in quarter hours, the passing of the four decades she lived there. It was a quiet part of town in those days, and the two-story frame house was one of the serene, substantial structures of my infancy and youth, for all its flimsy shabbiness."

If Thurber ever felt himself an unhappy castoff at the Albrights, no written mention of it by him is found. His several résumés of his life actually begin with Aunt Margery. In 1945, in his preface to *The Thurber Carnival*, Thurber writes that he was "brought into the world by an old practical nurse named Margery Albright, who had delivered the babies of neighbor women before the Civil War," and goes on to say: "Thurber's very first bit of writing was a so-called poem entitled 'My Aunt Mrs. John T. Savage's Garden at 185 South Fifth Street, Columbus, Ohio.' " [Mrs. John T. Savage was actually Mrs. Albright.]

At age ten or eleven, he found the Albright home—not the tense Fisher or noisy Thurber households—the place where he first decided to write creatively. The poem seems not to have been a lament of loneliness but a paean to the garden that he wrote of lovingly forty-five years later in his tribute to Aunt Margery.

In the 1935 *New Yorker* casual "Doc Marlowe," Thurber says of Aunt Margery (whom he calls Mrs. Willoughby here): "She had been a nurse in our family, and I used to go and visit her over week-ends, sometimes, for I was very fond of her." Life at Aunt Margery's was never lonely for young Thurber. The upstairs bedroom was always filled with interesting boarders, who came and went. There was Doc Marlowe (probably a fictitious name), who managed a patent medicine show. As a teenager, Thurber would pick up Doc's ingredients at the Wholesale Chemical Company, and Aunt Margery and Belle would bottle the stuff as "Sioux Liniment." The medicine show included a Mexican rope thrower, Chickelilli, and a banjo player, Professor Fields, who also boarded with the Albrights. Doc Marlowe would come out after the entertainment and harangue the audience to buy his liniment.

Though he knew that Doc, who passed himself off as a Wild West scout, was from Brooklyn, young Thurber never doubted at the time that Doc was the greatest man in the world. He even forgave Doc for cheating Aunt Margery at poker, for cheating Thurber himself out of the price of a soda with a two-headed quarter, and for selling two other roomers an old car rigged to get the couple no more than a few miles west of Columbus. Disillusionment easily loses out to understanding and forgiveness in his reflections on Marlowe.

On Saturday mornings, Aunt Margery would take young Thurber grocery shopping with her, buying carefully and selectively from the truck gardeners on Fourth Street, and ending up at the store of John Hanse, the neighborhood grocer. William remembers that when Thurber was a teenager, old man Hanse was amused by his original doggerel; whenever they entered the store, Thurber would make up limericks for the aging grocer, rhyming "Hanse" with "pants."

In 1950, amid his preparations for the "Album" series, Thurber wrote "The Figgerin' of Aunt Wilma," in which Aunt Margery becomes Aunt Wilma Hudson and Hanse, Hance. Hanse shared the cost of a telephone with the Hays Carriage Shop next door; the phone, set in a revolving cubicle in the wall, could be twirled around to serve both businesses. "When I was ten," Thurber writes, "I used to hang around the grocery on Saturday afternoons, waiting for the telephone to disappear into the wall. Then I would wait for it to swing back again. It was a kind of magic."

On this day, Aunt Wilma buys ninety-eight cents' worth of groceries, and gives Mr. Hance a dollar. (In 1905, "what she had bought for less than a dollar made the market basket bulge.") The grocer has no pennies, so he places a nickel on the counter and asks for three cents. Distrustful of all menfolk, Aunt Wilma protests that Mr. Hance owes her two cents. At the end of hopeless misunderstandings on Aunt Wilma's part, Mr. Hance wearily accepts the loss of five cents. "I don't know how the world gets along with the men runnin' it," Aunt Wilma complains afterward, as Aunt Margery so often did.

Earlier, Thurber had also drawn upon some of Aunt Margery's idiosyncrasies to paint "A Portrait of Aunt Ida." Aunt Ida sees conspiracy behind every public event—corrupt goings-on by the men of the world. She discounts reports that the men on the sinking *Titanic* waved goodbye with brave smiles and smoked cigarettes. She is convinced that most of them had to be shot by the ship's officers "to prevent them from crowding into the lifeboats ahead of the older and less attractive women passengers."

Aunt Ida believes she is psychic; she has premonitions. She predicts "that old Mrs. Hutchins would not last out the year (she missed on old Mrs. Hutchins for twenty-two years but finally made it)." "Most of Aunt Ida's dreams foretold the fate of women, for what happened to women was of much greater importance to Aunt Ida than what happened to men. Men usually 'brought things on themselves.' " "In telling the sex of unborn children she was right about half the time." She knows young men and women who lost the use of their legs from smoking cigarettes.

Thurber has Aunt Ida dying at age ninety-one.

> She tended to her begonias and wrote out a check for the rent the day she took to her bed for the last time. It irked her not to be up and about, and she accused the doctor the family brought in of not knowing his business. There was marketing to do, and friends to call on, and work to get through with. When friends and relatives began calling on her, she was annoyed.

Aunt Ida's deathbed scene seems Thurber's dress rehearsal for that of Aunt Margery, who died at nearly ninety. Six years after the Aunt Ida story, he was writing:

> When Margery Albright took to her bed for the last time . . . she gave strict orders that she was not to be "called back." She had seen too much of that, at a hundred bedsides, and she wanted to die quietly, without a lot of unseemly fuss over the natural ending of a span of nearly

ninety complete and crowded years. There was no call, she told her daughter, to summon anybody. There was nothing anybody could do. A doctor would just pester her, and she couldn't abide one now. Her greatest comfort lay in the knowledge that . . . there was money enough for a stone marker tucked away in a place her daughter knew about. . . . Then she gave a few more final instructions and turned over in bed, pulling her bad leg into a comfortable position. "Hush up!" she snapped when her daughter began to cry. "You give a body the fidgets."

Aunt Margery died June 6, 1918, just before Thurber departed for Washington, D.C. and his wartime job as code clerk. She was buried in Green Lawn Cemetery, some distance from the Fisher ground, in a plot she had paid for, a dollar at a time, through the hard years. The twenty-three-year-old Thurber attended the funeral of this woman who had nurtured him with care and kindness. After the service, he stopped by the place that had served him both as an occasional foster home and, in later years, a favorite retreat. "It seemed to me," he wrote of that moment,

> standing there in the dim parlor of the old frame house, that something as important as rain had gone out of the land. . . . Mrs. Albright . . . would enjoy the absence of night in Paradise only because everlasting light would give her more time to look after people and to get things done. I still like to believe, after all these years, that chalcedony is subject to cleaning, and that a foolish angel falls now and then and breaks a wing, for glory, as mere reward of labor ended, would make Margery Albright uncomfortable and sad.

In a February 7, 1949, letter to *New Yorker* fiction editor Gus Lobrano, Thurber makes further confusing references to the Albright story which appear nowhere else:

> I was farmed out with Mrs. Albright from the age of eight to the age of fourteen, and one reason I have taken so long to get around to this, my favorite story, is that the ancient relationship was at times a sore point with my own mother. It is an odd thing that in this same old frame house my father was raised by Mrs. Albright from the time he was six until he was fourteen. . . . When, at fourteen, I was taken with a high fever, I staggered from my comfortable bed and went back [to Aunt Margery], collapsing on the very stoop I have mentioned. I was in bed three weeks and nearly died. You will see how deep this all goes, and I

hope it is reflected in the story about the greatest individual I have ever known.

Of his "Album" subjects, Thurber selected only his mother and Aunt Margery—the two women most important to his formative years—to be reprinted in a later collection, *Alarms and Diversions*. His latter-day adoption of Aunt Margery and her house as mother and home seems incredible to Robert. But though Thurber the artist was often purposely at odds with Thurber the person, it is easy to be persuaded by "Daguerreotype of a Lady," with its lovely appreciation of Aunt Margery, that it was intended as Thurber's last word on the subject.

9

That Sullivant School

In seeking an adjective to describe the Sullivant School of my years —1900 to 1908—I can only think of "tough." Sullivant School was tough. The boys . . . came mostly from . . . a poorish district with many colored families and . . . white families of the laboring class. . . .

Most grammar-school baseball teams are made up of boys in the seventh and eighth grades. . . . Several of [Sullivant's] best players were in the fourth grade, known to the teachers . . . as the Terrible Fourth. In that grade you first encountered fractions and long division, and many pupils lodged there for years, like logs in a brook. Some of the more able baseball-players had been in the fourth grade for seven or eight years. . . .

The Sullivant School baseball team of 1905 defeated several high-

school teams in the city and claimed the high-school championship of
the state, to which title it had, of course, no technical right.

—from "I Went to Sullivant"

Some facts about Sullivant actually survive Thurber's skills in exaggeration,
though he did not, to begin with, start there in 1900. His first and second
grades were spent in the Ohio Avenue School, 1900–1902, but of all his
school years, the teachers and classmates who most frequently peopled his
dreams and memory were those at Sullivant.

The last piece he wrote, published in the *Columbus Dispatch* a few weeks
before his death, was about Sullivant. His fourth-grade teacher at Sullivant,
Miss Ballinger, Thurber says, first encouraged his drawing. She brought a
white rabbit to class and asked the children to draw it. Thurber's sketch so
impressed her she kept him after school the next day and asked him to try
again. Thurber's embarrassment at this unexpected attention, and the
strangeness of being alone with Miss Ballinger and a rabbit, resulted in a
drawing unrecognizable as a rabbit, and Miss Ballinger paid him no further
attention.

His fifth grade was made unforgettable by a teacher, Linnie Wood, who
each Friday afternoon would place curly-headed Elsie Bierbower atop her
desk to recite for the entertainment of the class. (As Elsie Janis, she went on
to a prominent acting career, patriotically entertaining the troops in World
War I and appearing at Liberty Bond rallies.)

Columbus citizens would have been happy to see Sullivant slip anonymously into history; few, if any, remembered the school with any affection
until Thurber made it immortal. Named for James Sullivant, the longtime
president of the city's board of education, the school was built in 1871 for
$73,407, an amount considered exorbitant by aroused taxpayers. The
nineteen-room, red-brick school was designed to be overcrowded, intended
for seven hundred pupils, or an average of nearly thirty-seven to a classroom.
The instructor/student ratio was enough to impede the effectiveness of the
teachers (all women), even when they weren't fighting for their pride and
physical safety against the growing percentage of aging unruly male students.

Three years after the school was completed, a private "visiting committee"
made its annual tour of Columbus schools and reported, "We find that the
three-story Sullivant building is very objectionable . . . and we trust that
no other of this character will be built in this city." In a sulk over Sullivant's

"high cost," the school board refused to allocate funds to put a bell in the belfry to signal the start of school or the end of recess. Out of Christian charity, the nearby Presbyterian church agreed to ring *its* bell upon school opening, checking the time each day with Savage's jewelry store. No recess bell was provided, and six years after the school opened, the annual visiting committee noted that the teachers risked contracting respiratory ailments in the winter by having to raise the windows or go outside to shake a dinner bell. The committee recommended "that a gong bell be placed on the outside of the building, operated by a pulley from within." No action was taken on the recommendation. William remembers that he and his classmates, instructed to stop immediately what they were doing when the dinner bell sounded, would freeze in exaggerated positions the moment the principal, Miss McLaughlin, emerged to ring it at the end of recess.

Sullivant's only boosters appear to have been the older pupils, who made up a dangerous gashouse gang. An ancient Columbus native, Carlos Shedd, who entered Sullivant in 1873, remembered years later that after-school fights were a daily practice from the beginning, thanks to partisan loyalties to opposite sides of a line described by Oak Street and Sixth. Weaponry was usually "Irish confetti"—rocks, packed in snowballs or not. Robert agrees that Sullivant was tough, but both he and William could hold their own in a fistfight, he says, and escape was possible by the dozen routes one could take between schoolyard and home.

The humorist Donald Ogden Stewart, eight days older than Thurber, was a year ahead of him at Sullivant, because of Thurber's lost school year in Washington. Stewart writes that he first remembers seeing Thurber in the group of boys watching him while he was hitting "Beans" Horne in the stomach during recess, behind Sullivant's outdoor toilets. Fighting went with the curriculum. "School never let out," writes Thurber, "without at least one fight starting up, and sometimes there were as many as five or six raging between the corner of Oak and Sixth Streets and the corner of Rich and Fourth Streets, four blocks away. Now and again virtually the whole school turned out to fight the Catholic boys of the Holy Cross Academy . . . for no reason at all—in winter with snowballs and iceballs, in other seasons with fists, brickbats and clubs." Territory, rather than race or religion, seems to have motivated the fights.

How did Thurber, the passive, studious, nonparticipant, get by? He would seem an obvious target for the usual bullying of boys of Sullivant age. And as he writes, "I wore glasses from the time I was eight, and I knew my lessons, and both of those things were considered pretty terrible at Sullivant." He was also a daydreamer. When he was in the fourth or fifth grade, a teacher's report card to his parents read: "I think James is deaf. He never seems to hear anything I say to him."

"Jamie was very shy and very quiet," his mother recalled. "He never had to study much, but he always got good grades. He absorbed more in half an hour than the other boys did in a whole evening. He was always very good and never got a bad mark in deportment."

In "I Went to Sullivant," Thurber's safety is assured when one of his classmates, "Floyd," adopts him. Floyd, a black center fielder on the Sullivant baseball team, is one of the fourth-grade teenage holdovers. Nobody knows his other name, including Floyd, and "he would grow sullen and ominous" when the teachers "insisted that he must have another name to go with Floyd." When a teacher tries to discipline Floyd, he breaks her switch and begins "to take the room apart, beginning with the desks." The janitor is called but Floyd wrestles him to the floor and won't let him up until the janitor promises to be good and says "Dat's what Ah get" ten times.

> I don't suppose I would ever have got through Sullivant School alive if it hadn't been for Floyd. For some reason he appointed himself my protector, and I needed one. If Floyd was known to be on your side, nobody in the school would dare be "after" you and chase you home. I was one of the ten or fifteen male pupils in Sullivant School who always, or almost always, knew their lessons, and I believe Floyd admired the mental prowess of a youngster who knew how many continents there were and whether or not the sun was inhabited. Also, one time when it came my turn to read to the class . . . I came across the word "Duquesne" and knew how to pronounce it. That charmed Floyd, who had been slouched in his seat idly following the printed page of his worn and pencilled textbook. . . . After that, word got around that Floyd would beat the tar out of anybody that messed around me.

It is a wonderfully touching scenario, but more likely it was Thurber's one-eyed, glasses-wearing condition that protected him; he was neither a threat physically nor a worthy challenge. Neither brother remembers a Floyd who "protected" Thurber, or that Thurber needed protecting. Joel Sayre, whose parents sent him to Columbus Academy partly to avoid Sullivant, attended Sullivant baseball games, and remembers that a black youth named Dick Peterson befriended Robert. Robert became an excellent player for the Sullivant baseball team, and Peterson, its captain, volunteered to act as Robert's bodyguard. Sayre thinks it is a probability—a moving one, at that—that a young handicapped Thurber, in Mitty fashion, invented Floyd as protector, as

Peterson came to champion Robert. Neither Robert nor Sayre knew if Peterson died in a saloon brawl when in the sixth grade, as Thurber writes, but given Sullivant's high enrollment of maturing, bellicose pupils, neither would deny the possibility.

After Thurber had finished sixth grade, his family moved a number of blocks farther east, enrolling the boys in Douglas School, a mile from Sullivant. Thurber is remembered there as always knowing the answers when called upon by the teachers, but shy, nervous, and red-faced with embarrassment at having to recite before the class. Margaret McElvaine, his eighth-grade teacher, expressed to Mame her concern over Thurber's excitability; whenever she called on him to recite, his Adam's apple bobbed so wildly that he could hardly speak. An inveterate doodler and jotter, his notebook was constantly with him, serving as a kind of security blanket.

In 1951, when *Time* was burrowing into his past in preparation for its cover story, Thurber characteristically volunteered facts of his own to the editors, and added: "In case I made myself out pretty much of a pussycat in grammar school, I was head of what we called the Fifth Street Army in 1906 and 1907, which consisted of a dozen boys around the age of twelve. We got into some fights but no crime."

Though Fifth Street included Aunt Margery's run-down neighborhood, Thurber's wild life as a delinquent seems to have amounted to an instance of dropping light bulbs on pedestrians from the upper stories of the State Capitol. His grade-school work is thought to have been consistently well above average (the Sullivant grades remain undiscovered), though none of his teachers later claimed to have identified him as marked for future success.

Outside class, he continued to tease the girls, performing tricks with his glass eye—acts of painful self-consciousness and disparagement, driven by the determination to laugh at himself before others did. That trait remained ingrained in his personality for his lifetime. With his peers, he could be witty and was generally liked, though considered a bit of an oddball. His writing (rated "E" for "excellent" both years at Douglas) and his popularity helped earn him election as the 1909 class prophet. The lengthy class prophecy, a story seventeen typewritten pages long, is his first available writing that contains a hint of promise. Its format would be familiar to most eighth-graders of the period, across the country, but the narrative has been properly hailed by nearly every Thurber scholar as containing the seed from which Walter Mitty would sprout thirty years later.

The story is of a few old-timers from "good old Douglas," class of 1909, collecting the others for a journey to Mars on a "Seairoplane" built by a classmate. Flying was an exciting novelty of the day and a natural topic for Thurber to choose. In the six years since Orville and Wilbur Wright had first flown their heavier-than-air machine, aviation had become a lively local hobby. The year before Thurber's prophecy, he had visited the airship built by Grandfather Fisher's brother, Jake, at Indianola Park. "In every backyard in Ohio, men and boys were building airships," Thurber says. Furthermore, the works of the nineteenth-century French writer of scientific romances Jules Verne—such as *A Voyage to the Center of the Earth*, and *Twenty Thousand Leagues Under the Sea*—were still immensely popular with young readers of Thurber's age.

Aboard the airborne Seairoplane, a piece of rope fouls the machinery "on the farthest end of a long beam, which extended far over the side." Unless it is extracted from "the curobater," the class is doomed. "What was our surprise to see James Thurber walking out on the beam. He reached the end safely and then . . . extricated the rope, but . . . his foot caught and he pitched head foremost. . . . His unusual length saved him for he landed safely on the Seairoplane. . . . We . . . learned that James was a tight rope walker with Barnsels and Ringbailey's circus."

His invented technical terms—the machine's "hythenometer" and "curobater"—come as easily to him at age fourteen as they do thirty years later in "The Secret Life of Walter Mitty," in which Mitty, as surgeon, saves a patient from "obstreosis of the ductal tract. Tertiary." Flying machines frequently turn up in Thurber's dream world. Mitty first pilots an "eight-engined Navy hydroplane . . . SN202 . . . through the worst storm in twenty years of Navy flying," and later prepares to fly a World War I bomber alone to bomb an enemy ammunition dump, though "Von Richtman's circus" is between him and his objective.

In "Mr. Pendly and the Poindexter," the timid Thurber Man, humiliated by his wife's superior knowledge of cars and how to drive them, dreams at night "of descending, in an autogiro, on some garden party she was attending: he would come down in a fine landing, leap out, shout 'Hahya, Bee!,' sweep her into the machine, and zoom away."

Thurber still found flying a natural subject for school essays when in college. Wendell Postle, later the dean of O.S.U.'s dental college, remembers dropping into a room at the Phi Kappa Psi fraternity, finding Thurber and Elliott Nugent there, and commenting that he was stumped for an English theme that was due. Thurber promptly reeled paper into his typewriter and said, "What shall we write about? How about a scenic tour in an airplane?"

"I've never flown," Postle replied.

"That's O.K.," said Thurber, who had never flown either. "We'll make it a flight from Columbus to Dayton." He quickly typed a first-person description of the air flight. Postle liked it. So did his English teacher. "It was *too* good," Postle says, and so believable that the professor read it to the class and called on Postle to tell them more about the trip. Trapped, Postle confessed all.

In reality, Thurber feared flying, necessity forcing him to make only two white-knuckled flights in his lifetime. Marvin Belt, in "Sex Ex Machina," a 1937 casual, can only be Thurber:

> Marvin Belt . . . had a complex about airplanes that was quite interesting. He was not afraid of machinery, or of high places, or of crashes. He was simply afraid that the pilot of any plane he got into might lose his mind. "I imagine myself high over Montana," he once said to me, "in a huge, perfectly safe tri-motored plane. Several of the passengers are dozing, others are reading, but I am keeping my eyes glued on the door to the cockpit. Suddenly the pilot steps out of it, a wild light in his eyes, and in a falsetto like that of a little girl he says to me, 'Conductor, will you please let me off at One-hundred-and-twenty-fifth Street?'" "But," I said to Belt, "even if the pilot does go crazy, there is still the co-pilot." "No, there isn't," said Belt. "The pilot has hit the co-pilot over the head with something and killed him."

In 1940, the Thurbers were suddenly obliged to fly home from Bermuda to Helen's dying father. Wartime submarine threats had suspended travel by cruise ship. Ronald Williams, Thurber's Bermuda friend, remembers Thurber giving the same jittery prophecy, the night before his departure, of what he expected to happen on his flight. "Given Thurber's ability to attract chaos wherever he was," says Williams, "he had Jane and me worried, finally. After he and Helen departed, it became wholly possible in our imagination that, in midflight, the pilot would shoot the copilot, walk out of the cockpit and ask Thurber to let him off at One-hundred-and-twenty-fifth Street. We were enormously relieved to get their cablegram reporting a safe landing."

10

That Container for the Thing Contained

Miss Groby taught me English composition thirty years ago. . . . You remember her. You must have had her, too. Her influence will never die out of the land. . . . I [see] her sitting at her desk, taking the rubber band off the roll-call cards, running it back upon the fingers of her right hand, and surveying us all separately with quick little henlike turns of her head.

—from "Here Lies Miss Groby"

According to Helen Thurber, Miss Groby represents "the teacher who first got [Jamie] fascinated by the English language, a fascination that always stayed with him, and got more intense after he lost his sight."

If so, Thurber rewards her in a peculiar way. True, from his four years at Columbus East High School (1909–1913) the pseudonymous "Miss Groby" is the only teacher to get the Thurber memoir treatment, but in it he seems to be punishing her for embarrassing him. She was a dedicated parser of sentences, one whose enjoyment of literature seemed limited to anatomically dissecting and labeling its segments, to Thurber's frustration. In 1942, when the eye operations had thrown his self-distractions inward and enlarged his preoccupation with the uses, sound, visions, pitfalls, flexibilities, and sacredness of language, he seems to have taken his revenge upon his former English teacher, who could well have been still alive and able to recognize herself:

It is hard for me to believe that Miss Groby ever saw any famous work of literature from far enough away to know what it meant. She was forever climbing up the margins of books and crawling between their lines, hunting for the little gold of phrase, making marks with a pencil. . . . Night after night, for homework, Miss Groby set us to searching in "Ivanhoe" and "Julius Caesar" for metaphors, similes, metonymies, apostrophes, personifications. . . . It got so that figures of speech jumped out of the pages at you, obscuring the sense and pattern of the novel or play you were trying to read.

Miss Groby is especially fond of metonymies—figures of speech in which the name of one thing is used for that of another, as in "Friends, Romans, countrymen, lend me your *ears*" rather than *"attention."* Her requirement that her pupils look for instances of the "container for the thing contained" starts Thurber reading literature for its makeup rather than its meaning. "At first," Thurber writes, "I began to fear that all the characters in Shakespeare and Scott were crazy. They confused cause with effect, the sign for the thing signified, the thing held for the thing holding it. But after a while I began to suspect that it was I myself who was crazy. I would find myself lying awake at night saying over and over, 'The thinger for the thing contained.' "

He thinks of an inversion: a woman threatening to hit her husband with a bottle filled with milk, saying, "I'll hit you with the milk." That would be "a thing contained for the container." Genuinely pleased with himself, he volunteers his thought in class. Accustomed to the wisecracking Thurber, the class laughs at the image of a man being crowned with a milk bottle by his wife. But Miss Groby saw it as mockery, and when she quieted the class, "she said to me rather coldly, 'That was not really amusing, James.' " Thurber feels unjustly treated. "I was eager and serious about it," he says, "and it never occurred to me that the other children would laugh."

That it's the wife threatening the husband with a milk bottle, rather than the reverse, may be a sign that Thurber already saw wife/husband roles according to those being acted out by a dominant mother and a passive father.

His women teachers were fond of him, as teachers usually are of a quick, bright student whose high marks and good behavior are seen as reflecting favorably upon themselves. In turn, Thurber felt more comfortable with them than with male teachers. "I am just a woman teacher's pet," he wrote in 1959, "and when I was assigned to Mr. Huesch's algebra and geometry class, I asked to be reassigned to Miss Gordon's instead. . . . Mr. Huesch's shoes squeaked and it got on my nerves." To meet his science requirement, however, he submitted himself to a chemistry class taught by Frank Gullum, and did well. Gullum went on to be a chemistry professor at Ohio State University, and when he retired in 1955 he was given a dinner party at which a Thurber cablegram was read, sent from Paris: Thurber remembered Gullum "affectionately and clearly," and credited Gullum, who had been coach of the East High football team, with discovering Chic Harley, Ohio State University's first immortal gridiron star. Thurber also remembered being nearly suffocated by pure ammonia gas, which had been mishandled by another boy in Gullum's class.

He did less well in physics, taught by another male teacher. In his breezy 1951 briefing of *Time*'s editors, he writes: "Only low grade I got was in Physics. Developed my own system of computing rate of momentum and after I demonstrated it on the blackboard, Professor Hambleton said, 'You would go from New York to Boston by way of Detroit.' "

Thurber was enrolled in East High's "Latin Course," which emphasized the classics and literary composition. He was to become reacquainted with one of his Latin teachers in 1959, shortly after the *New Yorker* published his "Midnight at Tim's Place." "Old sundials used to boast, in Latin," the piece begins, "and I suppose a few quiet gardens here and there still do, '*Horas non numero sine serenas*'—'I count serene hours only.' " A New Jersey high-school reader sent Thurber a postcard saying the use of *sine* was incorrect, taking, as it did, the ablative, and that the correct word was *nisi*.

Thurber was annoyed that the magazine's checking department had left his error to be caught by a teenager, and the editor, William Shawn, agreed to run an acknowledgment of the correction—rarely done in a matter so trivial. In it, Thurber says that "the late Miss Daisy Hare," who had taught him Latin nearly fifty years before at East High, would have been shocked at his carelessness. Clowning his way out of his embarrassment, he added that he probably wouldn't have admitted the error publicly except for a dream he had had in which he was excavating some Roman ruins and came upon a sign with Latin words freshly written in chalk: "Hic erat Kilroy."

The magazine promptly received another letter addressed to Thurber saying the Kilroy sentence should have read "Hic stabat Kilroy." Thurber declined further public confession of error, remarking privately, "I don't think Kilroy would know which verb or tense to use." Meanwhile, another letter had reached him, saying that, far from being "the late Miss Daisy Hare," Daisy Hare was alive and well in Columbus. Thurber, who by now was ready to consign his excursion into Latin to the pits of hell, wrote Miss Hare one of his warm masterpieces of goodwill and diplomacy. The matter, as always, was soon in the hands of the local press, and a *Dispatch* reporter, Patricia Gardiner McGuckin (daughter of Thurber's good Columbus friend, Ted Gardiner) tracked down Miss Hare, who did the rare and near-impossible on such an occasion: she outdid Thurber in graciousness.

"I keep in touch with many of my former students," she said, "and I'm very proud of James. I would say the mistakes James made in his Latin merely reflect on my ability as his teacher back then." Thurber chose to drop the matter there. When *Lanterns & Lances*, containing "Midnight at Tim's Place," was published the next year, the *New Yorker's sine* had yielded to the New Jersey high-school student's *nisi*.

Ralph McCombs, two years behind Thurber at East High, remembers that William and Robert used to "pester" him, while Thurber led an inoffensive life. Though Thurber's face no longer reddened when he was called upon in class, his quiet ways were still obvious. But outside of class he was finding himself socially and acquiring a few friends. Moreover, his ability to complete schoolwork in a fraction of the time it took his peers was earning him respect. Gradually, his wit and spontaneous comedy acts were winning him additional popularity. Joel Sayre was volunteering as water boy for the "Blinkies" baseball team at the Ohio State School for the Blind when he first remembers Thurber, by then of high-school age:

I was nine and a half years old when I first saw, and started laughing at, Jim Thurber. . . . At the [Saturday ball games] I would see Jim . . . William and . . . Robert. Robert was the flash Thurber brother at this time; handsome, a juggler, and a future baseball captain at East High. Among us kids he had the reputation of being a terrific fighter and a demon player of duckpins. William was only a so-so athlete, but a pretty good fighter. Jim could do nothing athletically. . . . He was known, however, as a rabid fan and sports critic and a rapid-fire comedian.

What got me laughing at him that summer was the way he would strike out with his big feet and long legs and do dance steps, flapping his hands in unison from side to side as he chanted:

"Root-el-ty toot, oh, root-el-ty toot!

We are the ones from the Institute."

That routine of his didn't just make me laugh, it strangulated me with laughter. I'd think I was going to die. . . . Pretty soon he realized he could make me break up any time he wanted to.

Once at a Blind asylum game when I was carrying a big bucket of drinking water across the infield . . . he came up beside me, covered his mouth with a hand and murmured, merely murmured, "Root-el-ty toot." It broke me up so, I dropped the bucket and spilled the water and had to go back to the power plant, where the faucet was, for more.

But if there is anything extraordinary in the Thurber story during his school years, it is its general ordinariness. His few contributions to his high-school publication hardly signal precociousness or promise. In later years, he cheerfully acknowledged that he was "a late bloomer."

Columbus was a city of more than a hundred and eighty thousand people by 1910, and Thurber's cultural conditioning through his school years was typical of its Midwestern, middle-class residents. Along with his brothers, Thurber saved his nickels to see the Columbus baseball team, the Senators, at Neil Park. He and Robert over the years would challenge one another's memory of baseball statistics.

He escaped regularly into the world of pulp-magazine adventure. "He was always reading," Robert remembers.

"In the tranquil period between McKinley and Taft," Thurber writes in 1947, "[there] was the nickel novel." He remembers buying his first, *Jed, the Trapper*, in 1905. " 'Jed' was a mild tale of wintry treachery, but it gave me a taste for the genre, and in a year or so I had a formidable collection . . . of 'The Liberty Boys of '76,' 'Young Wild West,' 'Fred Fearnot,' and 'Old King Brady.' " There were also those perennial staples, the Rover Boys and Frank Merriwell, "who pitched his way out of my life with his curve ball that broke in two directions." Wild Bill Hickok became a favorite when Thurber found him, in 1908, in a book about the Wild West that William had obtained from Sears, Roebuck for ninety-eight cents.

Westerns were also regular fare in Columbus's eight theaters of the day, where itinerant troupes of actors staged western melodramas, generally double-billed with silent movies—many of them westerns. Charles frequently took his sons to see them. In 1951, Thurber writes in *The Bermudian*:

> Before I was sixteen, my palms had sweated and my pulse increased at "The Round Up," "Arizona," "The Squaw Man," "The Flaming Arrow," and "Custer's Last Fight." I once saw William F. Cody plain, and in 1915, at the Dreamland Theatre in Columbus, Ohio, I shook hands with J. Warren Kerrigan, hero of "The Covered Wagon." I never missed a W. S. Hart movie. . . . I read "The Virginian" when I was so young the gun duel on the lonely street at sundown made me sick to my stomach.
>
> I remember the desert scene in a Flying A movie of nigh on forty years ago, in which the villain (Jack Richardson) put a rifle bullet (ka-rang) through Kerrigan's canteen; the rousing saloon fight in "The Night Stage"; Maclyn Arbuckle rolling a cigarette with one hand in "The Round Up"; Bronco Billy Anderson of Essanay films, who never

seemed able to breathe through his nose; and the time Bill Hart respectfully removed his hat during a gun battle when a woman appeared on the scene.

So long and deeply immersed in the genre was Thurber that when he undertook seriously to write two short stories, in 1913, at age eighteen, they were embarrassingly derivative. One, "How Law and Order Came to Aramie," never published, written in a fine, even hand similar to his father's, is so riddled with the clichés of the western pulps that, knowing the later Thurber, one half expects it to be revealed finally as hilarious parody. But the theme of manly strength versus the pussycat was already a grave and haunting one to him. Thanks to the self-plagiarizing nature of the arts and the entertainment industry, Thurber's plot is as old as a hundred years and as fresh as last night's TV western.

The hero is Sheriff "Big John" Oakes, actually small of stature—Mitty may be off and running here again—but bighearted. The sheriff hopes to keep the peace without using a gun, but he is challenged by the villains and called a coward by the townspeople. "John," the sheriff is told, "they're a sayin'—they're a sayin'—you're yellow. Now, o'course—"

"What!"

Getting the sheriff steamed up sufficiently to light out after the bad men takes nearly two-thirds of the story. Thurber backs away from describing the shoot-out. Another bad hombre riding through town learns that the little sheriff has sent the gang of outlaws skedaddling and he vamooses, too. One can only guess whether so striking a simile in the story as "the glint in his eyes like the flash of a polished filing in the sunlight" is out of Thurber's lively imagination or borrowed from one of his adventure paperbacks.

The first story of James Thurber ever to be published, "The Third Bullet," appeared in *The X-Rays*, the East High School magazine, in May 1913, a month before his graduation, at age eighteen. Another western potboiler, its hero's unflappable composure unnerves the villain so badly that he misses with all six free shots he's allowed to fire first. The principal character, a gold prospector named Harding (Harding, the future president, was already a local political hero to Charles Thurber), spares the bad man his life but berates him for his cowardice as, thirty-six years later, Kelby, in "Teacher's Pet," would berate the young Elbert for his refusal to face up to the bully:

"Get up, you miserable wretch," Harding tells the groveling scoundrel. "Why I couldn't have the heart to kill a helpless, cowardly thing like you. Get up! Here, be a man!" The popular short-story writer O. Henry had died in 1910, but his surprise endings were still the rage with magazine editors and writers of the period. Thurber comes up with his own: the prospector, who has been searching in vain for gold, finds that the villain's third bullet has exposed a vein of it in a rock wall.

We look at Thurber's high-school writing and press ourselves to remember what he is to become, though two senior-class English compositions that survived the family housefires demonstrate Thurber's growing fondness for the language and his early responses to the challenges it presented. In one, he describes a cyclone that struck the farm of a maternal relative in Licking County, Ohio, five years before. Though told as if witnessed personally, no later reference to experiencing a cyclone is ever made by Thurber, and it is possible that he adopted a family account, read of it in the press, or viewed the wreckage after the storm and reconstructed the event in his mind: Trees are snapped close to the ground as if they were saplings; fences are blown "helter-skelter into a mass of flying wood and tangled wire"; a galvanized tub flies past the window of the farmhouse and over the cow-barn. The "sickly yellow of the sky" gives way to "an awesome grayish black hue." "The orchard, the pride of our host, was literally blown away. Apples lay upon the ground thick as leaves in autumn. . . . The tin roofing of the post office, twisted in a marvelous way, almost entirely covered a large elm." Thurber compares the carnage to that of Port Arthur "after the Japanese bombardment there." The spelling is impeccable and the similes are constructed with care.

In the fall of 1912, he submitted an essay extolling the virtues of Theodore Roosevelt and the Progressive Party, whose fortunes would soon determine those of his father. He followed that, in early November, with a report on the three-way (Roosevelt/Taft/Wilson) presidential-election night in Columbus:

> Excitement was at a fever heat in Columbus . . . last Tuesday night. . . . High Street especially was a scene of great action and irrepressed [sic] excitement. A mighty crowd thronged the sidewalks brilliant with the myriads of electric lights strung along the thorofare in blinding array. . . .
>
> At several of the busiest corners, results of the poll in various states were being flashed upon large screens. . . . As the night wore on these places became black with people who shouted themselves hoarse with more or less volume as bulletins to the effect that "Wilson is ahead in New York" or "T. R. leads in Illinois" or "Taft had carried Cincinnati" were thrown upon the screen. . . .
>
> As ten o'clock rolled around and it was established beyond a doubt who was to be our next president pandemonium reigned in the street.

Millions of horns kept up an incessant and strident song of victory. One could scarcely force his way thru the struggling pushing throng and at best emerged with a mouthful of confetti and a pair of ringing eardrums. . . .

A Presidential election comes but once in four years and the people evidently try to become inoculated with enough enthusiasm and celebrating to last them until next time. If one can judge by the general actions of last Tuesday night they not only succeeded but should have enough left to give them a fair start Tues. night Nov. 5 1916. . . . There certainly was a "hot time in the old town" that night. And the reason was Wilson—that's all!

"Very good, James," his teacher marked on the paper. "You sometimes use quotation marks where they are not needed." (Hardly a help to Thurber, considering the disregarded misspellings, lack of commas, clumsy syntax, and indeed, the need *for* quotation marks around the famous whiskey ad: "Wilson —that's all!") There is no hint on Thurber's part of the crushing effect the election returns were to have on his father, who, with Roosevelt's defeat, would lose any substantial reward for his months of Progressive Party service.

Thurber enjoyed English, languages, and history in high school, Robert remembers. He even got good grades in math and science, neither of which interested him, and "though he took less time with his homework than William and I did."

To pay for his nickel novels and theater tickets, Thurber found odd jobs, beginning in 1909 after graduating from Douglas School. That summer, dressed in knickers and long stockings, he became a delivery boy for the Central Ohio Optical Company, his long thin legs pumping a bicycle throughout the city. During high school, Robert recalls, Thurber worked for part of a summer at the Buckeye Steel Castings Company, a job Edward Morris, his best friend at the time, may have helped him obtain. "Ed Morris was the only one close friend Jim had in high school," Robert says, "although Jim was well liked by all. Ed's father was the wealthy owner of a large steel and iron company in Columbus. Ed was proficient in higher math and later in engineering. I found him boring in conversation, taking much time to explain mechanical problems whether the listener was interested or not. But he and my brother hit it off."

During another summer, Thurber's father, who knew many city and state government people, may have helped find Thurber a temporary job with the State-City Free Employment Agency. Ralph McCombs has a dim impression that Thurber was hired at McClelland's bookstore, owned by McCombs's uncle, to deliver packages during the Christmas season rush, at ten cents an hour plus carfare. During his senior year at East High, Thurber clerked at a cigar store after school and on Saturday mornings.

If his years at East High were not when he discovered he would be a writer, despite his latter-day claims, there were signs of an emerging personality. He was gaining a reputation as an extrovert, and was sufficiently popular to win the senior-class presidency, outpolling his cousin, Earl Fisher, and also the son of a prominent attorney. He managed to get through his "President's Address" on the 1913 "Class Day" program, though speaking to a live audience of substantial size would always terrify him.

In later years, Thurber liked to say that his big disappointment in high school was not to have been made editor of *The X-Rays*, and that the reason he was not was Mame's asking the school principal not to permit it because of "Jamie's" fragile eyesight. This may have been a Thurber afterthought; Thurber seems to have had little interest in the magazine before getting his one story published in it shortly before he graduated. There is nothing to show that he was even a member of the magazine's editorial board.

Columbus was a baseball and high-school-football town at the time. Ohio State University's football team still awaited East High's Chic Harley to swing the interest of Columbusites from high-school athletics to university. The big rivalry was between East and North High. There were nightshirt parades and other shenanigans the night before the games, which led to annual tongue-clucking editorials in the city newspapers. Chic Harley was not only a football threat; two years behind Thurber, he played shortstop on the 1913 East High baseball team, whose star pitcher was Robert, a junior. ("We lost only one game that year," Robert says.) Harley had already made the high-school football team one to be reckoned with in the fall of 1912.

Thurber's lingering adolescent, sentimental worship of the athletes of his day continually trapped him into maudlin reporting: In 1923, at age twenty-eight, writing as a *Dispatch* columnist ten years after his graduation from East High, he reminisces:

> The hush that fell in the week before the North game, working up to rallies and songs and speeches and proud boasts, with a great undercurrent of unmentionable fear, made life worth living in a painful, bittersweet sort of way. It was the terrible, keen enjoyment of a man dicing for

his life. Nerves are never strung so high, hearts never break so often or with such a sad whanging note as when one is in his teens and high school.

On the day of the game the orange and black of East blazed out defiantly against the sullen, more impressive maroon and gold of North. There was something unbreakable, masterful, ineluctable in maroon and gold, something gay and brave as youth, and as finely futile, in orange and black.

One barely fathoms from this giddy flow the fact that East High lost.

In June 1913, with the Thurber family in attendance at the ceremonies, James Grover Thurber graduated from Columbus East High School. In his childhood, at times when the family budget was strained, he had occasionally worn hand-me-down clothes from William or his Fisher cousins. On this occasion, he wore a blue serge suit that cost approximately twelve dollars at Lazarus's department store, with a white stiff collar and tie, and a handkerchief whose folded points stuck neatly out of his breast pocket. One of his classmates, accustomed to Thurber's general indifference to clothes, which never seemed to fit him, is certain that Charles or Mame arranged the handkerchief for him.

11

That Day the Dam Broke

My memories of what my family and I went through during the 1913 flood in Ohio I would gladly forget. . . . If anyone ever wished a city was in hell it was during that frightful and perilous afternoon in 1913 when the dam broke, or, to be more exact, when everybody in town *thought* that the dam broke.

—from "The Day the Dam Broke"

During his high-school senior year, a number of local events might have been fair literary game for Thurber in the years to come: Columbus celebrated its centennial anniversary in August 1912, with a parade featuring four thousand suffragettes. A luncheon was held for all descendants of Ohio governors who could be tracked down. The city was filled with German singing societies, thought by some music critics to have made Columbus's support of the Allied cause in World War I an even easier matter. President William H. Taft, a former Columbus resident, spoke at the Fairgrounds, but nobody remembered what he said. Extreme heat caused several cases of prostration during the children's pageant.

Before the city's two hundred thousand residents had recovered from the week of celebrating the settling of Columbus, the evangelist William A. (Billy) Sunday and his troop of workers arrived to campaign for the salvation of Columbus souls in a spiritual blitzkrieg. Sixty churches closed for the several weeks' occasion so that their pastors and congregations could participate. In a tabernacle built for the event, seating twelve thousand in the audience and twelve hundred in the choir, ninety-five meetings were held. Throngs from out of town joined with local citizens clamoring to get in. Employees of stores and factories went en masse to the services. Sunday preached all but two of the ninety-five sermons, leaving with nearly half of the forty-five thousand dollars in offerings. According to the city historian Osman Hooper, "reconsecrations and conversions numbered 18,333, of whom 2,189 went forward on the last day of the meetings."

Columbus was obviously already accustomed to mass collective civic action by the spring of 1913, when the flood hit. Hard on the heels of evangelistic warnings of Armageddon's approach, there was good reason for the city to be jumpy about dams breaking. "The West Side was, at the time of the dam scare," writes Thurber, "under thirty feet of water—as, indeed, were all Ohio river towns during the great spring floods of [1913]. The East Side (where we lived and where all the running occurred) had never been in any danger at all. Only a rise of some ninety-five feet could have caused the flood waters to flow over High Street . . . and engulf the East Side."

Thurber, surprisingly, is fairly accurate on this point. His classic East Side story of 1933, "The Day the Dam Broke," depends largely on a West Side tragedy. Eleven times since the area's first recorded flood in 1798, the Scioto River had flooded the flatter lands of its west bank, the last one in 1898, when Thurber was three years old. Despite modest flood-control measures taken after that, the city's electric-light plant and waterworks were again under water. The flood began on March 25 (Thurber's date is March 13).

Hooper writes: "There had been heavy rainfall in the watershed of the Scioto and Olentangy rivers. . . . By 9 o'clock Tuesday morning [March 25] the water overtopped the levee [and] the submerged section [was] at the mercy of the river which raged beyond the capacity of the channel for nearly five days." Houses were bowled off their foundations, ninety-three lives were lost, four street bridges across the Scioto were destroyed, the entire city was without water for twenty hours, and all public schools were closed for three days.

It was the frightening spectacle of what was happening to the West Side that prepared the East Side for panic and "the great run," which did, in fact, take place. Thurber throws everything into his description of it, including the ironing board, which, he says, they had to use to stun grandfather, who thinks the crowd is fleeing from the Confederate cavalry of Nathan Bedford Forrest. "The only possible means of escape for us was to flee the house," Thurber explains, which requires knocking grandfather unconscious and carrying him with them.

> Black streams of people flowed eastward down all the streets; . . . these streams, whose headwaters were in the dry-goods stores, office buildings, harness shops, movie theatres, were fed by trickles of housewives, children, cripples, servants, dogs, and cats, slipping out of the houses past which the main streams flowed, shouting and screaming. People ran out leaving fires burning and food cooking and doors wide open. I remember, however, that my mother turned out all the fires and that she took with her a dozen eggs and two loaves of bread. It was her plan to make Memorial Hall, just two blocks away, and take refuge somewhere in the top of it. . . . But the seething throngs, shouting "Go east!," drew her along and the rest of us with her. When grandfather regained full consciousness, at Parsons Avenue, he turned upon the retreating mob like a vengeful prophet and exhorted the men to form ranks and stand off the Rebel dogs, but at length he, too, got the idea that the dam had broken and, roaring "Go east!" in his powerful voice, he caught up in one arm a small child and in the other a slight clerkish man of perhaps forty-two and we slowly began to gain on those ahead of us.

According to Robert, the Thurbers lived at 1104 Fair Avenue at the time, safely on the East Side. "Jim and his close friend, Ed Morris, were downtown that day," he writes. "They came out of a store on High Street and saw a couple of mounted policemen riding up and down the street shouting that the dam had broke and imploring everyone to go east to higher ground. . . . Jim didn't panic, but at the same time didn't tarry. He and Morris . . . reached home late in the afternoon. We were students at East High that year, but in those days school was out at 1:30 P.M. My mother and I were home. We first heard the rumor from a next-door neighbor. We were quite concerned and relieved when we learned the rumor was false. My father was at work in a downtown office building. I don't remember where William was."

Joel Sayre was eleven at the time. "I lived in the same part of town that Thurber lived in," he says. "People had just been reading about a big flood in Dayton. My brother and I and some other kids were playing ball in the street and suddenly a lot of grown-ups came striding by, some of them doing a dog trot. We said, 'What's the matter?' They said, 'The dam broke.' We thought they were drunk or crazy. But a neighbor of ours, a Mrs. Sangly, got very alarmed, took all her groceries with her up to her attic and stayed there about three weeks. It's really true that there was this stampede. Thousands of people did run."

Ben Williamson, a Columbus contemporary of Thurber's, remembers taking refuge with his father in his Ohio Tax Commission office in a tall downtown office building, safely above the threat of flood.

How did the panic start? Thurber writes:

> The Columbus, Ohio, broken-dam rumor began . . . about noon.
> . . . High Street, the main canyon of trade, was loud with the placid hum of business and the buzzing of placid businessmen. . . . Suddenly somebody began to run. It may be that he had simply remembered, all of a moment, an engagement to meet his wife, for which he was now frightfully late. . . . He ran east on Broad Street. . . . Somebody else began to run, perhaps a newsboy in high spirits. Another man, a portly gentleman . . . broke into a trot. Inside of ten minutes, everybody on High Street . . . was running. A loud mumble gradually crystallized into the dread word "dam." "The dam has broke!" . . . Two thousand people were abruptly in full flight. "Go east!" was the cry that arose— east away from the river. . . . "Go east! Go east! Go east! . . .
>
> All the time, the sun shone quietly and there was nowhere any sign of oncoming waters. A visitor in an airplane, looking down on the straggling, agitated masses of people below, would have been hard put to

Two Thousand People Were in Full Flight

it to divine a reason for the phenomenon. It must have inspired, in such an observer, a peculiar kind of terror, like the sight of the *Marie Celeste*, abandoned at sea, its galley fires peacefully burning, its tranquil decks bright in the sunlight.

In writing his story, Thurber may have remembered the Columbus *Dispatch* review of the incident published a year after the event, which states that it was a bootblack at the Neil House who imagined that the rampaging river down the slope was unexpectedly and rapidly rising. It was he, the 1914 story offers, who first shouted, "The dam's busted." Hearing the bootblack's cry (the *Dispatch* writer goes on), a man on horseback took up the alarm. Immediately stores and shops and stables were emptied. Cattle and horses were turned loose. People headed for the higher buildings in town. Some, the reporter recalled, were too winded at Grant Street to go on, but others made it to Washington Avenue, and a few to Franklin Park. (Thurber has some running all the way to Reynoldsburg, twelve miles to the east, but George Smallsreed, then on the *Dispatch* staff, doubted that anyone got that far unless the refugee was driving an automobile.)

The next day, the city went about its business as if nothing had happened, but there was no joking. It was two years or more before you dared treat the breaking of the dam lightly. And even now, twenty years after, there are a few persons . . . who will shut up like a clam if you mention the Afternoon of the Great Run.

"Jim is right," Smallsreed says. "There was silent agreement among us on the paper that the panic run was best forgotten. It wouldn't have done much for Columbus. It was a year before we broke that part of the story." Another 1914 *Dispatch* item in the anniversary coverage finally states that Griggs Dam, the one in question, was already inundated by the flood water. Had the dam broken, it wouldn't have affected the water level more than a couple of inches.

"Later," Thurber writes, "when the panic had died down . . . people had gone rather sheepishly back to their homes and their offices, minimizing the distances they had run."

Smallsreed confirms that, too. One reason for the press silence, he explains, was that a number of the local newspapers' staff members were among the many fleeing citizens who had publicly exposed so startling a lack of inner resource. Smallsreed, Gus Kuehner (then a nineteen-year-old *Dispatch* reporter and later Thurber's city editor on that paper), and another newsman, Bill McKeanan, were covering the flood on the West Side that day. When they recrossed the river on their return, the water was overflowing Town Street Bridge and up to the hubcaps of their car. The bridge was carried away twenty minutes later. Upon gaining the East Side and parking the car, they heard the shout "The dam has broken!" and joined the stampede to the east on foot, needlessly stopping to free horses from a livery stable, to their owners' later annoyance. "The last I saw of Kuehner that day," says Smallsreed, "he was running up the hill on Town Street between two white horses, all going like the furies." McKeanan caught a ride with some city detectives and ended up on the Parsons Avenue viaduct, some distance to the east, waited in vain for the floodwaters, and confessed to having "to walk all the way back."

"There are few alarms in the world more terrifying than 'The dam has broken!'," Thurber writes. "There are few persons capable of stopping to reason when that clarion cry strikes upon their ears, even persons who live in towns no nearer than five hundred miles to a dam."

During the panic, one woman, he reports, "managed to get up onto the 'These Are My Jewels' statue, whose bronze figures of Sherman, Stanton, Grant, and Sheridan watched with cold unconcern the going to pieces of the capital city." The statue was mentioned in 1962 by Donald Ogden Stewart, who tape-recorded his recollection of Thurber and Columbus:

> James Thurber's Columbus, Ohio, and mine were the same. I was born in the same year, 1894, and within five blocks and eight days of him. In those days, Columbus was quite small. We walked to school only six blocks from the center of town. That center was the State House, with a ten-acre yard filled with buckeye trees, squirrels, and statues of Civil War heroes who had been born in Ohio. There was one in particular which Jim and I used to stand in front of with ten-year-old admiration. It was a large, bronze Thurber Woman, representing Ohio, embracing with her arms two Civil War generals, under the carved words, "These are my jewels."

The statue, recently refurbished, still stands before the State House. The toga-clad "Thurber Woman" atop it, arms outstretched in an all-embracing gesture, is the Roman Cornelia, mother of Tiberius and Caius. When a wealthy lady showed off to Cornelia her many jewels and asked to see Cornelia's, Cornelia summoned her two sons and said, "These are my jewels, in which alone I delight." Both Thurber and Stewart fail to give the full roster of Cornelia's "jewels" after she was imported into the service of Ohio: in addition to Grant, Sheridan, Sherman, and Stanton, it includes James A. Garfield, Rutherford B. Hayes, and Salmon P. Chase.

"The Day the Dam Broke" made a permanent Thurber fan of General William M. Hode, the commanding general of the Fourth Armored Division, who read the story in the Armed Forces edition of *My Life and Hard Times*. He reports that during the Battle of the Bulge, the rumors of American positions being overrun and of other German penetrations grew to fantastic proportions. One of the general's duties was to visit the outlying units and counteract the rumors. After the crisis was over, he read "The Day the Dam Broke," and, touting it as the perfect example of the havoc unfounded rumor can create, required every member of his staff to do the same.

12

Those University Days

Ohio State was a land grant university and therefore two years of military drill was compulsory. We drilled with old Springfield rifles and studied the tactics of the Civil War even though the World War was going on at the time. At 11 o'clock each morning thousands of freshmen and sophomores used to deploy over the campus, moodily creeping up on the old chemistry building. It was good training for the kind of warfare that was waged at Shiloh but it had no connection with what was going on in Europe. Some people used to think there was German money behind it, but they didn't dare say so or they would have been thrown in jail as German spies. It was a period of muddy thought and marked, I believe, the decline of higher education in the Middle West.

—from "University Days"

In 1862, Congress passed an act, signed by President Lincoln, that would radically democratize higher education in America. It granted each state thirty thousand acres of federal land for each of its U.S. representatives and senators. Acceptance was on the condition that the state sell the land and use the proceeds to endow at least one college, "to teach such branches of learning as are related to agriculture and the mechanical arts" but "without excluding other scientific and classical studies, and including military tactics." The government also offered an annual support fund of fifteen thousand dollars to each land-grant college (raised to twenty thousand in 1890).

Until then, higher education was largely the province of those whose families had the financial means and social clout to get them into preparatory schools, colleges, and universities funded by church, foundations, or other private endowment. The spread of free or inexpensive coeducation at land-grant state universities transformed the children of farmers, shopkeepers, and mechanics into an expanding middle class of professionals in law, medicine, commerce, science, engineering, and education. Their fiscal and intellectual support, in turn, has kept the system self-perpetuating.

In Ohio, the public land sales brought in half a million dollars. Existing schools petitioned to have the money divided among them—a legal option. The state board of education favored one centrally located institution. The debate lasted six years, until Governor Rutherford B. Hayes successfully backed the state board's position.

Another dispute then arose among Ohio's counties as to the location of the new college. The railroads, already carrying state officials to and from Columbus, saw further benefits in transporting students there. Though other counties offered to raise more money for the college's operation, the railroad lobby helped influence the General Assembly's vote to select Franklin County, which contains Columbus. The Neil farm, two miles north of the city's center, was purchased as the campus site. The school opened in 1873 as the Ohio Agricultural and Mechanical College. Five years later, its name was changed to "The Ohio State University." It accepted for enrollment, tuition-free, any Ohio resident, male or female, certified to have graduated from an accredited preparatory or high school or to have passed qualifying examinations.

With Charles Thurber struggling to support a family and meet the medical expenses of his chronically ailing sons (throughout his childhood, Thurber's glass eye had to be replaced annually), it is unlikely that James Thurber would ever have continued an academic education except for the fact of Ohio State University. Any tuition payment would have been out of the question, as would the cost of transportation and board and room at an out-of-town college. As it was, the O.S.U. campus was a ten-cent trolley ride from the Thurber household, where board and room were free.

American literary history includes many distinguished writers who didn't need a college background to make their mark, but there is little indication that Thurber would have been one of them. Lacking direction, self-confidence, and adult guidance, at age eighteen he had only the vaguest of ideas as to what he wanted to do or be. O.S.U. proved to be his salvation—the right place at the right time. It was where he decided, once and for all, that he would be a writer; where he first drew for publication, first acted in theater, first knew in large measure the good feelings he would always get from making others laugh; where he acquired literary taste, and met the woman who helped get him out of Columbus and on with his career.

He may have been reluctant to take the plunge, or simply procrastinating, for after finding odd jobs that summer to earn spending money for the upcoming academic year, he still didn't apply to the university until it was almost too late. His application wasn't approved until September 10, 1913, six days before classes began.

At the time, the university had nearly four hundred faculty members and more than four thousand students. Its academic disciplines were divided into a graduate school and a dozen colleges, each with its own faculty and dean. Thurber signed up for English composition (obligatory for freshmen), American and medieval European history, Latin, general psychology, and the compulsory military science and gymnasium.

When his psychology professor, Albert P. Weiss, tested his students' ability to recall at later dates what they had read, it provided Thurber with the first evidence of his superior power of memory. He would proudly cite his Weiss test results to friends, strangers, and interviewers the rest of his life. Though there is undeniable evidence that Thurber's ability to recall was far from total, as he liked to boast, it unquestionably served to save his literary career, and possibly his sanity.

His freshman year got off to a bad start. Though he came through his thirty-three credits with good grades, he felt alienated and ignored on campus. His cheap clothes were ill-fitting, his lack of confidence showed up in nervous, awkward movements and mumbled speech, and behind his steel-rimmed spectacles "there was evidently something wrong with one of his eyes," writes his friend, Elliott Nugent, recalling his first meeting with Thurber, "as it did not always look in the same direction as the other one."

Fraternity membership was essential to any campus standing at O.S.U. The Chi Phi house quickly pledged Thurber's best friend, the well-to-do Ed Morris, but after briefly "rushing" Thurber, rejected him. No other fraternities were interested in him. Morris's new friends and fraternity life left him little time for Thurber. Two of Thurber's Fisher cousins were also selected by fraternities, including Earl Fisher, whom Thurber had defeated for senior-class president at East High. Being a "towner," he lacked even the casual associations of dormitory life. Classmates of that period remember Thurber as a "barb" (barbarian, in campus parlance) or a "wet smack"—lonely, unpopular, and introverted.

Two university requirements also plagued Thurber at the outset. Each afternoon, all male freshmen and sophomores attended military science and tactics, which included learning to march in close-order drill. Secondly, there was gymnasium, with swimming a requisite for graduating. Thurber despised undressing in front of strangers in the locker room and had Mame's fear of deep water. (Mame constantly reminded her sons that her grandfather, the father of Kate Fisher, had drowned in the Hocking River when Kate was seven.)

Military science and tactics was taught by Captain Converse, a West Pointer with a patch covering an eye he had lost in the Indian wars. Far from being sympathetic to Thurber, he seemed to feel the ungainly young man was a disgrace to the ranks of one-eyed persons. "As a soldier I was never any good at all," writes Thurber in "University Days." "Most of the cadets were glumly indifferent soldiers, but I was no good at all. Once General Littlefield, who was commandant of the cadet corps, popped up in front of me during regimental drill and snapped, 'You are the main trouble with this university!' I think he meant . . . my type . . . but he may have meant me individually."

Thurber began to cut military classes. "Why should I spend my afternoons walking around with a rifle on my shoulder?" he complained to his family. He knew his physical disability would disqualify him for military service, and he resented the reading time that the drilling exercises cost him. William remembers his brother putting a patch over his glass eye at home and performing wildly funny—and hostile—impersonations of Converse (renamed Littlefield in "University Days").

He was missing half his gym periods, too, he told Robert, because they bored him. He had begun to smoke, and boldly submitted to *The Sun-Dial*, the O.S.U. humor magazine, a poem proclaiming the fact:

> "The Best Part of a Class Hour"
>
> To stand out on the freezing step
> And freeze,
> Smoking a hasty cigarette,
> Freezing,
> Drawing deep drags
> Until it's a quarter after.
>
> Then go into class,
> Frozen
> 'Neath the professor's freezing eye,
> And let the warmth of the room
> And the drone of his voice

And the frieze of the chalk
Marks on the board
Lull you to sleep,
Less frozen.

The homophones "freeze" and "frieze" hint faintly of young Thurber's developing fascination with wordplay; and at least he was signaling his presence on campus, however weakly. The dozing referred to in the poem could well have been in Professor Weiss's class, for Thurber's psychology textbook flyleaf and margins contain the doodlings of a bored student. His natural brightness and quick grasp of ideas usually left him waiting for others to catch up. The scribbling reflects the aimless turns of mind that occupied many of his hours in the lecture room: the football score of the Ohio State–Western Reserve game; neatly ordered swastikas on four different pages (the emblem was not yet associated with Naziism, and the Freudians had yet to explain its sexuality); the sketch of an early Thurber Man (presumably Professor Weiss); a couplet: "The beaver is a working fool, who went to manual training school."

A lifelong master at recycling his earlier work in one form or another, Thurber refers to these classroom musings, penciled thirty-six years before, in a 1949 casual, "The Notebooks of James Thurber." He cites juvenile jokes he composed in the notebook he was to have kept during his psychology class. Example:

He: The news from Washington is bad.
She: I thought he died *long* ago.

He adds: "No literary executor is going to get his hands on *that* notebook." (The notebook, of course, is in the Thurber Collection at O.S.U., available to any Thurber scholar.)

Neither the campus newspaper, the *Daily Lantern*, nor the monthly *Sun-Dial* magazine used bylines in Thurber's day, but his disciples have identified a few *Sun-Dial* items that seem Thurberish in style. One, published his freshman year, is entitled "Eugene and Bob, A Moral Tale for Young Folks, from Our 21st Reader." It is a commentary on the Anti-Saloon League and other Prohibitionists, who were then mounting a telling drive for the abolition of alcoholic beverages. They had recently held their national convention in Columbus, their speeches sagging with innumerable case histories of men destroyed by drink.

In the first fable attributed to Thurber, "Eugene" is persuaded by "Bob" to enter a "riotous café." Eugene has a harelip and orders a nonintoxicant drink, a "Vin Fiz." The waiter, "who had been to college and could not understand English," misunderstands and serves Eugene a gin fizz, containing "the Serpent Alcohol which is undermining the youth of our country." Eugene staggers home "a drunk sot," is "dragged down step by step, and ten years after he first set foot into the den of infamy, was filling a drunkard's grave!" Bob, on the other hand, accustomed to drink, remained in the café "and conversed cheerily with the head waiter . . . who inside of six years died and left him an immense fortune."

"Moral: If you have a harelip, talk with your hands."

This is another piece the mature Thurber undoubtedly hoped nobody got ahold of.

His freshman year over, Thurber spent the summer working at Olentangy Park, selling and taking tickets at a Panama Canal exhibit. The park, with its ball- and ring-throwing booths, was a favorite place of Thurber's. In 1906, at age eleven, he and his cousin Earl had taken the trolley there, spent the day, and were down to their last fifteen cents—their carfare. They agreed to spend it on a loop-the-loop ride and walked the eleven miles home.

That fall of 1914, Thurber registered for a full semester program at O.S.U., taking English literature and composition courses and first-year French. The war in Europe had begun and a national military "preparedness" mood was in vogue, with an even greater importance attached to the Reserve Officers Training Corps requirements. A science was also mandatory, which added a new nightmare to Thurber's curriculum, joining his military and physical-education obligations. He had selected botany, as one of the more bloodless and congenial science options, but hadn't realized that it meant looking through a microscope:

I passed all the other courses that I took . . . but I could never pass botany. . . . I could never see through a microscope. . . . I never once saw a cell through a microscope. This used to enrage my instructor. . . . He would begin patiently enough, explaining how anybody can see through a microscope, but he would always end up in a fury, claiming that I could *too* see through a microscope but just pretended that I couldn't. . . . "I see what looks like a lot of milk," I would tell him. This, he claimed, was the result of my not having adjusted the microscope properly, so he would readjust it for me, or rather, for himself. And I would look again and see milk. . . .

I finally took a deferred pass . . . waited a year and tried again. . . . "Well," he said to me cheerily . . . "we're going to see cells this time, aren't we?" "Yes, sir," I said. Students to the right . . . and . . . left of me . . . were seeing cells; what's more, they were quietly drawing pictures of them in their notebooks. Of course, I didn't see anything. . . .

Only [once] did I see anything . . . a variegated constellation of flecks, specks, and dots. These I hastily drew. The instructor, noting my activity, came back . . . , a smile on his lips and his eyebrows high in hope. He looked at my cell drawing. "What's that?" he demanded. . . . "That's what I saw," I said. "You didn't, you didn't, you *didn't*!" he screamed . . . and he bent over and squinted into the microscope. His head snapped up. "That's your eye!" he shouted. "You've fixed the lens so that it reflects! You've drawn your eye!"

Oppressed by the need to meet three academic requirements that lay beyond his abilities and inclinations, and feeling himself a social outcast, Thurber dropped out of school, explaining later to a classmate that he wanted to read and browse around libraries and find himself. He frequented both the public and university libraries, "where," Joel Sayre writes, "he did little else but sit reading . . . with his hair in his eyes, looking like an emaciated sheep dog."

He had begun to keep his life his own, volunteering little about himself to his family. Not until after Thurber's death did Robert Thurber learn from Thurber scholars that his brother had not attended O.S.U. that second year. He had continued to leave each schoolday morning to catch the streetcar, as he had the previous year. "None of us suspected," Robert writes. "If a friend happened to run into him during this period, he no doubt had an acceptable excuse ready."

One excuse Thurber used was that he had been ill that year. In Elliott Nugent's memoirs, he writes that when he met Thurber, in the fall of 1915, he found him "a bit of a hermit and a loner around the campus," and that the situation may have been made worse "after a bout of bad health forced him to drop out of college for nearly a year."

But Robert writes: "He had no illness then, I am sure, and I can't believe it was a matter of finances. Somehow he had . . . money for his immediate needs, [if] not for luxuries. He was still pretty shy at that time and he probably had a difficult time adjusting to college life. . . . He was always secretive and whatever the reason, he wouldn't have told anyone in the family, anyway."

Though others label it a lost year for Thurber, it proved to be one important to his career. First, he was developing an interest in more demanding and rewarding books, moving away from the light literary entertainment of his youth. "I was a great reader from the time I was ten," he wrote the headmistress at Northampton School for Girls in 1950, which his daughter then attended, "but most of my [literary] enthusiasms in high school and college I found outside class. I am a rabid antagonist of the 'Silas Marner' kind of required reading. Neither this nor 'The Spy,' nor 'The Talisman,' nor 'The Return of the Native' stirred my interest as a writer and appreciator as much as the good books I read for myself."

The second development during his truant year was his realization that he wanted to become a writer of entertaining paragraphs, of light social commentary, in the manner of Robert O. Ryder, the gifted and gentlemanly editor of the *Ohio State Journal*.

13

That Man from Franklin Avenue

Newspaper paragraphing, the daily grinding of gleams and sparkles of humor and satire from the grist of human nature and the news of the world, is a special and demanding comic art. Its practitioners must keep regular hours, like the office worker, and they can't indulge in the relaxing frailties and postures of temperament. The best paragraphs, to be sure, come out of the quiet mind and the tranquil time, but the true paragrapher has had a tough training in reporting and editing, and he can write in any mood or weather. . . .

[Robert O. (Bob)] Ryder . . . was probably the best of all the genuine paragraphers, and his "output" . . . was more widely reprinted than that of any of his colleagues except [Ed] Howe [of the *Atchison Globe*]. The old *Literary Digest* used a great deal of it, and so did [Ryder's] favorite newspaper, the late New York *Morning World*, and a hundred others.

—from "Franklin Avenue, U.S.A."

By 1915, Thurber, now the inveterate reader of books, had also become an ardent follower of Robert O. Ryder's daily *Ohio State Journal* column and his popular syndicated feature, "The Young Lady Across the Way," illustrated by Harry J. Westerman. Ryder was a scholarly man, with great popular appeal as a human being and a facile writer. His copy was studded with classical allusions. He wrote in longhand. His Sunday columns, "Round About Ohio," dealt with the changing of the seasons, wildlife observed, and good-natured challenges to the points of view of other Ohio editors. In his daily features, he reported on an imaginary female cast of characters along with the Young Lady Across the Way, all of particular appeal to Thurber; there was "the neighbor women of Franklin Avenue," "a certain noble woman" (Ryder's wife), and "Mrs. Wilson, our dear mother-in-law," terms appropriated later by the nationally syndicated gossip columnist Earl Wilson, another Ohioan.

More than any other source of inspiration and motivation, Ryder's paragraphs of domestic, local, national, social, and political commentary, and his "Young Lady" ("a pretty but vacuous girl, symbolizing the American woman's indifference to what is going on in the world") set early and lasting professional directions for Thurber. Ryder's amused and patronizing treatment of the "Young Lady," which would result in a feminist boycott of his material today, helped solidify Thurber's own stereotyped notions of the female sex.

Writing in the early 1900s, Ryder comments on the neighbor women who live on his street, Franklin Avenue: "They always succeed in making a girl who is as pure as the driven snow sound less interesting than one who is no better than she ought to be." Thurber never forgot that one and adapted it to a 1938 *New Yorker* cartoon caption. As late as 1924, when Thurber had his own column in the *Columbus Evening Dispatch*, he was writing fond and complimentary references to Ryder, though Ryder was still editing the *Dispatch*'s rival newspaper, the *Journal*. Here are examples of lines Thurber printed in *The Thurber Album* as among Ryder's best:

"I say she used to be no better than she ought to be, but she is now."

"Our memory goes back to the time when another reason why we re-garded girls as of the inferior sex was because they never seemed to have any warts."

"About all a girl has to do to get engaged to a soldier is to be around."

"We suppose every woman who has been married a good long time has her moments of depression, as she cleans up after her husband, when she feels that she'd rather have the insurance money."

"The night has a thousand eyes, and the neighbor women at least twice that many ears."

And Thurber's favorite:

"A woman is either hearing burglars or smelling something burning."

In late 1914, with no classes to attend, Thurber began composing para-graphs in admitted imitation of Ryder. He may have first submitted them to

The Sun-Dial and had them refused on their merits or because Thurber was not matriculated. Or he may have sent them directly to East High School's *The X-Rays*. In his sense of isolation he had little affection for the university then and considerable nostalgia for East High, where he had enjoyed more social success. The paragraphs appear in the February, March, April, and June 1915, issues of *The X-Rays,* and here and there casually appropriate Ryder's own Young Lady as a compliment to the master: "We asked the Young Lady Across the Way if she used many theme tablets [notebooks], and she said, my! she wouldn't think of taking a drug to stimulate her mind, even if she didn't get high grades on her themes."

His addiction to puns and other wordplay is off and running; he has the Young Lady saying "her brother passed everything last semester but curriculum." Elsewhere, Sleepy Hollow is "a yawning chasm"; "Corporal Punishment, Major Premise and General Debility seem to bear charmed lives"; "Troy fell because it was a one-horse town"; "Next month: The Spoon, a stirring drama."

In "Franklin Avenue, U.S.A.," Thurber writes of Ryder:

> I met him only once, forty years ago, when I was a junior in high school. I had written some paragraphs for the school paper, in flagrant and callow imitation of the master, and sent them to him. He read them . . . and reprinted one in the *Journal.* Later my father introduced me to Bob Ryder and I still remember that great day.

Thurber may have met Ryder when a junior in high school but he had no paragraphs to send him until 1915, three years later, when Thurber was nearly twenty-one. As an autobiographical revisionist in his fifties, Thurber seemed to find it important to claim a precociousness that simply didn't exist. Nor do we know which item Ryder used; it was not among the examples of Ryder's writing Thurber chose to reprint. In any case, Ryder's interest must have been of immeasurable value to Thurber, helping to convince him that there was a promising field for him in humorous essays.

Reading Ryder today, one may sincerely ponder whether his contribution to written humor is less in what he wrote than in his influence on young James Thurber. Thurber, of course, tended to enshrine any who had been a factor in his professional life and, to the end, maintained that Ryder rates among America's great humorists, from Twain to E. B. White.

What appealed most to Thurber were Ryder's quotes and descriptions of his real and imagined ladies. Though he was delighted to identify the mildly scatterbrained women with his mother and his eccentric aunts, Thurber assumed an increasing impatience with women in general as the years rolled on, and didn't spare them when he discovered he owned the heavy weapons of art. In a 1946 *New Yorker* cartoon caption, the Thurber Man snarls at his wife: "How is it possible, woman, in the awful and magnificent times we live in, to be preoccupied exclusively with the piddling?" (Just as often, in his first-person pieces, however, he asked the same question of himself.)

Thurber never gave up certain attitudes toward women—attitudes that Ryder had helped inspire. As late as 1960, the year before his death, he was telling Harvey Taylor, of the *Detroit Times:* "Women are taking over the world because they are blandly unconcerned about history. I once sat next to a woman who asked why we had to purchase Louisiana when we got all the other states free. I explained to her that Louisiana was owned by two women, Louise and Anna Wilmott and that they sold it to General Winfield Scott provided he'd name it after them. That was called the Wilmott [sic] Proviso, and his closing of the deal was the Dredd [sic] Scott decision.

"She answered, 'Never mind the details. Why did we let them talk us into it at all?'

"I don't believe the canard that some women thought that Pearl Harbor was a movie actress. But one woman, asked to name the martyred presidents said, 'Yes, but how do you know what torture they inflicted on their wives?' "

Thus, the "lost" school year of 1914–1915 proved to be one of transition for Thurber. If he couldn't command recognition or find personal resolve in ordinary social competition, he would, like Ryder, develop a literary personality. Ryder was the proof that it could be done even in Columbus, drawing on material from the very environment Thurber inhabited.

14

That Night the Ghost Got In

The steps began again, circled the dining-room table like a man running, and started up the stairs toward us, heavily, two at a time. The light still shone palely down the stairs. [Herman and I] saw nothing coming; we only heard the steps. Herman rushed to his room and slammed the door. I slammed shut the door at the stairs top and held my knee against it. . . . There was no sound. None of us ever heard the ghost again.

The slamming of the doors had aroused mother: . . . "What was all that running around downstairs?" said mother. So she had heard the steps, too! We just looked at her. "Burglars!" she shouted, intuitively. . . . "We'll call the police." Since the phone was downstairs . . . she flung up a window of her bedroom which faced the bedroom windows of the house of a neighbor, picked up a shoe, and whammed it through a pane of glass across the narrow space that separated the two houses. Glass tinkled into the bedroom occupied by a retired engraver named Bodwell and his wife. Bodwell had been for some years in rather a bad way and was subject to mild "attacks."

. . . Bodwell was at the window in a minute, shouting, frothing a little, shaking his fist. "We'll sell the house and go back to Peoria," we could hear Mrs. Bodwell saying. It was some time before mother "got through" to Bodwell. "Burglars!" she shouted. "Burglars in the house!" Herman and I hadn't dared to tell her that it was not burglars but ghosts, for she was even more afraid of ghosts than of burglars. Bodwell at first thought she meant there were burglars in his house, but finally he quieted down and called the police.

—from "The Night the Ghost Got In"

Though Thurber was skilled at melding the apocryphal with actual happenings for the best comic effects, he insisted until the day he died that he did hear a ghost on a November night at 77 Jefferson Avenue, running around the dining-room table and up the stairs. William [Herman] and Mame [mother] were just as firm on the point.

"It was the only time the boys ever actually heard the ghost, but it was true they did, even though Jamie wrote it so funny," Mame told a *Time* reporter in 1950. Robert writes: "It's true that my father and I were in Indianapolis the night they heard the ghost, as Jamie writes. They really did call the police, too."

In his story, Thurber gives the house address as 77 Lexington Avenue, rather than Jefferson. "I deliberately changed the address," he told a *Dispatch* writer in 1957,

for the simple reason that there *was* a ghost in the house. I often wonder if it is still heard there or if it has finally been laid to rest. The family who lived in the house ahead of us moved out because of the strange sounds, [we] found out later. The corner druggist to whom I related my own experience, described the walking and running upstairs before I could describe it myself. They were undeniably the steps of a man. It was quite an experience to hear him running up the steps toward us, my brother and me, and to see nothing whatever. A Columbus jeweler is said to have shot himself after running up those steps. This is the only authentic ghost I ever encountered. I didn't want to alarm whoever might be living there when I wrote the story. I think it was a music school for girls.

Mame often explained that the jeweler had telephoned his girlfriend, was told their romance was over and, hysterical with disappointment, rushed up the back stairs and shot himself.

Cousin Earl Fisher, when in his seventies, said he doubted the authenticity of any such story told by Mame. "She could convince the boys that they had heard a ghost, whether they had or not," he says.

In a 1936 *New Yorker* story, "Mrs. Phelps," Thurber describes a Mrs. Jessie Norton ("an old friend of my mother's"), a psychic who reads fortunes in tea leaves—including Thurber's, when he is visiting Columbus. On one such visit, Mrs. Norton tells Thurber of a strange experience. On a recent "night on which the wind moans in the wires, and telephone bells ring without benefit of human agency, and there are inexplicable sounds at doors and windows," a neighbor of Mrs. Norton's, a Mrs. Phelps, turns up in tears at Mrs. Norton's door to report that her elderly father has just dropped dead. She asks Mrs. Norton to call the undertaker, while she goes back to be with her father. There are lights in Mrs. Phelps's residence when Mrs. Norton, who has called the undertaker, gets there, but nobody answers the door. The undertaker arrives; he and Mrs. Norton search the apartment; there is nobody there, living or dead. The next day a puzzled Mrs. Norton knocks on Mrs. Phelps's door. Mrs. Phelps, all smiles, is surprised to see her and cheerfully invites her in. No further mention is made of Mrs. Phelps's father, who is never seen in any form.

"I took the story for what it was, fuzzy edges and all," writes Thurber, "an almost perfect example of what goes on in the life that moves slowly about the lonely figure of Mrs. Jessie Norton, reading the precarious future in her tea leaves, listening to the whisperings and knockings of the ominous present at her door. Before I left her she read my fortune in the teacup I had drunk from. It seems that a slight, blonde woman is going to come into my life and that I should beware of the sea."

On a trip to Columbus, Mame introduced Thurber to Evangeline Adams, the astrologist. Was *she* Mrs. Norton?

Did Earl Fisher have any idea who Mrs. Norton might be?

"I'm certain it was Mame Thurber," Earl Fisher replied. "She read tea leaves. Jamie got a lot of his stories from her. She was an actress and a convincing one. Her children would believe whatever she'd tell them. She was apt to move the furniture around and tell them, 'Why, look, it must have been a ghost. Why, that clock was here last night and now it's over there.' Sometimes she'd turn to Uncle Charlie and say, 'Isn't that so, Charlie?' He'd just smile. He never contradicted her. She read fortune cards, too—though never in the Fisher household, even as a joke. My grandparents were traditional Methodists and cards were never allowed in the house."

Mame would cheerfully boost along any story containing the unexplainable, though it was Thurber and William who actually heard the ghost, not she. Thurber not only insisted on the reality of the ghost's footsteps, in his last months he became adamant if challenged on the subject and failed to see the humor in it that others did. "The only time he got angry with me was a few months before his death, when he was talking about ghosts," says Mark Van Doren, a Columbia professor of English and a neighbor of Thurber's, recalls. "He said he believed in ghosts and wanted to write about them some day. I attacked the idea. I said, 'Jim, I don't believe in ghosts and you don't, either. I do believe in imagination, but the supernatural is so trivial—a voice saying, "Ethel, you dropped a spool of thread behind the clock," or some such.' Thurber got suddenly angry and wouldn't let the subject drop. He was irrational. It wasn't until his fatal attack shortly afterwards that my wife and I realized in what bad shape he was that evening, physically and mentally."

Surprisingly, Thurber's lasting belief in ghosts began with his single encounter with one that November night in 1915 at 77 Jefferson Avenue. The experience literally haunted him all his life, and figured into his disjointed plans for an article on Houdini and aspects of the occult, in the days before his death. During those last weeks, when he could retain only an uncertain grip on himself, he told an interviewer:

> My careful researches more than forty-five years ago, revealed the story of a man who had lived in that house, had walked around the dining-room table, then ran up the steps and shot himself in one of the second-floor rooms. He left a note describing his final behavior, but it was destroyed by the family. I found out, and the police have never heard of it, and I promised I would not tell about the note. A strange voice, anonymous, had telephoned him at his office one morning and told him that if he went home around ten A.M., entered the kitchen door, and stood quietly in the dining room, he would hear his wife making her daily assignation with her lover and this is precisely what happened.

How had Thurber learned of a note? To whom had he promised not to tell about it, and why? His version seems to be among those sad, directionless mental wanderings of his final days.

In the 1920s, the house was home to the Wallace Collegiate School and Conservatory of Music. It later became a beauty shop and then a boarding house. When it was owned by a woman named Anna Bancroft, a state employee named Esther Reich rented a suite of the upstairs rooms. During her evening visits with Bancroft, Reich would hear footsteps running up the back staircase from the dining room. She supposed that they were coming from the neighboring house until William Thurber, whom she met at a dance, explained that the house was haunted. Esther Reich eventually moved, but on one occasion returned to visit Anna Bancroft and spent the night in the alcove off the living room. She says she awoke to see a figure seated in the rocking chair nearby, hunched over, his elbow on his knee. She lay back in bed, and when she sat up again the figure was gone.

In the late 1950s, the peripatetic Columbus artist and chronicler Bill Arter visited the place and inquired into the ghost matter with its owner, Mrs. Marie Madry, who had lived there for nineteen years before moving elsewhere, continuing to lease the house to others. With a firmness only an absentee landlady can adopt when speaking of a property she must rent out, Mrs. Madry pronounced, "No ghosts." Arter gallantly published his opinion that Thurber's writing about the night the ghost got in had exorcised any further evidence of it.

In 1984, a group of private citizens acquired the 1890 building, oversaw its restoration, and turned it into The Thurber House—a Thurber museum, bookstore, and site of a writer-in-residence program. The project was primarily sponsored by Ohio State University and the *Columbus Dispatch*, with support from the National Endowment for the Arts. Guest writers live in the attractive apartment recently converted from the old attic—where the bed fell on Charles Thurber one night, and where grandfather shot the policeman for a Union deserter. The house next door, through whose window Mame was supposed to have thrown a shoe, was later acquired and connected to The Thurber House as a conference center for scholars and authors' public readings.

Thurber's famous account of the haunted house became an item in a game of Trivial Pursuit. Playing the game with his family in 1987, O'Bear Thompson, who had boarded at 77 Jefferson Avenue years before, discovered the item and said he then remembered that he had heard footsteps creaking up and down the attic stairs, stopping at his door. After hearing that the house was haunted, Thompson said he still didn't believe it was a ghost.

Patricia DiPerna, a 1988 writer-in-residence, says she did see the ghost "as I stepped out of a car in the back parking lot. I happened to look up to the [attic] apartment and the ghost—a hefty, somewhat stooped, black torso shadow, apparently dressed in a raincoat with the collar turned up, moving at a silhouette's pace—made a single pass through the hallway lights just as my eyes travelled up the building wall, as if waiting there, set in motion by my glance." She also heard unexplainable clatterings in the kitchen cupboards. Investigation of both phenomena revealed nothing there, but Thurber would, by now, feel vindicated.

15

That Dear Old Confrère, Nugey

Time has not yet served to efface your blonde handsomeness from my retentive memory, old keed. . . . Every now and then I spare a moment for reminiscence on the college days. . . . Sounds like the mournful words of one bidding adieu to his youth, doesn't it? Well, not youth exactly, Elliott, but certain of the haunts and pastimes and ways of things connected with youth, such as the "keen, bitter-sweet days, blazoned against the night." . . . When I think of the old institution with its rich gallery of imperishable pictures by Memory, I can see now only a drab chromo of the well known Duke of Medina [Virgil (Duke) Damon, president of the Phi Psi chapter, from Medina, Ohio], studying in a far corner, a solitary figure in the old Phi Psi Castle. That is my vision of next year. I am not going back, Nugey.

—Thurber letter to Elliott Nugent, June 28, 1918

By the summer of 1915, Thurber was moody, withdrawn, unrecognized, and lonely; he had dropped out of the university's 1914–15 academic year; he was broke, unable to find full-time summer employment, and that July he accepted his father's offer to take him and William to Cleveland to work on one of Charles's promotional brochures.

"They published suggested answers to contests that were [frequently] running in newspapers," Robert says. "They advertised [the brochure] in the papers there and placed them on consignment in bookstores, large news-stands, and similar places. I don't know how successful they were but [there seemed to be] a good profit for all."

That fall Thurber was back on campus, again trying to outmaneuver the university's depressing requirements of military and physical conditioning. He again cut military drill—eleven times—though he completed the first semester's elementary French, survey of English literature, and advanced composition. Also enrolled in Professor Edwin L. Beck's composition course was Elliott Nugent, whose friendship would change Thurber's life forever. "Without Nugent," says Joel Sayre, "Thurber might have wound up as a sad old newspaper hack somewhere, or maybe, if he ever could get through college, a sad old professor teaching or doing little-noticed scholarly research. Nugent was unquestionably a catalyst."

Nugent, sometimes called "Nugey" by his friends, was from Dover, Ohio, a son of professional actors. From infancy he had traveled the theater circuits with his parents. By age four, he was part of the show, billed as "Master Elliott, the Boy Monologist," and paid seventy-five dollars a week—a sum few adults were earning at the turn of the century. When he grew to school age, his mother quit the stage and settled in their hometown of Dover to provide Elliott with a more conventional childhood.

In school, Nugent was not only way ahead of his classmates in maturity and poise but in literature, thanks to his playwright father. He wore clothes from Browning-King in Chicago, got excellent grades, was a teacher's pet, and had his own folding metal cup to avoid using the school's public drinking fountain. In summer, he continued to play vaudeville theater with his parents.

He carried his father's small typewriter as they traveled by train, having nurtured ambitions of writing from the time he was a toddler. At an earlier age than Thurber, he discovered G. A. Henty's historical books for boys, and other writers of juvenile fiction. Like Mame, Grace Nugent worried about the amount of time her son spent reading; in Thurber's case, Mame feared the overuse of his eye; in Nugent's, the concern was that a young boy alternating between the make-believe worlds of theater and fiction would eventually be unable to deal with reality.

His athletic ability and personal popularity earned him the captaincy of the football and track teams in high school. He played center on the basket-ball team and edited the high-school yearbook. He graduated second highest in his class scholastically. Though his mother had retired from her career to look after him, Nugent's father and a new stage partner, billed as "J. C. Nugent & Company," were flourishing. Middle-class life in Dover was comfortable for Elliott; he was driving the family's new car while in high school. He planned to attend Princeton, but his mother contracted what would be a long and incurable illness, and it was decided that he attend a college not far from Dover, in case of emergency. He selected Ohio State.

Competition for the potential "big men on campus" was fierce among the university's fraternities. Nugent's reputation as a near-celebrity had preceded him to Columbus. He was greeted at the station by a welcoming committee of Phi Kappa Psi, and taken to lunch at the famous old Neil House. He soon decided to pledge.

Nugent had promised his father to concentrate on English and writing courses, for, as they both agreed, it was the poets, writers, and artists who were "the movers and shakers of the world"—the words of an Arthur O'Shaughnessy poem they both liked. Though a freshman, Nugent had obtained special permission to take the sophomore-level advanced composition class. Freshman English composition was, in his words, "merely intended to help the students learn to write a short business letter." Professor Beck's condition was that Nugent revert to freshman English if he didn't perform satisfactorily. Seventeen-year-old Nugent not only did well, he talked his way into other advanced English and writing courses.

Student enrollment was at five thousand, classes were large, and Nugent became aware of Thurber only when Beck one day read a Thurber paper, "My Literary Enthusiasms," that humorously parodied the current dime novels. After class, on the steps outside, Thurber heard Nugent asking who had written the theme and bashfully acknowledged authorship. An unlikely friendship began between the seventeen-year-old urbane sophisticate and the awkward twenty-year-old "towner." Thurber's dropping out his sophomore year had meant that what few acquaintances he had made on campus as a freshman were now ahead of him, in third-year classes. Nugent describes Thurber in those days as a solitary figure wandering "about the campus on cold winter days dressed in an old pair of pants, an old coat, no vest, and no hat." (It might not have occurred to the young, privileged Nugent that Thurber could afford nothing else; both of Thurber's brothers had enrolled at O.S.U. that fall, and though they both dropped out soon enough for medical reasons, the Thurber family was especially hard-pressed financially.)

Their friendship "ripened slowly," says Nugent. Though he occasionally took Thurber to lunch at the Phi Psi house, the two saw little of one another during Nugent's busy freshman year, in which he went out for football and track.

Before the second semester began, Thurber received a letter from the president's office, dated February 4, 1916:

Dear Sir:

I beg to advise you that the President has protested your registration for the second semester of the current year owing to your continued absence from Military drill. The registering officers have been instructed not to register you except upon written authority from the President.

Handwritten on the file copy is a note: "Mr. Thurber called Feb. 8, 1916, was directed to see Capt. Converse and bring written note from the Capt. withdrawing protest." The school's requirement was for four terms of drill. Thurber eventually drew an incomplete in military in 1914, 1915, 1916, and 1917. He despised Captain Converse. "Commie," as the pompous martinet was called behind his back, was said by the students to be one of three men running the university at the time, along with the president and the athletic director, and Thurber's comrades in arms were fascinated by the apparent suicidal tendencies of the gangly young man who repeatedly deserted their ranks. Rather than beg the hated Captain for reinstatement, Thurber dropped out of school again, returning to a routine of reading books at the Ohio Union Building and the Columbus Public Library. (He was still using his juvenile library card to borrow books from the city library; on March 3, 1916, the librarian pointed out to Thurber that he was twenty-one years old, and more than qualified for an adult card. Thurber acquiesced.)

That summer, Robert recalls, Thurber worked with the Ohio Department of Agriculture in the State House, thanks to the help of a friend whose father supervised the department's clerical work. Thurber folded circulars and addressed and sealed envelopes. By summer's end, he had made up his mind to settle things with the university and get on with his education. He made an appointment to see William Oxley Thompson, the Presbyterian minister who had headed the university since 1899. Though Thurber in later years would make only lukewarm references to him, Thompson proved to be an invaluable friend to Thurber on at least three occasions. He now heard Thurber out sympathetically. "W. O. T. reinstated me on his own," Thurber proudly wrote James Pollard, journalism professor and university historian, in 1960, "without any letter from Converse. The great Thompson said to me, 'Don't let the military get you by the neck.' "

He signed up for the semester's full fifteen credits: American literature, nineteenth-century poetry, journalism, political science, and economics. He and Nugent were together again in the journalism course, which was taught by Joseph (Chief) Myers, an alumnus and former newspaper executive from

Pittsburgh. In the class, also, was a sophomore, Minnette Fritts, from Mt. Sterling, Ohio. An education major taking a minor in journalism, she was another woman Thurber would remain sentimental about through much of his life.

"His typewriter was next to mine," she says. "Jim would turn in his assignment very rapidly but then would continue to write, pulling out the pages and throwing them in the wastebasket. My curiosity got the better of me; we used to walk together from journalism to the English Department, but one day I made some excuse not to, stayed behind and pulled his crumpled pages out of the basket. They were wonderful. I showed them to Chief Myers and after that he and I made a habit of reading Jim's throwaways after class. They were written for his own amusement, but fun and so clever."

The idle exercises may have been akin to the compressed playlet young Thurber left on the inside cover of his copy of *Addison's Essays*, entitled "The Cribber, a lugubrious drama in four acts":

ACT I.
Sitting room of John Smith, XV. Enter nurse.
NURSE: Boy.
JOHN SMITH, XV: Joy. President some day.
NURSE: Should worry. Curtain.

ACT II.
Examination room in English. (Professor exits.)
JOHN SMITH XVI: Anybody know anything about . . . this stuff?
(No response)
JOHN SMITH XVI: Aw, well, hell.
(Produces textbook from each rim of tortoise shell specs.)
JOHN SMITH XVI: Now, boys, we'll get somewhere.
(Opens book. Enter professor, 139 pounds of pussycat.)

ACT III. Scene 1. President's office.
ENGLISH PROFESSOR: Cribbed.
PRESIDENT: Out of school.
JOHN SMITH XVI: Have a cigarett [sic]?
PRESIDENT: Out of my sight.
(John and professor exit from President's sight.)
Scene 2. (Out of President's sight)
JOHN SMITH XVI: Cigarette?
PROFESSOR: Thanks awfully.

ACT IV. Grocery store of Newt Bangs.

NEWT BANGS: Take this order out to Mrs. Fieldings, boy.

JOHN SMITH XVI: Yes, sir.

Curtain

It was either a testament to the importance of higher education or a mockery of those who considered it so.

As part of the journalism curriculum, the students got out the *Lantern*, the school newspaper, with a distribution of about thirty-five hundred copies, five days a week. Working with Thurber on the *Lantern* that fall of 1916, Nugent and his fraternity brother, Jack Pierce, one of the newspaper's rotating editors, became dedicated Thurber fans, increasingly taken by Thurber's "ability, wit, and charm," says Nugent. With Nugent's background as a performing artist, he knew the rare creative mind when he came across it, and he sensed Thurber's extraordinary potential long before Thurber, who still had a hard time imagining himself at all. But Thurber responded to Nugent's and Pierce's recognition like a flower transplanted from shade to sun. The two fraternity brothers began a campaign to get Thurber into Phi Kappa Psi, fully aware that the foundation of the Greek fraternities is elitism.

"There was the matter of Jim's looks and attitude," says Fritts. "He still had very little self-assurance, and that showed. He was awkward and poorly dressed. I remember the difficulty Elliott was having persuading his fraternity to offer Jim a bid."

Virgil (Duke) Damon, the president of the fraternity, lived in the Phi Psi house the seven years he was on campus as a premed and medical student. He would become a nationally known Park Avenue obstetrician to celebrities, delivering Rosemary, Thurber's only child, in 1931 in New York. "It took a year to get Thurber into the fraternity," he recalled. "The Phi Psis and Phi Gams were the two leading fraternities on campus then. They took college boys with money. It cost $50 a month for board and room and you were expected to have $4.50 a week spending money. Thurber simply didn't fit the picture; he had no money at all, it seemed. Nobody knew much about him. He was a towner but never mentioned his family, or invited anyone home to meet them. He seemed to have come from nowhere and some of the fellows thought that strange. I remember the big debate over whether Thurber should be taken in. The question was: would he be socially amenable, contribute to the *esprit de corps*? Thurber was such an improbable fellow, older than most of the boys, and not all that popular with the majority, so the vote was to postpone the decision for a year."

Nugent and Pierce would have none of that and, it has been said, put it to their fraternity brothers—"Take Thurber or lose us." On several weekends, Nugent invited Thurber to his home in Dover to visit his family. He realized that those not in journalism class with Thurber would fail to understand what a find he was. He and Pierce undertook a campaign to sell Thurber, persuading him to get a haircut and a new suit. (Nugent, according to some, paid for both.) He saw to it that Thurber was frequently at the fraternity house, getting acquainted with its members, studying, working on writing projects, or holding discussions with Nugent in Nugent's room.

"Only Jack Pierce, besides Nugent, seemed to understand and accept Thurber," says Ben Williamson, also a Phi Psi pledge when Thurber was an initiate. "Nugent both impressed and baffled his fraternity brothers by his sincere and obvious enjoyment of Thurber's company. Jim was a whimsical guy. He appeared shy, shyer than he actually was, wore those heavy glasses, and gave the impression of always being in an economic pinch. Those who watched Nugent's friendship with Jim witnessed the start of Thurber's self-confidence."

"Members who lived and ate at home were supposed to pay fifty cents if they stopped by the fraternity for lunch," Damon says. "The student who acted as steward took down the names of those not paying regularly, but somehow Thurber never was asked to pay. Maybe Nugent paid for him, but my feeling is everyone felt he paid his dues by entertaining us."

The fraternity matter was settled in the winter of 1916–1917. Damon, acting in his capacity as Phi Kappa Psi president, dropped in on Thurber one evening in the journalism building, where Thurber was working on the *Lantern*, and offered him the bid to join. Thurber accepted. "He still wasn't popular with a lot of the boys," Damon said, "but an influential group within the house thought he belonged. One thing in his favor, the fraternities put on skits at one another's houses, with all the men taking part, and Thurber was good at skits—writing or acting in them. He could be the funniest man on campus just making a remark about the weather. Thurber would put that patch over an eye and do imitations of Converse and bring down the house. He'd do other professors, too. The holdouts began to see what he could bring to the membership."

Thurber "cheerfully submitted to the semicomic tortures of 'Hell Week,'" Nugent writes. "Jim handled all his assignments with comic solemnity and soon endeared himself to everyone. I do not believe that he had any false ideas about the importance of fraternities, but he really liked most of the fellows and began to take more interest in social life."

The importance of the fraternity to Thurber, apart from a newly acquired social status and identity, was the opportunity to spend more time with Nugent at the house without feeling himself an interloper. In fact, he never forgot the Phi Psis' earlier repudiation of him, nor other humiliations of the fraternity system he had suffered at the hands of boys younger than he was. The Phi Psi house never became home to him, as it did to his brother members, in later years when he returned to the campus. At such times, as an emerging literary celebrity, he became irritated at the inability of any of the contemporary residents to recognize his name or to pronounce or spell it correctly.

In 1930, he was invited back as principal after-dinner speaker at a Phi Psi Founder's Day banquet, honoring the fiftieth anniversary of the O.S.U. chapter. It was held at the Deshler-Wallick Hotel. While his best Columbus friends, Ted Gardiner and other non–Phi Psis, were enjoying a lively drinking session in a suite upstairs, Thurber was forced to sit through dreary speeches at the banquet dais. When it was finally Thurber's turn, he got up, ignored his prepared remarks, and handed out an impromptu roasting of the fraternity system in general and the O.S.U. chapter of Phi Kappa Psi in particular. "I've listened to this ghastly bilgewater about the pure white flame of Phi Psi for two hours and fifteen minutes," he said. "The only reason I ever joined your fraternity was because of Elliott Nugent and Jack Pierce." He kept up the vituperation, topping insult with insult. Whether they mistook the remarks as rich Thurber humor or not, the speech was a big hit, and all present except a few of the fraternity's national officers applauded wildly and insisted on writing their initials on Thurber's white shirt.

Nor were fraternities of much use scholastically, he later decided. In the 1940s, wondering whether the roommate system at the Northampton School for Girls was conducive to his daughter's good study habits, he wrote the headmistress, Sarah B. Whitaker: "With one exception, the members of my fraternity who got the highest grades were the boys who lived at home and not the fraternity house itself."

Wendell Postle remembers Nugent's room at the fraternity, the floor littered with the discarded writings of Nugent and Thurber, two desks in the room awash with typewritten pages, the two friends working in their shirtsleeves and smoking cigarettes, enjoying one another's ideas. Nugent had copies of professional theater scripts written by his father, which awakened playwriting ambitions in Thurber. When not working on class assignments or reporting for the *Lantern*, they whiled away much of their time at the Phi Psi house or in the *Lantern* office making up satirical skits, limericks, and quatrains. Ralph McCombs, a classmate, remembers one that he, Nugent, and

Thurber collaborated on; it begins: "Don't never pinch a bulldog's balls, even if you're clever." (Thurber would forever keep risqué material out of his published work, but it was occasionally fair game among friends.)

Following Thurber's disillusionment with O.S.U. during the McCarthy period, he began to revise his recollections of his experiences there. When *Time*'s cover story on Thurber dutifully repeated his claim of indebtedness to Nugent for getting him into the fraternity and the university's social life, he felt too much was being taken from him and given to his old friend. He wrote the Whites:

> I suppose you have seen the Sayre piece in TIME. . . . Joe actually played down my unkemptness, but fortunately played up Elliott, which won't hurt his troubled ego. [Nugent, at the time, was suffering from manic depression.] The only playing up, however, would be obvious to fraternity men, who don't take a man in because he wrote a theme. I had brought and laid at the feet of Phi Kappa Psi the two editorships, or I would never have got in. But I deliberately said the sequence was right. . . . I loved, and was loved, by two wonderful men named Carson Blair and George Packer, who had charge of the humorous monthly and passed it on to me when it could have gone to a man in their own fraternity. They did this three days after I rejected their effort to pledge me to their fraternity. This is the real kind of story that can't get into TIME, but should.

It would have been an inaccurate story, for Thurber's positions as an editor on the *Lantern* and the editor of the *Sun-Dial* followed by a year his joining the fraternity. It isn't clear why he would wish to deprive Nugent of any credit for getting him accepted as a Phi Psi; Nugent even paid Thurber's initial membership fee. There is little doubt that, in McCombs's words, "Nugent was a sort of a Svengali for Thurber's Trilby," and a lasting influence on him in matters far more important than a fraternity membership.

Nugent led his own campus life where Thurber could not always follow. He became the leader of cotillions, the darling of the coeds; he liked hiking, tennis, golf, and swimming. He was elected president of his junior class, chairman of the May Dance Committee, secretary of Bucket and Dipper—an intrafraternity social group—and vice president of Sphinx, the senior honorary society of male superachievers on campus. He was also elected president of the Strollers, the dramatic club, and persuaded the hesitant Thurber to join. Thurber "was naturally a good actor," Nugent writes, "and retained a spark of ambition along those lines that was never gratified until . . . he played himself in A *Thurber Carnival* on Broadway." But, Nugent adds, "Jim made a stronger impression on Chief Myers, the head of the Journalism Department, than he did on our dramatic directors."

Nugent would go on to a career as an actor, producer, and director in theater and film. He and Thurber would remain friends and fulfill the promise made in their fraternity days to collaborate one day on a play about Ohio State. Meanwhile, Thurber's self-imagining by now encompassed even more than a career as a newspaper paragrapher; thanks to one English professor in particular, he now also dreamed of writing literature in the tradition of—of all people—Henry James. That master of elegant run-on sentences, wordy excursions into endless dependent clauses, and cautious parenthetical thought would now take up an unlikely residence in Thurber's hall of idols alongside Ryder, the artisan of quick, bright, economical sentences and paragraphs.

Such contradictions help make understandable the reply once given to a young woman who excitedly told a *New Yorker* editor one day that she had just met James Thurber. "Which one?" he asked.

16

That Man with a Pipe

He was round of face and body, with yellow hair, pink cheeks, and fine blue eyes. . . . He was a great pipe man, and once asked me, after I began to write for a living, if I smoked one when I worked. I told him that I did, although I didn't, and it seemed to please him.

—from "Man with a Pipe"

With Ryder his role model, and humorous paragraphing his professional objective, Thurber entered the fall semester of 1916 with only a limited awareness of the literary treasures that a pipe-smoking professor, Joseph Taylor, would help him unearth. In 1918, Thurber took Taylor's second-semester course in Victorian poetry (Tennyson, Browning, Arnold, Swinburne, A. E. Housman). He read the homegrown nineteenth-century poets in his *Introduction to American Literature*, too, remembered it all, and would quote from and parody those English and American poets ever after.

Thurber is thought to have laughed several of the lesser classics right out of the classroom poetry anthologies when, in 1939, his "Famous Poems Illustrated" series ran in the *New Yorker;* the poets' sincerity is turned to absurdity by Thurber's bizarre drawings. Can anyone, having seen Thurber's Barbara Frietchie waving the Union flag out the window while bawling out Stonewall Jackson, ever again be moved to anything but laughter by the Whittier poem? Or keep a straight face reading Longfellow's "Excelsior" in which The Thurber Man carries a banner while climbing the Alpine slope in a business suit and bow tie?

In 1917–18, Thurber took Taylor's two-semester study of the English novel (Richardson to Scott; Dickens to Meredith) and in the course of it the eager, father-hungry student seems to have adopted Taylor not only as his literary

mentor but his intellectual emancipator. Taylor's preferences in writers became Thurber's: Cather, Conrad, Housman, Meredith—and most important, Henry James.

Immature, sexually inexperienced, suspicious of the future, Thurber felt immediately comfortable in the protected world James created in his stories. He identified at once with James's "poor sensitive gentlemen." The middle-aged Thurber Men of his cartoons came to represent himself as a Jamesian victim in a culture dominated by women, with the men unable to understand or affect the matriarchal culture. *The Ambassadors* would remain his favorite James novel, and when Thurber arrived in France in 1918, he set about to see Paris and the French countryside through the eyes and emotions of Lambert Strether (the first "ambassador" sent to Paris to bring Chad home). Homesick for Ohio by 1920, Thurber would be torn by indecision, remembering Strether's conclusion that Parisian life was superior to that of contemporary America, and his final advice to Chad, who chooses not to return: "Live all you can; it's a mistake not to."

James's heroines became Thurber's, too, for similar, self-protective reasons: they were of a caste of woman who would spare him the embarrassments of worldly challenge, should they ever materialize in his life. *The Ambassadors'* Mme. de Vionnet became his feminine ideal. Thurber would quote lovingly, time and again, this James reference to Mme. de Vionnet: "When she touches a thing, the ugliness, God knows how, goes out of it." Mme. de Vionnet set the feminine criteria of character, tone, and fashion for young Thurber. The objects of his college infatuations took their turns atop his pedestal, whether they were aware of it or not. In New York, where women of the 1920s had taken full advantage of society's new permissiveness, those occupying Thurber's dreams found themselves still trussed up by his Victorian ideals, made to look and feel as out of place as the naked woman crouched atop a bookcase in Thurber's cartoon. It took the harsh facts of married life to melt his image of Althea as Mme. de Vionnet, and—in fairness to Thurber, the Jamesian gentleman—he blamed himself, not Althea, when she toppled from grace.

Though not surrendering his plan to write like Ryder, he now thought of becoming a novelist in the Jamesian tradition. That self-restricting idea would wither a few years later, when Thurber went broke trying to write a novel in France, but his fascination with James survived, stronger than ever. In his *New Yorker* stories, he often apes James's syntax and subordinated thoughts, making liberal use of dashes and parentheses. James was the subject of four parodies and several articles by Thurber. He exchanged long letters with his Columbus friend Herman Miller, then teaching at O.S.U., about turning *The Ambassadors* into a play.

"The professor . . . who influenced and encouraged me so much, was the late Joseph Russell Taylor of the English Department of Ohio State," Thurber wrote Frank Gibney of *Newsweek* in 1956. "His great belief in the novel and story of sensibility, and other things I learned from him in three years [actually two] had a direct bearing on my writing and show up in such things as 'The Evening's at Seven,' 'One Is a Wanderer,' and 'A Call on Mrs. Forrester.' "

Taylor was a feminist in an age when it was a heated issue around Columbus and the nation. He fancied himself an artist—he had taught drawing before teaching English—and a poet, but remained frustrated in not achieving the recognition awarded his mentor, the poet and Columbia University professor George Woodberry. He believed that the best work of Elizabeth Barrett and Robert Browning was done in the years of their marriage. Thurber, Nugent, and Herman Miller believed that Taylor's pretty but shallow wife had been a millstone around his neck and a reason that the Brownings' marriage seemed especially noteworthy to him. One of his favorite passages was Wordsworth's tribute to the "perfect woman, nobly planned; to warn, to comfort, and command."

Thurber remembered Taylor's classroom remarks as he did no others': "Art is revision." "You can't get passion into a story with exclamation points [or italics]." "A straight line can also be the dullest distance between two points." "A character of iron [in fiction] does not speak in words of tinfoil." "The only taste that is false is that which does not change." "Nothing genuine need fear the test of laughter." More important, Taylor reinforced Thurber's instinctive and essential reach for understanding the difference between literal fact and literary truth, a distinction that his professional life would rest upon.

It pleased Thurber that Taylor had earlier encouraged George Bellows to pursue a life of painting, and was a friend of Robert Henri, the art teacher and philosopher. Years later, as several photographs show, Thurber tried Taylor's pipe-smoking habit, but all the fiddling involved with cleaning, tamping, and relighting didn't fit Thurber's temperament, and he gave it up.

"Jim Thurber came to our house frequently," says Stafford Taylor, Joseph's son. "Sometimes he'd been invited; other times he'd just drop in for a chat with father. He had an elfish humor, but more often he was serious on those occasions. The dinner conversation might cover everything from literature to the newspaper comics. Thurber didn't strike me as a studious student—not

Phi Beta Kappa material. But he liked to hear father's thoughts on everything."

O.S.U.'s especially strong English Department left Thurber with a respect for professors of literature that lasted for many years. Of the people he collected in *The Thurber Album* as those of greatest importance to his Columbus development, three were English professors.

Thurber never completely divested himself of a sense of cultural inferiority. His gods were literary—to be worshipped, not argued with. His awe of them made easy his early beliefs that his own work was too concerned with the trifling to permit him the right to take off his overcoat in the hall of immortal letters. It was Taylor who broadened Thurber's range of literary aspirations and helped point him in the direction of a more serious and lasting self-realization.

In 1931, a bus struck the car Taylor was sitting in on the campus, and he died two years later from the effects of the accident. That fall, a tribute was planned "to the late Professor Joseph R. Taylor of the English Department for 43 years, who died March 30." The tribute took place in the Faculty Club on homecoming Saturday, with speeches by the O.S.U. president, "Professor William Graves, and James L. [sic] Thurber of New York," according to the program.

It was an ordeal for Thurber, who had to compete with the president and the popular, smooth-spoken professor, Billy Graves, neither of whom could have experienced the affection and gratitude for the departed that Thurber did. Faculty member James Pollard recalled that "Thurber was very nervous. I introduced him and said he had come at our invitation but at his own expense out of his devotion to Joe Taylor. He stood behind a davenport and kept pressing against it, moving it on the floor toward the audience and his hands fluttered while he spoke." Dissatisfied with his performance, Thurber then wrote a long letter to the alumni monthly on what Taylor had meant to him.

Shortly afterward, Taylor's wife brought some of her husband's poems to New York and asked Thurber to help find a publisher for them. "I showed them around to quite a few poetry editors and poets," Thurber says, "but her hope of publication was a disappointment. Although Joe Taylor thought of himself primarily as a poet, he lacked a basic gift which was best pointed out by E. B. White, who said, 'These verses do not sing.'" And when Thurber read Taylor's scholarly study "Taylor on [Henry] James," he regretfully concluded that his hero of university days simply "could never get it down on paper."

Thurber's suspicions as to the difficulties Taylor encountered in his marriage were, he felt, corroborated by the widow, who told Thurber that she considered the greatest American writer to be Paul Gallico—a sportswriter who became a prolific short-story contributor to the slick magazines of the 1930s and 1940s. ("I could hear Joe Taylor turning in his grave," says Thurber.)

Ludwig Lewisohn, who taught German and German literature at O.S.U. in Thurber's day, refers in his novel *Roman Summer* to a professor who can be no other than Joe Taylor:

> But it must not be supposed that John Austin was a fool. At college he had fallen under the influence of a teacher of intense but limited and stagnant tastes; a small ruddy gnome of a man who had, long ago, been a favorite pupil of George Edward Woodberry, a protégé of Richard Watson Gilder in the genteel days of the *Century* and had published a volume of late Victorian verse. His literary eminence was a legend in the city. Young Austin had taken all of the courses offered by his teacher. He was not unaware now of the man's limitations. What allied him to that teacher still was an unconquerable love of beauty and fitness and precision of speech.

Though Lewisohn couldn't have known it, in describing John Austin he neatly summed up Thurber as disciple to Professor Joseph Taylor.

Earl Wilson, the syndicated newspaper columnist, who had, like Thurber, edited O.S.U.'s the *Sun-Dial*, remembered when Thurber visited the campus in 1943, shortly after the death of another prominent faculty member, William Lucius Graves. Graves, by Thurber's admission, says Wilson, "was the most popular professor in the history of his university," if not with Thurber. "Asked to say a few words of regret about a very revered professor," Wilson writes, "Thurber told reporters 'I was never one of his great admirers.' Asked to say something lovely about the alumni, Thurber said he was tired of meeting Ohio State graduates who couldn't read or write." (Thurber could never forget the student whose theme about a ghost-ridden vessel was entitled "The Haunted Yatch.")

It isn't easy to explain why Thurber included Graves, whom he held in contempt, among his subjects of fond memory in *The Thurber Album*. He seemed to have had no intention of doing so at the beginning of the project. Writing Herman Miller's widow in 1951, he says: "I have now decided to devote one whole piece to Joe [Taylor] and to deal with [Professor Joseph] Denney and a few others in the second piece. The last half of the piece will be devoted to the best of them all, Herman Allen Miller." (He never wrote of Miller for publication.) No mention of Graves is made. And after the *New Yorker* published "Lengths and Shadows," in December 1951, in which Graves is handled gingerly and Denney is eulogized, Thurber wrote James Fullington at O.S.U.: "I got very little out of Billy's [classes]. He had the only short-story class, so I went to it."

But Graves was a campus phenomenon whose omission from Thurber's reminiscences would have been hard to explain. Thurber writes in "ΒΘΠ":

> Billy Graves was known for more than forty years as the friend of fresh-men, the confidant of seniors, and the chum of alumni. Every night . . . he wrote at least one personal letter [usually to] his former students, literally hundreds of them. They recognized the tall, well-groomed bachelor, forever young in heart, as a mere visitor in the intellectual world, like themselves, and not one of its awesome, withdrawn first citizens. They liked him because he never missed an issue of the *Cosmopolitan* magazine . . . and because he sometimes openly confessed his inability to understand certain so-called masterpieces of writing. . . . Billy Graves, his myriad young friends told people, was a good guy; he could go along with a gag; he was fun to have around.

Thurber states that "I entered [Graves's] short-story course in . . . September of 1916." Actually it was the spring term of 1917 that Thurber, Nugent, and Ralph McCombs sat in the rear row of Graves's class, snickering to themselves and noting his prissy manners for later mimicking. None of them suspected, until after signing up for the course, the method by which Graves taught the creative writing of short fiction. His preferences ran to the popular writers of the day, offered as models to his classes. "He stubbornly insisted on outlining ready-made plots for his students to follow in writing their 'original' short stories," writes Thurber. The plots were frequently of mother-dependent situations (Graves lived with his aging mother): the paralyzed woman begging her daughter not to marry and leave her; the cowardly youth who faces the firing squad bravely after his mother tells him the bullets are blanks. Thurber lost interest and never turned in the required number of assignments, receiving a deferred pass.

Graves knew art, music, and literature, played classical and ragtime piano, and was the perfect extra man at dinner parties. Though he didn't write fiction himself, for forty-two years he did write a weekly column, "The Idler," for the *Daily Lantern*—usually about his scenic walks through the countryside —and, for many years, a monthly article for the alumni magazine. Thurber seems to have recollected from Graves's "Idler" column, if not much else, a 1917 item that cited Professor Louis Cooper of O.S.U.'s English Department as the first champion of the split infinitive—a point of grammar whose defense Thurber took up lightheartedly in his 1929 *New Yorker* series "Our Own Modern English Usage." (His "Split Infinitive" begins: "Word has somehow got around that a split infinitive is always wrong. This is of a piece with the sentimental and outworn notion that it is always wrong to strike a lady.")

Following the German defeat of France in 1940, Graves used his *Lantern* column to attack the England he had long admired as a professor of literature for having "instigated" World War II. He criticized the U.S. "pro-British" Congress and praised, by inspired proxy, Parisian life under Nazi occupation. Charles A. Lindbergh, head of the America First isolationist movement, became Graves's hero. "The American masses" would never appreciate Lindbergh, Graves wrote, for he was too intelligent and had too much accurate information about the German military might.

Though his points were rebutted by others in the *Lantern*, Graves's anti-Allies sentiments continued to be reflected from time to time in his column until Pearl Harbor put an end to them. There was talk that Graves had come under the reactionary influence of the young woman, a former student of his, he had married late in life—to the astonishment of most, who had taken for granted Graves's neutered or homosexual disposition. All this was news to Thurber, until he began researching the Graves story for his "Album" series. In 1951, he writes Nugent: "I was astounded to discover that Billy was a vehement pro-Nazi in his late sixties, a hater of Britain and France, and a violent admirer of Lindbergh. He got married about the same time to a woman of identical views [and] lost a lot of friends when he wrote his political views in the Lantern." In *The Thurber Album*, Thurber writes: "Since few alumni had ever subscribed to the *Lantern* [including Thurber], Billy's host of graduate pals was largely ignorant of his strange transfiguration."

Thurber took care of this gap in their knowledge by distributing the news of Graves's pro-Nazi lapses through a half-million copies of the *New Yorker* and a book that was on the best-seller lists for weeks. Perhaps he intended to share his alarm at how easily a threat to an open society can be concealed by a cloak of learning, a façade of erudition.

Thurber did his best to clean up Graves before old friends of the professor walked in the door. "It must be reported, in fairness," Thurber writes toward the end of "BΘΠ," "that the well-remembered charm and affability of Ohio State's professor-plus has obliterated, like a ramble of morning-glories, his flaws and frailties. The Billy Graves legend remains as bright as ever, time having quietly erased its most prominent stain." So it had, until Thurber unveiled the warts on the Billy Graves portrait all over again.

Thurber bore another grudge against Graves. The dilettante professor avoided a lonely life not only by making himself socially available but through a fanatical allegiance to his fraternity, Beta Theta Pi. One of his Beta brothers estimated that Graves visited the chapter house five thousand times between Billy's 1893 graduation and his death in 1943. In "The Miracle of Brotherhood," which Graves wrote for his fraternity's national magazine, he says: "I have yet to hear from a Beta what I heard from a member of another great brotherhood who could not be sure of his fraternity's name, or from a second, only the other day, who told me he had not heard or thought fraternity for so long that he hardly knew what the word meant. . . . If I am glad of any one thing it is that for me the miracle of brotherhood has come to pass, and if I am proud of anything, it is that the badge on my breast is a Beta badge."

Thurber, who was frequently host to contradictory feelings and beliefs, questioned both the relative merits of the Betas and his own Phi Psis, and the value of the fraternity system in the first place. In a letter to a Manhattan couple who had written Thurber about the Graves article, he replied somewhat testily:

Some people, including a lot of Betas, seem to have got the remarkable idea from my piece on Billy Graves that I was a member of Beta Theta Pi. The Betas are notoriously stupid, and one letter of thanks was signed by seven old codgers who went to Ohio State years ago. "My God," a faculty member wrote me, "the Betas actually think you were praising Billy and the fraternity, and they are proud of the piece!" I had done my best, I had thought, to show the vapidity of a collegiate love of snobbishness that is continued into maturity, but I guess I just missed getting it over because I wouldn't underline my points.

My own fraternity history is not too good, since I have never been one who could believe in it, man or boy, and I think there is reason to fear the perpetuation into middle-life, on a national scale, of little snooty college clubs based on an idiotic theory of false superiority. I was not pledged until my senior year, just after I had rejected one offer from a frat I didn't consider smart enough. I wanted to belong to the one that Elliott Nugent, Jack Pierce, and Whitney Dillon belonged to. I don't know how it rates anywhere else, but at Ohio it had the editors and class presidents, and no athletes—it even turned down Chic Harley. One glance at an old Who's Who would have shown you that Dean Denney belonged to Phi Kappa Psi when he was at Michigan.

Here is the transparent Thurber revisionism at work. Nothing so thrilled him at the time as his acceptance by his fraternity—his pride of membership stands out in the above letter of denial. He was mailing sappy, sentimental letters to Nugent after leaving O.S.U. about his Phi Psi pin. Dreaming of "pinning" his sweetheart wraith, Eva Prout, he writes: "Boy, cant [sic] you see the lil golden shield, the greatest pin in the world, gleaming richly and austerely and yet debonairly from the folds of that Blue [navy-blue suit, popular with women then]?" And in the next paragraph he calls the Phi Psis "a great old bunch, Nugey, and till the stars grow dim on high it will continue to be."

However snobbish and elitist he felt the fraternity system to be in 1953, he was still a Phi Psi, and Billy Graves wasn't going to get away with suggesting that the Betas were "a greater old bunch."

17

Those Editorial Days

My memories of my editorial days [include] the night I was a column and a half shy on page one and was saved at three a.m. by the greatest aurora borealis since the Civil War, and the time when I had to write a four-column, 10-point editorial for the first page, to say nothing of the time my drawings of naked women were found in the office by an editor named Chambers, whose quest of the culprit was ended when Jack Pierce twisted his arm.

—Thurber letter to Lester Getzloe, 1950

During the 1916–1918 college years, when Chief Myers's journalism class was getting out the Ohio State *Daily Lantern*, Thurber is remembered as a hard worker and a stickler for accuracy as reporter and editor, though the *Lantern* carried no bylines and nobody has identified with certainty what he contributed. It was printed five days a week, under a different editor for each issue. During the 1917–18 year, Nugent and Thurber were among the five issue editors.

"I saw a lot of Jim Thurber that year," writes Nugent. "He was in charge of the *Lantern* every Wednesday, and I took over the Thursday issue. We often helped each other out, spending late hours at the office putting the paper to bed, then we'd drop into Marzetti's restaurant for sandwiches and coffee. Jim's family lived several miles from the campus, so he would often spend the rest of the night at the Phi Psi house, sleeping on a couch if he could not find a vacant bed."

Nugent and Thurber were also contributors to the *Sun-Dial*, the campus humor monthly begun in 1910. A picture of the unsmiling 1916–17 *Sun-Dial* staff in the *Lantern* shows Thurber positioned inconspicuously at lower right in his usual attempt to keep his glass eye from the camera. The staff included the journalism classmates who made up Thurber's principal social circle on campus: Nugent, Carson Blair, Jack Pierce, Maurice Mullay, Ralph McCombs, and George Packer.

Soon after the United States entered World War I in April 1917, Ohio's Governor James M. Cox issued an order permitting students to leave school with credit for the term if they were entering military or farm service or another war-supportive occupation. The student body, now more than six thousand, shrank within days as several hundred males—mostly juniors and seniors—packed up and left. (It was almost worth a world war to Thurber to see his nemesis, Captain Converse, called to Army service the following year.)

George Packer was the *Sun-Dial*'s editor in 1916–17; Carson Blair, who contributed art, was his assistant. "Thurber did so much to help us get out the magazine," said Blair, "George and I agreed he should be the next year's editor. Technically, the position had to be ratified by the publications board, based on the quantity and quality of the candidate's work, but in practice the editor always managed to pass his job on to a fraternity brother. Thurber wasn't in our fraternity but his work obviously met the first criteria and with so many of the guys leaving for the service, he didn't have much competition."

Thurber, Nugent, and Blair were elected members of the honorary journalism fraternity, Sigma Delta Chi, and were chosen for "La Bohème," a small literary seminar group of students and faculty. Blair remembers that the three of them, along with another student, William Dumont, put on a skit at the Ohio Union Building impersonating their professors. "Each May the Journalism Department was allowed to get out the *Columbus Citizen* for one issue," Blair says. "In the skit, we pretended to be our professors getting out the *Daily Lantern*, which we called the *Anti-Nocturnal Candelabra*. Nugent played Billy Graves as the desk man; Thurber was Professor Beck and Bill Dumont was Bernard Bergman, a recent graduate who was then on the *Dispatch* downtown —Thurber later helped him get hired by the *New Yorker*. Thurber sounded more like Beck than Beck did. It was a great way to close out the year before so many of us had to leave for the war."

That summer of 1917, Thurber worked as a publicity agent for Olentangy Park. Nugent stayed in town for a month as a cub reporter on the *Columbus Monitor* and spent the rest of the summer in Dover, working for the local newspaper.

With the world at war, Thurber's last year at O.S.U., 1917–18, was his most satisfying. Perhaps because of the war's interruptive effects on campus, he was somehow exempted from the military and physical-education classes. He could choose his courses. He and Nugent studied Shakespeare under the legendary Joseph Denney, Dean of the College of Arts, and signed up for another year of journalism. Thurber took both semesters of Taylor's study of the novel and, in the spring, the second half of Taylor's Victorian poetry course. He was enrolled for only ten credit hours of classes that semester, and in the fall of 1917 he was again hailed before President Thompson. Thompson pointed out that Thurber's editorial positions were reserved for those satisfactorily carrying fifteen academic hours per semester. Thurber explained that ten hours were all he could handle and still get out the school publications with only war-depleted staffs to help him. Furthermore, he told Thompson, he intended to become a magazine editor, and editing the *Dial* and *Lantern* was a practical course in itself. With so many exceptions to the rules being made at the time, Thompson seems to have had little trouble in agreeing with him.

Thurber was still selling his editorial experiences as viable substitutes for academic credits thirty years later when he wrote to Miss Whitaker of Northampton School for Girls, "I failed . . . to become Phi Beta Kappa, but I was editor of my college magazine, one of the editors of the newspaper, a member of the dramatic society, and I believe that I got as much out of these as out of my classroom work."

Thurber now had the *Sun-Dial* almost to himself and used it as his personal showcase of jokes, editorials boosting O.S.U. and its football team, drawings,

Sun-dial sketches

and Ryder-type paragraphs. In 1946, Carson Blair worked in public relations in Detroit. Michael Zeamer, who worked for Blair, was preparing an article on the boss's famous classmate and quotes from a Thurber letter:

> All the artists who had drawn for [George] Packer went into the service and I was left with the task of doing some ten or fifteen drawings an issue if I was to fill up the pages of the monthly. This was the first time that my line drawings appeared in print since this was the only magazine whose editorial policy I controlled.
>
> In the Christmas issue that year I contrived to save space by drawing at the top and bottom of each page a line drawing one inch deep, showing merely a skyline and some gaunt trees. Under each [strip] was a caption, "Christmas in Fargo, N.D.," "Christmas in Denver, Colorado," and so forth. Since the magazine had some forty pages, I saved eighty inches in this way which otherwise I would have had to fill up with writings. I had an associate editor named Elliott Nugent but he was too busy as president of this and that, and in going around to dances, to turn in very much copy.

Thurber, in his words, was "filling up all the white space, to the thundering applause of practically nobody." His name was on the masthead and on a handful of drawings, but most of the *Sun-Dial* signatures were of obvious invention. For the most part, he avoided drawing faces, but he worked harder than he ever would again at cross-hatching and filling in detail in his drawings.

Corrupted by Ryder, Thurber usually cast women in the Dumb Dora role in his He-She jokes and elsewhere. In the March 1918 wartime issue is a spread of cartoons under the title: "Americans Who Are Doing Their Bit at Home." The cartoons are not by Thurber but the captions probably are, one reading: "Miss Corinthia H. Dinger, of Purple Veil Falls, Wisconsin, who has written a personal letter to the Navy Department telling them how foolish it is to conduct a nation-wide appeal for binoculars when they can be scraped right off the hulls of old vessels."

Nugent that year forgot his mother's fiftieth birthday, which could have been that ailing lady's last, and wrote a depressing poem of guilt and contrition that Thurber loyally ran in the humor magazine. "Then, as now," Thurber writes, "the magazine was notable for mistakes and the nice sonnet by Nugent lost its final line, for which was substituted a sentence from another piece like this: " 'If that is all you want,' she said, 'I am going home.' "

Thurber cheerfully misrepresents his role as artist in his recollections of the *Sun-Dial* days. In a letter to Herman Miller years later, he writes, "I did pictures for the Sun-Dial when I was editor because all the artists went to war or camp and left me without any artists. I drew pictures rapidly and with few lines because I had to write most of the pieces, too, and couldn't monkey long with the drawings."

But most of the drawings in Thurber's issues are by other artists, and the few that are his show a time-consuming care for detail quite different from the quickly rendered ones of later years. And in a 1950 letter to the chairman of the *Princeton Tiger*, he confesses: "I was lucky enough to have the services of a *Cornell Widow* [a Cornell student publication] artist who was taking officers training at Ohio State."

He makes fun of inspirational one-liners popular in newspapers of the day and in the *Literary Digest*, which often reprinted Ryder: "Virtue is a text book lying next to the Cosmopolitan." "Pleasure is a novel with the last chapter torn out." "Death is the chance you take on a picture show being interesting."

He writes a gloomy tribute to Joseph Conrad:

> *His Fates are all Cruel*
> *His lives are a Duel,*
> *His Destinies from Granite take shape;*
> *His youth is a Flare*
> *That burns to despair,*
> *His Joy is enshrouded with Crepe.*
>
> *His World's just a Jest,*
> *Life's an unhappy Quest,*
> *And Love is a Wreck on a Shoal;*
> *His Hope is a Wraith,*
> *Chance far outweighs Faith,*
> *And Nothing, Nowhere is his Goal.*

Masked in anonymity, he puts his romantic nature on display, celebrating his grade-school crush on Eva Prout:

> *I held her in my arms,*
> *This one at present dear,*
> *And there came from out the past*
> *Your vision clear.*

The human touch is strong,
But close and warm as faith
Clings the memory of you,
My sweetheart wraith.

Also anonymous is his rhythmic "Reincarnation":

A million suns have shone
  And a million moons have died
Since I was a soldier with Cortez
  And you were the Aztec bride.

"When the Linotyper Falls in Love" may be a comment on the *Sun-Dial*'s frequent typographical errors:

Tell me not in mournful muxbuz
  Life is but an excvt bewtpfg
For the soul of dzzftt that spblizt
  And rubguppfg are not what they zboomwhoops.

The personable Minnette Fritts was the darling of the journalism crowd—in particular, Thurber, Maurice Mullay, Karl Finn, and Tom Meek. She preferred to play the field rather than limit herself socially. "All through school I kept them as friends," she says. "I was devoted to all of them." "Minnie" Fritts had attended a prep school in Illinois, and taught school for two years, before entering O.S.U. as a freshman in 1915. She was six months younger than Thurber and the first woman of his generation to express interest in him. Eva Prout was literally the girl of his dreams, out of touch and sight since the eighth grade. Fritts was a flesh-and-blood reality he could interact with, who praised his writing and kindled his romantic hopes.

Awkward around Minnette at first, by 1917 a remodeled Thurber, made confident by the recognitions his editorial and fraternity positions represented, was pursuing her. The women students had neither dormitories nor sorority houses but roomed off-campus. Several times, very late at night, Fritts would be awakened by Thurber and Tom Meek tossing pebbles at her window. (Meek planned a career in journalism but later became a Wall Street broker, eventually handling Thurber's investments.)

"There would be Jim and Tom saying they just put the *Lantern* to bed and they were hungry," she remembered. " 'Couldn't we go down to High Street and get some food?' So I'd go with them to an all-night restaurant on High

Street. Then they'd walk me back to the house where I lived and I always wondered how they ever got home at that hour in the morning; I guess there was always an 'owl' car [streetcar] running."

The Phi Psis ended their year with a May dance. It was a milestone event for Thurber. He and Minnette had shared many campus walks, library talks, and group get-togethers, but the dance was the first formal occasion at which Thurber could show off his own date—and a popular, attractive one at that. But it created a new problem. Unlike the suave Nugent, Thurber was no dancer. In desperation, he took lessons. Helen Thurber remembers her husband's reciting his experiences at Miss Naddy's Dancing Academy, located over a bowling alley on the poorer side of town.

"Most of the male students smoked cigars and packed guns," Helen writes, "but their teacher was pretty tough herself, and never daunted. 'All right, now we'll try another moonlight waltz,' she would yell, after three previous attempts, 'and this time I want you guys to stay out from behind them palms!' "

According to Fritts, Thurber was entitled to a refund from Miss Naddy. "Jim walked over me pretty much of the time," she says. "He was not much of a dancer."

Years later, at a Manhattan party attended by *New Yorker* editor Harold Ross, Thurber, and other staff members, there was the loud, tinkling crash of glass breaking on the floor. Without looking in its direction, Ross quietly asked, "Thurber?" His companion nodded. But Thurber's social mishaps were endemic long before his days of drink and blindness; at the Phi Psi dance, there was a similar crash, and several in attendance, though out of sight of the buffet table, immediately guessed correctly that Thurber had knocked the bowl of fruit salad onto the floor. It was something he joked about in later years, but it was a face-reddening humiliation in the presence of Minnette.

Nugent doesn't remember whether Thurber was a poor or good dancer. "We often teamed up in taking a couple of girls to a dance," writes Nugent, "and at least once he was able to borrow his grandfather's car so that we showed some style."

Just how and when Thurber learned to drive a car is a mystery. Thurber is of no help in solving it. "I had driven various cars since 1913, with only a few minor accidents," he writes in *The Years with Ross*. But in writing of Grandfather Fisher in the *Album*, he says: "The first car [Grandfather] bought . . . was an electric runabout. . . . He never learned to back 'her,' but once when I was fifteen, he paid me a dollar to drive her out in the country and show him how." That was 1910, three years earlier than when he later claimed to have first driven a car. That he was, at such an early age, in a position to instruct his wild-eyed grandfather in the mysteries of the automobile is a puzzle to his brother, Robert, who writes:

I first drove our first car, the Reo, prominently mentioned in some Thurber articles, and taught both of my brothers to drive it. This was in 1918. From then on William and I did all the driving. When [William] was away from home on trips or out-of-state jobs, all the driving fell to me. Neither my father nor my mother could ever master the art of driving, although I tried several times to teach them. James wasn't in Columbus, or at home, often enough after 1918 to permit him to drive very much.

The Reo "was unusual in that the clutch and brake were on the same pedal," Thurber writes. It may have needed special instruction to operate, and Thurber could well have been driving his grandfather's car before 1918.

When Grandpa Fisher bought a Lozier, "he never tried to drive it himself," writes Thurber, "but he liked to have his grandsons take him out in the country, so that he could 'scorch' [speed]." Grandpa had plenty of grandsons to drive him, and Thurber could well have been one of them. It was certainly the Lozier he was driving one of the nights he and Nugent were double-dating. The two had attended a dance, dropped off their dates, and stopped for coffee at a downtown restaurant. When Thurber pulled away from the curb, a car caught the left front fender of the Lozier, broke free, and kept going. The impact of metal on metal seemed to send Thurber into a state of shock; he sat there getting sick to his stomach over what had happened to the Fisher car. Nugent, a track-team man, leaped out of the Lozier, dashed after the other car, caught up with it at the next traffic light, and detained the driver until the police came. The driver, who was inebriated, owned a small business in Columbus, and Thurber, unable to pay for the damage to the Lozier, came up with a scheme the next day for getting a quick out-of-court settlement. Nugent went along with it. The seasoned actor, neatly dressed in a suit, called on the businessman, identified himself as Thurber's attorney, and said that twenty dollars would avoid the need of taking the case to court. The man paid. Thurber, waiting outside, pocketed the money and said that Nugent was now probably guilty of a felony: extortion through the impersonation of an attorney.

"But it was your idea," Nugent protested.

"No judge or jury will believe that," Thurber replied. If you chose to be Thurber's friend, you took the risks along with the pleasure of his company.

Everything was going his way. Writes Nugent: "One of the big events at Ohio State each year is 'Link Day,' when the graduating members of Sphinx, the senior honorary society, gather on the steps of old University Hall to select those who have been chosen from the junior class. These men are almost always leaders in campus activities." Nugent was chosen, of course; he was certain Thurber would be, too, "but as man after man joined the group on the steps I began to wonder. Finally the last man was marched up with scattered cheers, and that man was my friend Thurber. I asked him later where he had been hiding, and he told me that he had not been under a bush but simply standing well back so if he was not chosen he could quietly disappear."

For all his strengthened self-esteem, Thurber still distrusted his popularity; he saw himself as a puppeteer manipulating his comic talents for the entertainment of the public while hiding the real Thurber from sight. The fact was that he was prized by the end of his college years, not as a clown but as an interesting, talented, and contributing member of the university community. Through his constant reading, he had an expanded vocabulary that was the envy of his classmates. When he was drawn out, even those who didn't know him well found him congenial and enjoyable to be with. But all his life recognition, acceptance, and "belonging" would be more important to him than to most; he would wear his Phi Psi, Sigma Delta Chi, and Sphinx pins until he was twenty-five. Certainly, by the end of the spring term of 1918, "Jim was no longer the quiet, almost unknown boy that Jack Pierce and I had discovered," Nugent writes. "He was now one of the 'Big Men in School.'"

Thurber's credits were far short of those needed to graduate. Were the war not depleting the campus of friends and activities (publication of the *Sun-Dial* was soon suspended for the duration), Thurber might have gone on to graduate. The fact that he didn't seems to have mattered much more to him later than to anyone else. He tells Miss Whitaker of Northampton School that he "failed to become Phi Beta Kappa," implying that he had at least graduated; he would joke later about how he could easily have persuaded another student to pass the swimming test for him that was required for graduation; in 1939, in a *New York Mirror* interview, he says he didn't graduate because he couldn't pass botany ("I've always been allergic to daisy chains," he explained); on October 31, 1956, he writes Frank Gibney of *Newsweek*, "I was not graduated from Ohio State because I failed to pass military drill and gymnasium and quit in June 1918." In another autobiographical note: "Set out for Phi Beta Kappa and was on my way to making it through sophomore year, but dropped behind in studies to become one of the issue editors of the Ohio State *Daily Lantern* and to become editor-in-chief of the Ohio State monthly, the *Sun-Dial*."

What is remarkable about these defensive claims is that they were all made after Thurber was an international figure of letters and art; whether he held a college degree or not would be a matter of no importance, except for the significance Thurber pumped into it through his frequent and inconsistent explanations of why he failed to get one.

18

Those Draft Board Nights

I was called almost every week, even though I had been exempted from service the first time I went before the medical examiners. Either they were never convinced that it was me or else there was some clerical error in the records which was never cleared up. Anyway, there was usually a letter for me on Monday ordering me to report for examination on the second floor of Memorial Hall the following Wednesday at 9 P.M. The second time I went up, I tried to explain to one of the doctors that I had already been exempted. "You're just a blur to me," I said, taking off my glasses. "You're absolutely nothing to me," he snapped, sharply.

—from "Draft Board Nights"

The student population was down by a thousand by the end of May 1917, but there was a growing military presence on the campus, beginning with a school of aviation. A hundred military recruits were arriving each week, taking over university building after building. After working late on his Wednesday issue of the *Lantern*, Thurber was occasionally challenged by a sentry as he crossed the darkened campus. "I always halted promptly when he called to halt," Thurber writes. "I sometimes have my moments of depression when I wish I hadn't."

Because the *Lantern* was a morning paper, its staff had worked until after 11:00 P.M., when there were long intervals between streetcars. Now, with fewer men on hand, women were helping to get out the paper, and it was changed to an afternoon publication so they would not have to walk home in the dark. Other changes were taking place. When a class contained no more than a half-dozen students, it was cancelled. By the 1918 spring semester, campus celebrations had been eliminated. Women students acted as their own dining-room waitresses and rolled bandages in their home-economics classes.

The handicapped Thurber was increasingly depressed. Age twenty-three, in mufti, he felt more and more inadequate, as his classmates, fraternity brothers, and teachers left school to go to war.

"It was a ghastly time for Jim," says Minnette Fritts. "He was in despair. He tried to enlist and they wouldn't take him. He lied about his eyesight. I remember him as a very distraught young man at the time."

"Thurber tried to sign up to drive ambulances in France," Ben Williamson remembers. " 'It would have got me into uniform,' he told me." (No patriot acquainted with Thurber's driving skills lamented his rejection.) Meanwhile he continued to be summoned by the draft board:

> I had to take off all my clothes each time and jog around the hall with a lot of porters and bank presidents' sons and clerks and poets. Our hearts and lungs would be examined, and then our feet; and finally our eyes. That always came last. When the eye specialist got around to me, he would always say, "Why, you couldn't get into the service with sight like that!" "I know," I would say. Then a week or two later I would be summoned again and go through the same rigmarole.

Says Williamson: "Thurber told me every time he volunteered for a non-combatant, war-related job that would have excluded him from the draft, he was turned down. Each rejection had to be reported to the local draft board, which would then automatically summon Thurber to report for another interview and physical."

Another cause for failing Thurber was flat feet, a common reason for military rejection in the First World War; the Navy flunked the physically fit Nugent on such grounds until he tricked them, the second time around, by walking on the outsides of his arches.

In "Draft Board Nights," after a number of visits to Memorial Hall for his physical, Thurber picks up a spare stethoscope and joins the examiners:

> I passed most of the men that came to me, but now and then I would exempt one just to be on the safe side. I began by making each of them hold his breath and then say "mi, mi, mi, mi," until I noticed Ridgeway looking at me curiously. He, I discovered, simply made them say "ah," and some times he didn't make them say anything.

Writing in PM in 1940, Thurber notes the draft law passed by Congress that year, and offers another wild version of his own draft-board nights:

> Among the cripples who were constantly being called up in Columbus was me. Because I couldn't see anything at all out of my left eye, the draft board gave me exemption papers, which proved to be absolutely worthless. Every Wednesday I would be ordered to some camp or other, and every Friday night I had to appear before the board and explain why I hadn't gone. . . . I would get a new stamp on my exemption papers. . . . I always met the same draftees, men with only one leg or long white beards, and a very nice young woman whose first name was Sidney. Columbus doctors had never heard of a girl named Sidney, so she was ordered to camp every Wednesday, too, and came up for examination every Friday. The doctors finally got the idea that Sidney claimed to be blind and that I thought I was a girl. "It's absurd of you, Mr. Sidney," one of the more nervous doctors said to me one night, "to pretend you are a woman." . . . It was a period of magnificent confusion.
>
> I finally went to Washington . . . as a code clerk, but summonses and threats followed me. The records showed, I was told, that I had never appeared before the draft board. In October, 1918, I was ordered to proceed to Syracuse, N.Y., and help guard a bridge. Across the face of this communication I wrote the single word "deceased" and sent it back. I was never bothered again. The War Department records on me now read, "Sidney, James (or Jane). Draft evader. Died while guarding a bridge in Rochester, N.Y. Sight: normal." [As for] Miss Sidney . . . I imagine that by now she is listed in the War Department records as the father of four.

In January 1918, Thurber applied for a clerical job with the State Department, taking his cue from his friend Ben Williamson, who had been hired as a code clerk there. Thurber's father used his influence with two Washington-based journalists he had come to know through Columbus and Washington politics: Sloane Gordon, who knew the Capitol Hill denizens, and Charles's and Mame's old mischievous pal George Hugh Marvin. But the weeks went by without word from the government. Thurber's life seemed stalemated while the world around him was being turned upside down. Nugent was at home in Dover, working on the local newspaper and awaiting his call from the Navy (it would come on Armistice Day). By now, the Thurbers had moved to Gay Street, an address that, remarkably, they would keep for twenty years. Robert was back from five months in the service with a medical discharge. William was hopping from one draft-exempted job to another. Aunt Margery Albright died that spring, and a senile and ailing Grandfather Fisher would not live out the year.

The university closed a few weeks early, on May 25, in a ceremony featuring the unfurling of a giant service flag studded with 2,640 stars representing alumni and faculty members in service. By then Charles's work in his son's behalf had paid off. His newspaper friends learned of State Department openings for embassy clerks and advised Thurber to get in touch with Breckenridge Long, third assistant secretary of state, to whom they promised to write letters of recommendation.

Aware of his ragged college record, Thurber again asked long-suffering O.S.U. president Thompson for help. That good man came through again, his recommendation, dated June 14, directed to Long:

> Mr. Thurber has recently been rejected by the District Board for regular enlistment and assigned to Class I—clerical, the reason being the loss of the left eye when 8 years of age, through an accident with a bow and arrow by his brother. . . . Mr. Thurber will be 24 years of age next December; is a graduate of East High School, Columbus, Ohio; a member of the junior class in the Ohio State University, and was selected by the Sphinx Society as a member, which selection may be taken as the student judgment as to his all around quality and standing as a student. In his education Mr. Thurber has pursued courses in American and European History, the foundation courses in Economics, and . . . Political Science. He has given special attention to the study of English and also the courses in Journalism. He has made a creditable record through the three years in the University, and I am pleased to

commend him for favorable consideration to any position for which his educational and personal qualities would qualify him.

On June 9, twenty-five thousand men, women, and children marched in a Columbus Win-the-War parade: mothers of soldiers, military horsemen, women factory workers, Boy Scouts pushing a huge rubber ball behind a banner reading "Keep the Ball Rolling," and O.S.U. coeds carrying the great flag. Motion pictures of the parade were taken to send to the boys at the front to show them "that Columbus backed them all the way." If the city seemed defensive, perhaps it was because a large percentage of its population was German-American.

Moving through the sidewalk crowds, Thurber and Minnette Fritts spotted one another. They had not dated formally since the Phi Psi Christmas dance of 1917, though "I saw Jim frequently and we had many, many interesting discussions, often at the library," Fritts recalls. Socially, she was still playing the field, and Thurber, believing his evening of dancing with her had been a disaster, had not followed up. Though he remained attracted to her, he nursed a self-protective fear of the competition offered by several of their male student friends, all of whom, he felt certain, she would find more attractive than he: Karl Finn, Tom Meek, Maurice (Mullie) Mullay, and others.

Now, with the old college crowd breaking up, he asked her to go with him to see Marguerite Clark in *Prunella,* a dramatic fantasy then playing in Columbus. He borrowed the family Reo and took her for a ride after the show, ending up at Marzetti's for a meal at 1:15 A.M. Two moonlit nights later, he drove with her up the bank of the Scioto. They parked and hugged and kissed, in the contemporary college tradition of "necking" soon to be celebrated by the young novelist F. Scott Fitzgerald in his first novel, *This Side of Paradise.* Thurber responded by going overboard. Minnette had given a "perhaps" to Maurice Mullay, who had asked if she would wear his fraternity pin, and Mullie had begged his rivals to leave him a clear field. Thurber had agreed, certain he would get nowhere with Minnette anyway. But now Mullie had departed for the Navy, and Thurber, carried away by the moment, not only renounced to Minnette his pledge to Mullie but asserted that she and she alone was the object of his fancy.

Both Thurber and his friend Elliott Nugent were virgins—though that fall Nugent would finally "step aside" (from the straight and narrow, as the saying went) while at the Great Lakes Naval Training Center, in Chicago. Thurber would abstain for another two years.

"Along about 1920, I read Scott Fitzgerald's *This Side of Paradise,*" Nugent writes in his memoirs, and for some years afterward I wondered if we at Ohio State had really all been so innocent about sex and drinking during my college days, and if so, why were things so different at Princeton, where Fitzgerald spent almost the same years. To us there were two kinds of girls, "nice girls" and those who were "fast." . . . Necking seemed rather more prevalent in Dover than in Columbus, at least to me. Liquor or wine was not served at any of the dances or parties, nor allowed in our fraternity house.

A Jamesian idealist, Thurber neither wanted nor expected any sexual favors from Minnette, a "nice girl," and on several occasions he brought her home to visit with his family. She was genuinely taken by Thurber and knew how to please Charles and Mame, who grew particularly fond of her. Even after Thurber's departure for Washington in mid-June, Mame "often invited me to dinner," says Fritts. "Her chief subject of conversation was Jamie, and I was just as interested in Jamie, so we had much fun."

But Thurber was soon wondering what he really felt toward Minnette. "The only girl he ever talked about much at home was Eva Prout," Robert remembers. Thurber still carried the torch for his Douglas schoolmate, whom he hadn't seen since he was fourteen and wouldn't see again for another two years. She had left school after the eighth grade to become a child star in vaudeville and later in silent movies; she was featured with Francis X. Bushman and other Essanay Films stars. Before she was twenty-one, she appeared in a musical comedy at the Winter Garden, in New York. Her rapid rise to success beguiled Thurber as much as Nugent's would. An early Mitty and a romantic wooer of women, he had been haunted in his dreams by images of Eva through the years.

On June 21, carrying letters of recommendation from his journalist sponsors and President Thompson, Thurber and his father left Columbus for Washington, where they roomed at the New Ebbill Hotel. Thurber soon discovered the Post Café, at Thirteenth and "E" streets, where many of the Washington press corps dined. (The name of the assistant manager, Mrs. Rabbit, intrigued Thurber for life.) Newly full of himself, Thurber was interviewed at the office of Assistant Secretary Long, where, he wrote Nugent,

a dream of a brunette, just my type and not over 27, quietly informed us that she had charge of those appointments, that there was an opening and that I could have it, after my papers had gone thru the necessary channels. The Hague was the place. Then I mentioned about Bernie [Ben Williamson, who was already a code clerk in the U.S. embassy in Berne, where Thurber wished to be sent], whereupon she gave me another smile (there were several) and said she would very gladly shift the 6 or 8 fellows who were listed for Berne over to other places, and give that to me. It was all so quick and miraculously easy that I am dazed yet. The only ways I can account for the speed and certainty of her words is (if you'll pardon me and likewise God save the mark) that the lady was impressed with me.

He and Charles looked up old friends from the 1901–1903 days and toured the historic sites, Thurber not trusting all the unofficial "authentic relics" he was shown. Booth, he decided, must have been wearing six spurs on his right boot the night he shot Lincoln. "Imagine my sentiments," he wrote Nugent,

upon seeing, after 15 years, the old homestead here, the old corner drug store where we spent the hoarded nickels, and a tall, whistling youth striding by that was an 8 year old kid playmate o' mine. It sure has been an enchanting week, and what with my prospects and all, it well overbalances the shooting up of old John Sundial money. Which reminds me I gotta scrape together some coin of the Rellum before I sail, and mail it to Chubby. But that should be easy. $2000 a year I will get, you know.

Pleased with his first full-time job, Thurber reported for training at the Bureau of Indexes and Archives, the base for State Department cryptography. He first had to produce his birth certificate and draft release, but when the draft board in Columbus was queried, it sent him another notice to report for a physical examination. Thurber enlisted the help of his father, who had returned home after a week of getting his son settled. The draft board had no record of Thurber's previous visits, the board chairman told Charles, who managed to get matters straightened out.

While waiting for the necessary documents, Thurber received a letter from Nugent, still in Dover, informing him that Katherine Garver, a University of Akron student and a childhood sweetheart of Nugent's, had agreed to marry him. After several years apart, the two had met the previous summer and begun "going steady." The engagement "did not make much sense," Nugent writes in his memoirs, but with the men leaving for the service, "everybody was getting engaged or married."

Nugent's news had the effect of a hand grenade exploding under the theatrical-minded Thurber. He had followed Nugent into amateur theater and a fraternity-based social life, and if Nugent had rediscovered and won a "first love" from grade-school days, it was the very O. Henry short-story ending that Thurber was determined to experience, too. In one of a series of giddy, adolescent letters from Washington, larded with campus colloquialisms, he writes Nugent:

7/16/18

Dear old Pythias:

So a pair of Brown Eyes has wooed you away from old John Typewriter. . . . Little did I reck that your bosom treasured also a youngster love affair that you never quite forgot. [I use] "Also," advisedly, because the Romance of me life is, too, just such an affair as our well-meaning parents laugh to scorn. . . . Mine was one of the legended "school boy and girl" affairs. I played 15 opposite her 14 in the drama "The Seventh Grade," and ten years have passed, friend of me college days, and I love her yet. Surely I told you, if only briefly, the plot of the piece. My eccentric memory for the trivial calls up a scene in your handsome Phi Psi rooms, you lolling in your upper berth, I dragging on a Piedmont, just abaft the picture of the Rocky Mounts there on the mantel piece, when I spilled the tale. Your own story of Her Return after many years, gives me quite a pang. The story of my youthful affaire . . . is too long to rehearse, but, oh boy, I wish a certain pair of Brown Eyes would come back where I could dream life's sweet, sweet dreams agazin' into 'em again. She is the One Girl, old keed, but I guess the long and attenuated Jimmy is out of luck. However, I'm going to play one last long chance before I try the impossible method of forgetting and, quite crudely, giving the rest of the world's women a chance. I once wrote this wonderful girl a letter, 7 years after we parted back in the grammar grades,—or three years ago. I was lifted aloft to places where cherubims twitter by a 12 page answer from Colorado Springs asking me to write again which I did in a way that set me back 8 cents for postage of the Rellum, addressed, as she requested, care of her sister 203 Underwood St, Zanesville, Ohio. No response. And, quite like the lackadaisical Thurber, I let it ride from thence to nownce. She was beautiful as the Helens of Poe and Troy, graceful as Endymion etc. etc. since it's too hot to reach for classical similes. But her voice, Nugey, her voice! Keats' nightingale. Darn you, I told you she used to sing that song to me about "Love, I am lonely." At least you recall . . . the Nugent rendition of it a la like, of a quite often frequency, Back in the College Days. Hence, the stage for her. But she had ruined [her] voice when young. Thence, the movies. Thence, vaudeville. Now, Lord only knows. Ask your dad if ever in his theatrical circles he saw or heard of a certain little Dream named Eva Prout.

Thurber's gushy confessional took more than two hours to compose; he then takes up the Minnette "problem":

Of course, as you know, I at one time—and still—was rather attracted by the Fritts. You also recall the Dampers de Ardour you flung. Also, very confidentially, I stuck away, quite altruistically, because of a Mullie [Maurice Mullay] appeal with tears in his eyes. Not to be mentioned, of course. The Phi Psi Xmas dance was my first and only date. Until a week before I left.

Columbus, that week, heaved a huge Win-the-War parade. Thousands thronged the main travelled marts. In this vast crowd I upheld the basis of all O. Henry stories, by meeting Minnette. A date was inevitable. . . . Took her in old John K. Reo. . . . Date two nights later. Karl Finn, Tom Meek out of luck. Moonlight, Reoings along the Scioto, in brief, all the old paraphernalia and stage drops. And, deus ex machina, the Thurberian damn temperament or lack of balance. Oh, well, hell, Nugget, it's gone pretty damn far [and] a little hunch informs me I'm in. . . . I don't know what she wants, unless its my P.K.P. pin, surely not my Sig Delt Chi decoration. At any rate, I'll never be able to get back home with the suit-case I brought here, on account of Minnette's loving letters taking up so darn much space. And, Nugey, like a damn fool . . . I haven't the heart to appear less amourous than I was during the moonlight madness of those few dates. I like Minnette very much, more than any girl at school by far, as you are aware; she used all her tricks them nights,—and . . . I think we are engaged. Go ahead, you blonde Don Juan, and laugh your head off! Now I could learn to love the kid, and I'm sure that as married couples go, we would be domestically out there. But, Nugey, the blow that cools James is the Hope that Spouts eternal about the One Girl. Someday, somewhere I'll find her. I've quite an O. Henry philosophy and Faith. Oh, quite. I'm positive that me and the Eva are Hero and Leonidas, or Heroine and Alexander or whoever it was, those eternal destined lovers, that swam the Halcyon. . . .

So you see what a damn fool I still remain. And the hurt that hurts is Mullie. She told him "perhaps." And I've ruined him, one of my best friends, whom I promised I would step aside for. Ruined him. . . . But nuts, Nugey, I've got a clear field . . . and poor lil Seagoing Mullie is sunk. And, God help me, I don't want the girl that these others kids are dying for! Oh, Life, where is thy logic! Boy, page Thomas Hardy.

Enthralled as he was by the prospect of his best friend's setting off on the mysterious, scary, but fascinating adventure of life with a woman, Thurber saw the same threat to his friendship with Nugent that he would see when, at the *New Yorker*, Katharine Angell married Thurber's close colleague and officemate E. B. White. He writes Nugent:

I might wish for your philandering to cease, except that I want us both to be free to fling a few twosome parties when this man's war is over, without having to dodge friend wife to arrange them. Marriage is all right in its place and time, but the Paldomain of Men must not be jeopardized for a mere . . . quibbling of matrimony.

He bounces back, with ill-concealed delight, to the Minnette "predicament":

I really should shoot myself at sunrise, but moonlight and Minnette and 15 gals of gas leads the way that madness lies. I wouldn't dare show you the answers I send to her letters, simply because I believe I have compromised myself so that I cant get out of it, without being of the genus mucker or cad. I thought of course she would play around and toy a bit and let it go. Perhaps she yet will. But Nugey, her letters don't sound like it, and, if I lost on my chance that she would play with me as the rest, no matter what was said, I'm willing to pay and act the gent. She is really a fine girl, and of all the kisses I have ever kissed none can compare to the peculiar quality of hers. Like nothing so much as frozen roses on an August night. She used lots of tricks, but I'm afraid she has decided she now has the One & only case, and I believe she decided that since I left. I think she was willing for a while to let our respective lines go cum grasno salis [with a grain of salt], but now finds her heart was really on her lips. Gawd help me. I either want to be saved, or—garçon, a love potion, queek!

The flamboyant self-exposure reveals a playwright in the making, fashioning a script that would undoubtedly surprise the real-life principals he casts for it. But he is at a loss in dealing with his sexual longings, and, with giggles and titters, he prefers Jamesian fictional conjectures to realistic attempts at perspective. Thurber's posturing could be considered progress, however, given his years of feeling inadequate. As a Big Man on Campus, hung with pins representing social acceptance and academic achievement, he finally believes himself to be irresistible to Minnette, the campus favorite. But he is also frightened by the thought of what to do next; if there is truly commitment to Minnette, he distrusts himself to cope with it. He dreads the consequences of an illusion short-circuited by reality. It is more fun for him to suppose and speculate than to accept the obvious. The *New Yorker* writer Emily Hahn asks: "Given Thurber's family years with three other males and an eccentric mother, isn't it possible that Thurber simply didn't know what a woman was?"

One may wonder why, over the years, the younger but more sophisticated Nugent kept these "on the one hand this, but on the other hand that" immature flounderings of his friend Thurber. He believed in Thurber's potential, to be sure, found him an interesting and entertaining buddy, and, like many creative people, was a magpie in hanging onto material he might one day use in his plays. Indeed, in a short while Nugent and his father would write *The Poor Nut,* a play based on the Thurber Nugent remembered at O.S.U. He seems to have encouraged Thurber to write such letters by answering with satirical comments on them that delighted Thurber. Because Thurber used his memory for information storage and retrieval and was not a letter keeper, we can't know if Nugent's letters were that much more mature than Thurber's, for Thurber writes to Nugent: "Please answer soonly and at your usual delectable length and with the unfailing Nugentian style, which, I can't refrain from telling you, my love, makes the institution of correspondence something worth the living and waiting for."

Still watching his pennies, Thurber used hotel stationery filched from lobbies and, in one instance, pages bearing Martin's restaurant letterhead. He continues his private soap opera in a letter to Nugent five weeks later. Minnette has continued to write him letters,

> about two to my one, and more loving each time. . . . I haven't the heart to register coolness. I tried it once and it was misconstrued resulting in a binding confession of the old undying stuff from Minnette. Really I do like her very, very much, because she is to me, I am positive, what she has never been to any of the other luckless lads, I mean she has done with trifling, jipping et al and she's mine for life. Don't think me a credulous, blind fish. She's been writing for 2 months and I know. She told Mullie that she had only known one man she would marry,—I'm elected. The paradox is nice: I'm elected but I refuse the nomination. There it is in a Chestertonian nutshell. But now for the worst.

Thurber has written again to Eva Prout at the Zanesville address and, lo and behold, she has replied to him warmly. He had supposed she had found him "a funny sort of curiosity—or boresome," he writes Nugent.

> Minnette couldn't have held my thoughts for ten seconds . . . if it had not been that I had absolutely reasoned my one and only love was gone for good. I imagined her laughing at my last letter—4 years ago—and giving it to her maid to read. Ten years away from me and a gay life onstage. . . . Hence my forced attraction to the M. F.
>
> One night Mullie and I had a M. date together. Afterwards a cigarette at Mullies, and a confession from me as to my one and only, including the statement that Mullie was safe, as I couldn't fall in love with M. if I sprained 106 bones in the effort. Mullie, tickled to death, confides this in M. the next day. . . .
>
> Minnette used all her tricks. She was out for romance and love-stuff and—she won. She started it all with a delicate flagrant line that only a Kappa of 3 years standing could fling. Then she asked me about my schoolgirl love affair, mentioning Mullie's story of it. . . .
>
> I was still sure Eva was dead forever to me. 10 years is a cold grave, grass grown as an abandoned bear-pit. Moreover, I was rather bitter that she hadn't answered my letter. . . .
>
> So I told Minnette "nuts to the Eva," and I lied and said I kidded Mullie to relieve his fears about me. What else could I do—she had got by that time a tentative line of "I'm for you, Minnie" from me. I tried to

love her,—all the time telling myself that the kid of my dreams was dead and gone. And in the moonlite along the Scioto I did, Nugey, believe I was falling for M. I told myself I could "learn'—worst lie in the world. . . .

Yesterday I got two letters. One from M. ended with her jubilant over the fact that Mullie was wrong about my "grammar school" girl. The other, of course, from Eva. Wonderful letter,—must have taken her 2 hours to write. Wants me to come to Zanesville (O.) where she lives and see her before I go to Berne. In my letter I . . . mentioned Gleeson McCarty of [Columbus] . . . a mutual friend—and it seems that a week after she got my letter she got one from Gleeson asking her to come with another Zanesville girl to Camp Sherman and help in a Y.M.C.A. enter-tainment. Eva went. Naturally I know, she asked Gleeson about me.

Now, you see, when I was a bit of a lad in grammar grades and short pants I was a wreck—teacher's pet—grind—nothing for whose memory the Eva would fall. . . .

Gleeson is strong for me. He has handed her a nice line that I am really not an ass at all. Gleeson thinks, in fact, that I'm out there. He has told her I'm worthy of the name "Jim." She believed me a regular "James." I love to picture the scene in the Y.M. Hut when she said, "Gleeson, do you know a boy named James Thurber," and Gleeson (Bless his heart) answered, "*Jim* Thurber? Well, say—" All nice and lovely. Hence the really wonderful letter from Eva. Hence my almost 2000 foot altitude, and also my wrecked condition with the M. waiting for me with wide eyes and arms. Good Lord, aint it dramatic, Ezra! . . . I'm going to use up half of my time home playing in Zanesville. And I've got one awful great big hunch. I'm going to pledge Eva Phi Psi. I can't help what happens. I just feel it coming, big and sure as Destiny. For 10 years I've never absolutely in my subconscious mind given up hope. And I can tell from her letter no other guy has her as a parlor decoration yet. She quit the stage after last year's Winter Garden in N.Y. and doesn't want to go back.

Someway or other I'll square things with Minnette, like a gent. It was awful, but Lord knows it happened and it has to stop. I really believe Minnette is the kind who really can't be hit beyond repair. Heavens know also I'd rather face a firing-squad composed of Beta dentists rather than go back and see her, but once I get out of this dry town I'll get a shot of Old Something and prepare for the Scene. . . .

M. enlisted several weeks ago in the Red Cross, first college girl in Columbus to enlist. . . . Eva is the key to everything for me. . . . I knew all this 10 years ago and I've grown up to be a Sigma Delta Chi power. . . . I hope you have a trick of saving letters you get.

I leave the figuring out of that to you, my dear Watson.

In one way, the handwritten letters support the theory that shy individuals are often cruelly self-centered. Here is the looming ego, leading to self-adulation, susceptible to flattery, certain of its own worthlessness. It is an ego that can make life both interesting and hellish for others in its endless quest for reassurance.

As for Minnette, she may have been playing the patriotic role with all the romantic fervor that that uncertain period stimulated. She would have done her best not to cause any young man heading overseas in wartime to feel rejected. Says Sally Benson, the *New Yorker* contributor and screenplay writer: "All the men I was dating in those war years were leaving for overseas. They all asked me to marry them. I became engaged to every one of them in the morbid belief that they would all be killed. I was also playing the odds that at least one might survive and come back to me in the midst of what I supposed would be a man shortage. To my embarrassment, they all came back. I married 'Babe' [Reynolds] Benson because, as a decorated hero and flyer, he had probably come closer to getting killed than the others. If that doesn't make sense, very little in those days did."

The hot summer dragged on in Washington. Thurber trolleyed across the Potomac to Falls Church for a look at the house the Thurbers had rented in August 1902, where his monumental bad luck had befallen him. He snapped the pictures of the house which would be used to establish the address nearly forty years later when Elizabeth Acosta began her hunt for the place.

Ben Williamson, whom Thurber followed into State Department cryptography, remembers thinking how ludicrous it was that the government had cleared Thurber for coding and decoding. "I used to get eye-aches myself," Williamson says, "and wondered how a man with one poor eye that required a thick lens to see much of anything, could possibly be asked to decipher code." But Thurber was remembered by Stephen Vincent Benét, a fellow trainee in Washington, as a hard worker at learning to create and interpret the code's hieroglyphics, and good at it. Language was his love, and he was fascinated by the basic green code's strange-looking words, such as Golux, Nadal, and Todal, which he never forgot and three decades later would use in his children's book *The 13 Clocks*.

He lived in a rooming house and ate each evening at the Post Café, listening to the newspapermen who frequented the place. He was in his ninth week of training when he wrote Nugent again. He had been telling his family that he was certain to be allowed leave to go home in a very few days, but at the last minute his requests were always met by the bureaucracy with "All in due time." As interesting as Thurber found his work, it was never as important to talk about to Nugent as was the subject of girls. His romantic drama, starring Prout, was totally intertwined with Nugent's commitment to Katherine Garver. He predicts that the two of them would descend "the long trail" to the girls of their respective dreams. He envisages how "Nugey's" fraternity pin will look against Katherine's chiffon or georgette crepe. He still finds it hard to believe that the sophisticated Nugent would be so abruptly "overturned." He creeps toward that future battle zone where his "The War Between Men and Women" will take place: He understands, he writes Nugent, how "the mere curve of a girl's cheek" can "smash the philosophy of a young lifetime." The average girl is not to be trusted, he believes. She is . . . an actress off-stage, perhaps not understanding that she is. But she leaves it to the male to find out whether or not he has "dashed into a movie scene."

In a letter to Minnette, he confessed all about Eva ("with certain, sensible reservations," he writes Nugent), and concluded from Minnette's response, as he tells Nugent,

> that she is wonderful. . . . I told her I had written to this other girl, that she had answered, that I didn't know but what I loved her more than anyone else, and that I had a date with her in Zanesville, for the purpose of finding out. I added that I loved Minnette, which I do, so I didn't lie to her, because she has proven to be so wonderful and lovable in so many ways it is impossible for me not honestly to love her in a way she understands and which she is pleased to call "my way." Perhaps I love her letters. Perhaps it is certain ideas she holds. Perhaps it is her remarkable ability to understand. Perhaps it is a cleverness and "differentness" in her which I did not suspect until a month ago. Well, perhaps, then, it is her. I wrote her what under the circumstances, could not but seem a crude, smashing letter, rather contradictory, somewhat disconnected and certainly all the proof she needed to see . . . a basis for insincerity on my part.

It isn't nice, he goes on, to "smash a girl's heart," even though it seems a girl's privilege to smash the male heart "left and right." It all makes him sound "crazy" and "Thurberian." One should protect the "nice, only" girls, but it's hard to tell the breakable from the immune; they all play the same game. Sometimes they act. Other times they are real. "Ruth" can change into "Ruthless."

Minnette had replied to his confessions about Eva with "winsomeness, cleverness, charm, naiveté, wistfulness, truth, sincerity and whimsicality." Did that mean Minnette knows how to "play" him, or is she sincere? He thinks the latter. Minnette would be a girl, he tells Nugent,

> of whom I would not tire for, oh, ever so long, and a wife whom I could not fail to learn to love. She would be a wonderful pal, an understanding companion and all one might look for, if one were looking for things. . . . But I would have to shut up a certain part of me for life, reconstruct a few eccentric ideas and forget many things in order to chime with Minnette. And those things are the things that to me mean what we're here for. . . .
>
> Minnette may be just the medicine for my ills, Eva merely an irritant, —but the ills are mine and what's mine is me, and why try to be an electrical engineer, even tho' you could, if you'd rather starve in a garret. Tolerance of Luxury is a penchant for penury.

But, he cautions himself, he has yet to see, hear, and observe Eva. A decade is a long time. Grammar-school dreams may be mirages; romance can pall. Disillusionment or bad luck could await the Eva affair. The last chapter awaited the writing.

If the boyish—some would say girlish—redundant musings in his letters to Nugent suggest an overstayed immaturity in a man approaching twenty-four, he was sailing a rather normal course for a boy from a city with a small-town Bible Belt culture. He was baffled as to how to dispose of his glandular drives, caught up as he was in the biological mysteries that Columbus society of the period had helped to keep him from understanding. He was saddled with the popular notion that a sex life meant either marriage or else a corrupt and degrading pursuit of "fast" women, who were certain to give you a case of the "collapse"—as he thought, until long after puberty, the disease was called. The flow of his sexual desires was confined to the usual Victorian channels, its expression colored by the moonlight-and-flowers of popular song lyrics and informed by the poetry of the English Romantics. It has been argued that Thurber's naiveté in many matters that should long before have been settled, or at least understood, may have delayed his emergence as a major artist.

By early fall, the deadly flu epidemic that was ravaging the nation invaded Washington. Thurber credited gargling with Glyco-Thymoline three times a day with getting him through it. "All one sees here is nurses & hearses," Thurber wrote Nugent metrically in October,

> and all he hears is curses and worse. And such a heroic thing to pass out with,—Influenza! dying of influenza in these times of brave, poetical deaths. Allan [sic] Seeger was a lucky bird. I imagine him writing: "I have a tryst with influenzas, at daybreak in some pest-house ward." I'd just as soon go with house-maid's knee. However, fear no fears for the J.G.T. I am in chipper condition with the correct psychological attitude of chestnuts and baseballs towards all flu. The influx of Enza will have to select a clever rapier and twist an adroit wrist to pink me, altho' I am in the pink of condition.

Minnette may have been a game player but no less curious than Thurber as to what they had together was leading to. She courted his parents, who urged him to forget Eva and hang onto Minnette, of whom they heartily approved. Her "understanding" letter to Thurber about Eva may have been only artistry in face-saving. The shoe was being fitted to the other foot when Charles forwarded to him a newspaper clipping about Minnette's departure from Columbus for Red Cross training.

"I have not heard from M. for about 12 days," Thurber complained to Nugent in October:

> This is the longest delay she has allowed except the last letter I got came after an almost equal delay. Before that we wrote twice a week almost. However, her last letter was warmly cordial and nice as ever, and my answer was too. I cannot understand why she hasn't written me about her call [from the Red Cross] and where she is going and so forth. Really, I worry about it. It is useless for me to laugh Minnette from my thots. Sincerely, Nugey, I never have—and I never can. As time goes on I admire her and yes, damn it, love her more. . . . What to do with Minnette, I don't know. Do not be surprised if, years from now, I become even more deeply serious about her.

Thurber and Minnette stayed in touch intermittently in the years to come, but she denies that she ever considered herself engaged to Thurber, though she admits to having been immensely fond of him.

"Nugent advised Jim never to count on me having one boy friend, because I played the field," she told an interviewer in 1973. "That was true. All through school I had the same friends and I was devoted to all of them but never engaged to any of them."

As to their love letters, she recalls: "Jim was a prolific writer. I'm sure I had a letter every day. I had stacks and stacks of [them] from Washington and from Paris. I wish I had kept the letters from Paris. They were beautiful. He was an ardent admirer of Henry James and I thought we had a second Henry James with us. Jim had a sense of humor which Henry James did not have and one could see the development of his humor in these letters but I still felt that he was to be a writer of novels instead of what he became."

After marriage, Minnette was very ill throughout her first pregnancy, was certain she wouldn't live through it, and worried that Thurber's letters to her would be discovered, containing, as they did, references to her own declarations of love for him. "The night before my Sally was born I went down to the basement and burned all of Jim's letters," she says. "Probably a hundred and fifty of them. How I could have burned [those absolutely beautiful] letters I don't know. Isn't that tragedy?"

Minnette had dropped out of O.S.U. to serve in the Red Cross, and she returned to the university in the fall of 1919. She and Thurber resumed writing to one another while he was in Paris. At Christmastime, 1919, Minnette traveled to Chicago for a dental appointment. She had kept in touch with a former classmate from her prep-school days in Peoria, Illinois—Oscar (Ossie) Proctor, now a doctor interning in Chicago. She had agreed to a date with him and, to her own surprise, accepted his proposal of an almost immediate marriage, which took place over the holidays. When she wrote Thurber in early 1920 that she had "unexpectedly married," she says, "my last Paris communication from Jim was a cable of three words—'What the hell!' "

19

That First Time He Saw Paris

The *Orizaba* had taken a dozen days zigzagging across the North Atlantic, to elude the last submarines of the war. . . . Corcoran and I felt strange and uncertain on what seemed anything but solid land for a time. We were code clerks in the State Department, on our way to the Paris Embassy. . . . I can still feel in my bones the gloom and tiredness of the old port [St.-Nazaire] after its four years of war. The first living things we saw were desolate men, a detachment of German prisoners being marched along a street, in mechanical step, without expression in their eyes, like men coming from no past and moving toward no future.

—from "The First Time I Saw Paris"

An outbreak of the flu in Berne and a request for more code clerks at the American Embassy in Paris had led to Thurber's reassignment. Though Thurber was given a four-day home leave before sailing, he was apparently unable to see Eva. The reason may have been the flu epidemic, which had hit the Columbus area hard in October, taking several hundred lives in the city and nearby military posts. The university, public schools, churches, and "other places of public assemblage" were closed because of it, and people were urged to stay home and avoid public transportation. Robert believes that Thurber was unable to see Nugent in Dover for the same reason, though Nugent could have been in New York visiting his father. Nor did Thurber have much time at home; his four days included train travel to Columbus and, from there, to Hoboken, New Jersey, where he was to board the *Orizaba*. Minnette had left Columbus for Red Cross duty before Thurber's arrival.

His family took his picture on his last day home, and he comments on the photograph in "Exhibit X," in 1948, when the U.S. government was busy sorting out its citizens according to those considered American and un-American:

> The subject of the photograph is obviously wearing somebody else's suit, which not only convicts him of three major faults in a code clerk—absentmindedness, carelessness, and peccability—but gives him the un-wonted appearance of a saluki who, through some egregious mischance of nature, has exchanged his own ears for those of a barn owl. . . . His worried expression indicates that he has just mislaid a code book or, what is worse, has sold one. [The FBI's] dullest agent could tell that the picture is that of a man who would be putty in the hands of a beautiful, or even a dowdy, female spy. The subject's curious but unmistakable you-ask-me-and-I'll-tell-you look shows that he would babble high con-fidences to low companions on his third *pernod a l'eau*. This man could even find some way to compromise the Department of Agriculture, let alone the Department of State.

In Hoboken, though his trunk was taken aboard the *Orizaba* (a passenger ship converted to troop transport), his suitcase was left behind—deliberately, Thurber believes, because the crusty Merchant Marine captain refused to "take orders" from the State Department, and because Thurber's diplomatic passport hadn't been properly endorsed. "He finally let me stay on board after I had bowed and scraped and touched my forelock for an hour," Thurber writes.

Ed Corcoran, who had left Harvard Law School to become a code clerk, shared Thurber's stateroom. They were the only two civilians aboard. Thurber, seasick from the instant the ship reached deep water, had never really seen an ocean. During the entire voyage, he clung in fear and misery to his bunk, convinced that he would never make land alive. Meanwhile, Corcoran wandered in and out of the cabin, singing, joking, and smoking nearly the entire box of San Felice cigars Thurber had bought. Even some of the sailors were sick, but not Corcoran. The pitch and roll through the heavy November seas lasted a dozen days. When Thurber, pale and nauseated, was called on deck to attend a lifeboat drill in midvoyage, he was told that the life raft he had been assigned to was rusted to the deck and thus useless in case of emergency.

The armistice was declared before the ship docked in St.-Nazaire. Ashore, Thurber and Corcoran had their first cognac and walked around the port to get warm. They shared a sleeping compartment on the train to Paris with "a thin, gloved, talkative Frenchman who said he was writing the history of the world," and he awakened them in the middle of the night, "to explain that Hannibal's elephants were not real, but merely fearful figments of Roman hallucination."

The armistice celebration was still at fever pitch in Paris, Thurber writes, when he and Corcoran arrived:

> Paris' heart was warm and gay, all right, but there was hysteria in its beat. . . . Girls snatched overseas caps and tunic buttons from American soldiers, paying for them in hugs and kisses, and even warmer coin. . . . The Folies-Bergère and the Casino de Paris, we found a few nights later, were headquarters of the New Elation, filled with generous ladies of joy, some offering their charms free to drinking, laughing and brawling Americans in what was left of their uniforms. . . . Only the American MPs were grim, as they moved among the crowds looking for men who were AWOL. . . . Doughboy French . . . bloomed everywhere. . . . The Americans have never been so loved in France, or anywhere else abroad, as they were in those weeks of merriment and abandon.

His trunk was taken off the *Orizaba* but not delivered for weeks, leaving Thurber with only the clothes he was wearing. Even Thurber's hat was snatched off his head as a souvenir. Wartime prices were at their highest; he paid $4.75 for BVDs. A suit he bought "at a shop deceptively called 'Jack, American Tailor' . . . might have been made by the American Can Company. The hats looked like those worn by Ed Wynn," and he "went through that cold, dank Paris winter" hatless. Nor, when he could afford to, was he able to buy a properly tailored suit in Paris. He located a men's clothing store with a reassuring Scottish name but with French tailors, who took his measurements and gave him trousers so large that in trying them on he put both feet into one pant leg. "After six or eight revisions and alterations" the pants were down to a size suitable to the portly humorist Irvin S. Cobb, but "beyond this point the French tailor refuses to go," Thurber writes four years later in his *Columbus Dispatch* column.

Thurber's pay was about forty dollars per week, and in the winter of 1918–19 a franc was worth nearly twenty-five cents. Though its value later rose, he had to curtail expenditures. This benefited posterity by keeping Thurber in his *pension* on the newly named Avenue President Wilson, or late at the embassy, writing newsy letters home to family and Nugent, most of them preserved. He was writing love letters to both Eva Prout and—until her startling news of marriage at Christmas 1919—to Minnette. He wrote in longhand, though he used an embassy typewriter when he could. His family received letters from a folksy, parochial, corn-fed Thurber; those to Nugent were elaborately stylized and of a confessional mood that shared his every feeling, usually from a Thurber determined to experience Paris as he imagined James's "ambassador," Lambert Strether, had.

Two months after Thurber's arrival, the peace conference began in Paris, on January 18, 1919. The American mission to the conference was based at the Hotel Crillon, where Thurber was told to report for duty. But the mission had not, after all, requested any code clerks, and he was re-assigned to the American Embassy. Thurber believed the error was due to another frailty of the diplomatic code: "codebooks," which *were* needed, had been wrongly transmitted or translated as "code clerks." Code-dispatching at the Crillon was under the command of an American admiral who used Navy code, the only one he and his people understood, but which the State Department, receiving the messages in Washington, did not. The Department ordered that its own diplomatic code be used, so clerks, who had just been classified as superfluous, were suddenly in demand.

One coded request from Washington to Ambassador William Sharpe was for all information about "Big Bertha," the large-bore German cannon that could fling shells twenty-five miles, and which had accounted for the only artillery bombardment of Paris during the war. (The two shells did little more than kill a horse.) The Navy decoders delivered a wrongly transcribed message to a puzzled Sharpe that led him to send back a list of all American occupants of the hotel. The State Department took the names to be those with special knowledge about Big Bertha, and the Crillon inhabitants began to be queried by American military officials about the gun. The prolonged and confusing exchange about a cannon long since silenced by the armistice continued to jam the transatlantic cable traffic for some time.

American government codebooks were, Thurber thought, of a simple-minded order and had not been updated since the Grant administration. The principal reason for their longevity was economic—to save on telegraph costs—and an apparent unwillingness to perplex foreign governments. Rumor was that the Germans had had all the U.S. codes during the war, anyway, and that a missing U.S. codebook had been politely returned by the Japanese because either they had finished with it or already had one.

Thurber's Columbus friend Ben Williamson, assigned to Berne, visited Thurber in Paris. "I thought one thing that had given Jim great confidence was the way he had mastered the code," says Williamson. "The adhesiveness of his memory and his feeling for words were already with him. Thurber had miraculously memorized the whole codebook to save his eye. 'Golux,' for instance, which he liked the looks and sound of, was a word in the State Department's 'green basic' code, often used as a variant for a period. Or it might have stood for a whole phrase in another level of the coding system, such as 'George Fold Lucky Under Xenia.' Thurber enjoyed working with such words, and culled odd combinations of letters from the messages for his own use. Years later he wrote me when I was in Cleveland. His letter was interspersed with old code words I could barely remember and Thurber never forgot. There were archaic diplomatic phrases we used to have to handle: 'I venture to suggest that' was perhaps symbolized by the code word 'Hulip.' There could be a dozen variants on a code word like 'Monops,' or 'Pyrix,' all meaning the same thing.

"The codebook was a fat volume containing phrases arranged alphabetically, and so well known generally, their English translations could have been sent. As a gesture of security, 'green basic' was translated into hundreds of ciphers. To reassemble them in English you first deciphered and then decoded. It was almost too much for me to see the ease with which Thurber handled this maddening and chaotic job, and to realize that he *enjoyed* its 'Through the Looking Glass' overtones."

There was also fascination in living in a *pension*, Thurber wrote in early 1919 to Nugent, who was out of the Navy and back at O.S.U. Thurber's routine was to get home from work and after dinner take a good book to bed. He was currently reading Edith Wharton, the English poet William Ernest Henley, and a dozen of "the pale poets," but his life was "a mess." The charm of dank stairways and gabled windows had to be weighed against the lack of running water and the necessity of eating carrots three times a week to save money. With the savings, he treated himself to the cuisine of several famous French restaurants.

Ben Williamson recalls, "My sister, Donia, who later married John McNulty, had gone to East High with Thurber, and my mother knew his mother well. We were all part of the tight, East Side community, so small in area you usually walked to one another's house. For that matter, Columbus itself was so small then you could stroll Broad Street on an afternoon and meet half the people you knew. So Donia had learned before I did that Jim was in Paris, and wrote me about it in Switzerland. When I was transferred to Paris, I looked him up at the Hotel Crillon. What came through was what *fun* Thurber was having. He was then living at the Hotel D'Iena. His room was a garret on the top floor with the ceiling sloping into half-windows.

"Thurber was storing away notes about everything he saw and experienced. He seemed to be laughing at everyone and everything around him, including all the confused events that led to the Versailles Treaty. He was walking around museums, the flea market, reading a lot, living comfortably enough but actually not absorbing much 'culture.' He seemed more interested in his reactions to what he saw than in 'appreciating' the art and music he saw and heard, for example. At least those were my impressions the number of times I saw him. He was a loner. He never thought he was obliged to be with you even if you had gone out of your way to look him up. He'd say, 'What are you gonna do?' I might tell him I thought it would be nice if we did such and such, and he would say, 'Well, if you change your mind, come along with me. I'm going to see such and such.' It wasn't rudeness, or even absent-mindedness. He was merely too absorbed with stocking up on his own experiences in Paris to be tied to social amenities.

"One night Jim and I went to the Ritz for dinner. We ate in a long, narrow, beautiful room. It was a classic dinner the depressed franc barely put within our reach. We observed people. Thurber was a great *observer* of everything. He never wanted to draw attention to himself. He didn't move from place to place so much as he transplanted himself from one observation post to another. He acted like a spy, in a sense. And he wasn't just eating at the Ritz on this occasion; he was *experiencing* eating at the Ritz. Jim had discovered Pommard wine and loved it. He had had no real feeling for drink of any kind before coming to Paris. We had filet mignon, potatoes soufflé. I'd serve up the name of a mutual acquaintance and Jim would dissect him. Finally we had run out of people to dissect so we got up to leave. We were both proud of ourselves, young men from Columbus, dining at the Paris Ritz at our lovely small table. Then Jim tripped over a cord and pulled down a tall standing lamp with a great silk shade, and there he was, the center of attention, stared at by everyone. The captain came running up, and then I saw the great change in Thurber from his gawky, awkward days at the Phi Psi house. He struck a pose worthy of the Grand Duke of Russia and said to the captain, clearly and for everyone's benefit: 'Oh, what the hell!' and strode out, quite in charge of the situation. Outside, he laughed and laughed about it."

Carson Blair, in the Navy, looked up Thurber in Paris, and corroborates Williamson's impressions of a socially evolving Thurber. "He was a man of the world by then," Blair says. "We took in the Folies-Bergère and the Casino and drank at the Ponceon. It was hard to believe it was the old Phi Psi from *Sun-Dial* days."

"From Franklin County to Paris was a tremendous leap for Thurber," Joel Sayre adds. "Except for the few months in Washington, he'd never been anywhere but Columbus. He always liked Europe after that and when he was back home he kept remembering Paris in his writings and conversations."

Thurber purchased a two-volume edition of *The Ambassadors* in English for five dollars, which he read and reread, tracking down the Paris landmarks James mentions. He continually met up with O.S.U. acquaintances, including his old friend Ed Morris, now a first lieutenant in the Army. Another, "Buzz" Speaks, had chanced upon Charme Seeds, formerly a popular O.S.U. coed, now with the Red Cross in Paris, and told her that Thurber was attached to the embassy. She looked him up. Seeds had entered college in 1917; as a journalism major, she had worked on the *Lantern* and had known of Thurber, the illustrious upperclassman, without having been introduced to him. After Thurber became a celebrity, by the end of the twenties, Charme wrote of him in the O.S.U. alumni magazine, remembering him as quite a ladies' man on campus. In Paris, on his first date with her, he noted with pleasure that she was wearing, in place of the regulation Red Cross uniform, a "smart, cute, irregular, rakish blue toque on her head, the wide, cool, sweet Buster Brown collar," her only Red Cross identification the enamel insignia "pinned against the dark blue of her toque." They had tea in a Jamesian setting, and "one of the famous Duck Dinners at the Tour D'Argent, the famous restaurant . . . where Strether and Madame de Vionnet dined together," Thurber told Nugent. "Buzz himself didn't drop around until after Charme did, but he drifted in a few nights ago, big as a house and strong enough for two." (Seeds, who went on to a journalism career in the Midwest, married Charles (Buzz) Speaks; they moved to New York to become a part of the O.S.U. alumni contingent, along with the Meeks and the Nugents, who stayed in touch with Thurber through most of his life.)

He found the French ballads of the Black Cat pretty but the beer vile; was disappointed that the Moulin Rouge seemed to have closed its doors forever; marveled at the high speed with which guided tours were whisked through Notre Dame, a speed that "warmed" the natural "Gothic coolness" of the cathedral. He visited Reims, Soissons, and Verdun, toured the battlefields, clambered in and out of trenches and over barbed wire, ruined a shoe and a trouser leg, and finally even managed to set off a hand grenade fifty feet away when he tripped over a strand of wire; the episode left him unharmed but badly scared.

His provincial allegiances were instantly renewed when Eva Prout sent him her picture. Her "clear, sweet beautiful eyes" reminded him that there were no girls anywhere to equal the American. The writer Mark Sullivan, he noted in a letter to Nugent, had written in *Collier's* that the United States should get the troops home before "they acquire the European attitude toward women," but Thurber primly insists that, thanks to their observation of French women, the American Expeditionary Force had learned to worship the morality of American womanhood with "an undying flame that would never be extinguished." In fact, seeing Americans in Paris alongside thirteen other nationalities made one love America, he added. Americans were "cleaner and finer." Many had "slipped," yes, but their morals and mentality would forever keep them American.

In such letters to Nugent we have another disheartening glimpse of Thurber headed down a dead-end track in his approach to the opposite sex, a misdirection for which he would pay dearly. His particular ideal women, nameless, faceless, inhabited English drawing rooms in Henry James novels, in which Prufrock-style men stopped, started, hesitated, circled, wondered, dared, hoped, and withdrew—all out of a magnification of romantic possibility and a genuine dread of commitment. This was the perfect breeding ground for the impatient, practical Thurber Woman, an American woman Thurber did less to create than to define out of his own disappointments. He would never cease to blame and ridicule her for his own failure to hold up his impractical end of the contract. She would necessarily have to resist the Jamesian-Thurberian attitude toward her as lethal to her own fulfillment, fight back when attacked, and take over when he could not function effectively.

Robert and his mother—Charles occasionally—were writing to Thurber, Robert delighting his brother by reconstructing Columbus events with newspaper clippings and detailed reports, including what songs were popular. There was occasional homesickness in Thurber's letters to Columbus. His tenure of employment seems optional. "Often I decide to go home soon as possible," he writes Robert, "but then I redecide that as long as I am in Paris . . . I ought to [stay], as . . . Paris is . . . always interesting, and a wonderful field for study, of all kinds. Every now and then . . . I think I have seen enough of Paris. Because, on final analysis, there are more things to go back for, than to stay for. My heart is in Ohio."

Robert had begun in earnest his life of semi-invalidism, and was to be operated on again. "I understand you are about to have six or eight more cuttings," Thurber writes him.

As a ball player, you are quite a patient. . . . For Heaven's sake sign the pledge never to get anything else the matter with you. . . . You couldn't possibly get anything new, but stick away from relapses and lay off of setbacks. Decline to go into declines—and refuse to be flung amongst the refuse.

Ever generous financially, and still with a strong strong sense of family, Thurber enclosed ten dollars to Robert. "William is able to work, and you aint just yet," he explained.

In those days, Robert could readily join with Thurber in laughing at their family's antics. The ailing Robert, who could still drive the Reo but now couldn't hand-crank it, tried to teach his father how to start the car. The cranking so upset Charles that he could calm himself only by going to his room and fiercely brushing his hair with military brushes. Thurber to Robert:

> Your very clever dialogue of the O.M. [old man] learning to crank the machine . . . was one of the funniest things I have had . . . come over to cheer me up, your final touch about the use of the brush to calm the Thurberian temperament was true to life, all right. . . . Mama writes that papa is still an earnest advocate of putting his family to bed early, doubtlessly tucking them in securely also, and so I assume that you are getting your rest, which ought to help you recuperate in good shape.

With credits for his brief Naval service, Elliott Nugent received his degree from O.S.U. in June 1919, and left for New York to join his playwright/actor father, who introduced his son around and helped him look for a part in a play. That August, actors striking for recognition of their new union, the Actors' Equity Association, closed the theaters of several large cities. Nugent spoke a good imitation of Amish dialect, which got him a part in *Tillie, A Mennonite Maid*, playing outside strikebound New York. A letter from Thurber reached Nugent on tour, extolling his friend's genius and good luck, both as budding actor and playwright. (Nugent had sold an option on a book he had written for a musical play—it was never produced.) Thurber praised Nugent for having "managed everything just right," including being filmed while winning a track meet at O.S.U. the previous spring in a newsreel Thurber had just seen in Paris. Nugent's success clearly both impressed and saddened Thurber, in the way friendly rivalries do. He, himself, had been thinking of writing a one-act play but he was short of ideas, he went on. In fact, he added prophetically, he was afraid his range didn't extend past the "skit" kind of thing. Anything larger would require a "strenuous pushing" beyond his abilities. One thing the Paris experience had demonstrated to him, he told Nugent, was that there had to be an expansion of knowledge and skills, not just tricks of the writing craft. The realization had shaken his self-confidence, and that was "the most destructive thing imaginable." Castles in the air, he said, had to be razed in the face of reality, and slower and harder effort put into building on their sites. "Now and then I admit I sort of quail [through] the dark moments . . . I have had to fight against all my life, mostly to myself, all alone. For I have never had a natural invisible supply of supreme confidence or even of transcendental courage, and it keeps me . . . gritting the molars every now and then to keep the manufacturing plant going."

Nugent sent him a poem that Thurber showed the two Red Cross girls from Columbus he was dating. Thurber confessed to Nugent that he too had been dabbling in poetry, or at least "putting down sequences of words that rhyme now and then."

He visited Rouen, where he toured the city and the province of Normandy on his own. He was charmed by Normandy, to which he would return five years later in an effort to write a novel. "The chimes are always chiming in Normandy," he wrote Nugent, with an ear as receptive to bells and striking clocks before blindness as after. The September landscapes were "seemingly sculptured by the hand of a poetic giant." He wandered Normandy's "mossy manses, gray-stoned old castles, crumbling abbeys and fourteenth-century gabled houses." There was "many a castle and . . . stretch of ground that Fame played in, Hate raged, Pageant paraded, Glory shone." Everything in Normandy seemed richly old, "fairly palpitating still with the throb of history."

Inside the Church of St. Ouen, he found his own way up narrow stairs by candlelight. The stairs wound in such small circles that "had I started to run them I would sure have been inextricably fixed there, like a vine that has woven itself in and out of the palings of an old fence." Leaning through the gargoyle parapets, "it was no trick to imagine oneself back in the middle ages, and I stared with some surprise at the people passing below in modern mufti, whereas I half expected to see feathered, drooping cavalier hats on swaggering blades, and the cleft mitres of gloomy bishops stalking in the gardens of the church below."

He took a carriage to the Church of St. Gervais, where even his cautious footsteps "sounded like sabots in a silent street." Candle tips of light "flitted and darted gracefully in dark recesses" as if balanced and juggled "by some invisible sprite."

His kaleidoscopic similes at times seemed as much the by-product of his unreliable eye as of the sense of imagery that may have been influenced at the time by his fondness for the writing of Joseph Hergesheimer, a popular American novelist of the period.

In the fall of 1919, Thurber, nearly twenty-five, who had half-supposed he would preserve his sexual purity for his Jamesian ideal, for the first time "stepped aside." What exactly happened remains a mystery, but his reaction to the event seems to have traumatized him. He was too shattered to continue his correspondence to anyone for a time.

From Paris, Thurber had sent his fraternity pin to Eva Prout in Zanesville, with the plea that she wear it as a symbol of betrothal, though they had not seen one another for ten years. She refused, wanting to discuss the matter with Thurber in person, and not wishing to ostracize herself from a social life at home. But his letters had won her romantic interest.

"I'd been receiving beautiful love letters from Jim," she says, "and answering them all. Then suddenly his letters stopped coming. And evidently he stopped writing everybody, even his family. I was quite upset. So were the Thurbers. Mr. Thurber came down to Zanesville to see me and asked me, hadn't I heard anything at all from Jim? He was certain I must be keeping something from them. I really wasn't and I was just as concerned as they were. I was really in love with Jim."

Elliott Nugent, still on tour with *Tillie*, was equally alarmed; three of his letters to Thurber had gone unanswered. Finally he received a reply, on December 7, 1919; Thurber said that he had just "resumed communication with tout le monde":

> [Received] your last letter, from Battle Creek, concerning your Columbus visit and the revelation of my long silence. . . . I had long intended to tell the whole story to you, but . . . finally decided . . . with everything getting back to rights again, that I wouldn't . . . because there no longer seemed to be the actual need for it. . . . There is nothing in the world that I wouldn't want to tell you first, but since the affair looked finished and status quo, everywhere, once more resumed, I didn't see the need of bothering you with past troubles, until I should see you, when I most certainly would have unburdened myself. . . . Of all those who have touched on the subject of my silence you alone have perfectly done so . . . as only a real honest to God friend could—I must also add Eddy Morris my Chi Phi chum of longtemps who almost came up to your standard of friendship, too. . . . You cannot know how much I appreciate, in the face of everything, your simple statement that you will not lose faith in the James. . . . How readily I would bet my

life that you would do as much for me as I would for you, and that is, I believe, saying the ultimate. . . .

Rest assured that things have not been so bad as they seemed, that many a mountain was really a mole-hill, that through it all, though perhaps always wrong, I was nevertheless trying to be right, and that everything is once more back as it should be and that I am really happy and hopeful.

Only after returning to Columbus and learning, at the Phi Psi house, of Nugent's own "stepping aside" in Chicago while in the Navy did Thurber confide to Nugent his sexual initiation:

I hadn't been here long till I heard from several sources that one E. J. Nugent stepped out quite colorfully in Chicago. . . . Whether you did or didn't makes no damn difference. I just bring it in to pave the way to telling you that such things have a trick of getting around from which I was spared with my one or two affaires d'amour in Paris. I lasted a little over 12 long months in the gayest city in the world. I now have a picture of Ninette, the most wonderful dancer in the world, and memories of my first step aside, the pretty Remonde of Provins. The whirl when once it whirled went whirling so fast that I saw it as a reason for whirling home. Ninette told me once in the privacy of her cute Montmartre apartment, "Jeemy, at zee step which you step, you must last about two weeks." "Ah, non, ma chérie," I returned, lighting a Pall Mall from a huge red box of them which I had given her, and offering my glass for some more of her fine Porto, "Ah, non, vous vous trompez, you are very wrong, at this pace I will last all of ten days. Voilà."

But despite the lighthearted show of sophistication to Nugent, something associated with the experience had brought on a form of nervous breakdown and scared him into coming home. Had he led either of the girls on, getting himself into an awkward social scrape? Was there a pregnancy scare? Had he, after all, contracted a case of the dreaded "collapse," or thought he had? Did he take fright at the possibility that he could slip into irreversible debauchery? Was he overworked? (His letters of the period indicate long hours of decoding at the embassy.)

More likely, in his adopted role as James's Strether, he felt drastic self-betrayal; he had sullied himself, perhaps disqualifying himself, in his mind, for the Jamesian heroine—at the moment, the pure, innocent Eva Prout.

The ordeal, which his old friend Ed Morris helped see him through, lingered during his first weeks at home. "I am still a bit unsettled and uncertain yet," he wrote Nugent,

> and things are somewhat nebulous and a trifle worrisome. You see I am not in très excellent condition, having had a very bad time of it with nerves in Paris—which is a hint of the silence story—untold yet by the way. . . . I am picking up wonderfully. The ocean trip in itself was a wonder worker, and home and the way spring comes up Ohio ways, are keeping up the good work, ably assisted by Fellow's hypophosphites and new mental orientation.

Part of the orientation, presumably, was to retrieve some of his earlier Jamesian outlook toward sex. "I have no regrets, fortunately," he wrote a Nugent who could only be bemused,

> but I will say that I can't see it except as a passing experience once in— or twice in—a lifetime, providing there is no One Girl. I mean if there isn't One Girl, why then say six or eight passing experiences or nine or ten or . . . hell. The genus known as Gash Hound intrigues me not. Nor does it suffocate you with enthusiasm, either. But what have you to say as to how long your pace would have lasted? Come to think of it I never had your statement that you hadn't hunted forbidden berries long ago, but I at least imagined you hadn't. I don't believe I ever told you I got as far as Paris all right, either. It seems to have been . . . things which we naturally didn't consider worth the time for discussing. And God knows it isn't.

The experience lost its traumatic aspects with the years and softened into another sentimental Thurber memory. He tried unsuccessfully to locate one of the women on one of his Paris trips years later. And he appears to have written the incident into "The Other Room," one of his last stories, published posthumously in *Harper's* in 1962. It is set in 1959; an American veteran of World War I relates the experience as his own to a group of compatriots in a Paris hotel bar:

> There was this . . . French girl. She wasn't any older than I was. She spoke English, though, and was I glad for that! Well, we sat out in front of the Cafe de la Paix. We drove there in a taxi. She said she thought I should have something to drink. And so we had a couple of

drinks. Then she told me about herself. She came from some place in Southern France, and her father was a drunkard, and used to beat up the family on Saturday nights, so she ran away to Paris, and got some work in a garment factory, but all they gave her was a few francs a week, and she saw all these other girls in fur coats and things, and so she took to—well, making the boys feel better, she called it. . . .

The other day I took a taxi up to the street where [she] used to have an apartment. I remembered the street, and even the number. . . . They call it Rue Marcadet, and it's . . . in Montmartre. I didn't get out of the cab. . . . I just looked at the building, the windows on the second floor. . . . She would be sixty now, . . . twenty then. . . . There were pictures of guys [in uniform] all over her living room [including] a young Canadian soldier . . . and he couldn't have been more than twenty himself. He gets into my dreams, too, kinda banged up, with his uniform all bloody. . . . He had been killed in action. This friend of his brought her this note he had written her. . . . She showed it to me . . . the first and only time I ever went there. . . . I remember what it said, all right, every word of it. . . .

She had a bottle of port wine at her place, and we sat there drinking [it], too much of it, I guess. After a while, she went out of the room . . . and left me sitting there. . . . This good-looking boy on the piano kept staring at me, and looking sad, and awful young. . . . I thought of a girl back home. . . . Then I heard this French girl calling to me from the other room.

Released by the government, Thurber sailed for home in February 1920, after fifteen months abroad. Paris had truly been a city of light to him, a wide-screen, nonstop operetta, but "closing down" a bit, he thought, as the peace talks ended and the numbers of uniformed persons thinned, to be replaced by American expatriate students, artists, and writers. Thurber had seen the city at its wildest and now it was becoming tame, he said.

He reached New York on a cold, windy day. He had never been able to find a hat in Paris to replace the one he lost there, and one of the first things he did was to purchase one. From the inner hatband he discovered that it had been made in Paris.

20

That Sweetheart Wraith

October's burning on the hills
And rainbow leaves are falling,
And your blue eyes are in my dreams,
And your dear voice is calling.

June has charms of wide array,
And May can still a lover's ills,
But every pathway leads to you
When October walks the hills.

—to Eva Prout, 1920

The national prohibition of the sale of alcoholic beverages had gone into effect in January 1920, and Thurber came home to a dry country. He was still plagued emotionally, financially broke, and with no plans for the future. Visiting the Phi Psi house weighted him with nostalgia; he learned from the contemporary brotherhood that his imitations of Captain Converse and his and Nugent's antics were now part of the chapter's fonder legends. As usual, he tried to sort things out in a letter to Nugent:

Your . . . letter shows . . . you believe I am in school, but I aint. I got back too late for one thing and I didn't feel up to it for another, and there are also family complications,—the sickness of my younger brother and things financial. . . .

Very soon I will start out as you have on the old road of life, which in my case can mean but one thing, writing. It must mean that, win or lose, fail or prosper. But I intend to hit it hard and consistently and go in for the big things, slowly, perhaps, but surely. I have of course no assurance of success, even of ability, beyond the outer rim of mediocrity, but I have the urge, the sense of what it is and means, and a certain vague confidence which will grow, I believe, as I grow and work.

Minnette had returned to O.S.U. following her Red Cross stint, her husband still a hospital intern in Chicago. She obligingly spent time with Thurber, listening sympathetically while, in his nonstop fashion, he aired his confusions and an inexhaustible self-analysis that fed on itself. "Dating" a married woman, he realized, could compromise her, but there could be no reason for people to "talk." For if ever there was "a safe, a fine friendship in dangerous waters, it is mine and hers," he wrote Nugent. "Why, we would always do the Henry James thing—the Strether thing. . . . It isn't terribly comforting to feel that I know her better than anyone else does—that our plane is a thing Tommy Meek, Karl Finn and any other never reached. . . . She counts me her Great Friend [and] said suddenly 'Jim, you'll be coming to talk with me when we're sixty!' " (Her prediction was almost accurate.)

Determined to be in love, to have "a sweetheart," The One Girl, as Nugent had, Thurber continued to pursue the other object of his Edwardian sexual fantasy—his Sweetheart Wraith, Eva Prout.

Two months older than Thurber, Eva had shared his school classes and teachers from the third through the eighth grade, at Sullivant and Douglas schools. "Jim sat right across the aisle from me," Prout recalled in 1973. "We were always seated in the front row because of my being very small and Jim's eyesight. . . . He was smart, intelligent, brilliant and studied a great deal. He was also shy but kind and thoughtful; he helped many of us along the way. Nobody teased him because of his one eye."

Times were hard for the Prouts; her father, who named her Evebelle, died when she was eighteen months old; her mother ran a rooming and boarding house on State Street, from 1902 till 1908, to support her two daughters. Eva, or Eve, as she came to be called by friends, was in the first grade when a German choirmaster at Trinity Church in Columbus noticed that she had a deep contralto voice, unusual in a child of seven. He arranged for her to sing at Sunday evening mezzanine concerts in the downtown hotels. Her mother was asked by the manager of the local vaudeville theater, the Keith, if Eva could debut there. During her week at the Keith, she was heard by the booking agent for another theater circuit, and each summer thereafter through the eighth grade, Eva, chaperoned by her mother, toured and sang professionally, returning to school each fall. A starstruck Thurber developed his crush on her in the third grade, when the teacher, Miss Ferrell, would perch little Eva on her desk and have her sing *a cappella* to the class "Slumber Boat," "Rose in the Bud," and "Sing Me to Sleep." He became truly infatuated with her in the seventh grade. She was the first girl he kissed—during a birthday-party game, when he was thirteen.

Eva left school after the eighth grade to sing and act professionally. Thurber remembers their farewell after graduation at the Douglas School, and how his family kidded him about his infatuation: "I told her good-bye," he wrote to Nugent, "pulled my cap to pieces, and felt an ache and an urge in my heart too old for my years, but too eternal and . . . strong ever to be classed as 'puppy love.' . . . She was the One Girl."

He wouldn't see her again for eleven years. From time to time, young Thurber, nearly a daily patron of the local theaters, would thrill to see Eva in silent movies; she played children's roles for the Essanay studio—in *Goldilocks and the Three Bears, Cinderella, Little Red Riding-hood."*

"Louella Parsons was the head of the scenario department at Essanay," says Prout, "and used to find the right scenarios for me; she helped my movie career a great deal." As Eva matured, she was given adult parts in such silent movies as *The Perils of Pauline*. In 1916, at age twenty, she was booked into New York's Winter Garden in a Shubert revue. "When the war began, the theaters began closing around the country," she says, "and Mother thought we should go home, which, by then, was Zanesville, where my sister lived. I'd been acting and singing for nearly eight years. Jim had written me a couple of years before; he had read in *Billboard*, or *Variety*, where I was appearing; I got his first letter in Denver."

Having courted Eva solely through correspondence, Thurber dreaded, like Cyrano de Bergerac, the moment he had to appear before his love, but "the finest letter she wrote to me," he told Nugent triumphantly, "was one she sent after she had seen a recent picture of me." He had no sooner unpacked upon his return to Columbus than he got in touch with her. She invited him to dinner in Zanesville. They had last seen one another in 1909. "I loved her when I saw her," writes Thurber. "There were the 'rapid heart-beats' and all. I sat and stared at her as I never sat and stared at anyone." She was the One Girl, the girl of his dreams, "The Girl heroine of movie stories, and 'Prince

Chap' plays and pipe-dreams, the girl one's heart yearns for." Forget the Jamesian ideal woman; "the devil take Joey Taylor's neat philosophy and H. James' cool churches! The girl of Browning gondolas, of Lee Robert's songs, of Douglas Fairbanks fifth reels and of Harold McGrath's novels. [That's] the one, after all, we marry."

Thurber invited Eva and her mother to Columbus to see the local Follies, on April 1. They stayed overnight at the Thurbers on Gay Street. "Eve and I had but a very few minutes together this second time," Thurber reported to Nugent,

> not enough to make any progress towards knowing each other. . . . I have found . . . that Eve never in her life bumped up against or associ-ated with a personality just like mine or with a man of my interests and enthusiasms and my change of gait. I know that she is a bit puzzled, vastly interested, in a way fascinated and most of all half-eager and half-afraid about her own ability to find my plane . . . for she never went to college, has no idea then of that life, and about all we have at the start in common is I believe a mutual interest [and] an affection for the stage.

But Thurber was already feeling ambivalent toward Eva. He worried that she was not physically strong. "Her nerves seem to be mated with mine in many ways, which is a discomforting reflection," he told Nugent, and he thought she was against marrying because her mother felt it wouldn't do for her to have babies. That, of course, fitted with Thurber's plans never to have children, who risked inheriting "the Thurber nervousness . . . the three of us brothers having had a double heritage of it, and before I believed Eva felt that way I had decided that I would never marry either, if the girl did want children."

He was still attracted to other girls, he confessed, and Eva was not the girl of *all* his dreams. He had based those dreams on "a pretty little Bob-haired girl, an image . . . so wonderful that she couldn't, I suppose, live up to it." She was, he thought, "not so beautiful as I had been sure she would be." Her voice was less than the one he remembered. She was more sisterly than colorful and radiant. "How could I live," he wonders, "with the . . . girl who would be the most acute reminder always of what might have been. . . . If I had met her for the first time I would have been crazy about her, I think. . . . Maybe something bigger will take its place, but the little princess of mine who played about the willow trees on Yarrow [legendary river in Scot-land] is still there. I have never found her, I never will."

Then jealousy restored all his earlier desire for Eva, and more. Another man was dating her, Thurber learned. Ernest Geiger, also interested in the-ater, was from Zanesville. "My family had known his for a number of years," says Prout. "I'd met him at dances; there was nothing really between us at the time I was seeing Jim. But Ernest was in the picture and Jim knew about it."

Thurber learned of it when he turned up unannounced in Zanesville, causing Eva to break a date with Ernest. She assured an embarrassed Thurber that Ernest would get over it, but when Thurber writes her next, he is careful to ask permission to visit. "I ask so long in advance because I don't want to ruin another date of anyone else," he says, pretending to a worldly maturity in contrast to Geiger, who was younger than both Eva and Thurber. "I refuse flatly to cause any poor love-lorn kid to lie awake nights. Tell him I'm a fatherly old soul whose interest in you is like the interest of Whitcomb Riley in roses or at the worst like the avidity of Omar Khayyám for jugs. Tell him I had a bet that I would meet you someday, is all. And he'll 'get over it,' as you said."

He hints that he may not be around Columbus long; he is considering returning to France with Carson Blair to write syndicated material for Ameri-can newspapers—a suggestion made to him by Charles Thurber, who was beginning to worry about his second son's continued unemployed status. Thurber would like to show her his Paris, he adds, and lays out a three-day schedule of how he would do so, beginning: "1. Morning. A walk down the Champs-Élysées, with a half hour's rest under the flowering chestnut trees of the Élysées Gardens."

"Jim would come to Zanesville practically every weekend," Prout says, "and wrote me nearly every day; sometimes several letters a day."

One April Saturday, he arrived in Zanesville at noon, three hours before he was expected by Eva. He had learned that, because of power problems, the trolleys between Columbus and Zanesville that day might not be running later. He spent the three hours of wait in the lobby of Zanesville's Hotel Rogge, writing Eva nonsense verses on the hotel's stationery. He wonders, while watching the clock, whether "Rogge" is pronounced with a hard or soft "g" and tries it both ways in verses about the fertile guinea pigs the Thurbers once owned:

> The guinea pig's a funny hoggy
> (Twelve, thirty-one in the hotel Rogge)
> He's awful fat and short and podgy
> (Twelve thirty-two in the hotel Rogge)
> Of course he's not a sure 'nuf hog
> (Twelve thirty-three in the hotel Rogge)

His wife is a thrifty little drudge
We once had two named "Kewp and "Budge"—
(Twelve thirty-four in the hotel Rogge)

You should have seen the family grow
They had thirty children then, I know—
And hubby walked the ground at night
—Forty children, if I am right—
But his wife thought they were awful nifty—
These forty—or was it really fifty—
But she could sleep, land sakes alive—
And hubby up with all sixty-five—
Yet still he loved his little matey—
And him with the care of all them eighty!
He died at last one morn at eight—
Going on at such a sleepless rate
The funeral was very fine—
He left a wife and ninety-nine.

Thurber soon confessed his love to Eva. She didn't want to end the situation or (though she had never worn it) return his fraternity pin, but she was put off by his overwhelming, slightly frightening interest in her, mostly expressed in letters. He saw her hesitations as rejection. He suffered through the two weeks she visited friends in New York without writing to him, though she had given him an address there, where he continued to write to her. He was still mooching hotel stationery, once writing her at a desk in the Neil House lobby:

"Eve, the hope of you means so much to me that until I know what you want to be to my future I haven't any interest in things. I can't plan or go ahead at all with any happiness. So please help me quick." He threatens self-exile in the nature of a Conrad character, but to a place few would consider appropriate to Lord Jim's test of character:

I believe if I must never see you or write to you again I would go back to Paris . . . where the ghosts of red, unhappy days are. I don't believe it would help me, and if I went I wouldn't care much whether it did or not. Unless there is you to build things for, why should I care what happens?

I don't believe that a poor old sensitive dreamer like me who has cared so much for you could ever get over it and make anything of himself without you even if he tried.

Please Eve give the "James" every charity you can in deciding and always believe that no matter if your dismissal sent me to the farthest latin quarter café in Paris . . . your word would bring me back, and I'll never give up hope that some day you'll want me. Once a dreamer of dreams, always one.

And should she refuse him,

I would . . . go back to my old, old hopes of my little blue-eyed sweetheart and I'd die with your name on my lips. Robert Browning loved Italy so much that he said they'd find that name carved on his heart when he was dead,—just where if they cared to disturb such a nonentity as me they'd find your name written, too, Eva.

He filled four pages with love poems to her, and bombarded her with letters of increasing intensity. He was happy when he was with her, he said; depressed when he wasn't. "You must ask Freud or Bergson or the Ouija board or a heart specialist, then, to explain. . . . Your letter was so very wonderful . . . you showed me your character and flashes of your soul in such a contrite and ingenuous and delightful way that it taught me the lesson we men must all learn—the higher plane of woman's spirit."

He recognized that he might lose out to Ernest and even draws upon Mame's astrology to make his case:

If you love and marry "another" I will help you both along, and I *will* after twenty years, find consolation in Velvet tobacco, gold-fish, memories and a parrot and Victor records of Slumber Boat. But for at least a *while* I'll say mean things to my best pals, curse congress for the lack of strong beers and heavy wines, be glad if your babies keep *him* up all night. . . .

Do you think . . . that I just *want* you a little, and don't *need* you . . . ? A woman never wants to marry a man who doesn't in some way *need* her. "Sagittarius," it says in the book, "is the most deeply affectionate and loving of all the signs and the one which most needs love and the one of the twelve signs whose happiness in life is most dependent on love." . . .

I am not a mature, philosophical sort of man of the world. I am a boy, and I know of certain heart hurts which no balm of philosophy can stop hurting. A man is always a boy. A girl is always a woman. . . . Those are the reasons women suffer in silence and men make such a fuss about things. There is in you the spirit of all the mothers of all the years of time. . . . A real man does not love any quality half as dearly and intensely as he loves that "mother spirit" in the One.

As to Ernest: "He's gotta be as wonderful to you as the one who loses knows *he* would have been. . . . He can have my Overland [a make of auto] or my overcoat or my walk-overs—and I'll even play the overture,—*But* the organist must not play 'Sing Me to Sleep.' . . . Outside of that, my hand and my best wishes to the Luckiest Guy in the whole world. . . . You did give me a waiting chance and I did fear that you might not be able to give me any. . . . You couldn't have turned out the stars and blown out the moon, could you?"

Had Thurber suspected that certain of his letters to Nugent and Prout, composed out of his romantic innocence, would survive, it is likely that both could have effectively blackmailed him. With Mitty illusions of his future importance, he even imagined such a situation, writing Nugent in April 1920: "If anyone should ever want to compile my letters after I am famously dead, and should call upon you to furnish the most of them and of me, I fear you would have to censor and expurgate with a free wrist movement." But their value is in what they reveal about an early Thurber, who made his version of the war between the sexes a legendary part of literature and art.

In May, Thurber spent time with Nugent, who was in Dover visiting his ailing mother. Thurber used Nugent's typewriter to write "The Only Woman in the Whole World, Her Royal Highness Princess Eve of Yarrow," to invite her to a Phi Psi May dance at the Columbus Country Club. Eva worried that she would seem outclassed in a college environment, but simply said she didn't feel physically up to it. "Please, Eve," Thurber pleads, "aren't you well and strong and husky now . . . ? I won't have you miss it for anything." For one thing, he said, Nugent wanted to meet her. Nugent had hoped to visit his girl in Akron, "but Mamma Nugent is jealous and I guess she loves him most and anyway it's Mothers Day. God bless all mammas."

Eva gave in. The Saturday fraternity dance was lovely, she remembered. "I stayed overnight at the Thurbers. Elliott Nugent was at the dance and be-tween dances he and I went out on the terrace. It was a very [clear] night, the stars were out, and I noticed one in particular. I mentioned, 'What a lovely star! It looks green.' And he said, 'Oh, yes, it's definitely green.' Jim came out looking for us, and I [said] 'We're looking at that beautiful green star.' Jim didn't like it at all that I saw green stars with Elliott."

She worried that she had disappointed him in other ways, that she had seemed unenthusiastic about the people he introduced her to. He quickly reassured her: "I am not . . . disappointed in your so-called lack of 'enthusiasm.' I hate enthusiastic girls or women." But the green-star incident wasn't forgotten, and in spite of himself he wrote her a sarcastic letter about it. She told him that she found it so, and in his response, angry and suffering from a kind of hypochondria of the heart, Thurber pulls out all the emotional stops:

> So my letter was sarcastic. . . . Do you think it is a simple matter to give one's whole heart away, his whole being, his entire self,—to a girl who may be a little amused, somewhat pleased, and only on occasions seriously realizing what she has had given to her. . . .
>
> A woman is often a wonderful thing. And you are. But in you, as in all of them, is the indifference of Carmen, the joy in cruelty of Cleopatra, the tyrannical marble-heartedness of Katherine De Medici, and the cold glitter of all the passionless despots of men's warm souls since sex first originated,—since Eve broke the heart of humanity forever and laughed with sadistic joy at Adam sweating blood on the rack she made for him. . . .
>
> I'm not blaming you. I'm blaming the ages of women gone before you who handed such legacies down,—blaming the radiant and sparkling and fidgety ladies of history who kissed in a moment of coquetry and saw men die, kings dethroned and nations fight in blood because of that careless caress. Men are fools, weak, wine-blooded, deeply-devoted darn fools. What have women done for them half so intense and potent as what they have done *to* them? . . .
>
> Nothing is so near to tears as laughter is. That's all my sarcasm meant. Shouldn't I naturally, despite myself, want to hurt you if you never care for me? Whom the gods destroy they first make madly in love with a girl.

It was seeing her, wanting her, that had brought on his negative feelings, he said. The other Eve, she of his years of dreams, the Eve of letter exchanges, the Eve of imagery, "I could have given up with a sigh and a tear." But Eve in the flesh has kindled both physical attraction and enhanced his "spiritual love" for her.

"I will only give up with much raving and jealousy and smashing up of furniture and biting of lips and screaming," he adds prophetically. "I *want* you. I want you to be *mine*. . . . I want your blue-eyes and your smile and all of you. . . . Then I won't be jealous." When both physical and spiritual love is mixed in a man, "he loves with all the fire and passion of a poet and a cave man."

Three months after he has begun seeing Eva, Thurber has yet to kiss her. "I am ten times the affectionate nature you are," he writes her in another letter. "That frightens me. To be my wife a girl would have to want to be loved,—lots and very terribly. If I ever kiss you you'll know that,—and you'll know what a wonderful thing my love is."

Recently he has kissed another girl, he tells her, "many times. . . . I'm not engaged to you, and don't suppose I ever will be and I won't always be young and I do love to be loved,—now. . . . I crave much love. . . . That's Sagittarius. They must be petted and kissed every now and then or they can't write plays or sleep well or think life is fun.

"If I'm ever engaged to you I'll . . . never kiss anyone else. Your kiss, once given, would . . . make me your slave forever." Surely she understands all that, because she "has a woman's soul and a woman's heart, and lots of 'Mother' in her and therefore lots of 'wife.' "

Thurber's fictitious Walter Mitty is lovable because the frustrations and disappointments and pain he feels are suffered in a kind of heroic silence; he does his best to cope with the consequences of an entrapment he has brought on himself. But Thurber as a Mitty gone public can only impale poor Eva solidly on the horns of a dilemma. She couldn't bring herself to end his courtship, but its intensity worried her. She was being blamed for Thurber's self-inflicted anguish.

Given the repeated reservations Thurber expressed to Nugent about both Minnette and Eva, wooing them the while with outlandish protestations of love, it is probable that had Eva yielded it would have been her undoing. Like Groucho Marx, who wouldn't join a club that would compromise its standards by admitting him, an insecure Thurber would have found victory not worth the spoils. Both women seem to have sensed just that.

Indeed, Thurber showed that he recognized the strategic effectiveness of women who either play "hard to get" or are simply and honestly cautious. Nugent was falling out of love with Katherine Garver—for two years his fiancée—and now broke off with her. He sent her roses and a note, saying he hoped that they could be friends. Thurber, a few days later, was in Akron to look into a job possibility, and at Nugent's request visited Katherine to see how she was bearing up. He then lectures Nugent on his insensitivity, revealing a caginess in affairs of the heart that would have given Eva further pause. "You must understand the single-track mind of a girl who has loved, *who still loves,* and who was engaged two years," he instructs Nugent, in a letter to Dover:

Her mother is "disappointed" in you. She "thought you were different."
. . . Then she was big enough to say that she guessed a man has as
much right as a girl to change his mind. [Katherine] holds the idea that
if she hadn't so readily fallen in with your talk that "fatal" night about
marriage, she could have—shall I say—kept you "interested." . . . She
set me wondering . . . what your attitude would be now had she, that
night, set you down gently . . . as one she was not so damn sure of.

As it turned out, Eva was unwittingly but effectively working the hard-to-
get strategy on Thurber, as Kate did not, to her sorrow.

Minnette had returned from spring vacation, and Thurber used her in an
attempt to make Eva jealous: "I had Minnette home for lunch and it was the
first time she was ever here," he writes to Eva dishonestly. Minnette, still the
Thurbers' favorite of all his girls, had been an occasional visitor to their home
since 1918, with and without Thurber. And again, trying the you'll-miss-me-
when-I'm-gone approach: "I intend to come to say good-bye before I depart
to work hard far away from Yarrow,—which is Zanesville. . . . I hope I am
happier this time next year than I am now. . . . The thing which gives a
man most content and comfort is his work, and success in it and growth of it,
and a hold on the future."

He was cheered when she accommodated his schedule by breaking a date
with Ernest. "I am glad that Ernest was merciful about his date," Thurber
wrote her, "and really he seems to be either getting resigned to it or to be
growing older (or perhaps not)."

"Perhaps not" was correct. Thurber's emotional advances to Eva had challenged Ernest to make his own move, especially when, in early summer, Eva
seemed to be leaning toward "Jeems," her pet name for Thurber.

"One Sunday when [Jim] was down to Zanesville, we became engaged in a
way," says Prout, "not officially. I remember the very spot where we talked it
over. We had walked across the golf course—we lived very close to it—and
. . . stopped under beautiful big trees. He asked me if I would . . . wear his
[fraternity] pin. He had sent it to me [from Paris] but I had never worn
it. . . . I never did [but] kept the pin until after we broke up . . . in late
1920. . . . I think I really was in love with Jim [for a time]." But she realized
that Thurber's future was in writing, that hers was in the theater, and that "I
might hold him back; that I just wasn't for him."

Meanwhile, Ernest Geiger, who danced and played "a very good piano in
the style of Eddie Duchin," says Prout, was making a rebound. A distraught
Thurber writes to Nugent on June 9:

Three weeks ago Eve wrote me a letter which hurt bad. I tore it up, even. The gist was that she likes Ernest muchly and that there was just One man [never identified] who could have made her forget him and she never saw him again. She said she "probably will end by loving the wrong man." . . . I went up two days after her letter. . . . We fought a bit,—rather I "bawled her out." . . . She held firmly to not letting me come over on Sundays, since Ernest was given a standing Sunday date.

Minnette, about to leave for Chicago at school's end, consoled him, which made him realize that "the old interest [in Eva] is a bit dimmed," he writes Nugent, "and the old dreams a bit bruised." It was Minnette—he now realizes, too late—who was "enough of the Sweetheart of Dreams, after all, and much more than anyone else can ever be to me of a sweet, helpful, inspiring, sympathetic wifely type. The most contented marriage in all history failed when Minnette and I missed out. . . . Write for me when I am dead, 'Here lies one who died of dreams.' " But Thurber was to live and prosper from them, too.

It had been months since his return from Paris, and Mame was seriously worried about her second son, his run-down condition, and his inability to get going on a career. She felt Eva was a primary cause for both situations, and when Thurber was out of town she took the streetcar to Zanesville to have it out with her.

"She tried to persuade me that I had done the wrong thing [in turning down Thurber]," Eva said. "She got in somewhat of a temper because I [still] felt it was for the best."

Eva may be putting a better face on things here than is warranted; neither Mame nor Charles favored Thurber's involvement with her. Mame's scolding of Eva was less likely over Eva's spurning of Thurber than over Eva's inability or unwillingness to put a definite end to the affair and get out of her son's life. In 1929, Mame was writing to Minnette, by then a Seattle housewife with children, to tell her about Thurber's separation that year from Althea, his first wife. Thurber had resumed writing to Eva, and Mame worries that they might yet end up together:

"I do hope Jamie will not make another mistake. . . . Eva has left her husband [Ernest] and has gone home to her mother in Cincinnati—but she would never be the one for Jim Thurber—never! . . . I am so afraid Eva will hang on to him. . . . She seems very fond of Jim—but you know she would *never* be the one for him. Why there isn't anything on earth to her." As far as

Mame was concerned, it was still childish puppy love on the part of her thirty-five-year-old son. She may have been right.

Elliott Nugent stopped by the Thurbers shortly before he left for New York. Thurber was not home, and Mame unloaded on Nugent all her worries about her son. Nugent wrote a concerned letter to Thurber, who replied: "Not at all as de profundis as Madame Thurber's apprehensions led you to fear . . . this thing which she would have as blighting my life."

He had been given new hope in August that things would work out with Eva. Eva's mother favored the older, personable, entertaining Thurber over Ernest and invited him to Zanesville to visit her when Eva was again in New York. Jubilantly, Thurber passed on to Nugent what Eva's mother had told him. He calls it

> an adventure . . . pregnant with material for the short story of my life. . . . It appears that Ernest, my young, admittedly good-looking, but lead-headed rival, him with the dancing and singing ability whom Eva became interested in solely at first because he seemed "material" for the stage and worth while exploring, got her infatuated with himself, god knows how, after all. Last Wednesday he culminated a week of objection to her going to N.Y. by calling her thrice on the phone and making dire but unknown threats. Eva's first reaction was to tell him she was disgusted with him, refused to let him come out, and told her surprised mother that he was a "fool kid" or something. That was after his first call. His next one made her still more outraged at him, but his third call left her hysterical for the long balance of the day.

Earlier in the week, according to Eva's mother, Eva and Ernest had returned from a date to find Thurber's "last appeal" letter waiting for her. Ernest insisted that she say "No," but she wouldn't. She had written a reply to Thurber that he could only believe was an acceptance. The letter went mysteriously astray. Eva's mother, who had been divorced and remarried, had given it to Eva's stepfather, who may have failed to mail it. Thurber believed the letter was intercepted by his family.

He brings up the matter in a letter to Robert thirty-three years later:

"I found out from Mamma many years ago, that a certain letter had been withheld from me. . . . This was actually depriving me of a part of my own life and if it turned out well it was surely without my knowledge or help [from the family]."

There is no indication, in any case, that the letter was the one Thurber hoped for. Eva Prout told an interviewer toward the end of her life that she had always thought it best that she not marry Thurber, and still did. Decisions in such matters appeared to come hard for Eva; she did marry Ernest Geiger, but not until April 30, 1924, when she was nearly thirty, and two years after Thurber married his first wife. Perhaps she did consider Geiger too immature for marriage and waited until he had grown up a bit.

The Geigers eventually went into show business together, Ernest performing as Eva's piano accompanist. In 1928, Thurber, by then with the *New Yorker*, read that they were playing in New York and looked them up. He and his first wife, Althea, were estranged, and Thurber was a lonely man.

"We were staying at the Flanders Hotel on Forty-seventh Street," Eva remembered, "and at night [Jim] would be in the lobby when we would get home from the theater. We'd all go up to the room and listen through the open window to the merrymaking on the street outside, as all the theatergoers were leaving the theaters. Jim and Ernest would go up to a little speakeasy they called the Green Door. It was still Prohibition. Both men evidently liked gin pretty well and then they'd go across the street to a delicatessen and get delicious sandwiches and bring them back to the hotel for our midnight snack. We'd sit there and talk, the three of us. And many a night I would get so tired that I would just curl up on the bed and go fast asleep and Jim and Ernest would sit there talking to the wee small hours of the morning, possibly four or five o'clock. My husband would awaken me and say, 'Come on, Eve, waken, because Jim is going,' and the trashmen would be rattling the cans out on the street.

"We had a portable phonograph and Jim liked to hear our records. We had Gershwin's *Rhapsody in Blue* that Jim especially liked, and 'What a Day Was Yesterday, for Yesterday Gave Me You.' We loved to play music when we came home at night. The hotel didn't allow us to make much noise at that hour of the morning, so my husband would stuff towels in the speaker. Althea was in France the four to six weeks we were there, so the three of us got together just about every night."

The Geigers left for an engagement in Toronto, and Thurber immediately wrote up his sentimental encounter with his old Sweetheart Wraith in "Menaces in May," published just weeks later, in May 1928. It was his first serious story to appear in the *New Yorker*. (Harold Ross, fearful of losing one of his premier humorists, objected to Thurber's "going grim" or getting the idea he was a "serious" writer, but E. B. White enlisted Katharine Angell's help in persuading Ross to publish it.)

"Menaces in May" contains more than the nostalgic Thurber Man spending an evening with a former love and her husband; he feels menaced not only by his inability to find lasting emotional fulfillment but by the primitive threats of everyday urban life, in which death can strike suddenly and indiscriminately. Eva, years later, pronounced the story an accurate summary of their evenings together at the Flanders:

> The man standing at a window on the fifth floor of the Belgium [Flanders] . . . watches the vaudeville people coming out of the Somerset. . . .
> The sound of a quartet singing on a phonograph record, "Dear, on a Night Like This," comes from the room the man is in, and he turns away from the window. . . . Joe, the man notices, has become a little fat and his hair is thinning. Julia is exactly the same as eighteen years ago. . . . Once they had all been in an Ohio grammar school together. . . . "What a day was yes-ter-day for yes-ter-day gave me you-u-u."

If Mame was correct about the Geigers being separated in 1929, the year after they saw Thurber in New York, they were definitely together again in 1935, when Thurber unexpectedly stopped by their house in Zanesville, on his way from New York to Columbus. It was on the eve of his marriage to Helen Wismer, and he was in a confused and highly dramatic state of mind. He stayed only an hour, Eva remembers. It was the last time she saw him. By then, the Geigers had retired from show business, and two years later they moved to Miami, where they managed a music store. Before moving, Eva selected several "special" Thurber letters from her huge collection to take with her. She stored the rest in the basement of a friend in Cincinnati until she could send for them, along with pieces of antique furniture "and other very precious things that I didn't want to lose." But a pipe burst in the basement and the letters were destroyed in the flood.

For the next few years, Thurber sent her Christmas cards, including the famous one that features the disorganized Thurber dogs pulling Santa's sleigh. On it he had written: "I am sorry for so long a silence and at not having seen you two for so many years. Four to be exact." It was the last she received. She wrote to him in late 1946, once again in care of his family in Columbus, not knowing his address. Her letter wasn't immediately forwarded, but Robert informed Thurber about it, who at once wrote Robert from the Homestead, in Hot Springs, Virginia: "Be sure and send me Eva's letter as I want to write her." But he seems not to have written.

In 1973, Eva, nearly eighty years old and living in Coral Gables, Florida, sorted through the "special" letters she had saved and proudly showed an interviewer the poems Thurber had written his Sweetheart Wraith fifty-three years before.

"Jim was much more romantic than the man I married," she said, with a note of regret. She then read aloud Thurber's inscription in a copy of *Is Sex Necessary?*, which he had sent her in 1929: "For Eve, who didn't get into this book, not because I didn't think of her but because I thought too much of her. Jim Thurber."

And she agreed with her interviewer: "He always expressed things so beautifully."

21

Those Memoirs of a Drudge

I worked on the Columbus *Evening Dispatch*, a fat and amiable newspaper, whose city editor seldom knew where I was and got so that he didn't care. He had a glimpse of me every day at 9 A.M., arriving at the office, and promptly at ten he saw me leave it, a sheaf of folded copy paper in my pocket and a look of enterprise in my eye. I was on my way to Marzetti's, a comfortable restaurant just down the street, where a group of us newspapermen met every morning. We would sit around for an hour, drinking coffee, telling stories, drawing pictures on the table-cloth, and giving imitations of the more eminent Ohio political figures of the day. . . .

[Afterward] I would stroll out to the Carnegie Library and read the

New York *World* in the periodical room. . . . Only a little fragment of forenoon remained in which to gather the news, but I somehow managed the aggravating chore.

—from "Memoirs of a Drudge"

Well into the summer of 1920, Thurber remained at home, unemployed, nursing vague daydreams of a freelance writing career. In April he had rented a typewriter for a month and purchased stationery with a "James Grover Thurber" letterhead, but he used them mostly to write to Eva Prout and Elliott Nugent. Thurber also hoped to follow Nugent into the theater, as a writer if not an actor. His interest in dramatics seems to have been kindled two years before, when Nugent persuaded Thurber to join him onstage in Arnold Bennett's one-act farce *A Question of Sex,* produced by the Strollers, the student dramatic society.

Bertha (Buffie) Austin, a 1918 member of Strollers, remembers Thurber's first appearance as an actor. The Bennett play deals with a newborn baby girl whose father [Nugent] and his sister and sister-in-law are all trying to hide her sex from the father's wealthy uncle [Thurber], because his estate is to be left only to a male heir.

"The war was on, and in the middle of rehearsing for the play, our director was called to Washington," Austin recalls. "Jim arranged for his former English teacher at East High to act as substitute director. In introducing her to us, Jim assumed the character of the blustery uncle and said something like 'This dear lady has spent the whole day teaching before coming here to help us. The least we can do is learn our lines, listen to her, and follow her directions. Horsing around before and after rehearsal is fine, but when she says "Let the play begin," she means it!' "

Now, hoping to become active again in Strollers, Thurber visited the O.S.U. campus and discovered, to his instant fascination, that a men's musical organization called the Scarlet Mask Club had been formed. Its shows were patterned after those staged by such Ivy League male student groups as the Princeton Triangle, Mask and Wig, and Hasty Pudding. Its origin was "a one-act piece of nonsense called *Oh Splash,* put on by the men's glee club," says Ralph McCombs, a seventy-five-dollar-per-month student instructor at the time, who was the show's playwright, director, and one of its actors. *Oh Splash* made fun of Prohibition, which had just arrived, and the show "was immensely popular, to the grave disapproval of the dignified director of the glee club, who would thereafter have no more of us," says McCombs. "So in 1920 I became one of the five founding fathers of the Scarlet Mask, and did, practically single-handed, the first show, *'Tain't So*. Jamie was vastly taken by [it] and the whole farcical-extravaganza idea upon which Scarlet Mask was based. When, the next year, I went forth into the world to seek my fortune (didn't find it) he became playwright-inordinary to the club."

"McCombs' musical play ' 'Taint So' . . . was very good," Thurber writes Nugent in April. "His situations and plot were well done, his lines were poor, the music was fine, there were one or two clever scenes and one or two good musical-comedians." Thurber was, in another word, "hooked"; as a respected alumnus, he would involve himself in Scarlet Mask productions for the next four years, and in playwriting forever.

Thurber laid out for Nugent his freelance writing agenda, confiding for the first time his mental telepathy experiences:

> Some of the things . . . I am working on are: a book for next year's Scarlet [Mask]; an original sort of [Henry James's] Washington Square thing called "The Fourth Mrs. Bluebeard"—the other wife who gypped [him] but who was never written about—she beat him by modern feminine craft. "The Call" which is powerful in my mind, but which will no doubt fail,—a Henry James sort of thing with another special trick of mine as the basis, namely a gift I have at long but awfully vivid intervals of receiving mental telepathy messages from friends or family in trouble. Don't believe I ever told you that trick. It has really worked but five times in my life, one of which I will never tell but which is the most beautiful and complicated of all—and which, damn it, is the basis for my story, so I guess I'll have to do it under a nom de plume. Oddly enough, two of the five instances happened here since I returned, and one of them had nothing to do with trouble at all, it was just a freak working. My mother has had the same thing several times. Then I am working on a comedy about a French wife with a new twist—(. . . the story has the twist) an article along the line of "France and America, Last and First Impressions," which no American magazine would print, probably, since my status is about 67 to 33 favor France. And there are minor poems and things.

But he was soon driven to apply for gainful employment, as well. His old *Sun-Dial* colleagues Carson Blair and Maurice Mullay were both in corporate advertising in Detroit and urged Thurber to join them. "Jim told us he would," says Blair, "so Mullie and I and another associate rented a four-

bedroom apartment in anticipation of Jim's arrival. He never showed up."
Later, Blair and a partner started their own Detroit advertising agency, and
this time Blair dangled a tempting salary to lure Thurber away from the
Dispatch. Thurber's response was an agonizingly slow "no," one that again
kept Blair thinking he had bagged Thurber. (Blair continued to believe that
Thurber, with his lively imagination and penchant for linguistic gimmickry,
would have made it big in advertising.)

Thurber applied to a company called Magnetic Springs, and to the Goodrich Tire Company, in Akron, for a job in their advertising or public-relations
departments. He was invited back by Goodrich for a second interview, but
toward the end of June told Nugent that he had found out "finally that the
loss of the old left eye was a barrier." (This may have been a face-saver
offered the successful Nugent.) The turn-downs could only have meant further humiliation that, coupled with his losing fight for Eva's hand, kept him
despondent and ailing. He began to think of returning to "State" that fall—a
respectable place to hide from his failures. Or there was his "pet Ohio syndicate idea" of writing news articles for syndication—his father promised to
help arrange for their distribution and to solicit customers for his son—"but
I'm uncertain of the next move as yet," he tells Nugent, "even uncertain as
to returning to State, altho' I believe I will."

Though his parents indulged him, Thurber adds, home was a detriment to
his plans; his family had never really understood him, for one thing, he says,
though "they sympathize and have been wonderfully helpful in many ways."
He kept himself in carfare to Zanesville with odd jobs, clerking briefly at the
State Department of Agriculture and taking tickets at the State Fair.

Mame had reason to worry about his health. "I should use about six
months out of doors in some fine climate," he writes to Nugent on August 9.

> I am convinced that for a time I was so low physically and all the way
> from desiretude, flatulant ennui and God damn head over tailism [over
> Eva], that my reasons was akin to movie cogitation. But I have got a hell
> of a lot to worry about, and I'm one efficient worryer. . . . But, cheers,
> me lad, I've given over funk and folly and fol-de-rol about people, girls
> especially, in fact with the accent on women. My mind is getting single-
> tracked for health, success and money.

It did help matters when he finally decided that if he couldn't have Eva to
himself he would withdraw from the competition, even though, as with so
many past relationships, he would think of her frequently. ("I still know the
phone number of a girl who gave me the go-by in 1920," he wrote twelve

years later, in "The Civil War Phone-Number Association," "and now and then, as the years roll away, it flicks around the back of my head annoyingly, like a deer fly, upsetting my day.")

He thanks Nugent for helping him see the humor in his obsession with Eva and Minnette: "Your summary of my crazy insanity about both girls is so true it is refreshing. And it makes me giggle at myself, which widens all breaches and lessens much interest."

In August he applied for a reporting job at the *Columbus Evening Dispatch.* Karl Finn, Thurber's classmate and former rival for the affections of Minnette, had been the *Dispatch*'s student sports correspondent at O.S.U. and now was on the staff. The city editor, Norman (Gus) Kuehner, who would normally have handled Thurber's application, was on vacation; the managing editor, Charles (Heinie) Reiker, asked Finn about Thurber. Finn said he considered Thurber a kind of genius, though he couldn't be sure Thurber would become a good reporter. "But I urged him to give Jim a try," Finn recalls. "Reiker was hardheaded but a friend of mine, and he agreed to do it."

The *Dispatch* was the city's evening paper; its rivals were the *Ohio State Journal,* edited by Thurber's hero, Robert O. Ryder, and the *Columbus Citizen.* The Wolfe brothers, Robert and Harry, owned both the *Dispatch,* the strongest of the three papers, and the *Journal.* These, taken in conjunction with their wealth and other local properties, gave the Wolfes a sizable stake in the political, economic, and communications life of Columbus.

Thurber was hired at twenty-five dollars a week. It was a career milestone: at age twenty-five, for the first time he was being paid for what he wrote. His apprenticeship under the city editor was a rough one. Gus ("Dutch" to a few) Kuehner was of the fading breed of self-made editors who felt the need to exhibit their power and cloak their envy and self-doubt in cynicism, insult, and badgering—especially toward "colletch" graduates of "choinalism" schools. Thurber includes Kuehner in *The Thurber Album* as one of those important to his career development. One wonders why—for, despite his forgiving nature and the time-mellowed interval, Thurber, some twenty-five years later, is unable to show Kuehner as anything but another barrier to his anemic flow of personal confidence.

The son and grandson of German cigar makers, Kuehner broke with family tradition to become a newspaperman. He delivered the *Dispatch* door-to-door while in grade school and joined the newspaper as a copy boy at age fourteen, leaving school after the eighth grade. He wore a perpetual frown even as a youngster, and an editor nicknamed him "Gus" after the dour comic-strip character, Gloomy Gus, Happy Hooligan's brother. It stuck, and Kuehner, in turn, nicknamed—usually disdainfully—his newspaper subordinates: an ex-

Army lieutenant became "Loot"; a former farm boy, "Farmer"; George Smallsreed (eventually the editor-in-chief), a tall thin youth with a bespectacled studious face, was "Parson." ("I reminded him of a clergyman," explains Smallsreed.) All college hires were "Phi Beta Kappa" until Kuehner could find a more apt designation. When Kuehner learned that Thurber was writing the libretto for a Scarlet Mask production, he dropped "Phi Beta Kappa" to call him "Author," and, Thurber writes, "kept it up as long as I knew him." Those who didn't quit under Kuehner's harassment, and even managed to like him, chose to detect no derision or insult in the labels, or in his refusal to use their surnames. "Kuehner always called me 'Jew-Nigger' as a mark of affection," writes Karl Finn loyally and cryptically, "because I was always so tanned."

Kuehner harassed the new, put down the educated, tormented the gullible, and repaid courtesy with rudeness. Asked the time of day, he would snap, "Get a watch." He baited a rewrite man until the frenzied victim tried to stab him with a desk spindle. Kuehner knocked him out. He lamented the paper's policy of hiring college graduates, especially women, whom he called "slob sisters." Once when a woman reporter was at her desk, legs crossed, one shoe dangling from a foot, Kuehner snatched the shoe and threw it out a window. It fell through a sidewalk grating into a sub-basement. She was left to retrieve it with great difficulty, wearing only one shoe, and when she told Kuehner where it had gone, he said, "Good shot," without looking up from his desk.

As a former police reporter, he never got over his fondness for violent crime. He once took Smallsreed with him to the city morgue for the single purpose of enjoying the cub reporter's revulsion as they viewed a murder victim; a hole in the skull, made by a large-caliber bullet, had allowed the brain matter to drain out, Smallsreed says. Standing there, Kuehner said in feigned innocence, "What do you say we go get a hamburger?" " 'We' didn't," Smallsreed writes.

"Kuehner was merely hard-boiled, but his boss, Reiker, was sadistic," says James Pollard, an O.S.U. journalism professor who had reported for the *Journal* in Thurber's newspaper days. "None of us thought we'd like to work on the *Dispatch* then, and Thurber must have been able to absorb a lot of punishment to last nearly four years."

Thurber got off to a bad start the first day Kuehner was back from vacation. "When he spotted me . . . sitting at a desk in a corner," writes Thurber, "his eyes darkened, and he sauntered slowly over to me with the gait of a traffic cop approaching an incompetent and unattractive woman driver. He stood behind my chair for several moments, not saying anything. I said, 'Good morning,' and he still didn't say anything. I had been rewriting some brief items from the *Lantern* . . . and when he saw what they were, he swept them onto the floor with one swipe of his big hand, growled 'This isn't a college paper,' and strolled away. . . . He let me sit at my desk the rest of the day doing nothing."

Smallsreed, a few years younger than Thurber, had been the *Dispatch's* campus correspondent at nearby Capital University, and, after his graduation in 1919, went on the payroll a year before Thurber arrived. "I was on the rewrite desk by then," Smallsreed recalls. "As the man who often rewrote Thurber, it isn't surprising that I wasn't a close friend of his in the early years. Not that Jim showed outward resentment; it wasn't in him to in those days. He was a meticulous writer and liked to turn in colorful feature stories. Kuehner didn't like them. He'd begin reading one, stand up slowly, rip it in two, say, 'I don't like this stuff,' and drop it into the wastebasket. Thurber would look like a beaten dog. I can see him now, pulling on his hair, but bent over his typewriter undaunted. After six weeks on the job, Kuehner became less oppressive to Thurber and things got better for him."

But Thurber and Kuehner were never close. Though his anecdotal treatment of Kuehner in the 1952 *Thurber Album* was bracketed in claims of personal fondness, former colleagues of Kuehner recognized the piece as weighted on the side of Kuehner's disagreeableness. "But didn't you find," asked one former *Dispatch* hand of Thurber, "that underneath that crustiness, much of which must have been a continuous act, was a wonderful layer of kindness and humaneness? You touched upon it in the description of his home life." "I never saw his rough side," another Kuehner associate wrote in a rebuke to Thurber. And a lady reporter who preceded Thurber at the *Dispatch* protested that "he was always gentle and sweet to me."

Thurber was simply not Kuehner's kind of man. After his initiation period, Thurber kidded around at the office and found a great deal to laugh about in his work, and any boss feels threatened by an employee who makes light of his assignments. "Jim had a desk in the corner of the city room," Smallsreed says. "I remember how, whenever he came in, there was always a crowd around it. He had a great outgoing sense of humor and people loved to hear him talk about what he had just been up to. He always gave them their money's worth.

"He was sensitive, keen, and he wrote elegantly, but he wasn't appreciated by either the city or managing editor; they liked their news straight, with no trimmings. Thurber simply wasn't cut out for newspaper work. He wasn't brash enough, if that's the word."

That word will do. Nelson Budd, a former Columbus newspaperman, writes:

There was a period when . . . Thurber and I were . . . on rival newspapers [and] found ourselves on the same . . . murder case. We had the cruel and disagreeable task of obtaining a picture of the victim from the shocked and bereaved family, within a scant hour or two after the tragedy. With Jim was a member of his business staff, there only for reasons of his own morbidity, but relentlessly and callously pressing [the family for the picture]. Jim was outspoken in his abhorrence of his companion's tactics and behavior. He was just as outraged over the State House employee who boasted that he hadn't missed an electrocution at the Penitentiary in the last 15 years [though] he had no official reason for being present. . . . Despite Jim's later assertions that 'I'm a damned good reporter,' he was really too humane, too creative, too big to be a good reporter in the strictest sense.

"Jim did have one advantage over the other reporters," Smallsreed adds. "Things are always getting lost around a newspaper office and quite a few reporters made carbon copies of their stories just in case. Jim never did. He didn't have to. He could reconstruct a story verbatim if the first one got lost. He used to tell us proudly that he never took notes when on assignment; his memory for details seldom if ever failed him. He couldn't stand the slightest typographical error in the story he was writing; couldn't turn in a page with a crossed-out word. He'd make a typing error and begin again, no matter how far down the page he'd gone. When we were fighting a deadline this would drive us crazy. He was not only meticulous, he was studious and an excellent researcher and craftsman; just not much of a reporter in the newspaper tradition.

"Kuehner seemed to make a point of keeping Thurber's talent under his thumb. Of course, he didn't see it as talent. But it was Kuehner who kept Thurber from getting a real break on the *Dispatch* for a long time. He thought all college people interested in writing would be better off if they had been developed under the tutelage of a good old-fashioned editor. He considered journalism professors only failed newspapermen. We know that enterprise emerges only if it's encouraged. Not many of those under Kuehner got that encouragement. Certainly Jim didn't thrive under the browbeating."

As negative as Kuehner supporters found Thurber's profile of their old colleague, we now know that Thurber pulled many of his punches out of generous consideration for Kuehner's survivors—two sons and two sisters. "In 1936 [Kuehner] gave up his job suddenly for reasons that have never been clear to me," Thurber pretends in the *Album*. But nothing could have been clearer to Thurber; while he had plenty of time to make changes in his *Album* manuscript, he received a letter from Smallsreed giving the precise reasons Kuehner "resigned" his *Dispatch* position: Kuehner had risen to the rank of managing editor in the 1930s, long after Thurber departed the paper, but had become a heavy drinker and would disappear for days on end. The Wolfe family was kind to him because of the twenty-eight good years he had given the paper, Smallsreed writes. In January of 1936, he was offered a year's leave with a paid-for trip around the world. Kuehner refused, promised to reform, and asked for another chance. He performed well for another month, then went on a binge that lasted for several days. When the editor-in-chief asked him where he had been, Kuehner, either wickedly hung over or still drunk, replied with obscenities and was fired. (Smallsreed was promoted to take his place.)

Kuehner worked on the 1936 Alf Landon presidential-campaign staff in Chicago, and then for the Unemployment Compensation Commission in Columbus, a job he hated. In 1938, he wrote to Thurber at the *New Yorker,* citing a half-dozen former Columbus newsmen who had migrated to New York, and asked Thurber to "contact them and tell them I got to have a job. I'll do anything from turning a lathe to trimming ladies' hats." But it was still the Great Depression, and jobs were hard to find. With World War II's military build-up, Kuehner was hired by the Curtiss-Wright Corporation in Columbus, working on the midnight-to-eight shift in aircraft production. He died in his apartment of a heart attack in 1943 at age fifty. The heart that finally failed him had never left the newspaper business. Four months before his death, he had written in his last letter, to a sister, that he still had high hopes of going back to the *Dispatch.*

At the start of 1921, Thurber was assigned a regular beat: the city's council meetings. "Five days after I was put on City Hall," he writes to Nugent,

> I attended my second council session at 7 P.M. Wed. Jan. 12. At 8 P.M. the building burned . . . down. I remained in the ol' hall ten minutes after the councilmen and prominent city officials and local residents attending the session had beat it. . . . I was the last person out of the now swiftly burning joint. . . . When I came [downstairs] the council room doors had been shut and fastened to prevent drafts. My coat and hat were inside, so I bust 'em open.

Looking for something to save, Thurber picked up "three huge blue prints which were being used in street car extension discussions, and two letters to council from railway presidents. . . . Got said apparel and the letters and blue-prints, and made an easy escape although . . . within half an hour the interior was a furnace."

Outside, the city was aroused and all telephones were busy. Thurber hurried to the empty *Dispatch* offices, turned on the lights, and was soon joined by the telegraph editor, who "said he guessed we could do nothing" but yield the story to the morning papers, "whereupon I said nuts I got th' story, so he said write it, and I did . . . we shot out an extra, beating the . . . Citizen and Journal. We got on the street at 9:30, an hour and a half after the fire alarm and one hour after I wrote the story. I was complimented by both Editor in chief and managing editor . . . and all in all it was a gala night for James. I am now drawing 35 per week. I started at 25. Bin here six months."

In his later versions of the story, it was somebody else's coat—and a watch —that Thurber rescued. The "extra" edition could not be found among the *Dispatch*'s back issues but a full account was in the next day's regular noon edition. It lacked a byline but bore the Thurber touch: "The . . . structure burned like so much paper, and the fire at its height cast fanciful shadows against the [overcast] sky." By then he had learned that the blueprints and letters he rescued were safely duplicated elsewhere, something Kuehner kidded him about for weeks. The building, as it turned out, was only partially gutted, and in Thurber's news story he notes that "very few records were destroyed."

H. E. (Cherry) Cherrington, the *Dispatch*'s drama critic, had become a good friend of Thurber's, sympathized with his literary ambitions, and sponsored his contributions to the "Observations" column on the editorial page. These included humorous verse, "overheard" items of local gossip, and one-liners in the Ryder tradition. Cherrington also permitted Thurber to assist him in reviewing plays, movies, and books for the Sunday edition. Thurber received no extra pay for these pieces.

In March he was sent to Springfield, Ohio, to cover the putting down of a race riot. The 1921 economic recession was at its worst, and "floating, unemployed Negroes" had migrated from the South looking for work, their desperate condition creating tension in Springfield's black community. There had been a rape; "a [teenage] negro" had shot and wounded a policeman; a gun battle had broken out; a young black was wounded; troops were called in. Thurber interviewed the mayor, the chief of police, the military commander, and other officials and filed about three thousand words, which the *Dispatch* ran in two installments. Thurber was given a byline.

Typically, he visualized the near-tragic event as potential dramatic material, writing Nugent:

My most enthusiastic, ambitious and best effort now . . . is a one act play in two scenes, called "Riot"—and dealing with race-troubles. . . . No paper would carry it unless the revered but irreverent [*Smart Set*] took it on. I got the idea during my special assignment a week ago in Springfield where for three days I kept the wires hot with stories on the race-rioting there. . . . I was hauled out of bed at 12:25 and machined to Springfield towards dawn. I went 44 hours without sleep, but I beat the A P to the Saturday afternoon lead, shot in pictures in time for our noon edition even and generally had a great experience. My stories were spread all over the front page and the old name was set up in 12 point black-face directly under the head and over the stories.

But Nugent, as usual, was ahead of Thurber in their literary rivalry, having sold a short story to H. L. Mencken's and George Jean Nathan's *Smart Set* for forty dollars. The two popular editor/writers were the arbiters of American culture at the time, and their magazine was the toast of the younger generation. "So you beat me to the first sale after all?" writes Thurber. "Well, lay on, McNugent, and poverty-stricken be he who first shouts 'back to plumbing.' "

Thurber and an O.S.U. junior, Hayward Anderson, had coauthored the book for a Scarlet Mask musical, *Oh My, Omar!*. Through an H. G. Wells kind of time machine, Omar Khayyám finds himself at a college house party in 1921. Promoted by O.S.U. alumni chapters, the show played during the 1920–1921 winter season in Columbus and toured seven or eight other Ohio cities. (Thurber's work with Scarlet Mask over four years—either as librettist, director, lyricist, or substitute actor—paid him between three hundred and four hundred dollars a show, depending on box-office receipts and his negotiating skills.)

No longer the *Lantern* student editor eating a late-night sandwich at Marzetti's and listening with envy to the talk of the professional journalists near him, Thurber had become the hero of the late-morning hour there, when local reporters from all three newspapers met for coffee, cigarettes, and talk. Nelson Budd remembers that Thurber's "best stories . . . were not the ones . . . printed in the *Dispatch*" but his hilarious "versions of city-council meetings, or fires, or interviews [which] he shared with the group at Marzetti's."

Ray Lee Jackson, who had handled the costumes and sets for *Oh My, Omar!*, was co-owner of a photographer's studio in downtown Columbus that became a kind of salon for those associated with Mask and Strollers, including certain young faculty members and local journalists with an interest in the visual and performing arts. Thurber began to spend more and more time at the studio, where tea and pastry were served along with literary discussions of both a serious and frivolous nature. (Kuehner heard about the tea sessions and never forgot; years later, on a trip to New York, he telephoned Thurber at the *New Yorker* to ask caustically, "Where do you get your ladyfingers now, Author?")

Beginning in January 1921, Thurber's light verse and commentary begins to appear on the "opposite editorial" page of the *Dispatch*. It includes a lament over the disappearance of the early silent movies, and of his favorite film comedian, Maurice Costello. Here is a part of it:

Ballade of Missing Movies

What has become of the first movie men
 And the tricks of the first movie days,
Shall we never see our lost idols again
 With their flickering, gesturing ways?
And what of the comedy known as the "chase"
 With houses that tumble and ladders that fall—
And where in the midst of the Past's dimming haze
 Is Maurice Costello, the "King of Them All"? . . .

Folks, they are one with Decembers and Mays
 That are lost in Time's ever-echoing hall,
And somewhere above them, encircled with bays,
 Is Maurice Costello, the "King of Them All."

Temporary government offices had been set up on the second floor of the public library while a new City Hall was under construction. This put the library reading room on Thurber's official beat. He browsed each day through the nationally popular op-ed columns of the *New York World* and those of other out-of-town paragraphers, and through the monthly literary magazines then in vogue, such as the *Smart Set*, *Scribner's*, and the *Century*. His immediate goal was to follow Cherrington as a regular newspaper critic of plays and books, while freelancing in his spare time. He laid out his career plan beyond that in one of his headlong letters to Nugent, January 22, 1921:

I expect to stick with the Dispatch for two years [and] shall have tried my hand at every angle of reporting. . . . In my plethora of off hours, —comprising almost every afternoon and evening I am going to concentrate on free lancing. . . . I want at least to land three or four stories in two years . . .

After leaving the Dispatch I expect to line up a few Ohio papers for a weekly Sunday article, including the revered Dispatch; several trade journals for monthly articles; a paper in some eastern city for a weekly dramatic story; a semicontact with some movie magazine and a few other kinds of publications. . . . Then I hies me onto Paris . . . whence I shall ship many a glowing story of affairs European, French, English and etc.

Free lancing over there is soft,—few newspapermen in peace time go into it—few want to—fewer can—fewer yet know anything about it— and me, well, I gotta big drag with Embassy and other officials there, know the ropes and should get over big. In the interim between contracted for stories, I shall write many hits of inconsequent verse, short stories and my great American novel, of course.

He broke into the Sunday edition with a wordy review of Paris theater, rehashed from New York newspaper theater sections and trade publications. His labored lead: "Paris, where the writer tarried long enough after the late applauded armistice to observe things theatrical begin to unlimber their legs after four years of Rip Van Winkling, has now regained the old-time use of them and from the 'petitest' revue to the grand opera the joie de vivre of pre-war days is to be observed again, if one may take the word for it of various Paris correspondents of Eastern papers and dramatic periodicals." He didn't yet write comfortably and, even allowing for errors by the typesetters, one easily imagines Kuehner's disdain for Thurber's Sunday features.

His assignments didn't always work out. His editor gave him one question —Thurber doesn't say what—about a current local situation to ask the American war ace, Eddie Rickenbacker. Thurber waited for the Columbus hero to land at the local airport and asked the question, which required a studied answer. All Rickenbacker said was, "I don't think so," and walked away, leaving Thurber to wonder if it was a response to the question or if Rickenbacker meant he didn't think he would answer it.

"My shortest interview on the phone," says Thurber, "was with Harry M. Daugherty, then President Harding's attorney general [whom Grandpa Fisher, who couldn't keep names straight, had always addressed as "Mr. Dorothy" when they met on the streets of Columbus]. I asked him some question or other and he said, 'Go to hell' and hung up."

Several of Thurber's anecdotal paragraphs in the *Dispatch*'s Observations column are similar in tone and format to those the *New Yorker* would sandwich between its Talk of the Town stories during its first thirty-five years or so. Elsewhere, he uses the editorial "we," another device he would find familiar when writing for the *New Yorker*'s front-of-the-book section.

In a Sunday feature, he berates "money-grubbing" movie makers for buying good plays and books, changing the plots, and exhibiting them with sensational box-office titles. "Along comes Conrad's marvelously appropriate title, 'Victory,' with all its subtle and touching irony and it is emasculated into 'Love's Victory!' The excuse was that many would think 'Victory' a war film. . . . F. Scott Fitzgerald's clever 'Head and Shoulders' was metamorphosed by the thick heads of the film men into 'A Chorus Girl's Romance!' How weak, forsooth, is even the blackest exclamation mark."

In "Memoirs of a Drudge" he claims the City Hall beat was not that dull: that it was where he was taught to blow a tuba by a city employee bandsman, and where the dance-hall inspector told him of "the more dubious clubs about town," in which "the boys and girls contrived to two-step without moving their feet." "The Mayor's office was frequently besieged" by addle-pated characters: the man who claimed he was receiving a local radio station on his dental bridgework; "a woman who was warned of approaching earthquakes by a sharp twinge in her left side, and a lady to whom it had been revealed in a vision that the new O'Shaughnessy storage dam had not been constructed of concrete but of Cream of Wheat." (Five years later, in "Newspaperman—Head and Shoulders," Thurber recycles one of the characters: the woman who could foretell earthquakes through "a sharp twinge" could now predict them "by means of griping pains in her intestines"; but this time she turns up at the *Dispatch*, driving Gus Kuehner to hide in the men's room.)

One habitué of the Marzetti and studio gatherings was John McNulty, who reported for the *Ohio State Journal* and shared Thurber's propensities for mad-cap social antics. McNulty was an Irishman from Lawrence, Massachusetts, whose surprising imagination lent arresting life and color to the human-interest stories he specialized in during his forty-five years of writing for newspapers and magazines. He kept on tap a store of humor and charm that drew people to him. He described 1885 as "the year the owls were so bad," and stated authoritatively that "only people with Vincent for a middle name write about leprechauns." He avoided the pretentious and self-important, and often associated with characters considered the lowlife of both Columbus and New York. McNulty could make anybody he found engaging, interesting to everybody.

His father died when McNulty was two. His mother ran a small newspaper, tobacco, and candy shop, which provided the family living. In the First World War, McNulty took shrapnel in both legs in France, leaving him with deep scars and a slightly uneven gait. After the war he worked for several New York newspapers. In those days such work inevitably involved saloons and whiskey. Scraps of autobiography in McNulty's stories attest to his weakness for both. In "Two People He Never Saw," he writes: "God, I was sunk then! . . . I was drinking too much and I lost one job after another. . . . I was looking for a job and coming back every afternoon to the furnished room about four o'clock."

His drinking led to frequent job changes and within a few years he was finding work hard to come by. Friends rallied around, arranged with the *Ohio State Journal* to hire him, bought him a ticket, and put him on the train for Columbus. It was 1921. He soon met Thurber, and he was Thurber's kind of man. In McNulty's first year in Columbus, Thurber writes, "he knew more people in the city than I did, although I had been born and brought up there. They included everybody from taxi drivers, cops, prizefighters, and bellboys to the mayor . . . and the governor.

"John once explained to me, 'Two-thirds of the Irish blood is grease paint,' and he was a fine offhand actor and a raconteur rampant, who would jump from his chair in a living room and theatrically bring to life one of the characters he had so fondly collected during his wanderings."

The same could be said of Thurber. Both men delighted in plotting pretended misunderstandings and misrecognitions to take place in public, baffling passers-by. They loved words and embellished their vocabularies with nonwords to describe special situations that otherwise defied description. They shared books and phonograph records, played on the Victrola in the Thurber home. They competed for the floor in delivering their monologs. Both had quick tempers, and drink could cause them to flare, but neither could bear prolonged enmity and they always handled the restoration of peace without assistance from others.

Thurber introduced McNulty to Donia Williamson, sister of his old friend Ben, of Phi Psi and code-clerk days. She became the first Mrs. McNulty. "John and Jim were a couple of funny guys," Donia recalled, long after she had divorced McNulty and remarried. "They alternately outdid one another in their appreciation of the other's gags." Adds Ben: "They also had an affinity for sardonicism, and for laughing up their sleeves at other people."

The more worldly McNulty helped Thurber learn how to handle bootleg booze and overcome his puritanical, Jamesian aversion to "fallen" women. In July 1921, Thurber writes to Nugent, whose family had just moved permanently from Dover to New York: "I have had quite a mélange and compôte of romance—or call it philandering—since you left. I believe philandering would more closely apply."

Thurber also needed McNulty's tutoring in drinking the near-lethal concoctions that Prohibition gave rise to. Robert Kanode, a *Citizen* reporter of that day, remembers that in late spring of 1921 Columbus officials invited City Hall reporters to a possum dinner. "Near beer," moonshine, and white lightning were served, Kanode recalls. "For all his wit and worldly references to France, Thurber was extremely naive and unsophisticated in those days. He was about the only one at the dinner who had no experience in drinking strong stuff in any amount. He was to direct the Scarlet Mask production, *Oh My, Omar!*, at the state penitentiary that night after the dinner. When the Mask people came to pick him up, they found him standing in the middle of the dinner table delivering a speech to the councilmen, who were either too tired or drunk to understand what he was saying.

"A couple of us helped his friends get Jim to the penitentiary, where we tried sobering him by walking him up and down in front of the prison. But he got worse. Someone went in to explain the situation to the warden, who asked that they put the show on as best they could to avoid a prison riot. Another reporter, named McCoy, and I drove Thurber home. His parents had obviously never seen Thurber or anyone else in their family in that condition. Which was a good thing. I explained that the possum had made him sick and I think his mother accepted it, for all that Jim didn't act sick. He was singing by then. It's a wonder any of us survived that Prohibition stuff."

Mame talked about it for days, laying the poor quality of Columbus government at the time to "those awful possum dinners" the councilmen were always eating.

Thurber's apprenticeship as a party hell-raiser gradually picked up steam under McNulty's influence. During an office party at the *Dispatch,* he emulated Kuehner by dropping a woman's fur coat out the second-story window. But it didn't work out the same way. The indignant woman ordered Thurber to go downstairs and retrieve it, and he meekly obeyed.

In the friendly scramble between Thurber and McNulty for conversational domination fact often succumbed to invention. But one McNulty anecdote, which has been challenged, is true, according to Faith McNulty. When McNulty was finally fired from the *Journal* for drinking, "he went back the next day, sober and cleaned up, saying to the city editor, 'I understand there is a vacancy on the staff.' He was promptly rehired."

Later, McNulty went over to the *Citizen* and managed to survive there with colleagues who loved him and kept explaining away his more unacceptable behavior as absentmindedness. Once, when he was sent on assignment to Mt. Vernon, Ohio, forty-eight miles northeast of Columbus, he vanished for three days. As Smallsreed remembers, McNulty finally broke silence by calling the *Citizen*'s managing editor to ask, "Harry, why am I in Athens?" The editor said he didn't know, since Athens, Ohio, was ninety miles from Mt. Vernon. Talented writers, McNulty's associates explained to the boss, were almost always prey to that kind of absentmindedness.

The McNulty/Thurber friendship continued after Thurber left Columbus in 1925. Donia Williamson Karpen writes that "in the early 1930s Jim was visiting Columbus and persuaded John to go back to New York with him."

McNulty was still getting drunk, fired, and rehired, says Dorothy Miller. "Herman and I had rented a house we loved for forty dollars a month—from a man who was financially strapped and owed just that much as his mortgage payment. We gave a party at which John got drunk and insulted our guests. Jim was in Columbus shortly after that and I told him about McNulty and how angry his behavior had made me. Jim was about to go back to New York that very night and talked McNulty into going with him. He paid McNulty's train fare, helped get him a job, introduced him to Ross and kept urging Ross to let McNulty write for the *New Yorker*."

The year was 1935, and Donia McNulty remembers that when she followed John to New York in another unsuccessful attempt at married life with him, Thurber saw to it that they didn't lack for acquaintances and attention. Stanley Walker had just resigned from the *Trib* as city editor to become, briefly, managing editor of the Hearst tabloid, the *New York Daily Mirror*. Walker wrote Thurber in 1957:

> John McNulty is more your discovery than mine. I had met him briefly in a speakeasy around 1921, remembered him pleasantly, and then had lost track of him until you called me up in 1935 . . . and suggested that I hire him. I did so, rewrite at $50 a week to start, and he was great from the start. He was at this time, as you may recall, only a step out of the gutter, but he more or less pulled himself together. . . . I remember the day he came to work at the *Mirror* he [was] pretty dirty, and worse than broke, so I loaned him enough money to get his clothes out of hock, get cleaned up, and get a night's decent rest before he went to work. I recall he was puzzled when I hired him and asked, "Isn't there something else you want to say to me? . . . Aren't you going to caution me not to drink, and tell me I'll be fired if I take a drink—that's what they always tell me." "No," I said. "I'm not going to say anything about it." This hit him hard. He said: "By God, just for that I'm going to stop

drinking." Of course there were times after that when he DID drink, and plenty.

McNulty's move to New York would eventually put him among the literary greats, for though he resumed work on newspapers for four years, under Thurber's encouragement he began to submit pieces to the *New Yorker*. Thurber kept a proprietary eye on him. Even when abroad, Thurber's letters to McNulty wisely counsel him on how to write "Talk" stories, the biographical articles called "Profiles," and "A Reporter at Large" pieces. Thurber once wrote to Ross demanding sternly that the *New Yorker* editors leave McNulty's copy alone.

McNulty's heart began going bad in 1949, and in 1954 a hopeful Thurber tries to reassure Smallsreed and other McNulty admirers in Columbus:

> McNulty is in fine shape . . . He has a wonderful four-year-old boy, John, Jr. [by Faith McNulty, his second wife], and since my daughter is twenty-two, he points out that she is old enough to be his son's mother. This leads him to be very solicitous when he is with me. "What would you like, Jimmy?" he will ask. "A drink, or a crutch, or a wheelchair?"

McNulty's death in 1956 at age sixty hit Thurber hard. He wrote Smallsreed in bitter disappointment, "McNulty's heart condition went back six years but he took little care of it or he'd still be with us."

The string of McNulty *New Yorker* pieces stretched from December 1937 to the end of 1955. Thurber called Shawn and insisted on writing his obituary for the magazine. Shawn agreed:

> The days didn't go by for John McNulty. They happened to him. . . . He was not merely an amusing companion; he was one of the funniest of men. When he told a tale of people or places, it had a color and vitality that failed in the retelling by anyone else. . . . We grieve that such a man cannot be replaced, in our hearts or on our pages.

22

That Dog That Bit People

A big, burly choleric dog, he always acted as if he thought I wasn't one of the family. There was a slight advantage in being one of the family, for he didn't bite the family as often as he bit strangers. Still, in the years that we had him he bit everybody but mother, and he made a pass at her once but missed . . . He was sorry immediately, mother said. He was always sorry, she said, after he bit someone, but we could not understand how she figured this out. He didn't act sorry.

—from "The Dog That Bit People"

While Thurber was in Paris, his brother Robert purchased a tan Airedale pup from a litter born near Lenworth, Ohio. Mame wrote to Thurber with the news and asked his help in choosing a name for "our dog." "What kind of animal is he?" Thurber wrote back. "Collie, bull, . . . Spaniel, Iceland Seal terrier or what? Anyway, he'll probably always consider me as an intruder when I get back. Show him my picture, let him sniff an old suit of mine and tell him the story of my life."

Whether by family consensus or Robert's preference, the dog was named "Muggs." He *was* inclined to bite people not in the family. Says Thurber in *My Life and Hard Times*:

Mother used to send a box of candy every Christmas to the people the Airedale bit. The list finally contained forty or more names. Nobody could understand why we didn't get rid of the dog. I didn't understand it very well myself. . . .

One morning when Muggs bit me slightly, more or less in passing, I reached down and grabbed his short stumpy tail and hoisted him into the air. It was a foolhardy thing to do and the last time I saw my mother . . . she said she didn't know what possessed me. . . . He twisted and jerked so, snarling all the time, that I realized I couldn't hold him that way very long. I carried him to the kitchen and flung him onto the floor and shut the door on him just as he crashed against it. But I forgot about the backstairs. Muggs went up the backstairs and down the frontstairs and had me cornered. . . . I managed to get up onto the mantelpiece above the fireplace, but it gave way and came down with a tremendous crash. . . . Muggs was so alarmed by the racket that he . . . disappeared. We couldn't find him anywhere, although we whistled and shouted, until old Mrs. Detweiler called after dinner that night. Muggs had bitten her once, in the leg, and she came into the living room only after we assured her that Muggs had run away. She had just seated herself when, with a great growling and scratching of claws, Muggs emerged from under a davenport where he had been quietly hiding all the time, and bit her again. . . . Mother . . . told Mrs. Detweiler that it was only a bruise. "He just bumped you," she said.

"Actually, Muggs liked Jim and never bit him," Robert says, "but Jim never liked Muggs. Muggs really wasn't a mean dog but he got that reputation by not making up instantly with strangers. . . . When they came into the house, they'd try to pet him right away and he didn't like that, but most anyone could be friends with him with a little patience."

In 1918, when the Thurbers moved to 330 Gay Street, "a rather large house with extra bedrooms we could spare," writes Robert,

we had a roomer, sometimes two, to supplement the family income, up to 1930, when we moved to an apartment. One of the roomers didn't like Muggs. He teased him and . . . made faces at him frequently and that made Muggs a little nippy; he went after ankles. But he wasn't really vicious. Yes, there were quite a few people he bit—I don't know if it was forty, as Jim writes, but when Mother would come home and ask if anyone had called, we'd tell her that so-and-so had been, bit and gone.

"Lots of people reported our Airedale to the police," writes Thurber. "The cops had been out a couple of times—

Nobody Knew Exactly What Was the Matter with Him

once when Muggs bit Mrs. Rufus Sturtevant and again when he bit Lieutenant-Governor Malloy—but Mother told them that it hadn't been Muggs' fault but the fault of the people who were bitten. "When he starts for them, they scream," she explained, "and that excites him." . . .

I think that one or two people tried to poison Muggs—he acted poisoned once in a while—and old Major Moberly fired at him once with his service revolver. [Muggs] bit a congressman who had called to see my father on business. My mother had never liked the congressman —she said the signs of his horoscope showed he couldn't be trusted [and] "Muggs could read him like a book."

"Actually it wasn't a congressman but the mayor of Columbus Muggs bit," corrects Robert. "My father worked for him and the mayor stopped by the house to drop off something or pick something up. He tried to pat Muggs. It wasn't a bad bite; it just left Muggs's teeth marks. It scared the mayor but he didn't shoot at Muggs. I don't think anyone actually pulled a gun on Muggs."

Donia Williamson made the same mistake as the mayor when she and John McNulty, by then her fiancé, once visited Thurber at home. When she reached for Muggs, he nipped her in the ankle. Eva Prout had better luck. "That weekend of the country-club dance," she says, "when I stayed at the

Thurbers, being an early riser I got up before the others on Sunday morning. I went downstairs and saw Muggs lying in front of the fireplace. I knew his reputation and wondered whether he was going to bite me. I called to him pleasantly, 'Muggs, Muggs,' and he got up and shook himself and came over to me. I put my hand out and he licked it. I told Mrs. Thurber about it and she said it didn't surprise her at all because both Muggs and I had been born under the sign of Libra."

Mame sent Eva chocolates anyway, in appreciation of her *not* having been bitten by Muggs. ("She made the most delicious candy," Eva comments. "Very professional-looking boxes of fine chocolates.")

> We used to take turns feeding Muggs to be on his good side [writes Thurber], but that didn't always work. He was never in a very good humor, even after a meal. Nobody knew exactly what was the matter with him, but whatever it was it made him irascible, especially in the mornings. Roy never felt very well in the morning, either, especially before breakfast, and once when he came downstairs and found that Muggs had moodily chewed up the morning paper he hit him in the face with a grapefruit and then jumped up on the dining room table, scattering dishes and silverware and spilling the coffee. Muggs' first free leap carried him all the way across the table and into a brass fire screen in front of the gas grate but he was back on his feet in a moment, and in the end he got Roy.

"Jim has that wrong," says Robert. "It was William who hit Muggs with the grapefruit, not me, and I think he got out of the house before Muggs could get to him. I'm not sure Muggs would have bit him, maybe just snarled and snapped; after all, William was family."

In the story, Mame visits a woman mental healer to find out if it is "possible to get harmonious vibrations into a dog." The healer had never treated a dog but advised Mame "to hold the thought that he did not bite and would not bite. Mother was holding the thought the very next morning when Muggs got the iceman, but she blamed that slip-up on the iceman. 'If you didn't think he would bite you, he wouldn't,' mother told him."

In Muggs's last year, Thurber writes, it was hard to get him to come into the house, "and as a result the garbage man, the iceman, and the laundryman wouldn't come near the house. We had to haul the garbage down to the corner, take the laundry out and bring it back, and meet the iceman a block from home."

Thurber's dislike of Muggs was more than a comic literary convenience. In

1923, a year after he had moved out of the Thurber home to marry, he was proclaiming his "very special antipathy for Airedales" in his *Dispatch* half-page, "Credos and Curios." "Nothing is cuter than an Airedale leaning out of an automobile," Thurber offers as a Ryder-type one-liner, "or more deadly."

Robert explains the remark by showing a snapshot of Muggs, resembling remarkably Thurber's drawing of him, looking out of a 1919 Overland 90 touring car. "Muggs loved cars," says Robert. "We couldn't get him out of the Reo, or the Overland, which we got in late 1919 after the engine block on the Reo froze and cracked. He'd growl at you and bite if you tried to make him come out. If the windows had been left up, he'd stay in there even on a warm day, hot and panting. Sometimes we had to take food out to him. When we took him for a drive, Muggs would crouch on top of the back of the rear seat. The Reo had button-on curtains that were loose at the bottom, and twice Muggs fell out. The first time, he fell onto the road like a sack of flour, and the second time one of us caught him and held him by the ham until we could stop the car and haul him in. When I drove, he'd stretch out across my lap, but once he got up and blocked my view and we had a small accident."

> A few months before Muggs died, he got to "seeing things" [Thurber continues]. He would rise slowly from the floor, growling low, and stalk stiff-legged and menacing toward nothing at all. Sometimes the Thing would be just a little to the right or left of a visitor. Once a Fuller Brush salesman got hysterics. Muggs came wandering into the room like Hamlet following his father's ghost. His eyes were fixed on a spot just to the left of the Fuller Brush man, who stood it until Muggs was about three slow, creeping paces from him. Then he shouted. Muggs wavered on past him into the hallway grumbling to himself but the Fuller man went on shouting. I think mother had to throw a pan of cold water on him before he stopped.

"Muggs had a complication of diseases typical of a dog getting up in years," writes Robert. "He had been injured a few years earlier, hit by a car, which slowed him down considerably. It affected his back legs and might have hastened his death."

Airedales were a popular breed in the 1920s, and Thurber, in 1923, was continuing his crusade against them in the *Dispatch:* "Where we would chuck a bulldog under the chin or snap our finger against a lion's nose, we would run from the coffee-colored Airedale, whose name sounds like a country estate. . . . It is our misfortune to live in a neighborhood largely given over to Airedales." He is continually being bounded at by an Airedale, he adds, who serves only as an outrider for a whole Airedale band waiting for a victim. Airedales "are afflicted with a kind of nervous twitching of the teeth which they can only allay by sinking them into wrists."

Muggs lived from 1919 to March 1928. Robert loved him—Muggs was the only dog he ever owned—and thirty-four years afterward he still could not discuss the dog's death without emotion. Robert was visiting Thurber in New York when Mame telephoned to tell him that Muggs was very sick. He returned home at once and took Muggs to the veterinarian, who pronounced the case hopeless. "I left him there," says Robert. "Muggs didn't want me to go. I'll never forget his look as I was leaving. I guess he did bite a lot of people but he really wasn't a mean dog."

Thurber wrote Robert his condolences:

> I certainly felt badly about Muggs, on account of you and the rest, and the old dog himself. . . . That's the hell of having a dog. I still feel bad about Rex and often dream of him. They cant live long, and ten years is a long time for a dog. Why cant we have alligators as pets, which live to be 1500 years old, or crows which live to be ninety? Seems strange that God would pick such cumbersome and morose animals and birds to live that long and give a dog the bad break of a handful of moments, as the years go. Still, our family has been lucky about deaths and we got to buck up against them because the years are going on and people die and what the hell, a person simply must build up a philosophy that will endure it all. . . . I have always expected to find Rex in the company of some such guy as . . . Raoul Lufbery [World War I ace] and maybe Muggs will have Christy Mathewson [a professional baseball player whom Robert and Thurber idolized] with whom to scamper across the porphyry and chrysophase fields.

A perennial favorite book of children is Crockett Johnson's *Harold and the Purple Crayon*, in which little Harold creates his own world and adventures by drawing them in an endless purple line. He wishes to take a moonlight walk, so he creates a moon; then an ocean on which to sail a quickly drawn boat, a mountain he falls off, and a balloon sketched in time to ride safely to the ground. Similarly, blank paper was to Thurber the unstructured world around him, on which to stake out his role and place with pencil and pen. The renowned Thurber World was merely translated from the jumbled code of his imagination. In the process, the Thurber Dog became part of that world —the lovable, vulnerable, bewildered canine of indeterminate breed that he drew tens of thousands of times, and which became forever the Thurber trademark. A sentimentalist about dogs, Thurber came to love the one he had created, and was delighted that it pleased others (numberless people have named their dogs "Thurber"). In its most common form, it seems to be a short-legged bloodhound pup, though nearly everybody with a floppy-eared dog of whatever age is convinced that he or she owns a Thurber Dog. Dog owners are sometimes inclined to see the dog as symbolizing Thurber himself —the saddened artist as canine, in a perpetual cry for help, hoping for sympathy, affection, and understanding.

The dog's proliferation throughout Thurber books, and in countless unpublished sketches, is readily explained: The dog became Thurber's favorite subject for idle doodling, the rendering taking him only seconds and three or four strokes of a pencil. He drew it while thinking of how to begin a piece of writing, or while he was talking, or to start the setting for a cartoon. He gave out thousands of them to friends and strangers, conceived on the spot, wherever he happened to be. When blindness ended his career as an artist, he could still dash off a Thurber Dog instinctively, his wife inserting the eye and nose dots in the right places.

Thurber writes of the lithograph of six hunting dogs that hung in Grandfather Fisher's front hall, "who were to remain permanently in my memory for fond, if perhaps imprecise, reference later on, when I began to draw," he writes. But Mame Thurber was certain the dogs he had in mind were in a print she received as a wedding gift, showing the heads of eight dogs, including two bloodhounds. "James used to sit and look at it for hours," says Mame. Mame's melancholy flop-eared canines do come closer to the plump, wistful dogs of Thurber's cartoons than those in his grandfather's lithograph.

As the dog's fame snowballed over the years, Thurber used its popularity to gradually assert himself as a principal authority on dogs, pronouncing himself, finally, the patron saint of dogs, one who had owned seventy-two of them in his lifetime. No later claim of Thurber's as to what he was, or what it used to be like with his family in Columbus, baffled his brothers more than that pertaining to the family dogs. "Jim never showed any affection for Muggs, and not as much toward our other dogs as William and I," says Robert, "but you never could tell what Jim was thinking. Maybe he really did feel bad about Muggs dying."

In his foreword to *Thurber's Dogs*, Thurber refers to himself as "a dog man who owned his first dog before the battleship *Maine* was sunk." That tragedy was in February 1898, when Thurber had just turned three years old. The Thurbers' first dogs, Sampson and Judge, actually turn up in 1899, after the family moved to South Champion Avenue. This fairly remote location qualified for watchdogs, especially during the year when Charles worked in Washington. Thurber describes Sampson as "a restless water spaniel." ("Mostly mongrel," says Robert.) Judge was a pug. ("An ugly thing with loose fitting skin," says Cousin Clifford Fisher.)

Thurber had a vulnerable tenderness toward dogs. Like E. B. White, he delighted in assigning human thought to animals, and he consistently ranked canines higher than humans in intelligence, loyalty, and honesty. He did, however, resist being called a dog lover, arguing that the term can only designate a dog in love with another dog.

In his youth, Thurber became emotionally attached to two dogs. Scottie, Grandfather Fisher's collie, would meet the Thurber boys after school and spend time at the Thurber house. This ended when William brought home Rex, a Pit Bull. The two dogs had a fight in the Thurber house. "It was possibly the longest and certainly the noisiest dogfight ever staged in an American parlor," writes Thurber, "and there were blood and hair and broken Victrola records and torn lace curtains and smashed ash trays all over the place before we got the battlers separated." Scottie never came back to the Thurber home, but Thurber continued to visit him. Rex had been with them ten years when he and Scottie died at about the same time. Thurber was then in high school and poured out his heart in this tribute:

> *Somewhere beyond the brightest star*
> *That's always a-shining up there so far*
> *There's a heaven that no good life will bar—*
> *A heaven where Rex and Scottie are.*

> *The two best dogs that have ever been*
> *Steadfast and true through thick and thin,*
> *Innocent of human crime and sin,*
> *Some canine paradise has let them in. . . .*

> *I like to think it's a glorious hall,*
> *Where a doggie knows no sorrow at all—*
> *Where Scottie is chasing a pearly ball*
> *And Rex is jumping a golden wall.*

"In his grief over the loss of a dog," Thurber writes in 1955, "a little boy stands for the first time on tiptoe, peering into the rueful morrow of manhood. After this most inconsolable of sorrows, there is nothing life can do to him that he will not be able somehow to bear."

Thurber's insistence that he had owned seventy-two dogs in his lifetime begs for qualification. With his first wages from the *New York Evening Post* in 1926, he and Althea bought a Scottish terrier named Jeannie, whom Althea bred for gain and profit in early 1929. The first four pups were born in a shoe closet in the Thurbers' one-bedroom apartment on West Eleventh Street in Greenwich Village. Jeannie had the fifth and last unexpectedly at Fifth and Eleventh streets while Thurber was walking her.

"It was . . . just when the city was going to work, that the fifth pup made her appearance," writes Thurber. "I had been taking the mother for a walk, which both of us needed. I had a headache as the result of having had too much to drink the night before and not enough sleep. Quite a crowd gathered, which did not seem to bother Jeannie, but it bothered me. I put the newcomer in my pocket, told the loudly protesting mother to shut up and hurried home."

Thurber's sentimentality over Jeannie is prominent in one of his early stories for the *New Yorker*, "The Thin Red Leash." Walking the little dog in a working-class neighborhood, both he and the Scottie are greeted by guffaws. "They're scrappers, these dogs," Thurber tells the toughs defensively. "What d'they scrap—cockroaches?" is the caustic reply. Finally, a burly workman who knows Scotties attests, in front of the others, that they are "hellcats in a fight. . . . Seen one take the tonsils out of an Airedale one day." The other workmen are won over and all take turns patting the terrier, who has carried the day.

When Thurber and Althea were visiting friends in Columbus with Jeannie, shortly after Thurber had joined the *New Yorker*, the dog disappeared one morning. Had she been stolen? Thurber doubted it. "I knew that Jeannie was a strayer and it was getting harder and harder for me to conceive of anybody deliberately wanting to own her." She was found two days later, through an ad in the *Dispatch*.

His impatience with Jeannie's wanderlust later contributed to both his and Althea's disenchantment with the breed. But in writing Robert his sympathies over the passing of Muggs in March 1928, Thurber says: "I know what it would mean to me if Jeannie passed out and we've only had her a little over a year. When I lost her in Columbus I was nearly nuts. . . . I expect any day to find that she has wandered off and got lost upstate or been killed."

He extols over and over the Scottie's ability to outfight larger dogs and offers to give one to Robert to replace Muggs:

> They are tremendously expensive some of them but yours will be FOB nothing. . . . They are not only brave and intelligent but dignified and playful at the same time, easy to teach and easy to housebreak, tremen-

dously loyal and affectionate and noted for their fine disposition. . . . One day our dog, left here to her own devices too long—both of us were gone from eleven in the morning until eight at night—got fed up on having nothing to do and dragged down, or out, or up, everything we had, practically. The house looked like twenty-seven burglars had organized and gone through it hunting for money. Hats, coats, pans, rugs, spools, needles, cigarettes, clocks, overcoats, suitcases, pillows, pillow-slips, bedspreads, letters, bills, manuscripts, books, magazines, lamps, dish cloths, curtains and ties were strewn from one end of the house to the other. Many things were chewed but a lot were not. She had specialized on the cigarettes the match boxes and the bag that held Althea's sewing things, especially chewing the spools of silk thread. Only one book was gnawed and that was one we had borrowed from a lady and it was autographed by the author—the one book of our six or eight hundred that she should not have got hold of. Althea corrects her but when I come home alone and find the dog has got things out I always say, "For God's sake, dog, let's hurry and straighten up here or there'll be hell to pay." She is wise enough to know that I will not beat her (which I should). . . . She used to sleep on the bed and we spanked her, so that when she heard us coming she would get down and crawl under the bed, and then come out slowly looking sleepy and surprised. But she neglected to pat the pillows and smooth out the bedspread where she had been laying [sic]. This is a trick she has never learned but if I come in on her someday patting the pillows into shape I'll call the police, or a minister."

But the Thurbers soon wearied of Scottish terriers. Thurber, in fact, eventually became downright hostile to the breed, finding them inept as mothers, habitual runaways, and rather stupid in general. In 1948, he could write: "Jeannie had no show points to speak of. Her jaw was skimpy, her haunches frail, her forelegs slightly bowed. She thought dimly and her co-ordination was only fair. Even in repose she had the strained, uncomfortable appearance of a woman on a bicycle. . . . Jeannie did everything the hard way, digging with one paw at a time, shoving out of screen doors sideways. When she was six months old, she tried to bury a bone in the second section of the *New York Times*. . . . She developed a persistent, troubled frown, which gave her the expression of someone who is trying to repair a watch with his gloves on."

And elsewhere: "A female dog knows more about raising her own pups (I except only Jeannie) than any man or woman could teach her."

Althea had a black standard French poodle shipped to them from Chicago in 1929 and that summer persuaded Thurber to give up the city apartment and rent a farmhouse in Silvermine, Connecticut, near Westport, where she could more practically run a professional kennel. The two were having their problems, and the arrangement fitted into a kind of trial separation. During the week, Thurber worked and stayed at hotels, visiting the suburbs on most weekends.

Jeannie quickly suffered from comparisons with Medve, the poodle, whose intelligence and personality Thurber found approached, and often surpassed, that of humans. He became a poodle fancier the rest of his life. Medve was the perfect mother, too. Jeannie had another litter in Silvermine but Thurber —reflecting later on the event, and with Medve's ideal whelping experiences setting a cruel standard—found the Scottie's performance inadequate. "Jeannie . . . went around wearing a martyred look when she had pups to care for. . . . She responded to every call from the puppy basket with a frown of desperation, and I don't believe she could tell a yip, or a yap from a yowl . . . (she didn't even know how to snap an umbilical cord, and usually asked for human help). . . . Jeannie was as inept in a barn with her young as she was in [the apartment's] shoe closet, and once when she lost a pup under a floor board she trotted outside and began frantically digging, with one paw, at the base of the stone foundation. I estimated that she would have reached the skeleton of her pup, by that terrier method, in approximately fourteen weeks."

After Medve (Hungarian for "bear") delivered her first litter, of four males and seven females, Jeannie felt displaced and became noticeably disheartened. She began leaving the house at dawn and returning at dusk. Though she rarely ate at home, she was gaining weight. Thurber followed her one day and discovered that she was using her one trick—sitting up to beg—to get food from campers at nearby lake cottages. "She took to staying away for days at a time. I would have to go and get her in the car and bring her back." She continued to disappear. The mailman would inform Thurber as to where "your little dog is." Thurber would drive miles to pick her up. ("I opened the door and she climbed slowly into the car and up onto the seat beside me. We both stared straight ahead all the way home.")

After Rosemary was born, Jeannie grew increasingly jealous, and one day snapped at the toddler, biting her under the eye. Thurber's case against Scottish terriers was complete. Jeannie was given to a childless couple who loved dogs and doted on her until her death in 1935.

Medve the poodle became Thurber's kind of dog. She could do no wrong. Althea had decided on her because she was a professional show dog and

Althea wanted to raise and sell the best of thoroughbreds. Medve came through with two litters of eleven pups each and went Best of Breed at the Westminster Show. Thurber did his best to help out but revealed his ineptitude as a weekend country squire in various ways.

The barn at the Silvermine property was used as both a garage and kennel. One pitch-dark night, at 1:00 A.M., something roused the kennel of poodles, and Thurber investigated. "I had quite a time quieting the dogs, because their panic spread to me and mine spread back to them. . . . Finally, a hush as ominous as their uproar fell upon them, but they kept looking over their shoulders, in a kind of apprehensive way. . . . At that moment the klaxon [horn] of my car, which was just behind me, began to shriek. . . . Few people have heard [a horn] scream behind them while they were quieting six or eight alarmed poodles in the middle of the night in an old barn. I jump now whenever I hear a klaxon, even the klaxon on my own car when I push the button intentionally."

Nor did he have better luck with the assignments Althea gave him when Medve was being shown. Once Althea drove their Model A Ford coupé to a dog show in the rain while Thurber and Medve sat in the rumble seat, Thurber holding a parasol over the carefully groomed poodle, who was also wearing a red rubber bib, because she always got carsick. Althea suddenly turned off the road and into a large garage, with Thurber still holding the parasol over Medve. "Hey, get a load of this, Mac!" a mechanic called to another, scornfully eyeing the rumble-seat tableau.

During one show in which Medve and several of her male pups were entered, Medve refused to get up on the bench assigned to her and her family. "So I got up on it myself," says Thurber, "on all fours, to entice her to follow. She was surprised and amused, but not interested, and this was also true of my wife, who kept walking past the bench, saying out of the corner of her mouth, 'Get off that bench, for the love of heaven!' She finally got me off, and the dogs on."

By the early 1930s, the dog Thurber drew almost as a nervous reflex had captivated him. He decided it looked more like a bloodhound than any other dog:

> My dog is lower on its legs than a standard bloodhound, although I would scarcely put it that way myself. He got his short legs by accident. I drew him first on the cramped pages of a small memo pad in order to plague a busy realtor friend of mine given to writing down names and numbers while you were trying to talk to him in his office. The hound I draw has a fairly accurate pendulous ear, but his dot of an eye is vastly

over-simplified, he doesn't have enough transverse puckers, and he is all wrong in the occipital region. He may not be as keen as a genuine bloodhound, but his heart is just as gentle; he does not want to hurt anybody or anything; and he loves serenity and heavy dinners, and wishes they would go on forever, like the brook.

The dog of his drawings gradually assumed a permanent life of its own in Thurber's mind. His cartoons were first accepted by the *New Yorker* in 1931, and a year afterward the dog would appear in them more and more frequently, if only to balance the composition. Thurber began to feel proprietary, not only toward his dog of economic line and Orphan Annie eyes but toward bloodhounds in general. In 1932, he assigned himself a Talk of the Town story on the use of bloodhounds by the police, celebrating the breed. Four years later, browsing through a book entitled *The Outline of Science, a Plain Story Simply Told,* he came upon this passage, under "Domesticated Animals": "There are some [dogs] which seem to repel us, like the bloodhound. True, man has made him what he is. Terrible to look at and terrible to encounter, man has raised him up to hunt down his fellowman."

Thurber took the remarks as a personal attack on his Dog, commenting:

> Poor, frightened little scientist! . . . I have never liked or trusted scientists very much, and I think now that I know why; they are afraid of bloodhounds. They must, therefore, be afraid of frogs, jack rabbits, and the larger pussycats. . . . Out of my analysis of those few sentences on the bloodhound, one of the gentlest of all breeds of dogs, I have arrived at what I call Thurber's Law, which is that scientists don't really know anything about anything. I doubt everything they have ever discovered. I don't think light has a speed of 7,000,000 miles per second at all (or whatever the legendary speed is). . . . I have always suspected that light just plodded along, and now I am positive of it.

His pitch of hysteria on the subject had not abated nearly two decades later. "My indignation is still as strong as it was then," he writes in "Lo, Hear the Gentle Bloodhound," in 1955. But his opinion of the bloodhound's disposition didn't extend to the breed's intelligence. In 1940 he told a *New York Sun* writer that he wanted to own a bloodhound, but "bloodhounds are too dumb to keep in town."

The madness of the human act portrayed in Thurber's cartoons was all the more pointed when the Thurber "bloodhound" was present, waiting in puzzled, patient fashion for love and an explanation. Though Althea got them into the dog business, the cartoons usually show the Thurber Man and Dog in a warm alliance roundly distrusted by The Thurber Woman.

Articles have been written harping on the symbolic relation of Thurber's Dogs to the human predicament. Asked about it, Thurber's good friend Peter De Vries shrugs and says, "Thurber had an affinity for dogs. That's all."

Medve's death in 1940 inspired one of Thurber's finest memorials to a dog. He and Althea had been divorced for five years and Medve was living with Althea, as a companion to their nine-year-old daughter, Rosemary. Though Thurber would not have been present at Medve's death, he got the report of it from his ex-wife. He remembered the poodle fondly and mentally arranged her demise as convincingly as if he had witnessed it:

> She knew that the Hand was upon her, and she accepted it with a grave and unapprehensive resignation. This, her dark intelligent eyes seemed to be trying to tell me, is simply the closing of full circle, this is that flower that grows out of Beginning; this—not to make it too hard for you, friend—is as natural as . . . raising the puppies and riding into the rain.

"Will You Be Good Enough to Dance This Outside?"

In addition to Jeannie and Medve, Althea's kennels account for another sixty-nine of the dogs Thurber claimed ownership of. As he cheerfully admits in a 1944 article, "All but five or six of my dogs were disposed of when they were puppies, and I had not gone to the trouble of giving to these impermanent residents of my house any names at all except Shut Up! and Cut That Out! and Let Go!"

Thurber's "seventy-second" dog was another black standard poodle, named Christabel. "My mother bought her," says Rosemary,

> probably with money from my father—and she was given to me for my birthday. We named her Sophie, called her Poo. Christabel was her rather lofty kennel name. Poo lived with me, my mother and stepfather in Amherst for a number of years—until her daily barking and harassing of the postman caused him so much anxiety he refused to deliver the mail. Althea and Helen must have worked out the arrangement that brought Poo to Cornwall (where the mail was delivered by a man in a car at a box way out on the main road). She led a calmer, more pampered life in Cornwall and she and my father were indeed very happy together.

It was two years after Medve died, that Poo, or Poodle, became Thurber's pride and joy until her death in 1959. She wasn't replaced. So the honest number of Thurber's dogs comes to three, and their acquisition had been largely Althea's idea.

No matter. Thanks to his generous proliferating of the beloved Thurber Dog throughout the world, Thurber is more solidly identified with dogs than with any of his other creations, with the possible exception of Walter Mitty. Few would object to his anointing himself at least an honorary patron of canines. Writes Helen Thurber:

"My husband had a natural affinity for dogs, and they for him. [One June Commencement Day at Williams College] the outdoor platform where the officials and [honorary-degree recipients] sat was in the full glare of the sun. From my seat in the shade, I saw that my husband, in his hot . . . black robes, looked rather unhappy until suddenly out of nowhere, a [nondescript] dog . . . strolled up the aisle onto the platform . . . went straight to my husband and put his paw up. Not to shake hands, but to pat his knee and say, 'Don't let it get you, Mac. You're one of us, and we're all with you.' Everyone laughed, and all at once we felt better, and even a little cooler."

23

That Magic Mirror Girl

At a banquet given by members of the three Columbus newspapers, Althea was accounted by most the most strikingly beautiful lady in the 60 or more present . . . Not only beautiful is she but ravishingly intelligent with characteristics so much like mine in many directions you would of course find her fetching. But this night she was more beautiful than new snow with the light of stars upon it, or than cool flowers in the soft of dawning . . .

—Letter to Elliott Nugent, April 4, 1922

"I want to find The Girl," Thurber was writing Elliott Nugent in January 1921:

I have little or no desire to traipse back to France, much as I love Her, without the Girl. Just who she will be depends on Fate and the nice Gods and everything. I see few prospects right now. But I crave a Sweetheart, and must, in fine, have one before long. I am, I find, cut from the stuff which demands a Lady in the Case. . . . As I have told you . . . I lost the Only One after all, to Chicago. . . . I have already written [Minnette] asking her to suggest someone. She would know. . . . She will be here in May for a visit.

In Minnette's senior year at O.S.U. (1919–20), she had been elected president of her sorority, Kappa Kappa Gamma, and she returned in May for a reunion of the sisterhood. She claims to have justified Thurber's faith in her as matchmaker on that occasion by introducing him to a sophomore sorority sister, Althea Adams, the girl he married a year later.

Althea was born April 28, 1901, in New York City, the daughter of Paul and Maude Gregory Adams. Adams was a medical student in his last year of internship, and, the next year, moved his family to Los Angeles, where, after a brief practice, he became an Army surgeon. He was serving with the Fifth Cavalry in Hawaii in 1910 when he died of peritonitis. Althea was nine years old. "He seemed like an old man to me at the time," Althea remembers, "but he was only thirty-two."

She and her mother moved back to California, where Maude worked with the YWCA. Dr. Adams's sister and her husband, Professor Frederick Blake, dean of the Physics Department at O.S.U., invited widow and daughter to live with them in Columbus. Maude Adams became a home-economics graduate student at O.S.U., teaching at the Columbus School for Girls while finishing her last college year. Upon graduating, she joined the university's Home Economics Department as an assistant professor.

A 1918 graduate of North High School, Althea attended Western College for Women in Oxford, Ohio, for a year and transferred to O.S.U. in the fall of 1919. She was tall (5'9"), square-shouldered, and pretty, with dark brown hair. Her handsome picture graces a page of the 1921 *Makio* (Japanese for "mirror"), the university yearbook, as one of eight "Magic Mirror" girls, selected on the basis of womanly courtliness and bearing. Earlier she had been elected by the student body as one of nine "Rosebuds of the Rosebush," whose criteria were an outstanding "womanliness, brightness, fairness, and willingness to help others," and whose attitude "helped make the Ohio of today."

"I loved Althea," says Minnette, "that beautiful, lovely girl. We had no sorority house in those days but we lived not far from one another. We both liked to walk. We became very, very close friends."

After his day at the *Dispatch* was through, Thurber spent his evenings working on both a Strollers drama and skits for Scarlet Mask. Althea had joined Strollers but had not met Thurber, says Minnette, "and I remember discussing with Tom [Meek] whether he thought it was a good or bad idea to introduce them." They decided it was a bad one, "but Althea . . . so . . . wanted to meet Jim that I invited them to the house where I lived and introduced them. Or maybe it was an evening date, just the three of us. Being a married woman, I couldn't be seen with a male date of my own."

But Althea, some fifty years later, remembers first meeting Thurber at a Strollers rehearsal. One spring day in 1921, he drove the family car to the campus chapel, which also served as a student theater, to discuss with Ray Lee Jackson a scene he was writing for the next Scarlet Mask show, *Many Moons*. Jackson was directing a Strollers play with Althea in the cast, and Thurber's arrival brought a brief pause in the rehearsal and his introduction to her.

"It could have been either of two plays that Ray directed," says Althea. "I was in *The Importance of Being Earnest* and one of the three girls in *The Girl with the Green Eyes*. Jim had recently returned from the U.S. Embassy in Paris, a polished man of the world, and I was somewhat bowled over by him, I suppose. He was on the *Dispatch* and I was in college and at four P.M. on many days a group of us would meet downtown for tea at the photography studio that Al Callen and Ray Lee Jackson ran. We took turns bringing cakes. It was the nearest thing Columbus had to a Bohemian tea. We had a wonderful time in an innocent way. There was always good conversation."

Thurber was smitten but not ready to acknowledge it. He makes no mention of Althea to Nugent in a July 10, 1921, letter, but indicates that, though his attitude toward women may be more worldly, it is still Jamesian:

> I, as I grow older, seem to enter deeper and deeper into the spirit of this "age of discretion" thing. Discretion, my boy, is the practise of reasoning cooly [sic] while being hotly kissed. Woe unto the young man, Solomon might have said, who allows his breath to be taken away by a woman's words, who loses his head because of his heart, or has his feet swept from under him because of her legs.
>
> I may say, however, that I might well have heeded that maxim six weeks ago.

He was stimulated, as usual, by Nugent's precedent. Nugent was now playing the juvenile in *Dulcy*, the first Marc Connelly and George S. Kaufman collaboration. The ingenue was Norma Lee [stage name], and she and Nugent fell in love before the show was four months old. By summer of 1921, they were engaged. The marriage was on October 15 at the Chapel Notre Dame, Morningside Heights, New York. Thurber came from Columbus by train to be best man. He didn't see much of Nugent, because of the bridegroom's theater commitments. The newlyweds took only a weekend honeymoon.

The events in Nugent's career, which had gone off like a string of firecrackers, must have kept Thurber in flight from one emotional daydream to another, beginning with Nugent's sale of a short story to the *Smart Set*.

Standing up for Nugent at a wedding attended by the entire cast of a Broadway hit could only have reminded him that his nose was still pressed against the glass, on the outside looking in, yearning to be in love and married, to be published, produced, recognized, and an achiever, like his best friend.

Thurber and Althea saw each other more and more as the year progressed. Most of their acquaintances wondered why she was attracted to him. She was beautiful, popular, very much an extrovert. Thurber still appeared shy and aloof to those outside his special circle of colleagues and friends. "Jim worried about boring people," says Jake Meckstroth, a newspaper contemporary of Thurber's. "He'd seem almost apologetic about saying something witty in a group of people he didn't know well. It was in his nature then to be a bit reserved and reticent."

"I'll never know the right answer to sex and marriage," Thurber had written Nugent in 1920. But by the next fall, whatever his confusion, he was hinting to Althea of marriage. His serious intention toward the prominent and striking campus beauty seemed to the studio salon group a reckless Thurber fantasy, a guarantee of another heartbreak at the hands of Woman. But Althea, who had lived several years with her mother, aunt, and uncle, and now shared an apartment with Maude, yearned for a life of her own. She majored in Romance languages, with an emphasis on French, and was intrigued by Thurber's constant drumming on his theme of returning to France to live and work.

Althea was in on all the shows, says Ralph McCombs, an early Mask participant, "whether acting or involved with sets and costumes." Her interest in theater was a plus in Thurber's mind, he adds, but "I was not the only one who marveled at such disparate persons joining hands and hearts. The Adamses didn't have a great deal of money, but they had status in that Althea was a niece of the dean of the Physics Department. In North Columbus, where the Adamses lived, it mattered who you were, in the way that only a small Midwest city can insist on. The Adamses moved in socially respectable circles, both in Columbus and at the university. The Thurbers were considered raggedy pants by comparison. Althea was sheltered and simply not prepared to live through moneyless stretches the way Jim was. That's hard on any marriage; it would have been particularly hard on Althea. I wasn't surprised to hear they ended in a bitter divorce."

Duke Damon, Thurber's fraternity brother, thought Thurber's height was in his favor when courting Althea. "Men usually go for women smaller than they are," he says. "Althea didn't know that many men taller than she who interested her."

Carson Blair thought Thurber's attraction to Althea was rooted in more than looks and status: "She was very certain of herself, feminine but self-possessed. She had *stability*. Jim looked for that in a woman to offset what he used to refer to as 'the Thurber nervousness.'

"Most of those who couldn't understand what Althea saw in a high-strung, awkward, quiet guy like Jim, were men, who would be the last to understand the appeal Jim had for girls. But he had that appeal. He was entertaining, profound, erudite, a good listener, and he was functioning successfully half-blind, which could draw a kind of affectionate sympathy from a woman which the ordinary guy didn't merit.

"Jim was more adventurous when he got back from Paris, too. I know from my visits to his family's house on Gay Street that he was corresponding with a girl in France. And he had one date, at least, with a stripper at the Lyceum Theater. I don't think any of the rest of us would have had the nerve to ask her out."

Minnette offers her disapproval of the match as protecting Althea, though her fondness for Thurber may have surprised a latent sense of jealousy in her. "I felt that Althea was not quite the person for Jim," she says. "Jim was temperamental. I thought Althea should marry an older man who could take care of her more adequately than Jim would be able to."

Minnette's doctor husband had been offered a job at the Mayo Clinic, in Rochester, Minnesota, and Minnette, about to join him there, told Thurber she didn't think it appropriate for him to continue writing to her. Thurber agreed sadly, and kept his pledge—for eight years.

Even on his best days at the *Dispatch*, Thurber never regarded his reporting job as anything but a way station on a climb to the heights of literary and playwriting fame. He was open to any suggestions where the performing arts were concerned. In the spring of 1921, at a studio tea, he met Harold (Hal) Cooley, a pioneer movie cameraman who had worked at the early studios on Long Island and produced weekly "human interest" short films for Fox. Cooley was planning a short Civil War film called *Over the Garden Fence*, using a private estate in Bexley, near Columbus. He persuaded the principal creative powers behind O.S.U.'s stage productions—Thurber, McCombs, and Jackson —to join him, not only in making the feature but in supplementing it with a documentary of Columbus to be called *Twenty-five Minutes from Broad and High*.

"Am at work on what appears to stand a half way chance of being a successful local movie venture," Thurber writes to Nugent in July 1921. "I have already turned out a 3 reel comedy drama for the starter of the thing which hereafter will confine itself to news reels, features etc. . . . My picture, if any, will be an ad scheme and will involve a local popularity contest in selecting the leads. The more or less great R. L. McCombs is interested in the project."

It isn't known what became of Thurber's ad film. Local remnants of the Grand Army of the Republic were tracked down and hauled by truck, in their faded, outgrown uniforms, to the Griggs Dam to play soldier. (The GAR was to receive half the receipts.) Dynamite caps were placed in bags of flour and exploded during the battle scenes. The film shooting went on for days. The cast starred the local beauty whom Cousin Earl Fisher would one day marry, as well as Althea, William Thurber, and McCombs, among other Columbusites. Thurber helped write the captions for the silent film.

The show's premier was at Memorial Hall, where Cooley had been able to assemble a sizable orchestra. The premiere was a disaster. Rain restricted attendance. Cooley had nearly amputated his hand while cutting and splicing the film, was in Grant Hospital, and missed the show. In an attempt to repay the modest sums put up by the producers, it was run again in the Knickerbocker Theater, with even worse results in attendance figures and press comments. (All that Thurber had to show Nugent was a local review, which praised only the idea of making a film in Columbus.)

Nearly thirty-five years later, as Thurber remembers the episode: "[Ralph McCombs] died nobly in the Civil War battle scene, flinging his left arm before him as he fell. We irised out on Ralph's wrist watch. Said Cooley later, 'All we needed to make [the] Civil War background perfect was a Mack Truck for an ambulance.' "

To Nugent, July 10, 1921: "I am still turning out a lot of helpful and uplifting news for the Disp. The work has by no means begun to pall on me and I consider that it has been the most valuable training I have ever got, in school or out, for a life of literary crime in the future, if any."

But his only identifiable work the remainder of that year were Sunday reviews of the Broadway theater scene during the fortnight he was in New York for Nugent's wedding and short verses in the "Observations" column, one protesting the tendency of people to address strangers with disrespectful familiarity:

> *Indicate the exit.*
> *Point the way out,*

To the total stranger
  Who calls one "scout."

Allocate an island
  With hot winds to smother
The unknown questioner
  Who terms one "brother."
                —J. G. T.

J. C. Nugent, Elliott's father, had accompanied Thurber on his theater junket around New York, pointing out stage celebrities on the street and at the Friars Club, which Thurber proudly salts into his *Dispatch* pieces. He praises the senior Nugent and adds that "his talented family bids fair to equal the dad before long. Elliott, his son, has done fine work in 'Tillie' . . . and even finer work in the great comedy 'Dulcy.'" Thurber's reviews contain hard-to-follow, run-on sentences that often trip themselves into a jumble of confused syntax. ("When the deeply sensitive, very intelligent and greatly loved (by Greenough) wife does not immediately find her love for Julian die, one ceases greatly to feel for her.")

The underpaid Columbus journalists took outside writing jobs when they could, and with marriage on his mind Thurber was especially eager to do so. Captain H. Mowrey, a *Journal* reporter of that day, remembers when the Shrine circus came to town and "its manager spread word at the newspaper offices that they needed publicity writers. Jim and I got the jobs. We worked like demons and got the circus a continuous flow of good publicity from a month before the circus got to town to the day it closed. After it was over, Jim and I were called to the Shrine headquarters and given fifteen dollars apiece for our month's work. All we could do when we got out the door was chuckle together as two people who knew they'd been taken."

Carson Blair was in town with a new advertising agency. One of his first accounts was the city's water system. "I had to come up with human-interest stories about it," Blair says. "I needed help and I knew only one guy who could write imaginatively about a municipal water system. Jim wrote three or four pieces for me."

Thurber also wrote press releases for the Majestic Theater and Indianola Park, and completed the book for Scarlet Mask's 1921–22 production, *Many Moons*, a Thurber title he would use again for a 1943 children's book. The musical's plot: how the ruler of Polonia solves his political problems by "jazzing up" his government with chorus girls in the cabinet and "syncopation" in affairs of state. (The typical student pit orchestra of the day included piano, drums, banjo, tuba, cornet, and two saxophones.) Althea helped out with costumes and setting. The show, which "netted me $350," says Thurber, was highly praised by Billy Graves in the *Lantern*.

Althea consented to marry him. "She and I are set to kick off the single coils and face a ministerial barrage of nice sounding phrases in October," Thurber writes Nugent in April 1922. "Money has not flowed in fast enough to warrant a setting nearer of the date yet. But prospects look good. Two weeks ago I got the Columbus correspondence for the justly great Christian Science Monitor. . . . It means a lot in possible prestige and not a little in money since they pay the wonderful rate of 37 and one half cents the inch, or about 8 to 10 dollars a column, and since they use much academic, literary and educational stuff I plot many articles of length. Also I am set to handle occasional telegraph stories for the Cleveland News Leader." In the case of the *News Leader*, he had help from his Paris Red Cross friend, Charme Seeds, who was working on a Sunday supplement magazine for that newspaper's syndicate. He used the university faculty as authorities on such subjects as the discovery of "mound builders" in the area, and other local geological phenomena, sometimes selling the same piece to papers in Boston, Cleveland, and Wheeling. The *Monitor*'s small checks, he claimed, were made out to him as "Jane Thurber." (None of the newspapers have records of Thurber as a stringer, and bylines were not yet the fashion.)

In this period, Thurber, ever the hometown booster, begins to question the staid Victorian values he had been raised with and continued to defend in his reviews of plays, books, and art shows. His certainty of the superiority of Jamesian proprieties in American culture had first been shaken by his discovery of H. L. Mencken of the *Smart Set*, who saw American life dominated by the hypocrisy, stupidity, and bigotry of the "booboisie." Then Sinclair Lewis's *Main Street* (1921) attacked the prejudices and provincialism of small-town America, and *Upstream* (1922), the autobiography of Ludwig Lewisohn, who had taught at O.S.U., ridiculed the practices and standards of both the university and Columbus itself. Thurber was especially impressed by *Upstream*, writing Nugent:

> Ludwig Lewisohn, whom perhaps you knew better than I, has issued a new book . . . in which he takes up Columbus, under a name not that, and the university and subjects the whole scene to a searching north light, revealing with deft satire, much bitter pinking with swords and not a little hurtful truth, the ways of people and things as he saw them here. It is a smashing indictment of what he pleases to call the mental and intellectual vacuity of the region. I have read only quotations in

reviews and news stories so far, but suggest we both get the book and chuckle as we see his Menckian lunges leap past us at everybody else whoever went to school here.

Still under Lewisohn's persuasions, he writes that his outside press-agent work is intended to bring such distinguished artists as Sergei Rachmaninoff and Pablo Casals "and others to this God forsaken place to cudgel [sic] what passes for the artistic sense of the benighted heathen. That will mean 300 rocks for little effort over a period of two or three moons. I am, as usual, also, planning writing free-lance stories. . . . Look for me in the Century or the Smart Set or the Housemaid's annual."

He continues an effort to sell Althea to Nugent. "Althea has heard more of you than of any other living American she has not met," he writes. He quotes colleagues on the *Dispatch* who remarked on how pretty Althea looked at a journalists' banquet. His own opinions of her at times seem less important to him than those of others.

"Many of *my* friends were *our* friends," says Althea, "people of my age, actually, rather than the people [Jim] had known. It was a full and pleasant life." Althea and her mother were living in an apartment on Thirteenth Street by then, and Mrs. Adams owned a Ford coupé, which Althea drove most of the time. One evening, Althea drove Thurber to visit a married sorority sister of hers in Newark, Ohio. The four spent the night playing poker with milk-bottle caps for chips, and tossing the caps into a wastebasket from a distance. (Thurber remained excellent at these cards-tossed-into-a-hat games throughout his sighted life.) They drove home in the rain, arriving in Columbus the next morning, Althea late for class and Thurber late for work. The assignment waiting for him was "Man Loses Life in Storm, Leaving Widow and Nine Children," he tells Nugent:

> It was my task to worm from a heavy minded and wide breasted widow, her eyes rimmed with the redness of much crying, the thin story of their lives, and to line up all nine youngsters in various states of excitement and happiness, for it was all like a circus to them. . . . The raising of the [photographer's] flash above his head, precipitated a riot and it took a new half hour to drape them about the family horsehair sofa again. It's a hard but interesting life, working for the zest of pathos craving readers.

Having found The Girl to take with him, his plans to return to France were still very much alive and now included the cameraman Hal Cooley. Thurber was to write captions and leaders for Cooley's educational and weekly short feature films produced abroad and sent to American distributors. Thurber would also write a series of "literary letters" from Europe.

He and Althea decided on an earlier wedding date, perhaps recognizing that they would be as economically strapped in October as in May. He also wished to avoid the risks of mind change that go with delay, for he was convinced that Althea was The Girl to make his Jamesian illusions reality. Althea's mother, while not opposed to the marriage, felt that her daughter should wait until she finished college. The new May wedding date meant that she would not finish her third year; married women were not qualified to attend undergraduate classes. But Althea was in love, too. "I felt he was the complete man of the world," she recalled fifty years later. "He was so much better read than I. He introduced me to good writing. Nobody could talk me into delaying the marriage." Her determination strengthened Thurber's. He was delighted to have the full responsibility of decision in the matter lifted from him.

Two days before the wedding, one would suppose Thurber's thoughts would be on little else, but that day he read in the New York reviews that *Kempy*, the play Nugent, his father, and Russel Crouse had put together, starring the senior Nugent, son Elliott, and daughter Ruth, was a hit. He writes Nugent on May 18: "Bless God, the world is yours! . . . I have spent the whole day darn near, and me with a million pre-nuptial things to do, riding a mad machine over wet streets carrying the word to friends of yours and to perfect strangers. I have called up everyone you ever nodded to, spreading the news."

The Thurber-Adams wedding, he twenty-seven, she twenty-one, at Trinity Church, Saturday, May 20, 1922, was a big one. The church was Mrs. Adams's choice. The *Kempy* commitment prevented Nugent from acting as best man, so Thurber's old friend Ed Morris was drafted. Althea's uncle, Professor Blake, gave her away. The ushers were among the last to arrive. Of the six, only Ray Lee Jackson got to the church on time to help seat the guests. The others dressed at the Phi Psi house and rode in one car, which was delayed by a minor accident on the way to the church.

Robert Thurber boycotted the wedding, claiming to be on the sick list that day. Contrary to a disclaimer by Minnette, Althea *was* somewhat socially conscious, and the Thurber family felt it keenly. "Mrs. Adams was always very nice to us," Robert says, "but Althea was a snob toward us. She used to smile when she visited us in a way that said she was just being a good sport hobnobbing with Jim's family. If one of us ever mentioned somebody of prominence in Columbus, Althea was apt to say to Jim, in front of us, 'How would *he* ever know *him*?' As if we were just drawing attention to ourselves for no good reason. She was always criticizing someone in the family. Maybe she'd heard a lot about my illnesses from Jim, because when she'd hear I had a dental appointment, for instance, she'd say in a nasty way, 'Do you really have to go to a dentist?' We never felt comfortable around her." He was not speaking for Mame in this case, who, writing years later, says: "I . . . liked Althea but never thought she was the one for Jamie. . . . Althea was always wonderful to me; we never had a bad word."

Robert may have been a bit jealous, losing the brother he had been close to. But he knew better than to complain to Thurber, who appreciated Althea in every way, including the volume of womanhood her size represented. "It's a little like sleeping with the Statue of Liberty," he told his friend, Ted Gardiner, with pride and affection.

After the reception, the newlyweds drove to Washington, D.C., in the Ford coupé, which Mrs. Adams either loaned or gave them. Althea had perched her overnight bag on the car's running board, forgot about it in the excitement of the send-off and remembered it miles out of Columbus, too late to turn back and look for it.

Why they went first to Washington rather than straight to New York, where they intended to see the Nugent family in *Kempy*, is a mystery. Perhaps Thurber wished to show Althea the sites of his Washington experiences. Nugent had been forewarned:

> Althea and I leave here Saturday aft. for Washington to remain thru Wednesday, then running up to NY for a day or two. I will contrive to have a few minutes with you, famous though you be. Please leave word with all sub-assistant secretaries that J. G. Thurber, a friend of your lowly, only by comparison, days, is to be allowed the freedom of all your town houses, your five cars, your Long Island estates and your personal theaters. . . . Expect then, on Thursday or Friday, a word with me and Mrs. James G. Thurber.

From Washington, the newlyweds drove to Compo Beach, near Westport, Connecticut, where the Nugents had rented a small cottage. As houseguests of the Nugents, they saw *Kempy* and put in a solid week of playgoing. Thurber reviewed all the plays for the *Dispatch*, to help defray expenses. A major disappointment for him on the honeymoon was the obvious lack of enthusiasm his old friend Nugent had for Althea. Nugent, who knew and loved Thurber, simply felt that she was all wrong for him, and, in private, referred to her as "a bonehead." Thurber's letters to Nugent rarely make mention of Althea after their return to Columbus.

24

Those Credos and Curios

I am reading [Credos and Curios] with alarm, disbelief and some small pleasure here and there. . . . It was practice and spadework by a man of 28 who sometimes sounds 19, praises "clean love" and such books as "Faint Perfume" and "If Winter Comes" and practically any play or movie I ever saw, and attacks Cabell, Joyce, Hecht and Sherwood Anderson. I was a great Willa Cather man.

—Letter to Frank Gibney, October 31, 1956

Back from their honeymoon, the James Thurbers rented small quarters in southeast Columbus and, a few months later, moved to the Tionesta Apartments on Neil Avenue, near the O.S.U. campus. Where he had had an easy walk from the Thurber house on Gay Street to the *Dispatch* building at Gay and High, he now rode the trolley the three miles or so.

He still enjoyed the late-morning hour at Marzetti's with McNulty and the local newspaper brotherhood. A newcomer to the Marzetti fold was Joel Sayre, another of the half-dozen men who would remain close friends of Thurber for life.

Sayre, born in Marion, Indiana, had moved to Columbus at age nine. "I first really got to know Jim about 1922," he says. "He covered City Hall for the *Dispatch* and I covered police headquarters for the *Journal*. It was a pity Jim wasn't on our paper [edited by Robert O. Ryder, where] he would have been much more appreciated." Sayre believed it was Thurber's later literary distinction that led some of his Columbus contemporaries to decide, in retrospect, that Thurber was never meant to be a reporter. "Actually, he was an excellent newspaperman," Sayre says, "[though] nothing he was writing led us to believe he would become a celebrity." Thurber continued to write for Strollers, which led to his meeting Herman Miller, who would remain important to Thurber until Miller's premature death in 1949. (In 1952, Thurber dedicated *The Thurber Album* to the memory of Miller, "whose friendship was an early and enduring inspiration.") Miller, two years younger than Thurber, was a "towner" from the German South Side. He graduated from O.S.U. in 1920, joined the faculty that fall, and taught English, drama, and speech for the next twenty years. By 1940, he knew that he had an incurable illness and resigned from the university to write plays and literary criticism. He had Thurber's love of stand-up storytelling with dramatic embellishment. They played to one another's theatrical and comic sides. Both had attended Professor Joe Taylor's novel course, and, not surprisingly, were Henry James enthusiasts.

"I never knew Thurber well until 1922," Miller writes:

> Then, at Christmas time, we did some one-act plays for Strollers. . . .
> At the performance of ["A Night at an Inn"] one of our cast went stone cold with stage fright and could not speak a word. Thurber and I, working relays, had to sandwich in all of his lines with our own. Naturally, that didn't do the play much good, but it did begin our friendship. That friendship, nurtured by a love of good books, of night-long talks, and of Roquefort cheese with a bottle of milk, has persisted these many years.

Thurber coauthored the book of the 1922–23 Scarlet Mask production, *A Twin Fix*, Althea helping with lighting and sets. When he went on the road with Scarlet Mask productions, he said, often someone in the cast would be taken unexpectedly drunk and he would fill in. "I had acting in mind," he was to claim years later, and perhaps he had, for Nugent's stage success still haunted his fantasies.

In a September 1922 letter to Nugent, Thurber discusses a novel he plans to write, its theme hardly what one would expect from a man married only four months. It would be

> a chronicling of people in this thoroughly Middle Western town, largely autobiographical as we are told all good novels are and written from a University-Paris-Newspaper chronology of events, impressions and de-

velopments. It would be quite melancholy since the longer you live the more you see that life is a melancholy thing. . . . Nothing to get morose about, for there are many pleasures and lots of fun, if one has a sense of humor, to keep on going, but what a welter of futility, commonness, unenlightenment, frailty and insignificance life is made by the average person. Out of living here I get only an increasing conviction that America has no cultural or intellectual or even intelligent future. The signs of it are everywhere. It is all stocks and bonds, automobiles, real estate, super movies, business deals, pettiness and other junk, with one person out of 10,000 who seems inspired by any outside light at all.

Thurber concludes that he and Nugent must continue their correspondence, despite their "crowded hours . . . in the interest of a coming generation which is already jeopardized by a paucity of belles lettres. How would 'Hells Belles Lettres' be for a book of essays?"

With *Kempy* still going strong, Nugent and his father wrote another play, *A Clean Town*, which tried out in Washington in October 1922. It was a comedy satirizing Prohibition, and Nugent wrote to Thurber offering him a character role in it. The offer both excited and scared Thurber. He might have tried it had Nugent been in the play, too, he said, but Thurber knew the tenuous nature of any new drama, and perhaps Nugent's nonparticipation provided the excuse Thurber was relieved to take. Or Althea may have had a voice in his decision. As it turned out, the show was judged to be so bad, despite Charles Ruggles's good acting, that it closed in Stamford without reaching Broadway.

The heavy baggage of emotional immaturity that Thurber carried for so many of his earlier years is somehow reflected in his struggle to write coherent prose. His letter writing to Nugent was steadily pulling away from the show-off use of fatuous words, redundant synonyms, silly colloquialisms, labored humor, and the self-conscious use of classical literary allusions. Though we don't know how much editing help he received from Cherrington and others, Thurber's several *Dispatch* columns in 1922, called "Pallette & Brush," show a refreshing clarity of language in his reviews of paintings, music, and even an Oriental rug exhibit. His first profile article of any length makes its appearance in May 1922. The subject is Charles Schneider, an early Columbus photoengraver who made possible the first wood cartoon produced in a newspaper.

Ever the Ryder disciple, Thurber contributed more and more limericks, one-liners, puns, and anecdotes to the newspaper. He was paid no extra money for them but they sometimes got his name or initials in print:

The world has moved apace, my dear,
*   The young folks now are wild, I hear,*
And maidens kick the chandelier.
*   Times ain't what they used to be!*

But just between us two, my dear,
*   They're getting old, the ones who jeer,*
Let us be young enough to cheer:
*   "Times ain't what they used to be!"*
                                    —J. G. T.

In the Sunday edition, he protests moviemakers who goad frightened lions into appearing on the screen as fierce predators. The lion, says Thurber, is "as lacking in fortitude as a federal prohibition officer." He quotes from an article that says the lion does not even climb trees, a statement that leads into an early authentic Thurberism: "[The insinuation is] that it would climb trees but is afraid it couldn't get down." As for

the famous incident of Androcles and the lion . . . he had the brilliant audacity to tell the emperor that he once plucked a thorn from the [lion's] foot! Now anyone who has ever tried to pull a thorn from a lion's paw, or even to extract a tack from a pet Pomeranian's ankle, knows full well that if there is any time when a beast will fight back it is [then]. . . . There could be but one act more dangerous than approaching a lion and trying to pluck a thorn from its paw, and that would be in sneaking up upon it and trying to push a thorn in. A sick Belgian hare would kick a blacksmith in the face if he tried it.

He describes high society as depicted in the current movies: "An [heir] never works, no matter how much he wants to. If he refuses to work his father gives him a yacht and suggests a cruise with numberless girls and chorus men. 'My son,' he says, 'I am determined that you shall have all the disadvantages your father lacked. Go to it.' "

His and Althea's social agenda was more and more taken up with campus dramatics. Meanwhile, driven by the worry and guilt of a marginal provider, Thurber spent desperate hours at his typewriter, at home and office. Their food budget was twenty dollars per week, and some evenings were designated "onion sandwich parties," according to Dorothy [Mrs. Herman] Miller. Miller often brought Roquefort cheese and milk to the parties. He and Thurber would read to one another from their writings while Althea listened. "I didn't attend those parties," says Dorothy. "It was before I married Herman, or knew Jim, but Herman said Jim and Althea were very happy in those days. He thought she was the nicest, sweetest person, and a real lady."

At the start of 1923, Thurber and Harold Cherrington persuaded the *Dispatch* management to let them share a full page of the Sunday edition in which to gather their book, play, and movie reviews, verses, one-liners, anecdotes, Ryderisms, playlets, fictional skits, and commentary. Cherrington favored poetry. A staff artist, Ray Evans, illustrated Thurber's bottom half of the page with comic-strip figures. Thurber gave his half-page the title of "Credos and Curios."

It was a brave conglomeration of items that took its cue from Heywood Broun, Franklin P. Adams, Don Marquis, Ryder, and other contemporary newspaper giants of the clever turn of word. Cherrington, says George Smallsreed, liked Thurber and encouraged him to take on the feature. "Jim wrote his own titles and headlines," Smallsreed remembers, "and may have illustrated something he called 'The Captain's Dominoes.' The drawing looks less like Evans's style than like something that would evolve into Thurber's. He had been signing his regular newspaper pieces 'James G. Thurber,' but he dropped the middle initial so that his name fitted more neatly over that of Ray Evans's on the page."

Patches of Thurber's "Credos and Curios" read well today, though the criticism of theater and books still rambles in the fashion of the novice who seeks to hedge his bets through verbose and obscure writing. There is a pretending to urbanity that suggests Thurber was writing principally for his special circle of university friends and newspaper associates. But more and more in this apprenticeship period his literary reach is within his grasp.

A feature, "Dad Dialogs," is a device enabling Thurber to argue with himself over the book trends of the day. He picks a friendly quarrel with "Dad," who has trouble understanding the newer trends in books. Often, however, Dad is expounding Thurber's conservative and prudish sentiments. Dad is no expert in literature; he usually picks up the book in the doctor's office while waiting to be told "to give up smoking, or to walk to work."

Althea found herself drafted by Thurber to play his version of Ryder's "Young Lady Across the Way":

"A woman is a person who will advise you tragically, on any and all occasions, that she can't take her hat off because her hair is a wreck."

"No mere husband can ever quite comprehend why it is that a woman wants to keep the bathroom constantly looking as if it were a place where the foot of man had never trod."

"A woman will ask you a question from the next room just as you turn on the water in the bath tub and feel that you are beginning to neglect her when you ask her to repeat it."

Adapting Ryder's style to his own purposes, he begins his mockery of the female sex, developing a prejudice he would keep for a lifetime: He complains about women who talk all through a mystery play, trying to guess who the murderer is. He is most unforgiving of the women who punished the country with Prohibition. He was alarmed, he writes, when covering a Columbus meeting of the Women's Christian Temperance Union at Memorial Hall, at the ladies, "worn-faced, rushing in fanatic ardor about the platform," rehearsing a "sing-songy la-de-da which ended with the shout by everybody 'The whole world is going dry.'" What he really objected to, he said, was

> the singular gracelessness with which so many women, born into the tradition of reform, exhibit. For one with kindly eyes and gentle manners, there seem to be twenty-five in any gathering of reformers, with grim-lipped mouths, two bright eyes and nervously energetic manners.
>
> It is our . . . personal belief that there is more menace to this country in the destruction of the charm of women by their dedication to reform than in . . . the objects of reform . . . We live in dread of the day when there will not be a woman left who will refuse to take part in a parade.

He discusses his experiences in writing Scarlet Mask productions: "Laughs are born and not made. Your best comedy line . . . may not get a titter. A line . . . you wrote merely for furtherance of action, or to get a character off the stage, may draw a howl. There will be a general giggle at something that post-show analysis cannot account for. A thing that has fairly convulsed the actors in rehearsal will go by unobserved. The psychology of the theater laugh is worth a book." Years later, rewriting scripts for two Broadway shows, he would have no reason to change a word of his 1923 observations.

In the second issue of "Credos," he settles a score with a Columbus traffic policeman, who, he says, plays what had become one of America's great outdoor sports:

> We will say that you jaywalk while lost in thought as to what President Wojclochowski of Poland is going to do in the Memel imbroglio.

You are accosted by a policeman. "Stranger here, Mister?" he will ask. Don't be misled. He doesn't intend to tell you what President Wojclochowski is going to do . . . or what's a good restaurant. He has merely begun to play cat-and-mouse, taking the part of Ignatz.

"Yes," you answer.

"Crippled?" he will then inquire.

"No," you will say.

"Blind?" he will query.

You still say no, unless, of course, you are blind, in which case you win the game, which rarely happens.

"Ever try crossing the street at the crossing?" he will ask you.

"Why, sure," is as good an answer as you will think of.

"Well, do it then, pardner, or you will walk into the hoosegow," he will vouchsafe.

This play wins for him unless, of course, you lose your temper. . . . If he asks more than fifteen insulting questions, you should rap him in the eye or tear his badge off. You lose, of course, but it's worth it.

He is already the mimic studying mannerisms of speech, a custodian of the integrity of language, deploring the Midwestern contraction of "What's the matter?" to "S'matter?" and "going to" to "gunna."

His attacks on homespun legend have begun: Why blame the groundhog on Groundhog Day? he asks. Why not blame the sun? It takes the two to make a shadow.

He enjoys himself writing a twelve-part serial that parodies the new "psychoscientific" detective in fiction. His sleuth, Blue Ploermell, rings with Sherlock Holmes overtones, though Ploermell's trademark characteristic is the eating of animal crackers—a favorite snack of Thurber's. Thurber's idea for the serial came from an actual murder case in Columbus, in which a caged parrot was found in the kitchen of the house where the killing took place. Thurber says that at the time he was with other reporters trying to get an exclusive interview with the parrot, which chose not to reveal anything of significance.

He promotes the work of Edith Wharton, Henry James, and Joseph Hergesheimer. He borrows from the styles of Mencken and Nathan, then appearing in the *Smart Set*, as well as from Alexander Woollcott, the theater critic for the *New York Times*: "I ask heaven for forgiveness, but I find them [two novels by James Branch Cabell] a little dull." Cabell, Thurber decides, "is a circus trying to pass for a carnival." He resents Cabell's non-Jamesian treatment of the fairer sex: "He has the most nauseating attitude toward women of any writer I've ever come across."

Herman Miller was soon contributing lines to Thurber, who was now occasionally borrowing from other newspapers' paragraphs containing typos or gaffes for snide comment—another practice he would find in fashion when he joined the *New Yorker*.

He used "Credos" to rehearse material he would later publish in the *New Yorker* in finer form. He makes a modern mystery, for example, of *Hamlet*, suggesting that it was Horatio who killed the prince. The switching of rapiers in the final duel scene has never been carefully enough analyzed, he says, and he finds it significant that Hamlet dies in Horatio's arms. When Hamlet is turned partly from the audience and "gurgles . . . the rest is silence," indeed it is, says Thurber, because Horatio has shut his wind off.

Thurber's nagging age consciousness is already at work: "I am almost middle-aged," he writes one Sunday [he was twenty-eight], "and what I say and believe may be senile but it is not sophomoric." Like an old-timer remembering, he recalls Aunt Margery Albright's garden; the high cost of a luncheon at Voisin's in Paris; the Post Café in Washington, with its assistant manager and sometime waitress, Mrs. Rabbit; "Many Junes," a ballad he said had been dashed off for him in nine minutes by Stephen Vincent Benét.

At times he seemed to write without apparent suspicion that he had any readers besides his acquaintances. He quotes Joel Sayre, who defines the difference between the police attitude toward drunks in the U.S. versus that in London: the British bobbie calls a cab and sees the drunk home.

As many another hometown newspaper personality has done, Thurber jokingly offers to run for local public office. Part of his platform is to abolish the song "Yes, We Have No Bananas," because a South Side merchant said it tended to destabilize the banana market. He admires the public utilities for having "slipped something over on the public . . . and shall be inclined to favor their further demands if elected." He would increase Columbus's annual appropriation for [library] books "from its present equality with that of . . . Castle Rock, South Dakota, to an amount commensurate with decency, intelligence and Christianity."

John McNulty helped Thurber satirize newspaper clichés: "Old John lives in the hope that some day a recluse will die whose death will not be 'shrouded in mystery.'" McNulty has also bought a "missing-man's suit—that is, a dark gray mixture which, according to Mac, all men, missing out of New York, are wearing when last seen."

Dorothy Reid, a student in Herman Miller's poetry class (she and Miller would later marry), had founded *The Candle*, a campus literary magazine that immediately ran into financial trouble through lack of student and university support. "I never met Jim until after he left Columbus," Dorothy says, "but Herman told him about the trouble *The Candle* was in and Jim fought for it in three issues of his 'Credos and Curios' page."

"[It] has too much good stuff in it to last at the O.S.U. college for football players, Boost Ohioers and stock judging teams," Thurber writes. " 'Millions,' say Ohio State students, alumni and downtown fans, 'for football programs, but not one cent for literature [and] not a dime for Candles!' " Thurber's campaign failed, as did *The Candle*.

Thurber's boyhood friend Donald Ogden Stewart came to town with the galleys of a new book. Thurber interviewed him. Stewart had established himself as a humorist with *A Parody Outline of History* and witty short pieces in *Vanity Fair*. Stewart recalls that he and Thurber drank dubious Prohibition intoxicants during the interview and sang such songs as "Down by the Old Mill Stream." Thurber knew all the words of the songs they sang, Stewart recalls—the verses as well as the chorus.

Thurber learned that the woman who reviewed plays and movies at the *Journal* was retiring to get married; he aspired to the job but was told that it paid only thirty dollars a week, five dollars less than his *Dispatch* salary. Only later did he learn that Ryder, the *Journal* editor, had always surreptitiously paid her double that amount.

"Credos and Curios" served Thurber as a safe training ground on which to practice before showing himself to a more sophisticated readership. He still needed editing, although he would no doubt argue that he had a lot of space to fill each Sunday.

In 1951, George Smallsreed, managing editor of the *Dispatch,* photostatted all the "Credos and Curios" pages and sent them to Thurber in West Cornwall, Connecticut, asking permission for the *Dispatch* to publish them as a book. Thurber had them read to him and politely refused Smallsreed, rightfully claiming that their many evidences of an unmastered craft would hardly enhance his current reputation. Yet, there is no better hunting ground for the Thurber archaeologist than "Credos," for one sees the genesis of Thurber's first-person techniques, nonsense, wit, parody, and satire that would lay the base of his distinguished career and name. No guardian of self-image as alert as the 1950s Thurber would want his 1923 pages exhumed, even though here and there an item sparkles with greater brightness and comic value than several that would be accepted for publication in the *New Yorker* in his earliest days on the staff. There, Thurber was to credit the influence of his colleague E. B. White in shaping his own work. But bits of parody, verse, and observation in Thurber's *Dispatch* column suggest that he was traveling a course parallel to White's, and given the *New Yorker*'s general lack of format in its beginning days, he might well have come to a full and independent flowering there on his own.

The "Credos" page ended on December 9, 1923, after forty-two weeks. "I started this Sunday half-page called 'Credos and Curios,' for which I got no extra money," Thurber said in a 1950s British interview. "And then it was stopped because the man who wrote the top half of the page said something nasty about the town of Urbana, Ohio. . . . They gave me the excuse that they needed it for advertising space."

Thurber also told Smallsreed in a 1951 letter that the reason for ending the Sunday feature was a poem by Cherrington that made light of Urbana, and had caused irate residents of the town to write the paper's current publisher, Robert Wolfe. Wolfe ordered the page terminated. Cherrington, Thurber added, was also told by management that the Sunday page was needed for increased advertising. Smallsreed, who didn't know the real reason for the page's demise, was certain the full explanation was never given to either Thurber or Cherrington. Says Smallsreed, "You drop a feature if it isn't getting good readership, or if the management just doesn't like it, or public and advertising pressures are brought on management to drop it, and Urbana, Ohio, didn't have that kind of power, either political or in the number of readers. Furthermore, if something offensive is published, you run a correction or apology. Controversy builds readership. Or if half the page is pulling the other half, you lop off the poor half and keep the good. You don't throw the baby out with the bath water. If they told Thurber it was Cherrington's fault the feature was dropped, maybe they told Cherrington it was Thurber's."

Thurber, certainly, had engendered his own quota of letters to the editor with such items as the harsh attack on the ladies of that noble crusade, Prohibition, and sarcastic references to other sacred institutions of Columbus, delivered in his best version of Mencken-Nathan vitriol. Whatever the sin, the punishment was harsh. With his feature gone, Thurber was no longer the local metropolitan celebrity. He was relegated to regular features and infrequent bylines. The loss of "Credos and Curios" remained prominent among his reasons for wanting to get out of Columbus.

25

That Day Chic Harley Got Away

He was a tackle on the football team, named Bolenciecwcz. At that time Ohio State University had one of the best football teams in the country, and Bolenciecwcz was one of its outstanding stars. In order to be eligible to play it was necessary for him to keep up in his studies, a very difficult matter, for while he was not dumber than an ox he was not any smarter.

—from "University Days"

The fierce partisanship that still marks the annual football rivalry between Ohio State University and the University of Michigan may have been bred in 1835, when Ohio and Michigan both claimed ownership of a strip of land from Lake Erie to Ohio's western boundary, an area that included Toledo. Michigan's acting governor sent militia. The governor of Ohio sent a commission to survey the boundary, along with five hundred militiamen to protect the commission. Despite the protection, Michigan troops captured nine members of the Ohio surveying team. The Ohio General Assembly was called into special session and appropriated three hundred thousand dollars to field ten thousand troops for war against Michigan. President Andrew Jackson arbitrated, giving Michigan the northern peninsula and awarding Ohio Toledo and the rest of the disputed area. But bad blood between the states lingered for decades, and finally found expression in the annual football contest between the two state universities—still the most highly charged game of their seasons.

Columbus had little interest in college sports for forty years after the university's founding. The state funding of O.S.U.'s athletic program was meager and its football record lamentable. The 1892 season, for instance, saw Oberlin beat Ohio State, 50 to 0. O.S.U. began playing Michigan in 1897 (losing 34–0), and it wasn't until 1904 that the Ohio team even scored a touchdown against Michigan. In 1902, when Thurber was nearly eight, hated Michigan won 86–0. Other such records of humiliation are missing, and university historian James Pollard thinks they may have been deliberately destroyed. In 1910, O.S.U. finally managed to avert a loss to Michigan by tying the score, and the city went wild.

Ohioans remained "heartily ashamed of the poor, struggling school on the outskirts [of town]," according to writer Robert Cantwell. "Football history has rarely recorded such dogged determination by such persistent losers. In 21 years Ohio State scored three touchdowns and one field goal against Michigan, while Michigan piled up 369 points against Ohio State." Meanwhile, Columbus football fans focused on the "high-school games, which often drew bigger crowds than college games."

Thurber maintained a sentimental interest in the North-East high-school games even after Columbus had become a college football town. In an unsigned *Dispatch* story of November 1921, Thurber writes: "We went to the North-East game a week ago. It was like opening an old school book in which your name is written with a girl's above it and letters are mystically crossed out. You may have forgotten the girl in between but she will come back as radiant as firelight on snow. Nine years ago we saw a North-East game and North, with a great big swiftly moving line of men destroying interference, choked East." He was at it again in a 1923 fall issue of the *Dispatch*, remembering a 1914 game between the schools. ("East was always having its heart broken.")

Charles Wesley (Chic) Harley almost single-handedly turned a struggling O.S.U. team into a Big Ten football power. He played shortstop on the East High baseball team that Robert Thurber captained, and he entered O.S.U. two years after Thurber. "Until his last high-school game against Columbus North," Cantwell writes, "the football teams that Harley played on never lost. [East's athletic ground was later named Harley Field.] With Harley as halfback, Ohio State went undefeated in 1916, winning its first Big Ten championship and repeating it the next year. It did not beat Michigan [that would take place three years later] which was temporarily out of the Big Ten." Harley was picked by sports columnist Walter Camp for his All-American team all three years that Harley played varsity football—the first Ohio State player to be so designated.

In November 1922, Thurber drew up his own all-star team as only a man with a penchant for puns could, playing upon Camp's name:

Walter Cramp's All-American football team has been selected by that great authority of the gridiron. Its personnel is as follows:

L.E.—Tube of Colgate.
L.T.—Stick of Williams.
L.G.—Church of Notre Dame.
  C.—Gang of Tufts.
R.G.—Graves of Washington and Jefferson.
R.T.—Bust of Lafayette.
R.E.—Eyes of Brown.
Q.B.—Tomb of George Washington.
L.H.—Hart of Maryland.
R.H.—Purchase of Louisiana.
F.B.—District of Columbia.
  Substitutes: Hills of Kentucky, Lock of Yale, Auditor of State, Off of Centre, Banks of Wabash, Works of Carlyle, Poets of Indiana. Coach: Hale, Columbia.

A year later, the popular *New York World* columnist Franklin P. Adams ran in his "Conning Tower" almost an identical joke on the All-American team, reprinted from the old *Life*, a humor magazine. Though Adams was a much-admired role model of Thurber's at the time, Thurber, in his "Credos" page, strongly protested what he thought to be a case of plagiarism. But any thievery was by the *Life* writer, not Adams, who probably had never heard of Thurber at the time.

In 1919, nine years after the O.S.U.–Michigan tie, Harley, back on campus after a year of military service, finally led the Buckeyes to their first victory over Michigan, 13 to 3. When he was in Columbus, Thurber never missed a game in which Harley played, but he was in Paris on that red-letter day.

"Harley," continues Cantwell, "was slight, weighing only 145 in his senior year of high school. He was a good-natured, self-conscious boy with a lopsided grin, and was fast enough to break high-school sprint records. Often, when not on the playing fields, he wore a look of puzzlement that may have had something to do with the monumental eligibility problems he faced because of his grades."

It would have caused a student riot if any faculty member had disqualified the gridiron hero who put O.S.U. football on the map. In "University Days," Thurber disguises the slow-witted Chic Harley not as the lightweight running back Harley was but as "Bolenciecwcz," a heavy tackle:

Most of his professors were lenient and helped him along. None gave him more hints, in answering questions, or asked him simpler ones than the economics professor, a thin, timid man named Bassum. One day when we were on the subject of transportation and distribution, it came Bolenciecwcz's turn to answer a question. "Name one means of transportation," the professor said to him. No light came into the big tackle's eyes. "Just any means of transportation," said the professor. Bolenciecwcz sat staring at him. "That is," pursued the professor, "any medium, agency, or method of going from one place to another." Bolenciecwcz had the look of a man who is being led into a trap. "You may choose among steam, horse-drawn, or electrically propelled vehicles," said the instructor. "I might suggest the one which we commonly take in making long journeys across land." There was a profound silence in which everybody stirred uneasily, including Bolenciecwcz and Mr. Bassum. Mr. Bassum abruptly broke this silence in an amazing manner. "Choo-choo-choo," he said, in a low voice, and turned instantly scarlet. He glanced appealingly around the room. All of us, of course, shared Mr. Bassum's desire that Bolenciecwcz should stay abreast of the class in economics, for the Illinois game, one of the hardest and most important of the season, was only a week off. "Toot, toot, too-toooooooot!" some student with a deep voice moaned, and we all looked encouragingly at Bolenciecwcz. Somebody else gave a fine imitation of a locomotive letting off steam. Mr. Bassum himself rounded off the little show. "Ding, dong, ding, dong," he said, hopefully. Bolenciecwcz was staring at the floor now, trying to think, his great brow furrowed, his huge hands rubbing together, his face red.

"How did you come to college this year, Mr. Bolenciecwcz?" asked the professor. "*Chuffa* chuffa, *chuffa* chuffa."

"M'father sent me," said the football player.

"What on?" asked Bassum.

"I git an 'lowance," said the tackle, in a low, husky voice, obviously embarrassed.

"No, no," said Bassum. "Name a means of transportation. What did you *ride* here on?"

"Train," said Bolenciecwcz.

"Quite right," said the professor. "Now, Mr. Nugent, will you tell us—"

With Ohio State's first Big Ten championship in 1916, the major interest of local football fans swung from high-school games to college athletics in Columbus. It also prompted O.S.U. alumni, the city, and the state legislature to plan the mighty million-dollar Ohio Stadium, on the west side of the campus, near the river. (The city donated nearly six hundred thousand dol-

Bolenciecwcz Was Trying to Think

lars.) As intended, the stadium outdid the 1914 Yale Bowl in size, seating seventy-four thousand, with an additional ten thousand seats during the football season.

In September 1922, Thurber writes Nugent:

> Too bad you cant be here to whiff the football air and to see the Stadium dedicated. It is nearly completed now, a wonderful structure, set down in the pastoral back eighty of the OSU like a modernized Greek temple or a Roman coliseum born of mirage. Michigan plays here on Oct. 21, dedication day. . . .
>
> On football, I wonder if you have heard of the truly sad condition of Chic Harley. He has been in a bad way since last winter and is variously reported as hopeless, his case being diagnosed as dementia precox by a number of examiners, although the Harley mind, unless known of old, might bother any medical man. At any rate he has dropped out of life, and is now in a Dayton sanitarium. . . . Some middle western Henry James might "do" Chic in a really great story. The only immortal piece written about him so far is my own epic poem in three eight-line plunges . . . having as its refrain "Like the glory of the going when Chic Harley got away . . ." to grace a two column box in the state edition.

Here is a stanza from Thurber's "epic" poem, "When Chic Harley Got Away," printed in the *Dispatch* on the occasion of the stadium dedication, in the fall of 1922:

> *The years of football playing reach back a long, long way,*
> *And the heroes are a hundred who have worn the red and gray;*
> *You can name the brilliant players from the year the game began,*
> *You can rave how this one punted and praise how that one ran;*
> *You can say that someone's plunging was the best you ever saw—*
> *You can claim the boys now playing stage a game without a flaw—*
> *But admit there was no splendor in all the bright array*
> *Like the glory of the going when Chic Harley got away. . . .*

The stadium dedication took place at homecoming, October 22, 1922. Thurber was on hand, writing in the *Dispatch*:

> When the ticket-holder broke through . . . and rounded the open end of the giant horseshoe he got his first glimpse of the . . . crowded stands. The sight rooted him [to] the spot. . . . The highest line of

persons was a row of black dots against the sky. . . . Perhaps never again will the heart leap up quite so high and the breath come so swiftly as when, forming back of the north goal posts, the Ohio State band led by the wonderful "Tubby" Essington, the emperor of an undreamed-of Kingdom, went out upon the field, the sun gleaming on 110 pieces and 110 scarlet and gray capes, the strains of "The Spirit of Ohio" crashing on the air.

It hurt too much to put Michigan's victory that day into a headline without reminding the reader that O.S.U. had won the year before. Thurber's headline: MICHIGAN AVENGES DEFEAT OF 1921.

Thurber would remain a quick-change artist when it came to cheering on his alma mater's gridiron team one moment and lambasting the school's emphasis on football at the cost of academic quality the next. "As much as we love our dear old alma mater," he writes in "Credos," "far be it for us to refrain from telling the truth, namely, that it is a cockeyed and a lopsided school. In the one side of the scale there is the weighty stadium, in the other there are half a hundred persons interested in anything more important than the new Oakland; on one hand there is $40,000 a Saturday spent for football; on the other there is about $12.13 spent for the excellent lyrics, the clever articles and the really good stories of [*The Candle*]."

The university's curriculum still emphasized agriculture, a major clause of the school's original charter, and Jack Fullen, O.S.U. alumni secretary, recalls that Thurber once said of his alma mater, "It's a school dedicated to football and manure." Fullen offers a somewhat lame defense: "In the 1900s, O.S.U. didn't get the recognition that schools fifty years younger were getting. The thought behind spending a million on the stadium was to get the university recognized and to attract better professors."

Even when Thurber was loudly supporting the school administration in its struggle to de-emphasize football, he would continue in the next breath to reminisce admiringly about the football greats of the years he was on campus, when he sat in the huge stadium that Harley built and cheered the gray and scarlet.

During his early years in New York, Thurber occasionally arranged his return to Columbus to coincide with a football game. In 1936, Thurber brought his second wife, Helen, to Columbus for Thanksgiving and the Michigan game. He drew the cover for that Michigan–O.S.U. homecoming official program and wrote autobiographical notes for the back of it.

Thurber's heart kept sidetracking his intellectual directions regarding his alma mater. When in Columbus, he led the cheers for O.S.U. football. When elsewhere, he was quick to scold the university for its preoccupation with athletics over scholarship. In 1939, he and Nugent began writing *The Male Animal*. The play concerned itself with a mild-mannered professor's stand against a philistine threat to academic freedom and his domestic happiness. The villains were the trustees and alumni who favored big-time football over the educational purposes of a university.

Yet, just a decade after *The Male Animal* opened on Broadway, Thurber, discussing some of Columbus's better known sons and daughters in the *Bermudian*, singles out its athletes over such literary achievers as, say, William Dean Howells, who began his career as a Columbus newspaperman. In fact, he is back on his favorite O.S.U. theme, "the last and greatest, Charles W. (Chic) Harley, whose dazzling feats on the gridiron from 1916 to 1919 are as fresh in the memory of every Columbus resident as they were more than thirty years ago."

In February 1951, Thurber was complaining because O.S.U. had fired a football coach who had qualified the team for the Rose Bowl the year before: "A newspaperman I know said not long ago that one of our mottos is don't hit a man when he's down. Kick him." Yet he was behind Jack Fullen's effort to de-emphasize football at O.S.U. Fullen had boldly and publicly stated that an irreversible stampede, "informed by a special lunacy," had begun "to turn O.S.U. into a football factory of the first magnitude."

A few months before his death, Thurber wrote George Smallsreed, "I always stuck with Jack Fullen in his courageous stand against over-emphasis on football." But while Fullen was in the midst of his ideological travail, the ambivalent Thurber was proudly writing another alumnus about Ohio State's recent victory over the University of California in the Rose Bowl: "I bet even money on Ohio State to win, fortunately." Thurber's conflicts between mind and emotion left him in the dilemmas of ambivalence all his life, whether the subject was his family, his university, Columbus, the women in his life, the *New Yorker*, or humor in America.

Perhaps his contradictions demonstrate the ineffectiveness of the humorist in such instances. It is known that humorists please, elevate, fascinate, charm, and clarify, but too often, in the end, change nothing. As someone has said, in areas outside literature the humorist is often as powerless as a court jester dismissed from the throne room.

Deprived of his Sunday feature, Thurber concentrated on the 1923–24 Scarlet Mask production, *The Cat and the Riddle*. "[It is] the brain child of James G. Thurber of the staff of the *Columbus Dispatch*," reads a review of the show in the *Citizen* in February 1924, "a parody on the many mystery plays of the present season [such as *Seven Keys to Baldpate*, *The Cat and the Canary*, *The Thirteenth Chair*]. Thurber is fortunate in having as fine a cast as the Scarlet Mask affords for the interpretation of his satire." Besides writing the entire book, Thurber contributed clever lyrics to one number called "The Cat," which drew special mention in a couple of the reviews. The show's program has a picture of Thurber looking much like a bank teller, with steel-rimmed glasses, neatly parted hair, and a stiff collar.

Thurber's friend Herman Miller, writing in the university's *Lantern*, said: "It is a good book lifted above the level of parody into Thurberlesque by such pixie-pranks of the imagination as the amazing lantern scene, which reads like a passage from 'Alice in Wonderland.' " (Charles S. Holmes [in *The Clocks of Columbus*] believes Miller's review to be "the first critical comment on the essential quality of Thurber's comic imagination.") Althea, as always, helped out with costumes, sets, and lighting. Over the Christmas holidays, the show toured ten cities in three states and played to sell-out auditoriums.

After a three-day run in Columbus in February 1924, the show was history. Thurber was back on his old City Hall beat. In April, the year before, he and Althea had spent ten days in New York seeing plays, Thurber's reviews helping to fill his "Credos" page. They had visited the Nugents in Westport, where a friend of Nugent's, taken with Thurber's lively personality and literary ambition, offered him the use of his Adirondacks summer house in Jay, New York, eighteen miles from Lake Placid. Thurber, content with "Credos," didn't accept the offer that year but now inquired into it for the summer of 1924. "Corner Bright," as the farmhouse was called, was again available, free to a struggling artist. He and Althea decided that he would quit the *Dispatch* and begin his freelance writing career there. The *Dispatch* agreed to pay Thurber for reviewing another ten Broadway shows, and Thurber planned to convert a script he had begun for Scarlet Mask, called *Nightingale*, into a Broadway musical.

"It was a very exciting time," Althea recalled. "We lived in a little farmhouse miles from anybody, except for our landlords who lived in the next cottage. The country was beautiful. We got there in April and planted my first big vegetable garden. I remember it with a great deal of pleasure. It was my project. Jim wasn't as interested but was willing to help. It saved us a few bucks."

The same faulty eyesight that led Thurber to describe football games and other panorama as kaleidoscopic images was at work in Jay, to Althea's frustration. As he writes in "The Admiral on the Wheel":

It was me . . . who once killed fifteen white chickens with small stones. The poor beggars never had a chance. This happened many years ago when I was living at Jay, New York. I had a vegetable garden some seventy feet behind the house, and the lady of the house had asked me to keep an eye on it in my spare moments and to chase away any chickens from neighboring farms that came pecking around. One morning, getting up from my typewriter, I wandered out behind the house and saw that a flock of white chickens had invaded the garden. I had, to be sure, misplaced my glasses for the moment, but I could still see well enough to let the chickens have it with ammunition from a pile of stones that I kept handy for the purpose. Before I could be stopped, I had riddled all the tomato plants in the garden, over the tops of which the lady of the house had, the twilight before, placed newspapers and paper bags to ward off the effects of frost. It was one of the darker experiences of my dinner hours.

A songwriter, Frank Bannister, affiliated with radio station WJZ in New York, had published such songs as "Say It With a Ukulele," "Bringing Home the Bacon," and "Forget Me Not." William Haid, O.S.U. class of '24, who composed "Pretty Mary Ann," one of the best songs ever done for Scarlet Mask, knew Bannister and suggested that he consider writing the music for Thurber's *Nightingale*. Thurber was delighted at the prospect. He still thought his future might well be in the theater.

Says Althea: "At that point Jim was my father figure, literary man of the family. I was the housekeeper, the wife, the helpmeet. I was still a bit overwhelmed by this sophisticated man of the world. I wasn't involved in his work then, though I was later. At Jay, he wrote short stories and submitted them to magazines that rejected them. Then he finished this musical-comedy book, *Nightingale*, put on his plus fours, and started out with it for New York City. In no time he was back and said he'd lost the manuscript. Left it on a train. He was very upset and so was I. It was our whole future. He never recovered it. He rewrote the whole thing. Nothing came of it. There was no reason in the world for him to attempt so crazy a thing as starting out to make [his] name writing a musical comedy without any music and without actually knowing a single soul in the business."

Thirty years later, in a letter to E. B. White, Thurber places the blame on Haid for losing the manuscript:

The libretto of a musical comedy I wrote in 1923 was left on a subway train by a young musicker named Haid . . . who wrote nice music for

Scarlet Mask and who knew absolutely nothing else at all, including his ass from a hole in the ground, or how to button his own pants. That libretto was last heard of between Chambers Street and the Brooklyn Museum stop. It has been read by thousands of subway riders. Guy named George Choos had some idea of producing it and a guy named Bannister was going to supervise the music.

But Althea insists that Thurber had confessed to having lost the script without help from anyone else. The libretto, never produced but on copyright record at the Library of Congress, was well worth losing. It was thought by some that Thurber had originally written this paper-thin farce for the Scarlet Mask Club, which turned it down, surely a clue in itself as to *Nightingale*'s merits.

He and Althea had told family and friends that they planned to stay in Jay until November and then reside permanently in New York, but by September they were broke. In the five months at Jay, Thurber sold only a paragraph to Heywood Broun's column, "It Seems to Me," in the *New York World*; it was a comment on bullhead fishing and the abundance of nature, presented as an old-fashioned "tall tale." He and Althea did spend several days in New York going to the theater, and he was paid a few dollars for his reviews by the *Dispatch*, as well as for some copy he filed on the Democratic National Convention, held that summer in New York City. And the first story he ever sold, "Josephine Has Her Day," was written at Jay, though it took nearly two years and a dozen rejections before the *Kansas City Star* Sunday magazine finally printed it, on March 14, 1926. The story reflects Thurber's and Althea's dream of owning a Scottish terrier, but "Dick and Ellen Dickinson" buy a sickly bull terrier instead, the runt of the litter. Exasperated with its infirmities, they try to find a good home for the pup, but it ends up in the possession of the town bully, a hulking tough named Gibbs, who routinely beats the dog. In the town hardware store, Dickinson tries to buy back the dog from Gibbs, who will have none of it. A fearful Dickinson is transformed by anger from his natural disposition as pussycat into a pugnacious Walter Mitty: "In two bounds [Dickinson] was across the room, for he was lithe and quick, if no match for the other in strength." Dickinson throws boxes, cans, and racks at Gibbs and, with a lucky hit over the eye, brings down the bully.

There are the melodramatic overtones of his high-school short story, "The Third Bullet," in "Josephine Has Her Day," but there is also humor, and his love of dogs makes its first prose appearance.

Thurber had arranged to write the Scarlet Mask Club's 1924–25 production, and he and Althea used the commitment as their excuse for giving up New York for Columbus. "WELCOME HOME, JIM!" reads a friendly headline by one of his old newspaper friends. "Former student at Ohio State, author of the Scarlet Mask shows, has been picked again to write this year's production. He has been in New York, will arrive here today to start work on a play at once. This year's show will be a satire on modernists and the scenes will be laid in suburban Columbus."

Thurber gave the show a title borrowed from Longfellow: Tell Me Not. The project became his principal outlet from his exasperations with the public-relations work he had to take on, for his old position with the Dispatch was no longer available. Johnny Jones, who had known Thurber through childhood, college, and Dispatch days, was managing the Majestic Theater, and hired Thurber as a press agent. Thurber also resumed publicizing Olentangy Park, and such events as the Elks Circus and a Cleveland Symphony concert. He despised much of the work and was occasionally churlish. A clubwoman in charge of promoting the appearance of Pablo Casals asked Thurber how she might get the event on the front page of the local newspapers. Thurber told her that although Casals was the world's foremost cellist, her only chance of getting front-page mention of him in Columbus was to persuade Casals to bathe in Lazarus's department store window.

With her mother's sponsorship, Althea entered O.S.U. again for part of a semester. "I still had some idea of getting a degree," she says, "but I developed a thyroid condition, incipient for some time, and had an operation. That put an end to that notion.

"It was discouraging, having to come back to Columbus, but thanks to Jim's newspaper contacts he found freelance work and got me a number of jobs that fall and winter. One job I had was selling tickets to a well-known concert series downtown. I'd sold out the entire house for one famous opera singer, but she didn't turn up, so I had to refund all the money at the ticket office. In another job, I staged, wrote, and directed a pageant that featured three hundred schoolchildren. I tremble at my nerve and temerity at writing and costuming and directing three hundred girls in 'Famous Women of the World.'

"It was the type of thing I did all that year, anything that came to hand. We were living in an old house in the East End [Side] in one room. I remember it was a terribly cold and miserable winter. We were plagued with near-pneumonia and every other kind of illness, while trying to get a few dollars together. Money was always scarce with us, so those jobs I got were not only fun but helped considerably. It was a hand-to-mouth situation in no uncertain terms."

Tell Me Not was finished on schedule for the Christmas holidays. As in The

Male Animal, the play Thurber and Nugent would write sixteen years later, the scene is the home of a Midwestern college professor, but the show's volatile moments are not from the visit of a former football hero but of a French countess. The motif was derived from Thurber's earlier Strollers play, *Psychomania*, satirizing the effects of Freudian psychoanalysis on the new scientific detective gaining popularity in fiction. A musical number, "Kelley," shows a growing Thurber sophistication:

> *If a fellow killed his sister*
> *When dear old Dad was young*
> *A jury of his equals*
> *Had him sent out and hung.*
> *But the use of such rough tactics*
> *Is abolished in the land*
> *And we let 'em go if they can show*
> *A low pineal gland.*

The lively title song, "Tell Me Not," ends:

> *Silk pajamas may appear as smarty,*
> *Yet you bet the life of any party*
> *Tell me not that life is wrong my hearty*
> *Life is what you make it to be.*

Thurber directed, as well as writing the book, and collaborated with Ralph McCombs on the show's lyrics. Althea designed several of the male chorus costumes again and helped with scenery and lighting. The show made its Christmas tour and played the Hartman Theater in Columbus the second week of January, 1925. Thurber says it paid him three hundred dollars.

By now they were living in a small apartment at 76 Lexington Avenue, with no reliable source of income. The question of who and what got them out of Columbus and to France has been batted around for years. Thurber's dream of returning to France had occupied much of the letters he had been writing to Nugent. Yet most agree that it was Althea who made it happen.

"I saw quite a bit of the Thurbers before I left Columbus," Joel Sayre recalls. "I could see that Althea was ambitious for Jim in a good way. It wasn't that she wanted him to be successful for her sake alone, but for his, too. She believed in his abilities; she knew he had more than Columbus could bring out. Poverty wasn't driving love out the window at the time. Neither had had much money and they were used to that. Althea was certainly no shrew. She had pink cheeks, beautiful blue eyes, was good-natured and a nice lady.

"It's easy, in light of what happened later, to take sides, to argue that if the marriage was wrong in the late twenties, it had been wrong all along, and that Jim succeeded despite Althea, not because of her. But that isn't true. Thurber acquired his great drive only after he got going; he had acquired very little ego while in Columbus. I used to hear Althea tell a down-in-the-mouth Thurber, 'You can write and you must write. You are a humorist and Columbus isn't the place to do humor.' She was entirely unselfish about it. Jim was too good for his hometown, she felt. He was a worrier, timid and without confidence, and she responded as any person who loved him would. If she had believed he would be better off in Columbus she would not have persuaded him to leave. She recognized the large charge Paris had given him, and that was the reason it made sense to her to help get him back over there. Thurber himself kept presenting her with the contrasts: how great Paris had been and how awful Columbus had become. Next to Nugent and Miller, Althea was the principal believer in, and catalyst for, Jim back then. He didn't really begin to make the bell ring until he wrote about Columbus in the My Life and Hard Times series, and he would never have written about Columbus and his family that successfully if he had stayed there. How could any writer get perspective or lose a crippling self-consciousness if he decided to write about a family and city he saw on an everyday basis?"

Dorothy Miller, who had finally been introduced to Jim and Althea by Herman, remembers them as a happy couple, despite everything, though she felt Thurber's self-confidence was on the wane. "Herman recognized, as did Althea, that Jim ought to get out of Columbus," she says. "I got no impression that Althea was calling the shots. She was one of the nicest, sweetest persons I'd seen till then and I thought at the time how good she was for Jim, who used to talk to Herman in discouraged ways now and then. She was beautiful and gracious and Jim seemed to appreciate both those things as much as anything about her."

Helen Thurber, as a stricken widow of only a few weeks, can be forgiven if, in her reaction to Sayre's pro-Althea discourse, she suddenly saw Thurber's first wife as stealing the show. "That's a lot of crap," was her rejoinder to Sayre's comments. "Jamie would have left Columbus sooner or later with or without Althea." A decade later, she was conceding to Thurber biographer Burton Bernstein that Althea *was* behind Thurber's departing his hometown, but for strictly ulterior motives. "Althea thought—and it was very bright of her—that something in Jamie would be her ticket out of Columbus," she is quoted as saying. "It is possible she believed this all along and set a trap for him as the likeliest ticket out of town. Of course, you can never discount love as a motive, but Jamie in that period needed somebody strong to steer him, and Althea was strong."

Helen could only have received her impressions of the situation from Thurber, who in a Christmas letter to E. B. White in 1952 states in ungracious, dishonest—and unmanly—fashion: "Althea forced me to give up my good paying jobs in Columbus and sail for France."

For years, nobody thought to ask Althea about her and Thurber's departure from Columbus. "It *was* more my idea than Jim's," she says. "Ray Lee Jackson had gone to France the year before on a student tour. So had a number of people we knew. The student-tourist ticket class had just come into being and it started quite a trek of people, including some of my alumni friends from O.S.U. It was a great find. I'm sure Jim wanted to go but I was the one who felt we could actually do it. We had money from our jobs and from the Scarlet Mask show, and we made sure we bought our return tickets in advance and had a hundred and twenty-five dollars in savings. We had no job or commitments in Europe; Jim was going to write on his own."

Robert Thurber said that the family never expected James to leave Columbus, or to be anything more than a newspaper writer and editor. Robert, filled with poor feelings toward his sister-in-law, was certain that Althea was having her way in leaving, not Thurber's.

They sailed on the *Leviathan* from New York on May 7, 1925. Thurber couldn't let go of his security blanket, Scarlet Mask. He had obtained the organization's agreement that he do the 1925–26 show, and supposed that he and Althea would be back that fall to see it staged. As it turned out, neither of them would ever again return to Columbus as a resident.

26

That Grande Ville De Plaisir

[In Nice] one day in 1926 the mistral, that violent and unpredictable wind from the Alps, came to town, like a cavalcade of desperadoes drunk and firing from both hips. It knocked over chimneys, ripped off signs, tore shutters loose from windows. I was walking with [my wife, Althea] in the Avenue Felix-Faure when the terror descended. The lady walked, I am happy to say, very fast—so fast that we were able to step clear of fifty tons of bricks that suddenly roared and thundered to the pavement behind us. . . . I can still see with too great clarity the hand of a man who was killed in the wreckage, sticking up out of his tomb of bricks. A few moments before, I had been abreast of him. The lady, as I have said, was a fast walker.

—from "La Grande Ville De Plaisir"

On their departure date from New York, Thurber and Althea attended a "tea party," as cocktail parties in Prohibition days were called, given for them by Charme Seeds, who had moved to New York from Cleveland. In "My Trip Abroad," Thurber presents the disasters that can follow *bon voyage* parties. Once aboard ship, he gets lost in the engine room, carries the gifts of candy and flowers into the wrong stateroom, occupied by a lady unknown to him. His wife, meanwhile, has had their stateroom changed but hasn't told him, and he is sleeping in somebody else's quarters when Althea finds him. The first day out is torrid and he strips to his undershorts and works out with an Olympic track team that happens to be on board. By this time his wife isn't speaking to him, principally because he has come to dinner wearing only one shoe, a girl at the *bon voyage* party having thrown the other out a window.

Joking aside, Althea found that traveling with Thurber, and observing the nervous apprehension that would come over him when he was faced with packing, obtaining passports, tickets, porter service, and the thousand other things that go with shipboard embarkation, offered her the earliest legitimate excuse to begin to "take over." Perhaps the takeover could have been handled with greater face-saving to the husband—she and Thurber quarreled on the crossing—but it was frequently a matter of do-it-herself or miss all travel connections.

For three weeks in Paris they sight-saw and Thurber tried to line up free-lance article assignments from newspaper and feature syndicates in the States. The two researched material for a series of pieces on ambassadors and ministers which Thurber planned to write that summer. They traveled by train through the South of France: Carcassonne, Marseilles, and Nice. They stayed a week at the Villefranche, outside Nice, where they beached, bathed, got sunburned, and peeled "like church bells," Thurber wrote his old Columbus chum Ben Williamson.

In a letter to Columbus friends Ted and Julia Gardiner, Thurber writes: "We had some lovely bathing at Villefranche, and once I nearly drowned, which isn't as funny as you make out. The buoyancy of the water and not of my spirits kept me up, but I am proud to say that when a trawler man with a wooden leg named Raoul pulled me out, I asked him to save the women and children . . . after he got me out. Most of the women *need* saving too."

They visited the Milan Cathedral and went on to Berne. "It was the loveliest trip of all," he writes Williamson,

> and me and the wife are crazy about the well known Schweizcapetenhallenfussenfaher, which is, I think, the German name for Swiss capital,— at any rate its close enough. . . . We go on to Paris tomorrow. . . . What I want is anything you might think would fit into a sort of rambling account of the Berne legation, its doings, its specialties, its this and that. Of course I interview each minister and ambassador and the rest serves as sort of background. . . . I must have a hell of a sight more rapid action than you are accustomed to give, as a correspondent. The last letter I wrote you was in 1919 and it is still unanswered. . . .
>
> Well, toot de sweet with an answer . . . or as the Swiss . . . say, fuhngerhaltensprachetnbargenfunf.

In Paris, he writes the Gardiners, "we visited Napoleon's tomb, the Folies-Bergère, the grave of Washington Irving, and a hotel where Pershing spent the night."

In "Quick, the Other Side!," an article Thurber sold later that year to *The Detroit Athletic Club News*, he transforms the horrors of travel logistics into satirical advice to the American trying to figure out the French railway system. The proper traveling costume in France, he writes, is a track suit of durable material, cleated running shoes, and a headband for keeping the hair out of the eyes. The traveler should practice running up and down the hall of his hotel, carrying his luggage, to prepare for the ordeal of catching a French train the next day for Carcassonne.

If he is a good traveler the gentleman will have reserved his seat, and it is in looking for the seat bearing his number, on a tiny neat card, that the first need for the track suit comes in. It will be necessary to run up and down the narrow aisles of seven or eight coaches for approximately half a mile searching for his seat. At the end of this time he will discover that his seat has not been reserved. Whereupon it is the quaint custom of the country to tip the porteur. . . .

It is necessary to change at Bordeaux, for some reason, although Bordeaux is in the opposite direction from Carcassonne. At Bordeaux one misses connections and spends the night. There is no chance of not missing connections, so there is no need to hurry upon arrival at the station.

Once one's baggage is neatly stored above one's seat, he continues, it is customary to get off and inquire if it is, after all, the right train. A porter will ask the traveler where he wishes to go:

At the very mention of the word Carcassonne the porter will scream: "L'autre côté, l'autre côté!" That is the magic byword in all French travel. It means "The other side . . . !" The well-dressed man hurdles onto his train, hurries his bags off . . . and rushes for the other side of the station. . . .

As the traveler runs, the porteur keeps crying: "Vite, vite!" which means, "Hurry, hurry!" and is the only other word besides "L'autre côté" which the . . . tourist need know. He bangs up the steps just in time to see his train pulling out, tips the porteur, and spends the night in Bordeaux.

Thurber was finally gaining ground on his potential as an assured essayist.

He and Althea settled on his favorite province, Normandy, as a place where Thurber would work at his novel during July and August.

"Somebody must have told us about this farmhouse, way out in the countryside, in the little town of Carolles," Althea recalls. "We took an upstairs room and did our cooking on a little one-burner plate and tried to avoid spending any money. The farmer and his wife tried to tempt us into buying food from them, and I remember how hard we had to try to avoid spending one cent [wastefully]. We had to pay some rent, though it was almost nothing. The French couple wanted to sell us a rabbit to roast but I saw them hanging one—which is how they killed rabbits—and we didn't want one after that.

"We rented bikes and biked to the sea, about three miles away. It was wonderful country, beautiful gardens. We had a great many fleas in our bed and a great deal of rain. We were taken by the farmer to a typical farm auction. I did a little better than Jim in speaking French; it was my major—Romance languages at O.S.U. mostly meant French. . . . When we lived in Paris, both of us became more fluent."

In "Remembrances of Things Past," Thurber refers to their landlady, who griped constantly—about the weather, the crops, and "America's delay in getting into the war." The "large and shapeless" Madame had a toothy smile under a prominent mustache, a smile that "was quick and savage and frightening, like a flash of lightning lighting up a ruined woods." Her mercurial disposition probably helped explain her sulky little girl. Madame assumed that Thurber, like all Americans, was rich, that his spectacle rims were of solid gold, and that he carried a thousand dollars at all times for spending money. The woman scared Thurber. He imagined her entering his room at night with a kitchen knife, ready to commit murder for the money she thought he had. She was proud of her English phrases, which she used without sensible association.

"Sometimes," Thurber writes, "she gave me the shudders saying, apropos of nothing . . . 'I love you, kiss me, thousand dollars, no, yes,' her total inventory in English words." She presented Thurber with a bottle of bad wine he thought was a gift until he got his weekly bill. It was such bad wine that he soaked pieces of bread in it and threw them out the window to the chickens. The chickens got drunk and fell down a great deal, alarming Madame, who thought that, on top of the bad weather and poor crops that year, a new disease had infected her flock.

The hero in Thurber's novel was to be good-looking, urbane, and erudite Herman Miller, though Miller didn't know it. The setting was Ohio State.

(At about the same time, Elliott Nugent and his father had based the central character of their successful new Broadway play, *The Poor Nut*, on Thurber, as an inept O.S.U. botany student.) Thurber's writing style was satiric commentary couched in Jamesian stops, starts, conditional clauses, and parenthetical asides. Thurber said later he found himself so tired of his characters at the end of five thousand words that they no longer interested him. He showed the pages to Althea, who pronounced them "terrible." He agreed and never tried novel writing again.

In 1960, he wrote to James Pollard, the O.S.U. historian, "As Thornton Wilder has said, we are all influenced by other writers to begin with, but must throw off that influence as we mature. I had to throw off the influence of Henry James and Joseph Hergesheimer, and the tendency to write such a Jamesian sentence as this: 'First of all, it occurred to me, there was one thing, to begin with, to do,' and such a Hergesheimerism as this: 'He remembered a girl in a boat, on a river, when it was summer, and afternoon.' "

He used some of his Normandy time to work on the 1925–26 Scarlet Mask production, *Amorocco*, shipping the first act to the club members for their comments. (As it turned out, he and his contribution would have nothing to do with the final version.)

At the end of August, with little to show for their Normandy stint, they decided to return to the States. Their bags were transported to the local train station in a two-wheeled cart. Thurber gave the sulky little girl a farewell present of five francs, which set Madame off in angry pursuit of the child and the money. She didn't make it back in time to say *au revoir*.

"We had decided to go home," says Althea, "because we had our return tickets and didn't know what else to do. We returned to Paris and were seated on the terrace of a Left Bank café having a drink, and in a short time three people we knew turned up, joined us, and we had such a good time we decided not to give it up. It took just that one evening. We took a little apartment on the Left Bank and Jim got a job with the Paris edition of the *Chicago Tribune*."

The *Tribune* "was like no other newspaper on earth," says William L. Shirer, who was on the rewrite desk when Thurber joined. Colonel Robert McCormick, the owner of the *Chicago Tribune*, had started the Paris newspaper on the Fourth of July, 1917, as the home paper's "Army edition," "to provide the soldiers with a little touch of home: comics, sports and news." By war's end, a million doughboys were reading it; its modest profits were turned over to the American Expeditionary Force.

McCormick, who didn't regard New York newspapers as truly American, kept the Paris *Tribune* going after the war to compete with the *New York*

Herald's Paris edition, "to interpret America's [at least, the Colonel's] attitude toward Europe." Writes Shirer:

> But it never turned out that way. The Paris *Tribune* became the organ of the expatriates of the Paris Left Bank, mostly written and almost entirely read by the bohemians of Montparnasse, who scorned all the standards and values of America, and especially the colonel's dear Midwest. The Paris edition was concerned chiefly with the writers and the painters and the drunks of the Latin Quarter, reporting on their books, their little magazines, their paintings, their lives, their loves; more interested in literature, the theater, the art exhibitions, the concerts, the gossip of the Left Bank cafés than in the goings on of the Right Bank American colony, which was full of businessmen and social climbers, or in the politics and the economics of . . . Europe. . . .
>
> Had McCormick read its columns, or understood them, he either would have suffered a stroke of apoplexy or killed the paper immediately —perhaps both. It was far more "un-American" than the New York newspapers, which he despised.

There were dozens of American artists, writers, drifters, and hedonists— few newspapermen—constantly lined up at the American French-edition newspaper offices applying for work. The *New York Herald* turned down Thurber, who then applied to the *Chicago Tribune*. David Darrah, the *Tribune* editor, told Thurber that there were at least twenty-five applications ahead of his, and added, "By the way, what are you—a poet, a painter, or a novelist?" Thurber told him he was a newspaperman. Darrah hired him at twelve dollars a week as a rewrite man on the night shift and told him to come to work the next night.

O. W. Riegel, fresh from the University of Wisconsin and a year on a Pennsylvania newspaper, ran out of money in Paris and joined the *Tribune* a few weeks after Thurber. Most of the young Americans on the staff were there, Riegel says, not only because Paris was "the mecca of a large number of exceptionally articulate Americans," but because "to stay in America when *Main Street* was the best-seller was almost to suggest an acceptance of Babbitt's hypocrisy and phony values." The American expatriate groups were separated socially and economically. Few could afford the well-heeled, party-loving ranks led by the F. Scott Fitzgeralds and by Harry and Caresse Crosby of the international social set. Even the word men fell into two groups, says Riegel: the freelance writers, represented most importantly by such as Ernest

Hemingway, Matthew Josephson, and Malcolm Cowley, and the newspaper-men, notably "Eric Hawkins, Al Laney, and Ned Calmer."

"Our money needs were small," Riegel continues. "All the necessities of life, such as theater tickets, alcohol, and the entertainment of women were cheap. We were all poor, I suppose, but we had enough. It was a true economic democracy; we might criticize and satirize our contemporaries for various faults and foibles, but poverty and affluence were not among our criteria."

Though Althea and Thurber were able to stretch their francs like everyone else, their hundred-and-twenty-five-dollars' worth of savings was depleted early in the game and they were soon in debt to their landlord. "Jim was happy with the *Tribune* job," says Althea. "We lived the typical poor man's version of the literary life—nothing like the Hemingway set in any way, though we used to see them and were up on all their doings. Mostly we knew other young American writers in our situation."

The *Chicago Tribune* was "a lighthearted operation," Riegel recalls,

partly because there were few members of the staff whose major interests were not elsewhere. Even the pros were not inclined to look upon it as a vital stage in their careers. Our duties included a good deal of translation from the French press, editing and headlining telegraph and other copy, covering an occasional event or interviewing an arriving celebrity of interest to the American colony, and, of course, getting the paper made up. Our printers were all French.

While the mood of the staff may have been lighthearted, the product was not without merit, and considerably more lively and interesting than its contemporary, the Paris *Herald*. We worked in a large, bleak room on the third floor of the *Petit Journal* building. As a promotion stunt, the *Petit Journal* once installed in its lobby a cage that confined a cadaverous guru who had volunteered to show how long he could survive without food and drink. We had a French gastronomic contributing editor by the name of Rosetti. He was a florid and oleaginous glutton. He had just finished a large gourmet dinner when he came upon this starving creature on the way to the office. The spectacle so unnerved and saddened him that he returned to the restaurant and consumed another dinner the same size as the first.

When I was on the copy desk, the regulars around the rim included William L. Shirer and Elliot Paul. [Thurber had just left to work on the paper's Riviera edition.] Once Paul, when working on the *Herald*, went out for dinner, leaving his hat and cane on a hook. About a year later he reappeared for work after dinner as if nothing had happened, complaining loudly that his hat and cane weren't where he left them. He had been in the Balearic Islands writing *The Life and Death of a Spanish Town*. "The most magnificent moment in *Ten Nights in a Bar Room*," Paul used to say, "is when the drunken father pulls out a piggy bank and spends his little girl's last dime."

Our proof-readers included Henry Miller and Bravig Imbs. Imbs worked his way through Dartmouth as a waiter and by entertaining dinner guests at the home of the English Department head, George Lambeth, by playing the violin—until a visiting British novelist, Arnold Bennett, inquired irritably whether it was really necessary for the student to practice his violin while they were eating.

William L. Shirer, in *20th Century Journey*, remembers that getting out the *"Trib"* each evening was "primarily a work of the imagination." News sources were so meager that it was necessary to "embroider" or resort to "outright fiction" to fill the eight pages. An American newspaper was supposed to print news from home, but there were few American items in what the *Trib's* London bureau could steal from the British press and telegraph to Paris early each evening, and there was, Shirer says, "a skimp one hundred words a day from the New York correspondent of the home edition, which arrived by cable around 10 P.M. If used as received, they would have filled no more than a few inches of one column, but we had from eight to ten columns on the front page and inside to fill. So after our return from the coffee break we would pitch in to enlarge one hundred words of cable from home into several thousand words." And he continues:

That was where one's imagination came in. Especially Thurber's. He turned out to be a genius. The night editor would toss him eight or ten words of cablese and say, "Give me a column on that, Jim." And Thurber, his owlish face puckering up, would say, "Yes, suh," and he would glance at the cable and go merrily to work. That fall and winter he seemed to specialize on President Coolidge, whose inanities gave him so much pleasure that they seemed to tide him over all the dreary, cold, rainy days that season.

Early in October the President addressed the American Legion convention in Omaha and a cable duly arrived giving us these bare facts: "Coolidge to Legionnaires Omaha opposed militarism urged tolerance American life." That was all Thurber needed, and he set to work composing a column and a half of the finest clichés that had ever resounded from Washington . . . and most of which, I have little doubt, Coolidge actually used.

Thurber was at it again a few weeks later when the president spoke in Washington to the international convention of the YMCA and our cable merely reported "Coolidge tells international convention YMCA American youth needs more home control exparental action." The president's inane homilies, the state of America's wayward, rebellious, jazz-age youth, the worse state of their frenzied thirsty parents in an age of bootleg gin and dizzy paper profits on the bullish market—Jim put them all in as his imagination soared. The result was another classic.

Thurber would become impatient if Coolidge was silent for long, and unable to restrain himself, Jim would simply make up a dispatch about our great Yankee President. Once he had Coolidge addressing a convention of Protestant churches and proclaiming that "a man who does not pray is not a praying man."

Shirer remembers the night editor handing Thurber a five-word cable: "Christy Mathewson died tonight Saranac." Thurber "took the cable," says Shirer, "and muttered, 'Too bad. A great pitcher. A great man.' And he sat down and batted out from the recesses of his memory—we had no morgue of background clippings—one of the finest tributes I have ever read, replete with facts about the player's pitching records, stories of some of the great games he had pitched in World Series, and an assessment of his character on and off the diamond."

Mathewson was a Columbus boy who pitched for the New York Giants, and Thurber and his brother Robert knew his professional life by heart. On the other hand, Thurber had to fake the account of Admiral Richard Byrd's 1926 flight across the North Pole, of which Thurber remembered only one phrase: "with the ice of the North Pole clinging on their wings."

Joel Sayre, who was attending Oxford University but visited Paris often, remembers Thurber at the *Tribune* desk, his pocket French-English dictionary always at his elbow. Thurber translated editorials from *Le Figaro* with the aid of a French office boy and the dictionary, says Sayre. In 1954, Thurber recalled his *Tribune* days this way:

> One of my tasks was handling the international financial situation. "What casting!" as Joe Sayre said the other day about this. . . . I knew less about finance than anybody in the world. I was also assigned to do a series of articles on Poland, including the condition and history of the zloty, this series being mandatory because Poland took advertising in the

Tribune. I got my international finance stories by rewriting Le Figaro and one other so-called semi-official newspaper. . . .

I used to write parody news features mainly for the enjoyment of the other slaves, and one of these accidentally got sent down the chute and was set up, two-column headline and all, by a linotyper who didn't understand English. Dave Darrah found it on the stone and darn near dropped dead, since it involved fifteen or twenty famous international figures in an involved mythical story of robbery, rape, extra-marital relations, Monte Carlo gambling, and running gun fights. [Someone] later figured the Tribune would have to pay about eight billion dollars worth of libel if the story had appeared.

Darrah was always hollering up the tube for short filler items of a sentence or two, and I got away with a dozen more phonies which were printed.

Thurber had arranged for a New York literary agent, George Bye, to handle his freelance pieces. A product of his Normandy farmhouse days was "Tip, Tip, Hurray! The Battle Cry of Greedom," bought by the *Kansas City Star* Sunday magazine. It indicts French porters and taxi drivers who, spoiled by the big tips given them by wealthy American tourists, demand as much of "the poor student or teacher," who is trying to see France on a shoestring.

Thurber had met President Woodrow Wilson's Paris barber, Léon Barthélemy, on his first trip to France in 1918. Besides Wilson, Barthélemy's clients had included the revolutionist Aleksandr Kerensky, whose hair he could never cut evenly, because Kerensky, who had survived several political purges, would leap out of the chair whenever a door slammed or a manicurist dropped her scissors on the floor—so Thurber wrote. Seven years later, Thurber finally wrote up Barthélemy and sold it to the *New York World,* which printed it in September 1925.

Thurber had planned a series of articles on ministers and ambassadors, but the one Thurber came up with at the time is "The Evolution of an Ambassador; How Myron T. Herrick Won His Laurels As the Foremost American Dignitary in Europe," published in the *Kansas City Star* magazine (October 4, 1925). It had stuck in Thurber's craw that the American Legion post of Paris had put up a stone tablet commemorating Myron T. Herrick as the American wartime ambassador to France, when William G. Sharpe had served all but four of those wartime months between 1914 and 1918. (Thurber would later do two more pieces on the Herrick/Sharpe matter.) While admitting that Sharpe's service was less than distinguished, and his diplomatic effectiveness less than Herrick's, Thurber wanted the record set straight. (Both Herrick and Sharpe were from Ohio.)

Most of Thurber's freelance pieces, written in the afternoons before he reported to the *Tribune*, were an American's lighthearted complaints of Paris life, or a contrast of French social customs with American. One that appeared in the *New York Herald Tribune* magazine ("Balm for Those Who Didn't Go Abroad: If Compelled by Circumstances to Remain in the United States, This Confession May Reconcile You to Your Fate") assures those who didn't come to France that they escaped the frustrations of guided tours. (This has moments reminiscent of Twain's *Innocents Abroad.*)

Thurber's first significant freelance success came in December 1925, when he sold a humorous essay—slightly more than two pages—to *Harper's*, an even more prominent and influential literary monthly then than now. Thurber has reported the amount paid him as both seventy and ninety dollars. Titled "A Sock on the Jaw—French Style," the subject was inspired by a dispute between Paris cabdrivers, witnessed by Thurber on his way to work. In the essay, Thurber marvels at the French people's ability to argue, utter epithets, and provoke one another without anyone ever swinging a fist at an opponent, the American way of settling a street fight. Another time he sees a horse fall on the street. The angry driver curses the horse, and the gathering crowd takes vocal sides. A favorite and perennial character of Thurber's pops up in this early piece: the excitable woman. " 'He knocked the horse down; I saw him!' cried one passionate old lady, who had just arrived and was carried away [by the scene]." Thurber concludes that Frenchmen don't sock one another on the jaw because it would abort "the free exercise of community debate in France."

The *Harper's* check equaled at least six weeks' salary, and Thurber and Althea not only repaid their debts, they had enough left over to celebrate.

With many Americans wintering on the French Riviera, the Paris *Trib* sent Thurber to Nice to join a half-dozen others in getting out a small, six-page Riviera edition of the *Tribune*. The editor was B. J. Kospoth, Thurber was assistant editor, and Althea was made society editor. At the last minute, Althea purchased two Senegalese lovebirds at a Paris flower market and took them aboard the Blue Train for Nice. The birds, which hated one another, didn't sing but made fluttering sounds all night in their covered cage. This kept awake not only the Thurbers but a middle-aged Frenchman who shared the compartment with them. The Frenchman complained, but Althea placated him in her steadily improving French.

The newspaper's page dimensions were that of the Ohio State *Lantern*, which Thurber remembered well. The paper was set in ten-point type rather than the customary smaller eight-point, to accommodate the constant lack of legitimate copy. Most of the paper's content was from the Paris edition, telegraphed to Nice, where the principal task was layout and headline writing. The issues were padded by plagiarizing stories from *L' Éclaireur de Nice et du Sud-Est,* a local French publication given to bizarre news stories.

The workday began after dinner and usually ended before midnight, writes Thurber.

> It was then our custom to sit around for half an hour, making up items for [Althea's] column. She was too pretty, we thought, to waste the soft southern days tracking down the arrival of prominent persons on the Azure Coast. So all she had to do was stop in at the Ruhl and the Negresco [hotels] each day and pick up the list of guests who had just registered. The rest of us invented enough items to fill up the last half of her column, and a gay and romantic cavalcade, indeed, infested the littoral of our imagination. "Lieutenant General and Mrs. Pendleton Gray Winslow," we would write, "have arrived at their villa, Heart's Desire, on Cap d'Antibes, bringing with them their prize Burmese monkey, Thibault." Or "The Hon. Mr. Stephen H. L. Atterbury, Chargé-d'Affaires of the American Legation in Peru, and Mrs. Atterbury, the former Princess Ti Ling of Thibet, are motoring to Monte Carlo from Aix-en-Provence, where they have been visiting Mr. Atterbury's father, Rear Admiral A. Watson Atterbury, U.S.N., retired. Mr. Stephen Atterbury is the breeder of the famous Schnauzer-Pincher, Champion Adelbert von Weigengrosse of Tamerlane, said to be valued at $15,000." In this manner we turned out, in no time at all, and with the expenditure of very little mental energy, the most glittering column of social notes in the history of the American newspaper, either here or abroad."

The French composing room went on strike about one night a week, because the Americans would not subscribe to the French newspaper custom of "using whatever size type was handiest and whatever space it would fit into most easily." The quarrel was always carried to the bar next door and ended with the combatants singing French and American songs in renewed camaraderie.

Althea and Thurber spent the "long days of warm blue weather" climbing the Corniche roads, riding chairlifts up mountains, and sitting on restaurant terraces overlooking the Bay of Angels—once chatting with a young Englishman who, Thurber said, was convinced Henry James was still alive and in hiding in the vicinity, rewriting *The Golden Bowl.*

"It was a wonderful winter for us," Althea remembered. Helen Thurber, his second wife, was with Thurber when he revisited Nice in 1937, and believes, from hearing Thurber's fond recollections, that Althea and Thurber never had a happier period together than the 1925–26 winter in Nice.

There was little supervision of their newspaper work, few complaints, not much legwork, and a lovely winter climate. Thurber interviewed a number of celebrities wintering there or passing through, including Rudolph Valentino, the oil tycoon Harry Sinclair, Carl Laemmle (the head of Universal Pictures), and Isadora Duncan, all residing in the hotels along the Promenade des Anglais, overlooking the Bay. Valentino, who would be dead in a few months, looked healthy to Thurber, and proudly showed him the wardrobe lockers of shoes he traveled with. Harry Sinclair, Thurber writes in "La Grande Ville de Plaisir," grudgingly consented to an interview. One of the principal culprits of "the Ohio Gang" associated with the Teapot Dome scandal of the Harding administration, he never met Thurber's gaze but stared at him from the corner of his eye. His alleged three-hundred-thousand-dollar bribe to Secretary of the Interior Albert B. Fall was under criminal investigation at the time, and within three years he would be in jail for contempt of the U.S. Senate and for hiring detectives to follow members of the jury trying him on conspiracy charges. Thurber, the journalist, always felt proprietary toward the scandals of Ohioan Harding's administration.

One evening a wire came in from the Paris office of the *Trib* reporting that Sergei Esenin, former husband of Isadora Duncan, had committed suicide in Moscow. The editor told Thurber to telephone the famous dancer at one of the grand local hotels. He got her after 1:00 A.M. and asked her reaction to the suicide of her ex-husband. She hadn't heard the news, Thurber says, and repeating, "No, no, no, no!" she dropped the receiver. A frightened Thurber frantically called the hotel desk and told the night clerk, who could barely speak English, to "do something about" Miss Duncan. Nothing was "done," but she had recovered by the next day.

It was after an all-night session of argument, song, and drink that the Nice *Tribune* staff boarded a train at dawn for one of the most celebrated sports events that year—the tennis match between Frenchwoman Suzanne Lenglen and the American Helen Wills. Thurber tells of a drunken *Trib* reporter who canvassed the trainload of French passengers as to whether Edgar Allan Poe's famous poem "The Raven" would be improved if the raven quoth "*Jamais plus,*" rather than "Nevermore." The "reporter" could only have been Thurber. In spite of the shape he was in—or perhaps because of it—Thurber, who knew nothing about tennis and had only attended one or two tennis matches of that caliber before, found himself emotionally caught up as an American, as he watched Wills go down to defeat.

His poor eyesight again led to a typically kaleidoscopic impression of the match. His *Tribune* story was expressed in the style of the novelist Hergesheimer:

> A rush of people struggling around a livid woman in pink colored silk, a sudden rioting of flowers from somewhere, a bright glittering of silver in the sun. . . . The crowd that watched from the stands was a little stupefied. It had all been too swift and dazzling. . . . And then a girl in white walked silently away from the colorful, frenzied throne they were building around the woman in pink silk. The crowd that watched from the stands could comprehend it now. The silent girl in white detaching herself from the mad maelstrom, was a note of familiar sanity. Helen Wills had been defeated and was going home.

Looking through a Jamesian prism, Thurber seemed to be contrasting American innocence (the Californian, Wills, was barely twenty) with European worldliness. One might think, from Thurber's stricken account, that the match was Wills's finale as a ranking tennis player. Actually, Suzanne Lenglen, the victor, was six years older than Wills and disappeared from the headlines long before Wills did. Wills, in fact, took the British women's singles title in 1938, the year her former rival died. The experience began Thurber's interest in tennis. He would eventually take up the game, nearly driving himself mad with frustration on the court, and would cover tennis in a sports column for the *New Yorker*, which he signed "Foot Fault."

A Paris *Tribune* reporter, Leo Mishkin, remembers replacing Thurber on the Riviera edition in 1926, though the paper was suspended that June. Thurber, meanwhile, had written another couple of articles that his agent was able to sell to New York newspapers. An editor on the Paris *Herald*, Eric Hawkins, says Thurber once told him that he had sent copy to the *Herald*, "which you must never have used because I didn't get a check." "But that might not have meant anything," Hawkins said later, "because we could have used it and not paid him. I think he was wandering around on his uppers then and maybe didn't have the price of a newspaper to check to see if we'd used his copy. I remember he did write for the *Herald* at least once, an amusing interview of himself."

Back in Paris, Thurber was, indeed, on his uppers. Poverty had become more of a bore and a nuisance than a challenge. The let-down after the glamorous four months in Nice didn't help. And now he was unemployed: either his old job at the Paris *Trib* was filled while he was in the South, or he had resolved not to go back to a wage that paid less than basic subsistence. Althea felt the poverty more than Thurber did. He, at least, had been doing what he enjoyed, and money never was a concern to him or any of the other young American journalists, as Riegel points out. But Althea felt too poor to have fun, and Thurber, a frequent victim of inadequate feelings in those days, was rarely able to make things seem right for them. When Althea sued for divorce nine years later, she gave 1926 as the year in which they were first "separated" for lack of compatibility. She liked order and dignity in her life and companionship of a quantity and quality that Thurber, vacillating between hard work and his fraternity-house fondness for all-night bull sessions with the boys, was unable or unwilling to provide. Her early realization that his talent, which she conceded to be real, meant a good deal of picking up after him, was bearable only if the results made it worthwhile.

On the other side, the quiet but clear recognition, by both, of Althea's need to manage the details of their lives if they were to function adequately within any social structure, was the rub to Thurber. He was losing the Jamesian male's control. His dread was of becoming the domestic pussycat, and the dominant role Althea was assuming was doing nothing to alleviate the apprehensions. They both had learned how to aggravate an open wound in the other. She wanted the separation; she welcomed independence.

They agreed that he should return to New York, where he could be closer to his freelance markets and perhaps get a better idea of what editors needed. When he had things settled there, and money available, Althea would join him in the States, where they would lead comparatively independent lives. "I stayed in Paris two months after Jim went back," says Althea. "I got a job in the downtown office of the *Chicago Tribune*, in Rue Scribe, and worked there while Jim was away."

One reason for Thurber's and Althea's alienation at the time, says Helen Thurber, is that Althea was enamored of one of the *Trib*'s staff members. After four years, their marriage was suffering in another respect. In other accounts of Thurber's life, he has been called undersexed, and Althea oversexed. But sexual needs begin in the head and are affected by attitudes that may differ with every couple. Other of their partners could well have described the sexual needs and behavior of Thurber and Althea quite differently. The fact remains, though their happy Riviera life had been their first genuine honeymoon, sex was too frequently a frustration to them both.

Joel Sayre had promised Thurber that he would keep an eye on Althea after Thurber's departure for the States. One afternoon, when they were seated on a bench by the Seine, Althea began crying and told Sayre, "I've been married four years and I'm still a virgin." A startled Sayre worried that the remark was something of a come-on, and nervously walked her home. "I was a friend of both Thurbers," Sayre said, "and I worried about their marriage after that." Whatever the nature of the Thurbers' difficulties, we know the fuddy-duddy, sexless Jamesian standards Thurber couldn't help applying to "nice girls" like Althea would have been a heavy cross for any young wife to bear for long. Thurber had the gift of fantasy, of being able to soar neatly over the obstacles imposed by reality. Althea did not.

Thurber later claimed that the *Harper's* money went to help buy his passage to New York, but that had long since been spent. He left Althea living on borrowed money, and when he disembarked from the *Leviathan* in New York in March 1926, he had only ten dollars.

During the voyage, he tried to sum up his status as a writer in a letter to Sayre, finally grasping that his potential strength was in humor, and not Jamesian fiction:

> I write mostly soi-disant humor, since I haven't brains enough to write more solid articles and wouldn't if I could. I often worry about my future since I am no doctor and at best but a mean scrivener, but out of all the things one does, from pipe-fitting to testing seamless leather belting and from ceramics to statesmanship, I can do only one thing, even passably, and that is make words and space between punctuation points.

Thus ended Thurber's brief association with the so-called Lost Generation of Paris in the twenties. As Riegel puts it, "We had no intention at any time of becoming expatriates; the experience of Europe sharpened our sense of American nationality and our interest in the currents of American cultural and political life, of which the contrasts of Europe made us all the more aware. The time came when we felt that we had accomplished our mission; we had seen, lived, and felt what we had come for, and any more would be too much."

27

Those Violets in the Snow

"Here, get on this—lady says there are violets growing in the snow over in Red Bank." "Violets don't grow in the snow," I reminded him. "They might in Red Bank," he said. "Slide on over there." I slid instead to a bar and put in a phone call to the Chief of Police in Red Bank. A desk sergeant answered and I asked him about the violets. "Ain't no violence over here," he told me, and hung up. It wasn't much to hang a story on, as we say, but I hung one on it. But first I had a few more drinks with a man I had met at the bar, very pleasant fellow, captain of a barge or something. Shortly after the strange case of the violets in the snow, I left the newspaper game and drifted into the magazine game.

—from "Memoirs of a Drudge"

In New York, Thurber looked up a young woman he had met in Nice, borrowed twenty dollars from her, and took a room with cooking facilities, at five dollars per week, on West Thirteenth Street in Greenwich Village. He ate in doughnut shops and from canapé trays served at parties to which he managed to get invited—usually by Charme Seeds or Charles Speaks and their circle of friends. He walked to save carfare. He intended to return to France almost immediately, as he told Nugent, who was with a new play in Philadelphia:

I been in France ten years. Althea is still there. We're very happy, though. I mean together. I came over for just as long as [it] takes me to do what I want to do and get back. That may be two weeks. Again it may be a month. It won't be longer. I should admire to see you and Norma and the Annabelle, but suppose no. I'm used not to seeing people. I'm used to lots of things you aint used to. But I'm still young, though thinner. . . . I may be even hungrier . . . and quite tired, but what the hell. . . . Walking is good for the character.

But he wouldn't see Europe again for eleven years. He and his agent had parted company, and Thurber took his manuscripts to the Brandt & Brandt literary agency. Though it declined to represent him, someone there suggested he send his work to the *New Yorker*, then a struggling, fifteen-month-old weekly. One of his submissions was about Alfred Goullet, France's greatest six-day bicyclist, who was participating in a racing event at the new Madison Square Garden, completed the year before. The piece included Thurber's recollections of sharing a stateroom with Goullet in 1920, when returning from France.

"My pieces came back so fast," writes Thurber,

I began to believe the *New Yorker* must have a rejection machine. It did have one, too. His name was John Chapin Mosher, a witty writer, a charming man, and one of the most entertaining companions I have ever met, but an editor whose prejudices were a mile high and who had only a few enthusiasms. It was in the always slightly lunatic tradition of the *New Yorker* that he had been made first reader of the manuscripts of unknown writers. In the years that followed, we became friends, but I never had lunch with him that he didn't say, over his coffee, "I must get back to the office and reject."

(Reading this account of Mosher in *The Years with Ross*, Katharine White, fiction editor and a primary adviser to Harold Ross, took exception to it, pointing out that it was Mosher who "discovered" Thurber, after a number of justified rejections. Mosher, says White, discovered most of the magazine's early writers, including John O'Hara. Given the ratio of the acceptable to the unacceptable found in most "slush" mail, Mosher's principal work was indeed rejecting, and his lunchtime remark was one of his standing jokes, says White.)

The Goullet piece was taking longer to come back than Thurber's other submissions, and, like any novice freelance writer, his hope began to build along with his impatience. He stopped by the *New Yorker*'s shabby offices at 25 West 45th Street and asked about it. Mosher came to the small lobby to see Thurber. Thurber describes Mosher as "looking like a professor of English literature who has not approved of the writing of anybody since Sir Thomas Browne. He returned my manuscript saying that it had got under something, and apologizing for the tardy rejection. 'You see,' he said, 'I regard Madison Square Garden as one of the blots on our culture.'"

The year before, crossing to France on the *Leviathan*, Thurber and Althea, at some incompatible moment, had agreed to make shipboard acquaintances independently of one another. Thurber's interest was snagged by a professional gambler, in whose occupation Thurber thought he saw article material. Althea struck up an acquaintance with another young married woman traveling in the student passenger class, Lillian Illian, whose brother, Elwyn Brooks White, had just had his first poem and essay published in the fledgling, all-but-unheard-of *New Yorker*. "We saw a lot of Lillian in Paris," Althea says. "When Jim left for the States, I passed on to him her brother's name." Thurber jotted down the name as "Elton" White, with the additional information that the young man now worked part-time on the new magazine and might be able to help with advice and introductions. Thurber, on this disappointing June day, asked Mosher if White was available. Mosher obligingly checked and reported that White wasn't in.

Thurber next looked up the managing editor of the *New York Evening Post*, whom he had met in Paris the previous fall. Thurber was looking for writing markets, but all the editor could offer him was a job, which Thurber turned down. He was finding newspaper work a dead-end street. By July he was out of the money he had borrowed from friends, and he got in touch with Clare Victor (Dwig) Dwiggins, a successful comic-strip artist whom he had interviewed—and borrowed money from—in Nice, where Dwiggins had also introduced him to his family. The cartoonist was fond of both Thurber and Althea. For a time, Dwiggins penned two characters named "Jim" and "Althea" into his regular cartoon feature, "Reg'lar Fellers." (Dwiggins was also known for his syndicated daily panel called "School Days.") He invited the Thurbers to spend the summer with his family in the Adirondacks, at Green Lake, in Gloversville, New York, near Albany, where Thurber could write. Thurber borrowed two hundred dollars from his parents and wired passage money to Althea. She and Thurber arrived in Gloversville in July. "We lived in a tent in the Dwigginses' yard," Althea remembers.

Thurber was working up a book-length parody of four current best-sellers: *Microbe Hunters*, by Paul de Kruif; *Nize Baby*, by Milt Gross; *Gentlemen Prefer Blondes*, by Anita Loos, and *Why We Behave Like Human Beings*, by George

Dorsey. He called his finished manuscript, which ran to more than twenty-five thousand words, "Why We Behave Like Microbe Hunters." (He planned to use an illustrator to attain book length.) Parodies were extremely popular at the moment, and Thurber had been impressed by how well his old school-mate, Donald Ogden Stewart, had done with his *A Parody Outline of History* and *Aunt Polly's Story of Mankind.* There was also Ernest Hemingway's recent book-length lampooning of Sherwood Anderson, *The Torrents of Spring,* and a young humorist, Corey Ford, was in great demand by *Life* magazine and other publications for his short sketches spoofing the writing mannerisms of Theodore Dreiser and other literary giants of the day.

Dwiggins's son, Donald, remembers that that summer he used to play his favorite new song on his Victrola on the front porch, over and over, "Horses, Horses, Horses, Crazy Over Horses, Horses, Horses." Thurber, helpless in his tent, was unable to shut out the noise. "One night," says Donald, "Jim got out of bed, came up on the porch, shut off the Victrola, took the record and busted it over my head. Looking back, I really don't blame him."

Thurber experienced his usual quota of mishaps at Green Lake. Dwiggins had planned a deck off his gun room. The carpenters had installed the door, but the deck was still to be built, as Thurber discovered one day when he absently chose the door as a way out. He was not seriously hurt.

Commenting in 1936 on Mary Perin Barker's pamphlet "The Techniques of Good Manners," which advises that "the gentleman goes ahead to help [the woman] into a boat, up a slippery incline, or up a ladder," Thurber writes:

> I can think of no woman friend of mine who would dream of letting me step into a canoe and then try to hand her into it. Most of my women friends would be perfectly willing—and eager—to get into the canoe first, rules or no rules, and then help me in—with the aid of their husbands, a couple of ropes, and a board. My difficulties with watercraft began some fifteen years ago [sic] at Green Lake, New York, when in stepping into a canoe I accidentally trod on a sleeping Boston Terrier that I didn't know was in the canoe. I had a firm hold on [Althea's] hand, since I was about to assist her into the canoe. . . . What followed was a deplorable and improbable fiasco. . . . The woman I was assisting at the time and the women she has talked to about the happenings of that day—in other words, all my other women friends—would rather stay behind and burn up than follow me up a ladder. And as for a slippery incline, nobody who saw me try to recover a woman's English sheep-dog puppy for her one icy day two years ago in Sixth Avenue at

Fourteenth Street—the dog had slipped its leash—would want to follow me up a slippery incline. That goes for the dog, too.

Donald Dwiggins remembers that during a party at Green Lake Thurber was complaining about the difficulty of writing the kind of fiction currently in vogue because it meant having to think up "all that crazy sex stuff." "My father said, 'Jim, is sex necessary?' Thurber jumped up and said, 'Hey, that's a great title for my book!' "

Going back to his tent from the same party, Donald Dwiggins recalls, Thurber, having had more than one too many, slipped off the dock and fell into the lake, luckily in shallow water. He looked up at an exasperated Althea and said, "Here I am, honey, down among the goldfish."

They returned to New York in early September on a hundred dollars Dwiggins had loaned them, and took a basement apartment on Horatio Street "under the Ninth Avenue El," as Thurber describes it. His parody was rejected by three publishers, says Thurber, as were its six chapters when submitted separately to several magazines, including the *New Yorker*. (Years later Thurber claimed that Harper & Bros. and the *New Yorker* unwittingly used parts of *Why We Behave Like Microbe Hunters* that he rewrote into *Is Sex Necessary?* and *Let Your Mind Alone!* Though recycling his previous material was a common and practical practice of his, the original manuscript is lost and Thurber's claim cannot be verified.)

Althea found work in a bookstore, which only added to Thurber's sense of urgency and lowered self-esteem. "At that time Jim seemed to loathe New York," Joel Sayre reports. "He complained about its dirt, jostle, and the brash ways of its citizenry. He had lived in Paris, Nice, Columbus, and Washington, and none of them matched the rudeness and noise level of New York, he would say. Yet, I think none of that would have bothered him if he could have sold *Why We Behave Like Microbe Hunters* to a publisher, or just one or two of its chapters to a magazine."

Toward the end of September, Thurber was ready to throw in the towel. "I was about to go back to Columbus, thinking I couldn't make it in the big city," Thurber told Stephen Potter during a British TV broadcast in 1958. "[Then] I sent a *New Yorker* rejection to Franklin P. Adams of 'The Conning Tower' of the *Morning World*, and it occupied one of his whole columns. I think not more than ten times in his twenty-five years was there one whole column devoted to the work of somebody else and this gave me confidence, so that I decided to stay on and try it some more."

"The Conning Tower" was unquestionably the most prestigious of the op-ed columns in national journalism. In lieu of payment, contributors settled for the prestige of their name in print in the syndicated column with its large, sophisticated readership. Perhaps because his name was becoming associated with so many rejections, Thurber even chose to forgo that reward, signing his column-length satire on the tabloids "Jamie (his mother's name for him) Machree."

"If the Tabloids Had Covered the Famous Sport 'Love-Death' Scandal of Hero and Leander" appeared in "The Conning Tower" September 28, 1926. In this old Greek tale, Hero, a priestess of Venus, fell in love with Leander, who swam across the Hellespont every night to visit her. One night he drowned, and in her grief Hero drowned herself in the same sea. Here are a few of Thurber's headlines announcing the news as they might have appeared in the mythical scandal sheets the *Daily Tab* and the *Daily Glass*:

LOVE PACT IS BARED
AS LEANDER DROWNS!

SWIMMER MISSING IN
HELLESPONT CROSSING

HINT PUBLICITY STUNT
IN HELLESPONT "DEATH"

HERO SEES FOUL PLAY
IN LOVE SWIM DEATH

POLICE PROBE CHARGE
LEA HIDING IN GREECE

"HE SWAM TO SEE MAMMA
EVERY NIGHT," PENS HERO

Having decided to remain in New York, Thurber turned himself in to his acquaintance on the *Evening Post*, located on the waterfront in lower Manhattan, and accepted the job of "staff correspondent" offered him. "What are gaiety and vodka in the old sleigh," he had written Sayre, "when that thing bumping your elbow is a wolf?" The pay was forty dollars a week—his old *Dispatch* salary, but he was determined to add to it by freelancing.

Thurber's usual inability to report events without fanciful and whimsical interpretation soon left him trusted by the city editor to do little more than "color" features, or overnight stories not requiring a fast turnaround. One of his first assignments had been to cover a theater fire in Brooklyn. "I rode subway trains, elevated trains, and street cars," Thurber told Joseph Mitchell, then a reporter for the *New York World-Telegram,* in 1934. "I kept getting back to Chambers Street. They sent me out at 1:30. At four o'clock I got out at Chambers Street the last time and got into a taxicab. On the way over to Brooklyn I stopped off for a minute and bought a *Post,* and the story about the fire was all over the front page. So I told the cabdriver to turn around and take me home."

Robert Coates, friend and *New Yorker* associate of Thurber's, remembers how Thurber liked to tell this story, imitating the facial expression on the city editor's face as he cries, "A four-alarm fire, and this fellow just can't find it!" It was after "a standing order not to send [Thurber] to Brooklyn" that he was put on less timely stories. He writes: "When other reporters were out wearing themselves down in quest of the clangorous and complicated fact, I could be observed wandering the quiet shore above the noisy torrent of contemporary history, examining the little miracles and grotesqueries of the time."

He was sent to interview General John J. Pershing, the World War I hero, who was stopping at the old Waldorf-Astoria. "I found him in his room," writes Thurber, "a straight-backed, stern-faced man, who was brushing lint from the blue serge suit he had on. He pointed his eyes at me like two pistols, and there wasn't a single wasted word in what he said. 'I never discuss controversial matters,' he told me. I explained that the matter in hand, whatever it was, was not controversial. 'I see no need to discuss noncontroversial matters,' he said, and went on brushing, and I thanked him and left the room."

Thurber's specialty was the thousand-word, nontimely story. Cautioned once about too long a lead sentence, he typed out a phony item whose lead simply ran, "Dead." Next sentence: "That was what the man was the police found in an area-way last night." He showed it around the office as a joke. Years later, as a celebrity, he would tell an interviewer that he had turned in a story to the *Post* with just such a lead in response to a charge that his lead sentences were too wordy. By 1958, he was telling Eddy Gilmore of the Associated Press a more elaborate version: "The [editor] decided that all leads should consist of one word. . . . One night he said to me, 'Thurber, there's a real sexy play over at the such and such theater. Go over there and write a story about it.' My one-word lead was a word that neither my paper nor your paper would publish. . . . My second paragraph said, 'That was the word flung across the footlights yesterday.' 'All right, all right,' said the boss, 'Thurber and everybody else are starting to kid the hell out of it so we'll go back to leads that make sense.'"

"My mini-scoops on the New York *Evening Post* included one interview, a tough one, with Thomas Alva Edison, who had been sore at newspapers for years, or since they had made fun of his then celebrated written examination for would-be employees," Thurber wrote Beverly Gary, of the *New York Post*, in 1959. He leaves the impression that he managed to get an exclusive, one-on-one meeting with Edison. In fact, it was Edison's eightieth birthday and Thurber was one of fifty reporters invited to submit written questions in advance to the great inventor. The questions numbered about a hundred and fifty. Edison wrote out his answers in pencil and had them read. Henry Ford and Harvey Firestone were present for the hour-and-a-half session. Edison fudged on many of the questions. "James G. Thurber, Staff Correspondent of Evening Post," filing his story from West Orange, New Jersey, February 11, 1927, writes: "Mr. Edison advocated early marriage, prophesied that the machine age would not interfere with the production of art . . . , remarked that the theatre would go on about as now unless the motion pictures showed a great improvement. . . . He said that crime would eventually decrease because it does not pay."

By now Thurber was enjoying his *Post* assignments and his staff associates. They included "Russel Crouse, Nunnally Johnson, Bruce Gould, and a gal named Laura Mount, now known as Laura Z. Hobson," Thurber wrote Dale Kramer in 1951. "She didn't get any more money than I did, but Johnson got a hundred a week when he replaced McGuinness as conductor of a daily department, for which I was also a candidate. [James Kevin McGuinness was a New York *Evening Post* columnist, and nonstop talker, who worked for Ross part-time.] I don't know how much Crouse got then for his 'Left at the Post' column, but I doubt that any of us, including Charles J. V. Murphy, considered we were successful at that time or had ever been. . . . I think 1927 marked the beginning of success or failure for all of us."

On February 1, 1927, a Thurber *Post* story tells of Mrs. Harry Houdini, wife of the magician and escape artist who had died a few months before, delivering Houdini's forty-five books on crime and penology to Houdini's friend Lewis Lawes, the warden of Sing Sing state prison. Thurber interviewed Lawes and found himself on the train with Beatrice Houdini on the return trip from Ossining to Grand Central. They chatted and she asked Thurber if he would like to come to her home and select certain Houdini books for himself. "I said YES," Thurber writes in a letter to his family in Columbus.

> I went up twice to her house, the second time with Althea. . . . She gave me a rare Latin book on magic, dated 1648, to start with. One of

my prizes is a book presented to Houdini by Harry Kellar, the great magician, containing Houdini's signature and an inscription by Kellar. . . . There are also three first editions of James Russell Lowell's works, two volumes in German on German cities, with the bookplate of David Belasco on the inside front cover. . . . Many of the volumes are more than a hundred years old and deal with all sorts of subjects. I think one collection of thirty-two paper backed song books is perhaps a very rare and valuable collection. They are American song books, some of them printed as early as 1845 and all together they contain probably all of the American songs from Yankee Doodle to The Sidewalks of New York. . . .

A very rare book is one called "The Life and Death of John Wilkes Booth," published in Memphis. Houdini is said to have bought up almost every copy of this book to make it rare. I have the only copy outside his family. . . .

I have no doubt but that our collection will someday, if indeed not now, be worth upwards of a thousand dollars, maybe more.

Thurber, already interested in the occult, kept Houdini in mind as the subject of an article he would one day write. Until shortly before Thurber's death, he was still badgering William Shawn, the *New Yorker*'s editor, with a Houdini Profile proposal. Nobody knows what happened to the valuable Houdini books Thurber and Althea accumulated in early 1927.

"I got a $5 bonus for the Sing Sing books story,—since it was a beat," Thurber wrote his family. "I've collected several such bonuses, including one on trench mouth being epidemic here. Funny thing I had a slight recurrence of the trouble the day after I wrote the story and I went to the specialist whom I had quoted and he treated me for nothing and gave me medicine to use."

By February 1927, Thurber was back on heavier assignments, though still not any requiring a fast turnaround. He did a series on the city's water-supply problem, later claiming—falsely—to have predicted New York City's water shortage of 1950.

All his life, Thurber was unusually generous toward other writers trying to get started. Robert S. Harper, of the Ohio Historical Society in Columbus, recalls:

I never knew Thurber well, having followed him at O.S.U. by a few years, but I was in New York looking for work and looked him up at the *Post* in January or February, 1927. Thurber was wearing overshoes and carrying an umbrella that day. He was wonderfully kind and introduced me to the city editor, or someone fairly authoritative on the *Post*. There was no opening and I eventually got a job on the New York *World*, but I've always been grateful to Thurber for what he tried to do for someone he scarcely knew, and only because I was from Columbus and young and poor.

Thurber and Althea's basement apartment on Horatio Street was heated by pipes running through the rooms. "It's a nice sector," Thurber wrote ironically of Horatio Street to a former *Dispatch* colleague, "populated largely by poison liquor victims and old bed springs." The apartment had an unusually large, bright bathroom, which had been converted from a regular room, and at times Thurber set up his table and typewriter in there. "Thurber got lots of his good ideas for writing and drawing while sitting on toilets in bathrooms," says Joel Sayre. The mailbox was constantly filled with rejection slips from *Harper's*, the *American Mercury*, the *New Yorker*, the *New York Sun* and the *World*.

Joel Sayre had been studying medicine in Heidelberg, intending to be a doctor, until he realized he didn't like being around sick people. Back in New York, he often visited the Thurbers. "I was lounging on a sofa in the Thurbers' apartment one Sunday afternoon in January, 1927," Sayre says. "Thurber had been working away at his typewriter on something he hoped to sell the *New Yorker*. Althea said to him, 'Aren't you spoiling your stories by spending too much time on them?' She suggested, half in fun, that he set an old alarm clock to ring in forty-five minutes and try to finish his article within that time. Thurber did. Then he retyped it cleanly and sent it off to the *New Yorker*. He received a check for forty dollars. He had expected another rejection slip, he told me, and the check was a wild surprise."

Says Thurber, "I learned later that I had been writing about the very things Ross didn't want—my newspaper experiences, Broadway characters." The story, which the *New Yorker* ran as "An American Romance," was a bittersweet comment on the purposeless tests of endurance, then in vogue, submitted to by long-distance swimmers, flagpole sitters, marathon ballroom dancers, and practitioners of similar mindless exertions. A little man—the first appearance of the Mitty-Thurber Man anywhere—in a badly fitting overcoat, goes around in a revolving door of a department store and won't stop. He is grimly motivated by a fight he just had with his wife. A floorwalker tries to disperse the gathering crowd, police try to talk the Thurber Man out of the door, but a chewing-gum magnate offers him forty-five thousand dollars if he can keep himself twirling for two hours more. He does, setting a world's record, collapses, and never answers the psychoanalyst who asks him where his boyhood was spent, if he has ever been in a cyclone, and if he has ever had a severe shock while out walking. The little man gets more than a hundred thousand dollars in offers from vaudeville and the movies, and explains simply, "I did it for the wife and children."

The piece's brevity was vital to the *New Yorker*'s format of the day. Its issues were thin, and the ideal length of any text was a page, or "spread," with its tone the chatty style of a personal letter, emphasized by putting the author's signature at the end of the story, article, or casual. To stress the informal tone he was after, Ross coined the term "casual" to apply to short humorous or reminiscent pieces, such as this one by Thurber.

Thurber at the start signed himself "James Grover Thurber," in the prevalent fashion of three-name authors. He later cut it back to "James G. Thurber" when someone suggested that the contributors' names seemed in some instances to be running longer than the text.

He next sold the magazine two poems and another casual, this one about the embarrassment one had to endure when asking at a candy counter for Love Nests, Tootsie Rolls, or other cuddly candy-bar names. Thurber claims to have heard one muscular fellow first tell the candy dealer, "I fancy a lady has fainted yonder," and, when the dealer turned to look, saw the customer throw down a nickel and snatch "a Booful Biskit."

Now known at the magazine as a "contributor," his submissions were usually passed directly to Katharine White, and she liked what Thurber was sending in. "Some of my earliest stuff was more or less a kidding of the New Yorker itself," Thurber wrote Dale Kramer, "for having rejected some twenty longer casuals that I liked. 'I'll give them tootsie rolls and poems, since that's what they seem to want,' I once told my first wife." But in *The Years with Ross* Thurber expresses wonder at some of those early pieces having ever been accepted.

His poems "Villanelle of Horatio Street, Manhattan" and "Street Song" fitted the magazine's makeup requirements for the February 26, 1927, edition, as his first casual, "An American Romance," did not, and the poems became Thurber's first published appearance in the *New Yorker*. "Villanelle" was inspired by a walk along Horatio Street near the waterfront, and its verses elaborated on the letter of complaint he had written a friend on the *Dispatch* a short time before:

> Rusted bed-springs in the street
> And rowdy kids that fight and yell,
> All in a clutter at your feet.

No matter what the hour, you meet
  Brawling children and, as well,
Rusted bed-springs in the street.

Nothing here is clean and neat,
  What you'll find you can't foretell
All in a clutter at your feet—

Tawdry signs of life's defeat;
  Irate voice, supper smell,
Rusted bed-springs in the street.

A broken keg, a buggy seat—
  Stuff that junkmen buy and sell—
All in a clutter at your feet.

If your eyes lift up to greet
  The stars you fall on, sure as hell,
Rusted bed-springs in the street,
  All in a clutter at your feet.

The poem was drawn from experience. In his single-eyed existence, Thurber was already tripping, falling, and "bumping into things," a condition he would refer to in his written and oral recitations the rest of his days. These easily forgettable verses were his inaugural appearance in a magazine he would be identified with inextricably and forever. He still wasn't sure how his signature should look. "Villanelle" was signed "James Grover Thurber"; "Street Song" was signed "J. G. T.," the magazine's decision.

The first sale to the *New Yorker* seemed to give both Thurber and Althea a fresh resolve to make things work out, says Sayre. They used the forty dollars to buy Jeannie, the Scottie. "Althea did her share in those days, working in a bookstore and then a department store, selling children's clothes and ladies' wear. She was extremely good-natured and very entertaining about how to be a saleslady."

It was soon evident, however, that Thurber and Althea had declared their sexual independence of one another. "It was a strange sort of marriage," Sayre says. "I'd drop in on Jim after dinner. Both he and Althea would be glad to see me. Pretty soon another guy would come in and the four of us would sit and chat for a bit. Then Thurber would say to me, 'Come on, let's you and I go uptown. Althea and Fred—or Bill—or Henry—want to be alone.' He didn't sound bitter about it or even resigned. It was almost like good-natured needling. There would be friendly 'So longs' from everybody. It wasn't my idea of how to run a marriage but Jim never said anything about it to me."

But there came a time when he did. One snowy evening, Thurber walked with Sayre around and around Washington Square, talking of his marriage. Althea, Thurber said, thought she was in love with Sayre. An astonished Sayre followed Thurber back to the Horatio Street apartment, where Althea was waiting. Thurber left them together; Sayre says that he simply explained to Althea that he didn't like many people but he loved Thurber. That was the end of it, he says, and adds that the incident made it all the more difficult for him to write the *Time* cover story about Thurber.

While marketing his "Why We Behave Like Microbe Hunters," Thurber looked up Russell Lord, a young man who had taught journalism at O.S.U. during Thurber's final months in Columbus. Lord was in New York, an editor on a farm publication, *The Land*. He was married, lived in Greenwich Village near the Thurbers, and had been a classmate of E. B. White's at Cornell. White was living on West Thirteenth Street with three former Cornell classmates, including Gustave Stubbs (Gus) Lobrano, who would succeed Katharine White as the *New Yorker*'s head fiction editor years later. Kate and Russell Lord knew of Thurber's attempts to sell to the *New Yorker*. One rainy night at their apartment, White remarked that Ross was always looking for new talent. Kate Lord hurried in the rain to fetch Thurber and introduce him to White. Thurber told White he would gladly give up the *Post* job for a job writing for the *New Yorker*, and White said he would try to set up a date for him to meet Ross. "Andy showed Ross a clipping or two of Thurber's *Post* stories," says Katharine White, "and Ross told Andy to get Thurber in to see him." White did.

A 1962 interview of the Whites turns up a slightly different version of the circumstances leading to Thurber's hire. "I can't remember if I first met Jim at Russell Lord's apartment, or at the Thurbers', or Joel Sayre's," White said. "I think it was Lord's. I'd never heard of Thurber until then, and I wasn't acquainted with his stuff in the *Post*."

"Well, Ross was," Katharine White put in. "Ross showed me Thurber's clippings from the *Post*—perhaps Jim had sent them—and asked what I thought of them."

"I didn't meet White until five minutes before he took me in to see Ross," Thurber writes in *The Years with Ross*, whether from a memory lapse or from the Thurber practice of rewriting his personal history for heightened dramatic effect.

Apparently, Thurber's first sales to the *New Yorker* didn't impress Ross. To Thurber's disappointment, he was hired not as a writer but as an editor, and not a traditional editor but one who was supposed to serve Ross as a kind of chief operating officer. A long-impoverished Thurber stifled his objections when Ross offered him seventy dollars a week—nearly a 60 percent increase over his *Post* salary.

Thurber as the chief operating officer of a busy, growing weekly magazine? He wasn't really cut out for that sort of thing, was he? Althea was asked later. "That," she replied, "is the understatement of the year."

PART II

Those Years with Ross

I don't believe any editor actually develops a writer, but Ross did have a way of attracting and holding the people perfectly suited for his magazine, and he was determined to get new people and not depend on old and famous names. No man or woman can add to a writer's skill or talent but they can create a congenial atmosphere and help a great deal by not trying to influence or direct or insist. It was a nice place to work, and we were certainly on our own, and Ross was a great encourager by word of mouth, telegram and letter.

I remember your saying that some writer was said to have been "ruined by Ross" and I keep wondering how this is managed. I feel that a writer who is ruinable is not really a writer.

—*Letters to Dale Kramer, 1950*

28

Those First Years

Ross is still all over the place for many of us, vitally stalking the corridors of our lives, disturbed and disturbing, fretting, stimulating, more evident in death than the living presence of ordinary men. A photograph of him, full face, almost alive with a sense of contained restlessness, hangs on a wall outside his old office. I am sure he had just said to the photographer, "I haven't got time for this." That's what he said, impatiently, to anyone—doctor, lawyer, tax man—who interrupted, even momentarily, the stream of his dedicated energy. Unless a meeting, conference, or consultation touched somehow upon the working of his magazine, he began mentally pacing.

—from *The Years with Ross*

Thurber would hardly have achieved his success and fame had he not been hired by the *New Yorker* in its early years. The magazine's uncharted editorial direction and the consequent receptiveness of its founder to new ideas quickly opened for Thurber the unique chance to exploit his genius. He was influenced by other contributors to the magazine, especially E. B. White, but, through the accidents of time and circumstance, no one proved so central to his development as *New Yorker* editor Harold Wallace Ross. Ross looms continually throughout Thurber's memoirs and conversational reminiscences after 1926. Though just two years older than Thurber, Ross—gradually, unwittingly, unrealized by either man—took on for Thurber the shape and character of a father figure. (Thurber would nervously deny it.) Like anyone in such a role, Ross paid the price. Over the years, Thurber's recognition of the editor's importance to him would give rise to his affection and anger, admiration and ridicule, gratitude and resentment. His feelings were often understandable, for Ross was a contradiction in his own right—incomparably kind and cruel, brave and cowardly, insightful and obtuse, crude and charming. The wonder is that the Thurber-Ross forces collided and meshed to the ultimate benefit of both men. Thurber greatly accelerated the rate at which Ross's magazine attained its commanding lead and influence as an entertaining, intelligently written periodical, the envy of rivals for more than a half-century. Reciprocally, the *New Yorker* showcase displayed Thurber's work to an influential, intellectual, and appreciative readership that helped propel his life and career into the permanently illuminated reaches of literature and art.

Ross remains a surprising, even a hard-to-believe figure in magazine journalism. Some of those who worked with him in the *New Yorker*'s earlier days of stress and uncertainty remember the penalties he exacted through his eccentric trial-and-error seeking after a perfection too imprecise to be attainable. Some never forgave him the pain and humiliation—certainly not those who were summarily fired by a fickle, changeable Ross, who usually had his underlings swing the ax when he would not be on the premises to hear an appeal. Ross lived as a semiparanoid, according to survivors of the period. "I live the life of a hunted animal," he would frequently say. He was often and unfairly suspicious and cynical toward those trying to help, and always fearful of failure—even after the magazine had seen its worst days financially. Many of the people who worked with Ross in the early days of the magazine, kept as they were in a state of job insecurity, found him difficult to like. Ross was, from the start, protective and considerate of the underpaid outside contributors, but only when the magazine's future was finally secure did he express a similar concern for his employees.

"Ross didn't acquire the appreciation and affection he finally had for his staff until fifteen years after he began the magazine," says Rogers Whitaker, who was there from 1926 until his death in 1981. "Personal considerations made sense to him only if it clearly helped the magazine in the early days. All the firing of editors that Thurber writes about is funny now; it wasn't all that funny then. It was frequently heartless and cruel."

Brendan Gill, who joined the *New Yorker* as a staff writer in 1937, sees Ross as miscast from the beginning as editor of the *New Yorker*. Certainly a normal search for an editor to start a sophisticated periodical catering to the literate and moneyed class of the Eastern establishment would have overlooked Ross. Especially if the talent scout knew him personally. He was thirty-two in 1925 when he got the *New Yorker* off to a fragile start. Janet Flanner, who began writing the magazine's Letter From Paris just four months after its first issue, writes of Ross in that period:

> He was an eccentric, impressive man to look at or listen to, a big-boned Westerner from Colorado who talked in windy gusts that gave a sense of fresh weather to his conversation. His face was homely, with a pendant lower lip; his teeth were far apart, and when I first knew him, after the First World War, he wore his butternut-colored thick hair in a high, stiff pompadour, like some wild gamecock's crest, and he also wore anachronistic, old-fashioned, high laced shoes, because he thought Manhattan men dressed like what he called dudes. . . .
>
> Ross was a strange, fascinating character, sympathetic, loveable, often explosively funny, and a good talker who was the most blasphemous good talker on record. Once . . . at the *New Yorker* office I heard him chatting in the corridor. I called out to him that his profanity was really excessive, to which he said in surprise, "Jesus Christ, my dear, I haven't said a goddam thing!" His swearing was automatic, unconscious, always chaste, never coarse and merely continuous.

Ross's face, sufficiently disorganized to permit a fascinating variety of expressions, reminded Alexander Woollcott of a dishonest Abe Lincoln. He slouched when he walked as if he were following a plow. (Stanley Walker, one of the magazine's many managing editors, always believed that Ross had Indian blood, though Ross's father was from Northern Ireland and his mother was of old New England stock.)

Self-educated, Ross's favorite reading included Webster's Second New International Dictionary, encyclopedias, Fowler's *Modern English Usage,* and the works of Herbert Spencer, who preached rugged individualism and freedom from government and a matriarchal society. He distrusted poetry, even poetry he understood ("Don't ever leave me alone with a poet," he once ordered an assistant), and obscure or mannered writing, and he was neurotic in his watchfulness for factual inaccuracies. Ross, writes Gill,

> had the uneducated man's suspicion of the fickleness of words; he wanted them to have a limited, immutable meaning, but the sons of bitches kept hopping about from one sentence to the next. . . . Nor were the goddam dictionaries the allies he thought they ought to be; they nearly always betrayed him by granting a word several definitions, some of which were maddeningly at odds with others. That was why

Ross fell back with such relish upon Fowler's *Modern English Usage*—the work of a petty tyrant, who imposed idiosyncrasies by fiat. Ross was awed by Fowler; he would have liked to hold the whip hand over words and syntax as Fowler did. If words in themselves were not to be trusted, figures of speech were suspicious in the extreme. Metaphors and similes were Ross's adversaries.

Ross's limited knowledge of classical and current literature was always a matter of office gossip and amusement. One noon he stopped by his checking department to ask a surprised young man if Moby Dick was the man or the whale. ("I was so startled, I had trouble for a moment remembering," says the novelist William Gaddis, who put in a brief stint as a fact checker in the 1940s.) But Ross gradually and haphazardly learned how to attract to the *New Yorker* a concentration of talented writers and editors, and, finally, how to get the best out of them. Because of that, and because he instinctively recognized first-class quality in a product, he became the greatest magazine editor of his time. In the words of William Shawn, Ross's successor and his managing editor for a dozen years before Ross's death: "In the early days, a small company of writers, artists, and editors—E. B. White, James Thurber, Peter Arno, and Katharine White among them—did more to make the magazine what it is than can be measured. . . . But at the source, abounding in promise, was Ross."

Ross was born November 6, 1892, in Aspen, Colorado, to George Ross, a mining and demolition worker, and Ida Ross, a Scottish Presbyterian schoolteacher. Ida bequeathed her son the sense of morality and integrity few suspected lived in this profane and roughhewn man until it became evident in the guidelines he imposed on what his magazine would or would not publish. He fell in love with the newspaper business, and after his sophomore year in high school he dropped out to work as a reporter for the *Salt Lake City Tribune*. He is remembered as being born to the trade. "He could not only get it, he could write it," his friend, Herbert Asbury, remembers.

One of Ross's *Tribune* assignments, Thurber learned, "was to interview the madam of a house of prostitution. Always self-conscious and usually uncomfortable in the presence of all but his closest women friends, the young reporter began by saying to the bad woman (he divided the other sex into good and bad), 'How many fallen women do you have?' "

It was the era of tramp newspapermen, and Ross's wanderlust and restless curiosity led him to work on eight newspapers before he was twenty-five—in Marysville (California), Sacramento, Panama, New Orleans, Brooklyn, Atlanta, and San Francisco. His frequent changes of job location, often accomplished by hopping freight trains, earned him the sobriquet of "Hobo" Ross. He was fond of horseplay, was not by nature a hard drinker but became almost an addicted poker and cribbage player. He was convivial and well liked, and it was thought that his noisy, profane speech disguised both his poker strategy and an innate shyness.

He appreciated practical jokes but was as often the victim as the instigator of them. When seventeen and reporting for the *Sacramento Union*, Ross was ordered by his city editor to catch a freight train headed for the Sierra Nevada and write up a Sunday nature feature, an assignment so vague that Ross should have been on his guard. The editor had Ross followed to learn the number of Ross's boxcar, telephoned a friend, the sheriff of Placer County, and asked him to arrest Ross in Auburn on vagrancy charges. Ross was jailed, cursing and yelling that he was a newspaper reporter. At Ross's insistence, the sheriff called the paper and was told to tell Ross that he was unknown there. Ross, realizing he had been victimized, spent the night in jail successfully convincing the awed petty offenders in the cell with him that he was wanted in Salt Lake City for three murders.

When the United States entered World War I, Ross joined the Army and, once in France, got himself assigned to the *Stars and Stripes*, a newspaper published in Paris for the troops. By force of personality, Ross became the editor, though the staff boasted such college-trained stalwarts as Alexander Woollcott, former drama critic with the *New York Times*, John T. Winterich, and Franklin P. Adams (F.P.A.), whose newspaper column, "The Conning Tower," often written in the diary style of Samuel Pepys, would be prominent for more than two decades. The shabbily uniformed Ross, and the myopic and unathletic appearances of the others, led Woollcott to comment upon joining the staff that they were, "by strictly military standards, the least alarming soldiers I ever saw before or since." So was Woollcott.

In Paris, Woollcott introduced Ross to Jane Grant, an effective feminist from Joplin, Missouri, who was the first woman reporter on the *New York Times* to win equity with the men in pay and assignments. She had failed to be accredited as a war correspondent but made it to Europe with the Motion Picture Bureau of the YMCA. Watching Ross at a poker game at a bistro in Montmartre, Grant decided he was the homeliest and most disheveled man she had ever met, but she was more than impressed by the fact that "Harold Ross, a journalist no one had ever heard of before, had become boss of a whole pack of well-known newspaper men."

Ross was unimpressed by rank and status. Upon being introduced to Sherwood Anderson in the years that followed, he said, "Hi, Anderson," and began a long lecture to the famous writer on English usage. Later, when introduced by Thurber to the British artist Paul Nash, well known for his World War I battlefield paintings, Ross said, "Hi, Nash. There are only two phony arts, painting and music." He called people by their last names, a habit picked up by many on his staff with the prominent exception of Shawn, who courteously prefaced names with "Mr.," "Mrs.," or "Miss," regardless of the number of years he had known their owners.

In 1918, Ross was discharged from the Army in Paris, and arrived in New York. He roomed with John Winterich on West Eleventh Street. The Butterick Publishing Company offered Ross and other former members of *Stars and Stripes* funding to start a weekly veterans' magazine, the *Home Sector*, which first appeared in September 1919. Ross was editor, Winterich managing editor, and Woollcott, though back with the *Times*, contributed. A printers' strike put the *Home Sector* out of business, but its staff was offered positions on a house organ for the newly organized American Legion. Ross's contract paid him ten thousand dollars a year, the most he had ever earned. This gave him the courage to propose marriage to Jane Grant, who was back on the *Times*. Grant accepted, keeping her maiden name and her job after the marriage. New York was enduring a postwar housing shortage, and the couple moved in with another couple: Heywood Broun—a well-known newspaper columnist who dressed so shabbily that a stranger, moved to pity, once handed him a dime outside the Algonquin—and his wife, Ruth Hale, who refused to be addressed as "Mrs." (She was elected president of the Lucy Stone League, an organization seeking further rights for women. Jane Grant was elected secretary.)

Two theatrical press agents, Murdock Pemberton and John Peter Toohey, worn out from lunching at the Algonquin with the conversation-hogging, narcissistic Woollcott, whose favorable theater reviews they sought, began inviting their literary friends to counter him. Woollcott, in turn, invited Ross. Thus began the Algonquin Round Table, named after the large circular table reserved for them each noon in the rear of what later became the hotel's Rose Room. Its arch, witty, acidic membership (which never included Thurber or E. B. White—by their own choice) fluctuated over the next several years, eventually including *Vanity Fair* staffers Robert Benchley, Dorothy Parker, and Robert Sherwood, as well as F.P.A., Marc Connelly, George S. Kaufman and Edna Ferber. The fare was biting repartee and skilled witty insult, at which Ross seems to have been the least quotable. Nicknamed "the Vicious Circle," the Round Tablers "took charge of American humor in the 1920s and 1930s," according to Wolcott Gibbs, and their influence on American letters and theater spread across the country like ripples on a pond. Membership qualification was restrictively high. One outsider, trying to crash the circle one noon, ran his hand over Marc Connelly's bald head and said, "You know, it feels like my wife's bottom." Connelly thoughtfully ran his own hand over his pate and replied, "So it does." The gross aspirant was boycotted thereafter. More on the mark was Dorothy Parker, who, when Robert Sherwood's wife gave birth, wired her, "Dear Mary, we knew you had it in you." Ross initiated the Algonquin's Thanatopsis Literary and Inside Straight Club, a poker group that drew some of its gamblers from the Algonquin crew but welcomed other risk takers willing and able to stay up all night.

Though already dreaming of a magazine of his own, in 1924 Ross became coeditor of *Judge*, a national humor magazine of He-She jokes and short anecdotes. Ross soon saw why such a magazine could only fail: the time it took to distribute it throughout the country made it less than current, and its intellectual content was forfeited to the common denominator of a broad, lowbrow readership. Says Jane Grant: "Ross hoped he might revive the ailing *Judge* with some of his ideas for our [proposed] New York magazine. . . . He was at once in conflict with [the management]. . . . One of his first acts was to revise the He-She joke and use one-sentence captions on cartoons. His colleagues considered that heresy." Ross saw that the fatal problems affecting *Judge* also pertained to the humor weekly *Life*, which gave up the ghost in 1936 when Time, Inc., bought its title for $80,000 and made it a picture magazine.

Ross pasted up a dummy of his proposed weekly, which addressed in a hit-or-miss way the culture, people, and events of the New York metropolitan area—a magazine he believed could be supported by advertising bought by regional stores and services that catered to the wealthy and whose ad agencies shunned national publications as the least cost-effective message bearers. At a Thanatopsis poker game, F.P.A. introduced Ross to Raoul Fleischmann, an heir to the baking and yeast business. Fleischmann, dubbed "Royal Flushman" for his skill at poker, enjoyed taking risks, was part owner of racehorses, and speculated on Wall Street. Ross persuaded him that $50,000 was all he needed to get his proposed magazine airborne. Fleischmann agreed to put up $25,000; Ross and Jane Grant contributed the other $25,000 from their savings. (They had managed to live largely on Grant's income, while banking most of Ross's.) Ross quit *Judge* after six weeks and by late summer of 1924 had moved into a small office suite on the sixth floor of 25 West Forty-fifth Street, a building owned by the Fleischmann family. His cadre consisted of a secretary, a telephone operator, an editorial assistant named Tyler (Tip) Bliss, and the writer Philip Wylie, who was to put "momism" into the dictionary with his *Generation of Vipers* a couple of decades later. Wylie's small New

Jersey public-relations firm had been wiped out by bad publicity stemming from a paternity suit. Ross, says Wylie, was so intrigued by his story of the woman plaintiff delivering a normal-term baby five months after Wylie had first met her that he let him join the staff—at no pay. Wylie helped out editorially until he could establish the worthwhileness of publicizing the new magazine. He did, by arranging to have the first issue of the *New Yorker* publicly presented to New York governor Al Smith in Albany. Rea Irvin, the art director at *Life*, agreed to spend a few hours a week looking over the art submissions. The apartment Ross and Grant shared "was filled with copies of *Punch*, *Simplicissimus* [a German magazine], and other foreign magazines which we studied for layout," writes Grant. "We culled the old files of *Leslie's*, *Gleason's*, *Harper's Weekly*, and . . . old and new copies of *Life*, *Judge*, the *Smart Set*, and the *American Mercury*."

No name for the magazine had been settled on. "All our friends were asked for, and gave, suggestions," Grant recalls: "*Manhattan*, *New York Weekly*, *New York Life*, *Truth*, and *Our Town*, among others." John Peter Toohey came up with "*The New Yorker*" one day at a Round Table lunch. Toohey was given stock in payment for the idea. He would have given Ross the title free and "was as much surprised as anyone at the value of the stock a few years later," Grant says.

Two experiences firmly persuaded Ross that if he ever edited his own publication, he would throw out the publisher and advertising manager the first time they appeared on the editorial floor with suggestions: Running the *American Legion* magazine, he had been ordered often by the Legion's executives to print semiliterate articles so awful he couldn't even find humor in the situation. Secondly, Dorothy Parker was fired from her job as theater critic at *Vanity Fair* because she had been too critical of plays produced by friends of the publisher, Condé Nast. (Her Algonquin colleagues, Benchley and Sherwood, quit out of sympathy.) Ross would insist, as head of the *New Yorker*, that the editor alone determine what went into the magazine, including the quality of the advertising. Though blasphemous and not averse to off-color jokes, he began as and remained a prude in guarding his magazine from his version of what was risqué or indecent. Sex, which he considered "an incident," was off-limits in the magazine's contents, but because of its insidious nature its overtones crept into text and cartoons and kept Ross nervously believing that the writers and artists had "put one over" on him with each issue.

Fleischmann was soon having his doubts about the enterprise. "I felt that Ross had not had enough experience in publishing and editing," Fleischmann wrote Dale Kramer in 1951, "and that some of his brilliant friends might be valuable on an advisory board." Ross obligingly named some of his Round Table friends to such an editorial board: Ralph Barton, Rea Irvin, George S. Kaufman, Alice Duer Miller, Marc Connelly, Alexander Woollcott, Dorothy Parker. It was "the only dishonest thing I ever did," Ross said later, for few of the group would have anything to do with the flimsy new periodical in its first months of life.

Ross wrote his famous prospectus in such excellent and restrained phrases "that those who did not know him then—the later members of the staff [including Thurber]—have questioned his authorship [of it]," says Grant. "But it was his alone, for much of it was written in my presence and passages of it were read aloud to me as the work progressed." Ross ran a shortened version of it in the first issue's lead article, which consisted of two pages of paragraphs called "Of All Things." The principal significance of the prospectus today is historical, its inspiration and intent rooted in what Corey Ford calls "The Time of Laughter," which began with a postwar irreverence toward America's bourgeois, material, and puritanical fixations. This attitude flourished in a carefree period of bootleg gin and politically and sexually emancipated women. The magazine's lighthearted editorial approach continued to hold up even during the Depression, which deprived so many citizens of dignity and slowly wiped the grin off the face of America. World War II blew apart Ross's early assumption of a magazine that could remain focused on metropolitan personalities, issues, and trivia, and the nuclear balance of terror after the war finally left less and less for writers to find funny or for readers to chuckle over. But in 1925, with practitioners of humor in welcome abundance, Ross could optimistically, cheerfully, and moralistically run this statement based on his original prospectus:

> The New Yorker starts with a declaration of serious purpose but with a concomitant declaration that it will not be too serious in executing it. It hopes to reflect metropolitan life, to keep up with events and affairs of the day, to be gay, humorous, satirical but to be more than a jester.
>
> It will publish facts that it will have to go behind the scenes to get, but it will not deal in scandal for the sake of scandal nor sensation for the sake of sensation. It will try conscientiously to keep its readers informed of what is going on in the fields in which they are most interested. It has announced that it is not edited for the old lady in Dubuque. By this it means that it is not of that group of publications engaged in tapping the Great Buying Power of the North American steppe region

by trading mirrors and colored beads in the form of our best brands of hokum.

There wasn't, and still isn't, a masthead listing the management or editors. Ross, at the time, had deep respect for the British humor publication *Punch*, which kept its staff similarly anonymous. Originally he sought total editorial concealment, which, given the poor quality of the early issues, most contributors didn't mind for a time. Furthermore, some of Ross's famous friends were under contract to other organizations, and a number submitted rejects—work they realized was probably not in their best interest to sign. A few familiar names were disguised by pseudonyms, like Well Known Broker, Last Night, Sawdust, Golly-wogg, and Touchstone. Ross wanted "the New Yorker to project its own character," says Grant, but writers gradually insisted on being named after the magazine began to attain status and respect. The practice of signatures at the end of a piece was Ross's "reluctant concession after a long battle with contributors," Grant adds.

The only memorable and favorable feature of the first issue was Rea Irvin's cover of an aristocratic gentleman in early nineteenth-century costume examining a butterfly through a monocle. Until recently, the cover graced every anniversary issue, and the gentleman continues to appear each week, in different poses, on the contents page and the leading page of Talk of the Town. (When lack of advertising left the inside front cover bare, Corey Ford began a comic series about a similar dandy, whom he called Eustace Tilley; gradually the name was thought to apply to Irvin's cover character.) A gossip column, "In Our Midst," reporting the activities of the better known, was soon dropped in favor of short articles called Profiles, a name given them by James Kevin McGuinness of the *Post*, who contributed to the magazine on a part-time basis. Newspaper columnists and humor magazines such as *Punch* and *Judge* for years had run typographical errors or senseless sentences and paragraphs from other publications, tacking on a cutting comment at the end. Ross took up this practice of publishing "newsbreaks"—which continues today on a reduced scale. His first:

CHAUFFEUR HELD AS BANDIT
—Heading in the *Herald Tribune*.
[tagline] "The start of a long-needed crusade."

"Tip" Bliss, the editorial assistant, a Harvard man who had worked with Ross on *Stars and Stripes* and the *Home Sector*, was still wedded to the two-line joke and was held responsible for garbling a tired one in the first issue:

THE OPTIMIST

Pop: A man who thinks he can make it in a par.
Johnny: What is an optimist, pop?

Bliss was soon fired as an incurable addict of He-She captions, and Ross masochistically insisted on running the garbled joke every anniversary issue until his death, to the increasing despair of his later staffs. (One story is that Ross deliberately turned the joke upside down to kid the old-style humor magazines, but that point was hardly pertinent enough to be made annually as late as 1950.)

The kinks in the early, dreadful issues would have been worked out through experimental dummies if there had been enough funds. As it was, what got published kept the small staff acting as on-the-job trainees, eliminating and adding, and always soliciting contributors and ideas. Russel Crouse, who worked on the *Evening Post* with Thurber, and was one of the first Talk of the Town writers, believes that Ross's inability to articulate his ideas was a fortunate thing, "for there might have been a monotony of style if he had been more coherent."

Ross was nearly as wary of artists as he was of poets. Artists were children who never went anywhere or knew anybody, he believed, so from the start he yielded to the judgments of the few artists he trusted and felt comfortable with: Rea Irvin, Ralph Barton (who committed suicide in 1931, to Ross's immense grief), and Wallace Morgan. Irvin, who eventually became wealthy from his *New Yorker* association, remained an art editor there until he retired in 1955 because of poor health—a remarkable tenure of service, given that "Ross never understood pictures," as Irvin told Jane Grant, adding that "we disagreed on what was funny." But there was little doubt that in the early issues the art and cartoons were the magazine's strong suits.

Philip Wylie was officially hired at forty dollars a week, and acted as manager of the art department from 1925 into 1928. He writes in two letters to Dale Kramer:

> Ross' search for his "magic formula" was a vague, general, intuitive thing. He dreaded corn but corn, at the beginning, was all he knew, and the New Yorker was plenty corny. He had, I think, a sort of intuition, gained from an awed but sharp scrutiny of European satirical magazines, that there was a place for something of that sort in America. It was the artists, plus (to a lesser degree) a few writers, most of them not Algonquins, who originated and brought in the stuff that developed the tone,

style, and format of the magazine. And Rea Irvin led the whole parade. . . .

If you scan the first two years of New Yorker[s] you will find the magazine, textually, takes off with the old Life-Judge-Stars and Stripes corny humor. [The text] was routine jokes, wisecracks and parodies of the heavy, Corey Ford sort. . . . But . . . from the start, the art and drawings [had] that élan, that satiric sharpness and gusto, which the text lacked. . . . The late Helen Hokinson—a midwest fashion artist come east to seek her fortune, walked into the office the first time with water color drawings of two middle-aged ladies [drawn from the back] waving farewell to a steamship—the highlights on their behinds; the drawing skill instantly appealed. [Peter] Arno walked in in sneakers with some decorative drawings of energy and [craftsmanship].

Ross always knew what he wanted to achieve with his magazine; he never had a lucid and articulate sense of how to go about getting from a Judge-Life format to what he soon got. [But] Ross had the stamina to push ahead in all the early hard times. He had the charm and self-confidence to get the dough. He was extremely nervous, unbrave, dubious and jittery but now and then he did have the nerve to pioneer. He had plenty of gall in dealing with people. And he had a vision, that was like the bright backside of an enormous inferiority complex, of becoming the editor of a magazine that would be as novel and brainy for America as anything abroad.

E. B. White adds, in a letter to Dale Kramer:

> I think the New Yorker was bound to happen, just as another magazine is bound to come along sooner or later to overshadow it. Ross wasn't so much seeking a formula as he was trying to shake off the formulae of Life, Judge, Puck, Harper's, and all the rest. Jokes were mostly he-and-she, essays were tweedy, feature writing was at low ebb, humor was barber shop. The NYer took a fresh grip on the bat and swung at everything, unabashed. Ross was as enthusiastic as he was wide-eyed; and his uncompromising nature attracted a lot of good, if inexperienced, people to his side. . . . It was a lot of fun. And a lot of work.

Nor could Ross articulate what he was looking for in advertisements appropriate for the magazine to carry. Ad copy had to be submitted to him for "taste, clarity, and entertainment." By knowing what he didn't like he was usually able to back his way into accepting something that was "going in the right direction" at least. (He rarely conceded that any item in the magazine was perfect.) His censorship of ads "caused quite a stir in advertising circles," writes Grant. "Some [advertisers] refused to cooperate, declaring they'd take their business elsewhere—and did. It took a lot of courage for Ross to stand his ground, for we were desperately in need of revenue, but his Scorpio stubbornness sustained him."

"I have an utter contempt for businessmen," Ross told the writer James M. Cain, who took a brief turn as managing editor. "The trouble with them is, they don't know anything about business. Because if the magazine is right, anybody can sell advertising in it, and if it's not, nobody can. They understand everything but the magazine."

Elsie Dick, Ross's first secretary, and Grant compiled lists of potential subscribers and hired young debutantes and vacationing college girls to telephone them. It was the start of the circulation department.

Even prospering publications suffered lowered advertising revenue during the summer season, and Fleischmann suggested that the magazine—its circulation after a few issues at less than three thousand and losing $5,000 a week —be suspended during the summer of 1925. Nobody kidded themselves; suspension meant the end of the magazine. John Hanrahan, Fleischmann's publications adviser, agreed that suspension made economic sense, but, returning from a conference with Fleischmann, Ross, and Hawley Truax (Ross's housemate, friend, and financial expert) at the Princeton Club, Hanrahan sadly commented that it was "like killing a defenseless thing." The comment hounded Fleischmann the rest of the day. Meanwhile, that night, Grant vigorously protested the decision to Ross and Truax, and in a day or two, through a friend, located a wealthy oilman in Cleveland who would put up $100,000 to get them through the summer. Fleischmann, told of this development, obtained the $100,000 himself, from his mother. Part of it went into newspaper ads written by Hanrahan and Arthur Samuels, a Round Table composer and wit, borrowed for the occasion. The first ad asked:

"WHAT EXPLAINS THIS EXTRAORDINARY RECEPTION?"

The copy, bordering on the dishonest, read: "The New Yorker—unheralded and unpromoted—acquired almost overnight the largest metropolitan circulation of any class periodical." Later ads in the series featured testimonials by financial, political, and entertainment celebrities, including Robert Benchley, who said he liked the magazine because "my folks come from Dubuque, Iowa."

During the *New Yorker*'s first year, it spent $225,000, all but $35,000 of it Fleischmann's. An additional $485,000 was invested during the next two years. Of the total $750,000 that went into the *New Yorker* in its first three years, including a $40,000 loan, Fleischmann's investment was $550,000, making him the predominant stockholder and eventually a much wealthier man than he had been.

Though Ross has been criticized for working his small staff beyond reason at times, he worked longer and harder than any of them, putting in twelve-hour days seven days a week and, in frantic efforts at relaxation, playing poker, backgammon, or cribbage all night. The magazine was only six months old when Ross's father died, taking him out of the office for three weeks to tend to his mother in Colorado. He experienced far less sorrow over a father he had never got along with than over being away from the magazine. Still, Grant believes the loss of his father did affect Ross adversely. He developed chronic ulcers and signed into the Battle Creek, Michigan, Sanatorium for ten days, where he was put on a vegetarian diet and forbidden to smoke.

But the work had piled up in his absence, and the communal apartment life he and Grant lived with others at 412 West Forty-seventh Street got on his nerves—especially after the advent of their self-absorbed and tiresome cotenant Alexander Woollcott. "Ross found no peace," writes Grant. "He would lug his typewriter from one room to another in restless frenzy. It was either too noisy, too quiet, too many people around—and, finally, he was too far from the *New Yorker* office four blocks away."

These stressful circumstances so early in their marriage no doubt contributed to the divorce three years later. As in the case of so many who find their marriage partners incompatible but still deserving of fondness and respect, Ross and Grant hoped for an amicable divorce, but it became a bitter one. Ross, who earlier had lost $29,000 in one disastrous evening of poker, had no money for alimony. Grant's lawyer then insisted that Ross set up an escrow guaranteeing Jane a definite amount if her *New Yorker* stock lost value. Ross objected fiercely before giving in, for even by 1928, when the divorce took place, there was no guarantee of the magazine's success. Ross moved into an apartment on East Fifty-seventh Street to join Edward McNamara, "the singing policeman" turned actor. Grant moved to a suite in the Savoy-Plaza, forever looking back on her marriage to Ross as a casualty in the battle to get the *New Yorker* launched.

Ross thought his magazine might find some financial shelter in appealing to social snobbery in the beginning, rather than to the intellectual snobbery that characterized the *Smart Set* and the *American Mercury*. Some of his early hires reflected that bent: Fillmore Hyde, son of a famous capitalist known for his flair at riding to the hounds, and Ralph McAllister Ingersoll, grand-nephew of Ward McAllister, who had initiated New York's Social Register by selecting the "Four Hundred," society's elite, who could fit comfortably into Mrs. William Astor's ballroom. Ross hoped to put the magazine into the hands of the more affluent by getting it talked about, and in the fall of 1925 he got his chance. Ellin Mackay, a postdebutante of twenty-two, daughter of Clarence H. Mackay, the wealthy president of Postal Telegraph, had wearied of her ordained social life and decided to be a writer. Her handwritten manu-scripts, bound in expensive leather, were being sent to *Vogue, Vanity Fair,* the *New Yorker* and elsewhere—and rejected. But one amateurish piece was called "Why We Go to Cabarets—A Post-Debutante Explains." Her cousin, Alice Duer Miller, a Round Table member, mentioned the piece to Jane Grant, who, without bothering to read it, at once envisaged it as a means of promoting the struggling magazine.

Irving Berlin was secretly in love with Ellin, and she with him. Woollcott, who had written a book about Berlin, brought the couple home to meet Ross, Grant, and their other cohabitants on West Forty-seventh Street. Ross liked Ellin and put off reading her manuscript, certain it was no good and that he would have the painful task of rejecting it. Pressured by Woollcott, he showed the manuscript, without its byline, to Ralph Ingersoll, whom Ross had casually named as managing editor. The article was frightfully bad, Inger-soll told Ross, but he thought the subject would draw readers from Park Avenue. Ross gave in and asked Fillmore Hyde, hired to write Talk and handle other editorial tasks, to rewrite the Mackay article. Miss Mackay gave the rewrite to a Social Register executive, who protested Hyde's version. At Grant's insistence, Ross reluctantly published the original.

Grant showed the article proof to her friends and colleagues in the press. News stories about the item appeared in the *World,* the *Times,* and the *Trib-une.* Philip Wylie sent out press releases on the article. The wire services picked it up. When the Mackay piece was published, November 28, 1925, the *New Yorker* sold out for the first time. The article itself was a study in reverse snobbery: debutantes went to cabarets with high-society escorts of their own choosing, even though "we do not particularly like dancing shoulder to shoulder with gaudy and fat drummers [salesmen]." Why go to cabarets? Be-cause young men falsely claiming to be of the Social Register were being invited to the private parties of the rich.

It was a sorry publishing landmark, but it did get the magazine talked about within the nightclub set and the upper crust, a point not lost on advertisers. Another Mackay piece followed two weeks later: "The Declining Function, A Post-Debutante Rejoices." Unknown to most, in it she was indicating her intention to marry Berlin, seen by her father as only a Jewish songwriter from the Lower East Side: "Modern girls are conscious of the importance of their own identity, and they marry whom they choose, satisfied to satisfy themselves. They are not so keenly aware, as were their parents, of the vast difference between a brilliant match and a mésalliance."

Subsequent market surveys showed that New York's Four Hundred and their fellow blue bloods did not become regular readers of the *New Yorker* because of the Mackay pieces, as rumor has it. But the articles did increase the magazine's circulation among the speakeasy, café-society crowd. Ross expected more copy from Ellin Mackay, but she telephoned him from a booth in City Hall a few days after her second piece appeared to tell him that she had just married Berlin and wouldn't be able to get her next article to him on time. She went on to write novels later in life, but nothing more for the *New Yorker*.

That November the wire services carried summaries of the first Ellin Mackay piece, which were picked up by the international press. Thurber, sitting on the *terrasse* of the Café Dôme in Paris, reading the Paris *Herald*, came upon the item. It wasn't until then, Thurber writes, that he "first heard of the existence of a magazine called the *New Yorker*." This may be true, though one remembers that he and Althea met E. B. White's sister, Lillian, on the *Leviathan* six months before, and saw a good deal of her in Paris that summer, according to Althea. Lillian's references to her brother's association with the *New Yorker* may have failed to register with Thurber. From the start, Lillian was more Althea's friend than Thurber's. Althea's reminders to Thurber that he should look up White at the *New Yorker* when he returned took place in June 1926, seven months after his discovery of the Mackay piece. And he had White's name wrong, at that.

29

That Managing Editor

I told [Ross] that I wanted to write and he snarled, "Writers are a dime a dozen, Thurber. What I want is an editor. I can't find editors. Nobody grows up. Do you know English?" I said I thought I knew English, and this started him off on a subject with which I was to become intensely familiar. "Everybody thinks he knows English," he said, "but nobody does. I think it's because of the goddam women schoolteachers. . . . I'm surrounded by women and children. . . . I never know where anybody is, and I can't find out. Nobody tells me anything. They sit out there at their desks, getting me deeper and deeper into God knows what. Nobody has any self-discipline, nobody gets anything done. Nobody knows how to delegate anything. What I need is a man who can sit at a central desk and make this place operate like a business office, keep track of things, find out where people are. I am, by God, going to keep sex out of this office—sex is an incident.

—from *The Years with Ross*

The *New Yorker* had just purchased Thurber's two poems and casual when he was interviewed for a job by Ross. The poems appeared in February 1927, the month Thurber was hired. But given Thurber's skimpy writing portfolio at the time, it isn't surprising that Ross at first would consider him one of the run-of-the-mill writers who are, and always have been, a dime a dozen. Jane Grant believes Thurber might not have been hired if E. B. White had not accompanied him to see Ross, thus leading Ross to conclude that the two were old friends and that White's brief, mumbled introduction was an implied endorsement. Says Grant: "Ross had been skeptical about even interviewing Thurber until White said, 'Why not see him?'"

White was the apple of Ross's eye; his prose, verses, cartoon captions, his lighthearted but thoughtful and finely literate editorials, and his clever taglines for "newsbreaks" were all exactly what Ross wanted. White was setting badly needed standards of literary competence for the young magazine, contributing, in Marc Connelly's words, "the steel and the music." His lead-off paragraphs (Notes and Comment) were the only part of Talk of the Town that Ross, to his credit, shied away from editing or rewriting.

It has been assumed that because Ross believed Thurber and White to be friendly birds of a feather, he arranged for the two to share one of the magazine's closet-size offices, big enough only for two desks, two chairs, and two typewriters, but White says, "Jim and I simply got thrown together. We stayed together for several years, willing to make the best of whatever we were given to do. We never felt competitive, and we became good friends the while. Our primary interest was in making a living."

In his frequent party imitations of Harold Ross, Thurber would reenact the hour Ross hired him as an editor. "I want to write," Thurber, as applicant, would protest. "You'll start as managing editor like everyone else!" Thurber, as Ross, would shout in reply.

It was true that Ross routinely saw "the new man" as someone who might bring order to the organization. The dozens Ross found to feed successively into the revolving door of his unrealistic expectations all came to be called, by a staff grown cynical, "the new genius," or, by irreverent modification, "the new Jesus." Katharine Angell White comments: "Ross always found satisfactory editors harder to find than writers. I think that is still the case."

"A stranger was always walking into my office," says Rogers Whitaker, who joined the staff in May 1926 as a copyeditor, "and he'd say, 'I think we ought to do this or that,' and I'd say, 'Sure, but who are you?' It was always the latest assistant to Ross, a guy who Ross had thinking was the new managing, or executive, editor."

In Ross's fantasies, he saw a "Central Desk," or "Hub," controlling the operations. The miracle men hired to occupy it were nearly all destined to fail, for Ross seemed never to want them to win. He often stood in the way of his own high expectations. The surreal was sufficiently at war with the pragmatic to keep tempers and blood pressures high and the office in a perpetual confusion of job changes and firings. The more effective the new editor might prove to be, the more Ross felt threatened. A truly efficient operation would have ended the game Ross seemed compelled to play. For one thing, he was too dissatisfied with the magazine, as it was then evolving, to want it to be hardened into formula through capable management. He accused subordinates of being unable to delegate decision making, but he was the principal offender. He was The Boss and he couldn't for long share even the authority needed by his "central desk" man to accomplish what he thought Ross wanted. As long as he lived, excepting rare periods of sickness or vacations, nothing on either the editorial or advertising side of the business got into the magazine without Ross's consent.

Ralph Ingersoll, who was hired as a reporter five months after the magazine began, was still angry at Ross's treatment of him thirty-six years later, when Ingersoll published his memoirs, *Point of Departure*. (Few seemed able to retain a consistent attitude toward the enigmatic Ross; Ingersoll dedicates his book to him.) Having agreed to see Ingersoll to discuss his hopes for a reporting job, Ross, in the interview, hedged, saying that maybe a reporter was the last thing he wanted. Ingersoll describes the occasion:

" 'I'll tell you . . .' Ross suddenly began again, throwing his arms wide in a sweeping gesture. . . . The gesture included an open bottle of ink, which he sent flying, the blue-black stuff cascading down the front of a new Palm Beach suit I had bought for the occasion. . . . 'Jee-sus,' Ross snarled. . . . 'Okay, you're on. Hell, I hire *anybody!*' "

Ross, nervous by nature, may have been unusually apprehensive because of what he had heard about Ingersoll. Six feet, three inches, Ingersoll had been a heavyweight wrestler at Yale. As a reporter on William Randolph Hearst's *New York American*, he knocked down the city editor, who had used statements from an Ingersoll story out of context in a rewrite that dishonestly disparaged a government agency Hearst didn't like. Ross was fearful of violence and suspected all large men of sinking to an animal level in addressing grievances.

In the capricious environment of the magazine's first five years, Ingersoll could offer the best proof that if there *were* a managing-editor title it had been his. Never mind that Ross, during that time, brought in many others, including Thurber, who, he told them, had the authority to order Ingersoll around. (Thurber declined, "being sane at the time, or fairly so.") "Ross seemed to demote Ingersoll once a year," says Whitaker.

From 1925 to 1930, Ralph Ingersoll was listed as managing editor in the magazine's statement of ownership, published by postal regulation. "But Ingersoll was no more the managing editor than Thurber was," claims Jane Grant. "Ross was always telling this person or that, 'You're just the fellow I need,' but he would never give them a real managing editor's responsibilities. He considered Ingersoll the 'bug' editor—working at getting bugs out of the operation. The statement required by the Post Office Department, the first week of every October, was hard for Ross to deal with. At first he was going to list his friend Harpo Marx as managing editor, but I remember the night he came home, one hand over his mouth to cover that gap in his teeth that showed when he grinned, and told me he had listed Ralph Ingersoll as managing editor. Harold left it that way for several years, and Ralph probably used it to sell Henry Luce on hiring him as managing editor of *Fortune*. Ralph had been fighting with Ross for five years by then and Harold was relieved to see him go."

"But in fact," says Katharine White in response to Grant, "Ingersoll did everything a managing editor is supposed to do. He *was* the managing editor, though Ross never used the term. Ralph was a very good one. One of the best we ever had."

When preparing *The Years with Ross*, Thurber queried Ingersoll, who replied:

[Ross] sent my name in [to the Postal authorities as managing editor] and it was duly printed in the usual small type. He used to taunt me with it. Said I was about as qualified to be anybody's managing editor as Carmen [sic], our office boy. Later he added Katharine [Angell's] name and so listed us both for as long as I was there despite the comings and goings of Jesuses. . . . I used to be very touchy about whether I was or wasn't Ross' M.E.

With his penchant for anonymity, Ross refused to run a masthead and would have been hard put to know what to list. Members of the small staff performed a myriad of duties without titles. The hierarchy was easily summarized: there was Ross at the top and there was everyone else. (Even in the magazine's more structured environment, years later, the same would be said of Ross's successor: gentle, iron-willed William Shawn.)

When Ingersoll's career at Time, Inc., eventually led to a vice presidency, someone needled Ross about having let Ingersoll go. "Well," Ross replied defensively, "they say people grow, don't they?" Then, typical of his insistence on precision, he added: "Who the hell's 'they,' anyway?"

"It's true," says Grant, "Ross considered Thurber the new genius for about six months, but Jim was never told he was managing editor. Harold just didn't believe in titles in those days."

Thurber, in *The Years with Ross*, credits Ingersoll, more than anyone else, with helping him get settled on the staff. "He took care of a thousand managerial details that I was supposed to handle, couldn't have, and didn't want to, and Ross never knew about it." "Ross knew about it," says Grant. The Whites agree with Thurber, who writes:

> Ingersoll . . . was the best of all the Central Desk men, the very administrative expert Ross spent his life looking for. I think he knew this unconsciously, would not admit it even to himself, and spent a lot of time after he had let Ingersoll go trying to justify and rationalize his bad judgment.
>
> "He thinks he's a writer," he said to me when I told him he had lost his most valuable assistant. . . . "The top drawer of his desk was always full of medicine. If I'd given him a thousand dollars a week to sit alone in a room and do nothing, in five days he'd have had six men helping him. . . . He brought Hush-a-phones into the office. . . . He knew too many people."

Unswervingly loyal to Ross, Katharine White agrees with him that Ingersoll was no writer. "Whenever Ross was out with illness," she says, "Ingersoll *would* try to write for Talk [of the Town]. His pieces were dreadful and so was his writing. Ingersoll played the stock market, which is the reason he used a Hush-a-phone." And Ingersoll did keep his desk drawers filled with bottles of substances he had been led to believe would arrest his baldness.

"In just five months, every senior employee on the magazine had been fired by the time I was hired," says Ingersoll. "Within another five months the continuous job turnovers left me the senior editor." Though a managing editor's job is usually that of hiring, firing, assigning, scheduling, and getting the publication to press on time, Ingersoll found time for these tasks only when Ross was taking a coffee break or was on the phone trying to placate the most recent contributor he had insulted in a rejection letter. "The main part of the job was to listen to Ross . . . hour after precious hour while one's desk piled higher with chores that had to be done, despite him, in order to get the magazine out at all."

Indeed, the preliminary qualification the New Man seemed to need was a willingness to serve as Ross's conversational repository. Oliver Claxton, another Social Register member, whom Ingersoll introduced to Ross, was the first genius to be labeled a "Jesus." His brief professional experience had been as a Philadelphia bond salesman, but Ross was delighted to learn that he had no literary ambitions, and hired him. Claxton had no idea of his duties as Hub of the magazine and never did find out. He would be summoned by Ross who spent hours lecturing to him about his plans for the publication. As Claxton told Dale Kramer, he soon learned that Ross needed his presence only to get himself talking; that Ross could best clarify his ideas to himself through extended monologs. Years later, when Claxton heard that Ross had playfully brought into his office a store mannequin he named Sterling Finny, he was certain that Ross had finally found the Jesus he was looking for.

Charles Morton, a young reporter with a Boston newspaper, was invited to try out at the *New Yorker* in this period. His appointment with Ross was on a Sunday, when the offices were all but deserted. The eager and nervous Morton at once began talking, telling Ross what a fine publication the magazine was proving to be and how Morton believed he could contribute to it. Throughout Morton's sales pitch Ross stared at him, his face growing darker and darker, and finally exploded: "Jesus Christ! Let *me* talk!" Morton, who, as an *Atlantic Monthly* editor in 1957, persuaded Thurber to write the famous series of articles on Ross that became *The Years with Ross*, on this day scarcely got in another word, and soon returned to Boston.

As in the classic case of the blind men positioned around an elephant and asked to describe it, no two people who knew Ross can agree exactly on who the man really was, or whether the *New Yorker* could have found its stride sooner, spared his early eccentric behavior. What is indisputable is that there would not have been such a magazine, or so successful a one, without Ross.

"Ross enjoyed being intellectually rough on his associates," says Ingersoll. "His characteristic criticism was sardonic, sarcastic, hard, sharp, merciless. His rages were prolonged, intemperate, and recurrent; he would often beat people dozens of times over a period of months for the same mistake, sometimes keeping an offending piece of copy tacked up on the wall over his desk to remind him to get angry whenever he saw the perpetrator."

Having fired Tyler Bliss, his old friend and colleague from *Stars and Stripes* and the *Home Sector*, Ross hired Joseph Moncure March, a sensitive twenty-five-year-old who wrote poetry and believed himself an artist as well. Though he had tried unsuccessfully to sell his drawings to Ross, he had the advantage of being the nephew of a close friend of Jane Grant's at the *New York Times*, and he had edited a New York Telephone Company house organ. Through extrapolations unclear to others, Ross decided March could easily put together the *New Yorker* each week. There was little or no backlog of material in those days, and March, with Philip Wylie, had to rush every issue's copy to the printer, wait until the Linotype operators set it, and hurriedly proof the galleys, always jittery at the high risk of error. Inevitably there *were* errors, which would greatly disturb and excite Ross. Both the tight schedules and the stress Ross engendered told on both men, and Ingersoll states that March, after a comparatively short time on the job, was carried out in a straitjacket. (He returned to writing poetry and later disappeared into Hollywood.)

Ross's respect for the creative mind was most evident in his solicitous attitude toward outside contributors. "But without exception, he really didn't like anyone *on* the *New Yorker*," Ingersoll insists. "Even Katharine and Andy White, though he was in awe of them both. There was one month—no more —that he almost liked me. We had one or two meals every day together. I don't know what brought that on. The routine he put all of us through began between ten and eleven A.M., and ran to seven at night at a minimum. Then he would move some of us to a speakeasy—usually to the first '21,' on Forty-ninth Street, or the Bernays, 150 Third Avenue, a cellar with overstuffed sofas and chairs, with a restaurant in the front serving as a decoy. You walked through the kitchen and through a steel door to the speakeasy in back. We'd have five or six drinks, Ross still talking The Magazine. Some of us wanted to be home, but family life was out.

"The confusion of operation and organization was the direct reflection of Ross's confusion. Once, after I'd acted on orders he later regretted, he told me, 'Just because I tell you to do something is no reason to do it.' He was sincere.

"Ross was an invective guy. He liked to pit one man against another. He'd hire someone and keep him hidden upstairs until the man learned the job and then announce to some old hand that he had been replaced. For three years, I had to fire people for him, including the secretary who followed Elsie Dick, Ross's first secretary. Ross picked Christmas week to fire her; she was the sole support of her ailing mother.

"Ross couldn't even be relied on to be consistently mean, which somehow made it worse. He did have feelings. I'd point out some inhuman thing he had done and he'd get embarrassed and tell me, 'Go away, you son-of-a-bitch, you're breaking my heart.' And he wasn't kidding."

In 1934, Ingersoll wrote a thirty-five-thousand-word article on the *New Yorker* for *Fortune*. Ross's people, he said, left the magazine for sanitariums, had fits on the floor, wept, and offered to punch Ross. Old-timers remembered Katharine Angell consoling a sobbing makeup editor whose layouts Ross had ripped up just before they were due at the printers. Another makeup man had warned Ross that he was pushing him close to the danger mark. Ross took the warning to heart and prudently sent his male secretary to complain about that week's magazine design. The makeup man knocked him down, put on his hat, and quit.

Ross drove himself into nervous breakdowns from time to time, Ingersoll writes. Several times, an exhausted Ross checked into Riggs' Sanitarium in upstate New York—a retreat used by other shattered staff members from time to time. On one occasion, he was making progress toward recovery by weaving baskets. He took pleasure in telling editor Hobart Weekes that he decided he had to leave after the arrival at the sanitarium of one of Weekes's Princeton classmates who thought he was pregnant.

Ingersoll cracked up in 1926, after a period of running the magazine while Ross was laid up with an infected wisdom tooth and Katharine Angell was on vacation. One of Ingersoll's symptoms was the feeling that he had no legs from the knees down, even though they responded when he pinched them. He chopped wood on his father's farm for several weeks, chanting to the rhythmic swing of the ax, "I'll never go back, I'll never go back," working each day until he was so exhausted he fell to the ground. When he returned, he demanded a smaller salary so Ross wouldn't expect as much of him. Ross obligingly cut his pay but not his duties.

"Why did I put up with it? my friends kept asking me," muses Ingersoll. "For more than two years the undergraduate content of much of the magazine was an embarrassment. The newspaper columnists ridiculed it. But Ross's dream was infectious, for all that he seemed to be constantly undermining it. And Ross was always talking about starting other magazines, and I liked to be in on the start of things.

"Thurber was another reason I could tolerate the place. Ross's cruelties really brought us together as sympathetic allies. To me, the great thing about Thurber's arrival was that he was the first person, after nearly two years, I found I could have a close and personal feeling for at the *New Yorker*. It was through Thurber I got to know and like Andy White, too, though he was there before Thurber. Andy was a private person who kept to himself, and shyness is easy to interpret as coldness. I'll always feel one of Thurber's greatest contributions to the magazine was in what his warmth and gaiety did for the morale of the 1927 staff. He involved himself personally. We all needed friends in the hostile and anxious atmosphere Ross created. Thurber, with his enthusiasm, somehow enabled the Whites and me to grasp that we had adopted Ross's mission; that we had as much faith in his dream as he had. We saw our jobs as building an organization so strong that Ross couldn't break it with his eccentricities. We were determined to make the magazine a success even if it meant saving Ross.

"The *New Yorker* was doing well, critically and financially, by 1930 and its earlier challenge to an entrepreneur like me was weakening. When I heard about Luce starting up *Fortune*, I asked to join him. From the start I had a tremendous advantage over all those who found working for Luce difficult: none of them had ever worked for Ross."

In 1956, Thurber was telling Frank Gibney, *Newsweek*'s editor: "I found out that I was managing editor three weeks [after I was hired], when I asked my secretary why I had to sign the payroll each week, approve the items in [Goings On About Town], and confer with other editors on technical matters." This was only part comic exaggeration; Thurber *was* bewildered by all that Ross expected him to do, and he did the best he could without protest in the beginning. He had known his share of job insecurity, was grateful to be on a publication of his choosing, earning a living wage, and he knew Ross's first impression of him was no more durable than a stretch of fair weather. Ross reminded Thurber of Norman Kuehner, his hard-boiled city editor on the *Dispatch,* and his initial relationship with Ross was quickly conditioned by memories of those days of bullying and bluster.

"Ross assigned a secretary to me," says Thurber, "but I felt so self-conscious I wrote or typed out what I wanted and gave it to her to redo. Sometimes what I typed would have been adequate, but I couldn't stand to have her around doing nothing." In his casual titled "The Conscious vs. the Unconscious," he elaborates:

> I had never had a secretary before, and had, indeed, never dictated a letter up to that time. We got some strange results. One of these, in a letter to a man I hoped I would never hear from again, was this sentence: "I feel that the cuneo has, at any rate, garbled the deig." This was not owing to fatigue or indisposition or to resentment, although there *was* a certain resentment—or even to a young man named Cuneo or Deig. It was simply owing to the fact that my secretary, an Eastern girl, could only understand part of what I, a Middle-Westerner, was saying. In those days, I talked even more than I do now as if I had steel wool in my mouth, and the young lady just did not "get" me. Being afraid to keep asking me what I was trying to say, she simply put down what it sounded like. I signed this particular letter . . . just as she wrote it, and I never heard again from the man I sent it to, which is what I had hoped would happen.

The week Thurber began work, Ross was having the offices repartitioned. Ross, he writes, "seemed to believe that certain basic problems of personnel might . . . be solved by some fortuitous rearrangement of the offices. . . . There must have been a dozen Through the Looking Glass conferences with him about those damned walls." Thurber suggested putting the walls on wheels to make them more adaptable to Ross's restless plans. Ross considered it but decided "you could hear everybody talking. You could see everybody's feet." Thurber began drinking martinis at lunch to brace for the ordeal of hearing Ross resume his discussions of new partition arrangements.

"The confusion over partitions was really Ross's unconscious attempt to do away with them altogether," says Rogers Whitaker. "He kept himself and the staff in a stew by pretending that the magazine could be run like a newspaper, with everybody in one productive bull pen, with no walls at all, where we could all be visible to him; but he knew we'd all quit if that came about. We didn't have that much privacy to begin with. We worked in cubicles of leaded-glass partitions with a door, desk, chair, phone, and typewriter. The place was especially a mess after the weekly art meeting. The artists, who waited for the verdicts, scrambled for desk space where they could retouch their cartoons and spots according to what Wylie, or Katharine Angell, told them Ross wanted done."

In the rearranging of offices, Ross occasionally was without one temporarily and would use an end of someone's desk to work. Once, he had his office insulated to shut out the noise his own reconstruction plans created, but then began to believe, in his private silence, that a staff he couldn't see or hear was conspiring to put something over on him. He had the insulation torn out.

As to Thurber's administrative abilities, it was apparent to others, long before it was to Ross, that Thurber was adding to the very confusion that Ross was looking to him to minimize. Wherever he was or whatever he was doing, Thurber was the center of a localized distress area. His desk and the floor under it were awash with papers by the end of the day, and he often told Ross he had taken care of a letter from a reader, or had already processed a manuscript, to conceal the fact that he couldn't find it. Ann Scharff, Ingersoll's secretary, who had become good friends with Thurber, one day lost her patience with him after Thurber kept asking the busy woman for help in finding an interoffice memo, a letter that Ross had requested, his notebook, and his wallet. He took her rebuke in gentlemanly fashion and a few minutes later stood before her desk again, stripped to the waist. "Ann," he said apologetically, "I seem to have lost my shirt and I wonder if you could help me look for it."

"If anything about Thurber was to grate on Ross," says Ingersoll, "it was that they were so much alike. It's hard for one nonstop talker to be around another." Both men were nervous and unsure of themselves, and contemptuous and afraid of women who knew their minds and spoke them. Both were basically shy. "When Ross was in the company of his heroes, the Algonquin crowd," says Ingersoll, "he was almost tongue-tied, leaving most of the conversation to them." Thurber could even outshamble Ross. Both men were chain-smokers, played practical jokes, and kidded; both gesticulated with restless arm movements, and ran their fingers through their wild, unruly hair as they talked or thought. (Thurber's hair kept falling forward, almost obliterating his face, and George Kaufman insisted that the jungle scenes in the movie *Chang* were shot in Ross's three-inch-high pompadour.)

But Ross must already have recognized glimmers of Thurber's creative potential, a quality he sought and prized. As Thurber correctly points out, Ross's search for perfection was always and only through the gifted people Ross was able to attract and retain. Even an otherwise disapproving Ross would have soon viewed Thurber as a great editorial find. As a rewrite man, Thurber sopped up assignments like a blotter. He was beloved by Andy White and nearly everyone else in those days, and he was instinctively propelled by the Midwestern work ethic. His one eye was put to extraordinary demands as he edited manuscripts and galley proofs for all the departments and went over the agate print of Goings On About Town.

Whitaker was chief copyeditor in those days. He had left a job he didn't like on the *New York Times* and, following the suggestion of Lois Long, the *New Yorker*'s nightclub and fashion columnist ("Lipstick"), asked Ingersoll for a job. Ingersoll introduced him to Ross, who hired him within the hour. Whitaker was also in charge of making up the layout, which Thurber, as the new genius, had to approve.

"We used to come in on Sunday afternoon to write and edit the sports columns about events that had taken place that day and the day before," Whitaker says. "Thurber got not only the sports to edit, but theater copy that also came in on Sunday. He did the best he could with subjects he didn't really understand, including the racetrack, yachting, and court games.

"There was another last-minute chore just before press time. Ross perversely defied the Prohibition laws by having us collect current illegal-liquor price quotations for publication. We were assigned different kinds of bootleg booze to cover; most of us had an entrée into a speakeasy. I was the Cointreau and Vat 69 man. I can't remember what Thurber had to price.

"Ross's demands may be something to smile about today but they were no joke then. The staff was physically exhausted most of the time and there was little relief. The bulk of the book went to press on Friday. We'd finish up on Saturday morning, if we were lucky. That gave us off Saturday afternoon and night and Sunday morning. At three P.M. on Sunday, we'd begin again and wrap up 'A' issue, working till at least nine P.M. We had to get theater and sports written up while the events were still fresh in the columnists' minds. Our copy and layouts were sent to Blanchard Press, on Twenty-fourth street. When the Condé Nast outfit began printing us in Greenwich, our schedule was even tighter.

"The speakeasies were our only merriment, and the only places open when we got through. We often went to John Peron's, which later became El Morocco, in a brownstone in the West Fifties. But only if we went to press early enough. Thurber, Lois Long—she was doing our 'Tables for Two' then—and I used to gather at Peron's quite a bit."

When Thurber felt more secure in his job, he joined those who "often became bored or infuriated" with Ross, and plotted with the others to march on him in protest. "Sometimes," Thurber writes, "we sat for hours after work [in a speakeasy with] a bottle of Scotch or rye, planning just how to tell Ross where to get off."

On at least two occasions, staff delegates confronted Ross with their hardships. The first time they entered his office, he leaped for his coat and hurried out, pausing long enough to say, "I never thought the magazine would last, anyway." When it happened again, the delegation followed him to his home and cornered him there. Ross nervously seated them, gave them drinks, and delivered a two-hour soliloquy that began with, "I lead the life of a hunted animal," and took them through a catalog of personal and business problems that left the rebels limp with misery in his behalf. They shamefacedly apologized for having added to his troubles and left empty-handed. By the end of the next day of life under Ross, the mutinous gatherings had begun again. "When the revolution comes," said Dorothy Parker, "it will be everyone against Ross."

"We were badly understaffed back then," Thurber told an interviewer in 1949. "I was working seven days a week, sometimes twelve hours a day. A lot of us were. Ross, too. Ross had us all thinking that the only way a magazine could get published was to work ourselves to death. I was getting so run down and irritable, my wife [Althea] made me insist on taking off one day a week, and finally even got me to ask Ross for a vacation."

Already thin, Thurber was losing weight and becoming chronically tired and nervous. Several persons, including Katharine Angell, spoke to Ross about it. But "I was afraid of Ross," Thurber confesses. "He and I were growling bulldog and trembling poodle in 1927." When, finally, Thurber asked for time off, Ross grudgingly consented. The Thurbers traveled to Columbus, taking their dog, Jeannie. The day Thurber was due back, Ross received a wire from him explaining that he would be late because the dog was lost. This was high treason to Ross; The Magazine came before any personal considerations. Thurber was two days late getting back.

"Ross came home in a rage and showed me Thurber's telegram," says Jane

Grant. " 'He's out there playing fast and loose with his responsibilities back here,' Harold stormed. 'I'm going to fire the bastard. He can just stay in Columbus with his lost dog.' I told him, 'You can't keep on with this firing of people you need.' "

Grant believes her argument was all that kept Ross from immediately notifying Thurber in Columbus that he was finished with the *New Yorker*. But Ross was still angry. Thurber had dared to place a higher priority on a dog than his obligations to Ross. Late in the evening of Thurber's first workday back, after 9:00 P.M., Ross summoned him and asked if he didn't agree that his concern over a dog was the "act of a 'sis.' " Thurber had worked nearly ten hours that day and he went into a rage, threatening to fight the large-framed Ross on the spot. It was his first blowup at Ross, and Ross was appalled. While he merely stared in surprise at Thurber, Thurber yelled that he didn't think Ross was a match for him and told him to get one of his friends to help him. This immediately stirred Ross's curiosity. "Who?" he asked.

"Alexander Woollcott," Thurber replied.

The thought of the prissy, precious-spoken, bespectacled, rotund Woollcott taking part in a fistfight sent Ross into roars of laughter. Thurber, like any good comic, was immediately pleased by so rewarding a response, and that put an end to the argument. "From then on we were great friends," he says.

Ross took Thurber out for drinks, "our first extra-office get-together," says Thurber. There Ross confided to Thurber, by way of apology, that at age seven he had been fond of a "shepherd dog" named Sam. The dog had to be left behind when the family moved by stagecoach from Aspen, Colorado, to Salt Lake City. No story about Ross's past could have more quickly won Thurber's forgiveness.

Ross never quite knew what to make of Thurber, says Ralph Ingersoll, but he had the sense to see a promise of talent and to keep him around. Ross's reaction to Thurber's overstayed vacation was, nonetheless, a close call. In the course of working for two dozen newspapers, Ross had come to think of job migration as natural and beneficial to all parties. Though politically indifferent, he was conservative by nature and antiunion; he thought nothing of firing people for the most spurious of reasons. Writes Nunnally Johnson: "Sam Behrman told me . . . that Ross fired a Mr. [Bowden] Broadwater, husband of Mary McCarthy, because he couldn't hear him coming down the hall."

To make room for Thurber, Ross had fired a man named Hilles. "Ross didn't dare fire [him] to his face," Katharine White recalls, "but left a note [in the man's typewriter] on Friday saying he needn't return the following Monday." "I never met the guy," Thurber tells Ingersoll in 1957, "but most of the staff was cold to me for months because the guy had multiple daughters and I was blamed for ousting him."

"It's hard to remember all who came and went," says Rogers Whitaker. "The sad part of it—they were usually family men trying to make good on an impossible job."

Not everyone took their dismissals lying down. Herman Mankiewicz was one of the few from the Algonquin group who helped Ross with the early issues, becoming his theater and film critic for a time. When he was in Hollywood, he learned that Ross had replaced him without the courtesy of notification. Mankiewicz returned in a rage and informed his friends that he intended to take his malacca cane to Ross. Ross was warned. He had no lock on his office door, and when the receptionist called to say that Mankiewicz was on the premises, Ross hid in a supplies closet, dragging the giant Ingersoll in with him for protection. Mankiewicz took several swipes at Ross's deserted desk with his cane and returned to Hollywood for a screenwriting career that would culminate in his immortal motion picture, *Citizen Kane*.

Largely abandoned by his renowned Algonquin friends, Ross had little choice but to surround himself with what he termed "children"—eager young people, in their early twenties for the most part, a number of whom actually stayed the course under Ross and remained to put a new face on magazine journalism and enliven American letters.

Writes Thurber:

> I have done a lot of brooding about the mystery that some literary scholars have wrought out of, to quote one of them, the central paradox of Harold Ross's nature; that is, his magic gift of surrounding himself with some of the best talent in America, despite his own literary and artistic limitations. Without detracting from his greatness as an editor, it must be pointed out that the very nature of his magazine, formless and haphazard though it was to begin with, did most of the attracting. Writers and artists of the kind Ross was looking for decided that here was a market for their wares, and to say that the head of such an enterprise, personally unknown to most of those who came to work for him, was the attracting force is to say that the candle, and not the flame, attracts the moths. I think the moths deserve most of the credit for discovering the flame.

The parable is interesting, but not one of Thurber's most supportable. The flame that did the attracting existed only because Harold Wallace Ross had the native intelligence, vision, competence, and even the required peculiarities to light it, and to win the loyalty of those who were drawn there. No one else could have done it.

30

Those Miracle Men

I made deliberate mistakes and let things slide as the summer [of 1927] wore on, hoping to be demoted to rewriting "Talk of the Town," with time of my own in which to write "casuals." . . .

Ross banged into my office one afternoon. He paced around for a full minute without saying anything, jingling the coins in his pocket. "You've been writing," he said finally. "I don't know how in hell you found time to write. I admit I didn't want you to. I could hit a dozen writers from here with this ash tray. They're undependable, no system, no self-discipline. Dorothy Parker says you're a writer, and so does Baird Leonard. . . . All right then, if you're a writer, write! Maybe you've got something to say."

—from *The Years with Ross*

After six months as the Central Desk man, of stressful weeks helping the magazine to bed, of listening to Ross's repetitive insistence on an organizational tranquility he needed as protection from his own disordered ways, Thurber's physical fatigue was thought by Ross to be the result of his compulsion to write. "You're wearing yourself down writing pieces," Ross told him. Ross was partly right. Being that close to a readily accessible market for his work was more than Thurber could resist, after his long, barren months of article and short-story rejections. He wrote during the few hours the magazine spared him, staying on in the evenings and, on Saturday nights and Sunday mornings, typing in his Village apartment. Sunday noons, he took the subway back uptown to Sixth and Forty-second Street, three blocks from the office on West Forty-fifth Street, and began another seven-day week of work.

As more of his casuals were printed, he began to grasp his increasing worth to the magazine and to worry less about his administrative ineptitudes. At the end of one Talk meeting, Ross asked the woolgathering Thurber if he had anything to say. Thurber hastily served up the very matter the group had just been discussing. ("Thurber is the greatest unlistener I know," Ross commented.) In another editorial conference, when Ross demanded to know who was responsible for seven errors in the current issue Thurber cheerfully volunteered for the blame. Ross grouchily praised him for his honesty.

By June 1927, four months after Thurber had joined the staff, Rogers Whitaker had entered in a notebook a list of Thurber's administrative and editorial mistakes and given it to Elsie Dick to present to Ross. "I must have done it at Thurber's request," says Whitaker. "He wanted to show Ross documented proof that he wasn't the man for the job." Ross saw the notebook as a reflection of his own judgment and angrily ordered Thurber to fire Whitaker. Thurber talked him out of it. Ross, as it turned out, was going through a strange period of resenting the invaluable Whitaker, who stayed the course for fifty-five years, outlasting Ross by thirty. "I'm mistaken for him by some people, right here in the goddam hallways," Ross complained to Thurber. "It's embarrassing. People probably think he's me, too." (Ik Shuman, who became executive editor in 1936, came to believe that Ross, for reasons never unearthed, was always afraid of Whitaker, a man of considerable intellect.)

Thurber tells of the day when Ross laid on his desk a letter from an advertiser who felt he wasn't getting fair treatment in the "As to Men" department, and asked Thurber what to do about it. Thurber, still drinking martinis at lunch, swept it on the floor, saying, "The hell with it." Ross appeared to appreciate the prompt and direct action. "We can't please everybody," Thurber quotes him. (Katharine White is dubious about the anecdote; Ross, she says, sought only to please himself and cared not a whit how advertisers viewed editorial text as long as the New Yorker columnists were speaking their minds honestly.)

"Thurber dealt with his high office rather simply," writes Wolcott Gibbs. "Every evening on his way across the street for a drink at the Algonquin, he would take the day's accumulation of memoranda telling him what to do tomorrow out of his pocket, tear them up, and drop them in the gutter. It is a commentary on the rather casual methods of the magazine that this worked very nicely for quite a while."

Once Ross had recast Thurber in his mind as a writer, he abandoned all his earlier perceptions of him as an administrator. If a manuscript that involved Thurber was lost, Ross immediately suspected Thurber. He once accused Thurber of losing a typescript that was in Ross's briefcase, and, when he realized his mistake, said that if Thurber had had it he *would* have lost it. In the years ahead, Ross's respect for Thurber as writer and artist grew, while his sense of him as a sound, even rational, source of advice and counsel receded. In the late 1950s, in response to Thurber's thoughts on an editorial matter that Helen Thurber passed on to Ross, Ross unhesitatingly wrote in reply: "Your husband's opinion on a practical matter of this sort would have no value." This was hardly a put-down, since it reflected Ross's opinion of many of his more prominent contributors by then; he saw the imaginative and the practical incapable of effectively inhabiting the same mind, and he usually patronized the former. Thurber's position in Ross's firmament was finally and securely fixed.

Though Ross had offered Thurber seventy dollars a week—a salary the long-impoverished Thurber could hardly have turned down, Ross understood his disappointment at being hired into an ill-defined desk job rather than as a writer. To Thurber's surprise, his first weekly paycheck was for a hundred dollars. "If you write anything, goddam it, your salary will take care of it," Ross told him. That was fine with Thurber at the time, but in his senior years he would complain that he had been cheated of payment for the pieces published during those early weeks. (In different interviews, he listed their number as seven, eight, and twelve. The more likely figure is five.)

None—except "The Thin Red Leash," about Jeannie—were ever collected in a book by Thurber. With the exception of the successfully funny "My Trip Abroad," which had attracted the attention of Dorothy Parker and Baird Leonard (a popular woman writer of humorous poetry), Thurber quickly came to recognize their undergraduate level. "In re-reading some of the earliest [casuals]," he writes in 1958, "I marvel that Ross put his approving R on . . . a short parody called 'More Authors Cover the Snyder Trial.' "

In this piece, he tries to burlesque the styles of Gertrude Stein and James Joyce and to suggest how Ty Cobb might write about a trial occupying the headlines of the day:

WHO DID WE DID DID WE WE DID, SAYS MISS STEIN!
This is a trial. This is quite a trial. I am on trial. They are on trial. Who is on trial? . . .

JOYCE FINDS SOCKSOCKING IS BIG
ELEMENT IN MURDER CASE!
Trial regen by trialholden Queenscountycourthouse with tumpety taptap mid socksocking with sashweights by jackals . . .

OUT A MILE, WRITES COBB!
. . . It's not like the Cry Baby bandits—four bawls and a walk to Sing Sing. . . .

In "News Of The Day: And a Little Child—" he comments on the ghoulish practice of theatrical booking agents who bribe crime victims to discuss their painful experiences for public entertainment. Thurber's fictional exploited child is an eleven-year-old girl named Marjorie. Her father runs off to Canada with his stenographer, who murders him on the same day that Marjorie's mother chokes her lover to death with an oil mop. The little girl disappears. The world worries that she has killed herself in despair, but

the next day little Marjorie came back to her aunt's house in the Bronx.
"My precious!" cried her happy aunt, "where has Aunty's precious been?"
"I'm booked solid for twenty-six weeks in vaudeville at five grand a month," said little Marjorie.

New York violence continued to preoccupy Thurber. In "Another Mother's Day," an Irish mother, pleased at the attention being paid her son, who has killed a policeman, proudly shows the press his picture, boasting, "Joe banged the buttons off a bull." Even a rare Thurber poem comments on a murder trial in the news: "Portrait of a Lady [From Infancy to Murder Trial]" (April 9, 1927). Thurber plays with variations of the defendant's name —Evangeline Wordsworth. (He soon abandoned poetry, except for the amusement of himself and friends, yielding the field to E. B. White, his office companion, and clearly Thurber's superior in the medium.) He kids his recent employer with "The Youngsters as Critics [With Apologies to the Literary Review of the New York Evening Post]," suggesting how children might review books, currently in vogue, for that newspaper.

If Ross approved these shaky examples of early Thurber, Thurber thought it would have been on the recommendation of Katharine Sergeant Angell, who was head of the recently formed fiction department. Katharine, retired in 1972, confirms that all casuals of the period would have had her endorsement before they were given Ross:

> I was [Thurber's] editor and of course I encouraged him just as I did every writer I ever edited, but of all of them, he needed less encouragement to write than anyone I knew. Once he had an outlet, it was like spontaneous combustion. . . . You seem to imply that a lot of his early stuff was poor. I suppose it was, but so was everybody's and the magazine was desperate for material. The art of starting a magazine from scratch was to see potential talent in small beginnings and Ross was great at that.

Ross soon held respect, even reverence, for Katharine's cultural mandates. She was, writes Thurber in an understatement, "one of the pillars upon which Ross could lean in his hours of uncertainty about his own limitations. 'She knows the Bible, and literature, and foreign languages,' he told me that day I first met him, 'and she has taste.' " Given the near-hopeless prose that characterized the magazine in August 1925, the wonder is that a woman of Katharine's refinement and sensibilities elected to associate herself with it when she did. The wonder, too, given her early encouragements, is why Thurber would grow to detest her. He was eventually known to dislike nearly all his friends' wives in later years, but though they had been warm friends at the start, he would become especially vitriolic toward Katharine White.

When the tall and arrogant aristocrat Fillmore Hyde was hired to read unsolicited manuscripts, one of his summer neighbors at Sneden's Landing, on the west bank of the Hudson across from Dobbs Ferry, was the quiet but energetic and civic-minded young lawyer Ernest Angell, who was married to Katharine. As the incoming "slush" steadily increased, Hyde persuaded Ross to hire Katharine as a part-time reader at twenty-five dollars a week. Her quick eye for literary and comic merit, and whatever else would suit the young magazine, impressed Ross. Two weeks later, he hired her as a full-time reader at twice the salary. Hyde eventually moved on to write "Notes and Comment" and to edit newsbreaks, an arrangement that lasted until E. B. White appeared in late 1926.

Hyde remained until 1927, one of the few early employees who resigned without pressure from Ross—perhaps because of Katharine's loyalty to him. "He never thought the New Yorker was going to amount to much and went on to what he thought would be richer fields," writes Katharine in 1957. "I guess he still doesn't think it amounts to much." But as the man responsible for bringing Katharine Angell into the fold, when Hyde departed he left behind a lasting and indispensable contribution to the magazine he disdained —one that would forever shape its character and do much to ensure its success.

The mother lode of information about the remarkable Katharine Angell White (she divorced Angell in 1929 and married E. B. White) is a 1987 biography, *Onward and Upward*, by Linda H. Davis. Born Katharine Sergeant, her parents were from central Massachusetts and Maine. Her father was a railway executive, a position enabling him to bring up his three daughters in a well-to-do Boston suburb. Katharine attended Bryn Mawr College, 1910–1914, where she assumed leadership roles and graduated fourth in her class. She revived and coedited a biweekly school magazine, *Tipyn O'Bob* (Welsh for "a bit of everything"), to which she contributed editorials, fiction, and verse. She edited the college's literary annual, and helped to cast and direct student plays.

Bryn Mawr's president, Dr. Martha Carey Thomas, was against students marrying, or risking romantic distraction of any kind. "It is undesirable," she counseled, "to have the problems of love and marriage presented for decision to a young girl during the four years when she ought to devote her energies to profiting by the only systematic intellectual training she is likely to receive during her life." If a Bryn Mawr woman was irresolute enough to marry, Dr. Thomas believed she should be "both economically and psychologically independent" of her husband, if only to afford servants to do the housework. (Thurber, who eventually enjoyed needling Katharine in any way he could, refers to Bryn Mawr in several drawings.)

In May 1915, a year after her graduation, Katharine married Ernest Angell, whom she had known since childhood and had been engaged to throughout her college years. A Harvard Law School graduate, Angell, six feet tall to Katharine's five feet, was bright, athletic, literary-minded (he was on the Harvard *Advocate* with his 1910 classmates Conrad Aiken and T. S. Eliot), and passionate about advancing human rights. (He eventually became the head of The American Civil Liberties Union.)

Angell joined his father's law firm in Cleveland, Ohio. A year after their first child was born, America was at war. Ernest joined the Army and went to France to help organize the first insurance system ever devised for the American military at war.

Katharine seemed to gravitate to nurturing roles. In Cleveland she made door-to-door surveys of handicapped people's living conditions, and judged whether they qualified for work training. She worked for the Consumer's

"She's all I know about Bryn Mawr and she's all I have to know."

League, inspecting factories for unsafe working conditions. Ernest didn't return until ten months after the armistice. He had been gone twenty months and Katharine not only found him changed but found her feelings toward him had changed as well, for it became painfully evident to her that he had accepted "the French idea that a wife and a mistress was the way to live," as Davis puts it. They moved from Cleveland to New York, where, September 19, 1920, their second child, Roger, was born.

The marriage was soon in trouble. She and Ernest were living beyond their means, and the need for money provided Katharine with the excuse to work. Work, in turn, gave her a needed respite from an increasingly unhappy home with Ernest, whose continued infidelities were the cause of frequent quarrels between them. (Their unhappiness with one another came to worry Thurber, who, through Katharine, had become friends of both.)

She sold articles to the *New Republic*—severe indictments of America's imperialist policy toward Haiti and the Dominican Republic. She reviewed books for the *Atlantic Monthly* and the *Saturday Review of Literature*. She tried rewriting a book written in Germanic English by a female psychoanalyst but gave it up, she writes, when "I found out that she was more messed up than her patients were—having an affair with another woman, oppressing her son, et cetera."

The odds should have been against Katharine's becoming the creative force she immediately became on the struggling magazine. "Ross was furious that I was a woman," she says. Though Ross often spoke to her with pride of his mother's career as a schoolteacher, he was an unrepentant male chauvinist, believing that the immaturity and semiliteracy of the American male were the direct result of American motherhood and female schoolteachers. Women in the office worried him. They signaled the danger of sex crouched in the wings, ready to spring embarrassingly onstage, harming The Magazine's operations. When World War II siphoned off his male Talk reporters, Ross reluctantly hired women but insisted that all their copy be rewritten by a man. With the men's return after the war, Ross hounded William Shawn to get rid of the women reporters, though Shawn was able to rescue Lillian Ross and Andy Logan as staff contributors.

Katharine quickly defined the parameters of her own relationship with Ross. She would have none of his bullying. "It was never difficult to disagree with him," she wrote Jane Grant,

> and one could be frank. I could say 'you're crazy' and he could reply 'you're nuts' and there were no hard feelings. I remember that once in the midst of one of these verbal battles I exclaimed, 'All right, all right, but you needn't be so goddam rude about it.' He never was rude or violent in his speech to me again. He was profane, of course, and I picked up his profanity, as you see."

Colleagues and authors have celebrated Katharine's abiding worth to the magazine and American letters, including Shawn and her second husband, E. B. White, who told the *Paris Review:*

> She was one of the first editors to be hired, and I can't imagine what would have happened to the magazine if she hadn't turned up. . . . Katharine was soon sitting in on art sessions and planning sessions, editing fiction and poetry, cheering and steering authors and artists along the paths they were eager to follow, learning makeup, learning pencil editing, heading the Fiction Department, sharing the personal woes and dilemmas of innumerable contributors and staff people who were in trouble or despair, and, in short, accepting the whole unruly business of a tottering magazine with the warmth and dedication of a broody hen.

When *The Years with Ross* appeared in 1959, several at the *New Yorker* who had worked with both Thurber and Ross felt that, in Roger Angell's words,

Thurber presented himself as "having single-handedly saved the magazine from the country bumpkin who founded it." But few of them would have disagreed that Katharine Angell, in ways perceptible and imperceptible, came closest to doing just that. She prevailed with a caring, firm attitude toward Ross and everybody else on the staff.

Nearly all descriptions of Katharine sooner or later include the adjective "formidable." Nor is it always meant as a pejorative term, though it is one neither she nor Andy felt fairly applied to her. The *New Yorker* fiction editor William Maxwell, who learned his craft from Katharine, writes:

> Mrs. White was in part responsible for turning *The New Yorker* from what was originally a funny magazine advertising itself as "not for the old lady from Dubuque" into something more original, more ambitious, more literary, with a point of view that was immediately recognizable and that became widely shared. She went to considerable pains to train young editors who would otherwise have been left to sink or swim . . . "maternal" is the word that best describes her concern for the work and lives of writers and artists. They found themselves confiding to her. When they turned work in, they felt she was on their side, and in fact she was. Of the two kinds of editors, the no-sayers and the yes-sayers, she was a yes-sayer and if possible would find a way to save a manuscript that was almost but not quite right. She did not take kindly to some of the things Brendan Gill wrote about her in *Here at The New Yorker* but his summing-up of her qualities as an editor is entirely accurate: ". . . militantly proud (as the Bryn Mawr graduates of those days especially were) of her fitness to take part in matters of importance in the world, she . . . had not only a superb confidence in herself and in her eye for quality; she was as stubborn . . . in pushing for the acceptance of her opinion as some weighty glacier working its way down a narrow Alpine pass. She must often have intimidated Ross. . . . She certainly gave him what amounted to an intellectual conscience. . . . Always a resourceful opponent, when she was not the glacier, she was the narrow Alpine pass."

It wasn't the first time Katharine's means of exercising editorial power had been publicized. In his 1934 *Fortune* article, Ralph Ingersoll, still bitter about the hard times he had endured while on the *New Yorker*, writes that Katharine had undertaken Ross's education, "since he was without taste, either literary or good." She was, he added, "hard, suave and ambitious" and had "set the rigid formula" for Profiles, handled people smoothly "with a carefully studied courtesy and tact," took personal office problems on her own shoulders, "had frequent recourse to tears" to get her way, and created a *New Yorker* dynasty when she married White, all in the face of Ross's misogyny. In *Point of Departure,* Ingersoll describes one result of Katharine's influence: "the cleaned-up barrack and barroom corn which Ross had once appreciated soon began to be conspicuous by its absence from the magazine."

Brendan Gill's book, published in 1975 to capitalize on the magazine's fiftieth anniversary, devastated the eighty-three-year-old Katharine, ailing and retired in Maine. She had "discovered" Gill, had been his first editor, had endorsed his hiring by St. Clair McKelway in 1937, had admired his writing, and had trusted him to behave as a loyal and trusted member of the *New Yorker* family was supposed to behave. And here he was, his elegant prose fashioned into a rapier, leaving his entertaining, freewheeling narrative strewn with the bodies of the founding fathers—Ross, the Whites, Thurber, and Fleischmann—with that of John O'Hara found nearby. Especially troublesome to her was Gill's hint that she might once have been ready to lead a palace revolution against her beloved Ross.

"Roger told me his mother cried for two days after reading my book," Gill says, in a tone of disbelief. He does, as Maxwell points out, give her her full due as the one whose sensible, guiding hand was on the helm with Ross's.

"[Ross] never wanted a literary magazine," Thurber agrees, "but [thanks to Katharine] that's what he got." Given Katharine's insistence upon substance, taste, and quality, the matter was hardly a negotiable one. The magazine's emerging financial and intellectual supremacy was to prove her right, and Ross's gratitude—ever difficult for him to verbalize—may be indicated by his inscription on a 1928 photograph of himself that he gave her: "To Katharine Angell, god bless her, who brought this on herself. H. W. Ross."

"I was the first to credit her in print with being the intellectual conscience of the magazine," Gill points out. "She had the guts to force Ross to become a better editor than he was. She had a superior mind, and it was a marvelous accident of fate that she found herself on a magazine of humor working for Ross who, in the beginning, thought the wrong things were funny. She got O'Hara to give up writing silly pieces and to write real short stories. She was a marvel, the making of the magazine. I respected her enormously. But she was also a tyrant, wanted her way, and if she couldn't have it, deemed it unforgivable."

Gus Lobrano had been a Cornell classmate of Andy White's and a roommate in New York. Katharine and Andy persuaded Ross to hire him as Katharine's successor in 1938, when she reluctantly gave up the fiction department to go to Maine with White. ("She loved her job but she loved Andy more," William Maxwell puts it.) In his later years, Thurber was charged with creating much of the tension in the fiction department with his objections to how his work was handled. But the tensions were already there.

When the Whites moved back to Manhattan in 1942 to help Ross with his war-depleted staff, Katharine was technically under Lobrano in the fiction department. "She resented him," Gill says. "He and the Whites became desperate enemies."

In language much less extreme, Maxwell acknowledges that "it was not easy for [Katharine] to break herself of the habit of authority, and her relationship with [Gus] Lobrano, whom she had picked to succeed her as fiction editor, became increasingly tense. When his death, of cancer, created an emergency, she came back on full time briefly, but had to give this up [in 1957] because of ill health."

Gill believes that women trying to succeed in a man's world in the twenties and thirties had to suppress their senses of humor; that in Katharine's case she could recognize and approve for publication good humor, but always from behind a façade of sobriety, which she may have seen as essential to a woman's professional survival. It *was* Katharine's aura of seriousness and authoritarianism that, in later years, kept tempting Thurber into trying to unseat her from what he regarded as the high horse she was always riding. He resented her, too, for overcoming White's early hesitancies about marrying her, largely crowding Thurber out of a personal relationship with White that he would always remember as a fond and important one. What may have made matters worse for Thurber was that the marriage endured as a textbook one of affection, respect, mutual dependency, and contentment for forty-eight years.

There is little to support Gill's contention that Katharine forfeited humor for a firmer professional foothold. However stern her countenance in the *New Yorker* corridors, her letters show a joyous appreciation of others' humor, an appreciation that required a well-developed comic sense of her own. Examples abound. Katharine liked to tell of one woman reader who complained that a poem by E. B. White was irreverent and had offended her and her family. Ever defensive of White's work, Ross replied: "Dear Mrs. _____: You and your family are crazy. H. W. Ross."

Though Katharine's first marriage was already failing when she joined the *New Yorker*, she seems not to have found it more than she could bear until after she fell in love with White, an assumption Linda Davis finds credible if beyond proving. (Katharine forever insisted that one had nothing to do with the other.)

The youngest of six children, White was raised in the then comfortable and gracious Westchester suburb of Mt. Vernon, New York, a half hour from the city. His father was general manager of a piano-manufacturing company, White's ability to play the piano an inevitable consequence. In his introduction to *Letters of E. B. White,* he says he "was neither deprived nor unloved" as a child, but he was troubled

> about practically everything: the uncertainty of the future, the dark of the attic, the panoply and discipline of school, the transitoriness of life, the mystery of the church and of God, the frailty of the body, the sadness of afternoon, the shadow of sex, the distant challenge of love and marriage, the far-off problem of a livelihood. Being the youngest in a large family, I was usually in a crowd but often felt lonely and removed. I took to writing early, to assuage my uneasiness and collect my thoughts, and I was a busy writer long before I went into long pants.

He followed his brothers into Cornell on a scholarship in the fall of 1917. Like the collegiate Thurber, five years his senior, White was bashful, introverted, and bookish, but he managed to edit the campus newspaper—the *Daily Sun*—quite capably. He was nicknamed "Andy," as were all male Cornell students named White who held student office, a custom with reference to Cornell's founding president, Andrew Dickson White. Like young Thurber, White could emerge from his shell among friends he trusted. And like Thurber he could charm his classmates with original entertainment. He joined the honorary journalism society, Sigma Delta Chi (as had Thurber). At one meeting he enthralled the other members by parodying the classroom mannerisms of a Cornell professor seemingly unable to lecture without exaggerated body movements. White gave a deadpan delivery of a nonsense subject without interruption, while going through physical contortions that ended with his hanging by his legs from a trapeze. In later years, he avoided the risk of ever having to speak in public; the prospect of it alone made him ill. The only ceremonies he agreed to attend were a few college commencement exercises at which he was awarded honorary degrees without having to say anything. But unlike Thurber, White remained a recluse, hating large parties and most social functions. He had hay fever from age six and his lifelong concern with "the frailty of the body" encouraged a lasting hypochondria, a condition, Linda Davis conjectures, that Katharine loyally acquired out of love for him and the wish to share. ("I'll see you at the prescription counter," was often how the Whites were heard making their luncheon dates at the office.)

White's *Daily Sun* editorials led to the establishment of Cornell's student honor system; he won an Associated Press award for his precocious handling of the English language, and, like Thurber, finally came to understand that the broad reaches of his mind were not suitable for the disciplines and short-cuts of timely newspaper writing. Hired by the United Press after graduation, White was assigned to cover the funeral of a U.S. senator at Valley Forge. Describing the assignment in the third person, he writes: "They sent him to cover the funeral of a statesman, but he took the wrong railroad, missing the cemetery by a scant forty miles. This terminated his connection with UP, and almost turned him against statesmen."

According to his biographer, Scott Elledge, White was put off by UP's preference for speed over accuracy, and by the press's exploitation of human tragedy and indecent invasion of privacy. He took a job editing the house organ of a silk mill. He quickly wearied of it, and when asked to write horoscopes of the employees, mischievously identified one girl as destined to have three children without benefit of marriage. He preferred writing his way out of a job to resigning. He next worked for the American Legion News Service and, to ease his boredom, kept a journal. He wrote self-absorbed and melancholy letters to a Cornell girl from Buffalo, Alice Burchfield, who wore his fraternity pin.

The talent was there. Four poems by the twenty-two-year-old White were published in Christopher Morley's *Evening Post* column, "The Bowling Green." He had purchased a Model T Ford roadster, which he called "Hotspur," beginning his love affair with that car that found lasting expression in his *New Yorker* 1936 casual "Farewell, My Lovely!" In February 1922, when Howard Cushman flunked out of Cornell, White quit his job and the two friends loaded up Hotspur and left on a trip across the continent "in search of experience."

They saved money where they could, White playing piano at their fraternity chapters in one college town after another in exchange for lodging. They spent a month at Cushman's parents' home in East Aurora, New York. A rumor reached White that Alice was engaged, and when she returned from Cornell on spring vacation, White visited her in nearby Buffalo and found the courage to ask her to marry him. She was surprised—he had never held her, kissed her, or told her he loved her. She was not engaged, as it turned out, but she refused him, though keeping his pin. White fled the scene, writing Alice a long letter. Says Elledge: "It had not been so much his lack of money and of a good job that had prevented him from pursuing Alice [which

White offered as his excuse for dropping the pursuit] as . . . his fear of losing the independence and privacy he could not live without."

He and Cushman continued their American odyssey. White sold verses and pieces to newspapers on subjects spontaneously conceived, and peddled roach powder door to door. In Montana, Cushman pitched hay on a ranch and White played popular songs in a local café. There was occasionally money from home, but eventually they had to hock Cushman's typewriter.

In Seattle, Cushman had had enough, and he returned home. White took work with the *Seattle Times*, where he had trouble satisfying himself and his employer. He was sent to Everett to report a murder ("It was my first murder . . . and the four victims' first, too.") After viewing the burned corpses of two adults and two children, White telephoned the city desk and said, "This is White, on the Everett story." "What's it like?" the editor asked, wondering how much of the front page should be held open. "It's raining," White said, hung up, and vomited.

When he did write up a story it wasn't always in time, says Elledge. Every piece had to be a masterpiece, White recalled years later, "and before you knew it, Tuesday was Wednesday." As with the fanciful Thurber at the *Evening Post*, the city editor switched White from news reporting to features. He was asked to write a daily column of his own. Though without a byline, it would serve as an outlet for his poems and paragraphs—"capsule essays" running no more than ten sentences, commenting on what he saw, heard, or read. As White says, the columnist of that era was expected to be a poet and a scholar; the most successful ones were "gifted writers whose good sense and humor projected a personality and built a following." Though White's first-person paragraphs went unappreciated by the management of the *Seattle Times*, it was excellent preparation for his years on the *New Yorker*, where he set the magazine's editorial tone writing Notes and Comment. The first-person, singular and plural, became White's milieu. "I ramble terribly when I get talking about myself," he wrote Alice. "We all do." Which was fine with White, "if not carried to extremes. I hate people who are not interested in themselves."

But he wasn't right for Seattle journalism, and in June 1923 he was fired. He spent all his money on a one-way steamer ticket to Alaska, and worked the return voyage as a mess boy. Back in New York, he looked for work but seemed to hope not to find it; when he did manage to see Adolph Ochs, publisher of the *New York Times*, he couldn't bring himself to ask for a job. In the fall of 1923, he took work as a layout man at an advertising agency, living with his parents in the suburbs and commuting. He was unhappy in the advertising world, he says, "because I couldn't seem to make myself care whether a product got moved or not."

The dean of the columnists, Franklin P. Adams, began to accept nearly all of White's verses for publication in his *New York World* column, "The Conning Tower," a feature that also carried items from William Rose Benét, Dorothy Parker, John O'Hara, and Don Marquis. In Grand Central, on his way home to Mt. Vernon, White bought a copy of the first issue of the *New Yorker*—a friend had told him to watch for it as a possible congenial market for his kind of writing. His first piece, on the coming of spring, appeared nine weeks later. In May, his "Defense of the Bronx River" was published. These small successes sparked hope and an impatience with his advertising job. He quit the agency and moved into a Village apartment with three former Cornell classmates.

White describes this period as his "moping years." Without steady work, he ushered at the Metropolitan Opera House for the sake of hearing its music. He tried his hand at writing "a mail-order course in automobile salesmanship in ten easy lessons." But "when the first order arrived from a barber in Wisconsin," White resigned, "full of remorse." He sometimes sat on the benches in Grand Central studying the commuters, gazing "with aching insides" at "lovely, laughing women." (In his journal, he writes, "I walked in the paths of righteousness, studying girls.") In October he took a part-time advertising job at thirty dollars a week, which left him time to write. In the next two months, he sold eight more pieces to the *New Yorker*. The one that brought lasting attention to him, from Katharine Angell and Ross, was called "Child's Play," and it appeared in the last issue of 1925. It tells of White's having lunch in one of Child's chain of restaurants. A passing waitress spills a glass of buttermilk on him, exclaims "In the name of God!", breaks into sobs, and hurries away to get towels.

> The waitress came trotting back, full of cool soft tears and hot rough towels. She was a nice little girl, so I let her blot me. In my ear she whispered a million apologies, hopelessly garbled, infinitely forlorn. And I whispered back that the suit was four years old, and that I hated dark clothes anyway.

As Thurber once wrote, "The proof of humor is the ability to put one's self on awkward public record." But it was five months before White's next work was accepted—a piece about a homeless bum in Union Square and a cheerful drunk on a commuter train. At Katharine Angell's suggestion that White be hired as a staff writer, Ross dropped him a note to stop by the office. When he did, in May 1926, it was Katharine who came into the reception room and asked, "Are you Elwyn Brooks White?" White hadn't been addressed in that formal way in a very long time. He remembers only that she "had a lot of back [sic] hair and the knack of making a young contributor feel at ease."

White wasn't ready to commit himself to a staff job, however, and he joined a student tour of Europe, having been paid to write the script of a publicity film to be made enroute. When he returned, in August, he found six checks from the *New Yorker* waiting for him, which persuaded him, says Elledge, that "he could do what he had dreamed for twenty years of doing— earning his living by writing what he wanted to write." Job negotiations between him, Angell, and Ross began, but White, conscious of his newspaper failure, was reluctant to let go of the part-time job he then had with the ad agency. He finally agreed only to work part-time at the magazine, also for thirty dollars a week.

Ross was looking for someone who could satisfy him—or disappoint him less—at editing newsbreaks, rewriting Talk stories, and making cartoon captions funnier. White proved to be superb at everything he undertook, and Ross was ecstatic. "I can't remember a piece by anyone but E. B. White that Ross ever really thought just right," says Ralph Ingersoll. He "took to White instantly, sheltered him from the day of his bewildered arrival. . . . White could do no wrong." Which made life more miserable for the rest of the staff, described to Ingersoll by Ross as "those God-damned incompetent bastards that are all we have to get out this magazine with. Women and children, women and children!"

It was several months before White would agree to work full time. He was somewhat put off by Ross's personality; "he was a very different fish from me," White says. One development that is thought to have led him to sign on full time was the arrival of Thurber. Jammed together in one unit of the editorial floor's rabbit warren, two people could quickly learn to despise one another or become the best of friends. White and Thurber, allied in Ross's cause, each admiring the other's humorous interpretations of small and large events, became close and intimate friends. "Andy was fearful of life," says Ingersoll. "Jim was warm and involved with life. They were opposites who attracted one another."

White had kept his distance at first, insisting on time to himself, to contemplate, to continue to observe himself and his reactions to the world around him, convinced that few, if anyone, could improve on his own company at the moment. When Thurber first asked him to have lunch, White coolly replied, "I always eat alone."

But Thurber's ceaseless outgoing offerings of camaraderie and his wild humor finally won White's amusement, interest, friendship, and confidences. After Thurber died, thirty-four years later, White wrote:

> I am one of the lucky ones; I knew him before blindness hit him, before fame hit him, and I tend always to think of him as a young artist in a small office in a big city, with all the world still ahead. It was a fine thing to be young and at work in New York for a new magazine when Thurber was young and at work, and I will always be glad this happened to me.

31

That Slight Blonde Woman

> Before I left her she read my fortune in the teacup I had drunk from. It seems that a slight, blonde woman is going to come into my life and that I should beware of the sea.
>
> —from "Mrs. Phelps"

The moody White and mercurial Thurber shared a cubbyhole office from early 1927 until 1930. "We got on fine together," remembers White. "From the first we loved each other's stuff. We never felt competitive." White kept a journal until 1930, and on New Year's Day, 1929, writes despondently that he is considering quitting his job and leaving town, "telling no one where I was going." But two days later he confides to himself:

Yesterday hard at work, dutiful at the office, for all my great fuss the day before about going away. But I thought of a funny drawing [by Thurber], and so was reconciled to my lot. Besides, one of the persons I like best in the world is Thurber. Just being around him is something.

Charme Seeds had sparked the Thurbers' social life after their arrival in New York from Green Lake. She occasionally accompanied Thurber on a Talk assignment, such as tracking down the hotel and pub frequented by the legendary short-story writer O. Henry. She was keeping company with Charles Speaks at the time, the man she would marry.

"Charme was most helpful to us," says Althea. "She loomed large in our lives back then. We stayed with her for a while until we found an apartment nearby. Charme had lived in New York for a number of years and had sat at the Algonquin Round Table. That made her pretty high up on our list of famous people."

On Althea's list, perhaps. The comments underscore one of the troubling differences between her and Thurber. Thurber was interested in everybody and receptive to anyone who entertained him or was willing to be entertained by him. Althea was status-minded, which conditioned her dislike of Thurber's family and eventually led to her rejection of the zany crew on the *New Yorker* and Thurber's closest drinking companions. The two, already sexually independent of one another, were now following different social goals.

White worried about Thurber, who was working under severe pressure from Ross that summer of 1927, and he persuaded the Thurbers to join him and others in Amawalk, in Westchester County, for the Fourth of July weekend. It was there that Thurber met Ann (Honey) Honeycutt, with whom he fell instantly in love and would remain infatuated for a decade. Ann was a petite blonde, and, unlike Thurber's earlier Jamesian ideals, could outdrink and outfight him, releasing him, to his great delight, from the bonds of Victorian behavior and the guilt feelings that would ordinarily have followed their violation.

"Honey" was from Louisiana. After two years of finishing school, she learned typing and telegraphy at age sixteen and entered her father's business—exploring, or "wildcatting," for oil. Her father died when she was nineteen, and Ann then ran the El Dorado, Arkansas, office of a company of wildcatters who couldn't read or write. She kept the books and served as secretary and treasurer. "The work was simple," she says. "You just recorded what came in and what went out. Our strategy was to buy up leases all around an area we thought might have oil and drill in the middle of the property." While she was an employee, the company earned and lost two million dollars.

When she had saved enough money, she went to New York, staying at the Panasses Club, near Columbia University. She took voice lessons and acted in some Gilbert and Sullivan productions. To earn money, she worked for a mission that looked after homeless men on the Bowery. A friend got her into radio—the Columbia Broadcasting System—as a singer of semipopular songs. "But I had a limited repertoire, and I didn't like the theatrical life," she says. "I wasn't cut out to be a performer; I was better behind the scenes." Because she could type and correctly spell the names of musical composers—a rare talent in the early days of radio, she says—she was hired by CBS's music department as an assistant program director, editing scripts. It was there that she met John Gude, a young executive with CBS who later became an agent selling writing talent and properties to the movies, radio, and, eventually, television. Gude's nickname, "Jap," resulted from a youthful case of yellow jaundice. He would become the agent that Thurber and White used, and, by the end of Thurber's life, he was the friend Thurber loved most.

Ann—she was "Honey" to nearly everyone—was living on Washington Square North in a ten-dollar-a-month rental when she was invited by Montgomery Roosevelt Schuyler, another Village inhabitant, to spend the weekend of the Fourth at his Amawalk estate. Schuyler rented all the outbuildings on his property to vacationers. "I met the whole *New Yorker* in-crowd there," Ann says. "Thurber and Althea were renting the ice house, made over into a cottage; Bob Coates and Andy White had one of the barns; I had another. On a later weekend, I met Wolcott Gibbs there. It was instantaneous love all the way around. We all prepared our own food, using the outdoor barbecue grills sometimes, though there wasn't as much interest in food as there was in drinking. We brought books and read and wrote poetry down by the brook. There was a swimming hole, a deck-tennis court and ringtoss, which Thurber was excellent at."

In a courtship letter to Honey a few years later, Thurber describes their first meeting, referring to her in the third person, as Estelle Darlington, or "Darling."

> My first impression was of her smile, which was nice, and of her figure, which was nice, too, but, I thought, a trifle buxom. This may have been due to . . . the fact that I do not see very well, having lost one eye, a disability which sometimes causes me to look like a distraught

bird and militates, at such times, against any girl really looking upon me as a romantic figure. . . .

My next recollection of Darling is meeting her some hours later by chance in the moonlight outside the Ice House . . . and telling her that I intended to marry her. . . . I did not say this so much to startle her as because I really felt that I would like to marry her, a curious feeling when it is understood that, at the time, I was already married. Darling made the usual smiling and witty responses to my remark . . . making of it just a "line" that a drunken man (for I was a drunken man at the moment) would "hand" any pretty girl suddenly encountered in the moonlight at a gay party. I remember wanting to take her in my arms and kiss her and say those throatily sincere and eloquent things which, on such occasions . . . die in my throat and are succeeded by the . . . humorous and fantastic remarks of a facetious nature which it has been my custom to employ when I am rebuffed or think I am rebuffed or think I am about to be. My near-sightedness and lack of handsomeness, together with the fact that I am some thirty pounds under weight, always restrains me from going through with the mad, dashing, he-man tactics which I should greatly love to employ. . . .

Darling wandered away from me to show a rather definitely admiring attention to a friend of mine at the party named E. B. Brown [White], who at that time was a surly, almost morose man with a disposition to draw apart from the general gaiety and observe with a fascinating and sour detachment the antics and idiocies of foolish mortals at their play. . . .

The effect of this . . . was to make me both jealous and sad. . . . I determined to go over to the couple and try to win Darling away from Brown by another display of . . . light banter. . . . In so doing . . . I stumbled over one of those outdoor stoves constructed of rocks and a piece of sheet iron. I fell sprawling awkwardly. I was not grievously hurt . . . so I scrambled up and continued on my way amid a veritable uproar of laughter from Darling and Brown. Instantly I became a victim of my admitted egotistical desire for applause and . . . let go completely, fell over several more stoves, on purpose, and ended up by being put to bed by a disgruntled wife and several friends, only to get up out of bed several times to return to the scene of what, being drunk, I actually believed to be my triumph. . . .

When I saw Darling for the first time [the next] day . . . she laughed aloud as soon as she looked at me and said something about I certainly was a scream. I need not emphasize the disconsolate effect that this had upon me. I realized more and more that this woman was going to play a big part in my life and I realized that, at the very outset of this important affair, I had set up the almost insurmountable handicap of making myself, to her, essentially a crackpot and clown. Years later her memories of me, her first impression, were to pop up with a burst of laughter in the midst of my most intense moments. . . .

The next time I saw Darling was . . . a week or two later, at the same summer place. My heart leaped up when, in looking out of the door of the Ice House one morning I beheld her sitting in a chair in the doorway of the God Head wearing an enchanting sweater and reading a book. I wondered if by any possible chance her knowledge that I was at the Ice House that weekend had caused her to come back again. Later I was to find out that it had. She said she simply *had* to come back again and see me because I was the funniest person she had ever known in her life.

It was Honey's initiation into the social life of the small *New Yorker* clique. White took her to the theater soon after that. "When Andy brought me home," says Honey, "he said 'Good night' at my door, kissed me on the cheek and wrote me a letter the next day apologizing for having done so." (White by then, in his tentative way, was becoming interested in Katharine Angell.) Wolcott Gibbs, Stanley Walker, and St. Clair McKelway were other *New Yorker* men she would date over the years. Ross, who had trouble keeping track of who was who on his growing staff, saw so much of Honey on and off the premises that he eventually got the impression that she worked for him. "That was a good piece you did on the Philippines," he once told her. Honey thanked him, to spare him embarrassment. Gibbs dated her between his marriages. When he was the magazine's theater critic, his caustic reviews led several producers and playwrights to warn Ross that the magazine was not going to be issued opening-night invitations. "Wolcott hated Lillian Hellman's plays, especially," says Honey, "and when she threatened to bar him from her opening nights, Ross would call and ask me to meet Gibbs for an early dinner and not to let him get to the theater drunk, his usual preparation for reviewing plays."

Her favorite *New Yorker* companion for eight years was Thurber. "I'd been thwarted by much of life, and Jim opened doors for me," says Honey. "I found him more fun to be with than anyone else. He claimed to suffer from inferiority feelings and said it was why he needed to be seen with attractive women.

It *was* important to him that Althea was beautiful, and to get one of the campus beauties he had been willing to become her boy for a time. She was his badge of honor. His pride was hurt when she grew indifferent to him. It had been the princess and the frog, the campus queen marrying the ugly duckling. It was his subservience that caused her to lose interest, I thought, and she let him undermine so many of her original beliefs in him that she couldn't even place much value on his work, even when it began to reach a level of excellence recognized by everybody.

"There are men who don't have a great deal in physical or intellectual endowment but who do a great deal with what they do have. Jim was the opposite. He had much more to offer than the other men I knew and never grasped that. To him, he was a gawky hick from Columbus with a glass eye. He was more than a wit, who gets his laughs from picking on others' foibles. Jim was a humorist who could bring himself into a situation and take his lumps along with everybody else. You can't help but love a man willing to do that for your personal enjoyment.

"He'd pick fights, and I loved that, too. We played the fight act over and over, usually to an audience. It pleased him that I had a lot of men friends but he always pretended to be angry about it. He talked of marriage and for a long time I considered it. Then, when he got his divorce and could actually *get* married, I chickened out. I think he would have been less frightened of a wife than a mistress, but, in the end, I couldn't become either.

"We were both hams, a couple of vaudevillians, and that kept us good friends over the years. We'd let others goad us into a fight, even Helen, after he was married to her. Thurber never folded up on me. He'd keep fighting when I'd fight back. If he had folded, I'd have felt bad at the tactics I used. We were both tough in a fight. I wouldn't whine and cry, and he appreciated that in a woman, because he never really wanted to win his fights.

"I'm afraid we were a bit of a public nuisance at times. We fought at Tony's, and at the old '21' Club, and all over midtown Manhattan and the Village. He was a joyous man in his rages. Once at '21' we got into a fight over whether I had spoken to another man at the restaurant. Thurber slapped me and I threw my Scotch at him. We were evicted. It was lunchtime, but six hours later Thurber was proudly showing Gibbs his wet shirt and saying, 'Look at what Honeycutt did to me.' Thurber had to have splashed water on himself within the hour. Somehow it was a victory for him to have provoked me to throwing drinks.

"We never had sex together, and Jim always blamed me for that. But for a half-dozen years I had more fun with Jim Thurber than I'd ever had with anyone in my whole life."

Oliver Wolcott Gibbs, considered the fifth "founding father" of the *New Yorker*, joined late in 1927, commended to Ross by Gibbs's cousin, novelist and Round Tabler Alice Duer Miller, a close friend of Jane Grant. (Ross, says Gibbs, despite Gibbs's protestations over the years, couldn't get it straight that Miller was not Gibbs's aunt, or that her son was not illegitimate, fathered by one of the Marx brothers.) Earlier, Miller had persuaded Gibbs to give up his four-year employment as brakeman with the Long Island Railroad and take work on a Long Island country weekly. He joined the *New Yorker* as a copyeditor and soon became the art editor and an assistant to Katharine Angell. His genius as an editor, rewrite man, parodist, and critic emerged from a neurotic disposition that Ross, by then, had uneasily accepted as characteristic of the kind of talent he needed.

Katharine Angell's affinity for the afflicted soon had her expressing her concern to Ross over Gibbs—his nervous stomach, his discomfort in elevators, his occasional panic upon going into the street, his occasional suspicion that someone was following him. None of it surprised Ross. "Aberrations of the creative mind had [Ross] always on the alert," Thurber says. " 'They have *sinking* spells,' he would say. 'They can't ride on trains, or drive after dark, or live above the first floor of a building, or eat clams, or stay alone all night. They think automobiles are coming up on the sidewalk to get them, that gangsters are on their trail, that their apartments are being cased.' "

Gibbs, a misanthrope, admired the writing of White and Thurber, but he seemed to like little else about the magazine. Significantly, he was one of the few able to become friends with cantankerous, paranoid John O'Hara, whose fiction he eventually edited at the *New Yorker*. Unable to account for his own gifts, he attributed them to some mystical absorption of talent from those he worked near. He viewed the high-strung nature of his life with the same detachment with which he viewed the fine quality of his work, as if it had been provided to him by attendant spirits and was in no way to be credited to native endowment.

Poltergeist elements seemed to infest his person and at a party a drink would inexplicably fly out of his grasp, leaving Gibbs staring uncomprehendingly at his empty hand. One of his books was titled, significantly, *Bed of Neurosis*.

He was a grudge bearer of the first order. His brilliance was seen to best advantage in his acidic parodies and articles. His caustic *New Yorker* Profile of Attorney General Thomas E. Dewey, then running for the presidency against Roosevelt, led Dewey to have Gibbs's bank account impounded, convinced that Gibbs was in the hire of the Democratic Party. "As usual our bank account was overdrawn," said Elinor Gibbs, Gibbs's second wife. "Dewey didn't understand that Wolcott wrote best in a state of vitriol and sought out subjects guaranteed to put him in the negative moods he needed."

Gibbs's most famous parody was of *Time* magazine: "Time . . . Fortune . . . Life . . . Luce." In its early years, *Time* had briefly inhabited the same building as the *New Yorker,* on West Forty-fifth Street. For some time, Ross had been annoyed by *Time*'s "liberties with the language, factuality, and its invective," in the words of Luce biographer W. A. Swanberg. When Ralph Ingersoll wrote his 1934 *Fortune* article about the *New Yorker* and embarrassed Ross by alleging that his annual salary was forty thousand dollars, as well as making wrong guesses about other staff salaries, Ross authorized Gibbs to settle matters with Ingersoll, Luce, and Time, Inc., once and for all. The piece was written in *Time*'s style of the day; readers would repeat Gibbs's lines from it for years: "Backward ran sentences until reeled the mind"; "Where it will all end, knows God!"

Gibbs took his revenge on Ingersoll:

> Looming behind [Roy Larsen] is burly, able, tumbledown Yaleman Ralph McAllister Ingersoll. . . . Littered his desk with pills, unguents, Kleenex, Socialite Ingersoll is *Time*'s No. 1 hypochondriac, introduced ant palaces for study & emulation of employees, writes copious memoranda about filing systems, other trivia, seldom misses a Yale football game. His salary: $30,000; income from stock: $40,000.

When the profile galleys were sent to Luce, he angrily demanded to see Ross at once. Ross, who had attended a dinner party earlier in the evening, received Luce and Ingersoll at his penthouse on East Thirty-sixth Street at 11:30 P.M. The session, attended by St. Clair McKelway—he and Ingersoll, both helping themselves to Ross's liquor, nearly came to blows—lasted until 3:00 A.M. Among the facts Gibbs had made up was the average weekly salary that Luce paid his employees. "I'd put down an average of $45.6789 a week, using, of course, the numbers in order on the typewriter," Gibbs wrote Thurber, "and basing my facts on nothing whatever, but Luce questioned them severely. 'You including the Chicago mailing employees?' he asked. 'The Chicago mailing employees are in,' said Ross, and Luce accepted it meekly."

Ross refused nearly all the changes Luce requested. When Luce complained that there wasn't a positive thing in the piece about him, Ross told him that that was what he got "for being a baby tycoon." Ross sometimes came to regret what he had published, but he stood solidly and lastingly behind Gibbs on the Luce Profile. The day after the two publishers met, Ross wrote Luce that not only was *Time* considered anti-Semitic, it was "generally regarded as being mean as Hell and frequently scurrilous." He added that Luce was "apparently unconscious of the notorious reputation Time and Fortune have for crassness in description, for cruelty and scandal mongering and insult. I say, frankly, but really in a not unfriendly spirit, that you are in a hell of a position to ask anything."

Luce's more strenuous objections included the article's references to the "most drenchingly beautiful" Clare Boothe, whom Luce had married the year before. Gibbs footnoted the critic Richard Watts's criticism of Mrs. Luce's play, *Abide with Me:*

> One almost forgave "Abide with Me" its faults when its lovely playwright, who must have been crouched in the wings for a sprinter's start as the final curtain mercifully descended, heard a cry of "author," which was not audible in my vicinity, and arrived onstage to accept the audience's applause just as the actors, who had a head-start on her, were properly lined up and smoothed out to receive their customary adulation.

"Wolcott had never forgiven Mrs. Luce," says Elinor Gibbs. "Once when she agreed to be interviewed and invited him to her apartment, she kept him waiting more than an hour, made a flip remark about the *New Yorker,* suggested he do a profile on a celebrity she admired at the moment and abruptly dismissed him in favor of her current paramour, who had stopped by. It took him some time to get even but Wolcott knew how to bide his time."

Thurber was finishing his book about Ross in 1958 when Shawn wired him at his London hotel that Gibbs had died of lung cancer. Like so many of Thurber's generation, who turned night into day, ate improperly, smoked, slept too little, and drank too much Prohibition booze, Gibbs was only in his fifties when he died. He was, a saddened Thurber said of his old colleague and drinking buddy, "one of the most important figures in the career of Harold Ross and in the history of his magazine."

In Ann Honeycutt, Thurber had a new audience to write for, and, though by the end of 1927 he was the principal editor for Talk, he was still finding the time to submit casuals regularly to Katharine Angell. Her growing romantic interest in Andy White, and her awareness of White's fondness for Thurber, may have accounted in large part for her cheerful recommendations to Ross that he buy Thurber's short, chatty pieces. Gertrude Stein would become a recurring object of Thurber's parodies, with which he showed that short sentences can obscure meaning as much as long ones. He offered suggestions for adapting the game of polo to the home, including how to get "a quivering bright-eyed horse" used to an apartment.

"The Literary Meet," September 1927, lampooned *Liberty* magazine's practice of printing an average reading time for each story or article. Members of a ladies' literary society make boastful claims of setting speed records in reading *Liberty* and other publications:

> Mrs. Leeper, who finished "Evangeline" in 30 minutes and 18 seconds was disqualified for slurring her nouns. The long-distance match . . . was the reading of the New York *Times'* editorial page for September 18. It was won by Mrs. Goldie Trinkham, the mother of two lovely children, in one hour, 14 minutes and seven seconds. Mrs. Preen . . . was forced to drop out at the bottom of the second column.

He took off on the *Herald Tribune's* detailed reporting of President Coolidge—a favorite subject of his—by emphasizing the president's chronic silence about everything: "At breakfast the President ate a bit less than is usual with him and some concern was felt. He seemed in good spirits, however. Mr. Coolidge made no comment."

Though Ross was firm in insisting that his staff writers not offend the contributors, he O.K.'d Thurber's parody of Hemingway, who had recently sold Ross a parody of his own—of Frank Harris's autobiography. In the Christmas, 1927 issue, Thurber's first Talk story—finally released by Ross—and his first Hemingway parody appeared. Hemingway's tough and punchy style in *The Sun Also Rises* and in his short stories was being imitated by undergraduates and novice writers everywhere. Thurber strains "A Visit from Saint Nicholas" through his conception of how Hemingway might have written the famous poem in prose form:

> "Can you sleep?" asked the children.
> "No," I said.
> "You ought to sleep."
> "I know. I ought to sleep."
> "Can we have some sugar-plums?"
> "You can't have any sugar-plums," said mamma.
> "We just asked you."

The Golden Age of American Humor that began after World War I—the Algonquin Round Table was formed in 1919—lasted well into the Depression years, when it gradually lost literary ground to the rise of political ideologies erected against totalitarianism and national poverty. Hollywood's money and popularity neutralized such symbols of the humor age as Robert Benchley, mentor to and inspirer of so many literary comics of the period; nearly all the magazines containing humor, except the *New Yorker*, had gone out of business by the start of World War II, and the horror of the atomic bomb tended to smother at birth whatever new crop of literary humorists may have been in the offing.

But the late 1920s, even with its bootleg liquor, was an ideal time for Thurber to come on the scene. He was in time to be part of what John Updike calls "a spendthrift generation whose promise sparkled in speakeasies and glimmered through a long hangover."

Nathaniel Benchley, in his biography of his father, Robert, offers a typical stage-setting for the life after hours that Thurber began to know so well:

> The 1920s were, for the people in [Benchley's] general category (almost all of whom had come to New York from out of town), intensely vibrant and exciting. There was an air of daring, and rejoicing, and rebellion, and the main goal was to have as much fun as possible. It was a period of group activity, when people moved in groups, ate and drank in groups, loved more or less in groups, thought in groups, and kept going until they dropped from exhaustion; they then revived in groups, and were off and at it again, and the strongest and most durable were admired the most. . . . The lonely ones were those who fell behind or fell in hopeless love, and their anguish was all the greater because of the fun that everybody else was having. . . .
>
> The excesses were in the realms of fun and heartbreak. . . . Even the work was fun. . . . There was lots of money for everybody. . . . Creative talent fed and thrived upon itself and project led to project and success to more success. There was only one resentment, and that was against the Act, which many felt had been wangled through while all their backs were turned. So Prohibition was cheerfully and generally flouted, and society linked arms with the bootleggers and gangsters and everybody had a glorious time. . . . It was fun to drink and fun to mock the law, and it was considered rude not to accept a drink that was offered to you.

The need for the restorative alchemy of drink after a day under Ross, and the loneliness fostered by an unhappy marriage, found Thurber habitually with his colleagues in their favorite speakeasies. These were also frequented by the Algonquin crowd—the newspaper and theater celebrities. As Thurber's work became known and admired, he got to know them all.

In 1925, Herman Mankiewicz, the assistant theater critic of the *New York Times*, talked Ross into bringing to the *New Yorker* twenty-two-year-old Lois Long. "I was Herman's college girl," she says. A minister's daughter, she had been the theater editor and critic of *Vanity Fair*, earning thirty-five dollars a week. Ross called her and asked, "What can you do for this magazine?" He hired her at fifty dollars to write "Tables for Two," the nightclub column. She also began the popular shopping column "On and Off the Avenue." Lively and pretty—Philip Wylie lapsed into a long period of depression when she married cartoonist Peter Arno—Long was a dynamo and favored with a tireless ability to visit and write about all the better nightclubs and speakeasies.

"I was earning seventy-five dollars a week when Thurber joined the staff," she says. "The men I invited along on my nightclub beat wouldn't let me pay my bills, even though it was *New Yorker* money. This meant that only the better-heeled felt they could go out with me. My moneyed boyfriends scared Thurber away from me, I think. I began to see him more and more as he caught on to where the better liquor was served and developed the habit of pub crawling.

"Everybody belonged to a club in those days, and we were loaded down with the cards you were supposed to have, although the doorkeepers quickly came to know you. Tony Soma loved celebrities, and his back room and kitchen used to be crowded with theater people. It was where Thurber got to know Humphrey Bogart, who was still getting those 'Tennis, anyone?' roles on Broadway, before he became famous. The nightclub banquettes were excellent substitutes for the psychiatrist's couch, less expensive and certainly more fun.

"Everybody made scenes, terrible scenes, or else were moody, which was almost worse. A club was a good place to go to if you were badly off emotionally, because you usually wound up helping someone who had convinced you he was in worse shape than you. We talked out our troubles. There wasn't much chance to sulk. There was a reckless atmosphere we responded to. We women had been emancipated and weren't sure what we were supposed to do with all the freedom and equal rights, so we were going to hell laughing and singing.

"It worried Ross that I was only twenty-two. He was one of those Protestant Westerners who was certain no woman who drank, smoked, and cursed could be truly respectable. One night I took him with me on my nightclub tour and he never got over the shock. You never knew what you were drinking or who you'd wake up with, and in Ross's Western outlook if you slept with a girl you compromised her, and ought to marry her. There was an *obligation*. I always suspected there was a lot of Ross's Western attitude in Thurber. Problem men didn't bother Ross but problem women drove him crazy. He worried about all girls under thirty. He'd get so tense in a speakeasy with a girl that he'd get you tense; then he'd say something really funny and we'd all relax and have a good time. We'd start at '21' and go on to Tony's after '21' closed. Drinks were a dollar twenty-five. We thought brandy was the only safe thing to drink, because, we were told, a bootlegger couldn't fake the smell and taste of cognac. Usually we wound up in Harlem. They had Charleston dances at the Harlem Club, where the girls wore blue step-ins.

"We wore wishbone diaphrams that weren't always reliable. There was a woman doctor who handled abortions for our crowd. She would take a vacation at Christmastime to rest up for the rush after New Year's Eve.

"You were thought to be good at holding your liquor in those days if you could make it to the ladies' room before throwing up. It was customary to give two dollars to the cabdriver if you threw up in his cab. Wolcott Gibbs was always getting rolled when drunk. Margaret Case Harriman, whose job I took at *Vanity Fair*, wrote *The Vicious Circle*, about the Round Table at the Algonquin, which her father, Frank Case, owned. She was one of our regulars until World War II, when she became convinced that all the waiters at Longchamps were Nazis and stopped being much fun.

"Our favorite cabdriver was Charlie [Rosenberg], a former member of the Schultz mob trying to go straight. He was reverent about celebrities and adored Thurber after Thurber's cartoons began to appear in the *New Yorker*. Charlie would refuse fares and wait for Thurber to come out of a speakeasy so he could drive him home. I was walking past Tony's one evening when Thurber had just been thrown out and was pounding on the metal grille to get back in, threatening to clean out the place. Charlie was leaning out the cab window and pleading with him: 'Please, Mr. Thuba, use ya left hand; don't pound with ya drawin' hand.'

"I should say it was nothing out of the ordinary to get thrown out of those clubs. People were frequently brawling, and the proprietor usually made an arbitrary decision to put out a chronic offender from time to time just to show the other patrons that there was an intention of good order, even if it didn't exist in fact. Thurber threw drinks in the faces of people more famous than he was, for some reason. I never could understand what he was trying to prove, for he rarely got mad at the lesser-knowns. It created greater excitement for him, I suppose. He was a startling challenger. He always moved unexpectedly and took his victim by surprise. Nobody would suspect he was mad at something until he made the overt act.

"At heart he was a dear, sweet man, but he couldn't drink, especially the Prohibition stuff. It's a wonder we didn't all go blind from it right along with Thurber. Ross actually liked us all to go on binges. He had a theory that we would be so remorseful afterwards that we would write especially well the next day. He even set up a club for the staff and the contributors in the basement of a Fleischmann property on Forty-fifth Street, where he hoped we could drink and stimulate one another to come up with good ideas for the magazine. He thought if the magazine had its own speakeasy it would be safer for us and that the same general decorum could be kept that Mrs. White inspired at the office. Then Ingersoll came in one morning and found Arno and me stretched out on the sofa nude and Ross closed the place down. I think he was afraid Mrs. White would hear about it. Arno and I may have been married to one another by then; I can't remember. Maybe we began drinking and forgot that we were married and had an apartment to go to.

"Arno was doing the Whoops Sisters cartoons for the *New Yorker* back then—the two London charwomen who would make innocent but insinuating remarks you were supposed to find funny. 'Whoops, I lost me muff!' Things like that. Before he was cartooning, Arno was making twenty-five dollars a week playing the piano and living with a psychiatrist's wife. He came to hate the Whoops Sisters. When Thurber turned into a cartoonist, Arno hated him, too. Jealous.

"Loyalty to the magazine was a one-way street. Ross never returned the loyalty. We'd drink and knock Ross and try to figure out what kept the guy alive when obviously no blood reached his heart. I never did feel the remorse from drinking he hoped we'd feel. Once, I found myself drinking beside a priest who gave me the blazing-eye treatment and tried to convert me. I promised him I'd slash my wrists before I had the chance to die a natural death. I told Thurber the story and he drew a cartoon about it. Several of the girls were always attempting suicide. It was almost a fad. One of them wore huge diamond bracelets to cover the scars. Dorothy Parker wrapped her wrists with big red bow ribbons after she'd slashed herself over some man. Benchley noticed her ribboned wrists at a party and told her if she didn't quit doing that it would ruin her health.

"All we were saying was, 'Tomorrow we may die, so let's get drunk and

"Unhappy woman!"

make love.' Today's young people say, 'Tomorrow we may die, so let's get a Ph.D. or start a riot.' You aren't supposed to laugh at anything anymore. We were a much tougher generation than the current ones. One of the ladies who worked with me on 'On and Off the Avenue' recently told me she'd left her eighty-six-year-old husband drunk at the Princeton Club because he would have been embarrassed to learn that she had helped him home. She's in her late sixties."

Honeycutt notwithstanding, Thurber seemed still in love with Althea. She was frequently away on trips with others and although there was little companionship when she was home, he always missed her not being in the apartment. In April 1928, he wrote to his brother Robert, who had just been to New York to visit him:

> Althea will not be home [from Greece] before the 15th of April I think. She is scheduled to sail on the 8th. . . . I wish you could get back and stay till Althea comes, because it gets pretty lonely here. I don't like to stay alone at nights, even in an apartment house and on such nights as I see a mystery play or read a mystery story, I leave the light on in the bathroom.

His first serious story, "Menaces in May," appeared the next month. Though it was inspired by his visits at the Flanders with Eva Prout and her husband, Thurber's regrets over his marriage, the missing Althea, and his fear of the city at night also spill onto the pages. Before the story could be published, Eva Prout and her husband had moved on to a theater in Canada. Thurber wrote to them, pretending they were all part of a large family:

Dear Act:
    I took your key back to the old Flemish Hotel and felt very sad. The room clerk and I had a good cry together. "They'll never come back," I said. "Jesus, I hope not," he said. It was very affecting. . . .
    The twins are here, your uncle fell and broke his foot, your Aunt Emma is blinder than usual and lost her crutch, the top is gone off the percolator again, the cat is poorly—it's her liver—the last she got from the butcher's was spoiled, but we gave it to the colored maid who said she would cook it in vinegar and it would be all right, there's a hole in the front room curtains, the dog's been on the body Barusselle again and spotted it, I found George's cuff links, your cousin Arthur has the prickly heat, their child isn't going to be smart, I guess, he's two now but hasn't said anything since he was born. . . . I'm well and sunburned. I played deck tennis yesterday at which I turn out to be pretty good but it has made my joints all stiff. I'm not as young as Ernie used to be, I guess.

His ties to Columbus remained strong; he was still the hometown boy making good. A number of professional humorists like Frank Sullivan, Robert Benchley, and White, were still outwriting him, but his record was highly impressive back home, which he made known with letters to his family, Herman Miller, John McNulty, and friends on the *Dispatch*. Before the *New Yorker* had hired him, Thurber would later say, he had received job offers from *Liberty*, and *Time* magazine. Nothing is known of such offers. He did apply to *Time*—and was turned down. Henry Luce had taken him to the Yale Club for lunch and suggested Thurber might wish to try out as a *Time* writer of national affairs with a piece on the Farm bill. Thurber asked, "What is that?" Luce laughed and said, "Yes, I guess you're right about not being the man for national affairs."
    He fed McNulty nonsense items, including plans for a tabloid newspaper

in which to "bust loose with a big scandal story about a secret love affair between the Statue of Liberty and the Colossus of Rhodes, with the equestrian statue of Sheridan in Washington named as co-respondent." The story, Thurber adds, will be "monumental."

For a time, it is said, Ross couldn't be sure whether hiring Thurber had been smart or the stupidest thing he had ever done. But 1928 settled the issue with Ross, in Thurber's favor. His production was prodigious. Besides rewriting Talk of the Town nearly every week, he contributed Notes and Comment to four issues, while White was on vacation; nine Talk stories of his own; "Menaces in May"; thirteen casuals; a verse, and his only Profile—on the subject Thurber seemed unable to let go of—Myron T. Herrick, the Ohioan and Ambassador to France during World War I. Ross made him rewrite the article sixteen times, and Thurber would never again try another long article about a personality for any publication, until, twenty years later, he began his series on the Columbus figures who make up *The Thurber Album*.

Except for the first of his "Mr. and Mrs. Monroe" series, which appears in *The Owl in the Attic*, and nine of his Talk stories, collected in *The Beast in Me and Other Animals*, Thurber harvested none of his 1928 crop in book form. The first Talk story he selected for book publication was about the American Museum of Natural History and the thirty-six-ton meteorite that Admiral Peary brought back from Greenland and presented to the museum. ("Geezus, I hope they were expecting it," Ross commented.)

A *New Yorker* reject, "As Europe Sees Us," (how Europeans still considered the United States to be one big Wild West) was bought by *Sunset* magazine. He had easier going with "ADVICE TO AMERICAN LADIES WHO ARE PREPARING TO TRAVERSE THE ATLANTIC. IN THE STYLE OF MISS LESLIE'S HOUSEHOLD BOOK, 1854."

> If the ship "splits apart" great judgment should be used in determining which side to stay on. . . . The part containing the engines is likely to sink, or submerge, in such a manner as no longer to be above the surface, when it is said to have "sunk."

Thurber had brought with him from Columbus his fondness for animal crackers, to which his "Credos and Curios" detective, Blue Ploermell, had been addicted. In a *New Yorker* casual, "How to Acquire Animal Crackers," signed Childe Harold, he pleads that the little cookies be packaged in "man-sized" boxes, rather than the tiny children's carton with a string handle. He was, he wrote, embarrassed to ask for them in a store and had taken to slipping them under his coat, much as he hated to. The National Biscuit Company reprinted the story in its employee publication, this time signed with Thurber's name, and shipped him a huge carton of the cookies. In Thurber's letter of thanks, he said, "There remain about 10,000 [boxes] although they have been eaten steadily. One of the best rewards I've got out of writing. I've given one or two animal cracker parties. . . . Our Scotch Terrier . . . has learned to sit up and beg for animal crackers."

He returned to Columbus that fall. Elliott Nugent was in town, playing an Ohio theater circuit in *The Poor Nut*, the play based on Thurber's days at the university. Its opening night was attended by Ohio's governor, Columbus's mayor and the university's president. The head of O.S.U.'s athletic association presented Nugent with a red sweater with the "O" monogram, making Nugent, as he wrote, "the first Ohio State athlete to win his letter for typewriting." Columbus would give Thurber his day in the sun in another dozen years, but Nugent was the city's pride and joy then. The two friends watched the Ohio State–Iowa game together at the big stadium on the river.

Thurber had grown a mustache—to compensate for his small mouth, according to Robert Thurber. White soon followed suit. Gibbs already had one. For a year, White and Thurber had been sharing not only their close office quarters but their baffling experiences with the opposite sex. Scott Elledge tells us that White had been, in an adolescent sense, in and out of love since his boyhood. He had no sooner given up publishing love poems spawned by his infatuation with Mary Osborn—a Southern girl he had fallen for a year earlier—than he was in love with a nineteen-year-old *New Yorker* secretary, Rosanne Magdol. White's ardor waned when he learned that Rosanne was temporarily living with an older man. Rosanne remembers vaguely, says Elledge, that White wanted her to run off with him but that he never mentioned marriage; he was, she says, "afraid of being hemmed in."

Two persons "gradually changed the color and complexion of [White's] life," writes Elledge. "One was James Thurber, whose wit, wild humor and extravagant flights of fancy delighted him. The other was Katharine Sergeant Angell . . . to whom White found himself increasingly drawn in admiration and affection."

Katharine and Andy White discussed those days in a 1962 interview:

"We were all extremely close and happy," White said. "Even after I got my own office after 1929. Both Kay and I felt great affection for Jim in those days."

"Jim was a good friend of mine, back then," agreed Katharine.

"Life was both creative and emotional for him," said White. "He was having many troubles, married to Althea."

"She was a fine girl but an unhappy wife," said Katharine.

"They were both nice people who just didn't hit it off," White said.

"Jim's eye was beginning to bother him then, I found out," said Katharine. "One day in late spring of 1928, he called my office and said 'I'd like to ride home with you and talk about something.' It surprised me because he knew I was in a hurry; that I was getting ready to go abroad with my family and I guess that's why he asked for no more of my time than the cab ride. In the cab he said, 'I can't see very well. In fact, I can hardly see anything.' I looked at him and made sure he was serious. He was; he was a little frightened, too. I made him promise to keep the cab and go straight home. I told him I was going to telephone Ross about it. I did. When I got back from Europe, he seemed to be all right again. But it was the first time I understood that his eye might be failing. That he might even be going blind."

32

That Talk of the Town

My last letter, which crossed your rather depressed one, maybe didn't cover the main points of your depression (which was once also mine). Ross ran my stuff through his typewriter for months, threw it away by carloads, often rewrote the things so I didn't find a phrase of mine left. I would try to imitate his rewrites of my rewrites, keeping in mind what he always said, "limber it up, make it easy and off-hand. . . ." What came out often sounded like the table talk of Bindle stiffs. I was imitating the wrong man. Ross is a great editor but often writes with a hoe. . . . I listened too much to his descriptions of what Talk should be, too. Maybe it's just as well you haven't seen much of him. He's likely to fill you up with too many ideas and maxims and instructions. He could rattle off "Don't build it up . . . we dont have to know too much, we want goddam it like table talk, interesting stuff, full of facts, to hell with the facts, we dont have to be experts, let yourself go, thousand interesting things in the city, for Christ's sake, etc. etc." I got bewildered.

—Undated letter to John McNulty

The Talk of the Town, which led off each issue of the *New Yorker*, consisted of Notes and Comment (paragraphs of opinion and reflection), followed by articles from about eight hundred to a thousand words in length, usually written with playful overtones. The writer's anonymity was protected by use of the editorial "we." Humorous anecdotes (frequently invented) of urban and suburban life were sandwiched between the Talk pieces. Ross depended on the Talk pieces to make good on most of the promises contained in the magazine's original prospectus. Their timely references to the places, people, and events of New York also helped assuage a nostalgia for his old newspaper days. Except for his famous queries on galley-proof margins ("Who he?" "Hogwash!"), he rarely meddled directly with nonfactual features in the book, but for years indulged a proprietary attitude toward Talk. Until White and Thurber, nobody who wrote or rewrote the Talk department satisfied Ross—and Thurber was a long time convincing him that he was the man for the job. "Ross sometimes had as many as three men, in separate offices, writing pieces for Talk," says Thurber, "each one unaware of the competition of the others. Most of them 'went out like matches in the wind of Ross's scorn,' as Ralph Ingersoll once put it."

"White and Thurber wrote most of the Talk department from late 1927 on," says Rogers Whitaker. "But it was a small staff and everybody contributed to it—ideas came in from outside and inside. We all reported for it. Until Thurber and White took it over and gave it a lasting format, Ross kept bringing in an odd assortment of men to try their hand at rewriting Talk. My favorite was Thorne Smith, who wrote the Topper novels. Ross kept him hidden; after he left for good, we found a whole Talk department Smith had rewritten with a fountain pen but never submitted. Some weeks he wouldn't show up, or, if he did, he'd be plastered and spend his time working on the galleys of his next book. Mrs. Smith would collect him and he'd disappear for another week."

Without Ingersoll's "help and direction," Thurber states in *The Years with Ross*, "I could never have got 'Talk of the Town' off the ground." It was another claim that irritated some of the old *New Yorker* hands. True, after his "demotion," Thurber was the chief rewrite man for Talk until he left the staff at the end of 1935. White soon "owned" Notes and Comment, and though he occasionally wrote Talk pieces, that part of the department did come to belong to Thurber. He was the man who determined its character, monitored its quality, and set its lasting tone, with literate, easygoing, and entertaining treatments of the facts. As his friend Robert Coates wrote after Thurber's death: " 'Talk' was just made for him, as he was made for it, and it is no more than simple fact to say he 'made' the department . . . into its present image."

The early Talk was little more than a gossip column, signed "The New Yorkers," or "Van Bibber, III," Ross's idea of conveying a mock aristocratic panache. But in one form or another, and however ragged its origins, the feature had been published for nearly three years before Thurber took it over and improved on it. His claim to have gotten it "off the ground" points up the risk the memoirist runs of seeming overly self-absorbed; so many achievements of Thurber he immodestly offers in *The Years with Ross* should appropriately have been written elsewhere by others. In the end he is often unfair to himself, taking a step beyond the literal truth and requiring the kind of correction that risks taking more away from his record of accomplishments than is deserved. For others do have legitimate claims to getting Talk under way. Ingersoll writes:

"I came to the *New Yorker* in July, 1925, hired to assist the late, great James Kevin McGuinness [the New York *Evening Post* columnist who worked for Ross part-time]. He was supposed to invent a Talk dept.—did it—stormed out—and I inherited [it]—and did invent a formula for Talk . . . the only basic ingredient I *know* I contributed."

One night, after Thurber had taken over Talk, he was at "21" when McGuinness was there, boasting that he had "invented" Talk. "I don't know why anyone would boast about anything in the New Yorker during its first year," Thurber writes Nunnally Johnson. "[McGuinness] then said the New Yorker was edited by pansies and I charged him, boldly shouting, 'Why doesn't somebody separate us?' "

"I did many a Talk of the Town piece," writes Morris Markey, a rewrite man on the *New York World* Ross hired in 1925, whose principal writing was of Profile and Reporter at Large. (Ross finally wearied of Markey, explaining: "He thinks everything that happens to him is interesting.")

"Everybody did everything in the early days," Katharine White adds. "Ross was really the fact editor, and no one can be credited with doing Talk single-handedly, even after Jim took over."

For purposes of financial compensation, the *New Yorker* librarian kept scrapbooks of Talk items, with the names of those who contributed the idea, reported the story, or rewrote it to size, recorded in the margins. The books show White concentrating more and more on Comment and record Thurber's staggering amount of Talk production over the years. But there were dozens of other names, of people on and off the staff, handwritten in the scrapbooks. In those days, reporter hopefuls tried out by chasing down suggested Talk ideas, and were paid only if their stories were accepted for rewrite. Those who showed promise and stuck it out were hired at a below-subsistence salary—perhaps thirty dollars a week. Those were the conditions under which William Shawn, Eugene Kinkead, Charles Cooke, Haydie Eames Yates, and others, came to work for the magazine.

Ross had patterned Talk after the front-of-the-book paragraphs of the British humor magazine *Punch*. Whatever opinions or thoughts White chose to express in Notes and Comment were as close to a contemporary editorial policy as the magazine ever had. "I went to Notes early," White says. "The five dollars per paragraph tempted me. Jim and I did a lot of original [not needing rewriting] visit pieces, too." (Talk stories were categorized as "visit," "personality," and "fact.")

"I began writing Talk of the Town late in 1927 and kept it up for eight years," Thurber wrote the editor of *Newsweek* in 1956. "Ross had been sure I couldn't do it because I would never get away from journalese. . . . It took months to convince him. He made me rewrite a Talk piece about Billy Seeman, buddy of Jimmy Walker, six times. 'Now you got it,' he said. 'Write it the way you would talk to a dinner companion.' He meant the way *he* would talk to one, offhand, casual." ("I don't remember that Jim had any trouble catching on," White says.)

Russel Crouse, who, with Howard Lindsay, was to adapt Clarence Day's memoirs into the long-running play *Life With Father*, was another *Evening Post* newspaper columnist who worked part-time for Ross. He was the last to rewrite Talk before Thurber took over. Crouse writes Thurber, in 1957:

> I would go to a Wednesday morning conference where all the editorial staff met and swapped ideas—that is, until the ideas got to Ross. He made short work of most of them and talked so loud that before half an hour everybody else was quiet.
>
> I have always felt that my only contribution to literary history was

being eased off Talk of the Town to let you take over. I remember the
day when I got back from my vacation and called you to get back that
bale of stuff that was the nest-egg for Talk each week and you said:
"Haven't you heard?" I hadn't and when I called Ross and asked him
why he hadn't told me he said: "I was too embarrassed." I told him he
had never been embarrassed in his life [though] it was one of the curious
contradictions in Ross's character that he was always acutely embarrassed when anyone told a dirty story in front of a dame, any kind of a
dame.

It was at those meetings that I discovered what I, at least, thought
made Ross a great editor. He never knew what he wanted until he saw
it. This kept the magazine from becoming stereotyped.

Thurber estimates that he wrote more than a million words for Talk—
counting his own pieces and those he rewrote. He credits White, working
alongside him, with helping him find the proper approach to the department.
"The precision and clarity of White's writing helped me a lot, slowed me
down from the dogtrot of newspaper tempo and made me realize a writer
turns on his mind, not a faucet," he wrote the *Newsweek* editor. He would
generously describe White as his literary mentor until nearly the end of his
life, when he finally recognized that their bodies of work had moved too far
apart in subject, mood, and manner to be compared. "I learned a lot from
E. B. White's fine clarity and pure declarative sentences," Thurber reiterated
the year before his death. "The way I write now, however, is absolutely my
own, I think." Unquestionably so. "[Thurber's] work was largely unclassifiable
(it was simply Thurber)," William Shawn wrote in the *New Yorker*'s Thurber
obituary.

White from the beginning questioned Thurber's crediting him as a major
influence. A dozen years after Thurber's death, he writes to Helen Thurber:

> I've never known, and will never know, how much Jim was influ-
> enced by my stuff. It has always seemed to me that the whole thing was
> exaggerated. Jim himself exaggerated it, as he exaggerated other matters
> and events. . . . My memory of those early days was that Jim was writ-
> ing very well indeed and needed no help from me or anyone else. Of
> course, we watched each other's work, the way writers do watch what
> others write. . . . He was hep to a lot more things than I was, had had
> a wider journalistic experience, and was a few years older than me. . . .
> He and I hit it off well, but I was no Big Brother.

Given the reciprocal nature of their physical and mental closeness, an inevitable development—but one rarely mentioned—was Thurber's influence on White's writing. Though both men began to sound alike in their Talk stories, Thurber threw caution to the wind when writing his first-person casuals of misadventures, frustrations, and comic comments, and, as Elledge writes in *E. B. White*, "the Thurber effect began to show up in White's work."

Brendan Gill, who has startling opinions on nearly everything and everybody, believes that "White's final record leaves him as unquestionably a first-rate American writer, but that Thurber's affirms his genius." Says Gill:

"White could never attain the levels of abandon and fantasy that Thurber could. Like Twain, Thurber could reach that upper dimension of unrestricted imagination; could walk right into his subconscious. Andy was too timid for that, too cautious. He emerges as a nicer human being than Thurber, for Thurber, like Twain, was full of rage and hatred, while eager to be loved, accepted, to be made much of by the world that Andy shrank from. Their personalities affected what they wrote, but Thurber's work, even with all its score-settling, is the humorous writing that will remain timely. It's an exalted difference to have to define, between White's superb talent and Thurber's genius."

Housed with White, there was sanctuary for Thurber. Ross rarely dallied in any office White inhabited, worried that in some way he would keep a seed of inspiration from germinating in his favorite writer's mind. For years he paid White at a higher rate than Thurber. He responded to White's manuscripts with no more than cautious queries he felt were necessary to satisfy his curiosity and to clarify what he thought might be puzzling to the reader. He accepted meekly most of White's occasional, obscure literary conceits, which Ross couldn't have understood.

Together, White and Thurber explored an early spectrum of *New Yorker* possibilities, set standards for the rest of the book to follow, and helped liberate Ross from his dependencies on other publications. In the course of it, they helped complete the emancipation of American letters from the English, and from wearying nineteenth-century literary traditions everywhere. They raised humor from cracker-barrel philosophy to an art, wrote satire without smugness, and implied civilized tastes without arrogance. They also helped make the *New Yorker* likable and respected.

Ross continued to bring in "geniuses" he found through friends, staff members, and in speakeasies. As Ralph Ingersoll wrote in his *Fortune* article: "Ross has hired them out of advertising agencies, from behind city desks, from the Social Register, from the Players Club. He brings them back from lunch, he cables for them." Ross's reasons for their brief tenures of service were often desperate ones, conceived to deflect any suggestion that he had exercised poor judgment in hiring them. "I thought you were a genius, but you're not," Ross remarked bitterly to a surprised Oliver Claxton on the day he fired him. It's said that Claxton was partly responsible for Ross's elimination of any real reception room at the *New Yorker*, after Ross returned to the office late one night and found Claxton and a young woman on one of the couches. Also, says Gibbs, "contributors had a way of spending the day there," which annoyed Ross.

As Thurber wrote to William Shawn in 1957:

> When Harold Ross lost interest in a thing, an idea, a man or a woman, it was lost for good. Few people ever re-entered his good graces. Most of the enthusiasms of men diminish, and their ardor cools, but Ross was a special victim of these normal and natural dwindlings because he often read less into men, and more into women, than was really there.

The theatrical press agent Murdock Pemberton was the magazine's art critic for a short time. He resented any editing of his copy, and when Thurber was introduced to him as the newest hire, Pemberton sneered, "Are you the current punctuator?" Time was on Thurber's side. Ross became increasingly unhappy with Pemberton's messy copy, which Pemberton blamed on an electric typewriter that, he said, from time to time went out of control and took off on its own literary fancies. He was replaced as art critic by Thurber's good friend Robert Coates, with whom Thurber shared an office after White was given his own.

A particularly sad case was that of M. B. (Bill) Levick, with whom Ross had worked on a San Francisco newspaper. Unable to please Ross as a miracle man, he took on art makeup, though he disliked cartoonists and came to believe that Thurber was the only artist who could spell, read, or write. ("One day nearer the grave, Thurber," was his morning greeting.) Ross's reasons for letting Levick go: He called Ross "Sir," with a mocking grin, used "sked" for schedule and "pix" for pictures. "All he cared about was his goddam pianola rolls," said Ross. "You don't play the pianola every night unless there's something the matter with you." Ross was also convinced that Levick had knowingly married a prostitute, an act Ross would have regarded as a deliberate assault on his personal code of ethics. And, as fervently as Ross sometimes hated Alexander Woollcott, Levick's continuous references to him as Old Foolish was another mark against him.

Woollcott, a Round Table companion, had offered to do a column, "Shouts and Murmurs," for the magazine, beginning in 1929. Says Katharine White: "Ross said to me that he would only take Woollcott on if he had nothing to do with his copy and if I would take on handling him. . . . Every week Levick turned up in my office to ask, 'Old Foolish this week?' Woollcott had the privilege of writing a piece a certain week or not writing one, and he would phone me one day early in the week to let me know."

In *The Years with Ross* Thurber writes that when he told Ross that Levick had died, Ross said, "I didn't treat him right, goddam it." Katharine White disputes this. Ross was fond of Levick and "kept him on in spite of untenable behavior," she says. "He wanted to be an artist and he became one, and because his son was killed in Spain [in the civil war there] he became a seaman on a ship to prove that he could be proletarian. He went off the handle . . . walked out on his wife; on shipboard he developed lung trouble. Ross knew all this as it happened. It was Levick who treated himself wrong [not Ross]. He turned communist as a matter of fact."

The "miracle man" Ross disliked and distrusted most was Arthur Samuels, another Round Table member and a close friend of Fleischmann's. A Princeton man, Samuels had been a newspaper reporter, an advertising executive, composer, and, at Fleischmann's behest, worked on the early *New Yorker* promotional ads, which may have saved the magazine from extinction. He was witty and talented—he went on to become the editor of *Harper's Bazaar* —but, because of his connections to the business side and because Fleischmann idolized him, he could do no right in Ross's eyes. It isn't clear how Ross ever succumbed to Fleischmann's pressure to make Samuels the "number two" man in editorial. Samuels occupied an office larger than Ross's and furnished it lavishly with rugs and bridge lamps.

"I guess Art Samuels was the most dangerous man we ever employed," Wolcott Gibbs writes Thurber. "Samuels . . . told me once that Ross wanted to fire me but he, Samuels, had persuaded him not to. We had a good many half-assed Machiavellis around the office, but he was the worst."

Whether Samuels had anything to do with it or not, material scheduled to be published was being leaked to other publications and ad agencies. Somebody, says Mrs. White, was also selling the same cartoons to the *New Yorker* and *Punch*. Ross was especially sensitive to the danger; as a reporter in Atlanta, he had occasionally destroyed or pilfered the competition's stories at the printing shop shared by his newspaper and its rival. So Ross took defensive action.

(left) Mame Thurber's father, William M. Fisher *(above)* With "Scottie," 1912

Thurber's paternal grandmother, Sarah Thurber Hull

(*above*) Young Charles Thurber, secretary
(*left*) Wedding day of Charles and Mame
Thurber: July 12, 1892, at the Fisher
home on Bryden Road, Columbus

(*left*) His father's derby was a favorite
Thurber subject. (*above*) Charles, secretary to the mayor, 1920s

Thurber, left, at 18 months, with William (*Courtesy* Columbus Dispatch)

(*above*) Aunt Margery Albright with, from left, William, Robert, and James. She was the midwife to all three. (*right*) Aunt Margery's garden was the subject of Thurber's first poem, at age six.

(*above*) Thurber's birthplace, 251 Parsons Ave., in 1946. It was razed in 1962 to make room for a thruway. (*Photo by Gregg D. Wolfe*) (*right*) The house at 921 South Champion St., site of the "dog factory"

Eva Prout, in her twenties

Eva as a child star

Eva Prout Geiger, in her early seventies, 1973
(*Photo by Lewis Branscomb*)

(*above*) Thurber, *Dispatch* reporter
(*left*) Thurber at the family home on Gay Street before leaving for France

(*above*) Althea Adams
(*left*) Wedding photo, 1922

Muggs, 1919–1928

Muggs, William, and Overland

Thurber, right, visits his family on Gay Street, circa 1936.

Thurber and Ted Gardiner, 1950s

Dorothy and Herman Miller at "Fool's Paradise," their home in Worthington, Ohio

Thurber, Rosemary, Mame, and poodle at Sandy Hook, 1933

Sandy Hook, 1932: Althea with Rosemary and Medve, the poodle

Mame with 1940s portrait of Thurber by James Montgomery Flagg

Mame's eightieth birthday celebration, January 1946 (*Courtesy*
Columbus Dispatch)

While visiting Columbus, a nearly blind Thurber poses as a reporter at the *Dispatch*, 1942.

By late 1928, Rogers Whitaker was in charge of the checking department, and a new hire, Hobart (Hobey) Weekes, another Princeton man, was his assistant. "I edited sports, fashions, and Janet Flanner's Paris letter," Weekes recalls. "Technically I edited Robert Benchley—he typed single-spaced—White, and Thurber, but I usually just put 'follow copy' on their stuff and marked it up for typesetting.

"When Ross suspected people were stealing our ideas, he had a door to the checking department installed with a little panel in it that you could slide to one side, like an entrance to a speakeasy. We had to keep the door locked when copy for 'A' issue [the issue going to press that week] was being laid out for shipment to the printer.

"I was there late one night with a young male checker when I heard people singing 'Bye, Bye, Blackbird' outside the door. I opened the panel and looked into the faces of Thurber and Elliott Nugent. Thurber wanted Nugent to see the galleys of a casual Thurber was proud of. Both men were obviously inebriated and carried jugs of wine. Thurber said he and Nugent had overpowered the guards, had come to spring us from Ross's prison, and thought it called for a party. What a drinking Thurber could do to an 'A' issue ready for the printer was a frightening consideration. I refused them admittance, whereupon began such a pounding and thumping on the door as to make very nervous the young checker, who, like the rest of us in those days, was overworked. Then Thurber and Nugent sat on the floor outside and moved into Irving Berlin's earlier period: 'Remember the Night,' 'I'll Be Loving You Always,' and 'We'll Always Be Together.' Their singing was in pardonable harmony, and I had a somewhat hysterical thought that perhaps both men were in the wrong professions.

"The singing suddenly stopped; the two of us looked at one another warily. A Trojan Horse trick to get us to open the gate? I could see no one out the little window. I slipped into the corridor. Thurber was in Art Samuels's office at the end of the corridor. Samuels was one of those strong-minded men who was the current managing editor and scaring the tar out of Ross because he seemed to know what he was doing. Ross was afraid of anyone who knew his own mind. Samuels had offended most of the staff by rigging up his office as if he were an advertising executive—plush furniture, carpets, even a spittoon and etchings on the wall. He had strong connections with the business side of the house, which enabled him to get furnishings that were the envy of everyone—I think even Ross—and also accounted for the general suspicion the editorial staff held him in. I heard Thurber telling Nugent, 'This is the elegant tomb Art Samuels has built for himself.' The next minute he was behind Samuels's desk playing Samuels to perfection. Thurber was a flawless mimic.

Nugent played Thurber, the shy, stumbling, put-upon employee taking abuse. To put an exclamation mark to Samuels's bullying oration, Thurber hoisted the huge, inverted jar from the watercooler outside Samuels's door and smashed it on the floor of the hall.

"I retreated to the safety of the locked room and calmed the startled young man, new to the staff as he was, and unprepared by his Ivy League classical education for this kind of experience. We were witnessing, I told him, part of the price the magazine had to pay for the kind of genius we needed. Thurber pounded on our door again, said the guards he had knocked unconscious would be up and around and this was his last offer to spring us from the hoosegow. If we refused to open the door and let him show Nugent his story, they would stay there all night and see that the relief column never broke through to rescue us. They were soon seated in the corridor again, singing fraternity and Ohio State football songs. The rest of the office floor was deserted. My principal concern by now was that the broken glass and water happened to be near the door to Mrs. Angell's office and that Thurber and Nugent would keep us from cleaning it up.

"Most of us get through life with little trade-offs, and we can only hope they remain within the limits of conscience and integrity. For example, there are those who will work for a slightly dishonest organization before they will work for a vulgar one; and there are those who will accept the tawdry in exchange for ennobling activity. The uniqueness of Mrs. Angell was that there could never be compromise considered on either score. She was the source of power that provided energy, taste, direction, honesty and moral momentum for the magazine. As a kind of universal housemother she worried about members of the staff, their health and their personal problems. People unacquainted with this employee benefit would emerge from the elevators rattled because Mrs. Angell had been looking them up and down closely during the ride. They would learn later that she had heard they had a cold, or were scheduled to be operated on, and was only being kind and solicitous. This was easy for me to forget, I know, when I encountered her in the hall. I was never able to shake the feeling at such a time that either my nose was running or my trousers were open. When Whitaker explained to me that she was merely concerned for our health, things didn't improve. There were a few nervous people on the staff who would be feeling fine until Mrs. Angell's once over, but then go home and go to bed in a worried state, waiting fearfully for whatever it was she knew, and they didn't, to strike them.

"In return for all that this remarkble woman was doing to keep the magazine and its staff healthy, it was understood that we had only to preserve the illusion of a working environment that contained the semblance of gentility, idealism, sweetness, light, and love. This unwritten contract was to be honored by all at the insistence of Ross, for whoever in any way contributed to the discomfort of Mrs. Angell not only stood to lose his or her job at Ross's hands, but ran the risk of never working again anywhere.

"So it was imperative that I clean up the mess. Thurber and Nugent were drinking wine—it would be hard to say what they had been drinking prior to the wine course—nobody could be certain in those days. Mercifully, within the hour they became weary, stretched out on the floor and passed into unconsciousness. I sought help from the building-services people, who helped me get them across the street to the Algonquin for the night. The missing water bottle on our premises would have required an explanation I had no intention of attempting with Samuels, Ross, or Mrs. Angell. I sent my young assistant up the fire escape to pilfer another water jug from whatever organization he could gain entrance to.

"The *Saturday Review of Literature* inhabited one of the floors above us, and on its night-lighted premises he found a water jug easy to filch. But as he lifted it out of the watercooler, a slight stirring on a nearby sofa drew his startled attention. A well-known and distinguished male contributor to the *Review*, by the most innocent interpretation of the situation, was making love to one of the lady editors. When I returned with a janitor to clean up the glass and water, I found the young checker seated, pale and shaking. He had managed to make off with the water jug, but the incident had left him feeling faint. I had him sit with his head between his knees while he told me what happened; it seems that this one night had brought to a total of four the number of his idols of literature and stage—he had long admired the lady editor, too—whom he had witnessed in situations he could not have imagined in the days when his college yearbook had prophesied his certain and brilliant future in the magazine business. . . .

"In replacing the water jug, I discovered it was only half the size of its predecessor. It was exactly the sort of thing Mrs. Angell or Samuels would notice and ask searching questions about. Nothing happened, but I worried about it for the couple of days it stood there until the spring-water vendor replaced it."

Weekes, a bachelor and man-about-town, would not have been totally out of sympathy with Thurber's and Nugent's frivolous behavior. Ross referred to him as a middle-aged juvenile delinquent, and when Weekes died, in May 1978 at age seventy-seven, he had left instructions that there be no funeral service but that his friends have a drink on his account at The Coffee House.

Ross feared the inevitable confrontation with Arthur Samuels. When Samuels took a six-week leave of absence abroad, Ross saw his chance to fire him without a personal interchange, but, writes Thurber:

> He put it off until Art's ship was back in the harbor of New York. Then, just before Samuels disembarked, he got a telegram from Ross telling him he was through. Late that afternoon [Ross] . . . was sitting with his head in his hands, and he said, "Samuels was just in here bawling the holy hell out of me. No white man would have fired him the way I did, I guess."

Ross wasn't the iron man he wished people to think he was. The magazine's telephone system, which he kept redesigning, once led to one of his emotional collapses. His marriage to Jane Grant had ended the year before. He would ask his "blue-eyed, effeminate young male secretary," says Weekes, to get the comedienne Beatrice Lillie on the phone—she was his paramour at the time—but inevitably Ross found himself talking to the magazine's makeup room or the office boys' quarters. Roaring that he was the victim of a conspiracy to keep him from a phone line out of the building, he turned himself in to Dr. Riggs's sanitarium again. Katharine Angell had a discreet bulletin-board notice posted which raised more questions than it answered. Ralph Ingersoll and Art Samuels ramrodded the fact side of the book, while Angell "handled everything else."

Alterations of offices had been under way the day Thurber reported for work and seemed never to stop. Though Ingersoll arranged to have the workmen come in after hours, that hardly spared those required to stay late with Ross. Once when the racket was so bad that Thurber couldn't work, he disgustedly rolled metal wastebaskets down the corridor to add to the confusion. Daise Terry, who had been Katharine Angell's secretary, was selected by Ross as the "old hen" (his expression) he had been looking for to run the typing pool. She helped put a stop to the noise, Thurber and workmen alike. Thurber settled for a sign that he hung near the elevators, warning visitors, "Alterations going on as usual during business."

Most anecdotes concerning the early years on the magazine involve Thurber. Says Ingersoll: "Thurber had magnificent fluency and an ability to go through hours of monolog, darting in and out of a score of subjects and ending in double talk, so cleverly contrived that it might be minutes after you had lost the gist before you realized there was no longer any gist to follow."

Thurber was soon up to his usual tricks, dropping into offices while their occupants were out and filling their memo and telephone pads with his doodles that nobody then took seriously as art but did take seriously when they needed paper to make a note during a phone call. "You would rip off the Thurber dog on the top page," Ingersoll remembers, "only to find a Thurber seal on the next, and a man chasing a woman on the third—right on down to the cardboard back. It was funny but irritating."

Many stories associated with Thurber he later claimed to be apocryphal, not adding that he had begun most of them. There was the telephone-booth story. Because people shared offices, a pay telephone was installed in the hall for private calls. Interviewed by Joseph Mitchell, then a *World-Telegram* reporter, in December 1934, Thurber said he had tipped over the phone booth, glass doors up, powdered his face to look corpselike, and stretched out in it. "A great many people came in and looked at me," Thurber told Mitchell. "It was difficult to upset the telephone booth and the effort tired me. So I stayed in it most of the afternoon. At six o'clock I climbed out, dusted the powder off my face and went home." When Dale Kramer was preparing his book, *Ross and The New Yorker*, he queried Thurber about the story. Thurber said he had just stayed in the phone booth "a little while." Elsewhere, after Daise Terry reminded him that it had never happened, Thurber said the story wasn't true at all.

He never did forgive John Chapin Mosher for rejecting his early submissions. Once when Mosher, who shared an office with Wolcott Gibbs, complained about the lack of heat, Thurber set fire to his paper-filled wastebasket. When Mosher stayed late to interview an authentic Russian princess who hoped to write for the magazine, he was humiliated by the hammering, sawing, and drilling that took place after 6:00 P.M. Thurber, dressed in workman's garb, with mussed hair, and dirty face, repeatedly passed through the interview area pretending to be collecting tools and paint brushes. He called Mosher "Jack," and complimented him on the wild party he said Mosher had thrown in his office the night before, especially "the dame you were wrestling with on the sofa." By the end of a half hour, both Mosher and the princess were certain things would not work out for her at the *New Yorker*.

Years later, Thurber was outraged by Mosher's rejection of a story by Astrid Peters. Thurber sent it to Ross, who overruled Mosher and bought the story, "Shoe the Horse and Shoe the Mare," which was included in the 1944 *Best American Short Stories*. Mosher had found it "a tedious bit about an adolescent female." Katharine White writes in defense of Mosher:

"Someone else must have said no on it (probably Gibbs) and thus it never reached my desk. . . . Mosher had his limitations as a first reader, and Ross and I were well aware of them. At one time we put in Sally Benson as a reader of his rejections just to catch any love stories etc. that had not appealed to Mosher, but I can't remember that she turned up much of anything. . . . Mosher . . . discovered most of our early and most talented writers [including] Jim."

Gibbs told Thurber that his most uncomfortable period on the magazine was when he was sharing an office with the flamboyant Mosher, who was courting another man. But Gibbs was shocked when Mosher once returned from having had lunch with Mrs. Angell to report that she had asked him to try to curtail his homosexual behavior because it made Ross uneasy. Actually, says Gibbs, Ross loved Mosher's work and never registered an objection to his lifestyle. Though he complained to Thurber that he had acquired at least "three hundred scars" from working with "Mrs. White," Gibbs nonetheless admired how she could handle a social crisis at the office.

"One day, John Peale Bishop came in to discuss a ms. with Mrs. White and me," Gibbs writes Thurber, "and when he took it out of its envelope a couple of condoms . . . dropped out on her desk. Mrs. White just covered them with a blotter, and we went on talking about commas. Great poise, I thought."

Thurber had begun to court social disaster when he drank, but these were still the good days for him; no one minded that his emotional commitments could only be to himself and his writing ambitions, for outwardly he was funny, gentle, and kind when sober, and worthy of easy forgiveness when he was not.

Nor was he the only one who cut up in what one veteran refers to as "the screwball days." Though Ross pleaded for decorum at the office, he enjoyed a New Jersey retreat of the vaudevillian Joe Cooke called Sleepless Hollow, which featured a golf tee atop a water tower and a channelled fairway that ensured a hole-in-one. Ross found hilarious the telephone there that squirted water when you picked it up to make a call, as well as the butler at Cooke's parties who would seize and consume the drink a guest was about to take from his tray.

Even the burdened Ingersoll and the shy White behaved like kids on Halloween night if the challenge merited it. A Talk story reported that a Greenwich Village prankster had stolen the sign outside the New York Society for the Suppression of Vice and was using it as a cocktail tray. John S. Sumner, who headed the society, brought legal action to force the New Yorker to reveal the identity of the culprit and the location of his sign. He settled for a replica to be furnished by the magazine. White, Thurber, and Ingersoll connived in a speakeasy conference to rig the society's original sign as a false front that hid one featuring a scantily-dressed chorus girl kicking off Mr. Sumner's stovepipe hat. The art was provided by a *New Yorker* artist. But the sign was rehung by the society at a safer, second-story level. Ingersoll and White dressed as housepainters and propped a ladder on the building. They were challenged and fled. They returned after hours in firemen's uniforms only to discover that the cabinetmaker had nailed the false front too securely to be removed. White bought a hatchet and went back alone with the ladder, chopped the frame away, and telephoned the newspapers. He didn't specify the need for photographers, however, and though the sign received some publicity Sumner was able to get it down before the cameramen reached the scene.

"In most of our high jinx," Ingersoll writes, "Jim Thurber was a silent collaborator, but in one he played a leading role. His was the whole idea of the Sitting Bull hoax."

A Talk reporter, Haydie Eames—who contributed the classic "His love life seems as mixed up as a dog's breakfast" to the office lore—had the "swarthy coloring and the hawklike features of a handsome Indian brave," according to Ingersoll. She acted on Thurber's suggestion that she get in touch with the Junior League's entertainment committee, dress up like an Indian squaw, bill herself as Sitting Bull's daughter, and address the League's local membership on the plight of the Indians. White wrote the script, so subtle a one that no one in the audience suspected a joke. "Did you know you can't even hang a picture on the wall of a tepee?" Miss Eames challenged the affluent ladies. Weeping tears of remorse and pity, they collected money for the underprivileged squaw.

A frightened Haydie Eames returned to the office with hundreds of fraudulently obtained dollars. Ingersoll returned them. The League officers, shocked beyond coping, agreed that nothing should be said and that the money would be sneaked to charity somehow.

Thurber still seemed able to hold his liquor then. "We all liked him very much," says Whitaker. "Drinking wasn't really a problem. We were all a drinking crew in those days and Thurber would come in drunk every now and then, but he was never mean or destructive. He would simply have an extra drink at lunch he couldn't handle and make a valiant effort to get his work done but sometimes couldn't. He was very much one of us and a favorite drinking companion of us all. He was kind enough and funny enough so that we didn't mind taking his bad if we could be privy to his good."

A volatile person like Thurber operates at a manic high others have to drink to reach. Alcohol sent Thurber into outer space. Later, his blindness gave him the anger and his fame gave him the power to hurt. "It was one thing to blow up in a day and on a staff when everyone blew up," says Whitaker. "It was another matter to blow up after he became a celebrity. When you're an important writer and artist, blowing up carries a lot more megatons. I'm not sure Thurber understood that or why people got so mad at him in the later years when he lost his temper and carried on.

"He put a lot of his temper on, I think. He was a ham and loved to cause a scene. Underneath he was a reasonable man. He liked to bait, and I think of that as a typical Midwestern trait. I used to edit a trade magazine and attend business conventions in that part of the country. Everyone is his own humorist out there. It's kid and be kidded. So I never took Thurber seriously when he blew up. I don't think many of us did. Certainly not Ross."

In a three-ring circus, Thurber would still have been the most conspicuous of the cast. Katharine White remembers sitting in Ross's office when Ross's secretary, Elsie Dick, rushed in and said, "Quick! Quick! Mr. Thurber is trying to kill himself." Ross said to her, "See? That's my life."

"I rushed into the corridor," Katharine wrote Thurber,

> and . . . you had just smashed the green light shade and were bleeding awfully. You said, "I think I'm going to faint" and I pushed you against the wall and held my hands on your shoulders and said, "Jim, don't faint! Jim, don't faint!" I remember this, for I felt so silly afterward—as if telling you that would prevent your fainting, and as if I could have held you up if you had fainted! Very likely Ross said the "That's my life" line many times but he certainly said it then.

"The stories about Thurber's office behavior," writes Gibbs, "are manifold, peculiar, and perhaps as much as fifty-percent true."

Thurber and Gibbs, between marriages, were often men about town together. Emily Hahn, who reconnoitered the clubs with Gibbs and Thurber for a time, says: "Someone once told me Thurber had said he was sure he was the only man on the staff who hadn't slept with me. It was a lie on both counts; he *had* slept with me. In fact, he was too drunk to do anything *but* sleep. Hotel guests had to have luggage in those days, so the boys kept a suitcase at the *New Yorker* full of telephone books in case of an unplanned overnight. I think having to lug a heavy suitcase from the offices to the hotel tired out Thurber. But he proudly told Gibbs the next day that he had spent the night with me. Gibbs, of course, told me, and assured me that Thurber would henceforth always love me; I had been initiated into the Thurber legend as conceived by Thurber. He did treat me sentimentally when I got back from the Far East during the war years. He was practically blind but walked all the way from his apartment on East Fifty-seventh Street to my place in the East Nineties to tell me how much he admired the way I'd handled the ordeal I'd been through, with my child's father, a British officer, a prisoner of the Japanese over there. I think Thurber told Helen about our night together, too, because when he called her to tell her where he was, she arrived by cab in no time at all, very annoyed with him and a bit cool to me."

As time passed, the staff members aged, settled things with themselves, moved on, wearied, or died. In 1955, reflecting on articles and books about the *New Yorker*, A. J. Liebling, that durable and talented staff contributor of the magazine's second generation, comments: "People who try to write about the magazine remember the old stories and think they have to try to be funny about the *New Yorker*, and there hasn't been anything funny about this place in years. The screwballs either grew up or left. The atmosphere around here is as undisturbed as that of a geriatric hospital ward."

Thurber, at fifty, writing the preface to Mary Petty's book of cartoons in 1945, even disclaims the magazine's "screwball" reputation of the beginning years. The *New Yorker* was not, in fact, the violent loony bin it had been cracked up to be, he writes. One would have found

> in its plain, workaday office, shy and even timorous persons, given to flatulence, tremors, and mild melancholia, and absorbed by family worries and commonplace problems. A group photograph of its editors and resident contributors at that time would have moved the soft-hearted to send in contributions of food, clothing, money, and inspirational literature.

33

That Mr. and Mrs. Monroe

In his New York existence . . . more than any other thing [Thurber] was concerned with the relation between the sexes. . . . Appalled at the grave thrumming of sex itself in the metropolis, he was at once amused and frightened by its manifestations among his friends, many of them married. . . . Into the real quandary of marriage he read a droll sadness. Above the still cool lake of marriage he saw rising the thin white mist of Man's disparity with Woman. In his drawings one finds not only the simple themes of love and misunderstanding, but also the rarer and tenderer insupportabilities. He is the one artist that I have ever known, capable of expressing, in a single drawing, physical embarrassment during emotional strain. That is, it is always apparent to Thurber that at the very moment one's heart is caught in an embrace, one's foot may be caught in a piano stool.

—E. B. White's Introduction to *The Owl in the Attic*

When Althea returned from her trip to Greece in the spring of 1928, she and Thurber retrieved their Scottish terrier from a country kennel. "Jeannie went accommodatingly into heat the day we got there," Thurber writes Eva Prout and her husband, "so Althea is taking her to a professional dog husband at Hempstead L. I. today so she can become a mother."

They had moved from Horatio Street to a larger apartment at 65 West Eleventh Street, between Fifth and Sixth Avenues. Charme Seeds and Charles Speaks soon married, continuing as social mentors to the Thurbers, introducing them to Village residents who spent summer weekends in the Connecticut suburbs, where Thurber and Althea became frequent house-guests. The Speakses themselves bought a house in Westport. Though Thurber preferred the Amawalk compound, where Honeycutt was often a summer weekender, he also enjoyed the Westport area, with its actors, writers, artists, and editors. One of his friends was Richard Connell, a successful writer of humorous stories for such "slick" magazines as the *Saturday Evening Post*, and *Collier's*. He lived in Greens Farms, near Westport.

"We met the Thurbers at a party given by Kate and Sigmund Spaeth," says Louise Connell. "Ours was a crowd of working artists and writers, not people who pretended to be or just played at it. Our place at Greens Farms had one of the few tennis courts around. Thurber had just taken up tennis and that helped draw him to our place. No one was very good at tennis in our crowd and, by those standards, Thurber wasn't bad. When it was too dark for tennis, we'd dance to a phonograph and eat cold-meat sandwiches. We were all full of play in those days. Even after the Depression began, the innocence of the period continued; our group seemed to get by well enough financially and few of us had to learn to do without. We always gave a fancy-dress ball on the Fourth of July after a daylong tennis tournament, and I think Jim and Althea were there for the one in 1928.

"It was a rowdy crowd in and around Westport but nonetheless usually respectable and great fun. People would fall for each other and feel they had to divorce and remarry. Today I suppose they would say, 'Think of the children!' and settle for an affair. Prohibition made our event similar to the Boston Tea Party in our minds—defying the unreasonableness of the Act. It made drinking a cause. We used a cabdriver who would drive a practical nurse to our house. She wore a crisp, long, white shirt that hid a five-gallon can of alcohol, which she got from wherever she worked. I learned to make quite a good gin, 40 percent alcohol. You added oil of juniper drops to kill the harshness. An olive in the martini was important for its oil. Those who couldn't stand the martinis had ginger-ale highballs. The butler's pantry was full of gallon bottles and funnels and we made the gin in the bathtub for large parties.

"One night I got the ginger-ale jug mixed up with the gin, and the guests were wondering why they weren't feeling the usual exhilaration and why the party was so dull. A few never came back. Another time, I forgot to add the water and served straight alcohol with only the juniper drops. It was a wild night; all but one or two of the guests were knocked unconscious. Luckily, Thurber wasn't there. Jim liked to drink but was no alcoholic; drinking was strictly a social thing with him. It was only bad when he would get drunk for the benefit of people who simply weren't worth getting drunk for. Prohibition's awful stuff made nearly everyone look as if they couldn't hold their liquor, Jim in particular.

"Thurber wasn't a great dropper-in, as others were, and my husband, Dick, appreciated that. He and Thurber got along marvelously. Jim and Althea met Sylvia and Frank Godwin at our place one weekend, and we were all invited to the Godwins' summer home in the Finger Lakes area—on Lake Skaneateles. There, both Dick and Jim, as usual, began telling each other funny stories. We were all spellbound. We'd been served luncheon at 12:30 P.M., and at 3:30 they were still going strong. The servants were restless, waiting to clean up, and near rebellion.

"We all liked Althea. She wasn't someone you could be close to; she seemed almost cagey about not giving away what was on her mind. You could only know her surface. Thurber's mind was enchanting; Althea hid hers. But she was as socially attractive as Thurber; good-looking and responsive to other people. The men at parties flirted with her and she seemed to enjoy that. She struck me as not a self-sacrificing type, and I thought she saw Thurber's work as neither important nor interesting. But she was by no means the woman monster of Thurber's stories and cartoons. She didn't seem to care what Jim did as long as he made a living and didn't disgrace her socially. She apparently saved her real affection for dogs. I thought at the time that her enthusiasm for dogs was what kept Jim infected with his own fondness for them."

In 1926, Henry Watson Fowler, the English lexicographer, brought out his *A Dictionary of Modern English Usage*. Ross, its enslaved follower, usually gave a copy of it to the editors and writers he hired. By late 1928, Thurber was tearing into it, partly to espouse grammatical prejudices of his own, partly to needle Ross, but mostly to have fun. His nine articles on the Fowler tome, carried under the *New Yorker*'s running title of "Our Own Modern English Usage," were strung out from January to December 1929. The pieces are uniquely Thurber, with no suggestion of his earlier partial dependence on humorists who had gone before him.

He picks up his discussion of the split infinitive where he had left off in the *Sun-Dial*, but he now had his physical confrontations with Honeycutt to draw upon. To say using the split infinitive is always wrong, he now writes, "is of a piece with the sentimental and outworn notion that it is always wrong to strike a lady. Everybody will recall at least one woman of his acquaintance whom, at one time, or another, he has had to punch or slap." At a dinner party, one should be careful not to knock one's lady companion completely under the table, "because it would leave two men seated next to each other."

The problem of when to use "who" or "whom" is best met by avoiding both, says Thurber:

> The Buried Whom, as it is called, forms a special problem. This is where the word occurs deep in a sentence. . . . Take the common expression: "He did not know whether he knew her or not because he had not heard whom the other had said she was until too late to see her." The simplest way out of this is to abandon the "whom" altogether and substitute "where." . . . Unfortunately, it is only in rare cases that "where" can be used in place of "whom." Nothing could be more flagrantly bad, for instance, than to say "Where are you?" in demanding a person's identity. The only conceivable answer is, "Here I am," which would give no hint at all as to whom the person was.

"Which" clauses are to be avoided also, argues Thurber, who sees the chance to parody Hemingway again:

> Foolhardy persons sometimes get lost in which-clauses and are never heard of again. . . . Fowler cites several tragic cases . . . : "It was rumoured that Beaconsfield intended opening the Conference . . . in French, his pronunciation of which language leaving everything to be desired. . . ." That's as much as Mr. Fowler quotes because, at his age, he was afraid to go any farther. The young man who originally got into that sentence was never found. [Another Fowler example:] ". . . the leaders of which being the very people from whom an example might well be looked for . . ." Not even Henry James could have successfully emerged from a sentence with "which," "whom," and "being" in it. The safest way . . . is to follow in the path of . . . Ernest Hemingway. In his youth he was trapped in a which-clause one time and barely escaped with his mind. He was going along on solid ground until he got into this: "It was the one thing of which, being very much afraid—for whom has not been warned to fear such things—he . . ." Being a young and powerfully built man, Hemingway was able to fight his way back to where he had started, and begin again . . . : "He was afraid of one thing. This

was the one thing. He had been warned to fear such things. Everybody has been warned to fear such things." Today Hemingway is alive and well.

Ross once told A. J. Liebling, "I have never seen a good sentence beginning with 'however'." Thurber adds his own warning, that of starting sentences with "only," for the "o" has to be capitalized, he points out, and can cause a hurried reader to take it for a proper noun and confuse it with Richard Olney, secretary of state under President Cleveland. He is also against substituting pet names for the indefinite "one," although a sentence like "Mopsy loves Flopsy" often gets into the newspapers, especially if Flopsy turns out to be an ambitious blonde and Mopsy a wealthy mop-handle manufacturer. Thurber ends the piece on a note of heartfelt sincerity: "Nothing can be done about the verb 'to love'."

He is equally entertaining and unhelpful on when to use "bad" or "badly," "whether," the subjunctive mood, exclamation points (which, on the manual typewriter, risks accidentally striking the upper-case shiftlock key and unknowingly writing the next eight sentences in capital letters), and the perfect infinitive, a tense in which even the correct "We would have liked to find you in" sounds incorrect and keeps the frustrated visitor writing over and over the note he wishes to leave on the front door. One of Thurber's techniques is to drift into non sequiturs, changing from grammar to whatever subject is accidentally washed ashore in the sample sentence. The series brought an appreciative letter from Fowler's secretary, if not from Fowler, who lived nearly four years after Thurber's wacky satires on his book appeared. The secretary hinted, however, that Fowler, too, was amused. So was Hemingway.

None of these late-1920s writings were selected by Thurber for either of the retrospectives of his work published by Harper's: *The Thurber Carnival* (1945) and *Alarms and Diversions* (1957), but they were important to his development as a literary personality. The Fowler satires were among the best things published by the magazine at the time. They added to Thurber's self-confidence and Ross's interest in Thurber's emerging talent.

When the dyspeptic Wolcott Gibbs abandoned his job as chief copyeditor in the 1930s to become the magazine's theater critic, he wrote a guide labeled "Theory and Practice of Editing New Yorker Articles" for the benefit of his successor and the other editors. With regard to fiction he warns,

The average New Yorker writer, unfortunately influenced by Mr. Thurber, has come to believe that the ideal New Yorker piece is about a vague, little man helplessly confused by a menacing and complicated civilization. Whenever this note is not the whole point of the piece (and it far too often is) it should be regarded with suspicion.

It could be said that the Thurber Man was introduced to the world in the first casual Thurber sold to the *New Yorker*—the "helplessly confused" little fellow who set a record number of turns in a revolving door, motivated by a fight with his wife and the need to earn a living for the family.

By the end of 1928, Thurber's American male, put off by Woman's refusal to behave according to Victorian, Midwestern tradition, became a theme that White and Thurber took up in successful collaboration, leading to the publication of *Is Sex Necessary?* in 1929. During their time as officemates, they found they both looked upon the opposite sex in baffled contemplation. White listened by the hour to Thurber's reflections on Althea, whose growing indifference kept churning Thurber's ambivalent feelings of anger, self-pity, and wistful longing. White, in and out of love ("Too small a heart, too large a pen," he wrote in a self-indictment), was, by late spring of 1928, focused on Katharine Angell. ("I was half in love with her for a long time," White told Linda H. Davis fifty years after his marriage.) The Angells sailed for Europe that summer, and Katharine and Andy had agreed to meet in Paris. (Ernest planned to pursue his own interests and return by himself.) Their brief affair in France and Corsica seems to have been traumatic for them both. As Davis points out,

> For the rest of her life [Katharine] would suffer the psychological fallout of her own adultery, and seek to mask her guilt by denying that the affair had occurred. . . . But she was in love with Andy, and, as White later observed [after Katharine's death], she "had to become a bad girl in order to survive in her marriage." . . .
>
> Either because Katharine was not yet ready to give up on her marriage or because Andy was fearful of commitment and had proven fickle in love before, they agreed not to continue the affair. They would remain friends at the office. It was a hard, unhappy resolution for them both, and it could not last.

For Thurber, the Woman problem was the more complicated and painful one of a relationship with Althea that was winding down toward complete disconnection. Bickering and unhappy with one another, in January 1929 they agreed to a further declaration of independence, one at first confided only to such close friends as the Speakses, but which would end much of their socializing as a couple for a time. For financial reasons, they continued to share their Village apartment, along with Jeannie and her pups, until the summer. That June, they gave up the apartment and rented the farmhouse in Silvermine, Connecticut, within an easy drive of the Westport area crowd, where Althea began breeding poodles and Scotties in earnest. Thurber visited on an occasional weekend. Both declared the separation a friendly one.

Though they had been seeing others socially, and Thurber believed himself in love with Honeycutt, he simply couldn't get over his original Jamesian romantic feelings about Althea. "It was obvious to all of us that he still carried the torch for her after the separation," says Lois Long. Ralph Ingersoll agrees. "Jim seemed to adore Althea," he says. "She had large, classical, handsome features that Jim always described as beautiful. To Jim's friends she could seem unimaginative and intellectually inferior to Jim, but I'm sure her friends felt that way about Jim and his circle. Jim was always very supportive of her in the presence of others. Althea took up amateur theatrics in Westport that summer of 1929. Jim took me to see her in a play. Althea had the leading part. The show had barely begun when it was clear to me that the part was well beyond Althea's abilities. Not only was she struggling to make the best of a role unsuited for her, everything happening onstage was something the *New Yorker* crowd would have made fun of, including Thurber.

"I was embarrassed for Jim and didn't know how to let him know I understood what he was going through. Then he turned to me and said, 'Isn't Althea wonderful?' I thought he was being satiric, but I looked at him and realized he meant it. Perhaps I was biased; I was one of those who, because they loved Jim, resented his wife for the problems she was causing him. I thought Althea never respected Jim's work, or cottoned to the *New Yorker* people. We were all still nervous about making the magazine a success, and it didn't help that Althea seemed unable to take us or our work seriously."

But Althea had a better grasp of the situation than Ingersoll gives her credit for. In her seventies, she told an interviewer: "Three things, even as early as 1927, meant a writer had arrived: a mention in the columns of Franklin P. Adams and Heywood Broun, and getting on the *New Yorker* staff. It was already a prestigious magazine; it helped Jim's reputation and helped him get *Is Sex Necessary?* published. His *New Yorker* connections were important; knowing the people who could help him get a book published."

Though Thurber did his best to keep the news of the separation from his family, they heard about it through a friend of Charles's, who may have learned of it from John McNulty, who was still a newspaperman in Columbus. Mame and Minnette Fritts Proctor had remained in touch—Mame had even done the horoscopes of Minnette's two children. ("They didn't turn out to be exact, but they were very interesting," says Minnette.) Mame wrote Minnette the news of Althea and Thurber in September 1929; Minnette replied that she had known for several months, since Thurber had unexpectedly written her that spring. Stricken by unrequited love, he had resorted once more to fantasy, as if the confidential friendship he had once shared with Minnette, now a busy housewife and mother married to a prospering physician, could be resurrected.

Thurber had even asked to come to Seattle to see her. An astonished Mame responds to Minnette's revelation:

> I can't understand what he meant by insisting on coming out there— is he crazy? I think he wanted to talk matters over with you—you know you always had so many confidential talks. What else could it be? Surely he must know you are very happily married and have two lovely children. Why it baffles me, really. I am sure you did right when you wouldn't allow him to come. It would have been terrible. Dr. Proctor would likely had him judged insane.

One surprise that emerges from this correspondence is that Charme Seeds may have been romantically interested in Thurber, though no evidence has been found that Thurber was aware of it, or encouraged it. Minnette apparently still felt somewhat possessive toward Thurber, and jealous of other women who interested him. Though claiming to be fond of Althea, she had decided at the start that Althea was wrong for Thurber. ("Althea Thurber thounds thilly," she had taunted Thurber before his marriage.) Minnette had known Charme Seeds at O.S.U. and either disliked her personally or envied her her career and close friendship with Thurber. Not knowing Charme had just married Charles Speaks, she wrote Mame that Charme would "ruin" Thurber if they were to marry. Mame, who greatly admired Charme, was curious:

> *Please,* I beg of you tell me what you mean about saying Charme would have ruined Jim. . . . Why they have everything in common. . . . Of course [Charme] has no children . . . and how Jim did want children.
>
> I must tell you Althea and Charme are very good friends. . . . I would really like to know just what it is you've against Charme. . . . All the Speaks family [who lived in Columbus] just adore her. . . . I

really think and I've told Jim many times that Charme cared more for [Jim] than any one of the rest of the girls—and this means you also. . . . I am so sorry Jim has worried you as he has and I do hope you will write and tell him you are sorry as he is in trouble now. And I am sure he will also apologize to you. He needs friends now. . . . Now be kind to Jim but give him to . . . understand he must be out of your life forever.

Thurber's lovesick letter to Minnette, out of the blue, had caused a slight misunderstanding between her and her husband. She replied to Thurber in severe terms she might not have otherwise used. Thurber took her scolding as betrayal. When Minnette didn't hear further from Thurber, she worried about him, and that November she wrote to Mame about her concern. Mame replied:

[Jim] warned me in a letter not to let you especially . . . know anything on earth about him ever in any way or any of his business . . . and said you wrote him [a] most *terrible* letter in April and I guess he is pretty sore. . . . I'd not write him . . . I believe it would do no good and likely make matters worse. . . . It isn't likely you will ever see or hear from him again. . . . I understand and know you are interested in him—but he will never believe it . . . but he is doing wonderful— papers all over the country copy his articles. . . . I think he is a won- derfully bright boy and he has such a sweet disposition—also he has grown fleshy—and a friend of his says it is very becoming.

In his letter [to his family] he talks lovely about Althea—he says her mother wrote him [the] most beautiful letter he ever read—he says Al- thea sure comes from a great and high class family—very proud of their family tree etc. . . . It was only her disposition I objected to.

So also in Jim's letter he said Althea has made him what he is—and he said he loved to do things for her as she was so kind about it and didn't make any "demands" on him. . . . Charme told me when I met her here she lived near Althea in [Connecticut] and had learned to know her better and said she liked her better all the time. But as Jim said —as their temperaments were different, they were happier apart—and he goes to see her every week end and they have separated as good friends and he will always look out for her he said. We really admired the way Jim talked about her. He said we must blame *him* as much as her. But you know we can't get anything more out of him. . . . I never could get close to her, never [but] she has been fine to me. Last Xmas she sent . . . us all nice things. She gave me her lovely set of dishes before she left here . . . years ago—so we must give her credit for what she has done—but she is never [meant] for Jim Thurber, as you know, even if you won't say.

In the magazine's last issue of 1928, Thurber's "Tea at Mrs. Armsby's" appeared. The first of eight "Mr. and Mrs. Monroe" pieces, it starts the timid, ineffectual Thurber Man on his henpecked journey, which would end with "The Secret Life of Walter Mitty," that perfect summary of the arduous pilgrimage and the daydreaming techniques through which the Thurber Man survived it.

"Tea at Mrs. Armsby's" finds the Thurber Woman, tipsy on cocktails, indirectly punishing her husband in front of others for habitually leaving on her dressing table his handkerchiefs, the pencils he absently brings home from the office, match folders from his pockets, and towels from the bathroom. ("She frequently spoke to him disapprovingly about such things.") Inebriated, she tells hostess and guests that her husband collects pencils ("eight hundred and seventy-four thousand" of them). Though the Thurber Woman is often out of control in Thurber cartoons, she rarely is in his prose, as in this instance—(" 'Pull yourself together for the god's sake,' said Mr. Monroe.") It's a no-win game, the put-upon Thurber Man the loser even when he is the sober one and she is acting the fool.

The Monroe series (Althea and her mother had lived on Monroe Avenue in Columbus) draws almost literally on the Thurbers' married life. Writing to Herman Miller on September 22, 1931, Thurber says: "The Monroe stories were transcripts, one or two of them varying less than an inch from the actual happenings." But Mrs. Monroe is prudently disguised as Ann Honeycutt, small and blond, rather than the taller, brown-haired Althea. Though at the time Althea could not have cared less about Thurber's personal life ("Go ahead and call her," she would reply whenever Thurber voiced the wish to telephone Honeycutt or the actress Paula Trueman), divorce and remarriage were not yet on her mind, and she still depended on Thurber for material support and weekend help with the Silvermine house and the dogs.

In "The 'Wooing' of Mr. Monroe," written a short time after the Thurbers had separated, Thurber imagines Althea, as Mrs. Monroe, fending off the threat of another woman romantically involved with John Monroe. (Like Honeycutt, the femme fatale is a petite blonde.) Mrs. Monroe employs offense as defense. She calls on her rival to warn her that, among other ineptitudes, Monroe "is simply terrible with machinery." She describes a visit they made to Monroe's alma mater, where, in trying to take a shower, Monroe filled the shower room with steam, the water too hot to go near. Rushing back to their room naked ("He always forgets his bathrobe—and theatre tickets"), he could only make "Woo! Woo!" sounds. ("He always goes 'Woo! Woo!' when things go wrong with machinery.") Monroe, his wife continues, "pulled down a curtain rod, curtain and all," with which to reach the faucet handle, wearing only the negligée she had thrown on him. The university engineer had to shut off the school's entire water supply. And there was the time when Monroe, stumbling about backstage in a theater, managed to turn off all the power in the middle of a production.

" 'May I ask,' cut in the other woman, 'how long you have endured this?' "

" 'Eight years in June,' said Mrs. Monroe. 'Naturally, I feel that the—next lady—should know what to expect.' "

So ended the threat to Mrs. Monroe's marriage.

By coincidence, two years later, in 1931, the hot-water fiasco actually took place. Thurber and Althea (temporarily reunited) had arranged a party at the Algonquin for the English painter Paul Nash and several New Yorker cartoonists Nash wanted to meet. Thurber writes to Anthony Bertram, Nash's biographer:

Twenty minutes before Paul arrived at our hotel apartment, I had started to take a bath, turned on the hot water full force and filled the bathroom with steam. It was too hot there for me to turn off the water, and when Paul arrived—we had left the hall door open—the living room was dense with steam. The hotel engineer had to turn off the water for a while in the whole building. . . . When the fog had cleared, there was [New Yorker artist] Otto Soglow sitting on a chair.

Though the Thurber Man, his foolish pretensions underscoring his vulnerabilities, is solidly launched as the inept victim of self and circumstance in the Monroe series, the dominating Thurber Woman has yet to appear. Althea, as Mrs. Monroe, is spared for the moment. For Monroe misses his wife, feels protective toward her, is grateful for her kindnesses to him. The reader feels sorry for her, given what she endures.

The arrival of Medve the french poodle by Railway Express leads to another domestic flap, in "The Monroes Find a Terminal." It is Mrs. Monroe's persistence that leads them to the dog after one futile search, but she graciously permits her husband to lecture her pompously: " 'You see, my dear, . . . you have to go at these things carefully and calmly and figure out logically where a dog, shipped from Chicago, would most naturally—' His wife smiled . . . and kissed him. 'My great big wonderful husband,' she said, gently."

Preparing for his wife's return from Europe, Monroe, in "The Imperturbable Spirit," tries to adopt a more masterful attitude; he reads a book on God and morals and tells himself that his wife is no more than a child who has to be looked after. His heart leaps up at first sight of her but he remembers "(oh keenly) . . . how she was wont to regard him as a person likely to 'go to pieces' over trifles. Well, she would find him a changed man." He kisses her firmly, which surprises her, as if "taken aback by a sudden change in the tactics of an old, old opponent." It doesn't take her long to figure out he has been "reading something."

When he learns she has illegal bottles of Benedictine in her luggage, panic ensues, all thought of imperturbability washed away in the cold waters of reality.

A snapshot of the move from the city to the Silvermine farmhouse is taken in "Mr. Monroe and the Moving Men." Mrs. Monroe is "terrifyingly" away, "terrifyingly" because Monroe had no experience in moving household goods. He remembers his wife leading him from room to room, pointing out what was to go into storage and what was to be sent to Connecticut, but he isn't sure about anything. "All that he could recall was that she had spoken in the slow, precise way in which she always spoke to him in a crisis, as if he were a little deaf or feeble-minded." The movers quickly develop contempt for him when his uncertainties become evident. He plays Mitty, imagining himself telling them: "See here, my men, . . . *I'm* in charge here—get that!" ("He loved himself in that rôle, and was often in it, in his day dreams.")

As a lifelong city boy, Thurber found the lonely farmhouse in Silvermine alien territory. As Monroe, he proudly kills a spider that has frightened his wife but goes to pieces when he goes to bed and, in the dark, realizes there's a bat in his room. (The Monroes sleep in separate rooms.) "Mr. Monroe Outwits a Bat" is reminiscent of Thurber's "Credos and Curios" account of his father's attempts to get a bat out of their house in Columbus. Neither outwitted the bat.

One of the more successful Monroe stories—and one of Sinclair Lewis's favorite "Thurbers"—is "Mr. Monroe Holds the Fort." On a weekend at the farmhouse, Monroe is left alone for an evening by his wife, who is attending her ailing mother. Convicts have escaped from a nearby prison. The old house creaks in the night. Monroe turns on all the lights—which his economy-minded wife has forbidden—and carries around a pistol he finds in the house. To his relief, Mrs. Monroe calls with a change of plans. She will catch a midnight train home. Monroe, fearful of new noises in the house, leaves for the station two hours early.

Mark Schorer, in his biography of Sinclair Lewis, quotes a servant who said Lewis "was terribly afraid to be alone" in his Vermont farm home. When his wife was away, a servant "would often have to sit up with him in the living room until two or three o'clock in the morning. . . . There were several servants elsewhere in the house, but he wanted someone in the room." When Lewis met Thurber in Bermuda in the mid-thirties, he praised "Mr. Monroe Holds the Fort," adding, "All of us are afraid to be alone in a country house at night, but you are the first one brave enough to admit it in print."

As a thirty-five-year-old (Thurber's age at the time) Jamesian protagonist in "The Middle Years," Monroe plans to call a lady he thought had flirted with him at a party. Mrs. Monroe, as is frequently the case, is out of town, but her pervasive presence is always there. ("Little Mrs. Monroe's mocking face kept preceding him wherever he went.") Changing his clothes preparatory to calling on the woman, he sees himself in a mirror and decides that "a tall thin man looks like an ass in socks and garters." He procrastinates, dozes off reading *The Golden Bowl*, and goes to bed. The Thurber Man, plagued by indecision and lack of nerve, rescuing himself by daydreams, trying to save face in the presence of a collected and realistic wife, is now on Thurber's center stage. Matters would grow worse between him and Althea, and the Thurber Woman, in his fiction and drawings, would never again get off as lightly as Mrs. Monroe does.

Ernest Angell was aware of Katharine's dalliance with White, and in late February 1929, roused to uncontrollable anger in one of their frequent quarrels, he struck Katharine, knocking her down. Resolved on divorce, she spent a couple of days in the Thurbers' apartment on West Eleventh Street, while Andy and Thurber moved her things to the Angells' summer home at Sneden's Landing. She lived there, seeing the children on weekends. Both White and Thurber visited her frequently, Thurber staying a week there with Jeannie and her pups during Althea's absence. In May, Ross and White saw Katharine off for Reno and the weeks of residence required by Nevada's divorce laws, the nation's most permissive at the time.

Katharine had asked White to care for Daisy, one of Jeannie's offspring the Thurbers had presented to Katharine. (*Is Sex Necessary?* is dedicated to the two female terriers, with Jeannie's name misspelled.)

The most of what Thurber owes E. B. White professionally resides in the circumstances surrounding the publication of their book, *Is Sex Necessary?* Largely through Katharine Angell's influence with Eugene Saxton of Harper & Bros., White's first book of poetry, *The Lady Is Cold*, had been published in early 1929, establishing an easy entry at Harper's for the submission of *Is Sex Necessary?* White's stubborn admiration for Thurber's drawings, which he insisted must illustrate the book, led to the discovery by Thurber, Ross, Saxton, Paul Nash, and the world at large that Thurber was an artist of merit and popular appeal. Even so, in view of the skepticism at Harper's White felt that an explanation of the art should be included in the book. In it, he assumes the major responsibility for Thurber's drawings:

> The inclusion, in this volume, of some fifty-two drawings by James Thurber, was on the whole intentional. Because, however, of the strong feeling of suspicion which they will arouse in certain quarters, it may not be amiss to offer some explanation. For this task I feel peculiarly fitted, for it was I who, during those trying months when the book was in the making, picked up the drawings night after night from the floor under Thurber's desk [and] by gaining the confidence of the charwomen, nightly redeemed countless other thousands of unfinished sketches from the huge waste baskets; and finally, it was my incredible willingness to go through with the business of "inking-in" the drawings (necessitated by the fact that they were done in such faint strokes of a broken pencil as to be almost invisible to the naked eye) that at last brought them to the point where they could be engraved and reproduced.

In 1950, Harper & Row reissued *Is Sex Necessary?* It has outlasted all the "deep and lugubrious books on sex and marriage" it originally spoofed. White, in his new introduction, writes:

> Thurber and I were neither more, nor less, interested in the subject of love and marriage than anybody else of our age in that era. I recall that we were both profoundly interested in earning a living, and I think we somehow managed, simultaneously, to arrive at the conclusion that (to borrow a phrase from Mr. Wolcott Gibbs) the heavy writers had got sex down and were breaking its arm. We were determined that sex should retain its high spirits. So we decided to spoof the medical books and, incidentally, to have a quick look at love and passion.

The two men wrote their sections of the book independently of one another during the first part of 1929, exchanging their chapters to avoid colli-

"At a certain point in every person's amours, the question arises: 'Am I in love, or am I merely inflamed by passion?'"

sion of thought and phrase, but, in the process, seeming to spark mutual inspiration. The subject was made to order for them. Despite White's disclaimer, the potential calamities and rewards of sex and marriage were much on their minds during the several months of composition. White was still seeing the unhappily married Katharine; the Thurbers had agreed to separate. Althea remembers that the floors of their apartment that spring were covered with Thurber's drawings for the book ("most of them done with fountain pen on writing paper").

In White's Foreword, he puts his finger on why writers on sex are ponderous and lengthy: they "expended their entire emotional energy in their writing and never had time for anything else. . . . They had been home writing; and meanwhile what was sex doing? Not standing still, you can better believe."

Even when it is apparent that Thurber is having fun, one can still detect in *Is Sex Necessary?* the bitter self-mockery that provides the element necessary to a book of the classical humorous tradition. That tradition, we are told —and told—carries humor and tragedy along a double track, coming from the same place and going in the same direction.

His "Preface" is chock-a-block with Benchley-type madness: Men and women have always sought to be together, he points out, and, at first, being unicellular, there was no conflict.

Later the cell separated, or began living apart, for reasons which are not clear even today, although there is considerable talk. Almost immediately the two halves of the original cell began experiencing a desire to unite again—usually with a half of some other cell. This urge has survived down to our time. Its commonest manifestations are marriage, divorce, neuroses, and . . . gun-fire.

Though marriage is a perfect thing, he goes on, it can't be applied to present-day emotional relationships of men and women, and perhaps should be abandoned. The problem began when Man began to idealize woman, thus subordinating himself to her. "He fell down on his knees, the pitiable idiot, and grasped her about the waist."

The Frenchman's idea, Thurber writes, is to get the woman interested in him as a male; the American man's idea is to point out the beauty of the stars and hope the woman makes the connection. In the nineteenth century, because love, marriage, and children stood for progress, he continues in chapter 1, there was an absence of neurosis and nervous breakdown "barring a slight flare-up just before the Mexican and Civil wars." When the race between the sexes leaped from an economic to an emotional playing field, women resorted to such sex-evasionist and delaying tactics as fudge-making and playing charades, which kept other people in the room.

Because they were getting nowhere with women, "men began to act jumpy and strange." Woman took on "the proportions of an unattainable deity." There were "almost no achievements of value" in this period. "Outside affairs of all kinds were neglected. Men retired to their dens and were not seen for days. The panic of 1907 was a direct result."

In another chapter, Thurber discusses feminine types, among whom we may be glimpsing both Althea and Ann Honeycutt. The "Don't, dear" type seems an obvious reference to Althea:

> No matter what he does, she will say, "Don't, dear." This type is a homemaker. Unless the man wants a home made for him within a very short time, it is better for him to . . . depart. The type is common in the Middle West, particularly in university towns.

Althea also seems to fit partly the persuasive type tall enough to twist the buttonhole of his suit, demonstrative in her affections, but who can be "restless and discontented with the married state, largely because she will want to go somewhere that her husband does not want to go, or will not believe he has been to the places that he says he just came from. It is well to avoid this type."

Honeycutt seems to come in for her share of Thurber's vengefulness, probably qualifying as the

> phenomenal modern type, a product of these strange post-war years . . . the girl who gets right down to a discussion of sex on the occasion of her first meeting with a man, but then goes on to betray a great deal of alarm and aversion to the married state. This is the 'I-can't-go-through-with-it' Type. Many American virgins fall within this classification. . . . If involved with, or even merely presented to, a woman of this type, no man in his right mind will do anything except reach for his hat. Science does not know what is the matter with these women, or whether anything is the matter. . . . One thing is sure, they are never the Quiet Type. They talk your arm off.

White writes for both himself and Thurber in "The Sexual Revolution" chapter, for White was just as uncertain and insecure in the face of the opposite sex. Man, unable to make himself attractive to Woman, he writes, as the male lion and peacock can do, must "develop attractive personal traits to offset his dull appearance." He must say "funny things," learn "to smoke [and] earn money. . . . In the course of making himself attractive to Woman by developing himself mentally, he inadvertently became so intelligent an animal that he saw how comical the whole situation was." But White seemed to know where he was inevitably heading; he had already discussed marriage with Katharine Angell. "In order to contemplate marriage," he writes, "it was necessary for a man to decide on One Particular Woman."

A married man soon becomes claustrophobic, writes Thurber in the "What Every Young Wife Should Know" chapter. Here is the male's plea for succor from Woman's domestic tyranny, a cry for help from the husband who forgets to empty the pan of water under the refrigerator, causing the ceiling in the apartment below to fall, sending the woman downstairs into hysterics; who cannot distinguish between guest towels and those that are to be used; who walks on freshly painted floors, or doesn't know where things go when they move. "If she would only realize that things which are easy and uncomplicated to her are strange and mysterious to her husband," Thurber begs.

Is Sex Necessary? may have served only as a diversion for White—as Walter Winchell pointed out, columnist White gave his own answer to the book's title by marrying Katharine Angell a week after it was published—but it is the opening gun in Thurber's lifelong war between the sexes. Harper, caught bringing out the book in November 1929, a month after the stock market crashed, gingerly held the first printing to twenty-five hundred copies. But it jumped onto the best-seller lists and stayed there well into 1930. It went through twenty-five printings in four months and had sold around forty thousand copies by the end of the first year. It gained its authors national recognition and the most money either had earned from his writing. For its re-issue in 1950, Thurber and White were asked to write a new introduction. White agreed; Thurber declined, but wrote an amusing commentary that White included, ending the subject of the twenty-one-year-old book with a simple request from Thurber: "If you know anything about sex, let me know."

34

That Seal in the Bedroom

In the case of a man who cannot draw, but keeps on drawing anyway, practice pays in meager coin for what it takes away. It would have taken away even more but for the firm and impolite interference of Andy White, who came upon me one day fifteen years ago laboring over cross-hatching and other subtleties of draughtsmanship beyond the reach of my fingers. "Good God," he said, "don't do that! If you ever became good you'd be mediocre."

—"Author's Memoir," *The Seal in the Bedroom*

Is Sex Necessary? was not only the world inauguration of White and Thurber as humorists of a substance and potential to be watched, it first put Thurber's drawings—excellent ones—between book covers. To Ross's incredulity. "Where the hell did you get the idea you could *draw?*" he greeted Thurber with annoyance, after seeing the book. He disliked publishers, convinced that they all lived high off the hog with money unfairly withheld from their authors. And here were his two prize staff contributors on the best-seller lists, rewarding a publisher with drawings *not previously shown The Magazine*. (Katharine Angell and Ross had seen the book's text; the *New Yorker* published a short version of one of Thurber's chapters six weeks before the book came out.)

"Actually, Ross had seen a drawing of mine weeks before," Thurber says. "I used to pencil figures and situations on our yellow copy paper while thinking about what to write. I'd throw them away, most of them missing the basket. Andy was tidier than I was and would pick them up. One he liked showed a seal on a rock with little figures in the distance, the seal saying, 'Hmmm, explorers.' That was when Admiral Byrd and others were exploring the Polar regions. I guess the joke was that, with all the explorers there, they had become a common sight to the native wildlife.

"White was the first to see any value in my doodlings. He inked in the lines of the seal cartoon and sent it to the art conference. It came back with a note and sketch from Rea Irvin, the art director—Rea was trying to be helpful—showing how a seal's whiskers really look. White resubmitted mine, saying this was how a *Thurber* seal's whiskers looked, but Ross turned it down. After the book was a success, he denied that he had seen it. He asked me for it, but I'd thrown it away. He wanted me to do it again, but more than a year went by before I tried it. This time the rock the seal was on began to look like the headboard of a bed, so I finished it that way and put a man and woman in the bed. Ross bought it. By that time he'd published a couple dozen of my drawings. After this one ran, Benchley sent me a telegram saying it was the funniest cartoon caption the magazine had ever run. But it was the kind of accident in draughtsmanship that accounts for a lot of my drawings."

The famous cartoon, published in January 1932, has been explained by Robert Coates as the fantasized fulfillment of a man's desire to be right just once in an argument with his wife.

"Charles Poore once reviewed a book of mine in the *New York Times* and said that in my work I take my subconscious on benders," Thurber continued. "And another critic suggested that when I found I couldn't rise above my subconscious, I made a career out of it. A woman psychiatrist once told me she thought she could cure me of my drawings. I assume she had decided they come from a highly disturbed mind, and she's probably right.

"People have seen sinister symbolism in my drawing of the house that

"All right, Have It Your Way—You Heard a Seal Bark!"

merges into the head of a woman. I never know how those things turn out as they do, so we may as well blame the unconscious, I guess. The better ones seem to come like that, when I just start drawing lines, not knowing where I'm going, until finally I have something and then think up a caption to go with it. For instance, that drawing began with a woman's head. I didn't know it was going to be part of a house. When it came out that way, I put the man in front of it. Thirty percent of my cartoons are drawn like that. Those I draw deliberately, with a caption in mind, I have less luck with."

(In this 1948 interview, he still spoke of drawing in the present tense, knowing the while that his days of turning out marketable drawings were finished.)

In February 1929, Elliott Nugent accepted a Hollywood contract that began his successful career as motion-picture actor, writer, and director. "Talking pictures" had just been introduced, and Thurber, who felt that Nugent was betraying himself and legitimate theater, took a satirical swing at the primi-

Home

tive sound technology. "The Roaring Talkies" (*New Yorker*, August 24, 1929), written as a screenplay, directs the actors to talk inside bank vaults and into bathtubs and dishpans—thus accounting for their tinny voices.

It would be nearly a decade before the two friends of college days were reunited on the West Coast in writing *The Male Animal*. Over beers in a bar next to the Lamb's Club, they discussed the courses of their careers. Nugent defended his Hollywood contract by saying he wanted to follow Plato's counsel—to be a good actor, writer, director, husband, father, citizen, yes, but also "a happy fellow who made enough money to live well, enjoy life, play some tennis, and have some friends."

Thurber thought this impure motivation. He said he was an Aristotelian who believed in absolutes, and the essential thing he wanted to be was a very fine writer. To that end he was perfectly willing to sacrifice comfort and temporary happiness. "In a way," Nugent wrote years later, "each of us followed his philosophy through life." Probably so. Though Thurber obtained a share of good times, friends, professional recognition, and happiness, it was largely the by-product of his concentrated efforts as a writer. His drawing, he insisted to the end, came too easily for it to be anything but an accidental adjunct to his prose.

Until November 1929, Thurber had been in a sulk regarding Minnette; in forbidding him to visit her, she had also taken him to task for typing his signature to his letter: "If you can't write long hand why don't you [at least] sign your name?" But feeling expansive and forgiving from the publication of *Is Sex Necessary?* Thurber ended his boycott:

> After thinking it over for eight months, I have decided not to let you have the last word. . . . I was more hurt by your silly anger at the way I signed my letter than at anything you wrote. . . . Trouble is, I *never* have ink in my office—they dont allow me to because I used to spill it on manuscripts, visitors, suits, etc. . . . I can promise that I have grown very sane and mature . . . and will never write childish letters again. . . . Nor ever talk of love, tangles, life etc. . . .
>
> I have written a book with another guy. I'll send you one, and write in it, if you want me to. Elliott is in the movies for two years or more on contract . . . ; Althea is raising poodles, Siamese cats and Scotties.

He signed the letter in ink, in five different ways. Minnette sent a friendly reply and Thurber wrote her a few days later of the "beautiful defense of Althea" he had sent to his mother, putting to rest Mame's "silly and baseless suspicions, charges and dislikes, which a boy's mother has for the girl he marries." He enclosed several reviews of *Is Sex Necessary?* and told Minnette he was "all set up by being, suddenly, a really important figure about town!" As to Althea:

> Ours is a relationship at once charming, fine, and hurting. I get a great pain in the heart at times. But doesn't everyone somehow in life . . . make a great misstep, [and] go along with a big regret?" . . . It gives me a real reason to be courageous—and more and more I see courage as one of the finest virtues. But how hard it is. . . .
>
> Generally, I am pretty well confused, but also I have got discipline. I am the captain of my soul—but (as someone said) "I had more fun when I was cabin boy!"

Reminiscent of his early letters to Nugent, those awkward studies in self-exposure, he continues:

> In the place of indulgences I have got dedications. They are harder,
> and not so exciting . . . but they have a certain satisfying sweetness.
> . . . I live in dread only of hurting, in the hope only of helping. I really
> don't think of myself enough. I have had to make so many compromises.
> But now I rather like the man who has come out of them. He really has
> some of the splendidness now that once he merely thought he had! And
> yet . . . he has some of those terrible old weaknesses and irresponsibili-
> ties still.

Minnette responded warmly, and in a few days Thurber was recklessly writing her a letter of romantic come-on—as "childish" and larded with the very "talk of love, tangles, life etc" he had just vowed never to touch upon again. He couldn't be sure, he writes, if she were favoring or still opposing his coming to Seattle.

He was seeking a cure for the distress he was feeling over Althea, but a visit to Minnette, he writes her, could create a deeper malady, "which in turn would have to be cured." He doesn't know what he will do in his present situation, he tells her:

> I might do anything almost at any minute . . . if I ever get economi-
> cally free of responsibilities, which sometime soon I may. Me released
> from an anchorage would be a menace. Sometimes I want to see you
> because I want to see what you're like; sometimes because I want to see
> what you think I am like; sometimes . . . (and mostly) because (and
> you know it damn well too) I want to make love to you. . . . I am
> afraid to look on the shining face of that possibility; I am afraid the walls
> of Jericho would tumble down, that extras [newspapers] would be got
> out, that people would go to pieces, that the moon would never set and
> there'd be no noon-hour again—just nighttime or the memory of night-
> time. . . . Perhaps for a wife and mother of your standing and experi-
> ence, these things seem improbable . . . but you know what our words
> and glances can do to improbable things. (At this point the editor came
> in with a suggestion for a change in a [Talk] story I wrote about a man
> who deals in old used gin and scotch bottles. . . .) That . . . is a
> perfect instance of what happens. In the midst of moonlight on Jericho,
> a woman gets a pain in her stomach . . . or one of Althea's puppies
> gets a pain in its stomach. One is snapped back into his greatest reality

—the reality of a long marriage—the solidest reality we know. . . . We're always in the squirrel cage, going round and round, theorizing and knowing that theory is nothing. Thus we'll just let it go on until the force of life, or the inertia of it, does something to us, or doesn't do anything.

Isn't that so, Garfield 7844, and are you still home Mondays?

The signature, "Jim," was handwritten.

Though early in her marriage Minnette had destroyed the naive, innocent letters Thurber had written her from Washington and Paris, she now valued him as a budding celebrity and saved all but his letter that first asked if he could visit her in Seattle. Minnette's marriage would last fourteen years longer before she divorced and married, when in her sixties, a former O.S.U. classmate who, like Thurber, had never got Minnette, as coed, off his mind.

Thurber, from eighth grade on, had always been in love with love, a common affliction of fiction writers and poets. As White wrote in *Is Sex Necessary?*, possibly with Thurber—as well as himself—in mind:

I have seldom met an individual of literary tastes . . . in whom the writing of love was not directly attributable to the love of writing.

A person of this sort falls terribly in love, but in the end it turns out that he is more bemused by a sheet of white paper than a sheet of white bed linen. He would rather leap into print with his lady than leap into bed with her.

White would know; much of his courtship of Katharine was in the form of poems he sent newspaper columnists for publication.

More help had arrived for Thurber in the Talk of the Town department. By late 1927, there was Robert Coates, who worked as a Talk writer for a year before doing literary criticism. Coates was a novelist and intellectual who had made his name in the Dada movement in Europe. One of his books was the movement's first novel in English, *The Eater of Darkness*. In Paris he knew Joel Sayre, who introduced him to Thurber, who, when Coates returned to America, introduced him to Ross. He and Thurber became the closest of friends—he was Thurber's best man at Thurber's marriage to Helen Wismer —until Coates, in later years, left a wife Thurber and Helen loved and married someone Helen disliked. Coates, a sweet-dispositioned man universally prized, became literary and, later, art critic for the magazine and one of its better short-story writers.

"Thurber was always getting a new man hired," says Rogers Whitaker, "and they were usually pretty good. Ross was always hiring someone he had just met in a bar. They never lasted long."

Geoffrey Hellman joined in 1929, writing about court games. He also gave out Talk assignments and took the reporters' notes to Thurber and White. ("They were both gods to me," he says.) A socialite, Hellman strolled the halls in morning coat, striped trousers, gray tie, and boutonniere; he was a particularly incongruous sight when he was seated in his small dowdy office, with its battered yard-sale furniture.

Charles Cooke was so indefatigable and productive a reporter for Talk that he held the job from 1930 to 1942. His beginning salary of thirty-five dollars per week rose to only sixty dollars in twelve years, a testament of his devotion to, and pleasure in, his work, as well as to the New Yorker's general disinclination at that time to develop, encourage, and properly reward a farm team of homegrown contributors. Ross preferred raiding other organizations for established writers.

Talk ideas were discussed and passed upon in Wednesday-morning meetings; those accepted were put on index cards and placed in a file box. The reporters chose from what was left after the writers more firmly entrenched in the establishment had had their pick of the lot. When James M. Cain was there as a short-lived Miracle Man, he "set up a system of red and green tabs on the inventory card files," says Katharine White, "and gave them to Raymond Holden to operate. But Holden was color-blind, couldn't tell red from green, and the system collapsed for a time." (Holden was a poet whom Ross made a Talk editor.) Red was to indicate a message that was timely; green less so. Thurber's solution to the color-blindness problem, that the "urgent" tab be shaped like an alarm clock, was dismissed by Ross as another attempt to kid him.

Cooke was pleased to be rewritten by White and Thurber but smarted when second-guessed by what he calls "lesser talent." "Thurber would rewrite page one of a Talk story sometimes a score of times until it was letter-perfect," Cooke recalls, "then rewrite it again because, he would explain, a fly speck on the page, if it was over a period, could be mistaken for a colon. If it was somewhere near a comma, Thurber would worry that the proof reader would think it was a semicolon. He was hopelessly fastidious, which was why it was hard for him to take anyone's editing of his finished work. As far as he was concerned, his manuscript was complete when he passed it in. He knew if Ross had tampered with a single comma. Ross enjoyed applying his own natural nervousness to editing; he'd wrestle with a Talk story like a wild-animal trainer. But so would Thurber, who, by then, had an office personality nearly as strong as Ross's. They had terrible arguments. Ross was coddling him by then, for he realized Thurber's worth to the magazine. They both needed one another emotionally, I always thought. They were a productive symbiosis; two species living together uneasily but to their mutual advantage. Still, Ross always came out on top. In the end it came down to 'Whose magazine is this?' "

Ross enjoyed "the hot arguments" with Thurber, says Jane Grant. Ross spent more time on Talk than any other department, and Talk meetings interested him more than the art sessions; also, he disliked artists, except Rea Irvin, Ralph Barton, Peter Arno, and a few others. As a writer, he never could spell many words—his letters were proofed by his secretary; he used the dictionary to check others' spellings, but never his own. Though he regularly improved pieces by questioning their authors and challenging their statements, some of his changes in Talk copy were so awkward that Thurber rewrote them and forged Ross's monogram of approval to the manuscript. They argued over grammar. Ross was wary of any use of phrase or clause not specifically ruled on by Fowler. Thurber believed, for example, that to praise something as a "fairly good" thing—good enough only to be fair—was a kind of negative; "pretty good" was preferable, but Fowler hadn't covered the point. Often, in Ross's absence, Thurber sneaked "pretty good" into enough pieces to show Ross later and claim that its continued usage had gained it respectable precedent.

"Thurber rewrote at least a hundred of my stories," Cooke continues, "and got sore at only one—about a summer snowbank someone had seen on West Street. The snow had been cleaned out of some refrigerator freight cars. Trying to make a Talk story out of something that could be explained in a sentence infuriated Thurber. He sent it to Hellman with a note: 'Take this goddam thing the hell out of my sight.' Hellman passed it on to me.

"Thurber would often call me on the phone about a point in one of my stories. It might have been one about a flagpole sitter on top of Grand Central, or a cockroach race someone was holding. White was an elegant writer; Thurber was guttier; he took more chances. They both did originals sometimes; if they got their teeth into a good story, it was extra money for them."

The magazine, remembers Cooke, was dominated by two forces: the "powerful" Katharine White and Ross, who hated to be stopped in the hall for any reason but especially to be told about an idea. "How the hell would I know!" he would bellow. "Put it on paper!"

Thurber, Wolcott Gibbs writes, was "superb" at Talk writing, "since his mind worked on a queer secondary level, and while the facts were usually there, they had a way of suggesting something a little dramatic and deranged or supernatural about his subjects."

"Thurber was especially great at writing items to fit layout requirements," says Hobart Weekes, who eventually read each week's entire issue for error and repetition of phrase. "Once a whole Talk department for an issue was lost completely. Other times Ross would tear the whole thing apart. Thurber always had to put it back together and invent replacements. He was expert at it. 'How many anecdotes do you need?' he'd ask me. 'How big do you want this?' Nothing stung Thurber like an incompetent check of facts, or insensitive editing; he regarded either as personal and damaging interference with his life. As White became more interested in Notes and Comment, Thurber did more and more of the Talk pieces. White had a tank of guppies that he studied while thinking. I always thought that put him one up on Thurber, who had only a picture of Max Eastman on his wall."

"It was more than a picture," says Cooke. "Thurber had taken a grease pencil to it, blacked out a couple of Eastman's teeth, and pulled Eastman's pretty face into unsightly pouches. It looked worse than Dorian Gray's portrait."

"One Friday when Thurber turned in his Talk copy to me to process for the printers," Weekes recalls, "he gave me a number to call if I had a question. I did. I called the number, and to my horror, Katharine White answered. It was the Whites' apartment. Thurber wasn't there and wasn't expected. I learned later that he and Nugent had taken the train to Columbus without telling anybody. I'll never know if he had had a dinner date at the Whites and broke it, or if he deliberately wanted me to get into trouble. I did. Mrs. White made it known to me in no uncertain terms that she was not to be called at home on business matters. Though she was properly jealous of her privacy, she really cared about people and tried to put them at ease, even when she couldn't. Philip Wrenn used to provide Talk tips to us and became a sports columnist for the magazine later. He was very shy, and once when Mrs. White invited him to dinner at her home, she told him, 'Philip, please call me Katharine.' And Phil meekly replied, 'All right, Mrs. White.' I think most of us would have reacted the same way."

Thurber at times lent legitimacy to Ross's paranoid belief that his staff was always trying to "put one over" on him. Once, in Andy White's absence, Thurber was handling newsbreaks and invented an item he attributed to a nonexistent publication, simply to work in a pun he was proud of. The mythical paper's item was that Oswego, New York, General Sherman's birthplace, had no memorial to its native son, to which Thurber adds, "Oswego marching through Georgia?" Ross, too late, recognized it as a hoax, remembering that Sherman was born in Ohio, and gave Thurber an angry bawling out—with justification. Such shenanigans on a magazine admired for its accuracy were those of an employee on his way to being dangerous. Thurber realized it at once, took Ross's rebuke to heart, and never did it again.

In her bitter rebuttals of Thurber's *The Years with Ross*, Katharine White asks, "Why does [Thurber] persistently try to make Ross such an ignoramus?" There *are* hints in the book of deliberate mischievousness by Thurber, of his yielding his obligations as memoirist to get a laugh at Ross's expense. Here, Thurber describes Ross touring Paris with him in the summer of 1938:

> When it came my turn to show Ross my Paris, he said, "I don't want to go to Sainte Chapelle, I've been there," and he added something that comes back to me now as "Stained glass is damned embarrassing." He wouldn't get out of the taxi when we stopped in front of Notre Dame, but he opened the cab door and stared at it. "That cathedral has never been sandblasted," he told me.

In the June 8, 1929, *New Yorker* is an obscure Thurber casual, "Two Ships Bring Americans of Note and English Author [By Our Own Ship-News Reporter]." As the reporter, Thurber pretends to interview passengers on a ship just arrived from Europe. Thurber's casual predates the Babbittry of Senator Claghorn on the old Fred Allen radio show, who, on his return from abroad, complained that there were "nothing but a lot of foreigners over there." Here, Thurber's fictitious "former governor of Oklahoma," when asked what he thinks of Europe, reports that "the art galleries and buildings generally are old. Many of them occupy expensive sites at a great economic loss. Some cathedrals haven't been sandblasted for twenty years, I should say." (Thurber lets the English novelist off no easier; the author, in America for the first time, states that "there is no art in the United States to speak of," and that he will stay at the McAlpin Hotel and write a novel about Harlem life and return to England in three weeks.)

The similarity of Ross's know-nothing comments in *The Years with Ross* to those of Thurber's fictitious governor three decades earlier rates more than the *New Yorker*'s "Funny Coincidence Department"; it raises a troublesome question or two. Ross knew Paris from his months there in World War I; he took the usual doughboy tours of the galleries and cathedrals. If, indeed, he behaved with such cultural insensitivity, it might have been for Thurber's benefit. Jane Grant writes that Ross often played the dumbbell to watch others make fools of themselves:

> "Why did you make those zany remarks this evening?" I'd protest when I got him alone. I'd heard him making some ridiculous statements to the new "Jesus."
>
> "It built him up, made him think he was smarter than me. If he couldn't see through what I was saying, he's just a damned fool and I might as well know it first as last."
>
> He insisted so firmly that he never read anything . . . or "Who's Willa Cather?"—that some of them began to believe him. I warned him they would, but he took a fiendish delight in acting the goon or playing stooge.

Again, Thurber writes of Ross: "Neither I nor any other man ever heard Ross tell a dirty story." It was the most baffling remark in *The Years with Ross* to St. Clair McKelway. "Ross told lots of dirty stories," he says, "though he was embarrassed to hear a dirty story told in front of a woman. If he never told one in front of Thurber, he knew Thurber didn't go in for them." Katharine White, in her fierce record of rebuttal, even insists that Ross told *her* "funny, dirty stories." Nobody seems to have straightened out Thurber on the point after the book was published. Until his death he talked of Ross in just the anecdotal way he wrote of him. He could mimic Ross perfectly, but he may have misread several important aspects about the man. If Ross successfully teased Thurber throughout their twenty-four years together into believing he was the unsophisticated backwoods rube he probably suspected Thurber thought him to be, he paid for it by becoming the lasting literary victim of his own charade. And if so, the unfairness is twofold, for Thurber's genuine appreciation of his years with Ross comes through in too many ways to be questioned. In 1957, he writes Russel Crouse: "Surviving Ross was an ordeal and it took me a long time. Then it became a pleasure and a blessing, too . . . to work for him."

Thurber was his own best publicity agent after the appearance of *Is Sex Necessary?*. He accepted invitations to speak at dinner meetings. In "Memoirs of a Banquet Speaker," Thurber is gripped by an uneasy feeling that he is in the wrong banquet room. He inquires of those beside him and learns that each has a different idea as to what the occasion is. The first speaker worsens Thurber's fears:

His nervous condition and incoherent remarks obviously upset the toastmaster who, all we speakers were instantly aware, was not absolutely sure that he was at the right banquet himself.

He wrote a publicity item for the *Chicago Tribune* that appeared a few days after the publication date of *Is Sex Necessary?* in which he said that he and White believed there would be no more sex after the first of the year, "which is why we wanted the book brought out." Americans never understood sex or drinking, he explains, and tend to do away with what they don't understand —which explains their acceptance of Prohibition. Sex, which Americans work too hard to have time for, will be replaced by "games, anagrams, yo yo, puzzles . . . and football."

The stream of bread-and-butter casuals by Thurber flowed throughout 1930, some too lightweight for book collection, in Thurber's judgment, but even those have their moments: Thurber's inability to get a telephone bill paid; crime news in which there are so many names and addresses that the facts of the story are lost; satires of children's literature.

He offers his impression of a noisy "literary tea" that sounds like what today would be taken off a tape recorder left in a corner of a room crowded with people. (". . . tongue in his cheek I happen to know married the second wife of her third husband's biggest hoax that's been pulled in the last twenty years if you want to know in less than five hours by a girl down at Harper's never wrote a line before in her life I don't doubt that jumbled up the pages somehow so the whole book was published backwards author raised all kinds of hell but got such swell reviews they hadda keep it quiet if you can tie that . . ." (Thurber regarded the gag of mistakenly reading, writing, or printing books backwards as a particularly durable one, to be used again and again.)

By 1930, Admiral Byrd's airborne explorations at the South Pole were occupying the headlines, and Thurber pretends to cover the Rear Admiral's report to a U.S. Senate committee. The Senators wonder whether there is oil under the Antarctic ice cap. Byrd replies that if there were, "it would be impossible to get at unless the region became tropical or semitropical again, as it once was."

"How long would that take?" asked Senator Grosbeak.
"Several hundred million years," said Byrd. There was a long silence and all the senators looked slightly unhappy.
"It might take only *one* hundred million years," said the Rear Admiral, reassuringly.

Byrd tries to cheer up the disappointed legislators by discussing ocean measurements. "We found some very deep spots," he tells them. Inquires a Senator:

> "You have claimed one hundred and twenty-five thousand square miles of land for the United States, and we'd like to be able to give people some idea of what we've got down there. . . .
>
> "Ice is on it," said Byrd. . . . "We claimed one area of floating sheet ice which is as large as France."
>
> "That seems like a lot of sheet ice," said Senator Grosbeak. "We don't need that much sheet ice, do we?" . . .
>
> "There's a great deal more work to be done down there," said Byrd. "I'm going back again, of course."
>
> "Ah—yes, that's quite right," said Senator Vanfield. ". . . If I were you I wouldn't claim any more. . . . I think we have enough."

There is an early appearance of the Thurber Woman in "Mr. Higgins' Breakdown"; she drags her husband to a psychiatrist because, like Thurber, he forgets social engagements. The analyst decides that this reflects the husband's desire to evade responsibility.

Thurber imagines an American *coup d'état* in the manner of South American revolutions:

> The White House guards, several of them garbed in their old Civil War uniforms, beat off an attack by police who in turn beat off an attack by U.S. Marines under command of General Smedly O. Butler. General Butler announced himself as President. His action was later denied, and a report was current that Hoover had not resigned, but was fast asleep.

Thurber next needles the theater gossip columnists who track the restless movement of Broadway plays from one theater to another. He was an ardent theatergoer himself, kept late hours, and was usually awakened by the hotel maids in the morning, who always looked in on him and exclaimed, "My God . . . this bird's still in bed, if ya can believe that."

His first "Reporter At Large" piece, on a police academy, appeared. In it, he describes a fatally wounded policeman who manages to scrawl out the license number of his killer's car. Crime and the city's menaces, whether in May or any other time, were frequently on Thurber's mind.

Even his *New Yorker* rejects were selling. *Harper's* took "Thumbs Up," a carefree defense of the thumb as more useful than the fingers. In those last euphoric days of a boom economy running headlong for a fall, Thurber was selling humorous essays to *The Magazine of Business*, posing as a financial neophyte expert, at times writing Benchley-style nonsense. The 1928 presidential elections, he writes, clearly affected business and industry. "Business men everywhere were afraid that somebody was going to be elected and, as it turned out, their fears were well grounded." Thurber predates industrial concerns over worker fatigue at repetitive manufacturing tasks. To alleviate assembly-line monotony, he suggests that after every twenty-fifth auto part, something different is allowed to come down the line—a ship's keel, or a Scottish terrier.

He believes nothing inspires business confidence like large figures, and though he forgets what the figure originally applied to, he proclaims the business outlook is $97,000,000. A picture accompanying the article shows the author with a mustache, holding a Scottish terrier.

He was still writing to make a living, first and foremost, but a greater attention to quality, before he relinquished a piece beyond retrieval, was already setting in. Though much of the crop of casuals he sowed in 1930 was unharvested for book collection—a baker's dozen of them—the year produced a couple of Thurber perennials: "The Remarkable Case of Mr. Bruhl," and "If Grant Had Been Drinking at Appomattox."

Earlier that year he was invited to Columbus for the Golden Jubilee of Phi Kappa Psi—he and Nugent were among "the 10 or 12 distinguished alumni of the old frat's 50 years," he wrote Minnette. Nugent was unable to attend; his mother had just died suddenly in New York, bringing Nugent and his father from California by plane. Thurber's local volunteer press agent in Columbus was his friend McNulty, who wrote a column for the *Columbus Citizen* entitled "Ballyhoo," and kept central Ohio informed of Thurber's activities. He reprinted Thurber's letter to him, in which Thurber had listed the times Columbus appeared in current books—including Edmund Wilson's new novel, *I Thought of Daisy*, and Malcolm Cowley's book of verse, *Blue Juanita*, in which Cowley says "Columbus is a whistle in the night." ("Don't consider the impermanence of the sound," Thurber advises McNulty. "Consider its loveliness.") Thurber takes care to point out that Columbus is also mentioned in *Is Sex Necessary?*, promising to send McNulty an inscribed copy, "together with a picture of me in a straw hat and white duck pants, which is what I wore in part of my old vaudeville act, The Six Flying McNulty Brothers & Sons Company."

In Columbus, with *Is Sex Necessary?* a best-seller, Thurber received a celebrity's red-carpet treatment. Nevertheless, he later claimed that the students at his fraternity house recognized neither him nor his name, which they pronounced "Thorber." (His claim that everyone got his name wrong would become one of his frequent lines.) In his column, McNulty attributes to Thurber "a long-legged mind which continually straddles the fence between the serious and the ridiculous." A number of young ladies, now matrons in the Columbus area, McNulty continues, remember Thurber as

> Ohio State's greatest romancer. He's now widely known as the world's greatest romancer. Whereas he used to be mistaken for a psychology professor with his hair needing cutting, the new Thurber has his hair cut and wears a double-breasted blue serge suit, freshly brushed. He is one of Manhattan's bright young men. . . . He's the most wined and dined, sought after, and talked about young man in New York City. He is introduced night after night as "speaker of the evening."

Thurber spoke to a 9:00 A.M. journalism class and at a luncheon the Sigma Delta Chis held in his honor. In front of the students, he smoked cigarettes, stroked his mustache, looked over his horn-rimmed glasses, and told them that he had bought a lot of drawing paper and India ink when he heard he was to illustrate *Is Sex Necessary?*, but that White had taken them away from him and given him an envelope and a sawed-off pencil, remarking, "Who do you think you are, an artist?" One advantage of working for the *New Yorker*, he went on, was being able to parlay misfortune into profit. White had been fined two dollars for walking Katharine's dog, Daisy, without a muzzle, he told them; White wrote up the incident as a Talk anecdote and received twenty-five dollars, a net gain of twenty-three.

When a student from the *Lantern* asked Thurber if he thought sex was necessary for college students, he simply said he didn't know. He looked sad and added, "I've never given out a decent interview in my life and when I worked on a paper I used to hate people who couldn't talk. I suppose it is just punishment for me that I can't think of a darned thing to say to a reporter now."

Thurber couldn't relinquish his earlier dreams and hopes regarding Althea. Despite the weekends in Silvermine, he felt himself on the outside looking in, and blamed himself.

"Althea's lovely French poodle won first prize in the Westminster Dog Show," he writes Minnette in early 1930, "a triumph which unsettled her so she almost cried when the judges handed her the blue ribbon. I was as thrilled as the day I made Sphinx!" But things were not going well between them, and he confides that he may go to Europe to try to get over his unhappiness:

> Althea still plays a great part in my life. She is still, except for her dogs, unanchored. I wish she were not. We have some moments that tear me to pieces—for this after all was my undertaking, this girl. I have done more to her life, actually, than to anyone else's and I feel responsible about it. You see, one can't go back, one must go ahead on what he has built. And I live so much in what is past—the realized past and the unrealized, but we live by what we have been through, in accordance with the life of the person to whom we have given . . . those years when we were growing into final maturity. There is . . . no real starting over again; there are the shadows and the monuments of the past always. . . . My going away to Europe would be an effort to escape, to start over, to [find] a new happiness. I know that I could do that only partially. Sometime in France I would turn a corner that she and I turned, under such different conditions, five years ago. The emotions of that day would come back, and I would be that man for I dont know how long.

And a few weeks later:

> The Althea situation is as complicated as ever. The next man hasn't showed up for her. I'm standing by, bolstering, cheering, comforting. She's quite wonderful, but at times lonely, herself against the world on a Connecticut farm.

With Minnette's renewed interest in Thurber, she no longer discouraged the confidences he poured upon her. She had told him he would always have to have a dream girl in his life, he reminds her, and he agrees. She hears about Honey:

> I may be married again—although I'm not divorced yet—to the Louisiana girl I think I have mentioned once or twice; she is really exactly right for me—or shall I say, nearly so. What is exactly right for me would take too long to explain . . . but I do know that I was never cut out to be a bachelor and to live a sort of house-to-house life. . . . She is reminiscent of you—quite a lot—the contour of her face, her voice, and the way she moves about. Perhaps you dont want to know any more than that—perhaps not even that. . . .

When I was younger a dedication to some woman seemed enough. It isn't. Women find out sooner than we do, that a dedication to one person will not serve. It doesn't finally cover all the edges of our desires and our longings; our feet of clay stick out from under the covers and get cold, or else our shoulders do. . . .

Our friends—those few who know me best—are for her, because they know she understands me, because they know she appreciates what I need, what I ought to do (intellectually anyway).

It still mattered greatly what others thought of his choice of a woman. And it was certainly true—"a dedication to one person" would not serve for the distraught Thurber. A comely actress, Paula Trueman, had also drawn his ardent interest, he tells Minnette:

She is quite famous here . . . an actress of, as the *Herald-Tribune* critic said, "an infinite charm." . . . I've long liked her intensely from orchestra seats. Many times in the past year I've told Althea "I have the oddest desire to look up Paula Trueman." "Well, look her up," said Mrs. Thurber. Three weeks ago I got, in my office mail, a [note from Paula] asking if I had ever seen her, telling me what kind of things she did—as if anybody in N. Y. didn't know!—and asking if I would write a skit for her to use in a big Broadway revue soon to go into rehearsal. She said she took the liberty of introducing herself to me because she had long admired my "delightful sketches" in the New Yorker! . . .

She lives at 61 West 12, I at 65 West 11. I can see her front windows from my back ones—never knew she lived near.

I went down one May night and rang her bell (by appointment) (Incidentally, 3 people had told me she looks like Honey . . .) She lives in a top floor apt. with a big sky-light and a little cat. I knew when I saw her standing there that it was going to be just too bad. It was. In 3 weeks we've got really far . . . (nothing sinful . . .) There's a man, named Thornton Delehanty, a movie critic, nice fellow. [She's] been living with him two years or more. I met him one midnight—called her up because I couldn't sleep unless I saw her. She has a lovely voice. They had been on the roof watching the zeppelin fly over. "Delehanty says come on down and have a drink," she said. I went. I had never seen him before. . . . It was a swell night.

Then two nights ago we went to [a roof restaurant] in Brooklyn, which has the loveliest view of any place in America . . . a view of the harbor and the New York sky line lighted entrancingly. There was nice music. I fell horribly in love, awfully, madly. We stayed for hours. We got charmingly involved. I'll always hear her voice saying "oh, Jim!"—that was in the taxi, crossing Brooklyn Bridge, with the lights of ships moving mistfully below through the soft June night. She kisses as only one other lady I know. . . .

I told [Honey] . . . of my infatuation . . . She said nothing I did would change her opinion of me. I asked what if I married, or lived with someone else. "I shall expect to see you all the rest of my life, whenever I have to," she said. I explained that this other girl's warmth, her quick response—which Honey has never quite given (but is capable of) had overcome me, because it is so much what I need. And I said I didn't think she, Honey, really loved me. "I have," she said, "a deep and fundamental love for you." And few sentences have ever touched me so. . . . She's afraid, oddly enough . . . not of Paula, but of Althea.

Honey's fondness for Thurber was at its zenith, and Paula did worry her. Honey and Thurber spent a weekend in Westchester County with the Whites, and on the train ride back, she asked Andy, "Who are you for, me or Paula?" White replied that it sounded like a tennis match between "Tilden and Cochet," and added, "I'll read about it in the papers someday." The Whites "loved" Honey, Thurber tells Minnette,

but they are afraid of a lack of emotion between us. In two years, of much being alone, nothing has happened beyond a few cautious extravagances in caresses. That, in its way, fascinates me. . . . Isn't it just what I want, too—the non-attainment of the desirable? Is that why I am writing to you? If it is, why then is Althea so important? Do I want both —something I can have and something I can't? Then I won't ever "get anywhere," will I?

Said Honey one day, "When you are over your affair with Paula, I know the place where I want you to take me—a lovely inn at the end of Long Island." "You would just submit," I said, "you wouldn't really want to." "I would go with a great deal of pleasure and abandon," she said.

But Thurber was so drawn to the unattainable that he seems never to have pressed his sexual advantages with any woman. He may have disappointed the pleasure-loving Honey, not only in that regard but in his insistence that they marry; marriage, she says, never appealed to her, including an unsatisfactory year of it with St. Clair McKelway. In 1977, she was writing White: "I have always been scared to death of marriage, the claustrophobic terror of it to me."

The nature of his Woman Problem, Thurber insisted, was that he was never lover or husband, but a "friend" of the women he admired most. The dilemma frustrates him, as he tells Minnette:

> One of the results of the glorious fourth [of 1930] was the mutual discovery of Honey and myself that we were not in love, so now we are friends —a condition at which, you know, I always arrive. Friends with you, friends with Althea, friends with Honey, even friends with Paula, I think. . . . I figure myself as a man who is, in a certain subtle sense, rather more feministic (not feminine) than masculine, a quality in me which women sooner or later detect, but which is usually lost on men. As a result of this, I always become, in the minds (not in the hearts) of women . . . a symbol rather than a person; they discern a great capacity for understanding, sympathy, and entertainment in me, but in so doing they lose the unreasoning headlong affection which they have for the man they are in love with. I have never had such an affection—no woman has ever felt, I blush to say, a definite and authentic passion for me. I have just realized that. Yet all the women I have known intimately have been the kind who have wanted, needed, and eventually got the proper object for a really demonstrative love. The kind that cools, yes, but which, while it lasts, may sometimes be worth everything else in life. The kind which I have always wistfully longed for and, now I see, never had because of this damnable quality in me. I analyze too much, I talk too much, I am never the strong, silent man who puts this or that lovely lady to bed and causes her to remember the incident the rest of her life, or at least for the duration of the current month. Seeing in me the makings of an interesting and dependable friend, women always set out to bring us to that basis as shortly as possible. . . . Take Honey. She has said . . . that she hasn't any emotional feeling for me, but qualifies this by adding that, whoever she married would have to understand that she expected to see me three fourths of the time the rest of her life. That's the only necessity in a woman for which I can ever hope. It is rather nice, too, knowing that some lady just has to see you and brightens when you appear but since I am 100 percent male, despite this strange feministic aura of mine—this ruin of mine—it is also melancholy to realize that it is never because the lady wants to be kissed, fondled, mauled or anything else. She wants to sit and talk, she wants to listen; she goes forth satisfied and contented by the experience of a

kinship of spirits. . . . Then she may be tortured by other desires, by other necessities, by other fears, and pains and hopes—usually, however, for some man who is less kind to her, who understands her not at all, who is often not even interesting—but who has that strange, indefinable something I haven't got.

He asks Minnette to tell him whether or not she, herself, ever "could have imagined me as a lover":

> I want the truth about that. I want to have the courage to face my destiny, and the sense to understand myself, which I never have had before. . . . I want, finally, after much prayer and suffering, to be able to endure my fate. It's going to be hard for me to realize that I'm just god's friendship-gift to women, and to bring myself to accept that. . . .
>
> Well, I'll never marry, or even have an affair with someone, who doesn't want me in some other way. I'm really tired of this business of being the school girl chum of girls, their confidante, the sharer of their candy and their joys and their sorrows, the receptacle of the story of their heart-breaks, the guide and the mentor, the big brother, the beacon, the helping hand, the understanding soul, the pal, the best friend.
>
> Your old school girl chum,
Jim [handwritten]

If it were simply friendship, writes Thurber another time, and he was asked to take his five best friends to a desert island, he would take five men. If it's to be only friendship, says this emerging leader of the war between the sexes, "there isn't any girl I consider important, interesting, inspiring or anything."

During the 1930 football season, Thurber was back in Columbus, telling his troubles to Herman Miller. Dorothy—not yet married to Herman—listened as the two men talked late into the night. "Jim said his marriage to Althea was washed up," she says. "That it had never really existed except as a theory. While he was talking, Althea called. She was about to have a wisdom tooth extracted and wanted Jim with her. There wasn't a bit of hesitation on his part. He took the next train back. It didn't seem to me to be a marriage that was washed up. And the next thing Herman and I heard, a few months later, was that Althea was pregnant."

35

That Pet Department

My drawings are now coming into a strange sort of acclaim. The New Yorker is going to run a series of my animal pictures, and a concern wants me to do ads for it! Imagine!

My best work is an amazingly naturalistic capturing of the primary motives, with a hint of the unequal struggle of the soul against them. I'm enclosing a few, which you can throw away. They'll alarm you.

—Letter to Minnette Fritts, 1930

Less than three months after *Is Sex Necessary?* appeared, the *New Yorker* published its first two Thurber drawings—on Washington's Birthday, 1930. They were part of a Thurber series called "Our Pet Department," a takeoff on newspaper pet columns. White and Thurber both had a penchant for assigning human characteristics to animals and birds, and Thurber's Pet Department makes the most of it; his drawings had supposedly been sent in by the readers:

There's "William," a dog on its back, its owners worried that it hadn't moved in two days. Thurber, the pet expert, thinks the dog "is in a trance," and though its ears suggest that it is in happy repose, "the tail is somewhat alarming"; a police dog that is driven to hiding neurotically because its master comes home each evening and says, "If you're a police dog, where's your

badge," and laughs; the animal bought as a St. Bernard puppy that grew to resemble what looks to be a large bear. Its owners complain that it won't let them "have things," like bath towels it might be standing on.

Althea had added two Siamese cats to her menagerie in Silvermine. When she wasn't present, Thurber enjoyed tying up the cats with his bathrobe cord to watch them get loose. The cats also provided him with something else to draw. The Pet Department features a cat "who is thirty-five," in bed. "She follows every move I make, and this is beginning to get to me," writes the owner. "She never seems sleepy nor particularly happy." Thurber suggests lettuce, "which is a soporific," but he "would have to see the cat watching you to tell whether anything could be done to divert her attention."

A seal confounds its owner because it won't learn to juggle. Thurber points

out that seals don't juggle, they balance things or toss a ball to another seal, which would be difficult in the case of only one. Another letter writer finds an owl in the attic that may or may not be stuffed. Thurber, commenting on his own drawing, says it looks more like a stuffed cockatoo than an owl. "This is the first stuffed bird I have ever seen with its eyes shut, but whoever had it stuffed probably wanted it stuffed that way."

The series brought such favorable reader reaction that when Thurber collected the pet columns for publication, along with the Monroe stories, and the "Our Own Modern English Usage" pieces, his publisher agreed on the stuffed cockatoo as the basis for the book's title: *The Owl in the Attic and Other Perplexities*.

"All the time," writes Wolcott Gibbs, "[Thurber] was drawing the pictures which for a good many years were regarded by the rest of the staff, with the exception of E. B. White, as a hell of a way to waste good copy paper, since his usual output at a sitting was twenty or more, not to mention those he drew on the walls."

"I don't remember just when I began to take Thurber's drawing seriously," says White. "I didn't really know art, or draftsmanship, but the drawings seemed funny, above anything else. Now I think they're great. Maybe I took them more seriously than others because I knew they reflected Thurber's troubles as well as his sense of fun. Except for the accident of my sharing an office with him, a lot more of his drawings would have been lost to the world than were.

"I think Jim was tops as a writer, but I also think his art surpasses his writing. I was on the seventeenth floor [the *New Yorker* business offices] a few days after Jim's death. They had three of his *New Yorker* covers enlarged and framed on the corridor wall. I looked at them closely and after all those years I still thought his drawing has the touch of genius. He underrated himself as an artist because he didn't realize he was a natural who didn't have to work at it; he usually drew while thinking of something else. And despite his claims to the contrary, I don't think writing came that hard to him, either. He used to rewrite a lot, but so does every good writer."

White often discounted the credit Thurber kept offering him. Upon reading the *Washington Post*'s obituary of Thurber, White replies:

> The piece on Thurber in your Nov. 6 [1961] issue sounded as though he and his work would have lain unnoticed if I hadn't come along. This, as far as I'm concerned, is a pleasant theory but it is a preposterous one. I did nothing to get Thurber appointed to the staff of the New Yorker except drop his name one day when Ross was casting about for names.

. . . I knew nothing about Thurber at that time. I had met him at the apartment of a friend . . . and I thought he was a funny guy.

I did not "help him become an international celebrity"—he became one because he had what it takes. Nothing in the world could have stopped him. Even my much-touted admiration for his early drawings, although real enough, was touched less with perspicacity than with desperation. He and I needed some drawings to illustrate a book manuscript. . . . We thought we would stand a better chance with the publisher if there were some drawings. So we scooped up a few that were lying around in our office, and Jim drew others to fit the text. Harper & Brothers were bewildered, but they were game; they published the book not knowing they were launching a great artist. I didn't realize what was happening either.

Thurber's gateway was not me, it was *The New Yorker* itself. As soon as Ross saw Thurber's writing, he knew he had a humorist on the premises.

Though White and Thurber were both among the literary discoveries of the season, White shunned publicity appearances. It is said he chose the publication date of *Is Sex Necessary?* to marry Katharine to avoid Harper's plans to publicize him. Thurber, however, was more than willing to oblige the press. His former employer, the *New York Evening Post*, ran a sketch of the nearly thirty-six-year-old Thurber; a reporter, Mary Rennels, interviewed him:

Thurber says the real trouble with sex in America is our great effort to treat it as if it were as common as bread, while at the same time we react to it as if it were a violent toothache. This is a lot like trying to read Edgar Guest in a Martin bombing plane and is bound to lead to maladjustments.

This youth, with the long body and a smallish head, was Elliott Nugent's inspiration for *The Poor Nut*. He looks as though he would write a serious book on sex and not as parody. Everything is funny to him except his own emotions. . . .

"Grief is of all the emotions the one under which I work best," he says seriously.

Football is his favorite spectator sport, and he is "the only man in the world who likes parsnips and thinks there is not a single American actress of any consequence." (He had yet to meet Paula Trueman, or Ann Fordyce, another actress he courted.)

He was proud of his "ability to throw rocks, apples and the like with greater accuracy than anyone I know." He once bought four volumes of Augustin Thierry's *Conquest of England by the Normans* in the original French "because I thought 'conquête' meant 'coquette.'" Unlikely. Nor was the reporter taken in when Thurber said he had once sent a check for fifteen thousand dollars to the gas company, confusing the meter number with the actual charge. "I got a lovely letter from the president of the company," he claimed.

The reporter quoted Thurber as habitually going to the "smart *New Yorker* office without a tie on, which embarrasses him most when he happens to be wearing gloves, a muffler, and carrying a stick. Once, feeling for his four-in-hand and finding he didn't have one on, he went home by alleys and side streets, only to find he was wearing a bow-tie."

To further promote the book, and with the help of Honeycutt and Jap Gude at CBS, Thurber made his first radio appearance, on Bill Schudt's show, "Going to Press," at 6:15 P.M., February 3, 1930. "Last Wednesday I broadcast over a coast-to-coast network," he writes Minnette, "but didn't know it was coast-to-coast till I read about it in the Columbus papers which gave me far too much space for the crazy talk I made. I would have let you know just to see if you could have got me on your radio if I had known it was going so far. . . . My family heard me clearly on a small set Robert has."

The effectiveness of an author's publicity efforts are sometimes difficult to measure, but *Is Sex Necessary?* was on the January 1930 best-seller lists, along with such strong competition as Erich Maria Remarque's *All Quiet on the Western Front*; *Young Men of Manhattan*, by Katherine Brush, a book by Eddie Cantor, and *The Art of Thinking*, by Ernest Dimmet.

The humorist Will Cuppy called the book a classic. Its jacket carried an encomium by Heywood Broun, printed alongside a set of Thurber's briefly sketched, and ever sexless, men and women, innocently and ludicrously naked. Those who had first met the Thurber Man as John Monroe could now get an idea of what he and the female object of his perplexities may have looked like. Already the men pictured in the book are slumped in fear and dejection, the women steady of purpose.

The promise of the new decade was a mixed bag for Thurber. Despite the stock-market collapse, the magazine seemed on an irreversible, sound financial footing. His growing popularity with its readers and with Ross, reinforced by the friendly patronage of the Whites, amounted to a paid-up job-insurance policy. He had developed the Midas touch, for even his drawings, which he saw as "dreaming along with a pencil," were being talked about as art by those presumably in positions to know. He was still writing too quickly and too often but gradually getting a firmer hold on his craft.

There were a few turns for the worse. He had cherished his days with White when "the office we shared [had] just enough room for two men, two typewriters, and a stack of copy paper," as White wrote. As much as he enjoyed Thurber, White reluctantly recognized the difficulties of concentration with Thurber crowded next to him. With Katharine's assistance, it is assumed, as well as the addition of editorial space, Ross gave him his own office in 1930.

Thurber had warned Nugent in their single days that the marriage Nugent was then contemplating could easily impair their close friendship; similarly, he eventually became unable to accept White's marriage with sustained good grace. Thurber had liked both Katharine and Ernest Angell. After their breakup, in more than one separate talk with each, he tried to persuade them to patch things up. Whatever his reservations about the interruption of a status quo he enjoyed, Thurber continued for a time as a close friend of Katharine's, as well as of Andy's, after their marriage.

"Jim gave us a series of funny drawings called "La Flamme and Mr. Prufrock," White said.

"They made a superb wedding gift," added Katharine. "We still have them."

When, as a child, Roger Angell visited his mother and Andy on weekends at their Village apartment on Eighth Street, Thurber was often there. "I was ten or eleven when they enlarged the apartment to make room for a Ping-Pong table," says Angell. "Thurber and I played one another quite a bit. I liked him in those days. He was cheerful and knew how to please a young-ster."

The cultural significance of the White/Thurber relationship continues to this day. They achieved, together and separately, a lasting professional success, and, with Katharine Angell, a significant revision of the naive mandates in the magazine's early prospectus. Their minds were sensitive to what was funny and to the insupportables that lay beyond the laughable.

Thurber produced at a headlong rate, as if driven by demons rather than muses. He still lacked the winner's psychology, which had a mellowing effect that endeared him to many among his office family. As proof of talent piled up, he would use it to initiate greater tests of his power in careless, almost self-destructive ways, slightly alarming White from time to time. For though the two men often thought alike in their amused observations of the world around them, they were of differing cultures, upbringing, habits, and inclinations. Both men had tough cores of resilience. White's was seated firmly below the frostline, rarely subject to ground heave. Despite his timidity, he soon knew where his strengths lay, and his need to apply them left him seeking the quiet, private places of an independent life in which he could think and work. Unlike Thurber, he was content with the anonymity of Notes and Comment and newsbreaks, rather than a byline. He feared the consequences of modifying his early, modest self-assessments. "Nothing that has happened to me in the last thirty years has shaken my lack of confidence in my ability in the world of letters," White wrote Thurber in 1957, "which is why I hang on to newsbreaks."

Woods, farmland, and water were White's favorite topography for recreation and inspiration, reminiscent of Thoreau, who was his favorite spokesman for the laissez-faire philosophy White endorsed. White often kept with him a pocket-size copy of *Walden*, finding it the most suitable model of how good writing can spring from both a spirit of civil disobedience and a metaphysical rappport with nature. White was a primitivist in heart, an intellectual in mind. Thurber, to him, was another of nature's mysterious wonders, as unpredictable as wildlife, stimulating to be around, and, confessional and open as he was, an appealing object of study. Though White had a sympathetic interest in Thurber's melancholy concerns with life, he brought the same sense of order to his feelings that he did to his writing, and the spectacle of Thurber's disheveled state of mind was as fascinating to him as the shower of penciled Thurber drawings that floated to the floor in the office they shared.

The two friends saw less of one another as their personal lives took different courses, and even incidental meetings at the office all but ended when Thurber quit the staff at the end of 1935. ("I just didn't see much of him after that," White says.) After blindness helped turn Thurber into a shorter-fused personality, the Whites found it necessary to avoid him socially, for he was less and less able to control an animosity toward Katharine. ("Sooner or later," says Katharine, "Jim seemed, because of his deep antipathy to women, to attack his friends' wives when he was drinking.") Yet, few who read the Thurber/White letters today would suspect that anything had gone wrong between the two friends until, late in 1957, the Whites' unhappiness with Thurber's *The Years with Ross* became reflected in the guarded tone of Andy White's replies to Thurber.

Though a writer first learns from imitating, and Thurber began at the magazine writing for both White's and Ross's approval, he was soon breaking his own paths. While White tapped his unique set of inner assets, Thurber drew his material from outside himself, nurturing a useful state of self-distrust and willingly submitting himself to the buffeting of society's climates and vicissitudes. One reason he succeeded was that in the course of it, as Kenneth Tynan wrote of Noel Coward, Thurber "never suffered the imprisonment of maturity."

But in 1930 the Whites worried about Thurber, who continued to live alone at the 65 West Eleventh Street apartment, with Althea and the dogs in Silvermine. Andy and Katharine both considered health a tenuous gift from the gods, subject to instant recall if one disregarded it for a moment. Thurber violated all their tenets of self-preservation. He sometimes never made it home, or even to the Algonquin, and the morning after would be found asleep on the floor of strangers' apartments where he had attended a party.

"Everybody was giving parties in those days," says Jane Grant, "and everybody came, including those not invited. After Disney's *Fantasia* made its debut, Neysa McMein—one of our Algonquin crowd—was so enthralled by it she impetuously invited Disney—whom she didn't know—to one of *her* parties, never dreaming he would accept. He traveled across the country and stayed the entire weekend. The lively company, along with free food and drink, were even hard for celebrities to turn down back then."

One morning Daise Terry arrived at work to find a rumpled Thurber stretched out asleep on one of the long art tables in her area. The proper Miss Terry recruited her typists, receptionists, and secretaries—usually debutantes and Junior League members—from the graduating classes of the more elite women's colleges. (Others of a lesser social and financial standing may not have been able to settle for the meager salary, though it was a source of wonder to some on the staff that, in the heart of Manhattan, few, if any, Jewish girls could be found by Terry to qualify for the secretarial pool during her more than three decades as its supervisor.) The well-bred young ladies came to New York from college, shared apartments with former classmates, studied dictation and speed writing, and usually stayed no more than a year at the *New Yorker*, or until they realized that the prestige of being associated with the publication wasn't worth the grief of working for Terry, or the depressing pay. Most soon quit, left to tour Europe, returned to their families, and married the hometown boy. Terry provided them with the stern custodianship of a Mother Superior. Worried in this instance by the prone figure of Thurber on one of her tables, and the impending arrival of her cadre of young women, Terry jostled Thurber awake. Thurber painfully opened his eyes, looked at Terry and said bitterly, "Ann Honeycutt says sex is dirty."

He made the Fourth of July, 1930, "a gala three-day holiday," he wrote

Minnette, "during the course of which, at a great drinking joust, up in West-chester county, I definitely went to pieces. Some of the people at the office bought me a ticket and shanghaied me to Canada, where, in two weeks, I got on my feet."

In 1929, White had acquired part ownership of Camp Otter, a summer camp for boys in Dorset, Ontario. Thurber's state of mind worried White even then, for he had written Ross that year from the camp, saying, "I'm worried about old man Thurber and hope you can make him take a decent vacation. . . . Tell Thurber to write me."

The next year, James A. Wright, White's camp assistant, remembers, "Thurber was having marital problems . . . and was on the point of a break-down. So Ross phoned Andy and asked if he could send him up."

"[Thurber] takes things too hard," White wrote Katharine, who was at home on Eighth Street, pregnant with Joel. "If he thinks the *New Yorker* is complicated he ought to see a boy's camp."

Staff members saw Thurber off on the train for Bracebridge, Ontario, fol-lowing his debilitating Fourth. White acknowledged receipt of the shipment, writing Katharine:

> Jim is here, wandering aimlessly about camp, a tall misty visitor about whom nothing much is known. He arrived yesterday in Bracebridge, his suitcase collapsing on the platform just as he detrained. I found him picking up shirts and neckties, the blood rushing to his head. He brought your letter and also tidings.

"The camp was a rugged little place, on an island," says White. "The only way to reach it was by boat. I'd bought a 150-pound bell for calling campers to meals. It had just been delivered on the mainland when Jim arrived. I put the bell in the bow of the canoe and Jim in the middle. The canoe was low in the water and I may have made a remark about losing the bell and having to swim for it if we swamped. Jim told me for the first time he couldn't swim, and when I thought about it years later I realize I could have been responsible for losing a great world humorist to an overloaded canoe. He gripped the gunnels and started to talk even faster than he usually did. We made it. A season or two later, Kay and I invited Jim to our place in Maine. He said he wanted to go sailing with me. He still hadn't learned to swim, and was obviously scared to death. I don't know why he wanted to put himself through the ordeal."

Neither did Thurber, probably. "In the middle of a rushing brook," he writes in "Suli Suli," "I would drown faster than you could say 'J. Robbins.'"

Thurber, the city boy, spent two weeks at Camp Otter, White paddling him across the lake to Huckleberry Island to see a loon ferrying chicks on her back, and hiking with him to visit Sam Beaver, a Chippewa Indian. Thurber spent time illustrating the Monroe stories and the Fowler satires for *The Owl in the Attic*, scheduled for publication the following February. There was a square dance, but "Thurber didn't go," White writes Katharine, "because he was afraid of getting shot. . . . The first issue of the *Otter Bee* [the camp paper] was out Saturday, containing a special Thurber rotogravure section."

In it Thurber illustrates "Mrs. George I. Loon, and son, George Jr., who are making their summer home on Huckleberry Island—or trying to." There is a portrait of himself wielding a mallet and holding down a fish. The caption: "4-pounder—had to be beaten to death." A series of a man struggling with a canoe, and losing, has the cutlines: "Household Hints. Artist Shows How a Canoe Can Throw a Man Who Doesn't Know How." He draws his impression of the perilous voyage with the bell, showing himself holding it. "The bell was bought for $1.50," he writes under the sketch, "at a roadside auction. . . . As yet no use has been found for the bell in camp, but a committee is working on it."

He painted a picture of an otter on the side of the boathouse. White was to remember it with delight: "[The otter] is the only animal in the world that really looks as though it had been designed by you," he wrote Thurber in 1956. "You thought you were drawing a Thurber otter, but by God you were drawing an otter."

Wright, Thurber, and White Bring Large Bell and Not Much Else
The camp's new bell was paddled across. (The man in the middle "legs sprawled, chest pinned by an iron bell," is our boy James Thurber.)

4 pounder—had to be beaten to death.

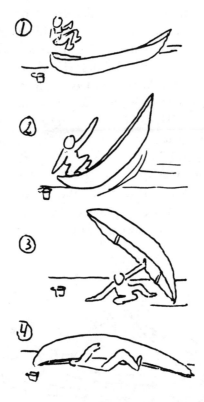

Household Hints: Artist Shows How a Canoe Can Throw a Man Who Doesn't Know How.

Thurber's renewed effort in 1930 to live a life with Althea ended the Monroe series, but soon new aspects of the relationship would find their way into more frightening literary and cartoon expression. He often quoted Carl Van Doren's "It is hard to write, but it's harder not to." Thurber's writing was so central to his life, he so seemed to need the chaos he said he recollected and processed in private tranquility, that one even holds suspect his proclaimed intentions to make a real try at holding his marriage together; a successfully romantic union with a woman would always run counter to his creative needs. His ideal lady, who would feel passion for him without spoiling matters by wanting a carnal relationship, simply refused to take up residence in Althea.

It is difficult to know if Thurber at times worked his marriage for a pathos more fancied than real. Althea's desire for a fuller sex life than he could provide remained an unhealed and hurtful wound, but, though the pain was real, his entertaining public confessions of disharmony often suggest an author determined not to do himself out of material. "Happy endings" are fallow ground for the conflict needed in good storytelling. He was also, without having to try, his own best subject; his disorganized life was prime grist for his mill. His best and funniest interviews and reports would always be of himself.

The office and its surrounding social landscapes continued to change with the new decade. The Algonquin Round Table dissolved, not because of the wrecked economy but because its members had acquired fame and wealth, which made their own demands. "By 1929," writes Gibbs,

> [Alexander Woollcott and friends had] moved their poker game from the Algonquin to the Colony where the check for refreshment was usually more than anybody had made in a week when the Thanatopsis Club began. Almost everybody bought a little place in the country . . .
>
> Hollywood got some of them and others moved to Connecticut, partly to escape the New York state income tax and partly under the sad old delusion that a man can write far more rapidly and beautifully while raising his own vegetables.

Though too late on the scene to be a member of the Round Table, Thurber was a favorite with many of them. He and White had attended only one of the legendary luncheons "and were so embarrassed by the trained system of insults that they used on each other, we never got used to it," Thurber remarked on a British talk show of the fifties.

His love sickness, whether contrived or real, continued. His letters to women seem like those of a homeless person, seeking emotional handouts. When he visited Althea on weekends, he lived on her terms. She was finding her own extramarital companionships, but she needed his participation in her world of suburban home and kennel. He resented the subordinate role she assigned him, but he still cared about her. Honeycutt had been right about who her own competition was—more Althea than Paula Trueman. Emily Hahn recalls:

"Paula looked a lot like Honeycutt, same turned-up nose, same profile. During a long, drunken luncheon with me, Thurber told me that he and Paula had decided he couldn't go on as he was; that he had to break with Althea. He said he had talked to Paula time and again about how Althea got in the way of his work, how unhappy they were together. It struck me that what he was mumbling about was what any drinking man might say about his wife—nonspecifics, about how awful she was, didn't understand him, tried to curtail his liberty, how she loved the dogs and didn't love him; that she was frigid and didn't want to go to bed with him. He used to tell all this to Paula, Thurber said. When he proposed to her, Paula told him marriage couldn't even be considered until he cut loose from Althea, and that it was high time he did. Thurber said, 'Very well, by God, I'll do it. Wait here. I'll be back and we'll discuss marriage.' This all took place in the green room of a Broadway theater where Paula was in a play. Althea was in the city at the time, and Thurber said he went straight to her and told her he wanted to leave her to marry Paula, that Althea looked at him horrified, went to pieces and then blew up at him, telling him he simply couldn't do it. 'I found I couldn't, either,' Thurber told me, 'and for all I know Paula is still waiting for me in the green room.'

"He was still pining for Althea, it seemed to me. He was always saying that she was the prettiest girl on campus. Come to think of it, Thurber wasn't 'always saying' anything; he never told things the same way twice. He needed to talk to women about himself the way a boy needs to talk to his older sister. Even as a woman, I found my older sisters very important to me, and I find it significant that Thurber, Philip Wylie—or, for that matter, Freud, Christ, and Marx—never had a sister."

The woe-is-me letters to Honeycutt continued. She was in as earnest a search for fun as everyone else in those days; she was fond of Thurber and on a couple of occasions came close to agreeing to marry him, which, she says, would have spoiled everything for Thurber.

"Jim, in his better moments, reminded me of Glen Hunter, the actor, or James Stewart at times—shy, moonstruck, wistful," says Honey. "And he could be so entertaining." In his letters to her, as well:

The report that goes around about me plaguing girls and women is entirely false . . . due to an unreasonable fear that, even if the lady surrenders, how can you gracefully get her things off so that she won't laugh and cause the whole thing to crack up? Few people realize that this inordinate fear of mine has spoiled what would have been otherwise a most adventurous career. There are, of course, several ways to manage the removal of a lady's things, none of them really successful. You can come right out, after she has yielded to your embraces, and ask her, with boyish gaiety, if she will now remove her clothes. This has to be done just right, however, and usually in the heat of things, the gentleman gets so wrought up, what with this and what with that, that he fairly barks it at her, thus either making her mad, hurting her [feelings], or shocking her sensibilities. Another method is to say to the lady, "Now I'm going to get rid of some of these crazy things we wear," and start taking off her shoes. No matter how expert you are, however, or how much you practice on department store window models, you are likely to get into trouble anywhere from the shoe buckles to the brassiere. Tearing things off is a system some people use, but you usually have to replace, or think you have to replace, the things you tear off, particularly if you begin with a new evening gown. I have known few men, however, who could remove the panty-waist and those things worn around the middle successfully. . . . You have to whisk them off quickly and adroitly, or the girl's mind will get on something else. If you try to whisk and the panty-waist holds, this is likely to lead to a grim and determined effort, in which the gentleman goes about the process much as if he were trying to fix a gasoline engine. He will mutter and swear and say, "How the hell does this dam thing fasten?"—which is fatal. The old theory that you really don't have to take off many things is fatal, too because nobody looks quite so funny as a person, or two persons, with practically everything on except pants and skirt. Each one is afraid to get up first for fear he—or she—will look comical. So someone says "Now close your eyes" and then he gets up, closing his eyes too, with the result that he is likely to forget that his trousers are around his knees and be thrown with great violence. I think the best way is to say "I'm going into the next room for a minute" and then go into the next room, leaving the girl to undress. In the next room you undress, always tortured by the fear that when you get back, she will not have touched a stitch but will be sitting quietly in a chair reading a book. This so worries a certain type of man that he gets himself into a frightful state wondering just what clothes, if any, he should wear when he goes back. I think the best thing to wear is shirt and trunks for if the girl is really reading when you re-enter the room where you left her, you can trot around, jump over canes, and pretend that you got undressed simply to go through some exercises. . . .

There has been an ominous silence about the pictures I handed in today and about the casual I wrote yesterday, so I am beginning to get my usual six p.m. depression. It would be a good time now to go to Tim's with Jap [Gude], but Jap has gone. . . . He is a nice boy and I wish I were he. He has a pretty wife named Helen, and a lovely baby named Joe. He was married before to Katherine White but divorced her because of a scene at Amawalk when she went away with Mark Prentiss. . . .

Wolcott Gibbs reports on Thurber's office behavior in that period. "It is extremely unlikely," writes Gibbs,

though often told, that he used to roll water coolers down the hall, making the sound of doom, whenever the editor decided to reject one of his pictures. . . . Once when the management declined to get him a new typewriter, Thurber is the kind of typist who can beat practically any machine into scrap in a week, he called up the Underwood-Elliott-Fisher Company and ordered that their most expensive machine be sent up that afternoon and charged to the company. He got it too, and so did several other members of the staff, who up till then had never thought in terms of direct action.

When the rental lease on the Silvermine house was up, in June, 1931, the Richard Connells offered their nearby summer house to the Thurbers for the next year, rent free. "Dick had accepted a Hollywood contract to write screenplays," says Louise Connell. "The Thurbers didn't want to tie themselves up with another lease—they had separated temporarily—but Jim insisted on paying us rent."

The Connell property, known as the French Farm, contained several buildings set around a courtyard with a willow tree in its center. There was a guest house and an artist's studio, "a large one," says Louise, "big enough for parties and dances. Thurber did quite a bit of work in it. It was uninsulated but heated by a stove. Above the telephone in the main house was wallboard that Thurber drew on as he sat talking. He worked in the attic at times and drew on the walls up there, too. Mutual friends later rented the place. Dick and I begged them to save the drawings but later owners had them covered with cream paint.

"Jim had drawn a large ship and a man in the ocean sweltering under a bright sun, his leg in a shark's mouth and being beaten by a woman treading water and wielding a club. People were happily diving into the water, ignoring the man. A rabbit and dog were standing nose to nose. I daresay there's great psychological significance in all this. I used to wonder if it got on Althea's nerves to see that large Thurber Woman always beating up the little Thurber Man. I never heard her discuss it. The child in Thurber gave a gentleness and charm to his work, and to him. He didn't drink during the day and did lots of good work at the studio. The studio had a balcony and at one party Jim began to drop empty whiskey bottles from it, smashing them. He also liked smashing lightbulbs. He gave you the impression of being easier to know than he really was. He'd pretend to be confessional in his conversations with women but he never gave much away.

"We partied and danced at the studio when we lived there. Thurber was both an asset and liability at such a time. He was a celebrity and very amusing on the one hand, but an unpleasant drunk on the other. He was unhappy with Althea and the way his life was going, I know. His work was his salvation."

The Connells soon found that a party of people too large for Thurber to dominate seemed to drive him to drink to excess. "You thought carefully about the size of a group you intended to get together, and who would be there, before you invited Jim," says Louise. "If you guessed right he made the evening a joy to remember. If you guessed wrong it could be a disaster nobody wanted to remember."

In 1951, Thurber wrote Anthony Bertram about Paul Nash: "He must have been capable of anger and temper because he was a fine artist." Though Thurber never assigned himself any aesthetic importance as an illustrator, as a literary artist he may have begun to justify his self-permissiveness with a claim of artistic temperament.

Friends of the Connells, Frank Godwin, an illustrator, and his wife, Sylvia, met the Thurbers one weekend in 1930 at a Westport party and were charmed by them. "We spent a weekend with Jim and Althea at their home in Silvermine, Connecticut," says Sylvia. "They had their first Standard French poodle there, and Jim told us so many nice things about it we bought one from Althea. Jim said poodles were like people, different from other dogs; they shake hands properly, and don't just give you a paw.

"We lived in Riverside, Connecticut, in the early thirties, but for ten years we summered on Lake Skaneateles, one of the Finger Lakes, eighteen miles from Syracuse. We kept the house filled with four guests at a time. The

Thurbers were there, along with the Connells, the summer of 1931, I think. We were two hundred and eighty miles from New York City, so it was common for guests to spend two weeks with us.

"We fished a good deal, from two motor boats. Jim wasn't fond of fishing; he made a mess out of a couple of efforts."

So Thurber confesses in "Suli, Suli," five years after the event. He shared Benchley's dread of confronting nature on its terms. "I tried casting in a stream only twice," he writes, "and the first time I caught a tree and the second time I barely missed landing one of a group of picnickers."

And, in the same casual, he corroborates Sylvia Godwin's recollection, writing:

> I went fishing on Lake Skaneateles with a group of people, including a lovely young woman named Sylvia. On this occasion I actually did hook a fish, even before anybody else had a bite, and I brought it into the rowboat with a great plop. Then, not having had any experience with a caught fish, I didn't know what to do with it. I had had some vague idea that a fish died quietly and with dignity as soon as it was flopped into a boat, but that, of course, was an erroneous idea. It leaped about strenuously. I got pretty far away from it and stared at it. The young lady named Sylvia finally grabbed it expertly and slapped it into insensibility against the sides and bottom of the boat. . . . A man never completely gets over the chagrin and shock of having a woman handle for him the fish he has caught.

"Jim would begin telling stories at breakfast," Sylvia continues, "and when Jim talked nobody left the table. Four hours later, the maid would ask if she should serve lunch, so we'd have lunch served, never having moved since breakfast. When Jim got wound up we were spellbound. He'd start with an aunt and uncle back in Ohio and build on that. He had a dry delivery and would laugh only when we all laughed.

"We played badminton and danced. Jim danced very well, the fox-trot and waltz. He loved parlor games. We played them at his Sandy Hook house—a simple, unpretentious place with a narrow staircase leading up to the bedrooms.

"Jim was shy, gentle, liked animals, loved talking—especially to women—and being with people, and I never saw him aggressive or drunk; always interesting. He could be caustic in his writing but he wasn't by nature. You didn't debate him, because once he got on a subject you didn't want to interrupt him.

"Once in that period, I asked Jim about Althea. He said she had gone to the Caribbean on assignment for the *New York Sun,* or some newspaper. He seemed vague about it, which made me wonder."

Althea and Thurber had reunited just in time for him to dedicate *The Owl in the Attic* to her. Published in February 1931, it was the first book whose content was completely Thurber's, though White, in a merry mood, contributed an introduction of skilled nonsense. Thurber, White said, had to sit on the left side of a person to make conversation with a minimum of head swiveling because of a missing left eye. Harking back to *Is Sex Necessary?*, he added that Thurber had given up trying to find out anything about sex in favor of worming puppies, and was both amused and frightened by the number of his friends getting married, a fear exhibited by the figures in the book, of "stooped" males, contrasted with "the erect and happy stance of the females."

The book had a modest sale—a first printing of 3,355 copies was followed by two smaller ones. The drawings received most of the attention. The reviews were friendly, as nearly all reviews of his books would be through most of Thurber's life. S. T. Williamson in the *New York Times* thought that "if not in a book of humor, some critics of modern art would be taking [the drawings] seriously." Will Cuppy—who also courted Ann Honeycutt—writing in the *Herald Tribune,* found the economically drawn Pet Department bestiary "animals plus," "springboards to the infinite," and possessed with sinister qualities. "Surely Ibsen at his worse never thought up anything half so horribly symbolic as Mr. Thurber's night prowling horse."

Harper's publicity people arranged press meetings. Thurber loved to be interviewed, he told John Forbes of the *New York Telegram,* removing his coat and vest for the occasion. Thurber, "slender . . . with a heavy mustache [and] thick shell-rimmed glasses," as Forbes saw him, turned in another nutty performance. Breakfast, he said, was his important meal. "Not that I eat a heavy breakfast," Thurber told the confused Forbes, "but the idea of breakfast appeals to me." He got the idea for the cast-iron animals in "The Pet Department" from Columbus, "whose lawns are overrun with cast-iron animals." He knew Paris like a book but couldn't direct anyone to Carnegie Hall or the Plaza Hotel. He wasn't partial to turnips. His illustrations? They amused him. "Several authorities, who call me master of the line," he said, "have told me I have something new."

Thurber explained that a tremor in his hands made it impossible to trace over his penciled lines accurately with India ink, so he began drawing in ink.

If he missed he began again, because he couldn't erase. But since that was what he had always done in pencil he wondered why he hadn't always been drawing in ink. ("I could do a hundred a week," he boasted truthfully in *The Years With Ross*, "but I usually submitted only two or three at a time." He had a sufficient grasp of economics to know better than to saturate the market.)

From the publication of *Is Sex Necessary?* Thurber had been prepared to laugh with the reviewers at his pictures and still suspected himself guilty of artistic fraud when critics treated them with respect. He saw them as fantasy beating reality to the punch, if he thought of their significance at all. He flirted with the idea of taking art lessons—he did take one or two—but his ultimate decision not to take himself seriously as an artist undoubtedly helped preserve the primitive purity of his drawing, keeping it a simple and easy adjunct to the creative process, devoid of thought, plan, or design. "To sit down and draw was like lighting a cigarette," he told Henry Brandon, a British newspaperman, years later. "A form of relaxation after writing, or when I got stuck on a piece of writing. A great many of the drawings I did, I was unconscious of doing."

An English edition of *Is Sex Necessary?* brought Thurber's strikingly original drawings to the attention of Paul Nash. Nash had attained eminence as a painter of the Flanders homes, villages, and fields left desecrated by the battles of World War I. He had become interested in American humor in art: in comic strips, magazine cartoons, and book illustrations. Among the comic artists he hoped to meet in preparation for an article he planned on the subject were Thurber, O. (Otto) Soglow, John Held, Jr., Milt Gross, and Walt Disney.

In 1931, Nash was invited to lecture at Carnegie Institute in Pittsburgh. Accepting, he told the head of the school's Department of Fine Arts that he would like to include Thurber in the list of artists to be invited to a luncheon Carnegie was giving in New York in Nash's honor. The department head notified Thurber, referring to Nash as "the leader of the new idea in British art."

In his letter to Anthony Bertram, who, in 1951, was preparing a biography of Nash, Thurber, writing from Bermuda, described the luncheon: Nash arrived at the Century Association, on Forty-third Street, wandered down the reception line, came to Thurber and stopped to chat, to Thurber's embarrassment, for Thurber knew very little about art by his own admission. Nash invited Thurber to sit next to him. Lunch was served before Thurber and Nash had time for more than one drink from the bottle of Scotch on the sideboard, and Thurber brought the bottle to the table, bringing raised eyebrows to the faces of the more serious, noncomic members of the art community present. He needed it, he said later, to get through that "amazing" lunch. Feeling guilt at monopolizing Nash's attention, Thurber reminded him that the other guests represented the forefront of American art. Nash replied that from what he had seen of their work, most of them were bringing up the rear of French Modernism. It was Nash, as art critic for the *New Statesman and Nation* in London, who first suggested the similarities of Thurber's art to that of Matisse.

Ross later dismissed Thurber's reports of the favorable reception his art was being given in Britain. "A passing fad of the British," Ross said. He never did know how to evaluate Thurber's drawings, and depended on the judgment of others. Two contributing artists whom Ross liked and trusted, Ralph Barton and Wallace Morgan, told Ross that Thurber's pictures had genuine merit, but Ross was still skeptical. When a frustrated cartoonist asked Ross why he turned down his work and printed that of "a fifth-rate artist like Thurber," Ross instantly replied, "Third-rate."

Even after Thurber's cartoon of the seal in the bedroom brought Benchley's glowing telegram of praise, Ross was still dubious. Don Wharton, another candidate for the "genius" position, remembers that his interview with Ross took place shortly after the cartoon appeared.

"Ross interviewed me in a bare little room, next to his regular office," Wharton recalls. "There was only a table and one straight-backed chair in it. One was brought in for me. He interviewed me for hours. Could I do this? Or that? Or the other thing? On and on. Over and over. Finally, he opened a scrapbook that the librarian kept of contributors' work and showed me Thurber's cartoon of the seal draped over the bedhead. I'd never seen it before. 'Do you think this is funny?' Ross asked me.

"I was a bit put out at the interminable, repetitive nature of the session and too tired to find anything funny, so I said, 'No,' not caring by then if I got the job or not.

" 'All right,' Ross said. 'You're hired.' "

36

That Approaching Fatherhood

Dear Ann:

I'm going to contrive it so that you won't have to see me or hear from me again for a year. . . . I don't dare continue to feel, as you do and as I do, that I am a horrible and ghastly person. Althea called me the same things, too. . . . My hands are cold from fear about myself. . . . If the trouble is my soul, and I'm just essentially awful—I mean like a creature born misshapen, I'll try to find the guts somewhere to get rid of myself. . . . But I have to go on making money and trying to be half way contented (so I won't go to pieces and can't look after the things I have to). . . . I have figured on dying in my double-breasted suit. I always look nice in it, I think, proudly, even when lying in the gutter or a field.

—Letter to Ann Honeycutt, circa 1931

In early 1931, Althea discovered she was pregnant. At first it was an embarrassment to Thurber, who had told his women companions that he and Althea were not sleeping together. "He turned up at my apartment quite upset," says Honeycutt. "He told me he hadn't had sex with Althea for a long time, and that she had told both Katharine White and him whose child it was. He could have fooled me, because, based on our relationship, I thought Thurber might well be impotent. We weren't much of a home-and-children group, so it took a while for him to adjust to the idea of fatherhood. But soon Thurber was bragging about the pregnancy. When his daughter was born, he was exceedingly proud to be known as a father. It did wonders for Jim. It helped correct some of the earlier, poor impressions he had of himself. It didn't necessarily improve his home life but he was charmed by the idea of a child of his own."

Thurber had, indeed, been guilty of his usual theatrical game playing. Rosemary Thurber, today in her sixties, has never resembled anybody but Thurber.

At the office, the procession of geniuses continued. In late 1930, Ross led Ogden Nash into Thurber's office and said, "I'm thinking of letting Nash here take a swing at running the Talk department." Young Nash, an advertising man who composed nonsense rhymes, was eventually known best for his "Candy/ Is dandy/ But liquor/ Is quicker." He had begun selling verses to the *New Yorker* in 1930. Later that year, he met Ross in a speakeasy. Nash writes:

> In many ways [Ross] was a strangely innocent man and he assumed that my presence in a speakeasy meant that I was a man about town. He was, I believe, still in mourning over the departure of Ingersoll, who had apparently been the ultimate in men about town, and was looking for a suave and worldly editor. He hired me practically on the spot. It took him less than three months to discover that it takes more than a collection of speakeasy cards to make a man about town. Besides this, he didn't need an editor anyhow, as anything he didn't do himself was capably handled by Raymond Holden and Mrs. White.

It was soon common knowledge at the office that Nash, the twenty-fifth "genius," or "hub," or "managing editor," wasn't working out. Morris Markey, hired from the *New York World* in 1925, had made himself important to Ross by creating "The Current Press" feature—later "The Wayward Press"—and "A Reporter at Large." Knowing of Ross's disenchantment with Nash, Markey persuaded him to interview James M. Cain, whose fame as a novelist (*The Postman Always Rings Twice, Double Indemnity, Mildred Pierce*) as yet awaited him. Markey and Cain had been close friends since their days together on the *World*, which had recently folded, leaving Cain unemployed. On the morning of the interview, as Markey escorted him to Ross's office, Cain remembers passing a door where Markey had told him Nash would be sitting. He looked in, he writes, and saw "a young man who looked away quickly with a little smile of relief, and a little pity, all of which told me a lot of what might be in store."

Cain was responsible for the budget and unhappy with the magazine's drawing-account system of payment to staff contributors, which he considered a form of indentured slavery. Regular payments to writers and artists were charged to them as debt, to be reduced by the magazine's payments for acceptable work. The modest fees, the rejections, and the usual slow pace of research and creativity inevitably left most of the contributors deeper and deeper in red ink. It was Cain's observation that this negatively affected morale and slowed productivity by causing everything from writer's block to several varieties of mental depression. Furthermore, Ross would advance extra money to certain writers without telling Cain. And when the financial straits of a particular writer or artist reached a crisis point, Ross often wiped the debt clean—again without informing Cain. (Under William Shawn, in later years, writers "on the draw" weren't expected to repay the magazine in money. Many died owing the New Yorker thousands.)

Another of Cain's complaints was Ross's favoring White over Thurber. He writes:

> I admired [Thurber's] talent, and carried on a running fight with Ross to get him put on a parity with White, he getting 15c a word at the time, White 17c, I contending he was at least as gifted as White, and entitled to an equal rate. Ross contended White was superior in subtle ways. I said: "Could it be his superiority consists in having a wife who is one of our editors?" No answer from Ross. (Oh, I made myself popular on that magazine.)

Cain left the magazine under his own steam after nine months.

Perhaps with Althea's encouragement—she was well into her pregnancy—Thurber bought a twenty-acre farm in Sandy Hook, Connecticut, in the summer of 1931. It was more than an hour's train ride from Grand Central, and Ross was against any of his staff members using time to commute that could otherwise be put to use for The Magazine. ("You'd spend all afternoon catching the 5:15 train," Ross said.)

In The Years with Ross, Thurber writes:

> Ross pretended to be frightened when he heard about my plans to live in the country. Timid, as usual, about taking up personal matters with a man face to face, he assigned Cain the task of trying to dissuade me from moving out of the city. Jim had approached the subject gingerly in my

office, with only a couple of sentences that I recognized at once as bearing the stamp of a Ross panic, when he suddenly stood up and said, "This is none of my business, or Ross's either. I'm sorry I mentioned it. Live where you want to and the way you want to."

But Cain clears Ross of meddling, in this case:

If Thurber sniffed Ross behind my effort to talk him out of the house, he was wrong: I am not the catspaw type, for Ross or anyone else. I assume I checked with Ross my intention to talk to Thurber—that would have been protocol. But it was my own idea, and mainly on Thurber's behalf, rather than the magazine's. Having myself directly and bitterly found out what it means, to be due with a check on the first of each month in payment for a dead horse, I went to him, in a somewhat avuncular frame of mind, as an older man to a younger, to plead with him not to get himself handcuffed to something that could be an old-man-of-the-sea around his neck. . . . The interview was a bit gritty, and in fact we didn't even sit down. He was standing up when I entered his cubicle, shuffling some papers, and we barely got started before I detected his hostility, not only to giving up his project, but even to hearing me out. . . . Suddenly . . . I asked "How old are you?" "Thirty-seven [actually 36]," he answered, in a surly, what's-it-to-you tone of voice. I had expected "Twenty-eight," or some such answer. . . . I was talking to a man almost as old as I was (I was thirty-nine at the time)—[which] left me with all the wind taken out of my sails. . . .

All I remember of it was my own tongue-tied stuttering on a mission I mortally hated, and his tongue-tied mulishness about it, and that curious delivery he had, as though his face had been punctured with novocaine, on the left side. . . . In person, he was damned hard to like. . . .

P. S. He got the money and bought the house.

It was to Cain that a grinning Ross reported the classic phone conversation he had just had with Dorothy Parker. Asked why her book review was late, she replied, "Aw, Harold, I've been too f——— busy. Or vice versa, if you prefer."

The Whites liked Cain; White remembers him as "a compulsively neat man, an ashtray mustn't have any stale ashes in it." Cain once had the Whites at his apartment for Thanksgiving Day. "The turkey was bigger than the platter," writes White, "and Jim delivered a monologue as he carved, while the slices of meat slipped quietly to the floor . . . an exercise in imperturbability."

Cain was known to be as hard to figure out as Thurber, and an old-timer, years later, confessed to Thurber that Cain was called Dizzy Jim, and Thurber, Daffy Jim. After Cain left the magazine to become a celebrated author, Wolcott Gibbs wrote to him asking him to contribute to the magazine. Cain outlined his own Cain mutiny to Gibbs:

> On the whole, I would rather be dead. You see, by the time I thought up a list of ideas and submitted them and found out the one I liked Ross didn't like, and then wrote one up and sent it on and then got it back again with 32 numbered objections from Mrs. White, and then rewrote it and sent it back, then considered the proposal to buy the facts from me for $50 and have Andy White rewrite it, and finally it came out as a "Reporter" piece by Markey—I would probably be dead anyway.

There was no love lost between Thurber and Cain, and when Cain's tough-guy yarn, *The Postman Always Rings Twice*, became a national bestseller, long after Cain had left the premises, Thurber pounced on it, calling his parody of it "Hell Only Breaks Loose Twice." He used a college campus as background rather than Cain's roadside diner:

> She leaned over the chair where I was sitting and bit me in the ear. I let her have it right in the heart. It was a good one. It was plenty. She hit the floor like a two-year-old.
>
> "What fell?" asked the Dean, peering over his glasses. . . .
>
> I walked close to her. It was like dying and going to Heaven. She was a little like my mother and a little like the time I got my hip busted in a football scrimmage. I reached over and let her have one on the chin and she went down like a tray of dishes. I knew then I would be beating her up the rest of my life. It made me feel like it was April and I was a kid again and had got up on a warm morning and it was all misty outdoors and the birds were singing.

"I never wrote him about it," says Cain, "as to tell the truth I didn't think it too good."

Cain was followed by Bernard A. Bergman, sponsored by Thurber, who had known "Bergie" from O.S.U. days. Bergman, several years ahead of Thurber, had majored in journalism, helped edit the *Daily Lantern*, and reported for the *Columbus Dispatch*. While working in public relations in New York, he proved to be a good "idea" man for Talk, contributing suggestions on a freelance basis from 1928 on. Thurber, overworked as usual, thought Bergman would be ideal as Talk editor, and when Ross agreed to hire him, begged Ross not to talk him into being Cain's replacement.

It was of no use. Though Ross swore Thurber to secrecy about his plans to offer Bergman the Genius position, Thurber immediately telephoned the news to Bergman. In a letter of reminiscence to Thurber, Bergman recalls: "I was to call you after [Ross and I] talked, [but] when I telephoned you told me you heard it all. [You] picked up a rug from the reception room, curled up in front of Ross's keyhole and listened to it all. Say, wasn't that also the night of your suicide?"

At the keyhole, Thurber overheard Ross loudly giving Bergman the usual treatment—the need to hold artists' hands, how he wanted the place run like any business office, and sex kept off the premises. Thurber's disgust and anger at losing Bergman to Ross was noted by somebody who followed Thurber into the men's room and saw him open a window, still muttering to himself. The unknown witness hurriedly reported Thurber's "suicide" preparations to Elsie Dick, who had long believed Thurber capable of anything. She interrupted Bergman and Ross with "Quick! Quick! Mr. Thurber is going to jump out a window!" As in Thurber's earlier "suicide" attempt, Ross simply looked at Bergman and said, "That's my life." Bergman was later relieved to see Thurber coming down the hall, still angry but alive.

Bergman lasted two years before he felt pressured to resign. It was in his administration that Ross hired Charles Morton on a try-out basis. "He had written some casuals," says Bergman, "and Mrs. White recommended we give him a try. . . . One afternoon Ross got all upset because Morton brought his wife in to meet him. Poor Ross didn't get over it for some time." Neither did Morton, whom Ross had Bergman fire soon after that.

Charles Cooke, who idolized Thurber, has only one poor memory of him: "I saw a sarcastic note he sent Bergman, a brutal attack on an honest attempt by Bergman to do something for the magazine. But Bergman was technically Thurber's administrative superior at the time, so I guess that made it O.K. Thurber never picked on underlings."

Bergman's most memorable service to Ross was in hiring Alva Johnston from the *Herald Tribune* in the early thirties. Johnston's Profiles improved the general tone of the magazine's nonfiction with a fine intelligence, wit, and artistry. Though his formal education stopped with a high-school diploma in Sacramento, California, Johnston seemed to know everything about everything, including how to write it up in entertaining and literate fashion. He had worked about eighteen years on the *New York Times* without a byline or much recognition. Finally deciding that the *Times* of that day was "The Dullards' Club," he offered to work for Stanley Walker of the *Trib* for a hundred and twenty-five dollars a week, fifty dollars less than the *Times* was paying him. His signed material in the *Trib* quickly drew attention. News of his voluntary salary cut circulated, and it was Johnston's apparent indifference to money that had Ross baffled as to how to lure him to the *New Yorker*.

"Ross tried to get . . . Johnston . . . for a long while," writes Bergman. "But Alva always refused. Said he was too old to change his field . . . and . . . take a chance on magazines. Ross said to me that if I could get Alva . . . that's all I'd ever have to do.

" 'How much did you offer him?' I asked.

" 'Oh, we never discussed salary,' Ross said. 'Alva just said he didn't want to gamble from a secured position in the newspaper business to magazines.'

" 'Well, let's offer him three hundred a week,' I said. 'That's double what he's getting. . . . He just won't be able to turn it down.'

"Ross said . . . 'I never thought of offering him money.' "

Bergman found Johnston watching the elevators in the lobby of the Vanderbilt Hotel for someone connected with the Lindbergh baby kidnapping—the hot news item of the day—and offered him the three-hundred-dollar weekly salary. "I can still see Alva turning pale," says Bergman, "standing up and saying, 'Gee, I'll have to think that over.'

"I went back to Ross and told him we got Alva. We had, too. [It] showed Ross's occasionally naive and charming impracticality, although he was the world's greatest."

Thurber came to admire Johnston immensely. They shared an office for a time. Thurber intended to dedicate *The Years With Ross* to him. ("Alva . . . was always after me to do the Ross story," Thurber writes.) But Johnston died in the interim and Thurber decided to honor the living Frank Sullivan instead.

Women, partly and indirectly, seem to have accounted for Bergman's quitting his job. Thurber believes that Katharine White's proprietary feelings toward Ross led her to an overzealousness in protecting him from the threat of newcomers. From the day of Bergman's arrival, Thurber remembers, she made much of the fact that he brought his own secretary with him. Bergman writes that Thurber

had warned me that Mrs. White was spreading the story that I had hired my mistress as my secretary. So silly I laughed it off. A big mistake to laugh Mrs. White off. . . . That [secretary] had never worked for me, but was one of Louie Weitzenkorn's asst. editors on the Sunday World.

. . . I, in my naive fashion, felt subeditors might make good secretaries. Hottest affair I ever heard of on the magazine was Mrs. W. and Andy.

I quit because I realized that I didn't live up to Ross's specifications as a Jesus. . . . He had that new fellow there, Francis Bellamy, in a vague sort of job. Mrs. White picked him, as I remember. I knew he was there to replace me. . . . I always felt that because I couldn't build partitions so Ross could walk from his office to the men's room, he lost confidence in me. That was one of his prize hopes. He dreaded meeting people in the hall on the way to the men's room.

Bellamy lasted only a few months. ("He smoked cigars," was Ross's only explanation for firing him.) Bergman married one of Lois Long's young "On & Off the Avenue" assistants and was later hired by Hearst's *New York American* to edit the "March of Events" page. He printed material by Benchley, Frank Sullivan, Clarence Day, Nash, Cain, and other *New Yorker* contributors. Thurber, too, sent Bergman some columns and drawings of the Thurber dog, until William Randolph Hearst himself wired his son, editor of the *American:* "Please don't let these gentlemen make a kennel out of our March of Events parlor." Later, Hearst objected to Cain's columns, as well, again wiring his son: "Get rid of Cain. I thought Abel had done it. Sorry he failed."

In *The Years with Ross*, Thurber says Ross thought Thurber had broken his *New Yorker* contract by allowing Bergman to use his drawings, and had Mrs. White send Thurber a note of inquiry on the subject. Thurber says he explained that the drawings had all been rejected by Ross. "Rubbish," Katharine White responds. Neither Thurber, White, nor many others were ever required to sign a contract, she adds. "Ross never in his life asked me to do anything like this or anyone else." Thurber, in his book, also wonders why Ross once praised Bergman for his newspaper page in the *American*, because it competed for some of Ross's favorite writers. Katharine says Ross explained that to her: "All those people were sending their good stuff to us and their bad stuff to Bergman," she says. "If we rejected a Sullivan, Day, or Thurber, it made Ross feel better if they still had a market for it. But if he felt something good was on their page, then he got sore. Mostly it was bad."

Before Philip Wylie got around to attacking American motherhood in his *Generation of Vipers*, Bergman published Wylie's attack on the horse "as a stupid, vicious animal." "We got bagfuls of mail attacking Wylie, the *American*, and other Hearst papers," says Bergman. "I always felt that this piece was the beginning of the end of the *N.Y. American.*"

After Bellamy vanished in a cloud of cigar smoke, Ross hired Don Wharton from the *Herald Tribune*. Stanley Walker, city editor of the *Trib*, remembers Wharton as "easily forgotten, but he was a pretty good man, rather stolid in manner, and not bad on detail. He and Ross drove each other crazy for some time."

"Ross had an unusual respect for writers," says Wharton, "less for cartoonists, least for editors." Wharton found that Thurber and White were in a special category. "Don't disturb them," Ross told him. "Get them to write but don't worry them." Gibbs wasn't yet fully appreciated by Ross, according to Wharton. He was no longer Mrs. White's assistant but he was still only an editor good at rewriting, in Ross's eyes. "Alva Johnston was revered by Ross and considered to be in a class by himself," Wharton remembers. "He was paid to produce twenty-six Profiles a year. He didn't come close, and when he reached an indebtedness of several thousand dollars, Ross would always write it off."

Though Thurber mocks Ross's editing of Talk pieces, Wharton says that "Ross rewrote whole paragraphs and always greatly improved them. I think it annoyed Thurber that Ross rarely challenged White's Notes and Comment, but Thurber was stuck with a much greater volume of work each week. The reporter's notes given him were often no more than research drafts, with no composition or organization. Thurber almost always had to start from scratch."

Wharton found Thurber hard to take at times. Once Thurber stalked unexpectedly into his office and asked, "Do you want to see an angel go to Heaven?" Without waiting for an answer, Thurber strode to the window, pulled down the blind, sketched a huge Thurber Man with angel's wings and snapped the blind back up. "This was quite out of the ordinary," says Wharton. "Thurber and I usually sent notes to one another regarding Talk ideas, and I didn't know him all that well. I can't say that the incident helped me know him any better." Another time, after a particularly exhausting office disruption by Thurber, Wharton said wearily to Eugene Kinkead, "Can you imagine having Thurber as your houseguest for a whole weekend?"

As to Wharton, Thurber writes Stanley Walker: "[He's] the only guy who ever told Mrs. White that she was silly. He didn't last long after that."

"I never did know what happened," says Wharton. "I heard that my work was being bad-mouthed to Ross and I asked him about it. He said, 'Tell every one of them to go to hell. Tell them all to go to hell.' Six weeks later, when he was in Florida, he sent word for me to be fired."

Wharton, who eventually became a *Reader's Digest* editor, is hardly mentioned or remembered in *New Yorker* history, but he made a significant contribution to it. Eugene Kinkead, who received his first check from the *New*

Yorker in November 1932, remembers that Wharton was his boss in 1933, when he and young William Shawn were the only two freelance reporters on Talk. "We were paid space rates on whatever we came up with that the magazine would accept," Kinkead says. "Sometimes we'd be given ideas to explore, but always on speculation. No payment if nothing came of them. Shawn was so slow and painstaking in what he wrote, and so shy about interviews and going on assignments, that he wasn't even earning a living. Wharton realized that Shawn wasn't going to survive, and also recognized that he was an ideal idea man. Wharton persuaded Ross to hire Shawn as an editor, to generate Talk ideas, and it became obvious that the desk was Shawn's milieu. He quickly showed he could apply his intelligence and sensitivity to other people's writing, and—most important to Ross—get writers to agree to changes with a minimum of trouble and encourage contributors to produce more."

Ross by then was fully accustomed to the peculiarities of staff members and contributors, and easily accepted Shawn's few, harmless eccentricities. Shawn suffered from mild claustrophobia. When he took the train to visit his family in Chicago, it is said, he slept with a hatchet in his Pullman bunk to chop his way out in the event of a train wreck. He hated elevators, and when, at long last, the manually operated elevators at 25 West Forty-third Street were automated, an attendant still ran one, at Shawn's request.

Shawn's demonstrated value to the publication eventually made him the logical successor to Ross himself, but, even after years on the magazine, he would seem the nadir of dark-horse entries for the position, given its flamboyant occupant. Where Ross was profane and so blunt-spoken that even his attempts at lightheartedness were easily confused with insult, Shawn was quiet, introverted, and compulsively polite in speech and manner.

He was born in Chicago in 1908, son of a well-to-do cutlery merchant, Benjamin Chon, whose store was located at the Union Stockyards. (Shawn later changed the spelling of his name because, as the writer he intended to be, he didn't want his byline to be taken as Oriental.) He attended a private prep school, graduating as class president. He put in two years at the University of Michigan and quit to report for the *Las Vegas* [New Mexico] *Optic*, thinking he would like the state's climate. It was where, in 1928, he saw his first copy of the *New Yorker*. ("I thought I was the only one who knew about it," he said.)

A few months later, he was back in Chicago, an editor with a news service, and married a newspaperwoman, Cecille Lyon. They lived in Europe for several months. In Paris he earned money as a jazz pianist while trying his hand at writing fiction and composing ballet music—the primitive work of an uneducated musician, according to his own assessment. He was an addicted reader of the *New Yorker,* and moved to New York to write a book about the magazine, but soon asked to try out as a Talk freelancer. He received two dollars per inch for his few accepted pieces.

"In some instances, Thurber rewrote me," Shawn says. "In 1933, when I joined the staff, he was an established part of the *New Yorker* generation ahead of me, one of the founding fathers, already much more than a Talk rewrite man; he was known internationally, and an important writer. I didn't really have much to do with him until years later, when I managed fact pieces and helped Ross edit Thurber's series on radio soap operas."

At the start of 1931, Thurber was alternating between hopelessness and resolve, his lifestyle remaining the same in either case. Living in town during the work-week, his part-time bachelorhood was crammed with the clutter and happenstance of a disorganized life: dirty laundry, skipped meals, and an inability to keep from overdrawing his account at the Fifth Avenue Bank, where Ingersoll had helped him open one. The bank once called him to ask why, if he entered his check amounts on the check stubs, he couldn't reconcile them with his deposits. He replied that he didn't record his expenditures, and as to his balances, "I just estimate them."

Though he was excited and curious about becoming a father, relations with Althea worsened. "I never thought Althea or Jim were guilty of anything but hard luck in their ill-fated marriage," White wrote Helen Thurber years later. "For many years both of them gave it the old college try, but it was obviously beyond anyone's power to save. It just didn't work. The only good that came out of that marriage was that it made Jim so miserable he doodled to take his mind off his troubles. And from the doodles came the drawings that enchanted the world."

Now drawing in India ink without pencil foundation, Thurber saw his first regular cartoon with caption published in the *New Yorker* on January 31, 1931. It shows a cluster of ludicrous-looking men, with a detective saying to a colleague: "Take a good look at these fellows, Tony, so you'll remember 'em next time." The freakish assortment of Thurber men could hardly be forgotten by anybody.

The path broken by his illustrations for *Is Sex Necessary?,* and his direction set by *New Yorker* acceptances, Thurber was off on one of the most unusual art careers in the history of graphics. It would be one of the briefest, most prolific, popular, unorthodox, and enduring in modern art. It has been said that Thurber's emergence as an artist to be taken seriously was the fortunate coincidence of his work with Duchamp's Dadaist revolution. He was, in fact, a one-man movement, original, inimitable and in league with creative forces beyond his own understanding.

"Bergie" Bergman had met George Grosz, the German painter with radical ideas in art and politics, who, in 1932, abandoned Germany for the United States. Learning that Bergman was with the *New Yorker*, Grosz asked him to arrange a dinner date with Thurber, "whose work began where the other cartoonists' left off," in Grosz's words. Bergman arranged the dinner and later told Thurber: "Grosz told me the reason the New Yorker was a great magazine was because it published your drawings. If I didn't tell you that before, I'm sorry."

As Thurber began to explore his newly discovered strength as illustrator in 1931, the number of his written contributions began to shrink. His published cartoons ran to twenty-three that year; his signed text pieces, thirty-three in 1930, dropped to twelve. His Talk output increased; with White on vacation at the time, Thurber is credited with the entire department for June 13, 1931, including Comment and five stories, a rare grand slam, though it may have included "bank" pieces—Thurber items already prepared and held for scheduling.

He had begun writing the casuals treasured by posterity:

Scribner's magazine had been running a "What if?" series, which speculated on the outcome of current history if certain of its events had ended differently. The young Winston Churchill, a war buff, had written for *Scribner's* "If Lee Had Not Won the Battle of Gettysburg," in which a victorious Lee sets up headquarters in Washington, abolishes slavery, and forms an alliance with Britain. Others of the series were "If Booth Had Missed Lincoln" (Lincoln has a stroke in 1867, and is incapacitated anyway), and "If Napoleon Had Escaped to America." (Napoleon liberates the South with the aid of the British military, gained by marrying into England's royalty.) To Thurber, the series begged to be parodied: His "If Grant Had Been Drinking at Appomattox" supposes that the Northern general, hung over from a night of drinking, tries to surrender his army to a surprised General Lee, whom Thurber always regarded as the better man anyway.

Another casual, "The Remarkable Case of Mr. Bruhl," is about an insignificant little Thurber Man who happens to have a facial scar similar to that of a notorious gangster, who is at large and wanted, a fact widely publicized in the press. Bruhl's departure from reality and into psychosis is caused by a prankster friend who, knowing the nature of Bruhl's distress, telephones him—as Thurber was wont to do—pretends to be a hit man, and tells Bruhl he's "cooked."

What if Lindbergh hadn't been made to order for the ideal national hero? Thurber comes up with the answer in Jackie Smurch, of "The Greatest Man in the World," a crude, greedy bum who somehow manages to fly a patched-together airplane around the world for the first time. His mother, a short-order cook in Iowa, is quoted as saying she hoped he drowned. Refusing to behave like "that _____ _____ baby-face Lindbergh," Smurch is hidden from the public and pushed out a window to his death, with the president's approval.

"The Funniest Man You Ever Saw" is an obvious bore who, his friends insist to the narrator, is a delightful wag and clown, whose routine is to produce variations on a vaudeville joke, where you walk on with a piece of rope and say, "I've either found a piece of rope or lost a horse."

Thurber often became a prisoner of his partial freedom from Althea. Until learning that she was pregnant, it was a particularly low point in his life, says Jap Gude. His level of near-total despair is delineated in "A Box to Hide In" (January 24, 1931). The desperate Thurber nonhero, isolated in his hotel room, decides to look for a box large enough to get into and hide from the world. No grocer he asks has one. "Whatta you mean you want to hide in this box?" one grocer asks. "It's a form of escape," the Thurber Man replies. "It circumscribes your worries and the range of your anguish. You don't see people, either." But nobody has a box big enough, so he hides in his hotel room again.

> I turned out the light and lay on the bed. You feel better when it gets dark. I could have hid in a closet, I suppose, but people are always opening doors. Somebody would find you in a closet. . . . Nobody pays any attention to a big box lying on the floor. You could stay in it for days.

The cleaning woman wakes him the next morning.

> She looked at me with big, dim eyes. There's something wrong with her glands. She's awful but she has a big heart, which makes it worse. She's unbearable, her husband is sick and her children are sick and she is sick too. I got to thinking how pleasant it would be if I were in a box now, and didn't have to see her.

Asked about the piece, Thurber was reluctant to discuss what led to it, but said, "The symbolism there is pretty deliberate, isn't it? I'd read some Freud and knew that rooms, closets, and boxes were womb symbols. At first I thought of having the man hide in the closet and frighten the cleaning woman. Then I decided to keep it simple. At times I still want to hide in a box."

When he was not trying on his new reputation as artist, he was busy with what he cherished most: writing serious humor. Like yesterday's Benchley, or today's Art Buchwald and Russell Baker, he seized upon something in the news, threw the spotlight on its absurd or weak spots, and enlarged them to an entertaining form of social protest. Too contemporary at times to survive the passage of time, some of the pieces have been forgotten, such as "Why Mr. Walker Went to California [If Everything That You Heard Was True]". He not only rounds up the diverse rumors posed by the newspaper pundits as to why the secretive, popular, playboy New York mayor Jimmy Walker visited the West Coast, but offers some of his own, wackier than those in the press.

Like many of the lighthearted observers of the social scene before him, he plays out his helplessness with man's mechanical devices that seem more apt to impede civilized progress than promote it. The telephone company always plagued him. In "Subscriber's Nightmare," Thurber imagines that the phone company is changing the names of its subscribers as well as their numbers:

"Is this Mr. Joseph C. Barrell?" a telephone caller asks. "I'm sorry, sir," the subscriber replies, "but my name has been changed. Will you please ask if this is Mr. Charles O. Hinge." "Is this Mr. Charles O. Hinge?" "Yes."

A Navy inquiry into the causes of a fire aboard the presidential yacht ("The Burning Deck") is conducted by a doddering Thurber admiral, who is deaf and keeps talking about the Navy's glory of yesterday. Nothing whatsoever gets accomplished.

Menace forever threatened Thurber, and the world's arguable insanity was always crowding in on his consciousness. Thurber reported it in terms of his, and others', personal survival strategy. "Cholly" (a familiar pronunciation of his father's name) seems to be a literal account by Thurber of a newspaper vendor at a subway stand. Cholly lost his wife and children in a fire and was shot accidentally by a policeman when a hold-up man got behind the counter with him. Yet, Cholly, a survivor, was a man "curiously at peace with his inferno of noise and color and jostling crowds," Thurber writes. "In some strange way his stand in bedlam was sanctuary."

Thurber's distrust of science is behind "The Future of Element 87," which has just been discovered, leaving only one element not yet found. Thurber treats the missing element as a temperamental person in hiding, refusing to come out, despite the scientists' entreaties.

Thurber was proud of his Sandy Hook farm, the first real estate he had owned. But it settled very little of what continued to bother him. Sitting on the porch of the farmhouse in late September, he writes his old friend, Herman Miller, and his fiancée, Dorothy:

> I've been leading a mixed-up and fretful life, with the heat, approaching fatherhood (although Althea is unquestionably the world's most patient and finest mother-expectant), office work, meditation upon the probability that I shall never write anything really as good as I should like to . . . , the thoughts of a man of thirty-six. Anyway, here I am now at my country estate, having a few weeks' vacation (Althea's mother is here, which is a kind of sanctuary) and sitting for hours at a typewriter thinking muddled thoughts and putting down absolutely no words that are interesting or novel. I did write the first chapter of a novel to be called Rain Before Seven, but I am afraid all of my novels would be complete in one chapter, from force of habit in writing short pieces and also from a natural incapability of what Billy Graves would call "larger flight". . . . So I try to write and dont and then I read something, now and again dropping a pencil or rattling some papers so that Althea, reading in the next room and thinking the softly confused, half-ethereal, half-economical thoughts of approaching motherhood, will not know that my mind has become a blank and my creative talent, such as it was, gone.

There were distractions from his writing, he continues, even in the country: an apple falling from a tree; his neighbor's sheep, which gives him the raspberry with its strange blat. Two of their five female dogs are in heat. But the environment could not be more pleasing to him: a house a hundred and twenty-five years old, overlooking a valley that leads to an old Connecticut town "that was flourishing when Washington was seducing the Mount Vernon chambermaids." He has arranged croquet wickets all around the house and hopes to beat his present record of twenty-three.

Rosemary was born the morning of October 7, 1931. The obstetrician was Dr. "Duke" Damon, Thurber's Phi Psi brother at O.S.U. "We came down to New York [from Sandy Hook]," says Althea, "two weeks before the baby was due, to be on hand in plenty of time for the delivery. It was the week of the Forest Hills tennis tournament, so every day several friends, Jim, and I took the train . . . and watched the entire [tournament]. I didn't find out till afterward that I had completely ruined the time of all the others . . . because they were so terrified . . . that something would happen to me.

"When the baby was overdue . . . Dr. Damon consented to induce it. I . . . felt so justified in my having chosen . . . a person of his skill because there were complications."

Damon had put in five years of resident specialization, was in his first year of practice, and had already delivered one of Nugent's children. "There was a loop of umbilical cord around the baby's neck," says Damon. "It's one of the things that can go wrong at delivery and nothing an obstetrician of any competence can't fix quickly and safely. But for years Thurber told people I had saved his daughter's life. 'She wouldn't be here if it wasn't for you,' Jim would tell me on the phone, on Rosemary's birthday. He liked to dramatize, to see everything in his life as unique or unusual."

The observation was also White's. "Jim found it very important to his ego that everything and everybody connected with him was the greatest," White wrote Helen Thurber. "You, being his wife, not only had to be the greatest woman editor that had ever come down the pike, you had to be Marilyn Monroe times three."

Nearly four years later, when, under the strict divorce laws of Connecticut, Althea had the painful duty of presenting worst-case scenarios of life with Thurber to the court, she told of Thurber's arrival at Doctors Hospital the morning following Rosemary's birth. He had been out all night, a tabloid quotes her, and told her he had been in a fight in which he had driven his hand through a taxi window. She noticed blood on one hand when he finally arrived at the hospital.

Honeycutt affirms that she and Thurber had spent the evening in speakeasies "celebrating" the impending birth, and that later, at her apartment, he had gone into one of his sudden, drunken rages and put his fist through the glass of a French door.

Still bloody, Thurber took a cab to the Jap Gudes, who lived in an old converted carriage house behind 112 Waverly Place in the Village. Gude was on a business trip and his wife, Helen, alone, was startled to hear the doorbell ring "at two or three in the morning," says Gude. She "bravely armed herself with a fireplace poker," walked across the little courtyard separating the carriage house from the back of the main house and through the ground-floor hallway of No. 112.

> There was enough light from the street so that she recognized Jim's silhouette, and let him in. Our studio was just one large, handsome story-and-a-half room with sleeping quarters on an open balcony; she

had to maneuver Jim up a narrow flight of winding stairs in order to bathe and bandage his hand. She put him into our bed and she . . . bedded down on the living-room couch. The really terrifying part came when he woke up and, confused about where he was, started to fall down the stairway. Helen, who had visions of a broken neck and headlines in the tabloids, "Writer Found Dead in Village Love Nest," made a dash from the kitchen where she had been washing the bloodstains out of his shirt, yelling, "Don't die, Jim; please don't die." Somehow he righted himself halfway down the stairs and slid down the rest of the way unharmed and laughing. Helen knew then that he was all right, and she got him off to the hospital the next morning, brushed, groomed, and cheerful in spite of a sore hand and a bad hangover.

Damon remembers Thurber sitting in the delivery room, agitated and nervous, but not drunk and disheveled, or with a bloody hand, as Althea would testify in court.

"Some of their friends thought the baby would improve matters between Althea and Jim," says Damon, "but in all my experience I've never known having a child to save a bad marriage."

37

Those Destructive Forces in Life

I suppose that the high-water mark of my youth . . . was the night the bed fell on my father. It makes a better recitation (unless, as some friends of mine have said, one has heard it five or six times) than it does a piece of writing, for it is almost necessary to throw furniture around, shake doors, and bark like a dog, to lend the proper atmosphere and verisimilitude.

—from "The Night the Bed Fell"

"Everyone knows about Thurber the writer, and Thurber the artist, and Thurber the dramatist," wrote Frank Sullivan after Thurber's death, "but only those privileged to enjoy his company knew Thurber the storyteller. He was a great raconteur."

Thurber's fondness for spontaneous acting, for entertaining, for mimicry, was often only a prelude to writing. Mentally, he would draft a piece over and over, and usually part of the process was to hear himself telling it. It was less the technique of a prose writer than that of a playwright or poet who tries out spoken lines on a live audience before committing them to print. But he *was* a ham actor; he needed to occupy the center of attention and gained it by performing as a comic spellbinder. Most writers suppose that by talking out an idea they will lose the urge to write it, or that someone will make off with it. But nobody else had Thurber's eye, ear, and imagination; his pieces could never belong to anyone else. Wolcott Gibbs, Lois Long, Dorothy Parker, St. Clair McKelway, and dozens of others who inhabited Manhattan's apartments and speakeasies in the early thirties repeatedly heard the early versions of Thurber's experiences in Columbus that would eventually make up *My Life and Hard Times*.

"I first heard Thurber tell me those stories at Martin & Mino's speakeasy," says Gibbs's wife, Elinor. "Helen Wismer was with him—I think it was their first date together." ("It was," Helen affirms.) And when the *New Yorker*'s obituary of Thurber stated that his Broadway appearance in his revue, *A Thurber Carnival*, was a recent accomplishment, McKelway took issue. He had personally witnessed Thurber, he said, exhibit a fine acting ability from nearly thirty years before.

"I'd just met Thurber. I had an apartment on Tenth Street in the Village, and one night Thurber dropped in and told a group of us about the night the bed fell. He threw himself into the act. He'd climb under the table to illustrate the bed falling on him, would slam doors and change his voice to imitate his mother, brothers, and the barking dog. If you missed one Thurber show, there was plenty of opportunity to catch the next." Thurber's performances, McKelway writes, ran intermittently at night for months in houses where every seat, including those on the floor, was occupied. These houses were usually brownstone ones and were mostly in Greenwich Village. . . . Thurber was engaged on these evenings in telling—and acting out—stories about his family in Columbus. . . . He hadn't, as far as I know, given a thought to writing these stories, and none of us . . . recall having advised him to do so. The lot of us were too racked by mirth on those evenings to make such a constructive suggestion. . . . The lines and actions of all the characters played by Thurber were continually being rewritten and switched around.

The thing might open with a performance by a character who really had no part—Aunt Sarah Shoaf, for example, who was obsessed by a fear of burglars, and who, waking in the night, would cry "Hark!" . . . throw one of her shoes in one direction and its mate down the hall in the other. . . . Since Aunt Sarah . . . didn't live in Thurber's house in Columbus . . . she had to get off the stage after throwing her two shoes. . . . One after another, and sometimes more or less simultaneously, he would play the parts of his mother, his father, his grandfather (offstage), his brother[s] . . . and a dog . . . in addition to playing himself. . . . This memory of the young Thurber getting ready to make all the world laugh is something his death cannot take away.

Another member of those audiences remembers joining a party just as Thurber, playing his mother, was bellowing "He's dying!" while pulling on a closet door he pretended was stuck, a door his audience was convinced led to an attic where Charles Thurber was asleep in a bed. "Let's go to your poor father!" Other latecomers would walk in to the sound of Thurber's muffled voice from inside the host's wrap closet, presumably his father demanding that "someone get me out of here!"

"Once my mother came to town and either I invited Thurber to the apartment, or he just dropped in," McKelway remembers. "He'd often call to say he was just around the corner and thought he might drop in. So there was my Presbyterian mother from Washington, D.C., and Thurber, in my apartment. Naturally I was a bit apprehensive. The Dionne quintuplets had just been born in Ontario, and after a few drinks Thurber became Dr. Defoe assisting at the births. He could sound just like a crying baby, because his own had been born not long before. As the country doctor, he'd flop in a chair from exhaustion after delivering twins. Then he would sit bolt upright and say, 'My God, there's another one!' He'd brace his foot against the foot of the couch and yank another baby into the world. By the time the fifth was born, my mother had to be helped to her room. The fare was too rich for her and she was so weak from laughter she was worried about herself. Thurber was never obscene. He used swear words in the way Ross did and sparingly.

"At the time, Thurber was famous, but mostly to those who read the *New Yorker*, and the circulation wasn't that big in 1933. He was sure he wasn't going to be a big literary figure and I think that's why he needed social recognition, a need that paid so many dividends to those of us who invested in a relationship with him. He gave of himself freely and seemed glad that he could please the people he respected and liked. When he finally got all the Columbus stories on paper, it turned out to be the biggest thing he'd done, and I think nobody was more surprised than he was that *My Life and Hard Times* became an all-time success."

New Yorker staffers couldn't get enough of Thurber's imitating Ross. He would run his hand through his hair, as Ross did, and might begin: "Jeezus Christ! Nobody does any work around here but me." Once when Ross was told that Thurber had been imitating him at Dorothy Parker's apartment the night before, he summoned Thurber to his office and sullenly invited him to repeat the performance, but Thurber needed a more congenial audience.

Though he probably didn't recognize himself, Ross, as editor, had to have read Thurber's imitation of him in such a casual as "How to Adjust Yourself to Your Work": "Russell . . . I want to see a dive, a hideout, a joint. I want to see these gangsters in their haunts. I want to see them in action, by God, if they ever get into action. I think most of it is newspaper talk. Your average gangster is a yellow cur."

"When I had the checking department, Thurber would call me on the phone and pretend to be Ross, angry about something already in the magazine or about to go in," says Rogers Whitaker. "He did his homework. The points he'd bring up were always timely and plausible. He usually fooled me."

Though shy in many respects when he was growing up, Thurber liked to put on one-man home shows for the family. One of the Fisher cousins tells of a grade-school Thurber at home reciting funny items from magazines to his relatives and acting out stories he had read. One evening he ran out of magazines, asked his audience to stay in their seats, ran over to Grandmother Fisher's and came back with more material so that the show could go on. (Or, as he used to say before making his appearance onstage in *A Thurber Carnival*, "The show-off must go on.")

The British writer Alan Sillitoe writes that he couldn't help mimicking his own parents and others as a youth, and was often punished for being impertinent. Later, his propensity to mimic his supervisors cost him job after job. He makes the point that good mimics often are introverted people wishing to escape from themselves, who sometimes become so caught up in their disguises that they cease to have a life of their own. This can also be true of the better actors. But it can put off self-awareness, and could partly explain the despairing, muddled, and adolescent self-impressions in the letters Thurber continued to write women who interested him romantically, until he was nearly forty years of age.

Mimicking his O.S.U. drill instructor had helped Thurber gain social advantage and confidence with his fraternity and classmates, something he never forgot. Impersonation was an easy path to popularity for him. At times, hostility probably informed some of Thurber's furtive antics. He did seem intent on trying to drive Katharine White out of her mind, telephoning that busy, worried woman and pretending to be a Negro laundress who had lost the Whites' laundry, had scorched some of the garments, or had been forced to watch helplessly while a drunken husband tore the laundry to shreds before her eyes.

But neither friend nor foe was safe if Thurber had their telephone number. Once, Joel Sayre had just published an article on college football greats in the *American Mercury*. He was working on the *Herald Tribune*, didn't go to work until 1:00 P.M., and was home when the phone rang one morning and a strange voice said, "Is this Mr. Sayre?"

"Yes."

"Mr. Joel Sayre?"

"Yes."

"You wouldn't remember me but I'm Fike Eichenlaub," the caller said. Eichenlaub was All-American in 1912–13, and had helped Notre Dame beat Army with a last-second forward pass. Sayre had written about him in the article. He also knew Eichenlaub was then a coach and that there was a football coaches' association meeting in New York that week. It all made sense. So he said, "Of course I remember you, Mr. Eichenlaub. All-American fullback."

"Gosh," Eichenlaub went on, "that's swell of you to remember that."

"It was Thurber, of course," Sayre says, "sounding exactly like a big ex-football player, a low, awkward voice trying to say something impressive to thank me for the write-up I'd given him. He kept it up until I began to wonder if I would get to work on time. I fell for it completely. Finally Thurber couldn't stand it and began laughing."

In "Preface to a Life," Thurber wrote, "I have known [middle-aged] writers . . . to phone their . . . offices from their homes, ask for themselves in a low tone, and then, having fortunately discovered that they were 'out,' to collapse in hard-breathing relief." The "middle-aged writers" he refers to is

James Thurber. He sometimes called the *New Yorker,* asked for himself in a disguised voice, and left outlandish messages, often cryptic threats expressed in the language of the underworld. When he arrived at the office and was given the message by a worried, novice receptionist, he would play out the drama, looking alarmed, sinking into a chair, clutching his heart, and gratefully accepting a glass of water.

As usual, he translated the chaos he created into casuals. In "The Advent of Mr. Moray," the office boy leaves a message on Mr. Gregg's desk: "Mr. Slug phoned and will phone again."

> Mr. Gregg . . . was extremely susceptible to the beating of the mythical drums of doom. He was always expecting that something was going to happen. He was always considerably surprised at night that it hadn't.

Gregg is so convinced that Slug is after him that he takes his swivel chair with him at lunchtime as an excuse to ride the freight elevator. Another message ("Mr. Axkiller phoned") increases Gregg's anxiety, and it is followed by a receptionist's call that "A Mr. Moray phoned and said he would be in to get you." Moray, as it turns out, is a former forgotten college chum who had a date with Gregg, which Gregg didn't remember. Moray bursts into Gregg's office with their old school yell, "Kill 'em all!" "Mr. Gregg jumped from his chair, screamed, and fell over backward in a faint."

Long after Thurber left the staff, he was still telephoning from his home to harass old colleagues, his voice disguised. Among his victims were members of the second *New Yorker* generation, including Brendan Gill—Thurber unaware that Gill distrusted him. "The cruelest jokes are those in which information is withheld from the victim," says Gill. "Thurber's telephone mimicry could cause worry and pain to innocent people." It is possible, Gill thinks, that it was Thurber's revenge on a life that had left him handicapped.

Thurber's daughter, Rosemary, remembers "getting fooled several times thinking there was a looney on the other end of the phone. Being a basically timid type, I would start to hang up and then my father would reveal himself. He would call radio stations and confuse the operator, demanding the quick loans a bank might be advertising. I was fascinated at how he could show up their silly ads for what they were."

To most of Thurber's friends, his stunts were, in the end, both funny and forgivable. They went with the Thurber territory. "They were usually harmless pranks," says Sayre. "Jim wasn't the obnoxious practical joker, who employs props. He used only his imagination and theatrical skills, and if he had taken the time to develop some of the situations he hatched with the telephone, he could have disrupted the whole bloody world. Everybody was nervous and guilty about something in those days, and Thurber always sensed what it was and hit it every time."

Thurber's Columbus friend Ted Gardiner says: "You didn't get mad at Thurber, because the fun he had with you was always a unique experience; there was the element of genius in it."

Gardiner sold theater supplies and distributed films to theaters in the Columbus area. "Thurber was absolutely psychic in knowing when to call and pretend to be someone else," he says. "Once when I didn't know he was in town, he telephoned and pretended to be an irate manager of a convention hall who had rented a couple thousand chairs from us. He was mad as hell and wanted to know why my people had set up all the chairs facing the rear instead of the platform. As it turned out, just the day before I'd contracted to set up two thousand chairs in a convention hall. I had new help I wasn't sure of and it all could have happened the way Thurber described it. I had a dreadful time calming Thurber who wanted his money back, was threatening to sue and to take the matter to the Better Business Bureau. I was still trying to build my business and he nearly gave me a heart attack.

"Another time he called as the manager of a local theater. He was slightly hysterical but rational enough to point out that although a Clara Bow movie was being shown, the marquee was advertising a William Hart film. 'You're sending people into my theater expecting to see Bill Hart when I've got Clara Bow on the screen,' Thurber shouted at me. Actually I'd just been through an identical mix-up with this same theater and I thought I'd straightened it out. He seemed to sense what would work. He took me in every time, even when he made a big scene because my employees had delivered equipment to 165 and 7/8 Main Street instead of 165 and 1/2. It took me a few minutes to realize that no Columbus street number contains a 7/8 fraction."

When Gardiner was in New York, he always called Thurber, who wanted to share everything going on in his life with his friends, Gardiner says. But sooner or later the sublime would be replaced by the ridiculous.

"Once, he kept me in a bar drinking until just prior to my train departure, and I had to dogtrot to Grand Central. Thurber let me get a head start and then began running frantically after me, shouting, 'Stop that man! That's my suitcase!' Luckily, that sort of thing doesn't even draw attention in New York and I made my train. They closed the gate right after I got through, leaving Thurber shaking the bars and shouting that I'd never get away with this. He put everything he had into a gag and it was plenty. There's no one around now who could make the world the wild and funny place that he could."

When the Gardiners knew Thurber was in Columbus, even the children were ready for him. Their telephone number was a Kingswood exchange. Thurber used a deep, gravelly voice and would ask, "Is this Gardiner 3-7503? Is Mr. Kingswood there?" The Gardiner children would scream with laughter.

"Thurber always knew what delighted a child," says Nora Sayre, daughter of Joel and Gertrude. "About 1940, Helen and Jim had a cook, an Irish lady who talked to herself. She'd say things like 'Get off my back and get away from my eyes. I haven't got time for you or Dewey.' She said she was talking to her 'familiar,' or 'spook,' a witch with whom she helped cast spells. Jamie would tell me about it, and we'd laugh and laugh."

"My father had a good voice and strummed a ukulele; Thurber could imitate him perfectly, singing "Redwing," and songs with Thurber's own lyrics—something like 'Oh, my freckle-faced, consumptive Sarah Jane. Some say that you are crazy; I say you're just insane.'"

Thurber took special and nonmalicious delight in malapropisms, whether those of servants or children. "I was shy as a child," says Nora. "I'd get words mixed up, scream and clap my hand on my mouth, but Jamie would laugh, pat me on the back and say, 'No, it was better the first way you said it.'" To Thurber, children were like noncombatant ships in a war zone, never to be fired upon and always to be escorted to safety.

During one visit to the Sayres, Joel came upon Thurber and Nora, age six, at the breakfast table. Joel writes:

> She hated the milk she was supposed to drink, and he was telling her how much his brother Robert hated milk, too. He was also giving very loud imitations of the horrible noises Robert would make to register his hatred.
>
> "BAAAAAUP!" Jim would go, screwing up his face dreadfully. "BUUUUURP!" And there was my child, gasping and strangling with laughter, precisely as I had done at his antics a whole generation before. . . .
>
> What an entertainer Jim was, what a charmer! A lot of bum amateur psychology has been put forth arguing that he was *compelled* to entertain and charm—and compete ferociously for attention—to compensate for his visual handicap and inability to excel as a sports hero. Jim would have been entertaining and charming—and attention-getting—if he had had the eyes of Babe Ruth and all the skills of the last Heisman Trophy winner. . . .
>
> Had he been interested, he could have earned his living as a professional mimic. Jim looked no more like Harold Ross . . . than he

looked like Ulysses S. Grant; yet when he got going on his Ross imitations, he *was* Ross."

Thurber didn't talk all the time; he could listen with a special concentration to how others talked. His best sources for his written and acting material were servants, usually first-generation immigrants or others with difficulties in handling the English language. In "The Black Magic of Barney Haller," Barney is the hired man at Thurber's Sandy Hook farm. Thurber pretends to take alarm from Barney's garbled efforts to communicate in a language not native to him. "Once I see dis boat come down de rock," Barney might say, meaning —as it later turned out—he had seen a bolt of lightning come down the lightning rod on the house. In an effort to counter Barney's black magic, Thurber confronts him with an aggressive rendering of a Frost poem ("I'm going out to clean the pasture spring . . ."), and when Barney, intending to go up to the garret to clean out the wasps, tells Thurber, "We go to the garrick now and become warbs," Thurber decides "The hell we do!" and launches another counteroffensive, ranting to an astonished Barney in a Lewis Carroll mode:

"Listen!" I barked, suddenly. "Did you know that even when it isn't brillig I can produce slithy toves? Did you happen to know that the mome rath never lived that could outgrabe me? Yeah and furthermore . . . even if I were a warb, I wouldn't have to keep on being one if I didn't want to. I can become a playing card at will, too; once I was the jack of clubs, only I forgot to take my glasses off and some guy recognized me."

Convinced of Thurber's insanity, Barney quits on the spot.

Negro patois was big in the Thurber inventory in a day before it connoted heartlessness toward the conditions that had given rise to it. Thurber's puritanical, self-appointed guardianship of his beloved language left him fated to note every misuse or mispronunciation. His reaction was annoyance, if the mishandling was done by the reasonably educated, who should have known better; it was one of delight if done by an innocent. In 1929, he told a New York *Evening Post* interviewer, "My favorite line in all literature is in the play *The First Year*, when the wife says to the colored maid, 'Did you seed the grapefruit?' and the maid answers, 'Yes'm, I see'd it.'" He built an entire casual around the maid who reported that "they are here with the reeves [wreaths]." "Only Lewis Carroll would have understood Della completely," he writes.

Sayre says that Thurber figured out, and correctly, that anyone in New York who had hired a maid had hired seventy-nine maids. "He could call any married woman he knew and say, 'Dis is Beulah,' and the woman would say, 'Of course, Beulah, how are you?' Beulah would always be starving, or turned out of her house by her no-good husband, or her son would have been in a shooting scrape with the cops. It was the Depression and lots of people were starving and asking for help, so Jim's impersonations were easily believable. Nobody got their maids' names straight and Jim sounded like all of them."

Thurber made his skits a joyous thing, and if Beulah was ever treated roughly at the other end of the phone, Thurber took it personally and was known to harbor a grudge, to the bewilderment of the victim, who never did learn that it was Thurber on the phone. For in playing Beulah he became Beulah, complete with all the intolerable burdens her race had had to endure.

"Dick and Louise Connell lived in a hotel apartment," Joel Sayre recalls. "One Sunday Thurber stopped by the hotel lobby and telephoned the Connells. Much of what happened—but not everything—he wrote up."

In "Destructive Forces in Life," the Connells become the Conners, and Thurber is Bert Scursey:

> . . . for some strange reason, when Louise Conner answered, Bert Scursey found himself pretending to be, and imitating the voice of, a colored woman. This Scursey is by way of being an excellent mimic, and a colored woman is one of the best things he does.
>
> "Hello," said Mrs. Conner. In a plaintive voice, Scursey said, "Is dis heah Miz Commah?" "Yes, this is Mrs. Conner," said Louise. "Who is speaking?" "Dis heah's Edith Rummum," said Scursey. "Ah used wuck for yo frens was nex doah yo place a Sou Norwuck. . . . "What is it you want, Edith?" asked Mrs. Conner, who was completely taken in by the imposter. . . . Scursey—or Edith, rather—explained in a pitiable, hesitant way that she was without work or money and that she didn't know what she was going to do; Rummum, she said, was in the jailhouse because of a cutting scrape on a roller-coaster. . . . Louise . . . said that she could perhaps find some laundry work for Edith to do. "Yessum," said Edith. "Ah laundas."

Louise tells Edith to take the elevator to the seventh floor, apartment 7A. Thurber then began telephoning every few minutes pretending to be lost and wandering into other people's apartments. Louise tries to direct her: ". . . you took the elevator, didn't you?" "Dass whut ah took."

Louise tells Edith to ask the elevator operator to help her. Thurber hung up and soon called the Connells again, wanting to prevent Louise from checking with the elevator man. Dick Connell answered this time.

"Hello," shouted Conner, irritably. "Who is this?" Scursey now abandoned the role of Edith and assumed a sharp, fussy, masculine tone. "Mr. Conner," he said, crisply, "this is the office. I am afraid we shall have to ask you to remove this colored person from the building. She is blundering into other people's apartments, using their phones. We cannot have that sort of thing, you know, at the Graydon." The man's words and his tone infuriated Conner. ". . . please come down to the lobby and do something about this situation," said the man, nastily. "You're damned right I'll come down!" howled Conner.

Sayre is able to fill in what little Thurber left out of the piece. Dick Connell was already in one of his depressed states that Sunday and had determined not to see anybody until he was out of it. He took the elevator to the lobby in a murderous mood, to confront the manager. In the lobby, while storming at the surprised manager, Connell spied Thurber, as Edith, talking on the phone to Louise again; he was jackknifed over the house-phone counter, rear end protruding, yammering in dialect that the people in the apartment she's now calling from never heard of the "Commahs." Connell, says Sayre, delivered a quick kick to Thurber's rear, shaking his glasses loose. Thurber didn't miss a beat. Still Edith on the phone, he at once complained to Louise hysterically, in a high, thin voice: "Miz Commah, yo know wha yo husban jes done? He *kick* me, das wha he done!" Louise could hear her angry husband cursing at the other end of the line and fearful that in his depressed state he was assaulting an unemployed laundry woman, hurried down to find the hotel manager trying to calm a belligerent Connell and restore order. "I don't know this gentleman," Thurber was explaining coldly to the manager. "He just came up and assaulted me. I was thinking of moving here, but if this is the kind of place . . ."

In "Destructive Forces in Life" Thurber has Conner moving from New York to Oregon "for a less important position," but one that was still not far enough away from Scursey. As always, says Louise, her husband, Dick Connell, soon saw the humor of it and forgave Thurber.

"I once asked Jim how he knew when to call and pretend to be somebody, or an agency or institution that, as it turned out, you were expecting to hear from," says Sayre. "He said both he and his mother had the ability to sense things like that, and he didn't understand it, either."

Sayre was right that Thurber rarely used props in the tradition of practical jokers, but colleagues remember the ancient derringer he once brought to the office. Driving through Winsted, Connecticut, he stopped to windowshop and bought the old firearm. According to his "Guns and Game Calls," Thurber pulled the trigger so often that he had to have a gun shop replace the firing spring. It is the derringer he was carrying when, according to St. Clair McKelway, copy editor Rogers Whitaker looked up from his page proofs to see Thurber "staring at him wild-eyed." "Are you the S.O.B. who keeps putting notes in red ink on the proofs of my Talk stories?" McKelway reports Thurber as saying. Whitaker acknowledges the fact, whereupon Thurber points the gun at him and pulls the trigger. Whitaker is supposed to have fainted and never used red ink after that. The apocryphal anecdote has even made its way into serious biography.

Whitaker points out the absurdity of the story. He and Thurber had worked together for nearly eight years; he was used to Thurber's office capers; Thurber certainly knew who copy-edited his Talk proofs. The chances were good, Whitaker says, that Thurber improved on the story when he told it to Freddie Packard, head of the checking department, who passed it on to Mc-Kelway. McKelway never checked the truth of it with Whitaker.

The feud between Packard and Whitaker had gone on for years, so long that few on the staff could trace it to its origins, though when Whitaker, head of the checking department at the time, hired Packard, it is said that they took an instant dislike to one another. Once, when Packard allowed an error to get into print, Whitaker made him memorize the entire piece containing the oversight and recite it to him. Whitaker's disdain for Packard persisted for decades, though Packard spoke foreign languages, teemed with classical knowledge, and, when Whitaker was promoted, succeeded him as chief fact checker. Freddie was a thick-set man who shuffled when he walked while continually scratching the back of his left hand. One staffer remembers Whitaker standing in the corridor, watching Packard move past him at his usual slow gait, and sneering, "And what does this float represent?" Whitaker could well be right in believing that Packard passed on to McKelway a Thurber-embellished story that left Whitaker the patsy.

When Wolcott Gibbs read in Max Eastman's *Enjoyment of Laughter* Thurber's statement that humor was emotional chaos, remembered in tranquility, he took issue, writing in Book-of-the-Month Club *News:*

> This quite possibly is what Thurber thinks about humor but it comes a little oddly from someone who has never remembered anything tranquilly in his life. A great many hilarious and profoundly discouraging things have happened to Thurber during the past half century but his

recollection of them is never precisely what you call detached . . . [including] the memory of old arguments, generally of a literary aspect and nature and late at night . . . . Thurber all in all is an intense man, which may or may not explain his talent, but it certainly doesn't entitle him to go around talking about tranquility.

By World War II, a growing national conscience had put an end to dialect in magazine fiction, with its haunting reminder of a century of economic and educational neglect of blacks and other minorities. In the 1940s, the *Saturday Evening Post* stopped running Roark Bradford's popular fiction, which employed the Negro patois; with the changing national attitudes, it was ruled to be in poor taste and no longer funny in a family magazine. (Remarkably, the radio comedy "Amos 'n' Andy," featuring two white men in blackface, remained popular with both blacks and whites, defying racial attitudes, until the 1950s, when the show went on television with African-American actors, at which point several organizations successfully objected to it.) Thurber was still protesting society's judgment call on the issue in the fifties, when he appeared on a British talk show:

THE HOST: The New England colored girl . . . who'd say "Do you want cretonnes for the soup tonight?" or "The lawn is full of fletchers." These wonderful words . . . you can't have made those up . . .

THURBER: No, those were all genuine. I would feel if I made them up that somehow the validity would go out of the thing. . . . I was exasperated . . . during the period when the word "stereotyped" came in. You mustn't say anything about colored people, it is all stereotyped. . . . I don't think it is at all. . . . Humor must not have any bounds except those of libel and I suppose in a sense, taste, although what taste is I don't know. It is what each person decides is what he can say or what he shouldn't.

As if to prove the point, in 1949, Andy White and Thurber were reminiscing over a gin and tonic in the Algonquin lobby for the benefit of an acquaintance.

"Back in the thirties," said White, "a Buick I owned was stolen from a garage here in town, and used in a robbery and a police chase. There were bullet holes in it. The cops traced the car's license to me and decided I was the brains behind the robbery. They were in my office questioning me off and on for a week."

"They had Andy's telephone line bugged," Thurber said, "so I'd call Andy and say [speaking now in a loud, tough voice], 'Hiya, Lefty, this is Dutch. When the heat's off I got another job for ya.' "

"And they'd say, 'All right, who's Dutch?' " White picked up.

"Whenever they'd be about to drop the case against Andy," said Thurber, "I'd call in as another underworld character, which would keep the cops watching Andy for another day."

White chuckled. Though the two no longer saw much of one another socially, they both cherished memories of their early days together.

38

That Admiral on the Wheel

Mr. Pendly hadn't driven the family car for five years, since . . . the night . . . when he mistook a pond for a new concrete road and turned off onto it. He didn't really drive into the pond, only hovered at the marge, for Mrs. Pendly shut off the ignition and jerked the emergency brake. Mr. Pendly was only forty-two, but his eyes weren't what they had been. After that night, Mrs. Pendly always drove the car. She even drove it during the daytime, for although Mr. Pendly could see in the daytime, his nerve was gone. He was obsessed with the fear that he wouldn't see the traffic lights, or would get them mixed up with lights on storefronts, or would jam on his brakes when postmen blew their whistles. You can't drive toward a body of water thinking it's made of concrete without having your grip on yourself permanently loosened.

—from "Mr. Pendly and the Poindexter"

The first gasoline-powered auto in the United States appeared two years before Thurber was born, and he grew up in the decades when the nation was shifting from a dependence on animals for transportation to machines. The dilemmas that his relatives ran into during the transition was enough to scare even those with a sounder nervous system than Thurber's from ever setting foot in a horseless carriage. During the Christmas season, one of his aunts steered her primitive auto impartially through all the red and green traffic lights in Columbus, believing they were part of the holiday ornaments.

Like Pendly of "Mr. Pendly and the Poindexter," Thurber submitted himself to the agonies of hell when he drove a car, but unlike Pendly, Thurber was determined to meet the challenge, forbidding as it was. He saw operating a vehicle as the essential symbol of manhood and domestic masterfulness. He resented, as much as anything in his life with Althea, her taking over the driving, though he well knew that she did so for no more humiliating a reason than that she wanted both of them to live. Ever since Robert taught him to operate the family Reo, and though he occasionally pretended to be a better driver than he was, he continually confessed in print to his traffic misadventures, blaming his poor vision. Yet he persisted in driving until failing eyesight put an end to it in 1939.

It was during his university days that Thurber, on a drive to Goodale Park, mistook the smooth surface of the moonlit lake for solid pavement, stopping just in time. Once, he drove his Grandfather Fisher's Lozier into a tulip bed, and another time, trying to park, with a fraternity brother and two girls as passengers, he drove into a clump of trees. Usually, his passengers seemed unaware of the perils of riding with Thurber, knowing him to be a clown and believing that his auto antics were deliberate attempts to scare them. But Minnette Fritts says she was amazed that Thurber's family would let him drive the Reo to the campus to see her. "We went up on sidewalks," she says, "and I think once hit a telephone pole."

With the move to Silvermine, in 1929, Althea began shopping for a used car. She already did the driving. Thurber, as Mr. Pendly,

> was not particularly unhappy about the actual fact of not driving a car any more. He had never liked to drive much. It galled him slightly that his wife could see better than he could and it gave him a feeling of inferiority to sit mildly beside her while she solved the considerable problems of city traffic. . . . He [knew] very little about any automobile. He knew how to make them go and how to stop them, and how to back up. Mrs. Pendly was not good at backing up. When she turned her head and looked behind her, her mind and hands ceased to coördinate.

It rather pleased Mr. Pendly that his wife was not good at backing up. Still, outside of that, she knew more about cars than he ever would. The thought depressed him.

At the Poindexter showroom, Pendly worries that the salesman will find out he "didn't know anything at all about automobiles. . . . A husband whose wife drove the car!" Tommy Trinway, in "Smashup," is another whose history of vehicle accidents and fear of driving deliver him into the hands of a Thurber Woman who has a maddeningly efficient way with cars. After a harrowing drive from the suburbs to the city, with Trinway at the wheel, they relax at their hotel.

"Well," Trinway says, "nobody got killed."

> "No, thank God," said Betty. "But somebody *would* have if I hadn't jerked on the hand brake. You never think of the hand brake. You'd have hit that pillar sure, and killed both of us." Tommy looked at her coldly. "Oh, *yeah?*" he said. She raised her eyebrows in surprise and indignation at his tone; the match she was about to hold to her cigarette went out. "What's the matter with you?" she asked. . . . "Nothing is the matter with me," said Tommy. "I'm fine." She stared at her husband over the cigarette and, striking another match, still stared. He stared back at her. He tossed off his Scotch with a new, quick gesture, set the glass down, got up, and lounged over to the desk. "We'll want two single rooms tonight, Mr. Brent," he said to the man at the desk.

Published in the *New Yorker* a few months after Thurber's divorce from Althea, "Smashup" appears to be a parting shot at her. "The near-accident is faked," says Helen Thurber. "The rest true." "Smashup" refers to the fate of the marriage, not the car.

Althea settled for a used Ford roadster, not a Poindexter. This was the car she left at the South Norwalk station for Thurber to drive to the Silvermine house when he got off the train one evening. He writes Herman Miller:

> Dinner was to be ready for me twenty minutes after I got into the car, but night fell swiftly and there I was again. Although I had been driven over that road 75 or 100 times, I had not driven it myself, and I got off onto a long steep narrow road which seemed to be paved with old typewriters. After a half hour of climbing, during which I passed only two farm boys with lanterns, the road petered out in a high woods. From far away came the mournful woof of a farm hound. That was all. There I

was, surrounded by soughing trees, where no car had ever been before. I dont know how I got out. I backed up for miles, jerking on the hand brake every time we seemed to be falling. I was two hours late for dinner.

Helen Wismer, whom Thurber married in June 1935, had once learned to drive but was out of practice. When they bought a used 1932 Ford V-8 a month after their marriage, Helen debated whether to take a refresher course. She finally decided that to drive was to risk assuming the hateful role of the Thurber Woman in cartoon and story. She was aware of Thurber's Mitty dream, to drive a car at sixty miles an hour, cap reversed on his head like Barney Oldfield. "Driving meant so much to him," she says, "I decided to take my chances."

In a way it was almost an offer to sacrifice her life in the name of love for Thurber. He praised her to the Millers for being "patient, gentle, and kind" while he groped along in his Ford, honking, waving, being honked at by long lines of cars behind him. The only thing he thought ever got to her about his night driving was his tendency to whimper in self-pity. Night driving was his nemesis, as he wrote the Millers:

Helen Thurber and I have just returned from dinner at the Elm Tree Inn in Farmington, some twenty miles from our little cot. It was such a trip as few have survived. I lost eight pounds. You see I can't see at night and this upset all the motorists in the state tonight, for I am blinded by headlights in addition to not being able to see, anyway. It took us two hours to come back, weaving and stumbling, stopping now and then, stopping always for every car that approached, stopping other times just to rest and bow my head on my arms and ask God to witness that this should not be.

Farmington's Inn was built in 1638 and is reputed to be the oldest inn in these Untied States. I tonight am the oldest man. You know my sight of old, perhaps. I once tried to feed a nut to a faucet, you know, thinking it was a squirrel. . . . A further peril of the night road is that flecks of dust and streaks of bug blood on the windshield look to me often like old admirals in uniform, or crippled apple women, or the front end of barges and I whirl out of their way, thus going into ditches and fields and up on front lawns, endangering the life of authentic admirals and apple women who may be out on the roads for a breath of air before retiring. . . .

Whereas I was anguished and sick at heart, Helen must have felt even worse for there were moments when, with several cars coming toward me, and two or three honking behind me, and a curved road ahead I would take my foot off of everything and wail "Where the hell *am* I?" That, I suppose, would strike a fear to a woman's heart equalled by almost nothing else. We have decided that I will not drive any more at night. Helen . . . is going to get back into it again. She can see. She doesn't care to read, in the Winsted Evening Citizen, some such story as this:

"Police are striving to unravel the tangle of seven cars and a truck which suddenly took place last night at 9 o'clock. . . . Although nobody seems to know exactly what happened, the automobile that the accident seemed to center about was a 1932 Ford V-8 operated by one James Thurberg. Thurberg, who was coming into Winsted at 8 miles an hour mistook the lights of Harry Freeman's hot-dog stand, at the corner of Harmer's lane and Route 44 for the headlight of a train. As he told the story later he swerved out to avoid the oncoming hotdog stand only to see an aged admiral in full dress uniform riding toward him, out of the old wood road, on a tricycle, which had no headlights. In trying to go in between the hotdog stand and the tricycle, Thurber[g] somehow or other managed to get his car crosswise of all three roads, resulting in the cracking up of six other cars and the truck. Police have so far found no trace of the aged admiral and his tricycle. The hotdog stand came to a stop fifteen feet from Thurberg's car."

[Helen] is as calm as ice when I am driving at night, or as cold anyway.

A year after writing this letter, Thurber recycled some of it for the *New Yorker* casual, "The Admiral on the Wheel." When a *New York Times* article urged more stringent drivers-license tests, Thurber, in "The Character of Catastrophe," argued that most accidents were caused not by inept drivers but by family arguments and mistakes, such as when the wife turns to the driver and shouts: "Oh, Don, I threw your glasses away instead of the peanut shells!"

In the fall of 1936, *Stage* magazine accepted Thurber's offer to review Noel Coward's *Tonight at 8:30* in Boston, a hundred-and-forty-five-mile drive from Litchfield. Thurber was at the wheel. He and Helen dined with Coward; Thurber found him "a swell fellow," though, as an aspiring playwright himself, he was discouraged to hear that Coward had dashed off all the one-act plays that summer.

They started back that night, when Thurber supposed the traffic would not be as heavy. Yet, as he expressed it to the Millers, it was still Thurber driving at night. When Helen thought they had passed a turn they should have made, Thurber put the Ford in reverse and backed up to see the road sign in his headlights, went off the highway and got stuck. It took a crew of men to pry out the Ford after a long interval in which the Thurbers sat in the dark waiting for help to come.

When they went to Europe in 1937, they took their 1935 Ford V-8 with them. Thurber continued to place great masculine store in operating the car for thousands of miles from Italy to Scotland, Helen gamely riding the passenger seat, doing what she could not to deface his self-image as the head of household with a stubborn claim on driving prerogatives. They drove only by day and Thurber got the most fun and satisfaction from driving he had ever had, or would have again. Flavoring the news he wrote to the Whites, McNulty, and Nugent was his pride in getting around the continent by car. Having negotiated the southern coast of France, he wrote McNulty: "God, what a place to drive a car in! You're always a mile high looking down at the sea, or on a valley floor looking up at a town a mile above you." In *My World and Welcome to It* he tells proudly of turning the Ford around on a narrow mountain road in the foothills of the Pyrenees. In Dijon, Thurber writes White: "We got back a little while ago from Arles, which is 45 miles away, over roads known to me as the motorist's Paradise; you can drive 50 mi. an hour for an hour without passing a car or swerving an inch; no curves. . . . We travel with, in Helen's lap as I drive, a few of the indispensable guides to restaurants and hotels, all of them French."

London had been their first stop and where Thurber first got lost driving. There were seven streets leading into the same square and Thurber eventually returned to the square by way of all seven. He says he didn't know he was coming back to the same square until he realized it was the same policeman he was accosting each time.

> The address I had been hunting during my first three or four hours in London was No. 5, Derby Street, and, at the end of the fourth hour, I finally found it, only to discover that it was the wrong No. 5, Derby Street. There is a Derby Street in W.C.1 and a Derby Street in W.1. I found the wrong one on my tenth trip across Blackfriars Bridge. . . .
>
> "I am looking for No. 5, Derby Street," I told [another policeman]. "As a matter of fact, I just came from there—but it isn't really the place I want."
>
> He thought this over for a moment, said that he was frightfully sorry, but that life was like that; one never really wanted what one wanted, after one got it, and he went back to directing traffic.
>
> I went back to Blackfriars Bridge.

He never did acquire the instincts of a driver comfortable with his car. While in a garage waiting for a small repair, Thurber happened to glance at the dashboard dials and noticed with horror that the needle of one registered a high of 1560. Expecting an explosion, he showed it to the mechanic, his finger shaking in fright, he says. The mechanic explained, "That's your radio dial, Mac. You got her set at WQXR."

Probably the closest Thurber came to a fatal disaster in a car was in 1938, when he and Helen were renting a villa on the Riviera. The gardener, Olympy, was the Russian husband of the French caretaker, Maria. Thurber offered to teach Olympy to drive the Ford so that he could take Maria in style to the Nice Carnival. Olympy and Thurber tried to converse in French, a language alien to them both. It was the near-blind leading the inept.

In "A Ride with Olympy," the Russian at the wheel nearly runs down an elderly couple walking on the road, "unaware of the fact that hell was loose on the highway."

> Ahead of us now was one of the most treacherous curves on the Cap. The road narrowed and bent, like a croquet wicket, around a high stone wall that shut off your view of what was coming. . . . There was a car coming, but it was well over on its own side. Olympy apparently didn't think so. He whirled the wheel to the right, didn't take up the play fast enough in whirling it back, and there was a tremendous banging crash, like a bronze monument falling. . . . We were still moving, heavily, with a ripping noise and a loud roar. "Poussez le phare!" I shouted, which means "push the headlight!" . . . I shut off the ignition and pulled on the hand brake. . . . The right front fender was crumpled and torn and the right back one banged up. "Il fait beau," I announced, which is to say that the weather is fine. It was all I could think of.

After her husband's death, Helen confessed to something Thurber never had, or would have: it was Thurber at the wheel, not Olympy.

Thurber, in *The Years with Ross*, tells of meeting Ross in Paris in the summer of 1938, and implies that Ross was unreasonable and silly in refusing to have Thurber chauffeur him about Paris in the Ford. "I had driven various cars since 1913, with only a few minor accidents," he writes, "but Ross would have none of Thurber at the wheel." "We'll take taxis," Ross told Thurber. "I'm not going to drive with you." Having read Thurber on driving, Ross needed only a modicum of wisdom to take Thurber at his written word.

In 1939, when Thurber and Elliott Nugent decided to collaborate on *The Male Animal*, the Thurbers booked passage on a ship, through the Panama

Canal, to join the Nugents, who were in Hollywood. Nothing would do for Thurber but to take his beloved Ford with them. It was on that trip that the eye problem became critical and failed to improve. As proud as he was of driving a car, with all its masculine status, he had to give it up by that fall. Fortunately, *The Male Animal* provided Thurber with the first sizable income he had known. It enabled him and Helen to buy a large, comfortable Cadillac and to hire a competent chauffeur to drive them. Though Helen would never admit it, she had to have felt relief.

After the *New Yorker* accepted his drawings, Thurber drew in ink whatever he intended to submit for sale. The rest of the time, he continued to "hum along with a pencil":

> I prefer pencil because you don't have to keep dipping it in ink or, as I sometimes do with a pen, in the ash tray, my glass of Scotch, or Helen's hand. Once, at the Algonquin, where I used to draw, I spilled a whole bottle of India ink all over the room and that very night, in going to the bathroom in the dark, I cut my forehead open [on the edge of a door], so that the room was also covered with blood. It was an indescribable shambles.

His illustrations in *Is Sex Necessary?* and *The Owl in the Attic* served to support the text, but by the summer of 1932, Thurber had contributed nearly fifty "stand alone" drawings to the magazine, and he quickly drew another eighty-five to fill out a book, *The Seal in the Bedroom and Other Predicaments*, published by Harper in November. It was the first to feature his drawings exclusively.

The title, of course, derives from the famous picture of the seal draped over the headboard of a Thurber couple, the drawing that Benchley championed. Thurber had sent the original to Benchley in gratitude; it was borrowed from Benchley for a Thurber art show in 1934, and then lost for seven years. When Thurber heard about the loss, he tracked it down and returned it to Benchley and asked why he hadn't told him about the missing drawing earlier. Benchley said he had come to assume that it was "on permanent loan."

Thurber supplied art for the book's jacket, as well, and for the broad green paper band that protected the book from impecunious bookstore browsers. On the band, a Thurber seal peeked through a keyhole, the promotional copy reading, "What does the seal see? How does the cow go? Who's in that room? Where do men get the strength to go on? Is there any life after marriage?

Give the nice man (or nice lady) $2 and get James Thurber's plain, blunt answers to these involved and daring questions."

Dorothy Parker, who enjoyed Thurber's party humor and went weak with sentiment over his penciled dogs, wrote the introduction. People had begun to go around looking like Thurber drawings, Parker insisted. Ten minutes for a drawing, she says, Thurber regards as drudgery. "He draws with a pen, with no foundation of pencil, and so sure and great is his draughtsmanship that there is never a hesitating line, never a change. [True, for if Thurber made a drawing mistake, he always started over, rather than try to correct.] No one understands how he makes his boneless, loppy beings, with their shy kinship to the men and women of Picasso's later drawings. . . . And no one . . . knows from what dark breeding-ground come the artist's ideas."

But one suspects. Thurber was enduring his uneasy weekend marriage to Althea and an unrequited romantic obsession with Honeycutt. A confused mixture of misery and longing, brewed by his inconclusive relations with women, saturates most of the drawings. Thurber felt himself adrift and lonely that summer of 1932, and the book is his only one during his lifetime not dedicated to anyone. In it, somehow he manages to transform private pain into caricatures of people and situations—often inexplicable ones—that resemble life just enough for the reader to find among them the disturbing, the relevant, and the funny.

Marriage is portrayed as betrayal and disenchantment. A husband walks through the door to find his wife holding the little Thurber Man on her lap. ("I'm helping Mr. Gorley with his novel, darling," she explains.) "When I realize that I once actually loved you, I go cold all over," a tall, chilling Thurber Woman tells the small, paunchy man, who is smoking a cigar and looking up at her. After a party, she scolds him in bed: "Everybody noticed it. You gawked at her all evening." Two women sit on a sofa, their lack of physical appeal underpinning the hilarity, as one confesses to the other: "I yielded, yes, but I never led your husband on, Mrs. Fischer!" Thurber's growing anger with women kept pace with his fundamental fear of them. A wild-haired lady appears at the door of a neighboring apartment with a gun, asking the frightened Thurber Man in pajamas and his wife: "Have you people got any .38 cartridges?"

The women get sore at sports or simply go out of control—at croquet, skating, Ping-Pong. Thurber remained convinced that women, as nurturers, were conceived to outlast men. "The Race of Life" has the female carrying the fatigued man, protecting him from menace. Though the child in the picture may make the symbolic summit with the woman, the man is clearly too exhausted to try. (All three are in innocent nudity.) More and more

"I Yielded, Yes—but
I Never Led Your Husband On, Mrs. Fischer!"

often, the lovable, gentle dog comes front and center as a solace to man, innocent of heart. The Thurber bloodhound trails a bug to a hole in the baseboard with only curiosity in mind, then wanders back and falls asleep. Thurber offers several versions of one cartoon in which the man is staring past the woman he's talking to, at a female that Thurber does his best to make look sexually daring. Only the femme fatale changes from picture to picture, either going nude or wearing revealing clothes. Each caption contains the name of a different male friend of Thurber's.

A henpecked man lies on a sofa, across a lady's lap, saying, "You're the only woman I ever knew that let me alone." But as a seeker of female companionship, one of Thurber's problems was that women too often did. Ann Honeycutt was as frequently the object of his frustration as Althea. "Jim and I would argue and argue about whether to get married," Ann says, "and I might finally give up, saying something like, 'Jim, you're driving me crazy.' Then in the *New Yorker* his next cartoon would be the man saying to the woman, 'With you I've known peace, Lida, and now you tell me you're going crazy'." (His women's first names often ended in "a," like Althea's.)

His unfamiliarity with children shows; Thurber's tots seem aberrational, the Thurber Man and Woman drawn in miniature and decked in children's clothes. His most reliable cast of cartoon characters are the small, bald,

"A Penny for Your Thoughts, Mr. Coates"

plump man with spectacles and the larger, dowdy woman. The difference between them, Marc Connelly pointed out, was that "the Thurber women have what appears to be hair on their heads." The dogs are neutral, harmless, and lovable and often serve as little more than ballast, to keep the composition of a cartoon from tipping over from a lopsided cargo of chairs and lampshades elsewhere in the picture. Thurber gradually began to arrange the humans to make room for the dog, the Thurber trademark he grew to love as much as did his followers.

James Geraghty, former art editor of the *New Yorker*, says that during Thurber's heyday as a cartoonist a proud mother would send in a drawing done by her child with a note pointing out that because it was so similar to a Thurber, the magazine should publish it. Thurber replied to one such mother, agreeing that her little boy's drawing was technically as good as his, but "he hasn't been through as much," he explained. He was only partly kidding. The torture he endured at his own and others' hands was what accounted for much of the content of that strange phenomenon that—in White's words— joined Thurber's mind to pencil and paper through the finest connective tissue anywhere.

For years, Thurber was the only cartoonist-writer in residence at the *New Yorker*. Katharine White persuaded Ross to let him write the introduction to the *New Yorker*'s 1932 volume of cartoons. Also published by Harper, it was automatically in competition with *The Seal in the Bedroom*; a few Thurber cartoons appeared in both books. But it was a prestigious showcase and he did

"With You I Have Known Peace, Lida,
and Now You Say You're Going Crazy"

well by it. He notes the distinction between how women and men are treated
in the cartoons. One cartoon shows a little man pushing among guests at a
party, pleading that somebody "pick a card, any card." This, to Thurber,
shows the male's "inescapable consignment to a sublime loneliness." The
female, with her "inexorable demands upon awareness," would never be
found in such a situation, he says. "If a woman asks somebody to pick a card,
somebody is going to pick a card." The cartoon women live in a place of trim
lawns and straight streets, adjacent to "Jeopardy," "the haunt of the male," in
which he becomes "inextricably entangled."

Thurber's interest in his new role as parent shows up in the copy. Unable
to pick out a toy for his infant daughter at F.A.O. Schwarz, he is handed a
little woolly lamb by a saleslady and asked if a "soft animal" would help him
decide. His own childhood yearnings took over, he says; he kept the stuffed
animal at his office and got Rosemary something else.

Harper & Bros. was in financial straits, soon to ask its employees to take a
10-percent cut in salary to help the firm shovel its way out of the mud of the
great Depression. Its cautious first printing of two thousand copies of *The Seal
in the Bedroom* soon sold out, and there were three small, subsequent printings
before the year's end, to Harper's delight. Lisle Bell, in the *Herald Tribune*,
found the drawings conceivably influenced by what may have been found in

Egyptian tombs or abandoned telephone booths, the man-woman cartoons saying more in one panel of domestic strife than Ibsen could have said in a four-act drama. "He is very cruel to human beings, and very kind to dumb animals," Bell writes. Others praised the book as well. Thurber, the primitive, the "impure" artist, had not only arrived, he was to remain for good.

In debt to the *New Yorker* by several thousand dollars—much of it the borrowed down payment on the Sandy Hook property—Thurber was selling his original drawings, after the magazine had used them, to a smart art dealer on Forty-seventh Street, for five or ten dollars. The dealer, in turn, was selling them to a wealthy client who sent them out as Christmas gifts. Thurber was reciting this story at Tony's one night to Benchley, the film actor Roland Young, and a friend of Benchley's whom Thurber didn't know, but who announced that he was the man buying Thurber's art. Thurber learned later that the man was Jock Whitney, the multimillionaire. The *New Yorker*, though growing rich right through the Depression, was paying Thurber twenty-five dollars per cartoon.

Like other *New Yorker* cartoonists who moonlighted, Thurber was engaged by advertising agencies to illustrate sales messages—for the French Line and the *New Yorker* itself, promoting subscriptions. In several mass-circulation magazines one could find the Thurber Man holding a flower pot and pointing at the Thurber Woman, who sits at a table with a cooking pot, all in the service of Heinz soup. For the American Radiator Company, the Thurber Woman is seen bawling out the Thurber Man and Dog. "Don't you think the subconscious has been done to death and it's high time some one rediscovered the conscious?" a Thurber caption reads in an advertisement for S. N. Behrman's play *Rain from Heaven*.

"Just what I feel about my Art, I can't say," Thurber writes Herman Miller:

> I have refused to allow it to be used on sofa cushions or as ornaments for automobile radiator caps. On the other hand I have drawn a dozen pictures for the Vacuum Oil Co's advertising campaign for Bug-a-Boo . . . in the Saturday Evening Post. I have yet to meet anybody I have ever known, even casually, who hasn't got at least one of my drawings. It seems that at times I have drawn as many as thirty pictures for drunken ladies at drunken parties, drunken ladies whom I had never seen before but who now pop up here and there and remind me of our old intimacy.

He was considered for the commission to do murals for the new Louis XIV restaurant in the recently opened Rockefeller Center for a five-figure fee. He wrote home as if the assignment had been sealed and delivered, but the job went to fellow cartoonist William Steig. Thurber did do a large mural in white chalk on a blackboard surface for the circular back wall of the Café Français at the Center. It was ninety feet long, a snow scene with skaters, tobogganers, and skiers. Thurber did it in two hours. (It has long since been replaced.)

At the office, the former stream of Thurber drawings into the wastebasket had been redirected to the walls. Lois Long remembers that when the stairway was being built connecting editorial floors at West Forty-fifth Street, the architects drew lines on the fifth floor for the construction men to follow the next day. Thurber redrew the lines that night, but this failed to bring the new stairway up through Ross's office on the sixth floor, as Thurber intended. (Thurber gave Ross many of his reasons for tyrannical management; once Thurber broke into Ross's office at night and forged his "R" of approval on three Thurber cartoons Ross couldn't make up his mind about.) The new construction provided Thurber with fresh mural space. As one climbed the new steps, the struggling little Thurber Man kept pace on the wall alongside, ducking huge rocks and other missiles raining from above, clinging to trees and finally reaching the top where, on the wall around the corner, the ferocious Thurber Woman waited for him with club upraised. On another wall, the Thurber Man stood under a clear sky, unaware that a menacing Thurber Woman leered at him from behind the sun, ready to resume her day's persecution of him. It could be thought of as Thurber's Paranoid Period, but occasionally the Thurber Man fights back: on one side of a steel filing cabinet, he fires a gun; on the other side, the Thurber Woman is dropping dead.

"Thurber drew on the office walls of a number of people," the Whites remember. "Every time someone went on vacation, his office usually got a fresh coat of paint and the workmen would brush over Thurber's murals. This always shocked the occupants when they returned. Ross finally gave orders that none of Thurber's drawings be painted over, but that didn't always work, either."

39

That Hiding Generation

I hoped that some day somebody would ask me if I belonged to the Lost Generation, so that I could say no, I belonged to the Hiding Generation. . . . About ten months ago I got around to the idea of writing a book called "The Hiding Generation," which would be the story of my own intellectual conflicts, emotional disturbances, spiritual adventures, and journalistic experiences. . . . I sat down at the typewriter, lighted my pipe, and wrote on a sheet of paper "The Hiding Generation, by James Thurber." That was as far as I got, because I discovered that I could not think of anything else to say. I mean anything at all. . . . I wondered if I had already said everything I had to say, but I decided, in looking over what I had said in the past, that I really hadn't ever said anything.

—from "The Hiding Generation"

If Thurber's generation of New York journalists, essayists, actors, playwrights, critics, and fiction writers was too self-absorbed to be concerned with world affairs, or even with much of a life outside itself, it can still hardly be thought of as hiding; no noisier and more verbal, vocal, and socially restless a crowd was ever known in Gotham before or since.

The *New Yorker* continued to prosper in the thirties, to the wonder and envy of those on the foundering newspapers and magazines of the period. Its tone remained playful even toward many of the troubling social issues of the day; it made its readers feel they were members of an elite club, sharing a world of urbanity, intelligent criticism, satirical comment, tasteful writing and editing, delightful cartoons, and contributors with an innate posture of "We've got the funny answer to everything, and what more do you want?" Its reporters posed as all-knowing, and superior to what they reported. The less shy staff members and contributors were a presence on the cocktail circuit.

"Most intellectuals weren't successful materially," the critic Gilbert Seldes says of those times. "The *New Yorker* crowd had it both ways; they were intellectual—not about the sociological things that had begun to obsess a lot of the writers and artists, but intellectual nonetheless—and fairly prosperous, too. They were envied.

"Once, when I wrote in praise of something Thurber wrote, he visited me at the *New York Journal* to tell me he liked having his writing admired over his drawing. He left me with the impression that he felt out of step with the times, irrelevant, that he was on the outside looking in at contemporary society. I saw him and his associates on Forty-fifth Street as just the opposite."

Thurber and Ann Honeycutt continued as highly visible members of the Hiding Generation. He flooded her with descriptions of his hours and interpretations of himself:

> At night I dream about cats . . . or catastrophes, rarely about women, and when I do dream about women they are not sexual dreams but anxiety dreams; six women are going to go with me, separately, to the same show on the same evening. I wake up in perspiration . . . and am glad to be alone. . . .
>
> Over my coffee in the morning, I think clean colorful thoughts of creative work, I plan stories, I think of plots. I make little lines. Up until noon I am at my best, I get things done. At noon I exchange ideas and thoughts with my friends and if, among them, there be a woman, I content myself with a casual and faintly interested examination of her wit and her intellect. If she be rather more witty and superficial than intellectual and weighty, I like it better. . . .
>
> About 3:30 in the afternoon, Sex begins to creep in. It knocks at my door, it rears its ugly head; from behind the radiator, in calls on the phone, it whistles in the wind. I drink water, sharpen pencils and write, but Sex comes between me and the page. . . . Erotic revery . . . is usually reminiscence on departed scenes, memories of certain amorous

moments, certain exciting gestures, certain yielding words, certain astounding and indefensible actions. . . . It is scarcely revery, because
instead of thinking back on women I have "been with" . . . I think
forward on women I want to be with. . . .

At 8 p.m. after a few drinks, there forms in my mind one crystallized
desire, one intention: to get some individual woman around to the the-
atres and speakeasies as fast as possible and to get her home and to bed
before my wit and my strength and my finesse are so atrophied by liquor
and carousing that I begin to get mean rather than loving. I have never
yet met a woman who would rather go quietly home with me, at a
decent hour, such as 11 o'clock, even for the purpose of talking, or
communing. Always, she wants to sit in Tony's till she has had her glut
of liquor and of seeing people and of wild talk and of being seen. By this
time it is a quarter to four and everybody feels like a 1906 Newfound-
land dog rug. . . . Everybody has had his belly filled with . . . the glut
of our modern New York nights. Lips begin to ooze out over faces, hair
gets wrassled, eyes grow dim and wavy, finer sensibilities are drowned.
This is no time for love, but if you're going to get love this is when
you're going to get it. . . . The whole thing is rather unlovely, and just
around the edge of the next hour (for by the time you get the girl in her
apartment or hotel, it is 4:30) lies the damp gray face of morning, morning the charwoman, morning the street-cleaner, morning the housemaid, clearing up yesterday's dirty glasses and cigarette stubs, sweeping
away last evening's blithe hopes and happy dreams and wistful desires.
. . . The only time I had ever called on a girl, at her home, in the
decent early hours of the evening, has been when she was sick in bed
from being in the gutters the night before. Speculations upon this . . .
at times, cause me to become morose, and now and again to break
glasses, slap ladies down, and sit glumly in taxicabs while doors are
slammed on me. Of course, if girls want to go to Tony's I'll show 'em
how to go to Tony's.

Had Ann agreed to marry him, would Thurber have then changed his
mind about wanting to? "Well," Ann replies, "he was skilled at reversing
things and making the fault others'." He was good company, she said, "until
he'd lose his mind over the smallest things. There was a wildness about him I
liked in the earlier years; I never knew how we were going to wind up; there
was always violence, danger, and excitement in the offing, and times when I
wondered if one of us would get killed."

Honeycutt came to believe that in her case the fights Thurber so enjoyed, the angry reactions he got from her, served him as a substitute for sex; that he emerged from such displays of strong emotion in a state of orgasmic relief.

Althea and Thurber had lacked the naturally acquired loyalties of a married couple for a half-dozen years. Though they were now, in 1932, making something of a new try for the sake of the baby, Thurber couldn't throw off the smothering burden of loneliness an unsatisfactory marriage sentences one to. It was never that Althea held the baby hostage in order to keep him.

Bar

Thurber's sentimental longing to belong, to be a husband and father, was enough to prevent his abandoning the arrangement permanently. Eventually it had to be she who made the move that gave them both a second chance.

Understandably, Althea, busy with a baby and dogs during the week, was eager to talk to Thurber when he finally arrived in Sandy Hook. Thurber is unsympathetic. In "Listen to This, Dear" he writes that "the small annoyances of marriage . . . slowly build up its insupportabilities as particles of sediment build up great deltas." One of the worst annoyances, he says, is "the female's habit of interrupting the male when he is reading." Woman has always found ways to stand in the way of Man's thoughts and creativity as well, he insists:

> Where once woman shook man, or struck him with a rock, or at least screamed imprecations at him, when he sat down to draw pictures on the walls of the cave, she now contents herself with talking to him when he is reading.
>
> "I must tell you what happened to the base of the Spencers' child's brain," a wife will begin when her husband has just reached the most exciting point in the . . . account of a baseball game. . . . Or she will say, "I want you to listen to this, dear," and she will read him a story from *her* section of the evening paper about a New Jersey dentist who tried to burn up his wife and collect her insurance. Telling the plots of plays and speculating as to why a certain couple were drawn together, or drifted apart . . . are other methods a wife frequently uses to interrupt her husband's reading.
>
> Of the various ways of combating this behavior . . . open resentment, manifested by snarling or swearing or throwing one's book or newspaper on the floor in a rage, is the worst, since nine times out of ten it will lead to quarrels, tears, slamming of doors, and even packing suitcases. . . . The husband . . . will no longer be in the proper frame of mind for quiet reading. He will find himself wondering where his wife is, whether she has gone home to her mother. . . . He will then fall to recalling miserably the years of their happiness, and end up by purchasing a dozen roses for his wife, and five or six rye highballs for himself. . . .
>
> The best way . . . is to pretend to listen . . . to murmur an interested "yes?" or an incredulous "no!" . . . He must . . . be on guard against "inner-quote queries." . . . If a wife should say . . . "So I asked her, 'What time is it?'" the husband is lost if he . . . replies,

"About a quarter after eight, I think." This is bound to lead to accusations, imprecations, quarrels, tears, slamming of doors, etc.

When he arrived late at Sandy Hook on a weekend, Thurber often slept in most of the next day, ignoring both her and the baby, Althea later complained at the divorce hearings. (In a 1932 cartoon, the Thurber Woman glares at the disheveled man sitting on a bed in his underwear, smoking cigarettes and drinking whiskey, and asks disdainfully, "Why don't you get dressed, then, and go to pieces like a man?") Althea may have been intrigued by the power over him that he seemed to grant her most of the time—a power he allowed her by default, by his reluctance to make the overt moves toward a divorce that, in his Jamesian outlook, would be embarrassing to him —an admission of a failure he was not up to.

So the game went on, Thurber drawing upon his discontent and Althea's, too, to amuse the world. It was awful and bewildering to those who knew, but universally funny to those who didn't. Reality and fantasy were interlocked for him. The men in his half-imagined world fought back ("That martyred look won't get you anywhere with me!") but generally they became more dejected, especially as Thurber's disillusionment with Honeycutt steadily came into play. The women remained bossy ("I don't want him to be comfortable," she tells a clothing clerk fitting a suit to her husband, "if he's going to look too funny"). In one way Thurber set the tone for *New Yorker* cartoon themes through nearly all of Ross's and William Shawn's editorships—70 percent of all cartoons submitted, says cartoon editor Lee Lorenz, continue to be of a husband and wife, one scolding the other. But Thurber's went over the edge, conjuring up a violence always in the offing. His women are seen as a physical threat, pointing a gun at the husband, having him arrested by the police, beating him up in a speakeasy, arguing, petulantly ordering his loyal and lovable dog out of doors and putting the male in such a state of disconsolation that he's known at parties as "Lida Branscomb's husband—he's frightfully unhappy."

Appearances always mattered to Althea. Knowing this, in "The Private Life of Mr. Bidwell" the Thurber Man holds his breath at parties, to his wife's annoyance. " 'What do you suppose people thought—you sitting there all swelled up, with your eyes popping out? . . . If you can't stop blowing up like a grampus, I'm going to leave you.' There was a slight, quick lift in Mr. Bidwell's heart, but he tried to look surprised and hurt."

Althea's family, the Adamses, were thought to have descended from the first Adams to settle in Massachusetts. In "The Indian Sign," the Thurber Man is the unwilling witness to documents his hated wife has dug up to prove that a woman ancestor named Cora had killed nineteen Indians in colonial times. His little girl has been named Cora as a result, though he had wanted to name her Rosemary, after a dream he had had. After weeks of coming home to hear about his wife's ancestors, he tiptoes into his wife's bedroom one night and stands in the dark until she asks what the matter is. His reply is a sudden, wild, rebellious Indian war whoop.

Given his half-crazed feelings toward a stubborn Honeycutt, he undoubtedly has her in mind when he draws a man choking a helpless woman, smaller than he, while another man protests, "Have you no code, man?" There is an innate promise of bloodlessness in all Thurber's work; no one supposes that anything gory will actually take place.

In one letter to Honey, he regrets having telephoned her on her vacation at a Pennsylvania resort to bawl her out. Better, he says, that he had stayed at Martin & Mino's speakeasy and spent the money on Tom Collinses; by 5:30 P.M. he would have lost track of what he was broken up about and begun screaming "that I am a greater writer than White."

He sends her poetry; an excerpt reads:

> I count the raindrops as they fall
> But even that wont work at all;
> Whate'er I try to think or do,
> I'm walking in the rain with you.

He was either working late into the night, or drinking, when Honey came to mind, too late for him to telephone her, and so he wrote letters to her and drew the cartoons she inspired.

In February 1932, Althea talked Thurber into accepting Morris Markey's offer to them to join Markey and his wife, Helen, in Florida for a vacation. (Markey was the *New Yorker*'s principal Reporter-at-Large writer at the time.) She pointed out that it would give Thurber a rest from his hard days at work and hard nights at play. They arrived in Miami by ship. The nurse for Rosemary was seasick the entire voyage. They were met at the pier by the Markeys. Markey, a man six feet tall, weighing two hundred pounds, with a Southern accent that could be sliced with a knife, was fond of Althea, and eventually sided with her against Thurber. The Markeys had visited the Thurbers in Connecticut, once attending the Danbury Fair. The Thurbers, in turn, spent an occasional weekend at the Markeys' Long Island home. The Whites were present when Thurber got into one of his wild arguments with

Markey, and White remembers that "Morris suddenly turned to [his wife] and said in his high, clarion voice, 'Helen! Thurber has lost the power of discussion.' "

In Florida, in a rented bungalow, Thurber continued to write to Honey. (Though Althea brought this up as a mark against him during the divorce proceedings three years later, she had been told by her lawyer to think of anything that would impress the judge in favor of her petition; she and Thurber had given one another permission years before to see or write or telephone whomever they wished, but her lawyer knew what a judge wanted to hear.)

His heart isn't in the Florida trip, he writes. His mind is on whether she likes him—whether, with all his peccadilloes, she forgives him. He misses her and thinks of her every minute. He promises to return with a ready explanation for all his misdeeds she will have heard about in the interim.

Dreams continued to haunt him. One afternoon, with Althea and the Markeys at the races, Thurber wrote to Carson Blair about a bad dream he had just had, one involving Blair and Thurber's free-floating dread of menace:

In the dream, he was living with his Columbus family when he was brought a note saying that a policeman would stop by the next morning at eight to shoot Thurber, because of some law he had unknowingly violated. Thurber's father said he would get things straightened out through the mayor but returned at midnight extremely nervous because he had forgotten to. Thurber moved to the Neil House, planning to escape from Columbus the next morning, but when he got up at 6:00 A.M. he found Carson Blair seated near the front door of the lobby, hand in his coat. Blair handed Thurber a card that read "Carson Blair, Shooting Cop." Blair asked Thurber to step down the alley to get the matter over with, but Thurber said it was a mistake, crossed to a traffic policeman, told him Blair was bothering him, and handed the cop Blair's card. The policeman made Blair move along and Thurber caught a train back to New York.

Thurber ended his letter by asking Blair, who hadn't heard from Thurber in several years, to let him know at once if he had any explanation for hounding Thurber with a gun.

His letters to Honey are weighted with his boredom in Florida. He reads from the encyclopedia about President Wilson's messages to the Imperial German Empire ("I thought for a time that the United States was *never* going to get into the war. They finally did, however. . . . Germany was defeated in the end.") The Everglade swamps were afire at the time. (" 'There's a little bit of muck still burning and yearning, down in my swamp for you'—remember? Ah God, the old songs were best!")

She had written him that the novelist James Branch Cabell had been interviewed on the air at the CBS studios where she worked. Thurber replies: "Cabell knows that a wistful man, with a great sense of the beauty of love in his heart, is usually married to a woman he doesn't want to sleep with, but who wants to sleep with him, and that he wants to sleep with a woman who doesn't especially want to sleep with anybody. . . . Almost nobody makes a practise [sic] of having lunch with somebody they dont want to have lunch with, while somebody they do want to have lunch with is having lunch with somebody that doesn't want to have lunch with them."

He quotes to her from his fan mail. Paul Nash has seen *The Seal in the Bedroom* and writes Thurber: "You have done some superb drawings lately. The seal one and the dog and bug are two of the best humorous drawings I have ever seen of any period or country—my sincere congratulations."

He finds Honey's silence alarming and wonders if she has decided not to have anything more to do with him ("which would kill me—which I deserve"). She shouldn't believe all the things she hears about him. "I aint hoarding the nation's money; I didn't take the Lindbergh baby."

> I am a fish, I'm afraid, whose waters are New York. Here I am, stranded on a sunny beach, wondering how goes everything in the cool speakeasies, which are one's undoing and one's solace. . . . My companions here speak very high and mightily of how they never hope to set foot in Tim's or Mino's again, to which I say nothing, since I hope to. There is, of course, something in a broad expanse of blue water over which clouds and flamingos aimlessly drift, but there is also something to a stuffy room and a damp bar and a seventy-five cent drink of mediocre rye, and a companion who is pleasantly cocked.

Joel Sayre, when on the *Herald Tribune*, had written of Legs Diamond and other New York gangsters. In 1930, his novel *Rackety-Rax*—a title borrowed from Aristophanes' *The Frogs*—appeared. It portrays gangsters muscling in on college football. The book sold well. Sayre soon married a *New York World* reporter, Gertrude Lynahan, from Corning, New York, whom St. Clair McKelway, also on the *Trib*, had dated a few times and introduced to Sayre.

The Sayres moved to Bermuda in the spring of 1932, where Joel wrote *Hizzonor the Mayor*, about two corrupt New York mayors. News that the movies had paid a thousand-dollar option on *Rackety-Rax* brought Thurber (sans wife and baby) to Bermuda for a month to help celebrate. He and Sayre enjoyed singing together, Sayre a baritone, Thurber a thin tenor. They knew all the barbershop harmonies, which included "Moonlight Bay." Thurber's musical preferences ran to popular love songs: notably "Who" (which he featured in the dance scene of *The Male Animal*) and "Marie." But "Bye, Bye, Blackbird" remained his favorite from the day it emerged in the mid-twenties; the melody and words held an almost mystical fascination for him. One of the plays he never finished was titled *Make My Bed*, from the lyrics of that song.

One evening Joel, Gertrude, Thurber, and a *Trib* sportswriter named Don Skene made up an all-night singing quartet. Skene, who had sung professionally, had made popular "Honey, Honey, Bless Your Heart" (which Thurber adopted as his frequent musical tribute to "Honey" Honeycutt.) The quartet was joined that night by a young couple, Ronald and Jane Williams, living nearby. The Williamses became lifelong friends of Thurber, and Jane became another remote love object for Thurber to worship and dream about in the years to come.

"Jim was red hot to play any game he could be good at," says Sayre. "Small games of skill. Deck tennis, for example. He'd play at it all day in shorts, in the sun. He could throw things well—he'd throw an ice pick at a bull's-eye on a barn door at his place in Connecticut from a line he'd draw a specific number of yards away. He could flip playing cards into a hat better than anyone else, but anyone else often didn't have the enthusiasm for it that Jim did. Usually he challenged you to things only a one-eyed man would be good at—throwing rope rings over a stake. He loved throwing for accuracy. He was just good enough at tennis to get mad a lot of the time. If you hit the ball to his blind side, he'd lose it, so we'd try to hit it to his right, but if he suspected you were catering to his handicap he'd get mad at that, too. They all played the match game at Bleeck's, each player trying to guess how many matches the others held in their fists. Jim was a determined player at everything and that, of course, made him a pretty bad loser. It wasn't fun to beat Thurber at anything."

"I had lunch at the Algonquin today with Helen Whimser [sic]," Thurber had written Honeycutt on the eve of his departure for Miami, "who is a nice and calm girl. It is easier to have lunch with her than with most anybody else because she works at the corner of 44th and sixth, which is as far as I can get nowadays."

Helen Wismer was an editor on such pulp magazines as *Daredevil Aces*, and other World War I air-combat fiction. She worked in the Fawcett Building, next to the Algonquin. Her father was a Congregationalist minister who had moved his family from Nebraska, where Helen was born in 1902, to Bangor,

Maine, where he began his training for the ministry. He became pastor of churches in New Haven and Bristol, Connecticut. Helen graduated as valedictorian of her Bristol high-school class, and entered Mt. Holyoke, where she became friends with Helen Howard, Jap Gude's future wife. Helen, who had literary aspirations, majored in English, and after graduation in the mid-twenties she and a classmate moved to New York, sharing a furnished room on Charlton Street in the Village. "We had to go upstairs to [a community] bathroom," says Helen. "Cooked on a one-burner electric plate (creamed tuna fish mostly), had bedbugs, and paid, the two of us, twelve dollars a week. Ah, youth!"

She clerked in a YMCA bookshop, which turned her against religious books, read scripts for Universal Pictures, and then got into pulp-magazine editing, eventually becoming responsible for three of them at the same time. By then she and her roommate were living better, at 47 Charles Street, next door to Ann Honeycutt's apartment. In early 1930, she was invited to an afternoon party at Honey's and when she knocked on the door, Thurber opened it. She recognized him from his pictures and said, "Mr. Thurber, is sex necessary?" The book had been published just a few months before, and Thurber laughed and said, "Come right in!" Though she hoped he would get in touch with her, she didn't see him for another year.

Helen, however, was into the activities of the Village literary crowd. She dated a village artist, Aristide Mian, and Reynolds Benson, or "Babe," as he was called, Sally Benson's husband. "My recollection is that Helen was determined to marry somebody on the *New Yorker*," says Sally, who began writing fiction for the magazine in 1929. Sally's mother had brought her to New York from St. Louis to study ballet dancing. Sally married Benson, a World War I ace. "He was strong, silent, and handsome," she says, "and I read the most unimaginable wisdom into his silences. After a few years, I realized he really didn't have anything to say to me, so we went our separate ways. We didn't bother divorcing; we just took up with other people."

Babe Benson was a great fan of Helen's pulp magazines about war aviation, and he provided her with a social life. Helen was brown-eyed, worrisomely thin, tall, lantern-jawed, flat-chested, knock-kneed (as Honeycutt enjoyed pointing out), and wore glasses, except on dates, when her nearsightedness led her, at the place of rendezvous, to peer closely into the faces of strangers until her escort arrived and rescued her. Yet there was an attractive "cuteness" about her. Though her intelligence and wit vastly outranked Benson's, he was an entrée into the Village life. John O'Hara and Wolcott Gibbs were part of that crowd, but because Honeycutt couldn't stand O'Hara's "arrogance," Thurber usually joined her in avoiding them, to Helen's disappointment. Thurber would have felt at home in Helen's group; at one party at the Bensons, Helen remembers, Benson threw O'Hara's guitar out a window. It caught in a tree and nobody could reach it. After another party, Benson found O'Hara's overcoat, didn't know whose it was, and gave it to the janitor, who refused to give it up. "O'Hara was still poor at the time and couldn't afford another coat," says Helen.

Gibbs, who played with both groups, always hovered close to that twilight zone in which comedy and the near-tragic merge. He sometimes set himself on fire in bed, falling asleep with a lighted cigarette in his hand—which, sadly, is how his wife Elinor died. Gibbs would always awaken in time to call the management and announce that his bed was on fire.

Gibbs liked few people and had a bitter tongue. He knew it, and blamed it in large part for the suicide of his previous wife, Elizabeth, in 1930, according to several associates. Gibbs, twenty-eight years old, was at a table in their Manhattan apartment reading, drinking, and quarreling with her one night. She was in another room, upset. They were calling nasty comments to one another when he said something she didn't reply to. "I knew," Gibbs said. "Right away I knew." He hurried into the other room and found the window open and his wife gone.

"Gibbs and Thurber were almost more than I could bear together back then," says Emily Hahn. "Thurber was so mean in print to female writers, when the group of us were out on the town I'd say nothing about my work. Just listen. He had the drunk's philosophy, speaking for posterity. He was straight and open. His emotion was raw and unprocessed. He passed on all his feelings. He wasn't flip but was colloquial, and that somehow took the agony out of it. Thurber was *sweet,* we'd agree. He mumbled. I got the Althea treatment along with the others. The dogs had never been his; they had always been Althea's. Then I had to hear from Gibbs about *his* woman problems. He was madly in love with a beautiful girl who was madly in love with Sam Behrman, the playwright."

After a party in Robert Benchley's suite at the Royalton, Thurber took off his shoes, fell asleep, awakened in the night and put on Benchley's shoes which were so small they left Thurber's feet swollen. He didn't realize they weren't his until he received a wire from Benchley asking him to return them. On another night, Benchley's secretary and sidekick, Charles Mac-Gregor, got drunk with Thurber and slept in Thurber's room at the Algonquin. MacGregor awoke first, failed to recognize where he was and telephoned the operator to ask. The operator thought it was Thurber and giggled, "You're funning me, Mr. Thurber." Still confused, the hungover MacGregor went back to sleep. Later, Thurber awakened, also hungover, didn't recognize MacGregor, and called the same operator to ask if he was in his own room. "Please, Mr. Thurber," she said, "enough is enough." Though the comment baffled him, that she knew his name was reassurance. He went back to sleep, too.

If there was a tendency for Thurber to turn night into day, to ask more of a social occasion than should be asked, it was not unusual then. He and his fellow revelers, writing, drawing, or acting professionally in the midtown Manhattan of that period, worked hard as well. The remnants of the Round Table, which continued to gather in the Rose Room in the early thirties, never drank at lunch during Prohibition. The hotel's owner, Frank Case, religiously obeyed the law and furthermore, after the repeal, could not bear to see promising talent abusing itself with alcohol on the premises of his "inn." He was a liberal giver to the Salvation Army, and though his staff handled drunken clientele with discretion, it pained him to witness it. Thurber was of particular concern to him.

There never was a Hiding Generation. In 1950, Thurber told a reporter that neither had Thurber's been a lost generation. "We knew where we were all right," he said. "Ours was the generation that stayed up all night."

40

That Middle-Aged Man on the Flying Trapeze

I [don't] believe, for your own good and mine, that we should see each other again. I know you believe that, too, but you are too generous and too really, at heart, appreciative of me, to say so, finally. You have had only suffering with me not only lately, but always. . . . It isn't your fault—or mine—but the fault of an impossible union . . . We are bad for each other so long as I persist in insisting on a love interest which you never asked for, which at times you felt you could go through with, but which we both know you couldn't finally.

—Undated letter to Ann Honeycutt

Thurber's state of mind regarding Honeycutt in the fall of 1932, when he was spending more and more time in town, less at Sandy Hook, is presented in "The Evening's at Seven" (the title a play upon Browning's line "Morning's at Seven"). The canvas of the story bears a few brush strokes in the style of Henry James: Leaving the office with less than an hour to be at his hotel for a predictable dinner and a routine evening with his tiresomely predictable wife, the lonely Thurber Man impulsively stops by the apartment of a woman he is still in love with, or thinks he is.

"She would want to know (but wouldn't ask) why he was, so suddenly, there, and he couldn't exactly say . . ." runs a Jamesian sentence. The few precious minutes with her are spent in idle chatter and, on his part, clock watching. He explains that he must be at the hotel by 7:30 or he will miss dinner. She asks what will be served. At Thursday dinner the hotel serves clam chowder, he replies. She wonders whether that's how he knows it's Thursday, or that's how he knows it's clam chowder.

With less than ten minutes to get to the hotel, he finally makes his move, striding toward her to force the moment to its climax, but both are saved by the doorbell as her sister arrives. Probably fearing the consequences all along, the Thurber Man, a procrastinating J. Alfred Prufrock, has watched the clock tick away the time in which he could have learned what, if anything, the relationship still held for them. Again he has momentarily stretched the rubber band that binds him to a colorless and futureless circumstance, but cannot break it.

The sad short story took Thurber followers by surprise, as "Menaces in May" had four years before. It was a startling change of pace within a string of his rollicking short pieces—parodies, satires, and comment: In "No More Biographies," he urges that authors who publish any more biographies of Grant, Lee, and Lincoln be fined. If all biographies in print were laid end to end, he explains, it would stop traffic and the raising of foodstuffs, necessitating a war of aggression to get extra space in which to park the biographies still coming off the presses.

"Guessing Game" resulted from a hotel management informing him that he had left an article in his room, an article he had to describe in order to claim, or it would be disposed of after two months. He takes inventory and realizes he is missing a number of things, none of which was he likely to leave in a hotel room, and wonders if somebody else occupied the room without either knowing the other was there. ("Perhaps he always arrived just after I had left the room and got out each time just before I came back. It's that kind of city.")

He skewers the memoirs of Elsie Janis, whom he knew in the Columbus grade schools, and whose theatrical career he had watched with admiration as a youth. But "Isn't Life Lovely!" spares her nothing. If some prominent autobiographers wrote the way Miss Janis did, he sneers, it would come out like this: "James liked Crane but he didn't like Swinburne. Swinburne liked Conrad but W. H. Hudson didn't like Swinburne. I liked Hudson . . ."

As to the Depression's spread of bank closings, Thurber felt that bankers, like ships' captains, should go down with their banks when they failed; stay inside and prowl about as a heroic gesture.

"A Farewell to Florida" finds him in a bookstore, hoping not to be bothered, but, because of a similarity of names, he is mistaken for "Thalberg," husband of Norma Shearer, and his day is ruined.

Besides rewriting Talk throughout 1932, Thurber reported three Talk "originals" himself, published twenty-seven casuals, and wrote two Reporters at Large. Half the pieces were substandard Thurber—sixteen were never collected by him in book form. His efforts to satirize the *World-Telegram*'s account of a temporary halt in New York's crosstown-bus service are nothing short of wretched; nobody else could have gotten it past the first echelon of editors.

In "Some Notes on the Married Life of Birds," he compares the behavior of wildlife to that of human society, an analogy that culminated nine years later in the play he wrote with Elliott Nugent, *The Male Animal*, whose instinct is to fight to keep its mate. The promiscuous birds are the prettiest, he decides. The warblers are "the happy hearts, who each year have a different mate."

Upon the birth of Rosemary, he was commenting on how modern woman responds to motherhood. In "A Preface to Dogs" he writes that as soon as a woman has a child "her capacity for worry becomes acuter: she hears more burglars, she smells more things burning, she begins to wonder, at the theatre or the dance, whether her husband left his service revolver in the nursery."

The Christmas season of 1932 was nearly a bankrupt one, inspiring newspaper stories of poor children who had tried to be good and had hung their stockings hopefully in anticipation of a visit from Saint Nick, only to be disappointed. It was more than Thurber could bear. He composed a brief playlet, "A Farewell to Santa Claus; or, Violins Are Nice for Boys with Chins." In his North Pole workshop, Santa, with patches on his suit, is doing his best to make wooden toys with a gouge, his other tools having been sold to make ends meet. Mrs. Claus is dying of grief, and a student in the workshop is contemplating suicide. A door opens and all are machine-gunned in gangland fashion, leaving not a creature stirring, not even a mouse.

Some of the uncollected pieces of that year are scarcely useful in tracing Thurber's professional development, but smiled upon by Ross, the Whites, and Gibbs, he could do no wrong. His published drawings, which offered none of the creative resistance to him that writing did, and were increasingly popular, more than doubled in number, from twenty-three in 1931 to fifty-seven in 1932. They include his first "spots"—decorative drawings without captions "spotted" on a page of text. His cartoons were becoming more filled in—"heavier," in Helen Thurber's words—than the earlier "lighter" ones of fewer lines. They were also becoming more populated with the flop-eared dogs that appear to be bloodhounds on basset legs.

With pen and typewriter, Thurber was cementing into the New Yorker format and the American scene his classical little man, whether called Walter Mitty, John Monroe, or Mr. Pendly. Largely because of the Thurber Man's appeal, the New Yorker was deluged with submissions of short stories about timid men. Thurber's popular model wasn't the only one. Dorothy Parker's "Such a Pretty Little Picture," in the Smart Set of 1930, for example, features Mr. Wheelock, a wimp who longs to flee family and home but remains to trim the hedge while his wife and daughter look on. Her message: there isn't much we can do with our lives.

Wolcott Gibbs, though an admirer of Thurber, was against his imitators, and was soon pleading for an editorial rule against any more "Thurber husbands" pieces. Ross granted one. Frances Warfield, who launched her own little man, Mr. Wilcox, on New Yorker waters in the early years, says that Ross's ban of apprehensive little men from his magazine's fiction just about put her out of business. "There is no doubt in my mind," she writes,

> that I came by my little New Yorker man, Mr. Wilcox, quite naturally. How naturally I discovered with surprise and pleasure, when I was writing my two autobiographical books. . . . Surely most people have a little man hidden away. Thurber gave us the notion of exploring them— and before long, I expect, we were exploiting them. The times—late Twenties, early Thirties—had a great deal to do with it. I wouldn't take

anything for Mr. Wilcox, but he is definitely a period piece for a corner of the mantel.

That the Thurber Man dwelt within women as well as men wouldn't surprise Thurber, who often suspected many of his own feelings at times as being "feminist" in the gender sense, a suspicion that would have done little to abate his self-doubts and fears regarding women. But he also came to credit such feelings for much that he accomplished in the course of living and inventing. The condescending "tea and sympathy" treatment he often attracted from women, he attributed to the feminine qualities in his emotions and perspectives as often as the masculine.

Thurber had the last word on the subject of the bumbling, fearful Thurber Man in *New Yorker* fiction with "The Secret Life of Walter Mitty." This truest, most cosmic and enduring survivor of the little-man species made his historic appearance in the *New Yorker*'s March 18, 1939, issue. Mitty, who escaped a henpecked life through fantasy, was the perfect closer of Thurber's long parade of sad, comic losers. As Frances Warfield implies, the changing period was making the case for the daydreamer an increasingly hard one to win. Thurber got in under the wire with Mitty; literary fashions were being changed by the threats of fascism and war. The new public appetite, even among the sophisticates, had become one for fictional heroes of sterner stuff.

Long before blindness turned him further adrift in a disconnected world, Thurber was plagued by dreams day and night. He once discussed his "Back to the Grades" (*New Yorker*, June 11, 1932), in which he imagines taking his fifth grade of school over again: "I made it the fifth grade," he said, "instead of the sixth to spare my sixth-grade teacher, who I thought was still living. The fifth-grade desks would have been much too small for me to sit at. I'm sure Freud would see it as a wish to return to the womb."

But perhaps the piece didn't connote merely rejecting life; it could mean the wish to start over and get things right this time. He considered the comment. "I was talking to a woman psychologist at a party the other evening," he said. "I mentioned wanting to crawl inside a sixth-grade school desk. Having learned a bit about me through our conversation, she said it probably reflects my guilt at not having written a novel or a play. I was trying to hide from myself and my fancied failures. Evading responsibility."

For the more than seven years he wrote to Honeycutt, Thurber's letters describe, in their rambling, lovesick way, his lamentably immature state of mind regarding the opposite sex. Honeycutt occasionally dated Benchley—"No sex" she insists—and once compared the two prominent humorists:

"Jim," she says "saw the potential in an experience or a joke and enlarged it, wrote himself into it, played it out to the applause of the public. But you're supposed to get out of costume when the curtain comes down, and become a citizen of the world again. With Jim the curtain stayed up; he found the daydreams and the acting too vivid and pleasant to become himself again. He had trouble making the return trip from fantasy to reality; a humorist who can't do that can get into terrible trouble, and I think Jim did. Every good actor has to have a love affair with himself for the sake of his stage career but often suffers from self-dislike when he takes off his mask and makeup.

"Benchley filled fifteen books telling us good-naturedly about all the banana peels he slipped on. But when he got up from his typewriter he was back to wonderful old Benchley as he really was. He didn't force his humorist's world on his friends. Benchley essentially liked himself while recognizing, and joking about, his human vulnerabilities. Thurber didn't like himself and didn't want people he admired to know who he really was. So he'd write ludicrous roles for himself on the spot, act them out, and insist it was the real Thurber. Everybody knew it wasn't and he knew we knew, and that's when the rages would start. He thought if anyone suspected what he really was, they couldn't like him."

Everyone agrees that Thurber could be the kindest and gentlest of friends until—as Gibbs has so often been quoted as saying—after 5:00 P.M., or a number of drinks. "After six drinks he was as mad as the next guy," says White, "and usually a little madder. Or at least more violent, vocally. Jim was never an alcoholic—just a bad drinker on occasion."

Thurber drank to become someone other than the someone within himself that he disliked, but the change was from Jekyll to Hyde, turning him into a someone his friends dreaded. His unhappy and lonely days led to an after-hours life of fights, throwing drinks and other objects, being ejected from bars, and insulting those who stood by him. Like Mame sending chocolates to those Muggs had bitten, Thurber always made amends. "You couldn't stay mad at him," says Gibbs. "He was so funny about describing what he was apologizing for."

Thurber's was a recklessness of attitude and behavior that his friends felt he was lucky to survive. It might be suggested by nothing more than his tapping a cocktail glass against his glass eye. Or when "a group of us left the old '21' Club," Ted Gardiner remembers, "and took a bottle of sauterne back to the *New Yorker* to drink it in Thurber's office. We were passing it back and forth with the greatest finesse—the way a waiter would handle it, with towel and everything. But after a bit of this, Jim said, 'Aw, the hell with it,' smashed the top off the bottle and poured from the broken neck."

Robert Benchley, like Frank Sullivan, was an atypical humorist—ever kind and forgiving; "Sweet Old Bob," he called himself, "or, if you prefer, you can use the initials." He moved across the street from the Algonquin to the Royalton to avoid the distractions of friends who dropped by his room or waylaid him in the lobby. (The situation was quickly duplicated at the Royalton.) Once in Benchley's Royalton suite Thurber "was off on some tirade," says Nathaniel Benchley. "My father took it for a while, and then said, "Look, Jim, we were all having a good time until you arrived. Why don't you be a good boy and run along?" Thurber left, muttering about suicide, but "his conscience hurt so much the next day that he did a drawing for my father called 'Thurber and His Circle.' "

It shows a wild-eyed Thurber, drink uplifted, hair over his face, ranting on to a living-room group of three men, a woman, a dog, a portrait, a stuffed owl, and a plaster bust, everybody and everything with their eyes closed in either sleep or boredom. "Hold the picture up to the light," says Benchley, "and you see that they're all glaring at him with deep hatred. He'd drawn the angry eyes on the reverse side."

The late Margaret Case Harriman remembered receiving another version of "Thurber and His Circle," for similar reasons. But Thurber was usually great theater, and few saw much need for his morning-after contrition, unless there had been insult and near-violence, as at the Royalton.

Donia McNulty remembers a dinner party at which Thurber kept the host David Lardner, and other guests up to an ungodly hour. As they left, Thurber undoubtedly reflected Lardner's thoughts as he was finally closing the door after them, Thurber saying in a loud voice, "I thought we'd never get rid of those people." And Thurber writes of another host who told him, as Thurber was leaving, "It's always a pleasure to say 'goodnight' to you." "I thought that Thurber fellow would never shut up," Thurber would announce loudly after a party, for the benefit of the other guests waiting on the sidewalk for a taxi.

His schemes were unpredictable. When the McNultys arrived in town from Columbus for a visit, they had agreed to meet Thurber at the Algonquin. They were late and when McNulty checked his hat at the cloakroom, Thurber, behind the counter, took it politely and said, "Mr. McNulty, a Mr. Thurber has been asking for you. Where the hell have you been?" "He had had the hat-check girl hide behind the coats," says Donia.

Thurber, usually in Robert Benchley's company, occasionally visited Polly Adler's combination speakeasy and brothel. This has been presented in snickering prose as evidence of Thurber's hopeless debauchery. Actually, Adler ran an illegal but elitist bar and restaurant at which businessmen often met in conference and completed financial deals. The women were an option if any customer so chose. Adler, who paid off the police and building managements, set up in good neighborhoods and was able to stock a good quality of liquor. Benchley sometimes kept a room there where he worked, avoiding the hangers-on at his Royalton suite. Peter Arno once took Ross to Adler's; Ross had a briefcase full of manuscripts with him that he spent the night reading.

"Polly Adler had become a kind of freak celebrity," says Jap Gude, "and it became fashionable to drop in at her establishment . . . , have a drink or two with one of the girls, or with Polly herself, and see and be seen. It was strictly a snob thing, like being at opening night of the opera season even though you loathed opera. It was also something to drop casually at '21' the next day: 'You'll never guess who I saw at Polly's last night.' "

Polly stood for no rowdiness at her place and her establishment was presumably a once-in-a-while safe haven for Thurber. In 1952, when Adler was writing her memoirs, *A House Is Not a Home*, she wrote him, asking of "my old friend Jim Thurber" permission to use an insignificant anecdote involving his drawings. Thurber refused. "My mother is a hundred years old and would drop dead," he wrote Gibbs, "and . . . the eyebrows of my daughter, a senior at Penn, have risen high enough because of me."

In one of Thurber's most brilliant parodies, "Something to Say," may probably be seen the prose equivalent of his "Thurber and His Circle." It was inspired by Henry James's "The Coxon Fund," in which Frank Saltram, a man of advanced intellect, fails to live up to his promises as a writer, putting most of his creative energy into spellbinding conversation. He ceases to write at all after he inherits money. The Elliot Vereker (the name is taken from another James story, "The Figure in the Carpet") of Thurber's casual is a wild conversationalist whose literary pretensions completely take in his trusting, hopeful circle of friends. Vereker's outrageous behavior is related by a gullible observer, who reads the most significant meanings into Vereker's drunken or sadistic behavior. (The narrator in James's "The Coxon Fund" is as sympathetic as Thurber's, but understands the situation throughout.) There are unmistakable similarities in "Something to Say" to how Thurber often saw himself in his own knockabout life of the period.

Vereker continuously stimulates his friend, the narrator, "to the brink of a nervous breakdown." He comes on the scene "in Amawalk, New York, on the Fourth of July, 1927 [the date and place Thurber first met Honeycutt]." "Vereker was a writer; he was gaunt and emaciated from sitting up all night talking." He likes to throw burned-out electric lightbulbs against the sides of houses and the walls of rooms.

> He loved the popping sound they made and the tinkling sprinkle of fine glass that followed. . . . He had no reverence and no solicitude. He would litter up your house, burn bedspreads and carpets with lighted cigarette stubs, and as likely as not depart with your girl and three or four of your most prized books and neckties. He was enamored of breaking phonograph records and phonographs; he liked to tear sheets and pillowcases in two; he would unscrew the doorknobs from your doors. . . . His was the true artistic fire, the rare gesture of genius. When I first met him, he was working on a novel. . . . He never finished it, nor did he ever finish, or indeed, get very far with, any writing, but he was nevertheless, we all felt, one of the great original minds of our generation. That he had "something to say" was obvious in everything he did.

Vereker has never read Proust but can still make that author's meanings "more clear" and "less important" than anyone else can. When he is drunk, he belittles "in strong and pungent language" the achievements not only of Proust but of Goethe, Voltaire, and Whitman. "Santayana," he says, "has weight; he's a ton of feathers." He sticks folded newspapers into electric fans so that he has to shout to be heard. If he is asked what he said, he shouts " 'You heard me!' . . . his good humor disappearing in an instant." At Tony's, a Thurber hangout, Vereker flounders into the kitchen "insulting some movie critic on the way," repeats his line about Santayana to whoever is in the kitchen and comes "roaring back."

> You would invite him to dinner, or, what happened oftener, he would drop in for dinner uninvited, and while you were shaking up a cocktail in the kitchen he would disappear. He might go upstairs to wrench the bathtub away from the wall . . . or he might simply leave for good in one of those inexplicable huffs of his which were a sign of his peculiar genius. He was likely, of course, to come back around two in the morning bringing some awful woman with him, stirring up the fire, talking all night long, knocking things off tables, singing, or counting. I have known him to lie back on a sofa, his eyes closed, and count up to as high as twenty-four thousand by ones, in a bitter, snarling voice. It was his protest against the regularization of a mechanized age. . . . He never believed in doing anything or in having anything done, either for the

benefit of mankind or for individuals. He would have written, but for his philosophical indolence, very great novels indeed. We all knew that, and we treated him with a deference for which, now that he is gone, we are sincerely glad.

Thurber gives Vereker some of his own lines: "American women are like American colleges: they have dull, half-dead faculties." "If there had been no Voltaire, it would not have been necessary to create one."

None of us ever left Vereker alone when we came upon him in one of his moods. . . . "You have so many things left to do," I said to him. "Yes," he said, "and so many people yet to insult." He talked brilliantly all night long, and drank up a bottle of cognac. . . .

I had gone to the bathroom for a shower, the time he invited me to his lady's house, when he stalked into the room. "Get out of that tub, you common housebreaker," he said, "or I shall summon the police!" I laughed, of course, and went on bathing. I was rubbing myself with a towel when the police arrived—he had sent for them! Vereker would have made an excellent actor; he convinced the police that he had never seen me before in his life. I was arrested, taken away, and locked up for the night. A few days later I got a note from Vereker. "I shall never ask you to my house again," he wrote, "after the way I acted last Saturday."

(Thurber put this last line aside for recycling; a few months later, after throwing a tantrum at Honeycutt's apartment, he writes her, "I acted so badly I shall never let you ask me to your house again.")
Like Thurber, Vereker's repentances "were always as complete as the erratic charades which called them forth."

He was unpredictable and, at times, difficult, but he was always stimulating. Sometimes he keyed you up to a point beyond which, you felt, you could not go. . . .

His entire output, I had discovered, consisted of only twenty or thirty pages, most of them bearing the round stain of liquor glasses; one page was the beginning of a play done more or less in the style of Gertrude Stein. It seemed to me as brilliant as anything of its kind.

Vereker's friends get together their own Coxon Fund—about fifteen hundred dollars—to send him abroad to write.

We knew that it was folly for him to go on the way he was, dissipating his talent. . . . "Here, but for the gracelessness of God," he would shout, "stands the greatest writer in the history of the world!" We felt that . . . there was more than a grain of truth in what he said: certainly nobody else we ever met had, so utterly, the fire of genius that blazed in Vereker, if outward manifestations meant anything.

He wouldn't try for a Guggenheim fellowship.

"Guggenheim follow-sheep!" he would snarl. . . . "Don't talk to me about Good-in-time fellowships!" He would go on that way, sparklingly, for an hour, his tirade finally culminating in one of those remarkable fits of temper in which he could rip up any apartment at all, no matter whose, in less than fifteen minutes.

At the going-away party, Vereker gets frightfully drunk and denounces everybody at the party.

He combined with his penetrating critical evaluations and his rare creative powers a certain unique fantasy not unlike that of Lewis Carroll. I once told him so. "Not unlike your goddam grandmother!" he screamed. He was sensitive. . . .

Thus the party went on. Everybody was speechless, spellbound, listening to Elliot Vereker. You could not miss his force. He was always the one person in a room.

When it is time to get Vereker aboard ship, he is found on the roof of the apartment building, mercifully murdered.

"The world's loss," murmured Deane, as he looked down at the pitiful dust so lately the most burning genius we had ever been privileged to know, "is Hell's gain."

I think we all felt that way.

Vereker is actually Mitty looking the other way, toward dreams of being a hell-raiser and public nuisance, resisting the American hero stereotype. One suspects he is among Thurber's favorites of all his fictional characters.

Though some of "Something to Say" may reflect Thurber's suspicions as to how others regarded him socially, the overwhelming evidence is that, at the time, most of his circle preferred Thurber as he was to no Thurber at all.

However out of control through drink he became at times, he had redemptive originality, wit, and theatrical presence. He also had the admiration of many for what he was producing professionally. And at the core he remained a "sweet" man, by Lois Long's definition, for he still retained the humility fostered by an insecurity that never left him. And like most good writers, he knew how to gossip entertainingly, especially about himself.

By 1933, Thurber had begun putting on paper his parlor stories about life in Columbus, which would make up My Life and Hard Times. Joel Sayre believes he was galvanized into doing so by the appearance of Clarence Day, Jr., on the literary scene. In 1931, Harper's and the New Yorker had begun publishing Day's humorous reminiscences of his nineteenth-century, upper-middle-class New York family, later collected in his books, such as God and My Father (1932) and Life With Father (1935). Day also illustrated his poems and text with a technique that was less surrealistic than Thurber's, but resembled his free style. He drew animals with the looks and behavior of men and seems to have held the same suspicious views toward women that Thurber did.

Thurber describes to a graduate student his reaction to discovering Day for the first time:

> I picked up a copy of [Day's] "Thoughts Without Words" in a bookstore and sweated at the close similarity there is, both in line, and in the attitude toward men and women. On further examination I was convinced, however, that this was more apparent than real, and Day and myself are the first to insist on our difference. I am far closer to him, however, than to anybody, in drawing, in our concept of the animal world, and in our separate studies of our families. His stories about his mother and father arrived at the New Yorker about a month ahead of the first six chapters of "My Life and Hard Times."

But Thurber's wild manipulations of events in the Thurber family could have passed, in part, as a parody of Day's material. In the end, My Life and Hard Times became a classic that established Thurber, once and for all, as the country's leading literary humorist. Harper & Bros.' timid first printing of three thousand copies was followed by twelve editions by public demand over the next few years. It has rarely been out of print, if at all. Reviewing a 1961 reissue of the classic, Russell Baker called it "possibly the shortest and most elegant autobiography ever written." "Nearly every week I get requests from youngsters who have just read one of Jamie's stories from My Life and Hard

Times in an anthology," Helen Thurber said years after Thurber's death. "They ask how old Jamie is and if he's written or drawn anything else."

Kenneth Tynan writes that the book can serve as a child's introduction to adult laughter, as it served as his. He was a young child, he said, when he read "The Day the Dam Broke" and collapsed in laughter for the first time at adult humor. The book also caught the early and favorable attention of T. S. Eliot and Ernest Hemingway. "I find it far superior to the autobiography of Henry Adams," Hemingway wrote the publisher after receiving an advance copy. "Even in the earliest days, when Thurber was writing under the name of Alice B. Toklas, we knew he had it in him if he could only get it out." Thurber distrusted the encomium, pointing to the recent, well-publicized break between Hemingway and his former Paris mentor, Gertrude Stein, close companion of Toklas. Hemingway, Thurber said, was merely using his book as an excuse to annoy Miss Stein. Perhaps, but Hemingway's admiration was also sincere. Thurber's was one of the names he offered Lillian Ross, who had written a Profile of Hemingway, as subjects he thought she should write about.

White and Dorothy Parker had written introductions to Thurber's previous two books; this time he wrote his own: "Preface to a Life," as well as "A Note at the End." One reason for both essays, says Helen Thurber, was that Harper considered the book too thin, which also led Thurber to write "The Dog That Bit People"—one of the best stories in the collection—at the last minute, rushing it to the publisher without submitting it to the *New Yorker*.

Thurber's friends and admirers volunteered to review the book. Frank Sullivan, in the *Herald Tribune*, wonders if Thurber has not become "a state of mind," suspects that the Thurber servants had worked earlier for William Faulkner, and wasn't at all sure Rousseau's *Confessions* didn't suffer from not having been written by Thurber. Robert Coates, in the *New Republic*, points out that Thurber wasn't trying to lead anybody anywhere; only trying to escape.

The book's success led to another round of interviews, their results as innocuous as the earlier ones. Thurber said he spent a generous portion of every week on his Sandy Hook farm, was fond of tennis, bowling, Ping-Pong, and "all sorts of manufactured games." The interviewers reported that Thurber was "lively and fun-loving" but worked and played intensely—true enough. He received letters from about forty present and former Columbus residents, most of them telling Thurber of their experiences in the 1913 flood.

He was a gossip-column celebrity by now. The second Mrs. Hemingway, in *Vogue*, June 1933, praised life in Cuba, where, among all its advantages, there was no one who had heard of Tony's, "21," Noel Coward, Cole Porter, Mrs. Parker, Mr. Thurber, or Mr. Benchley. The old humor magazine *Life* ran a cartoon in September of 1933 showing a man with a dowdy-looking Thurber Woman saying to the receptionist at the *New Yorker:* "I'd like Mr. Thurber to do a portrait of my wife."

My Life and Hard Times sold to the movies, with the result a cinematic horror called *Rise and Shine*, starring Jack Oakie as the slow-witted football player, "Boley" Bolenciecwcz. Oakie leads "Clayton College" to a national football championship when someone capitalized on his fear of floods by shouting "The dam has burst," galvanizing Oakie the necessary distance for a touchdown.

The response to the book enabled Thurber to begin taking himself seriously as a writer, though, in later years, he downplayed its importance. He worried that he would be best known for its stories, a victim of professional arrested development. Privately, he may have fretted over whether he would be able to surpass the ingenious combination of comedy and art achieved in the collection.

Later, when he was told that Ross had remarked that, had he done nothing else with the magazine but publish the works of Clarence Day, the whole enterprise would still have been worth it, Thurber felt a sibling's jealousy. In 1957 he was writing William Shawn:

> Am I right in thinking that we now get away from Ross's old fixation that everything in [Talk] should be about New York? I managed to write about an outdoor symphony orchestra in Connecticut and to do a visit piece on the Morro-castle [a burned cruise ship] at Asbury Park, but usually Ross fretted his head off about "how are we going to hang it?" . . . This was one of his craziest obsessions, especially since by that time it was the Talk of the World and we were no longer provincial. However, his liking of Clarence Day's stuff as against my Columbus reminiscences and Sally Benson's St. Louis memories [*Meet Me in St. Louis*] was due to locale as much as anything.

In July 1933, Mame Thurber came to New York, on her way to visit friends and relatives in Boston, Providence, and Philadelphia. Thurber was delighted to show her off to Ross and others on the staff. Her zany, nonstop babble lent a validity to Thurber's Columbus pieces, which were running in the magazine at the time, says Emily Hahn. Mame was scandalized by the number of dirty shirts that Thurber had piled up in the closet of his room at the Algonquin. Thurber simply forgot to send out his shirts to be laundered and would buy a new one on his way home from work. While dressing for dinner one night, with Mame in the room, a shirt he had laid out on the sill of an open window slid out and floated to the bottom of an air shaft. Mame, expense-minded, saw the event as a near-calamity. "It could be worse," Thurber reassured her. "I could have been *in* the shirt."

Though in debt from paying for the farm and the support of a wife and child, things were looking up for Thurber financially. The price Ross paid him for his cartoons had been rising from $25 to $40, $50, $75 and, by the end of 1933, $100. The year was a tremendously productive and lucrative one for Thurber in money and fame. Besides fifty cartoons and spots in the *New Yorker*, Thurber's drawings were appearing in magazine advertisements for the French Line and Fisher Body. One of his "spots" adorned a page of Alexander Woollcott's book *Shouts and Murmurs*.

The magazine's permissiveness was still occasionally working against Thurber, making it too easy for him to get into print with second-rate casuals. "The Threefold Problem of World Economic Cooperation (By Six or Eight Writers for the 'Times' Magazine Section, All Writing at Once)" ends by being duller than the style and content it tries to parody. An excerpt:

> There will be much shrewd give and take, with the ever-present likelihood that the Anglo-Saxon delegates, in conceding to the Latins old-fashioned lace doilies, monk's-head match holders, and burnt-leather table runners, will discover, too late, that they have conceded with these any hope of a successful and permanent solution of England's sheep-lands problem!

There was a rash of newspaper stories at the time about kidnappings in which the victim grows fond of the abductor and asks leniency for him after his capture. Thurber's candidate is "Tom the Young Kidnapper; or, Pay Up and Live: a Kind of Horatio Alger Story Based on the Successful Kidnapping in Kansas City of Miss Mary McElroy, Who Had a Lovely Time, Whose Abductors Gave Her Roses and Wept When She Left, and Whose Father Said He Did Not Want the Young Man to Go to the Penitentiary." Thurber has the gangster-kidnapper win the sympathy of the girl victim by explaining to her how he needs the money for his gang. The girl pleads his case to the judge, who not only sets the gangster free but marries him to the girl.

In March 1933, Joseph Taylor, the beloved professor of Thurber and Herman Miller, who had introduced them to the work of Henry James, died. The two men wrote one another, lamenting the destructive influence of Taylor's marriage on his potential as a writer. Miller planned a book or play based on

Taylor's life, and Thurber later wrote Miller at length as to how they both might adapt *The Ambassadors* to the stage, a book both Taylor and Thurber especially admired.

Three months after Taylor's death, Thurber wrote his "Recollections of Henry James." The excuse for his parody, he said, was that for the past four or five years all autobiographies he had read had had a chapter devoted to reminiscences and impressions of James. Thurber pretends that he, too, has met James, and his mockery of the ponderous Jamesian style is mixed nicely with an obvious, lingering affection for the author and his work. Thurber writes:

> James' great gift, of course, was his ability to tell a plot in shimmering detail with such delicacy of treatment and such fine aloofness—that is, reluctance to engage in any direct grappling with what, in the play or story, had actually taken place—that his listeners often did not, in the end, know what had, to put it another way, "gone on."

Joseph Conrad, Thurber suggests, in discovering James could only have felt that his own novels "had made things too preposterously clear and that too many things happened." Conrad is so taken by James's "The Beast in the Jungle," in which nothing happens to the central figure, that "it was weeks before I could calm [Conrad] down, before I could dissuade him from a monstrous idea that had taken possession of him; namely, to write a novel in which not only nothing happened but in which there were no characters."

Ohio was becoming aware of its native son. The Cleveland Museum of Art acquired one of Thurber's cartoon originals and handled it like a Rembrandt. John McNulty continued to get Thurber publicized in the Columbus press. Were the local citizens to follow the *New Yorker*, runs one newspaper story— probably by McNulty—they would see High Street, or the State House, mentioned "every week." Thurber, the item goes on, was still living "on a remodeled farm in Connecticut with Mrs. Thurber and their daughter, Rosemary."

That was fine for hometown consumption, but things were going poorly for Thurber, back at the remodeled farm. He disliked himself most when he was there, guilt-ridden by his disloyal behavior in town and at home. He was quarrelsome with the handymen, nervous about country life, and fearful of checking out the dogs in the barn at night.

He was asking women to marry him when it was obvious to them, if not to Thurber, that he would never be the one to seek a divorce. He was, however, weighing the consequences of one, in his seriocomic fashion. In "Behind the Statistics" he presents what he often sees following the breakup of a married couple: "George is asked to drop the Bascoms because Ella (George's divorced wife) expects to go around a lot with Bert Fliebling, Grace Bascom's sister's husband's brother."

Among William Shawn's objections to *The Years with Ross* was that Thurber had implied that he was still on the staff, in on the editing and decision making, long after he had left the magazine. Shawn chose his obituary of Thurber to set the matter straight: "From 1927," Shawn writes, "two years after the magazine began, until 1933, he was on the editorial staff."

In fact, Shawn hurries Thurber off the premises two years too early. All that happened at the end of 1933 was that Thurber went from a salary to a drawing account, the arrangement that sets the writer gambling with the magazine against himself and his productivity. It was a seamless change, of interest only to Thurber and the financial office. He continued coming to the office daily. His Talk reporting and editorship remained, and he submitted his drawings, casuals, and short stories as he always had. The success of *My Life and Hard Times*, its sale to the movies, and growing revenue from his cartoon advertisements had helped to persuade Thurber that he no longer needed the security of a salary. He was given the drawing account at his request.

Thurber was now being paid a hundred dollars for every thousand words of other people's copy he rewrote for Talk—approximately the length of one Talk story—and better than double that amount if he reported and wrote up a Talk story himself. He fell behind, payments to him soon exceeding accepted work (a common occupational hazard at the *New Yorker*), but was furious when Ross passed on to him the accounting department's notice that he owed the magazine three thousand words to balance his account. He sent a tart note back asking Ross which he wanted: three thousand words torn out of the dictionary, or extracted from a children's book that the auditing department could understand. Ross chose not to make an issue of it. Ross disliked scenes, prized Thurber by now, and was probably already aware of how little the magazine had, over the years, paid Thurber and the other founding fathers who had helped put the magazine on the road to prosperity.

41

That War Between Men and Women

America is a matriarchy. It always has been, it always will be. It became obvious to me from the time I was a little boy that the American woman was in charge. . . . I think it's one of the weaknesses of America. . . . The mother dominates the son. . . . He . . . says: "Hey— Mom! Can I do this—can I do that?" Permission from "Mom" is the big thing. . . . I don't think there will be [any revolt by the American man]. In the series I did, "The War between Men and Women," the woman surrenders to the man, but you'll notice in the drawings that each woman has a big rock . . . behind her back. In other words, the war is not over.

—Thurber interviewed in the *New Republic*, May 16, 1958

Thurber's fifteen drawings making up "The War between Men and Women" ran in the *New Yorker* serially from January 20 through April 28, 1934. They seem more likely to have been inspired by his arguments with Ann Honeycutt than by his marital conflicts. The violence breaks out when a man throws a drink in a woman's face. Battles rage, prisoners are taken, and the men rout the ladies; a scowling Thurber Woman on horseback hands over her club to the Thurber Man in surrender.

"I give [W. H.] Auden credit for being the first to spot something in one of the drawings that must have come out of my subconscious," Thurber told an interviewer in 1949. "Remember the map on the wall in the women's head-quarters?"

The state of Maine had apparently been lopped off, the interviewer replied.

"So is Florida," Thurber said; he spoke almost as if someone else had done the drawing. "Auden points out that the women seem to have emasculated the whole country."

No major humorist before Thurber or since has exploited as extensively and intensively the natural conflict between men and women. He seems to have found both satisfaction and safety in going public with his domestic and romantic dilemmas. Despite the women's battlefield surrender, in Thurber's prose and cartoons, the men lose more frequently, highlighting the unlikable and dangerous character of the females.

"Are you looking for trouble, Mister?" the huge Thurber Woman with an oversize dog belligerently asks the tiny Thurber Man and his minuscule canine. "If you can keep a secret," another tells him, "I'll tell you how my husband died." The Woman is used to dominating any situation, however alien: "What have you done with Dr. Millmoss?" she angrily asks a Thurber hippopotamus, which is standing next to a few of the ill-fated doctor's belongings. She is also a menace at a cocktail party: "One more of these," she says, holding a drink, "and I'll spill the beans about everybody here." She is silly in her promiscuity: "You owe it to your glorious body, Mr. Cambodia, to eat at Schrafft's."

Thurber's cartoons were becoming favorite topics of discussion for psychologists and psychiatrists, from whom he heard occasionally. Frank Sullivan recalls:

> In the early days of the *New Yorker*, almost everyone on the staff, from Ross on down, went slightly cuckoo every once in a while. It was almost expected of you, and since I wanted to be in the swim, I took my turn one year and went to a psychiatrist to have a kink in my ego ironed out. About this time, Thurber's drawings of his remarkable men, women, and dogs were beginning to delight America and England. My doctor was flatteringly interested in my problems until he found I knew James Thurber. At that news he dropped me and my troubles . . . and would talk only about Thurber. He saw great significance, with a capital "S," in Thurber's work, and he was right. The next time I saw Thurber, I told him how he had alienated the affections of my analyst and suggested . . . he . . . pay half my doctor's bill. He was highly amused. He took a sheet of paper and in a few moments had covered it with drawings of

Women's G.H.Q.

Thurber characters . . . to . . . present . . . to my doctor. I did, and the little fellow was as delighted as a boy on Christmas morning when I gave him the Thurber original, direct from the master.

Thurber's latter-day protests that he really liked women were not deliberately misleading, for his root feelings toward the opposite sex remained obscure to him. But he did know why he preferred women's company at parties to that of men; the men were often as inclined to hog the spotlight as he was. "I saw quite a bit of James Thurber," writes the British writer Alec Waugh, "but I never knew him well. At mixed parties—and it was always at mixed parties that we met—he preferred talking to women. So do I. . . . I liked Thurber a lot; but [for this reason] I never had a real talk with him."

Those who knew Thurber best, however, agree that he resented not only the wives of his friends but most women in general. "He hated their goddam guts!" Thurber's close friend Joel Sayre assured an interviewer, slamming his shot glass on the bar for emphasis. Still, Thurber's handling of the issue is so consistently entertaining and harmless in appearance that he earned the adoration of women in the process. When asked why Thurber's resistance to McCarthyism didn't make him a prime target for a congressional investigation in that period of national suspicion, a congressman replied that his wife and daughters would not have stood for it.

"What have you done with Dr. Millmoss?"

Thurber's public never took his war against women seriously. One explanation may be that, as Wilfrid Sheed points out, humorists generally attempt to appear helpless. Confessions of inadequacy are certain to elicit a motherly response, even from the enemy. A man who is both funny and unhappy can make off with near-universal sympathy and affection.

"Great comics tend to be bastards in their personal lives," says Emily Hahn. "Chaplin. W. C. Fields. Humorists like Benchley, Sullivan, the early Thurber, stayed lovable by dealing in inconveniences rather than in serious social commentary and tragic emotions. You've got to be tough-mean to tackle those. Thurber later got into some of that, but his attitudes toward women, however painfully arrived at, always remained boyish, harmful to nobody but himself. His treatment of women in his books is too bizarre to be anything but funny."

As Thurber's mistrust of man's handling of the world's affairs increased over the years, he saw women's natural resistance to men as perhaps civilization's only hope. Yet he was against the political equality of the sexes, if that meant woman's surrendering her natural role as creator and preserver to play the men's game. Who, then, would be left to save the race? Thurber never found a comfortable place for himself in the shell-pocked, no-man's-land between men and women; much of his artistic energy was generated by the friction of his ever-changing, ever-conflicting beliefs on the subject. ("I love the idea of there being two sexes, don't you?" the predatory Thurber Woman asks the timid male, who is still thinking about it.)

In January 1934, in a benevolent mood, Ross published a critical essay of Thurber's which compared Eugene O'Neill plays with the work of Henry James; this was a one-of-a-kind *New Yorker* piece for Thurber. "The difference," writes Thurber, "between the indirectness of James and that of O'Neill lies in the fact that whereas James got farther and farther away from his central character through the perceptions of other people, O'Neill achieves his remoteness of contact by having his central character get farther and farther away from himself through splitting up into various phases of view point and behavior." Luckily, Thurber was not tempted again to get that far away from what he did best, nor was he encouraged to by Ross.

A piece that Ross rejected, and Thurber placed with the *Nation,* makes a sincere plea to Walt Disney to produce Homer's *Odyssey* in cartoon form. The version that was forced upon Thurber in high school, he wrote, was "cold and gray in style and in content." Disney could bring a liveliness to the story; his version would be one Thurber "should like my daughter to know . . . when she gets ready for the 'Odyssey'."

The *New Yorker* was thriving financially in an otherwise depressed 1934, and *Fortune* asked its *New Yorker* alumnus, Ralph Ingersoll, to try to explain the phenomenon. Ingersoll's explanation for leaving the *New Yorker* had been: "After five years under Ross, sanity dictated that I gravitate to less terrible people."

The *Fortune* article featured pictures of the editorial principals. The caption under Thurber's describes him as "a telephone-book scribbler." Ingersoll's article elaborates:

> His art grew out of fits of melancholy, rescued by his collaborator, E. B. White, and succeeded despite the adverse judgments of his editor. More important to the *New Yorker* have been his anonymous writings and his famous Talk of the Town Department. He is wonderfully adept at throwing missiles such as ice picks, rocks and electric light bulbs, despite the fact that he has only one eye. He loves to disguise his voice on the telephone and is so good at it that his colleagues rarely know to whom they are talking. A mad raconteur, his wit is not forced. For several years he shared with White the distinction of being the magazine's number one contributing editor. His *New Yorker* earnings: eleven thousand a

year. . . . My *Life and Hard Times* was the *New Yorker*'s best prose in 1933.

White, Ingersoll continues, along with Thurber, was "the wheel horse to the *New Yorker*'s wit," and earned twelve thousand a year. Visitors to the editorial offices, on the sixth floor of 25 West 45th Street, were met, according to Ingersoll, "with a little sign on the right of the receptionist's window saying, 'If no attendant is present please ring bell.' There usually isn't."

> The *New Yorker*'s editorial offices are the soul of inhospitality. The inside is bleaker. Ross is impatient with office design. . . . Men left the *New Yorker* for sanitariums. They had fits on the floor. They wept. They offered to punch [Ross's] nose. Ross is terrified of physical violence. . . . He kept on hiring and firing blindly. By hit or miss, he found the individuals who could articulate his ideas, and who could stand the pace of his temperament.

Ross, who disliked working with women, resented Katharine Angell at first, Ingersoll wrote, but had grown to depend on her as "his most indispensable executive." She was paid eleven thousand a year. (All salary figures are approximately 15 percent of what they would amount to today.) Ingersoll's disclosure of salaries especially infuriated Ross, who posted a bulletin-board notice that he was not, as *Fortune* claimed, earning forty thousand dollars a year. Rivalry is built into any enterprise, and nothing can more quickly bring dissension and disruption of morale than for employees to know what their deskmates are being paid. In his days at the magazine, Ingersoll did indeed know what everybody earned, but he had been gone for more than three years, and the *New Yorker*'s claims of his inaccuracy are doubtless valid. Thurber, who had remained a friend of Ingersoll's, was suspected as a source, though probably without reason; not since his first six months as the new "genius" had he known who was paid what, nor did he care.

Wolcott Gibbs, whom Ingersoll never liked, is described as Katharine Angell's right-hand man; "slim, handsome, macabre." All the *New Yorker* editors were neurotic, Ingersoll noted, and if they were not, Ross soon made them so. Having bowled over its staff, Ingersoll tried to pick up the magazine and dust it off. It had been aped, he said, by collegiate editors from coast to coast and had changed the wit of a generation. "The delicate, barbed quill has battled nobly if ineffectively with the world in its far from perfection."

Written in the irritating, staccato "Time style" of the day, the article rocked the *New Yorker*'s people, who were touchy about their privacy and conditioned to anonymity as a near-constitutional right. In the next week's *New Yorker*, White had a bitter one-line rebuttal to Ingersoll's piece: "The editor of *Fortune* gets thirty dollars a week and carfare." The Whites were particularly upset at Ingersoll's mention of their shared hypochondria, believing it hardly worthy of a man they had championed against Ross, and it was Katharine who suggested the parody Profile of Luce and *Time*, which followed a year later.

Thurber elected never to understand or accept the *New Yorker*'s insistence on privacy, a policy honored by nearly all staff members. The magazine's reporting, after all, was fueled by snooping into the affairs of others. But a buttoned-up staff was part of the mystique, arrived at not by charter but as the consequence of a founding hierarchy of gun-shy senior editors, especially Ross. Long after Ross, younger staff members, innocently replying to journalist friends who wanted to know whom to ask for a job at the *New Yorker*, were summoned to the office of the editor in charge of hiring, Leo Hofeller, and chastised for giving out his name. Thurber, unhampered by peer pressure or modesty, all his days cheerfully volunteered whatever was on his mind to outsiders, and candidly answered the questions of anyone writing about The Magazine. He saw no reason not to publicize himself and his works, or the magazine he worked for. He was a promotion department's dream, and a menace to his colleagues, who clung to secrecy like a security blanket. "Don't tell him those things," Ross once sharply commanded his mother, who was visiting New York, had just met Thurber, and was talking to him about Harold's home life as a young boy. "He blabs everything."

Thurber was pleased at how he emerged in the *Fortune* piece; even his picture was a good one. It also made excellent reading in Columbus, and it still very much mattered to him what Columbus thought.

In March 1934, Althea took three-year-old Rosemary on a cruise to the Bahamas. Thurber's work and love interests led him to find excuses not to accompany them. And perhaps Althea preferred it that way. However, the next year, she would claim in her divorce petition that Thurber had neglected to send her money in Nassau for the return passage or the hotel bill until barely in time for her to check out and get aboard ship, and that he failed to meet them in New York when it docked. This, her lawyer held, comprised legal abandonment. Althea had plenty of such transgressions to choose from to make her divorce case. Two years before, Thurber had left mother and child in Florida to get back to Ann Honeycutt and the speakeasy circuit, writing Honeycutt:

I am . . . leaving my wife and child here for two weeks. That will enable you and Pricey [Honeycutt was sharing her Charles Street apartment with Antoinette (Nettie) Price] to get many a meal for me at night in exchange for me making you fried eggs in the morning. I ought to be able to fry seventy or eighty eggs in two weeks. . . .

EDITOR CHARGED WITH FRYING EIGHTY EGGS/ Police Arrest 'Hen Fiend' in Charles Street Love Nest.

New York, April 6 (AP)- Police yesterday arrested James Thurbird, alleged egg-fryer, in a Charles Street love nest, on complaint of neighbors who had not been able to buy any eggs in the vicinity for three days. Detective Charles Crupper broke down the door of the elaborately furnished apartment, which was protected against raids by two locks and a crowbar. . . . Lolling on a luxurious chaise-longue in the one room of the lush apartment, which was redolent of illicit love and eggs, Crupper discovered two Village women, clad only in pajamas of an extravagant and voluptuous design. The women had plates of fried eggs, and others were "coming up" from the "kitchen" from time to time. Crupper counted more than seven dozen eggs, in and out of shells, in the nest. No reason could be assigned for the deed.

In April, Alexander Woollcott went into the hospital for a rest, and to help fill in his weekly half hour on WABC radio, Thurber was selected to broadcast for fifteen minutes on Thursday nights, at 10:45. As usual, Thurber was his own best publicist. When asked by a reporter, "Are these broadcasts of yours to be serious, Mr. Thurber?" he replied, "Well, as they stand now, it begins to look pretty serious for WABC." What had he done to prepare for the upcoming broadcasts? Thurber replied that he had bought a new suit. He wrote his own press releases, in the third person: "Once he decides what to do, Thurber thinks radio will be all right. 'I think radio will be all right,' was the way he put it." Thurber also promised to clear up "a situation that's arisen in the war between men and women," referring to his series, which was then appearing in the magazine. He claimed that he had gone into radio to obtain more wall space for his murals, having filled the walls of his *New Yorker* cubicle, those of other people's offices, and those of his hotel room. He was currently consigned to drawing on restaurant tablecloths, he added, but he felt the medium lacked permanency.

Despite his seeming nonchalance, he kept revising his script for his debut until the last minute, listening anxiously to studio advisers ("Now, don't read; just tell the thing"). He got reasonably good notices from the critics, several of whom liked his stories about the cook he and Althea currently employed and his imitation of her dialect; and his ruminations about the dogs at Sandy Hook, his family in Columbus, and a famous old prizefighter named Sam Langford. The *World-Telegram* radio editor approved. ("It was chatty, pleasant diversion. I for one am counting on it to make my next few Thursday nights a little more diverting than usual." The *Boston Transcript* delivered itself of a sentence that would have stunned Ross: "This stuff is pretty terrible but we still think he ought to be pretty good."

The show's director soon became a nervous wreck worrying over Thurber's well-known carousing and his habit of appearing only seconds before airtime. He assigned someone to watch Thurber through the cocktail and dinner hours—at the Algonquin bar, at Bleeck's, at Costello's—and to let him know if it looked like Thurber would fail to get to the studio on time. Thurber discovered that he was being followed and became angry; he had never missed a professional deadline except for the Brooklyn fire assigned to him by the *New York Evening Post,* and that was because he couldn't find the subway that went to Brooklyn. He evaded the spy one Thursday evening and had Jap Gude telephone the program director shortly before airtime to announce that Thurber was drunk. The director howled at Gude to get Thurber into a shower and taxi and to the studio immediately; meanwhile, he arranged for fifteen minutes of organ music. Thurber, who had smashed his hat and ripped his shirt collar open, burst into the studio, hair in eyes, tie under one ear, suit coat half off with one sleeve dragging, and reeled toward the mike. "Sh'O.K., sh'O.K.," he told the director, "Lemme go on. I'll tell the SOBs." The director screamed at Gude to get Thurber out of the room. At the last minute, Thurber reappeared, sober and neatly dressed, script in hand, fully in command as he took his place at the microphone. The director collapsed in a chair a whimpering shambles, and promised afterward never to spy on Thurber again. Thurber's vengeance wasn't complete. During one broadcast, he pretended to fumble in his pocket for his script and then, having found it, let it tumble helter-skelter onto the floor. The director and the engineer were horrified, but Thurber had memorized the material and launched into his monolog without a glitch.

He was now the established man about town and a celebrity of not immodest dimensions. A picture of him taken that April shows him in a tuxedo, feigning interest while the stout Major Bowes, father of all radio amateur hours, tries to fit a pair of two-hundred-and-fifty-dollar shoes on a pretty young lady at the Cinderella Ball. The caption identifies Thurber as one of radio's newer humorists, "popular for his subdued absurdities and his air of resignation."

Thurber soon gave up the weekly broadcasts. He was later to claim that

Ross objected to them, because they siphoned off material that The Magazine could use. Jap Gude, who was the publicity director for both the red and the blue network, disputes this:

> Thurber had a genuine curiosity about the potentialities of [radio as a new medium for him] that continued to fascinate him through the years. To be sure, his later interest was partly due to his blindness, which was progressive and which made him turn more and more to radio as an important source of news and entertainment. I doubt that Ross ever worried, or even protested about [Thurber's] brief little fling with broadcasting, or was even aware of it; in fact I doubt if Ross was even aware of the existence of radio. . . . Thurber was not "fired" from the job. . . . he found that it involved more work than he had bargained for, and he was not interested in doing something unless he could do it well.

"I worked across the hall from Edward R. Murrow, who was in his mid-twenties and director of 'talks' in CBS's public-affairs division," says Honeycutt. "Once when Thurber stopped by my office I introduced him to Murrow. Thurber at once demanded of Murrow equal time for his political party on CBS's 'talk' programs. Murrow asked what his party was, and Thurber said it was the Bull Moose Party. Murrow said he thought that party was long dead, and Thurber went into one of his tirades: Too many people thought the Bull Moose Party was dead. Did Murrow know how many members it still had? Millions! If Murrow was in public affairs, why didn't he at least know that?

"Thurber didn't like to leave an argument, even one that he had begun and was based on nonsense. He ranted and raved until I dragged him out of there. Murrow didn't know what to make of Thurber; Thurber sounded so sincere and so often came close to making sense. Later I explained things to Murrow and when they met again, Thurber apologized. Murrow laughed and told Thurber it had all been enjoyable."

Thurber teased Gude and Honeycutt with phony letters of suggestions for CBS programs—letters signed by "Mrs. Joe Knicple," "Mrs. Madge Blue," and other pseudonyms. Mrs. Knicple threatens to "spill the beans" about the antics of radio executives. ("All of them gather together with employes and drink whisky sour and about midnight are having whoopy I can tell you, if I wanted to make trouble." As "Mrs. Gertie P. Quickly," Thurber writes:

Dear [Columbia Broadcasting] System:
    I have a little daughter aged seven who is a marvel on the violin and

would appreciate it if she can begin playing for you on some "hour," starting next week; we would prefer having her on the best hour you have, such as Lucky Strike hour, with Ted Husing as her announcer if he is possible. Do you think he is possible? If she can play for you [I] would be able to accompany her myself although I am not a professional accompanyist still I am her mother and unless I am in a room when she plays she becomes frightened and cannot control her kidneys; this was very painful to us all at the First Methodist Church social last month when I could not be there to quiet her.

If Mr. Husing is impossible, I should like to know at once.

By the time Althea returned from the Bahamas, Thurber had moved temporarily into an absentee friend's apartment, on Madison Avenue, across from the J. P. Morgan mansion and library.

In Columbus, the Thurbers had moved from the house at 330 Gay Street to an apartment building on the same street. In February 1934, the apartment had caught fire. Some of the stacks of clippings and publications collected by Charles and Robert Thurber for their newspaper-promotion activity had been too close to a hot chimney pipe. Robert discovered the fire and awakened his parents, but Mame, instead of leaving the building, went upstairs to awaken the Kimmeys, the building's owners, who had already fled. She became trapped by the smoke, and her screams brought firemen to her rescue. No one was hurt. The family moved into temporary quarters, but Thurber invited Robert to visit him for a while, putting him up at the Algonquin. Robert stayed for several weeks. Asked his impressions of Thurber's circle, Robert submits a classic letter of its kind:

Most of the social gatherings I attended were comprised usually of members of the New Yorker staff, either in the lobby of the Algonquin or on a few occasions at "Tony's" or "21." They were usually informal talks about a variety of subjects and only occasionally any heated debate. Everyone had their say and opinion, but invariably it was on a friendly basis. Frequently, with the aid of a few rounds of drinks, many were talking at the same time, and it was difficult to follow the discussions. . . .

The New Yorker bunch was a very friendly and down-to-earth group of writers. They did not try to impress you with their knowledge and status. . . . This is true particularly of E. B. (Andy) White, Bob Coates, Dick Connell, Wolcott Gibbs, and Morris Markey.

Markey was probably the most talkative and Coates the most quiet of the group. Alva Johnston was more of the serious type, seldom joining in the general talk. . . . Dick Connell was a congenial and fun-loving type. When he first met me, his first words were: "Another Thurber? It can't be!" Gibbs, I believe, was the only native New Yorker of the staff. He advised me to visit but never live in New York and to retain my non-drinking status. Harold Ross was a little difficult to know and you didn't feel too comfortable around him at first, but after a period of time, this wore off.

My brother took me to his [borrowed] apartment one night. [It] was the last word in luxury and security.

Ross and my brother got along very well. Jim understood him and knew how to handle him. I believe my brother was closer to E. B. White than any of the others, although they all were a pretty close-knit group. . . .

[Morris Markey] was rather a wild driver behind the wheel of a car. The few times I rode in his car it was always a case of thanking your stars when you finally reached your destination. He really scared you. . . . I recall one time when he needed about $800 to settle some business matter and proceeded to write an article for the Sat. Eve. Post for which he was paid just about that amount. This always amazed me.

I met Benchley only twice and John O'Hara and Dorothy Parker once, all at one of the favorite night spots of the *New Yorker* staff ["21"].

Bob Benchley was always congenial, smiling and ready for a fast quip and a continuous flow of jokes and humorous stories. You just couldn't envision him as ever being ill-humored or upset about anything.

Dorothy Parker and John O'Hara seldom opened their mouths the whole evening . . . holding hands and continually whispering in each other's ear. She had little expression in her face.

Morris Ernst, the famous lawyer, was an especially good friend and admirer of my brother. He was . . . as easy to talk to as your favorite barber. He loved to bowl and on two occasions, he, my brother and I tested our skills. . . .

I met Marc Connelly once . . . on . . . a trip to a movie titled "Viva Villa," starring Wallace Beery. Althea . . . and Connelly walked together followed by Jim and me. I can't . . . recall that the four of us sat together to see the movie.

I met Max Eastman, the controversial figure only once, and briefly in the Algonquin lobby. He was quite friendly and very handsome and well-groomed.

I recall a couple of occasions when my brother managed to avoid meetings with Katharine Millay, sister of the famous Edna St. Vincent Millay. She was rather excitable and boring, I guess, as he found out on previous occasions.

From time to time I saw other famous persons, in the lobby, the elevator or eating in the Algonquin dining room, including H. L. Mencken, Helen Hayes, George Kaufman, Elsie Janis, Hendrik Van Loon, Blanche Bates, the once-famous actress [who starred in *Girl of the Golden West*], and Bessie McCoy Davis, actress and widow of Richard Harding Davis. Unfortunately I never had the opportunity to meet any of them.

I did meet J. C. Nugent, Elliott's father, and Ross invited us to his apartment once. I don't know how Jim kept up the pace. He introduced me to Harold Lloyd, Lowell Thomas and Tom Mehan. He had Marc Connelly autograph a copy of his play, *The Green Pastures*, for me.

When Jim had things to do, as he put it, he'd buy me a ticket to the theater while he took off. The tickets were always for the third and fourth row orchestra seat, just about the best in the house. Ordinarily I'd go to bed at 10:30 or 11 p.m., but Jim would sometimes come into my room at four or five in the morning to sleep, and on Wednesday mornings, when he had a Talk meeting at 10 a.m. at the *New Yorker*, he sometimes wouldn't bother going to bed at all. John McClain, the theater critic, was staying at the Algonquin and we saw quite a bit of him. I couldn't keep up with Jim and never understood where he got all the energy.

We'd sit in the Algonquin lobby from 10:00 a.m. to 5 p.m. lots of times. Have lunch there. People joined us. The crowd kept changing as some left and others came in. It was never boring as long as Jim was there. Once at "21" Andy White and Bob Benchley sat with us for two or three hours. White didn't drink much. I sampled champagne and got a hangover; never did smoke or drink. Jim had us playing mental games —Categories; name a category, call out a letter and the others have to come up with something in that category and beginning with that letter. Morris Markey wouldn't stop fidgeting, a very restless man. Ann Honeycutt, Wolcott Gibbs and Dick Connell's wife were at "21" another time. I never could figure out how all those people could drink all that stuff and stay so sharp. You can't bluff your way out of a situation like that; you have to be able to hold your liquor. We'd order dinner and then we'd leave in the middle of it to see a show and have a late supper afterwards. I don't think I finished one dinner on theater night before curtain time; so much time was spent on cocktails.

Marc Connelly was one of the Round Table charter members Thurber admired, and those Thurber admired usually saw him on his best behavior. "I met Thurber through Elliott Nugent, when he was acting in my first play, *Dulcy*," Connelly recalls. [The *Dulcy* cast had attended Elliott Nugent's 1921 wedding in New York, at which Thurber acted as Nugent's best man.] "I saw him off and on by merit of his frequenting the Algonquin. He was in and out, pleasant, gay, wildly humorous, and had the same enthusiasms we all did for theater, books, food, and drink. Jim would sit and make mental notes, listening to the rest of us. In the early thirties I asked him for some of his sketches and he spent half a day on them, brought them to me and said, 'Try these on for size.' It was the first time I ever heard that expression, and I think Thurber began it. We had a common interest in the *New Yorker*, of course. Ross put six of us from the Algonquin group on the masthead at the start of the magazine, and I edited two pieces Ross wrote when Art Samuels was managing editor. Thurber in the early thirties, when I knew him, was a thoughtful person with an adult mind, but he hadn't had the adventures of growth, the chance to develop the clearer, definite values. This doesn't mean that a writer's productivity necessarily improves when he acquires those things, but in Thurber's case it did. The more physically handicapped he became, the clearer and leaner his work, it seemed to me. He was a highly civilized man. He didn't see himself as humorists usually do—carrying spotlights around, as Twain and Will Rogers did. Usually they're exhibitionists, at home anywhere in the world, but not Thurber."

Connelly's profile of Thurber would astonish most of Thurber's other friends, but he could apparently turn himself off and on, like a light switch. When he was around those he felt he could learn from, or before whom he feared exposing his vulnerabilities, he was a listener. Not only Connelly but several others found the normally tempestuous soul of Thurber in genteel repose, and perhaps never knew of the fun they missed. Dame Rebecca West, the distinguished British journalist and one of Ross's favorite *New Yorker* contributors, acquired a more negative impression of Thurber:

> I only met Thurber four times. Each time, I think, when I had gone on to a party after a theatre and he was always very drunk, and once he was being a Thurber drawing. It was in some very luxurious apartment, I think on Park Avenue, where there was a huge living room with some good pictures in it. It was lit entirely by concealed lighting and by spotlights on the pictures. I was put down to sit next to Thurber who spoke to me just four times in an hour. Each time he said the same thing. He asked me, "Did you think that lamp shade was moving?"

I must have talked to him on some occasion because I was aware of the very large advances that Ross gave him—and certainly Ross did not tell me. I have an idea that at one of these meetings he complained that Ross was being impatient because he (Thurber) owed the New Yorker some thousands of dollars in advances.

I have a strong feeling that Thurber did not like me, but I cannot say it worried me. It was like hearing that a heraldic animal disapproved of one.

In the end, Rebecca West didn't like Thurber, either, if one can judge from her angry review of the British edition of Thurber's The Years with Ross, finding it an insufferable ego trip on Thurber's part at the expense of Ross's reputation. As to his comments to her about the moving lamp shade, they could pertain to Thurber's recurring eye trouble. During his New York visit, Robert remembers seeing Thurber frequently taking off his glasses to wipe his good eye as though it were bothering him. The surrealistic visions conjured up by his distorted and failing sight throughout the thirties are the subject of several of his casuals.

One night at Tony's, Thurber introduced himself to F. Scott Fitzgerald. "Why should I talk to you?" Fitzgerald responded. Because, Thurber replied truthfully, he regarded The Great Gatsby as one of America's outstanding novels. That sufficed, but few writers like to discuss their previous work, and Fitzgerald talked of his newest novel, Tender Is the Night, as his real master-piece. Fitzgerald's wife, Zelda, was under psychiatric treatment in an institution up the Hudson, and much on Fitzgerald's mind. A show of her paintings at a New York gallery had recently opened, and Fitzgerald had undertaken its publicity personally, handing out leaflets and catalogs of Zelda's art.

After a number of drinks, Fitzgerald told Thurber that he wanted to meet a "nice" girl, just to talk to, and Thurber obligingly telephoned Honeycutt, who, though not unaccustomed to Thurber's late-night calls with strange messages, was disinclined to invite two drunken men to her apartment at that hour. ("I spoke to Jim's companion briefly on the phone," says Honey. "I'd never met Fitzgerald, but this man didn't sound like I thought Fitzgerald should; I thought he had a Southern accent; I still think it was Faulkner, and always wondered if Jim had the right novelist.") Helen Wismer also declined to entertain the two writers, but Paula Trueman was more sympathetic, and curious to meet Fitzgerald. Thurber kept vigil in one room while, in another, Fitzgerald talked himself out to Paula, whose tolerance of a man compelled to talk about himself for hours on end had been honed to an art by her association with Thurber.

Fitzgerald's *This Side of Paradise* had electrified Nugent and Thurber when it appeared just after their college years, and this memory, enhanced by his admiration of *The Great Gatsby*, was presumably enough for Thurber to settle for his unusual, passive, secondary, intermediate role in the night's mini-drama. It was his only encounter with Fitzgerald.

That year, 1934, Wolcott Gibbs married again and began summering on Fire Island. Thurber was relieved—Gibbs and Honeycutt had occasionally dated and once had talked marriage—but he was also saddened to see the ranks of his fellow bachelor-boulevardiers diminished. Gibbs's bride was Elinor Mead Sherwin, who had been introduced to Gibbs by John O'Hara. To nobody's surprise, she was an actress. Not only had the twenties brought thespians into respectable society once and for all, but actors and actresses were now considered a distinct asset to any occasion. Ross, Gibbs, McKelway, Thurber, and other *New Yorker* men enjoyed being seen in restaurants and nightclubs with a woman of stage or screen.

"I'd floated in from Hollywood," Elinor Gibbs recalls. "I first met Thurber on a double date: Gibbs and I, Thurber and Helen Wismer, at Tony's. It was at the start of 1933. Helen was a very gay young woman, who drank along with the rest of us and didn't worry about anything. She was dating an assistant to the newly elected mayor, Fiorello La Guardia. Thurber made a big thing out of that.

"Thurber was amiable, and amused us with his *Life and Hard Times* recitations later that evening at Martin & Mino's. He was a very funny actor. He acted out *Tobacco Road* one afternoon in Gibbs's apartment. He arrived around one p.m., and it was dark before he finished. Things were always lively around Thurber. I didn't understand at first why Wolcott was wary around him, but I soon found out. Gibbs disliked scenes and Thurber enjoyed making them. With Thurber, the scene was always in the offing. He'd soften you up and then spring like a rattlesnake, but without the warning. He attacked both men and women; your sex was no protection. He could pick on you in a feline, catty kind of way. At such a time, it made him a very feminine kind of man. He needled. 'You think she likes you,' he'd say to Wolcott, referring to some woman Gibbs admired, 'but you should have heard what she told me about you.' It may not have been true, only a trick, but Thurber left you wondering. Or he'd say to Wolcott from time to time, 'You think you can be as good a writer as Andy White but you never will be.'

"TOBACCO ROAD"

"Gibbs was doing Notes and Comment then, but he didn't feel competitive with White. If he had to be measured, he felt he made up in volume what he may have lacked in White's special quality. Gibbs said he wrote over a million words for the *New Yorker*—more, he believed, than any other staff member at the time. He had handled all the departments, working with Ross, the art editor, contributors, Mrs. White. He not only wrote Comment but theater criticism, and during World War II, with a staff shortage, he took on movie reviews, too. Thurber was judging a race Wolcott wasn't even running.

"Thurber was an endless telephoner, so no one ever lost track of him, although Gibbs stayed on at Bleeck's when Thurber became the pillar of Tim Costello's, on Third Avenue, in the early forties. We didn't see that much of him after that. The remaining hard-core match-game players at Bleeck's broke up after Ogden Reid died, and Mrs. Reid began firing so many of the good men off the *Herald Tribune* in the 1940s."

"Before his vision got too bad for it," says Gibbs, "Thurber was the worst poker player in the world." The poker games were usually held at Honeycutt's Charles Street apartment, and when these games were not scheduled, Thurber joined the men at Bleeck's speakeasy to play the match game. Bleeck's, or the Artist and Writers' Club, conducted its illegal trade in booze behind a

Greek coffee shop on West Fortieth Street. It was a hangout not only for the staff of the *Herald Tribune,* next door, but the *New Yorker* staff, eight blocks away, including such former *Trib* reporters as John O'Hara, Joseph Mitchell, and Alva Johnston. Women weren't allowed inside, until after repeal, in late 1933, when Jack Bleeck, a political conservative, was legally obliged to give in. His new sign read "Formerly Artist and Writers' Club," leading the match-game players to label themselves "The Formerly Club." Stanley Walker, the Trib's city editor, who eventually worked a year for Ross, introduced Honeycutt to Bleeck's and the match players. She was soon considered one of the boys.

Bleeck was a conservative Dutchman who served German food. The pub's faded mahogany-paneled walls and clustered light globes were termed "early Butte, Montana." The *Tribune* staff not only ate and drank there but sometimes practically laid out the next day's issue of the paper on one of the tables. Regular match-game players were O'Hara, John Lardner, the press agent Richard Maney, Gibbs, Thurber, McKelway, Walker, Richard Watts, Honeycutt, Lucius Beebe, Leslie Midgley (a *Trib* editor), John Crosby, and Walt Kelly. Robert Benchley occasionally turned up, though in playing the match game he said that he felt like a skywriter who couldn't spell. The match game was perfectly suited to accommodate an ever-changing number of participants, for a game could begin after an issue of the *Herald Tribune* was put to bed and continue till 4:00 A.M., when the tavern closed, people joining in and dropping out the while. Leslie Midgley explains how it worked:

> Each player is equipped with three wooden matches. He puts both hands behind his back, then puts one clenched fist on the table. Inside the fist can be anything from three to no matches. The players guess, in clockwise order, the total number of matches in all the hands. If a player guesses the total correctly, he drops out and collects any side bets he may have made. The game continues until all have dropped out except two, who then play two-out-of-three. The loser pays off all the others, usually a drink and one dollar. But there can be many side bets between players contesting which one of them will get out first. . . .
>
> The game got a little out of hand over the years and the side bets got into the $10 and $20 range.

Most of the laughs were from insult humor. Thurber commemorated the match game in ten drawings, which he left on one of the tables and Bleeck confiscated, had framed, and hung on a wall over the famous suit of armor and a stuffed fish that J. P. Morgan had caught, its presence at Bleeck's never explained. The miniature Thurber "murals" became to Bleeck's what a chalice is to an altar arrangement. Numbered by Roman numeral, several pictured the tall, lean, mustached Thurber with a strand of hair falling over his glasses. His titles included: "Onslaught School"; "Coming Out Fast and Furious"; "The Plunger"; "Fifty Fish" (Thurber is looking aghast at the side-better here); "The Fair Intruder" (a Thurber Woman, either Honeycutt or Tallulah Bankhead, another frequenter of Bleeck's, sits in while the men glower or look unhappy); "Possible 27" (a waiter with a tray of glasses stares entranced at the nine players); "Opening Guess of Zero Wins" (the woman is the winner, eliciting further distraught looks from the men); and "The Maney Terror System: 'I'll Burn You Up!'."

Bleeck, described as "a pathological conservative," and never as popular as his tavern, sold the place in 1953, retired to Long Island, and took the Thurber murals with him. There was a general outcry from the match-game stalwarts, though Thurber had long since given up Bleeck's for "21" and Costello's. When Richard Maney's autobiography, *Fanfare,* was published, Bleeck got in touch with a former regular customer, Hugh (Meathead) Beach, a sportscaster, and said he would swap the Thurbers for an autographed copy of Maney's book. Maney agreed and met Beach at noon in a saloon, Maney paying for the drinks. They rented a chauffeured Cadillac and made the long trip to Bleeck's home in Manhasset. The seventy-five-year-old Bleeck tried to welsh on the deal, offering the sodden visitors an autographed picture of Mickey Rooney instead of the Thurbers, thus moving Maney and Beach, who were still drinking, to threaten physical violence. The frightened Bleeck relinquished the Thurber pictures. Maney hung them on the wall of his Manhattan office, which led to new outcries from the old Bleeck's crowd, who wanted them back in the pub.

"It was a campaign of terror," Maney said afterward. "I was menaced by telephone by members who had not even been appointed to the committee to menace me. My arguments were that I had donated my book, paid fifty-three dollars for the Cadillac and chauffeur, and I was the only one Thurber mentioned in any of the pictures' titles. I told the others they were just anonymous swine as far as Thurber was concerned. This seems not to have helped matters in the least. There was talk that the game players would pay me off at fifty cents a week to compensate me for my expenditures, but nothing came of it. The telephone threats were beginning to include my family, so I took the Thurber gems back. I did it after consulting Thurber, who said they belonged on the tavern wall. After they were rehung, Walt Kelly, Pogo's creator, inspected them and pronounced them fake Thurbers.

There were fresh threats to my well-being until Kelly withdrew his judgment and the matter was settled."

Maney handled publicity for Thurber and Nugent's *The Male Animal*. He was described by Wolcott Gibbs as "the greatest press agent since St. Paul." "Maney and Thurber were hilarious together," Nora Sayre recalls. "Dick had the tough mind and wits to keep up with Thurber and give back as good as Jim gave. Jim liked somebody who was very good at repartee, someone joining him on the stage, much more than he liked a worshipful audience. Dick would interrupt a Thurber monolog with little asides: 'No good can come from that,' he'd say, as Jim would keep talking. Maney was strictly deadpan. Even Thurber would break up before Maney would."

Thurber once tried to get John McNulty and Maney together, thinking they would find one another stimulating, but when the two did meet, McNulty decided any man as unwilling as Maney to surrender the floor to him would be hard to get along with. He wrote Thurber as much, when Thurber was abroad. Thurber defended Maney as a great guy who had stood solidly by him the night Maney's wife had thrown Thurber out of Maney's house in Westport.

"Thurber and I shared a common thirst," Maney recalled in 1962, "and a common fondness of sports—baseball in particular. We discussed sports all the time by yelling at each other in Bleeck's. Bleeck's began as a *Herald Tribune* hangout, but then Ross began hiring away the best staff the *Trib* ever had—Walker, the city editor, A. J. Liebling, McKelway, Sayre, Alva Johnston, and a lot of others. Then it became a kind of *New Yorker* hangout, too, by default.

"Thurber loved controversy; he'd take both sides. He could be a tenacious bastard on either side of an argument. If he decided he was winning too many people to his point of view, he'd switch viewpoints and begin attacking those who had been agreeing with him. Differences were settled at Bleeck's in the Western tradition, and many a man, insulted on the street, was wont to cry out, 'You step inside Bleeck's and say that.' The only violence Bleeck felt strongly about was if a playwright dropped in after his opening night, and the reviews were out, and assaulted a critic who had panned his show. Bleeck figured if that practice ever became tradition it would seriously cut into his clientele, given the number of theater critics who hung around Bleeck's. Bleeck blackjacked one playwright who had just pasted Richard Watts, a *Trib* critic at the time, for lambasting his play. Some of the critics could be pretty rough, and I think a few came to Bleeck's for protection after their reviews were turned in. Ogden Reid, the *Trib*'s publisher, had warned Bleeck that if he didn't protect the *Trib* staff from violence, Reid might switch the *Trib* from Republican to Democratic. This terrified Bleeck, whose hero was Westbrook Pegler and who considered us all Communists to begin with. The Reid threat kept him a vigilant, protective custodian of *Trib* people on his premises.

"Everyone thinks Thurber was always trying to start trouble, but all he really wanted was for someone to yell back at him. He enjoyed yelling, which was more acceptable at Bleeck's than gentlemanly behavior. Alva Johnston, one of the world's great reporters at the *New Yorker*, was the only one who refused to yell in Bleeck's. He was a one-man dullard's club. He'd walk in and begin an intelligent, rational discussion in a natural tone of voice and would empty the bar within an hour. Bleeck was fond of him, not only because he was quiet but because he was the only conservative fellow who seemed to turn up.

"Jim was a great gambler, and the match game was made to order for him. He'd bet on everything. If two waiters went downstairs to the wine cellar, Thurber would bet on which one would come up first. Back then, after eleven p.m., you could go to Bleeck's and meet fifty people you knew. But after Bleeck sold the place in 1953, the new management let it be known that all the debating and games and arguing were not liked. That put a hush on the festivities, and all the cloak-and-suiters from the garment district nearby, which all our shouting and fighting had kept out, began to take over. Thurber had pulled out for Costello's a decade before. He had gone completely blind and claimed we were cheating him at the match game and it frustrated him that he couldn't see who to hit."

Carson Blair, on a 1934 visit to New York, looked up Thurber, who dazzled him with a tour of the night spots. "At '21,'" Blair says, "I met Charles MacArthur, Mike Romanoff, and the son of William Randolph Hearst, among others. Thurber knew everybody and everybody knew Thurber. I met Ann Honeycutt and spent an evening in Jim's Algonquin room with him and Helen Wismer. Jim was telling Helen, largely for my benefit, reminiscences of our old days at O.S.U., in which Jim made himself the fall guy, the patsy, the drunk. He liked to poke fun at himself, to play the dumb guy. He was a lot of fun, and Helen was obviously fond of him."

Helen Wismer was seeing more of Thurber. She wasn't yet one of the front-runners among his women friends, but she could be seen as a dark horse with good prospects. At the end of one letter to Honeycutt—dated February 19, 1934—Thurber drew a map of his heart. The largest area was labeled "Honeycutt." Ross, Joel Sayre, Ann Fordyce, Paula Trueman, the 1922 Althea, Ohio, Martin & Mino's, Sally Benson, Mary Pickford, and the song "Who?" are all allotted portions of Thurber's illustrated affection. To the far left is a stingy sliver of Thurber's heart initialed "H. W." Helen Wismer barely makes it, but, four years after meeting him at Honey's 1930 party, she's firmly aboard Thurber's heart and on his mind.

42

That Man on the Train

He was sitting tensely on the edge of the seat across the aisle, one hand lying limply on his knee, the other clutching tightly the back of the seat in front of him. The train hadn't yet begun to move out of the darkness and closeness of the Grand Central cavern. I had the feeling that the man wanted to jump up and get off the train, run off; but he just sat there, one hand clutching the seat-back, the other lying limply on his knee. . . . "Ja notice that fella was sittin' opposite you?" [the conductor] asked me [later]. . . . "Poor fella just lost his little girl," he said.

—from "The Man on the Train"

In 1948, a student exploring the psychological significance of Thurber's work asked him about "The Man on the Train," which appeared in the *New Yorker* of April 20, 1935. Death in a dream, Freud writes, is frequently seen as a journey, such as a train trip—an image formed in childhood, no doubt, since children are often told that someone who died has "gone away."

Thurber: "I got the idea when my daughter was an infant and quite sick once. She's seventeen now. But with the neurotic's way of imagining the worst, I thought how awful it would be if she died, and then decided maybe I'd get that thought out of my head by writing about it. I had to have the man on some public conveyance where the operator or conductor would know him, so I put him on a train as a commuter familiar to the conductor. Interesting that Freud ties death to a train trip; as a child I always thought of someone riding away on a horse when he died."

Thurber, actually the stricken man on the train, was not just a "neurotic" imagining the worst. He had learned, just before writing the casual, that Althea was suing for divorce in order to marry someone else. Whether Rosemary was also ill at the time isn't known, but Thurber became frantic at the thought of losing "his little girl" to Althea's custody, with only vague visiting rights offered him. He worried that she would grow up in another man's home, not really knowing her father.

By the summer of 1934, Althea had wearied of a marriage that was more in name than in fact. A mutual attraction developed between her and Francis Comstock. Comstock was in the printing business in New Haven, but gave it up shortly after meeting Althea to go on a Yale archaeological expedition to the Middle East. He and Althea had exchanged letters of increasing warmth and commitment, and in late summer she told Thurber that she was filing for a legal separation. Most of the terms of the separation, handled for Thurber by his friend and *New Yorker* lawyer Morris Ernst, would serve for the divorce settlement, including alimony. In exchange for deeding the Sandy Hook property to Althea, Thurber was not required to pay child support, though he became Rosemary's principal financial provider when she reached her teens. Althea was undoubtedly hopeful that things would work out with Comstock, but couldn't be certain, and neither she nor Thurber spoke of divorce for the moment.

The separation was inevitable. Both had tired of dragging the corpse of a marriage behind them. Well before Althea had met Comstock, she and Thurber were engaging in bitter and unretractable argument. Each needed to be disappointed in the other to explain their unhappiness and the public embarrassment of a failed marriage. Thurber had taken to quoting Clarence Day's antiwoman verses, which insist "it is the wife, it is the home" that keep the man tied down, not free to roam and create.

"You're a millstone around my neck," Thurber had once raged at Althea. In a summer cottage, he had thrown a kerosene lamp at her. ("I blew it out first," he later defended himself when she brought it up.) Althea gave as good as she got. Robert Thurber, during his visit to New York, says of Althea, "I thought she was being pretty nasty to Jim."

They had long before agreed that their extramarital relations should be of no concern to each other, but after the Sandy Hook purchase and the birth of Rosemary, Althea had needed more of Thurber's presence and help with the large property and the baby, and the time and attention he gave other women became an issue.

"Althea had to make the move," says Honeycutt. "As miserable as he was with her, Jim was scared at the thought of being alone and losing his child. I think he would have gone on preferring an emptied, collapsed marriage to no marriage at all. And not just because it provided him with material. He had plenty of other conflicts to use for that, nearly all of them of his own making."

So it seems. He closed out 1934 with three sad and bitter drawings published in December, that traditional season of peace and goodwill. The bald, plumpish, despairing Thurber Man is told by his unhappy wife: "The magic has gone out of my marriage. Has the magic gone out of your marriage?" At a bar, listening to nearby women gossips, the drunken Thurber Man snarls at them: "You gah dam pussy cats!" And the insignificant-looking husband, seated across from his large, forceful wife, tells her heatedly, "I assume, then, that you regard yourself as omniscient. If I am wrong, correct me!" Ross, who enjoyed Thurber's war every bit as much as the magazine's readers did, was publishing one of its pictorial battle reports almost once a week.

With each issue, Thurber was a new source of wonder to Gus Kuehner and other former *Columbus Dispatch* colleagues. "I knew him when he couldn't

"You gah dam pussy cats!"

draw a line!" Billy Ireland, the *Dispatch*'s editorial cartoonist, exploded to Milton Caniff, another O.S.U. graduate suffering Kuehner's persecutions as a "nightside" *Dispatch* employee. Caniff, who would attain national prominence with his cartoon strip "Terry and the Pirates," was fired by Kuehner in 1932 and went to New York, where he worked for the Associated Press while "trying to break into the freelance gag field," he writes. Caniff, who didn't know Thurber but had "crossed his path" while on the *Sun-Dial*, sent some of his drawings to Thurber, who recommended several to the magazine's art conference. They were all rejected, and Thurber returned them to Caniff with sincere regret, explaining that he had no role in the selection process. He added that it was hard to break in to the *New Yorker* but he hoped Caniff would keep trying, hoped he was selling elsewhere, and that everything was all right with him and his wife. Caniff, then the unknown, never forgot the effort on his behalf by the celebrated Thurber. A side of Thurber few knew about, he says, was his eagerness to help young writers and artists and any of his friends in trouble. Both he and Caniff had

> shared John NcNulty's stormy confidences. . . . Without a doubt, Thurber . . . kept [McNulty] a luminary in spite of McNulty's efforts to destroy himself. . . . Even those who did not become well-known were lifted by [Thurber's] touch.
>
> I did not meet him until the night Terry and the Pirates started publication in the *New York Daily News*, October 17, 1934. He was single then, so he joined Mrs. Caniff, Charles and Charme Speaks, and me at dinner to celebrate the occasion.

Shortly after Althea's legal action, Herman and Dorothy Miller visited Thurber in New York. He was living in yet another friend's apartment, on lower Fifth Avenue. "We were getting ready to go out to dinner when Althea stopped by to get something," Dorothy says. "She was very polite and glad to see Herman, who had taught her at O.S.U. There was no squabbling, and I wondered why Jim didn't invite her to join us for dinner. I feel she would have accepted.

"Jim and Herman were in their zany mood. We walked to the Charles restaurant in the Village. Thurber had loosened the laces of one of his shoes and would suddenly kick it ahead of him on the sidewalk. It annoyed me, because Herman and Jim both laughed like fools when considerate people, including one sincere, little man, retrieved the shoe for Jim."

Robert Coates and Thurber drove to Columbus that spring. Coates, Thurber's closest companion on the staff at the moment, was curious to see the breeding ground of the characters in *My Life and Hard Times*. As for Thurber, his latest separation from Althea had put him in another panic of insecurity, and his first stop was at Eva Prout's home in Zanesville. Eva was upstairs when someone called to her that there was somebody to see her.

"I went down the steps," Eva remembered, "and as I stood in the doorway Jim was sitting in a chair and we both just simply flung ourselves into each other's arms . . . we were so happy . . . to see one another. He asked me if I was happy . . . and was going to remain with Ernest. I said, 'Well, of course.' "

The questions surprised her, for she hadn't seen Thurber for six years. Thurber, who still hoped to marry Honeycutt, and hadn't decided to marry Helen, told Eva that he was separated from Althea but was going to remarry. "But my impression," says Eva, "was that he first wanted to know if I was going to remain with my husband." It was the last time she saw Thurber.

The impending divorce drove a frightened Thurber into a search for the old possibilities once more. Minnette Fritts Proctor also heard from him. "He was phoning me several times a week," she says. "I realized he was mentally and emotionally disturbed. [As in 1929] he insisted on coming out to Seattle —which my doctor husband would not have understood *at all*. I knew that I could not help him."

Mame was expecting her son and Coates, but for three days she didn't know where they were. She called Eva Prout to ask, "Eve, did Jim stop to see you?" Eva recalls telling her, " 'Oh, yes. He was here yesterday.' And [Mame] said, 'Well, he hasn't arrived home yet.' And I said, 'Well, certainly he wasn't going anyplace else.' And then the next day she called me [again]. They couldn't imagine where he was . . . for three days. . . . He just sort of disappeared."

Thurber and Coates had spent those days visiting the offices of the *Dispatch*, the Millers, and the Ted Gardiners. As Columbus inexorably outlived Thurber's era, in his mind it remained as it had been when he lived there, a place frozen in memory, to be treated as a literary trademark and resource. But his warmth toward Columbus was sustained less and less by his family, which gradually became more a source of worry than comfort and pleasure to him. The city's lures were by now his friends, principally Herman Miller— until his untimely death in 1949—and Ted Gardiner. Visiting these lively, sophisticated men, who were of Thurber's mind and humorous bent, compensated for the duty-bound ordeal of visiting his family when he was in town. While he owed much to his mother for her wild and original lessons in conspiracy against the world's dullness, she had always been self-centered and unaware of what her second son had experienced in their family life. As a compulsive talker and telephone addict, she could completely shut out her family, and, to Joel Sayre, "was always a damned bore, a show-off; expected applause for her pranks the moment she sat down." Whatever his thinking about his family, Thurber's love for the city came to be anchored by his fondness for the Millers and Gardiners.

"As far back as I can remember," wrote Patricia McGuckin, Gardiner's daughter,

> the pattern of our family life was marked and brightened periodically by Jim Thurber's visits. [The] visits were always awesome occasions for me. . . . Though I was then too young to appreciate his writing and mind, I instinctively knew that this tall, kind friend of my father's, with his restless gestures and his rapid-fire, sometimes incomprehensible manner of speaking, was no ordinary man. . . . Evenings at our house usually followed the same pattern—the dinner, then long hours of talk and laughter, most of the talk by Thurber, who was once called by a friend "a night-blooming monologist."

Because he had mentioned to Mame that he was coming to Columbus, it is probable that Thurber and Coates made it to the Thurber apartment—restored after the fire—to see the family before their return East. "Jim would come to town and we'd never know he was here," Robert says, "until he'd walk in the house unexpectedly. 'Hi,' he'd say to us, as if he'd just been down to the corner drugstore for a pack of cigarettes."

As a gag, Thurber would insist that his old friends in Columbus were unaware of his career in New York, says Donia McNulty. "He'd say that some greeted him with 'Have you been out of town? Haven't seen you around lately.' But Thurber talked freely about his projects and plans, often implying that they were as good as completed, though most would never materialize. *My Life and Hard Times* had been sold to the movies, and Thurber said he was debating whether or not to accept an offer to work on the screenplay for three months at seven hundred and fifty dollars a week. In which case, the *Columbus Citizen* reported, Thurber would quit his drawing-account arrangement with the *New Yorker*, and his Talk duties, to accept the offer, occasionally contributing to the magazine on a freelance basis. The newspaper also reported that Thurber had completed a picture book on sports in collaboration with Robert during Thurber's brief stay in Columbus. Actually this book, which Thurber had promised to write with Robert, was never even begun, and Robert ended his life still feeling let down by his brother on that score.

Smith College had exhibited drawings by Thurber and George Grosz in the winter of 1933, and in December 1934 the Valentine Gallery in New York opened the first one-man show of Thurber's art. The catalog blurb, obviously written by Thurber, states:

> He never plans out an idea. He merely gets angry or bewildered by something and begins to draw. He draws for pleasure but with grim intent. He strives to catch the humor, sometimes fantastic, sometimes grotesque, sometimes sad, that appears upon the surface of simple situations and elaborate involvements in which men and women, wives and husbands, constantly find themselves trapped.

An accolade from Paul Nash is included, along with a shower of dropped names of people who possessed Thurber originals, and a somewhat spiteful mention—clearly bearing the mark of Thurber's ego—that though the Cleveland Museum of Art had bought two of his drawings, the Columbus Gallery of Fine Arts had none. Nor, it was added, did the Columbus Public Library still have a copy of "his successful book," *Is Sex Necessary?*.

The *New Yorker's* prosperity through the Depression continued to leave Ross both pleased and incredulous. One day he opened the door to E. B. White's office to say in wonder, "We've got a hundred thousand readers." The imperturbable White replied, "That's fine. How are they all?"

Thurber's abundant production in 1934 was achieved within a lifestyle that would have destroyed a man of lesser resilience. "As for staying up all night and working," he writes in "A Dozen Disciplines," "I know all about that: that simply turns night into day and day into night. I once got myself into such a state staying up all night that I was always having orange juice and boiled eggs at twilight and was just ready for lunch after everybody had gone to bed. I had to go away to a sanitarium to get turned around." He never did get turned around, and one hopes that his fondness for nightshade made his blindness easier to bear when it came upon him.

Rather than fill out requisition forms for his office supplies, Thurber used a stolen passkey to get into the stockroom and take what he needed. The business office eventually audited the inventory and discovered the shortages. New locks were placed on the doors, but Thurber smuggled the master key to a locksmith and had twelve keys made from it, which he distributed to his friends. Thurber embroidered the incident in "Thirteen Keys." The timid little Thurber Man this time is named Mr. Kimmey—the name of the landlord of the Thurbers' apartment house in Columbus—who

> always wrote his own letters, being too self-conscious to dictate to anybody. He simply didn't have the strength to phone Miss Williams, the office manager, to send an office boy with a requisition blank. He always ended by going out for a malted and going to a newsreel theatre and going home.

Finally, Kimmey, desperate for supplies, steals the key off its hook, has twelve more made, returns to the office at night, opens the stockroom, and loads his desk with supplies. Then he panics, imagines "the keeper of the keys" has put the police on his trail, and takes all the supplies back and replaces the master key on the hook after crawling over the transom. But he still has the dozen keys, and his fear of being caught with them is so great that he can't eat dinner. He walks across the Manhattan Bridge, periodically dropping a key into the river until they are all gone.

Thurber marvels at a *New York Times* feature about how radio gagmen thought nothing of twisting old jokes a thousand ways for use after use. In "How to Relax While Broadcasting," Thurber finds that magazine writers are simply not that versatile. He, for one, can think of only twenty-seven variations of "Who was that lady I saw you with last night?"

In December 1934, the *Herald Tribune* reported Admiral Byrd's claiming of the land beneath the Antarctic for the United States. Thurber finds the *Tribune*'s account so confusing that he decides that Byrd was lost most of the time and refused to admit it. As to Byrd's donation to the country, he asks, "Are we landowners or ice dealers?"

In "Has Photography Gone Too Far?" he wonders whether a photographer-artist has the right to monkey with the negatives or prints of a photograph in the name of art. He finds extreme a photograph of a horse's mouth taken while the photographer lay in the street. The dilemma, to Thurber, is whether the artist or the camera is in control. "Once the camera itself gets the upper hand," he warns, "the Lord Himself only knows what might happen."

He fractures the French on wine-bottle labels ("How To Tell a Fine Old Wine"): "The phrase '*mise du* [sic] *château*' means nothing more than 'mice in the château,' just as it says."

An R. A. Barry column in the *Tribune* about stamps and envelopes sets Thurber off on a discussion of what he gets in the mail. It's a forerunner to his famous 1949 casual, "File and Forget," in which his book publisher repeatedly sends books Thurber didn't order to obsolete addresses. In this mid-thirties piece, he is amazed that a letter sent to him at 65 West Eleventh Street reached him. "Going back to places where he used to live makes him sad," he writes in the third person. He remembers the "colored" maid there who called him "Jack" and said his bed always looked as if he had danced in it.

During the thirties, Robert Benchley was spending more time making movie shorts and reviewing theater for the New Yorker, and writing less and less humor. He gave as one reason his worry that Thurber had already done any piece he was thinking of doing. Benchley and Thurber did occasionally overlap in subject; both, for example, got around to attacking pigeons. Benchley, who disliked all birds (songbirds had been known to attack him) writes, "I am awakened every morning by a low gargling sound, which turns out to be the result of one, two or three pigeons walking in at my window and sneering at me. . . . It is a war to the death and I have a horrible feeling that the pigeons are going to win."

Thurber got onto that subject one afternoon in the fall of 1934, when he went to a newsreel theater and heard Gertrude Stein read from her works, including the line, "Pigeons on the grass, alas." It was made to order for the Thurber lunacy that Benchley envied. Pigeons were definitely not alas, Thurber writes. "A number of pigeons alight from time to time on the sill of my hotel window when I am eating breakfast and staring out the window. They never alas me, they never make me feel alas."

He couldn't stop. He pretended to be out of control on the subject. He poured feeling and energy into resisting the notion that pigeons are capable of making one feel at all.

> When a pigeon on my window sill ledge becomes aware of me sitting there in a chair in my blue polka-dot dressing-gown, worrying, he pokes his head far out from his shoulders and peers sideways at me, for all the world (Miss Stein might surmise) like a timid man peering around the corner of a building trying to ascertain whether he is being followed by some hoofed fiend or only by the echo of his own footsteps. And yet it is *not* for all the world like a timid man peering around the corner of a building trying to ascertain whether he is being followed by a hoofed fiend or only by the echo of his own footsteps, at all. . . . A pigeon looking is just a pigeon looking. When it comes to emotion, a fish, compared to a pigeon, is practically beside himself.

More than Benchley, Thurber not only had the "sure grasp of confusion," but he could work himself into an awesome frenzy over nothing in the name of comedy as art.

The week his discourse on Gertrude Stein's pigeons appeared in the *New Yorker*, Thurber attended her book-signing session at Brentano's bookstore and wrote it up as a Talk story. Thurber stood in line, but he didn't submit his name to her on a card, as the others did. "We just handed our book to her," Thurber writes, "and she glanced at us with her keen, humorous eyes and, seeing that we didn't have a name, simply put her own name on the flyleaf, and the date. She signs herself always 'Gtde Stein.'"

Thurber's nightlife, as illustrated in his cartoon series "Parties" in *The Seal in the Bedroom*, had hardly changed: "First Husband Down" (man passed out); "Love" (man flirting with woman while wife glares); "The Brawl" (trying to separate two men fistfighting); "Berserk" (man running wild); "When You Wore a Tulip" (group singing at a piano); "The Bawling Out" (woman scolds man in chair); "Four O'Clock in the Morning" (everyone at a party asleep).

"I usually argue with people when my clothes are rumpled and my hair is in my eyes," Thurber writes in "Footnotes on a Course of Study." He adds, in "Thoughts from Mr. Tierney," "I can never remember names or faces, a misfortune which is intensified by the fact that I am always sure I have met everybody I see." Thurber's social misadventures have consistently drawn attention, but there are those who fondly remember other occasions, such as his singing George and Ira Gershwin's "Lady Be Good" at the Gershwins' apartment, with George accompanying him on the piano.

He could have avoided the trouble he got into at another party had it not been for Harold Ross, a prankster in his own right. David O. Selznick, the producer of *Dinner at Eight*, was bragging about its financial success one night at the apartment of the songwriter Howard Dietz. Ross and Thurber were there. Ross asked Thurber to pretend to be the *New Yorker*'s treasurer and to tell Selznick that the magazine had grossed ten million dollars that year, a figure that dwarfed the receipts of Selznick's movie. It should have been a good-natured put-on, but somehow it turned into a fight between Selznick and Thurber, the former offering to punch Thurber in the mouth. Ross, who couldn't stand violence, immediately departed, leaving others to separate the two men.

Thurber was holed up at the Algonquin by December of 1934, collecting his pieces and drawing their illustrations for a book to be called *The Middle-Aged Man on the Flying Trapeze;* the title was a parody of William Saroyan's best-seller, *The Daring Young Man on the Flying Trapeze.*

Joseph Mitchell, who had lately become a feature writer for the *New York World-Telegram* and would shortly become the *New Yorker*'s premier chronicler of the city's contemporary life, real and fancied, used Thurber's Valentine Gallery art show as a peg on which to hang a Thurber interview for his newspaper. Mitchell was from tobacco-farm country in North Carolina. (He continued to spend vacations farming his father's land, into his eighties.) He had applied for work at the *Herald Tribune* in the early thirties and was hired by Stanley Walker. ("I thought the world of him," says Walker.) Walker also hired Richard O. Boyer, from St. Louis, who got Mitchell in trouble. Though Boyer "did some good work for us, very good work," says Walker,

> he was a surly, nasty problem child. . . . I fired Boyer and Mitchell the same night, with much regret, especially as to Mitchell. They had got drunk . . . and . . . had come . . . upstairs [in the HT building], thrown inkwells around [and] desecrated Ogden Reid's desk. . . . I kicked them out. The next day they came in, contrite, but they were fired for good. I got Mitchell a job on the World-Telegram and sent Boyer to Boston to work . . . on the Boston Herald.

Arriving for the interview, Mitchell found Thurber's Algonquin hotel room filled with dirty shirts (seventy-eight of them, according to Thurber) and packages wrapped in holly paper, though it was several days after Christmas. "I always wait until two or three weeks after Christmas to send my presents," he told Mitchell. He didn't like office telephones, he continued, ever since

> I worked on the old *Evening Post*. Sometimes all hell would break loose somewhere and all the telephones in the office would begin ringing. Maybe it would be a jail-break at the Tombs. Or . . . a subway wreck. . . . I would know a big story had broken and I would grab my hat and go home. I never cared for big stories. . . .

In 1962, Mitchell was asked his thoughts about the Thurber he had interviewed twenty-eight years before: "I was surprised in later years when Thurber began to tout himself as a hot-shot newspaperman," Mitchell said. "In *The Years with Ross* he would have us believe he had been a newspaper reporter par excellence. I don't think he can have it both ways. I rather suspect his earlier assessments of himself were closer to the truth, even after one eliminates the exaggerations." Which didn't lower Thurber in Mitchell's estimation one bit; asked recently his opinion of the *New Yorker*'s pioneers, Mitchell replied that "Thurber was the only true genius."

During the interview, Thurber was still chewing on the Hollywood screen-play offer, not certain he could write for the movies but eager to see the Nugents and to play wintertime tennis. He repeated to Mitchell his stock interview offerings: rye and water was his favorite drink; he had turned out a hundred and fifty thousand drawings for his own amusement; his American public was far less appreciative of his work than his English public. This last platitude was one he would repeat for the next thirty years. He never forgot that it was Britisher Paul Nash who first gave his art international recognition. There is little question that the British have hugely enjoyed Thurber's humor, and his work seemed sufficiently anti-American to give British admirers an early lead in Thurber worship. But over the years the loyalty of his American readers provided most of his income, and it continues as the largest source of revenue to his estate. The book reprints, television and stage productions, movies, operas, and ballets that derive from Thurber's original work have been principally American.

Thurber contributed eighty pieces of work in text and drawings to the *New Yorker* in 1934. Much of it reflects the maladjustments of the thirties. "The period led to some of Jim's funniest man-woman cartoons," says Jap Gude, "but it was a bad time for him. Within a span of weeks, the two most important women in his life at the time, Althea and Honey, rejected him."

Unable to remember to send out his shirts to be laundered, there is little wonder that Thurber couldn't begin to set any part of his life in order. When not at his typewriter or drawing board, he had come to fear his own decisions regarding all matters large and small. As the prospects of a future without a woman partner loomed, he sought the most impractical and impossible solution: the winning of Ann Honeycutt.

Honey's popularity drove him to distraction. She, Edward Angly of the *Herald Tribune*, and Thurber had leased a cottage at Martha's Vineyard in the summer of 1934, but Thurber had returned to New York early, pleading his work demands but actually in a sulk over the amount of attention Honeycutt was paying Angly. Thurber found the city steaming in as bad a heat wave as the one that had driven them to the Vineyard. He wrote Honey, "It's *still* terrible down here and I earnestly advise you to stay where you are." He continues:

> One of those sulky twilights is falling over New York. Worn and pasty people are drinking Tom Collinses downstairs [at the Algonquin]. Waiters are staring damply into space, men are removing their collars and shoes and cursing. Women are patting their sticky hair and wriggling moistly out of their damp pants, children are whining, radios are crackling insanely, automobile brakes are shrieking, and away off a swan is flying, wings outspread, into Hell, screaming like a cowardly, condemned man. . . .
>
> All my old doubts and depressions are back. I found them in my unsent laundry and my unanswered mail, in [John] Mosher's facetious remarks, in Gibbs' sharp comments, in Ross's swagger, in Mr. [Frank] Case's glib "Welcome back! Welcome back to Hell!"

Thurber was still on a crusade that he knew had been lost a long time before. He chose to view Honeycutt's indecisiveness as deceit, and he couldn't end his letter without angrily punishing her for telling him to depend less on her and the need for women:

> I sit and ponder your advice to stand on my own feet. . . . I never become so smug as you do in my pronouncements—violent and adolescent, but not smug. . . . You stay there and write me a few sharp admonitions about standing on my own feet. . . . Man is born and dies alone. Why shouldn't he live alone? You tell 'em, baby, you know the answers.

"Though we never talked about it," Honey says, "I thought Jim's experience with Althea made him question his potency. And that that accounted for his rages. He seems to have had his share of sexual affairs, so either I made him feel impotent or, at such times, he was able to overcome the self-doubts his life with Althea seem to have created."

Here lied Annie

God bless you & keep you!

43

That Great Heart Analysis

Dear Miss Honeycutt:

. . . I believe that if you understood [my patient] more thoroughly you would treat him with greater consideration and would not be so shocked and disturbed by the liberties he sometimes attempts to take, the reprehensible proposals he makes, and the so-called poison-tongued dinner talks with which he favors you. He is . . . what we call in my profession a Nervous Talker, but deep down behind that golden tongue is one of the greatest and most remarkable hearts I have ever examined. . . . I am taking the liberty of enclosing a copy of my chart of his heart, for your information.

—Letter to Ann Honeycutt, February 19, 1934

In late 1933, Thurber had escorted Honeycutt to a party at Wolcott Gibbs's apartment, where she first met the polished, courtly, worldly St. Clair Mc-Kelway. McKelway was with his second wife, but he seemed endowed with a talent for legally and efficiently disposing of a marriage when another woman caught his fancy. Of a Southern Presbyterian morality, McKelway preferred marriage to illicit affairs. Eventually he was married five times. Honeycutt would be number three, and was probably the least satisfactory of any of them for McKelway, she says. But she was taken with him from the start.

"As a person, Mac seemed everything Jim was not," she says. "He was ever a gentleman. No tantrums. Good-looking. Self-possessed. He could hold his liquor. To me, the most important thing about our relationship, once we began seeing one another, was that he didn't wear me out arguing all the time, as Jim did."

McKelway was a newspaperman who, in the late twenties, left New York for Siam to edit an English-language newspaper in Bangkok for five years. He returned in 1933 and had been on the *Herald Tribune* for six months when Ross persuaded him to join the *New Yorker* on a drawing account.

"I was to edit for two days a week, and to write Profiles and Reporter at Large articles the rest of the time," McKelway says. "I first met Thurber at the magazine, and got acquainted with him over drinks at the Algonquin. That was a fairly new experience at the Algonquin; Prohibition had just been repealed. When I began dating Honey, Thurber felt betrayed by both of us. He had the attitude that I had broken into his premises and made off with his personal property. I considered any unmarried woman legitimate, fair game."

After several months with Ross, even McKelway's collected disposition and balanced demeanor were under pressure. One of their early collapses was at the magazine's tenth anniversary party, at the Ritz-Carlton Hotel, in February 1935. The party was sponsored by Raoul Fleischmann. As usual, with liquor flowing, the hostility index steadily rose—not between the business and the editorial employees, who didn't know one another, but between the writers and the editors who massaged their copy. Carefully nurtured animosities lay in wait to ambush the unsuspecting. This touchy situation, staged annually at the magazine's Christmas party, led both Ross and Shawn to make only short, token drop-ins. (After Christmas parties were replaced by annual anniversary parties, Shawn came only to the fiftieth in 1975.)

There was no managing editor at the time, McKelway says; Katharine White and Gibbs both worked directly under Ross. McKelway immediately found himself rewriting and editing volumes of material, leaving him little time for his own writing. The pieces that gave him the most trouble were Morris Markey's. Markey, a large, hot-tempered Virginian, had a mottled face that made him appear to be in a rage even when he wasn't. He worked fast—for a time he had a Reporter piece published each week—but he sacrificed accuracy for quantity, and McKelway and the checkers were working overtime cleaning up the facts and the grammar in time for the printer's deadline. Once, Markey turned in an article about the old city morgue, based on his recollections as a newspaperman. Rogers Whitaker, who lived down that way, told Ross that the morgue had been torn down. Ross found Whitaker was right and killed the piece. Markey angrily promised to kill Whitaker. Whitaker and McKelway had similar plans for Markey, who nearly got into print, week after week, with inaccuracies bound to reinforce Ross's paranoia and make life additionally miserable for everyone. Thurber had cooled toward Markey, because Markey was siding with Althea in their running fight and because in Althea's presence at a Danbury Fair concession Markey had swung the sledgehammer with enough force to ring the bell and win a cigar, a feat Thurber couldn't match.

Honeycutt had come to the magazine's 1935 anniversary party with Stanley Walker. They were joined at their table by McKelway, Thurber, and others. Markey stopped by and said cheerfully, "Ah, here's Mac, surrounded by beauty as usual." This pleasantry, says Honey—coming from a man who left fact checkers and editors to pick up after him, and who seemed to be echoing Thurber's gibes at McKelway for being "a ladies man"—pushed McKelway over the edge. Always quick with his fists in those days, McKelway said later, he leaped up and began swinging at the startled Markey, to Thurber's surprise and delight. Bewildered, Markey backed away, saying, "Mac, if you keep this up, I'll have to knock you down." But McKelway was out of control, and in self-defense Markey hit him in the chest, sending him backward over one table and against another with enough force to upset it. (Ross, certain that any physical violence by staff members somehow involved him, was heard to say, "Geezus, what now?" before hiding in the men's room until things settled down.)

The day after the party, the inner circle, along with Russell Maloney, who had just joined the staff, and John Chapin Mosher, met at Gibbs's apartment in a customary effort at physical and mental recovery. Everyone was hungover and irritable, says Honeycutt. Elinor Gibbs was very pregnant with her first child, and was passing the hors d'oeuvres when Thurber looked at her bulging figure and said, "You ungainly creature, you." It could have been meant lightheartedly, but Thurber was known to attack his friends' wives, and McKelway thinks it was said hatefully. This time it was Gibbs's turn to explode. Gibbs hated scenes as much as Ross, and, although he had taken boxing lessons in school, he had never swung a fist in anger. A short man, he danced about the tall startled Thurber, rotating his fists like tricycle pedals, and let fly with a one-two punch. He managed to reach Thurber's face and draw blood at nose and mouth.

McKelway took Thurber back to the Algonquin. Typically, Thurber called everyone the next day and delivered so hilarious a description of what he was apologizing for that everybody forgave him. "Jim's real trouble at the time," says Honeycutt, "was that Mac and I were seeing quite a bit of one another by then, which Gibbs and his wife were all for. Gibbs had become McKelway's number-one admirer, which further annoyed Jim. I think he was trying to hurt Elinor to get at Gibbs."

Gibbs remembers that whole period as one of chronic discordance on the staff. Raymond Holden, the Ross "genius" who, according to Katharine White, had brought down the color-coded filing system with his color-blindness, was married to the poet Louise Bogan, who reviewed books of poetry for the *New Yorker*. She one day announced to friends that Holden was "a New England robot" and cut his dressing gown into tiny pieces with her manicure scissors. They were divorced shortly after that.

And there was Russell Maloney, a Bostonian and Harvard graduate, who joined the staff as a reporter, became a contributing writer, and caught on so quickly that he replaced Thurber as principal Talk of the Town writer and editor after Thurber left. For some reason, Maloney antagonized such stalwarts as Whitaker and John O'Hara. When Whitaker wasn't bullying Freddie Packard, he was cruelly out-dueling Maloney in daily corridor repartee. John O'Hara "drove Maloney crazy by requesting him to call him 'Mr. O'Hara,'" Gibbs told Thurber. "I drove him even crazier through mistaken kindness. One night, when he first came to town, he told me he didn't know any girls, so I said 'There is nothing easier,' and called up [a girl] who was

570 • JAMES THURBER

working then in a show called *Mulatto*. I'm afraid I told him in effect that she was a sure lay, which was a persistent rumor at the time, and she came running right over to '21' [when Maloney called her]. A month or so later, I remembered to ask him how he made out and, of course, he never spoke to me again because they were married."

Those who staffed the magazine during its first dozen years contributed more to its anecdotal history than did the total of all those who followed. When a "genius" named Scudder Middleton stopped coming to the office after lunch—he was said to have wooed women into bed in the afternoon by quoting Browning—Gibbs had to learn to forge "SM" on the payment slips so accurately that Ralph Paladino, who handled financial matters for editorial, couldn't tell the difference. There was Harold Winney, the secretary who handled Ross's finances and bilked him out of more than seventy thousand dollars and, when it was discovered, committed suicide. When Maxwell Bodenheim, the Village Bohemian poet, and novelist, down on his luck, stopped by the *New Yorker* offices with a clutch of inferior poems for sale, he settled for a loan of fifty cents. Baird Leonard, who did book reviews for Ross for a time, sent in her copy via her husband, the copy usually scrawled drunkenly on the backs of bills and envelopes, says Gibbs. To cover for her, Gibbs was obliged to do the actual reviews and sign her name to them, augmenting both his store of self-pity and his contempt for Leonard.

Dorothy Parker would insist, on a Friday, that her book review was finished except for the last paragraph, and then call on Sunday to say that it was so terrible she had torn it up. Gibbs would stay up all night to fill the space, usually resorting to Leonard's scrawls. ("In many ways," Gibbs told Thurber, "the *New Yorker*'s debt to me is enormous.")

Benchley was consistently guilty of missing deadlines as drama critic. He often called Ross to explain that he was in Worcester tending his sick mother —who hadn't seen him in months, Ross would later discover. On one occasion, Benchley phoned the office to say that he wouldn't have that week's theater review in on time because he was in Philadelphia, where there were no typewriters. He was, of course, next door at the Royalton.

When Katharine White finally invited St. Clair McKelway to call her "Katharine," a worried McKelway consulted with Gibbs, who had worked with her for more than six years. "You ever able to call her 'Katharine'?" McKelway asked him. "I never could."

"No," Gibbs replied, "I always had a feeling it would [be] like taking your finger out of the dike."

Philip Wrenn, a sports columnist for the magazine, and Elinor Gibbs cohosted a party at Wrenn's luxurious place overlooking the East River.

Among the guests were the ideological leftists Dorothy Parker and Lillian Hellman, and Sanderson Vanderbilt, of no known relation to the rich branch of the family. "Sandy" had left the *Herald Tribune* for the *New Yorker* after Katharine White drew Ross's attention to his fine newspaper writing. Vanderbilt wrote one memorable piece for the magazine, then took up editing, became Shawn's assistant, and gave up writing. At Wrenn's party, Vanderbilt passed out in the shrubbery, "giving enormous pleasure to Dotty Parker and Lillian Hellman," says Gibbs, "who thought he was a real Vanderbilt and consequently a fine example of upper-class depravity." It was at that party that Raoul Fleischmann got off his chest a resentment that had been building for years. Referring to Ross, Thurber, White, and Gibbs, he exploded to Gibbs: "I never understood why I have to treat all you sons of bitches as if you were Shakespeare!"

At a Christmas-season party given at a restaurant by playwright Philip Barry (author of *The Philadelphia Story*), Ross, who was inexplicably carrying a Christmas tree, got stuck in the building's revolving doors with it and had to be rescued. It was at that party that McKelway accidentally set fire to Joel Sayre's wife, Gertrude, with his cigarette; the fire was extinguished by Burgess Meredith with a brandy and soda. It was at a similar party that Ross, in a devilish mood, flicked a lighted cigarette at a group of women, and set the dress of one of them on fire, an incident that helped turn Brendan Gill against him.

The mad drunken whirl, his Talk responsibilities, Honey's interest in a half-dozen men, and Althea's threatened divorce were too much for Thurber.

He was, at the same time, writing "One Is a Wanderer," that rare and lasting public exposure of his anguished soul. It appeared in the magazine of March 2, 1935, and seems meant as a personal and final plea for Honeycutt's attention and sympathy. He is at the office:

> The dark was coming quickly down, the dark of a February Sunday evening. . . . He didn't want to go "home," . . . It would be gloomy and close in his hotel room. . . . He couldn't read any more, or write, at night. Books he tossed aside after nervously flipping through them; the writing he tried to do turned into spirals and circles and squares and empty faces.
>
> I'll just stop in, he thought, and see if there are any messages; I'll see if there have been any phone calls. . . . I don't want to sit there in the lobby again and drink brandy. . . .
>
> He . . . walked . . . to the elevator, and . . . began to sing . . . "Make my bed and light the light, for I'll be home late tonight,

blackbird, bye bye." He walked over to his hotel . . . and sat . . . in the lobby, without taking off his overcoat. . . .

He . . . began to think about calling up people. He thought of the Graysons. He saw the Graysons, not as they would be, sitting in their apartment, close together and warmly, but as he and Lydia [Althea] had seen them in another place and another year. The four had shared a bright vacation once. . . .

Marriage does not make two people one, it makes two people two. . . .

He said to himself . . . don't tell me you're not cockeyed now, because you are cockeyed now, just as you said you wouldn't be when you got up this morning and had orange juice and coffee and determined to get some work done. . . .

Look here now, he told himself . . . you're getting into one of those states that Marianne [Ann Honeycutt] keeps telling you about . . . when people don't like to have you around. . . . He . . . thought about Marianne.

She doesn't know how I start my days, he thought, she only knows how I end them. She doesn't even know how I started my life. She only knows me when night gets me. . . .

Now look, the Mortons had said to him, if you and Marianne would only stop fighting and arguing and forever analyzing yourselves and forever analyzing everything, you'd be fine. You'd be fine if you got married and just shut up, just shut up and got married. . . . Well, it would be, too, if you were twenty-five maybe . . . and not forty.

He remembers the Browning line he had written in a book for Lydia. He has another drink, lies in his room until after midnight, changes his clothes, and goes to drink in a bar until 3:00 A.M. His usual cabdriver is waiting for him, and he goes back to the hotel and to bed, singing "Bye, Bye, Blackbird."

A few days after "One Is a Wanderer" appeared in the magazine, Thurber commented on it to Honeycutt: "What a symptomatic, tight, egocentric, constipated piece *that* was! (but good technically). I wonder at it and at its acceptance by editors instead of its rejection by doctors."

That March of 1935, Thurber finally caved in to depression, nervous anxiety, and the consequences of a lifestyle of unrelieved self-administered abuse. At Honey's insistence, he admitted himself to Dr. Fritz Foord's sanitarium at Kerhonkson, in the Catskill Mountains. Thurber had "discovered" it, after hearing that O. Henry had used it as a drying-out place, and later Thurber's psychically exhausted colleagues would periodically turn themselves in there, too.

Thurber's reflections on what the previous months had put him through, expressed in letters to Honeycutt, seem similar at times to those of F. Scott Fitzgerald, whose confessions of emotional depletion and mental anguish in "The Crack-Up" were soon to be published in *Esquire* for the world to see— as Thurber's were not. At Foord's, he writes Honey, wallowing:

> Life alone to me is a barren and selfish and pointless thing. . . . But that's me, not you. You are, in some ways . . . the best aloner the world has ever known. . . . In eight months you will be married. I don't know who to. The situation has nearly wrecked us, maybe it has.

In a less morbid letter, he thanks her for her help:

> Now that I'm on my feet again, instead of yours, I'm ashamed to have depended so on you to get me here. . . . After this you will observe with awe my self-reliance. I need hold on to no woman's brassiere.

He proclaims to Honey that he is not only well on the road to recovery but to becoming a changed man she would find worthy of her continued interest:

> I have not only got away from New York but from writing, and it's bad to think I'll always have to get back to *that*, anyway. But I'll want to, finally; and I *always* seem to want to write you. . . . It's nice here, the place, the people, the country. I have gained 2 pounds and feel better than I have since June-November, 1918. Already, I do not accept that lank, sick, nervous man who for years wandered from the N. Yorker to the Algonquin to Tony's. I don't accept the things he said or did. I never want to see him again. I don't marvel that you and everybody else avoided him.
>
> I get to sleep at 10:30 & up at 7:45. Long walks, lots to eat; and my mind is slowly getting back to where it belongs. I don't miss drinking at all—as if there had never been any such thing as drinking. My nervousness is wearing away, with slight reactions such as now when I try to make sense in writing. . . . The state I was in, I can see, was not only awful but perilous. I'll be saved in

the nick of time. I was writing & drawing on sheer nerve force or something. The humor was purely mechanical like a six-day rider sleeping as he rode. I'll never get back to that state. I'll never stay so long in NY again. I dread coming back to the income tax, the [divorce] court judgments, the grind for money, but I'll be able to do it when I do. . . .

I'm a little drugged by the peace & quiet, the release from that hell down there where no one can, or has, lived a decent, motivated life of which he can be proud. Your "living from day to day" is not so good as I thot it was when you said it. It's another escape mechanism, another justification for a life without beauty, purpose, or meaning & I want you out of it, too. . . .

Don't tell me about any people except yourself. Keep well & sober. There's nothing in drinking & carrying on. There's a purpose in life.

Have faith in Ohio.

As always (only better)
Jim

And later:

. . . I'm not completely whole yet—but it takes time. I'll always have to fight to hold what I get up here, but I believe I will, even in the welter of obligations (which first cracked me up). . . . I'm still thinking about myself a lot but that will wear away, too. . . . I can't ever be a strong, silent type. . . .

You have never really had the Jims. And I don't blame you for guarding against them.

Honey promises to visit him.

You'll love it (ah, but for a day!) up here. It's like a Longfellow inn . . . with the kittyskills in the distance. (If the mountains of Nebraska look like a woman's breasts, it is unfortunately true that under certain lights the far Catskills look like montes venris [sic] shaved for an operation. (I am terribly sorry). . . . There is no vista in tony's and where there is no vista the people perish.

She writes a faintly sarcastic letter, telling him that since he has been out of circulation, his friends in New York were now "finding freedom of expression." He protests:

I am no longer like that. You refer to a period which is past and gone.
. . . All I can do is accept, and try to be a good, fine Christian boy,
hoping that the animus of people will fall off my back like a duck's
water. . . . I seem to have managed it all very badly, as you know. I
dont know anybody who has managed so badly.

Thurber's difficulties with Honeycutt were far from being all of his own
making; they were exacerbated by her confused and guarded defenses against
involvement. "I always preferred the company of men to women," she says. "I
enjoyed being one of the boys. For eighteen years, John Lardner and I took
turns having Saturday poker games at our homes. . . . I knew I could never
survive on the company of just one man."

At one time or another, Honey, in her eagerness not to disappoint, or be
ignored, had led Gibbs, Willie Coleman—a journalist on the *Trib*—and
Thurber all to believe that she was willing to marry them. Thurber kept
reminding her of it:

Perhaps no one ever gave a clearer insight into her strange and misty
intentions than you did in the failing days of the old year when you told
Ed [Angly] you were going to marry me, but discussed a trip to Europe
with Willie. . . . And yet you could "break with" Willie easier than
Ed, and make up faster. . . . A person has to pick up clues about you.
. . . I'd never believe[d] you were going to marry me (if you were) until
I heard you tell Willie.

Honey told Thurber she was content "to be the last of the mad
Honeycutts," to which Thurber replied: "Real egoists want to live alone, and
die alone." He refers to "statistics" that show unmarried women worse off
than married ones, mentally and physically. "What you have," he writes her,
"is a general basis for maladies growing solely out of your unique and unrealistic personal life at 33."

Notes [on the subject] I have been making for years to be enlarged some
day for my book whose working title is "The American Woman." They
are my own interpretations and indubitable facts. I expect the volume to
be a monument to me and a boon to womankind. I will make it as
simple and truthful and well-written as Emerson's essays on Nature and
the Spirit. . . . Perhaps I shall go in for the practise of my own theories
and set up an office. I would take only the cases of sensitive intelligent
people with humor and imagination. They get into worse spots than

most, but the way out, although difficult, is surer—under my care. I'll charge $3,000 a patient. At 50, with gray hair, I'd be a prepossessing consultant, radiating confidence. I know at least six people I'd like to work out on now. Eminently you.

Thurber was counting on his restoration and redemption at Foord's to win Honeycutt after all. She visited him there one weekend and agreed to accompany him back to New York, upon his discharge. His excitement at the prospect of seeing her is boundless:

Now don't you fall down on me about coming here Saturday. . . . my heart leaps up at the thought of seeing your wide blue eyes and golden hair again. I think of you as my "Blue and gold girl." You will find me calm and poised and altogether a charming, if slightly aloof and reserved, companion. The leaping jitters have left me. . . . I am almost ready for the world again. . . . Ideas, plots, plans, phrases, thoughts set [my mind] to bounding out of bed in a fever of creative fancy. . . . The sheer intensity of my interest in life and in writing acts on me a little like liquor. The hand shakes, the eye gleams, and I twitch. . . . Please do not confuse these things with the old, dead twitches. . . .

I am first of all an artist. . . . Secondly to ink and paper I am your devoted admirer.

They have run my ass off up here but the discipline has been fine. . . . I expect my Forties to be fine. What a name I shall leave behind for future ages to search for in vain. Fox tracks in the snow, but boldly made.

She had replied by phone to his arguments as to why she should marry, refuting most of them, and asked him to consider if he could even afford a wife, given his financial commitments to Althea. He replies:

I anticipate with some misgivings the letter you said you were writing, for I supposed you will deny everything. . . . *Live* alone, then, goddam it, and see if I cease to care! . . .

Who said I had no money. I make enough for you to bathe in, you and ed and willie. . . .

P.S. I have just been hosed and pummelled . . . Not a word have I wanted to write for the N Yer. Each of these is worth 17 and $1/2$c, so be proud and hold your head high . . .

It's like this, being hosed. First warm then cold as a son of a
bitch, as my aunt Caroline used to say. . . .
Jamie.

He sensed, but chose to ignore, that the time and trouble she took to
telephone, write, and visit him were only symptoms of her chronic inability
to cut off their relationship—of her helpless tendency to leave men believing
they had the inside track, with reason to continue to hope. He knew better,
but continued to build his house on sand:

The thing is to quit talking and do something. Live and have a
lot of laughs. I've gone back to the theory of laughs: that's the
thing. I have taken things too heavily. I'm going to be quieter and
funnier. After I marry you, which I am pretty sure I will. . . .
I'm never again going to let lawyers and taxes & McNulty and
my family & Tony's & the Algonquin get me down. Even when
they did I wrote & drew more stuff for the N Yer than anyone
else. . . .
With love and assurance.
Jim.

Did Honeycutt, in retrospect, feel that she ever misrepresented her situation to Thurber—that she had led him on?
"Thurber always accused me of that," she replies, "but you can't lead
anyone on unless he's leadable and wants to be led. He was, and did, but
blamed me. We were mutually convenient."
Upon his return to New York, though filled with resolve, Thurber was
again consumed by the Honeycutt dilemma, and in battling it he returned to
the old pub-crawling ways he had forsworn. One of the many miracles of the
Thurber story is how he could wall off the storms raging within him, set off by
rejection, disappointment, and other emotional trials, long enough to turn
out work of notable quality. In that awful period of angst, only "One Is a
Wanderer" was woven directly from the threads of his misery. He turned out
ninety-one pieces of text and drawings in his tormented year of 1935, eleven
more than in 1934, with thirty-two cartoons and twenty-one uncaptioned
drawings appearing in the *New Yorker*, an average of better than one drawing
per week. They included one of his classics—the lady crouched on the bookcase, with the Thurber Man benignly saying to a guest: "That's my first wife

"That's my first wife up there, and this is the present Mrs. Harris."

up there, and this is the *present* Mrs. Harris." Thurber had planned the crouching lady to be at the top of a flight of stairs waiting for her husband, but the stairs collapsed through an unexpected switch of perspective, becoming the shelves of a bookcase and leaving the woman stranded on top. ("It was a great deal of fun," Thurber told British reporter, Henry Brandon in 1958, "not to know what you were going to end up with.")

Besides Talk rewrite, he produced two original Talk pieces and a Comment, and thought up the caption for another artist's cartoon showing a barroom filled with women drinkers, the bartender yelling at the one male customer: "Take your hat off! Try and remember where you are, will you?" The cartoon was drawn in the mood of resentment felt by Bleeck patrons at the admittance of women to the former all-male speakeasy.

Ever since *My Life and Hard Times*, Ross and others, including many readers, had pressured Thurber to write more about Columbus, and, in the mood of nostalgia his marriage breakup may have provided, Thurber obliged. In "Snapshot of a Dog," he again honored the memory of Rex, the bull terrier, and produced the immortal "I Went to Sullivant." He presented to his reading public Doc Marlowe, the charlatan medicine man who had boarded with Aunt Margery Albright, and closed out the literary record of his marriage with "Smashup."

The national and international events of the 1930s provoked Thurber into casuals too dated for current interest, but which contain flashes of his best humorous writing: A Japanese man had been caught during the Christmas season of 1934 photographing American Naval property at St. Petersburg,

Florida. Thurber, in "The International Spy Situation," wonders why the Japanese would go to the bother, when photographs and statistics of all military vessels of all nations were available in *Jane's Fighting Ships*, in newsreels, and in movies like *The Fleet's In*, with Fred Astaire and Ginger Rogers. He answers his own question: Japan wanted the U.S. to think it didn't have pictures of our ships, or else wanted to scare the country into fortifying St. Petersburg while the Japanese planned to attack Perth Amboy. On the other hand, he ventures, it could have been merely a tourist taking pictures for reasons any tourist takes pictures. (In those pre-Pearl Harbor days, the joke was an innocent one.)

Broadway gossip columns reported that Joan Crawford and Franchot Tone would like to act the leading roles in a dramatization of James M. Cain's *The Postman Always Rings Twice*. Partly to kid Tone, one of Thurber's drinking buddies at Tony's, Thurber, in "Producers Never Think Twice," writes that Tone and Crawford are simply too sophisticated to play the story's hard-boiled characters. Thurber offers his services as scenario writer to provide words appropriate to the level of gentility he felt Crawford and Tone occupied. For Crawford he would write: "I love you as a child loves its first snowfall, a soft white dreamy love that will never vanish." Tone, Thurber felt, would find it hard to belt a lady talking like that, regardless of what the script called for. [The movie version of Cain's book didn't appear until 1946; neither Crawford nor Tone were in it.]

Thurber's final six letters to Honey in early 1935 track his mood from one of optimism regarding their future together to the sad realization that he has lost her. Following his return from Kerhonkson, he took Coates to a party at Honey's along with a gift of chocolates. There he went berserk again at her seeming contradiction in feelings toward him. In his frenzy, he denounced his friends and Althea—the divorce terms she was demanding had been made known to him—and began to throw nearly every loose object about Honeycutt's apartment except the candy. He wrote her an apology that she later decided was one of his funniest:

> Out of the shambles one bright consolation looms up: I did not throw the three pound box of assorted chocolates. I remember having the tendency to throw it—it attracted me more than anything else in the room, including the wooden Russian people, the dog, the tumblers, and Coates. But, crazy as I was, I knew that

if I threw that candy, the last spark of manhood in me would be gone. It was bad enough to revile my friends, traduce my wife, and compromise the neighborhood, but it would have been unsupportable to have thrown the candy. Picture to yourself, a gallant arriving at 8 p.m. with a ribboned box of sweets, bending over the charming girl. Picture, then, this same [swain] several hours later, she slapped down on a couch, he going around like a mad plumber, wrenching off fixtures, plucking out pipes, screaming. . . . It was impossible, in the old days, to produce so great a change of pace—to step from a sweet little picture, innocent enough to serve as [an ad] in the Atlantic Monthly, to a scene comparable to a gang shooting in Brooklyn—and done by the same cast!

> We will now sing, She Broke My Heart so I Broke Her Jaw.
> With love and curses,
> Jamie

Mame, who had met Honey two years before, and had long been aware of her son's infatuation, wrote to him asking where the relationship stood. Thurber pretended to summarize his answer to Mame in another letter to Honey, charting their ups and downs and concluding with: "[My mother] has always wondered why I would rather be unhappy with you than happy with somebody else. So have I."

He chose writing to her, late at night, to telephoning, and often liquor contributed bile to what he wrote. He upbraids her for being "so righteous," and for not having "the guts to take a chance." He mimics her accent: "Ah wouldn't, though, says you. Ah let people down at the first thing they do that ah, for one reason or another, cant or wont or wouldn't do."

Fiercely bitter at her refusal to give up other men in favor of him, he resorts to what, in his 1937–38 cartoon series "The Masculine Approach," he would call "The I-May-Go-Away-for-a-Year-or-Two Move"—a tactic he himself had once employed with Eva Prout. Writing late at the office ("The Letter-Writing Method"), he sets down his version of the maddening Honeycutt situation for her benefit, pretending to address the letter to Wolcott Gibbs. His indictment of her builds to what would seem intended as a bridge-burning denouncement. There remain only two persons in the world "to whom I give everything"—his mother and daughter. "As recently as when I went to Kerhonkson," he goes on, "I had some hope of saving something else, too. On coming back, I found I couldn't." He proceeds to reach beyond what he knows to be the facts, in the interests of what he believes to be a greater truth:

> When I was in Kerhonkson, I wrote only to Honey, I talked on the phone only to her, I thought only of her, as I have for some seven years. . . . She is the only woman, since I was first married, I ever asked to marry me. She has said she loved me and that she would marry me. This as long ago as seven years. In those seven years, the person I was, the person I could be, has been slowly and deliberately destroyed by her. . . . I offered her all that a man can offer a woman. . . . It was to her the same as a letter from Will Cuppy or a dinner date with McKelway. . . . It began to get me: it curdled my humor, it stopped my imagination, it drove me crazy. . . .
>
> She made it impossible for me to go on with my wife and child and farm and dogs. She made it impossible for me to go on with any other woman. . . .
>
> McKelway is her new triumph—since I think I drove [Stanley] Walker off. One night when I asked her out she said "I havent stayed home alone in months and I am going to stay home alone tonight." She went out with McKelway.
>
> She loved humiliating me at your house that day. I should have left immediately. I should never have come, but I felt low, too, and I wanted to see people. I saw her and McKelway, I heard her witty little flirtation on the phone with Walker, and her announcement to the whole room that he had asked her out that night and Sunday and Monday night. All the [encouraging] things she had said to me in between time, nobody knew but her and me. . . .
>
> I wish, naturally, I had never seen her.

He turns from addressing Gibbs in the letter to confronting Honey: "I wrote this to Wolcott but didn't send it to him. . . . I wrote it here in the office two hours before going to 21. . . . My feeling for you has turned into a desperate and implacable hate."

He knew he had gone too far and soon, in another letter, expressed his regrets to her: "I know how unutterably bad I have been, but that was not really me. Love makes even men of humor and imagination . . . crazy, at the worst times." He planned to join Elliott Nugent on the West Coast, where "I know I will get myself back." He suggests that they not see one another for several months, in which time he would "make myself the man you were once proud of."

As to those bad scenes I ask you to remember only this one thing. Before I was married to Althea, a woman I did not really love, because I have only loved you . . . , I was as bad and as bitter and as awful as I have been with you recently. But after we were married she was able to say, at the end of *five years* . . . when somebody asked her what kind of a husband I was, "He is an angel."

Just weeks before marrying Helen Wismer, he is writing Honey:

If, in Paula Trueman, Ann Fordyce, and Helen Wismer I have not found the girl, then in no girl besides you will I ever find it. . . . They are three of the most marvelous persons, men or women, I, or anyone else, has ever known. They all three know, to their dismay, that I cannot, as hard as I have tried, for your sake and mine, give you up for them —even if they were all three rolled into one woman. . . .

I am being divorced next week, or the week after, Morris [Ernst] tells me.

But McKelway was in the picture, and she told Thurber that something McKelway had said to her the night before—she didn't specify it—prevented her from giving Thurber the answer he craved. In a postscript, Thurber writes, "I still would like to know what Mac said to you last night. Apparently, I have underrated the young man's skill and ability."

He had, and when he realized it, it led to a bridge-burning letter to Honey, in late April of 1935. It was of the stiff-upper-lip kind, parts of which anyone suffering along with Thurber is relieved, and even proud on his behalf, to read:

I have come to the conclusion that any luncheon date for us would not be much fun for either one of us. . . . You have already been told all my latest jokes etc. by those colleagues of mine whom you see (I hope they give me credit for the gags that are mine—there's been a lot of stealing of gags in this city), and neither one of us wants to talk about *us* again as the sweet child Jesus—as McNulty calls Him—well knows. . . . You get as much satisfaction reasoning with me as you would with an eighteen-year-old suitor, and I get as much reasoning with you as I would with my four-year-old daughter. All we had together was our rather cultivated sense of the better wisecracks. . . .

I have ranted and raved and had middle-aged man's rye hysterics when I was with you, and you have had spinster's booze-gloom and would tell me how you had the window up and almost jumped, how you have no feeling, and simply live from day to day, how you are incapable of happiness. . . . As Markey would say, there aint any sense in us being together. . . .

I need not hide the fact that the last three weeks have been frightful; filled with anguish and real deep suffering. I wouldn't try to conceal from you the fact that the final realization that you didn't want me was the hardest thing I have ever had to bear. There were moments when I actually thought I could not go through with it. . . .

I feel mostly hurt because of the pitying attitude that I thought I discerned in some people who know us . . . that they thought that I had never actually, in these years, been in your heart to the extent that you ever considered marrying me. . . . I believed they were convinced that I kept trotting after someone who had always wanted to get rid of me. . . .

I expect to be married, in due time. I'm not in any hurry. . . .

I would rather you didn't let people imagine you "threw me out," but that we mutually agreed, in all good humor and with the best of feeling for each other, not to go ahead with something which was not right for either of us. . . . You need never fear that I will put on any scenes again. That's as gone as my marriage. . . .

One other thing. . . . There is only one thing I have ever given you that I would like to have back and that's the decanter which I gave you last Christmas time. Everything else I would appreciate your always keeping but somehow, when I bought that, it was with the feeling that someday it would be both yours and mine and that in our house we would pour drinks for our friends out of it, including McKelway (who can always have a drink in my home, regardless of my persistent feelings about certain things). I have visions of people picking that up and saying "This is very nice, where'd you get it?" and I dont want my name and the intimate associations of six [sic] years to fall into the pause that follows. . . . It is only that one thing. If you will let me know where to get it—I could call for it some afternoon if you left it at the hotel desk. I want to keep it, not destroy it, as the solidest memento I have of the deepest feeling I have ever had for any woman in my life, and the highest hopes, and now the very best wishes.

Honey and Thurber chose never to get completely out of one another's life, but after they married others, she faded into a wistful reminiscence he could live with comfortably as the years passed. Seventeen years later, Thurber wrote Andy White: "When I married Helen I had three pints of rye and no money and owed $2,500. But I had proved I could make money if I put my mind to it and quit sitting around thinking up new ways to kill Ann Honeycutt. She told Helen the other day that she had finally decided I didn't like her. She is right and I have figured out why. Our love never ripened into friendship."

44

That Mental Cruelty

I should like to ask you not to go into the details of the divorce, since there is nothing in them except grounds developed, at the suggestion of lawyers, in order to prove mental cruelty in Connecticut, which is a tough state and demands a lot. All the newspapers in New York City were friendly to us, knowing the situation, and in deference to another newspaperman. The Mirror, under Stanley Walker in one of his son-of-a-bitch moods, made a pretty terrible thing out of it.

—*Thurber, in a memo to* Time, *1950*

The public divorce proceedings—the hearing took place May 24, 1935—were hard enough for Althea to get through, but their reports in the media resulted in trauma for Thurber, who was not present at the event. A thirteen-year, stop-and-start marriage had to be summed up in a collection of its worst moments to persuade the judge that it was intolerable, unsalvageable, and deserving of a merciful end. The proceeding was covered by the wire services and given brief notices in the *Herald Tribune*, the *Times*, and *Time* magazine. But the tabloid *Daily Mirror* turned loose on it a feature writer, Ruth Phillips, who apparently had encountered Thurber on her own nightclub rounds. Her story employs the schoolgirl touch Thurber would have abhorred even had it dealt with matters of no interest to him:

> The upper classes wept into their demi-tasses [sic] yesterday when the stark truth about James Thurber, the *New Yorker*, owlish humorist, artist, night-blooming monologist and amateur boxer, came out.
>
> Mr. Thurber, whose drawings, "The War Between the Sexes [sic]," raised mayhem to high whimsy, was divorced in Bridgeport, Connecticut, yesterday by Mrs. Althea A. Thurber who said she had had all that she could stand.
>
> "I was simply amazed," Mrs. Thurber explained to Judge Ernest Inglis, "at the number of affairs he was carrying on with different women at the same time."
>
> Her testimony caused strong men to blanch at the "21 Club" and "Tony's" a few hours later, and women to scurry for cover. In a nut shell, Thurber was faithless, habitually drunken, extremely cruel, and was rumored to have breakfasted more than once in his evening clothes. . . .
>
> "I married him . . . in 1922," said his wife, "but we separated three years later. In 1930, however, he persuaded me to return to him." [There was no mention of the 1929 separation.]

Phillips quotes Althea as saying that Thurber often got into fights that he invariably lost; that "after a long spree, he would return home to have a damaged jaw or eye nursed. Once, up in Sandy Hook, he got licked by a farm hand." Althea tells the judge:

> When I realized that he had become involved with a number of women in New York I took him to Miami. . . . But it was useless. He wrote and telephoned them. Finally I induced him to buy a farm at Sandy Hook. Even there he kept in touch with them. On the night of October 7, 1931, when my . . . daughter . . . was born, my husband got drunk. He came to see me the next day with his clothes torn and his face black and blue.

Althea stated that Thurber lived beyond his means, which was true, but so did she; no wonder her "life was harassed by bill collectors." In the summer of 1934, she testified, Thurber told her that she was "a millstone around his neck" and suggested that she "get out." Phillips goes on:

Mrs. Thurber asked no alimony, but was awarded the Sandy Hook farm. She was also given custody of Rosemary, now four. Thurber did not contest the action.

Althea was required to produce corroborating witnesses. Several friends of theirs refused, but Louise Connell agreed to help out. She told the court that Thurber liked to show off how much he could drink, and often got out of hand, though he was not an alcoholic. "I was convinced they both wanted the divorce," says Louise. "Both had their faults; Althea was hard-boiled, but not abnormally so under the circumstances, and Jim was temperamental and needed someone special. Divorce is never pleasant, but I felt I was doing them both a favor, and Jim stayed friends with my husband and me afterwards."

The day the *Mirror* story came out, Geoffrey Hellman, at work in his *New Yorker* office, heard a tremendous crash of glass in the corridor and the sound of slopping water. He walked to the door and saw Thurber, who had apparently just thrown and smashed a large jug from one of the watercoolers, angrily pacing the corridor, hair in his eyes. Thurber then seized another water jug and threw it against the opposite end of the hall. "The bottle didn't break," says Hellman, "but the water was gurgling out of it. Thurber was howling, 'All hell's broken loose!' Andy White was walking along with him, hanging onto Thurber's arm, saying, 'I wouldn't do this if I were you, Jim.' And Thurber yelled, 'I didn't do it. Stanley Walker did it, and I'm just trying to cover up for him. These things are important, Andy.' "

Walker had just left the *Herald Tribune* to become managing editor of the *Mirror*, and Thurber would always hold him personally accountable for the gossipy article. Though he had recently been competing with Thurber for Honeycutt's attention, and had reason to disparage Thurber, Walker insisted that he had known nothing about the story until it was too late to edit it or stop it.

Thurber was usually able to laugh off adverse comments about himself, but these haunted him ever after. They failed in every way to reflect the person he knew himself to be. He probably still nurtured lingering hopes that Honeycutt would, after all, see him as a reliable marriage partner. And here was the *Mirror* "libel," which she was bound to read. Even more upsetting was the prospect of a maturing daughter who one day might read as gospel this lopsided characterization of her father.

Althea regretted the nature of the hearing—in which the wife had to make accusations that the husband, if he was not contesting the action, could not refute in a comparable forum. For example, though both had committed their share of infidelities, it wouldn't have served the legal case for hers to be mentioned.

The reference to Thurber's fiscal carelessness has a ring of authenticity, but it was his impatience with bookkeeping that kept him overdrawn at the bank —a situation that plagued him until his marriage to Helen, who immediately became the money manager. Althea had never shown interest in a similar role.

Perhaps for Rosemary's sake, Althea and Thurber both did their best to stay friendly after the divorce. Thurber still valued Althea as a symbol of an earlier, romantic stand—a memorial to a younger judgment he was determined to defend. Nor did he get over his sense of guilt; he continued to harbor a protective feeling toward his first wife. "Years later, he'd be annoyed to learn his friends had visited Amherst [where Althea's third husband taught college] and hadn't looked her up," Ted Gardiner says. Robert Thurber recalls that even during the hostile last days of the marriage, "anything I said negatively about Althea, when I was visiting Jim, he'd give a short little laugh, which meant he wasn't going to forget that. When we heard about what she'd said at the divorce hearing, I got off my chest a pretty stiff letter to her that the family in Columbus didn't think was strong enough. Jim said nothing about it for fifteen years, but once when he was mad at us over something about *The Thurber Album*, he brought up that I'd written that bad letter to Althea."

When Thurber was in the hospital for eye surgery, Ross stopped by to see him. It was 1940 and the Battle of Britain was raging. Ross paced the floor beside Thurber's bed and said, "Goddam it, Thurber, I worry about you and England." Thurber never forgot the characteristic way Ross covered his embarrassment by lumping worries over his star contributor with his fear for the fate of Europe, and later emulated him: After Althea's third divorce, Thurber often wondered how she was doing, with her child by Allen Gilmore to raise alone. Once, when Egypt's president Gamal Abdel Nasser, was causing turmoil by nationalizing the Suez Canal, Thurber was visiting the Gardiners. Ted Gardiner remembers Thurber remarking, "I worry about Althea and Nasser." Nobody doubted it.

In 1951, fifteen years after the divorce, Thurber went over galley proofs of Dale Kramer's *Ross and The New Yorker* (he had volunteered considerable information), and wrote to Kramer that only one line distressed him: a reference to Althea as being "large, amiable and firm-minded." When he married her, Thurber told Kramer with typical factual looseness, "she was rated as one of the most beautiful girls in the country," and their nineteen-year-old daughter would now appreciate at least another adjective "for the old girl." Kramer obliged.

Thurber threw a party celebrating the divorce, to which all his current women friends were invited. Althea turned up uninvited—to make the point, it was felt, that there were no hard feelings on her part. But she fell out of touch with Thurber's friends after the divorce, and nearly everyone in his inner circle lost track of her. Thurber did not, of course; Althea from time to time asked him for money, and in a few years Rosemary was on a visiting schedule with him.

Althea would occasionally come to town and drop in on Thurber and Helen after their marriage. "Jamie would often go to bed and I'd sit up over a drink with Althea, talking," says Helen. "They had both remarried by then, they wanted to forget the past, and there were no bad feelings between them. She and I got along fine." The Thurbers also entertained Althea during the war, when hotel rooms were expensive and hard to get, and Althea needed to visit Dr. Duke Damon, her obstetrician.

Sacha Guitry once wrote that "a man must marry only a very pretty woman in case he should ever want some other man to take her off his hands." Althea qualified. Francis Comstock, the archaeologist, returned from the Middle East after Althea's divorce, and they were married late that summer. "Soon after that, we set off for Syria during the next academic year, on another archaeological expedition, taking Rosie with us," Althea says. "We stayed until the latter part of May, 1936, when it became too hot to work, and came home." ("As I understand it," Thurber told Ted Gardiner when he asked what Althea was doing, "her husband digs up the bones and Althea scrubs them.")

Rosemary didn't see much of her father for several years. She went by Comstock, her stepfather's name. "I thought Franny Comstock was my father," she says. "I was somewhere around eight when my mother, who was about to divorce him, told me he wasn't."

Comstock moved Althea and Rosemary to Cambridge, where he studied for an advanced degree in history at Harvard. For several years, says Althea, "that was our life: Cambridge during the school year, Sandy Hook in the summer." She sold the Sandy Hook property in 1938. In Cambridge, Althea met another Harvard graduate student, Allen Gilmore, who was majoring in medieval history. In 1939, she divorced Comstock, and the next year married Gilmore. Whatever else she may have been, Althea was not material-minded, having married three men when they were unrealized professionally.

"I remember stories from my mother's and father's early years together, of their standing in front of a bakery window and wishing they could afford one of the pastries," Rosemary says—

> And her ironing on the bed because they had no ironing board. I don't think she ever felt nurtured so how could she do that for others? But, like most of us, she needed to be needed. I think she also had a terrible need to be in control. She became in later years claustrophobic and then agoraphobic. Her greatest fear was that she'd lose control, and/or 'go crazy.' Of course she never did, but I don't think she had any joy in her last decades either. (Personally I vote for a little madness!)
>
> I appreciate her intelligence, taste, humor and love of animals, flowers and natural beauty. She always hated her first name. Her father died when she was eight years old. I think this was the basis for her problems over the years. As an 'abandoned' child she toughened herself.
>
> Neither of my families (Althea [and Gilmore] or James and Helen) was a touching family and we rarely expressed any deep person to person feelings that I remember. I was in my forties before I told my mother I loved her. Then she told me she loved me. That's the first time I remember hearing that. My father was dead by then so I never got to tell him I loved him. I guess we all just *assumed* that we loved one another!
>
> When my mother married Gilmore, I was given a choice of last names—Gilmore or Thurber. Some instinct told me to go with Thurber, and then I promptly spelled it wrong my first day at school.

At the time of Althea's marriage to Allen Gilmore, Thurber's *Fables for Our Time* had just been published—in September 1940. "When I read 'The Little Girl and the Wolf,'" Rosemary says,

> somehow I connected that and the other fables with knowing that my father wrote them, but it was a rather confusing time.
>
> My first memory of my father was in Cambridge, this tall man coming to visit and bringing me things. It's my only memory of his visiting me there. I have a very clear picture of his throwing a tennis ball over our house at 51 Walker Street—a two-story house—and thinking that was pretty spectacular. My father later told me he kept asking my mother when she was going to get around to telling me that he was my father. But why didn't *he* tell me?

In November 1939, Thurber published *The Last Flower*, the sad but hopeful picture book that followed the outbreak of war in Europe. Rosemary, who had just turned eight, wasn't even aware that the book was dedicated to her. "I was a good deal older before I knew he had done that," she says. "I think they kept that from me so that I wouldn't be any snippier than I already was."

Althea never discussed her marriage to Thurber with Rosemary, except to refer to early troubles with Mame and the Columbus family, possibly over their asking Thurber for money. Rosemary adds:

> If Robert resented my mother because she seemed to act as his intellectual "superior," it was probably because he realized she was. She was very bright.
>
> I don't even know if my mother knew she was thought of as "The Thurber Woman," though she said she thought one or two of his cartoons were based on their experiences. My father used to tell me that it was all his fault that his marriage to my mother broke up. I know it was not *all* his fault. My mother was always attracted to men who wrote, to intellectuals, and liked to help and be part of the scene, but she wasn't too successful with any marriage. Neither was she the villainous heavy!

Rosemary remembers her mother regretting that she didn't ask Thurber for child support as part of the divorce terms,

> but I guess she asked when there was a need, for school, for example. Comstock left some money in a savings account for me when he and my mother were divorced "in case" my father didn't help out. He always did. My father would tell me that even though they were separated and it was a "mistake" that I was conceived he was very glad that I happened. I certainly believe that. He cared a lot about me. *And*, it was hard to be a "mistake."

Gilmore taught at Amherst College during the war. (His and Althea's daughter, Linda, was born in 1942.) Thurber and Helen rented apartments in New York in those years, and in the summers they rented one house after another in several Connecticut towns in the Berkshire foothills. As a teenager, Rosemary began to spend parts of her summer vacations with them, sometimes bringing classmates with her. Thurber had developed a full parental claim on her by the time she was enrolled in the Northampton School for Girls. He not only footed the tuition; in 1947, in one of his letters to the headmistress, he recommends that the students' summer reading list include certain of his favorite books and authors: *Babbitt,* by Sinclair Lewis; *Daisy*

Miller, by James; *Gentle Julia* (Booth Tarkington); *Linda Condon*, *Java Head*, and *Wild Oranges* (Joseph Hergesheimer); *The Wanderer* (Alain-Fournier); Fitzgerald's *The Great Gatsby*; Hemingway's *The Sun Also Rises*; *Invitation to the Waltz* (Rosamond Lehmann); *This Simian World* and *God and My Father* (Clarence Day); *The House in Paris* (Elizabeth Bowen); *A Lost Lady* and *My Mortal Enemy* (Willa Cather); *A Handful of Dust* and *Decline and Fall* (Evelyn Waugh); *Heaven's My Destination* and *The Cabala* (Thornton Wilder); *February Hill* and *The Wind at My Back* (Victoria Lincoln); *Blue Voyage* (Conrad Aiken); *The Bitter Tea of General Yen* (G. Z. Stone); *Lady into Fox* (David Garnett); *How to Write Short Stories* (Ring Lardner); *The Return of the Soldier* (Rebecca West); *Miss Lonelyhearts* (Nathanael West); and "E. B. White's *One Man's Meat*, whose perfect writing should be on every reading list."

These, Thurber wrote the headmistress, "interested, inspired or excited me and most important of all affected me as a writer." Thurber hoped that they would also "stimulate a young lady's interest in good writing." He had his reasons, but Rosemary, who dutifully read most of the books, says, "My father never got over the fact that I didn't want to be a writer. It was really a difficult blow for him, I think."

Upon her graduation from Northampton in 1949, Thurber gave Rosemary twenty-seven books he thought she would like. "He apologized afterward all the time for that present," she says, "saying it was a terrible present to have given a girl, but I loved them; they were wonderful."

In 1948, Allen Gilmore had joined the History Department of Carnegie-Mellon University, in Pittsburgh, and moved Althea and Linda there. Rosemary remained in the East, and attended Skidmore College for a year before transferring to the University of Pennsylvania, where she earned a degree in English. When she was still a junior at the Northampton School, Thurber began writing her letters that any daughter or son would treasure. They helped her to develop a special appreciation of her father's work; she found clues in his letters to what turns up in his drawings and writing. She believes that a sketch in one of his letters was a model for his drawing "Stop Me!", showing a huge Thurber Woman on ice skates, out of control and about to run down a frightened little Thurber Man.

Elsewhere, Thurber writes her:

> The only Tri Delt I ever met was one so powerfully built she could throw me and during dances when I tried to turn her I sometimes found both my feet off the ground. At that time, thirty years ago, the large girls were spoken of as stylish stouts.

He relates an anecdote involving Ronald Williams, the publisher of the *Bermudian* and a longtime friend of his. "Ronny," says Thurber,

> had lectured his five year old daughter on good behavior while he was lying in bed in his pajama bottoms. He told her about a prince looking for a good princess and rejecting the bad ones and she said she was going to be a good princess. He was pretty smug until he found that she had stuck a wad of gum in his navel. They had to get it out with rubbing alcohol. Never torture your father.

Rosemary thinks the incident gave Thurber the idea for his fable "The Godfather and His Godchild":

> A wordly-wise collector, who had trotted the globe collecting everything he could shoot, or buy, or make off with, called upon his godchild, a little girl of five. . . . "I want to give you . . . any three things your heart desires. I have diamonds from Africa, and a rhinoceros horn, scarabs from Egypt, emeralds from Guatemala, chessmen of ivory and gold, mooses' antlers, signal drums, ceremonial gongs, temple bells, and three rare and remarkable dolls. Now tell me," he concluded, patting the little girl on the head, "what do you want more than anything else in the world?"
>
> His little godchild . . . did not hesitate. "I want to break your glasses and spit on your shoes," she said.
>
> Moral: Though statisticians in our time have never kept the score, Man wants a great deal here below and Woman even more.

In November 1947, Thurber wrote his sixteen-year-old: "Helen has just gone up the road to buy some pot holders and luncheon sets from a young woman who appears at the edge of the woods on cloudy Saturdays accompanied by a violet-colored dog who shines at night and whose name, unhappily, is Floyd." ("You can see why you'd wait around to get letters like that," says Rosemary.) She sees this passage as a carryover from the mood Thurber created in the opening of *The White Deer*, two years before, when near-blindness frequently cut him loose from the confinements of reality to roam a more congenial landscape of fantasy:

> If you should walk and wind and wander far enough on one of those afternoons in April when smoke goes down instead of up, and nearby things sound far away and far things near, you are more than likely to

come at last to the enchanted forest that lies between the Moonstone Mines and Centaurs Mountain. You'll know the woods when you are still a long way off by virtue of a fragrance you can never quite forget and never quite remember. And there'll be a distant bell that causes boys to run and laugh and girls to stand and tremble. If you pluck one of the ten thousand toadstools that grow in the emerald grass at the edge of the wonderful woods, it will feel as heavy as a hammer in your hand, but if you let go it will sail away over the trees like a tiny parachute, trailing black and purple stars.

When she was at Penn, Rosemary, who like Mame wanted to be an actress, was in a play of which an otherwise favorable review found the overuse of her hands distracting. She sent the review to Thurber, who commented:

When I first acted at Ohio State, I discovered that I had three hands and only two pockets to put them in. This is a thing that goes away and by the time you are twenty-one you will have two hands like everybody else. Maybe [more people will come] if you put on *Tobacco Road* and let me play the part of Jeeter Lester. You could play the part of Ellie May. . . .

Ellie May has what was meant to be a hairlip [sic] but Bob Benchley said it looked to him from where he sat as if the ailment were more deep seated.

He enclosed a poem:

The critics have made a small sensation
About my daughter's intonation.
They liked her poise and her acting style.
They liked her voice and her pretty smile.
The flaws they found were three small flaws,
One in each of her lovely paws.
See my daughter where she stands,
Trying to manage her three left hands.
But here is my love, and its loaf and its crumbs,
And a kiss for each of her fifteen thumbs.

In February 1953, in the middle of her senior year at Penn, Rosemary married Frederick Sauers, a student at the Wharton School of Finance. Rosemary was twenty-one, Althea's age when she married Thurber. Sauers was also interested in the theater—he and Rosemary had met as actors in a school play. While living in a Chicago suburb, after Sauers' required Army service, the two became involved in community dramatics, including the forming of a touring children's theater troupe. Even the birth of their three children didn't keep Rosemary from realizing part of her ambition to act. For several years, she gave public readings of her father's works. She played Mame in *Jabberwock*, a stage adaptation by Jerome Lawrence and Robert Lee of My *Life and Hard Times*, which had its premiere at the dedication of the Thurber Theatre at O.S.U. in the fall of 1972. The following spring, Rosemary returned to give a lecture at the university, showing slides of Thurber's drawings and reading excerpts from his letters to her.

In a letter acknowledging her twenty-first birthday, Thurber admonished Rosemary to pick out a husband "with great care and have him tested by doctors, psychiatrists, and old experienced wives," though he confesses, "I have found out little about marriage after 30 years of it."

A woman's greatest problem is this: How to make use of her uterus without losing the use of her brain cells. Since God and Nature made woman the creative sex and remind her of it every 28 days, it is natural that talent should be a subsidiary thing in her case. A man has to keep his talent alive even if it kills him. But a woman can let hers die like a rose in a book. It often dies in the shade of a man but she has her children to compensate for this up until the time the oldest boy backs away from a filling station with a gun in one hand and the day's receipts in the other, and the prettiest of the twin girls runs away with a gambler from Memphis. . . .

If you are married, never let your husband keep his service revolver in the bedroom because recent news events have proved that if he doesn't shoot you on your way back from the bathroom in the dark, you will shoot him in his sleep because he has begun to get on your nerves and you're pretty sure the babies don't like him. . . . I've already bought you a pearl-handled submachine gun that once belonged to Al Capone's mother and I'm trying to locate her bullet proof Lincoln town car.

When Rosemary sprang the news that she wanted to marry at the end of the first semester of her senior year, she says she could "feel the anger" in her father's written responses, though he grudgingly agreed to "back you kids in whatever you finally decide to do." The "kids" had made up their minds. Thurber talked to Althea, now separated from Gilmore, her third husband,

and they agreed to limit their wedding invitation lists. (Guests, mostly Thurber's, totaled a hundred.)

The fact that Rosemary was taking on her mid-term exam, the lead in the university's spring play, and marriage, all at once, worried Thurber. Also, Sauers was scheduled for two years in the Army, and had no prospects of a substantial income:

> The dreadful variety of tests that you and Fred are putting marriage to reminds me of the guy that took off his wristwatch in Tony's kitchen and handed it to the drunken Benchley and Dorothy Parker saying proudly, "It's indestructible. Do anything you want with it." They threw it on the floor and stepped on it and Dotty finally whammed it against the stove. When they gave it back to its owner, he said in surprise, "It's stopped." The culprits looked astonished and then Bob said, "You probably wound it too tight."

But Thurber was soon writing cheerful references to the marriage—to friends, and to Rosemary. In 1955, when the Sauers' first child, Sara, was two months old, Rosemary told her father that whenever Fred picked up the baby it screamed. Thurber reassures them:

> Tell Fred that the feminine sex should start off in proper terror of the males. It shows that nature is preparing the girls to do something about the other sex before it is too late. By the time you get this letter, of course, your daughter will be in love with [him] as much as her mother. It takes time to adjust to the greatest menace on the earth, the male of the human species.

That letter is especially prized by Rosemary, who inexorably developed the feminist point of view. Whatever her father's personal problems with women, she believes that his public statements imploring women to save civilization from male-dominated cultures and governments are heartfelt.

Thurber's fondness and respect for his daughter can be found in his inclusion of her among the friends of his generation as a correspondent worthy of his best. This, from a letter written to her from Bermuda, in 1957:

> I woke up early this morning thinking of this paraphrase: "Last night, ah yesternight, betwixt her lips and mine, thy shadow fell Ida Rappapour the night was thine." You can see the effects upon my artistic invention brought about by the charm of this ring on England's finger, as Andy

White called Bermuda. He is now in Maine with his hypochondria, having had a dreadful three weeks in Florida. They [Andy and Katharine] had a termagant of a landlady and Andy developed a fixation about her. He was sure she had buried her husband in the backyard. Never bury your husband in the backyard. Never bury your husband in or around the house. The place to bury your husband is on a heath. Cops never look there; they always look in the woods. Getting him up on the roof to fix the spouting and then pushing him off is not a good idea. This is much too common and the police suspect the wife at once. Push him off a neighbor's roof and let them suspect the neighbor's wife or husband.

From the early 1940s on, Thurber kept trying to follow the success of *The Male Animal* with another play. It became a lifelong obsession with him. He writes Rosemary that he "has developed the character of Elliott Nugent's daughter" for "the play," with Nugent to play the lead. The actress

believes in love in the afternoon so that you can get up for cocktails and wine instead of love at night which ends in ascorbic acid, boiled eggs and sometimes waffles. . . . The loyal wife is both blind and deaf. A jealous wife sees and hears what's not there. The discontented wife neither looks nor listens. Thus the American wife does not have the vaguest idea of the truth of her husband's behavior or what his friends think about him. A woman cannot swear in court to the truth of what her husband did the night before but she could describe with absolute accuracy all the details of every gown worn by every woman there. . . .

Now is the season for the so-called panty raids in America, another unique American substitute for love and sex in which the pants are taken from a bureau drawer instead of off the girl. This is a complete change of the procedure in my own day.

Did I ever tell you about Roger Angell, Katharine White's son now 40 and an editor of *The New Yorker?* When he was 10 he stole the pants of a 10-year-old girl on the way home from school and threw them down the sewer. His teacher told the parents he must be punished and so they made him write the girl a letter of apology. It went like this: "Dear Sarah, I am sorry I took your pants off and threw them down the sewer. Love, Roger." He is now married and has two children. . . .

My mother was sure if you slept with French girls you got the leaping jitters and she used to write me of this in Paris. So when I came home after nearly two years I entered the house and greeted her shaking like a leaf or like the cup and saucer you carried across the stage that time.

The French girls know more about sleeping with a man before they are fourteen than the average American woman learns by the time she is 44. Science does not understand this problem and has practically given it up. As my cousin once told me when she was 18, "They were caught doing what you do when you're married." This is clearly a song cue and may be put in the next O'Hara musical comedy. He is the man who made love a three-letter word. Or did he make sex a four-letter word?

Though proud of being Thurber's daughter (she reassumed her Thurber name after divorcing Sauers), for years Rosemary kept to herself the trauma she experienced at the departure of her first stepfather, Francis Comstock, of whom she was fond; the realization that she hadn't known who her father was; and her father's years-long delay in claiming her as his own. "I never really discussed it with anyone until I was in my forties and in a profound depression," she says. "If my father were alive, I would let him know my anger. Still I know that he did the best he could, given his own experience."

Rosie's wedding reception at a Philadelphia hotel was the last time many of those who knew Althea from the old days saw her. When her second daughter, Linda Gilmore, moved to Scotland, Althea followed her there. She lived twenty-five years after Thurber's death, becoming a recluse, and died in Aberdeen on July 6, 1986, at age eighty-five, of an embolism following a fall that broke her hip.

When Thurber heard that Ann Honeycutt and St. Clair McKelway were to be married, he took the face-saving step of marrying first. He had found Helen Wismer adoring, witty, bright, supportive in all his difficulties, and a good listener. She was full of gaiety, and had a fine sense of humor and an appreciation of good writing. Her frequent dates with Babe Benson, Sally Benson's husband, seemed to intrigue Thurber, whose sexual interest was often piqued by jealousy. He needled Helen about Benson after their marriage. "Let's give a party and have old Babe Benson up here," he would say in front of others.

Physically, Helen was no Honeycutt, though there was a pertness and cuteness about her. She was brown-eyed, bespectacled, and skinny. Honeycutt, who remained oddly jealous of Helen, was rarely able to refer to her, after the marriage, without sounding snide. She delighted in repeating earlier careless remarks by Thurber—that Helen was not only knock-kneed but that her bony body seemed "put together like the insides of a tool kit." But Thurber soon enough proclaimed Helen the ideal soul mate.

Helen knew that Thurber was marrying her on the rebound. "I have you to thank," she told Honeycutt on several occasions. "We would never have married if he hadn't heard about you and Mac planning your wedding."

Thurber's proposal—in the Algonquin lobby shortly after his divorce—was typically impulsive but only partly booze-conditioned. Helen was so surprised that she immediately went to the ladies' room to collect herself before returning to reply, "Of course."

The inner circle was amazed, and the engagement was a principal subject for discussion at Costello's, Bleeck's, Tony's, "21," the Algonquin, and the *New Yorker*.

"It was a good swap that Helen made," says Joel Sayre. "Her father was a minister—and what clergyman of conscience could pretend to any material affluence in the Depression? In a sense, Helen grew up living out of a Salvation Army barrel. Jim was famous and pretty well off, despite some big debts, and had good potential. He moved in exciting circles of well-known personalities Helen wanted to be a part of. She obviously loved and admired him and, in the bargain, saw marriage to him as an all-around good deal. She got his finances in order for the first time. Jim wasn't even aware of how much money he owed. And what was she giving up? Editing magazines like *War Aces* and *I Confess*." (It grated on Katharine White when Thurber exuberantly noted that Andy and he were both married to "lady editors." But Helen's sensitive editorial assistance to Thurber suggests that she would have done perfectly well at the *New Yorker*.)

Helen had worked to help put herself through Mt. Holyoke, and she shared apartments in the Village with other women, while living on subsistence wages. But in no way was she looking for a way to take life easy. She recognized Thurber's need for the very help she felt qualified, by skill and temperament, to give him, and she knew it would be far more than a full-time job. While those who had made their own assessments of what life with Thurber would be like looked on with mixed emotions of gratitude, admiration, amusement, and apprehension on behalf of both of them, Helen took the plunge—"convinced," in Honeycutt's acid-soaked words, "that Thurber was a great find."

Helen had felt especially proprietary toward Thurber even before their engagement. When she put a Thurber biographer in touch with one of her former roommates as a possible source of anecdotes, the woman shrieked with laughter. "When Helen was going with Thurber, she wouldn't let any of her women friends near him," she said. "I don't think I was really allowed to talk to him until after they were married."

As for Thurber, he had misgivings about marrying Helen until the last moment, as we have seen. Shortly before the marriage, he fled to Columbus. When she finally tracked him down at the Thurbers, she angrily asked him, "Where are you, someplace in the gutter?" He reported this to Mame, who, besides telephoning Eva at the time of Thurber's visit, went with Robert to Zanesville to learn if Thurber had stopped off to see Eva Prout, and to be sure Eva knew about Thurber's wedding—Mame still not trusting her son where Eva was concerned. She told Eva what Helen had said to Thurber, and wondered if it boded well for the marriage. "I told her I was sure Helen didn't mean that," says Eva, "but I don't know." Mame took consolation from Helen's birth date (June 26, 1902), which, she declared, squared with the stars in a workable way.

In February 1934, Harold Ross was married a second time, to Marie Françoise Elie Clark, a Frenchwoman whom Ross called Frances. Thurber had climbed up a stepladder and drawn a woman's head high on Ross's office wall, with a star above it and a caption proclaiming that second marriages were made in heaven. At the time he could hardly have suspected that his compliment to Ross would have relevance to his own life within the next year and a half.

Ross, who believed the better writers wrote best when emotionally stricken, worried about Thurber's getting married and becoming happy. He asked Benchley to talk Thurber out of it. Benchley made dutiful daily calls to his own wife in Bronxville, but he remained in town and led the self-indulgent life of a boulevardier, quite independently of her. Like Ross, he suspected that the strictures of a traditional marriage ran counter to creative expression. He treated Thurber to cocktails at his suite in the Royalton and presented Ross's concern. When he met Helen, however, he recognized that she would provide many of the supportive strengths that Thurber lacked. "What are you waiting for, Ross's permission?" he asked, forgetting both his and Ross's arguments. This from a humorist whom Thurber had long idolized helped to dispel further doubts.

Thurber and Helen began drinking at "21" the day before the wedding and continued the celebration at the country home of Bob Coates—Thurber's best man—most of that night. Helen's father, the Reverend Ernest Wismer, officiated at the ceremony, June 25, 1935, at his summer cottage in Colebrook, Connecticut, near the Massachusetts border. Hung over, the principals tried to restore themselves with a round of Manhattans an hour before the nuptials. Most were prepared for Thurber to act the part of the nervous bridegroom in some fashion, but "when my father pronounced us man and wife, Jamie burst into tears," Helen told Burton Bernstein. "My father said to me afterwards, 'What kind of a man is this?' I honestly didn't know what to answer."

Thus began one of the most unusual man/woman, husband/wife, writer/editor, artist/business manager, listener/reader, performer/critic, hell-raiser/protector, patient/nurse, and even child/mother relationships that modern times have profitably played host to. Of the twenty-six years they were together, Thurber was legally blind through twenty-one of them, and that he kept going as long and as well as he did may be credited in large part to Helen's care and her commitment to the partnership.

"Helen rarely visited the magazine except on business," Daise Terry says, "but Thurber brought her to the office right after they were married. She was in a pink dress with white shoes and very thin, I remember. Thurber was very proud of her and led her about, introducing her to everyone. It was a great day for him and for us, really, who had seen him go through so much over the previous months."

Helen made certain the partnership worked. "She always went along with Jim," Sayre says. "Whatever Jim thought, felt or said was almost always O.K. with her." Peter De Vries graciously commented that with all Thurber's troubles at least he had been "spared being married to a Thurber Woman." Certainly Helen's efforts were always in Thurber's interests, which, from the start, were also hers.

So empathetic was Helen to Thurber's moods over time that she seemed to gain or lose weight when he did, and to have cataracts and other eye problems that he had; her glasses over the years gradually approached the thicknesses of Thurber's. She loyally stayed up with him for most of the night when he refused to go home or to bed; endorsed his positions and beliefs if they were challenged by others; subscribed to his self-conceptions and self-deceptions with consistent fidelity; worked, traveled, and played in tempo with his changeable disposition; and for twenty-five years after his death continued to contribute to his legend and to guard faithfully the image she knew he would want preserved. "Gallant" is how Morris Ernst, their attorney, described Helen. ("Life wasn't easy with Thurber," he says.)

When Jap Gude left CBS at the end of 1943 to form his own talent agency, Stix & Gude, Thurber became "a client by virtue of long friendship," he says. Gude sold Thurber's work to radio, television, and motion-picture and play producers. But Helen, as Thurber's de-facto business manager, joined Thurber in his negotiations with magazines, book publishers, and bidders for first and second serial rights. She set up a filing system for Thurber and for the first time kept copies of the letters he wrote to friends.

"It was the best thing that could have happened to Thurber," says Daise Terry, who handled his office correspondence and requests for permission to reprint his stories and art. "Helen had business sense. She knew publishing and was frugal. I'd tell Thurber some professor was getting together an anthology and offering fifty dollars for the right to reprint something, and Thurber would say, 'Those people don't make much money, Terry. Let's just take fifteen dollars. Better still, let's give it to them.' Helen put a stop to all that, and it was about time. He was much too generous for his own good."

Yet Helen, who was half Scottish and stubborn and logical in money matters, was no less generous than Thurber in all the important ways. "No one was quick enough in a bar to buy the Thurbers a drink for the twenty-six years they were together," says Joel Sayre. "That made them a powerful magnet to freeloaders." Helen was a sympathetic and fully-qualified drinking buddy. "When you love someone like that," Sayre poses, "what is there to do but drink along with him, go along with him, even on unsupportable points? Helen rarely tried to discourage Thurber from attacking others. It wouldn't have done much good, maybe, but also she seemed to recognize his need for the attacks. She sided with him if the counterattacks were more than he seemed able to handle."

And reflecting on those years after Thurber's death, Donald Ogden Stewart said of Helen: "Her tender, patient understanding, protection, and guidance of a blind genius deserved the gratitude of all who loved James Thurber, which must include all who have ever read a word of his."

45

That Wedded Life

I weighed 164 pounds the last time I was weighed—which is six or eight more than I weighed before I was married and four more than I ever weighed before. My lovely, charming and noble wife has gained only one pound, but she is younger than I am. Did I tell you I suggested calling our cottage at Martha's Vineyard "The Qualms" but Helen said she hadn't any and I said I hadn't either—and we haven't, either—so we just called it Break Inn, since once Mrs. Max Eastman came and stole half a bottle of rye and a honeydew melon.

The first two months of our wedded life has been serene and fine. It took me just forty years, six months, and sixteen days to arrive where I should have been when I started.

—Letter to the Whites, late summer, 1935

In the *New Yorker*'s June 22 issue, three days before the wedding, a Thurber spot drawing shows a woman, accompanied by a Thurber hound, sailing beatifically through the air, carrying a sleeping Thurber Man and reaching for a star. A few see it as Thurber's artistic blessing on his marriage: others see an aggressive woman who knows what she wants making off with a vanquished male. Both viewpoints may be supportable.

After the wedding night at a Litchfield inn, and a night with Bob and Elsa Coates, in Sherman, Connecticut, the Thurbers returned to New York. Ann Honeycutt threw a party for the newlyweds. "It was embarrassing," says Mc-Kelway. "Jim got drunk and flew into me in front of Helen, saying I'd taken away from him the only girl he'd ever loved. On other occasions, he'd bring up the same thing, with Helen present."

But Helen's love for Thurber was grounded in acceptance, and she often seemed more entertained than humiliated by such scenes. She understood Thurber as nobody else did, was tough-minded, ambitious for them both, and sensed the fitness of the match. She had known well in advance what went with the bargain she had struck. It all helped make her one of the few women he didn't fear.

From New York, they took the Fall River Line to Martha's Vineyard for a honeymoon/vacation near the Gudes, who owned a cottage there. Thurber, eager to show off his restored privilege as a car owner and driver, writes the Whites:

> We had to buy a car in Martha's Vineyard because you simply couldn't get around to the beach and places without one. . . . Jap had an old Packard he bought at a rummage sale but we could hardly keep calling on them. Before we got the car we had to walk to their house, half a mile away. I picked up a Ford V-8—a 1933 they told me, but it turned out to be a 1932—the year that ate up the oil like a baby eats mashed bananas. . . . I have to get oil every 100 miles. . . . I drove it around the vineyard for three weeks and got back into my old easy driving style, reminiscent of the days when I was the terror of the roads in Ohio and my mother wouldn't drive with me because I went around the wrong side of street cars and shouted at the motormen. I find that I am just as natural born a driver as Morris Markey, Public Enemy of the Highways No. 1. We left the vineyard on the last day of July . . . and drove to Colebrook. . . . I made it in six hours, and we had to drive through Providence and Hartford. Bob Coates had told me that Providence was the damndest city in the country to drive through, what with trick light signals, twisting streets, etc. I made it gracefully and calmly. Last week we drove over to Newport for the tennis there, and once again took Providence and Hartford in our stride . . . so I have no fears left. Didn't so much as collide with a bus full of schoolchildren.

At the Vineyard, Thurber's checks for both the cottage rent and the Ford were returned for insufficient funds. He dashed off "The Departure of Emma Inch," a fictitious account of a neurotic woman whom the narrator and his wife hire as a cook. When the ferry docks at Woods Hole, she decides against going on to the Vineyard, because her sickly dog, Feely, has taken a turn for the worse. The narrator tries to talk her out of returning to New York by herself. "I told her people sent sick dogs to Martha's Vineyard to be cured. But it was no good." He gives her money and leaves her smiling and waving good-bye to them from the pier, clutching Feely. It was the first casual Thurber sold after his marriage to Helen, and the first to cast her in her new role as the Thurber Wife. She emerges unscathed. Thurber routinely wired Ralph Paladino at the *New Yorker* for money, but his advances had far outstripped his sales at the time, and the new casual was needed as collateral for a loan extension.

They spent the rest of the summer in the Wismers' cottage in Colebrook. Regaining the driver's seat had put Thurber in an exuberant mood. At Colebrook, he finished "Smashup," "about a husband who is afraid to drive the car and then gets so he isn't afraid," he writes the Whites. "It's called 'Smash Up' [sic]—which has a symbolical connotation."

As to his former life, he tells the Whites:

> The hazards and honeycutts along the way were rather disturbing for a time, but all that is a faint mist far behind me as I roar along at fifty miles an hour, passing the mckelways and shouting at them to get over. . . . When we arrived at Matty's Vineyard, the only cottage available was the one Honey and Ed Angly and I had occupied last year, in a perfectly stainless (at least as far as I am concerned) but confusing (to the neighbors) way. I told Helen . . . the quaint and tortuous story of its previous occupancy, but she took it like a good sport with a laugh— she always referred to it as the Old Honeycutt Place. . . . We had a nice time there, without any ghosts from the past to haunt us. . . .
>
> Except for these private notes I am making, my past has long been decently and thoroly buried. Ahead of us stretches Route No.1 [they planned to visit the Whites in Maine], clear and long and curving. (I hate straight roads.) There is the promise of elms and unexpected lakes and mountain coolness over the rise. You'll find us an agreeable couple. We hardly drink anything at all any more. The hold of 21 and Tony's has been broken, headlock though it was.

Ross agreed to let Thurber cover five tennis matches for the magazine that year; he signed "The Tennis Courts" feature "T.J.G." or "G.T.J.," a scramble of his initials. Helen accompanied him to Newport, Chestnut Hill (Mass.), Forest Hills, and the sites of other prominent tournaments. After the Chestnut Hill matches, the Thurbers drove on to North Brooklin, Maine, to visit the Whites. Thurber's house gifts, as usual, were more of his drawings.

For years, the sedate Whites kept their Thurber art collection to themselves, forbidding reproductions even after donating the drawings to the Cornell library in 1963. A drawing of the magazine's art conference was for Katharine alone: In one, Thurber, with mustache, glasses, and tousled hair and holding a pen, has drawn himself, long legs under the table, bent over drawing paper in concentration. In a possible reference to her past rejections of his work, Thurber has Katharine saying to another woman: "He's trying to think of something that would amuse the art conference but there isn't anything." In a nod of questionable sincerity to Katharine's interest in fiction, Thurber draws an elderly woman describing to her elderly husband the novel she is reading: "When he finds out she's a pervert, he disembowels her with a tire tool." It could well be a comment on *The New Yorker*'s quiet fiction.

The Whites' *pièce de résistance*, of course, is Thurber's 1929 wedding gift to them, "La Flamme and Mr. Prufrock." Thurber's presentation note:

> Dear Andy,
> I'm making you and Katharine a present of these drawings known as The Embrace Series. These, as far as I'm concerned, catch better than any other of mine, the grotesqueries, the mad delight, the pathos, the fun and the beauty of love. You will note that it would be practically impossible to hang the last drawing upside down or sideways.

The drawings develop a narrative path a bit bold for Eliot's conservative J. Alfred Prufrock: The wife, leaving the house, tells her husband, "Now be sure and empty the pan under the refrigerator." Alone, Prufrock thinks,

Mr. P. is bored by all the aesthetics.

"Now to call up La Flamme and get her over here for a little de l'amour." He phones La Flamme. La Flamme agrees to come over and play, trips to the toilette to take a quick bath and "make herself sweet." "Mr. P." prepares for his "little visitor." His greeting sweeps her off her feet. There follows "The Improper Proposal. La Flamme prepares . . ." She admires herself in the bathroom mirror; Prufrock, in bathrobe, looks impatiently at his watch. In the bathroom by herself, La Flamme, nude, goes into a self-admiring dance before the mirror. Prufrock bangs on the door; La Flamme had almost forgotten the host, who bursts in. Her mind still on dancing, she tries to interest him in a platonic romp. Mr. P. tries to interest her in bed by bouncing up and down on it, but La Flamme goes into her *pas seul* again. He is about to use force; she kicks him. Angered, he angers her in turn by ordering her to leave. She takes him at his word. There is a disgraceful scene at parting, she thumbing her nose; he sticking out his tongue at her. This is followed by several drawings of a glum Mr. P. in bed alone.

How the Whites could be expected to extract "the beauty of love" from the drawings remains Thurber's secret, locked into his private feelings about the Whites' marriage.

In September, the Thurbers rented a furnished apartment at 8 Fifth Avenue, on the southwest corner of Eighth and Fifth. It was a part of the city they both knew well. "You have to walk up three flights," Thurber writes Herman Miller, "since the Rhinelanders, who own the house, lost their elevator in the market crash."

No longer alone, Thurber worked more frequently at home, often staying up all night to write. He still did Talk rewrite and put in his time at the office, usually arriving there in the afternoon. At five, he would often have a drink with friends and colleagues at the Algonquin, catch a bus down Fifth Avenue to the apartment, take an hour's nap at six o'clock, and sit down to Helen's dinner at seven.

As if afraid to be alone together, nearly every evening they either entertained or sallied forth to close up bars, sometimes impulsively inviting home celebrities or strangers who struck them, while in their cups, as being inordinately clever. They were usually sorry afterward, including the time they brought home a drunken Thomas Wolfe. Wolfe's physical and elocutionary bulk made every room he was in look too small. This behemoth of a man, a much-talked-about novelist in his middle thirties, playing the literary-cocktail-party circuit, was game for a drink and a good time at the pop of a cork or the lift of a skirt, to paraphrase Thurber. He could be fun to have along if one was part of the literary crowd living the high life. On one such night, he was at a nightclub in the company of McKelway and Hobart Weekes, all in collective pursuit of drink and the study of belly dancing, the club's specialty. The sedative effects of booze lulled Wolfe into a head-on-the-table sleep and rendered the judgment of the others questionable. One of the lady dancers swung her pelvis tantalizingly close to McKelway, who was deep in conversation and carelessly flicked a hot ash from his cigarette into her navel. Her strident protests brought two bouncers to the scene and the ensuing hassle aroused Wolfe, who unfolded himself to his full six feet and seven inches and asked the bouncers why they were bothering his friends. The bouncers, with uncharacteristic courtesy, asked the three men to leave. "Because the show had been put out of action temporarily," says Weekes, "there seemed little reason to stay."

Wolfe made a lasting enemy of Thurber the night Thurber and Helen invited him home. He sneered at the *New Yorker* writers collectively and told Thurber that his "short pieces" didn't qualify him as a writer. (His own story collection, *From Death to Morning,* had just been published.) Lurching about, Wolfe was a potential wrecking ball, and Thurber warned him against damaging furnishings and fixtures, because "this place belongs to the Rhinelanders." Finally, upstaged and insulted—and by a man too big to knock about except on Walter Mitty terms—Thurber went to bed, grumbling at the late hour and muttering sarcastically that he wished the author of *Look Homeward, Angel* would take his own advice. Helen tried to hold the fort after Thurber's abdication, but Wolfe, as his biographer Andrew Turnbull attests, simply tried to claim any woman he wanted when inebriated. Helen resisted gamely, leading the heavy-footed Wolfe around the sofa in her flight. The thumping and commotion aroused Thurber, who told Wolfe to get out of his house. "It isn't your house," Wolfe reminded him. "It's the Rhinelanders'." He had Thurber there. Wolfe next wanted to use the phone to talk to someone in Hollywood. "I cut the telephone cord," Thurber told Miller later. "I wasn't going to let my phone be used for a call to California by any writer who needs three pages to describe a pot of coffee percolating."

Thurber, made to feel like the contemptuous pussycat, never got over the incident, and shortly afterward drew on the wall of Tim Costello's Third Avenue saloon the mural reproduced below.

Thurber wouldn't let it go. In the *New Yorker* of November 23, 1935, a Wolfe-size man appears in a Thurber cartoon, huge and overwhelming, at a party. One guest is saying to another: "He looks a little like Thomas Wolfe, and he certainly makes the most of it." Two weeks later, another Thurber caption has a flirtatious female, seated on another man's lap, who tells the

"This is my house, Mr. Wolfe, and if you don't get out I'll throw you out!"

meek Thurber Man, "You can't *make* me go home!" And when Ross tired of Thurber's Wolfe references, Thurber sold another to the *Saturday Review of Literature:* The party scene is again overshadowed by a Wolfean figure, one man gesturing toward the giant and saying to another, "He says Thomas Wolfe has no real stature."

Thurber, who rarely attacked other writers in print, dedicated one of his columns in Ralph Ingersoll's short-lived tabloid *PM* to a final public roasting of Wolfe in 1940, two years after the novelist's death. Reviewing Wolfe's posthumously published book, *You Can't Go Home Again,* Thurber writes, "I am simply not strong enough to battle my way through Wolfe's thunderous tides and swim out to the [quoting Wolfe] 'confused but intuitive sense of the apparent meaning and patterns of life . . .' "

In 1953, the head of the English Department at the Washington Square College of Arts and Science wrote Thurber looking for anecdotes for a paper he was writing about Wolfe, who had once taught there. Thurber was delighted to reply:

I met Thomas Wolfe only once . . . when he came to cocktails one day and stayed till nine the next morning. For an hour he was very amusing and then he became a drunken writer and exactly as disagreeable as all drunken writers. Knowing him for sixteen hours [Helen says nine] was one of the great strains of my life. . . . I have never been able to do much with Wolfe's writing, for which I have the same feeling that Fitzgerald had when he wrote Wolfe, "You are a putter in and I am a taker out." Wolfe did not seem to regard anybody as a writer unless his books were so heavy they were hard to lift. At four in the morning he said to my wife, the three of us being alone, "Oh, neither of you know what it is to be a writer!" to which my wife, a Scotch drinker, replied, "My husband is a writer," and Wolfe said in genuine surprise, "Is he? All I ever see is the *New Yorker*." . . .

It seems that God, knowing my strength, only lets me meet great writers once: Wolfe, Lewis, Fitzgerald, Faulkner, Hemingway.

The professor replied that Thurber had been fortunate to get away with only an overnight visit from Wolfe; Sherwood Anderson had earlier told him that Wolfe once moved in with him uninvited and stayed a week, depleting Anderson's larder.

Herman and Dorothy Miller came to New York that fall to fill up with Broadway plays; Miller was teaching drama at O.S.U. Thurber was offended to learn that they planned to stay at the Woodstock Hotel, in the theater district, rather than at his apartment, and told them he would not allow it:

> You will be shot as soon as you enter the portals of the [Woodstock] by my bodyguard and sensibilities-protector, a taxi driver named Charlie Rosenberg, who carries a short length of lead-pipe as well as a pistol. . . .
>
> You can stay up as late as you wish and go to bed as early. Our bedrooms are so far apart we have to phone each other or write, so that it really isn't like moving in with anyone, if you dread that. Just the other evening I practised throwing the javelin in the living room and, standing at my bedroom door, I could not quite spear the guest room door.

The Millers did check into the Woodstock, but Thurber, who was watching for them, went up to their room before they could unpack, seized some of their luggage, and forced them to check out and move to his apartment. It was the first time they had met Helen, who was the finest of hostesses, says Dorothy Miller.

"A woman came in who prepared everything," she says, "but Helen served the excellent dinner. We were both impressed by how Jim had changed. He was better organized, more practical than some of his friends we knew, and worried about everybody he liked, especially McNulty and his drinking. After dinner, Babe Benson, Helen's former escort, dropped in. Jim was particularly nice to him, perhaps for Helen's sake, and because Jim liked athletes, having wanted to be a sports hero himself. But Benson was boring everybody stiff; he couldn't talk about books or anything anybody else was interested in. He didn't leave until four or five a.m. Jim had considerately sent us to bed at one-thirty, knowing we were worn out from a day of sight-seeing.

"When I saw *The Male Animal* five years later, in which the ex-football player, former boyfriend of the professor's wife, returns to the campus and continues to pursue her, I remembered that night at the Thurbers. I'll always believe Babe Benson was the model for Joe Ferguson."

The Whites gave a cocktail party, Katharine wishing to honor G. D. Stern, an English contributor to the magazine. "Andy always tried to avoid such parties," says Dorothy Miller, "but he couldn't this one, since Katharine was giving it, which gave Jim great amusement. It was Helen's first 'big' introduction to Ross and others, and she was more scared than I was—Jim had insisted that Herman and I go along."

The party was in a narrow brownstone in Turtle Bay Gardens, in the East Forties, where the Whites had recently moved from the Village. Ross, in a brown tweed suit, was holding forth in the entryway. Miller was soon answering his questions about the Millers' hideaway, called "Fool's Paradise," in Worthington, north of Columbus, and Ross talked about living in a little apartment and saving money to build a house on a farm he had bought outside Stamford. Dorothy had submitted items to Franklin P. Adams's newspaper column, and she was delighted to find F.P.A. conducting his own cocktail seminar in the next room. Thurber spent time with the guest of honor, who asked Thurber to draw some dogs for her. He did.

Bea Lillie (Lady Peel), with whom Ross was said to be romantically involved, was there with her understudy, Paula Trueman ("a tiny thing," says Dorothy, "an unusual understudy for the tall Bea Lillie"). Thurber proudly pointed out Paula to Miller as one of his ex-flames. White, who looked for any excuse to get away from people and associate with animals, acted on Thurber's understanding suggestion and led the Millers to the top floor to show them Minnie, the dachshund pup the Whites had just acquired.

In *The Years with Ross*, Thurber speaks of Ross's relief at receiving "A

Couple of Hamburgers," the first Thurber casual after his marriage to feature a married couple as hostile toward one another as those in his pre-Helen fiction and art. Thurber's War between Men and Women would rage on, to Ross's delight. In "A Couple of Hamburgers," the Thurber Man is driving the car again, and, tired, hungry, and out of sorts, is deliberately using such slang as "dog-wagons" for roadside diners, and other terms he knows his wife abhors. Both want to stop somewhere, but she is fussy about the looks of the diners along the way. They come to Torrington.

> "Happen to know there's a dog-wagon here because I stopped in it once with Bob Combs [Coates]. Damn cute place, too, if you ask me." "I'm not asking you anything," she said, coldly. "You think you're *so* funny. I think I know the one you mean. . . . It's right in the town and it sits at an angle from the road. They're never so good, for some reason." He glared at her and almost ran up against the curb. "What the hell do you mean 'sits at an angle from the road'?" he cried. He was very hungry now. "Well, it isn't silly," she said, calmly. "I've noticed the ones that sit at an angle. They're cheaper because they fitted them into funny little pieces of ground. The big ones parallel to the road are the best." He drove right through Torrington, his lips compressed. "Angle from the *road,* for God's sake!" he snarled finally.

Ebba Jonsson, a Swedish-born spinster, ran the *New Yorker*'s library from 1934 until 1970. She brought to the job an impeccable memory for every item the magazine had ever run. She scissored the pieces from each week's issue and pasted them into large scrapbooks under the handwritten names of their writers. It was Jonsson who, book after book, found and collected the writings and drawings that Thurber selected for publication. Her rewards, little more than notes of gratitude and inscribed books from Thurber, were all she ever wanted, she said. Thurber was a particular favorite of hers. ("You walk like a sylph, Ebba," he once remarked to her when he could still dimly make out shapes and movement in his growing blindness. She never forgot the compliment.) From the time Thurber quit the staff until his death, Jonsson and Daise Terry continued to wait on his every whim, even in his periods of alienation from the magazine.

During the late summer of 1935, the *New Yorker* moved from 25 West 45th Street to larger quarters in an arcade building a block south, at 28 West Forty-fourth Street (25 West Forty-third Street), a location it would occupy for more than half a century. The Forty-fourth Street entrance was diagonally across from the Algonquin, and a few doors east of the Royalton. Ross was against the sofas and couches making the move, and Jonsson obtained a motheaten Victorian settee that had been in the old reception area. She had it reupholstered and moved to her apartment in the East Fifties. The settee held sentimental charm for her, she said: at the old offices, she had occasionally found Thurber, limp and hungover, curled up on it in the morning. When Jonsson told him she had confiscated the settee, he said, "Thank God. If I'd ever spent another night on that thing, I'd be in traction today."

Despite the hectic social schedule that Helen permitted herself to be drawn into with Thurber, she brought substantial order to his life. Among other things, she kept him in an overcoat in cold weather. It wasn't that easy. In one apartment building where they lived during the 1940s, Thurber, now blind, groped his way through an unlocked door into the wrong apartment, which had a floor plan similar to his own, hung his coat in the coat closet, remembered a package he had left in the hall, and this time returned to the right apartment. Helen had bought another coat for him by the time they learned what happened to the first one.

Thurber usually drank to get away from the very personality that people liked and to move toward a fantasized and less likable persona of his own making. But even in that role, Helen provided him with support that other spouses only dream about. More so than Honeycutt, Helen was one to whom he could say absolutely anything he wished without fear of embarrassment, reprisal, tears, or other unsettling consequences. She is the only one to whom he dedicated two of his books—twenty years apart.

When Hemingway attacked William Saroyan in *Esquire* for writing "like a sloppy drunk," Thurber, in full agreement, had already parodied Saroyan's best-seller *The Daring Young Man on the Flying Trapeze* with the title of his collection *The Middle-Aged Man on the Flying Trapeze*. It was published November 15, 1935—in time for the Christmas book-buying season. The original printing of four thousand copies was followed by four reprintings and heralded by Harper & Bros. as Thurber's second best-seller in a row—following *My Life and Hard Times* two years before.

Thurber had considered including "Menaces in May" in the collection, he wrote the Millers, but found it "too sugary and fuzzy." He hadn't been able to resist drawing the Thurber Dog sniffing around a wooden box at the end of "A Box to Hide In," he writes, though "Mrs. Parker" had told him to keep his pictures separate from his writing. Thurber's favorite of the collection was "The Black Magic of Barney Haller." He gloated over the *New York American*'s review, which found the book superior to the latest works of Wolfe, Hemingway, and Sinclair Lewis, although the *American*'s Sunday editor, Ber-

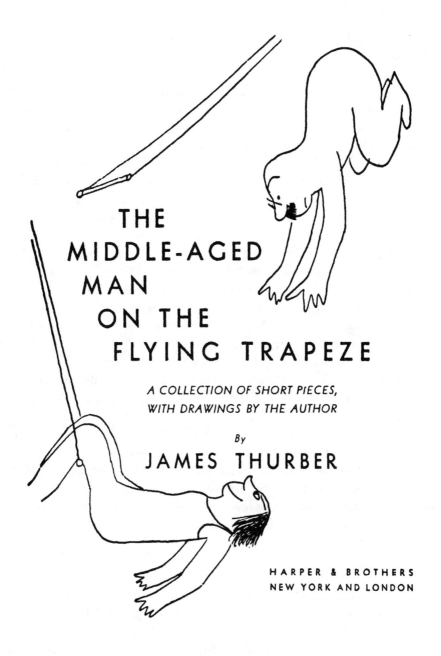

THE
MIDDLE-AGED
MAN
ON THE
FLYING TRAPEZE

A COLLECTION OF SHORT PIECES,
WITH DRAWINGS BY THE AUTHOR

By

JAMES THURBER

HARPER & BROTHERS
NEW YORK AND LONDON

nard Bergman, was an old friend. The viewpoints were those of a respected critic, but Bergman had selected the critic.

The book, dedicated to Bob and Elsa Coates, remains one of Thurber's best, containing uncollected short stories, with original drawings, spanning 1930 to the summer of 1935. It records the Althea years when he gained as a professional and lost as a family man. Throughout, one glimpses the pattern of dead-end streets that made up his social life during those years, leading him nowhere.

In "How to Listen to a Play," he explains that people were forever trapping him in the Algonquin lobby and reading their plays to him. "I don't know why they select me to read plays to," he says, "because I am . . . one of the worst listeners in the United States. I am always waiting for people to stop talking . . . so that I can talk." Sleepy, bored, or inebriated, he would find himself inadvertently answering questions being read to him from the script. "How've you been, Jim?" the playwright might read aloud from the manuscript. "Fine," the half-conscious Thurber would reply. Thurber was too well known about town to have to work at publicizing the book. Newspaper items about it refer to Thurber's "frolicsome evenings," when he was "likely to leave several cafés hurricane struck." Critics found him a "cold-blooded dissembler" beneath the humor, "intent on pulverizing the human race." "He is a rousing spirit in the cafés," the columnist O. O. McIntyre wrote, "where he lends himself to the warming gesture of applying the 'hot foot' as well as giving a yank, *en passant*, to the occasional bright beard of a serious thinker."

Lisle Bell of the *Tribune* found Thurber "as blithe as Benchley, as savage as Swift," kind to dogs, waiters, and taxi drivers, but mistrustful and destructive toward other manifestations of life. Charles Poore, of the *Times*, warns that "Mr. Thurber's manias are loose again," and calls Thurber "a James Joyce in falseface," who arranges for his characters to take their subconscious out on benders. His final conclusion: it is the funniest book of the year. The *Manchester Guardian* saw in Thurber something of the imaginative quality that recalled T. S. Eliot's Sweeney or Joyce's Bloom. His life work, said the *Guardian*'s critic, "may be described as the adequate revenge of the American male upon the American female."

The office move had added to Thurber's sense of dislocation and a restless yearning to change his professional as well as his personal life. He would pursue his old duties at the new offices only until the end of 1935. Russell Maloney was Thurber's understudy as chief Talk writer and editor. (Maloney had also joined the *New Yorker* bowling team, which included Thurber and Morris Ernst; "Thurber preferred duckpins," Ernst says.) In later years, a chronically cynical Maloney would give his ungracious impressions of the man he replaced and of a Talk of the Town department that for years to come would bear the Thurber imprint:

> Thurber brought the neuroses to English prose. . . . A tall, thin, spectacled man with the face of a harassed rat, Thurber managed to convey to his office associates something of his own sense of impending doom; [he contributed a] Gothic atmosphere. . . . But for that matter, any subjective writer, certainly any humorist, is a potential neurotic.

In his years of piloting Talk, Thurber had walked the byways of the city from early 1928. He had visited the newly opened Reptile Hall of the American Museum of Natural History, describing in fascinated detail the fat Brazilian horned frogs. (His interest in them and other odd animals, such as the raccoon bear, would show up in slightly different form in his "Our New Natural History," drawn from the same "sheer figment of . . . craftsmanship" that he believed lay behind nature's own living compositions.) He had reported the finding of seventeenth-century cemeteries in lower Manhattan; visited the hotels, restaurants, and bars frequented by William Sydney Porter (O. Henry), Richard Harding Davis, and Stephen Crane. He had written authoritatively of the Empire State Building, which he visited while it was under construction, and the new Hotel St. George in Brooklyn; he had composed vivid accounts of Mayor Walker and Admiral Byrd making early radio broadcasts; told of a zeppelin landing in Lakehurst, New Jersey; of the last day of the old Waldorf on Thirty-third Street; of the hysteria of women struggling to get through the doors of a department store on bargain day; and of a Simon & Schuster tea party for Robert Ripley and his new book, *Believe It or Not*.

He had spent ten minutes behind a screen trying to watch the Culbertsons, Lenz, and Jacoby play bridge. He had heard a Connecticut whippoorwill providing a clear obbligato during an outdoor symphony concert near Weston. He had interviewed Huey Long in his room at the Hotel New Yorker; toured the Pulitzer mansion; and inspected the burned-out cruise ship *Morro Castle* in Asbury Park, New Jersey.

At the end of 1935, he opted to leave the staff and embark on a freelance arrangement with the magazine. He would no longer work closely with Ross, though there would be editorial conflict between the two in the decades ahead.

"The atmosphere of the office was never the same after Thurber quit his desk job," says Rogers Whitaker. "He was always blowing up, or pretending to blow up—usually because Ross wanted him to change something in one of his drawings, or in a casual. Ross always smoothed it out, and Thurber always eventually agreed to make the change."

"Thurber made himself larger than life in his writing," says Charles Cooke.

"Ross saw himself as smaller than life. That was all it took to keep the two men from really being friends."

"Ross thought there was only one way a sentence should be written—clearly," says Eugene Kinkead. " 'What's meant here?' Ross was always marking on a Thurber manuscript. Thurber was more than adequate when handling facts, but his forte was putting in flashes of color and warmth. Ross had a corny love of the dramatic that Thurber had the sense and courage and wit to resist. And he was too creative not to be annoyed by Ross's realistic queries that centered on literal meanings. Ross gained considerable experience over the years with people who turned out to be great writers, drunks, or both. Thurber helped him acquire some of the experience, and certainly Ross taught Thurber a lot. The two of them, out of conflict but mutual respect, made up the principal force behind Talk for eight years."

Thurber's last Talk story, for which he received a hundred and fifty dollars, then the going rate, appeared in the Christmas issue of 1935. Strolling Fourteenth Street, he wrote:

> When we crossed Fifth to go east on Fourteenth, a gentleman airing his brace of Scotties got into momentary trouble with a vendor who was making his small mechanical dogs scurry about on the sidewalk. The vendor didn't care—it attracted a laughing crowd; the gentleman was deeply embarrassed; the Scotties were highly indignant. East of Fifth, on such a night, you come upon the chestnut men, and the pretzel women who look exactly alike, dumpy, bell-shaped, wound about with brown sweaters and brown mufflers. . . .
>
> We missed this year the vendors of those old-fashioned German Christmas cards with the tinsel snow and the rich colors. There used to be several of them around, and a sad man who played "O Little Town of Bethlehem" on a flute. Nobody seemed to know what had become of them.

The year had been a watershed one for Thurber. Honeycutt had married a man ten years younger than himself; he had experienced divorce, marriage, and the end of an eight-year office life at the New Yorker, which had been a second home to him. Somewhat ambivalently, he heralded the beginning of 1936 with an inscription in his brother William's copy of The Middle-Aged Man on the Flying Trapeze: "Off with the old crap, on with the new."

46

That Leftist Assumption

The Leftist assumption . . . has always been that writers should deal only with proletarian problems. . . . In my many meetings with the Leftist minds, I have pointed out that, ideology or no ideology, it must be apparent to any critical mind that the kind of thing I do cannot be made over to fit a dialectic.

—Letter to Dale Kramer, August 5, 1950

By the mid-1930s, the *New Yorker* had become unique in periodical publishing. Its circulation remained small (125,000 in 1934) but it was favored by advertisers, and held, at campuses and other outposts of elite readership, an avant-garde position in literature, journalism, and criticism. It was far from what Harold Ross, or anybody else, had thought it would be, but Ross had learned along the way and developed a strong grasp of what was right for the magazine. He never completely surrendered his early commitments to a comic content: Talk stories and the departments were usually written in a playful mode; funny first-person experiences were encouraged in casuals; cartoons were sprinkled generously through the pages, and out of respect for E. B. White's fascination with newsbreaks—a hand-me-down from turn-of-the-century newspaper columnists—they were featured as column fillers long after Ross's death. (The present *New Yorker* uses newsbreaks only infrequently, presumably for old time's sake.)

The carefree tone of the magazine in its first five years suited the majority of readers, who were unaware of or uninterested in the growing malfunctions within their society. But changes in the intellectual weather were becoming felt as the Depression highlighted the apparent breakdown of laissez-faire capitalism. As early as the end of 1929, 60 percent of American families already earned less than was necessary for basic human needs.

The hard times provided a rich seedbed for social protest and its literary reflection. Political doctrine was making its way into novels and dominating literary quarterlies. Marxism, seen as redemptive change, was claiming the interest—however temporary—of a number of distinguished intellectuals. They and their adherents were a passionate, vocal, pragmatic, and intolerant group, and the *New Yorker* soon came under their fire as an annoying and irrelevant distraction.

Ross was apolitical and on guard against any use of his magazine's pages to foster a cause. For years, he worried that A. J. Liebling had a leftist ax to grind in his writing, though no one could find much evidence of it. Thurber had it right when he wrote in *The Years with Ross*:

> Harold Ross, inherently cautious, fundamentally conservative, stuck res-olutely to his original belief that the *New Yorker* was not a magazine designed to stem tides, join crusades, or take political stands. He was not going to print a lot of "social-conscious stuff," because his intuition told him that, if he did, he would be overwhelmed by it. He has been accused of timidity—and he had a lot of that—of evasion of responsibility, and the loss of his chance to turn his magazine into a voice of protest and rebellion. The *New Yorker*, he stanchly contended, was not the *New Republic* or the *Nation*; it wanted superior prose, funny drawings, and sound journalism, without propaganda.

The pages were protected by the professional experience and instinct of their editors and contributors, whose biases centered on producing the best in writing and art with clarity and accuracy. Submissions continued to be rated on their literary merit alone.

The *New Yorker* sailed triumphantly through a decade that saw the older humor magazines, *Vanity Fair*, *Life*, and *Judge*, sink from sight. (Luce bought the *Life* title for a new picture magazine in 1936, and *Vanity Fair* was folded into *Vogue*, its circulation list sold to *Judge*, which went out of business in 1939.) The need for relief during those years of financial and psychological depression spawned excellent film and radio comedies, and the *New Yorker* found an increasing following attracted to writers and cartoonists who still seemed to be having fun.

"Are we important?" Ross once asked Thurber.

"We're just a fifteen-cent magazine," Thurber replied.

But though political and social considerations never deflected Ross's editorial direction, they had begun to bother White, whose Notes and Comment passed for the magazine's editorial position—and that did cause Ross concern.

Had White been less given to self-doubt, he could have dismissed as unimportant the complaints that the magazine was out of stride with the times. In 1934, White's old friend Ralph Ingersoll, in his *Fortune* article on the *New Yorker*, wrote:

> If you complain that the *New Yorker* had become gentler and gentler, more nebulous, less real, it is the Whites' doing; Andy's gossamer writing, in his increasingly important "Notes and Comment," [and] in his flavoring of the whole magazine with captions and fillers, [and] Katharine's . . . civilizing influence on Ross.

Scott Elledge notes in his biography of White that Andy took hard and painfully Ingersoll's attack on the magazine's anemic sociopolitical stands, on its being "irresponsible in ignoring the issues of the Depression," and of not "speaking out forcefully against poverty, greed and injustice." Ingersoll was managing a procapitalist business magazine and hailed from a conservative social background, but he had developed Marxist leanings.

In a 1937 Comment, White, though favoring the New Deal, protested Roosevelt's attempt to pack the Supreme Court with judges favorable to his proposed recovery legislation. Roosevelt's good intentions, wrote White, have "at last got out of hand. . . . America doesn't need to be saved today; it can wait till tomorrow. Meanwhile, Mister, we'll sleep on it." Ingersoll, who favored Roosevelt's move, wrote White in anguished response:

> I am no one to defend Roosevelt whole—too many things about him enrage me. But, so does your gentle complacency. "Let us sleep on it . . ." Andy, Andy!!
>
> Doesn't that well-fed stomach of yours ever turn when you think what you're saying? Let us sleep on suffering, want, malnutrition. Let us sleep too on young men who are so fond of phrasing things exactly that humanity never troubles them.

White may not have known that Ingersoll's political philosophy had moved much farther to the left, encouraged by the screenwriter and playwright Lillian Hellman, who was of stubborn and lifelong Communist persuasion. They had met in 1935 on a plane trip from California and slept together that night, according to William Wright's biography of Hellman. It was love at first acquaintance for Ingersoll. Hellman's principal paramour of many years, Dashiell Hammett, the renowned writer of detective fiction, was undergoing treatment for alcoholism and was temporarily out of the picture; she began an affair with Ingersoll that lasted more than a year. Ingersoll was then developing *Life* into a picture magazine and afterward was the publisher of *Time*, but to please Hellman he became a Communist for a short while. It was on beliefs borrowed from her that he founded *PM*, a leftist, prolabor New York tabloid, in 1940. Both White and Thurber occasionally contributed to the paper, out of their fondness for Ingersoll. (Hellman had thought up the newspaper's title.)

Elledge believes that the classical White/Ingersoll argument—the claim to freedom versus social conscience—helped a disconsolate Andy decide to take a year's leave from the magazine. Another reason may have been that Thurber had by then left the staff and rarely came to the office, depriving White of a working companionship he had long enjoyed.

Thurber had his own difficulties with the doctrinaire leftists. He saw politics as little more than the perfect playing field for a humorist. He is vague about how he voted prior to 1952—though while in Columbus he undoubtedly favored his father's Republican tickets, locally and nationally. He mentions having voted for Woodrow Wilson in 1916; though he was barely of voting age, he was a Republican poll watcher on that occasion. The 1920 presidential election was of interest to him only as an Ohioan: two Ohioans, Harding and Cox, were the candidates, and Thurber claims that, unable to make up his mind on election day, he tossed a coin, didn't bother to read what came up, and left without voting. In the 1932 campaign, he made fun of letters written to newspaper editors in support of Hoover, but one's impression is that he simply found the election a bore.

He had known hard times and had lived on coffee and doughnuts when he first came to New York from France, but, like White, he was now living in comfort. Ann Honeycutt says that politics was rarely on Thurber's agenda; she herself had been a conservative Republican, "even during the F.D.R. madness," and later was "secretly to the right of Goldwater." After the breakup of her marriage to McKelway, Honey took up with Bruce Barton, the rightist advertising executive who, as a congressman, joined with his colleagues Joseph Martin and Hamilton Fish to bitterly oppose all of Roosevelt's programs. (F.D.R. spoke scathingly, time and again, of "Martin, Barton, and Fish.") Honeycutt was holding Barton's hand when he died.

The Communist party had its strongest American showing in the elections of 1932, when it registered only 102,221 voters, though many members didn't register, not wishing to attract FBI interest and a threat to their livelihoods. Whether members or sympathizers, they were a noisy lot. In 1932, White had lightly dismissed all of them in a Comment: "We have decided that Communists have bad manners." And Thurber adds, to Dale Kramer, "White and I have always regarded the leftist attitude toward us as being arrogant, pretentious, and snobbish in the strong tradition of the intellectual bias."

Kyle Crichton, writing for the *New Masses* under the name "Robert Forsythe," joined in attacking the *New Yorker* for its complacency. In the early thirties, he recalls, he felt that the *New Yorker*'s people "were still living in their cream-puff towers, with the world crashing all around them." His attack led to what he considers overreaction by the *New Yorker*.

> They were lacerated by every whisper of criticism; they cherished their resentments endlessly. Even in the days when the fate of the magazine was in doubt, the staff had acquired an arrogant air which held that when the *New Yorker* had spoken, the last word had been said.

In his book *Total Recoil*, Crichton adds, "James Thurber is the only *New Yorker* regular who could mention the magazine without crossing himself."

Both the Spanish Civil War (1936–1939), in which communism was on the side of the democratically elected government, and the rise of Fascism in Europe gained some sympathy for the far-left movement, and further encouraged the American literary proletariats, who wanted a worker's society modeled on that of the Soviet Union. Beginning in the early thirties, there were few cocktail parties Thurber could attend without being forced to defend the *New Yorker*'s above-it-all attitude and his contributions to it. Like Robert Benchley, Thurber was not yet ready to worry about the world. To do so would result, he and Ross believed, in what Ross called "grim" writing. Thurber also felt strongly that the true writer disavowed his craft and himself by hiring out his typewriter to a cause.

His position got him into an argument with Lillian Hellman at Tony's that led to his throwing his drink at her. Her escort, Hammett, quickly stepped in and pushed Thurber against the wall, saying, "That's enough." He thought he had calmed Thurber and turned away, but Thurber promptly seized another drink from a table and threw it at him. Hammett ducked, and the drink hit a waiter, a brother of Tony's. Tony called the police. They were all taken to the station, where Thurber finally apologized, and the charges were dropped.

His anger could have been fed by a sublimated fear. Entertainers usually live by a determined innocence of significant issues. Thurber and his fellow humorists were the products of a period that demanded wit and comedy and provided a lucrative market for it. Thurber eventually saw beyond the limits of his mandate as comic artist, but at that time Lillian Hellman's insistence on writing for social change would have annoyed and scared him. It seemed that more and more of the intellectuals he knew and admired were moving toward her position, and he sought to protect himself from a literary trend that could endanger his career. His "impure" (as he called it) vocation had lastingly defined him in his mind. He lived his professional life in terms of anecdotes, the quick piece, the quicker drawing. Privately, he could debate the grave issues, but his art had to be kept separate. His lashing out at the literary proletariat was less from stricken conscience than from a sense of threat posed by the earnest doctrinaire writers who were attracting so much attention at the time. If they were right, then his work, his bread and butter, was useless. Like the other intelligent humorists, all he had contracted to do was entertain. Later he would try playing Hamlet; for the time being, playing an exceptionally good Falstaff was an enjoyable living and a part he was sure of.

The circle of Algonquin wits had been breaking up. ("There is less here than meets the eye," Tallulah Bankhead told Alexander Woollcott after attending one of the famous luncheons.) Social politics was one reason that the circle's members drifted apart, according to Gibbs's murderous Profile of Woollcott in the *New Yorker*:

> It was an exciting and gratifying time for everybody, but its very magnificence spelled the end of the Algonquin group as a local phenomenon. . . . Those who didn't move away were by now temperamentally unfit for the old close association, since there is nothing more enervating to the artist than the daily society of a lot of people who are just as famous as he is. The new conscience, born of dark doings abroad [Hitler's rise to power], also had some bearing on it. Mr. Woollcott's friends, who had no political convictions worth mentioning in 1920, began to think rather intensely and presently occupied conflicting positions ranging all the way from mild liberalism to the ultimate hammer and sickle.
>
> They grew apart, meeting only occasionally and usually by accident.

Woollcott initially thought the Gibbs Profile of him was favorable; when his friends convinced him it wasn't, he decided never to forgive Ross. A few of his supporters, like the Alfred Lunts, canceled their subscriptions, and

Noel Coward nursed a grudge against the magazine throughout his life. Once, when Woollcott thought he was dying, he wrote Ross asking that they meet and make up. Ross felt it was the least he could do for a dying man. But Ross's agreeable response so improved Woollcott's physical condition that he called off the meeting.

In a 1934 casual, "Notes for a Proletarian Novel," Thurber takes a swing at the literary proletariat, lamenting the disappearance of "ironic and satirical novels" that "made fun of Everything, in a nicely polished way,"

> but you can't do that any more because Everything has become sombre and important in the last few years. Authors privileged to live in this age must write novels about the workingman, with a drab economic background—and don't let me see any of you sneaking into fine old Edith Wharton drawing-rooms. . . . There is a hint implicit in literary reviews that unless authors give up monkeying around with well-to-do characters who fritter their time away on Love, something is going to happen. There is no place for Love any more, either.
>
> As much as I care about Individualism and Love, I'm not so dumb but what I see that I'll have to settle down to a book about factory life if I'm going to keep up with the times. Unfortunately, the only factory I was ever in in my life was the Buckeye Steel Castings Company, in Columbus, Ohio, [about which] I can't remember a thing except that I stumbled over a big iron bucket and was lame for days. . . .

He tries to remember his associations with the working class. During a summer job with the State-City Free Employment Agency, an unemployed cleaning woman seeking work simply stared at him and asked if he had been saved. ("I lied and said that I was. . . .")

> I did have . . . some slight connection with the recent waiters' strike in this city as a member of a committee interested in their welfare . . . but I doubt very much whether I could make a novel out of it. In the first place, I haven't the slightest idea what waiters do when they go home.

Thurber was certain that the proletarian writers knew no more about the home life of waiters than he did. He felt that the leftists he knew and liked—Dorothy Parker and Heywood Broun, for example—made little sense on social issues. Broun was a newspaper editor and columnist, and a Socialist who earned twenty-five thousand dollars a year—twice Thurber's income. All of

Broun's two hundred and fifty pounds were dedicated to the underdog. Broun suffered from claustrophobia and gave up his job as a theater critic because sitting in theaters nearly suffocated him. He couldn't ride on trains. His hypochondria led him to suppose that he had a bad heart, and he used to bring so many of his cardiograms to the Algonquin luncheons that Woollcott suggested he hold a one-man show of them. Broun's support of Lewis Gannett's efforts to form the Newspaper Guild got him in trouble with the management of the *World*, which carried his column at the time. The *World* folded in 1931, but Broun carried on.

Thurber had indeed been on a committee, at Broun's invitation, formed on behalf of the city's striking waiters. The committee met at the home of Norman Thomas, the country's leading Socialist. Broun told Thurber not to take a taxi, for the cabdrivers were also on strike. Thurber, who had written an angry piece on the crosstown-bus situation and was still sore about it, took a cab, driven by an independent, nonstriking hackie, to within two blocks of the Thomas residence and walked the rest of the way. Broun arrived in the borrowed limousine of a millionaire friend, driven by a liveried chauffeur whose name was actually James, and who later drove Thurber and Broun to the Players club for martinis. There was, Thurber told Broun there, "a thin line of crap running through the whole thing." One evening Broun and Thurber met for drinks, beginning at Tony's and going on from there. At 2:00 A.M. Broun reminded Thurber that he wasn't to cross the picket line at "21." Thurber pointed out that at the moment they were seated at the bar at "21" and therefore must have already crossed it.

Word reached Broun that Robert Benchley had volunteered to serve meals to Algonquin diners during the strike. The charge was false, but Broun chastised Benchley in his newspaper column and said that if the charge were true he would give up humor. Benchley wrote to Broun and said that Broun had nothing to worry about, since he had obviously given it up already.

Thurber was impressed by the political ineffectiveness of the liberals. When Broun ran for Congress in 1930 on the Socialist ticket, his friends attended a rally for him at which Groucho Marx interrupted Alexander Woollcott at the lectern to inquire how many of the two thousand Broun supporters present actually came from Broun's voting district. Three raised their hands. Ruth Pratt easily won that congressional race.

Aligned against Broun on most of the labor issues were Benchley and Ross, who cheered White on when, in a Comment, he attacked the campaign of the CIO and the Newspaper Guild for a closed shop. White communed with the spirit of Thoreau and was against any organized authority that complicated or in any way rent the tie of man to nature. His stand for simplicity of life, world peace, and individual freedom remained consistent. As the times changed around him over the years, he relented to the point of favoring a world government, and his insightful and poetic observations became a consolation to latter-day liberals without White's having moved much in either ideological direction.

Thurber was against the derogatory use made by the *New Masses* of Dorothy Parker's reference to humor as a shield and not a weapon. No day went by without "my crazy species," as Thurber put it, needing a shield. Thurber believed that he used his humor as both shield and weapon, but would probably have been hard put to say which was which most of the time.

As early as January 1928, less than a year after joining the *New Yorker*, Thurber was spoofing the *Nation*—with primitive nonsense, to be sure—on its tendency to relate "the common man" to every current event, including foreign affairs. In "After an Evening Spent in Reading the *Nation*," he pretends that a service-station owner named Burtz, "a liberal working man," has been persecuted by big business:

> On December 19th, the Standard Oil Company of New Jersey cut off Burtz's supply of oil for his filling station. He was forced to order his oil from Russia. Great Britain took this as a direct implication that Russia condoned the murder of aged Glasgow women. Russia immediately went to the Geneva conference to make trouble. Five persons were killed and scores of others were wounded. Milwaukee had again paid in blood for its political dominance by the oil interests.

Nor did Thurber spare the rightists. The Hoover administration kept promising a business upturn, and Thurber drew a man with glasses, lying on his back, top hat and cane on the ground, feet in the air. The man is labeled "Business," and the cartoon is entitled "The Upturn."

The *New Yorker* carried an entire page (March 18, 1933) of Thurber drawings and captions entitled " 'Don'ts' For the Inflation"—hints on how to survive the business crisis: (1) "Don't shout over the phone"; (2) "Don't run"; (3) "Don't lie down"; (4) "Don't keep saying 'hark!' "; (5) "Don't scream"; (6) "Don't offer money you printed yourself." The comedy was in the looney postures of the Thurber Man.

Thurber had long shared White's disdain for the Communist literary movement. He was therefore geared for combat when, in 1934, Robert Coates, the most intellectual of his friends, took him to a party where the guests included a number of Marxist writers and critics, including Michael Gold, a contributor to the Communist party's *Daily Worker*. Thurber, seen as one of the bourgeois effete, promptly got into an argument with Gold. Cooler heads prevented a brawl, but the inoffensive and gentlemanly Coates was humiliated by Thurber's behavior.

Coates's patience and friendship with Thurber had been tested innumerable times. Two years before, he had taken Thurber to a party given by Matthew Josephson. Coates and Josephson, a literary biographer, were fellow revolutionaries in the cultural experiments of the Dada movement during the early postwar years in Paris. By 1932, Josephson was back in America and had rented a barn for the summer, near the Coateses' house in Connecticut. Hart Crane, who had just returned from France and was still at work on his most famous poem, "The Bridge," was present. In *Life among the Surrealists*, Josephson writes that Coates's "thin long-legged friend, Thurber, who under normal circumstances was the most entertaining and lovable of men," did not get along with Crane, "who was likely to be unruly." Josephson continues:

> Thurber, though well-read and knowledgeable, used to pretend to be a simple middlebrow with no taste for such obscure poetry as Crane's. Evidently Hart said something that gave offense to Thurber; there were high words and they began to brawl. I heard Thurber cry: "Hold me back before I hit him." Crane had drawn himself up in fighting posture, while two persons seized Thurber and held his arms as he had requested. Then Thurber stepped backward, and one of his legs went into a big bucket filled with water and ice just behind him. He howled with surprise at the cold and wetness, then hopped about on one leg so that all the fight went out of him. He laughed at himself; we all laughed until the tears came.

Thurber had later regrets when that same year Crane took his own life.

One evening, sitting in the Algonquin lobby, Thurber read Malcolm Cowley's review in the *New Republic* of Joseph Wood Krutch's newest book of essays. Krutch was an intellectual of the proletarian school, and the review moved Thurber to write a fifteen-page letter to Cowley, who was editor of the *New Republic*. He knew Cowley through Coates—the two lived a mile from each other. The marathon letter was mailed in a manuscript envelope, and Cowley, thinking it was something being submitted for publication, set it aside unopened for several weeks. In it, Thurber asks Cowley for help with the

> great many things concerned with economics, communism, writing, proletarianism, life, happiness, love, and whatnot. . . . I am not so tied

up in my own interests and in the peculiar field of my own thought and writing that I have not observed that Great Changes . . . are taking place. My essential weakness, in this regard, is that I am not, in certain subjects, well enough read to be able, conscientiously, to set myself up as a spokesman, a student, a protagonist, or even a sound and well-documented opponent of many of the great and important factors that now enter into national and international life. . . . I have argued, even fought, with certain literary people who espouse Marxism, Communism, etc. . . . They have usually . . . won the arguments, but they have never won me. . . .

I refer . . . to my unhappy and, in some ways, deplorable set-to with Michael Gold some months ago at a party to which I wasn't even asked. Even Bob Coates, who took me there, was disgusted with me and as tolerant and generous as he has always been with me, in my cups and my moods, he told me, out in the street afterwards, that I had made a horse's ass of myself and he disappeared into that New York night he loves so well, leaving me to get home as best I could. . . . After every such scene I always wake up in remorse and regret and real anguish. . . .

I regard Mike Gold as a literary communist. He and various others like him are enough to make me turn against the whole idea of communism, the worker, Russia, proletarianism. I think that what communism needs is . . . more communists and fewer writers. . . .

These men give their own ideas. I have never yet seen one of them quote, directly, a worker or a leader of workers. . . . I have read Gold himself on the subject of Ring Lardner and . . . Thornton Wilder. Am I to believe that before Communism can get anywhere all writers must cease to write anything that isn't proletarian? . . . We have largely let the world go to pieces around us, thinking it would all blow over like the Civil War and take its little place in history. We know now it won't. . . . It is our own fault that we have thus been caught out of life, fishing in our little stream . . . planning our vacations, making love to a girl, writing silly little pieces about timid men afraid of the night that comes with sundown, oblivious of the night that comes with revolution. . . . It seems to me that the literary communists have almost got to the point where they believe . . . that you must be a communist to make even your private life important. . . . I remember that when Gold and I were arguing—and by the way he started it by saying to me (whom he didn't know then, even my name) that the New Yorker was edited by "College punks." . . . Of course I called him a non-college son-of-a-bitch. . . . Instantly he took the sweet martyred attitude that all Bourgeois people want to fight, to use bad words, because, as he said, they are all inferiority complex people. . . . What Gold emphasized was that if I understood Marxism I would do better and truer and more important stories and . . . pictures. For . . . I deal, in my stories and pictures, only with this strange amorphous indescribable group known as the Bourgeoisie. . . . It was my contention that my stories and my pictures were about relationships between men and women which are entirely apart from any consideration of economics, politics or anything of the sort. . . .

I don't see how anybody could fail to see, in [Gold's] writings on Wilder and on Lardner and in his talk to me . . . a desire to subject the individual to the political body, to the economic structure. . . . It is this desire to regiment and discipline art . . . that some of us are afraid of.

Thurber tells Cowley that he believes his own inability to figure out what the leftist critics are talking about is the fault of their obscure writing.

The struggling reader . . . puts the whole works down and goes out and gets cock-eyed at Tim's bar and asks Tim . . . what he thinks of things. "It's all balls," says Tim, and the reader goes to bed, sure of only that one thing. . . .

One of my favorite characters . . . was a mythical figure named Tristran. He was born in a land called Lyonesse which sank into the sea. . . . There is no trace and proof of the men he fought with . . . , no sign left that ever a woman named Iseult lived. Yet he was wont to say . . . "I come from Lyonesse and a gentleman am I." . . . I get a kind of solace out of repeating a line never said by a man who never lived from a land that never existed.

It must be almost dawn.

Yours,

Jim Thurber

Cowley replied that to answer Thurber's letter properly "I'll have to get mildly cockeyed and sit down at a typewriter after three o'clock in the morning and let myself go." He attributed the "narrowness, intolerance, [and] sectarianism" among the Communists to "a sense of uneasiness in the air as if everybody had the idea there is going to be serious trouble within the next few years" and "everybody wanted to get his own ideas straightened out while there was still time for thinking. The world would be a much more unpleasant place if it weren't for the *New Yorker* and the stories and pictures you do for it. Anybody who wants to abolish the *New Yorker* isn't on my side of the argument."

Impressed by Thurber's passion on the subject, Cowley persuaded Thurber to review *Proletarian Literature in the United States*, a four-hundred-page anthology edited by Granville Hicks, for the *New Republic*. The book was an important publishing event for the literary leftists, and getting one of America's leading humorists to write about it at the *New Republic*'s nominal fee was an editorial and public-relations coup for Cowley. Thurber took the matter to heart, spending, he told Cowley in a nine-page covering letter, at least fifty hours writing fifty thousand words in fifteen attempts at the review.

The piece appeared in the issue of March 25, 1936. In Joseph Freeman's introduction to the volume, Thurber finds bitterness and neurosis in the references to bourgeois love as lechery and narcissism and as the preoccupation of the nonproletariat. Michael Gold's attack on Thornton Wilder "seems as dated as the Dempsey-Carpentier fight." Philip Rahv's essay "loses its points in a mass of heavy, difficult and pedantic writing."

> For what some of these proletarian writers need to learn is simply how to write, not only with intensity, but with conviction, not only with a feeling for the worker but a feeling for literary effects. . . .
>
> Many of the stories are simply not convincing. . . . You don't always believe that these authors *were there*, ever had been there; that they ever saw and heard these people they write about. They give you the feeling that they are writing what they want these people to have said. . . . It is not the subject matter, but the method of presentation . . . which has raised the bourgeois cry of "propaganda."

Thurber rubs salt into the wounds he has opened by holding up the *New Yorker* as an example of writing that the leftists should follow. Some of the proletarian fiction writers and journalists, he observes, "might profit by an examination into the way Robert Coates or St. Clair McKelway handle such pieces." John O'Hara and Ring Lardner had abandoned the leftist movement after a brief flirtation with it, and Thurber says he "can understand why the Communist literati bewail the loss" of two people who knew how to write.

Almost all the literary criticism could profitably have been left out of the book, Thurber goes on relentlessly. "There is . . . not a note of humor in the anthology." Along with other revolutionary targets, literature can also die on the barricades, he reminds the Marxists. A doctrinaire writer is committed to a body of work that literary judgment later usually discards; the need to fit one's own experience into an ideology is a self-defeating one.

The review came to less than two thousand words; the covering letter to Cowley explaining Thurber's position came to four thousand words. His manuscript had been influenced by nothing but his own feelings as a "bourgeois" writer—"a hell of a goddam loose word," he writes, adding somewhat dishonestly, "After all my grandfather had a stand on Central Market." (The wealthy Fishers would have raised their eyebrows at the implication that their prosperous, large, produce warehouse was a roadside vegetable stand.) He smoldered over Freeman's contention that lechery and narcissism were middle-class sins, and that true love was the monopoly of the proletariat. Sex is obviously a force behind most of literature, Thurber agrees, and the writers of both camps were phallic narcissists at times. "The workers themselves probably didn't bother about such things," he writes. "They simply made love without self-conscious broodings or much introspection. The vulgar, derogatory terms for sexual love were proletarian, not bourgeoise." Proletarian and bourgeois writers in America were living essentially the same life; the differences were arbitrary, not real. Contributors to the anthology, he tells Cowley, wished for a world in which it would be "all right" to work for the *New Yorker*. The proof was that they clearly didn't know the first thing about portraying the actions, idioms, and gestures of a proletariat; they didn't really want to write about the worker; they merely felt that they had to, and this accounted for much of the bitterness they express against the sex life of the bourgeoisie.

John McNulty had once remarked to Thurber that the farmer knows that the city man has better women than he does; Thurber wondered whether the proletariat believed that the bourgeoisie had lovelier and more passionate women, and if that was the basis of the worker's resentment toward the upper class. Thurber, drunk, had told Gold that most literary Communists were personally and physically unattractive—a judgment that a later generation of beleaguered male writers would use against feminists. Thurber's specialty was the relationship between men and women, and it was the factory workers, the soldiers, the shopworkers who invented most of the dirty stories that degraded and laughed off love. Sex, he writes, was in back of every intellectual or literary cause; it had little to do with worker or capitalist but a lot to do with the artist.

"I don't think the revolution is here or anywhere near here," he concludes. "I believe the only menace is the growing menace of fascism. I also firmly believe that it is the clumsy and whining and arrogant attitude of the proletarian writers which is making the menace bigger every day."

Thurber throws more light on himself than on his subject. He lays claim to knowing as much about workers' troubles as anyone, offering the slightly absurd credential that he had been poor as a boy and as a newspaperman. In truth, he had been given a college education, comparatively rare in those days, known few menial jobs, and, even before the *New Yorker*, had enjoyed the low-paying but prestigious white-collar status of the journalist. If, as he insists, sex was the hang-up of proletarian writers, it seems also to have been his, however he sublimated it through humor and art.

Thurber wasn't wrong in not taking the leftist writers seriously. They mistook American labor for true revolutionaries, and volunteered themselves as its articulate representatives in an effort to win to their side not only the masses but the intellectual elite that every political movement has needed in order to succeed. As Thurber assumed, few workers understood either the language or the principles put forward on their behalf—they didn't want revolution, but security. In the next round of antiestablishment violence, starting in the 1950s, the worker would not only be of no help, he would join the vigilantes in beating the liberal protesters in the street. All he had wanted was the right to join a union, to strike, to get his share of what the system produced, and then to preserve the status quo. When the aging, disillusioned former Marxist intellectuals were being humiliated and harassed by government in the McCarthy period, the workers joined in throwing rocks and jeering them as "lousy Commies." Thurber, though he had disliked the leftists of the thirties, was angered over their political persecution by Congress and the Justice Department.

Following the publication of Thurber's 1936 *New Republic* review, Cowley invited Joseph Freeman and Thurber to dinner, followed by a party designed to fail. In 1950, Thurber writes to Dale Kramer about it:

> Joe Freeman wrote a ten thousand word preface to "Proletarian Literature" and I took a crack at it. Cowley thought it would be amusing to have us both to dinner without knowing about it in advance. All kinds of writers dropped in after dinner, including J. T. Farrell, Kyle Crichton, and one or two admittedly fascist editors. I represented the New Yorker, capitalistic, liberal middle class, and whatever. With a wonderful chance for argument, the Leftists turned on one another, Freeman cornering Farrell in the dining room and saying, "You have no implementation." The New Yorker and the fascists escaped without scars, not having been attacked once. Edmund Wilson—not there—had liked my review, but

Farrell called it "One of the dumbest things I ever read." This did not lead to debate, since I challenged him to name one piece written in English over the entire range of history, that he admired. After three minutes of thought he said, "A poem Cowley wrote about his mother." It was a drinking evening in the bourgeois manner with the best Scotch. Expressions like "but he's a Lovestonite" flew about. In an essay in the old LIFE, Crichton had said that I wrote in a vacuum. Cornered by my wife on this point, he said, "But it's a very nice vacuum." . . .

When I said to one amiable guy that I would have to continue what I do, he said, "We would make certain concessions,"—that is to say, in a Leftist America, certain humorists and comedians would be suffered. . . .

Dwight MacDonald, in the Partisan Review, 1940, said that "My Life and Hard Times" was good humorous writing by a Know Nothing. I tried to argue with him at [Edmund] Wilson's, but the arguments of my class are considered proof of inferiority complex which would rub off on anyone who replied in kind.

Kramer later asked Cowley about Thurber's letter regarding the party. Cowley replies:

Party to which Jim Thurber referred was probably early spring 1936. I had the idea—still have it—that people were laying too much emphasis on opinions in the abstract and not enough emphasis on personal values; so I had a party and invited people of all opinions, thinking they might get along together better than they expected. There were liberals, Stalinists, Trotskyists, even a mild fascist (Seward Collins of the *American Review*)—Mike Gold, of proletarian literature, Jim Thurber, who had unfavorably reviewed the anthology—a whole collection that would have been impossible to assemble two years later. Party wasn't very successful. I was caught in a corner with Seward Collins, who was pouring out his soul, and missed a lot that was going on—but Thurber was partly right, the Marxists did fight among themselves. . . . and he was partly wrong, because I heard they got round to insulting him too, or at least Mike Gold insulted him.

Gold charged Thurber with being "an impotent bourgeois . . . with nothing in his pants," Cowley says, "and that really rankled him. In those two long letters to me he kept circling back to this subject of what's the difference, if any, between bourgeois sex and proletarian sex? He was . . .

sensitive about the domineering ways of the literary communists although his sympathies were liberal and leftward . . . but he was also furious with the literary communists for their attacks on the *New Yorker*. At a later stage he was standing up for freedom of speech during McCarthy's years when the ex-communists weren't. He hadn't changed; society had."

Following White's editorial against F.D.R.'s tampering with the Supreme Court, Kyle Crichton, in the *Nation* (March 20, 1937), wrote nastily that the *New Yorker* "hitherto aloof from the political struggle," had now "stepped down to join the free-for-all among us old and hardened gladiators." Crichton pretended to lament the passing of "the last and best of our ivory towers." In the past, he added, when troubled by events, "we would awake and reach for the *New Yorker*. There in the odyssey of Hyman Kaplan, the drawings of Thurber . . . we'd find calm and refreshment until the dawn came. . . . No longer." Elsewhere he adds, "Throughout the entire career of the *New Yorker*, they have produced only three names that mean anything in a world sense: James Thurber, John O'Hara, and Salinger."

Thurber didn't let Crichton's jab against the *New Yorker* go unpunished. A month later, he came out with "What Are the Leftists Saying?" in which he pretends to take a worker with him to a meeting of socially conscious leftist literary critics.

> The critics themselves believe, of course, in the education of the worker, but they are divided into two schools about it: those who believe the worker should be taught beforehand why there must be a revolution, and those who believe that he should be taught afterward why there was one. This is but one of many two-school systems which divide the leftist intellectuals and keep them so busy in controversy that the worker is pretty much left out of things.

In the casual, "Kyle Forsythe" joins the meeting late, thinks the analysis of Sinclair Lewis is about Upton Sinclair, and begins to talk about "escapism," which "means the activities of anyone who is not a leftist critic or writer." When the protagonist attempts to explain further to the worker what some of the leftist terms are—"dialectical materialism," for example—the worker flees the meeting, followed by Thurber calling, "Hey, worker! Wait for baby!"

A month later, he gets even with Joseph Freeman in "How to Write a Long Autobiography." Freeman had just published *An American Testament*, filled with correspondence and running to three hundred thousand words, Thurber estimates. Freeman quotes three hundred words from a letter to him from Irwin Edman, Columbia University professor and philosopher. "It is followed by a thousand-word letter Mr. Freeman wrote to Mr. Edman in answer to his," of which the opening sentence is: "It was my idealistic, religious, artistic bias which made me blind to pragmatism."

That is the topic sentence of a letter which somehow does not sound like a letter to a friend at all. It sounds more like an essay written to save in a file and someday print in a book. You get the inescapable feeling that the original was sent to a friend in order to get a well-written essay in return, which also could be used in the book. . . . I could never keep a carbon copy of a letter for fifteen or twenty years, the way Mr. Freeman can. If I keep a letter two weeks, I am doing fine. Then, too, my friends never write me long letters dealing with profound subjects. Their letters are usually hurried and to the point, and they sometimes deal with matters . . . I wouldn't want to have exposed in a book even after I was dead. . . .

I have got a few letters from well-known writers in my time [but] none of them would be usable in a book even if I could find them. Some of them are both illegible and illiterate, as if they had been written at a bar. . . .

I have one at hand now . . . which came just a day or two ago and hasn't been lost yet. . . . (the letter is written in black India ink on aquamarine paper):

"Dear Mr. Thumber:
For agree blest you've been out of my perine parasites. The obline being in case you're interested, a girl whose name escapes me, but merits swell pecul, and I know you'd know who she is . . ."

I'm afraid I'm not going to be able to use any letters . . . in my own 300,000-word testament, unless I . . . sneak a few out of Mr. Freeman's book. He'd probably never miss them.

The decade moved on, the *New Yorker* continuing to treat the cataclysmic issues of the times mostly as social embarrassment, the quarreling Communists losing membership following Stalin's nonaggression pact with Hitler and his savage purges of his own people. As Anatole Broyard pointed out in a *New York Times* column, reading Farrell, Dos Passos, and other social protesters of that period is like seeing old movies on TV late at night. And as Archibald MacLeish said to his fellow poet and Thurber's friend Mark Van

Doren, in the fifties: "Anybody who takes the Americans too seriously certainly doesn't catch their temper, which is why the Marxists were always wrong."

"I tell you there isn't going to be any insurrection."

47

Those Lovely Youngsters

Last night we started with Manhattans at our little cottage and then went dancing at the Bermudiana with Ronald and Jane Williams, two lovely youngsters I met when I visited the Sayres here. He edits *The Bermudian* magazine. Jane is one of the world's prettiest girls (Helen says I kept telling Jane last night she was *the* world's most beautiful girl). We sat up all night and drank Scotch—the first time we have misbehaved really.

—Letter to the Whites, April 1936

In March 1936, the Thurbers, worn down by their debilitating Manhattan lifestyle, fled to Bermuda. Thurber remembered the good times he had had four years before, when he and the sportswriter Don Skene visited Joel and Gertrude Sayre there. The four had specialized in barbershop harmony; Skene, who wouldn't get up in the morning until he had been served a cup of rum, particularly liked "Honey, Honey, Bless Your Heart." During one night of singing, "we ran out of tunes," says Thurber, "and our host suggested that we recruit a couple of 'youngsters' from Shorelee Cottage, a few yards away." The youngsters were "a blown-away Welshman," as Ronald Williams referred to himself, and his wife, Jane. He was thirty-two; she, twenty-seven.

In his last days, when Thurber was dying of a hematoma, or a blood tumor on the brain—Helen and others supposed it was simply his thyroid condition taking a turn for the worse—he was often in a semicrazed state; on one occasion, he persuaded his old friend Jap Gude to fetch him from Cornwall and take him to Manhattan. He had to "get away from Helen," he told Gude. In confiding this to her dentist, a sad and resigned Helen added, "He's talking about going to Bermuda to see Janey Williams. She was the only one who could deal with him during his hyperthyroid periods."

As of that spring of 1936, Jane, an American girl from Geneva, New York, permanently replaced Minnette Fritts, Eva Prout, and Ann Honeycutt in Thurber's Mitty-like romantic illusions. She was a safe repository for his daydreams, fourteen years younger than he, happily married to a man Thurber came to like very much, ever gracious, proper, and funloving, and eventually a mother of five daughters and a son. ("If he really was in love with me," says Jane, "he was 'nicely' in love.") When Thurber's eyesight finally left him unable to distinguish faces, he took with him into the dark the bright memory of a thirty-one-year-old Jane Williams. "You always have lighted candles in your eyes," he would tell her after his blindness, "so I'm still able to see you." He was never heard to speak unkindly to her or of her, which makes her unique in Thurber's coterie of women. Ronald Williams, protective of his marriage, and quite aware of the find he had in Jane, accommodated Thurber's years of infatuation with his wife with great amiability, recognizing, no doubt, that little untoward can happen to a woman on a pedestal.

Williams, who had gone to sea at age sixteen for six years, worked for the Furness, Withy shipping line in Bermuda. An extremely erudite man, he was largely self-educated. He began the *Bermudian* in 1929. Its design was influenced by the *New Yorker*, which he admired, and his editorial comments, patterned after Talk of the Town, were entitled "From the Crow's Nest," complete with the first-person plural.

Jane and Ronald met when she and her mother came to Bermuda on vacation. Jane had recently graduated from Shipley, a girls' preparatory school in Bryn Mawr, Pennsylvania. Williams came to the States to court her; they were married in Princeton, in 1931. A friend, T. S. Matthews—later managing editor of *Time* magazine—was the best man.

As editor of the *Bermudian*, Williams became a kind of clearinghouse for literary people visiting the island. He had met the novelist Sinclair Lewis and his wife, the political columnist Dorothy Thompson, in 1934. In the spring of 1936, Lewis was back, accompanied this time by his male secretary of thirteen years, Lou Florey. Dorothy Thompson was in Moscow, working on a book.

"Jane and I had just had dinner with Red, as he insisted we call him, at the Elbow Beach Hotel," Williams recalls. "Lewis didn't drink for six months at a stretch when working on a book, but when he did finish he'd hit the bottle hard. Unfortunately, he was off the wagon on this occasion. He had had a piano hoisted into his hotel room and paid a young couple to sing to him such songs as 'The Keeper' and 'Sweet Molly Malone.' We found him sitting on his bed drinking and sobbing sentimentally as the confused young couple continued to sing. We got through dinner together and he told us he'd heard that two men he'd always wanted to meet were on the island: U.S. Senator Bronson Cutting, who had fought the harmful Hawley-Smoot tariff legislation, and James Thurber. I told him I'd do what I could. I never did reach the Senator.

"The next morning I was riding the horse-drawn bus—autos were banned then—into Hamilton when I spotted Thurber strolling [with Helen] beneath a hibiscus hedge. When I got to the office, I tracked him down in Paget and told him Lewis wanted to meet him. He and Helen were delighted. I called 'Red,' and he invited us all to dinner the following evening.

"When we arrived at the hotel, Florey warned us that Lewis was quite drunk; he'd received a letter that day from his wife, in Russia. The marriage was beginning to break up, and Florey explained that Lewis often went off the deep end when he got a letter from Dorothy.

"As he led us down the corridor, two men came out of Lewis's suite— Hugh Baillie, president of United Press, and his father. They weren't ten paces down the corridor when Lewis began shouting curses at them, and accusing them of having stolen information his wife had collected for her book. They must have heard every word, but they kept going. He was still cursing until he saw Thurber. He grinned boyishly, stuck out his hand and said, 'Hello, Jim, I'm delighted to meet you.' We went downstairs for dinner. Lewis had engaged the entire grillroom and the orchestra for the five of us. He complained that the bass fiddle was missing. Then he began to tell the story from Jim's *The Owl in the Attic* about the man in a country home being frightened by noises in the basement ["Mr. Monroe Holds the Fort"]. He recited most of it verbatim. Lewis was almost as good a mimic as Jim was, and would change his voice with the characters. Thurber was amazed and abashed; Lewis was the first American to have won the Nobel Prize for literature.

"The first course he had ordered for us was oysters on the half shell. Lewis tried to swallow one and started to gag, making a horrible face. He excused himself, said he was going to take a nap, and disappeared. The rest of us finished dinner and went back to Lewis's room for our coats, where we found Lewis in fine shape, as if he had never had a drink. His talk was witty and entertaining. We all got to singing old songs—'Molly Malone,' again, and

Lewis began to sink once more, tears running down his face. 'They don't write songs like that anymore,' he sobbed. It was an amusing evening, one Thurber never forgot."

At one point, Williams remembers, Lewis said that he wanted to read aloud a large backlog of newspaper columns written by his wife—whether in the spirit of love or hate was not clear. This gave Thurber the idea for a cartoon that appeared in the *New Yorker* a few weeks later: the perturbed-looking Thurber Man is writing at his desk furiously, while his wife tells another Thurber Woman, "He's giving Dorothy Thompson a piece of his mind."

It was the only meeting of Lewis and Thurber, both of whom eventually added permanent male stereotypes—Babbitt and Mitty—to the language. One couldn't know, Thurber later told Lewis's biographer Mark Schorer, whether Lewis's drink at 7:00 A.M. was his first of the day or his last of the night.

The Thurbers were staying at a cottage owned by Ada Trimingham, who catered to visiting *New Yorker* editors and writers; the Whites had once rented from her. Thurber writes:

> Dear Katharine and Andy:
> Helen has put on five pounds (she weighed almost nothing when we came here), and she looks better than ever I saw her. So do I. We are both tanned. . . . We went . . . to see [Ada] and I read her your message of love, which pleased her. She thinks a great deal of you and Andy. And of John Mosher and Benchley and Gertrude Benchley. . . . The Williamses [and we] . . . all went to dinner with [Lewis] one night. Your dinner with him, my sweets, was nothing. Nothing. . . . We decided . . . he would be quite a swell guy sober. Maybe because he can, and did, recite most of the Owl in the Attic. The only drunken writer I ever met who said nothing about his own work and praised that of another writer present. He was poured onto the boat that took him home. . . .
> Andy once said I looked like a third-rate British novelist in a dressing-gown when my hair was long. I don't know what he would think I looked like in my mess jacket. It didn't hike up in the back or anything, though. I weigh 165 now. . . .
> We have got up every day at 8 and eaten 3 great meals and gone to bed at 10:30! This is the first time Helen has ever eaten

anything in her life. It has turned us around fine and I hope we keep it up. . . . I got $35 for the proletarian review [in the *New Republic*] and spent weeks on it, but I enjoyed doing something different for a change.

Mrs. T [Trimingham] has . . . all of Benchley (which I have re-read in toto). There is no doubt that Benchley is our No. 1 humorist. He has simply said everything. I think his "Pluck and Luck" . . . is the best collection of humorous pieces in the country, my colleagues. . . .

I have found it nice to work here. I also found out that it is better to work in the day time than at night.

Thurber was to claim that it was on this trip that he first tried to play tennis, though Louise Connell remembers his attempts at the game in the earlier Connecticut years, and Williams says Thurber and Joel Sayre played in Somerset during Thurber's visit in 1932. "He used to wonder why he couldn't hit a good backhand or serve well," says Williams. "He was tall, lean, and had tremendous grace until he got blind, but he was never in first-class health, and was no athlete." But tennis with Helen was a fresh challenge, as Thurber wrote the Whites:

Ada has a tennis court, on which we played ten sets in two days, me cursing every second stroke. . . .

However, I am much better every time I play. Helen is really very good, although she hasn't played for ten years. She used to win cups and things. She trimmed the panties off papa, too. Once in a while I got in a fine forehand drive down the line. But in making a backhand I look and act like a woman up under whose skirts a bee has climbed. I will get over this. I must get over it.

Helen was already giving him helpful comments on his writing—comments that he was heeding: "Helen says I have used too many 'my pals' etc. in this letter, so you can cut them out. She is always right."

Ross had begun a series called "Where Are They Now?" about people formerly in the news but now long out of it. As in Talk, the reporting was done by others, with Thurber the rewrite man. The seventeen articles ran from April 18, 1936, to September 17, 1938. Because they were not timely, they could be sent to him when he was off the premises. He had turned in the first two before departing for Bermuda, and when the proofs were held up, he wondered whether Ross had changed his mind about the series. The subjects of the first article were Jack Kilrain and Gertrude Ederle; Ederle, in 1926, was the first woman to swim across the English Channel. He writes to the Whites about his concern and, characteristically, doesn't wish to be given credit due others:

> I got the proofs of the Where [Are They Now?] stories, two of them, and will send them back. . . . I will make what changes I can. . . . I want to thank you for getting some action on those pieces. I was pretty gahdam low about it all when we came here, because I thought nothing would ever be done and I said to Helen that I hoped Kilrain and Ederle would have a suicide pact and ball up the whole dam works. I know it will be a big hit (the series, not the pact). I signed the piece on Kilrain Jared L. Manley for no sane reason. [He would do the same for all seventeen.] There ought to be another name. I don't want mine used because as I have said I don't feel I have a right, or would want, to take full credit for pieces on which [Eugene] Kinkead and others have done so much work. Please see to it that Kinkead knows how fine I thought his reporting and writing of the last four pieces I got was. . . . I want him and Ross to know that I appreciate it. . . .
>
> Give my best regards to everybody, and kiss Ross. He is, as my mother said, a mighty splendid man and, as his mother said, I hope some day he will become connected with the Saturday Evening Post. He deserves a future and I think he will go far.
>
> Special love to you both, from both of us,
Jim & Helen

The Thurbers got along so well with the Williamses that they gave up the guest house and joined them as cotenants of Felicity Hall, a historic mansion owned by a retired admiral, in which Hervey Allen had written his best-selling novel *Anthony Adverse*. Thurber was fascinated by its former slave quarters and the handmade furniture, which included the cheap, old kitchen table used by Allen, who had stipulated, in leaving his furniture there, that nothing associated with him was to be sold. Thurber used the table as his own work station. The house was a stop on guided tours, and he was frequently interrupted in his writing by tourists calling to him through the open window to ask what he was doing. Thurber invariably told them that he was writing *Anthony Adverse* backward.

Williams was getting out a special issue of the *Bermudian* on ocean yacht racing, with articles by several experts. "I had a twenty-two-foot sloop," says Williams, "and I took Thurber out in it for a Sunday sail. He wore shorts for the occasion, but he was awkward and uncoordinated and once got hit in the head by the boom. He was so entertaining in talking about it afterwards that I persuaded him to join my experts in an article for the special issue, though he didn't know the bow from the stern. Jim took the encyclopedia we had, looked up diagrams of full-rigged ships and wrote the first of many pieces he eventually did for me."

According to Thurber's "The Story of Sailing," sailing is the favored topic of conversation in Bermuda. Once at dinner, he writes, the lady next to him asked, "Do you reef in your gaff-topsails when you are close-hauled or do you let go the mizzen-top-bowlines and cross-jack-braces?"

> She took me for a sailor and . . . of course I hadn't the slightest idea what she was talking about.
>
> One reason for this was that . . . "gaff-topsails" is pronounced "gassles," "close-hauled" is pronounced "cold," "mizzen-top-bowlines" is pronounced "mittens," and "cross-jack-braces" is pronounced "crab-apples" or something that sounds a whole lot like that. Thus what the lady really said to me was, "Do you reef in your gassles when you are cold or do you let go the mittens and crabapples?" Many a visitor who is asked such a question takes the first ship back home.

A study of the early Norse vessels, Thurber says, shows that they could make the ship go ahead, turn right, or left, but not completely turn about, which is "the reason the Norsemen went straight on and discovered America." As to the frightening trip in Williams's boat:

> This type of so-called pleasure ship is not only given to riding on its side, due to coming about without the helmsman's volition (spelled "jibe" and pronounced "look out, here we go again!") but it is made extremely perilous by what is known as the flying jib, or boom. . . .
>
> Helmsmen will tell you that they keep swinging the boom across the deck of the ship in order to take advantage of the wind but after weeks of observation it is my opinion that they do it to take advantage of the passengers.

"Thurber never accepted pay for the forty or so pieces he did for me over the years," says Williams. "He did accept some shares of stock in the enterprise and was technically on the board of directors—hardly your average board member, of course." Helen adds that Williams, in another effort to compensate Thurber, once offered to pay a Bermuda artist to paint Thurber's portrait, but Thurber wouldn't sit still for it.

Refusing another ocean sail, Thurber agreed to a canoe trip close to the shore. "We put out off Cambridge Beaches at dawn," says Williams. "Thurber sat in the bow, I paddled at the stern. I had enough sense not to go too far out to sea with Thurber the cargo. I hugged the coast around Daniel's Head, which was then a farm. In the early morning light, Thurber spotted a cow. He wanted to hug the cow. He got out of the canoe in three feet of water and waded ashore, waving at the cow in friendly greeting. The cow backed away from him until it realized it was at a cliff with a twelve-foot drop and could go no farther. It stopped and submitted to Thurber's affectionate embrace."

Except for the war years, the Thurbers visited Bermuda nearly every spring. "We never shared the same rental again," Williams says, "but they always took a place within a stone's throw of us, and were often our overnight guests. In later years, they would stay at an expensive hotel and still spend most of the time at our place—even when their hotel room and meals were already paid for."

In his 1936 piece, "An Outline of Scientists" in which Thurber castigates the scientist who found bloodhounds repugnant, he writes:

> Having been laid up by a bumblebee for a couple of weeks . . . in the cottage I had rented in Bermuda, [I] finally was reduced to reading "The Outline of Science". . . . The bee stung me in the foot and I got an infection (staphylococcus, for short). It was the first time in my life that anything smaller than a turtle had ever got the best of me, and naturally I don't like to dwell on it.

Actually, says Helen, it was some kind of sand fly, and he scratched the bite and infected it. "Jim was a bit of a hypochondriac," says Williams, "even before his serious medical problems began. When the sting had swollen, a Dr. John McSweeney, who had a terrible bedside manner, looked at it and told Thurber that he'd had a patient in Nova Scotia who had been stung by a bee on his finger and that he'd had to amputate the finger. Thurber was very cross at the doctor for frightening him, and wrote a poem, 'Bermuda, I Love You,' dedicated to John P. Sweeney. Its point was that visiting Bermuda could be lethal." An excerpt from the poem:

Maribel Smith scratched her hand with a stick.
She didn't bleed much and she didn't feel sick.
There was just a small cut on one of her paws
But in forty-eight hours she could not move her jaws.
In five or six days they were lighting the candles,
And they bought her a box with bright silver handles.
Or consider the case of Herbert A. Dewer,
Healthy at noon and by nighttime manure.
Herb would have said you were certainly silly
Had you told him that *he* would be soil for a lily;
Or list to the tale of Harrison Bundy,
Here on Tuesday, gone on Monday;
And over the grave of Beth Henderson sigh;
She died from the bite of a common house fly.
And here close beside the murmurous sea
Lies a tall nervous writer stung by a bee.

They had planned to stay only a couple of weeks in Bermuda, but despite the leg infection the Thurbers were having too much fun to leave. They finally boarded the *Queen of Bermuda* for New York on June 3. Thurber had proved he could get his work into the *New Yorker* from a Manhattan apartment; the Bermuda experience showed that he could meet its requirements from more remote locations.

He and Helen returned to the Wismer cottage in Connecticut and began a leisurely search for a house rental in the Berkshire foothills. ("We are happy and calm here in Colebrook," he writes the Whites. "It is a truly lovely spot, for miles and miles and miles. My favorite part of the world.")

An editor at the Alfred A. Knopf publishing house saw book possibilities in the "Where Are They Now?" series, and wrote to Jared L. Manley, in care of the magazine, unaware that it was Thurber's pseudonym. The query stimulated Thurber to get back to reporting, as he told the Whites:

> I'd like to do . . . a kind of Talk of the Country, instead of the Town. I want to see the drought country. My God, this nation is rapidly being covered by sand! I would start my journey with a piece on the New York City water supply problem. There aint going to be any water to drink or bathe in there in about 50 years, my friend, and nobody seems to care. What ever became of tea-pot dome and the oil reserves? What does the million dollar memorial to Harding, in Marion, Ohio, look like now? Do they keep it up? I'd like to spend a day with Clark Gable, or some other

guy making $10,000 a week, while the water is running out and the sand is creeping nearer. What really goes on in Salt Lake City? Are there any communists in Tulsa? I want to go to a luncheon of the Kiwanis club in Akron, Ohio, once the big boom city of my part of the country. . . . Books like this have been done, but Jared Manley would like a crack at it. After all, Knopf is interested. The old urge to report something again, to go to the scene of something, and find out about it, has come back on me.

But Ross was more interested in Europe than in Middle America. Even after World War II, when A. J. Liebling told Ross that his reporting had been focused on overseas stories and he now wanted to look at the interior of America, Ross waved the idea aside, saying, "You wouldn't like it, Liebling." Similarly, Thurber could avoid New York tie-ins only by sending articles from Italy, France, and England.

White was still on the premises and kept Thurber informed of what was happening on the staff. "Did you know," Andy writes him, "that [Hobart] Weekes was compiling a *New Yorker* style book which is longer than *Gone with the Wind* and more complete than Mencken's *American Language*? . . . He has come across one note (when Levick was managing editor) which says: '*Night club* not to be used any more as symbol of gaiety.' "

Ross was still looking for the perfect genius. He knew Stanley Walker's reputation for hiring and training a number of good writers at the *Herald Tribune* and had offered Walker a job on several occasions. By 1935, through a management change of attitude at the *Trib*, Walker had become unhappy there, as he wrote Thurber years later:

Most of my better men had been slipping away to the magazines . . . and I was finding it almost impossible to replace them. The Reids seemed to think that I could get out a good paper with an old rewrite man, two aged semi-pensioners, and some pin-headed and feckless scions of decayed old families that they had foisted on me. My great cavalrymen, Alva Johnston and Beverly Smith and all the rest of that fine group—were gone, and I could not offer good new men enough money to attract them. So I went with Hearst [at the N.Y. *Daily Mirror*] for a few months, quitting in August, 1935, because . . . I could never find out what I was supposed to do, and spent most of my time in interminable and pointless conferences.

St. Clair McKelway heard about the final showdown between Walker and Arthur Brisbane, the *Mirror's* editor, and he and Katharine White persuaded Ross to hire Walker. "It was a vague arrangement," Walker told Thurber, "and I honestly did not have much hope for it. About all [Ross] said was that he hoped I 'could make some sense out of the joint.' Well, no one could do that, as you know."

Before offering Walker the job, Ross first checked with Thurber to learn if he still had a grudge against Walker for the *Mirror's* coverage of Thurber's divorce. Thurber assured him that the matter no longer bothered him enough to throw water jugs.

Walker and Ross never understood one another, McKelway says, and though Walker "had been a crackerjack copy-handler as city editor of the *Trib,* he never learned how to handle copy on the *New Yorker* in the way it had to be handled." Ross realized it, too, and saw to it that the fact pieces Walker planned and assigned went through Katharine White and Gibbs, and back to them for editing. He lasted a year before Ross announced to McKelway that Walker "wasn't making any sense and that something had to be done about the factual end of the magazine."

Much of the administrative chaos, Walker later decided, could not be corrected, because it was the way Ross wanted it. At the *Trib,* "I had been in a position of almost complete authority," Walker says,

> getting things done with a minimum of red tape and monkey business. Therefore the rigmaroles at the *New Yorker* were foreign to me, and helped give me a feeling of impotence.
>
> I think Ross's Army experience influenced his actions on the *New Yorker* to a great extent. He could call the military "idiots" . . . but he loved military systems, the endless memos, the buck-passing. . . . That was why . . . he brought poor Phil Hoyt, a man of no ability whatever, to the magazine. Hoyt had been the youngest lieutenant-colonel in the Army during the war, and Ross thought this meant something. . . .
>
> I encountered an old newspaperman on the street [who] said he wanted to do something for the magazine. . . . I gave him [an assignment]. . . . With a little reworking it made the magazine, and Ross liked it fine. Then it occurred to him that the suggestion and the assignment had not gone through the regular channels . . . cleared and approved in conference. . . . He brooded about this for days. It meant that the military system had been flouted and that something was wrong somehow.
>
> Toward the end of my captivity, Ik Shuman came in one day, having

been parted from Paul Block [newspaper publisher], and suggested that he was in acute distress for quick eating money. I assigned him to a Reporter idea on an old motorman. . . . Ik . . . got the story that afternoon and evening, and wrote it the next morning. It required virtually no rewriting, or even editing, and Ross was so pleased with it that he gave Shuman a job. . . . But, after some time, Ross began to worry about the story. . . . How long had Shuman worked on it? Shuman told him the truth, and Ross was shocked and hurt. He thought such a story should have required at least a week's work and painful lucubration. Then . . . he wondered if he were not being cheated by the writers who took too much time. This way, of course, lies madness.

Ross had earlier offered the managing-editor job to McKelway, who had refused it, wishing to keep some of his time for writing. Knowing that Walker was unhappy and thinking of quitting, Ross approached McKelway again in late 1936, and this time McKelway said he would take on "fact" pieces (articles, Talk, and the weekly departments), if fiction, art, and poetry would continue to be handled by Katharine White and Wolcott Gibbs. He had, in effect, been working for Katharine as an editor and contributor, and Ross agreed that in his new capacity McKelway could report directly to him. McKelway signed a three-year contract at fifteen thousand dollars per year. His two assistants were Sanderson Vanderbilt and William Shawn.

A Thurber cartoon appearing at the time may have been intended to kid McKelway. (The University of Chicago's president, Robert M. Hutchins, expressed such delight with the drawing that Thurber sent him the original.

"He doesn't know anything except facts."

He thanked Thurber for "the man who does not know anything but facts. I am placing him on display so that all members of the faculty will see him and take warning.")

"Thurber was rarely there when I was handling fact," McKelway says, "but we had a good working relationship, mostly by mail and telephone." Thurber turned in his tennis columns, now signed "Foot Fault," to McKelway, as well as the "Where Are They Now?" pieces. "We got the facts for 'Where' through Kinkead and Edward O'Tool," McKelway says, "and sent them on to Thurber." Thurber had warmed toward McKelway over the year; he was pleased by his life with Helen, and Honey, feeling suffocated by her marriage to "Mac," was arranging for a divorce after only a year. She had kept her maiden name.

Ross lost his enthusiasm for the "Where Are They Now?" articles when, in July 1938, one subject, a former child prodigy who passed Harvard's entrance examinations at age nine and matriculated when he was twelve, sued the *New Yorker* for libel and unlawful invasion of privacy. The suit dragged on for years. The magazine was cleared of the privacy-invasion charge—once a notable public figure, always one, it was held, with publicity part of the price of fame. The decision was appealed to the U.S. Supreme Court, which refused to review it, to the relief of the media. The libel charge was upheld, however —though the settlement was small. Thurber's writing, described by the court as "a merciless and ruthless exposure of a once public character who had sought privacy," was held to be only barely libelous. In *The Years with Ross*, Thurber says that the judges missed the point of what he was trying to do: point up the wrongness of parents' pushing precocious children into the glare of public notice, which so often worked to the later disadvantage of the child. Thurber's self-justification sounds lame, a bit like claiming to have hanged a man to show the awfulness of capital punishment. No one doubted the psychic discomfiture of the former prodigy, who was forty years old at the time of the article's publication, at seeing his brilliant childhood potential publicly matched against the mediocrity of his adult life. The suit wasn't two months old when Ross ended the series, publishing only two more that Thurber had already sent in.

Much has been made of Ross's effort to physically insulate the editorial from the business side of the magazine, but the partition had plenty of holes. Raoul Fleischmann often enjoyed taking to lunch, separately, the Whites, Thurber, McKelway, and other editors or contributors he admired. Ross never objected. He had to deal with Fleischmann at board meetings, but avoided him socially when he could. Despite his editorial concentration, Ross was not blind to the realities of the business. An editor's independence and job depend, in the long run, on the publication's financial success, mostly determined by its advertising revenue, which, in turn, is affected by the quality and numbers of the readership. Readership, of course attracted by editorial content, was steadily increasing under Ross, who rarely experienced job insecurity. "He was continually quitting or threatening to quit," says McKelway. "It was his big stick."

His leverage over Fleischmann came not only from the popularity of the *New Yorker* but from the loyalty of a talented staff that might not stay if Ross were let go. Yet, there was the personal satisfaction of achievement behind Ross's gleeful reports to the staff of increased circulation. He often agreed to run material whose literary worth he couldn't judge, on the basis of its promotional value. He was said to have bought Shirley Jackson's "The Lottery," a short story he didn't understand, because he believed it would "get the magazine talked about"—a favorite expression of his. It was partly for the same reason that he acceded to Shawn's request that John Hersey's account of the atomic bombing of Hiroshima be given an entire issue, and for his agreeing to Lillian Ross's controversial Hemingway Profile. His delight in S. N. Behrman's articles on Duveen, the art connoisseur and dealer, was enhanced by his conviction that it would draw further attention to the magazine. An ancillary to his primary goal of a magazine unexcelled in quality, clarity, and accuracy, free of advertising influences, was one of making sure that the appeal of what he printed kept the business department uncomplaining and at bay.

Ross worried about advertising volume, and not only in the early days of the magazine's fragile prospects. "Did you know," Stanley Walker writes Thurber in 1957, "that Ross, for many years, was exceedingly doubtful of the wisdom of printing book reviews of any sort, or hoping for any appreciable income from book advertising?" One reason, of course, that book publishers avoided the *New Yorker* was Dorothy Parker's reviews, which not only tore apart one book after another but usually maligned the author and publisher in the process. When Parker gave up the job for Hollywood, Clifton Fadiman took over the column, setting a longevity record for the position—from May 27, 1933, to November 20, 1943. Fadiman writes that his "column was liked and the book ads came in at a gratifying rate. . . . It seemed to please Ross, even when he was bored with what I wrote."

Gus Lobrano, who replaced Katharine White as fiction editor in 1938, remembers that Ross once asked him four times in one day if a passage in a short story would lose the magazine a cigarette advertiser. Lobrano, for the fourth time, said "No." "If you're wrong, you're fired," Ross told him.

Though Ross has enjoyed a reputation of principled professional purity, largely deserved, his disdain was never for the advertisers but for the magazine's business side, and that largely because of his hatred of Fleischmann, who had done the classic unforgivable thing of saving Ross's magazine for him time and again in the early years and helping Ross, the reckless poker player and hopeless manager of his finances, avoid personal bankruptcy. Whatever else lay behind it, Ross especially disliked being beholden to Fleischmann, and taunted him unmercifully.

McKelway remembers that "I used to have lunch with Fleischmann at the Ritz a lot" and that at the end of the first year of McKelway's contract, Fleischmann

> told me he was arranging for me to have some "units" which would be the same as owning some stock in the magazine . . . and I would get the benefits . . . only as long as I remained in that job. I told Ross about this and he hit the ceiling (the ceiling was a battered one, as we all know). He said, "What you ought to have is some dough, goddam it, a bonus." He jerked his typewriter to him, stuck in a sheet of paper, and wrote to Fleischmann that he demanded that McKelway be given a cash bonus of three thousand dollars. "If this demand is not met, I quit," he concluded. Then, "How will that do?" he said to me with a grin.

McKelway read the note and said that the money sounded fine but he didn't think Ross needed to offer to quit over it. "Ah, nuts to them," Ross replied.

In 1937 Ross was going through a strange phase of his life that none of his friends and colleagues could understand but that worried them all. It was what became known as Ross's "don't give a damn" period, says McKelway, "which simply resulted in everybody else working harder, which may very well have been what he intended." Others disagree; the malady was real, and some thought it was partly because Ross was having trouble with his second marriage. His behavior became nothing short of bizarre. He suddenly sold his *New Yorker* stock, estimated to be 10 percent of the magazine's total shares, to Time, Inc., explaining, to the bafflement of everyone who learned of it, that an editor shouldn't be an owner of the magazine he edits. (Time, Inc., later decided it shouldn't be part-owner of an outside magazine and sold the Ross stock at a handsome profit.)

Ross had dropped off the *New Yorker*'s board of directors, at whose meetings he did little but fight with Fleischmann. As the majority stockholder, Fleischmann controlled the board, which could have voted Ross out of office had Fleischmann so directed, but he feared the consequences. With Ross's retirement into a state of near lethargy, Fleischmann thought the moment might have come for safely ridding himself of his tormentor. He seems to have given Ik Shuman the idea that he thought McKelway should replace Ross. ("I was . . . sick of Ik . . . taking me to lunch and whispering that everybody felt I was the logical successor to Ross," says McKelway.) Joel Sayre writes:

> several members of the editorial staff decided that Ross had lost interest in the magazine. After a great deal of debate and soul-searching, they went to Raoul Fleischmann, who had founded the *New Yorker* with Ross. . . . When they had explained their doubts in detail, they asked Fleischmann to find a replacement for Ross.

Sayre had to have obtained this from Thurber, and McKelway partly agrees with it: "Ross was drinking at the time," he says, "used to get drunk with me and tell me he was going to quit and start a true-detective magazine and that I could be the goddam editor of the *New Yorker* if I wanted it."

In his 1975 memoir *Here at The New Yorker*, Brendan Gill says, "There *was* talk of replacing Ross in those days, and one story holds that it was Katharine White, who was prepared to lead a palace revolution." McKelway comes to Katharine's rescue in an earlier letter to Thurber:

> One time K. [Katharine] and Andy took me to lunch at the [Algonquin] and the gist of their conversation, most of it K's, but Andy agreeing, was that Ross needed a long vacation . . . and that an editorial board ought to be set up to handle the magazine on a temporary basis. . . . I said I'd have no part of any such idea. I think now that I probably *thought* K. was plotting to get Ross out, when actually it was just one of her feminine *notions*—and that for some reason Andy was sore at Ross that day, probably over a semicolon. Anyway, Gibbs was sounded out and also discouraged the notion. Nothing came of it, whatever it was. K. was like the rest of us—she would complain and moan about Ross and his unreasonable behavior but if anybody else said anything against him she'd claw his eyes out.

In preparing *The Years with Ross*, Thurber asked Katharine about the rumors of mutiny. She writes,

> About Fleischmann and his constant threats over the years to fire Ross, I had the same experience as you did and gave the same answer: No Ross, no magazine and no staff—we'd all leave with Ross.

Thurber next reminded Fleischmann of the episode, and asked for clarification:

> Dear Raoul:
> . . . You took me to lunch to the Coffee House and forthrightly put the proposition to me that Ross must either do something or get off the pot. I said that if he got out, I would go, too, and you said you hoped he deserved the loyalty so many of us gave him. There were various conferences at the time on this subject, one of them held at Ross's apartment, where he was sulking, and attended by Katharine, Andy, Gibbs, and me. It got nowhere and said nothing. I don't know what was the matter with Ross at that period, but it may have been unrequited love. . . . Morris Markey was on the side of ousting Ross. I know that Gibbs, McKelway and I were dead set against losing him and would have quit if he had been thrown out. . . . I don't know who you had in mind to put in as editor, if Ross had left, and that was and is your business. There is . . . a stubborn faction which believes that Katharine and Andy wanted him out. . . . She once discouraged Woollcott when he sent for her and said, "What would you think of me as editor of The New Yorker in place of Ross?" . . .
>   Anyway, Ross got back to work and the magazine went on as before.

Fleischmann had been reading Thurber's fond descriptions of Ross, which began running in the *Atlantic Monthly* in November 1957, and replied that the Ross Thurber knew and loved was not the Ross he knew. "I took too much of a beating over too long a time," he writes Thurber March 28, 1958, adding:

> Harold just had a great distaste for business people, or anybody who was not creative. For creative people he had the greatest respect, but the

business office was made up of people who did "chores"—(which was one of his favorite words involving our labors) and we were beneath contempt.

Ross and the *New Yorker* enjoyed a degree of loyalty from the contributors I imagine unparalleled in the publishing world, and that is why we are where we are today.

Fleischmann wished Ross had not behaved "so boorishly" toward the business people, marring the pleasure they all took in the magazine's success. "He just didn't give a good goddam what any of us thought, as long as the creative people thought well of him and kept on submitting their contributions."

A new monthly theater magazine, *Stage*, had come upon the scene, edited by Scudder Middleton, one of the many geniuses Ross had fired from the *New Yorker*. The publisher was Fleischmann's old friend and adviser John Hanrahan, a roly-poly little Irishman. Ross despised him, for Hanrahan's promotional suggestions to Fleischmann on editorial content had been forced on Ross in the early days, when Fleischmann's deep pockets determined whether the *New Yorker* lived or died. Now Fleischmann was backing *Stage*, with which he hoped to repeat his earlier success with the *New Yorker*. Its losses eventually deprived the *New Yorker*'s operational reserve fund of nearly a million dollars. When the fiasco finally became known to Ross, it led to a shoot-out between publisher and editor that nearly ended Ross's career at the *New Yorker*.

Having quit the board, Ross was ignorant of its action in subsidizing *Stage*. Fleischmann tells Thurber:

> He was very resentful of our unsound investment (very largely my doing) in "Stage" Magazine, and when we finally gave up the struggle in 1938, and the unhappy facts became a matter of public record, his resentment was almost boundless. At this point Ross and I really had our first serious breach, which was never healed. We had lost quite a few hundred thousand dollars of the company funds in this unfortunate investment, and because I owned well over half the company at the time, in the final analysis I took over half the beating—and fair enough. Harold owned about 10% of our stock at the time, and from his point of view—especially since he had never liked Hanrahan anyway—this was tantamount to my taking the money out of his pocket.
>
> At this juncture—it was early Spring of 1938—Harold made some fantastic demands upon me, which I could not honor, so I offered the job of Editorship to Andy and Katharine White. After "thinking it

over" for about forty-eight hours, they very charmingly and gracefully turned me down, saying that they were loyal to Ross and the *New Yorker* and could not entertain any such idea and were going to Maine to live anyway—which they did.

I had no intention of trying to find some Editor from the outside. . . .

So the months drifted by and Ross and I vaguely compromised his demands and we went lamely on until . . . his death.

Ross was entitled to his anger over *Stage*. It competed for almost the same advertisers as the *New Yorker*, and Middleton solicited manuscripts from *New Yorker* writers at rates better than Ross was allowed to pay. Even Gibbs and Thurber contributed to the new magazine, neither they nor Ross suspecting that it was being underwritten by Fleischmann. Thurber illustrated one of Gibbs's articles in *Stage*, as well as his own review of the Mae West film *Klondike Annie*, which ran in the April 1936 issue.

Thurber appeared again in *Stage* that fall, after his wild drive with Helen to Boston to see Noel Coward's collection of plays, *Tonight at 8:30*. He and Helen dined with Coward after the show. He sent Coward tearsheets from *Stage* of his flattering review of the play, lamented to Coward the negative criticism the show drew from critic Gilbert Seldes, and told him of his and Helen's plans to visit London the next year. Coward responds:

Dear Jim:

. . . I would not mind signing a contract with you to do reviews of anything I write.

I haven't paid any attention to Mr. Seldes' charming little article. I intend to rise above everything, because I have a lovely spirit and I am going to try to grow to love him. I have started in quite a small way by saying very loudly every morning and every night, "oh, dear, I do love Gilbert Seldes."

Let me know when you arrive. Love to you both,

Noel

The man caught in the middle of the fight between Ross and Fleischmann over *Stage* was Ik Shuman, Walker's discovery, who became, in effect, the executive editor in 1936, handling all administrative editorial matters outside the editing process itself. The conflict crested in April 1938. Shuman refutes

Fleischmann's claim that he had never considered bringing in an outsider to be editor.

"Ross came charging into my room," Shuman writes Thurber, "and asked whether I knew the *New Yorker* owned *Stage*. I said I did not. He said, 'Well, by God, we do; we've put a million dollars into it. I learned this last night. I'm not going to work myself to death so we can lose money in a magazine that competes with us. I'm going to tell Fleischmann he has to get the *New Yorker* out of *Stage*.' He added he was going to write a note to Fleischmann and wanted me to read it before it went upstairs."

The note read, "Unless I have your written assurance by Friday at 5 p.m. that we are out of *Stage* lock, stock and barrel my resignation takes effect immediately."

It was Tuesday noon. There was no answer Wednesday or Thursday morning. Ross worked steadily at his desk but looked grim. Shuman, worried, telephoned Fleischmann, who was home with a cold, and asked to see him. Fleischmann protested that he was sick, but Shuman insisted. He found Fleischmann in his Manhattan apartment drinking orange juice. Shuman asked him what he intended to do about Ross's note. Fleischmann said that he had decided to accept Ross's resignation. Shuman asked him to consider that Ross was simply trying to protect the *New Yorker*—asking nothing for himself, only that the magazine's capital be conserved.

"Ross is so bad-mannered," Fleischmann complained.

"Lots of people we do business with are bad-mannered," Shuman replied, naming two or three cantankerous advertisers, "but we continue to do business with them because we make money off them. You're making money off Ross."

Fleischmann then said that he had already picked Ross's successor—Arthur Krock, of the *New York Times*. Krock would make the magazine more political, said Fleischmann, with political cartoons; he would "keep up with the times." Shuman urged him to stick to the editor who had already found his readers. He cited the profit figures and reminded Fleischmann that any other editor would mean a different magazine, and perhaps having to start from scratch. "You're a logical little son of a bitch," Fleischmann sighed. "Tell Harold he's won again."

Fleischmann's note to Ross arrived the next day, Friday, before 5:00 P.M. All connections were cut between the *New Yorker* and *Stage,* which soon folded.

48

That Spider Trap

I just finished for the Saturday Review a piece on a book they sent me called "Be Glad You're Neurotic." I am doing—have done four chapters already and the NYer has taken them—an inspirational book of my own, to be called "Let Your Mind Alone." . . . I've had to read the most incredible crap—dozens of books like "How to Worry Successfully"—but filled with such a walking into my spider trap as you wouldnt believe. Or maybe you would.

—Letter to the Millers, October 1936

Back from Bermuda in June 1936, the Thurbers got their Ford out of winter storage, loaded some things into it from their Fifth Avenue apartment, and set out for the Wismers' cottage at Colebrook. Helen's devotion was never more sorely tested than when sharing Thurber's misadventures with his car:

At 164th Street the radiator began to steam [Thurber writes White]. It turned out water was getting into the oil. . . . I kept filling the radiator and changing the oil. . . . The only sure way I have of reaching Ridgefield is to turn right, left, right, and left through New Canaan, coming out behind a car barn onto a road only I ever travel. In Greenwich . . . I could sense bearings frying. . . . I put in the sixteenth quart of oil and the 20th gallon of water and we were off again. I reached the Coates' house exactly six hours after we left . . . travelling mostly at 22 miles an hour to keep the water from boiling over and the gaskets from frying. I took the car to Coates' favorite garage man who [discovered] the block was cracked. This is what carried off Coolidge.

They sold the old car for junk and bought a used 1935 V-8 Ford Tudor sedan for three hundred and seventy dollars. Thurber hadn't recovered from his financial setback following the divorce costs and settlement, including Althea's past bills, which he was obliged to pay; they put eighty dollars down on the car. Thurber fell in love with it and took Helen on a tour of the Northeast. In Saratoga Springs, they visited the *New Yorker* humorist Frank Sullivan. "Jim made a big hit with everyone here," Sullivan says. "We spent most of a night gambling with George Ball, president of the Saratoga Racing Association, who had wanted to meet Thurber. Jim fried eggs for all of us at four a.m."

They drove through the Adirondacks and crossed Lake Champlain into Vermont, staying for a week at an inn to visit Helen's sister and brother-in-law, who ran a children's camp nearby, then through New Hampshire to Quebec and Maine. After three days in Martha's Vineyard, they went to Boston, where Thurber wrote up a tennis doubles tournament, and then to Forest Hills to cover the U.S. Open. "It meant a lot to Jamie to do all that driving," says Helen.

Thurber wrote White that Metro-Goldwyn-Mayer had sounded him out as a screenwriter, and that he had asked for ten thousand dollars a week. He never heard further and said he didn't much care, though he probably did. Robert Benchley, Elliott Nugent, and other friends were doing well in Hollywood; Joel Sayre was adapting a picture for movie star Ann Shirley, and George Kaufman was rumored to be having an affair with an actress, moving Thurber to write White, "Whenever I realize George Kaufman beat me to a movie star's admiration, I begin imagining what I could do. It's hard to imagine Kaufman taking off his shoes in a boudoir; he looks so permanently clothed."

That summer they moved out of their apartment to the Colebrook cottage. It was a nostalgic occasion, for 8 Fifth Avenue had been their first home as a married couple. Their windows had looked across the rooftops to a sign which, in letters four feet tall, spelled the name of an upholsterer, "O. Charles Meyer." In "Goodbye, Mr. O. Charles Meyer!", published that August, Thurber immortalized the doubtlessly amazed Meyer—if he still lived —referring to him as one who had become a friend, and speculating on the kind of man he might be.

Later that summer, they found a house to rent in Litchfield. The owner was a woman in her eighties who had never heard of the eleven-year-old *New Yorker* and demanded another reference from Thurber. She was satisfied when Thurber listed Harper & Bros. and *Harper's Magazine*, both more than a hundred years old, though their combined earnings fell far short of the *New Yorker*'s. In 1936, the magazine carried the largest advertising linage of any American national weekly—135,921 lines. The two mass-circulation giants were runners-up: the *Saturday Evening Post*, with 127,389 lines, and *Time*, with 95,895.

> We have taken the most charming house in Litchfield [Thurber writes the Millers], the loveliest of towns. . . . We have three bedrooms, three baths, three everything. Acres of elms and maples. Across the road is the house in which Henry Ward and Harriet Beecher were born. Down the road is the birthplace of Ethan Allen. Around the corner is a house built by a Colonel Talmage of Washington's staff. In it the colonel's great grand-daughter lives, now 96. It is all the most beautiful place!

His plan was to "put down roots" in the country and give up the New York night life forever; only about once a month, he said, were he and Helen driving into New York to see some plays. He sent snapshots of the house to the Whites and told them he had joined the local men's forum and "will probably open my trap again during one of the discussions. . . . This first time it was Morals in a Changing World. Pretty funny. Sinclair Lewis [as Babbitt] wrote the whole meeting."

They entertained—the Coateses, the Connells, and the Malcolm Cowleys were frequent guests. Cowley remembers from his visits with Thurber at both Sandy Hook and Litchfield—as well as at his own home in Sherman—that Thurber "was a man who loved to talk at parties and organize word and drawing games.

> The drawing games were variations of charades: . . . One side would select a polysyllabic word and then instead of acting it out, as in charades, they would draw it out. This was perfect for Thurber, of course; he could draw everything so fast. For Peter Blume, too, who lived at the Matthew Josephson house a mile down the road from the Coateses. And for Coates, who was also a draftsman. It wasn't so good for me.
>
> [The game players] were literary people, many of them from the *New Yorker*; Joel Sayre and John McNulty, for example. One morning after [a] game. there was a great pile of drawings by various people, including

[those by] Peter and Jim. [My wife] Ebie, cleaning up the place, just pushed them all in the stove. A while later Jim was having an exhibition of his drawings. He phoned Ebie and asked if she'd saved those drawings. Ebie had painfully to explain that they'd all been burned.

There was singing at the parties, says Cowley. Thurber "had an enormous repertory of popular songs of the 1910s and 1920s, all the choruses and even the verses." After neither Thurber nor Helen could drive, because of Thurber's fading vision and Helen's nearsightedness, there were no more of these evenings. Cowley and some of the others would visit the Thurbers in Cornwall in later years, but the old "Litchfield/Sherman group" broke up in 1940, not only because of Thurber's eye problems but because Coates left his wife, Elsa, whom the Thurbers loved, in what they thought was a high-handed and cruel manner, and married a woman whom Helen had disliked from her days in the Village.

During that first summer in Litchfield, the Thurbers drove to Sandy Hook to pick up the set of Henry James books that Althea had once given him for Christmas, only half of which he had read.

I had never, God bless my soul, read The Spoils of Poynton [he writes Miller]. What a nicely glowing point of honor he put upon two people for giving up Love for a principle! It seems so far [a]way in this day when we give up principles for Love—and somehow the Love they gave up seems, God help us all, rather more worth the having, and the principles not so much. He would have been most unhappy now, I'm sure, in an age when the male sometimes doesnt even take off his hat or the woman her overcoat.

Thurber added a twist on the theme of a Dorothy Parker poem: the candles of Jamesian lovers burned at only one end and would definitely last the night.

While they were at Sandy Hook, five-year-old Rosemary brought him some of his dog drawings, which were lying around the house, and asked him disapprovingly, "Did you draw these?" Thurber said he had. "Why?" she asked. He said he had to think about it. He drew her more pictures with the dog in it. Impatiently, she pointed to a calendar with a picture of an Irish setter and explained to him, "That's a real dog."

In November, Thurber drove Helen to Columbus for Thanksgiving with the family, intending a week of play to include the Millers and Gardiners. He had drawn the cover of the program for O.S.U.'s homecoming football game with Michigan. The pamphlet's blurb, defensive and a bit overboard, could only have been written by Thurber. One line reads, "Many American artists have been critical of Thurber's work, but British artists consider him to be a successor to Matisse and Picasso."

Carl Sandburg, the poet and Lincoln biographer, came to Columbus to participate in a concert series at Capital University while Thurber was there. He and Thurber had never met, but each admired the work of the other. Earlier that year, Sandburg had sent three poems to Thurber, which he hoped the *New Yorker* would take. Thurber was in Bermuda, and the poems were given to Katharine White. She didn't like them and asked Andy's opinion. Andy didn't like them either, and suggested to his wife that "we might mention to Mr. S. that we admire his poetry, but not these poems. Maybe he's cooked. He sounds cooked." Katharine set Sandburg straight:

> Since Mr. Thurber is in Bermuda, and has been there for some months, your poems were turned over to the regular editorial department here. Mr. Thurber doesn't buy manuscripts in any case, but we shall see that he gets your letter when he returns from Bermuda next week.
>
> To our very great regret we don't think that these three poems belong in The New Yorker. It is hard to have to say this because we all of us admire your poetry so much. . . . One of the difficulties is that we find them hard to understand, and we do try not to print any poetry that we don't understand ourselves.

In Columbus, the Thurbers were invited to a dinner at which Sandburg would be a guest. The Thurbers extended their stay at the Deshler-Wallick Hotel to attend. "The evening lasted to early morning," says Dorothy Miller, "as Sandburg and Thurber talked and talked." Herman Miller observed that it was the first time he had seen two famous men trying to sit at one another's feet. The party lasted until 3:00 A.M. Thurber was at his best, as he always was with those he looked up to. Though Thurber made good on his reputation as a night-blooming monologist, observers say that Sandburg outlasted him in pontification. He talked of his own literary career and went into detail about why he thought the Chicago newspapers of that day were the worst in the world. (He had worked on one.) He also delivered a scornful lecture on the Midwestern poet Edgar Lee Masters, with whom Sandburg was feuding. He then strummed a guitar and sang for them; Thurber, unable to resist, joined in.

Thurber was forever grateful to Herman Miller for the evening. He sent both him and Sandburg drawings commemorating the event—portraying himself as a small figure and Sandburg as very large. In one drawing, Sandburg and Thurber dance together while Sandburg looks down at Thurber benignly. In another, Thurber and Sandburg are seated on the floor, reading to one another, typical Thurber characters scattered about in the background. Thurber drew it after Sandburg's *The People, Yes* was published, and labeled it, "The Other People, No."

Earlier that year, there had been a small dust-up among Thurber, Ross, and Andy over one of Thurber's "Where Are They Now?" articles, which had been given White to fix up. White worked without the research notes, and, humble as Thurber was wont to be when it came to the prose master White, he didn't hesitate to tell White when he thought White was wrong. In this instance, he was put out with Ross and Andy both:

> Look, I couldn't agree with you all the way on the changes you made [he writes White]. . . . I wish I could have talked it over with you. . . . I changed some of it right back, raising hell with Ross for keeping a story four months, then sending me the proofs the day before the office closed, marked Rush. . . . I am a little touchy about those pieces be-

cause I have done them with a hell of a lot of thought, research, and care. I certainly don't object to your helping on them, but I object to Ross's not letting me know. I left in some of your lines, they were better than mine but I couldn't see the "death and destruction" even as hyperbole.

He had further trouble with Ross and the fiction department, over his casual "The Wood Duck," which John McNulty declared to be his favorite Thurber story. Thurber tells an interviewer:

> It was the last piece of mine that the old editorial setup monkeyed with (1936) by sticking in a line to "clarify" the piece. [The "new" editorial setup would later give him even greater grief.] I had a sentence that went something like this, "They're not allowed to shoot wood ducks in this state anymore." This was amended to read something like this, "Hunters haven't been allowed to shoot wood ducks in this state since the Connecticut legislature passed a law in 1932 putting those birds on the protected list." What I had to say about that cost the New Yorker seventeen dollars in one collect phone call from Litchfield. Needless to say I saved the piece from the wreckage of clarification. This clarification was on behalf of that fourteen-year-old girl who is supposed to be a composite of New Yorker readers. God help us all.

Thurber had struck a vein of rich ore in the spring of 1936, when Wake Up and Live, by Dorothea Brande, was published. It was part of the rash of books in the dispirited thirties designed to give the discouraged citizenry, waiting for the economic upturn, something to think about besides jigsaw puzzles and playing Monopoly. The "how to succeed" books argued that there was much one could do for oneself despite the miserable social environment that was beyond one's control, beginning with "understanding" oneself, exercising self-discipline, and changing habits and personality traits. For many, these books, including the classic How to Win Friends and Influence People, by Dale Carnegie, comprised a poor man's religion—a do-it-yourself revival service.

Thurber dealt with the books unfairly, of course, to make his comic points. It was shooting fish in a barrel. He began the search for other books of this order, intending to do a book-length parody of them. He showed the first four chapters to McKelway and Ross, who bought them as a series called "Let Your Mind Alone."

An earlier example of the genre, "Wake Up and Live, Eh?" cites Mrs.

Sneden's Landing, 1929: *(above)* Throwing a stick for Jeannie *(left)* Katharine Angell, Thurber, and Jeannie's pup *(Courtesy Joel White)*

E. B. White and Thurber

AN OLD LADY ASKS A FIREMAN FOR A MATCH AT A BIG BLAZE.

One of four Thurber drawings to kid the weekly art conference; the drawing was still on Ross's office wall at the time of his death. (*Courtesy Alice Leighner*)

Lois Long, 1920s (*Photo © Harold Stein*)

Harold W. Ross (*Photo by Fabian Bachrach*)

Ann Honeycutt, circa 1950
(*Courtesy Joseph Mitchell*)

Emily Hahn, 1930s

Helen Thurber, 1941

Robert and Elsa Coates with Helen,
1935

Bermuda, 1936: The Thurbers, flanked by Ronald and Jane Williams

A late honeymoon, Bermuda, 1936

(clockwise from top) John "Jap"
Gude, circa 1950 (Courtesy
Elizabeth Gude)
Rogers E. M. Whitaker, 1966
(Courtesy Sara Lippincott)
Joseph Mitchell (Photo by
Anne Hall)
Ralph Ingersoll, early 1930s
(Courtesy Ingersoll Collection,
Boston University)
John McNulty in Hollywood,
mid-1940s (Courtesy Faith
McNulty)

Wolcott Gibbs,
1946 *(Photo by
Hilde Hubbuck)*

Wolcott and Elinor Gibbs, Fire
Island, 1950 *(Courtesy Elizabeth
Gibbs)*

The Sandy Hook house, 1931

Thurber at Sandy Hook, early 1930s

Thurber and Rosemary at Sandy Hook, 1933

Joel Sayre, 1950s *(Courtesy Nora Sayre)*

Nora Sayre, age twelve, when she visited the Thurbers frequently in New York *(Photo by Sylvia Salmi)*

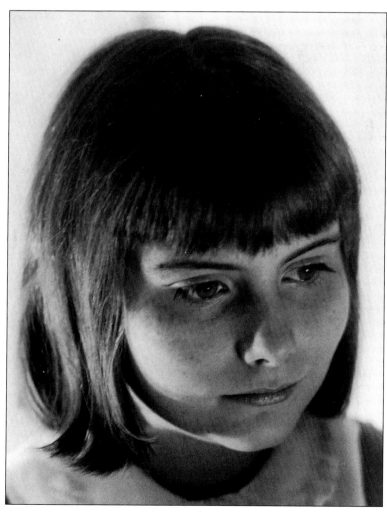

Thurber in his London flat, 1938

As a guest speaker at a Paris function, 1938 (*United Press International Photo*)

Thurber gathering wood at Villa Tamisier on Cap d'Antibes, France, 1938

Algonquin Hotel, November 29, 1938. Top row, from left: Alan Campbell, St. Clair McKelway, Russell Maloney, Thurber. Seated, from left: Fritz Foord, Wolcott Gibbs, Frank Case, Dorothy Parker. (*Courtesy Bettmann Archives*)

(left) Brendan Gill, 1970s (Photo by Nancy Crampton)
(above) William Shawn, 1946 (Photo by Hilde Hubbuck)

Peter De Vries at the New Yorker, 1964 (Courtesy Jan De Vries)

Eugene Kinkead, who reported much of Thurber's "Where Are They Now?" series (Courtesy Katherine Kinkead)

(*above*) The West Cornwall house, purchased in 1945
(*right*) Summer 1943, at a rented house in Cornwall, Connecticut. The mandolin was Helen's Christmas gift.

1945 party: from left, Mrs. Elliot (Lee) Nugent, Mrs. Jap (Helen) Gude, Ann Honeycutt

(left) Earl Wilson interviewing Thurber and Nugent upon revival of *The Male Animal*, 1952 (*Photo by Leo Friedman*) (*above*) Tim Costello and the Thurber murals (*Photo by H. F. Sozeo*)

Rosemary's wedding, Philadelphia, 1953: *(above)*
Father and daughter *(right)* From left, Mark Van
Doren, Thurber, and E. B. White at reception

Caught between his first and
second wives. Althea is at left.

(*above*) The Williamses and Thurbers in Bermuda, 1947 (*below*) London, 1958: Thurber being interviewed by Eddy Gilmore at the Stafford Hotel, where he completed *The Years with Ross*

(*right*) Thurber at work in his Algonquin suite, 1950s (*below*) Thurber at the *New Yorker,* 1959, dictating to "office temp" Margot Speer (*Courtesy* St. Louis Post Dispatch*)*

thought that she ought not to go on with her writing because it was mediocre."

In "Sex ex Machina," he discusses Dr. Bisch's scenarios describing how
three men react when they have started across the street against a red light
and got in the way of a car. Thurber thought it worthy of note that the doctor
used men as examples. Had they been women, he says, "all three of them
would have hesitated, wavered, jumped forwards and backwards, and finally
run head on into the car if some man hadn't grabbed them." And he adds:
"Only one woman in a thousand really knows anything about the mechanical
principle involved in an automobile." But nearly all of these charges against
women could be made against Thurber, a clue to his hostility toward the
feminine traits he believed were part of his own makeup.

He "hated" women, he goes on, because they never got anything exactly
right, used terms like "all righty" and "yes, indeedy," and threw objects with
the wrong foot advanced. He resents Woman's "quiet air of superior knowledge which makes a man feel that he is out of touch with all the things that
count in life." His use of women in his art and literature, he acknowledged,
had been influenced by "The Young Lady Across the Way," an empty-headed
lass with zeroes for eyes, in Robert O. Ryder's Columbus newspaper column.

His distaste extends even to Eleanor Roosevelt, whose "My Day" column
he parodies ("with Apologies"): "I sat in my office for an hour or so without
turning on the lights. It wasn't as lovely and peaceful as it should have been."
He "falls to wondering" what little animal gave its life to provide a cover for
his typewriter. He discusses a letter from the organization sponsoring the
Cleveland Dog Show, asking him for a letter of good wishes for the event; it
is signed "William Z. Breed." His wife refuses to believe that such a name
exists and insists the letter is a hoax. "We wrangled about this matter late
into the night. Of such unfortunate differences of opinion and unfounded
suspicions is married life in this country made up."

However well things may have been going with him and Helen, his professional pose required him to go on playing the put-upon male, discontented in
marriage, plagued by women not quite worthy of him. There is little Woman
can do that will please him.

Women go on forever, he writes; no five males could have survived as had
the Dionne quintuplets. Social scientists should stop including women under
the generic term "man." While men are going to hell at a breakneck pace, he
points out, women often live to be well over a hundred, celebrating their
centennials by dancing, playing kettle drums, and chinning themselves.
"There is Man and there is Woman," he concludes, "and Woman is going her
own way."

Thurber's draftsmanship was at the zenith of its power. Sometimes he would draw as many as thirty pictures for drunken ladies at drunken parties, he writes Miller. Over the years, some of these have been trickling into the Thurber Collection at O.S.U. One typical set is drawn on the backs of stationery with the letterhead "Far Horizons," a summer camp in Vermont. Nobody knows their provenance; they were sold to the collection by a woman requesting anonymity. The pictures show the firm, self-confident detail of the mid-thirties period. A meteor in the form of a woman's head races down from above toward an unsuspecting man holding a drink and reading a book. Caption: "Women want security. After they get it we'll ask the men what they want—Walt Whitman." One of the "Far Horizons" drawings plays on the "Marriages are made in Heaven" theme, but another shows the nude Thurber Man toasting Satan, while a woman's head glares at him through the flames of Hades. Caption: "Divorces are okay in Hell." Another shows the looming female with a firm grip on a little Thurber Man; it is entitled, "The Unexpectant Father." "Birth of a Love Affair" is a statuette of Man and Woman meeting, heads and arms separate but bodies melded into one. "Death of a Love Affair" is a series of panels in which a couple start drinking together, the smiles getting deeper on their faces. By the third and fourth drinks they are talking seriously. By the fifth, they are touching noses; after the sixth, they are prone. A close-up of two pairs of feet dominates the final panel; the sated lovers are on their backs, their sexual interest in one another exhausted.

Thurber's "Art and Marriage" represents the struggle between the artist's obligations to his craft and his marriage—a theme Clarence Day championed. Thurber has drawn an oblong body on its back, the head at one end male, at the other, female. The male is looking longingly toward a young and attractive woman with a flower and a star in her hair, labeled "Art."

His sketches continued to draw an occasional letter from psychoanalysts inviting him to become their patient. He burlesques that, too. In "My Memories of D. H. Lawrence," he says he has written to Lawrence ("I had some ideas about sex which I thought might interest him."):

> Lawrence never received the letter . . . because I had . . . put it in the wrong envelope. He got instead a rather sharp note which I had written . . . to a psychoanalyst . . . who had offered to analyze me at half his usual price. This analyst had come across some sketches I had

made. . . . I had told him that if he wanted to analyze somebody he had better begin with himself, since it was my opinion there was something the matter with him. As for me, I said, there was nothing the matter with me. . . . I never heard from Lawrence and . . . I kept hearing from the analyst.

Though he still wasn't taking himself seriously as an artist, others were. The one-man shows of his pictures at the Valentine gallery in New York had been followed by one at the Howard Futzel Gallery. Several of his drawings were included in the Dada-Surrealism show at the Museum of Modern Art in 1936. But there were longer-lasting Thurber art shows on the walls of his favorite watering holes. Among the most celebrated was that in Tim Costello's bar, on Third Avenue near Forty-fourth Street.

John McNulty worked nearby at the *Mirror,* and when his casuals began to get accepted at the *New Yorker* their setting was frequently the Third Avenue pubs that McNulty patronized. The stories, later collected in his book *Third Avenue,* helped build a loyal clientele of *New Yorker* staff members at Cos-

They're going to Costello's Restaurant!

TIM COSTELLO --- THIRD AVENUE AND 44TH ST.

tello's—Wolcott Gibbs and John O'Hara were drinking buddies there. Thurber's personal friendship with Tim Costello developed through McNulty, Costello's fellow Irishman, in the mid-thirties.

Costello's became Thurber's regular bar, his frequent hangout after he had abandoned Bleeck's, in the forties. Tim Costello left standing orders that the pub was never to close as long as Thurber was there—an order that in later years occasionally brought sighs of despair from Emil Stahl, the headwaiter, and others among the help, as Thurber, guided by Helen, would come through the door at 2:00 or 3:00 A.M., prepared to talk and sing until dawn. Tim Costello had begun his beer and steak pub in 1934. Because of Tim's charm and his esteem for artists and writers, his bar became the rough and rowdy equivalent of Mme. de Staël's salon.

Costello had emigrated from Ireland with little education, but he was well informed, dressed in fine style, and, as George Frazier wrote of him in *Esquire*, was sensitive to all nuances of the English language. He was no run-of-the-mill publican; he was apt to leave unattended an artist whose works he didn't particularly like. Costello communicated his literary preferences much in the manner of a professor conducting a seminar. Thurber occasionally read a manuscript of his to Tim for his comments before turning it in to the magazine.

A demeaning rumor as to the genesis of Thurber's famous murals on Costello's beaverboard walls keeps cropping up: that Thurber drew the murals to square a liquor and food debt from his salad days. On the contrary, his drawings were freely rendered, in enthusiasm and appreciation. Costello tried to make them a gift to the ages, having the drawings inked in and coated with a preservative varnish. He had the panels carefully dismantled when he was forced to move his pub from the corner of Third and Forty-fourth to 699 Third, next door, where they were lovingly remounted.

John McNulty felt Third Avenue changed for the worse when they began tearing down the elevated railway, whose pillars were a great aid in getting across Third Avenue safely when you were drunk. (The last of the El disappeared in 1956, the year McNulty died.) Costello, who passed on in 1962, a year after Thurber, regretted the disappearance of speakeasies, which enabled owners to select whom to admit. (He once refused to serve Marilyn Monroe vodka and orange juice because he didn't like her looks, claiming he had no fruit juices on the premises.) He was stricken at the news of Thurber's death. "Well, poor Thurber," he said in his Irish brogue. "God rest him. He was a great man. Aye, he was a decent man."

Costello's is gone—his son could not persevere against the crushing development of skyscrapers on Third Avenue. Thurber's drawings survive only in reproductions from photographs. They still tell us Thurber's view of marriage and New York society in the thirties. They are from his Helen period, and a "Marriages Are Made in Heaven" features a freefloating man and woman whose arms flow into each other's to form a circle. There's the endearing, cowardly dog running downhill, inexplicably pursued by three rabbits. There are male and female fencers and male and female skiers; dogs inhabit the corners of almost all the panels. "Quit acting like Katherine Cornell. All you've got is spinster's booze gloom," a man scolds a woman. In another panel, the Thurber Woman tackles a Thurber Man uselessly dressed in a football uniform. Caption: "Mt. Holyoke [Helen's college]-17, Yale-5." There is what may be a final, impressionistic farewell to Althea: the little Thurber Man, in the fierce clutch of a towering Thurber Woman, tells her, "I'm leaving you, Myra—you might as well get used to the idea." Another panel pictures the Thurber Man hiding atop a tree while the Thurber Woman searches for him below.

Over the years, cigarette smoke darkened the drawings, until the lines were barely distinguishable in the dim light of the saloon. The fact was noted by artists who had staffed *Yank* magazine, which was around the corner from Costello's during World War II. Art Weithas, *Yank*'s former art director, rounded up some of the magazine's veterans, and together they brightened the murals, lightening the backgrounds and retracing the lines. But they didn't survive the final closing of Costello's in 1994. Though their photographed reproductions exist, Rosemary Thurber believes the originals are lost.

The Thurbers were saving money to go abroad, so Thurber continued to hire out his pencil to advertising agencies. Thurber women turned up in *Liberty* and *Collier's* at club meetings at which the speaker refuses to take the podium until all the insects have been sprayed with Bugaboo. His characters also promote whiskey and remind people to subscribe to the *New Yorker*. Though other editors occasionally talked him into doing something for them, the *New Yorker* remained his principal vehicle.

Psychiatrists continued to intrude on his territory. Using *Forum and Century* as his platform, Thurber took Dr. Paul Schilder, of New York University, to task. Dr. Schilder had characterized Lewis Carroll's *Alice's Adventures in Wonderland* and *Through the Looking Glass* as full of cruelty, fear, and "sadistic trends of cannibalism," and had declared it unwholesome as children's literature.

Thurber felt especially possessive toward Carroll's works. He saw the mispronunciations of his domestic help as unconscious throwbacks to Carroll, and delighted in them. ("We once had a cook with whom he would maneuver an entire conversation in order to hear her pronounce the word 'Poughkeepsie,'" Helen told Milton Caniff.) Thurber uses Carroll-like words throughout his writing. In "The Car We Had to Push," "tires booped and whooshed, the fenders queeled and graked." He begins a letter to White in a "Wonderland" mood: "The corms are gittin our thrips already, but none of the thisbies has yit bin torn from the zatches. The gelks are in the pokeberries agin, though, and grandma has lurbs in her hust. Look out for drebs." He was to carry on the Carroll tradition in his children's books, as well. Why pick on Carroll, he asks, in "Tempest in a Looking Glass." There's the farmer's wife who cut off the tails of three blind mice, and Hansel and Gretel burning the witch. As for cannibalism, there's "The Rose-Tree" from *English Fairy Tales*— a collection of folk tales edited by Joseph Jacobs circa 1895—in which the stepmother cuts off the little girl's head and serves a stew of her heart and liver to her unsuspecting father. He quotes "a truly intelligent psychologist," Dr. Morton Prince, who could well have been defending the folktales of the world: "Far from being mere freaks, monstrosities of consciousness, they are in fact shown to be manifestations of the very constitution of life."

> I am having a show of my drawings in London . . . during the [King's] coronation [he writes Miller]. Also one in Hollywood next month and in San Francisco in March. I have on hand enough drawings left to have several more. . . .
>
> The New Yorker gave me 100 shares of stock to keep me quiet, or shut my mouth . . . and Helen and I may sell some of it and go to Europe in May for my show—and for other things.

The San Francisco exhibit was at the Gump Art Galleries. He wrote the gallery director a lengthy note about his drawings, which was published in *Art Digest*. Those who "explain" and "exclaim" over his drawings, writes Thurber, "invariably miss the fact that essentially most of them are . . . supposed to be funny." He continues to downgrade himself as an artist:

> Being essentially a writer, I find that I do not . . . share the emotions and mentality of artists who draw and paint. They, to me, are as alien and difficult to understand as Sally Rand. I have, as a matter of fact, no community of anything with artists. I originally drew, I think, to satirize and poke fun at the more pretentious artists. Once I began to share the temperament, the phony profundities, the ahing and the ohing, extravagant praise or denunciation of this and that, the language of art criticism, exceeded in monkey business only by the criticism of music, I would be lost.

Perhaps Thurber's tendency to downplay his talent as an artist, to withhold an investment of ego in that side of him, enabled him to overcome its later forfeiture to blindness, and may explain the handicaps he set in the way of those who tried to make knowledgeable evaluations of his drawings—which many, including White, continued to believe would be the best guarantee of his permanent reputation. He played the country hick, expressing in sophisticated but self-deprecatory language the prejudices of the know-nothings against the art world. He considered connoisseurs of music, the dance, painting, sculpture, and photography as, more probable than not, phony and pretentious.

The art critic of the *San Francisco News*, Amelia Hodel, visited the Thurber show at the Gump Galleries and refuted his assessments of his work. His art was, she said, "very strange and insane in its own inspired way. . . . Despite Mr. Thurber's protestations about his work, we call it art."

Meanwhile, Thurber and the editors at Harper & Bros. concluded that the "Let Your Mind Alone" series would not make a big enough book. He added twenty-eight casuals and essays—all but two from the *New Yorker*—and a slew of his illustrations, and the book, to be called *Let Your Mind Alone!* was scheduled for publication that fall.

In May 1937, the Thurbers sailed on the *Île de France* for Europe, shipping Thurber's favorite symbol of masculine competence, his beloved 1935 Ford V-8. He took with him three books he hoped would bring him up to date on contemporary France: Alexander Werth's *Which Way France?*, John Gunther's *Inside Europe*, and a book by the French Socialist Léon Blum. Thurber couldn't understand the Blum book, so he gave it to his steward, who happened to be a French Royalist and after that refused to answer when Thurber rang for him.

49

That Journey to the Pyrenees

Helen and I got the car out for the first time since my memorable advent in London, and drove to a beauty spot in Hampshire sixty miles from London. . . . Three or four couples who are painters, writers, editors, rented a great estate there with thirty rooms, tennis court, bowling green . . . for $45 a month. We had a swell time, for they are all very nice people. Our contacts with the English have been very nice and maybe we've been lucky. [I received a] letter . . . from Miss Dawes, who used to be Ingersoll's secretary, asking me did I remember the time I threw an alarm clock out of Mac's window onto 45th Street. She lives in Bath or Flinders Bottom, or Horsey Rinse. I think she has ferret bite.

—Letter to E. B. White, summer, 1937

They disembarked at Le Havre on May 25. Thurber took Helen on a ten-day tour of his beloved Normandy in the Ford. It was her first trip abroad, and she was curious to see the places that had significance for Thurber while he was there with Althea. They spent three weeks in Paris and were taken in hand by Janet Flanner, who wrote the "Letter from Paris" column in the *New Yorker*, signed "Genet"—Ross's mispronunciation of "Janet," which she elected to keep as a pseudonym. Among the Americans in Paris they met up with were Lillian Hellman and Dorothy Parker. The Spanish Civil War was on, and at a little bistro one evening Parker sobbed inconsolably over the deaths of "the little Spanish babies." On another evening, Hellman argued with Thurber once again about the writer's obligation to improve the world regardless of what he felt he owed himself as an artist. Thurber wrote White about it:

> What we need is writers who deal with the individual plight and who at the same time do not believe in [Walter] Lippmann. It came to me today . . . that the world exists only in my consciousness (whether as a reality or as an illusion the evening papers do not say, but my guess is reality). The only possible way the world could be destroyed, it came to me, was through the destruction of my consciousness. This proves the superiority of the individual to any and all forms of collectivism. I could enlarge on that, only I have what the French call "rheumatism of the brain"—that is the common cold.

And in a later letter to White:

> It is the easiest thing in the world nowadays to become so socially conscious, so Spanish war stricken, that all sense of balance and values goes out of a person. Not long ago in Paris Lillian Hellman told me that she would give up writing if she could ameliorate the condition of the world, or of only a few people in it. Hemingway is probably on that same path, and a drove of writers are following along, screaming and sweating and looking pretty strange and futile. This is one of the greatest menaces there is: people with intelligence deciding that the point is to become grimly gray and intense and unhappy and tiresome because the world and many of its people are in a bad way. It's a form of egotism, a supreme form. I've toyed with it myself and understand it a little.

White replies: "I, too, know that the individual plight is the thing. . . . If you have the poetic temperament you go on groping toward something which will express all this in a burst of choir music, and your own inarticulateness only hastens the final heart attack."

After three weeks in Paris, the Thurbers crossed the channel, the first visit of either to England, where Thurber was traumatized by driving in London traffic. The principal purpose of the visit was to see a collection of his drawings on exhibit at the Storran Gallery. He continued to credit the English painter Paul Nash with having "discovered" his art, and to believe that the

English valued his work more highly than his own countrymen did. In 1951, he wrote that his drawings

> have, for some reason, been more popular in England than in the United States. I had four or five shows in New York and in other cities in the United States but the single show I had in London in 1937 brought me in $2,000, or ten times as much as the American shows put together. . . . I was so surprised at the prices the drawings sold for that one of the directors of the Gallery said, "When you go to the show, please do not whistle or exclaim at the prices the buyers are paying." I promised to take it all very nonchalantly.

In an early thirties review of Thurber's work, says Thurber, Nash saw Thurber's drawings as "in the early fashion of Matisse." References to this somehow became transformed into the rumor that Matisse admired Thurber's art. In a letter to Nash's biographer, Anthony Bertram, Thurber writes:

> One of the Gallery men discovered that Matisse was in London, and called the old boy's secretary to arrange a meeting between Matisse and me. I didn't know about this until later. The secretary disappeared from the phone for a moment and returned to say, "M. Matisse has never heard of The New Yorker or of Mr. Thurber." I loved it. It still has not put an end to the legend.

The Matisse/Thurber comparison continued to be passed around—Thurber saw to that—but it served largely to underscore his own sense of incredulity at the effects his so easily rendered pictures were creating. He saw Matisse's response as less a put-down of himself than of Ross and his magazine, and he gleefully sent word to Ross that Matisse had never heard of him, the *New Yorker*, or Thurber, adding in an interview later that it evened things up, since Ross had probably never heard of Matisse. As to his drawings, he publicly hewed to his familiar party line: they were, he said, "no more than a minor nervous condition that any competent psychoanalyst ought to be able to clear up in twenty minutes."

The exhibit at the Storran included Benchley's loaned seal-in-the-bedroom cartoon and Tallulah Bankhead's "Well, *I'm* Disenchanted, Too. We're *All* Disenchanted." Thurber, characteristically, offered his services as publicist for the show. So many awful things had happened to him the day he was born in Columbus, he wrote for the art catalog, that he was unable to keep anything on his stomach until he was seven years old, though he had grown to be six feet, one-and-a-half inches tall and to weigh 154 pounds when fully dressed for winter. "Quick to arouse," he writes, "he is very hard to quiet, and people often just go away."

The show had run during Coronation Week, when George VI succeeded King Edward VIII. The *Sunday Observer* found Thurber "brilliant" as a humorist-artist, Thurber's mind "up-to-date" and "beautifully ironic." Art critic Anthony Blunt compared him to the famous English cartoonist Sir David Alexander Cecil Low, the creator of Colonel Blimp, whose work was on display elsewhere in London. Ten years ago, Blunt said, such "impure" artists would not have been permitted a showing like this one, but "the obsession with pure form is passing."

Nash visited the gallery, and with his wife, Margaret, entertained the Thurbers in Hampstead, in a house filled with paintings, collages, montages, and lithographs, where Thurber met Conrad Aiken. Thurber was quite well known to the English, thanks mostly to Hamish Hamilton, who remained his British book publisher throughout Thurber's lifetime and after. Thurber found himself sought out, a number of distinguished literary figures inviting him to visit them; his thank-you letters usually carried penciled illustrations of the occasion.

One of Thurber's London acquaintances was the London *Times* correspondent John Marks—a sophisticated, clever, sometimes lazy correspondent, according to one of his college classmates, Alistair Cooke, who had just settled in New York but was back in London that summer of 1937. Marks thought Cooke should meet Thurber.

"I was twenty-eight years old," Cooke says, "and scared of the prospect; for me, Thurber was Socrates and Aristophanes. It was a pleasant relief to find that he was only gentle and kind. We hit it off at the start, primarily because I have the same kind of flypaper memory he had. We were obsessive about dates. We had a terrible row over which ship Lord Kitchener was drowned on. 'All right, Mr. Know-it-all,' he told me, 'when was Paulette Goddard born?' As luck would have it, I'd just had reason to look it up and could tell him it was June 6, 1911, in Great Neck, Long Island. Not to be outdone, he told me that Charlie Chaplin had been born April 6, 1889, and Hitler was born April 28. He was wrong; Chaplin was born April 16, Hitler four days later. But having the pump primed in this way, he'd throw dates at you for the next three hours. I became one of the exclusive members of his club by offering my share of dates in return. Thurber could remember a lot about his schoolteachers, the date he took a certain quiz, where the textbooks had been wrong: Longstreet was *not* the corps commander on this day or that; how another book had misspelled Warren Harding's middle name.

"I told him I had seen him in person once before, while on a Commonwealth Fellowship to Yale. The dean of the Yale Law School, Eugene Rostow, had given a party for undergraduates. Thurber and his first wife were there. He was thirty-nine; I was twenty-four. He pretended to remember me but didn't. I first knew him through his drawing, not his writing. The first of his cartoons I saw was of the seal in the bedroom, in a copy of the *New Yorker*. I thought it was an editorial aberration, but when I came to America and Yale, I was amazed to find a drawing of his in nearly every issue.

"My impression of the physical Thurber at Marks's apartment was that of a grasshopper finally come to earth. He had a spiderly stance, enormous feet that may have been only the type of shoe he wore, and he had glasses as thick as binoculars. When I first saw Harry Truman, his glasses reminded me of Thurber's. They gave both men a Martian quality, and I used to think, when I saw Truman as president, that he could well be the president of Mars and Thurber the poet laureate. There was a terrific gentleness to Thurber, sitting there on the couch. He was flattering. He and Helen had heard a talk of mine on the BBC, where I had worked for three years as a film critic.

"The reason we were all there was that John Marks was about to start a London magazine, a frank imitation of the *New Yorker*. It involved some good people. Cyril Connolly was the editor; Graham Greene was film critic; Evelyn Waugh reviewed books; I was to send them a New York "Letter from the States" and Thurber agreed to do some things for it. It was called *Night and Day*, after the Cole Porter song, so popular just then, and contained a few good features."

Thurber gave Marks five drawings and his cartoon series entitled "The Patient," all of which Ross had turned down. The series ran from the October 21, 1937, issue of *Night and Day* to December 23, almost the life span of the short-lived weekly. He also contributed a casual, "A Night with the Klan," about his experiences with the Columbus chapter of the Ku Klux Klan as a newspaper reporter. He writes White:

> I have been selling drawings over here and we live very nicely on that. *Night and Day*, the London imitation of the *New Yorker*, bought a flock of rejected drawings yesterday, which Miss Terry shipped me, and when they are printed there will be a hell of a kick from the Art Conference, which will not remember ever having seen them. The only drawings they remember vaguely are the ones I send in three or four times until they are bought to shut me up. *Night and Day* bought "The Patient" series, which I did in Bermuda and which you liked, but nobody else liked but me.

"Actually, *Night and Day* was killed by Shirley Temple," Cooke states. "Graham Greene reviewed *The Little Colonel,* and wrote about it out of his bile duct. He suggested that in the scene when the sergeant lifts his hand to slap Miss Temple's 'plump little rump,' the 'squalid audience' around him, including cashiered colonels and vicars who had crept in from Tunbridge to see the movie, might be aroused. Well, there were tight libel laws in England. If you sued in England for something written in England, chances are you would be successful. MGM knew this and brought suit against Graham Greene and *Night and Day.* It not only killed the magazine, it planted the anti-Americanism in Greene, who, as an accessory, had to pay six hundred pounds. I saw him in the States that fall. He was still sore at Americans, in general, and Shirley Temple, in particular. It was also the end of my professional association with Thurber, whom I didn't see again until after the war."

In "Pepper for the Belgians," (*New Yorker,* December 18, 1937), Thurber thinks the trouble in international relations is that of language. "We avoid the unfamiliar where we can," he writes, "and when we can't we twist it into patterns we are used to," all of which leads to misunderstandings. For some reason, the piece brought him a startling letter from Rebecca West attacking the *Night and Day* staff. The reason Graham Greene "writes such offensive muck about the Americans," she asserted, was his conversion to Roman Catholicism. "All *Night and Day* stinks of the peculiar miasma which is exhaled by such—Christopher Hollis, Evelyn Waugh and all the Woodruff set," said West. "Their hell results from the possession of real talent and the lack of guts." They were determined to make an aristocracy of mediocrity and thus had to look for people who were their inferiors, she went on. The Roman Catholic Church "at once gives the privilege of despising all Protestants." Greene was a gifted young man, West adds, and the shame was in the effect that their religious conversions had on such writers, including T. S. Eliot; Greene's contempt for the Protestants had led to the anticlergy comments in his review.

Thurber made no recorded response; he rewarded her for "the clarification" with some drawings.

While in England, Thurber appeared on television—an experimental medium in 1937—drawing his standard cartoon characters on large sheets of paper for the British audience, he reported in a letter to the Williamses in Bermuda. He described how he had covered the Budge-Parker tennis match for the *New Yorker* by watching it on an eight-by-ten-inch TV screen twelve miles from the action at Wimbledon.

"England was way ahead of us then technologically," he told an interviewer years later:

When we knew very little about television they had sets in railway stations and hotel lobbies and they were putting on things that it took us two or three years to catch up with. I was once riding in a cab with T. S. Eliot and he asked me what I thought about television and I asked him what he thought and he said, "Well, I hope it doesn't become the ruination of our country here."

The Thurbers traveled to Scotland in mid-August, returned to London in September, and were soon off to the Continent again. In an interview with Art Buchwald in Paris in 1955, Thurber said that the London art sales in 1937 had given them

enough money to live here for a year and a half. We lived in a very nice hotel on the Right Bank. Then we had to move to a slightly beaten-down one on the Left Bank. . . . You know how wives are. In New York your second wife wants to stay in as good a hotel as the first wife, and in Paris your second wife wants to stay in as bad a hotel as your first wife. In this way your first wife will never be able to say to your second wife that she couldn't see the real Paris.

Actually, Helen was concerned with their budget. Thurber had lost some of their passage money in side bets on the match games at Bleeck's before their departure, and they had had to sell some of their New Yorker stock to finance the trip. True, the sale of Thurber's drawings had brought in about seven hundred dollars, but he was required to keep a flow of casuals and articles to the States to survive. The New Yorker ran two dozen of his prose pieces during the fifteen months he was gone, and nearly fifty of his drawings.

One of the cartoons was of a plump woman offering the Thurber Man chocolates, and cooing "Sweets?" A graduate student once asked him if it was tied to Freud's theory that candy was a substitute for sex. The question amused him. "I got the idea from a luncheon conversation with Joel Sayre," he replied. "We thought up words we hated and that men should never use. Like 'tasty,' or 'pranks,' 'petting,' and 'spooning,' or calling candy 'sweets.' My brother Robert looks for words like that and sends them to me. People seem to find them funny in my captions, whether the men or women use them. In several of my cartoons, the joke depends on nothing more than words and phrases I can't stand."

The British novelist David Garnett invited the Thurbers to visit him, after Thurber had thanked Garnett for describing him in an essay as "the most original writer living." (Thurber was soon describing Garnett's Lady into Fox

"Sweets?"

as one of his favorite novels.) Thurber passed on the quote in a letter to White. White let him down gently:

> I saw the David Garnett piece about you. . . . I doubt if you are the most original writer living, but I doubt whether anybody is. I am the second most inactive writer living, and the third most discouraged. The greatest living writer is Morris Markey.

Markey had begun to get on everybody's nerves at the magazine.

White, "the third most discouraged" living writer, had for some time been in a state of discontent with his life. The departure of Thurber, his friend and colleague, from the office and the country, could not have helped. Of his proposed year's leave of absence from the magazine, Andy writes Katharine—she was in New York and White in Maine—

> I am quitting partly because I am not satisfied with the use I am making of my talents; partly because I am not having fun working at my job—and am in a rut there; partly because I long to recapture something which everyone loses when he agrees to perform certain creative miracles on specified dates for a particular sum. . . . A person afflicted with poetic longings of one sort or another searches for a kind of intellectual and spiritual privacy in which to indulge his strange excesses.

His Comment in the August 7, 1937, *New Yorker* would be his last for several years as an employee of the magazine. After vacationing in Maine with Katharine and their son Joel in August, White remained to sail, meditate, and write poetry, while Katharine and Joel returned to the Turtle Bay apartment. The news of White's restlessness had reached Thurber, and he wrote Katharine in August, in care of her office.

> Dear Katharine:
>   . . . I reckon you all are in Maine now and probably having a fine time. When Andy gets enough of that tell him he better contact us about spending the winter on the Riviera with us. Are you going to leave, too, or go back to work? Seems to me I've heard that Thurber and White might leave New York for a year at the same time, but that Ross would never let you escape, too. Let us know the plans, anyway—and come with Andy if you can get away. . . .

Ross was distressed by White's abandonment of the magazine. "He just sails around in some goddam boat," he complained to Gibbs. Gibbs wrote White, "It's a crime that you should be out of this book altogether, and wish to God you'd write something—verse, casuals, fables, anything at all." But White was raising turkeys at the North Brooklin farm he rented in Maine. He would eventually buy it. He tried writing there, but was dissatisfied with everything he turned out. To the despondent letter he wrote Thurber in London, Thurber, not yet understanding the depth of White's sense of failure, replied in an effort to cheer him up:

> As far as I can make out, what you have is sheep blast. It comes from an admixture of Comment writing and whisk broom catchings. . . . I have it myself. It causes one to say, "Hello, George," to himself in the mirror of a morning. Over here everybody turns Catholic when anything is the matter, and perhaps you should try that. T. S. Eliot turned Catholic and so did Evelyn Waugh and they look fine.

In September, Thurber again suggested that White, no longer tied to deadline writing, visit them in Paris. White replied by postcard that he couldn't leave the farm until the "wood is all cut, cranberries harvested," and added, "I'm not a writer any more myself." Thurber wrote back:

Dear Andy:

You may be a writer in farmer's clothing but you are still a writer. You are a writer and go about saying you are not a writer. . . . This is not a time for writers to escape to their sailboats and their farms. . . .

I started to make a list of all writers living but the names blurred on me. Of course, if you are no longer a living writer you don't belong in the list, which ought to cheer you up. Garnett [says] that in one miserable place I sound like Mark Twain talking from the grave, which ought to cheer you up, too. . . . He thinks I ought to give up ideas and institutions, which I have long suspected, as after a great deal of study of them I feel that I do not know anything at all about them. This leaves me with only the dog and the wood duck and my own short-sighted blundering into other people's apartments and tulip beds, to deal with. Which is just as well. Garnett points out that Twain ended up by telling everybody there is nothing at all in art and music . . . and I guess he feels I will end up by telling everybody there is nothing in science, whether natural, organic, inorganic, or Freudian. It's high time I shut my trap and was reminded of the time my father got locked in the men's room on his wedding night. . . .

You are not the writer who should think that he is not a writer. Let [James Branch] Cabell do that. . . . Meanwhile the bacteria are working quietly away. The sheep tick in England has just about got sheep and man, too, where he wants it. . . . The sheep tick knows what he is doing. Up in Warsaw, owls attacked an old woman who was just walking along. Owls know what they are doing, too.

In Paris, Thurber took Helen on a tour of whatever landmarks he could find from his two previous trips. In "The City of Light," a *New Yorker* casual he never preserved in a book, we find the narrator ridiculing his fellow Midwestern tourists. He follows a middle-aged American couple. The man and woman are impressed by nothing they see; the boorish woman dominates her docile husband in all their conversations. Their cultural insensitivity, straight out of Lewis's *Babbitt*, seems so predictable that one wonders whether Thurber constructed the dialog beforehand and then looked for a situation to apply it to.

Thurber was determined to practice his French, but the room-service waiter at his hotel was equally determined to show off his English. Each day, when the waiter brought the food, Thurber would say, "Mettez l'assiette là-bas, s'il vous plaît." The waiter would reply, somewhat contemptuously, "Certainly, sir, and will there be anything else?" One day, he tried luring Thurber into more treacherous linguistic waters. "And what do you think of the weather today, sir?" he asked. The answer was beyond Thurber's reach in French, and, annoyed, he replied, "It is extremely difficult to predict exactly what my conception of today's atmospheric pressure is. Partially because I've not taken the trouble to observe and partly because the areas of high atmospheric pressure which I noted with interest in last night's weather report are moving with accelerated pace Southwest from Bourges, making any sort of a prophecy a sheer mockery. Anything might happen, to quote that beloved old philosopher, Dr. Johnson. Now, goddam it, mettez l'assiette là-bas, s'il vous plaît." The waiter thereafter served the Thurbers in silence.

Let Your Mind Alone! was published in September, dedicated to Helen, with a modest first printing of five thousand copies. Five additional printings followed by year's end. The collection consists of casuals and drawings, taking its title from his series on self-improvement books. The book's tone was Thurber at his most acerbic. Hamish Hamilton published the book in Britain a month later, but Thurber had sailed for France and missed that event, too. It was the first time he had not been on hand for the christening of one of his books.

The *Boston Transcript* reviewer thought Thurber's writing would be like Harpo Marx's if Harpo ever became articulate. The *New York Times* called it intelligent humor appealing to "the adult and sophisticated mind." *Time* casually noted it in conjunction with Wolcott Gibbs's own collection of *New Yorker* pieces, *Bed of Neurosis*, which happened to be published at about the same time. Thurber's mind, said *Time*, was "tough-fibered" and "analytical." Richard Lockridge, who had worked with Thurber on Talk in the early days, remained his admirer; after "One Is a Wanderer" had appeared in the magazine, Lockridge wrote Katharine White that it was the finest piece of fiction he had read anywhere. He now reviewed Thurber's new book for the *New York Sun*, quoting Max Eastman's assertion that Thurber had brains, "rare among humorists." The Thurber method, said Lockridge, was to be extremely reasonable in an unreasonable world: the drawings showed things as they were, and the prose showed what Thurber thought of things being that way.

The *Herald Tribune* reviewer supplied (anonymously) the heartiest tribute to Thurber as person, writer, and illustrator:

He understands clearly that life is pretty tough going and that very little
. . . can be done about it; he proves his case with charm and conviction. What a lawyer the man would have made if circumstances had not
turned his high talents to writing and drawing. He is one of our great
American institutions, and the sooner more people realize it, the better
off they will be.

One finds in this collection both the Thurber habits of old and the start of
new tendencies he would enlarge upon in the years ahead. His pessimism
about man ever working out matters satisfactorily on Earth was growing:

Working quietly through the ages, the insects and the rodents, at once
specialists and collectivists, have prepared themselves, I believe, to take
over the world. I see no reason to believe that they will not make a
better job of it than man.

His stand against technology and the social sciences as both dangerous and
ridiculous was firmer than ever. He achieves his literary absurdities through
both reduction and amplification, making a situation more complex than it is
or simpler than it is.

Walter Pitkin, a Columbia professor, had published a self-help book, *The
Psychology of Happiness*, in 1929. In it, he stated that six or seven people out
of every ten could attain a happy life, given the proper guidance and motivation. Using the 1930 population figure of 130 million Americans, Thurber
figures that only 130,000 of them were happy in 1929, by Pitkin's theory, but
that between 78 million and 91 million *could* have been happy.

Thurber would have been a fine screenwriter for Groucho Marx. In discussing "How to Develop Your Personality," by Sadie M. Shellow, he writes:
"I wouldn't dwell on this at such length if Dr. Shellow's publishers had not
set her up as a paragon of lucidity, precision, and logical thought. (Come to
think that over, I believe I would dwell on it at the same length even if they
hadn't.)"

Two of his lesser-known classics are contained in the volume: In "Nine
Needles," he wakes up at two-thirty in the afternoon in a friend's apartment,
starts to shave, rummages in the medicine cabinet, and manages to scatter a
group of needles into the washbowl, which is filled with soapy water. He
retrieves seven of them but can't get them off his wet hands, so he wipes
them onto a towel and then dries his hands on the bath mat. He can find
only five needles in the towel, leaving two missing and two still in the
washbowl. Worried that someone will use the towel with the needles, he

wraps it in a newspaper. He wants to leave a note of explanation but can't find a pen and decides to use a lipstick from the medicine cabinet.

> I got two fingers around it and began to pull gently—it was under a lot of things. Every object in the medicine cabinet began to slide. Bottles broke in the washbowl and on the floor; red, brown and white liquids spurted; nail files, scissors, razor blades, and miscellaneous objects sang and clattered and tinkled. I was covered with perfume, peroxide, and cold cream.
>
> It took me half an hour to get the debris all together in the middle of the bathroom floor. I made no attempt to put anything back. . . . I left a note saying that I was afraid there were needles in the bathtub and the washbowl and that I had taken their towel and that I would call up and tell them everything—I wrote it in iodine with the end of a toothbrush. I have not yet called up. . . . I suppose my friends believe that I deliberately smashed up their bathroom and stole their towel. I don't know for sure, because they have not yet called me up, either.

Also, in *Let Your Mind Alone!* is the hilarious casual, "No Standing Room Only." When the play *Victoria Regina,* starring Helen Hayes, completed its first fifty-two weeks, The *World-Telegram* reported that Hayes wished to celebrate the occasion by allowing only fifty-two standees admittance to the anniversary show. Thurber finds this a strange way to celebrate the occasion and wonders if the management misunderstood her actual request to let the first fifty-two standing-room-only patrons in *free.* He wonders what happened when the fifty-third person showed up, saw that there was plenty of standing room, offered to pay, and was told he wouldn't be allowed in.

"Every year, of course, is a Thurber year," a British book reviewer said, after leafing through Hamish Hamilton's edition of *The New Yorker Album* of 1937 cartoons.

The Thurbers spent six weeks in Paris, visiting art galleries and the French Exposition. In November, they drove from Paris to Aix-en-Provence, leaving the northern rain and cold weather for sweltering heat. They led a gourmet's life along the way, sampling snail, coq au chambertin, pheasant, partridge, wild boar, and "the finest of wines from 70 cents to two dollars." He wondered, he writes Elliott Nugent, whether he could ever again bring himself to pay as much as forty cents for a Scotch and soda in the States.

They drove to Italy, where Fascist bureaucracy and the people's fear of Mussolini kept Thurber grumbling in protest. A package of Christmas cards he had designed in Paris, to be forwarded to him in Italy for seasonal mailing, was held up by Italian customs. The card pictured a child lighting a candle in front of a decorated Christmas tree; to the right of the tableau is an unexplained Thurber rabbit, which Helen believes is what puzzled the Italian authorities, ever watchful for anti-Mussolini propaganda in subtle forms. Helen was later to say that Thurber was amused by the confusion his card caused the Fascists, but that seems unlikely, given Thurber's contempt for the government, his being deprived of his personal handcrafted cards, and his quick temper.

They spent Thurber's forty-third birthday in Rome. "We loved Rome, Sorrento, Amalfi, but not Naples," Helen writes. On December 16, he sent cartoons and caption ideas to the *New Yorker* art conference from Italy. One is of a teenage girl weeping while her mother tells a visitor, "She's reading some novel that's breaking her heart, but we don't know where she hides it." He sent along a spot illustration, too, offering a typical Thurber explanation to the art meeting:

The spot shows, as Bob Coates will see at a glance, the influence of the Roman phase. Just what the allegory is, if there is any, I dont know. I call it "Hope after Hannibal," I think. I am very fond of lions, and of

angels with wands—if this is a lion and an angel with a wand. I do not see how you can use it in the magazine, nor do I see why you can't.

In October, Andy White had returned to Manhattan from Maine to join his wife and son, but things were no better for him there. "I got back from Maine a week ago," he wrote Thurber, "but all this week I have been looking around and wondering why I came away." The gloomy tenor of the letter led Thurber to better understand that White's depression was more than a temporary setback. On December 22, writing from Naples, Thurber again invites White to join them at the villa they plan to rent at Cap d'Antibes, on the Mediterranean:

Dear Andy:

You could take an Italian ship . . . get off at Nice and there we would be . . . to meet you. At your age another New York winter would just about do you in.

We came down from Rome today over the old Hannibal route, a route I've always wanted to follow. . . . It has always been a sad thing to me that after crossing the Pyrenees and the Alps with those goddam elephants, [Hannibal] lost all but one in his first battle—on the flats. He reminded me of Rex, my old bull terrier, who, as a pup, worked for three days trying to get a telephone pole in through our kitchen door, only to have it taken away from him, with some effort, by eight linemen who had been wondering where it was.

We'll be here for Christmas—brought our presents with us. . . . Like Englishmen dressing for dinner in the desert, we will bravely carry out a Connecticut Christmas in the midst of these palms and olives and oranges.

White was still in a melancholy state, made worse by the recent death of one of his heroes, Don Marquis, the creator of archy, the typing cockroach; moreover, one of his articles had been rejected by an old friend, Joseph Bryan III, at the *Saturday Evening Post*. In a long reply to Thurber, White says:

I have made an unholy mess out of this "year off" business. I haven't produced two cents worth of work, have broken my wife's health, my own spirit, and two or three fine old lampshades by getting my feet tangled in the cord. Kay is restless when I go away, and I am no bargain when I am around, either. Gibbs quit his desk job rather abruptly, and Kay has had a lot of extra work deriving from that. She got grippe before Christmas, and I got it, and we celebrated the 23rd of December by fighting over what Xmas was all about anyway. This left us in a limp beaten state—one of those periods from which one can't escape by merely taking a boat and watching somebody balance a 20-gallon water jar on her head. We're going to have to balance our own jars for a while.

Thurber's marathon reply is from the Villa Tamisier, at Cap d'Antibes, where he and Helen would spend the first four months of 1938. He agrees with White's "sound" conclusions about things, except for the one about not being able to escape from "beaten states" by taking a boat. That, it seemed to him, is the only way to escape such things.

I felt I could not leave New York and my trips to Cambridge [Rosemary remembers seeing her father there only once] and my nervous overnight post looking toward Columbus where hell of one kind of another pops every few minutes, or did. But my daughter and I have established a new and strong tie; we engage in a fine and remarkable correspondence, notable for her ability to say everything that is necessary in two sentences without punctuation and my own surprising ability to write that hardest of all things, a letter to a girl six years old. My family seems to have taken on new courage and strength now that I am away; my mother's letters, while no funnier, are more cheerful. William is coming along all right, Robert has never been better, my father is doing all right. And nine months have gone by, all quite easily.

He knows there's nothing to laugh about consistently, given the troubled times, but "those of us who are able to do that must keep on doing it, no matter who or what goes to hell." And what was White doing sending his writing to the *Saturday Evening Post?* "What was the matter with that excellent weekly called the New Yorker? . . . Harpers, Scribners, the Forum, maybe, if you must get outside the New Yorker. . . . It is my carefully arrived at and calmly studied opinion that the New Yorker is the best magazine in the world." He tries to reassure White:

I doubt very much that your "year off" has been any less productive than mine. . . . My output in nine months would discourage you if you were me. The thing is to keep your hand in. Nobody can write anything who doesnt. . . .

Enough of the goddam lecturing or whatever it is.

The case of a swell guy like Don Marquis is enough to depress anybody. . . . There must be some kind of strange law about disasters pil-
ing up on certain people. Take my brother Robert. He not only had
goitre, but pleurisy, t.b., eye trouble, soft teeth, permanent rheum, and a
dozen other things, including duodenal ulcer which he seems to have
been born with; also he broke his right arm in two places, his left in
three, sprung out the spool pins of one ankle, fell out of a bus on his
head as a child, was run over by a milk wagon, and so on. I got shot in
the eye . . . and they called it a day. . . . Ten million men out of ten
million and two would have lost the sight of both eyes as a result of what
I stepped into. . . . I often wonder what I would be like now if I had
gone blind at the age of seven. I see myself as kind of fat, for some
reason, and wandering about the grounds of a large asylum, plucking at
leaves and chortling.

He notes that while White is thinking of leaving the city for the Maine
farm, the Coateses are thinking of selling their country home and of moving
into the city. Thurber thinks the Coateses are making a mistake:

They have got to the city after too long a time at a stretch in the
country and have fallen under the city's spell—a pretty strong one at
first—but in a year or so they would be exactly where you are, only they
wouldnt have a home they own to go to. . . . The New York life will
get them sooner or later, probably sooner, as it gets everybody. . . . It
has been interesting to see the perfect picture drawn in a few sentences
in each letter we get, of New York life. "There has been a steady traffic
to Foord's and back among the Gibbs, McKelway and unstrung group."
. . . And wonderful stories of how Louise let everything burn or get
cold so she and Jack didnt get any dinner at all, and how they left
Merton asleep under the piano, and the whole crowd went over to
Spitty's on Third Avenue for steaks but didnt eat them when they were
brought. And Mike finally got Bill told off about his wife and she
screamed that she loved Mike and Bill just sat down and cried, only on
the overturned chair, so Mike stayed on and Greta made scrambled eggs
for all three of them. . . .

Your problem about the city house is not so easy. What's the matter
with renewing the lease and kind of living there half the time, Maine
the other half? Or anyway, your three months in Maine (make it four).
Eight months in New York, with visits to the Thurbers in Connecticut is

bearable, and anyway you like New York and except for walking into cars you dont let it get you so much. I also think you should go back to comment, without letting it depress or kill you, because it was the best column in the country and something to find satisfaction in doing— with periods off now and then. I also think the magazine will rot from the base up if you never do any more newsbreak lines.

By March 1938, the Whites had decided to give up the Turtle Bay apartment and move to the North Brooklin farm. "Kay loved her job and it was difficult for her to give it up," says William Maxwell, "but she loved Andy more." White contracted with *Harper's Magazine* to write a monthly column called "One Man's Meat." Ross begged him to continue contributing to the *New Yorker, Harper's* column or not. White resumed his newsbreak work for Ross in June, and occasionally contributed casuals, poetry, and Comment as a freelancer. But when Ross asked why he preferred writing twenty-five thousand words a month for *Harper's* and not the *New Yorker,* he explained that with a signed department, in which he could use "I" instead of "we," he could "cover new ground, which is necessary at this stage." Furthermore, a monthly department gave him three weeks off, "which I can devote to a sustained project, like shingling a barn or sandpapering an old idea."

Ross took whatever he could get of White's. He paid him seventy-five dollars a week for his newsbreak editing, a new rate of twenty-five cents a word for whatever prose he contributed, and fifty shares of the magazine's stock each year. The *Harper's* column would continue for nearly five years, and then the Whites moved back to the city during the war years, and back to the *New Yorker* full time, though they had bought and winterized the Maine house and continued to vacation there.

At Cap d'Antibes, the Thurbers threw semimonthly parties, the warmer climates of the southern coast luring Janet Flanner and others from Paris. Maxine Elliot, a hostess who entertained royalty, and other members of international society, invited the Thurbers to tea at her nearby villa. Winston Churchill was downstairs playing mah-jongg when they arrived, Helen writes. Reminded of who Thurber was, Churchill said, "Oh, yes, that insane American and depraved artist." They were given the grand tour of the house during tea, shown Churchill's watercolors and told of Churchill's remark, which Thurber would treasure thereafter. Thurber fixed Churchill a strong Scotch and soda, which he took upstairs to bed with him.

The thirties were Thurber's golden years as man and artist. He may have seemed to reduce most of his equation of perplexities to a common denominator of men, women, dogs, liquor, and party talk, but there would be no easy resolutions as long as he saw the numerator as the multiple and insoluble mysteries of life. For the moment, he was handling those superbly.

50

That Man Who Knew Too Little

We want to go up into Vienna and Prague if we can get passports in May. . . . I am sorry I missed the chance to see Vienna as Viennese and it's terrible to think of it in the hands of the worst bastards the history of the world has ever known. . . . I wish there were no Czechoslovakia. That noble little country annoys me the way Ann Harding does [in] the movie we saw called "Green Light". . . . France will have to hurl herself against Germany with about as much chance of winning as a 15 year old Ohio virgin in a West Fifty-eighth street night club. It's been pretty discouraging to watch England kissing all the bottoms in Europe, France squabbling like a bunch of neighbor women, Russia executing all their prominent men in a way that makes pulp stories seem like Atlantic [Monthly] essays, while Hitler goes in and does whatever he wants to.

—Letter to Katharine White, March 24, 1938

The Spanish Civil War was crowding the ideological itinerary of the political and literary left at home. Hemingway, Dos Passos, and even Dorothy Parker had journeyed to Spain to report on the stand being made by the Loyalists against Franco's coalition of the military, Church, and Royalists. But Thurber, for all his hand wringing, stayed away from events of those proportions. He was sympathetic to the Republican side but, like George Orwell, a bit bored by it all, and he recognized that a literary commitment to ideology would numb his imagination. He felt that his Communist colleagues still didn't understand life under Stalin. Beyond that, humorists, as he had stated, "pulled the blinds against the morning," and crept "into smoky corners at night." What the world was up against they learned only by coming upon an old copy of *Time* on a picnic ground, or in the summer house of a friend.

He did join the League of American Writers in the winter of 1937–38; neither he nor anyone else imagined that in the McCarthy period a few of its members would be investigated for sedition. All Thurber knew about the organization was that Hemingway and others of celebrated stature in his profession belonged.

His "The Man Who Knew Too Little," published in the fall of 1937, sums up Thurber's potential danger to America as a leftist. It features a disappointed organizer of an espionage ring who assesses the Thurber Man's personality and explains to his wife, at a Paris café, that her husband is simply too nervous to be a joiner of organizations with revolutionary designs.

He wrote voluminous, chatty letters—to the Whites, McNultys, Williamses, McKelways, Coateses, and Nugents. Perhaps through McKelway or McNulty, Leonard Lyons, a gossip columnist for the *New York Evening Post,* learned that Thurber was mailing tempting advertisements of European liquor and drinking establishments to those friends who were struggling to stay on the wagon at home. (McKelway and Gibbs, who had planned to write a play together, were currently residents of Foord's sanitarium.) Lyons's item was part of an emerging tendency of columnists to try to tie Thurber to "funny" anecdotes that bore little resemblance to the way Thurber's humor operated, and a custom whose hash he tried to settle in "The Ordeal of Mr. Matthews":

His secretary brings him a folder of newspaper clippings labeled "Things You Have Said." Reading the unfunny misquotations leads him to believe "the practice of wit as a fine art is one with the carriage horse."

> Freddy Wakeman . . . told the [Chicago] *Sun*'s Spectorsky an anecdote about me when I was in Bermuda. A dewy young thing . . . asked me why I had sold a certain piece of mine to the movies. Quick as a flash, I answered, "M-o-n-e-y." . . .

A *Time* reporter got me on the long-distance phone. . . . He said, "Do you know Jo Davidson?" . . .

The files of *Time* . . . reveal that I shot back, "I met him once. He has a beard."

As keen as my famous Davidson quip was . . . I was to top it. . . . Earl Wilson, the . . . columnist of the New York *Post*, called on me at my office. . . . I was drinking black coffee. My greeting was what I can only describe as a staggeroo. "I'm having some formaldehyde," I'm supposed to have said. "Will you join me?"

I resent . . . what has all the appearance of a conspiracy to place on my shoulders the mantle of Calvin Coolidge.

He lamented the disappearance of a day when genuine wit flourished, and was accurately reported. He envied Benchley, whose witticisms seemed to circulate flawlessly. When a teetotaler told Benchley the whiskey he was drinking was slow poison, Benchley replied, "So who's in a hurry?" When Ross once asked Benchley why his play review was late again, Benchley said he was having trouble with the ablative accusative. Benchley's remarks got around intact; Thurber rarely had such luck.

One of Thurber's most popular pieces, "The Macbeth Murder Mystery," appeared in the *New Yorker* of October 2, 1937: The narrator meets an American woman at his hotel in the English lake country. She has purchased a copy of *Macbeth*, thinking it is a detective story. Having read it, she decides Macduff killed the King, for when the body is discovered, she says, Macduff "comes running downstairs and shouts, 'Confusion has broke open the Lord's anointed temple' and 'Sacrilegious murder has made his masterpiece' and on and on like that." An unrehearsed, innocent man, she says, would say, " 'My God, there's a body in here!' " The British coauthors of a mystery novel written as a parody of *Macbeth* charged Thurber with plagiarism. The *New Yorker*, however, confirmed that Thurber had submitted his piece before the book appeared.

He continued to have run-ins with Ross over the editing of his material. A Reporter at Large by Thurber, subtitled "La Grande Ville de Plaisir" and mailed from the French Riviera, contained a reference to the Hotel Ruhl. The magazine's fact checkers enlarged it to the "Hotel Ruhl et des Anglais." Thurber, when he saw this in proof, cabled Ross: "Where shall we meet for five o'clock tea—at the Waldorf-Astoria or the Ritz-Carlton?"

"The guidebooks listed it with the "et des Anglais," says Freddie Packard, who was the head of the checking department at the time. "A *New Yorker* reader wanting to look up the hotel might not have found it under Thurber's casual form."

"Thurber was one of our sacred cows by then," says McKelway. "You were very careful what you did to his copy. He once cabled Ross accusing him of putting a comma in a sentence where it didn't belong, and said if Ross insisted on sticking commas somewhere, Thurber had an excellent recommendation." When the Riviera piece was collected, in *My World—and Welcome to It*, the hotel emerged as the "Hotel Ruhl et Anglais," the "des" having been sacrificed through some unexplained compromise or mistake.

The Thurbers stayed at the Villa Tamisier on Cap d'Antibes from the first of 1938 until April 30. The servants were the Russian gardener, Olympy Sementzoff, and his wife, the housekeeper, Maria. Thurber's frequent references to the *New Yorker* led Maria to believe that he worked for the city of New York. In "A Ride with Olympy," as we have seen, Thurber makes that poor bearded White Russian the fall guy in a car accident during a driving lesson being provided by Thurber. Competing with French motorists was a sobering challenge. "The thing to do," says Thurber, "is stop when you spy a French motorist out of control or about to go out of control. . . . One should lie low when the French begin to bang into one another, and wait until the desperate design is disentangled and the highway is quiet again." Thurber was driving defensively years before the phrase gained currency.

News of changes at the magazine reached them. Gibbs had given up editing to replace White as the principal writer of Comment, and to review plays. McKelway and Katharine White were jointly encouraging promising young writers fresh out of college—Brendan Gill and E. J. Kahn, for example. Russell Maloney was working out as Thurber's replacement on Talk, Thurber thought. ("An Irishman named Russell," McNulty told Thurber, "is the wrongest thing I know of.") Katharine White had reluctantly agreed to quit as fiction editor to move to Maine with Andy in the summer of 1938. Their good friend Gus Lobrano, another Cornell man, had replaced her. Robert Henderson, who had been Katharine's assistant, now sent manuscripts to her for her consideration and editing. Other newcomers were Jack Alexander, Sanderson Vanderbilt, John and David Lardner, and Richard Boyer. Ross and McKelway even lured the *Times*'s cherished feature writer, Mike Berger, to the magazine, but Berger almost immediately got claustrophobia in his private cubbyhole, missed the companionship of the city room and, when he asked somebody next door to him at the *New Yorker* where he might get a drink of water, he found one of the famous watercoolers being set up outside his door. He soon returned to the *Times*.

Art Samuels, the former managing editor, died unexpectedly in 1938 but Thurber, in France, was unable to learn from what. "There seem to be as many changes in the New Yorker as in the European situation," Thurber writes Katharine, "both of which may lead to war." But Richard Boyer remembers that "they weren't really replacing people; just adding people." Among those being added, to Thurber's delight, was John McNulty. As McNulty's mentor, Thurber writes Katharine:

> I'm glad McNulty has been taken on and sure do hope he stays. I know he is crazy about it and will work very hard. Of course my rating of him is as one of the great people. What he knows about journalism, New York, Jews, Irish, cops, waiters, bartenders, city editors, Columbus, war, soldiers, social figures, bums, millionaires, is all there is to know. He's a fine reporter, the best mixer I know—he can get in with anyone anywhere—and has a sense of humor, a turn of wit, and a gift for phrase absolutely his own. I think that more and more he will be able to write what we want back there. But I dont want him to lose his marvellous original genius for phrases, sentences and ideas. About a third of the things I like to remember when I lie awake are things John said, found or revealed.

He offers McNulty further assistance, reminding him of the "idea" books at the office

> containing two or three thousand suggestions for Talk stories. . . . Every time Ross or anyone thought of something that might make a Talk story, it was entered with notes describing what it was. . . . You might get some ideas of Talk pieces you could slip out and do now and then.

But McNulty, who would make his name writing about his choice of subjects in his own style, was initially discouraged by Ross's editing of his fact pieces. He wrote Thurber a despairing letter. Thurber reassures him, reminding him of the difficult time he himself had getting started with Ross, and offering an example of Talk's style:

> I finally figured out what [Ross] wanted, in a way: "A man we know was telling us the other day about gaskets. Seems they are little funny kind of what's-its names. Fellow named Pritch or Feep invents them, or

imports them, or something of the sort. Otto H. Kahn has ninety-two and a Mrs. Bert Geefle of the Savoy Plaza seven. Nobody else has any, except Madame Curie who was presented with four thousand by the city of Nantes for telling the city what time it was one night when it called Meridian 1212 and got her by mistake." There you have an easy, off hand statement, full of facts, presented with a nonchalant, almost insolent disregard for facts, highly informative but sounding like my mother on the subject of Einstein's theory. Talk thus has a style. . . . You are not imitating Maloney if you write like that—or in any one of the half dozen other veins that fit the goddam thing—nor are you imitating White or me. Maloney probably went through the same half-depressed, half-angry period of wondering if he had to imitate me—just as I did about Andy. . . . No use worrying about that. John Steinbeck, Walt Whitman, Evelyn Waugh, and Shakespeare would all have to get the knack of it, if they got any stories printed. I can see Ross calmly running the copy of all of them through his typewriter, too. . . . I can hear Ross saying of Will Shakespeare, as he edits his copy, "Son of a bitch falls into a kind of goddam sing-song only it don't rhyme." As far as Talk goes, he would be right, too. . . .

People sometimes speak of a New Yorker Style, but they are either thinking of Talk or of the form and shape of the casuals. It takes a knack to do things in from 1000 to 3000 words. . . . I find most of my stories, after I have typed them, run to 6 and a half or seven pages. I havent tried for that. My brain has unconsciously formed that kind of mould for them. In a way this is bad, because everything I start—play, two-volume novel, or whatnot, finally rounds itself out into 6 or 7 pages—seems complete, too. The Saturday Review recently spoke of Gibbs' and my pieces as being of a special New Yorker form, neither essay nor short story but a little of each. It really is a form of its own, too. Slighter than the short story, stronger than the essay. . . . We have invented, or perfected, something that is neither a happy ending nor an unhappy ending. It might be called the trailing off. . . . We seem to find a high merit in leaving men on bases. We dont like to have a guy doubled off second on a line drive; too rough and abrupt. . . . More people are left standing and looking in ballets and New Yorker casuals than in any other known art forms.

I try to end a casual so that you know what the characters are going to do next. (This is not true of the drawings which end in a situation in which nobody could possibly do anything else . . .) Dont read the magazine too consistently. If you read it from cover to cover its like eating a two pound box of candy. . . .

Get the New Yorker slant or attitude or whatever it is, but take nobody's style. Be a little egotistical, remembering that nobody in the world can tell a story better than you and that all of us experts in story tellers know that. . . .

There's nothing more you have to learn from the New Yorker—the rest is what it's got to learn from you.

Katharine wrote Thurber about his submissions to the art conference, sent from Italy. ("I didn't expect them to use the lion and angel, really," he tells her in reply.) A cartoon had been rejected, said Katharine, because it was thought the point of the joke was that the man in the picture had no hair. "None of my men have hair," he answers her. "Hair on one of my figures denotes a woman. . . . The point [of the humor] was . . . in the caption; the man could have lots of hair."

He still finds it hard to accept her and Andy's decision to move to Maine for a year:

> Both of you like New York and get so much out of it. Andy, I know, really loves the place; nobody who didnt could have written the piece he did for the Saturday Evening Post which said in effect that you couldn't make him stay in Maine the year around. . . .
>
> It is pretty hard from a distance to figure out just what actuates you and Andy. When I am with you two I can always tell the fact from the supposition because you both have bad poker faces. . . . With you and Andy it is your pauses. You also throw lateral passes at each other that a blind end could break up. The health argument sounds okay, but some-how not okay enough. No decisions made by old New Yorker editors are ever as simple as all that. Retreating to Maine with a handful of news-breaks, the untimely comment, and one third of an editorial job may work out all right but it sounds a little temporary. . . .
>
> Well, in another twenty years we would all have to give up anyway, for a newer generation of Bryn Mawr, Cornell, and O S U girls and boys.

He gets into what he thinks is wrong with *New Yorker* casuals, taking part of the blame:

> The thing that marks us most, I think from here, is the pussy-cat quality of most of the males in most of the casuals. That's awfully deeply rooted

now, I'm afraid, and I had more to do with it with Mr. Monroe than Andy did with Philip Wedge, too. But who was to know that there would follow a Sally Benson, a [Richard] Lockridge, and, as good as he is, a [William] Maxwell, all members of the same school, all devoted in their separate ways to what Henry James called "poor sensitive gentlemen." . . . And yet all around us roars and thunders the maleness of the characters of Hemingway, Cain, Horace McCoy, and others. We are up with the times in going in for foreign pieces, and I'm glad of it, but the male characters of our casuals live in Admiral Dewey's time. We got to give 'em pokers to bend, women to lay, guys to smack in the puss. What ever became of John O'Hara?

But thinking all that over, he adds a postscript taking back what he had just said:

I have decided that the Little Man, the bewildered man, the nervous, beaten, wife-crossed man, is a realer and stronger thing in American life than the Cain men who lay Mexican women in churches or the Hemingway men that choke guys to death. American life being what it is, we couldnt leave the Little Man out of it. It has been interesting to notice the American ads over here, as against the French. The French picture-ads show the male dominant, the wife asking permission, etc. The American ads show a woman, full page, frowning, saying "I wont go a step with you till you shave!" and "If you think you can wear that messy shirt, you're crazy."

Thurber worked hard at his writing during the four-month stay at the Cap d'Antibes villa. They took time for a thousand-mile sight-seeing drive around Southern France. "You got to watch the person five cars ahead of you and five cars behind all the time," he writes Katharine. "Their favorite hazard is passing a car that's passing a car. This is apparently considered great sport, like skiing. You have to learn a new traffic signal here, that is: waving your left arm and hand madly in a gesture meaning 'Stay back there, you feeble-minded son of a bitch!' "

Katharine kept him posted as to her and Andy's current physical travails, and Thurber, who found it hard to take the Whites' chronic infirmities seriously at the time, writes Katharine:

I have long thought [Andy] suffers mainly from Repression of Writing Instincts, which can be a much worse repression than that of sex. I think now that he is writing more he will find that street dizziness and the ear trouble vanishing. Like his fallen stomach and paratyphoid I believe they are merely symbols of Writer's Repression.

They said good-bye to the Villa Tamisier and drove to Paris. They stopped at Lourdes, which, despite its international fame as the site of religious miracles, was described by the guidebook only as specializing in *chocolat*. Thurber was pleased to be mistaken for a French native and says that he was frequently complimented on his English by Americans asking directions. "Ees because," he would reply on these occasions, "I am leeving for forty-three years een New York and Ohio."

Though Paris was his favorite city, the British were his favorite Europeans. He was amused by London newspaper stories. In "Laughs from London," he quotes from the *Daily Telegraph* an account of a trial in which the judge got off a number of wisecracks—all incomprehensible to Thurber—and he marvels at the number of times the courtroom audience is reported to have laughed.

He wrote McNulty in June a carefree account of the landlord who operated the apartment building off Piccadilly where he and Helen were staying. The man knew all about horse races, a subject always dear to McNulty's heart. McNulty, in turn, wrote Thurber news from the magazine, including the fact that Maloney had wallpapered over one of Thurber's drawings at the office. Thurber assured McNulty that he would do a better cartoon and paste it over "the son-of-a-bitch's wallpaper" as soon as he got back. "We live in a nice flat," he tells McNulty. "Whores frequent this part of Mayfair and often six or eight are prowling up and down before the house. At 3 or 4 in the morning they play together, toss, catch, pig-in-a-poke, kitten-for-a-corner, you-chase-me, etc. . . . . Their approach: 'Would you like to talk with me?' "

Ann Honeycutt had sent him the manuscript of *How to Raise a Dog*, which she cowrote with a veterinarian, Dr. James R. Kinney, and asked if Thurber would illustrate it. He agreed. He drew thirty-one full-page drawings for the two-hundred-page book, and it was published later that year.

"I had got my first dog," says Honey, "and had read some awful books on how to raise it. Kinney was the chief vet for the Ellin Prince Speyer Hospital, in New York, and for the Westminster dog show at Madison Square Garden. Clifton Fadiman, whom I knew from CBS radio days—he emceed 'Information, Please'—was at Simon & Schuster and got us together with Jack Goodman, a nice Englishman, who was an S&S editor. Jack paid Thurber a flat fee for the illustrations, which satisfied Thurber but I don't think Helen. Thurber used to tell me it was really his book, that my text was simply the captions for his drawings. Helen seemed to resent his doing them, and when the book was a best-seller for a year, I think Helen thought I had used Jim unfairly. But I had two or three other artists willing to do it, and Jim said he wanted the assignment. Besides, Jim met Goodman through all this, and they became great friends. It was Jack who eventually persuaded Thurber to switch publishers, from Harcourt Brace to Simon & Schuster."

In London, John O'Hara invited the Thurbers to his flat for a Fourth of July celebration. O'Hara later recorded the affair: "The flowers were red, white and blue. The invited guests were Americans in London. There were the inevitable crashers and one of them, an Englishwoman, said, 'What *is* the Fourth of July?' That was all James Thurber needed. He made the best July Fourth oration I've ever heard and I can't remember a thing he said. He can't either."

The Thurbers were also with the O'Haras when they attended Ladies Night at "an eccentric dining club—Ye Sette of Odde Volumes, of which I was then Vice President," writes Alec Waugh. And Waugh remembers that a Thurber admirer, Lawrence Meynell, brought the Thurbers to his box at Lords for a cricket match between England and Australia:

> Thurber had been commissioned by the *News Chronicle* to write an article about the match. I was afraid that he might be facetiously patronizing about cricket, in the same way that some English writers are about baseball; but to my relief and amusement, he wrote an entertaining comparison between cricket and the match game that was at that time popular in Bleeck's. The Thurbers made themselves very popular in London.

Joel Sayre agrees. He remembers attending a formal dinner in ceremonial robes at Oxford, where he had been a student. He noted with apprehension at his left "a figure of imposing grandeur and monumental scholarship" who, he felt, would hopelessly outclass him as a conversationalist. But the distinguished educator put him at ease by leaning toward him and saying abruptly, "Now tell me all about this remarkable man, Thurber."

The Thurbers dined with Charles Laughton, who, according to an article by Alva Johnston, believed that Thurber, as pen-and-ink artist, was "the great comic genius of the time.":

> [Laughton's] greatest ambition is to play the Thurber man. . . . No other modern work, according to Laughton, equals the Thurber draw-

ings in their serious criticism of the world in their arraignment of the bad craftsmanship that went into the making of the human race.

Ross was in London with his second wife, Frances, a pretty woman a dozen years Ross's junior, whom he had married in 1934. Thurber proudly introduced several of his new English friends to Ross at the Dorchester Hotel, and met up with the Rosses again in Paris, where the Thurbers had gone in preparation for the voyage home from Le Havre. The two couples shared some sight-seeing. The Thurbers departed on the *Champlain* on August 25, arriving in New York seven days later, to the relief of Mame Thurber, who had been worried about the threat of war abroad.

With Thurber's drawings still legible here and there on the walls of the offices, it was difficult for some at the *New Yorker* to remember that he wasn't there, which was all right with Joseph Mitchell.

"Ross and McKelway had met me at the Blue Ribbon restaurant for lunch when I was one of several newspapermen trying to get on the *New Yorker*," Mitchell says. "Ross told me I could join if I wanted to but it would probably be a foolish thing for me to do. That was my welcome. The *New Yorker* offices weren't spread out the way they are now, but it was still a fairly inhospitable place. Thurber was in Europe when I joined, but his drawings covered parts of the corridor walls of the nineteenth floor. The walls were dirty, and the sketches gave them a strange and interesting life. Arrows pointed to certain words, with a doomful phrase here and there as some kind of warning to himself and to others. Russell Maloney used to scribble on walls, too, but I didn't think they worked; Thurber's did.

"There were always tensions in the office because Ross put such importance on unimportant things. The echoes of Thurber around the place helped. His graphics used to make me feel more cheerful, and I needed cheering. So a Profile I was working on went to pieces? It didn't matter, you felt, reading Thurber's fatalistic words, or seeing a Thurber Man in much worse shape than you felt you were in. Thurber had that sixth sense about disaster that talented people have. The professional dilemmas he wrote about, if they hadn't already happened at the office, inevitably would.

"When he came back from abroad I found him easy to get along with. He had a special feeling about ex-newspaper reporters, and remembered my *World-Telegram* article about him. As one of the old-timers with a lot of influence, he never pulled rank, or was in the least standoffish. I appreciated that."

A. J. Liebling also joined the staff in 1938. "Just before the War, I moved into a small office that [Thurber] had occupied for a while," he writes, "and . . . on the wall, just above my desk, he had drawn a Thurber tombstone, with a Thurber flower at its foot, and beneath the picture the following dialogue:

" 'He loved but once, and then too late.'

" 'Q—How late?'

" '—43.'

" '—Too late.' "

The wall writing would have been from late 1938, more than three years after Thurber's marriage to Helen.

Liebling became an admiring friend of Thurber's—particularly in 1955, when they saw much of one another in London. But he cooled toward him when, he felt, Thurber reneged on a promise that Liebling and several other *New Yorker* veterans would contribute their experiences with Ross to *The Years with Ross*. Nor did Liebling like what Thurber "did to Ross" in the book.

"It is interesting," Liebling writes acidly, "that at forty-three he should have loved 'but once.' That is one more than I would have given him credit for, if we except his crush on James Thurber, a lifelong passion. It is interesting, too, that he should have thought forty-three too late. When *I* was forty-three . . . I thought I was still hot stuff. (I no longer do.)" Barbara Lawrence, one of the many who worked briefly at the *New Yorker,* and who occupied that same office later, found Thurber's penciled regrets fading to near invisibility and carefully traced new life into them.

In deciphering Thurber's graphic codes, his age consciousness cannot be overlooked. The bells that tolled for him were the bells of clock towers, measuring the passing of precious years. In the East Side apartment of Dick and Louise Connell, there hung a magnificent cartoon by Thurber, presented on Dick Connell's fortieth birthday. There is a setting sun, a dying flower, an overturned glass, and candles that have burned low. A man sits before a typewriter, unable to lift a hand. It is Thurber's version of a writer turned forty, and as much a self-portrait as anything else. "For Dick, October 17, 1933," Thurber signed the picture, "with cheery wishes."

Once, in 1949, he was discussing with an interviewer the problems he was having writing a play. "I'm not sure I'll live long enough to finish it," he said. Was he aware, the interviewer asked him, of how much in his writing he seemed preoccupied with age? In his mid-thirties he was writing of himself as a man ready for a nursing home. He nodded. "Age is one of the phobias I've had to deal with. When I was twenty-nine, I used to get depressed worrying about turning thirty. I felt I'd lived my life and had nothing to show for it. Women are even more like that. My first wife cried all night on her thirtieth birthday. My thirties and forties were bad in that regard, too, but I'm enjoying my fifties."

But even in 1938, at age forty-three, he was feeling the weight of the years, as he wrote Katharine White:

> I wish I hadn't passed my prime for writing New Yorker stuff. I feel one's thirties are the best for it and that we'll all have to give up at 45. I think I am going through a mental menopause, with my mind and intellect at its lowest. . . . Let us all try to hold on a little longer. I got to see what Ross is doing about Arno and Fleischmann and all the little payment problems when he is 65. I got to see that. Please God let me see that.

He dreamed of ways he could hold down the relentless passage of time. "At age sixty-five," he told Glenna Syse, of the *Chicago Sun-Times*, shortly before his death, "it occurred to me: if there were fifteen months in every year, I'd be only fifty-two. That's the trouble with us—we number everything. Take women, for example. I think women deserve to have more than twelve years between the ages of twenty-eight and forty." And when *Newsweek* interviewed Thurber on his sixty-sixth birthday, the last he would live to see, Thurber was still in character, finding it hardly a day to celebrate. "After all," he said, "I'm now within fourteen years of being eighty."

Following his return from abroad, Thurber wrote the Whites a note, remembering to send White "Merry Birthday Greetings":

> We have been as busy as a turkey fancier since we got home 2 weeks ago, looking for a place to live. . . . Found one yesterday—near Woodbury [Connecticut], a dream, a poem of a house 225 yrs. old but complete with all facilities, one of the nicest places in the world. . . .
> Busy illustrating Honey's dog book & looking forward to EBW's Harper's pieces. . . . Driving to Columbus in October in new Ford I just got. No trace of Althea & my daughter yet—she's gallivanting I guess.

Though office space was always made available to him at the *New Yorker*, after fifteen months away he sensed a difference there. At Woodbury, he wrote White about it:

I feel pretty far away from the arms, the councils, and the understanding of the New Yorker. It's not the place I worked for years ago, when you and I removed Art Samuels' rugs and lamps in order to draw pictures and write lines for Is Sex Necessary. This is perhaps because I am an older man, with my youth definitely behind me and fifty around the corner. There is an air of college halls about the place; people bow to you; there is a faint precise ticking sound; an atmosphere of austere incoherence dwells there. . . .

Except for dear and wonderful Miss Terry, I feel that I am looked upon as an outsider, possibly a has been. She sends out letters and packages for me, handles mail etc., but I feel nobody else thinks I really have any right to any such services. With my name no longer on the list of editorial folk and no room of my own to go to, this is only natural. . . . The aging humorist I suppose is bound to be a sad figure. They go in for the fleeting smile down there and the neatly pressed pants and I have the notion that they shake their heads politely over what I think is funny. Of course, I withdrew from the actual halls but I never considered myself as withdrawing from the magazine. If only one person had asked me what I thought of one idea in the [dozen times] I was around the place I would have felt less like a waiter in the Beta house.

The fierce 1938 hurricane had just struck the Northeast. With telephone lines down, Thurber was unable to reach Althea and Rosemary in Cambridge for two days, but "I'm to see Rosemary this Saturday at Sandy Hook," he is able to tell White. "I have always had a feeling that nobody close to me is going to be ended by a flood or earthquake. . . . Fly-paper is something else. Althea says there is not going to be a war."

When in Europe, Thurber wrote White that he had agreed to do an article about him for the *Saturday Review of Literature*. When it appeared, in October 1938, it put White "into one of my wincing moods," he writes Thurber, "but I'm damned if I didn't come through in good shape." Thurber describes White as shy, unfamiliar to his public. But the reason he isn't recognized in the Algonquin, White tells Thurber, is that no one "can remember a single thing I have ever said that was either amusing or informing. I am a dull man. . . . Nobody ever seeks me out, not even people who like me or approve of me; because after you have sought me out, you haven't got anything but a prose writer. I can't imitate birds, or dogs; I can't even remember what happened last night."

He recognizes the financial sacrifice Thurber made in doing the piece for the *Saturday Review*. "Last spring in Bermuda," Andy writes, "I put in 53 hours doing a book review for them, and got nine dollars, or 17c an hour. That's small pay even for a Cornell man."

Thurber proudly drove with Helen to Columbus in October. In contemporary summer snapshots of her, Helen looks girlish and attractive in skirt, blouse, bobby sox, and saddle shoes. She wears a spit curl, with her hair gathered in back so that her ears show.

They stayed at the Deshler-Wallick Hotel and visited the Thurber family, the Gardiners, and the Millers. They saw the O.S.U.-Purdue football game with the Millers, and Thurber spoke to the students in one of Herman's classes. He held forth at the hotel and at the Mills coffee shop for an ever changing audience. "Talking to Jim Thurber," wrote one reporter, "is like talking to somebody who has just run a mile race. He's breathless all the time. He's so full of stories they stumble over each other in the telling. He starts one, turns around, forgets it and starts another:

" 'Did I ever tell you about the girl at O.S.U. that I advised seven years ago against trying to sell anything to the *New Yorker?* That was Ruth McKenney, whose stories in the *New Yorker* last year were published in *My Sister Eileen* and outsold everything I ever wrote.' "

He reflects on the number of Ohioans he saw in Europe; Ohioans were particularly gripped by wanderlust, he thinks. Joel Sayre was writing for the movies and John McNulty still put on a tuxedo to get fired in. Walter Winchell had broken the news in his column that Thurber was the Jared L. Manley who had signed the "Where Are They Now?" series. (It is believed that Harold Winney, the secretary who defrauded Ross, was selling *New Yorker* secrets to Winchell.) He explains to his coffee-shop audience that "Manley" stood for the manly art of self-defense and that "Jared L." was from the first two initials of John L. Sullivan.

Despite Thurber's complaints about the art conference's frequent rejection of his cartoons, his 1938 crop was a good one, even given his absence from the country: sixty-eight in all. Though three thousand miles away, he had continued to use his penciled man and woman to code improbable situations in tune with the season: skiing, figure skating, fencing. They still confront one another, visit analysts, get drunk ("Here's to m' first wife, darling," a besotted Thurber Man toasts the woman he's with but can scarcely make out. "She only wore one hat, God bless 'er!") He still uses the medium to deliver private messages. "My heart has been a stick of wood since May, 1927," says the Thurber Man, almost the date on which Thurber met Honeycutt. Drawing was his way of keeping a diary.

The "cute" words women use, which Thurber and Sayre had ruled out of line, are trotted out. The giddy woman comes home to find visitors and coos, "Oooooo, *Guesties!*" "Woolgathering?" she asks the Thurber Man, who is sitting pensively by himself. It's another word banned by Thurber from mature conversation. He never used the word "doodle," especially in reference to his drawing. "It always reminds me of a housewife at the telephone," he told Henry Brandon. Whereas cartoonists Helen Hokinson and George Price mainly used others' caption ideas, no more than twenty of the captions on Thurber's hundreds of drawings were suggested by others.

After his "The Masculine Approach" series of cartoons appeared ("The I'm-Drinking-Myself-to-Death-and-Nobody-Can-Stop-Me Method," for example) McKelway suggested that Thurber undertake a series called "The Feminine Approach." Nothing came of it.

At poker games at Bleeck's, John Lardner's, or Honeycutt's, Thurber was always ready to disparage the women players. As usual, Thurber portrays them as airheads: "Why do you keep raising me when you *know* I'm bluffing?" an indignant lady asks a male player. "What do four ones beat?" an infuriating young woman asks a startled circle of men at the poker table.

It was at this time, too, that there had been speculation that Dorothy Parker and one of her lovers had had stars tattooed on their thighs. Thurber pounces on the idea for a cartoon.

His drawings mattered more than the captions, though he didn't always

"Her maid told ours that she has a heart tattooed on her hip."

realize it. He couldn't stop kidding himself about his art. Herman Miller, asked to write an essay on Thurber's art, wrote to him for help. Thurber's reply, though seemingly playful, is probably not without significance:

> I just made a sound which caused Helen to look up and say "That didn't sound like you; it sounded like a phone being dialed somewhere." I suppose that I am rapidly becoming, in her ears, like a phone being dialed somewhere, and I daresay that I am the only husband in the city who has been so characterized by his wife this night. It seems to me that she has enunciated as clear a definition of me and my art as anyone could think up of. In "a phone being dialed somewhere" there is, I go so far as to say, the utter implication of everything I have done, and try to do.

In February 1937, in Litchfield, Thurber had written his former fraternity brother, Dr. Virgil (Duke) Damon, the Park Avenue obstetrician, a letter with foreboding overtones:

> I wonder if you would have a moment . . . to suggest a really good eye man to me? He can be an expensive one, because I havent got any disease that needs treatment. I havent any million dollars to spend, but I have become a bit wary of $10 or $15-an-examination men. Have you got anything around $50 or a hundred? I may have to have my glasses changed, and I may not. Oculists seem to disagree. I have just had three separate pairs of glasses made, none of which I seem to be able to stand wearing. You can imagine me with three pairs of new glasses and one old pair.
>
> I can promise any eye man one of the remarkable clinical eyes of the country. All oculists agree on that. They start out by deciding I shouldnt be able to see anything but moving shapes, end up with me reading two lines below normal on the chart, and finally discover a tiny hole left on a lens which otherwise is covered with "organized exudation." . . .
>
> Can you drop me a brief note, giving me the name of a good eye doctor . . . ?

Dr. Damon recommended Dr. Gordon Bruce, of the Columbia Presbyterian Medical Center. Bruce found a growing cataract in Thurber's remaining eye, which clouded the lens and tricked Thurber into seeing things that weren't there, but Thurber wished to show Helen Europe before any operation could be scheduled.

In late 1938, however, driving from Woodbury to Waterbury in broad daylight, he saw the countryside begin to blur and he couldn't keep the car on the road. He would continue to drive for nearly another year, but not as frequently. He knew the eye surgery couldn't be postponed much longer, and that according to Bruce the chances of seeing well enough to draw afterward were no better than fifty-fifty. He fought that day, now drawing his pictures in a mood of near desperation and mentally preparing for the hell he knew awaited him.

51

Those Fables for Our Time

When the little girl opened the door of her grandmother's house she saw that there was somebody in bed with a nightcap and nightgown on. She had approached no nearer than twenty-five feet from the bed when she saw that it was not her grandmother but the wolf, for even in a nightcap a wolf does not look any more like your grandmother than the Metro-Goldwyn lion looks like Calvin Coolidge. So the little girl took an automatic out of her basket and shot the wolf dead.

Moral: It is not so easy to fool little girls nowadays as it used to be.

—from "The Little Girl and the Wolf"

Before leaving for Columbus in the fall of 1938, Thurber had brought the Whites up to date in a long letter from Woodbury:

It is nice to be back under the 200-year-old maples and apple trees. . . . Cows from up the road get into the yard when I leave the gate open and their owner comes for them around one a.m. on a motorcycle. . . . One morning . . . I heard a cow eating apples under my bedroom window. It was 7 o'clock. After she had eaten 27, by actual count, I got up and chased her home in my nightgown. I figured she must have eaten a couple of hundred during the night; she is up and around, though, giving cider and apple jack, I suppose.

I sold the newyorker an onward and upward on which I spent a week of days and nights: a report on Punch for 1889–91, and 1863–65. The house here holds all the bound volumes from the first one (1841) to 1891.

Thurber had been to New York for physical examinations:

My bottom doctor, Robin Hood, told me he had had a man in his office who "almost exsanguinated." My favorite expression now for bleeding to death. Fellow had just let his rectum go for twenty years, taking a little iron and liver compound from time to time. . . . Asses to ashes, I said to him, dust to dust. . . . My dentist says I will have my teeth for "quite a while." My ophthalmologist says I wont need reading glasses for "a time." My rectologist says, well—

Margaret, our cook, is rounding nicely into a casual. She says one of her sons works into the incinerating plant where they burn the refuse; has had the job since the armitage. I'm going to have to combine her with another lady of the vicinity who pointed out a flock of fletchers on her lawn and who also told me of a young man who had passed his civil service eliminations. As far as real estate values goes she says there is great disparagement.

Margaret lost a daughter to tuberculosis, she tells Thurber. "She got it from her teeth. Went all through her symptom." The casual that Margaret's malaprops rounded "nicely into" is "What Do You Mean It *Was* Brillig?" (*New Yorker*, January 7, 1939).

His article on White had been published in October, and he comments to Andy:

I was by no means satisfied with my piece for the Sat Review but was caught between all the millstones you get caught between writing a piece about a friend. . . . Little apt sentences come to you in the night, paragraphs reshape themselves, ideas take off their dancing shoes and sit down so you can see what they are. Meanwhile the piece has been locked in the forms and there you lie remaking the living room of the story, putting in a rock garden, selecting new bedroom wallpaper. . . .

I helped move in here one Saturday, then drove to Sandy Hook and helped Althea move, then took a walk in the woods with Rosemary and helped her move fallen trees out of the path, a thing which it seems had to be done. I share her conscientious compulsions in these matters, which sets me off for her from all the other adults in the world, I guess. She has the most calm and poise of any child of seven I ever saw. But there's a lot of sparkle, too. I was overwhelmed by her. She came running out of the house and threw her arms around me, and I saw she wasn't a baby any longer. Always it used to be that I had to win her over, with skill and patience. She played me two pieces on the piano and read to me. She is inclined to think that Hitler will not be satisfied with what he has got. She pressed the bags out of the knees of my spirit and combed my spiritual hair. . . .

We all loved both your pieces in Harpers (J. Mosher is virtually incoherent with praise). Helen is very fond of the hens who can sit around singing and whoring. The Sat Review is right when it says you are among the great living essayists.

We still hope you will be able to come down for Thanxgiving.

By the start of 1939, he is engaged in a frenzy of drawing. Pen and ink at the ready, he doesn't allow his marriage to Helen to disturb in any way the war between the sexes that he seems compelled to wage. One would not know from the cosmopolitan themes of his drawings that Thurber had retreated to the country and was firing ammunition stored from previous years. In the pictures, the old Thurber circle of drinkers and party goers seems intact and self-perpetuating—a circle characterized by Benchley, a paid-up member, as "exclusive," meaning, he said, that no diphtheria cases were allowed. "Welcome back to the old water hole, Mrs. Bixby," an insincere Thurber Man greets a woman at the bar. The pointlessness of cocktail chatter is underscored by one inebriated celebrant telling another, "One of us ought to be a Boswell, taking this all down."

Unclothed Thurber figures in ink dance without words, their innocence too pronounced to be out of character in a magazine guarded by Ross's prudery; Thurber's people seem clothed even when nude. Male weakness is juxtaposed against female power: "Yoo-hoo, it's me and the ape man," she announces, leading her nervous, abashed husband into a roomful of people.

Self-delusion is still rampant: "It's our *own* story *exactly!*" the lumpish wife tells her enervated husband as she looks up from a novel: "He bold as a hawk, she soft as the dawn." She is as ominous as always: "What do you want me to do with your remains George?" she asks her startled spouse.

It was as if he knew his time for drawing was running out, that the gods that had granted him his gift had decided to place him on a final, measured mile before they emptied his life of light. He took on art assignments at an almost frantic pace. He contributed sixty-three titled drawings to *In a Word,* a book by Margaret S. Ernst, wife of his friend and attorney Morris Ernst. It was a labor of love for the word-obsessed Thurber, for Mrs. Ernst discusses five hundred or more words commonly used but whose meanings and origins are little known. When the book was reissued in 1960, Thurber, in the preface, warns of "the Oral Culture in America," an era of television and radio "babble" with its attendant dangers. "No woman, for example," he writes, "should call another woman 'fastidious' unless she has looked up the meanings of that word and knows which one she has in mind. It is just possible that the other woman may know the word and never speak to her again."

Fifteen Thurber drawings were published in *Men Can Take It,* by Elizabeth Hawes, a book on men's fashions and customs. (Thurber's men obviously can't take it; they swelter in too-heavy clothing while the women flit about comfortably in light dresses.)

"*What do you want me to do with your remains, George?*"

canary

Latin canis, *a dog. The word* canary *no doubt means, to you, a bird, the color of the bird, a wine, or the islands from which all these get their names. But* canary *itself means pertaining to dogs, because what Roman navigators found remarkable about the Canary Islands was the huge wild dog population. Pliny mentions* Canaria insula, *isle abounding in large dogs.*

Tales of a Wayward Inn, by Frank Case, the Algonquin's owner, published in 1938, has a full-page drawing by Thurber, who promoted the book with three illustrated advertisements in the *New Yorker*. Other Thurber sketches appeared in support of *Poetry* magazine. (Lowell Thomas, president of the Advertising Club of New York, presented Thurber with a medal for "the most artistic continuity in 1938 advertising" at an exhibition of advertising art at Rockefeller Center.)

The New York World's Fair opened in 1939, and Thurber constructed a *New Yorker* cover of a throng of people staring agape at the perisphere (the fair's centerpiece) and other attractions. It is the second of six Thurber covers the magazine eventually ran.

A reporter from the *Waterbury Republican* found Thurber drawing at his Woodbury home and interviewed him there in January 1939. One's life work, he told the reporter, should be something that involves difficulties. "Everything I write I work over and rewrite at least ten times, but if I touch a drawing after the first sketch, I ruin it."

"Thurber was a Civil War buff," says McKelway, "and in the winter of 1938–39 he was in Frederick, Maryland, visiting the home of Barbara Frietchie. He sent me a copy of [Whittier's] poem, with a drawing to illustrate it, and a very funny letter. I showed them to Ross and we agreed Thurber should illustrate other famous poems for us."

Nine of these caricatures of heroes and heroines from nineteenth-century poetry ran from March through October, 1939. The poems—by Longfellow, Charles Kingsley, and Sir Walter Scott, among others—luckily were in the public domain, beyond any legal reach of the poets' estates. Ross was delighted with the series. Upon seeing Thurber's illustration of Leigh Hunt's "The Glove and the Lions," Ross sent him a note reading: "It's the goddamdest lion fight ever put on paper." A few years later, he wrote Thurber again, asking, "Why in God's name did you stop doing the illustrated poems? There are forty million other verses in the English language, many of them unquestionably suitable for Thurber illustrations." But Thurber had become discouraged with the project, after illustrating nine of the poems, when he tried to draw Poe's "The Raven," and the raven, he said, kept turning "into a common cornfield crow."

In early 1939, Thurber thanks White for sending him a copy of his new book, *Quo Vadimus, or The Case for the Bicycle*, a collection of casuals and essays. Writing the Whites from Woodbury, Thurber mentions three things of significant portent: the start of "The Secret Life of Walter Mitty," a prophecy of his blindness, and the beginning of his collaboration with Elliott Nugent on *The Male Animal*:

Dear Andy and Katharine:
    Last night I finished the drawings for Curfew Shall [Must] Not Ring [Tonight], the 5th of the series I have finished, and tonight I am working, or going to, on the Secret Life of Walter Mitty. . . .

This noon Quo Vadimus arrived. . . . It is just as I expected it would be . . . a lovely and funny collection by my favorite author. I must do a piece on you some day, White, my boy. [Thurber's piece on White had been published six months before.] I am already planning a little essay on Style. Everybody, when he is in his mid forties plans a little essay on Style. In his fifties he lectures at Sarah Lawrence, I think. In his sixties he goes blind and has to give up whisky at the same time. I hate the prospect of running my hands over my grandchildren's faces to see which side of the family they resemble. I had to have reading glasses a few weeks ago, and keep taking them off and putting them on. I have an idea I dont see as well or as far as before; I am teaching Helen to drive. It may be the mist in the air or the dirt on the windshield, but it is probably that Change. . . .

We spent a week in New York having me examined. I took a metabolism and came out 12 above and old Chick wanted me operated on right away, but Helen and all her friends know people who have been from 65 to 1150 above and just went right on same as ever. He x-rayed my lungs and found nothing at all, not even a lung, I suspect. . . . I suppose I will go to a thyroid man and breathe through that tube again, and see what he says. I am growing a little dubious about the clowns. Very likely all I have is Aspergillosis. It goes, in man, when April comes. . . .

We look forward to seeing you in New York in a few weeks. We are going down next week for a few days because Elliott Nugent is coming on. He intends to get this play done which I suggested he and I do together. He would have arrived earlier but his wife went over a cliff in an automobile, with her mother. Norma parked it on the edge of the cliff, without brakes on, and got out with two of her little girls. Then the car started rolling and Norma jumped on the running board and over it went. A jut of muddy earth caught the car 20 feet down or it would have gone a hundred. They got bruises and cuts and sprains and wont be around on their feet for a month, but they were very lucky. Norma and her mother are named Cassidy. That seems to help.

I got to get at Walter Mitty now. Let us hear when you will arrive in New York. We will get roaring drunk and then make plans for the future. And what is all this about you looking for another job? It sounds silly to us.

In late 1939, McKelway told Ross he was quitting as managing editor for fact at the end of the agreed-upon three-year period. "I frequently drank too much and went to Dr. Foord's a good deal," says McKelway. "Ross was pained and once or twice angry [about it]."

"Ross didn't put up much resistance when McKelway said he wanted to quit editing and go back to writing full time," says Eugene Kinkead. "Mac wasn't all that reliable at the time; he was going through a bad period. Vanderbilt and Shawn were his two assistants and Ross picked Shawn to replace Mac. Shawn was totally dedicated to the job. Most of the young men on the staff worked for money to have fun with, and Ross knew he couldn't get out the magazine without people of Shawn's self-discipline and commitment. Shawn was more than an editor; he was a natural force. He even attended the art meetings when Ross was out of the office. The art meetings were stag affairs by then. Daise Terry had been the stenographer, taking notes for Ross, but Ross kicked her out so he could more freely belch and swear."

J. M. (Jim) Geraghty was named the art editor, a position he would hold for thirty-four years, editing, along the way, nine of the *New Yorker*'s cartoon albums. Gus Lobrano had replaced Katharine White as the fiction editor. "He was an excellent one, too," says Kinkead, "but Gus lacked the limitless energy Shawn had, and there was never any doubt in anyone's mind—except Gus's, I guess—as to which man would replace Ross after his death."

McKelway and Honeycutt had long since divorced, amicably. Mac's first assignment, in his new capacity as full-time writer, was an extended Profile of Walter Winchell, most of it written at the Riggs Sanitarium. It ran for a half-dozen issues. After McKelway returned from the Air Force following World War II, Ross greeted him with "Hi, Mac. Those Winchell pieces were too goddam long." Ross had once vowed never to run any item in the magazine that exceeded two thousand words. "It wasn't that Ross changed his mind," says Kinkead. "It's that his writers gradually felt surer of themselves, which was reflected in what they wrote, and which Ross found too good not to print."

The deadly thrumming of a world moving toward war led Thurber to take up fables as his "shield and sword"—to escape into protective fantasy and to protest the contemporary totalitarian tendencies of both left and right. His first fablelike piece seems to have been in 1938, when he reported on unusual newspaper stories in the British newspapers, for *For Men Only*. In "The Strange Case of the Pensioned Tramcar Conductor," published in January 1938, he tells of a strange war between bees and wasps near Birmingham. During the summer of 1937, Thurber writes, wasps "decided that the bees were not making proper use of their natural resources and they ought to be 'civilized.' They therefore descended on one of the hives in order to wipe it out in the interest of world peace." This was, of course, parallel to Goebbels's explanation of why the Nazis had found it necessary to occupy their neighbors' territory. Then in a swipe at the leftists, Thurber reports that it was the "worker bees" that successfully bore the brunt of the wasps' attack, "ignoring, I am sure, the exhortations of a lot of communist literary critics."

Thurber had long shared his personal sense of impending doom with his public. But now man at his historic worst was gaining ascendancy in Europe and the Far East, and even at home, with semiparanoid congressional subcommittees, "superpatriot" private organizations, and a few university trustees straining at the First Amendment leash to muzzle alien ideologies. The leftists took a more erudite and literary route but arrived at the same objective as the far right: a need to rule, ruin, or both.

The series began running in the *New Yorker* in January 1939. Thurber tackled the growing menace of intolerance and inhuman behavior in his own way, with beasts and birds. "Fables for Our Time" (the later book was dedicated to Herman and Dorothy Miller) stands as the first important, artful expressions of Thurber's anger with man's misdirections and misuses of his heritage, interspersed with clever parodies of Aesop. There is a concerned earnestness to what he offers lightly, for he knew there was nothing more seditious of a dictatorship than to point out something amusing about it.

As usual, some of the stories are grounded in his personal dilemmas. He had once ridden the train past Snedens Landing—Katharine Angell's temporary home at the time—and had to wait two hours for a return train. In "The Mouse Who Went to the Country," the mouse takes the train, finds that it doesn't stop at Beddington on Sundays and waits three hours in Middleburg for a train back to Beddington. There the mouse finds the last bus for Sibert's Junction has just left; he runs and catches it only to find it is going in the wrong direction. The mouse then says, "The hell with it," and walks back to the city.

If you live as a human being, it will be the end of you, one fable preaches. There's no safety in numbers, or in anything else, as the fly learns when it joins many others on flypaper. That pride goeth before a fall is proved again, by the lion who steals an eagle's wings and, convinced he can fly, leaps off a rock, crashes, and burns.

"The Very Proper Gander" reflects both the state of affairs in Nazi Germany and in America, where the House Un-American Activities Committee's search for Communists plotting the government's overthrow was taking bizarre turns, often at variance with Democratic principles. A gander struts and sings in the barnyard; a passerby comments that the bird is "a very proper gander." An old hen tells her husband that the passerby had said "propaganda." Her husband spreads word that the gander is a dangerous bird; a small brown hen remembers seeing the gander talking with some hawks in the forest. The barnyard inhabitants form a mob and expel the gander. Thurber's moral: "Anybody who you or your wife thinks is going to overthrow the government by violence must be driven out of the country."

Most of the fables were written before the outbreak of World War II and catch Thurber's accurate reading of the times. The dangers of the world in 1939 are summed up in his account of the little old man who is nearly bitten by a black widow spider, almost crippled by a grandson who pulls a chair from under him, tripped by a hoop rolled at him by a "grim" little girl, robbed in broad daylight, and deprived of shelter in the park because bugs and blight have killed the trees, leaving the man a clear target for a flight of bombers overhead.

Thurber as the new fabulist—George Ade's *Fables in Slang* was his only American precedent—also provides a fresh and liberal share of fun. Unrequited love is the fable theme of the male crow attracted to a female oriole. He pleads his cause to her, or, as Thurber would have it, "caws his pleas." She rejects his citation of his virtues with "I don't see how that could interest anybody but another crow"—a borrowing from the anecdote of the lady at the Central Park Zoo who asks the attendant what sex the caged hippopotamus is and receives a similar answer.

Thurber's fables usually support the pleasure-loving creatures and those who often deviate from their heritage over the hardworking and conventional. Here is the moth who refuses to fly around candle flames, like its suicidal siblings, thus living to a great old age. His war between male and female continues: In "The Shrike and the Chipmunks," the female chipmunk leaves her mate because of his indolent ways. The shrike can't get at him, because his doorway is clogged with soiled laundry and dirty dishes. The female returns, cleans up the house, and takes him for a walk; they are both killed by a shrike. "Moral: Early to rise and early to bed makes a male healthy and wealthy and dead."

In September 1939, Germany invaded Poland; France and Britain declared war on Germany, and World War II was under way. Thurber's "The Birds and the Foxes," published several weeks after that event, describes a bird sanctuary, surrounded by a fence that is denounced by the foxes as an arbitrary and unnatural boundary. The foxes "liberate" the birds by eating them. Thurber's conclusion: "Government of the birds by the foxes and for the foxes must perish from the earth."

When the Germans accused the Poles of having started the conflict, Thurber came up with "The Rabbits Who Caused All the Trouble." In this fable, the wolves threaten to "civilize" the rabbits if they continue to cause trouble. The rabbits want to leave, but other animals (Britain and France), "who lived at a great distance," shame them into staying, where they are devoured. (Thurber's bitter admonition to the rest of the world: "Run, don't walk, to the nearest desert island.")

His most famous fable, "The Unicorn in the Garden," is a rare instance of a Thurber Man besting Woman: he reports seeing a unicorn to his wife, who tries to have him confined, only to be confined herself when the man denies seeing the mythical animal and suggests that his wife is the demented one. (Moral: "Don't count your boobies until they are hatched.") This rare reversal of domestic fortune is repeated three years later in his casual "The Catbird Seat," in which a timid middle-aged male employee brings about the downfall of a pushy female management consultant, who is bent on an office reorganization that would put the little fellow out of a job.

The unicorn fable became one of Thurber's most widely reprinted pieces and the subject of ballet and other theater performances. In 1948, Charles Weidman used it, along with "The Owl Who Was God" and two other Thurber fables, in a dance recital that he took on a national tour. "The Owl Who Was God" posed a staging problem, because the blinded owl leads the animals and birds onto a highway where they are run over by a truck. Weidman wrote Thurber asking if he would object to having the owl lead its followers over a cliff instead. Thurber replied that he "was faced with the consideration that winged creatures fall off cliffs without damage to themselves," but wouldn't stand in the way of a ballet that "has its more flexible advantages."

Thurber was no longer above (or below) the political strife, as were Benchley and other humorists, nor had he ever hesitated to deal with philosophic concerns. Clifton Fadiman, editing the anthology *I Believe*—a collection of the credos of distinguished people—solicited a Thurber piece for the book. In his preface, Fadiman apologizes, while trying not to apologize, for including Thurber. "No special apology," he writes, "is needed to explain the presence of James Thurber in the company of such names as Mann and Santayana and Romains and Maritain. . . . Mr. Thurber, whether he writes or draws, is a first-rate humorist, which means that he is an important writer and an important man."

Thurber's chapter in *I Believe* ran first in *Forum and Century* as "Thinking Ourselves into Trouble," a title he hated and blamed on "some goddam woman editor there." "Where are we going, if anywhere, and why?" he asks. ("It will do no good to call up the *Times*.") He sees Man's ability to reason as of less benefit to him than that which the animals gain from instinct.

> Unfortunately, I have never been able to maintain a consistent attitude toward life or reality or toward anything else. This may be owing entirely to nervousness. At any rate, my attitudes change with the years, sometimes with the hours. Just now I am going through one of those periods when I believe that the black panther and the cedar waxwing have higher hopes of Heaven than Man has.

There is always Browning's "grand Perhaps," he acknowledges, and if it's hard to grasp and hold onto belief, it may be just as hard to guard our "unbelief" in a world beyond this one, as other sages have said. But he has his own doctrine of comfort:

> What is all this fear of and opposition to Oblivion? What is the matter with the soft Darkness, the Dreamless Sleep?
> "Well, folks," the cheery guard may say, as the train rushes silently into a warm, dark tunnel and stops, "Here we are at good old Oblivion! Everybody out!"

On March 18, 1939, the *New Yorker* published the most durable and successful case for the daydreamer: "The Secret Life of Walter Mitty." There was nothing new about the theme; indeed, Thurber was sued—unsuccessfully—by a novelist who was convinced that Thurber had stolen the idea from one of his books. Subliminally, Thurber could have been nurturing the idea from several sources. For example, he was an admirer of Joseph Conrad's *Lord Jim*, and this description of Jim, still an undistinguished sailor, appears early in the novel:

> He saw himself saving people from sinking ships, cutting away masts in a hurricane, swimming through a surf with a line; or as a lonely castaway, barefooted and half naked, walking on uncovered reefs in search of shellfish to stave off starvation. He confronted savages on tropical shores, quelled mutinies on the high seas, and in a small boat upon the ocean kept up the hearts of despairing men—always an example of devotion to duty, and as unflinching as a hero in a book.

And like Lord Jim, Mitty faces his execution with imperturbability.

Mitty figures turn up in Thurber drawings, as well: "Who are you today—Ronald Colman?"

Though the theme was far from new, Thurber handles it with a greater universal application than anybody before or since. It was reprinted twice by the *Reader's Digest*, by *Life, Scholastic, This Week Magazine*, and recorded on tape by Charles Laughton. Mitty quickly attained the timelessness of folklore. Six of Thurber's books were printed as Armed Services editions for the American military forces in World War II, giving Thurber his first mass distribution and guaranteeing him a permanent, large-scale following. Of all the Thurber treasures, service personnel found "Walter Mitty" the most memorable, its broad circulation among them augmented by its 1943 first reprinting by the *Reader's Digest*:

> "We're going through!" The commander's voice was like thin ice breaking. . . . The pounding of the cylinders increased: ta-pocketa-pocketa-pocketa-*pocketa-pocketa*. . . . The crew, bending to their various tasks in the huge, hurtling eight-engined Navy hydroplane, looked at each other and grinned. "The Old Man'll get us through," they said to one another. "The Old Man ain't afraid of Hell!" . . .
>
> "Not so fast! You're driving too fast!" said Mrs. Mitty. "What are you driving so fast for?"
>
> "Hmm?" said Walter Mitty. He looked at his wife, in the seat beside

"Who are you today—Ronald Colman?"

him, with shocked astonishment. . . . Walter Mitty drove on toward Waterbury in silence, the roaring of the SN202 through the worst storm in twenty years of Navy flying fading in the remote, intimate airways of his mind. "You're tensed up again," said Mrs. Mitty. "It's one of your days. I wish you'd let Dr. Renshaw look you over."

It was classic Thurber, the henpecked man fleeing into fantasy, the practical woman anchoring his external life. Thurber had rehearsed Mitty earlier—as Mr. Monroe, Mr. Pendly, Tommy Trinway, and others. Three years earlier, Thurber plays Mitty in "Anodynes for Anxieties." When he discovers he has only sixty dollars in the bank just before Christmas, he takes to his bed ill. He imagines J. P. Morgan visiting him to ask what his trouble is:

> "I'm not really sick," I told him. "I just need money." "Well, well, well," he exclaimed heartily. . . . He took out a checkbook. "How'd a hundred thousand dollars do?" he asked, jovially. "That would be all right," I said. "Could you give it to me in cash, though—in tens and twenties?" "Why, certainly, my boy, certainly," said Mr. Morgan. . . . "Thank you very much, J. P.," I said. "Not at all, Jim, not at all!" cried my ghostly friend. "What's going on in there?" shouted my wife, who was in the next room. It seems that I had got to talking out loud, first in my own voice and then louder, and with more authority, in Mr. Morgan's. "Nothing, darling," I answered. "Well, cut it out," she said.

Helen always denied she was ever a Thurber Woman, but, nonetheless, was made to play Mrs. Mitty time and again. It may have come more easily for her husband than she cared to realize. "Helen is one of the greatest proofreaders, editors, and critics I've ever known," Thurber tells an interviewer. "She's often rescued things I've thrown aside. If there's something she doesn't like she pulls no punches. When I wrote 'The Secret Life of Walter Mitty,' I had a scene in which Mitty got between Hemingway and an opponent in a Stork Club brawl. Helen said that it had to come out [as too topical]. You grouse around the house for a week and then you follow her advice."

Walter Mitty, as romantic hero, Navy pilot, surgeon, a "crack shot with any sort of firearms," became the hero of everybody, men and women alike, who inevitably yearned to be something other than what they were. World War II flyers used "pocketa-pocketa" in radio code; planes and vehicles were named "Walter Mitty"; airmen formed Walter Mitty clubs; troops used "Walter Mitty" as passwords. Confined within the military hierarchy, servicemen and women at once bonded with Mitty in his inner struggle to defy and rise above the system.

In 1945, Robert Benchley acted in a radio adaptation of Mitty, which Thurber considered to be its best realization. He wired Benchley his appreciation, and Benchley replied:

> Dear Jaime [sic]:
>
> . . . we all thank you for your wire re. Walter Mitty. It was the first radio job I ever enjoyed doing, and probably the last. . . .
>
> I had them send you what is known as a "cutting" of the show. We would call it a "recording". . . . I had it sent to The New Yorker. . . . I suppose that Ross has eaten it by now.
>
> I understand that you have sold it to a motion-picture concern. Does that mean that you will be out here to give it a Treatment, or will you just shoot yourself on the East Coast? . . . You may use my room at the Royalton if you like. Everyone else seems to.

Another old Round Tabler, Franklin P. Adams, wrote a friend that his son, "Tim, who is a freshman at Bowdoin, reads 'The Secret Life of Walter Mitty' aloud to me every time he comes home. Also to every visitor who comes to the house."

The story's popularity had, as Benchley noted, attracted the attention of Hollywood. Stretching a two-thousand-word casual into a two-hour Technicolor movie was challenge enough; that the subject was a man trapped in a dull, Maggie-and-Jiggs, exitless marriage, playing the no-win evasionist's game of disappearing into his own thoughts, posed a filming problem that resulted in internal disputes at the Goldwyn studio and eventually involved Thurber himself.

When Samuel Goldwyn announced that he was exercising his option to film Mitty, says Ken Englund, who, with Everett Freeman, worked on the film adaptation for a year and a half, Thurber began receiving letters from Mitty fan clubs telling him that they had already ruined the story. Not a line of the screenplay had been written.

Goldwyn bought the property for Danny Kaye, who, as Mitty, is dominated by his mother (the movie Mitty is young and unmarried), engaged to a shrew, further doomed by a nagging prospective mother-in-law, and finds his release in dreams suggested by the pulp adventure magazines he edits for a living. But whereas Mitty's external life was humdrum, Kaye's is entangled with international jewel-and-art thieves, led by Boris Karloff, who wants to kill Mitty. Even Mitty's dream girl (Virginia Mayo) turns up in real life. The dream sequences have Mitty as a fearless fighter pilot, a riverboat gambler, a gunslinger, and braving a typhoon as a windjammer captain. *The Secret Life of Walter Mitty*, which appeared in 1947 and is still seen on late-night TV, is an entertaining Danny Kaye romp, but in the end Goldwyn used only the title and a hint of an idea from Thurber.

The story editors, writers, and production staff had been divided on whether to preserve as much of the original story as possible or simply use it as a Danny Kaye vehicle.

After ten months of unsatisfactory attempts to adapt Mitty to the screen, Ken Englund was assigned to work with Thurber at the Thurbers' apartment, at 410 East Fifty-seventh Street. Englund's weekly salary was seven thousand dollars, and William Herndon, acting as Thurber's agent, arranged for Goldwyn to pay Thurber a thousand dollars for each day he worked with Englund or contributed ideas. Englund, a sophisticate, was one of the studio's pro-Mitty group—generally opposed by the pro-Kaye faction—but was told by Goldwyn, "Outside of a few thousand people in Manhattan, you are the only one in the rest of America that ever reads that *New Yorker* magazine!" Englund told Goldwyn about the moving letters from tailgunners and others in the military who had written to the *Digest* to say what the Mitty story had meant to them. Goldwyn insisted (correctly) that for the movie to make money it had to appeal to more people than the readership of the *Digest* and *New Yorker* combined.

John McNulty had left the *New Yorker* to work in Hollywood ("God bless you, McNulty, goddam it," was Ross's warm but gruff farewell to him), and Englund found Thurber angry with Hollywood and Hollywood agents because McNulty was being paid only a hundred dollars a week more than his last newspaper salary. But Thurber liked Englund and the two spent ten days at the end of 1945 making changes in the script. Thurber soon went along with the melodrama, and in a letter to Goldwyn he tried to sell the movie tycoon on changes that he and Englund had made:

I believe we have accomplished what you had in mind, which I am confident is also what I myself wanted to achieve. . . .

There is nothing that can be done at this late date about the melodrama, as such, except to blend it more realistically and more humorously with the dreams and with Walter's day to day life with his Mother and his fiancee. The melodrama still remains the spine of our structure, but I feel . . . that it no longer sticks out, but that it has been more ingenuously interlaced with The Dreams and the private life of our Hero. . . .

I profoundly believe that the characters in their relations to Walter and to the story are right the way they are now. I should like to have you dismiss those early suggestions of mine as being merely thoughtless ideas, thrown off by a man who was not yet quite familiar with the story and its problems.

I feel that I have learned a great deal in a short time about some of the problems that face a motion picture producer and . . . writer.

Thurber's placating letter would come back to haunt him. "When I left New York . . . after our ten-day think session," says Englund, "I had a brief-case crammed with my handwritten notes, and some in Jim's large scrawl, scribbled on both sides of his favorite unlined yellow paper." Both men were in complete agreement on what Mitty daydreams should be used, and how. But back in Hollywood, Englund found that Goldwyn had asked another film writer to help "funny up the dreams" to be sure they got laughs. Meanwhile, Thurber heard that a production clique was for downplaying the dreams in favor of the real-life scenes, and on April 1, 1946 he wrote Goldwyn's vice president, Pat Duggan:

> The last fifty pages should not skimp the dream element. To say that dreams slow up the story is to say the locomotive slows up the cow. The dreams are the best Kaye and the best audience appeal. They are new, unique and universal. . . .
>
> I will personally undertake to thrash anyone who mangles the dreams. They are wonderful.

Thurber's favorite scenes in the script, the "firing squad" episode and a new daydream in which Kaye sings one of Thurber's favorite songs, "Molly Malone," were not mangled—they were eliminated altogether. Englund says that Thurber bombarded him with "new dreams I might have ready to re-place those that fell by the wayside," referring to the last fifty pages of the screenplay as a

> long stretch of almost unrelieved melodrama to the final Fade Out. What we get too far away from, is Walter the ingratiating little guy to whom nothing ever happens except the humdrum—except in his dreams. These romantic, heroic dreams are funny, and touching, because

they happen to a man who, in reality, is in an office or tending a furnace or playing bridge badly, like Any Man.

When he heard that the firing-squad scene was in trouble Thurber wrote Englund asking him to urge Goldwyn to let them take another crack at it. He had some suggestions:

> Arriving in Perth Amboy, [Mitty's] mother remembers she has run out of "toothpaste" and this gives us the chance to have Walter stand against the drug store wall in the rain and go into the Firing Squad Scene. In a Close Shot of his standing erect and brave we hear the footsteps of passersby fall into the tromp, tromp cadence of the approaching firing squad.
>
> Mrs. Mitty's need for "toothpaste" is just a ruse, and we Cut inside the drugstore for a moment to see her and Irmagard [Mitty's future mother-in-law] covertly buying a sedative from The Druggist . . . that will calm "the disturbed Walter."

Had all Thurber's inventory of alternative Mitty dreams been acted upon, Englund says there was a good chance that the picture would have run longer than *Ben Hur*. Still, Thurber kept suggested rewrites of the dreams flowing to Englund, in his huge scrawl. Thurber's scenario for "The Cowboy Dream" is reminiscent of his high-school short stories of the Wild West:

> It is a big night at Death Gulch Saloon. We see Gertrude [Mitty's fiancee] dressed in the flashy get-up of a saloon entertainer. At a table sits Calamity Irmagard Griswold, with a holster and gun slung around her waist.

In the spring of 1946, the Thurbers were at the Homestead, in Virginia, and Goldwyn, still hoping for Thurber's endorsement of Goldwyn's movie, began mailing Thurber mimeographed script pages containing its daily changes. Helen dutifully read each change to Thurber, which inspired Thurber to suggest more changes. He offers a dream sequence in which Mitty heroically tries to save Holland by holding his finger in the hole of a dike, the water nonetheless rising rapidly around him.

Goldwyn's worry that some of the scenes were too sophisticated and unfunny infected Thurber, who, in a reversal of attitude, rushed some jokes to Pat Duggan that Englund and others of the pro-daydream forces thought too lowbrow. "The scene between Walter and the Psychiatrist . . . opens rather flatly," Thurber writes Duggan. "We can get more laughs and make more of a character in just a few lines of dialogue."

PSYCHIATRIST: "Now, just how often do you see this enormous silver fish floating around?"
WALTER: "I-I don't see any fish.
PSYCHIATRIST: "Hm? Oh, sorry—I was thinking of another patient, a Mr. Ingleby. He's coming along splendidly.

Though paid for his submissions, none of Thurber's material was used, but, says Englund, Thurber had come a long way since their first session, when Englund had had to point out to Thurber that Goldwyn needed to appeal to an audience of millions to show a profit on the picture. Thurber had replied, "All I care about reaching is my twenty thousand readers." Now he was seeing the task more from a producer's point of view—although his responses to the script remained on the high road: "My original strong objection to the characterization of Gertrude still stands," he writes Duggan. "My wife, my daughter, my two other closest friends and myself all feel that Gertrude is too close to the famous silly girl in Tarkington's 'Seventeen.' "

In an effort to co-opt Thurber before the shooting script was completed, Goldwyn took the most recent version of the screenplay to New York for Thurber to consider. Helen read the script to him and at a tea party in Goldwyn's Waldorf Tower suite, Thurber told Goldwyn that he found the screenplay too melodramatic. "You're absolutely right, Mr. Thurber!" Goldwyn exclaimed. "It's much too blood and thirsty!" Recapping the discussion for *Life* magazine, Thurber said he was "horror and struck" by Goldwyn's observation. (Legend has wrongly attributed the Goldwyn/Thurber remarks to an exchange of letters between the two men.)

The Secret Life of Walter Mitty opened at the Astor Theater in New York on August 14, 1947. After seeing it, Thurber, who recognized nothing of his material, asked his companions, "Did anybody get the name of that movie?"

The movie was a commercial and (mostly) a critical success, and is one of Danny Kaye's better vehicles. Even the *New Yorker*'s savage film critic, John McCarten, was entertained by it. Nobody expected Thurber's Walter Mitty, a mouse who remains a mouse, to survive in a nine-reel musical that requires a love story and the emergence of the mouse as a true-life hero. The fierce debate between the Goldwyn Productions sales force on the East Coast and the home studio on whether to change the title itself ended with the decision to keep it—a wrong one, since it opened the door to those critics who wanted the film to make good on the title's promise.

Goldwyn was stung by *Life*'s review, which said that Thurber "grows almost profane when he thinks of how his story has been corrupted." "Either Mr. Thurber has been misquoted or has in the past year done as complete a switch as ever Walter Mitty did from real life to dream world," Goldwyn wrote to the editors, in a letter that *Life* published.

Dishonestly, Goldwyn quotes from Thurber's letters to the studio approving of scenes that were later deleted from the script. "The original story," Goldwyn writes, "is a pure gem, which added great luster to the little magazine in which it was first published. However, in order to convert such a gem into a feature-length motion picture, it is necessary first to elaborate it into a screenplay."

Thurber was outraged by Goldwyn's slighting reference to the *New Yorker* and by his use of "that obsolete weapon of controversy, the excerpt-lifter." Creative work on the film had begun January 2, 1945, Thurber pointed out, in his published letter of reply, and it was ten months later, about November 25, that Goldwyn first showed him the script. "During this vital period," writes Thurber, "my counsel, criticism, and collaboration were never once sought." Upon Goldwyn's showing him the script,

> I was confronted by a set story line appallingly melodramatic for poor Walter. . . .
>
> Ken Englund and I worked six hours a day for ten days on an impossible assignment. We could not take out the melodrama but we could attempt to cover it up with additional dream scenes and other devices. . . .
>
> Next to the worry about our new dream scenes, the greatest fear of Mr. Englund and myself was the possibility that this movie might be spoiled by one or more of Mr. Kaye's . . . famous, but to me, deplorable scat or git-gat-gittle songs. Mr. Englund . . . and myself had strongly suggested that Mr. Kaye's song in the RAF scene be *Molly Malone.* . . . Mr. Goldwyn lifted the song and substituted what is to me an utterly horrifying, shockingly out-of-taste-and-mood piece of scat. . . . Another dream scene was written and shot, in which Mr. Kaye did sing *Molly Malone* [but] the scene was cut, along with the courtroom dream and the firing squad dream. My defeat was complete. . . .
>
> Sorry, Walter, sorry for everything.

In a *Time* interview, Ken Englund was asked about Thurber's contributions to the screenplay.

"They were many and wonderful," replies Englund. "I remember him telling me that Mitty must always be carrying something; it's the sign of the dominant female and the dominated male." The plot change also appealed to Thurber's attitude toward women, says Englund. Substituting Mitty's mother for his wife and introducing a stupid bride-to-be and an aggressive mother-in-law gave Mitty three female villains to fight instead of one. "Thurber was pleased by that," says Englund.

"Jim and I corresponded from time to time," he adds, "and he once suggested I do a Broadway musical dramatization of Mitty, but we never saw each other again. That's fate and show biz." He is grateful to Goldwyn, he admits, "for giving me the golden opportunity to work with and know James Thurber."

Meanwhile, "The Secret Life of Walter Mitty" continues to live a robust life in all its pristine, two-thousand-word integrity. Its commercial success helped accelerate Thurber's own self-transformation from daydreamer to recognized achiever. Emily Hahn, certain that success eventually spoiled Thurber for many of his friends, urges that all future dramatizations of Mitty leave him in his secret world, hiding from reality. "Had Walter been able to realize even some of his dreams," she says, "he would have been impossible to live with."

52

That Male Animal

I have tried a couple of plays and I always run into appalling problems. . . . It is . . . difficult to get characters on and off the stage dexterously. It may look easy, but it isn't easy. I have frequently had to resort to dogfights. "I must go out and separate those dogs" is not, however, a sound or convincing exit line for someone you have to get off the stage. Furthermore, you can only use the dogfight device once unless the dogs are total strangers who have been tied up together in the back yard, and that would have to be explained. You can't explain the relationship of two dogs, particularly two dogs your audience hasn't seen, in less than thirty seconds, and thirty seconds is a long time in the theatre.

—from "Notes for a Proletarian Novel"

For years, Thurber, more than Elliott Nugent, had talked of their doing a play together. In October 1938, Thurber wrote Nugent from Woodbury that he had an idea for a play whose setting was the Ohio State University community. "The idea came to me one day . . . while I was standing on top of a garage," Thurber writes.

Nugent, directing and acting in films on the West Coast for eight years, replied that he was too busy to coauthor a play. But he missed the theater, and when Thurber wrote him again in January 1939, there were a couple of scenes from the proposed play and a brief outline enclosed.

"It sounded good to me," says Nugent. "I wrote him at once, agreeing to the idea." After a travel delay caused by his wife's near-fatal auto accident, Nugent and his father, who was still active in the theater, came East and took a suite at the Algonquin. The Thurbers had already checked in. The two old friends spent two weeks plotting the play, which Thurber called *Homecoming Game*, with Helen and J. C. Nugent offering suggestions. Only a few lines remained of Thurber's two scenes by the time they had finished the new outline. Nugent's suggested title, *The Male Animal*, was agreed upon. Nugent writes:

> Thurber's original basic plot was for a comedy of married life in a college community such as we had known at Ohio State. Tommy Turner, a professor of English doing moderately well in his academic career but living on a modest salary, is afraid that his wife [Ellen, a name perhaps suggested by "Helen"], who ten years before had been the prettiest co-ed at the university, married him on the rebound after a quarrel with her former fiancé, "Whirling Joe" Ferguson.

Ferguson, a former campus football hero, now a prosperous businessman, returns for the homecoming game with Michigan. Ellen plans a party for him; Tommy is apprehensive. "Thurber had plotted . . . this half-serious, half-comic love story as far as the second-act climax," says Nugent, "with the resolution in Act III still to be worked out." Nugent felt "that since 'social significance' had become almost obligatory by 1939, even in a comedy, our young professor should blunder his way into some fight over academic freedom." Tommy was not to be "political," but simply intent on reading something of literary value to his class that a conservative trustee would find controversial. The writings of Karl Marx were considered, but in 1939 Marx was read and discussed in O.S.U.'s political-science classes. Thurber remembered the last letter of Bartolomeo Vanzetti, one of the two executed Italian immigrants whose murder convictions were based on meager evidence. Thurber thought it "a beautiful piece of writing by an uneducated man."

Nugent, a political conservative, had never believed in the innocence of Sacco and Vanzetti, but Thurber made him read Arthur Krock's account of the case "that had so damaged the reputation of Massachusetts and of America around the world," and Nugent was persuaded.

Nugent and his father worked on the play on the train back to Los Angeles, where Nugent had contracted to direct Bob Hope and Paulette Goddard in *The Cat and the Canary*. Thurber planned to join them on the Coast that June. He was busy, meanwhile, with his fables and "Famous Poems Illustrated," and Helen didn't wish to give up the Woodbury house before the lease had expired. The death of Thurber's father, Charles, at Easter required a hurried train trip to Columbus for the funeral. In April, Thurber writes McNulty:

> Your letter found me in the midst of death, illness, funerals, loss of sight, diminishing sex desire, hyper-thyroidism, etc., also a hundred thousand things to do, to keep mah baby in shootin dice and drinkin liquor. Helen and I are now up to our asses in barrels and trunks, moving out of here. . . . We leave for the All Is Not Gold Coast of California sometime in mid-May.

Told they would need a car to get around in Hollywood, they booked passage on the SS *President Garfield* along with the Ford. It was a mistake. The voyage, by way of Havana and the Panama Canal, was a long one, and the tropical sun worsened Thurber's eyesight. "Jamie was terrible on the trip," says Helen. "A young girl kept beating him at Ping-Pong, and he kept losing his temper with everyone, including the captain." Before the ship's arrival at Los Angeles, Thurber made it up to the captain by typing out a one-sheet newspaper he called "The Ship's Cat (The unofficial and uncalled for paper of the SS *President Garfield*)." In Manila, the ship, sailing westward around the world, had taken aboard forty-one thousand Chinese wooden chests filled with silver coins, which were being sent to a San Francisco bank by the Chinese government to reinforce its credit rating, a fact Thurber made the most of in his ship's paper:

37 MONEY CHESTS ARE MISSING

Every time the ship's counter counts the chests of Chinese [coins] in the hold, or wherever it is, he comes up with a new figure. In Manila the total was 41,000 even, in Boston (where men were put on guard) it fell to 40,989; in Havana it rose to 41,029. . . .

It is thought that the Marseilles stowaways who live below hatches on Chianti and fine Italian cheese may be using the money for buttons.

"I haven't made a personal count of the chests myself," admitted Captain Aitken, "because I make it a rule never to count higher than 25,000. No use in a man counting himself to death."

KAHN'S RETORT

When he was reminded by one of the more nervous passengers that the ship on which he is riding must be unlucky because it was named after President Garfield, who was shot, Eddie Kahn, the Texas cotton tycoon said, "It might be worse. I'm glad it wasn't named after President Hoover, who was sunk."

Upon arriving in Los Angeles on June 5, Thurber wrote Captain Arthur Aitken a note of apology for his temperamental behavior during the trip, and thanked him for a Chinese coin the captain had given him:

In return for your Chinese coin, this Roman one, as token of esteem and a lucky mascot. I bought this in Chester, England, where it was dug up. The head is of one Antoninus, date about 59–63 A.D. . . . It's not a valuable coin but it's 1876 years old! Remember that when *you* feel old.

We had a fine time, are sorry for my bad moments, and hope to be with you again.

At the Nugents, the worry continued over Thurber's worsening eyesight. He writes Dr. Gordon Bruce, his New York ophthalmologist:

I guess you better give me the name of a good man out here who can get me some reading lenses. The old eye is the same as ever for distance but I'll be goddam if I can read—except . . . under a big umbrella outdoors in a bright sun; under those conditions I see to read . . . exactly as well without my glasses as with my *distance* ones. . . . If I use my right lens as a magnifying glass and pull it away, I can see as clearly for a fifth of a second as I did in 1896. I can also do a lot of other tricks, but I am getting crosser and snappier and sadder every minute straining and struggling to type and to read and to draw (the latter is the easiest). I'd rather atrophy those muscles in two years than by god go through life like a blindfolded man looking for a black sock on a black carpet. . . . Life is no good to me at all unless I can read, type, and draw. I would sell out for 13 cents. Seems to me the eye began to dim slightly on the third day at sea—anyway I had been able to read for two days and then it got slightly harder.

There was a two-month wait before the specialist Dr. Bruce recommended could examine him. ("I won't be able to see the *doctor* by then," Thurber protested.) Nugent got him an early appointment with Nugent's own eye doctor, Julian Dow. For a time he was again able to read—in bright light— type, and drive the Ford. For two weeks, Thurber and Nugent sat around the Nugent swimming pool discussing the play's scenario, Nugent's secretary taking notes. Helen found a small house in Beverly Hills for her and Thurber, where he began to write dialog. Nugent wanted the play to have "a genuine Thurber flavor," and Thurber was to write the first draft of each act, with Nugent to rewrite and edit, but at the end of two weeks, "Jim, with his meticulous rewriting and revision, had finished only ten pages," says Nugent, "so I convinced him that I had better start writing Act II."

They worked from six to eight hours during the day and socialized in the evening. Thurber's professional reputation was known and admired in Hollywood, and he was lionized by the film colony and the local press. He gave entertaining interviews on the sunny terrace of Nugent's Bel-Air home. He laments being forty-four, "a terrible age because there's only one way out— through the fifties." "If you can write plays for college boys in women's clothes, you can write anything." "I told Vincent Price not to go to New York and he got the role of Albert opposite Helen Hayes in *Victoria Regina.*" The beautiful weather in Hollywood? "Monotonous. The sunny skies look as though they had been done by the Pittsburgh Plate Glass Company." He discusses events in Europe that are leading to war, events the Western Alliance was paying little attention to. The day the Nazis invaded Austria, he remembers, the headline of a Paris newspaper read, "Lily Pons Says She'll Spend Three Days in France." With Armageddon in the offing, all Thurber could make out from the excited conversation of Frenchmen in 1938 when he was in France was, "Marcel, don't let your dog get into the rosebushes."

He was taken to one of Hollywood's colossal movie premieres, and asked Nugent afterward what he thought of the film.

"I thought it stank," said Nugent. "What did you think of it?"

"I didn't think it was *that* good," said Thurber.

Even in Hollywood, citadel of eccentrics, Thurber quickly attained the rank of "character." Once, forgetting to put on shoes and socks, he joined Helen at a Peggy Hopkins Joyce party in his bedroom slippers. At one of Nugent's parties, a male guest told Thurber that he didn't think Thurber's cartoons were funny. "Will you tell me what's funny about them, Mr. Thurber?" Thurber, refilling his highball glass, replied, "When I was younger and more patient, I might have said that I don't think they're so funny myself. But right now my eyes are troubling me and I don't have time to talk to dumb sons-of-bitches." The outraged guest sought out Nugent to complain. Nugent only laughed. "I didn't like him much either," he says.

On June 26, Thurber sends a report to Ross and the *New Yorker* staff on his first three weeks in Hollywood:

> I enjoyed that telephone talk with you, but didn't understand it—that is, who paid, and why we had to go into the steam room to talk. So many things amaze me out here, though, that a $45 phone call seems unimportant. There is more social life . . . than in a rabbit warren during the rutting season, and it is this which may drive me crazy first. We have seen all the best patios, the largest swimming pools, and the more famous Glogauers. Jack Warner wanted to know yesterday if I was any relation to Edna Ferber—was I her husband? I spelled my name and then pronounced it. Zane Ferber? he said. Any relation to Zane Gray? Elliott Nugent patiently explained the whole thing and Warner nodded. On his way out of the party he stopped and shook hands. Good-bye, Ferber, he said. So long Baxter, I said. It's a great place.
>
> For lunch yesterday we were asked to the Chaplins and stayed for tennis and tea. He told us all about his dictator picture—which sounds swell—and gave a long talk at lunch on capitalism, culture, and the disappearance of the individual craftsmen with the coming of the machine age. There are weeds in the garden of his thought but he is a sincere little guy and a fine fellow—plays tennis left-handed. . . .
>
> Chaplin started right off at our introduction by saying that he was a [great] admirer of my work, particularly of one thing I wrote—and as far as he was concerned that was all I had to write. This one thing turned

out to be Andy's description in Max Eastman's book of why he became a writer of humorous pieces. I usually disclaim these false honors but I was afraid to this time; I just stood there grinning and silent. He thinks I'm feeble-minded, I guess. Well, the two drawings of mine which Broun likes best were both done by Steig. I am used to these things. . . .

I intend to write to the old farmer [White] some time, if my eyes hold out. They have been having their ups and downs out here. Sometimes I see as clearly as a barefoot boy; at other times the atmosphere seems to be composed mainly of milk; today I can read a little but sometimes I can't read anything smaller than a quarantine sign.

Benchley was going to take me out to see three pretty girls at his studio, but he failed me, the dog. It seems that as he was about to start out for the Nugents the day they gave a party for us, he mentioned it to three honey babies, Rosalind Russell, Vivien Leigh, and one other, who shall be nameless only because I can't remember who it was. Anyway, they all wanted to meet me, as you might guess, and Benchley says "Well, I'm bringing him to the studio tomorrow as a matter of fact." So he . . . asked me not to let him down, but to come to the studio as he had promised I would; said he'd send a car for me at 11 the next morning. I was all pomaded and macassared up and wearing my velvet suit with the frilled cuffs when 11 o'clock came. The phone rang, and it was Benchley's secretary saying he "had to go out on location."

In discussing the Chaplin party with Dale Kramer in 1951, Thurber says that Chaplin told him that the White anecdote mistakenly attributed to Thurber was "one of the two funniest things in the world."

I naturally asked the funniest man in the world what was the second funniest thing in the world. His eyes lighted up and he said, "A man is bending over tying his shoe, and a stranger comes up and kicks him in the bottom. 'What did you do that for?' asked the man. 'Well, you were tying your shoe, weren't you?' " This seemed remarkable to me, because it is surely not the second funniest thing in the world, and Chaplin had 6,500 gags that were superior. As a matter of fact, it isn't funny at all.

They visited the San Francisco Fair and Treasure Island at the end of August; Thurber drew a quick self-portrait for newsmen in the Bay Area.

In the 1950s, Patricia Stone, a graduate student, asked Thurber about "wall murals" he had drawn. In his reply he refers to pictures he drew in Dave Chasen's Hollywood restaurant. Chasen was a former comedian and a friend of Harold Ross; the two had roomed together at 77 Park Avenue, when Ross was between marriages. When Chasen moved to Hollywood, Ross put up some of the money that enabled Chasen to open his first restaurant there. Thurber replies to Stone:

> I drew some (not dirty ones) on the walls of [Chasen's] men's room, and they were wiped off by the scrubwoman (before they could be painted in permanently). However, I subsequently did two large wall panels for the restaurant, and these, as far as I know, still hang on the walls. Dave Chasen is a friend of mine, and I have been in his restaurant many times during the months I spent in Hollywood writing and seeing produced *The Male Animal,* with Elliott Nugent.

In September 1961, shortly before Thurber's death, an entertaining writer, Stanley P. Friedman, who was a United Press reporter at the time, interviewed Chasen, who told him that contrary to Thurber's—and later Helen's —denials to Friedman, Thurber had indeed drawn a bawdy cartoon on his men's room wall: a couple is fornicating, while the man looks in alarm at his wristwatch and says, "My God!"

Chasen, Thurber, and Charles MacArthur—Helen Hayes's husband, and playwright—had spent the night drinking at the bar, Chasen told Friedman, when, about midnight, Thurber went to the men's room and drew the picture in charcoal. When Chasen came in the next day, intending to have the drawing preserved in shellac, it was gone. The scrubwoman told him that not only had she cleaned it off, she was quitting rather than work in "a place like this."

Thurber laughed when, the next day, a grief-stricken Chasen called him to tell what happened to his drawing. Thurber replaced it with one that Chasen placed under glass and later hung on the men's room wall in his second, larger restaurant. It shows a nude Thurber Man, his huge, private part in full view, striding confidently into a nudist colony, suitcase in hand, the men looking at the new arrival in consternation, the women with surprise and delight. The caption: "The New Man—or Howdy Folks."

Many Thurber drawings exist of men and women in compromising positions, but none are as sexually specific as the nudist's arrival. Chasen kept a half-dozen conventional Thurbers in a private drawer of his office desk. One, of pure comic aspect, is of a nude male advancing upon an unclothed female, saying, "You want love, eh? I'll give you love!" In another sketch, of an inert, bedded couple, the woman is telling the glum male, "I ran into Peter Arno this afternoon." (Arno's indefatigable promiscuity was well known, and presumably the woman has nothing left to offer her bed partner.) In another cartoon that provides fodder for speculation, a young woman confides to another, "He wanted to live in sin even though we were married."

In 1959, for Thurber's amusement, Friedman sent him a copy of a large picture Thurber had done for Chasen entitled "Idea of Heaven," in which the men, separated from the women by some electronic barrier, are singing, drinking, fishing, golfing, and playing poker. Thurber thanked Friedman for the picture, "which brought back that occasion and the people; even though I couldn't see it, my wife described it to me, and there we all were again."

Can any of Thurber's cartoon characters—what Brooks Atkinson called his "limp homo sapiens"—be seen as ever behaving "improperly"? Diana Trilling may have given us Thurber's answer when she writes of the treatment of sex in literature: "It is the style of the agent which makes for the moral meaning of the act."

Nugent and Thurber worked on the play over a three-month period, "between parties," Thurber says. The two writers complemented one another: Nugent knew structure; Thurber rarely worked from plot outlines, or understood precisely where he was going when he began to write. It was what kept him from attempting another novel, or ever completing a play on his own, though he always had one dramatic script or another that he worked at through the next two decades. He has said that while he was writing *The Male Animal* he solved stage problems by sitting at his typewriter and searching for the answer by trial and error.

When the rough draft was completed, the two men revised each other's work—a process that often led to bitter arguments. While still living with the Nugents, Thurber stormed out of the house at one point, vowing he would never reenter it. (Nugent found him in the garage asleep in the car.) Thurber later illustrated the Thurber/Nugent blowups in a cartoon he labeled "Second Act Trouble"; it shows Helen and Norma Nugent joining in the brawl.

After the show opened on Broadway, both Nugent and Thurber, as part of the play's publicity, sketched what life was like working with one another. Says Nugent of Thurber:

> Unstimulated, he is one of the mildest of men. . . . Even with friends he is shy and reluctant to disagree. . . . The whirlwind comes later. . . . Suddenly the mild patient Thurber is gone like a forgotten zephyr, and a new, piercing hurricane is upon you, piling up waves of argument and invective, racking you, springing your seams, forcing gallons of cold

saltwater through your fondest pretenses. Listing badly, you man the pumps, you head your nose into the gale, you mix up a new batch of metaphors. . . .

Next day, while you are patching your sails and cutting away wreckage, Thurber appears in a canoe, bearing fruit and flowers.

"Was I bad last night?" he mutters, with a sheepish smile.

Too weak to hurl your last broken harpoon, you invite him aboard and borrow his ukulele.

Nugent, of a calmer nature than Thurber, stormed out of the collaboration only once during their many differences of opinion. Thurber writes of him:

> After ten years in Hollywood Nugent can still write clear English sentences. . . . Hollywood rolled over his even disposition like ducks over a waterfall.
>
> The only disagreeable thing about Nugent is that he is never disagreeable to his friends. There comes a time in your day or your week or your collaboration when, if a person doesn't snarl back when you snarl at him, you feel like going out and throwing stones at wounded lions. . . . He only gets mad on the second Sunday in October of the even-numbered years which are divisible by four. At these times he will defy the lightning. You would never believe then that he could assume that death-mask-of-Thomas Jefferson look which he wears in the play, or speak in that underwater tone of faded perplexity.
>
> His rage raises a lot of hell but abates rapidly. . . . When it is over Elliott goes quietly to sleep without moving on his right side till morning. . . . Me, I am chased by things in my sleep, I can't get my feet out of the sand, doors are locked against me, and the train has pulled out of the station. But Elliott [asleep] sees the kind of things that make people smile . . . as if they were greatly pleased.

The wives helped, their suggestions often winning the acceptances of their husbands. Thurber's eternal concern that he would be taken for a pussycat, and his jealousy of the muscular ex-beau of Helen's, Babe Benson, may have been what led him to treat Whirling Joe Ferguson as plain stupid. Helen argued that it wasn't fair, and Ferguson was touched up to show a bit of intelligence. Norma Nugent thought the professor was being made to be so mean to his wife that he would lose audience sympathy. That led to other changes.

If pure Thurber is to be found anywhere in the joint effort, it is in the drunk scene, in which the professor and the undergraduate, in their cups, discuss the need of the male animal of any species to defend his territory. It is, of course, one of Thurber's principal themes.

> Tommy (the professor), drinking: "I know I'm not a tiger, but I don't like to be thought of as a pussycat, either. . . . Let us say that the tiger wakes up one morning and finds that the wolf has come down on the fold. He does not expose everyone to a humiliating intellectual analysis. He comes out of his corner. The bull elephant in him is aroused. We are male animals, too. . . . The sea-lion knows better. He snarls. He knows that love is something you do something about. He knows it is a thing that words can kill. You don't just sit there. All the male animals fight for the female."

Tommy sees his wife dancing with Joe smoothly, as he cannot. "A woman must not go on living with a man when she dances better with another man," he says in self-pity. He challenges a reluctant Whirling Joe to a fistfight and is beaten up. Ed Keller, the powerful university trustee, threatens Tommy's job if he reads the Vanzetti letter in class. Keller has never read the letter, because "I don't read things like that."

> Tommy: "My God, you don't even know what you're objecting to!"

Ironically, the McCarthy period, so cruelly abrasive to those who held viewpoints the Senator disagreed with, created, in its backlash, a hunger for the freedom-of-speech theme of *The Male Animal*. A decade after its first appearance on Broadway, it was welcomed back for a successful and extended rerun, a rebuke to the Red-baiters in both the public and private sectors.

In September, the Thurbers, low on money and tired of Hollywood's pace and the playwriting strains, loaded the Ford on a train and returned to New York for a brief respite at the Algonquin. The world was in for another global conflict, and a discouraged and restless Thurber began drawing on his favorite yellow $8^1/2'' \times 11''$ paper sheets one evening after dinner. "After Mrs. Thurber had gone to bed in our suite at the Algonquin," Thurber writes, "I set about doing some drawings in the next room, and after an hour's silence she called to me, 'What are you doing?' I said, 'I've just finished a book.' *The Last Flower*. It took some three hours, of course, to ink these drawings in."

At the time of the book's publication, however, he told an interviewer that in that seventy-five-minute interval he had drawn only twenty-three of the fifty-three drawings. No matter, the book, a strangely moving comment on the inevitable cycles of war and peace, appeared at just the right time to appeal to a worried public suddenly facing the day of the Apocalyptic biblical prophecy of "wars and rumors of war." Strung on a narrative thread of about four hundred words, the pictures forecast the destruction of the Earth, when love disappears along with mankind's art. The few human survivors include aged, doddering generals, who can't remember what the last war decided. One sickly flower in the world remains, which young survivors discover and nurture to health. Much of civilization is restored, only to be demolished by yet another war. "This time the destruction was so complete . . . that nothing was left in the world . . . except one man . . . and one woman . . . and one flower." The drooping stalk and blossom, which end the book, represent Thurber's slender hope that nature will inevitably offer itself as humanity's only and ultimate salvation. (A biographer found a potted flower, remarkably similar to Thurber's drawing, resting on his grave in Columbus a year after his death. The flower is also etched on his grave marker.)

The book is dedicated to Rosemary, "in the wistful hope that her world will be better than mine." The drawings and text, presented to Eugene Saxton at Harper & Bros., took him by surprise. Harper's had already prepared Thurber's *Fables for Our Time* for a 1939 Christmas season publication. The November 4, 1939, issue of *Publishers Weekly* notes that

> a recent brainstorm on the part of James Thurber in the shape of a brand new book entitled "The Last Flower" has caused a sudden and drastic change in publishing plans regarding Thurber's fall book. Harper had already manufactured and announced for publication on November 15th Thurber's "Fables for Our Time." Suddenly Mr. Thurber telephoned to announce that he had a new book, a parable in pictures, which 100 people had seen and which he claimed inspired them to make affidavits before notaries public that nothing like it had ever come from the hand of Thurber before. . . . Harper . . . promptly ordered its manufacture for publication in place of "Fables for Our Time" on November 15th. The manufacturing job was done in a week despite the dangers of delay when the whole office staff clamored for extra proofs to read. "Fables" will be released in early 1940.

The first printing, of fifty-five hundred copies, was followed by seven more over the next few years. In interviews, Thurber typically corrupted his reason for doing the book by pleading a need for money. The need was real. Travel expenses to and from the Coast, and the Hollywood cost of living, had been draining. The death of Thurber's father had left him a major supporter of his family. In June he had repaid Nugent a ten-thousand-dollar loan. True, his *New Yorker* sales were holding up; in the seven months of 1939 following his departure for Hollywood, not only were his "Famous Poems Illustrated" and fables continuing to run, but the magazine carried fifteen Thurber drawings, eight Thurber advertisements of others' books, and three casuals. He was also selling to *For Men* (formerly *For Men Only*) and *Forum and Century*, and his work was being reprinted in a dozen anthologies. But the payments in all those instances, including those from the *New Yorker,* were far below those of the "slick" market; his thousand-dollar advance from Harper's against *The Last Flower* royalties was welcome. Even so, his dismissal of an important work like *The Last Flower* as something done hurriedly for money is another instance of Thurber's strange feigned and studied flippancy about his art. *The Last Flower* is deeply felt. It elaborated Thurber's long-standing disenchantment with man and his moral inferiority to animals—epitomized in an earlier drawing of a Thurber Dog watching a man, woman, and child cross a field and sneering to his fellow canines: "There go the most intelligent of all animals."

Reviewers found *The Last Flower* "a happy miracle," and "full of alarmingly acute vision, profound pity and innocent beauty." Thurber sent the Richmond novelist Ellen Glasgow, whom he admired, a copy of the book. She replied:

> That parable contains not only the last flower, but the last word about war. I put everything else aside and went over the book, from beginning to end. Though I had remembered perfectly the dogs and the soldiers and the drooping blossom and the sad lovers, I found that I had forgotten your wonderful birds. How is it possible to put so much expression into a single curve? Or in a multitude, for that matter.

The permanence of the book in American literary legend was assured when E. B. White, in his Thurber obituary, proclaimed it his favorite of Thurber's twenty-six volumes, an opinion he stuck to. White always favored Thurber's art over his writing, and it was easy to anticipate what would follow when White blessed *The Last Flower* in his elegant eulogy of 1961:

> Although he was best known for "Walter Mitty" and "The Male Animal," the book of his I like best is "The Last Flower." In it you will find his faith in the renewal of life, his feeling for the beauty and fragility of life on earth. Like all good writers, he fashioned his own best obituary

notice. Nobody else can add to the record, much as he might like to. And of all the flowers, real and figurative, that will find their way to Thurber's last resting place, the one that will remain fresh and wiltproof is the little flower he himself drew, on the last page of that lovely book.

To no one's surprise, Harper & Bros. reissued the book shortly after his death, and Helen Thurber, who had never previously declared her preference for one Thurber book over another, sent complimentary copies of this memorial edition to a number of people, with an inscription stating that it was "my favorite Thurber book." She also let it be known that in his later years Thurber had decided that it was his favorite, too.

The Thurbers' financial leanness led them to reflect on whether both Ross and Harper & Bros. had been shortchanging him over the years, and when Harper's rushing of *The Last Flower* to press resulted in a mismanaged production, Thurber decided to change publishers. *Fables for Our Time,* published in September 1940, would be his last book with Harper's for seventeen years. In November 1939, he wrote the Whites:

> I am about five pounds lighter than when I saw you, on account of the play and Harpers.
>
> In addition to reversing cuts and leaving blank spaces in The Last Flower, Harpers has got out ads which sound as if they might have been written by some of the old ladies Mary Petty draws. I am sure they would stir Mrs. William Tecumseh Sherman, or the late Mrs. William McKinley.
>
> They lead off at the top in black type with "The Book That Captured a Hundred Over Night" leading you to guess what that means. I guessed it meant maybe people they had sent advance copies to (including Mrs. Roosevelt, I see by Saxton's list—I once wrote a bitter parody of My Day when it wasnt as good as it is now). . . . I am always buttoning Harpers pants and seeing that they have lunch money and a clean handkerchief before they start out in the morning. Then they get lost in Central Park and I have to go out and find them. You cant turn your back on that ancient firm. Gene [Saxton] also wanted me to put the $500 LIFE money into a fund—with $500 of their own money for ads! [*Life* magazine printed part of the book.] I had a long talk with him today and said My God no. It's too bad that nice gentlemen like Harpers have to be so bad at publishing books or rather promoting them. They couldnt sell a bottle of pop to a man dying of thirst. S&S would plug this book with thousands of dollars and probably sell a hundred thousand. I feel that if

it sells 20,000 that will pleasantly delight the boys down there. They have no guts and they have no courage—about as much gambling instinct and real blood as a clay pigeon.

You got to choose between gentlemen who know the nice places to eat and the guys who sell your books. I havent much cared till now, but this book I want to see sell. (The Times Book Review ran an unsigned review under Children's Books—along with Patty, the Pacifist Penguin, etc.) . . .

(By the way, the hundred who were captured over night turned out to be secretaries, editors, Lee Hartman, printers, Rushmore, Mrs. Rushmore, phone operators, engravers, Saxton etc. Well, your guess was as good as mine. I pointed out to dear Gene that when you run a big boast about a hundred copies on the same page with boasts by other publishers running into the 27th edition and the 234,000th copy, it's like saying "Fifty People Jam Carnegie Hall to Hear Gluck.")

They've got me signed up for the Fables, but after that I think that the clause in the contract where it says "on terms to be mutually agreed upon" will be the stumbling block. . . . Do you think you could get Gene a job at Simon and Shusters [sic]?

While Thurber was still in Hollywood, Nugent had convinced him of the need for a West Coast tryout of the play to find any weaknesses. Arthur Beckhard, a New York producer who was running a stock company in Santa Barbara, read the play and eagerly staged its tryout runs in San Diego, Santa Barbara, and Los Angeles. Nugent caved in to Thurber's pleas and played the lead, Tommy Turner—it was his first stage appearance since 1931. His father filled in as Keller, the trustee, when the actor scheduled for the part pulled out for a better offer. Thurber was in New York during the rehearsals but returned for the San Diego opening, October 17. After that performance, Nugent and Thurber cut the play extensively, but when it opened in Santa Barbara the next night they realized they had to restore much of what had been deleted. On October 24, it came into Los Angeles for a nine-day run, where it got good reviews—though Marc Connelly shook up Thurber by recommending that the domestic conflict be shortened to make more room for the issue of academic freedom, which Connelly thought was the important point of the drama. Connelly, who has been described by Charles MacArthur as "an instantaneous orator," was the wrong person to have turned up at the theater. "Nugent and I made the mistake of asking him what he thought of *The Male Animal* in Hollywood," Thurber said later, "and it took all night to find out. He said we couldn't bring a play to New York called *The*

Male Animal, and then came this wondrous line, 'You have Brahms' Fifth in your hands and have given it to a man with a mandolin.' "

Nugent disregarded Connelly's comments, which helped restore Thurber's confidence and self-esteem. But the night after the Connelly episode, in the Nugents' living room, Robert Montgomery's wife, Betty, said she liked the third act the best. (Montgomery, a close friend of Nugent's, wanted to put up half the money to bring the play to Broadway.) It was the act that Thurber liked the least, in which a wealthy and influential alumnus, who never appears onstage, solves Tommy Turner's problems over the telephone. Thurber blew up at Nugent for permitting such "incredible naiveté" to get into the act. This time it was Nugent's turn to explode. "It had been a long hot summer," says Nugent, "and we were both no calmer than four or five Scotches had made us. I told him off with some crude and not very original advice about what he could do with the play. Then I angrily stalked out of the room and went upstairs to bed. This was a novelty, because when there was any stalking out done, it was always Thurber who did it."

It was the last fight that ended in either man's stalking out. They walked in the garden the next morning, and decided to close the play and take some time in rewriting it. The Thurbers returned to New York, the Nugents following. For three weeks in New York, Thurber and Nugent made daily changes on their own and met to discuss them afterward. The experience bordered on the alien for Thurber, as he reports to the Whites:

Second Act Trouble

For a writer in his middle years, who has learned to write slowly and not too often, who sometimes puts a piece by for a year or two because he doesn't have the slightest idea what to say on page 3, and has no desire to say it even if he could think of it, it is not the easiest thing in the world to have someone whirl around and say, "Give me a new line for Joe right here." "Hm?" says the middle-aged writer. "You don't mean today, do you?" "I mean right now!"

In this familiar theatrical crisis a curious psychological thing happens to me. The only lines I can think of are lines from other plays: "Please God, make me a good actor, good-by, Mr. Chips! Hey, Flagg, wait for baby! Aren't we all? The rest is silence. It only seems like never." It is needless to say that these lines do not get you anywhere; but, as I said before, I never was really going anywhere. . . .

After you have worked on nothing but dialogue for five months, you wonder if you can ever learn to write straight English prose again. . . . Just to get back into the swing of the thing, you try to set down Lincoln's Gettysburg Address. And what comes out is this:

Four score and seven years ago, our fathers brought forth . . .

Your fathers! Always *your* fathers!

I said ours.

You mean yours!

. . . on this continent, a new nation, conceived in liberty . . . I know! I know! and delegated to the proposition . . .

Not delegated! dedicated!

. . . that all men are created equal.

Ellen (bitterly)

All men are created equal! That sounds fine coming from you!

Enter Joe

"What's the matter with that tall, thin man at the typewriter, mamma?"

"Hush, child, he's going crazy."

Herman Shumlin had recently produced two popular hits, *Grand Hotel*, based on Vicki Baum's novel, and Lillian Hellman's *The Little Foxes*. He was Thurber's choice to produce and direct *The Male Animal*. The Nugents were staying at the Chatham Hotel that November. Thurber's friend, the press agent Richard Maney, arranged for Shumlin to stop by the Chatham one night. Nugent and Thurber showed him the West Coast reviews and, as Thurber writes the Whites:

Elliott and I have spent ten days rewriting the play and last night read it
—Elliott did—to Herman Shumlin. Took three hours. He had never had
a play read to him before, but since Elliott had acted in it and it had
been produced, he wanted to hear it. Warned us he would just listen and
then take the script home and go over it by himself. But at the end of
the reading and a short discussion of changes he wanted made, he said
he would do the play. This is pretty near a record, I think. Selling a play
in three hours to the producer who has the biggest record for successes
in town and who can have his pick of the play crop. He gave us our first
advance royalty check today. . . .

We both liked Shumlin a lot. He is a quiet, solid gentleman very
polite but straightforward, not a bully and bastard like Jed Harris. I was
prepared, if he didn't like certain parts, to say no, but he liked the
important things and objected only to the last part of the third act,
which I hadnt liked anyway. It got trite and hurried, and seemed heavily
plotted, and fixed things up too patly. I can do it and get it right. He
counts on opening the play here New Year's Week, even that is rushing
it a lot. We'd have to play Xmas week in a tryout city. I am confident
that we have a swell play now, and that it will be a big hit. I think as big
as Life with Father. . . . It was wildly received in San Diego, Santa
Barbara and Los Angeles, even when it was full of dull spots and bad
writing and some gags that creep in when your back is turned. The
theatre would drive you nuts in a week, White. I did some fancy screaming myself. Shumlin wants Elliott for the lead since we cant get Leslie
Howard or [Burgess] Meredith. . . .

Everybody wants to change this or that or . . . suggest lines. When
I got out there the play had lines in it . . . suggested by secretaries,
cousins, mothers, bat boys, doormen, and little old women in
shawls. . . .

We are now in two lovely rooms . . . at the Grosvenor. . . . I
could throw a rock in any direction from my room and hit some old
misery of mine.

Shumlin asked only that Tommy's job remain threatened at the end of the
play. Agreed. Shumlin and his backers were to put up 60 percent of the
investment, Nugent 25 percent, and Robert Montgomery 15 percent. "I
wanted the Thurbers to take a share of this forty percent," says Nugent,
"which cost only eight thousand dollars altogether, but Jim had no capital
available and refused to accept another loan from me. Also, someone had

told him not to risk his savings in his own show—usually sound advice, but I knew we had one of the exceptions."

The cast included Gene Tierney as the ingenue, the teenage undergraduate sister of Tommy's wife, Ellen. A product of Greens Farms, Connecticut, and a finishing school in Farmington, Tierney had made her stage debut the year before. The only two plays she had so far appeared in were unsuccessful, but *The Male Animal* would bring her to the attention of Darryl Zanuck, who lured her away from the show after a few weeks and off to Hollywood.

At one rehearsal, Thurber, onstage and backing away to see all the actors, tripped over the footlights and fell into the orchestra pit. He was annoyed but unharmed. After three weeks of rehearsal and revision, both he and Nugent were tired, nervous, and ailing, and aware that there was still something wrong with the play's ending. Helen, a constant smoker and worrier, like Thurber, was losing weight along with her husband. They left for the country for a brief rest, but the play was still on Thurber's mind, and the next day he sent a new ending by special delivery. Nugent and Shumlin liked it.

The play tried out in Princeton. Thurber got there in time for the dress rehearsal—Helen was to join him the next day. It was December, the theater was unheated, and Thurber, Shumlin, and Maney huddled in their overcoats during the performance. Walking back to the inn, Shumlin remarked that the play still needed work and that he was worried. Nugent recalls the conversation that followed:

> "I'm worried too," said Jim. "I'm worried about all the laughs we're going to get tomorrow night. They'll make the play run thirty or forty minutes too long."
>
> Herman stopped and stared at him. "You're worried about too many laughs? . . . Maney only laughed twice tonight!"
>
> "That's Maney," Jim answered. "Besides, he's read the play; it isn't new to him. Elliott has never seen it from the front. . . . I've seen it fifteen times in four different cities. The laughs are like a goddam grass fire! The main job is controlling them and weeding some out so it doesn't play like a farce!"

Nugent and Thurber drank Scotch that night, Thurber finishing up the gin on top of the Scotch; it was a combination that, to Nugent's wonder, never seemed to bother him. The Princeton opening went exactly as Thurber predicted. The laughter was so constant that the play ran thirty minutes too long. One woman had hysterics during the hot-water-bottle scene and had to be removed from the theater. The new ending seemed perfect, but the authors realized that now the play needed to be cut. "It was heartbreaking to toss out nice lines and scenes," says Helen.

Much of what Thurber experienced in helping get *The Male Animal* launched he put into a warning letter to Wolcott Gibbs a decade later, when Gibbs's own play, *Season in the Sun*, was about to open:

[Dick] Maney is likely to phone your wife, the way he phoned Helen from Princeton, and growl, "Stay where you are. Only one funny scene." He had watched dress rehearsal with six other guys wearing hats and overcoats and smoking cigars. One of the actors fumbled every line and kept saying "Balls," so that fifteen speeches ended with this word. It was the night before opening [in Baltimore] and we had to cut twenty lines from the first act; sitting up too late; drinking too much; eating too little. There was the usual last-hour panic. Shumlin wanted to put spectacles on the villain to make him comic and Nugent wanted to put his father into the part. Someone had quietly rewritten the charm out of the dancing scene and it had lines like, "What do you say we shake a leg?" . . .

During rehearsal you discover that your prettiest lines do not cross the footlights, because they are too pretty, or an actor can't say them, or an actress doesn't know what they mean. There comes the horrible realization that phrases like "Yes you were." or "No I won't" are better and more effective than the ones you slaved over. . . . On the thirteenth day of rehearsal, the play suddenly makes no sense to you and does not seem to be written in English. You wonder why you wrote it and have a wild intention to ask the producer to postpone it a year. In this state you are likely to fall into the orchestra pit or find yourself taking an actress to Jackson Heights in a cab. She will praise Benchley and Perelman and ask you if you believe there are people in real life like those in Tobacco Road.

On the opening night in New York you will decide not to see the show, but you will; standing in the rear, expecting door-knobs to come loose, lights not to light, entrances not to be made, and actors to put in new lines. . . . None of these things will happen, but you will go out for a drink when the scene comes up that never was done right in rehearsal or out of town.—It will be done perfectly. Some actress will tell you, at the bar, that she always gets diarrhea on opening night because all actresses do. You will then decide to watch the second act back stage and guys you haven't seen before will call you "Mack" and

"Buddy" and push you around. Watch out that you don't pick up an important prop from the prop table and forget what you did with it. Don't walk through any door, or you will find yourself on stage. . . .

At the beginning of the third act you will be appalled by the fact that everyone is whispering and that the crosses have been slowed down. You will then be sure that they are doing the first act over again. This is because of third-act ear drum, which makes everything sound dim and causes important lines to sound like "Did you find the foursome in the two green bags?" It is now time to go to the bar again where you will find a large man in a tuxedo, who walked out on the play. . . . Whatever happens, avoid Marc Connelly. He told Nugent that we had given Brahms Fifth to a man with a mandolin. Fortunately for us, there isn't any Brahms Fifth. This is the only real comfort I can give you. Best of luck and God bless you.

The tryouts moved from Princeton to Baltimore. Despite the frantic revising of the play, Thurber looked up Ogden Nash, a local resident. Nash invited the Nugents, Thurbers, and others from the cast to a midnight supper at his home. H. L. Mencken was there, having wanted to meet Thurber. Mencken had been interested in a *New Yorker* article Thurber wrote about old copies of *Punch* he had found in the Woodbury house. The two men had exchanged friendly letters on the subject, and would continue to correspond in the years ahead.

The show opened on Broadway at the Cort Theater on January 9, 1940. Except for the *Wall Street Journal's*, the reviews were favorable.

The toughest critics, of course, were Thurber's cynical *New Yorker* colleagues, who were ever suspicious of one of their number getting ahead of them. Daise Terry kept Katharine White informed of what was happening on the magazine while Mrs. White was in Maine. Of the opening of *The Male Animal*, Terry wrote:

Well, the great event has happened. We were all there with bells on, except Mr. Ross. Don't know why, but do know that Mr. Thurber didn't send him seats, which seems odd to me. By now you've read the critics, or some of them anyway, and know they all say it's a hit. Office opinion seems divided. I didn't think the play was very funny, didn't get more than a smile or two [from me]; it all seemed like an unfunny Thurber drawing acted out. Cleota, the colored maid, gave me my laughs; she sounded just like Mr. Thurber when he's imitating a colored maid on the phone. Mrs. [Sally] Benson, Mr. McKelway and the Gibbses didn't think it was a knockout by any means. Mrs. Thurber told me today that everybody except the New Yorker crowd thought it was a marvelous play. . . . The house was a sellout last night and tonight and Mrs. Thurber has just been in raving about it, said Leland Hayward says he can get $100,000 for movie rights. Both she and Mr. Thurber are so excited they are about to collapse. Mr. Thurber made a curtain call; was pushed onto the stage, looking very pale and bewildered. Said "I'm all out of breath; I thought the curtain was down [when I stepped out here] but I'm glad it isn't. I just want to say that we're glad you liked us; we like you even better"; or something like that. . . . All the friends and fans of the New Yorker were there. And many parties afterwards. I was so sorry you couldn't make it as you'd have loved all the excitement before and after.

A day or two later, in another letter to Katharine, Terry describes the very kinds of incidents that Thurber feared would happen during a performance:

Mr. Thurber is excited about your coming and is arranging for tickets. He finally arranged for tickets for Mr. Ross for tonight. I'm sending you a preview of Benchley's [New Yorker] review. The "jerk" he mentions was sitting just in front of us; he was either drunk or crazy or thought he was at a football game; he had an empty pipe in his mouth the whole time and stood up and waved his arms and yelled at every line.

A funny thing happened last night, which Mr. Geraghty told me about. He sat with Maxwell and the Lobranos. At a very tense moment in the second act, a woman just across the aisle from them screamed, "Jack, Jack, speak to me! My god, he's dead!" The curtain went down and Nugent came out and said there would be a moment's delay. The lights went on and the house doctor came down to Jack. The woman said, "It's his stomach." The doctor escorted Jack and his lady out and the play went on. Sounds like a Thurber prank, but it was a genuine incident, I guess.

Thought you might like the Grosvenor at the corner of Tenth and Fifth. The Thurbers live there and have a nice, light, sunny (when the sun shines) suite and they like it very much. The manager told me they would give you the finest suite in the house—bedroom and sitting room —on the Tenth Street side, top floor, for $60 a week. They are very New Yorker conscious since the Thurber success. He said it would be a privilege to take care of any New Yorker people. . . . You'd be foolish to buy a new evening dress. . . . At the Thurber opening the 1930 models looked just like the 1940 ones.

After the opening, the financier Tom Meek, Nugent's and Thurber's college classmate, threw a theater party for them jammed with other O.S.U. alumni Meek had corralled. The Nugents and Thurbers went on to the Waldorf and a party held in their honor by the Robert Montgomerys, and wound up at Bleeck's. If Thurber neglected to send Ross tickets, it would have been at Ross's request. He didn't wish to be on hand if the play flopped. He had stayed up for the newspaper reviews and tracked down Thurber at Bleeck's by phone to congratulate him. "Ross," he identified himself in his usual gruff, abbreviated manner. "Well, God bless you, Thurber. Now maybe you can get something written for the magazine."

53

That One Year of Brightness

My mother says everybody will be bad off till 1940 and then there will be a good year till 1941 when the war comes, as prophesied by Evangeline Adams.

We must make the most of 1940. . . . Let's start planning it soon, that one year of brightness.

—Letter to the Millers, spring 1939

The success of *The Male Animal* enabled Herman Shumlin to sell the film rights to Warner Brothers for $150,000. Forty percent went to Shumlin; 30

percent, or $45,000, to each of the authors, payable at $15,000 annually over three years. With his share of the box-office royalties as well, it was the first time Thurber could remember being free of debt. When Herman Miller gave up his teaching job at O.S.U. to try his hand at writing, Thurber remembered his own salad days in Columbus, when Miller had brought him and Althea cheese, crackers, and onion sandwiches: "If you need any money for cheese and crackers until the checks begin coming in," he wrote Miller, "there is no one you know who would more happily, or could more easily, thanks to Broadway, send it. *Don't forget that.*"

He and Nugent were the toast of New York, and newspaper columnists found both to be excellent interview subjects. Thurber, at forty-five, is described as "tall, thin, gray-haired, gray-mustached, quiet, nervous, chain-smoking, serious"; elsewhere, "six foot one, with shell-rimmed glasses and an angular face," and having "a pleasant voice and an exceptionally narrow mouth." One reporter was told by Wolcott Gibbs that Shumlin had telephoned him, after agreeing to produce *The Male Animal*, to learn what to expect from Thurber when Shumlin suggested script changes. Gibbs wasn't encouraging. He told Shumlin that whenever Ross rejected a Thurber article or drawing, Thurber would storm out of Ross's office and push over the watercooler, claiming that he hadn't seen it. Once, when *New Yorker* editors were mangling one of his pieces, Gibbs said, Thurber marched into Ross's office without his coat and announced that the editors were not only stripping away his best copy but his clothes; he had already lost his coat. Later, he came in without his vest, then without his trousers, and finally stood before Ross clad only in his underwear.

With the press, as elsewhere, Thurber was the all-time master of exaggeration. As Nugent said of him, "Thurber has both a prodigious and accurate memory and the true poet's unconcern with facts." Thurber had simply dropped out of O.S.U., but he fibbed to one interviewer that he didn't graduate because his poor eyesight had kept him from passing botany. During his revisions of the play, he claimed, he found himself writing sentences like "The silver ear trumpet is the sole guardian of the old-fashioned clam bake," an impulse he tried to restrain, he said, if he hoped to remain at liberty long enough to see what happened to the play. At other times he decided the plot read like *Lady Windermere's Fan*.

Nathaniel Benchley wrote in the *Herald Tribune* that Thurber had frightened friends, cast, and critics before the play opened by announcing that playwriting was easy and anyone could do it. He was told that if he had jinxed the play with such talk, he would be barred from Bleeck's for two weeks. Thurber at once accepted a bet that the play wouldn't last seven months. He barely won; it ran slightly longer. But there were writers, even those who knew Thurber's propensity for loose generalities, who were willing to take him at his word about the ease of writing a play. Rumor had it that, for a time, the tabs on nearly all the *New Yorker* typewriters were set halfway across the carriage because everyone was writing dialog.

Thurber got back to his casuals with a spin-off from *The Male Animal.* "Courtship through the Ages" traces "the sorrowful lengths to which all males must go to arouse the interest of a lady," harking back to the marine annelids. Alistair Cooke has remarked that "though Thurber surely didn't invent the War between Men and Women, he is its bravest war correspondent." But it was Thurber who seemed compelled to continue the war and to report it.

The Thurbers never felt that they belonged in Hollywood, and they remembered their three months there with distaste. "I'll never go back to Hollywood," Thurber told a reporter. (He never did.) "Too many people have to be too nice to people who are not nice," he explained. "They live on canned air, too."

"We lived on an avenue that we called Ghastly Drive," Helen put in.

"The sanest guy out there and I," said Thurber, "sat down one night and mapped out logical plans for a movie. All night we met. Next day I met him in the street and he said, 'Hi, Jim. What are you doing out here?' That's Hollywood." Thurber got much of his hostility toward Hollywood off his chest with a casual called "The Man Who Hated Moonbaum." The protagonist, Tallman, meets a manic-depressive movie mogul at the Brown Derby who invites him to his mansion for a brandy. The producer, unacquainted with the classical stories his movies are based on, drunk and raving, has it in for "Moonbaum," who he thinks is always sending the wrong props to his movie sets. Tallman escapes the Faustian scene by an early departure.

The Male Animal continued at the Cort well into the summer, when attendance fell off. Shumlin shut it down for a month and opened it in Chicago; this run was followed by a road tour, which lasted into the spring of 1941.

"Herman and I went to New York shortly after *The Male Animal* opened," says Dorothy Miller. "Jim learned we had bought our tickets and was furious with us for not arranging with him for complimentary ones. He, Helen, and Nugent met us after the play, and we ate in a little bistro before Elliott had to catch a train to the suburbs. They were excited by the play's success, but they all looked tired."

The cumulative strenuous effects of getting the play to Broadway, the publicity (Thurber provided text and illustrations to help press agent Dick Maney get the show talked about), and the interviews all took their toll on both Thurber and Helen. Worse, Thurber's eye was giving out—fading, partially recovering, fading. Dr. Bruce told him that the cataract forming on the eye would have to be removed soon. It was all too much, and the Thurbers left for Bermuda. From there, Thurber confirms Dorothy's earlier diagnosis of their physical condition in a letter to the Millers:

> Helen and I both went to pieces physically at once, nervously, and mentally, too, I guess. I have been until just a few days ago a shadow of my former self, a shell, a relic, and an old pooh-pooh. . . .
>
> Helen's collapse was fast and bad; she was taken to the hospital where she stayed two weeks with a blood count so low they were scared to death of leucoemia or leuchoemia or whatever it is. She only had six red corpuscles left and four white ones. They jabbed her full of liver extract and she gradually came up out of the vale. Meanwhile I was down in bed in the hotel, running a fever, seeing mice with boxing gloves on, and the like.
>
> They finally bundled us on a ship for Bermuda and we are just now beginning to get some color in the cheeks and some flesh on the bones. . . . We have rented through May a lovely old house down here on a turquoise bay with birds and flowers all about. The weather has just got fine and the light bright enough for me to see by—for my eyes took a header with the rest of me and for a while all I could see was the larger Neon signs and 45-point type. That also kept me from quill and typewriter. . . .
>
> The only ideas I have had down here havent been much. I'm going to do a book of animal drawings for young and old, with text describing them: the bandicoot, the platypus, the coatimundi, Bosman's potto, the aardvark, and half a hundred others. The kind of easy and soothing idea that a broken down playwright gets.

His restless mind and imagination were always engaged, and one remembers, from "What Do You Mean It *Was* Brillig?", what Della, the cook, told Helen: "His mind works so fast his body can't keep up with it." It would prove to be prophetic pathology.

The Whites were busy editing *A Subtreasury of American Humor*, which was to be published in 1941 by Coward-McCann. Thurber writes them from Bermuda on March 10, 1940:

Liberty Hall
February 22.
1940.

James Thurber

I've been reading Faust, Emerson, Voltaire, and Ring Lardner. The other boys date a lot but Ring's "Some Like Them Cold" is as fresh as ever, and "Golden Honeymoon." He wasn't as stuffy as Goethe, after all, or as glib as Voltaire, and he was too much of a realist to believe that Everything Is Going to be Just Dandy, the way Emerson did. I looked up the Emerson piece I mentioned on visiting Coleridge, Wordsworth, Carlyle, etc., and while it's amusing in spots . . . it doesn't belong in your anthology. . . .

Althea had to have poor old Medve, the 13 year old poodle, destroyed. I know it was a blow to her and I worry about its effect on Rosemary. The poodle was in the house when she was born—more than eight years ago—and that's a long time to have a dog, and such a sweet dog. I knew she was dying when I saw her at Christmas time, but she lay there with that same quiet dignity, waiting for the angels as she would wait for dinner. Dogs are on to the fact that it's all a part of life, this dimming out, and is as necessary as the last movement in a symphony. My mother's family have never got on to this and for three hundred years have lived in the sublime belief that when everybody else was dead, they would still go on.

I think that my eyesight is improving and that it rises and falls with my state of health and my weight. At first I bumped into horses by day and houses by night but now I only hit the smaller objects, such as hassocks and sewer lids that are slightly ajar. . . .

The play seems very far away but it also seems to be doing well, even better than before, because one weekly check was as high as $750.

I'd like to have you see the play again, as you mentioned, because I really believe people get more out of it the second time—and my best friends are less nervous, too.

Word reached Helen in Bermuda that her father, the Reverend Ernest Wismer, was dying. As a British colony, Bermuda was at war with Germany, and shipping was threatened by submarines. The Thurbers, readily confessed "sweaty-palm" air passengers, swallowing hard, were flown by seaplane to Flushing Bay, New York City, where they took a train to Newport, Rhode Island. A letter from the Whites, expressing concern over Thurber's upcoming eye operation, was forwarded to him at Newport. He replies that a cataract operation is "as simple as tying a shoe lace." For a second opinion, Dr. Bruce had sent him to a Dr. Dunnington, who agreed with Bruce that a cataract was forming and surgery was indicated. He tells the Whites:

It is in a very early stage now and I can see to type and to read and could get around alone all right but Helen wont let me. They think it will form fast but I notice no change in the week we've been here [at Newport].

Bruce will do two operations, instead of one. . . . The first in June maybe, the next in the fall. In between I will be able to see better. I will have to be in the hospital for five days, he said (probably means 7) but all that worries me is whether they will let me get up and go to the bathroom, as I do not care about using jugs and bowls, but I am a great hand at chaffing nurses and may learn to knit or make little pin trays and bread boards like McKelway. Almost everyone on the magazine is in a sanitarium now, some of them fishing with bent pins in washbowls, others coloring comic strip figures with penny crayons, still others tatting or simply playing Lotto.

> There was an old fellow named Ross
> Whose staff became covered with moss
> And lichens and splotches
> And soft fuzzy blotches
> And mouldy old green stuff, and floss.

Helen's father, poor sweet soul, cannot live and it is a sad vigil we are holding here. . . . Since he has always been fond of me I think it is a good thing that I can be here. . . . He has a coronary thrombosis, hardening of the arteries, and his kidneys are going—which is what happened to my father. . . . He and I had a very interesting argument, all in good fun, about life after death when he was in New York and he more than held his own and was very witty and penetrating. I said good bye to him that night and never really saw the same man again.

Mame Thurber, escorted by Robert, came East for a skin-cancer operation, with travel and medical costs paid by Thurber. Mame had never met her eight-year-old granddaughter, and Althea brought Rosemary to New York for the occasion. Robert and Mame apparently kept their antagonisms toward Althea in check. Thurber took them all to see *The Male Animal,* and reports to the Whites:

I managed the week with Rosemary and my mother and Althea and Robert all right and everybody was satisfied, but it was a strain I was glad to get over. I took my mother to a specialist and while she has a skin cancer it is not by any means serious and can be excised, as the doctors (or clowns, as Robert still calls them) say. It does not need immediate operation, either so I can space these things out. My main problem is to keep her away from quacks, crystal gazers, layers on of hands, salves, ointments, wall mottoes, radium water, snake oil doctors, swamis, etc. She and Robert listened to a lecture from me on quackery and next day looked up one Dr. Jutt in the west Fifties who cures all by making you eat meat three times a day. Robert had found and bought for a dime a pamphlet by the good doctor on the bargain counter of the book department of a drug store.

Rosemary is fine. I took her to the Central Park zoo, which she has always loved and we got there on the first warm day of the year when all the animals were cutting up, giving each other the hot foot, playing leap frog, and what not. The polar bears were wonderful, ducking each other in the water by getting hold of each others ears, jumping in and pulling down. The seals were even better. Even the bengal tiger came out and said well, well. (A bengal tiger has long droopy ears) I tossed a penny from a bridge among some people, so exciting Rosie that she swallowed her Beman's gum. My mother brought her a little mother of pearl box containing a small diamond and sapphire ring which my mother had when she was 12, and a hundred year old silver bracelet. Althea is as strong as a female moose and looks fine.

The Whites had asked Thurber which of his stories he would most like to see included in their anthology of humor, as well as his favorite stories by other humorists. All his books were in his father-in-law's Newport house and Thurber said he had "been looking them over."

I think Emma Inch is as good a short story as any of mine, and maybe Tea at Mrs. Armsby's from the Mrs. Monroe stories which I like even after ten years for some reason. I dont like Menaces in May much any more. . . . It is apparently impossible for me to remember stories, even my own, unless I have a book of them before me. . . . Helen agrees on Walter Mitty, or Emma Inch, or the Greatest Man in the World. . . .

I got a copy of [John] Mosher's book with the fine Petty drawings. I wish all my crises with people, particularly women, could have been no larger than Mosher's, an unfortunate phrase at tea time, a page missing from a phone book, a moment of anxiety at Schraffts. No drunken lover trying to get his key in the lock while you frantically hunt for your other shoe and the girl cant open the window leading to the fire escape. He is, however, a minor Henry James—amazing sometimes the style—and a Forty-fifth street Proust whose bête noirs are no more fearsome than a sea horse. . . . He is a very sensitive artist and he was in such a dither when he held his first book in his arms—I happened to be in the room— that it was wonderful to watch. Exactly like a father with a baby. As the tired father of seven books—or is it eight?—I tested the binding roughly, criticized the blurbs, spoke pessimistically of low royalty rates . . . before I was really aware of his condition. He almost had a seizure. Ruth, Helen's sister, first met John . . . when he came nervously into a large party we gave at 8 Fifth Avenue, was presented to her, bowed, sat down, and said to Helen, "I *must* have a lozenge." . . . Helen got him a lozenge.

The war I try not to think about. I have become, I think, an interventionist, because I cannot imagine living in a world with a Germanized France and a destroyed England. The American intention to live on a hemisphere instead of a planet seems to me a bit unworkable. I have an awful hunch the Allies cant win without something. I dont know whether we could help. I wish we could stay out, but I dont like the looks of things. Trouble is, I like France about as well as I do America. Pretzels and beer in those great restaurants is a picture I cant dwell on. Cant you just see a German captain drinking a bottle of chambertin 1915 right down, out of the bottle, in one swig? . . .

One thing that has cheered me up is a line from one of Agatha Christie's books in which a character says, "The guilt lies between one of us." She hasnt had no schooling; should be *among* one of us.

Earlier Thurber had sent to the Whites in Maine two poems he wrote in Bermuda, asking, "If you think they are all right, for the New Yker, would you send them on?" They did. While in New York, Thurber stopped by the office to check on them, and told the Whites:

> I have put my poem aside for a while since it is not right yet. It is fun to have Ross, the Mark Van Doren of Forty-third Street, critize [sic] poetry. He and Gus [Lobrano] agreed that we had to excise the last stanza and what they would do to the triolet and other repetitive poetical forms would be worth watching. . . . Ross was 37 before he had read any poetry except Comic valentine verse, and I am thinking of giving a little dinner for him and Edna Millay and Muriel Rukeyser. . . .
>
> I am thinking of copying out on yellow paper and handing in something by Swinburne or Coleridge, to see what they want excised before they print it. I have an idea Gus lives in constant dread of Ross and of disagreeing with him and I watch Gus every day for signs of sanitarium fever. The gentle, quiet type that never screams is likely to go out like a candle one day.

The poems were never published in the *New Yorker*.

McKelway, Ross, and Shawn were accelerating the hiring of young men with apparent potential, but minimum experience, as Talk of the Town reporters, hoping the farm team of hopeful and earnest tryouts would yield an occasional big-league candidate. In his letter to the Whites, Thurber notes the three latest recruits: two of them didn't long remain, but the third, Philip Hamburger, as of this writing, fifty-three years later, is still a contributor. ("Does he have to be called 'Hamburger'?" Ross petulantly asked McKelway, when Hamburger was hired. A rumor, perhaps a foreseeable one, has it that another promising prospect in that period was turned down because his name was Frankfurter and Ross said he didn't want his staff sounding like an Automat menu.) Thurber is critical of the new faces but acknowledges that most young men of that day were living in dread of a war that seemed less and less avoidable and into which they would be drafted:

The office, as you know, is filled with sad, slow-moving young men of twenty, old emotionally as hell itself, taciturn, laconic, who seldom speak. No more does anyone set fire to his waste basket or pour glyco thymoline into the envelopes of rejected newsbreaks. The younger generation is non-plussed and cautious and definitely alarmed. They stand staring at the headlines for hours on end, then move carefully away. They keep their overcoats and hats on, like men in a flooded area. They turn over for several minutes in their minds what you say and then murmur something politely. I find myself speaking slowly and loudly to them. They are all on the verge of weaving baskets. There is about them all the air of a man who has lost his wife and four children in an outboard motorboat accident. I dont know what has come over youth. You have probably not met Felsch and Wittman and Harberger [Hamburger]. They turn ashes over with their paws and sigh. They chew gum, drink coco [sic] cola and sit facing the door, with their hats and overcoats on. I think they wear garters. They call me sir and give me lots of room. They have lost something that they never had. I suspect that they get up before dawn to lean carefully out on the sill and study the street. I suspect they are better prepared for this Thing they see coming than I am.

Two weeks after the death of Helen's father, the Thurbers flew back to Bermuda. Thurber's eye continued to play tricks on him. He was scheduled to have his first eye operation at the Columbia Presbyterian Medical Center, on June 12. He was nervous but still hopeful, and his courageous cheer shines in the letter from Bermuda he wrote to the surgeon, Dr. Bruce:

What I allude to laughingly as the "power" of my eye seems to be about what it was when I saw you. I probably see as well as the water buffalo, reputedly the blindest of all large jungle animals. It is interesting to note that the water buffalo can lick a tiger in spite of his opacities and indifferent, if not, indeed, detached retina.

My opacities, or spaniel hair, as I like to call them give me lots more annoyance than my buffalo sight. Since I cant see very far beyond them, I sometimes just sit and look at them. I am familiar with all the new shifts they make and could draw an accurate map of the whole dirty brown constellation. (If I actually did, the Bermudians might think it was a map of the islands and put me in the military jail.)

I was thinking the other day that you might be interested in the charts of my eye kept by the late Dr. C. F. Clarke of Columbus and now in the office of his son (or nephew) a younger Dr. Clarke. I think there are about forty feet of readings, findings, and soundings. I could not have been more than 10 when he first examined me and I went to him off and on for fifteen or twenty years, I think. I thought this might be of some help about the time of appearance of the opacities. I remember how Dr. Clarke, who was supposed to be a good eye man (as eye men in Ohio go), was all during the years I saw him astonished that I could see as well as I could, and would call in other eye men and show me off to them, whereupon they would all exclaim, as if they had been watching a contortionist. He said there was a "veil" or something through which I saw. That may have been something else again. There are more things in my eye than were dreamed of in Horatio's day, anyway, or maybe Hamlet had opacities and thought they were ghosts. This would also explain Macbeth's looking at nothing at all in the banquet scene and shouting "Take any other form than that!" I think I know how he felt, if it was opacities he saw and not Banquo.

While in Bermuda, Thurber wrote three informal essays for Ronald Williams's magazine; one, "The Story of the Bicycle," was partly in support of Williams's losing editorial crusade to keep automobiles off the island. Another was "Extinct Animals of Bermuda," which presents some of the strange creatures Thurber had told the Millers he intended to make a book of.

Thurber's fascination with oddly named and strange-appearing animals probably began with his 1934 cartoon of a Thurber woman imperiously confronting the stolid, block-shaped animal—Thurber's version of a hippopotamus—that had consumed Dr. Millmoss. (Thurber's friend and Cornwall neighbor Kenneth MacLean, a Yale professor and Thurber scholar, believes that Millmoss feels happier and safer inside the Thurber hippo than outside with Mrs. Millmoss.)

Thurber explains the animal as his attempt to draw a hippo to amuse three-year-old Rosemary. "Something about the creature's expression," says Thurber, "convinced me that he had recently eaten a man. I added the hat and pipe and Mrs. Millmoss, and the caption followed easily enough."

He followed his illustrated account of Bermuda's extinct animals with "Prehistoric Animals of the Middle West," two years later. In the latter piece (published, surprisingly, in *Mademoiselle*), Thurber resurrects Dr. Wesley L. Millmoss, explaining in a footnote that "while on a field trip in Africa in 1931, Dr. Millmoss was eaten by a large piano-shaped animal, to the distress of his many friends and colleagues."

Millmoss builds models of prehistoric animals from fossilized remains, with such absurd results—drawn by Thurber—that Dr. Wilfred Ponsonby, another Thurber scientist, insists that Millmoss's animals were dreamed up, rather than dug up. For example, Ponsonby "asserted that the Thake bones which Dr. Millmoss had found were in reality those of a pet airedale and a pet pony buried together in one grave . . . *circa* 1907." (Millmoss's confusion could be attributed to the fact that his first wife was divorcing him at the time.) Asked if Man had got up off all fours before Woman did, Millmoss "gave me a pale, grave look and said simply, 'He had to. He needed the head start.' "

The Thurbers returned to the States in early June. Helen rented an eighteenth-century house in Sharon, Connecticut, not far from her mother, who had moved from Newport to Lime Rock after her husband's death. Florence Edwead [Butcher], a maid they were taken with in Bermuda, had agreed to return with them. She remained in their employ for more than ten years, largely denying Thurber a homegrown source of malaprops by being educated and articulate, as well as devoted. ("I consider my years with Mr. & Mrs. Thurber very sacred," she writes, "as we had grown to love and respect each other very highly.") They could also now afford a handyman to chauffeur and work around the house and grounds.

In mid-June, Thurber was admitted to the Institute of Ophthalmology at the Columbia Presbyterian Medical Center. As Dr. Bruce explained to a *Time* reporter years later, Thurber's wounded left eye had not been removed until after the right eye had become bloodshot. By medical dictates, Thurber claimed, he should have gone blind then, for he had developed sympathetic ophthalmia, a disease in which the uninjured eye takes on the symptoms of the injured one. Surprisingly, the right eye got better, and served Thurber reasonably well until 1928, when it first began to fail. By the time he got in touch with Dr. Bruce, in 1937, his vision was seriously deteriorating. A cataract, a delayed reaction to the old injury, had developed. "Because it was a dangerous eye to operate on," says Bruce, "I decided to do the operation in two stages." That June, he performed a preliminary iridectomy. This, says Helen, "cut an exploratory slit in the cloudy . . . lens, partially and temporarily giving [Jamie] a little bit more vision." Thurber's sight improved enough so that he could see to read and write during the summer, Helen adds, "at least until about the middle of September."

At that time, Thurber's vision receded again, and it was no longer safe for him to walk outdoors by himself. It was when he began to "bump into things." Bruce scheduled the second operation, in which the cataract was to be removed, for October 22.

In a letter to the Williamses from Sharon, painful for them to read, Thurber types:

I have not had a very good summer in my mind, it being full of dark gibbering figures dressed in black bombazine with lamb's blood on it, whilst in the background scamper the gray wet bodies of dozens of little cheeping wailwice and grunting chudhubs and small round mailbacked creeblies whose scales come off in your hand and stick to you like wet onion skin. . . .

It is almost time for me to go back to Hospy-wospy [hospital] for more monkey business. I can't see any better but I dont see much worse and can write on the typewriter with ease, having just finished and sold a 7500 word story to the Sat Eve Post, a baseball story . . . which wont be printed until next year because I got it in too late. Ross wrote me when he found this out that for two months he has been going around in his stocking feet shushing everybody and talking sadly about how I couldn't see anything smaller than the sign made of flowers reading ELYRIA to guide the airmen flying over that Ohio town. Now, he says, I find you are writing serials for the Saturday Evening Post. He wants me to get to work on that Bermuda story. . . . I think I will send it on to you, as it is interesting, and you can send it back, and I hope the censors dont get it but if they do I'll just say, "Ross, the censors got it." Got what? he'll say. The piece on Bermuda, I'll tell him. I dont know what you are talking about, he will then complain, for he no longer remembers anything for more than five, six weeks. [The Bermuda piece never materialized.]

Of course I get into some trouble on acct of not seeing too good. Do you raise them? I said to a lady on a bus. Raise what? she says. Those chickens like the one you have in your lap, I said. She pulled the emergency cord and brought the bus to a halt and got off at the corner of Mobray and Pineberry Street in Jersey City. What she had on her lap was a white handbag. I may be put away any day now. . . .

We went to Marthas Vineyard for a week and felt fine, since we had to get up for breakfast at 8:30 every a.m. hangover or no hangover.

The *Saturday Evening Post* story is "You Could Look It Up," a one-of-a-kind Thurber work. Its narrator is the semiliterate of Ring Lardner's stories, whose scrambled syntax and other grammatical offenses are intended to buttress the humor:

It all began when we dropped down to C'lumbus, Ohio, from Pittsburgh to play a exhibition game on our way out to St. Louis. It was
gettin' on into September, and though we'd been leadin' the league by
six, seven games most of the season, we was now in first place by a
margin you could 'a' got it into the eye of a thimble.

But nothing by Lardner matches Thurber's wild plot. The baseball team's
manager, faced with a crucial game, hires a midget to pinch hit. The midget's
diminutive chest-to-knees strike zone practically guarantees him a needed
base-on-balls, but the midget can't resist swinging at an easy pitch and is
thrown out at first base. The angry manager throws the midget bodily into
the air, the center fielder making a difficult catch of him. The story was
written in Sharon that summer following the first operation, says Helen,
"influenced by the fact that he couldn't read and used to listen to baseball on
radio a good deal."

The story gained immortality when, in 1951, Bill Veeck, colorful owner of
the now-defunct St. Louis Browns, was inspired by it to try the same tactic as
a publicity stunt. (The midget he hired did what he was told and was walked,
but the Browns still folded.) "You Could Look It Up" delighted sports reporter Grantland Rice and his friend, Harold Ross. Ross wrote Thurber that
while watching a World Series game with Rice, Rice had talked about the
story during two innings and said he thought it should be sold to the movies.
"By God, I do, too," Ross wrote Thurber. "Do you want me to start selling
it?"

Ross was genuinely moved by Thurber's threatened vision, both out of
compassion and out of worry that the productive career of one of his premier
contributors was in jeopardy. He visited Thurber in the hospital several times
in 1940 and 1941, throughout the five eye operations.

Helen had added her own letter to the one Thurber wrote the Williamses,
explaining his eye problems and that he was scheduled to enter the medical
center again on October 15, six weeks away:

Jamie saw better for a while, but it is beginning to go again, I think.
Here, in a house with which he is familiar, it is hard to tell, but at
Martha's Vineyard, on country roads and in strange houses with lots of
rocks and steps and ditches and such, it was rather difficult. He has been
simply wonderful, cheerful pretty much all the time, but occasionally it
gets him and then, more than at all times, I wish you were here, Janey,
to hold his hand and play word games with him, or were those word
games you two used to play? It will certainly be God's blessing when it is

over and he can see again as well as before. He hates being driven around in the car, and gets so bored with not driving that we haven't been down to N. Y. much, which is probably all to the good. . . . Our chauffeur-butler is so correct that we have finger bowls every meal except breakfast and would have them then if I hadn't put my foot down. Jamie hates the chauffeur because he is too soft-spoken, and turned on him fiercely one night when we were being driven home from the Coateses, very late and very drunk. I thought he would leave, as Jamie fierce is as fierce as any ten given tigers, but he forgave us. I guess that made Jim dislike him more. He is a fine butler and a fine driver, though, and I can't fire him because he speaks too soft, can I?

After the first operation, when Thurber could see slightly better for a time, he was high with hope. That summer, recuperating, Thurber heard from Ralph Ingersoll, who by then had taken an unpaid leave from Time, Inc., to start *PM*, a daily tabloid that refused advertising in the name of editorial purity. Ingersoll couldn't have approached Thurber at a better time. Thurber writes in *The Years with Ross*:

> When Ingersoll began publishing *PM* in 1940, I wrote a brief column for it, called "If You Ask Me," twice a week until I went into a nervous tail spin following my fifth eye operation. Ross read a few of these columns and objected because, he said, "You're throwing away ideas on *PM* that would make good casuals." But I was out from under the strict and exacting editing for which the *New Yorker* was and still is famous, and I needed this relaxation and the hundred dollars a column Ingersoll paid me.

This is a curious explanation, taken by itself. When he began the articles on Ross, in 1957, he was angry with *New Yorker* editors both for their rejection of some of his current work and for what he considered arbitrary changes in his copy that they did buy. As for payment, in 1940 the magazine had 166,000 readers and earned two million advertising dollars. It paid less than the slicks but far better than the other quality literary magazines—certainly better than *PM*'s hundred dollars per column. Furthermore, at the time, Thurber's relationship with fiction editor Gus Lobrano was friendly and satisfactory, as far as anyone knows.

The probable fact was that Thurber's frustration with his sight had led to an anger with the world, a rejection of all the familiar institutions of his life. Perhaps he was still annoyed with the negative reaction to *The Male Animal* of so many of his old colleagues on the *New Yorker*. Though the eye surgery was costly—the magazine offered no medical insurance then—royalties were continuing to roll in from *The Male Animal*, enabling him to subsidize his rebellion against Ross. After his fables series had run their course, and he had settled scores with Hollywood in "The Man Who Hated Moonbaum," his "Footnote on the Future" (June 15, 1940) was the last piece he would do for the *New Yorker* for fourteen months. The fifteen captioned Thurber drawings that the *New Yorker* ran in 1940 were mostly holdovers, as were five spot drawings. In 1941, the count was down to three captioned drawings and five dog spots. What writing he could or would get done during his trying period of eye operations went to *PM* or, free of charge, to the *Bermudian*. Other old loyalties went by the board as well. He had given up his first and only book publisher, Harper & Bros., after a dozen years, for Harcourt Brace. He even chose to live at the Grosvenor Hotel for a time, rather than the Algonquin; the Joel Sayres were living at the Grosvenor then, which may have influenced his decision.

Thurber began his semiweekly *PM* columns following the June operation. Many of the subjects are, in the Thurber manner, mock-serious complaints. It was a presidential-election year, and a campaigner telephoned Thurber to ask if he would sign a writers' petition for Wendell Willkie, to be rushed the hundred miles to Thurber by automobile. Thurber said he hadn't made up his mind, but a few days later signed on with Roosevelt supporters. *Their* request had been by night letter, and Thurber explains, "There seemed such old-fashioned simplicity, such abiding dignity, in this leisurely telegram," as opposed to a speeding auto, that it won him over.

The telephone company's constant changing of familiar numbers to those with additional digits irritates him. He decides that the man responsible is a phone-company bureaucrat in Hartford whose name is Rudwooll Y. Peffifoss. Peffifoss "has had to go through a lot of hell" because of his name ("the Y is for Yurmurm") and is determined to get back at the world by complicating telephone numbers.

He comments on a 1926 book by Will Rogers, acidly noting Rogers' doting references to Mussolini. He protests the long-windedness of Thomas Wolfe, and radio baseball broadcasts that are interrupted by family serials, like "Scattergood Baines." He wonders why women who write him never change their typewriter ribbons, though he is certain that by not being able to read what they write he is spared "feminine exhortation, accusation or complaint." He ridicules Anne Morrow Lindbergh's book, *The Wave of the Future*, for suggesting that the democracies take a cue from the nationalist "spirit" prevailing in the Fascist countries, and while he is about it he kicks her "America First" husband for his isolationist stand.

He got around to Medve, the poodle, in a lovely eulogy—frequently reprinted, and preserved among Thurber classics as "Memorial." During the summer, he sent Ronald Williams a riotous account of a fictitious Bertram Curvey, who is given to the same maniacal people-bothering as was Thurber's Elliot Vereker, of "Something to Say"—but without Vereker's presumed promises of artistic redemption. "Meet Mr. Curvey," which appeared in the *Bermudian* of September 1940, has somehow avoided the more permanent status of book collection, but it is Thurber, one painful operation behind him, at his wonderful manic high. There are, as usual, touches of autobiography to it:

> His first wife left him when, on the occasion of their first wedding anniversary, he brought her what turned out to be a cardboard chair with rubber legs. In sitting on it, [she] was precipitated into the fireplace. "You're lucky," laughed Bertram, as she scrambled to her feet, "that there wasn't a fire in there." His second wife divorced him for bringing to her on *their* first anniversary a box of wooden chocolates, which cost her a front tooth. This Mrs. Curvey was already pretty much annoyed because Bertram had showed her mother up to a "bedroom" on the first night of the old lady's visit, the "bedroom" door turning out to be one that gave upon the outdoors. Bertram had gone to the vast trouble of spreading a net under the door such as is used to break the fall of trapeze artists in a circus. "I save the old girl from breaking her fool neck," complained Bertram, "and she wants to have me put in jail. There's gratitude for you."

Thurber's *PM* column stopped abruptly for three months, following the second operation, on October 22. This was "the big operation, the removal of the cataract, which had developed completely by that time," Helen writes the Williamses:

> The doctor had said hopefully two weeks in hospital, two weeks more in town, and then we could leave. Things didn't turn out as planned. Dr. Bruce told me afterwards it was touch and go for the fifteen minutes of the operation. His eye was so stuck up with old scar tissue from the bad iritus [sic] he had had as a kid . . . that he thought the whole thing was gone. However, he got the cataract out without taking everything, through sheer skill, but Jamie [got] iritus bad, was in the hospital five

weeks, at the end of which he developed a bad case of hospital phobia or nerves, and we brought him down to the [Grosvenor] hotel, where we had day and night nurses for some weeks more. It was the first experience I have ever had with a nervous breakdown, so-called, and it was awfully hard on him. He pulled himself out of it through will power, though. We went up to our rented house [in Salisbury], for the eye looked better.

Helen's mother and Bob and Elsa Coates were guests at the Salisbury house during the Christmas holidays. But "when Jamie's operated eye turned bright red, we rushed back to New York and the hospital," says Helen. "From then on things were bad. Everything happened to the eye that could." She again rented a suite at the Grosvenor Hotel. Daise Terry kept Katharine White, in Maine, fully informed:

When I got in this morning, [I was] told Thurber had been calling me so I rang him [at the hospital] and he was all pepped up over the prospect of leaving the hospital for the Grosvenor today. Mr. Ross, his bride [Ariane Allen, a young and pretty artists' model from Texas, whom Ross married on November 10, 1940] and sister-in-law were up to see him last night, which pleased him. After his outburst yesterday about being deserted by all his "old and what he thought *best* friends" I scolded Mosher, Flanner and McKelway and Shuman and sent a message to Mr. Ross. . . . Mosher telephoned at once. Flanner is going to see him today. He's particularly sore at McKelway and Gibbs who have never once communicated with him in spite of all my nagging. Thurber said the nearest Gibbs came was Mrs. Gibbs saying to Mrs. Thurber at lunch that they were so sorry about it all. He rambled on and on this morning about his "impending breakdown" and dozed off while he was talking. He does this all the time; starts out very peppy and then falls asleep.

A few minutes later Mrs. Thurber phoned. They had a consultation last night and Dr. Bruce agreed to his leaving the hospital. They called Dr. Damon and he called in Dr. Russell, a general practitioner, who will take charge of him through this nervous business. Bruce of course will continue with the key treatment. Bruce says he had definitely turned the corner, he has had no pain in the eye for three days, but the infection remains. . . .

I thought it would please him to have a bouquet from the Whites to greet him when he arrives at the hotel, this p.m., so I sent a dozen lovely tea roses—his favorite flower, Mrs. Thurber says. You mentioned doing this earlier so I thought it would be all right. He's still limited as to food so flowers were the next best thing and he does like them. He's very self-conscious about having to be fed and not being able to get around without assistance, Mrs. Thurber says. He has almost no sight; he said yesterday (when he had his first tub bath in the hospital) that he could see the mirror in the bathroom, but Bruce was skeptical. He also said he could see large dark objects like the bed. Bruce may be a good eye man but he's certainly no psychologist. Mr. Thurber says he is positively inhuman.

Shortly after that Helen writes the Williamses:

I . . . closed the house in the country and rented an apartment on Washington Square . . . , brought my servants down, and the car, for we had to drive up to the hospital every other day, even when he wasn't in it, for treatments, and the Medical Centre is a five dollar's taxi fare from where we lived and I am Scotch and that killed me.

Still, Thurber determinedly refused to yield any of his writing plans. At the Grosvenor, he and Sayre worked on a movie scenario based on *My Life and Hard Times* (nothing came of it). Daise Terry writes the Whites, who were in Florida:

Mr. Ross is back looking very well in spite of his ulcer. He is on a diet, of course, and seems to be getting along all right. His face looks thin and drawn but he seems in excellent spirits. He was just here at my desk asking about Mr. Thurber, who, by the way, has never set foot in the office since you were here. The chief reason is that he and Joe Sayre are working hard on the scenario, which is about finished. I stopped in to see him on Sunday. Mrs. Thurber was at the movies and Sayre and Thurber were working. He's still going to the hospital every other day for treatments to keep down the "bulges" that keep popping up. Mrs. Thurber told me that he demanded that the doctor tell him definitely whether he was ever going to see again—of course the doctor didn't say anything definite, told him on Friday that the film they had been hoping would split and disappear is at a standstill; that he thought he would now try cutting a hole in it through which he might be able to see a little. The poor man [Thurber] is in a very nervous state and who wouldn't be.

Mrs. Thurber doesn't come into the office ever but calls up most every day. You're absolutely right about her ignoring the many, many things people do for him. She was having fits yesterday when she called me. They had been told that their income tax this year would run between $15,000 and $20,000 and she was raving. . . . She said they had paid around $6,000 for hospital this year.

Thurber began his PM feature again in the January 27, 1941, issue. It would no longer be illustrated. A note headed the column:

James Thurber has been absent from the columns of this paper for three months, due to an eye operation. Now he is sufficiently recovered to dictate his copy to a stenographer, but he has not yet found a way to dictate Thurber drawings.

Nor was the column semiweekly any longer. The start-up money that Ingersoll had raised was gone by September 1940, when he lost control of PM to Marshall Field II, who persuaded the floundering tabloid's eighteen stockholders to accept twenty cents on their investment dollar. Field's political philosophy was similar to Ingersoll's, and Thurber was content to remain with the new management. But he was having trouble with deadlines, and by the end of March "If You Ask Me" had become a Sunday feature. It now more frequently struck a misanthropic note, though still larded with the humor and fantasies of a tough and indefatigable Thurber.

A third operation, on March 21, was for secondary glaucoma—hardening, or swelling, of the eyeball—and iritis. Daise Terry sent Katharine White frequent (expected but unrequested) reports, filled with staff gossip:

Mr. Thurber went to the hospital for three days last week and they punctured that "bulge" that had been pressing on the retina and he has recovered from that. It had nothing to do with the film, which is about the same. The split widens very slowly and he sees no more than he did when you were here. He has been all keyed up since this last operation and lambasts the New Yorker more than ever. I told him yesterday he ought to be ashamed of himself calling us bastards, louses, rats, etc. He said he wasn't coming [into the office] any more because he couldn't stand having everybody asking him why he didn't write for the New Yorker instead of for PM.

Mr. Mosher was down to their new apartment (37 Washington Square) for dinner last night and stayed until four o'clock this morning.

He said Mr. Thurber ranted the whole time about his old friends, and was in a very nervous state.

Another iridectomy was performed on April 18, 1941, in which the scar tissue over the lens was slit to allow light, and, in May, the final operation, to drain fluid that was pressuring the optic nerve and retina.

Helen reports further to the Williamses:

> Each operation was harder on his nerves (no general anesthetic was allowed, only a local . . .), and he was [in] pretty bad shape. [After] the last one, he refused to stay [at the hospital] so down we came nurses and all, and one got measles the first day, and the second one got cramps, and we finally settled for a flat-footed old maid who has never been sick a day in her life but was as dull as an old copy of the Christian Herald. Well, we got through that, and the last operation, we hope, was scheduled for June, as an anniversary present, but as soon as Dr. Bruce saw that the eye was at last safe, and nothing new or awful could develop, he advised us to get away for the summer, and save the final thing for fall. It is the cutting of the film that never went away. Was supposed to split or something. It has a few pinpoints of holes in it, and it is through them that Jamie sees what he does see, which is an amazing amount, everything considered. Only he cannot go out alone, has to be led around, except indoors, where he is very agile. And the worst is that he cannot read or draw. He writes in longhand on yellow paper, but cannot see what he writes, and you know his painstaking method of writing and rewriting. He felt at a great loss, and still does, but did a casual, a long one, for the New Yorker a short time ago and they are crazy about it ["The Whip-Poor-Will"]. He had to do the first version, and the revision, in his head, then write down the second revision. And it came out swell. He does a weekly column for PM . . . and very well, too, but it is hard to get ideas when you can't read. He is a wonderful man. . . . I cannot think of anyone else, at least among our little group in New York, who could have gone through it and come out sane. But of course his brand of sanity was always different from anyone else's, and probably helped.

By July 1941, Ronald Williams had joined the British Navy and Janey was to return to her family's home in Geneva, New York, for the war's duration. Williams planned to sell the *Bermudian*. Thurber, recovering from the trauma of surgery, writes from Martha's Vineyard, where he and Helen had taken a house for the summer:

> The idea of selling the Bermudian saddens us terribly. I wish you could arrange somehow to keep one hand on it, so you can get it back when the war is over. . . .
>
> I have had five operations on the lone lim since I saw you, and I still can't see. They dragged old Jamie through all the corridors of hell, where I left most of my weight and two thirds of my nerves, but things have quieted down now, and after one more operation in the fall, I should be able to see again, normally.

There were no more operations.

In 1939, as noted, he had written Dr. Bruce from Hollywood: "Life is no good to me at all unless I can read, type, and draw. I would sell out for 13 cents." He was now destined to do none of those things, and the usual self-centered life of a writer would become, in Thurber's case, a nightmare-haunted existence of semi-isolation. He not only didn't sell out for thirteen cents, he did angry battle with the milky lightness that enfolded him, armed solely with a resolve that defied the unfair odds and contributed further literary treasures to posterity's enjoyment and enlightment.

54

That Whip-Poor-Will

I'd had five operations on my good eye, and after the fifth, the eye seemed worse than ever. I cracked up. I'm told most patients crack up from shock after the *first* such operation—and usually lesser operations than mine were. So I had a pretty bad case of nerves. Some of what I went through is in "The Whip-Poor-Will." I didn't have to draw on

[Freud's or] anyone's theories. The nightmares I describe were some of the nightmares I had.

—Thurber to Harrison Kinney, 1948

"They performed these very painful operations on his eye," says Joel Sayre, "and he had to lie there absolutely still. He was . . . strapped down in bed and in great misery. But the London blitz was going on and he was getting this over the radio. He . . . kept saying to himself, 'This is pretty awful but think of all those poor people in London and what they're going through.' This [he said] at least enabled him to hold still.

"After the operations, he suddenly just fell apart. I was sent for and went up [to Martha's Vineyard] and stayed a weekend or so trying to cheer him up, to get him to laugh a little. The Gudes were up there and they were very helpful and staunch."

It was to be near the Gudes on the Vineyard that Helen rented a house in Chilmark in the summer of 1941. As Helen told the Williamses, Thurber now scrawled words he couldn't see on yellow copy paper with a soft lead pencil, getting about twenty words to the page ("a hundred pages to a pencil," Thurber says); these efforts were transcribed by Helen, and, after a time, a secretary. His columns for *PM* were now almost all based on what he heard, on radio or in conversation, or from what was read to him. He has fun with "Maisie," a maid who tells him that "the timekeeper" is watching over him, ominous information for a man nearly blind; with the radio programs he now listened to frequently; and with presidential candidate Wendell Willkie's English. Following the March 1941 surgery, a deepening misanthropy, reflecting the war abroad and the bad time he was having, steadily soaks into his writing. The superiority of animals to humans is a recurring subject. One piece features a giant caged fulmar that, while being fed, bites the keeper's hand. A Thurber scientist asks the bird why he bites the hand that feeds him: "Couldn't reach his throat," the fulmar replies. "Interview with a Lemming," one of only three *PM* columns Thurber collected in a book, ends with that scientist telling the lemming, "I don't understand why you lemmings all rush down to the sea and drown yourselves."

"How curious," said the lemming. "The one thing I don't understand is why you human beings don't."

Thurber had been frightened by the thought that, sightless, he would not be able to write, and it helped to learn that the sprawling symbols he drew could be deciphered as words and published. Despite his emotional and mental turmoil, his irrepressible store of humor kept bubbling up—on such subjects as the eyesight of the water buffalo, and the parachuting of Rudolf Hess into Scotland. (The latter inspired a Thurber plan to further unseat such Nazi gods by spreading word among the Germans that Joseph Goebbels parachuted down over Liverpool "clad only in socks and garters and an opera hat.")

Helen had brought to the Vineyard some of Thurber's haphazard files, which she had been sorting through since their marriage—odds and ends that Thurber had kept as possible essay subjects—and found an item that Thurber made into a *PM* column, and which he later used to describe, in *The Years with Ross*, the *New Yorker*'s early Talk of the Town modus operandi:

> It was a letter from a woman reader, and on it was clipped a pink memo reading "Must go this week" and signed with the initials of Arthur Samuels [in] 1929. . . . The item was not only a dozen years old, but . . . Samuels had been dead for three years. Ross read that *PM* column . . . but all he said to me was, "God knows how we got out a Talk department when you were writing it."

He missed only one *PM* column after the March operation, but the April surgery put him out of business for a month. He drove himself to write something—anything—for publication, in a pitiable effort at self-reassurance, ruminating in one column that when young he had wished to be Hannibal, because he, too, had been blind. Helen, regarding the *PM* output as a lifeline Thurber was clinging to, worked as stenographer as well as nurse, encouraging and consoling. Both "servants," as Helen refers to them, were on hand to help.

But his July 20, 1941, column was his last, another that he never collected in a book. It was funny on one level but ominous on another. It begins with Lester Wedge losing a fight with a cigarette machine in a little store on Martha's Vineyard:

> Wedge had nothing but a $5 bill, which he had to get changed. This upset him and in trying to insert the proper coins he dropped 95 cents on the floor. His hat fell off while he hunted for the money and he got his hands dirty scrambling around on the floor. When he finally got a pack of cigarettes from the machine, it was wrapped so tightly in double cellophane that he broke his thumb nail getting the thing open. And, as

it opened, three pennies rolled out and fell on the floor. The people in the store laughed at Wedge. . . .

"There seems to be a conspiracy in this country," Wedge said to the Ralstons, "to keep a man from getting any cigarettes." They noted that he was flushed and wild eyed but they thought little about the incident.

Wedge is an overnight guest of Mrs. Van Fix, and over cocktails in the drawing room, Wedge puts out his cigarette in an ashtray containing a box of matches, which had been left partly open. The matches flare up, burning Wedge's fingers (which happened to Thurber more than once). "He hated women who put match boxes in ashtrays. Match boxes did not belong in ashtrays. Ashes belonged in ashtrays." Wedge retires to his bedroom, needs a cigarette badly and sees two cigarette boxes.

> He picked up the box on the table by his bed. . . . It wouldn't open. He struggled with the thing and broke his other thumb nail, but still it wouldn't open. Then he noticed that there were letters on it [that] read "If you my treasure trove would see, just press the spot that opens me." Wedge shook the heavy box savagely. There were cigarettes in it alright. . . . He . . . began pressing various parts of [the box] with his thumb. Nothing happened. He tried pressing each letter in the legend on the box separately, but still nothing happened. The lid stayed tightly closed. Wedge beat on the box a couple of times with the heel of his right hand and then gave up. After all, there was the other box.

He couldn't solve the key to that box, either. It was too much for Wedge in his nicotine fit, and though the mystery was never solved, "Mrs. Van Fix was found strangled to death in her boudoir on the second floor of her charming country place."

He had begun other writings, including "The Whip-Poor-Will," the only Thurber prose published in the *New Yorker* in 1941—the first in fourteen months and the last for another five. It reveals a glimpse of the terror and suffering endured by Thurber through his travail. In a Martha's Vineyard setting, the protagonist, Kinstrey, is being driven insane by the calls of a whippoorwill, and the nightmares the bird's calls induce. In his dreams, trios of little bearded men roll hoops at him. The bird's "dawn" call "pecked away at [Kinstrey's] dreams, like a vulture at a heart. It slowly carved out a recurring nightmare in which Kinstrey was attacked by an umbrella whose handle, when you clutched it, clutched right back, for the umbrella was not an umbrella at all but a raven." The problem turns on a very neat point, Kinstrey reasons. "William James would have been interested in it; Henry, too, probably." But with no relief from the torment, Kinstrey is pushed to madness, murder, and suicide.

A student pointed out to Thurber that Freud believed a psychosis begins at times with a dream and holds to a delusion that originated there. Yet in "The Whip-Poor-Will" Thurber seems to associate Kinstrey's fatal psychosis with William James. Thurber had earlier indicated a fondness for the elder James, whose insights, he felt, had been preempted by Freud's widespread popularity. But he replied simply by saying that the nightmares he described in "The Whip-Poor-Will" were nightmares he had recently lived through, and were not suggested by anyone's theories, his reference to James notwithstanding.

Was that also true of "A Friend to Alexander," his next *New Yorker* story? In that January 10, 1942, piece, Henry Andrews has nightmares in which he tries to hide Alexander Hamilton from Aaron Burr, but the famous duel is reenacted, with Hamilton again fatally wounded. Hamilton had become Andrews' dead brother and "practically every other guy I've ever liked," Andrews tells his wife. Feeling responsible for Hamilton's death, Andrews resolves to avenge him. He practices with a pistol, and the morning that his wife finds him dead in bed his empty hand is frozen in the pistol-firing position. The doctor can find no cause of death. Mrs. Andrews, who has accepted the reality of her husband's nightmares, wails to the doctor, "Aaron Burr killed him the way he killed Hamilton. [He] shot him through the heart. I knew he would."

Thurber shook his head, in answer to the question. "I may still have been under the weather emotionally when I wrote that, but I got the idea from a friend of mine [Herman Miller] who was doing a study of Hamilton. He called me one day and said, 'This is Aaron Burr.' It occurred to me that you can become so engrossed in a historical project of that sort, you might become a part of it."

"A Friend to Alexander" was the first story Thurber ever dictated. He had never learned "touch" typing, having used the journalist's hunt-and-peck method. It was a long while before he felt comfortable composing in his mind and dictating to a secretary, and even after he did, he would pencil the first draft of a story on paper, committing it to memory the while, wait for the hieroglyphic scrawls to be typed out and read back to him, and then talk through the revisions. His phenomenal memory enabled him to retrieve a story in his mind almost in its entirety.

"When I knew there wouldn't be any more [operations]," Thurber told a *Time* reporter, "and there was nothing [to hope for] to look forward to, I broke down. It took about three years to get over this."

Thurber was given to telling interviewers in the years ahead that though he lacked the apparatus of sight, he still could see more than science could explain. But science subsequently may have explained Thurber's "vision" as blindsight, the unconscious combining of perception, memory, and judgment through which the blind person perceives things he cannot see—an easy thing for a man of Thurber's imagination to achieve. Discovered about 1980, blindsight often enables a blind person to sense, or "see," something, though he doesn't know how he is able to. Thurber explained it by crediting himself with "one-eighth," or "one-fiftieth" vision, which Dr. Bruce never believed.

It was after "The Whip-Poor-Will" was completed that the lifeline snapped, and Thurber went to pieces from what is thought to be cumulative and delayed reactions to all he had endured on the operating table, as well as the realization that he would never read again, would have to compose with handwritten words he would never see, and deal with the physical world through sound, touch, and the sensory perceptions. It was the beginning of what Thurber called "a five-year nervous crack-up," during which he could work only spasmodically.

He went through a period of rejecting his worried, attentive, and gallant wife. Helen could well have been Mrs. Van Fix, whose cigarette boxes frustrated him. Her efficiency occasionally annoyed him,—an annoyance evident in the fable of the shrike, whose mate kept things intolerably organized and picked up. There was an edge of hostility toward her as early as April 30, 1940, in a letter to the Whites, again having to do with ashtrays:

> Good old Helen Wismer, one of the women from whom the verb to wismer or to wismerize is derived. There were only three Wismer women ("thank God," as undisciplined husbands who were afraid of having their affairs put straight, used to say). These three, however, could put a house to rights three times as fast and three times as competently as all the birds and animals in Snow White. If a man should bring into the house a brass cap from the rear axle hub of a dismounted 1907 Chevrolet, to use for a cigarette tray, a Wismer woman would, even through sleet and snow or fire and heat, carry it back to the stable and replace it on the wheel where it belonged.

On one occasion at the Vineyard, he rejected Helen completely, resenting his dependence on her, insisting upon moving in with the nearby Gudes for several days. In "The Whip-Poor-Will," Kinstrey is dangerously antagonistic toward his wife:

It struck him that perhaps Madge had no subconscious. When she lay on her back, her eyes closed; when she got up, they opened, like a doll's. The mechanism of her mind was as simple as a cigarette box; it was either open or it was closed, and there was nothing else.

("Helen, for all her gaiety, wit, and education, could be tiresome," says Ann Honeycutt. "She too often expressed herself in uninteresting ways, and I used to think that grated on Jim's sensitive ears.")

Reading that the haunting call of the whippoorwill drove Kinstrey to murder the servants and his wife with a knife, "several friends called us on the Vineyard," says Helen, "and wanted to know if I was all right."

Thurber's condition got worse. He threw up his drinks, got the shakes, needed people around him, exhibited sexual anxieties, and worried that he would be "put away" in an asylum. ("Please, Jap, please, don't let them put me away," he pleaded with Gude.)

He was desperately sick, says Jap Gude, adding:

> It's rather strange how few people—even his closest friends—ever knew how close he had come to a crippling breakdown. I don't believe that anyone but the two Helens [Thurber's and Gude's wives] and myself— not even Coates and Sayre, who were there through some of it—realized what frightening shape he was in. . . . With all due credit to other people involved, and the remarkable good luck of having Dr. [Ruth] Fox on the island, it was mostly Thurber's extraordinary strength of charac- ter and pure guts that pulled him out of the quick sands into which he was surely sinking.

The distinguished poet and teacher Mark Van Doren and his family were on the island. Van Doren recalls:

> I had just met him on the beach; there was a party, and nothing much was said. But the next afternoon he arrived at the house where we were staying and said he wanted to see me. That surprised me. . . . I led him out, and we found chairs and we sat down and I looked at him and he was weeping. . . . I said, "What's the matter, Mr. Thurber?" He said "This . . . blindness is a punishment." I said, "Why, what for? How could it be a punishment?"
>
> He said, "Well, in my writings I have always dealt with meanness and stupidity. . . . My subject has never been goodness and strength. I

"They're going to put you away if you don't quit acting like this."

have always talked about poor, terribly weak people; I made fun of them. And so this is a punishment. I have been stricken blind."

I said, "You know, everyone who's ever read you knows that you are for goodness and strength. . . . You are a satirist and you deal with the opposites of those things in order to reveal your true belief. . . ." He never forgot that, and he always thought of me . . . as a kind of oracle.

In an interview, Van Doren elaborated: "I told him humorists see the discrepancies of life more sharply than the rest of us, and a discrepancy is either terrible or wonderful, but must be identified. No one can do it better than the humorist." (Van Doren, as he talked, was stroking the family cat, black with white paws and chest, named "Walter Mitty.") "He was worried about the person as writer and the writer as person. 'Maybe I'm not doing enough,' he seemed to be saying. 'I should do more.' I told him that his satire was the reverse language of scorn, for it attacked what should be attacked—those things that fail to serve goodness and strength. I pointed out other writing he had done, the pleasure he had given people with 'Walter Mitty.' 'That's just cheap humor,' he replied. In the center of his gizzard he wanted to be the greatest writer that ever lived and not held to standards he had already set. Mitty was an old race run and won, and he felt he could run better and win a brighter victory tomorrow. He had the highest of standards.

"Why had he singled me out for help? It seemed to me that Thurber had an uncalled-for reverence for college English professors. Over the next twenty years that we remained friends—he and Helen eventually moved to the Cornwall, Connecticut, area, where we lived—he seemed to accept my offerings, my suggestions, my adventures into an idea, as gospel, not to be challenged or assailed. But often I said things to get his responses and thoughts. It was one of the few ways Thurber could frustrate me.

"After the Vineyard incident, he seemed to retain an embarrassingly high regard for me. 'Why won't you fight me?' I'd ask him when he would acquiesce to something I said that I hoped he'd find challenging. 'You treat your real friends by fighting with them.' Thurber credited an O.S.U. professor, Taylor, with getting him started both intellectually and socially, and I suppose he tried to identify me with Taylor.

"Every good man is a man, woman, and child; the child asks, 'Please love me.' Thurber, the child, was speaking to me at the Vineyard. He was most vulnerable when showing his serious side, and he was trusting me with that side. But he soon recovered and consented to his own existence; to like being Thurber; to enjoy playing the role of Thurber, even the blind Thurber. He had more vitality than a thousand other men. What do people do with vitality? It leads them to be more than themselves; it flares into other personalities. Out of his joy of being Thurber, he became more than himself. Given the state he was in when we first met, it was a miraculous thing to watch, this man who emerged from a lifeless family to become a blazing genius. As a humorist, he remained a very serious and sensitive man, with a rich and complicated mind."

But Thurber's character would be forever changed by the blindness. "His rages—terrible, fantastic," Van Doren agrees, "could be traced to it."

It was Thurber's old nemeses, women, who pulled him through the ordeal with the talk he needed to hear, with nursing and medical ministering—the two Helens and Dr. Ruth Fox, a neurologist. Even the psychiatrist, with whom a still shaky Thurber spent two hours following his return from the Vineyard, was a woman—Dr. Marian Kenworthy, a friend of Sayre's. Yet, throughout, the War between Men and Women became even more real to Thurber. When at last he had the freedom and independence that money grants, he went blind and was delivered into a complete reliance on the enemy—women handled his affairs and even took down the words he was obliged to dictate.

Daise Terry had dispatched a favorite New Yorker secretary of Thurber's,

Margaret Thurlow, to the Vineyard to help Helen with the dictation for a day or two. They would work together over the next few years, at the office and at the Thurbers' New York apartment.

In late August, he could write his surgeon, Dr. Bruce, in his large, floppy handwriting:

> Four weeks ago today I went into a tailspin, crashed, and burst into flames. This is to let you know that I am rapidly getting into shape again. B-1 injections, haliver oil and luminol have helped tremendously. It seems that the nerve exhaustion [Dr.] Russell detected just wasn't being helped enough by Vita-Caps. I have to have more help than that, for I had been hanging on by my fingernails for a hell of a long time. Even through the worst days, I began to gain weight, which I had not done. The Lord, who keeps doing all He can for me, sent in Dr. Ruth Fox, who is a gal with a fine background in neurology, and she pulled me out of it with great skill and understanding.
>
> The things that inhabit the woods I fell into are not nice. I never want to crash there again. . . . Helen, my Scotch wife, has been like three nurses rolled into one, and has stood up under it all like the Black Watch.
>
> I paid little attention to the eye during the battle of Chilmark, and strained it in the sun. . . . Well, we found that uncle [Dr.] Arnold Knapp was up here, so we crashed in on him, knowing you would approve. He was very kind and helpful, suggested scapalomine [sic] and compresses, once a day. The eye began to whiten and is almost all white now. I saw him three times. He even made two little jokes, too. We said little about the nerves, as all he would say to that was humph-humph. . . .
>
> I began writing a play in the midst of all the hell. They call me Iron Man Thurber. . . .
>
> Look out for bows and arrows.

In the fall of 1941, the Whites' anthology of humor was published. White writes in the preface:

> A great deal of modern humor has been born and is growing up which would never have seen the light . . . if it had not been for the receptive attitude of the *New Yorker* toward new writers, and for its solid conviction that humor is an art form and not a barber shop fitting. We have a speaking acquaintance with *New Yorker* pieces, a parental feeling

about some of them, and a high regard for the magazine and its editor and as contributors. It would be odd indeed if our book didn't show this attachment.

Thurber had a larger share of the anthology than any other humorist, present and past, turning up in four of the book's thirteen classifications of humor with four of his fables, the burlesque "If Grant Had Been Drinking at Appomattox," "The Greatest Man in the World," and "The Night the Bed Fell." Thurber took pencil in hand to trace out in his cumbersome handwriting his thanks to the Whites: "I like the selections of mine you are using in your book, and am very proud to be so lavishly represented."

For the rest of his life he would be at work on a play, in mind or practice, never to finish one. He tells the Whites:

> I have a swell idea for a play which I want to get at. I need someone to help me on it, though. I want to do most of the actual writing, but talking it out with someone is important to me, especially now. . . .
>
> I wish I could sit around and tell the idea to you. It's a little hard to do it in pencil in a semidarkness. . . .
>
> The whip-poor-will story was quite an achievement technically, since I wrote it longhand, on some eighty pieces of yellow paper, and since I had to use a new form of composition, doing all the rewriting in my head, before putting the final lines down. We—Helen and I—did a little cutting out later, but no rewriting. I was glad you liked it. Ross wrote me probably his longest known letter about it—some 800 words. He has been very good to me. The new word rate for casuals was partly my work, and the letter told all about that.

The Whites had bred Minnie, their dachshund, and had offered the Thurbers one of her pups:

> We would, of course, love to have a Minnie puppy, and it breaks our hearts that we wouldn't be just right for a dachshund just now. It has long been our dream to have six or eight variegated dogs when we buy our house in the country—a dachshund, a poodle, a water spaniel, etc. There is a wonderful black male poodle up here [Martha's Vineyard], name of Hugo. . . .
>
> I hope you can read this, but I dont see how the hell you can. . . . God knows I have been down in the bowels of terror, but I have climbed out of it with what Dr. Fox thinks is remarkable speed.

I wont go on any further, because this will be task enough for you, the way it is. It's my first finished work of any kind in two weeks. It gives me lift and confidence to get back at my writing table. Helen will go over this and translate the most horribly garbled words. We love to hear from you, about your life and Minnie's and all. . . .

There is nothing pathological about me, babies, just nerves. I used to think nervous breakdowns were not so terrible. I know now how wrong I was.

In mid-September, they sublet an apartment on East Fifty-fourth Street. Thurber worked at home, Margaret Thurlow coming over each afternoon to take his dictation. He produced "A Friend to Alexander" and two book reviews for the *New Republic*—of F. Scott Fitzgerald's *The Last Tycoon*, edited by Edmund Wilson (favorable), and of John Steinbeck's *The Moon Is Down* (very critical of Steinbeck's trying to portray sympathetically a Nazi officer in occupied Norway). The books, of course, were read to him.

Though he had just praised Ross's recent kindness, Thurber was scolding him a few weeks later, following the editor's well-meant suggestion that Thurber try writing captions for a sheaf of Mary Petty drawings. Thurber was annoyed when one of his suggested Petty captions was rejected, and took Ross to task over cartoons in the October 18 issue, using a formal salutation sarcastically:

Dear Mr. Ross:

. . . I got to thinking that it wouldn't be a bad idea to let me spend, say, two afternoons a week in the office not only trying to write captions to pictures, but also having a look at the captions to pictures which have been bought. Since I haven't sent in an idea drawing of my own for a year and a half, my beloved art meeting could hardly say that my criticism were based on a sheaf of my drawings having just been rejected. [Thurber's typos were now attributable to the dictation and proofreading process; no longer to his typing.]

You already have filed away for your autobiography some 50 or 100 blasphemous notes from me on what is the matter with the magazine. Most of these were written, I suppose, just after I got 3 or 4 of my best drawings back. Now we are on a new basis, since I am a blind, gray-haired playwright who still has a great affection for the magazine and is still capable of indignation. It seems to me that something is the matter when the first 3 drawings in the magazine turn out the way they did in the issue of October 18 [1941]. . . . The really great New Yorker drawings have had to do with people sitting in chairs, lying on the beach, or walking along the street. The easy answer the art meeting always gives to the dearth of ideas like the ones I am trying to describe is that they are hard to get or that nobody sends them in any more. It seems to me that the principal reason for this is that the artists take their cue from the type of drawing which they see constantly published in the magazine. Years ago I wrote a story for The New Yorker in which a woman who tried to put together a cream separator suddenly snarled at those who were looking at her and said, "Why doesn't somebody take this god damned thing away from me?" I want to help to take the cream separators, parachutes, fire extinguishers, paint brushes and tomahawks away from four-fifths of the characters that appear in The New Yorker idea drawings. . . .

It must have been 6 years ago that you told me drawings about psychoanalysts were terribly out of date. The next week I turned in one in which the analyst says, "A moment ago, Mrs. Ridgway, you said that everybody you looked at seemed to be a rabbit. Now just what did you mean by that?" . . . But you can't publish a drawing about an analyst and a woman with the caption, "Your only trouble is, Mrs. Marksham, that you're so horribly normal." This is one of the oldest, tritest, and most often repeated lines in the world. If you will look up a story of mine called "Mr. Higgins' Breakdown," published more than ten years ago, you will find that the first sentence is as follows (I quote from memory): "Gotham P. Higgins, Jr., was so normal that it took the analyst a long time to find out what was the matter with him." Just after that story appeared, the editor of Redbook sent for me and said he wanted me to write something for him because he had been so enchanted by that line. At that time, I have the vanity to believe, it was not old. But the years roll on, Mr. Ross, and turn into decades. So what you probably need is an old blind man sitting in one corner of Mr. Gibbs's office and snarling about certain captions which you are too old to remember helped make certain issues of The New Yorker way back before the depression.

Another fault of the art meeting, it seems to me, is your tendency to measure everything with rulers, stop watches, and calendars. I told Andy White the caption I sent in for Mary Petty and he laughed more wholeheartedly than he has since his teeth began to go and arthritis took him in the back of the neck. I understand the art conference decided Mr. Swope was not old enough to be known to the old lady in the suggested drawing. She certainly would know old Jacob Swope's boy, Herbie, just as a woman of your mother's generation would know about Mrs. Ross's boy Harold. Furthermore, there are at least a dozen variations of the caption I could have suggested.

If you ever write a comedy for the theatre you will discover that the best laughs invariably follow some simple and natural line which the characters involved would normally say. . . . To show you what I mean, let's take the specific example of the drawing which appeared in the issue of October 18th in which the salesman says to the lady at the door, "Couldn't we go inside and sit down? I have a rather long sales talk." This is such an extravagant distortion of reality, it is so far removed from what any salesman would ever say, that to be successful it has to be fantastic. But since the situation is not fantastic, it ends up simply as a bad gag. All salesmen that get into drawings in The New Yorker ring the changes on cocksureness, ingenuity, or ignorance. When I was a little boy, in my early 20's, in Columbus, my mother opened the door one afternoon to a tall, sad salesman with a sample case, who said, "I don't suppose you want to buy any of my vanilla. Nobody ever does." There is such a thing as a tired, sad, defeated salesman, but even if there weren't we could use one. I can hear this salesman in the October 18th issue saying, "I just want to say to begin with, madam, that I have been through a great deal today." . . . In an hour's time I could get 2 or 3 perfect captions for the particular drawing. . . . No salesman ever said to any housewife what you have him saying in the cartoon I am talking about. That is a gag man's idea.

I'll talk this all over with you any time you say. I can't go on any kind of salary basis on account of the [New York] State Income Tax, but I am willing to be paid by the caption. You must feel free to reject my ideas if you don't think they are right. I just want somebody to listen to them.

Love,
Thurber

"You said a moment ago that everybody you look at seems to be a rabbit. Now just what do you mean by that, Mrs. Sprague?"

Thurber was already demonstrating a characteristic of many people who dictate, spared the penalty of physical writing: a reluctance to be brief. But the letter reveals the unconquerable core of his humor.

Ross wasn't in the best of shape to be taking lectures from Thurber. That same month, Frank Sullivan writes Katharine White from Saratoga Springs:

> I just got back from New York. Was at the New Yorker one afternoon, and saw Terry, Thurber and Ross. Had a drink with Ross later; at least I had the drink and he sipped milk, as he has had a recurrence of his stomach trouble. Ross has got some curious views about things. He's very bearish on the future of humanity. Says he doesn't think Dotty Parker or myself or you or any of us can do much about it; says he hasn't got much faith in us. Regards all of us who are rather excited about the state of the world with a mixture of amusement and scorn. If he had been in better health I would have kicked him in the slats. Our discussion was amicable. I love Ross. I thought of a lot of remarks I could have made to him about his pessimism and do-nothingness after I left him, but will write them to him.
>
> Ross said Jim [Thurber] can now read the title "New Yorker" on the cover, which is an improvement. I saw Jim for only a minute. Sally Benson came along and caught us in her orbit, disrupting conversation.

Sullivan, Thurber, and the Whites were interventionists, believing America should come to the rescue of Great Britain, which was fighting the Axis powers pretty much on its own. Ross seemed to think nothing was going to save the democracies. The Japanese attack on Pearl Harbor that December didn't help the mood of anyone, especially Ross, who worried that he would lose many of his valued editors and contributors to the war. (He did.) The state of a wartime America scraped on Thurber's already frayed nervous system.

Through the recent ordeals with Thurber, Helen had become extremely thin and fragile. She had been highly protective of him; she had to be, for Thurber always thought he had more vision than he did, got into trouble with furniture, matches, and doorways, and, frustrated by sightlessness and world events, was frequently out of temper with others.

Between Christmas 1941 and New Year's, the Thurbers ran into Ann Honeycutt at Bleeck's. Thurber's emotional state had worsened, and though it was Helen who was probably more deserving of Foord's sanitarium, the next best thing was agreed upon in an impulsive moment: that Honeycutt accompany Thurber there. Explains Helen: "Among other things, I was exhausted from the holidays, going out every night or having people in for drinks and dinner." Ann was going through a bad period herself; her affair with Bruce Barton was not going well; he was pressing her to marry him, but Honey's brief marriage to McKelway had increased her psychological hangups regarding the institution. "Bruce was an advertising executive who got me in with advertising people," says Honey. "They were nice, but I was also missing the wildness of the old *New Yorker* crowd."

The Foord venture ended in a fiasco, and made Daise Terry's next gossip report to Katharine White:

> We've seen neither hide nor hair of Mr. Thurber since just before Christmas when he was in the office feeling pretty high. You've probably heard of his escapade at Foord's. He and Honeycutt went up there at Christmas and when they arrived they were both absolutely stinko, Thurber shouting and waving bottles, Honeycutt hysterical and screaming. They just about scared the pants off the old ladies gathered in the lounge having tea. Foord would have none of them and kicked them right out, threatened to get the police, to which Mr. Thurber shouts, "That's just what I want you to do. You're selling dope up here and I want the police to know it. . . ."
>
> It ended up their being thrown out and having to spend the night at an inn. They came back to town the next day, very meek, and Mr.

Thurber promptly got a heavy cold and then some intestinal upset, which he quickly got rid of, but he's never telephoned or turned up in the office since—about two weeks.

Mrs. Thurber was pretty sore about the whole thing—said she thought he was safe with Honeycutt, etc., etc. She stayed in New York during the fracas. Gosh, poor man, he'll probably be in for a severe depression now.

Ann remembers that Thurber had agreed with Helen, at Bleeck's, that he should go to Foord's. "But he wouldn't go alone," Ann said, "so I said I'd go with him. Helen said, 'I wish you would.' She'd had enough of his behavior. She made the reservations for us.

"On New Year's Day, Thurber picked me up in his Cadillac, driven by a chauffeur. At the last minute, I took a bottle of whiskey I'd just been given, from the top of my piano. I explained to Jim that it was necessary because we were going into snake country. Just beyond the George Washington Bridge, we decided we were in snake country. We drank the whole bottle. We got there when the ladies were having tea. Foord's didn't take drunks; just exhausted, postdrunk people for whom the tempo of life had been too advanced. The chauffeur tried to help Thurber, who was literally blind drunk, and Jim yelled at him, 'Take your hands off me, you Methodist c____ s____!' It definitely disrupted the tea hour. We were rushed to our rooms by an attendant before Dr. Foord knew about our arrival. I had the empty bottle under my coat for some reason, and halfway up the stairs the bottle dropped and rolled back down the steps. I was barely in my room when I was told not to unpack but to get out. Then Thurber said he'd been thrown out, too.

"It was snowing out. We went to a café, told the proprietor that Dr. Foord had thrown us into the snow. He directed us to the Ellenville Inn, which seemed to be open—at least the bar was, but the water taps wouldn't work in the rooms and they wouldn't take the colored chauffeur until we raised hell. We called Helen and Gibbs and insisted that we'd had reservations and Foord had no right to throw us out as patients. Gibbs, quite coincidentally, had written a casual about a fictitious man who had been thrown out of Foord's and we knew he would be interested. Jim had been the first in our group to find Foord's; after that, every one of the *New Yorker* crowd would go up to rest there for a couple of weeks. Jim thought Foord was ungrateful, after all the business he'd steered Foord's way."

Thurber continued his gradual disconnecting from the reminders of his former life. He even began to forgo his beloved match games at Bleeck's. Says Stanley Walker:

He loved to play the match game and was pretty good at it. A few persons, (including, I'm sorry to say, Helen Thurber) seemed to think that when he happened to lose that there was something crooked about it—that someone, or several, was taking advantage of his blindness. On the contrary, great pains were taken to see that he got an honest count. So far as I know there was only one man in the match-playing set who tried to cheat at all times. . . . When this man was in the game we all watched him and saw to it that he didn't cheat Thurber.

One night Thurber came into Bleeck's alone and proposed that he and I play a marathon game. . . . He fancied we were of about the same skill, or luck. We played for at least four hours, just the two of us, at $5 a hand. We had set a definite time limit . . . and at the end we were exactly even. It is possible, looking back at it all now, that this time might have been used more profitably in many other ways, but it seemed a splendid idea at the time.

Nathaniel Benchley remembers another time at Bleeck's, when Thurber got into an argument with a friend. In the heat of the fray, Thurber thought he heard his opponent threatening to take action if Thurber kept it up. Benchley says, "Thurber suddenly leaped for the friend's throat and toppled him to the floor, shouting 'So you'd strike a blind man, would you?' He later told me that his violent temper had been due to some glandular imbalance."

55

That Catbird Seat

It was just a week to the day since Mr. Martin had decided to rub out Mrs. Ulgine Barrows. . . . She had, for almost two years now, baited him. In the halls, in the elevator, even in his own office, into which she romped now and then like a circus horse, she was constantly shouting these silly questions at him. "Are you lifting the oxcart out of the ditch? Are you tearing up the pea patch? Are you hollering down the rain barrel? . . . Are you sitting in the catbird seat?"

It was Joey Hart . . . who had explained what the gibberish meant. "She must be a Dodger fan," he had said. "Red Barber announces the Dodger games over the radio and he uses those expressions—picked 'em up down South. . . . "Tearing up the pea patch" meant going on a rampage; "sitting in the catbird seat" meant sitting pretty, like a batter with three balls and no strikes on him.

—from "The Catbird Seat"

Thurber was still battling the humiliating conditions of near sightlessness in 1942, but the scant half-dozen pieces he wrote for the *New Yorker* that year demonstrate, again, that a humorist's defiance of obstacles often is at the heart of good entertainment. Several of his stories set compass directions he would be following from then on. Having to be read to impeded the flow of ideas for casuals. All but cut off visually from the current world, he began turning to his past. He remembers his prim grade-school teacher who was imprisoned by the barren disciplines of grammar for its own sake ("Here Lies Miss Groby"), his legendary ancestor, Jake Fisher ("A Good Man"), which begins the profiles of those who would inhabit *The Thurber Album* a decade later, and his newspaper days ("Memoirs of a Drudge"). A core of benign narcissism at his center was becoming more evident; he would play himself to the end, constructing the personal drama of James Thurber from its beginnings, and watching with an almost obsessive and defensive curiosity to see how it might come out.

It was still easier for Thurber to draw than to write, even given that he had, by his estimate, only an eighth of his vision; he would not be completely dependent on "blindsight" for another eight years. Richard and Louise Connell returned every winter to Manhattan from California, and Louise remembers visiting the Thurbers at their apartment. "We found Jim on his hands and knees on the floor drawing on big, heavy, six-by-five-foot sheets of paper that were too big for the table. He was covering the paper in heavy crayon with figures large enough for him to make out. I was so touched by the sight it filled my eyes with tears."

Hobart Weekes remembers the difficulty the magazine had reducing Thurber's drawings to scale for publication. He once found Thurber drawing in his office on the backs of wallpaper sheets that were hung on the wall for him. "He always had an office reserved for him," Weekes says. "Once I was with him when the phone rang. He needed to take notes and asked me to place his finger at the top of a sheet of yellow paper; he felt his way along as he scribbled his big words on it. I wondered why he bothered; he could remember just about everything he was hearing and if he needed his written words, they would have to be read back to him. It was embarrassing for him; he didn't like to ask for help."

Fifteen of his captioned cartoons were published in 1942, along with one of his six *New Yorker* covers, though the cover and several of the drawings were holdovers. The war now frequently imposed its commanding theme on the magazine's artists. Civil Defense measures were urging the citizenry to attend first-aid classes. Thurber's cartoon characters make an ominous most of it: "In first-aid class today we learned eleven different ways to poison people"; "Well, you're not going to try the fireman's lift on me!"; "I think he's stopped breathing. What do I do now?"

"There was only one war for Ross," says Lois Long, "the First World War. The second one was simply an imposition on him—as Thurber writes, Ross really was always saying, 'God, how I pity me!' Pearl Harbor set him quivering with anxiety over what was going to happen to his magazine. The last time he'd gone through anxiety trembling, that I remember, was when his second wife was in Reno, waiting to get her divorce, in love with an Englishman named Wilkins. Ross later wanted someone to do a Notes and Comment on the immorality and constitutional illegality of alimony, but no attempt at it, if there ever was one, came off. After Pearl Harbor, quivering anew, he went to Washington to declare everyone on his staff important to the war effort and to request their exemption from the draft. He had no more luck with that than with his alimony cause. He was offended that so many of his editors and writers saw a greater loyalty to the country than to the magazine. Sandy Vanderbilt joined the *Stars and Stripes* staff; Weekes was commissioned an Army officer; Whitaker got into military transportation; McKelway joined the Air Corps." ("It was the war that brought a change in [my] relationship [with Ross]," says McKelway. "He considered that I was a deserter because I accepted a commission.")

But Ross's worries had considerable merit: Thurber was nearly blind, often out of sorts, a sporadic and temperamental producer. White was writing his "One Man's Meat" column for *Harper's Magazine*, with only an occasional Comment paragraph for the *New Yorker*. Charles Cooke, whose reporting had underpinned the Talk department for more than a decade, also joined the Air

"How's about going somewhere and trying traction splints on each other, Miss Bryson?"

Corps, leaving Ross desperate enough to let Shawn hire women as Talk reporters.

Picnickers were making noise near Ross's Stamford estate. The state of Connecticut planned to make some land next to his a public park, and Ross thought that that would open the floodgates to residents of Harlem and the Bronx. He was suffering from a duodenal ulcer when he wrote a letter, in the spring of 1942, to Governor Hurley of Connecticut:

> I address you in a state of considerable panic and alarm. . . . Stamford is on the verge of becoming the playground of the Borough of the Bronx and the dark, mysterious, malodorous stretches of Harlem. . . . I do not mean to be undemocratic, but you couldn't choose a more alarming bunch of people in the world. . . . I write in sheer terror.

The letter became public and reaction to it immediately worsened Ross's ulcerous condition. The Bronx was then predominantly Jewish, and Harlem was almost entirely black. The liberal *PM* publicized Ross's ill-considered letter, the writer finding Ross's crude words and thoughts a surprising deviation from the urbane, sophisticated, and careful prose of the magazine he edited. Ralph Ingersoll still had an interest in *PM*, but he was by now in the

Army, and was unaware of the incident until after the letter was printed; he didn't believe that Ross was a racist or, given the ethnic makeup of his staff and regular contributors, in any way anti-Semitic. Henry Luce, still smarting from Gibbs's profile of him, saw that *Time* printed Ross's letter. Ross allowed a *Times* reporter to interview him and told him that he had been "taken aback" by the wild reactions. "I don't care whether they're from the Bronx or from Indianapolis," he said, "they are extremely numerous and noisy." Ross was bawled out by the Bronx borough president and others, who in effect reminded him that his very right of ignoble free speech was, at the moment, being defended on the battlefield by many from the Bronx and Harlem. Walter Winchell, still angry over McKelway's relentless *New Yorker* articles about him, gloated over Ross's embarrassment, referring to him as "Harold 'I don't mean to be undemocratic' Ross."

Stanley Walker thought that although Ross had brought it on himself, he was taking a bad rap from what Walker termed "the idiots' house organ, *PM*." He writes Thurber years later:

> It was the sort of dig that Ross could hardly answer. I leaped into the battle with a fine, long, vigorous editorial defending Ross and sneering at *PM*. Geoffrey Parsons, who liked Ross and was editor of the [*Herald Tribune*] editorial page, made it the lead editorial—a very unusual play. It shut *PM* up completely, and Ross was delighted [and] wrote Parsons a very fine letter of thanks.

A few weeks later, in June, the *New Yorker* announced that it was refusing all hotel ads that mentioned restricted clientele.

Paper was now rationed for civilian use, and Jane Grant, Ross's first wife, who was still a substantial stockholder in the magazine as the result of their marriage settlement, joined the promotion staff and, in Washington, obtained the hard-to-get paper for the *New Yorker*'s overseas edition. She also talked Ross into going along with an Armed Services edition, which brought the magazine to the attention of thousands of military people for the first time.

At Christmastime, 1942, Daise Terry writes Katharine White:

> This is about the gloomiest Saturday I've ever experienced; pouring rain, cold, air raid sirens screeching, and practically a full office staff trying to get out a humorous issue. . . .

The office seems fairly calm aside from putting in long hours. The air raid warnings (which I think they are overdoing a bit) seem to make people nervous. Gosh, if they start pulling in all the men up to 45 it will clean us out almost entirely. It's a terrible ordeal keeping office boys as those not of draft age can get such good wages working in defense projects. It would indeed cripple the old mag if they take our writing and editorial staff.

Among those willing to serve as an office boy that year was eighteen-year-old Truman Capote. "He was always trying to sit on my lap," says librarian Ebba Jonsson. "I'd have none of that, but Daise Terry adored him." Indeed, Terry took him to plays, concerts, art shows, and movies on the press passes issued to the magazine. Capote admired Thurber's work and asked Terry if he could be Thurber's secretary. But "Capote gave Thurber the creeps—me, too," says Helen, "although I think he is a brilliant writer." Capote never forgave the Thurbers for rejecting him not only as a secretary but as one of the boys assigned to guide Thurber to the Algonquin and back. A vengeful Capote "waited a long time for his tiny triumph," says Helen. The "triumph" was a savage lie that Capote was given the opportunity to put into circulation. Burton Bernstein quotes him:

> I worked as a boy in the Art Department then, and one of my jobs was to take Thurber to his girl friend's apartment. She was as ugly as sin, so it served him right. I would have to wait for him at the apartment till he was finished, and then I'd dress him. He could undress by himself but he couldn't dress by himself, couldn't even cross the street by himself. Now since Helen Thurber would dress him in the morning, she knew how he looked. Well, one time I put his socks on wrong side out, and when he got home, I gather Helen asked him a lot of questions. The next day, Thurber was furious at me—and he said I did it on purpose. But I was still assigned to lead him to the girl's apartment—back and forth, back and forth. Also, he was a terrible drinker. He breathed fire when he was drunk. Very jealous man, too, of other people's fame.

Naive reasoning by the most gullible should render this story by Capote incredible, even if it was unknown that Ross finally ordered Capote fired for mischievous story-telling, or that Capote's addiction to malicious gossip cost him most of his friends by the end of his life. Why would a romantic woman turn a nude, blind lover over to an office boy in her apartment to be dressed? A Thurber, who actually couldn't dress himself, would never have allowed it.

The story casts near libelous allegations on an innocent party: At the time, Margaret Thurlow, a *New Yorker* secretary—and a pretty one—served as Thurber's secretary, both at the office and at the Thurbers' apartment, where Helen was always present; never at Thurlow's.

"The entire Capote story is a lie, and a typical form of private revenge for being turned down by us for a job as Thurber's secretary," says Helen. . . . "The affair was not with a *New Yorker* secretary, but with his own secretary, years later, at East Fifty-seventh Street. . . . Thurber was a bad liar, and told me everything, usually very soon. [His actual affair is] quite a funny story (in retrospect), but I won't tell it. . . . That story about my noticing the reversed sock is an old Broadway gag. . . . It's unimportant except as a matter of taste, but I hate to see Capote get away with such a corny lie."

But it was important, for the Capote anecdote was gleefully pounced upon by a fair percentage of the Bernstein book's reviewers, and picked up as gospel by Gerald Clarke in his 1988 Capote biography. Writes Rosemary Thurber, in reference to what she calls "this silliness":

> My father did *not* need anyone to dress him. Helen did select and lay out his clothes each day. He bathed, shaved and dressed himself. (He would have picked out his clothes, too, but probably no one would have wanted to be seen with the result!) My father would *never* have let Truman Capote dress him. . . . I'm sure it was a lie for a laugh, as Ebba Jonsson suggested.

Katharine White also writes that she believes the story was an untruth.

Thurber's aversion to Capote, or to any office boy, was a most exceptional instance. Except when insanely drunk or tortured by thyroid troubles, he was universally kind to, and loved by, those who served him—bellhops, office boys, secretaries, cabdrivers, waiters, family cooks. If he was a troublemaking needler after a drink or two, he almost always picked on those more than capable of handling themselves, and usually he was relieved when they replied in kind. He could be a bully with those who tried to revere him, for he gradually came to live within the dichotomy—again, usually while drinking —of being an expert practitioner of self-adulation but resenting any fawning over him by others.

Daise Terry, of whom Thurber was fond, confirms his gentleness with the *New Yorker*'s lower-ranked staff. "I never personally saw him blow up at anybody," says Terry, "maybe because I only saw him during office hours. When he was at the Algonquin, he'd call me every morning for a boy to bring him over to the office. He never wanted to be treated as a blind man, so I'd tell the boy, 'Don't you take Mr. Thurber's arm; he'll put his hand on your shoulder.' When he was due to arrive, I tried to get the halls clear of tables and chairs. I'd meet him at the elevator and take his hat and coat. He worked in a little office next to me; he'd sit all afternoon smoking and writing his big words on yellow paper. I'd hold his hand to the stack of paper to get him started. He always tried to sign his name on what I'd have typed for him, because he knew people wanted that, but sometimes, if he was tired, he'd just say, 'Oh, you sign it for me, Terry.'

"He had a funny remark for the benefit of everyone, no matter who. He'd say to an office boy, 'Here's old Grandpa Thurber. Don't give me the wrong hat—aren't you the one who gave me the wrong hat last time?' The office boys would fight for the chance to lead him to and fro, because he talked baseball with them and was interested in where they went to school and what they planned to do. When he got to know a particular office boy, he'd call him directly, when it was time to go back to the hotel, and say, 'Come up and get your old pal, Thurber.'

"If one of his men friends wasn't available, I'd go shopping with him. He'd stumble into Black, Starr & Gorham and bump into a table, and he'd say, 'Terry, let's do some shoplifting; they'll never suspect me, being blind; I'll knock stuff off and you pick it up and put it in your bag.' People would push him aside, not realizing he was blind. He never reacted; he understood. Saks Fifth Avenue for a time catered to men shoppers, serving them cocktails. Mr. Thurber and I were there once when two men were getting blind drunk waiting for their wives. He never forgot the scene and wrote it into his theater revue, A *Thurber Carnival*.

"He'd make these heavy jokes about his blindness. Sometimes he'd sit at my desk and telephone: 'This is the blind writer'; 'This is old man Thurber'; 'This is the boy wonder.' He was always so considerate of me and my staff that I used to think one reason he tried to act so little like a blind man was because he didn't want to impose upon us any more than he had to. He dictated long and exciting letters and never wanted you to read them back. He'd have a galley proof read to him and know at once where a change had been made; his memory was phenomenal. He'd come in with a stack of letters people had written him at his home and dictate answers to all of them, no matter how mean or silly some of them were.

"He'd drop into the Tuesday afternoon art meetings now and then. He'd stumble in on his own, and Mr. Ross, who was very sympathetic to Mr. Thurber's condition, would say, 'Hi, Thurber, come in.' He'd sit on the table and swing his legs and Mr. Ross would ask him, 'What do you think about this caption?' and describe the cartoon. Sometimes he'd come up with something Mr. Ross liked.

"I never heard him make snide remarks about anyone on the staff; if he did, it was in fun. He loved telling stories on himself in which he came out poorly. Did you read what old so-and-so wrote about me in such and such a newspaper or magazine, he'd ask me. You couldn't be casual about him; you either knew everything about him or nothing.

"During the war, he once invited me to breakfast at the Algonquin. Because of the butter shortage, they served cottage cheese. He got his fingers in the cottage cheese on his bread plate and said, 'Jesus Christ, Terry, what is this stuff?' He had black coffee and scrambled eggs, which were so well done he insisted that the chef had dropped a rubber heel from his shoe into the eggs. They served us warm popovers; he expected toast and finding a popover in his hand surprised him. He said, 'This feels like a kitten that has been dead an hour.' Gee, I miss him."

That year, John Mosher died suddenly, another blow to Ross, for Mosher was, by then, not only his film critic but a contributor and an editor with a sensitive nose for new talent. In *The Years with Ross*, while referring to Mosher as "a witty writer, a charming man, and one of the most entertaining companions I have ever met," Thurber describes him as "a rejection machine," apparently still smarting from Mosher's returning his earliest submissions. But Thurber shows no evidence of resentment in 1950, when he writes the writer Clinch Calkins of Mosher,

> whose death in September, 1942, at the appalling age of fifty, was a tremendous loss to all of us. He was the most delightful companion we had ever known. I remember about the time Ross found himself at a trough adjacent to Mosher's in the men's room. "Why don't you write some more pieces?" Ross asked. "Because I've lost the slight fancy that sustained me," John told him. I'm collecting Mosher stories and heard one from a couple we met in Nassau last year. Seems they had driven him home in New York but had stopped, by accident, two blocks from his house. John got out of the car and wouldn't listen to their protests that they should drive him the two blocks. "Nonsense," said John. "There's a bit of the Daniel Boone in me."

Thurber's *The Years with Ross*, as noted, began as a series of articles for the *Atlantic Monthly*, and when Katharine White read there Thurber's negative reference to Mosher, she wrote to Thurber in Mosher's defense. But Thurber was unrelenting, replying:

I loved John Mosher, one of the most amusing men in the world, and I always wished he could write it half as well as he could talk it. He may have been a hopeful first reader, as you say, but he was not a good one. Naturally I believe that some of my first twenty pieces deserved more than a rejection slip, and that there was New Yorker stuff and promise in the chapters of "Why We Behave Like Microbe Hunters" which came back the same way. If he sent any of my early stuff on, then the fault lies higher up, but let's not worry about thirty years ago, for God's sake. Some of the chapters were later worked into New Yorker pieces of mine and into "Is Sex Necessary?" I used to tell John to his face that he was not a good first reader, and once wrote him, on his birthday, a letter quoting his [Thurber-invented] one-sentence rejections of Conrad's "Youth" and "A Piece of String," "Markheim" and "The Turn of the Screw."

"What is it ends with friends?" Thurber quotes William Ernest Henley, referring to the breakup of Ross and Alexander Woollcott. But he may also have pondered the question in reflecting upon his lost friendship with Robert Coates. Thurber had introduced Coates to Ross; the two had been office-mates, Talk of the Town coworkers, intellectual and social companions. The Thurbers and Coateses were frequent weekend guests at one another's Connecticut country homes. Coates had been best man at Thurber's wedding; The Middle-Aged Man on the Flying Trapeze was dedicated to "Bob and Elsa Coates."

Elsa was a favorite with the New Yorker crowd, and was beset by medical difficulties when Coates divorced her to marry another in 1940. "I had known (and not much liked) the new Mrs. Coates [Astrid Peters]," says Helen, "in her previous marriage to an actor in the Village. It was the cold, cruel way Bob dumped Elsa that we disliked." It was atypical of Thurber to cool toward a male friend because of a fondness for that friend's wife; quite typical for a friend to resent Thurber's hostility to his new wife. The social links were broken between the two men and never mended. "Years later, Jim asked me to patch things up between him and Coates," says Joel Sayre. "I told him I wasn't his nursemaid."

"Not enough is made of that very close friendship between Thurber and Coates," says Malcolm Cowley. "I knew Thurber essentially through Bob Coates. [One reason people know little of the friendship is that] Coates did not save correspondence, which is another tragic thing, because he corresponded with people of interest in France and in the United States. 'We'd like to have your correspondence with Gertrude Stein,' said the Yale Library, and Bob said, 'I didn't save it.' So Yale said, 'Well, that's funny. She saved *your* letters.'"

A Coates novel, *Yesterday's Burdens*, published in 1933, features a protagonist, Henderson, says Cowley, who "is either Coates himself or Jim Thurber. He's Coates as he would have been if he had stayed in New York, but at the same time Coates told his second wife that he always identified Henderson with Thurber. . . . Thurber was very much impressed by the novel. After he quarreled with Bob, he wasn't so much a visitor in these parts [Sherman, Connecticut]. He used to come around to see Elsa Coates, though, in the winter of 1942. We were living with Elsa in New York that winter."

Thurber never did make up with Coates, though Coates wrote a friendly obituary of Thurber. In 1966, five years after Thurber's death, Coates wrote Cowley:

> Hemingway—well, he is one of those problems that have always defeated me—like Jim Thurber; the man who gets worse, both as an artist and as a person, when he should be getting better. Jim when I first knew him, and he was then my closest friend (and, as on the *New Yorker*, my helper and benefactor) was, without listing attributes, just about the all-round nicest guy I've ever known. And then—what was it: blindness? drinking? something physical?—he got to the stage where Joel Sayre in a piece for *Time* could say he's the nicest guy in the world—'till around nine o'clock in the evening. And then, finally, well, outrage. And why?

Outrage, of course, at what made little sense to Thurber—a fate of blindness when early prophylactic measures might have prevented it; outrage at his loss of independent action, of the ability to read, type, and draw; outrage at being unable to see his friends. Asked once what he would most like to see if his sight were restored, he replied that he was sure he knew what Marilyn Monroe looked like and would rather see how his old acquaintances were aging. His good nature was further eroded by a thyroid condition, the effects of the medicines for its relief often as troublesome to him as the ailment.

Ralph Ingersoll also came to grief with Thurber, though he blames Helen for the rupture of their friendship. An Army private (he would soon be granted a commission) awaiting his service call, Ingersoll lived in Lakeville, Connecticut, not far from Cornwall, where the Thurbers rented in the summer of 1943. "I partly guessed what to expect when I visited Jim in Cornwall," says Ingersoll. "I'd gone to see him in the hospital after one of the operations. It was hard to see someone you loved, as I did Thurber, suffering. In Cornwall, he was still suffering, in his way, more than two years after the last operation. He must have experienced castrative feelings. Drink made him both sentimental and argumentative. My going to war seemed to frustrate him, too. Helen seemed to do her best to break us up that night. She had told me privately that if Jim hadn't married her he'd be a drunken bum, which didn't seem to leave Jim much credit for surviving what he had gone through. We stayed up till four a.m. that night, arguing. Helen got Jim and me fighting one another. 'Are you going to take that kind of remark from him?' she'd say to me, and, to Jim, 'Are you going to take that from him?' We parted on a sour note. In England, on D-day, I was certain I wouldn't get out of the war alive and wrote two letters, one to a woman, the other to Thurber, to square our account. He replied as only Thurber could, and in theory we were friends again. But after the war, we'd meet for a drink a couple times a year but were never close again. In my journalism work, I drew on his remarkable memory; I'd call him for dated slang terms: when was 'swell' popular? Or 'skidoo'? He was always delighted with the queries and always came through.

"I became a convert of Helen's; Jim couldn't handle his handicapped life by himself, and, with all her brittle hardness, she helped keep him productive and interested in life. I was saddened, when I saw him once, during the last year of his life, to hear him turn on her, to attack her with great sarcasm. Her world fell apart when he died, but at the same time it had to have been something of a relief to her to become a professional widow, running Thurber, Incorporated, without Thurber."

Ordinarily, writers run into difficulties trying to be friends with other writers. Writing is one of the more Darwinian professions, in which an author works with one eye on his script and the other on who may be getting ahead of him. But Truman Capote's claim that Thurber was jealous of others' fame was baseless; only at the end, when he saw the rewards of immortality too often being denied humorists, did he begin to keep a competitive score—how many awards and honorary degrees was White getting compared to his? But through most of Thurber's developing years, he wrote from such a sense of inadequacy that every success left him feeling ahead of the game. Until his blindness, he magnanimously, sincerely, cheered all the achievements of his colleagues.

E. B. White thought that if Thurber competed with any writer, it was with the ghost of Mark Twain. Speaking of the latter-day Thurber, White remarked, "He just didn't want any humorist to be better than he was," including Twain. Reflecting on his comment later, White said, "I should have added that I preferred Thurber as a humorist to Twain, who was awfully uneven and sometimes downright annoying."

Whether from envy or not, Thurber took an instant dislike to the work of

William Saroyan, which seemed to grate on him. When Thurber parodied the title of Saroyan's *The Daring Young Man on the Flying Trapeze* for his 1935 collection, there were those who didn't make the connection, including Saroyan, who thought he had an admirer in Thurber. Once, Saroyan tried to publish a book of rejected stories—not just his own but those of others—to be called *An Anthology of Lousy Writing*. He was having trouble getting rejected manuscripts from published authors, and although he had never met Thurber, he solicited a "lousy" specimen from him, in a letter beginning "Dear Jim" and signed "Bill Saroyan." When Thurber ignored it, Saroyan sent another letter, with a "Dear Thurber" salutation and signed "William Saroyan," hoping the more familiar name would ring a bell. When Thurber failed to reply to that one, Saroyan sent Thurber a cartoon idea, to show there were no hard feelings; Thurber couldn't use it, and never acknowledged it.

By the summer of 1941, E. B. White had come to believe that the *New Yorker* should take an editorial stand supporting the Allies. Ross told him that he thought the press should take its cue from Roosevelt, who hadn't yet made his position clear on the subject. Ross pointed out to White "that even Thurber, who favored America's going to war at once, doubted that the *New Yorker* should try to become a leader of opinion 'at this time.' "

The president had, along with British Prime Minister Winston Churchill, declared his commitment to a world blessed by "the Four Freedoms"—freedom of religion and speech, and freedom from fear and want—in his 1941 State of the Union address. Roosevelt then asked for a pamphlet on the subject. White was one of several prominent writers chosen for the job by Archibald MacLeish, who was then the director of the Office of Facts and Figures. White ended by rewriting the four other pamphlet writers. Holed up at the Hotel New Weston in Manhattan, White spent most of February 1942 on the project. In March, after completing *The Four Freedoms*, White wrote a *New Yorker* Comment recommending that the various federal information agencies be combined and managed by the news commentator Elmer Davis. Subsequently, seven writers—Howard Lindsay, Russel Crouse, William Shirer, John Marquand, Henry Fisk Carlton, Clifton Fadiman, and Rex Stout —petitioned the president to appoint "a co-ordinator of word-warfare," and recommended Davis. The petitioners sought "a hundred additional signatures from nationally known writers," including Thurber. Thurber agreed but thought it strange, indeed, that none of the seven, according to them, had seen White's Comment, which had earlier suggested Davis for just such a position. A dubious Thurber writes White:

Here is a copy of the petition together with the letter they sent to me. I have written them, enclosing a clipping of your Comment and suggesting that your name be asked for and giving them your address in Maine. I said I thought your name should be high up on this petition. It is hard to believe that none of these writers saw your piece and I guess they just decided to take up the idea and the hell with credit to The New Yorker.

Love,
JIM

That year, a movie version of *The Male Animal* received favorable attention by the critics and the moviegoing public. It starred Henry Fonda as Tommy Turner, Olivia de Havilland as his wife, and Jack Carson as the former football star. The movie, directed by Elliott Nugent, had been filmed at Pomona College, in Claremont, California. It had a happy Hollywood ending—the conservative trustee, Keller, repents; Tommy Turner is carried off in triumph by cheering students, his marriage forever intact—but the story still emerged as recognizable Nugent and Thurber.

Though both authors insisted that the setting for *The Male Animal* was not necessarily that of O.S.U. and could be "any Midwestern college," nobody believed them. The university, the Variety Club, Ohio civic groups, and state and city officials pressured Warner Brothers to hold the movie's first showing in Columbus. Warner's was delighted with the free promotion. It was the first world premiere of a movie ever held in Columbus. The Thurbers arrived on March 10, 1942, two days early, accompanied by June Fleming, *PM*'s selection as Miss Average Girl. A committee headed by Columbus Mayor Floyd Green met the Thurbers at Union Station. Governor John W. Bricker was on hand. An embarrassed Thurber told the committee, "I don't see why we should be the center of this. We're just simple people. I feel like I ought to be covering it; it would be a lot more fun."

He explained his tinted glasses to the press: his vision was "temporarily impaired." He was working again, he said, drawing on a board four by three feet, but couldn't read anything but the headlines, "and they're all so bad that I'm glad they're all I can read." He was working on a new play with Joel Sayre (never completed). The glasses, he said, were actually an asset: "People walk up to me and say, 'Hello, Jim.' I ask who they are. When they tell me, I say, 'Of course, I'd have known you if it weren't for these glasses.' "

At a Phi Kappa Psi dinner, Thurber was introduced by a former state attorney general, then was led to "The Male Animal Ball," which was broadcast over national radio and featured Cab Calloway's orchestra. The following noon, Thurber attended an O.S.U. faculty club luncheon. He was asked to speak before the student body, and to emphasize to the students that "our war effort needs the rah-rah spirit." A nervous speaker to begin with, he firmly rejected the request.

When asked by the *Columbus Dispatch* to do an interview with himself, he came through with his usual resourcefulness, complete with age-consciousness:

JUMPY CO-AUTHOR OF MALE ANIMAL REMINISCES
By Jim Thurber, former Dispatch reporter

"Good to be back in good old Columbus town," said the tall, aging, jumpy co-author of "The Male Animal," as he arrived here yesterday morning, supported on one side by Miss Average Girl and on the other by Mrs. Bewildered Wife.

Mr. Average Co-Author instantly began a long, rambling, inaccurate and disconnected series of reminiscences about his life in Columbus some years ago, to which nobody listens as they are busy with the pretty ladies who accompany the old gentleman on his trip home.

"I shook hands with Admiral Dewey or Farragut, I can't remember names anymore," quavered Mr. Co-Author. "It was right here where we're standing right now, or was it out at the Columbus riding park? In those days, if memory serves, Tubby Essington [drum major for the O.S.U. marching band in Thurber's day] stood at the corner of Broad and High, but he was later torn down to make room for the State House. A great many people considered this a mistake.

"Yesiree," continued the aged co-author (to whom now only a lone colored porter and a small boy were listening), "those were the golden days. It was just a few years after this that the Western Conference was torn down to make room for Chic Harley." The co-author looked about him and saw that now only the porter was listening.

"What do you want?" asked the co-author querulously.

"What I want to know," said the porter, "is what they made room for when they tore you down." The old gentleman didn't answer. He started off in a dazed kind of way, still talking to himself, in the general direction of Hoster's Brewery.

It was time for the movie. Sorority girls served as special hostesses at the theater. Fifty soldiers from Fort Hayes, designated as the Army's "male animals," were guests. Jack Graf, a Big Ten football and basketball star, was named Ohio State's "Male Animal" and was presented onstage with the girl chosen by the students of Western College for Women, in Oxford, Ohio, as "the Animal's Mate." The Ohio State Concert Band played, the university's Men's Glee Club sang, there were several short speeches, a pair of prize animals from O.S.U.'s Animal Husbandry Department were led onstage; Thurber took a bow from his balcony seat. It was all considerably more than he had bargained for. Nugent had the sense to remain in Hollywood.

That same year, Metro-Goldwyn-Mayer offered to buy both "The Secret Life of Walter Mitty" and "The Catbird Seat." Thurber held off, hoping to sell "Mitty" to Rodgers and Hammerstein as a musical, but finally agreed to the MGM purchase two years later. At that time, he also agreed to write a screenplay for "The Catbird Seat," in which the jeering, domineering Ulgine Barrows, an efficiency expert, plans to reorganize Mr. Martin's department to the point of leaving him unemployed. To her amazement, the mousy Mr. Martin, who doesn't smoke or drink, calls on his hated nemesis, lights his first cigarette, accepts his first whiskey, refers to their employer as "that old windbag," and tells Mrs. Barrows that he takes heroin and is making a bomb "which will blow the old goat higher than hell." When the shocked woman reports this bizarre incident to their employer, who has known the sedate and prissy Martin for twenty-two years, he is convinced that Mrs. Barrows has gone berserk from overwork and fires her. It is "The Unicorn in the Garden," of three years before: the oppressive female judged ripe for the booby hatch when she reports that her husband told her he had seen a real unicorn in the garden. The male has only to deny it to get her confined.

Thurber accepted a ten-thousand-dollar advance to write a film script of "The Catbird Seat," with an additional forty thousand dollars promised upon delivery of an acceptable fifteen-thousand-word scenario. He soon ran into trouble with the screenplay, as with his playwriting. He returned the ten thousand dollars to MGM.

Earlier that year, after Thurber's disenchantment with Harper & Bros., Coates had persuaded him to go with Harcourt Brace, which brought out Thurber's new collection of stories and drawings, My World—and Welcome to It, in late October 1942. The critics, as usual, were both pleased and baffled by Thurber's prose and drawings. Time called it "the weird Thurberian world —that closed circle within which the male animal plods foolishly round and round." All Thurber characters "are mentally on all fours," the magazine added.

Stanley Walker put in a word for his match-game partner, writing in the

Herald Tribune: "People who are morose, quixotic, off-center, troubled by deep but somehow indefinite tragedies—these are his particular meat." As is "the improbable behavior of women, their exasperating lack of understanding and their downright dullness. . . . He has a peculiar brand of wisdom, not untouched with madness."

Thomas Sugrue, an intellectual graduate of the *Trib*, writing in the *Saturday Review of Literature*, found Thurber "a realist, like Ring Lardner, Laurence Sterne and Henry Fielding. . . . It is the spirit with which the true realist (or humorist) is concerned: the spirit trapped in flesh, wandering about in an absurd and awkward garb, at the mercy of animal appetites, constrained by time and space, hunted by worms, stalked by death."

If Sugrue caught a glimpse of Thurber's recent agony, John Chamberlain, in the *New York Times*, missed it by a mile: "I read Mr. Thurber's chronicles of woe . . . quite callously, laughing uproariously every time the mournful hero got another bop on the head. Thurber's adventures with the whipporwill [sic] had me holding my sides."

Harcourt printed seventy-five hundred copies of *My World—and Welcome to It*, and reprinted it eight times over the next two years, its sales having been stimulated by two Armed Services editions. The book was dedicated "to Norma and Elliott Nugent."

Thurber's Columbus friend Herman Miller was having trouble with his freelance writing plans. He submitted his Alexander Hamilton manuscript to Harcourt Brace, at Thurber's suggestion, and simultaneously to Thurber, who was sympathetic, hopeful, and desperate to help. He writes the Millers:

> Helen read the Alexander Hamilton profile to me, correcting the few errors in punctuation and spelling that happen on the best type-writers, so that it came out to me just as it must have to Harcourt Brace. I called up Stanley Young [Thurber's Harcourt Brace editor] and gave a 15 minute talk about you and asked him to look up the story. That same afternoon I wrote him a long letter concerned with your achievements and again urging him to read that piece and ponder it as a suggestion for a book. . . . I shall think about other possible figures to go in your book and one or two you had picked from the Civil War period. There were a great many generals, not as famous as Lee and Jackson and Sherman, but in their way just as interesting, such as James Birdseye MacPherson, whom both Grant and Sherman considered to be the most talented general in the North. MacPherson was shot in the bottom and killed in Vicksburg, after calling on a southern girl, I believe. . . .

Meanwhile, if you have got your piece back from Harcourt Brace, don't be discouraged, but send it back to me and I'll try it out on another publisher.

Dorothy Miller had sent a clipping about Thurber from *Who's Who*. Thurber acknowledges it in his inimitable way:

The Who's Who boys certainly went out in a wholesale manner to get names this year. They had begun to write to me about ten years ago because Dick Connell sent my name in—Dick is a great wag. Their letters finally became threatening, but I still refused to send any facts about myself. Therefore, they looked up my record in old copies of the Ohio State Journal and talked to my deaf Aunt Edith, and sent me a galley proof of the write-up. The gist of this was that Jacob Thurman was born in Toledo, Ohio in 1904; he married Theo Madison in 1920 when he was only 16 and she was 8, apparently. Helen corrected this proof, since she is a stern editor of the old school, and sent it back.

56

Those Many Moons

"I have worked a great deal of magic for you in my time, your Majesty," said the Royal Wizard. . . . "I have made you my own special mixture of wolfbane, nightshade, and eagles' tears, to ward off witches, demons, and things that go bump in the night. I have given you seven league boots, the golden touch, and a cloak of invisibility—"

"It didn't work," said the King. "The cloak of invisibility didn't work. . . . I kept bumping into things, the same as ever."

—from *Many Moons*

While on Martha's Vineyard in the summer of 1941, Thurber had begun *Many Moons*, his first fairy tale. When he was blind in only one eye, he had still tripped regularly over such low-lying furniture as coffee tables and hassocks, and over doorsills, rugs, steps, and sleeping dogs. But on the Vineyard, all but sightless for the first time, "bumping into things" became a more serious and nagging nuisance—one that would always be with him.

The severity of Thurber's emotional collapse that summer was so great that both he and Helen forgot the *Many Moons* manuscript, which he had completed in his awkward handwriting; it was discovered the following spring at the Gudes' summer home by a caretaker. Published by Harcourt Brace in September 1943, it is the first Thurber book not illustrated by Thurber. Louis Slobodkin's galaxy of impressionistic, understated watercolors helped win the book the American Library Association's prize for the best juvenile picture book of 1943, and it continues in print as a perennial favorite of young people.

The princess in the book is named Lenore. "The name combines that of Lee Nugent—Elliott's daughter—and mine," Nora Sayre explains. "It was at a time when I was having the best of two worlds—with my parents and when Helen and Jim would invite me to visit them when Rosemary was living elsewhere with her mother. The Sayres and Thurbers were particularly close at the time. Later on I think Jim invited me frequently because of my mother's illness, but also because he was lonely for Rosemary.

"How I loved that man! He helped me understand that we were both basically shy. He drew pictures for me and told me stories, inventing characters that now and again would turn up in something he wrote. His children's books weren't merely word games, nor therapeutic exercises, just because they followed his eye operations; they were written with children in mind, which is what makes them both wonderful and permanent.

"He gave my parents a series of drawings of a man and woman clumsily and ineffectually trying to make love, unable to figure out how to get their arms and legs into proper position."

Thurber, an insistent disbeliever in the value others placed on his pictures, and indifferent to the general avarice of the human species, ended by owning very few of his own drawings, many of them having been bestowed by him on friends or celebrities he admired. In 1946, he recalls:

> Such good drawings as I still possess were caught in London by the war and are still there. Some seven years ago, at the behest of a friend, I sent forty drawings to an art gallery in Hollywood whose director sold ten of them, paid me for five and somehow could never find the remaining

thirty to return to me. . . . A great many of my [published] drawings, say one hundred, have disappeared one way or another. I used to give them out for reproduction to any well-spoken person who asked me to lend them a drawing for, say, the Art News and in this way I lost forever the drawing of the woman and the house entitled "Home."

Thurber was not through drawing, though the cartoons were now "lighter," with much less detail, and the construction was looser. In 1946, he could still explain gamely:

> Since I only have about one-eighth vision, I now have to draw with the assistance of a thing called a "Zeiss Loop" which was invented a few years ago for precision workers. I now draw with a black grease crayon on yellow paper, and the drawings come out about 2′ square. As you may know, black on yellow is the most highly visible combination of colors, and that is why all American highway signs are black on a yellow background.

His last one-man art show—there were nine of them—was in 1944 at the Arts Club of Chicago.

Thurber no doubt protests too much that the world was, in effect, being duped by his art because it was so easily rendered. When sight began to be denied him, he accommodated the tragedy by continuing to insist loudly that the truly important thing in his professional life had always been his writing. But he had to have respected the importance that critics of distinction assigned his drawings; even to suspect that his most immediate and easiest public recognition would always be from what he drew.

He did work at his writing with a concentration never spent on his pictures, though White believes writing came to Thurber a lot easier than he claimed. In a phase of self-rejection, Thurber even pretended to subscribe to Ross's stereotype of artists, telling *Newsweek* that he was glad he never took art lessons and adding, "God, but artists are dumb!" Yet Thurber had counted on his drawings to support his prose, and must have sensed that they were almost always closer to his inner self, to "pure" Thurber, than the self-portrayals he offered in prose or conversation. For his writing was frequently at the mercy of his intense presence and personality and of the unreliabilities of any author whose principal subject is himself. His growing anger after his blindness had to have come in large part from the fear that a public denied his art would, in some measure, deny him. He did not yet realize that he had accrued an unpublished inventory of drawings sufficient to keep his art before the public for the rest of his professional life. He resisted pity and kept himself sufficiently in emotional balance to continue producing stories, fables, essays, and articles, all the while proclaiming that drawing had never been a truly essential part of his talent. But it was, and perhaps what helped rescue him from dwelling on it was that critical intelligence that supplies people of talent, deprived in one area, with sufficient alternate interests to want to continue.

Thurber was still experiencing his moody ups and downs, and at Dr. Fox's recommendation, in the spring of 1942, Helen found a house to rent in Cornwall, Connecticut, to get him out of the city. It was next to the summer home of Kenneth and Sara MacLean; Kenneth MacLean was a professor of English at Yale, and after Thurber tumbled unexpectedly into his orbit he was soon lecturing and writing about Thurber and his work. "On an outside backporch of the house we have spent summers in," writes MacLean, "there is a crude old wooden table . . . made out of a great slab of oak. . . . In an antique-conscious world, everyone has commented upon this table, but only Mr. Thurber could say really what it was. 'It is a sacrificial block, obviously.' "

Cornwall became the heart of Thurber's literary and artistic friendships after 1942. The Van Dorens, Carl and Mark, lived in the area, as did Lewis Gannett, venerable book critic for the *Herald Tribune*. There was Armin Landeck, several of whose paintings, of a lonely New York without people, eventually hung on the walls of the Thurbers' living room, along with prints by French Impressionists Dufy (a sea piece), Rousseau (White Horse), and Seurat—most of the French works were bought in Paris in 1938. There was Marc Simont, the personable artist who illustrated Thurber's *The 13 Clocks* and *The Wonderful O*, and there was Rose Algrant, who taught French at Rumsey Hall, a private school in Washington, Connecticut. Her accent and linguistic mixtures delighted Thurber as much as those of any servant, and her home was frequently the gathering place for the Cornwall/Thurber crowd, at which Thurber was always expected to preside. Algrant and Thurber came to depend on the enjoyment they both derived from a special rapport that lasted the remainder of his life.

Thurber's friendship with Rose Algrant supports Malcolm Cowley's assertion that despite his public hostility toward the feminine sex, Thurber was "very, very fond of women." Granted that "his attitude toward women is not always clear to everybody," says Cowley, "he was at home with women, often closer to them than to his men friends, and yet continually full of resentments at [any woman's] attempt to dominate him." Rose Algrant was one of the few women in Thurber's world who succeeded in pleasing him while somehow keeping him free of threat. Their adoration of one another was warm, lasting, and a thing of joy and wonder to the Cornwall group.

From June 1940 through the first half of 1942, Thurber had fought what his wife called "the Thurbs." He tortured himself with sentimental memories of his former days on the *New Yorker*. He missed White, who was in Maine, and the days when he and White were young and shared an office. A simple letter of inquiry from a woman regarding *Is Sex Necessary?* washed Thurber overboard into a sea of nostalgia. The old worries and apprehensions, he decided, had been reduced to insignificant perspective by the world's current chaos. He writes White, addressing him as "Dear Tithridge"—Walter Tithridge and Karl Zaner were White's and Thurber's mythical "deans of American sex," in *Is Sex Necessary?*. The woman's letter made him sad, says Thurber; it was only thirteen years since Zaner (Thurber) and Tithridge (White) worked together on that book after office hours in Art Samuels's big office, Thurber's drawings spread over the floor. A moody Thurber continues:

The chief dreads we had in those days were little dreads indeed. . . . I'm sure that Zaner . . . has lost his quick, light step. His life work was really to no end; he might just as well have devoted it to making deal tables out of sawdust or scrawling names in white ink on little red glasses for visitors to a county fair. The only hope I see is that there are bright strong girls in Sioux City and Lincoln capable of wrapping a thousand bandages a day or shellacking struts on those thousand planes a day as they move by on the assembly line, if you can call that hope, Walter.

In those days, Philip Wedge [a fictitious character in a White short story] worried mainly because of his feeling that the phone was ringing when he was half way downstairs to the door or that his canary had caught one claw in his little wooden swing, and was hanging there cheeping. . . . Ross growled because your office and mine were too far from his; Ingersoll counted the girders that fell from buildings under construction. . . . Katharine and I worried whether Ernest or Althea would ever get married to anybody else . . . great worries that made us pale and thin. . . . Ross and Fleischmann did not speak for weeks. Markey and Lippmann did not speak for months. Times of stress and strain. One wondered a little uneasily not what Mussolini was going to do next but what Margaret Speaks was going to do next. I was browbeaten into buying a mouse colored belt and was prostrated for days. One was depressed by remarks made by William Rose Benet in the back room at Tony's. Mrs. [Dorothy] Parker's chief concern was whether the hotel would put another bottle of gin on the cuff or not. Benchley laid awake at night wondering how to get rid of Betty Starbuck. Ross bought a new checked gray hat to go down the bay and meet Madge Kennedy. Everytime you got on a ship you were afraid, not that it would be sunk by a torpedo but that somewhere aboard Vivian [Mrs. Arthur] Samuels lay in wait, combing out her little dogs' hair. Miss [Helen] Hokinson woke up one morning to find a Scotty with a big red bow at his neck standing there looking at her. Dey sing; dey cry; dey bark; dey so hoppy. A tall, thin man [Thurber] took off his shirt on a cold day and spread it over a lot of warm Scotties. A tall dark woman [Althea] brought 8 little bottles of milk to feed eight little puppies already so gorged with milk they couldn't keep their eyes open.

One did not speculate as to whether Chamberlain would ruin us; the question was, would James M. Cain ruin us? The menace was not that Stalin and Hitler would get together; the menace was the probability that Bergman was sleeping with the new office manager he brought in. The news that depressed the whole city was . . . that the Morning World had ceased publication. We didn't know how we were going to survive that. The thing that paled our cheeks when we heard it on the phone was that Aunt Crully was lost in Grand Central. What sent Ross home to bed was not planes and tanks in Holland, but the sight of two old cuffs and a pair of sox in my outgoing basket.

What in the name of god were we going to do about covering art? The one ray of hope was when Ross found a barber who could cure dandruff and a doctor who could cure piles. . . .

Joe [Joel White] and Rosemary were both born with the gift of hearing, their stomachs right side up and the right number of fingers and it seemed that there was nothing else to worry about. . . . I could read the fine type in the New York, New Haven, and Hartford time tables and thought nothing of it. Ross discovered that you could sleep with a woman without setting her up in a Park Avenue apartment with a five year lease and was so cheered by it that he spent the Talk conference hour telling amusing anecdotes. . . . We gave Ingersoll as a hostage to FORTUNE and there was nothing left to worry about except that White set the office on fire and I was caught playing with dolls. [Thurber had bought a doll for Rosemary; the secretaries unwrapped it and perched it on Thurber's desk, leading Ross to complain that Thurber was now playing with dolls.] Woollcott rode out of the office on an old 1903 high dudgeon, leaving Shouts and Murmurs to die and we all wondered what in the world would happen, but nothing did. . . .

Eva Prout Geiger called me on the phone one day and Andy ran into a Miss [Alice] Burchfield on the street but again things quieted down. Margaret Speaks married an Englishman and turned to Christian Science. Paula [Trueman] got a job . . . and the world quit shaking and turned evenly on its axis again. So they came up and they went away, the old terrors that walked by day; the old perils of the night. If advancing age hadn't given us a sterner and calmer viewpoint of things, the war would. The question: what will the both of them together do to us? I have an idea that I will begin to write a cross between Carlyle at his gloomiest and Gertrude Stein at her lowest. I speak of the style; not the content.

White worried about Thurber and when Thurber wrote inviting him to cowrite a play about Ross and the *New Yorker*, White replied from Maine in a manner meant to cheer up his old friend:

About that play that you and I are writing, I have only got as far as "A House in the Country" and am thinking of changing that to "A House in the City." Haven't anything prefigured except it occurs to me that if you and I write a play, it ought to be about love. . . . We would be on solid ground. . . . It should certainly contain Jap Gude . . . Scudder Middleton, Tim [Costello], Hannah Josephson and the waiter at Charles's who told you that duck was out and you said, "What, in all this rain?" My fear of writing a play is so great that whenever I think about the matter at all . . . I immediately dream up a bunch of characters all of whom play some instrument in a swing band, so that when the worse comes to the worst and there seems to be no other way to keep the action up, the people on the stage can open up collapsible music racks and break into a number. . . .

Let's write a play about the difficulty people are experiencing in the decline of snobbery. . . . The war is bringing a lot of stuff to a head. People with liberal ideas feel that all the fighting is just a lot of nonsense, unless the world comes out of it feeling different about negroes, Jews, etc., and with a new concept of equality. Sensitive natures have an inkling that big times are at hand and that unless people march hand in hand, like Walt Whitman with his arm around somebody, the whole thing is for nothing. . . . I remember that when Ingersoll got back from his trip to England, he said that in ten years there will be no such thing as Vogue or Harpers Bazaar, which you and I know is an exaggeration. . . .

What the hell am I talking about?

Oh, yes, playwriting. . . . The only way you and I could write a play would be the way we wrote Is Sex Necessary? which was to get thinking about the same thing in the same way, and then each withdraw into our separate orbits and write it. Only in the case of a play, you would probably have to do the whole thing because I can't seem to think of anything for anybody to do on the stage, except I have always wanted to have a scene on the stage when a piano tuner was tuning a piano while a couple of the characters were having a very important little talk about something. My childhood was filled with piano tuners. They make a wonderful sound. It is like no other sound in the world—full of a dark and troubling melancholy, and sweetness. My father had a piano store on Fifth Avenue near 18th Street, and whenever I went in there, a piano was being tuned somewhere in the basement. . . . But that is as far as I have ever got with playwriting. . . .

Why don't we start . . . by just picking a place, such as a three-room apartment, in which anything at all might happen. . . . You will have to figure out what is going to happen, though. . . .

I suppose the first act has to pose some sort of situation or "difficulty," as well as introducing the characters, but you and I have been in enough difficulties so we ought to be able to think of one. Anybody in love is in terrible difficulty right from the start, anyway,—so as long as we keep Love for our theme the difficulty ought to swing into place naturally enough.

White had made his point; he wasn't interested. But Thurber persisted, writing White on May 15, 1943:

I have finished Act I of a play for this fall. It takes place in the room at the New Yorker occupied by Terry, who figures largely in it. So does Ross. So does a guy named Jeff Crane, who could be you. Everybody comes out well. Nothing to worry about. Helen and I are pretty excited about the first act, which is very funny. The second act will be funnier. Almost everything that ever happened is in it.

The second act ends with Ross (Walter Bruce) holding in his arms a Scotty with a red ribbon on its neck, as pneumatic drills roar off stage, and saying "God, how I pity me."

I have been working it out in my mind for a year.

White viewed any public kidding of the *New Yorker* tantamount to fouling his own nest, a view Thurber either didn't comprehend or wouldn't accept.

Thurber pursued the play project on his own, noising about town that he had a play nearly ready for production. "Elliott [Nugent] is in Hollywood doing a Danny Kaye film for Goldwyn," Thurber writes the Herman Millers. "A thankless task. I'm trying to finish a play for him to star in next winter, a comedy about the New Yorker magazine." Nugent dutifully read draft after draft of disconnected scenes and acts over the years and expressed discouraging criticism or lack of interest, but Thurber kept at it. Earlier, *Variety* had taken him at his word and announced a new Thurber play called *Make My Bed*, to be produced in November 1943. It never was, and never would be. The play changed with every rewriting, year after year, and each draft shifted focus on a different set of colleagues and family members, and even took on political coloration. The project became a near obsession with him and a tiresome topic of his monologs over the next eighteen years. He wanted another *Male Animal* success, and he was determined to feature Ross in it.

Two weeks after America's entrance into the war, Prime Minister Churchill, with his wife, visited President Roosevelt at the White House to discuss their countries' new, allied effort in the war. In a waggish mood, at dinner, Roosevelt told Mrs. Churchill that the brussels sprout was America's favorite vegetable, and that there were thirty-four ways to cook it. Pursuing the joke, he ordered a pamphlet made up containing the recipes. Those assigned the responsibility for the pamphlet asked the *New Yorker* for an illustrator to design the cover. (In one of Thurber's versions of the incident, he has Roosevelt specifically requesting Thurber; this may be so, for Morris Ernst and others of Thurber's acquaintance were then often part of the president's inner circle.) Thurber got the assignment, in any event, and, harnessed to his Zeiss Loop, drew a long table bearing a large glass bowl of brussels sprouts with human faces, and a line of eager diners, forks in hand, descending on the bowl. The ubiquitous Thurber Dog, the only living thing Thurber could make lovable in his drawings, is at the near end of the table, on hind legs, one paw reaching for a brussels sprout. The pamphlet was sent to Mrs. Churchill.

At a diplomatic dinner in London, Mrs. Churchill told John Winant, the U.S. ambassador to Great Britain, that she understood that Americans especially prized brussels sprouts as a vegetable. Winant said he was certain she had been misled. "But your president told me it was the great American vegetable," she replied. Winant immediately and diplomatically agreed, insisting that he had been thinking of parsnips. The anecdote became one of Thurber's favorites.

In the autumn of 1942, Thurber shook off "the Thurbs." "Mr. Thurber has at last come out of his terrible state of depression," Daise Terry writes Katharine White at Christmastime; "the past two days he has been in the office telephoning to everybody doing his colored-maid stunt."

His buoyancy was heightened by a spate of recognitions in 1943: Martha Foley selected "The Catbird Seat" for her *Best American Short Stories of 1943*. Jack Goodman, of Simon & Schuster, had edited Honeycutt's *How to Raise a Dog*, and, through her, become a friend of Thurber's, eventually luring him to his publishing house. Goodman picked Thurber's "The Dog That Bit People" and "Snapshot of a Dog" for his *Fireside Book of Dog Stories*, a selection of the Book-of-the-Month Club. Two months after "The Catbird Seat" was published in the *New Yorker*, Thurber's "The Cane in the Corridor" appeared, and was included in *The O. Henry Memorial Award Prize Stories of 1943*.

Thurber had begun "The Cane in the Corridor" at the Washington Square West apartment, shortly after returning from the Vineyard. He had resented Gibbs for never visiting him at the hospital (Gibbs couldn't stand hospitals, Elinor Gibbs explains), and the story is of a former hospital patient who wreaks vengeance on just such a neglectful friend. Thurber had put the story away, unfinished; Helen found it more than a year later and read it to him, resurrecting Thurber's former bitterness over Gibbs's seeming indifference to his suffering, and the motive for finishing it.

Thurber tries to disguise the real-life prototypes by describing Joe Fletcher (Thurber) as a short individual, and George Minturn (the short-statured Gibbs) as having long legs. In one exchange between Minturn and his wife, Minturn says: "Why can't we go home now, Nancy?" and Mrs. Minturn replies, "We *are* home, dear."

Ever the recycler of his own material, Thurber, after his blindness, often pretended that he didn't know he was in his own home while entertaining guests late at night. Marc Simont, of the Cornwall group, remembers being host to Thurber, Helen, and two mutual friends of theirs—Red Smith, the sports columnist, and Alistair Cooke. "If the Cornwall group had one thing in common," says Simont, "it was their devotion to the English language, and a capacity for Scotch. In addition, Thurber loved treating Red Smith to a fountain of information about baseball. About three or four a.m. Helen finally said to Thurber, 'We really have to go home, Jamie.' Thurber looked surprised and said, 'I thought we *were* home.'"

In January 1943, the Thurbers closed down the Cornwall house and moved to the city. Both heating oil for the house and gasoline for traveling to and from the city were rationed. Apartments were in great demand, but a friend whose mother was in real estate found them a sublet on East Fifty-seventh Street.

On January 3, 1943, the *Herald Tribune* Books section ran a picture story of Thurber—drawing at his easel, writing at his card table, eating one of the maid's cookies in the kitchen, listening to the old-fashioned console radio, and strumming the mandolin Helen had given him the previous Christmas. (White, an accomplished pianist, on a visit to the Thurber apartment, further enhanced Thurber's admiration of him by playing the mandolin for him.)

His favorite radio entertainers were Amos 'n' Andy, Henry Morgan, and Fred Allen; he also listened to newscasts and baseball games. On January 23, he was listening to a talk show featuring Ross's old nemesis, Alexander Woollcott, who suddenly ceased his harangue against the Nazis and the *Chicago Tribune* and fell silent. Thurber was among the thousands who wondered what had happened. Woollcott had scribbled a note to the show host, "I am sick," and died of a heart attack hours later.

The John Duncan Millers had met the Thurbers in 1937 at a *Night and Day* magazine party, in London. They got on well together from the start and the Thurbers had spent several weekends at the Millers' country home in Hampshire. "It was on a tennis court there that Jamie won the only set of tennis he'd ever won in his life," says Miller.

> The other thing he got very interested in there was the French game of boule. We had a set of boule balls . . . and he got so excited playing this that nobody could stop him. . . . It's played on rough ground with metal balls. . . . You don't roll the thing . . . you throw [it] and try to knock [someone else's ball] out. . . . I remember evenings when we used to have to get everybody's cars out and focus the headlights on the little bit of an area so that we could go on playing after dark.

In 1941, Miller was posted to the British Army Staff in Washington, and the Millers resumed their friendship with the Thurbers on visits to New York. "I remember his wonderful discovery that there was one word in the English language, 'facetious,'" says Miller, "which had all the vowels in the right order. . . . He loved to go out; he enjoyed hearing noises around him." One evening in 1943, when the Millers were staying with the Thurbers for the weekend, they were preparing to go to dinner. "The doorbell rang," says Miller,

> and there was the first Mrs. Thurber, Althea, who had missed her train back to Amherst and was there with her luggage and wanted a bed. We all went out to dinner. Only three weeks before my wife had gone to see Noel Coward's *Blithe Spirit* with the two wives in it. And she felt that

what was happening at this party at "21" was almost the same—to be seated between [Thurber's] two wives. Jamie was enjoying it immensely, throwing in the kind of remark that would make them get at each other.

In 1941, Thurber and Johnnie Miller got an idea for a book to be called *An Alphabet of Class Consciousness,* consisting of rhymes, one per letter in the alphabet, each to be illustrated by Thurber. Miller supplied the twenty-six verses; Thurber did a dozen sketches, writing Miller in September 1943: "I want to send a copy of what we have to Andy White, a brilliant critic of such endeavors as ours. He might have a helpful category or word. As Helen read the verses to me I felt the old glow of certainty about the book."

Miller took the unfinished manuscript and Thurber's drawings and correspondence with him when he was transferred to India. On the way his ship was torpedoed, and although he survived the sinking, his verses and Thurber's drawings and letters to him did not.

As for the Herman Millers, Thurber hadn't heard from them in half a year, and on May 28, 1943 he writes them:

> At 48, going on 49, I am getting along as well as might be expected, seeing a trifle better. I draw now with a Zeiss Loop, and look like a welder from Mars. . . .
>
> I'm getting out a Fairy Tale in the Fall. . . . It's called "Many Moons" (no relation to the Scarlet Mask play of the same name—1923).
>
> Also a book of drawings, since I havent had one in eleven years.
>
> Neither had Althea had a baby for eleven years, but on April 16, after several years of trying ending in 2 miscarriages, she gave birth to Linda Adams Gilmore. Nice going.

Eugene Saxton, intent on getting Thurber back to Harper & Bros., queried him on reissuing *Is Sex Necessary?*. Thurber writes White in his rough but still mostly readable script:

> Here is the letter from Gene. Says he has been thinking about sex. I dont know—I was 34, separated, and able to see in 1929. I'm not sure I wouldn't want to do my pieces over or throw them out. I'm neither so light-hearted nor so oblivious of what was going on in the world as I was then. You have to listen sharply to hear the lonesome bell of sex now.

The Thurbers returned to Cornwall for the summer, where they began selecting Thurber drawings for the book that would be published that fall, to be called *Men, Women, and Dogs*. Thurber sounded out White on writing an introduction, because the book "would be sadly incomplete without your explanation of what the hell it's all about and how it got started, if you don't mind still taking that blame."

White declined in his friendly, sedative manner, but allowed Thurber to dedicate the book to him:

TO ANDY WHITE

who picked up the first of these restless scrawls from the floor fifteen years ago and bravely set about the considerable task of getting them published, this book is gratefully and affectionately dedicated

Thurber sent White a dummy of the book, put together by Helen, for his comments. He had thought of calling it "The More I See of People," but, he writes White on June 9, 1943: "We abandoned that title . . . since it sounded too much like a retired lady librarian's sketches about her three spaniels."

White had suggested that Thurber's "bravery" in continuing with his drawings in the gathering twilight of blindness be somehow indicated in the introduction. Thurber replies: "I cant very well call my own bravery wonderful. People would say, 'There goes proud-ass Thurber—calls himself What-a-Man.' "

Harcourt Brace's first printing of *Men, Women, and Dogs* was an optimistic 27,500 copies—fully justified, for it went into a second printing two months later and remained in print through 1951. Dorothy Parker was pleased to be asked to write the introduction—she had also written that of *The Seal in the Bedroom*, Thurber's 1932 book of collected drawings. Twice so honored, she writes in this introduction, she has changed her plans for her burial and now wants to

be buried in a prominent place on a travelled thoroughfare through a wildly popular cemetery. Above me I want a big white stone . . . on which I want carven in clear letters: "Uncover before this dust, for when it was a woman, it was doubly honored. Twice in life, it was given to her below to introduce the work of James Thurber. . . ."

I like to think of my shining tombstone. It gives me, as you might say, something to live for.

William Schlamm, writing in the *New York Times*, decides that Thurber has reduced the basic elements of our civilization to men, women, and dogs, "and the rare appearance of a child carries always the implication that something utterly abnormal must have happened. . . . The dogs don't seem to get the joke of it and look constantly sad."

A full-page Bonwit Teller ad ran in the *New Yorker* featuring a young woman modeling a spring dress whose pattern is packed with Thurber dogs, the designer announcing in fine script, "B. H. Wragge does 'Men, Women, and Dogs'."

Time heralded the book of the "greying, railish six-footer" Thurber:

> *The New Yorker's* famous comic master of neurasthenia . . . who has been prolific of achievement in the face of physical handicap . . . has published a dozen books of prose and pictures which have already taken their place among the humorous classics of the U.S.
>
> One of Thurber's simpler secrets is the dismaying fact that the maddest laughter is often provoked by no laughing matter. Thus, one twin-bedded, book-reading wife asks of her mate, in the other bed: "What the hell ever happened to the old-fashioned love story?"

In November, following publication of *Many Moons* and *Men, Women, and Dogs*, the Thurbers were again at the Homestead, in Hot Springs, Virginia, with Helen recovering from diverticulitis. Then Mame Thurber underwent an operation, and the Thurbers found themselves in Columbus for a ten-day family Christmas visit while Mame recovered. Thurber continued work on his next children's book at the Deshler-Wallick Hotel. As usual, the local press made much of him, and he responded, as always, confessing that he "came down a flight of stairs [at the hotel] the wrong way but landed standing up. I imagine people thought I was in vaudeville."

Of his old Columbus friends, he reported, Joel Sayre was in Iran making movies with the Army; Nugent was acting on Broadway in "The Voice of the Turtle," and John McNulty was directing radio news broadcasts. Photographs taken of Thurber by the local press gave him, as he himself pointed out, the look of a frightened gray-haired rodent disguised in glasses and a lion's mane.

Except for "The Cane in the Corridor," Thurber's prose production in 1943 was hardly noticeable. In that time, he was busy getting two books published two months apart, and tenaciously learning to draw large-scale, with a minimum of vision and the Zeiss Loop. The *New Yorker* published eighteen of his captioned drawings that year. Of his three *New Yorker* casuals, he declined to include one, "1776—and All That," in a book collection. College freshmen of the day, Thurber writes, citing an article, know nothing of U.S. history or geography. He suggests using movies and popular songs, which young people rarely forget, as teaching aids. Gene Saxton, still trying to get Thurber back into the fold, has been urging him to let Harper bring out a "best of Thurber" anthology, but Thurber writes White, "I can't have three books in one autumn, and guess I'll ask Gene to wait a year."

"I got a proof of the fairy tale [Many Moons] and its beautiful," Thurber writes White. "The color work is wonderful [he had to have Helen's word for it]. The plates cost $3,000. Hot dog. [Cass] Canfield [of Harper & Bros.] doesnt believe there is that much money."

Many Moons tells of how the common sense of the court jester—with whom Thurber clearly identifies—combines with the wisdom of a ten-year-old girl to settle a problem that has baffled all the king's counselors—how to grant the wish of the young princess to possess the moon. Perhaps Thurber had been subtly influenced by what White had recently written in his preface to A Subtreasury of American Humor:

I think the stature of humor must vary some with the times. The court fool in Shakespeare's day had no social standing and was no better than a lackey, but he did have some artistic standing and was listened to with considerable attention, there being a well-founded belief that he had the truth hidden somewhere about his person. Artistically he stood probably higher than the humorist of today, who has gained social position but not the ear of the mighty. (Think of the trouble the world would save itself if it would pay some attention to nonsense!) A narrative poet at court, singing of great deeds, enjoyed a higher standing than the fool and was allowed to wear fine clothes; yet I suspect that the ballad singer was more often than not a second-rate stooge, flattering his monarch lyrically, while the fool must often have been a first-rate character, giving his monarch good advice in bad puns.

Many Moons was fashioned from the substance of Thurber's dreams and set him off on another creative road not previously taken. In this fairy tale, the little princess is ill and her father, the king, believes her only chance of survival is to grant her wish to have the moon, which, she says, is made of gold. None of the king's wise men can come up with a solution. The jester asks the princess how large and far away she thinks the moon is. Smaller than her thumbnail, she replies, which she can measure whenever the moon gets caught in a tree outside her window. The jester has a small gold ball strung on a chain for her. The king worries that she will see the moon the next night and know she has been tricked. The chamberlain suggests dark glasses.

"This made the King very angry, and he shook his head from side to side. 'If she wore dark glasses, she would bump into things!' he said, 'and then she would be ill again.' "

The jester than asks the princess the next night why the moon is shining if it's around her neck. "That is easy, silly," she replies. "When I lose a tooth a new one grows in its place, doesn't it? I guess it is the same way with every-thing."

And so Thurber proved. If the sense of sight was taken away, a myriad of new sensitivities seemed to grow in its place, enabling him to go on listening to the world and interpreting it as he was somehow obliged to do. Malcolm Muggeridge, an admirer of Thurber's, has written: "There is no such thing as darkness; only a failure to see."

57

That Comic Prufrock

Dear Peter:

You put the right color to it when you said Black Saturday. Last night I got to fussing so profoundly about my coming ordeal that I developed a sharp pain in my stomach. Sensing that I was going around in a panicky circle Helen woke up in the middle of the night, got pencil and paper, and wrote down some ideas for me. Her notes together with your letter and some thought of my own have helped me to work out a kind of plan which I think will get me through this. . . .

I will certainly want you up there on the platform beside me. I also fervently hope that there will be some kind of lectern to kind of hide behind and lean on since this would give me added confidence and help me to stand up for an hour.

—Letter to Peter De Vries, April 4, 1944

Over cocktails at the Algonquin in 1962, Helen Thurber was stubbornly insisting that her late husband had been too fundamentally kind, sweet, and shy to have fought with *anyone*. "I should know," she said fiercely, "I was married to him for twenty-six years." Thurber suffered from toxic thyroid, its principal symptom—neuritis headaches—attacking him severely in the early 1950s. His uncontrolled, aggressive outbursts at such times, or when drinking, were familiar to many, and the matter of his intemperate behavior had arisen innocently, as incidental to another point entirely. Lois Long, who was present, looked at Helen in disbelief. "Oh, he was a dear," she told Helen, "but like Ross, he did have his eccentricities." "Well," replied Helen in calm retrenchment, "he never fought with Pete De Vries."

Helen, newly widowed, and worried about Thurber's place in literary annals and her own financial prospects, was right to summon forth the generous, self-effacing Thurber of his routine days of hard work—a Thurber of hesitant, considerate, kindly, and nervous manner, eager to like and be liked. He held himself to a disciplined agenda of labor wherever he was, and drank mostly only in the company of others. ("How do you think Thurber got out all those books?" Helen asks defensively.) Unfortunately, a social drinker by definition is on public display, so Thurber's comparatively short hours of drinking and misbehaving always had witnesses glad to titillate others by broadcasting his latest verbal assaults and tantrums.

By singling out De Vries as a solitary example of one spared Thurber's drunken rages, Helen, in a way, was conceding her own argument—unnecessarily and unfairly, for there were dozens of men and women friends with whom Thurber never quarreled seriously or with malice aforethought, including Gude, White, Jane Williams, Emily Hahn, John Duncan Miller, Alistair Cooke, Daise Terry, and most of his British acquaintances. What brought De Vries to Helen's mind was no doubt the specially preserved regard Thurber held for the younger man. De Vries had introduced the work of Thurber to the world of serious literary criticism, and Thurber, in turn, introduced him to Ross and the *New Yorker*.

"Thurber was two people," De Vries remarked, twenty-six years after Thurber's death. "Of the after-six sadist I had only the meagerest inklings—a sudden contentiousness midway the third martini, barbed retorts, jabs and jibes, these alone hinted at the redskin who should not be given firewater. I was spared the bruited shambles made by the legend in action. He never turned on me at a quarter to eleven, never disguised his voice on the telephone as a darky whose daughter had given birth to my pickaninny. His pranks and practical jokes were also hearsay. Maybe he never forgot that I was the first to give him high critical regard, in my *Poetry* essay. Who knows?"

De Vries was a longtime admirer of Thurber, and was a coeditor of *Poetry* magazine when it published his imaginative, interesting musings on Thurber's work ("James Thurber: The Comic Prufrock") in December 1943. He justified the critique in a magazine dedicated to poetry by ingeniously finding the body of that work aglow with identifiable poetic aspects, particularly those of the postwar symbolists. He saw Thurber's hapless middle-aged man as "the comic counterpart" to T. S. Eliot's J. Alfred Prufrock:

> There is, for instance, the same dominating sense of Predicament. The same painful and fastidious self-inventory, the same detached anxiety; the same immersion in weary minutiae, the same self-disparagement, the same wariness of the evening's company. And the same fear . . . that someone . . . will "drop a question on his plate."

De Vries mined from Thurber's drawings and prose similarities to much of what informs the writing of not only Eliot but Proust, Yeats, and Joyce:

> I do not know whether the critical landlords of Axel's Castle—our customary symbol for Symbolism—list [Thurber] among the occupants or not, or whether they are aware he is on the premises. . . .
>
> His inner state and private convolutions are, if not as profound, as skilfully projected as any.
>
> He may be the least of the family—indeed perhaps just a quizzical lodger cutting up in some remote corner of the premises—but this is the address all right.

Other intellectuals, such as Thomas Sugrue, had earlier and earnestly laid out Thurber's humor as serious literature and sociology in their reviews of his books, but De Vries's piece can be regarded as the first significant published ushering of Thurber from the back row reserved for most writers of humor to a seat up front in the company of the established great.

De Vries sent an early copy of the article to Thurber, who replied with such effusions of appreciation that De Vries, encouraged by his new wife, dared to ask him to appear publicly in Chicago at a fund-raising event on behalf of the chronically impoverished *Poetry*. It was subtle blackmail: *Poetry*, founded in 1912 by Harriet Monroe, was one of the earliest and most influential of the small literary magazines in America. It had published—in some cases for the first time—Eliot, Vachel Lindsay, Carl Sandburg, Amy Lowell, Ezra Pound, Hart Crane, and other emerging voices of early twentieth-century poetry. And now De Vries had argued publicly and effectively that Thurber belonged there. How could Thurber refuse?

Dear Mr. De Vries:

I am practically moved to accept your invitation not only because of my feeling for the magazine but because of your swell piece about me. It isn't often, as I shoot craps with Merlin below stairs in Axel's Castle, that anyone stops long enough to explore what I am up to. One of my regrets that I brought home from two years in Europe is that I missed meeting Eliot. Some one told me that he was fond of "My Life and Hard Times" which of course pleased me greatly. I think he particularly liked the preface, which he thought was a pretty fair statement of the nature of the artist. . . .

Back to the lecture proposition, it is quite true that I don't go in for that, partly because of my bad vision, partly because of a tendency to shake all over when I face a group of people and partly because I am not sure I really have anything to say. However I am going to give it my most serious thought and if I can coax Mrs. Thurber we may be able to make it sometime between January and April, since I plan to visit my home town, Columbus, about that time. Another reason for coming out which I omitted is that I would very much like to meet you.

It seems a contradiction that Thurber dreaded speaking formally before large audiences—this show-off who could dominate a roomful of people conversationally by the hour, who had had his own radio show, who had just heard Mary Margaret McBride tell him he had been "a knockout" on hers, and who would one day appear on Broadway in a musical revue. But the stage fright was real, Helen says. When he appeared as a guest on radio and, later, television programs, he got by because there was rarely a studio audience. He had struggled through a short speech in a war-bond drive as a literary panelist at Catholic University in Washington, D.C.—an experience that gave him little hope for success before a large audience. Milton Caniff writes:

> I shared what I think was Jim's first *big* radio appearance. At a table in a small studio, he was at ease—but in an NBC barn, with a studio audience before which he had to be *led* (then to have the announcer face him toward the mike) was traumatic.
>
> It was a rough night for Jim.

De Vries was born in Chicago in 1910 to Dutch immigrant parents. His young psyche was battered by the guilt and other feelings of personal inadequacy stemming from a stern Dutch Calvinistic upbringing and the humiliations of poverty. He developed a childhood stutter, which he manfully overcame by volunteering for his high-school debating team. But he had been driven in on himself by the affliction, and he attempted to fight his way out of the entrapment through writing. He knew almost from the start that the unfunny circumstances of his life could be best dealt with by being funny about them. His parents, who wanted him to become a minister, lost much of their interest in him when his literary ambitions surfaced ("They never read anything I wrote"). He attended Calvin College, in Grand Rapids, Michigan, spent a summer term at Northwestern University, and, as an avid reader, steadily educated himself to an erudition of awesome depth and range. His challenges of conventional wisdom and his deliberately snarled allusions in more than two dozen books helped build a reputation as America's premier comic novelist.

He stepped from college into the bear trap of the Great Depression. While in his twenties, he published three novels, which he later disowned. Though he sold occasional poems and humorous essays to magazines, he supported himself by servicing peanut-vending machines, selling taffy apples and Tupperware, editing a community newspaper, moving furniture, lecturing to women's clubs, and playing, in a radio serial, both a mad scientist and the wounded gorilla terrorizing the scientist. His poetry helped land him a job as associate editor at *Poetry* in 1938. He became coeditor in 1942. The position paid twenty-five dollars a week, and he continued to take menial work on the side.

"Editorial toils on that monthly," he writes, "regularly alternated with time-outs to beg, borrow or bludgeon our tiny salaries out of civic-minded persons. I say civic-minded because Chicago has always been proud of Poetry's deficit. The magazine's annual critical financial illness was always reported in the newspapers somewhere near the obituary page."

Katinka Loeser, an Iowan reared in Chicago and a graduate of the University of Chicago, had been writing poetry since she was fourteen. In 1943, she was awarded *Poetry*'s Young Poets Prize. She was notified by a telegram from De Vries, who hadn't yet met her. They were married that October, a month before De Vries's treatise on Thurber appeared. De Vries was thirty-three years old, Katinka thirty. Nobody but another poet, he believed, would have married him on his salary.

There was no money for a honeymoon, but when Thurber continued to be uncertain about journeying to Chicago for the fund-raising event that both De Vries and his wife saw as critical to the magazine's fortunes, they decided to invest in a trip to New York to persuade the Thurbers. They called it a postponed honeymoon. By prearrangement, they knocked at the door of the Thurbers' apartment on East Fifty-seventh Street one late afternoon. De Vries remembers his first sight of Thurber, "picking his way through the dusky foyer, with his arms out like the feelers of an insect." The couples got along famously, and the Thurbers capitulated. De Vries remembers:

It was a few months later, on an April day in Chicago, that we met again, this time in a room at the Ambassador East, to make final arrangements for the plan we had hit on in his New York apartment for lightening the miseries of public speech.

It was a rather shabby little stratagem that we cooked up.

Thurber had declined to give a formal lecture but would not mind answering questions. To make it even more foolproof, I myself made up the questions the audience would ask: questions for which the remarks he was smoothly and eloquently getting off in the relaxation of the hotel room—about men, women, dogs—would serve beautifully as answers. . . .

It was a quiz show in reverse. I scribbled down the queries, hastily tailoring them to fit the gems dropping from his lips. I wrote all these questions out in advance on slips of paper of different sizes, shapes and even colors, to bolster the fiction that they had just been jotted down by members of the audience.

The event was held on a Saturday morning in the Arts Club, located in that pastry chef's dream, the Wrigley Building. What any veteran of Thurber's conversation would have known would happen, happened. With the first question he took the bit between his teeth and galloped off on as fine a formal lecture as the audience had ever heard and they had heard Frank Lloyd Wright, Robert Penn Warren and Rudolph Ganz.

When I had called for him at the hotel, an hour before, he had given me a hand to shake as clammy as my own. Now, face to face with the invisible cloud of patrons, he underwent the transformation he always did in a pinch, because the phenomenon known as Thurber had two contradictory sides: apprehension and mastery of any given situation. . . .

He never to my knowledge mounted a public platform again, but he occupied that one just long enough to show that he might have borne comparison with Mark Twain on that score too, had he cared to add it to his list of accomplishments.

It was a public triumph for De Vries, as well. He was shy, taciturn, and soft-spoken, and had the woebegone look of a bloodhound. Even for a serious humorist, he seemed so self-repressed and unadventurous conversationally that many didn't realize that he had muttered something truly funny until they thought about it later. Despite having got the better of his introverted ways, he was nearly as fearful of public appearances as Thurber, and his occasional bashful, lackluster participation on a radio or television program in later years usually spared him a second invitation. He was grateful for that, because he placed his highest premiums on the time and privacy he needed to write. After he joined the *New Yorker,* he avoided socializing at the office, usually lunched alone (on Tuesday it was deviled beef bones at the Blue Ribbon, on Forty-fourth Street near Times Square), and wrote almost constantly, wherever and whenever he could. He commuted between the city and Westport, Connecticut, and one saw him seated on the crowded noisy train, briefcase lying flat on his lap supporting the notebook in which he steadily scribbled.

The popularity of his Thurber introduction at the *Poetry* event nearly equaled the response to Thurber's. His remarks were larded with the De Vriesian puns, inverted clichés, surprising analogies, and poetic conceits. He described the Thurber Man as having "a spine like a stalk of boiled asparagus," and Thurber as adept at "hitting the male on the head." Thurber had expressed concern that some woman would ask him his artistic credo, and De Vries headed that one off in his remarks, too:

> Thurber does not talk, and he will draw anything but a conclusion, so his being here is not only a local, it is a national, phenomenon. What rash mood made him consent, not only to lecture, but to submit to this mass interview before three hundred people, I do not know. Perhaps some profound sense of sin, some obscure impulse toward public self-immolation. . . . Who knows but that woman may be here, to ask him

what his artistic credo is. And what is he to say? Where in the name of heaven is he to get himself an artistic credo.

De Vries earned so many laughs that some thought he was Thurber. Both men were delighted with the results. They became instant and permanent friends. The Chicago Arts Club, freshly aware of Thurber, soon put on a one-man show of his drawings. "We want you and Katinka to select, as a small gift from us," Thurber wrote De Vries, "whatever drawing in the coming exhibit out there you would most like to have. . . . Thank you for everything. With fond memories, I remain, tall gaunt and melancholy."

Thurber became De Vries's promoter. Though De Vries thought so little of his three published novels that he refused to list them with his later books, Thurber insisted that they be sent to him, along with a copy of De Vries's introduction of Thurber at the Arts Club, writing:

> Thanks very much for your copy of what I like to think of as the speech of the day—not to say the speech of the season. I am afraid you are too late about "The Handsome Heart" [a De Vries early novel]. I came home from the office to find my colored cook, a Bermudian woman of intelligence and discernment, lost in its pages. She insisted on reading aloud to me from a book which turned out to be yours. She read your remarkable description of hands. If this small passage is any indication, you are wrong as hell about the thing. "The Bugle" [*But Who Wakes the Bugler?*, another disowned De Vries novel, published by Houghton Mifflin] hasn't arrived yet but is on the way.
>
> This is really an official communication soliciting in my own name and that of the *New Yorker* whatever pieces you might have on hand or in prospect for us to look at. I have spoken to the editors about you and they asked me to implore you to send something along.

When De Vries's material arrived, Thurber thought it was on the mark and gave it to Ross, who wrote De Vries, two days after the Allied invasion of Normandy:

> Mr. Thurber gave me the Comment items and the art ideas you sent him and I have gone over them and find, to my astonishment, that they are what can readily be described, in the language of this office, as very promising. This is an unusual experience. It is rare to read anything from a new writer and find him both literate and amusing. . . .
>
> You don't want an editorial job, by any chance, do you? Our desk staff

has been ravaged by war, and we have had less success in replacing editors than in anything else. That has ever been the way. Men who can handle copy and see it through to the final proof are extremely rare, war or peace, but we are especially short-handed now. You *are* an editor, and if you should want to go on as one, God forbid, I'd like to know about it.

Thurber was shown a copy of Ross's letter and wrote the De Vrieses, jubilantly playing his role as patron. His triumphant remarks, written in his sprawling, childlike handwriting, took up fifteen pages of copy paper:

By this time you have Ross's dazed and adoring letter. . . . I had handed the whole sheaf of your stuff to Ross who had said, sighing, "I'll read it, but it wont be any good." Half hour later he called me in and said, "Jesus Christ. It *is* good!"

Thus, in 1944 the advent of P. de Vries. I went over the heads of the art editor and the Talk editor, otherwise your stuff would have been scattered and its shape & impact lost. Hot dog. . . . Now that Ross has taken you over [as your editor], I suggest you send stuff direct to him. Art ideas . . . in letters to me confuse Ross. . . . Casuals, or fiction as they used to be called, should not go to Ross first, but to me or to Gus Lobrano, a tall, sweet guy you will like.

Ross would take you on as an editor at once, at, say, $12,000 a year, but I am of several minds about that, as follows:

You would like the people and, finally, the work, after you have been allowed to settle down to what you want to do, can do, and like to do. First, however, Ross would decide that you are god, Donald Nelson and Barney Baruch, all in one, a man capable of handling and running everything—from the arrangement of offices to the private life of the contributors. I started out that way. We all did. But he has more sense now, and he also has me to set him straight. I would be around like a mother dog, to snarl and snap in your defense. . . .

It is a considerable thing to recommend so abrupt a change in a friend's life, and I hesitate to do it. But I have confidence in your success whatever you do. . . . I should have introduced Peter [in Chicago] and sat down.

It was not only the start of a binding relationship, but the liftoff of De Vries's rocket into orbit. Thurber fussed over his promising protégé like a mother hen. When Ross invited De Vries to New York for a job interview, Thurber was on hand at the Algonquin lunch. When Thurber introduced De

Vries to Ross, Ross said, "Hi, De Vree. Can you do the Race Track department?" De Vries, warned by Thurber that Ross was given to the unexpected,
replied, "No, but I can imitate a wounded gorilla." "Well, don't imitate it
around the office," said Ross. "The place is a zoo the way it is."

Ross, who had so often hired the wrong people over the years, wasn't at all
sure he hadn't made the same mistake with De Vries. A few days after De
Vries's move East, when Thurber wrote Ross in further praise of him, Ross
replied:

> His talent is yet to be proved, or at any rate, yet to be classified. He
> has done some good Comment. . . . He turned in a flock of art ideas
> which were in or near the groove but not one of them was right to have
> drawn up. Of two fiction pieces I have read, one wasn't good, and the
> other wasn't as good as it ought to have been. . . . He unquestionably
> has a sense of humor and resembles White in what the Saturday Evening
> Post once called the "masterful use of the unexpected word." I wouldn't
> have rushed De Vries here at all if it hadn't been for the damned dead-
> line about job changing. I had to act before July 1st, or face going
> through the red tape of the United States Employment Office which, I
> was advised, might take weeks. Anyhow, as De Vries himself says, he's
> mainly in the peanut vending machine business now, and editing is not
> a much meaner occupation than that. . . .

De Vries more than justified Ross's gamble. He began by proving to himself, and others, that he could work effectively within the New Yorker's traditions of humor. He first screened and edited poetry submissions part-time,
which left him time to contribute material of his own to the magazine. Soon
he was a frequent writer of Comment. Before long, his ideas for cartoons and
captions won Ross over. He began attending the Tuesday art meetings and
going through drawings piled high in the rough basket, offering improvements of the comic situation or its caption. This, too, was supposed to be
part-time, but though he eventually commuted to the office only two days a
week, he carried a briefcase jammed with drawings with him on the train
home. During his more than forty years with the magazine, scores of his art
suggestions were farmed out to the cartoonists to follow. Over a drink at the
Algonquin, De Vries suggested to Charles Addams the famous cartoon of
ghoulish people pouring boiling oil from the rooftop onto the Christmas
carolers below. (The nonhero of his novel The Tunnel of Love is the art editor
of a metropolitan magazine similar to the New Yorker.)

His early casuals are in the self-victimized pattern made popular by Benchley and Thurber. He later credited the *New Yorker*'s literary standards with conditioning and heightening his own. "But where do you find better writing?" was his retort to a staff member who once complained to him about the too frequently dreary subjects and the run-on length of recent articles in the magazine. The civilized refinement of the edited copy was reward enough for him. "Manner over matter" became his own successful formula as a novelist. Painting his comedy onto the larger canvases, he learned to manage book-length narratives, which few writers of literate humor—Twain, P. G. Wodehouse, Evelyn Waugh, Kingsley Amis, and Anthony Powell (a favorite of De Vries's) were exceptions—can handle.

"Pete's earlier novels weren't Jamie's cup of tea," says Helen. "He worried about their plot deficiencies." But perhaps Thurber was also uneasy at seeing his young protégé strike out on his own in another milieu, culminating in a permanent independence of the *New Yorker* casual. De Vries seems to have sensed that he had been aiming at a disappearing target, that the old carefree era of humorous writing was fading, and that he could never overtake, on their grounds, those who had fashioned it—the Thurbers, Whites, Gibbses, Perelmans, Benchleys, and Sullivans. Forever influenced by their comedy and satire, he became an original in his own right. Though parts of early De Vries novels appeared in the *New Yorker* as casuals, he gradually stopped writing for the magazine. His cartoon work became his only connection with it. But he was making his own mark a significant one. As one reviewer noted: "Peter De Vries does for schizophrenia what the late James Thurber did for paranoia. Under the flesh of comedy are the bones of psychosis."

Over the years, whenever the Thurbers came to the city, there was almost always an Algonquin lunch with De Vries. "Pete always began by sitting down and saying to the waiter, 'No rolls,' " says Helen. "They charged $2.85 extra for the rolls." The two families visited one another's suburban homes occasionally, word games being the order of the evening, for Thurber could not play cards or board games or any longer challenge guests to dart-throwing or tossing cards into a hat. The word games were carried on by mail or telephone days after they had been begun. Thurber, De Vries, and Berton Roueché, another *New Yorker* contributor, once competed for the most words containing the five principal vowels; the assignment kept Thurber awake at night. He writes De Vries:

> Sequoia and its friends: discourage, precaution, precarious, auditioned, unintentional, aeronautics, mountaineer, permutation, emulation, unconscionable, disfiguration, figuration. I got six or eight more last night, but they left me. Damn Roueché & you for bringing this up! I

even got 2 5[–]vowel names . . . Louise Macy, Benjamin Clough. God!

Love, Jim Thurber.

Automobile, maneuvering. I'm going nuts, nuts! do you hear? NUTS ha, ha, ha, ha, ha, ha.

Their letters swapped thoughts on literature, accommodating such musings as those on age and death. "Autumn is the mellower season," De Vries quotes to him from Samuel Butler's *The Way of All Flesh*, "and what we lose in flowers we more than gain in fruits." De Vries thinks there is both truth and consolation in the quote "provided you don't spend your autumn days stricken with Parkinson's disease or a rickety bladder." After he sent Thurber a poem about death, by Maxwell Bodenheim, Thurber replies:

> Thanks for the book and the Bodenheim poem, which takes me back to the old Penguin book store on West Eighth Street, where he used to sit with his eyes closed, running his iambic hands over the breasts of imaginary women. I have a feeling that the image of death as an idyllic or droll fellow arises only in the healthy mind, that is a mind attached to a healthy body. I have observed for a long time that death seems more awful the closer you approach it and that at a long distance it has something of a romantic air. . . . Thirty years ago—my God, it was thirty-five—I used to sit around . . . discussing death in terms of the then extremely popular "Ivory Apes and Peacocks" of old James Huneker. I remember the vision of death as a long room lit only by a single gas jet. Ah, what a dusty answer gets the soul.

As for Thurber's work for the magazine, in 1944 only two of his pieces ran. One, "The Cherboors," an inconsequential commentary on radio announcers misquoting poetry and mispronouncing "Cherbourg" when reporting the Allied invasion, never qualified for a Thurber book. In 1945, the tally was down to one ("Fairy Tales for Our Time: The Princess and the Tin Box"), and to nothing in 1946. Despite his faltering craftsmanship, his art fared better; the magazine reran Thurber spots from time to time, and seven of his original cartoons appeared in 1944. In 1945, Thurber's "Our New Natural History" began, [in *The Beast in Me*, the title became "A New Natural History"] with Ross's encouragement. Thurber's weird plants and creatures took their shape from his visualizing how timeworn expressions might look: The Hopeless

Quandary, the Early and the Late Riser, the Barefaced Lie and the White Lie; a Scone and a Crumpet peering out of the Tiffin.

Though Thurber began submitting his "Natural History" parts in 1944, Ross let them accumulate, to be certain that he had a continuing series. He was writing Thurber about them in December 1944, apparently not to persuade Thurber to change anything but to show off the results of having prowled through encyclopedias and dictionaries. Rea Irvin, Ross writes Thurber, happened to know there was an actual fish called the pout, and adds:

> You have a bird called a shriek. In real life there is a bird called a shriker and also one called a shrike. I should think the approximation here does not matter.
>
> There is a bee called a lapidary, but you have drawn an animal.
>
> You have a clock tick. There is, of course, a tick. No matter, I say. There is a bird called a ragamuffin. You have drawn a ragamuffin plant. No real conflict.
>
> H. W. Ross

Two widely distributed rodents: the Barefaced Lie (left) and the White Lie.

Elsewhere, Ross writes, "There might be a name . . . in 'Lazy Susan,' a flower or a butterfly, or something. Would 'antimacassar' be possible? I guess not."

The "Natural History" ran in sixteen parts from March 1945 to May 1946. Meanwhile, Thurber's stream of captioned drawings in the magazine dwindled to a trickle—two in 1945 and in 1946, barely enabling him to continue his war against women.

On July 6, 1946, his final series of drawings, "The Olden Time"—Thurber's graphic impressions of the medieval period—began. The series ended January 18, 1947, and on November 1, his spot of two men boxing appeared; it was the last original drawing he would do for the *New Yorker*.

Thurber's unique drawings could hardly serve as a benchmark for other cartoonists, but they had become part of the magazine's legend that readers looked for, and this fact, together with a genuine humanitarian concern on Ross's part, led to a scheme to publish reversed Thurber car-

"How is it possible, woman, in the awful and magnificent times we live in, to be preoccupied exclusively with the piddling?"

"Supper" from "The Olden Time"

toons from the past with new captions. In *The Years with Ross*, Thurber writes:

> In the last seven years of his life Ross wrote me dozens of letters and notes about my drawings. In one he said he had found out that the *New Yorker* had published three hundred and seven of my captioned drawings, of which one hundred and seventy-five had been printed in one or another of my books. He wanted to know if I would permit new captions by outsiders on those rearranged originals of mine. "There is a caption here on a sketch by an idea man," he wrote me, "that it is thought might do for a re-used drawing of yours, as follows: (two women talking) 'Every time she tells a lie about *me*, I'm going to tell the truth about *her*.' Now that I've got it on paper, it may not sound so hot, but it might do. The women in your drawings used to say some pretty batty things." He wanted to pay me the full rate I had got for originals, but I said no on a project in which I would have no real creative part.
>
> The whole idea was abandoned after I told Ross that I didn't grieve about not being able to draw any longer.

But Thurber hurries through the episode too fast. De Vries was the idea man who persuaded Ross and art editor Jim Geraghty to rerun Thurber cartoons. He writes:

The whole thing was my idea. "After all," I said to the authorities in proposing it, "so many of Thurber's drawings are of two or more people in a room that a fresh caption can easily be slipped into a character's mouth."

After its approval and adoption I never had anything more to do with it—choice of cartoons, etc. Don't know what Ross's motivations were in adopting the practice, or why it was scrapped, but I always suspected uneasiness, the feeling that it was a form of cheating, pretending they were offering new Thurber pictures.

What had given De Vries the idea? "I don't know," he answers, "except possibly the thought of all those potential captions locked up in Thurber's head with no other release than this device—seen in retrospect not to have been such a good one."

Why hadn't Thurber credited De Vries when discussing the matter? "His knowledge of the matter may have been partial," says De Vries; "he may not have known of my role in it, or, knowing it, may not have considered it worth mentioning in his account. . . . Of course Ross would have had to be featured in the decision to reuse drawings. I can't remember how I proposed my notion to Ross, whether directly or indirectly through Geraghty."

Thurber eventually went along with the scheme. In 1947, the year before the reruns began to appear, he sends some of his old cartoons to De Vries, writing:

> I thought you might look these over and then discuss them with Ross. I told Ross at lunch more than a month ago that I had talked over new captions for the old drawings with you. This seemed to gratify him, for he said you are the best idea man the magazine ever had. [Helen and I] are sending . . . new captions for four old drawings, and have selected about twenty-six other drawings that would seem to lend themselves well to new captions. Helen has a list of these, numbered from our scrap book which Miss Terry got up, and will send you a copy if you'd like to know the ones we selected as best.
>
> I don't want to jump over Geraghty's head on this, but I know you will be able to handle it with the discretion you are famous for.

The first of the captioned reruns appeared September 11, 1948 (Man to woman: "What did those flying saucers turn out to be, George?"), and ended five months later with another antifemale broadside, the Thurber Man saying to his wife, "What do you expect to do when I'm gone, may I ask—live by your wits?" Though the titled cartoons ended, scissored parts of his previously published drawings continued to turn up in the magazine as spots as late as 1958. Presumably, neither Ross nor Thurber objected to reusing Thurber's old art, if they lacked captions.

There was beginning to be little about the *New Yorker* that pleased Thurber, especially after Ross died in late 1951. Less than a year after that traumatic event, Thurber was taking up with De Vries his objections to the magazine's current run of cartoons—objections similar to those that, earlier, he had made to Ross. With his cartoons no longer being run, he risked falling into the role of the old-timer who can't forget the good old days. Nor does he resist showing off for his younger friend, writing in 1952:

> I've been brooding about the kind of change that seems to have darkened the magazine's funny cartoons recently. There is much too much stuff about the man and woman on the raft and the two beachcombers. The first should have ended twelve years ago when the man said, "You look good enough to eat," and I thought I had ended the other one in the Ohio State Sun-Dial in 1917 with:
>
> 1st Beachcomber: "What did you come here to forget?"
>
> 2nd Beachcomber: "I've forgotten."
>
> I'm beginning to worry a little about Shawn's sense of humor and I hope you will tell me if it is simply a case of an old magazine passing through the tail of a comet. I cannot believe the old magazine has begun to cackle, and I don't want to believe that [Rea] Irvin is back. I wish to Christ Ross were. He would never have allowed these two stereotypes in the same issue. There is a definite carelessness at the New Yorker, for the fear that comes out of true respect is gone. Helen and others join me in my worry.

De Vries thought he had reassured Thurber earlier as to Shawn's sense of humor, having written him three months after Ross's death: "Shawn seems to be doing fine, judging from the contact I have with him in the art department. The first few art meetings were interesting for the paradox in the thing: this is probably the only magazine where you would find yourself breaking in your superior."

Thurber had announced to the world the year before that his art production had ended—a self-portrait for *Time* that year was his last published drawing, though he would continue to trace, from memory, feel, and habit, the sitting Thurber Dog. He tells De Vries on November 16, 1952:

I had hoped to do a few drawings based on captions I have dug out of hell in the past two years, but I think the strain would be too much for me now. Maybe [Whitney] Darrow, who drew the picture for my "When you say you hate your species do you mean everybody?" could do this one about a long married middle-aged couple. The wife is saying, "You're always talking about how dark the future of Man is—well, what do you think I got to look forward to?" This is two years old in my head. I can't do anything now since my humor sounds like that of an assistant embalmer. . . .

The psychiatrists say that there is always as much relief as grief at the passing of any great or beloved figure [Ross], and the relief comes first. Maybe this explains the loose ratchets at the New Yorker, and I have no doubt, and every hope, that time will tighten them. . . . P.S. How about this? There is a double page spread of cows moving from left to right, and then another double page, and then another . . . , all moving from left to right. The right half of the third spread shows the leader of the cows, a defeated biblical king who is presenting the cattle to a victorious biblical king, as reparations after a long war. The defeated king is saying; "Oh, I thought you said payment in kine."

He and De Vries waged friendly duels, with puns the weapons. Thurber:

I wonder what became of the lawyer who opposed counsellor Elihu Root forty years ago in a court case in which Root represented the Budweiser breweries. Said the other lawyer, "It used to be Hires' root beer, and now it's beer hires Root. . . .

It took me two years to get over my paraphrase of "And may all your Christmases be white," which was "Edna May Oliver Christmas E. B. White." More complicated than O'Hara's "There's a soft Helen Hayes on the meadow." It's all a matter of sourness of the stomach—I come from Columbus, acidity in Ohio.

Ross hated puns [and] broke Frank Adams' heart by cutting out his "Red Budge [Don Budge, a tennis hero] of courage." In my "New Natural History" I failed to draw a mother grudge nursing her young, and was chagrined.

People usually worry about this disease [punning] when they are younger than you, or about its variants: a phrase that won't leave the mind, the meaninglessness of words like "spool" when repeated all night, and all the Freudian tricks that pop up in nightmares—one of mine was "as important as the 'r' in shirt". . . .

P.S. What are you going to do if Katinka answers the doorbell some morning, turns to you, and says, "It's the Board of Health. They have come for the body of your work". . . . The neighbors are complaining about the body of my work, too.

In 1952, De Vries collected his casuals in a book called *No, But I Saw the Movie*, the first book he was willing to list in the front matter of his later novels. "I started to do a novel with that title," he writes Thurber, "and the title crept into publishers' conversations and literary columns, and I've got sick of publishers asking whether they could see it." Represented by the Ann Watkins literary agency, he signed up with Little, Brown—the publisher he would remain with almost to the end. Thurber had offered to write a preface, but when De Vries gave him the opportunity to get out of it, Thurber took it:

One thing you over-looked about that preface is that I suggested it quite a while ago when you had published only a few pieces in the magazine, but now everybody knows and talks about your stuff, and I'm thinking of asking you to do a preface to my next book. You don't need any introduction now. . . . Under all the circumstances, I humbly take back my offer and apologize for it. I think the title is a good one, and Little, Brown are probably as good as any publishers, which coming from me is little praise, or maybe little brown praise.

Two years later, the pun competition was still going strong between them, Thurber writing:

I don't know how you got to the Cantharides, but the Spanish fly. . . .

I wonder if you have ever visited the Hormones, the Eumanides, and the Valkyries. I may write about my own voyages . . . to the West Undies, whose dreadful caste system produced the Unmentionables. It was settled by men of Middlesex, and I believe DiMaggio, the great center feeler, colonized the place in spite of the Monroe Doctrine of hands off. . . .

I have thought of a title for Katinka's memoirs: "For the Love of Pete."

He was, he said in another letter, planning a novel about extramarital goings-on among the top brass in an Army post, to be called "Officers' Mess." De Vries suggested they "pour new blood into that most difficult of all word forms, the palindrome"—a word, phrase, or sentence that reads the same from either end. His initial candidate: "deified."

Thurber shared with De Vries the restless developments of the play he was working on. De Vries offered occasional material in support of Thurber's frequent changes, along with encouragement. As it turned out, it was De Vries whom play producers had begun to court. By 1956, De Vries had written a play script, based on his *Comfort Me with Apples*, which he sent to Thurber. The producers holding the option were inclined to turn it over to tested playwrights. "You must insist that you collaborate on the play," Thurber writes De Vries. "Your touch is unique and nobody is going to get it right without your help." As to his own play, now called *The Welcoming Arms*, Thurber tells De Vries:

> I want to have my play make some sense about the predicament of the American writer, while at the same time basically dealing with two men and a woman and two younger men and a younger woman. The man of action against the man of sensibility and thought. I have always been up against this in my own life, not only with [Gus] Kuehner and then Ross, but with friends of old girls of mine."

The De Vries play opened on Broadway the next year. Thurber led the applause. De Vries, in turn, welcomed the start of Thurber's series on Ross, in the *Atlantic Monthly* in the fall of 1957:

> I'm glad to see the reminiscences of Ross commencing, at long last, and so auspiciously. Not only to have his memory transfused with the right man's mirth and love, but to be able to remind ourselves again that America's great contribution is not plastics but quarter-sawed oak. For one likes to think of Ross as belonging in that native homespun tradition that gave us Lincoln, Darrow, Sandburg, Frost.

In September 1960, tragedy struck the De Vries family; ten-year-old Emily died a cruel, lingering death from leukemia. De Vries and his wife—whose short stories were appearing in the *New Yorker*—dealt with their grief by writing about it, De Vries in his wrenching novel *The Blood of the Lamb*. An aging and ailing Thurber, who had but a year to live, was overwhelmed by the pity and sorrow he felt for his friend. He writes the De Vrieses:

> There aren't any words of comfort that don't sound tiny and trivial. Pete told me on the phone once that infinity isn't out there, but in our pocket, and . . . I kept thinking about it. . . .

You have to know that Helen and I have been in despair and hopelessness with you. There has not been a day or night that this wasn't
true. . . .

There is and will be no day or hour of our life that you cannot call on
us for anything whenever you feel that you want to. You are precious
and important [and] have our everlasting love.

The heartbreaking words in reply were typically De Vriesian, diminishing
the awfulness of the occasion through mental strength and perfected art:

Your words are of the kind that remind us that words are not necessary, that we are all side by side through all these things without it
having to be said. We needn't look far for the cue to courage. When
Emily no longer had any spine left she supported herself on her sternum.
We can do no less. We all have to climb out of the pit of desolation, or
what is more likely, manage to live in it, planting our flowers among the
ashes and squirting them with our gaiety. No less so because in the end
the universe spits on us. Or so it seems. I shall not now add to the
heaped up question marks of the world, but close by thanking you for
your love . . . in Emily's name.

Thurber had been unable to talk on the telephone to De Vries, during the
wasting away of Emily's young body, without breaking down. After Thurber's
death the next year, De Vries wrote: "The only time he complained was on
your behalf. Shortly before the end of his life, hearing of the tribulations of a
friend [De Vries], he shook his head and said, 'It's just too much to bear.' He
was never tempted to that conclusion by his own ordeals."

Small wonder that Helen, driven from the position that Thurber had
never fought with anybody, would regroup her arguments behind the fact
that "he never fought with Pete De Vries." It was as if she felt that the
relationship—mutually respectful, affectionate, lasting through seventeen
years—carried by itself the weight necessary to square Thurber's social account, and perhaps to win the argument after all.

58

That Great Quillow

The people fled from the streets, and behind the barred doors and shuttered windows of their houses they listened and trembled. The baker, the butcher, and the candymaker hid under their beds. They had prepared no meal for the giant and they were afraid for their lives. But the brave little toymaker, his white hair flowing like the dandelion clock in the morning wind, ran through the cobbled streets and across the green valley and stood at the giant's feet.

—from *The Great Quillow*

As Charles Holmes tells us in *The Clocks of Columbus*, Thurber's five fairy tales, *Many Moons* (1943), *The Great Quillow* (1944), *The White Deer* (1945), *The Thirteen Clocks* (1950), and *The Wonderful O* (1957), are really the same story, in which "the man of imagination and love," a lightly disguised Thurber, solves the problems by outwitting both the tyrants and the kingdom's wisest men. It isn't the man of action who prevails, but the court jester in *Many Moons*, the toymaker/storyteller in *The Great Quillow*, the sensitive brother in *The White Deer*, the minstrel in *The Thirteen Clocks*, the poet in *The Wonderful O*. If blindness had cut Thurber off from competing in the physical world, he would have his private triumphs in fantasy.

He had worked on *The Great Quillow* in Columbus, at Christmastime, 1943. While there, he visited the Strollers, the O.S.U. dramatic group Thurber and Althea had once been part of, which was planning to present *The Male Animal*. Thurber is pictured in a *Dispatch* story talking to the amateur thespians. Nugent, starring in *The Voice of the Turtle* on Broadway, now lived in Manhattan, and the two friends had provided an original skit for a Columbus radio program, "From the Army," associated with a local war-bond drive, according to the *Dispatch*. No record of it seems to have survived.

It was at his Manhattan apartment that Thurber finished *The Great Quillow*. He and Helen remained in the city through July 1944 ("Rosemary is with us now. She is almost 13, tall—5'4½"—and, I am told, beautiful") and vacationed with the Gudes at the Vineyard in August. In September, he and Helen attended the christening of Thurber's three-year-old goddaughter, Dinah Jane Williams, near Geneva, New York. Her mother, Jane Williams, was living there with her family, the Palmers, while Ronnie was on sea duty. During the Thurbers' visit, Thurber came down with lobar pneumonia. Two Navy doctors at the Sampson Naval Training Station, across Lake Seneca, answered the Palmers' appeal. The two officers, who were ferried across the lake, may have arrived intoxicated. One fell in the water while disembarking, and the other listened to Thurber's chest through a stethoscope, threw it aside and announced, "I never could hear anything through that goddam thing." Thurber came through, anyway.

Back in their rented house in Cornwall, Thurber thanked the Palmers and Janey, in his laborious scrawl, for their hospitality and care:

> Well, here I am again, home safe and unsound. We will never be able to express our love and gratitude to the Palmers, so I wont even try. It was the best time a pneumonia patient ever had. I feel stronger today—I could easily crack an English walnut. . . .
>
> The porter on our train finally showed up after I had dropped the big suitcase in the aisle and Helen had carried it the rest of the way. He was a very old man and asked us to call him at six. Seems he oversleeps.
>
> We were only 20 minutes late, owing to the engineer, who had belladonna in his eyes. The conductor was a pleasant little man who had never made this run before and had the feeling he was going backward.
>
> At Grand Central we could not get a cab but Helen told a redcap I had pneumonia. "Ah'll get yor father a cab right away," he said, and he did.
>
> The porter woke by himself, I forgot to say. "How are you, George?" he said. "Morning, boss," I said.

Nine days later he is writing more clinically to the Whites about his illness, knowing of their interest in medical matters:

The Navy doctors . . . who knocked out my 105 degree fever in 2 days with sulpha say it is the first time on record a godfather failed to rally after a baptism. . . . I had one 42-minute chill which outdid the earthquake, knocking plates off the plate rail downstairs. . . .

I was up in five days, and am better than ever. . . .

There will soon be enough [penicillin] for us all, and we will live to be 130, they say. In this way we will one day have 13 living ex-presidents. White will live to celebrate the 200th anniversary of the Monroe Doctrine—think of it.

The only thing to worry about is the Mok-Mok—a weapon which will be invented for the next war. Four Mok-Moks will destroy the U.S. Look out for the KM10 also and the horrible ZU58.

To be bumped off in Maine by something that lands in Michigan is not pleasant.

Zeeeeek!

BLONG!

The Zo-Zo 40 is absolutely silent in flight, but has a range of only 2500 miles.

See you soon

J. G16 Thurber

Thurber's prediction of a doomsday machine was made less than a year before the first atomic bomb was exploded.

The Whites, who operated as one when on the magazine, had yielded to Ross's plea to supplement his war-depleted staff. They returned from Maine in late 1943 and were living in an apartment that Daise Terry had found for them in the midst of a local housing shortage. Lest the magazine's favorable treatment be lost on them, Thurber handwrote the Whites on September 30, 1944 of the difficulty he and Helen had just experienced in getting an apartment at their previous address on East Fifty-seventh Street:

There has been a revolution in the housing economy of New York City. The lessee now pays the renting agents' fee. You must bring a four-leaf clover, a rabbit's foot, and your husband's birth certificate with you. An agent told Helen people offered as high as $300 bribe to be put at top of the list of apartment hunters. Building superintendents are now accepting bribes, too. We were lucky enough to get an apartment in the same building as last year, through the superintendent. We had tipped him last year with money and canned goods. It is almost impossible to get a phone, too. This is just to tip you off to the new housing economy.

Thurber no longer took White's physical ailments as anything but hypochondria. That summer he agreed to illustrate an article in *Harper's Magazine* —"Who Are You?" by Aldous Huxley—and used Huxley's subject to needle White, who had just written Thurber that he was beset by spells of dizziness and a buzzing in his head—perhaps suggested by a Thurber cartoon that had recently appeared in the *New Yorker* (Woman to two men: "Some people glow inside when they're happy, but I buzz."). Thurber to White:

> If you saw the Huxley piece in Harpers on Varieties of Human Physique, you know you are sitting pretty. I have read Sheldon's book [Sheldon, a social scientist, photographed college students nude for classification under a theory eventually discredited] and it's all about your tough . . . vitality. You are a cerebretonic ectomorph, a man of powerful testicles and firmly rooted hair, capable of orgasms of a pretty high order and equipped with a curious kind of zingless lasting power. You may be dizzy and weak and you may buzz but you will outlast the Lou Gehrigs who run past you up the stairs three at a time. Pale and teetering slightly, you will help carry the coffin of many a mesomorph and endomorph, like Christy Mathewson, Young Stribling, Red Grange, Sayre, and Coates.
>
> Most of the Rudolph Valentino types you know are as good as laid to rest now. Cheer up, man!

Thurber's prediction wasn't far off the mark. When White died in 1985, at age eighty-six, he had not only outlived Sayre and Coates by a good decade, but nearly all his professional contemporaries—Thurber by twenty-four years.

In 1949, a new employee at the *New Yorker* confided to White his intention to write a literary biography of Thurber and hoped that he could count on White, a friend of Thurber for more than two decades, for assistance. White's face took on a sad look. "Thurber and I are no longer the friends we used to be," he said. "He was so rude to my wife we had to pretty much stop seeing him socially."

When had the break occurred?

"I'd guess about 1944," White replied. It was the last thing the Thurber/White admirer wanted to hear that day.

With the Whites and Thurbers again living in Manhattan, the expected gestures had been made at getting together. The Whites were apprehensive, for it was known that, since Thurber's frustrating blindness, his frequent animosity toward friends' wives—women editors and women fiction writers, in particular—was floated to the surface by alcohol in an increasingly deadly manner. "He was rough on women when drinking," says Dr. Virgil Damon, Thurber's and Nugent's O.S.U. Phi Psi brother and the Park Avenue gynecologist for their wives. "Jim had a quick mind and could be vindictive. He was always the last to leave a party, in some cases because he'd driven all the other guests into leaving first. Jim thought I'd been taken in by the second woman I married. He had made up his own mind about her and had even written me warning me against marrying her. As it turned out, Jim was right.

"One night in the nineteen-forties, we were all at the Nugents' penthouse on East Ninetieth Street. Jim could hardly see by then, and my wife, a fluffy little thing, seated herself at his feet and told him how sorry she was about his poor eyesight. It was partly an act; at times she liked the center of the stage as much as Jim. It threw Jim into a rage. His voice was penetrating enough to stop all conversation in a room. He told her, 'Your husband works hard every day and you float around spending his money. You're nothing but a Park Avenue butterfly; a social climber.'

"It didn't bother me because by that time I was in agreement with Thurber, but it crushed my wife. Norma Nugent led her out of the room to a bedroom and told her, 'Pay no attention; this happens all the time.' Jim couldn't always remember what he'd done the night before, and when Helen told him what he'd said to my wife he was terribly embarrassed, because he knew it would cut us off socially for a time. He sent her an apology and a book, or maybe it was flowers. I've always wondered how many unhappily married men, as I was at the time, Jim secretly pleased by telling off their wives."

Thurber needed intelligent praise and respected recognition, but couldn't resist responding rudely to strangers, or people he didn't like, who behaved toward him in what he thought was a superficial, self-serving way. He was always sorry and showered his victims with apologies the next day. Often his diatribes were meant as insult humor, not to be taken too seriously. "One evening he picked on my wife," says one Cornwall weekender who attended a Thurber party. "It wasn't the first time, but it was always the kind of thing you could take seriously and resent or put in the best light and forget. That night we decided it just wasn't worth it, and we never accepted another of his invitations."

"When Thurber throws a party, it always hits someone," Helen would say. Rosemary believes that many of the women Thurber cut down had it coming to them. Men came in for their own raking over by Thurber, but argument among men at parties is expected and usually goes unnoticed. Rosemary's conclusions are based on "just watching him at parties and in a group," she says, and it seemed to her that when women were "overbearing, or feather-headed, or obnoxious," it angered him more than when men were. In part, she believes, it was because her father actually appreciated women and felt they could have done much more about the serious problems of our time. For example, she says, Thurber believed that if the human race were ever to stop preying upon itself, it would be the women who brought it about, given the centuries of failure on the part of men. So foolish and empty-headed talk from a woman made him feel more let down than that sort of talk from a man. He probably wasn't all that sure, himself, what his feelings were toward women, Rosemary adds. "Helen told me that when anyone asked him what he *really* thought of women, he would leave the room." Rosemary, however, wasn't a witness to many of her father's attacks on women. "He was always on his best behavior around me; he never scolded me for anything," she says.

Mark Van Doren had seen Thurber's rages at Cornwall parties: "He would be suddenly angry if a man he didn't like intentionally uttered a tired cliché to be funny. A laugh, he felt, ought to be honestly earned. Once when the party was at our house, a man tried to wisecrack with 'Some of my best friends are Jews.' Thurber got furious, picked up a chair and smashed it on the floor. He not only hated the cliché but felt it had taken on overtones of anti-Semitism. All-male men don't please us; we like some woman in them. All-female women don't please us; we like some male in them. There is also some of the child in us. In this case, Thurber was behaving as a real man. My wife, Dorothy, never took his attacks seriously and he liked that, as any first-rate humorist would.

"He had the tables turned on him one evening at the Cornwall Inn. A girl at our table told him off—said that he was preoccupied with himself and a bore. Thurber left and told Helen he never wanted to see that girl again. The next morning he called her and told her she was right, and that he didn't want her to be embarrassed by what she had said. I think he was consistently for love and truth. Most of us are vain folk who haven't the gift to be anything but our plain, unvarnished selves. Thurber's gaffes, his stumbling over himself, was out of a willingness to expose himself in a way the rest of us cannot."

No one knows why Thurber seemed least able to control his disdain when it came to women editors and women fiction writers. The editors, he seemed to feel, were biased arbiters, with whom he was growing out of favor; the authors were unworthy competitors, enjoying undeserved endorsement from the editors of their gender; both, he believed, were refashioning the literary scene so that male writers, especially those writing humor, would soon be unneeded. In "The Notebooks of James Thurber" he sketched out a story in which a middle-aged novelist named Julian learns that his wife has been selling short stories under a pseudonym.

> Julian sarcastically says [to her] no female writes without using 'it was as if' all the time. Real rift begins when he finds her hangout over garage and reads sheet in ivory-colored typewriter. Tells her at dinner she can't use sentence 'The wind ran scampering up the street like a laughing boy.' You've got to use either 'ran' or 'scampered.' Rift widens.

Katharine White, who developed mutually caring and treasured relationships with the women contributors she edited, was a logical, handy, and long-suffering target of Thurber's. She had made off with his beloved Andy White, breaking up an office relationship he cherished. Now that she was back as a fiction editor, he suspected her of being behind what he viewed as new and sterner judgments of his casuals and art, and their occasional rejections. The writer Jean Stafford remembers a supper party given her by her publisher, with Katharine and the Thurbers in attendance. (Andy, perhaps suspecting what might happen, had refused to attend.) "The only woman Thurber was meaner to that night than me was Katharine," says Stafford.

Yet if Andy White bore grudges, he apparently believed their expression had no place in his personal letters. Thurber supposed that others forgave and forgot as quickly and unequivocally as he did, and seems never to have suspected White's change of heart toward him. Certainly he could not have been given a clue in White's correspondence with him, which went on as before. In her old age, Katharine chose to cover her relationship with Thurber with a protective gloss, harking back to her days of divorcing Angell: "Jim was a dear friend in the early days," she writes, "and always a friend until he died. He was very kind to me (with a couple of exceptions when he was drunk) and he helped me greatly in many ways."

In 1944, on one of their few social get-togethers with the Thurbers, the Whites introduced them to Maria's restaurant, on East Fifty-second Street. Thurber liked the food, the manager, and his wife and promptly confiscated the place, according to Val Fanfoni, the manager. "He'd bring in two or three couples, and always closed up the restaurant," says Val. "The Nugents, the Gudes. Nugent would take him to the men's room and have to talk him out of doing the walls with drawings. He was one of our biggest boosters. He called Ted Patrick, editor of *Holiday,* and asked for an assignment to write us up. Nothing came of it. He and his table companions would talk politics and theater. Thurber liked fettucine and buttered egg noodles and veal kidney sautéed in wine. He'd start with a V.O. old-fashioned with a cherry, no other fruit. One night he had a disagreement at his table and insisted that I sit with him at another one. 'Those theater people,' he said to me. 'I can't stand them. Would you believe what they were just telling me?'

"Helen did a good job at keeping him under control. He never misbehaved in my place. He was nice, greeted in a lovely way strangers who wanted to meet him. He and Helen were here two or three times a week during the late forties. The only thing was, I was proud that the Whites liked my place, too, but once they realized Thurber had become a regular, they stopped coming."

Thurber's bout with pneumonia proved to be only in remission. When it recurred, he was confined for three weeks at Doctor's Hospital, Helen fearing for his life. Once Thurber recovered, with Bermuda inaccessible because of the war, they returned to the Homestead, in Hot Springs, Virginia. There, in late November, his appendix burst and peritonitis set in, his third major illness in three months. He was taken in an undertaker's hearse to the Chesapeake & Ohio Railroad Hospital at Clifton Forge, Virginia. The emergency operation was successful, and two weeks later he was back at the Homestead. But meanwhile Helen had been enduring a primitive commute between the Homestead and the hospital, writing the Herman Millers:

> We wanted you to know that Jamie is fine and they've taken him off that glucose & blood plasma diet, with no parsley or watercress to make it look pretty. . . .
> I've been commuting by a slow freight, half a day to go 33 miles, spend the night in a dreary hotel in the railroad yards . . . then half a day to get back. After my last trip, when one man got in with whooping cough & another locked himself in the men's can & had the screaming D.T.'s . . . I hired a guy to drive me over & back each day. The hell with expense—my sanity is worth something.

But there was considerable expense, and she wrote Ross asking for an advance against Thurber's "Our New Natural History" drawings, which hadn't been paid for. Ross replies:

> I got your note . . . I was slightly worried by the peritonitis version carried in the newspapers. The word from you was a great relief. . . .
> As to dough. Under our peculiar system we can't figure up finally the amount coming Jim on the Natural History series . . . but I am having

a check for $750 deposited to your account. . . . If that isn't enough dough—and it very well may not be—let me know and I will have the business office deposit any amount you can think of. Just get me a word.

When the money was not immediately forthcoming, Helen wrote him again, getting a response in Ross's own misspelled typewriting—perhaps a gesture of contrition:

I didn't break my neck. The way things are these days I either do a thing instantly or don't get it done for days or weeks, as it gets sidetracked. One hour's relaxation and my desk, couch, table, chair, and everything else is covered with papers.

Keep him down there until he can walk. Wheeling him through town might have a permanent effect on him. Also, he might get cold and wet. The weather is lousy here.

The day after his fiftieth birthday, December 9, 1944, still at the Homestead, Thurber wrote the Millers:

I had a great surgeon, an excellent hospital, and a little help from God & Mother Nature; my appendix was behind my SECUM, and this helped to localize the peritonitis. [A case of "Hide and Secum," he would wisecrack later.]

"Since the Lord wouldnt let me go blind either, I figure he has something in mind for me to do. . . .

My wound still drains after three weeks, but I'm okay and we go back tomorrow to 410 East 57th St. . . .

Have you seen the stories about France by Mary Mian in the New Yorker? I urged her to write when she was past forty with three daughters.

In a letter sent to both the Sayres and McNultys, he becomes the clown once more:

I had a swell time. It was my remarkable wife who took it on the chin, waiting all night in a dreary hotel for the news of general peritonitis.

When I got onto the operating table I told the docs I was in fine shape. When they [w]hisked off the hospital shirt, they must have wondered what it's like when I'm in bad shape. I was picked for a "breakdown" of the incision and 2 weeks more in bed, but the chief said my recuperation was "remarkable." He ought to see Mamma and Robert and the Uncle Jake who lost 9/10 of his insides and sold pamphlets about it for 35 years.

I told Dr. Emmett that my great-grandfather could lift a horse, and he said, "The effects of thes[e] hypos will wear off in a few days now". . . .

I left Garfield Jett an envelope of money [so] he probably won't show up for a week. One orderly named Daniel would take a swipe at my bottom from the floor grunting "Dah!" each time and nearly killed me. Sounded like Dick Peterson cutting at a high curve ball. Nettie Jane had to change me twice like a baby, orderlies being busy. Now I can take anything. . . . I heard a keystone comic shuffling along the corridor, breathing slow and hard. This ancient negro . . . said his name was Garfield. . . . Full name—Garfield Jett, no kin to the propulsion of the same name.

Next day I asked my day orderly, Charley, how come this Garfield. "My name is Garfield, too," said Charley, coolly. . . . Full name—Charles Garfield Thompson—no kin to Jett. He was born in 1881, the year Gar[f]ield was shot. Now when you know that my eye was removed in 1900 at the Garfield Hospital in Washington, you can see how I lay there and brooded. I just call everybody Garfield now. . . .

Some reporter called my nurse one morning and said, "Phone me the moment he dies. Don't monkey around the bed—get on the phone!" She hung up on him. Put me in mind of old Red Dolan on the phone badgering secretaries. . . .

P.S. I listened to Hildegard's program one night. Guest star: John Garfield.

The news of Thurber's near-fatal illness made the wire services, and answering telephone calls and mail from friends and concerned strangers kept Helen busy; there were as many as thirty calls and letters a night. They returned to New York in time for Christmas, where Thurber recuperated in the East Fifty-seventh Street apartment.

He had begun reviewing his past work for "an anthology of all my books," he had written Minnette Fritts in June. "I keep in only the stories and drawings I like best. I expect from now on to do things a little longer and I hope better. Maybe a play by myself or a novel."

The "anthology of all my books" would be *The Thurber Carnival*, one of his three all-time best-sellers. Its genesis began several years before. In early 1939, Eugene Saxton of Harper & Bros. assigned a reader, Marguerite Hoyle, to compile the best of Thurber's published pieces and drawings to present to Thurber as part of a proposal for the anthology. Then news that Hamish Hamilton was that year publishing a similar volume in London, *Cream of Thurber*, led Saxton to postpone his own project. Thurber's *The Last Flower* and *Fables for Our Time*, appearing in late 1939, meant that an anthology would put three of his books in competition with one another in the same calendar quarter. In 1940, Saxton resumed work on the anthology, intending a 1941 publication. He was aware that Thurber had not been too pleased with the way Harper had managed the publication of *The Last Flower* and *Fables for Our Time*, and hoped a successful anthology would even matters. He was unprepared for Thurber's letter of January 8, 1941. Encouraged by Bob Coates to change publishers, Thurber had scrawled his large words into a blunt letter that shocked Saxton:

I have decided to go over to Harcourt Brace and am signing contracts with them today. Since I am still unable to write or draw, I have to make changes of all kinds in order to keep my mind occupied. I shall probably shift from The New Yorker to Liberty.

In view of my very slow recovery [from the eye operations], it doesn't appear that I will have a book of any kind for *anybody*, for a long while yet. I should think, at any rate, that ten years of me would be enough for any one firm. I am just learning to dictate, but not learning very rapidly, so that letters of this kind are extremely difficult. I should like to talk to you and hope that you can drop around some afternoon. I leave Harpers [sic] with the very best of personal feelings. . . . I know that I can explain my shift to you in person better than in this way. Anyway, I should like to have a drink with you some afternoon.

Saxton replied, in a hurt but reasonable and gentlemanly fashion, that "I could have wished (that old Harper sentimentality and Victorianism cropping out again!) that eleven years of publishing together might have come to a finish with a talk and a drink before the fact, rather than behind it."

He didn't give up his plan for the anthology. In June 1943, Saxton, a dedicated professional to the end, ill, and dead before the month was out, gamely wrote Thurber that at a Harper sales conference it had been suggested that a book to be called *The Thurber Sampler* be added to the Autumn list. "The volume would be made up of material taken from earlier works and I enclose a suggested Table of Contents which I would like to have you look at and see if you don't think it holds some possibilities."

Thurber handwrote a reply five days later, one of the last letters Saxton received:

> Dear Gene:
>   I'd like nothing better than an omnibus of the old pieces and pictures, but this seems the worst possible year, since I have two books coming out this fall,—a Fairy Tale, and a book of drawings.
>   I'm afraid a third project would not work out so well. . . .
>   A week before he died Heywood Broun told me he wanted to see a Thurber anthology, and I began to think about it. Maybe the fall of 1944 would be all right—if the world goes on. . . .
>   I agree in the main with your choices, although you include a couple I am trying to forget, and leave out two or three I still rate high ("Something to Say," "The Greatest Man in the World," "The Black Magic of Barney Haller").

The Thurber Carnival, a fifteen-year retrospective of Thurber's best work, was published by Harper & Bros. in February 1945. It includes "The Pet Department" from *The Owl in the Attic*; a selection of cartoons from *The Seal in the Bedroom* and *Men, Women, and Dogs*; parts of *Fables for Our Time*, *My World—and Welcome to It* (including Mitty), *Let Your Mind Alone!*, *The Middle-Aged Man on the Flying Trapeze*; the entire *My Life and Hard Times*; and six stories not previously published in book form, among them the prizewinning "The Catbird Seat" and "The Cane in the Corridor." (Harper paid Harcourt Brace 1 percent of the book's retail receipts in exchange for material from their two Thurber volumes.)

More than any other of his books, the *Carnival* brought him his first international fame and set his star permanently in the firmament. Critics, struggling to justify their fascination with Thurber casuals and cartoons, managed a collective and lasting assessment of him as a master of American prose and art. His literary friends volunteered to review the book. They were spared the need to fudge their opinions, for it was a winner in every respect. William Rose Benét, in the *Saturday Review*, described it as "one of the absolutely essential books of our time." Malcolm Cowley praised the *Carnival* in the *New Republic*. Thurber wrote Cowley, thanking him and congratulating him on his review of a Gertrude Stein book, writing, "Last summer, Mark Van Doren brought Mortimer Adler to our house one evening and Adler was wonderful on the subject of Stein's visit with [John K.] Hutchens [a literary critic]. After 5 hours of conversation, mostly by Gertrude, and during which

[Alice] Toklas just sat listening, the ladies arose to go, and Alice said to Adler: 'Gertrude has said things tonight it will take her ten years to understand.' "

Dan Norton, in the *New York Times Book Review*, said of Thurber, "The man, or at least his work, is here to stay. . . . We can no longer be content simply to laugh at what he produces; we must make a determined effort to understand him as man and artist." Thomas Sugrue, in the *Herald Tribune*, wrote that the *Carnival* proved that Thurber was "a satirist and prophet, a Jeremiah in fool's cap," comparable to Ring Lardner as a master observer of the American culture. "There was always a certain amount of suspicion that the man was greater than he seemed, but it became fashionable not to explain him, not to interpret him, not to explore the meaning of his work. The fad was inspired, of course, by the people about whom he was writing, and, since one of them was himself, he helped the notion along."

Time believed that the Thurber Male could be compared to Joyce's Bloom and Mann's Hans Castorp. Ellen Saltonstall, a columnist for *The Constant Reader*, saw the book as proof that Thurber was unequivocally a misogynist:

> There isn't any doubt about it. James Thurber does not like women. To begin with, he doesn't trust them, and any possible allure they might have is to him just a snare and delusion. Whether he is writing about them or drawing them, he portrays them as selfish, driving, demanding and thoroughly unlovely. If you need any further proof of Thurber's antipathy toward the female of the species you need take only one quick glance at his men. They all have the furtive, haunted look, as if they were trying to run away from something. You don't need two guesses to figure out what, or rather, whom they are trying to escape.

But of those who wrote him praising the book, women outnumbered the men. To the letter of an exuberant female admirer in San Francisco, he replies: "My effect on many women is so slight as to leave them staring at my words or drawings with a look of blank disapproval, and I am always delighted to hear from some lady who has really enjoyed some of the small labors of this tired old mind."

It was White, as usual, writing in *PM*, never allowing personal feelings to condition his professional outlooks in such circumstances, who summarized the book and its author with an artistic completeness:

> The Carnival will stagger those who meet Thurber for the first time, and delight veteran Thurberists who own all his other books but who

need a convenient new arrangement. Years ago, when Thurber was a controversial figure in the literary scene, one of the criticisms leveled at him was that his canvas was too narrow. This book ought to take care of any survivors who might still be clinging to that leaky raft of thought. Here in the Carnival are mood pieces, reminiscences, social satires, fables, dilemmas, some of the best short stories in the language, by all odds the funniest and most extravagant family memoirs ever written, political and literary comment, parody, burlesque, Americana, fantasies, casual essays, portraits of people and animals, tributes, travelogues, illustrations of famous poems, cartoons, spots, picture sequences, and a lot more stuff so original or strange that they can't be classified.

The characters in Thurber's drawings are against the backdrop of the ages. They're without nationality. Some of them are without clothes. The canvas, in short, is as wide as the universe, as high as the sky, as deep as trouble.

Like most good clowns, Thurber writes short and draws quick. . . . The book contains . . . the picture of the woman speaking into the telephone, saying, "If I called the wrong number, why did you answer the phone?" I've been thinking about that particular Thurber situation for many years; it seems to me just as alive and as funny today as when I first saw the drawing. Certainly, for many American males, it will stand as the perfect tribute to the sweet unreasonableness of the feminine mind, as well as the last word on the miracle of telephonics. It is the funniest, the most haunting caption I ever read under any picture. . . .

[The book] does not contain The Last Flower, which is too bad, since that is one of the most moving of the Thurber series.

Most writers await their subject with a certain expectancy, or go around looking for it. Much humor is produced knowingly. Thurber, on the contrary, has never seemed to be on the watch for anything to write or draw but has always seemed tortured by unreleased material. . . .

Thurber's work might be neurotic were it not that he never isolates the nervous system from the circulatory system. . . . His characters and ideas are developed with sympathy, with love, with compassion. If his people were not lovable and universal, they would be insupportable. The childlike and absent-minded quality in his drawings, which give them distinction, is also the quality which would have been quickly lost if there had been any affectation in them.

Thurber is now almost blind, but blindness, instead of mellowing his character, and destroying his ability, has rendered him if anything more tempestuous than ever, and has improved his writing. He still draws pictures, not as easily as in the days when he could see but wasn't looking.

After Thurber has lived with an imaginary experience long enough, the experience becomes as real to him as though it had happened. In this he is like the moth in his fable—the one who had set his heart on a certain star. "He never did reach the star, but he went right on trying, night after night, and when he was a very, very old moth he began to think that he really had reached the star and he went around saying so. . . . Moral: Who flies afar from the sphere of our sorrow is here today and here tomorrow."

I suspect Jamie Thurber is going to be here tomorrow.

Carnival was a Book-of-the-Month Club selection—which emboldened Harper & Bros. to have fifty thousand copies ready for distribution to book-stores—followed by four editions over the next ten weeks. Thousands of readers discovered Thurber for the first time—and wondered where he had been. Wolcott Gibbs, writing in the *Book-of-the-Month Club News*, did his best to tell them:

He has a great many friends, almost all of whom vow at least once a year that they will never speak to him again, but all of whom do, usually the next day.

Physically he is tall . . . and very thin. His clothes, though dashing in color and design, fit him only whimsically. His hair, now almost entirely gray, has a way of hanging down over his eyes, which are obscured by very thick glasses. Altogether he looks very much like the pictures you've seen of the early James Joyce. None of this, I realize now, has anything to do with what Thurber's really like but it seems to be about the best I can do.

Though few of his new fans read the *New Yorker*, with its circulation of about one hundred and seventy thousand, Thurber didn't forget that the magazine had been the wellspring of his best-seller; he dedicated the book to Ross "with increasing admiration, wonder and affection." Nor did he forget who had thought of the anthology and, sadly, had not lived to see it published. Thurber writes in the Foreword: "Most of the books represented here were published under the supervision of the late Gene Saxton, and this anthology was his idea. I salute the memory of a good friend and a wise and kindly counsellor."

Carnival was on the best-seller lists for nearly a year, but it was the Armed

Services edition that led to Mitty clubs in the military and requests for Thurber drawings. Thurber's popularity soon spread beyond the contents of *Carnival* when readers consulted his earlier work. One *New Yorker* spot, published May 29, 1943, is of a big-eared dog smelling a flower with his eyes closed. Thurber writes Michael Zeamer, January 5, 1946, who was preparing an article on Thurber:

> For some reason or other, that spot drawing became a favorite with soldiers and I got so many requests for copies of it that I used to draw eight or ten dogs smelling flowers on a long sheet of paper, cut them out with scissors and send them to the boys. I must have shipped seventy-five of these in the past three years.

Soldiers and sailors wrote asking what his favorite books were. (One of his replies: *I Thought of Daisy*, by Edmund Wilson, *The Last Tycoon*, by Fitzgerald, and *Daisy Miller*, by Henry James.)

"I would be more than pleased to have The Carnival put into the Overseas Edition," he writes Ed Aswell, who had replaced Saxton as his editor at Harper. "In connection with the boys in the service, I would like to contribute a couple hundred copies of Carnival to the hospitals, but I don't know how to go about this. Maybe somebody at Harpers would know."

The *Carnival* brought to the depleted Thurber coffers even more money than had the royalties from *The Male Animal*. In the preface, Thurber had written of himself: "In the past ten years he has moved restlessly from one Connecticut town to another, hunting for the Great Good Place [a Jamesian phrase], which he conceives to be an old Colonial house, surrounded by elms and maples, equipped with all modern conveniences, and overlooking a valley." He and Helen must have already had their eye on the house they were soon able to buy with the *Carnival* royalties. It was in West Cornwall, up the mountain from the villages of Cornwall and Cornwall Bridge, still close to Rose Algrant, the Gannetts, Van Dorens, and others of his exurban literary clique. It was surrounded not by a hardwood forest but by cathedral pines, which a blind Thurber would never see but could sense and smell.

Ross, busy with his magazine, wrote Thurber about the proofs, layouts, and captions for "Our New Natural History," remembering to add: "I have been intending to write you a nice letter regarding the dedication in your book; and I will do this sooner or later. . . . Meantime, God bless you."

He did write a letter later, acknowledging *Carnival* briefly. The book seems to have reminded Ross that he had at times forgotten, or overlooked, Thurber's value to the magazine's past and present: "Looking over your latest book, as I do from time to time, I get to realize your full stature more fully and, also, I get to realizing that the full potentialities of some of your earlier series were never realized." It was always "back to business," for Ross. "Our New Natural History" was about to be serialized, and Ross, aware that Thurber's new success could distract him and that his contributions to The Magazine had slackened, did his best to keep him interested, writing:

> Have you any objection to our canvassing the office for more words to use as names of birds, beasts, and flowers in the Natural History series? This series is going to be a very funny one, though, and I would like to do everything possible to realize what I will term its full potentialities. There *must* be a lot of other words that will fit in and keep the series going for a considerably longer time. There is, of course, a book in this, as your publishers have already told you.

Income from the *Carnival* also resulted in 1944 and 1945 income-tax bills totaling seventy-four thousand dollars, which horrified Helen and drove her to a Madison Avenue tax accountant, Jules Englander, who remained their tax adviser.

In February 1940, in anticipation of his first eye operation and a possible future as invalid, Thurber had turned over all rights to, and benefits from, *Fables for Our Time* to Helen, and though she was behind his progressively sharp queries to Ross and to his publishers about money matters, he seems to have retaken charge of his finances, unless letters on the subject were composed by Helen for his signature. When, in early 1946, the question of publishing rights in England came up, a harassed Thurber writes Dorothy Fiske, of Harper's, in a tone he would often adopt when dealing with publishers:

> I am just recovering from a severe attack of pneumonia [it had been over a year] and one of the things I simply am not strong enough to handle is the recurring headache about who deals with what rights of mine in London. It comes as something of a surprise to me that your London office has ever handled any rights of mine since I have no recollection at all of ever arranging any deal through that office. Curtis Brown usually gets the requests and therefore has usually handled them. It all amounts in the long run to such small change that I feel I am losing by going through so much fuss and using up so much energy on something which sometimes appears to me to be more hopeless than the international situation. . . .
> I feel that if it were not for all the hours I put in on permissions I

would get three more books done and live five years longer. At the moment I just don't care what Curtis Brown or anybody else does about anything. . . . I will probably feel better about it in another month. . . .

Best wishes to you as always, and don't mind the fussiness of a convalescent.

Thurber's best-seller revived old correspondences and created new ones. Elmer Davis, the radio commentator he admired, recovering from an operation at the Naval Hospital in Bethesda, Maryland, tells him: "I have been reading the Thurber [Carnival]. Everytime I experience a belly laugh the gash in my abdominal wall reopens and I start bleeding again. I figure you have set back my recovery at least a week, but it was worth it."

George Grosz wrote to tell Thurber he was "one of the finest writers alive today." If Schopenhauer had been a poet and writer of short stories, Grosz said, he would have written "The Unicorn in the Garden," "a masterpiece." As to his drawings, Grosz says, "They once told me, when old man Matisse came down to New York to collect a huge fee from old sourpuss Barnes for a so called mural . . . reporters asked him who he thought was the best draftsman in USA. As the story goes . . . Henri answered, 'the only good artist you have in New York is a man named Thurber'. . . . and that goes for me too."

Two seniors at Smith College decided, on the basis of the *Carnival*, that Thurber was "the funniest man in the world" and that they would like to marry him, or, if he was married, his son. Thurber answers: "I always reply promptly to girls who want to marry me or my sons. Unhappily I do not see how our families can be joined since I am married and much too old—50— for you anyway. My only child is a daughter of 14. . . . No doubt the boys who want to marry her will never go to the trouble of writing me about it. I wish I had a couple of sons for you two girls but it's much too late to do anything about it now."

A heart-wrenching letter arrived from a newspaperman; he and his pregnant wife had found such delight in the *Carnival* that they had decided to name the baby after Thurber. Then, frightened and desperate, he writes Thurber:

My first child, James Thurber ___, is making a creditable fight for life at the age of three days. He was born prematurely. . . . He is receiving oxygen constantly and the odds are no better than even that he will survive.

I should have considered it fatuous to let you know that a baby had
been named for you, sincerely though the compliment was meant, except that Jimmy needs prayers now and his mother may be right in
believing that yours would have a special claim to be heard. Will you
consider the request?

As with the case of Emily De Vries, the vision of a child's life ending
prematurely was among the few things Thurber couldn't bear. Though the
outcome in this instance isn't known, and though Thurber had never submitted his many stout moral beliefs to the formal framework of religious doctrine,
one can be certain that, like Quillow the toymaker, he would have drawn
upon a substantial store of compassion and understanding to help another
sufferer to beseech a baffling and mysterious god for merciful mediation.

59

That White Deer

The Getzloes wired me:
>   You would get well quicker
>   If you had voted for Dewey & Bricker
I replied:
>   The world would be a whole lot sicker,
>   If I had voted for Dewey & Bricker.

> —Letter to the Herman Millers, November 16, 1944

A half-dozen years had passed since he had heard from his old O.S.U. love,
Minnette Fritts. She had written him in 1941, Thurber tells the Herman

Millers in 1943, and "I had waited a year after hearing from her before replying. She is now waiting a year herself. At this rate we'll be 70 before we exchange many letters. . . . I'll send her a querulous, middle-aged note, stomping my cane at her, too." She wrote him again, a long letter, in the spring of 1944, explaining that her son, David, would be in New York and that she hoped Thurber would see him. He replied in his semilegible scrawl:

> As bad luck would have it, I couldn't reach New York when David did. He phoned me at home, and at least I got to talk to him a little. . . . I got tickets to Elliott's play [The Voice of the Turtle] for him, possibly not the perfect play for a young man, but I thought he would like Elliott and it's the only play I can get tickets to, on short notice. As bad luck would have it again, Margaret Sullivan [sic] was out of the cast that night . . .

Along with a group of writers who had declared for Roosevelt, Thurber had met F.D.R. at a Hyde Park presidential campaign meeting in 1940. Though Thurber casually claimed to be a political independent, he had become, and would remain, a liberal Democrat. When Minnette teased him about it, in one of her letters, he replied a bit defensively: "I was born a Republican of a long line of Republicans on both sides. . . . I voted for Hoover in 1928 and I am a registered Republican voter in Connecticut as a result. I do not see how any person in his right mind could vote for Dewey."

After nearly twenty-five years apart, Thurber and Minnette met in New York on January 5, 1945. He had reserved a room for her at the Algonquin and arranged for tickets to *The Voice of the Turtle*, to meet the Nugents after the show, and for a matinee the next day. Helen, judiciously allowing Thurber to pursue an aging dream on his own, put Thurber in a cab for the restaurant where he was to meet Minnette. Minnette realized he was almost totally blind, took his arm, and helped him to a table. She hadn't brought her glasses and neither could read the menu. "I was very upset," says Minnette, "until this nice middle-aged waiter saw my dilemma and said, 'Madam, allow me.' And he took off his spectacles and handed them to me, and I was able to read the menu to Jim."

Thurber took her to the *New Yorker* offices afterward. Minnette was a subscriber and "was so excited about going to the office to see where the work was done. I was a little amazed when I found out it wasn't a plush office at all [but] very, very plain. I was dying to meet E. B. White, so we went into [his] office and Jim introduced me, saying, 'Here is the only girl I ever wrote poetry to.' I'd brought his poems with me, from 1920; Jim had them in his pocket

"All right, all right, all right. You're for Roosevelt. I don't go around trying to win you over to Dewey all the time, do I?"

and pulled them out, and handed them to White and I was afraid I'd lose them, and said, 'Oh, no, Jim. Don't let him read them.' I got them back."

But the bloom was off the rose for Thurber. When, a year later, Minnette invited Thurber to visit her in Seattle, to meet a producer in need of writers for a project of his, he replied somewhat stiffly:

> Because of my difficulty in getting around, and also because of the work I have laid out for this year, it would be useless for me to plan to go so far away, even for such high and interesting rewards. . . .
>
> If this letter sounds a little formal and awkward, it is because I am completely unused to writing to my special friends without a pencil in my hand.

On February 17, 1947, when she wrote to once more arrange a meeting between Thurber and her son, who was studying medicine at Temple University (they again missed one another), Thurber took a light swing at physicians, in another dictated letter, though he was doubtless aware that Minnette's husband was one:

I dislike hospitals so much that I constantly wonder how a man can bring himself to become a doctor. A young doctor in Virginia told me that he hated to go home for lunch because "something wonderful" might happen at the hospital. By this he meant some lovely accident or some beautiful disease. It is a comfort to know that doctors usually make very bad patients. I was in Doctor's Hospital a year ago today, and in the room next to mine a patient recovering from a gall bladder operation sent his nurse from the room for cracked ice and jumped out the window. He was a forty-year-old doctor. The man in the room on the other side of me died of a heart attack, but as usual I got up and dressed and went home. . . .

Do you have any hope that Bricker will be nominated [as the 1948 Republican presidential candidate]? You may sleep in the White House yet, but it will be without my vote, if Bricker is the candidate.

In the spring of 1948, Minnette caught up with him again in New York, on her way to Europe. The reunion seems to have further corrupted Thurber's youthful memories of her, abetted by observations that, of necessity, were Helen's. Writing Katharine White an apology for being unable to visit her in the hospital, Thurber adds:

I took [Minnette] in to see Andy. . . . Three years ago he met her when she was wearing white overshoes in 21 because of the danger to life and limb in a blackout that no longer existed. In college I mysteriously identified her with one of Henry James's worldly and intelligent women, which gives you some idea of my perspicacity about the opposite sex in those days. She has managed somehow in the intervening years to unhook her own intelligence like a telephone receiver. Her transmitter works but the connection is bad. "Do you mind if I talk about my baby?" she asked Helen who wanted to know how old the child was. "She will be twenty-six in June," said Minnette. Letters I wrote her thirty years ago she has still preserved, it turns out, and they are done up in a packet marked "For Sally," the twenty-six-year-old infant who is supposed to read them after her mother is dead. This is the kind of thing that happens to me. . . . You will get some idea of the innocent contents [of the letters] when I tell you that before I was engaged to Althea I once presented [Althea] in the presence of her mother with a prize I had won for winning the horseshoe pitching contest at a Fourth of July picnic. "You and your mother may have some use for these," I said. "They are a dozen sanitary napkins." I was shocked when her mother clutched at her heart and staggered. I thought the things were for picnics, of course. I was going on twenty-seven at the time.

But a sentimental Thurber found it difficult to retire permanently the residue of what once had mattered to him romantically. Though he was four months late in answering a letter she wrote to him in June 1951, he reminded her that the delay was in "impolite disregard" of a woman who had once given him a lock of her hair. "The last such lock I got," he writes, "was from Eve Prout when we were both in the sixth grade, and it shocked and dismayed me. At that time I knew nothing about the etiquette of tresses, but I did carry a watch whose back opened, and I kept the lock for six weeks. I still have yours [unlikely]. I lost track of Eve ten years ago, but she is in Miami somewhere, and her hair is probably grayer than a badger's, for she will be fifty-seven a week from today."

Minnette says that Thurber sent her copies of his books after that, but there is no indication of any other communication between them. For Thurber there were occasional local peccadilloes and flirtations, but his Jamesian dream girls of the past were gone; there would remain only the lovely illusion of Jane Williams to adore, as she had looked when he could last see her.

In 1945, the beloved Robert Benchley died in New York City. Thurber and a number of other master humorists, fortunate to be around in an era so hospitable to their kind, regarded Benchley as the pioneering standard-bearer of their art. Wolcott Gibbs, writing in the New York Times, said of this departed hero: "I can't honestly say that he made me laugh more than any other humorist writing in his time—some of Thurber's maniacal experiences in Columbus, Ohio, still seem to me incomparable as examples of comic genius operating in what must have been an extremely favorable environment—but I think he was, by far, the most brilliant and consistent of the school, originating with Leacock."

Benchley had been finding writing humor harder and harder by the time Thurber had begun to hit his full stride. The ideas he came up with didn't seem worth exploiting, or reminded him of something he had written in 1921, according to his son, Nathaniel: "It occurred to him that very few humorists remained funny much beyond the age of fifty, and he resolved to quit while he was still ahead. In December of 1943, at age fifty-four, he announced that he was through with writing and resigned to being a radio and movie comedian." But Benchley never forgave himself for having forsaken his writing for Hollywood, and managed to drink himself to death by age fifty-six. (The screenwriter Herman Mankiewicz had led the exodus from New York to Hollywood, cabling his colleague Ben Hecht: "There are millions to be grabbed out here and your only competition is idiots. Don't let this get around.")

Benchley's idol had been George Ade, who was of the previous generation of literary humorists, but had died only the year before. "The night Ade's death was announced," writes Nathaniel Benchley, "Benchley got out of bed and went on the town. 'When a great humorist dies,' he said, 'everybody should go to a place where there is laughter, and drink to his memory until the lights go out.' "

Jock Whitney obligingly held a wake for Benchley upstairs at "21," where Benchley's New York friends commiserated and drank to his memory. (A plaque is still over his favorite table there; it reads, "Robert Benchley, His Corner, 1889–1945.") At a similar wake at Romanoff's, in Beverly Hills, Dorothy Parker, Marc Connelly, Donald Ogden Stewart, his first wife, Bea Stewart Tolstoy, and other survivors of what Groucho Marx called "that intellectual slaughter house" (the Algonquin Round Table) telephoned the "21" contingent to tell funny stories about Benchley through the tears. "Who will listen to our troubles now?" Frank Sullivan remembers Thurber asking at "21" that evening. Thurber took a West Coast call from Bea Tolstoy. "Jim didn't get her name and gave the phone to me," says Sullivan. "Afterwards, he asked, 'Who was that?' When I told him it was Bea Tolstoy, Thurber said, 'I suppose the next woman out there to call will be Betty Lou Dostoyevsky.' "

The Great Good Place in West Cornwall, a fourteen-room white colonial, "was very ordinary," writes Helen, "shabby, furnished with odds and ends left from the previous owners, scraps from my mother's old house, and a few miscellaneous items we'd picked up for our badly furnished [rented] house in the village [Cornwall]. The bathroom[s] had old clawfoot tubs and very bad plumbing. . . . Slowly and gradually through the sixteen years (1945–1961) my husband and I lived there we improved it." With the *Carnival* royalties, the improvements began at once, and the Thurbers bought a new Cadillac as well.

A violent crime, rare in those peaceful parts and one that was never solved, touched on the Thurbers. A Cornwall widow named Harriet "Hat" Higginson, who was a friend of the Thurbers, was so savagely bludgeoned that she spent the next twenty-five years in a nursing home, where she died. The Thurbers' chauffeur had joined the military service and no replacement could be found, so the Cadillac had been stored. "So I called Hat [one] morning about [driving me on] a shopping trip to Torrington," says Helen. "One of her young sons said she was lying on the floor. We got Mrs. Frost [a friend] to drive [Thurber and me] over, where we discovered the body, called the police and Dr. Walker."

A few Thurber books and drawings, inscribed by him to Mrs. Higginson, were found in the house by the state police, and because the Thurbers were among the first adults to find the injured woman, the police notified them that they would be questioned. Thurber expected the worst, or said he did.

"Helen said our best alibi was that I was blind," says Thurber, "and for god's sake, when the police arrived, not to go running around the house the way I do, leading people to think I have 20-20 vision. 'If you're upstairs when they come, *grope* your way down,' she told me. I tend to come downstairs fast, because I know the house so well. She said I should tell her when I wanted to get out of my chair and she'd pretend to lead me. We talked about what we could be doing when the police got there. I said I could be dictating a letter to Helen, but Helen said we'd be too nervous to be making any sense and what she wrote down might be held against us.

"When they arrived, one trooper said to Helen he assumed she'd driven us to the Higginson house. Helen said no, she didn't drive. The cop looked at me and said, 'Jesus, you let this blind guy drive you?' Helen said no, neither of us drove; we used to have a chauffeur but he'd gone off to the war, so we weren't using the car. Later, he checked that story with the local garageman in Cornwall, where the car was stored.

"And sure enough, I forgot everything we'd agreed on. I'd light a cigarette, flick the ash in the ashtray without missing, excuse myself to go to the bathroom and leap out of the room. The trooper wouldn't believe I was blind. 'You're looking right at me when you talk,' he said to me. 'How did you know your cigarettes were in that spot and where that ashtray was? And when to step over the dog lying there?' I told him I was acting on conditioned reflexes —the doctors call it 'accommodation'; that blindness somehow seems to transfer greater sensitivities to the other senses; nature's way of compensating. The officer tried to write this in his report but gave up and went away. They still haven't solved the case. We think the butler did it—the houseboy, really."

Thurber agreed that year to write the preface to a volume of Mary Petty drawings, and suggested the title, *This Petty Pace*, from *Macbeth* ("Tomorrow, and tomorrow, and tomorrow, creeps in this petty pace from day to day"). Much of Thurber's preface was a précis of the *New Yorker*'s beginning, which would turn up, in anecdotal mode, in *The Years with Ross*. His emphasis here is on Talk of the Town:

Into the midst of this carnival sauntered the young *New Yorker*, uneasy and a little bewildered, in spite of its jaunty strut and eager eye. The
new magazine reflected the reckless detachment of the period. It wore
no armor and it sought no grail; it did not carry a sword cane or even an
umbrella. Since neither trumpet nor banner had called it into existence,
it was not going anywhere to do anything about anything. It was just
walking along, like any other visitor from out of town, looking into the
expensive store windows, gazing up at the tall buildings, widening its
eyes and dropping its jaw at impressive statistics or unusual facts. The
amiable periodical tiptoed away from disputes and disturbances, since it
had nothing particular in mind to prove or disprove, to attack or defend.
Now and then it jostled the celebrated, or thumbed its nose at the
powerful, but all in a spirit of gay mockery. The New Yorker was not
really angry. It just didn't give a good goddam.

If there was little in the preface about the reclusive Mary Petty, it was
because there was little Thurber knew about her:

The biographer who attempts an extended study of this charming but
reticent lady has my sympathy. I can put down in no time at all the few
facts I have been permitted to glean. Mary Petty was born in a brownstone house on West End Avenue. Her father was a professor. She did
not have a particularly happy childhood. That's all, brother.

Joel Sayre, who was by then reporting the war in Germany, asked Thurber
to write a preface to *his* book that year, a collection of his wartime Persian
Gulf reports, which had first run as a series in the *New Yorker*. Sayre's *Persian
Gulf Command* describes the mighty logistical challenge of getting war maté-
riel to the Russians through Iran. Thurber was enthusiastic about the way
Sayre observed and wrote about it. Ross kidded Thurber in a letter about
writing book prefaces for two *New Yorker* contributors in one year: "We have
up the Christmas list of books by New Yorker authors and you have written a
foreword for practically all of them. We are meeting this situation with a
touch of wit."

Whether feeling newly empowered by the *Carnival*'s success or going
through postpublication Thurbs, Thurber had begun writing complaining letters to Ross. One of his large drawings had been trimmed too much, he felt,
and he suspected the magazine of lacking respect for his work. Ross replies:

I'm sorry that that drawing was cut as much as it was. I do not think it is
too small for framing. . . . As for the caption being pasted on it, that, I

am assured, is of no consequence. Rubber paste was used and the paper is supposed to be readily detachable. I have not attempted to tear it off myself, however. The engravers notified us that they could not handle the large sheets of paper that your drawings were on, and I told Peppe [Carmine Peppe, head of the makeup department] that he might trim them. . . . The truth is that I thought Miss Terry would guard and protect these drawings from start to finish, she being ever vigilent [sic] about art in general and you in particular. . . . A large part of her duties are [sic] to look after people like you around here.

I have never heard anyone in authority around here disparage your art. I have never heard anyone say, ever, "There are drawings and those things Thurber does."

Ross, in fact, had never been more supportive of Thurber, using his influential friends to try to sell Thurber's work. He suggested Walter Mitty to Rodgers and Hammerstein as a musical, writing Rodgers that Nunnally Johnson wanted the story as a movie, starring Jack Benny. Ross sent a copy to Thurber:

Dear Richard:

. . . by a coincidence, I happened to see Jack Benny the other night and I asked him about [the Mitty story]. He was very vague about the whole thing. He had been given the story to read, but apparently had got bewildered by it. I gathered that this might be due to overwork. In the course of the conversation, Benny said that he wanted to do a New York show, and it occurs to me now that you, Hammerstein, Benny, and Thurber could all get together. . . . You could do the show and then sell it to the movies afterward, and everybody would be intensely happy. . . .

I don't know whether you fellows would be interested in a story that has already been done in the movies. I shouldn't think it would matter, for, from my viewpoint, most stuff that goes into the movies might as well go into the wastebasket as far as the great public is concerned.

I am referring this whole business to Thurber, for it is getting beyond my depth. I only crashed into this business as a fan of the story and as an admirer of you and Hammerstein. I have always thought it had great stage and screen possibilities.

Though Helen insisted that Thurber acted as his own agent and negotiator, she was keeper of the household books, kept Thurber apprised of their finances, and raised no objections to Thurber's letters of complaints to Ross about *New Yorker* payments. In *The Years with Ross*, Thurber believes Ross conceded his own unfairness to his writers in a March 23, 1945, letter that Ross wrote to him: "What I can't do is say to publishers that they are robbing authors, because I am not an author, and they can come right back at me and say I am robbing authors, too, or am a party to robbing them. It is true, at least, that I have been a party to robbing them, for I unquestionably sat around this joint for years and didn't see that authors were done right by."

Thurber seems to take credit for a Ross conversion here, for he writes, "He began seeing that they were done right by from then on, and bonus money flowed like water. There was no system to these bursts of generosity, and some old-timers were inadvertently left out of it."

Katharine White, who regarded Thurber's book as treasonable and despicable, insists that Ross was merely "mollifying" a disturbed Thurber. What Ross meant, she says, is that he should have resigned if he couldn't get his writers better pay. Ross tried, says Katharine, to make up to Thurber, White, Gibbs, Benchley, and others the poor pay of the early years.

Thurber also quotes Ross as having told him, "Goddam it, I want writers to get paid well. It isn't my dough, it's Fleischmann's. But if you pay a writer too well, he loses the incentive to write." Katharine has an answer to that, too: Ross paid all he could, fought Fleischmann to get more, and underpaying writers to stimulate their creativity was a regular joke of Ross's.

In a sense, Thurber does take out of context Ross's March letter. Ross, at the time, was upset not by how the magazine paid his contributors but by his belief that publishers and reprint magazines were shortchanging them. E. B. White had recently learned that the *Reader's Digest* was planting in other magazines articles that reflected the political and economic conservatism of its cofounders, DeWitt and Lila Wallace. These articles, authorized and paid for by the *Digest,* were offered free to magazines of small circulation and tight budgets. The bribe was not only the donated copy but the knowledge that the magazine's title would be listed on the cover of the mighty *Digest,* with its millions of readers, when the *Digest* condensed and reprinted the renegade article. White had exposed the practice in Notes and Comment. Ross, who had always disliked what *Digest* condensations had done to *New Yorker* copy in the first place, was so incensed by what White had learned that he assigned a young writer, John Bainbridge, to do a five-part Profile on Wallace and elaborate in damning detail on the *Digest's* misleading and unethical practice.

For years, the *Digest* had reprinted *New Yorker* Talk items, cartoons, casuals, and articles in cut-and-pasted form. The practice began about 1930, when Wolcott Gibbs, then an assistant to Katharine White, had inexplicably been sent to the reception room to deal with a tall stranger named DeWitt Wallace, who asked if he could reprint condensed Talk stories free. Gibbs, not aware that the *Digest* was already a fast-growing cash cow for the Wallaces, gave DeWitt permission "just because he struck me as such a pathetic hick."

Moved by conscience, apparently, by 1936 Wallace was paying the *New Yorker* eighteen hundred dollars a year for reprint rights to a selection of its cartoons, Talk stories, and articles. Ik Shuman, the magazine's first executive editor, learned that Wallace was paying the Crowell, Hearst, and Curtis publishing companies twenty thousand dollars each for first reprint rights. Ross was incensed at the news, realizing—he hadn't thought about it before—that the *Digest* was using the *New Yorker*'s own material to compete against it on the newsstands. At Shuman's request, Wallace stopped by the office and cheerfully agreed to pay the magazine the *Digest* rate of five hundred dollars a page, with a guaranteed minimum of fourteen thousand five hundred a year, for first reprint rights. When Shuman asked about the years of underpayment, Wallace offered fifteen thousand for the previous two years. "I'd have paid the *New Yorker* more," he told Shuman, "but nobody seemed interested in talking to me. This is the first time I've ever been beyond the reception room. I've always dealt with a young lady [Daise Terry] in the hall." Wallace asked Shuman if he could meet Ross someday. Ross's response: sure, he'd like "to meet the man I'm working for, but, goddam it, I'll have to read a copy of his magazine; I've never seen it." When Ross did arrange to meet Wallace at the Ritz, he asked him, "Well, boss, are we working hard enough for you?"

In a legitimate reprint transaction, the *Digest* would pay a given amount to the originating magazine to reprint one of its articles, with only a few token dollars to the writer, who had been paid by the parent publication. But Ross had insisted that the *Digest* money paid to the *New Yorker* go directly and entirely to the writers whose material was being reprinted. When he heard of Wallace's covert planting of articles, however, Ross called some of his writers together and asked if they would join him in boycotting the *Digest*. Only Thurber and Cornelia Otis Skinner refused. "The *Digest* pays me five times more for a reprint than the *New Yorker* pays me for the original," Thurber protested. When, in 1948, Thurber wanted to sell reprint rights to certain of his pieces to the *Digest*, A. J. Liebling recalls, Ross, who "had made a hard rule against *Digest* sales, made an exception for Thurber because, he said, Jim was a sick old man and needed the money. Ross was several years Thurber's senior."

Katharine White says that Ross was bothered not only by the way *Digest* condensations were ruining good writing but by its efforts to control the press. *Harper's*, which was receiving twelve thousand dollars a year from the *Digest,* was what Wallace wanted to make it, Katharine explains; ditto the *Atlantic*. "It was a big corporation getting its tentacles into little ones and ruining the independence and freedom of the press," she says. Soon after the Bainbridge series appeared in the *New Yorker*, the *Digest* quit the practice of planting articles elsewhere to be condensed. (Today, only half its content is of condensed pieces; the rest consists of original articles by freelancers and the *Digest*'s own "roving editors.")

When Ross wrote the March 23 letter quoted by Thurber, he was still on a crusade against all reprint magazines. Thurber passed on to Ross a query from Ed Aswell, of Harper & Bros., regarding a request from *Omnibook* to reprint parts of *The Thurber Carnival*. Ross replied vehemently:

> I am now completely bewildered by these digest and reprint magazines. . . . There was a day, and I remember it, by God, when a magazine printed a piece and that was that; there wasn't a whole sky full of vulture magazines ready to pounce. It has got to a point where the greatest initiative shown in American publishing is in behalf of finding a story to be reprinted. Holy Jesus. Nobody can tell me that these magazines are not the enemies of the magazines that are stodgy and old-fashioned enough to go in for original publication. They sell on the same news-stands, side by side, and that is competition, and also they are likely to be better in their literary value, issue for issue, for they have a selection of all stuff written for all time, whereas poor bastards getting out a magazine like The New Yorker have to run what's written that week.

Thurber quoted Ross's paragraph to Ed Aswell, adding that "I'm a son of a bitch if I don't agree with Ross, by God and by Jesus. I have never believed, furthermore, in the publisher's right to the 50 percent they take out of all reprint money." He sent a copy of the letter to Ross, who blanched at Thurber's use of him as a cat's paw, writing Thurber:

> I am a little terrified by your letter . . . to your publishers after reading the duplicate you sent me. I have a vague feeling that I'm getting beyond my depth, and I shrink from being made the spearhead of the effort to overcome all the evils of the publishing business. I'm not in a good position to do this. It ought to be done by the writers themselves. I could be enormously helpful to a bunch of writers who would get

together and do something, God Knows, but I'm not a writer, and sooner or later I'm going to get called for being in the wrong swimming hole.

It was in this context, in the belief that he could have done more for writers regarding serial rights, that Ross wrote what Thurber quoted in *The Years with Ross*. Katharine's guess that it had nothing to do with *New Yorker* payments was probably correct.

Thurber had started his next book in the East Fifty-seventh Street apartment, writing the Herman Millers:

> My new fantasy, or whatever, which runs to 15,000 words is called "The White Deer" and is a new version of the old fairy tale of the deer which, chased by a king and his three sons, is transformed into a princess. Suppose, I said, that it was a real deer which had saved a wizard's life and was given the power of assuming the form of a princess? Most fun I have ever had. I even go in for verse now and then, such as,
> When all is dark within the house,
> Who knows the monster from the mouse?

Thurber's King Clode is against hunting deer in an enchanted forest, for the deer there too often turn into tiresome princesses who set difficult tasks for the king's sons in a competition for the princesses' hand, and who must then be returned to the kingdoms of their fathers, who always serve the rescuers inferior wine. Clode himself had wedded such a princess, now dead. She was pretty enough, he said, but she had "a way of fluttering up behind a man before he knew it."

In *The White Deer*, Thurber is back to turning linguistic handsprings. The sentences often contain alliteration ("this false flux of fact and form"). There seem greater splashes of color in his descriptions than before his personal world went dark. Reading the book, one thinks of a feature-length Disney animation, in shimmering hues, of a Lewis Carroll wonderland.

Ross's idiosyncracies turn up. When a comet is reported to have just missed the earth, Clode says, "They aim these things at me," and elsewhere proclaims, "done and done," a Rossism. Clode's insulting references to his royal assistants could be Ross denigrating the men he had hired and turned against.

The ghost of Thurber's Aunt Margery Albright haunts the pages. The king orders the royal Recorder to "stop your whinkering," an Albright expression. Aunt Margery warned that promiscuous men would sooner or later come down with "the blue boars." Here, Prince Thag must overcome a monster called the great Blue Boar. There are shreds of Thurber's favorite popular songs: One prince is given directions to "Turn to the right and follow a little white light." The Mok-Mok, the destructive weapon Thurber had warned the Whites against, is a monster who must be dispatched by one of the princes. Jorn, the sensitive and poetic son, is, of course, chosen by the princess.

Thurber's enjoyment is obvious. Since his blindness, he had been writing more and more for his own amusement than for others'. One lifestyle had ended for him, and he was using fantasy in charming and proprietary ways to work out his salvation. His interpretations of the world had often come to him through his ears anyway, which is how he became a mimic. The resumption of his vivid production after his blindness had awaited only his emotional acceptance of what had happened to him. The transformation is noted by an admiring White, to whom Thurber sent a prepublication copy of *The White Deer*. White sends him a rare handwritten note:

> It is not only a wonderful book but it is Exhibit A in the strange case of a writer's switch from eye work to ear work. I can't believe that anybody could make such a switch and live. The King is a magnificently funny character, I think, and ought to last forever—which is more than you can say for Ross. . . .
>
> One thing that tickled me was that your drawings in the Deer came out so well. It is very funny to have them in juxtaposition with the color pages of [the illustrator Don] Freeman and to see how all the colors of the spectrum turn pale alongside Thurber's wispy grey genius.

As if to mock his fairy tale's predictable ending, Thurber wrote "The Princess and the Tin Box" for the *New Yorker* a few weeks before *The White Deer* was published. In it, four suitors offer a princess elaborate gifts, including "a great jewel box made of platinum and sapphires. . . . The fifth prince was the strongest and handsomest of all the five suitors, but he was the son of a poor king whose realm had been overrun by mice and locusts and wizards and mining engineers. He came plodding up to the palace of the princess on a plow horse and he brought her a small tin box filled with mica and feldspar and hornblende." The princess selects the present she likes the most—the platinum-and-sapphire jewel box.

"Moral: All those who thought the princess was going to select the tin box . . . will kindly stay after class and write one hundred times on the blackboard, 'I would rather have a hunk of aluminum silicate than a diamond necklace.' "

Betting on momentum from the *Carnival*, Harcourt Brace printed thirty-five thousand copies of *The White Deer*, which Thurber dedicated to the three Sayres: Gertrude, Joel, and Nora. (The princess's name is Rosanore, a loving fusion of Rosemary and Nora.) Another printing soon followed. Don Freeman's three lushly painted illustrations are at the book's center. There are more than forty pencil drawings by Thurber; they were done "at the suggestion of the publishers about three days before they had to be sent to the engravers," Thurber writes the Millers. "They were all done in one afternoon and evening."

Though a fairy tale, *The White Deer* drew considerable and serious critical attention. The critique that mattered most to Thurber, of course, was in the *New Yorker*; it was written by the eminent Edmund Wilson, who replaced Clifton Fadiman as *New Yorker* book reviewer at the beginning of 1944. ("There will be more fun and confusion in these illiterate halls," Thurber wrote De Vries with the news of Wilson's arrival.)

Wilson discusses the *Deer* along with *Many Moons* and *The Great Quillow*, finding them "a phase in [Thurber's] rapid elimination of the last vestiges of the conventional humorist, and his emergence as a comic artist of the top layer of our contemporary writing." Wilson felt the fairy tales to be "the best things of their kind since Frank Stockton's, which in certain respects they resemble. Thurber . . . like Stockton, takes the characters and properties of the traditional fairy tales and by introducing at moments, unobtrusively, a contemporary point of view, makes them produce unexpected results." But "Thurber is more poetic, wittier and more unpredictable" than Stockton.

Then Wilson got into trouble with Thurber by daring to find fault. The *Deer* fell short of being one of the best things Thurber had written, or one of the best modern fairy tales, because the narrative "gets a little cluttered and the style sometimes runs off the track." Furthermore, "blank verse should not, as it occasionally is, be allowed to get into the prose of the narrative."

Wilson's conclusion, that *The White Deer* "has the essence of poetry and it ought to be read in preference to almost any best-selling novel," did not mollify Thurber. Another author would have happily settled for this endorsement by a prominent man of letters, but although his correspondence with Wilson continued in a friendly enough way, Thurber didn't forgive him for some time. Three years later, he was reminding a student author of a thesis that credited Wilson with a Freudian interpretation of James's "The Turn of the Screw," pointing out that Wilson had borrowed—albeit with a credit—

the idea from another author. The student, not knowing of Thurber's resentment toward Wilson, found it bizarre—and uncharacteristic—that Thurber would quibble over a footnote point.

In 1956, Thurber was chiding Hamish Hamilton, his London publisher, who was reissuing *The White Deer*, for listing it in his catalog under "For younger children": "Among these younger children we must therefore count Edmund Wilson, W. H. Auden and Elizabeth Bowen. I wrote only two books for young children, *Many Moons* and *The Great Quillow*. Wilson, he went on, "liked the first third" of the *Deer*—Wilson liked much more than the first third—and later "told me, in surprise, that Auden liked all of it and thought [Wilson's] review was wrong. 'Well I wonder what's the matter with him!' I exclaimed."

At fifty-one, Thurber, who had been concerned with age for twenty-five years and more, found himself still endowed with the aura of celebrity that attracts women. There was another chance to learn about himself, as a middle-aged man, and he indulged himself in a mild and short-lived summer affair with a book publisher's wife. It was an embarrassment to Sayre, who was talked into acting as a mail drop by Thurber, and who later wondered why. "I had never before driven a blind man to an assignation," he says. "It was messy. The woman had a husband, and Helen, who knew what it took to get a blind, romantic, drinking Thurber through an evening, was more worried about his physical well-being than losing him to another woman. There was one evening when I drove and Thurber sat in the backseat with his lady love, singing "These precious days I'll spend with you" from "September Song," and Helen sat in the front seat to make sure he got home all right. I don't know how it all came out. I got out of it right after that."

In November of 1945 they were back at the Homestead, in Virginia, and in January they went to Columbus for a delayed celebration of Mame's eightieth birthday, which Thurber held at the Deshler-Wallick Hotel. He had told Mame to make a list of the guests she wanted. Mame came up with nearly a hundred and fifty names. Thurber, with Robert's help, cut the list to fifty-five relatives and close friends. "Mame was equal to the hundred and fifty, but we weren't," Thurber told a reporter. "Five years ago, she visited us in New York. We kept her up at a night club till 4:30 A.M. Two hours later we saw a light in her room. She was reading a detective magazine."

Mame wore a powder-blue evening dress with an orchid, cut the cake, and opened the gifts, which included a pair of hard-to-get nylon stockings. She glanced at the younger women and said, "See? You have to be eighty to get nylons nowadays." When she was told that Thurber had paid sixty thousand dollars in taxes in 1945, Mame, says Thurber, was so indignant that she tried to call President Truman. "She was going to tell him, 'My son is not very strong and can't see and is getting old, and he can't pay all that.' But the White House circuits were all busy."

60

That Call on Mrs. Forrester

I first met Marian Forrester when I was twenty-seven. . . . . It is my vanity to believe that [she] had no stauncher admirer. . . . I took not only her smallest foible but her largest sin in my stride; I was as fascinated by the glitter of her flaws as by the glow of her perfections, if indeed I could tell one radiance from the other. . . . Even in her awfullest attachment I persisted in seeing only the further flowering of a unique and privileged spirit. As I neared her home, I remembered a dozen florid charities I had invented to cover her multitude of frailties: her dependence on money and position, her admiration of an aristocracy, half false and half imaginary, her lack of any security inside herself, her easy loneliness.

—from "A Call on Mrs. Forrester"

In January 1946, returned from Mame's eightieth birthday celebration in Columbus, Thurber was fighting off depression. The last of his series, "The Olden Time," was turned in that year. He knew there would be no more. His spot of two men boxing, a hold-over, appeared November first. His meager percentage of vision continued to dwindle. That month he wrote his eye surgeon, Dr. Bruce, who was back from military service. Typically, Thurber tries to spare the doctor by camouflaging with humor his own bitter disappointment:

I never have counted on any further monkeying with what is left of my eye, so you can rest in the tranquil knowledge that I am perfectly satisfied to let well enough alone. It is going to be harder to get an instrument in my eye again than to find you for the next war. . . .

I'll be seeing you one of these days.
Yours, Jim
The blind humorist
Ha, ha . . .

He faced away from what lay before him to revisit the world of Henry James. Playing a literary Walter Mitty, he had written several imitations of James over the years—an unusual match, given James's verboseness and Thurber's economic prose. Nor could the socially active Thurber have felt particular kinship with an author who revealed himself in his fiction as indecisive and reclusive. Indeed, Thurber often wearied of the way James's cautious characters tiptoed around their emotions. He once became so impatient with *The Golden Bowl* that he threatened to throw the book across the room.

But a young collegiate Thurber, worried about his physical and emotional limitations, had been especially vulnerable to the Jamesian ideal, which championed the safety of passive observation over the risks of action and clothed timidity in respectable manners. It may have been his belief that blindness would sentence him to a Jamesian life of social restriction which drove him to reembrace his old hero. In the winter of 1944, Thurber had begun work on a "pastiche" of James. This was not the mocking parody of the early *New Yorker* but an ambitious and respectful tour de force in the master's style. He worked at it steadily for four months, put it away, and returned to it nearly two years later, writing Herman Miller that he found "there are far too many poetic quotations and allusions of the kind our poor dear friend would most surely not have indulged in." A love of James bonded Thurber and Miller, and Thurber encloses a draft of the pastiche, asking Miller's opinion. He has shown it to Edmund Wilson, he says, who was all for shipping it off to the Atlantic Monthly but I still want to perform a few minor operations. . . . I would like your feelings in the matter. During the four months I worked on it . . . I was a nuisance around the house because I was unable to get out of the Jamesian phraseology in talking to Helen, and cook, or our guests.

He promises to write Miller about dramatizing *The Ambassadors*, which he had read four or five times, "but not since about 1933." Lapsing into his mimicry of James, he adds:

It will be interesting to set down the scenes and episodes that I remember after so long an absence from the company of our poor, sensitive gentleman and his circle. It is quite possible, of course, that when I make this analysis what will stand out sharply and clearly for both of us is the impossibility, not to say the inadvisability, of attempting to transfer to so harsh a medium the last final distillation of what is, need I say, in its original form, the perfect, God save us all, statement of the precious dilemma.

He did write the letter—three single-spaced pages—on how *The Ambassadors* might be adapted to the stage, adding:

It must have been about twenty years ago that I first began to think of [*The Ambassadors*] as having the stuff of a play. About that time, I told Andy White I wanted to write a play but was too busy answering bells and kissing girls and, as you may remember, he wrote a poem on the subject, called "The Young Man Wants to Write a Play." Very likely I attempted to describe the plot of the James book to him over a glass of gin and gingerale, and it must have been a remarkable and confusing afternoon since it is practically impossible to describe successfully anything by the old boy to a person who hasn't even read DAISY MILLER.

Six weeks later, he writes to Miller that he has given up "the incredible idea" of making a play out of *The Ambassadors*. While waiting for Miller's comments on the pastiche, Thurber kept rewriting it ("I may be working on it when I die"). He also began work on a related parody, "A Call on Mrs. Forrester (After rereading, in my Middle years, Willa Cather's 'A Lost Lady' and Henry James's 'The Ambassadors')." His preoccupation with James left 1946 nearly devoid of published Thurber, except for "What the Animals Were Up To." This feather-light piece contained his amused comments on a compilation of newspaper and radio anecdotes about dogs, other pets, and wildlife during the war years. It had been requested by his friend Jack Goodman of Simon & Schuster, who was editing a book aimed at the returned service veterans called *While You Were Gone: A Report on Wartime Life in the United States*. Helen sold the Thurber chapter to *Life*, adorned with Thurber drawings. (In 1941, the Thurbers had their lawyer incorporate Thurber's freelance business for tax purposes; Helen was paid an annual salary and acted as his literary agent; Gude continued as his "radio" agent, handling Thurber properties that were dramatized on radio, in movies, in live theater, and, later, television.)

Helen and Gude mostly stopped giving permission for Thurber men, women, and dogs to be used on clothing and souvenir items, after the B. H. Wragge print dress crowded with Thurber dogs became popular and was advertised in the *New Yorker*. His friends kidded him about it. "I don't want women at Schrafft's sitting on my dogs," Thurber said, in renouncing the practice. He also sharply limited his product endorsements in advertising. This may have reduced the cash flow of Thurber, Inc., but he never cared about money, says Helen; he "just liked a few little luxuries to make up for his rather deprived youth." Helen had had "an unluxurious youth," too, but neither of them, she says, had "high ideas of high finance."

In the period of letdown following *The Thurber Carnival*'s exhilarating publication, Thurber, still adjusting to his increased blindness, felt adrift. Though he had enjoyed a laugh-filled evening in Columbus with the Millers, they were concerned over his subsequent gloom, and glad to get a cheerful letter from him in March:

> I am fit again, and getting fat as a result of a high caloric diet, which for a month, involved 42 eggs a week. . . . I actually have a paunch and weigh 163 just after lunch. Outside of sweaty palms, cold feet and a touch of nervous apprehension for a day or two as a result of pondering my case history, the state of the world and chiefly, the illness of friends —almost all of whom are down—I am fine.

Ross corroborates Thurber's report on all the illnesses, writing Thurber: "At the moment the journalistic end of the magazine is practically shut down. Flu has been through the office, and you'd think it had been the Four Horsemen."

There were distractions for Thurber that year, some of his doing, some not. Robert and Mame visited him in West Cornwall in the summer of 1946. Thurber tried to capture his mother's nonstop chatter on a wire recorder, but whenever she was given the microphone, Mame could only giggle hysterically.

Jack Fullen, the O.S.U. alumni secretary, had been badgering Thurber, "as an alumnus worthy of note," to join the alumni association. Thurber felt he had largely outgrown his college, although he remained sentimental about one or two English professors and the campus publications he had been associated with. Fullen used Thurber's name regularly in publicizing the university, "as probably its most illustrious alumnus," but by 1946 Thurber had come to distrust a university board of trustees that included the conservative John W. Bricker, a former Ohio governor and 1944 vice-presidential candidate, whose political views he heartily disliked. Thurber's worst beliefs about O.S.U.'s backwardness had been verified for him in October 1944, when the publication of his beloved Sun-Dial was suspended by President Howard L. Bevis, who found the publication obscene. A female student from Cleveland was fired as editor. The magazine's cover had advertised the issue as "Filthy with Fun," and carried the photo of a seminude woman student. There were, as was usual with college publications of the day, wild parodies of such popular magazines as Time and Life, and a "Fun in Bed" spoof. Before its distribution could be prevented, three thousand copies were sold. After a student petition for the publication's restoration was presented to President Bevis, the magazine was revived as Scarlet Fever—a title chosen in a student poll. (The school's colors were gray and scarlet.)

Not until Thurber was in Columbus for Mame's party, more than a year later, did he learn of the incident. Fullen, who had no apparent appreciation of where Thurber stood ideologically, replied to Thurber's protest by blaming the controversial magazine on a student "gang of unhealthy Jews from Cleveland." The name change, he said, was because the Sun-Dial would carry "unsavory memories."

Thurber had already been in touch with other alumni "worthy of note" who had worked on the Sun-Dial—Gardner Rea, Dudley Fisher (syndicated cartoonist of "Right Around Home"), the columnist Earl Wilson, Ruth McKenney, Milton Caniff, Nugent, and the screen star Jean Peters, asking that they join him in trying to get the monthly's title restored. He then wrote to President Bevis, pointing out that

> the title itself was not at fault and the quick and easy abandonment of a
> university literary tradition seems to me to represent a deterioration in
> the principles and ideals for which a university should stand. . . .
>
> As this affair has dragged on, various rumors of a disturbing nature
> have arisen, as is bound to be the case when anything so drastic in the

way of censorship takes place. It has been suggested to me that an article unfavorable to Mr. Bricker was one cause for the kicking of the magazine off the campus, and what seems even worse the question of social discrimination has also been flatly stated [Fullen's reference to Jews].

Thurber then indirectly threatens blackmail, informing Bevis that "this kind of thing [the ethnic slur by Fullen] is bound to creep into the press finally if the matter becomes an issue so large that everybody from Mr. Rea and myself in New York to Elliott Nugent in Hollywood is forced to take a hand in it."

Thurber overreaches, perhaps another consequence of his 1946 "idle mind"; the magazine had not been kicked off the campus, only renamed. Student editors had earlier been warned several times to avoid offensive copy and pictures. That the magazine was published and distributed bespeaks of little previous monitoring and censorship by the faculty. Thurber hints at overwhelming opposition from empowered allies, when, it seems, only Gardner Rea was sufficiently interested in joining him in his quixotic quest.

Thurber wanted to believe that the publication's unfavorable references to Bricker were what had led to its suspension, making the issue one of First Amendment rights, but James Pollard, the chairman of the publications committee and later a university historian, says that the editors had been warned about obscenity after the September issue, and that the next one was even more obscene. Looking down the barrels of Thurber's heavy artillery, the administration restored the magazine's name, the *Sun-Dial*, presumably overriding the majority vote of the students. "Thurber made a mountain of a molehill," Pollard says. "I thought the new name superior to sleepy titles like the *Sun-Dial* and the *Lantern*."

Thurber remained unrepentant. When he was working on *The Thurber Album* three years later, he paid Pollard to research the background of Bob Ryder, Thurber's early hero and former editor of the *Ohio State Journal*, where Pollard had worked. In a letter to Pollard, he reminisces about "the terrible case of 'Scarlet Fever' . . . 'after the magazine fell into the hands of a bunch of Cleveland Jews,' as a prominent, and even powerful Ohio State man wrote me, apparently taking for granted that any good alumnus would share his vision. I regret that I promised to make no public issue of this if the name of the Sun-Dial was restored. It was restored so fast that it was hard to believe."

In the thirties, Aristide Mian, a French artist whom the Thurbers had known in the Village, married an American girl named Mary Shipman, and moved with her to France, to live among his friends and relatives in the region of Creuse. Her graceful, humorous letters to friends at home seemed to the Thurbers of *New Yorker* potential. Thurber enlisted the Whites in getting Ross interested. Mary Mian's descriptive, entertaining essays began to run in the magazine in 1943 and were collected in a book, *My Country-in-Law*, in 1946, for which Thurber proudly wrote the introduction. She dedicated the book "To Jim Thurber."

He seemed, that year, to be looking for excuses not to write. He was sending to Ross Talk ideas and anecdotes—those paragraphs of doubtful authenticity sandwiched between Talk stories at the time. After Ross accepted a Thurber Talk idea on "wrongly dated checks," Thurber bombarded him with more, including the exploring of who now lived in the Park Central hotel room where Arnold Rothstein was shot; or in the apartment in which Two-gun Crowley was captured; or in the room of the Hotel Monticello in which Jack Diamond was shot for the first time, cautioning that "the hotel is, I think, largely given over to elderly ladies, and I doubt very much if the management would care to discuss the subject."

The *New Yorker* got fooled from time to time by submissions of anecdotes either known to everyone but the editors or published years before in the magazine and forgotten. When Thurber sent Ross such an item, one a friend had told him, Ross replied: "That anecdote about the boy whose father's hat blew off in the automobile and who couldn't tell about it because he was eating cookies is old—been in here twenty or thirty times in last couple of years. You can't trust your friends in these matters."

Robert Thurber, who was operating a rare-books store in Columbus, found a 1930 letter from Calvin Coolidge to the Pullman Company, complaining that the sleeping-car porter had carried off his nightgown with the linen, and asking that it be retrieved and mailed to him in Northampton, Massachusetts. Thurber passed it on to Ross, who came up with his usual list of nitpicking questions for Robert to answer: How did the present owner of the nightshirt come to have it? What value did the owner place on it? Was it for sale? Was it made of flannel, or what? Was Coolidge traveling in a lower berth or a drawing room? A confused Robert did his best but was unable to answer Ross's questions, including "whether the Pullman Company got the nightgown back from the laundry."

After the war, the *New Yorker* continued to hire Talk reporters on a "tryout" basis, and Thurber was soon tweaking Ross about so large a staff doing what Thurber and one or two others had done effectively in the early years. When Ross complained of no longer getting good Talk ideas, Thurber sent him several more, writing that it would be a profitable idea, to assign one of your numerous assistants to the congenial if tedious task of going over ancient Talk of the Town departments and getting ideas from bringing some of the old items up to date. It used to be a habit of ours, at the end of a piece, to add, "If we hear any more about this we'll let you know"—or words to that effect. I feel sure that the passing of time has in some way enriched the interest of hundreds of those old visit and personality pieces.

I submit this flux of talk ideas directly to you because if my suggestions get lost in the amazing machinery of your factual department, you would always contend that I never did get them down on paper, because you look upon me as fallible though remarkable, and upon your factual department as infallible and remarkable.

Ross denied that he had "many assistants," in another letter to Thurber that Katharine White would regard as meant to mollify his valuable contributor, now of failed eyesight and uncertain temper:

The fault with Talk is mainly ideas. When you were doing the rewrite, we were getting better ideas. Shawn (peerless as an idea man) was on the job, and if I do say it myself, I was sparking some too. I was younger then. I've been very uneasy about the idea end of Talk for some time, now that the war is over and things aren't so obvious. I look over the ideas every week and am discouraged.

Give me you, Shawn and Cooke and I'll get out a Talk department. . . . It's up to god to send some young talent around this place, and He's been neglecting the job. That's the trouble.

One thing that may have been troubling Ross was that his tradition of lighthearted journalism—picking up rocks and playfully reporting in Talk what lay under them, posing as visitors to the city who "didn't give a good goddam" about much of anything—was now being practiced alongside the Notes and Comment of E. B. White—pieces that were giving grave consideration to the state of postwar civilization. The juxtaposition of statesmanlike counseling to the world and Talk trivia made the department seem both schizoid and out of tune. The war, while it lasted, had had to be taken into account in nearly everything being written and drawn in the magazine. Its dominance and seriousness had helped push White away from his meditative, self-absorbed "One Man's Meat" columns in *Harper's* and back to the *New Yorker*, a more immediate platform for his views. White believed that only a supranational government could prevent another global conflict, and he was single-handedly committing the magazine to that utopian ideal. Ross was too cynical to believe there could be any such solution to man's belligerence, but he so admired White's Comments that he encouraged their publication, and readily agreed to White's covering the San Francisco conference at which the United Nations Organization was established, in June 1945.

In a June 1, 1945, Comment, White compares the uncertainty of the world with that of Thurber characters:

> The earth, scratching its statesmen as though they were fleas, heaves and rocks with big new things. This is one of those times. The people feel the disturbance. They know it's here, they fear its consequences, and they live in fear. Living in fear, they act with suspicion, with ten-sion. If anyone were to run out into the Square and shout, "Go east!", like the characters in the Thurber story, there is a good chance you would see an eastward movement in the panicky noontime.

That summer, Ross gave in to Shawn's proposal that an entire issue of the magazine be given over to John Hersey's book-length description of the atomic bombing of Hiroshima. It ran in the October 31, 1946, issue and took even the staff by surprise—it is said that only Hersey, Shawn (who edited it), Ross, and Carmine Peppe, the makeup man, knew what was coming up. With such departures from the magazine's twenty-year formula in mind, Thurber replied to Ross's gloomy complaints about Talk by plumping for at least a partial return to the old days of Talk, while expressing an understanding of what had changed it. He saw in the frightening times a reason for the *New Yorker* seeking out whatever touches of lightness could still be seen within the developing madness:

> What has happened to Talk has many facets. First, none of us is as young and gay as he used to be and neither is the world. It was much easier to deal with trivia before Hitler. Second, something happened to the general tone of the department when we made over for Colen Kelly [war hero] and the first days of the war, and later when we devoted the department to the funeral of President Roosevelt. There are several reasons why I should like to see it get back to, say, a talk with the Missing Persons Bureau about the number of letters and calls which still come in about Judge Crater, and things like that. Not only has humor pretty well gone out but Talk of the Town now finds itself wedged in between highly serious and important world reporting and the comment page of a man who has become the most distinguished political philoso-

pher of the day. We all read and discuss the heavy subjects but we all spend a great deal of time on the same interesting facts, persons and places that we used to. Anybody, including me, could get up two hundred old-time talk ideas in a week. The thing is to get away from the portentous tone, or whatever it is, and this could be accomplished by a little relaxation of mind and spirit and does not necessitate a tremendous staff.

But Thurber was largely out of daily editorial touch with the magazine, as Ross, time and again, had to remind him, in replying to Thurber's ideas for the Talk section: "We have been swamped with cab anecdotes of recent years," Ross writes him; "that's all we get except letters left by maids and the peculiar things children say. I put a stop order on the cab anecdotes when the bank got to sixteen. We don't get the anecdotes we did when you were on the job."

And when Thurber suggested a Talk story on the late writer Max Brand [pseudonym of Frederick Faust] and his hundred and twenty books that would be published posthumously, Ross replied a bit brusquely, "Everything you told me . . . has been printed, and printed over and over. The papers had it in their obits, The Publisher's Weekly had it, and Time had Publisher's Weekly piece, boiled down."

Thurber's reverence for White as a writer had never flagged. When Henry Seidel Canby, the secretary of the National Institute of Arts and Letters, informed Thurber in late 1945 that the Institute's Department of Literature had elected him a member, Thurber stunned him with a blunt rejection, primarily because White had been passed over.

> It is only fair to state honestly my inveterate reluctance to join literary organizations. Perhaps this grows out of the fact that I have been for so long associated with Harold Ross' magazine whose editors and chief contributors are more or less dedicated to staying on the outside of organizations and looking in, or even occasionally tossing something through the window.

To Canby's further insistence, he responds:

> I find it bewildering . . . to discover that any group . . . devoted to the best in literature could overlook the ability and achievements of White. . . .
>
> I should . . . prefer to be selected at the same time as Mr. White, or

even after Mr. White, but I find that something . . . resolute inside me keeps me from . . . accepting a distinction which has been denied to this important figure, not only in American letters but in my own literary life and career. Since White makes no personal appearances, and so far as I know has never joined anything since college, I am pretty sure he would . . . run a thousand miles to avoid being found, and he would not consider this letter a friendly act if he knew I was writing it. This, however, is not the point. I just do not believe that there are a hundred or even five American writers who are anywhere near as fine a literary craftsman and artist as he is.

Canby replied that "I put up E. B. White, with as great an enthusiasm as yours, for the Institute two or three years ago . . . but so much of his work has been anonymous, and so unaware of literary talent are our colleagues in the other arts, that each year he has missed election by an inch or two. . . . I shall place him in nomination again for next year, and I can, I believe, guarantee that he will be elected, particularly if you'll help me." White, as Thurber said, wasn't interested in joining any organization.

When Whit Burnett asked Thurber to select one of his stories for Burnett's *The World's Best* [short stories], Thurber scolded him for not including any piece by White, "one of the great living prose writers."

A dispirited Thurber that year seemed to look for things to complain about. Charles Cooke, out of the Air Force, had discovered that either Ross or Shawn—he wasn't sure which, and perhaps both—didn't want him back at the *New Yorker*. After brief unsatisfactory stints as an associate editor at *Esquire* and *Holiday*, he began writing speeches for government officials in Washington. One day in 1946 he visited the *New Yorker* offices. "Thurber was there working in shirtsleeves," says Cooke. "He tried not to appear blind, but his eye was in bad shape. I said, 'How are you, Jim?' 'Low,' he answered. 'Me, too,' I told him. 'No, not that kind of low,' he said. 'A cosmic kind of low.' I was saddened, because I remembered the old Thurber who, despite all his troubles, would cheer up the whole staff in the course of a working day."

By October 31, the Thurbers were back at the Homestead, in Hot Springs, where Thurber was repossessed by The Thurbs. He writes Miller: "This turned out to be a bad summer for every writer I know, including myself, and I think I averaged eight words a day."

He was still down in December—though, when writing the Millers again, he tried his best not to be, for Miller was one of Thurber's favorite audiences:

> I feel like one of those charred carbon sticks we used to pick up under
> street lamps in the days when all technics were still clumsy and life was

fun. . . . I have not been able to write a Goddamned word for eight months . . . which I guess combined with a cold and a gloomy view of man makes me feel like an empty raspberry basket, frail, stained and likely to be torn to pieces by a little child. . . .

Elliott [Nugent] was here for 4 days and we were braced in the bar by a drunken gent . . . who thought Elliott was me. . . . To add to the confusion the man's name was Furber.

He asked Helen and me to lunch . . . and turned up with the Dowager Mrs. Cornelius Vanderbilt, who told me she had a funny mind, and proved it by urging us all to join hands and make the Russians like us. She then related how she had called, all alone, on the Gromykos to tell them about her dear friends, the late Czar and Czarina, and their nice, charming circle. The ten days that shook Mrs. Vanderbilt. . . . Mrs. V. also referred to the Russian Revolution as "that time they shot all my nice friends" and said she refused to speak to the Kaiser after 1914 because "he was so deceitful."

Dudley Fisher, the Columbus cartoonist of "Right Around Home," arrived in Hot Springs with his wife. At the movies one evening, they spotted Thurber squinting up at the screen in the front row, trying to make out the figures. Thurber invited them to cocktails the next afternoon. A short time before, a Columbus physician, Jack Frost, when leaving Hot Springs, had died when his car slipped on an icy road and went over the side of a mountain. "When we were about to leave," says Fisher, "Thurber and Helen walked us to the front porch. Thurber sniffed the air, and said, 'You know, Helen and I were the last ones to see Jack Frost alive. We had drinks with him right here in the hotel the day he was killed, and then we came out here with him to say good-bye. It was just such a day as this—the roads were beginning to ice up; it was getting cold and raw, just like now. Well, good-bye.' " (The nervous Fishers made it home.)

Whatever else was bothering Thurber, it was hardly from lack of recognition. His last *New Yorker* cover, littered with his dogs, had been published the previous February, to tie in with the Madison Square Garden dog show of 1946. His "Our New Natural History" and "The Olden Time" series ran intermittently throughout the year. The *Ladies' Home Journal* featured him in a major article ("The Legendary Mr. Thurber"). Two dozen of his writings and drawings were collected in anthologies—in one (*I Wish I'd Written That: Selections Chosen by Favorite American Authors*), the dour, anti-Labor arch-conservative columnist Westbrook Pegler, whom Thurber detested, chose Thurber's "One Is a Wanderer" as the story he would most like to have written. The Ohioana Library Association honored *The White Deer* as "the best juvenile book of the year"; Mame proudly accepted the award for her son in his absence, and Thurber's written remarks extolling Robert Ryder were read to the audience by a staff member of the *Ohio State Journal*.

The great and famous were claiming Thurber as one of theirs. "We meet far too seldom," H. L. Mencken writes. "I hope you drop off in Baltimore some day and let me show you the remains of a once great medieval city." Carl Sandburg wrote him in May, "It is long since that dandy all-night session in Columbus Ohio and you keep growing all the time, gathering a permanent audience that cherishes you as very real to them. . . . May you go on." S. J. Perelman responded warmly, in his inimitable style, to a Thurber note praising one of his books:

> I was particularly heartened by the theory you relayed about the reservoir of humor we're all supposed to possess. Candidly, mine seems at the moment to have shrunken to a greenish hog-wallow dotted with kerosene cans and old shoes. . . .
>
> One person, at least, continues to wear the old cap and bells vivaciously, and that's Bennett Cerf. Among his other exploits this winter, America's sweetheart [Cerf] got out a Modern Library anthology of humor with a dust-jacket representing you and me which is going to take some intensive forgetting. One of these days when we're not too busy worrying, what say we sneak over to Random House and clap a commode snugly down over his ears?

The education of fifteen-year-old Rosemary was on his mind. In response to a progress report from the faculty of the Northampton School for Girls, Thurber writes Headmistress Sarah Whitaker a long letter. Rosemary often wore a melancholy face that had one or two of her teachers concerned, he had been told:

> I don't think you need to worry about Rosemary's troubled expression since this is definitely familial. I am told that I wear, most of the time, a distressed expression which has been described by one of my friends as "the troubled look of a dog who has forgotten where he has buried his bone." Rosemary's own troubled look may be intensified by worries of her own, and heaven knows there are enough to go around in the era we are living in.

There had been mysterious fires breaking out at the Southern Hotel in Columbus, where Mame and Robert had an apartment, and where there were no fire escapes or fire stairs. Thurber, now the principal support of his mother and brother, wrote George Smallsreed, of the *Dispatch*, about the hotel situation, wondering if his paper might campaign for better fire-prevention techniques in Columbus. "The Southern" is all his mother and brother can afford, he explains to Smallsreed, and adds that Mame "lives now in a state of apprehension bordering on panic and this had extended, naturally, to me and Helen." Smallsreed took the matter under advisement, the results unknown.

Thurber was by now embroiled in his negotiations with Sam Goldwyn over Mitty and "The Catbird Seat." He told friends that he had been offered thirty-five hundred dollars a week to go to Hollywood to work on the screenplay, but that with each offer he would wire Goldwyn that Ross had met the increase. When Goldwyn started all over again with a lower figure, says Thurber, he wired Goldwyn that Ross had met the *decrease*. (As White said about Thurber's Columbus reminiscences, the Goldwyn exchange "largely took place in little Jamie's head.") Thurber liked to tell of F. Scott Fitzgerald's experience in converting his short story "Babylon Revisited" to the screen. Fitzgerald had persuaded the producer, Lester Cowan, a compulsive rewriter of scripts, that his own treatment was perfect and that nobody should try to revise it. Cowan reread it, and said, "You're absolutely right. I'll pay you two thousand dollars a week to stay out here and keep me from changing a word of it."

While at the Homestead in 1946, daily dictating letters and works in progress to the hotel's public stenographer, Thurber received a letter from John Hersey telling him that the British writer and editor Cyril Connolly was on his way to the States. "I gather that you're an admirer of his," writes Hersey, "and so wondered if you two would join Frances Ann and me [in meeting Connolly]."

Thurber was delighted. At the meeting with Connolly in New York, Thurber told him about the James pastiche and Connolly, who had founded the literary magazine *Horizon*, made him promise to send the piece to him if Ross refused it. It seems to have been one of the things that helped propel Thurber into 1947 full of drive and optimism.

In February they sailed to Bermuda for the first time in seven years and got reacquainted with the Williamses. They remained there until April 10, Janey Williams being credited, as always, with helping to make Thurber a new man. He writes Jap Gude: "Bermuda, like the French Riviera, is excellent for nerves; and for the first time in several years I have taken no luminal for two weeks. . . . If you see a photograph of Charles Jackson [author of *The Lost Weekend*] and me, the glass on his table contains coca cola." The Williams's daughter Dinah remembers that "Uncle Jim brought Mother a bouquet of flowers, got down on a knee and sang the lyrics of 'People Will Say We're in Love.' When he came to 'Don't throw bouquets at me,' Uncle Jim threw the bouquet. It bounced off the screen door and Mother jumped on them, presumably to help squelch any rumor that they were in love."

His first story for the New Yorker in eighteen months, "The Waters of the Moon," is one of Thurber's best. After reading it, the playwright Maxwell Anderson wrote Katharine White that "for sheer wizardry, for writing and construction, I think Thurber's Waters of the Moon is the best I've ever read in The New Yorker, and I read it pretty constantly. It's my guess that he's never written better prose any time, anywhere."

Thurber was writing by ear now, and his stories depended for their development on cocktail talk—usually misunderstood by one of the conversationalists—wordplay, marital tension, and literary allusion. When he learned that both Helen and Althea had played Rosalind in Shakespeare's As You Like It in high school, he wrote "Am Not I Your Rosalind?", featuring two wives goaded by one of the husbands into reading from the part into a wire recorder in the course of a drinking evening. The rivalry not only results in tension between the two couples but between husband and wife, as well.

"A Call on Mrs. Forrester" was a dress rehearsal for his James pastiche. In "Mrs. Forrester," the male persona, standing in the rain, brooding, is "a frightened penitent, come to claim and take away and burn the old praises he had given [Marian Forrester], standing there in my unbecoming middle years, foolishly clutching reasons and arguments like a shopper's husband loaded down with bundles." He will tell Mrs. Forrester that he is returning to Paris, to his present love, Madame de Vionnet,

> and I could hear her pitiless comment. "One of those women who have something to give, for heaven's sake!" she would say. "One of those women who save men, a female whose abandon might possibly tiptoe to the point of tousling her lover's hair, a woman who at the first alarm of a true embrace would telephone the gendarmes."

As though worried by his own seriousness, Thurber arranges a pratfall for his hapless Jamesian male:

> I would bow to my hostess, open the door and walk, not out into the rain, but into that damn closet, with its junk and clutter, smashing the Easter egg with my shoe, becoming tangled in the table tennis net, and holding in my hand, when I regained my balance, that comic parasol. Madame de Vionnet would ignore such a calamity, she would pretend

not to see it, on the ground that a hostess is blind—a convention that can leave a man sitting at table with an omelet in his lap, unable to mention it, forced to go on with the conversation.

Written in the subjunctive mood of unexplored supposition, one cannot be sure that the Jamesian prototype got up the nerve to as much as knock on the door of Mrs. Forrester, but he does plan to carry lilacs, "one of these summers," to Madame de Vionnet.

Two years after Thurber's death, Helen took credit for having sold Ross "A Call on Mrs. Forrester." Writing the introduction to Hamish Hamilton's British collection of Thurberiana called *Vintage Thurber,* she says that the parody "almost didn't get printed in the magazine," and adds, somewhat superciliously, that when Ross read it,

> he puzzled over it for a long time and left it, day after day, lying deject-edly on his desk. When I finally cornered him in the hall and demanded a decision, he blurted out, 'It's *literary.* I don't understand a goddam word of it.' Never shy with Ross, I followed him down to the water cooler, told him that just because he didn't understand the story was no reason to think it wasn't good, and pointed out that it was a brilliant pastiche of both Willa Cather and Henry James. He stared at me blankly for a minute, then went scowling back to his office, where he put a surly 'R' on the manuscript and sent it through. I've always wondered if it was 'pastiche' that did the trick. It was the kind of word he skirted around cautiously, not knowing what it meant and probably (I hope I'm not misjudging him) connecting it with a kind of ice cream served in fluted cups at children's birthday parties.

Emancipated from her wearing role as Thurber's "seeing-eye wife," Helen still preferred to play his surrogate rather than reclaim an identity of her own. She didn't hesitate to add to Thurber's earlier mischievous portrayal of Ross as an all but unlettered editor, but she lacked Thurber's palliative touch. Ross did begin as a novice in literary matters; Katharine White gave his magazine the cultural value that he could not. Ross's abiding interest was in the maga-zine's art and factual content; he depended on others' judgments of poetry, book reviews, and much of the fiction. But by 1947, after twenty-two years editing the magazine, he was in no way put off by the "literary" content of the magazine's fiction. That "A Call on Mrs. Forrester" was a parody of Cather and James is stated in Thurber's subtitle, and in the unlikely case that Ross didn't know the meaning of "pastiche," he would immediately have, on conditioned reflex, consulted the huge dictionary he kept in his office and used constantly. He wrote Thurber that the story itself "comes over," and in defending to Thurber the magazine's contract calling for a first look at his work, writes him that it wasn't the business department insisting on the requirement:

> It is we, the editorial department, who want the first clause. Christ, if we hadn't had that we would have missed the Mrs. Forrester story, which you only showed to us because you were obliged to, and at that you ran it down with talk of having written it only with the *Saturday Review* in mind, that Maxwell gave it back to you, evidently considering the act as perfunctory. It would have been a hell of a note if we'd lost that, which we would have if Lobrano hadn't just happened to get back from vacation then, or sickness, or something.

Before the Mrs. Forrester parody ran, Thurber was hard at work on the larger James pastiche for Cyril Connolly.

When not working or being read to, Thurber now listened to the radio for relaxation; if football or baseball was not being broadcast, he had to settle for daytime serials. He gradually sensed the enormity of the soap-opera industry and its importance to housewives. "Thix," one of his *New Yorker* casuals of 1947, hints of his first interest in the medium—an interest that would lead to his five-part report the next year, called "Soapland." In "Thix," he compares the paperback books he read as a youth to what the children are hearing in 1947 on the radio; Captain Midnight, for example, whose "every plight and peril is shared by . . . a little boy and a little girl. . . . What their parents can be thinking of I don't know. I do know that when these children should be in bed or in school, they are usually at the point of a flame, or lying bound and gagged somewhere."

He longed for a change of pace in what he had been writing—to return, however briefly, to reporting—and was soon dictating letters of inquiry, telephoning, and otherwise researching the soap-opera business for a series of *New Yorker* articles. He writes to Ross:

> My pieces on soap opera are progressing well in spite of the tremendous research I have had to do and am still doing. My letters and literature on the subject run to half a million words. . . . I am even more interested in it all than I was. . . . the *New Yorker* can put on a soap opera for $104,000 a year. . . . It could be called "Katharine Takes Over." . . . I wanted to do this as a hard job of reporting in my oldtime

manner when I was just that man from the newspaper, but I find that I can get in as the comic artist and writer. The reticent Hummerts who own fifteen soap operas and half a dozen other radio shows, refuse to see reporters so I plied their press man, a Thurber fan, with a long list of questions. Hummert replied through this man that he and his wife had been delighted by the letter, and he then proceeded to answer most of the questions.

He was still working on the series that fall, back at the Homestead. When he put off writing his regular letters to Rosemary at the Northampton school, she wrote: "Well, what's the matter—are you still up to your ears in soap?"

Ross was backing Thurber's work, writing, "I think it is astonishing that you undertook such a journalistic job, and admirable beyond my powers of expression. I am told that the office has agreed to pay for a secretary, or part of a secretary. It should do this."

As managing editor of fact, William Shawn found himself, for the first time, editing Thurber. It was a horrendous experience for the shy, peace-loving Shawn, for Thurber resisted changes. He had always challenged Ross's queries, often at the top of his lungs. When, in one editing session, with Shawn present, Ross, suffering from ulcers, impatiently told Thurber "If you could see, you would know what we mean," Thurber went out of control with rage. Ross apologized.

Ross's respect and care for Thurber continued. He writes Thurber at the Homestead that "I have heard great acclaim on all sides about your last piece ["Am Not I Your Rosalind?"], which several people have said is the funniest you ever wrote. A certain number of people always say that, every time a Thurber piece comes out, and maybe it's true, although I still cling to some of my old favorites."

When *Life* published Thurber's exchange of letters with Samuel Goldwyn, in which Thurber took umbrage over Goldwyn's slighting reference to "the little magazine," Ross was pleased and grateful, writing Thurber:

> I got a great deal of satisfaction from your answer to Goldwyn. Selznick pulled that "little magazine" stuff on me, too. I think several of them may have that phrase in their bean. It's a funny coincidence, anyhow. I'd like to know who wrote Goldwyn's letter, or how it was got together, but I'm not enough interested to devote any time to finding out. There's something funny there, though—the idea of Sam Goldwyn writing a letter. I'll buy you a meal for coming back at him on behalf of the organization, however.

A Sally Benson short story in the *New Yorker*—probably the one about the meeting of a man gone blind with a former lover—was criticized on the one hand for disparaging the blind, and praised, on the other, by an organization in support of the blind. Thurber sent Ross a letter he had received which castigated the story, and with which Thurber concurred. Thurber's ongoing posture was never to appear blind, and he felt that Benson's story was directed at him, and wrote Ross as much. A contrite Ross replies:

> I got that letter you sent in but I showed it to no one, not even Lobrano, who was as completely taken in as I was, or who was as innocent and ignorant. He goes around clutching his heart as it is, and I spare him. . . . Both Lobrano and I should have had our tails kicked hard for the piece. . . . What irks me most is that it was bad business to run it as is regardless, blindness being too serious a subject. I have heard nothing more about the thing . . . and my conclusion is that people generally, and people around the office in particular, did not suspect any personal motive in it. Regardless, I ask the forgiveness of you and Helen, and I will say that your attitude has been generous and understanding. . . . Your piece on the drunks and the word game ["Here Come the Tigers"], as I said [on the phone], is causing talk all around—worth the price of a year's subscription in itself.

61

That Beast in Me

A writer verging on his middle fifties, when he should be engaged on some work dignified by length and of a solemnity suitable to our darkening age, is a little surprised to find himself coming out with still another collection of short pieces and small drawings. He toys for a while with the idea of a prefatory note pointing out that all this is a necessary and natural rehearsal for the larger project that awaits the increase of his patience and the lengthening of his view. Then, in re-examining his material for evidence to sustain this brave theory, he finds little to support his argument and a great deal to contradict it. Take the imaginary animals in this book, for example. No labor of ingenuity could fit them into a continuable pattern. They emerged from the shameless breeding ground of the idle mind and they are obviously not going anywhere in particular.

—from the Foreword of *The Beast in Me and Other Animals*

After months of thought and revision, Thurber's pastiche of James, which he called "The Beast in the Dingle," appeared in the September 1948 issue of Cyril Connolly's *Horizon,* in England, the same month that it appeared in Thurber's newest American collection of prose and art, *The Beast in Me and Other Animals.* While the Jamesian gentleman couldn't bring himself to make a call on Mrs. Forrester, here, a mannered, cautious Charles Grantham engages Amy Lighter in conversation appropriate to the Edwardian period. Sly Joycean tricks of language, along with flashes of comedy, gleam in Thurber's dense verbal undergrowth. With reference to James's mysterious servants and children in "The Turn of the Screw," Miss Lighter accuses Grantham of expecting "me to say that perhaps the servants are, in truth, agents of a special kind, assigned to keep a sharp eye on the children, who are in reality midgets, possessed of a police record as long as your arm." And Grantham addresses James's moment of truth from "The Beast in the Jungle" with:

"If I should strike . . . at every rustling in the undergrowth, a high heroic stance, sword drawn from cane, and cry, 'Come out, come out!' and if there should advance . . . on veritable tippy-toe, the most comical of beasts, about its neck a pink and satiny ribbon tied in the fluffiest of bows, what, dear lady, in the name of Heaven, would become of me?"
Well, there it was, then, his beast in the dingle.

It is an elaborate, hard-won mockery of James, and of the painful realization of his narrator in "The Beast in the Jungle" that his existence had been lived on the edges of a life he never dared enter. Thurber would reduce that revelation—the tiger that springs—to a harmless purring kitty cat, denying James's poor sensitive gentleman even a menace worthy of his fears.

The James exercise was a catharsis for a time; a decade later, Thurber was telling an interviewer that he admired James "as a craftsman very much, but the more I reread Henry James, the more I realize he didn't have a great deal to say except in skill and in the relationships of sensibilities—rather than the clash of anything more important." But less than a year later, in 1959, after he had finished his memoirs, *The Years with Ross*, he was researching recent efforts by playwrights to dramatize James's 1902 novel, *The Wings of the Dove*, and writing of the James revival that began after the author's centennial anniversary, in 1943.

By this time, the going was rough for all parties in getting a Thurber piece serenely edited and published in the *New Yorker*. Hoping to find a compatible match, Shawn had given Thurber's 1958 Henry James article to Roger Angell, Katharine White's son, who had left *Holiday* for the *New Yorker* a few years before. Thurber had considered Ross and Lobrano worthy of his mettle in editorial disputes, but now they were gone and he felt misunderstood and unappreciated by their successors. They felt the same about Thurber. The subject of Henry James was a sensitive one, too, for Thurber felt proprietary toward it. In the 1958 James article, he included another parody of the master, which Shawn and Roger Angell felt—probably correctly—was out of place. Thurber acquiesced on the point, but fought to save other parts of the piece, writing Shawn:

> I gathered that [Roger Angell] was also for my taking out my brief description of the plot of "The Wings of the Dove." . . . I can't very well discuss [others'] mutilations of this plot without stating the plot and The New Yorker cannot kid me into believing that its erudite readers, or more than four percent of them, know the story of the novel. Anyway, from this particular position I shall not budge an inch. . . .
>
> I still think the piece is for "Onward and Upward with the Arts" and that it should now be called "The Wings of Henry James." [Both points were granted.]
>
> I refrained from taking a crack at such eminent authorities on literature as Edmund Wilson and Clifton Fadiman, who, like so many others in the Forties seemed not to have read James until the great Revival. . . . I went on "Invitation to Learning" with Mark Van Doren to discuss "The Ambassadors," which I did without having reread the book for more than twenty years. [Fadiman] and I discussed "What Maisie Knew." . . . If you are a true Henry James student you would know

which one [of us] has to be right. If you have to look it up, you ain't no Jamesian. . . .

Ross would have put 703 queries on this piece. I am willing to deal with 84. . . .

When I let Wilson read my pastiche, "The Beast in the Dingle" . . . he assured me that Henry James never went into sentences beginning with "We" in the last few pages of any of his stories told in the third person. I always keep my temper with such experts, and didn't even tell him he was full of crap. . . .

All this is put down to assure New Yorker checkers and editors that, in matters of fact and opinion, about Henry James, I recognize few peers and even fewer superiors. This is to avoid any possible editorial comment such as "Fadiman says" or "Wilson says" or "Anthony West says."

I am having lunch with Leon Edel [James's biographer] at the Century Club on Monday . . . and I am going to let him see a carbon of my piece. He is a lot more superior to me, or anybody else, when it comes to knowledge of H.J.

Seven months went by before "The Wings of Henry James" was published. Though Shawn was an excellent hands-on editor, as Ross often was not, an ailing, mentally distressed Thurber had so abused Shawn during the piece's processing that on one or two occasions Shawn's secretary was in tears. In October 1959, Roger Angell writes Thurber that "Shawn did the editing on this one, but he has asked me to shepherd the piece into print," and added, "Of course, this doesn't mean that you can't complain about it if you want to. . . . The piece is going to run next week. . . . Please call me if this seems impossible to you, or if you have any other questions."

To everyone's relief, it did run the next week. Though Thurber now and then mentioned James in interviews after that, James's ghost, which had haunted a special chamber of his subconscious for forty years, seems finally to have been laid to rest.

In April 1948, Katharine White was in the hospital, recovering from an operation. In a get-well letter to her, Thurber discusses his forthcoming book:

We are trying to get a title . . . that will take in all the animals both in drawings and prose. Helen thought of "The Beast in Me" which Doris Schneider at my publisher's likes. . . . Other titles I have put down are, Thurber's New Natural History, Of Man and Beast, It's Not a Fit Night, They Are Neither Beast nor Human (a line from Edgar Poe).

When I got to This is My Bestiary and The Bestiary Years of My Life I began to fade. . . .

My mother says everything is going to pick up after October 3rd.

Harcourt Brace published five thousand copies of a first printing of *The Beast in Me*, with its dedication "For Ronnie and Janey Williams/In memory of the serene hours at Felicity Hall." The book was a smorgasbord offering, described in the *New York Times Book Review* by Rex Lardner, a *New Yorker* staff writer, as containing "four short stories, a number of satirical essays, some excursions into natural and preternatural history, a couple of autobiographical vignettes, several parodies, a gallery of caption and captionless drawings, a fable, and [the report on] soap opera." Thurber also included most of the Talk stories he generated and wrote from 1928 to 1936, in a style, Lardner comments, markedly different from the one being used at the *New Yorker* in 1948.

Thurber's birds, plants, and creatures, real and fancied, discovered within the botanical gardens and game preserves of his imagination, were the last he could see well enough to draw, even using a powerful Leica lens. Some were among the best he ever did. Some art critics continued to find Thurber principally a caricaturist, vaguely related to Edward Lear and William Thackeray. *The Beast in Me*, Thurber writes the Millers, "is such a hodge podge that practically no two reviews were anywhere near the same."

In Cornwall, Thurber's secretary was now Elfride (Fritzi) Von Kuegelgen, who lived in nearby Sharon. While he was living at East Fifty-seventh Street or the Algonquin for an extended time, one of his secretaries was Patricia Stone, who offers a précis of her working life with the Thurbers:

"My hours were from two-thirty to five p.m. He was wonderful to work with. If he didn't take a suggestion from me, he'd explain why. If he thought a word should be changed, he'd rewrite the whole sentence, explaining that the change interrupted its original rhythm. He'd dictate letters but always wrote material to be published in soft pencil on yellow copy paper. I'd take his handwritten stuff, bring it back typed the next day, and read it to him. He had a photographic memory and would tell me precisely where to find something he wanted to revise. He worked hard all day—practically a recluse.

"Helen would read his mail and tell him what he should answer. They had an efficient working relationship. She was like a good secretary—helpful but never in the way. She was a straighten-upper. He was always knocking over a pile of book matches she would put on a plate near him for his cigarettes. She'd always say, 'Oh, Jamie, you knocked all those matches off and I have to pick them up again.' I sometimes wondered if it was a game she played, a way of reminding him of his need for her. Why did she heap the matches so high?

"I remember when Helen bought him a second hat and overcoat from DePinna's, after he had left the first ones in the apartment next door by mistake. When he finally got those back, and would be complimented on his hat or coat, he'd remark, 'I'm glad you like them. I have more just like them at home.' They were both generous with money—Helen was acquisitive but never stingy. Sometimes at five o'clock, he'd stuff some of the letters to be answered in his pocket and go to the *New Yorker* to work with Miss Terry, pick up mail, or autograph books she had waiting for him. Then he'd go to the Algonquin for a martini.

"He was also working on new captions for his old drawings that the magazine had begun to reprint. I remember one that was turned down had a child saying to the Thurber Woman, 'Mother, are you a mammal?' He used to say that people confused his name with that of Edna Ferber, and that he was going to use a pen name, Jacob Thrasbie.

"He remembered colors of things vividly after blindness. For a while, he could still dimly make out yellow. Harcourt Brace printed the jacket of *The Beast in Me* in yellow for that reason. He was interested in my problems; I had personal troubles at the time, and, after detailing them to Thurber one day, he summed it all up for me, saying, 'What you're telling me, Patricia, is that your husband is a cad.' That helped, because it was what I knew but couldn't say.

"Now and then he'd call someone he knew and pretend to be a former colored maid or laundress of theirs. Usually his line was that she couldn't deliver their laundry. Her husband was in jail for cutting someone with a razor and she'd had to sell the laundry to help raise bail. He could keep it up for long minutes at a time. I don't know why they never caught on.

"Sometimes he'd worry because the *New Yorker* wasn't developing new humor writers. I worked with him on *The Great Quillow, The White Deer,* and 'The Beast in the Dingle.' When I went on to graduate school at the University of Florida, I did my thesis on his art. He and Helen both cooperated."

In a letter to Stone addressing her thesis queries, Thurber seems willing to accept one of his classifications by the art critics as a caricaturist:

> The early drawings are done in insecure and fewer lines, and the later
> ones showed the detail and too great care that comes from practice
> which cramps and confines the early lack of inhibition. I suggest that
> good draughtsmanship is not essential to caricature, but the power of

getting what you want is essential. Thackeray, Carruthers, Gould, Max Beerbohm, are examples of this. We are sure about the drawing of a Daumier, a Garan d'Ache, a Charles Keene—we are not so sure of what Max Beerbohm does, but it does not matter, for we know that few great caricaturists are so certain of saying, with a few strokes, precisely what they want to say.

In her thesis, Stone suggests the psychological correlation of wit to dreams, both considered by some social scientists to be an escape from pain. Thurber writes her that "the analogy between dreams and wit rests on a similarity more superficial than basic, and the psychic explanation of wit fails to take in the selectivity of the artist whose powers of rejection and perfection are greater than his vulnerability to impulse."

"The letters were dictated, of course," says Stone, "and I felt a bit nostalgic getting them, somewhat envious of whoever was working with him. Several years later, when he was with his revue, A Thurber Carnival, the Thurbers took me on again as secretary to help with his correspondence when he was on tour with the show and later in New York. When I heard he died, I called Helen to ask if I could help her get his letters and unpublished material sorted out, but she seemed to resent the offer. 'I don't need you for that, Pat,' she told me rather coolly. I suppose, now that he was gone, she felt he wasn't to be shared with anyone."

In the spring of 1948, Herman Miller was ill—few, if any, knew how seriously. The Thurbers planned to visit Mame over Mother's Day, and in writing to the Millers of their plans to see them, too, Thurber includes a brief parody of Tennyson: "Take, dears, my little sheaf of wrongs—for old and new. Now of my three score years and ten it seems that only about 56 will not come again. Fair as stars when only two are always in the sky, and even the weariest Thurber winds somehow safe to thee."

They stayed at the Deshler-Wallick. "He'd memorized the number of hotel steps," says Dorothy Miller. "We hadn't realized how blind he had become. 'Watch out for this last step,' Helen would tell him. He acted so independently, other people probably thought he was simply an absentminded professor from the university who couldn't keep his mind on what he was doing."

Much of Thurber's correspondence that year was with Ross, who, at the time, was involving himself in nearly every detail of the magazine's editorial operation and often answered letters that Thurber had addressed to James Geraghty, Gus Lobrano, or Hawley Truax. Ross was delighted at Peter De Vries's suggestion that old Thurber cartoons be rerun with fresh Thurber captions, and adopted the idea as his own. This led to exchanges between him and Thurber that went on from June 1948 into the next year. The correspondence, fermenting for decades in the dusty annals of the magazine, leaves its reader of today heady with bemusement.

> *Ross:* Through the instrumentality of Mr. De Vries, several photostats of old Thurber drawings with new captions arrived on my desk. I am putting three of them through, to be regarded as new drawings . . . and we are committed to this project. . . .
>
> My viewpoint is that they are worth as much to us as new drawings would be. . . . Meanwhile, and henceforth, keep your mind on captions.
>
> Our postage bill will go up. Kip Orr will have to answer a lot of letters from people who get onto what we're doing. . . . My idea is to say that Mr. Thurber's eyesight not permitting him to draw at this time, we are giving our readers the pleasure of looking at some of the old ones again —or maybe *privilege* should be the word. That will have to be thought through.

Ross then thinks of cutting up Thurber's cartoons and rearranging the parts, rather than simply running them intact with new captions. His enthusiasm led him to write Thurber four letters—two on the same day, before he had time to receive Thurber's answer to the first.

> *Ross:* We're doubtful about the drawing of the doctor with the rabbit's head, because it's so distinctive that it will be remembered by most everybody. Geraghty has an idea that he could amend the drawing by taking an animal head out of some other drawing of yours and stripping . . . it onto the doctor, and then put in a different woman, making an entirely new drawing. . . . It opens up all kinds of possibilities. Readers then wouldn't recognize old drawings, and art historians of the future would have a fine time trailing down the original source of some of your characters. Let me know what you think, please.

Thurber wasn't agreeable to carving up his old drawings, but continued to send Ross captions for those left intact. He was satisfied with the payments— a hundred dollars per cartoon plus COLA (cost-of-living adjustment)—but felt that Ross was rejecting some of his captions without consulting other people on the staff; he recommends that Ross share them with White, Gibbs, and Mary Petty before making his final decision.

Thurber: I have got about seven more captions which I will send directly to you, but I am vaguely worried about the process of selection and rejection. I feel that since these are drawings with captions they should be submitted to the art meeting just as if they were originals. I hold your own judgment inferior to no man's and your experience wider than any but a one-person opinion is bound, by the nature of the human being, to be subject to that singularity which grows out of personal taste and private prejudice.

I do not hold a tremendous brief for the two you rejected, but I am interested in the grounds of the rejection. If you don't know that "taut" is a well-known cliché of dramatic criticism the line is lost through no fault of its own. . . .

I suggest that you make your own selections but that you get an outside opinion on those which you do not think are suitable. . . .

[Helen and I] have found only about twenty-eight old drawings that lend themselves easily to new captions, but this might be brought up to thirty-five . . . by the exercise of some remarkable ingenuity. I want to get up my own captions, since an old drawing of mine with somebody else's line would leave me completely out of the picture and could be just as easily done if I were dead.

Though Thurber had made up his mind that he was through drawing for publication, Ross's excitement over the old art briefly revived his interest in trying it once more.

Thurber: Several persons have suggested that modern scientists who have done wonders with lighting might contrive a . . . table drawing board, with glass instead of wood to draw on. The proper suffusion of light behind the glass and the right quality of paper might make it possible for me to draw with more ease than ever. I just don't know.

Ross liked the Thurber Woman's annoying comment to her harassed writer husband: "What's the matter, angel, have you lost the old know-how?" But the only Thurber cartoon containing a man at a typewriter had one woman saying to another, "He's giving Dorothy Thompson a piece of his mind." The extra woman made the new caption unusable.

Ross: The man . . . is sitting before a sort of card table, and there is no evidence that he is a professional writer. If he isn't a professional writer, the idea doesn't work. We are . . . consolidating the man at the type-writer with the woman of the picture that came with the caption. . . .

You expressed yourself as against consolidating pictures from different drawings, but I thought . . . we would make a try at it and send a photostat up to see what you and Helen think. . . . I think . . . it will save that caption for you, and that in the course of time a great many others could be made usable, too. I think that one reason I didn't give you action sooner on the pending seven captions is that, subcon-sciously, I was waiting to show you this photostat.

Many Thurber fans recognized the recycled drawings in the *New Yorker,* and soon the *London News Chronicle* published its own discovery of them.

Thurber: The . . . revelation . . . shows that people will recognize the old drawings, but this makes no difference. If we try to conceal it by avoiding some of the better known, but not the best known drawings, we would cramp our freedom. . . . It might be better if the audience were frankly let in on the secret and they might even enjoy it more. . . .

Here you are looking for a typewriter to fit a caption, when the caption should be fixed to fit a drawing without a typewriter.

I am keeping an open mind about the pasting up of parts of drawings into a new whole . . . but it well may be that you would be tampering with one of the basic principles of artistic integrity. Would you consider pasting new dresses on the women in Ralph Barton's "The 1930's" and calling them "The 1940's?" If I could have a hand in the permutations myself which I can't, it might be different.

Ross: I don't know now how we would go about letting the audience in on the secret . . . unless we ran an announcement in the magazine that we are reprinting Thurber's [drawings], which I don't think would be artistic. The fact is . . . and from my viewpoint there isn't any secret to be let in on. My idea is that if asked about it, we merely say yes, we're reprinting them, and that's that.

Thurber: I keep taking a dimmer view of the project to cut up and rearrange the old drawings. Some future day this operation would ham-per and confuse the historian who is bound to write the definitive study of the New Yorker artists under the title "Peter Arno and His Circle," in which I will be briefly discussed in Chapter 12, "Steinberg and The Others." It would be impossible to tell my work from [Geraghty's].

I also find that I am a little apathetic to the idea of beginning again with the aid of General Electric. Under the best circumstances it would still be a strain.

Only six Thurber cartoons were rerun with Thurber captions before he tired of the game, but Ross continued to have his old drawings scissored into captionless spots, and they ran with some regularity in the magazine until shortly after Ross's death. Thurber banked the money but no longer considered himself an active *New Yorker* artist.

The two men continued to fight over Ross's refusal to let the *Reader's Digest* reprint any text or drawings from the *New Yorker*. Thurber followed the rule, allowing the *Digest* to reprint his material only from books or other magazines. Thurber's claim to Ross, if true, that he could get five times more for a *Digest* reprint than what Ross paid him for the original could mean only that the *Digest* had made a special deal with him; at that time, the *Digest* paid writers just fifty dollars a page for reprints. It was the principle, Thurber told Ross—the freedom to do what he wished with his material. But Ross held his writers to the magazine's contract, which forbade condensed reprints of *New Yorker* content, insisting that the "ruined" text unfairly represented the magazine and helped its newsstand competitors compete.

Relations with all his publishers had long been a cause for Thurber's grousing. Books were still sent to the Thurbers' East Fifty-seventh Street apartment, for example, after they had moved back to Cornwall, or to the Homestead, in Virginia, when they were in Bermuda. Thurber's revived belief that he had been underpaid over the years by his publishers added to his resentments, and he tried to get it all off his chest with "File and Forget," the classic piece in which he complains that a publisher is shipping unwanted copies of *Grandma Was a Nudist* to houses he and his family had inhabited in Columbus years ago. "I have just read in proof your series of letters to and from the publishers," Ross writes him, "and got laughs all the way through. This is an exceedingly funny piece, and I predict that it will accumulate a considerable degree of fame."

John McNulty had given Thurber a recording by the Mills Brothers of "The Java Jive," containing the lyrics, "I love the Java Jive and it loves me." In November 1948, Thurber used "Java, Java"—a riff from the song—in "A Couple of Snapshots," the start of his Album series. Ross read the proof and writes Thurber, "I am advised that *jada jada* are the words in that famous American song, not java java." Thurber protested that the phrase was not from "Jada," a song of World War I vintage. Among Ross's ten queries on the proofs he next sent Thurber are: "Nobody at all has got this Java Java business. The latest I've had is a note from a checker saying the song is *Java Jive*, indicating that he's recalled that combination in some song or other. Apparently *Java* is a popular word with lyric writers, which astonishes me."

It got straightened out, but when Ross heard that Thurber was passing around Ross's confusion over the matter, he defended himself with annoyance in a letter to Thurber: "As to that phrase *Java Java*, I always, as I have done for many years, query everything I don't understand, and I do not know what all the shooting is about in this instance."

Thurber was still trying to interest Elliott Nugent in coauthoring a play about the *New Yorker*, but Nugent, besides preparing to direct the first movie version of *The Great Gatsby*, had become subject to depressions and periods of hyperactivity, and was, in his words, "seriously neurotic and . . . filled with terror about what I had done or left undone." At times, he would telephone Thurber drunk and incoherent. Rosemary, who was by then a senior at the Northampton School for Girls, spent part of her summers with her father and Helen. "Nugent came to visit us that summer [of 1948]," she remembers. "We met him at the Danbury airport; he had chartered a plane from New York. My father and Helen hadn't realized how sick he was. He insisted on stopping at a bookstore and buying a lot of books for no reason at all. At dinner, he and my father got into a terrible fight. Nugent looked at me and said, 'You shouldn't be hearing this. Go to your room.' My father told me quietly that I didn't have to go, but I was outraged to be ordered about by a man I didn't know. I learned later what the trouble was."

Ross, who knew of Nugent's problem, wrote Thurber a cheerful letter, meant to reassure him concerning his old friend, and proving again that Ross could clown with the best of them:

> I had dinner [at "21"] last night with Nugent, who had had some drinks . . . and he swayed and swung and was very expansive. . . . Morris Ernst was there, having been found friendless and alone in the place. . . . Nugent told about a dispute with you arising from your spurning of a financial proposition he had put up to you to work on a play. I never understood the deal. It was more complex than New Yorker finances. . . . Ernst . . . then interjected an anecdote about your throwing $28,000 in Goldwyn's face. They both agreed you were an odd character, and unwordly [sic] and impractical beyond human credence. When it was all over, I said I thought you were right throughout. You should have seen them. Instantly, I retreated to a corner and unsheathed

my rapier. I stood them off for about thirty minutes, at the end of which time they were worn down. I told them businessmen would never understand artists, many many other things—thrust after thrust. Remind me of this and I will tell you more when I see you. Nugent was affectionate toward you throughout, of course, and also toward me as far as that goes. I had a good time.

Ross was still going through his period of worry and warmth regarding Thurber, which had started with the eye operations. When H. L. Mencken visited Ross at his apartment in New York, Ross knew of Mencken's interest in Thurber and invited Thurber to an after-dinner get-together, along with Mencken's old magazine colleague, George Jean Nathan. Mencken had been writing for the *New Yorker* for a dozen years. He and Ross—old newspapermen and fairly close in their conservative view of politics and the world—dominated the conversation, leaving Thurber and Nathan largely nonparticipants.

Thurber was also present at the cocktail party Ross gave for Rebecca West that year, when that prominent contributor arrived from England. She remembers that Thurber and another *New Yorker* writer were "terribly drunk." At one point there was a crash of overturned furniture and a falling body, but, contrary to Ross's instant supposition, "the crash was not Thurber," says Helen, "but [the other writer], sprawled across my lap."

Joel Sayre had developed a form of writer's block, leading Ross to inform Thurber, who was Sayre's close friend and informal sponsor on the magazine, that he couldn't go on giving Sayre advances against a piece he seemed unable to finish. Thurber replies, sympathetically:

> I can't remember when any situation involving friends has upset me so much, unless you could count the strange interlude of Mr. Nugent. . . . You have said countless times in twenty years that extremely few persons can successfully become free-lance writers. . . . What the hell people do about it as they get older I don't know. I have enough to write to last me at least five years and I do not foresee any circumstances that would constitute a block.

By midyear he wrote Nugent, who seemed improved, that he had "at last got well under way . . . the version of the New Yorker play." His new working title was "The Chadwick Profile"; Nugent was to play Thurber; Leon Ames would play Ross. "All I know about Act III right now is that it ends with Bruce [Ross] taking up the frustrated art meeting. . . . The tag line is Bruce's 'God, how I pity me!' "

Thurber was soon writing Ross about it: "There is a character named Walter Bruce in the play who has certain resemblances to yourself, but the fellow comes out as a likable, if tortured, gentleman who triumphs in one of the finest hours of the magazine's history." Ross, who still suffered from ulcers, replied, "I haven't got time to discuss your New Yorker play. I'll have to reread your letter in a more relaxed mood and give my emotions time to organize themselves. Do those casuals."

The Cornwall Civic Club put on a benefit performance of *The Male Animal* that summer, with Rosemary as Cleota, the maid, Charles Van Doren as Tommy, and other members of the younger set participating on and off the stage. Marc Simont, the illustrator of Thurber's *The 13 Clocks* and *The Wonderful O*, painted the backdrops. Thurber writes Nugent that "the kids put on the best performance . . . we have seen outside the Cort and they were wildly acclaimed at both shows. . . . Rosie was a triumph as Cleota." (Thurber had told Carson Blair that it was "a constant source of gratification to me that my friends, almost all of whom are younger than I am, have older daughters. In this way, I can pass myself off as thirty-eight.")

An alarmed Mame Thurber wrote Thurber that she had dreamed that he and Rosemary died. "Rosemary and I are both all right," Thurber writes Mame. "We'd like to have you stop worrying about dreams. If you will make a list of the dreams you had about people dying who really died, you won't find many items. Dreams usually represent an anxiety about something other than the dream itself and science has discovered that they are usually about people other than those in the dream. Thus, Rosemary and I, according to Freud, were surrogates for the ones you were worried about."

Jap Gude was producing *I Can Hear It Now*, recorded radio broadcasts of world events. The narrator was Edward R. Murrow. The many recordings had to be reduced to forty-five minutes, and Gude asked Thurber for help. Thurber wrote a three-thousand word critique over a weekend, recommending condensations and a faster opening. Murrow had earlier read some Thurber fables on the air, which Thurber thought had been poorly done. Word got back to Murrow, who wrote Thurber: "If I butchered your fables please regard it as belated revenge for the time in 1936 when you almost persuaded me to allocate to you fifteen minutes of network time for the Bull Moose Party."

Thurber's livelihood depended on his use of language, and he became one of its most vociferous protectors and practitioners, fighting any sign of its pollution, in speech or text, caring for the tools of his trade as fervently as any artisan. The alphabet and English grammar served, as well, as his playground. He was a linguistic stunt flyer, competing in word games with others, and adding his own lexicon of phrases and syllables to the language. Blindness granted him the privacy and concentration—day or night were the same to him—to work and toy with his vocabulary. The results showed up more and more frequently in his writing and conversation, after he stopped drawing professionally. Kenneth Tynan, a later friend, says of Thurber:

> He lived in [an interior] universe, entirely inhabited by words which he would play with, dismember, anatomize, dissect, reassemble in strange and odd combinations. His mind was a sort of seething kaleidoscope of word forms, word shapes, abused words, misused words, neologisms, old coinages reshaped. He was enormously proud of this . . . elaborate verbal architecture that was going on inside his brain.

Thurber was ahead of most in his largely apolitical circle of colleagues in seeing another threat, not only to his own livelihood and career but to artistic freedom in general. The House Un-American Activities Committee had been formed in 1938, anticipating a period of domestic and international threat. The term "Un-American" rankled with Thurber, who felt that so loose a label could be stuck on any person whose ideas or behavior displeased a congressman. It was used to define patriotism and, he felt, made the country look foolishly nationalistic. He pointed out that no other country had such terms—un-French or un-Belgian, for example. He describes an unpublished skit he wrote, in which a husband and wife in a bar get into an argument with a man with an accent:

> The husband says: "You must be un-American." He says: "I'm a citizen of Oslo." "Then he's un-Swiss," the wife says. "No, I think he's un-Danish." The man finally says: "No, I'm just Norwegian."

"Un-Americanism" was coined in government ranks by a liberal Jewish congressman named Samuel Dickstein, who was worried about Fascism abroad and the anti-Semitism of the pro-Nazi German American Bund. In 1936, he had proposed a House committee to monitor the trend. In 1938, funding for the committee was agreed upon only if "Radicals" and "Socialists" would also be investigated. The committee was chaired successively and ineffectively by the conservative Democratic congressmen Martin Dies and John S. Wood.

The end of the war left the nation jittery about a victorious Soviet Union pledged to the undoing of capitalism, and there was a growing acquiescence by the majority of Americans to governmental policing of thought and political behavior. The 1946 midterm elections resulted in the first Republican Congress in sixteen years, and a conservative Republican, J. Parnell Thomas, became chairman of HUAC.

With the spread of Communist governments abroad, Republican politicians, abetted by J. Edgar Hoover's partisan FBI, became convinced that the executive branch teemed with Soviet spies and subversive Americans in sympathy with Communism. Truman, shaken by the 1946 elections and the discovery of Soviet espionage within the American, Canadian, and British governments, set up a loyalty program along with the Central Intelligence Agency. The program authorized the Civil Service Commission to conduct loyalty investigations of government employees, measures not in effect even during wartime. No specific charges were necessary, only that "reasonable grounds exist for belief that the person involved is disloyal to the Government of the United States."

The witch hunt was on. Names were named; blacklisting began. Former Communists who recanted became the government's expert witnesses, in the belief that because they were once wrong, they must now be right. Bertrand Russell commented that the United States would do anything to fight Communism, including imitating it. Mort Sahl was soon telling audiences at the Hungry I in San Francisco, "Every time the Russians throw someone in jail, we throw someone in too, just to show them they can't get away with it."

Private opinions—what one read, wrote, or once said years before—or the most fleeting of associations could be made a reason to end a career. One could be imprisoned on contempt charges for refusing to name names. The entertainment field was the first in the private sector to come under suspicion; it was said to be creating films sympathetic to Communism. The conservative libertarian Ayn Rand, novelist and screenwriter, testified before the Thomas committee that the movie *Song of Russia*—which had been made during the war, when Russia was an ally—was deliberate Soviet propaganda, because it showed Russians smiling. When a committee member asked her whether anybody in Russia smiled anymore, she answered, "If they do, it is privately and accidentally." Robert Taylor, who starred in the movie, indulged in a self-flagellation exercise before the committee and agreed that movies should only entertain, not propagandize; but when asked if he thought the motion picture industry should make *anti*-Communist pictures, he said he thought it should.

Thurber, who had scorned the leftists and the intellectual American Communists and sympathizers for nearly two decades, was appalled by this turn of events. So was E. B. White. Ross, a social conservative, continued to see his magazine as entertainment, not a medium for political stands. But in his eyes White could do no wrong. In the November 1, 1947, issue of the *New Yorker*, White, in a Comment, reacts to the HUAC activities and, perhaps, to Truman's loyalty program, under which the FBI had begun fingerprinting government employees the month before:

> This magazine traffics with all sorts of questionable characters, some of them, no doubt, infiltrating. Our procedure so far has been to examine the manuscript, not the writer; the picture, not the artist. We have not required a statement of political belief or a blood count. This still seems like a sensible approach to the publishing problem, although falling short of Representative J. Parnell Thomas's standard. . . . We sit among as quietly seething a mass of reactionaries, revolutionaries, worn-out robber barons, tawny pipits, liberals, Marxists in funny hats and Taftists in pin stripes as ever gathered under one roof in a common enterprise. The group seems healthy enough, in a messy sort of way, and everybody finally meets everybody else at the water cooler, like beasts at the water hole in the jungle. . . . If this should change, and we should go over to loyalty, the meaning of "un-American activity" would change, too, since the America designated in the phrase would not be the same country we have long lived in and admired.

A *Herald Tribune* editorial appeared within the month, stating that all employees should declare their political beliefs as a condition of employment. White, Coates, Angell, and others wrote the *Tribune*, protesting that this would violate the Bill of Rights. The newspaper ran White's letter, along with an editorial denouncing White's position as quixotic and dangerous. Thurber, at the Homestead, wrote White that "Helen read me your letter and the editorial reply . . . and I stayed awake for hours getting madder and madder. . . . The blow is also aimed at The New Yorker and the battle and investigation are on."

He enclosed a copy of a letter he had just sent the *Tribune*, in which he said its editorial "could be used as a preface to a book on how to set up a totalitarian state under the bright banner of the security of the nation. . . . This is the familiar way in which all such states have been established. . . . But why should I instruct your editorial writer? He seems to have a natural gift and a peculiar facility for writing the handbook."

Ten days earlier, Thurber had written Mencken, warning him that the annals of the *American Mercury*, of which Mencken had been cofounder and coeditor, would come back to haunt him, with their "light regard for Congress."

> I am anticipating the gruelling problem of my own iniquities in a forthcoming issue of . . . the New Worker, as it will soon be known to one and all. It has long been known that Ross has long planned to overthrow the government and only two considerations restrain him: his finicky complaint that revolutions cannot be sound-proofed, and his strange absorption in a program to eliminate the comma entirely. With this in mind, he has engaged in some agile and unfortunate wrassling matches with the prose style of my colleagues and myself. We have recently got him down and have broken his pelvis, and made him desist. [He has turned] his attention to a daring attempt to rid the language of the word "which." . . . I have been known to refer to Ross' present plan as a which hunt.

"I hope you escape the noose," Mencken replies. "I have been threatened myself at monthly intervals since 1914 when I came out for the Kaiser in a large way and damned democracy as a decaying superstition. When and if you are jailed, I hope it will be in the north. The southern hoosegows, as I can well testify, are extremely uncomfortable."

The "seditious" casual Thurber must have had in mind was "Exhibit X," in which he compares the laid-back security rules of his State Department days with the contemporary ones:

> Waking up at night and looking back on it, I sometimes wonder how I would have come out of one of those three-men inquisitions the State Department was once caught conducting. Having as great a guilt sense as any congressman, and a greater tendency to confession, it might have taken me hours to dredge up out of my mind and memory all the self-indictments that must have been there. I believed then, and still do, that generals of the Southern Confederacy were, in the main, superior to generals of the Northern armies; I suspected there were flaws in the American political system; I doubted the virgin birth of United States senators; I thought that German cameras and English bicycles were better than ours; and I denied the existence of actual proof that God was exclusively a citizen of the United States.

He approved of Truman's efforts to contain Soviet aggression—the Marshall Plan and the Berlin airlift. Worried about the effects of world events on

Rosemary and her classmates, he writes her that the present tensions resulted from the American attempt to build a bulwark against aggression. It would be more ominous, he writes headmistress Sarah B. Whitaker, if everything were serene, "as would be the case if the democracies permitted Russia to have her way."

To Thurber, the new threat was from within—not from un-American Americans, but from those who appointed themselves the official definers of the vague term "loyalty." Where White dealt with the issue in Comment, Thurber hoped to address it in his *New Yorker* play. One problem was that he wanted Nugent as coplaywright, and Nugent was of the politically conservative ranks and saw nothing wrong with flushing out "subversives" in both the public and private sectors. Thurber describes the play's plot in detail to Nugent in a letter, hoping to borrow from *The Male Animal* its liberal/reactionary conflict to use in a magazine setting. The magazine in his play plans a profile of "George Lincoln Chadwick (R.–N.Y.)" who is in the city to "case the situation":

> Chadwick has become the new J. Parnell Thomas and, in accordance with threats you are familiar with, his committee has decided to investigate, among other things, that hotbed of subversion, the magazine of opinion published in New York. . . . It is obvious from his interviews that the *New Yorker* is to be a target.

He finished the first act, but was dissatisfied with it, writing Nugent:

> I realize that the play might be called "Tommy Turner [from *The Male Animal*] on a Magazine" in that the part of the editor-writer is a badgered intellectual up against a Congressman who is a magnified Ed Keller, and that the wife is the same kind of sympathetic woman as Ellen. . . .
>
> The idea of the girl writing a thesis about Tim Norton is realistic. There is a young man from Columbi[a] going through my scrapbooks at the office right now preparing just such a thesis. . . . Tim is not me but a composite and he comes out more like Nugent on the *New Yorker* than anything else, but here are a few things about myself she [the student researcher] could have found out: I joined the League of American Writers in 1938 without knowing it was a communist front and I never resigned but merely ignored their letters; I am an honorary vice chairman of the Progressive Citizens Committee in Connecticut; and my name appears on a letterhead with Paul Robeson. Helen and I were

innocent contributors to the Anti-Fascist League which we thought was merely an anti-fascist league; but most amusing of all, "The Thurber Carnival" was praised in the New Masses as the work of a man who was boring from within and doing a lot to hold the middle class up to ridicule.

Nugent felt that the *New Yorker* was too specialized a stage setting, that Communism was a real threat that something should be done about, and that nothing entertaining could be made from mocking the un-American Activities Committee. A dogged Thurber makes one last try to persuade Nugent, before giving up the play. "I see that I have not explained to you the basic passionate and angry feeling and idea that prompted me to start this play. I agree with you that communism-cum-The Thomas Committee can be dreadfully boring on the stage . . .":

What I am afraid of, and mad about, is the possible growth of the malignant nature of committees. . . . I am trying to do in this play a basicly [sic] comic forecast of a possible increase of the present conditions. . . . One of our great weapons is no secret. It is the Bronx cheer, or raspberry. Long may it wave the sons-of bitches out at first base. My American Activities Committee is a justifiable caricature, but I want to show how foolish it is as well as dangerous. I want to kid it rather than tear it apart.

Thurber was never a comfortable joiner—of alumni associations, literary societies, or political groups. When asked by a *Time* reporter why he belonged to the Independent Citizen's Committee, an organization with ill-defined objectives, which his friend Humphrey Bogart had joined, the interview went like this:

Q: How did you become associated with ICCASP?
JT: What's that?
Q: You know—the Independent Citizen's Committee.
JT: Huh?
Q: Jo Davidson's outfit.
JT: Oh, yes, I think I belong to it. . . . I think they sent out a letter or something. . . . I think I'm an honorary member.
Q: What should the organization stand for?
JT: Well, I've been awfully busy and I suppose someone has formulated its ideas better than I could.

Thurber had discussed the play with both Nugent and Herman Miller. He sent both men duplicate letters on October 28, 1948, saying that he was having so much trouble with the play that he had given it up for the time being: "This is something that takes more than a few months, and a man who spent eight weeks on a piece called 'The Secret Life of Walter Mitty' is no hand at tumbling things out . . .":

> I think Elliott is unhappily sound when he says that any satiric play about a Congressman, however innocent and rightfully angry, runs the risk of seeming to be on the wrong side in the horrible and unbelievable state of black and white into which this fearful world has whipped itself. . . .
>
> I do not care to get involved in writing a play on any subject on which my statements are likely to be judged by a nation of people who are at present in a hypermanic condition. . . .
>
> Will it be any better in the first year of Dewey's administration?

Along with many others, Thurber was certain of Truman's defeat in the 1948 election. In Truman's own party, Strom Thurmond had declared his candidacy for the presidency on the Dixiecrat ticket, as a protest of Truman's civil rights stand, and Henry Wallace, former vice president under Roosevelt, was challenging Truman as the Progressive Party candidate. Wallace was opposed to the nation's joining the North Atlantic Treaty Organization or aiding Turkey and Greece in their fight against Communism—actions he felt were confrontations designed to provoke the Soviet Union into war. Thurber allowed his name to be listed as honorary vice chairman of Connecticut's Progressive Citizens Committee, perhaps persuaded by his friend, Mark Van Doren. Van Doren, as strong a man of peace as he was an anti-Communist, campaigned for Wallace. Added to these Truman opponents was the Republican Party, which had won both houses of Congress two years before. Thurber would make the claim later that one version of his play depended on Dewey's winning. However that may be, Daise Terry remembers the morning after Truman's stunning upset victory. "Mr. Thurber stuck his head in my office door," she says, "and simply said, 'What happened?'"

62

That Letter from the States

We have had wonderful weather and a wonderful time here, including a drinking and dinner party at the [John P.] Marquands along with
John Dos Passos. . . . With all this we have been able to get rest and
sunshine. . . . I have finished two acts of a play and all but one paragraph of a New Yorker story, about a woman writer of esoteric novels,
full of unmeaning and unmethod. At the end after her death, the butler
says to me "I was to have been the uncharacter of a nonbutler in one of
her books." "Didn't you appear in any of them" I asked. "Oh, but, no
sir" he corrected me proudly, "I did not appear in *all* of them." This is
less than I have not been able to do. Don't miss it, if you can.

—Letter to Jap Gude, from Nassau, March 3, 1949

The "New Yorker story" referred to is Thurber's glorious satire "A Final Note
on Chanda Bell (After Reading Two or Three Literary Memorials, to This or
That Lamented Talent, Written by One Critic or Another)," which moved
Wolcott Gibbs to send his often-quoted tribute, citing Thurber's "grasp of
confusion."

Ross turned fifty-six in December 1948, shortly after reading that "man
reaches his peak at fifty-five and then starts downhill," he complained to
Robert Sherwood. He was soon in more trouble—with the age-obsessed

THE
NEW YORKER
No. 25 WEST 43RD STREET

EDITORIAL OFFICES
BRYANT 9-8200

Monday —

Dear Jim —
I just finished "Chanda
Bell". It's a marvellous piece.
I wish to Christ I had your
grasp of confusion.
Loss to Helen

Ross

Thurber, who had just turned fifty-four and was suffering from a flare-up of his
malfunctioning thyroid gland. After reading the proofs of Thurber's "The
Notebooks of James Thurber," Ross writes him, "I go on record as saying I
love it. It's wonderful. You are still at your top, or maybe you haven't got
there yet. Anyhow, all the recent pieces seem to me to stand out like light-
houses." Then Ross, with all good intentions, blunders into Thurber's war
zone—financial compensations and contracts:

Lobrano has told me about the piece you are doing for *Holiday* ["What Every Traveler Should Know"] and the price you are getting. That isn't so much for such a wealthy outfit. . . . I also think that, under the first-reading agreement, you must have our permission to write this piece for *Holiday*. I herewith give it to you, on the grounds that it is a fact piece, and hence is excepted by the agreement. Anything you do is all right, and I'll fight for that, and I wouldn't say that to more than two or three people.

Perhaps because it was Katharine White's son, Roger Angell, then at *Holiday*, who had persuaded both Thurber and E. B. White to write articles for that magazine, or because *Holiday* paid Thurber so well, Ross sent Thurber a testy letter of self-justification. He had computed the average price paid by the *New Yorker* for Thurber's last five pieces at almost fifteen hundred dollars per casual, "which isn't bad for us. We're not the Curtis Publishing Company." Possibly aware of what he had stirred up, five days later Ross wrote Thurber yet again, complimenting him on a new casual, "What a Lovely Generalization!": "I think it's a funny, and a wonderful, and a masterly, and a sweet piece. Unless I'm getting feeble-minded, which is by no means unlikely, your recent stuff has been just about at your peak. You're amazing."

But on the same day, Thurber was writing his response to Ross's earlier letter:

A magazine that has bought twenty-two pieces in as many months [from me] does not seem fair or generous when it objects to one or more sold outside. I strongly favor a new form of contract, specifying that I may if I wish sell two out of every ten pieces anywhere without submission to you. I will always prefer and insist on selling you the eighty percent. . . .

The Holiday price was not by any means the only factor in that sale. . . . However, a piece of money like that occasionally is necessary in the case of a man who has been a free lancer for fourteen years. White and Gibbs are both on salary, and so is almost everybody else. The successful free lancer, and there are few of us, must be allowed reasonable freedom and not be bound by the same contract that applies to the salaried man. . . . I have written more pieces for you than White and Gibbs put together, and let me be the first to say that I am intensely opposed to the idea of any universal contract that applies to me. I drive a tougher bargain with publishers than any of the other boys or girls. I even get one hundred percent of all reprint rights and sole control of them. I surrender no part of any subsidiary rights. After fourteen years I have taken to making my own contracts. I am in a position to do this. I cannot be swayed by problems of bookkeeping . . . or a feeling about the inalienable equality of all New Yorker writers. . . .

I am willing to keep any contract secret from the youngsters and the slaves.

He ends on a snide note: "My total wordage for the past two years is about ninety-three thousand words. This does not count fifty thousand words written in letters. What do you get done?"

Thurber had his way. Ross, continually in awe of Thurber's prolific production from within his world of starless nights, writes:

I will say that I recognize the value of your heroic and distinguished service, past and present, agree with every point you make, and the arrangement shall be as you propose. Your contribution to this magazine has been enormous, and you write your own ticket. . . .

Keep this letter about in case I get hit by a truck, or forget the details.

In Nassau, the Thurbers met the vacationing Alfred (Fritz) Dashiell, a senior editor of the *Reader's Digest*, and his wife, Sara. Dashiell had been an editor at Scribners during its heyday, when it published Fitzgerald, Hemingway, and Wolfe, and he now handled relations between the *Digest* and the authors whose work it wished to reprint. Not knowing the Dashiells would also be in Nassau, Thurber had just written Dashiell an outraged letter, blasting him and *Digest* editor DeWitt Wallace. Wallace had rejected Thurber's soap opera series for condensation, calling it a rehash of what was generally known. After a party at the British Colonial Hotel, the Thurbers and Dashiells found themselves together in the elevator.

"It was a bit awkward," Sara Dashiell remembers. "The dining room was closed, so we four found ourselves going to the grill. The Thurbers were polite but very cool toward us, so I said, 'Mr. Thurber, I hear you are put out with the *Digest*. Fritz had nothing to do with it. Why can't we have a good time?' It worked. After dinner we invited them to our room for a nightcap and they stayed till four a.m. We had a lovely time. Thurber could still tell night from day; he could tell if there was a car at the curb, for example, but saw it only as a dark mass. He said another eye operation would either result in his seeing better or going completely blind. But the operations had caused him to have wild dreams in which he saw strange and terrible things, and the pain of it all had led him to decide against further surgery.

"We saw them several times after that. We came home on the *Mauretania* together. Thurber sang 'Bye, Bye, Blackbird' with the ship's orchestra. Alfred's job kept him in touch with Thurber. Andy White wouldn't let even his non–*New Yorker* pieces be reprinted by the *Digest;* he said they couldn't be, and shouldn't be, condensed. Thurber, on the other hand, would almost always send back the condensations with an O.K. Once, Fritz called him at his home, at eleven a.m., and woke him up. When Fritz told him what the *Digest* was paying for a particular piece, Thurber said, 'My God, is that enough?' and hung up. Helen called back and said it was acceptable. When the *Digest* wanted to use parts of *Many Moons* in an anthology, Thurber blew up at the price offered him per line. Fritz, who sometimes met with Thurber for lunch at the Algonquin, was asked to handle the matter. Fritz agreed with Thurber and got him more money.

"Thurber judged people—liked or disliked them—according to their voices. He told me, 'You must be very young; you have a young voice.' How could I not like him? Thurber was a Gilbert and Sullivan fan; I'd sung with an amateur G. and S. opera company, so we used to recite libretto passages to one another. His memory was astonishing. You had only to mention a subject and he would seize and build on it."

The Laughing Lion Society, whose members were former editors and managers of the *Jester,* Columbia University's humor magazine, held a banquet at "21," at which their 1949 Award for Humor was presented to Thurber, Fred Allen, Frank Sullivan, and Ross. Ross was disinclined to attend, until he heard that Allen was to be present. Thurber had told Ross that Jack Goodman, of Simon & Schuster, was after Allen to excerpt the best of his radio scripts for a book, and that some of the material would be suitable for the *New Yorker.* Hoping to press Allen, Ross agreed to attend the banquet, and then heard that Allen might not be there. He passed on the rumor to Thurber, who replies:

> I was going to write Fred Allen and ask him to get out from behind that indecision, and let us know if a couple of amateurs like us are going to have, or have not, his support that night. . . . They might ask Henry Morgan to accept for Allen. . . .
>
> Morgan is not a humorist, because he hates people. He hates his sponsors, his audience, and his friends. He wishes everybody were dead, but not in heaven with the angels. I don't think he has mellowed at all. I think he is clucking to the turkey, while he holds an axe behind his back.
>
> The trouble with these youngsters like Morgan and . . . Jack Parr

[sic] is that the lint of the high school magazine sticks to the blue serge of their talent. . . .

Are we going to dress that night, or is it just cocktails? I have a beautiful new dinner jacket, complete, for once in my life, with trousers.

Allen turned up at the award ceremony, but the fact was nearly lost on Ross, who usually avoided public appearances and was horrified to note that as each honoree received his trophy he was expected to offer a few remarks. When it was Ross's turn, he stood, took the award, nervously snarled, "Jesus Christ!" and sat down. Frank Sullivan, seated next to him, whispered, "Too long, Ross. I was bored after the first syllable."

Ann Honeycutt still haunted the peripheries of Thurber's sightless life. As a radio executive, her help had been enlisted to get Allen to the banquet. The Thurber ambivalence toward her, a mixture of lingering interest and resentment, shows up first in a letter to Ross: "Letting Miss Honeycutt in on this was not too wise. . . . As a middle-aged part of the New York scene, her projected memoirs trouble the sleep of a hundred men of high literary eminence or exalted public office. Her book is to be called, I believe, 'They Told Me Everything.' "

Yet upon his return from Nassau, he had written her: "At the Marquands I heard two different groups of people discussing you. They included Dos Passos, Sarah Murphy, and my wife. I could tell that Helen was beginning to feel her rum when I heard her assuring somebody that you are the only old girl of mine for whom she gives a good Goddamn. This praise of her most dangerous rival is either neurotic or a darned nasty trick."

Thurber never did quite get over Ann. "When I guided him to the men's room, he usually asked if any of his friends were there, and how they looked," says Emil, the headwaiter at Tim Costello's. "But he would always ask about Ann Honeycutt in particular—when had she been in, and who with?"

Honeycutt's and Thurber's friend Jack Goodman had been working hard to get Thurber away from Harcourt Brace, succeeding only after Frank Morley, with whom Thurber worked well, had left Harcourt to live in England. But Thurber was a worry to any publisher, and Goodman never took him for granted. He was aware that Thurber's popular "File and Forget" had been inspired by a mix-up in correspondence between Thurber and Simon & Schuster.

Phyllis Levy, who began at Simon & Schuster as Goodman's secretary, recalls, "Jack told me, anything that goes to Thurber, send it yourself; don't trust the mail room or a messenger or anyone else. There was a big demon in the midst of our dealings with Thurber. It was always his royalty statement—out of two thousand—that got lost."

"There was always some legitimate reason for Thurber to bawl us out," remembers editor Peter Schwed. "Now and then he'd get us sore, too, with his abuse, though we carefully kept our tempers. We were all proud to have him as an author and really tried to do our best by him. He had to have realized that, but never gave us credit for it. It was a vicious circle: worrying about getting things right for Thurber seemed to lead to more mistakes." Still, Thurber remained with Simon & Schuster until Goodman's sudden and premature death, at age forty-eight, in 1957.

In April of 1949, the Thurbers were chauffeured to the Northampton school to pick up Rosemary for a three-day weekend in New York. She would graduate that June and attend Skidmore College in the fall. Thurber's last clear visual impression of his daughter dated to 1940, when she was eight years old. He continued to hope that she would be a writer, though Rosie was clearly more interested in the theater. He had written the Millers during her junior year:

> She gave up writing when she was twelve to become an FBI agent on the ground that writing is too hard, but now she seems to like it again. I wrenched away from her an essay she had done on Thoreau. At sixteen, American girls do not like Thoreau and she went to great length to look up criticism unfavorable to the old boy and built her piece around a basic objection to the validity of his philosophy. On this last point she was supported by the Britannica. She also included a couple of apt quotations from Andy White's piece in "One Man's Meat."

On April 16, the Thurbers sailed for Bermuda, Helen having begged the Columbus Thurbers to stay healthy, and of no bother, which Robert resented. "Do keep well, all of you," she ordered, "so we can all have a peaceful, serene spring." Robert was further incensed at Helen's first letter to them from Bermuda:

> Jamie is eating fiercely, putting on weight, sleeping ten hours a night, and has finished two New Yorker pieces since we arrived. He wants to work on the play, but also wants to get enough money ahead to pay for the new car when we get back. We're hoping to get it in time for Rosie's Commencement, the 12th of June. . . .
>
> Now keep well, all of you, we pray. We both hate to fly, & would have to at sudden notice.

The year proved to be an emotionally trying one for Thurber. Herman Miller died unexpectedly in April. His death came as a shock to Thurber, though Miller had not been well for several months. Thurber had recently written his ailing friend, assuring him that at their ages "we all have bruises and flattened batteries and bearings but we will all keep running for years." He received the bad news in Bermuda. Beginning his letter of condolences to Dorothy, Thurber found that it hurt even to put down the date:

> It is hard to write down the day after Herman Miller's death, for it marks the end of my oldest friend, and in so many ways my closest. No matter how long it had been since we saw each other, an old communion was easily and instantly reestablished. There was no other man who knew me so well, and I took pride and comfort in his sensitive understanding. He remembered everything over thirty-five years, and brought it out with his special humorous soundness. There was more depth and pattern to our friendship than to any other, and I have nothing that can take its place. It was more pleasure to have his laughter and appreciation than anyone else's because he was the one who completely understood all the references, sources and meanings. . . .
>
> One of the nicest things about him was that genuine shyness which at first couldn't believe that the ones he loved, loved him. His happiness was all the greater when he found out. There was never a moment when he wasn't important to me.

Then there were Elliott Nugent's recurring symptoms of mental illness, and the health of Helen's mother was worsening. Later that summer, Rosemary was a passenger in a roadster whose driver took a curve at high speed and turned it over. As Thurber explained to his family:

> Rosie had to crawl out and was the only one injured. She got a cracked pelvic ring and was six weeks in bed, but is now completely recovered and getting around on crutches. . . . She was very calm when they took her to the hospital in a police ambulance. She was there six days and then at Althea's cottage near Gloucester where it happened. We have better facilities here, so we brought her down by ambulance.

The two Thurber casuals that Helen had referred to were "The American Literary Scene" and "Joyeux Noel, Mr. Durning," a title suggested by Helen, which Ross thought would be funny in a July issue. A Christmas gift, a bottle of Cointreau, had been sent to the Thurbers by their servants of Southern

France days, Maria and Olympy Sementzoff. It took nearly five months of bureaucratic correspondence to get the bottle through customs, which Thurber made use of in his piece.

Stephen Spender had reviewed for Cyril Connolly's *Horizon* a British book called *The Americans*, which gave Thurber the idea for "The American Literary Scene (After Reading Several Essays, in English Magazines, on the Plight of the American Writer and the Nature of the American Male")." Thurber pretends to be a British writer reporting on writing in America. He visits the *New Yorker*, "a weekly journal of capricious opinion published, with massive drollery, in an enormous hotel of the same name." ("The strenuous Mr. William Rose . . . was not in when I called at *New Yorker*.") He adds:

> The social intercourse of the American writer is realized, almost exclusively, in public houses or private homes and flats, between the hours of 5 p.m. and 4 a.m. the following day. . . . The superficial observer might regard these nocturnal meetings as a sign of gregariousness, but they are, in reality, gloomily planned assemblages of separate lonelinesses. Friendship in America is indicated and proved by a steady flow of insult and contumely between friends, who smilingly accuse each other of insanity, depravity, spiritual damnation, duplicity, conspiracy, and the stealing of flowers from the graves of mothers.
>
> Some American writers who have known each other for years have never met in the daytime or when both were sober. The coming together of writers in the home or flat of one of their number is invariably a signal for trouble to start.

Ross wrote Helen in Bermuda that he had read the piece, "a couple of parts of it damned self-consciously. At this moment, my skin is still creeping. Good God, I'm not William Randolph Hearst. Naming the magazine didn't bother me, but the use of the name Rose did, and does." But he allowed it.

Ross had inquired into the lighted drawing board that he hoped would help Thurber return to drawing, but Thurber replies that "it might be too much of a strain and I might not get the perfection that would make it worth while. I appreciate your interest in me, old boy."

Ross was in London in July when *The Male Animal* opened there, and wired Thurber: "Hot review of 'Male animal,' London pleased." Thurber, in *The Years with Ross*, quotes the wire as a kindly exaggeration by Ross, and adds that the reviews "could scarcely have been described as hot." But in fact, they could be. *Time*'s London bureau reported that the play was the biggest success the Arts Theatre Club (where it opened) had had in seven years, and that at the New Theatre, where the play moved to, critics called it "gloriously funny" and "as satisfying entertainment as London has had for many months."

In those troubled days, "I now know," Thurber says, that "the onset of a hyperthyroid condition made me irritable and often unreasonable," and that Ross "was far less the snarler than I was." Indeed, *The Years with Ross* too often portrays Ross as an intolerant grouch. ("If that book had had Ross 'snarling' one more time, I'd have thrown it out the window," says Lois Long.) Actually, Thurber never received more sensitive consideration from anyone than he did from Ross after his blindness had set in. Whenever Thurber came to the *New Yorker* to discuss an editorial matter, Ross almost always walked the long L-shaped corridor to meet him at the elevators and guide him back to his office. Thurber's well-being was frequently on his mind. "I admonish you not to show up at the office for the next few days," he writes Thurber. "Painters are at work in several offices and the halls look like a second-hand store. You'd kill yourself."

The magazine paid on the basis of galley proof inches; if a piece was then added to or subtracted from, the author's compensation changed accordingly. When Thurber wrote Lobrano, fiercely objecting to a reduction of sixty dollars after "Daguerreotype of a Lady" was further edited, Ross took the responsibility, writing Thurber:

> I can understand an author's dismay at being thus docked, especially on a piece he has put in years on, and is especially fond of, but at the same time I have sympathy with myself, for the financial side of such an undertaking as this is a most brutal thing to be up against. It damned near killed both me and the magazine in the early days and why I remained and still remain up against it, I don't know. I must be crazy to go on in the spot I am in. . . .
>
> I am having a check sent you, but want to improve any impression that I am a damned fool—although I am one, or I wouldn't be mixed up in this kind of goings on when I might be out in the open air or cultivating my mind with a good book. I'm crazy, all right, but you can't say that most of my mad acts haven't been in behalf of writers.

In all this, there were hints of a growing paranoia on Thurber's part, regarding the *New Yorker*. Always possessive toward his protégé, John Mc-Nulty, he accused Ross of allowing the editors to compromise McNulty's originality:

I wanted to tell you what a triumph McNulty's ["Back Where I Had Never Been"] was. . . . The surprise comes from the fact that it was not run through our formidable prose machine, in a desperate and dedicated Ross-Shawn attempt to make it sound like everybody else. . . . The machine has left almost no differences in tongue or temperament or style. . . . since there has to be so much rewriting of most of the authors, this dreadful similarity is hard to avoid.

I understand that McNulty had the usual terrible battle to survive as the magnificent individual he is, but he made it. The curse of our formula editing is that uniformity tends toward desication [sic], coldness, and lack of vitality and blood. . . . We are afraid of warmth, as we are afraid of sex and human functions. Our only true boldness lies in the use of "Jesus Christ" to show we're not afraid of the Catholic Church.

The attack on Shawn incensed Ross, for McNulty had become discouraged while writing the essay, and wanted to give it up. It was Shawn who urged him on, accepted it in pieces and assembled it into a splendid whole, as only Shawn could. "You understand as wrong as a man can understand," Ross wrote Thurber heatedly in reply. "Whoever told you that McNulty 'had a terrible struggle for survival' is a liar or a spreader of outrageous slander. . . . Shawn was the obstetrician, the midwife, and the godfather of that piece, and it never would have been done without him."

Thurber also worried about the threats of a nuclear age. The past became more important to him, as if in compensation. He feared the future, with, he believed, its dwindling need for humorists, its insane humiliations of creative people in the name of "un-Americanism," and all the cold-war tensions that degraded hope and spirit in a world his daughter would soon be entering as an adult.

His sightlessness seemed to help him to retrieve the past, for his powers of recollection were better than ever. He could, he claimed, remember the birthday and middle name of every child in his grammar-school class, the phone numbers of several of his high-school classmates, the christening date of any of his friends' children, and the names of all the people who attended the lawn fete of the First Methodist Church in Columbus in 1907. The puzzle was, he added, that even though he was able to recall a ragbag of precise but worthless information, he had always had trouble remembering the brake pedal from the clutch. He especially regretted no longer being able to make out the *New York Times* Sunday crossword puzzle, with which, he said, he used to increase his word power.

And so began the reminiscences that resulted in *The Thurber Album*. He not only enlisted the research services of his brother Robert and others in Columbus, but of George Smallsreed ("I didn't charge him," says Smallsreed. "I knew it would result in free publicity for the *Dispatch*.")

And then came news that a play about the *New Yorker* was to be produced that year, while he was still rewriting only the second act of his own. The competitor was William Walden, a *New Yorker* staff member for seven years. The play, *Metropole*, was produced in the fall of 1949. It featured Lee Tracy as Ross, and had the helping hand of George S. Kaufman. Thurber, asked for his reaction, simply wished Walden luck. But the play didn't survive opening-night criticism—the consensus was that portraying Ross onstage didn't work, because it seemed to be caricaturing a caricature.

Ross, of course, ignored the play. He had his own problems, and visited the Lahey Clinic in Boston that fall. ("They couldn't find a thing wrong except that my acidity is high," he told Thurber. "The ulcer scar is reported as conspicuous on the X-ray plates, and rather a beauty.") But ulcers were not now the problem; he would be dead in two years from lung cancer.

Brendan Gill, who had succeeded Russell Maloney as rewriter of Talk, acquired a sudden, fierce, and, as it turned out, unjustified hatred of Thurber that would continue for forty years, nearly thirty years after Thurber's death. It was based upon a grave misunderstanding:

In 1949, Gill wrote a negative review of John O'Hara's *A Rage to Live* for the *New Yorker*, finding it, among other things, "sprawling" and "discursive," with "recurrent passages of maudlin sexuality." O'Hara, whose paranoia was well known, withheld his work from the *New Yorker* for eleven years after that. Gill says that a few months after the review appeared, at the magazine's twenty-fifth anniversary party at the Ritz, "I was informed that Thurber had told O'Hara that he had 'documentary proof' that Gibbs had written the review, but hadn't wanted to sign it because O'Hara was his friend. O'Hara's paranoia was content, for he *wanted* Gibbs to have betrayed him. Conversely, he broke into tears when he was honored by the Institute of Arts and Letters, for that left his paranoia frustrated.

"I felt that Thurber always needed some expression of power, and, because he could forgive himself, expected all others he offended to forgive him. I couldn't, and neither could Bob Coates, an angelic man I can only suppose Thurber wounded in some way. I consider Thurber a genius; I reviewed his books favorably. But he was excellent at creating a wonderful catastrophe; it was a game with him, like fooling people on the phone with his mimicry."

In 1975, Gill got the matter off his chest, pillorying both Thurber, dead for fourteen years, and O'Hara, who had died five years before. His best-selling *Here at The New Yorker* casts Thurber in a villainous role:

Thurber, that incomparable mischiefmaker, informed O'Hara that he had documentary proof of the fact that the review had been written not by me but by Wolcott Gibbs. Now, this was a master stroke on Thurber's part; as Lobrano once told me, Thurber was never so happy as when he could cause two old friends to have a falling out. . . .

With the invention of a single bold lie in respect to my review . . . Thurber had done two things: one, he had ensured that O'Hara would see me as a jackal, willing to let my name be used for a nefarious purpose and therefore a person permanently unworthy of forgiveness; and, two, he had ensured that Gibbs and O'Hara would quarrel. Moreover, the most painful of O'Hara's paranoid fantasies would thus have been caused to come true—his oldest and dearest friend stood revealed as his worst enemy. Iago-Thurber took care to point out to O'Hara that my review contained the adjective 'discursive,' which O'Hara was surely aware was one of Gibbs's favorite words. This was a lucky shot in the dark on Thurber's part; unbeknownst to him, O'Hara had sent Gibbs an advance copy of the novel, and Gibbs, on finishing the book, had written a letter to O'Hara, conveying his disappointment in it and employing that very word "discursive."

Sadly, Gill's impressions were mistaken. Thurber had nothing to do with the incident. After hearing Gill's review of *A Rage to Live* read to him, he wrote Ross a letter gently reprimanding him for publishing it, and defending O'Hara, whom he still considered his friend:

> Several persons told O'Hara that Gill said he was going to "get" the O'Hara book before it was published. All I know about Gill is the report that he is hipped on the subject of novel writing and that he has told strangers no writer is any good if he hasn't written a book before he is thirty. The strangers always tell him he is right, since he has the look of a man who will brook no disagreement. O'Hara happens to be the man whose books started the New Yorker type of facetious review. After Fadiman reviewed "Butterfield 8" under the title "Disappointment in O'Hara", some of us felt that he had taken enough and should have been spared [Gill's review]. I have nothing against Gill except that, as the Talk of the Town writer for eight years, I resent a man who whistles while he rewrites it.
>
> Keep pitching, but not at O'Hara's head. We've had enough violence.

Ross responds that Gill couldn't have said he was "going to get O'Hara," because he didn't know he was going to do the book. Ross explained that

O'Hara had detected in the review a couple of sentences almost identical with sentences in a letter Gibbs wrote O'Hara before the book came out. (Gibbs never knew Gill was reviewing the book.)

The matter rested there until May 1958, when Thurber wrote O'Hara for material for his upcoming *The Years with Ross*. O'Hara was still in a sulk, less over Gill's review—the book had been O'Hara's first best-seller, despite it—than over Ross's having published it in the magazine that O'Hara felt, with some legitimacy, he had helped to build. He writes Thurber that "it was ironically appropriate that the most dramatic event in my association with the magazine was a review written by a snotnose who told an acquaintance of mine he was going to 'get' the O'Hara book before he'd even read it."

In reply, Thurber quoted Ross's 1949 statement that Gill hadn't known that he was going to review the book. "I'm sorry you let that old goddam review still grind at your soul," Thurber writes O'Hara. "It wasn't worth it and nobody remembers it." Not so, O'Hara insisted; Gill had already been assigned the book when he told someone at the Colony bar that he was going to "get" the O'Hara book. "I have absolved Gibbs from influencing Gill," O'Hara tells Thurber. "I based that suspicion on word coincidences that looked bad at the time, but Gibbs has convinced me they were coincidences and nothing more."

Never was Thurber implicated in the strange collision of miscomprehensions that led to O'Hara's split with the *New Yorker*. Apprised of this newly unearthed correspondence of Thurber, Ross, and O'Hara, Gill conceded his error, writing on July 10, 1991, sixteen years after his published castigation of Thurber, "You have convinced me that my account of the mess in my book 'Here at The New Yorker' is in error and that you have sorted out the facts correctly."

Who had told him Thurber had created the trouble?

"After forty-odd years . . . I remember the exact emotion with which I heard that Thurber had used the words 'documentary proof,' and how they stuck in my craw as being so obviously indefensible—but I don't remember who spoke the words. Life is a minefield: I never forgave Thurber for an offense he didn't commit and in the course of describing the offense I myself committed an offense against Thurber. Hell and damnation!"

After Ross's death, Gibbs did his best to reunite O'Hara and the *New Yorker*, but O'Hara insisted he would begin submitting his work again only if paid fifty thousand dollars, a form of punitive damages. The standoff held until after Gibbs's death, in 1958, when William Maxwell was successful in getting O'Hara to submit "Imagine Kissing Pete." Shawn paid ten thousand dollars for it, which seemed to placate O'Hara.

Despite Thurber's support throughout, O'Hara came to resent him, principally because Yale University gave Thurber, and not O'Hara, an honorary degree. Though O'Hara had never attended college, Yale was the school he admired most. He gave his typescripts to the Yale library, when asked, "but at commencement the Yale Fellows always had a date with Thurber," he wrote petulantly in a newspaper column. He also, typically, believed Thurber had bad-mouthed him, writing:

> In his last years he had some rather unpleasant, and not necessarily true, things to say about me. . . .
>
> When you consider what Thurber had to go through, you may be inclined to be charitable. A lot of us were, and were not merely charitable. We were fond of him. But his was not the only back with a monkey on it. . . .
>
> I could write a true and very devastating piece about Thurber, but I won't. I refrain from doing so out of respect for the good times, and there were many of them.

O'Hara, who died in 1970 at age sixty-five, must have been aware of the favorable help Thurber had given a *New York Post* reporter in 1959, who was writing a story on O'Hara. Thurber writes her:

> You can say I said this. John O'Hara, being both Irish and artist, is doubly interesting, twice as complicated and maybe three times as difficult as he would be if he were only one of those volatile beings. He likes to admit he is wrong when he is but he doesn't like to be told it. Being ambivalent, even dichotomous, he would go through the smoke and flame for a friend, and often has, but he has a quick Irish-artist tendency, now and then, to strike friends "off the list" as he calls it. This is sometimes a permanent consignment to limbo, but oftener just a temporary term in Coventry. I have been a friend of O'Hara's for 30 years, off and on, but mostly on. The only tough argument we ever had occurred about 1945 because of a certain name applied to O'Hara, not by me, but by him. He called himself this ugly name, and I told him he was a liar and he was not that, and this annoyed O'Hara, O'Hara being O'Hara. He can almost always tolerate a major aggression, but takes fire about minor misunderstandings, and thus gained the name of being "Master of the Fancied Slight." I did not apply this to him and do not know who did. He writes wonderful letters and I've got quite a few . . . but have apparently been off the list for some months now. I don't know why.

. . . He is, of course, one of the major talents of American literature. He brings into a room, or a life, the unique presence that is John O'Hara. If he sometimes seems to exhibit the stormy emotions of a little boy, so do all great artists, for unless they can remember what it was to be a little boy, they are only half complete as artist and as man. Who wants to go through life with only easy friends? Nothing would be duller. That reminds me of Meredith's

> Would we through our lives love forego,
> Quit of scars and tears?
> Ah, but no, no, no.

O'Hara, being O'Hara, would undoubtedly have read this lovely encomium and interpreted it as a personal attack.

In August 1949, Thurber agreed to write a front-page essay on Robert Benchley for the *New York Times Book Review*. The occasion was a posthumous collection of Benchley's pieces. He prepared for it as conscientiously as a Ph.D. candidate readying his dissertation, writing White, Gibbs, Donald Ogden Stewart, and Nathaniel Benchley for their memories and impressions of Benchley. It was a loving testimony to the legendary humorist, in which Thurber tells of first meeting Benchley. He had been sent by the *New Yorker* to Benchley's Algonquin suite to pick up overdue copy. Benchley greeted him warmly, and made it a social occasion. When the magazine phoned to ask where Thurber was, Benchley took the blame, saying he was having the devil's own time with a cognate accusative.

In the fall of 1949, Thurber began his "Letter from the States" in the *Bermudian*. Ronald Williams, who had turned over the magazine to others when he went to war, regained control after the war, and Thurber was made a member of its board of directors, a position that paid him nothing but amused him greatly. Out of a fondness for Williams and a continuing romantic infatuation for Janey, Thurber contributed, free, more than two dozen of the columns, further demonstrating to Ross his independence of the *New Yorker* and its first-refusal agreement. Many of the columns were idle musings, of little interest to anyone but Thurber, but he was too good a writer not to score highly with a number of them. The pieces ran, irregularly, from October 1949 to July 1952, accompanied by spot illustrations from Thurber's tremendous backlog of drawings. Seven were collected in *Thurber Country*, his selection of writings from 1949 to 1953.

The media had discovered that Thurber could always be counted on for a good interview. Thurber turned each one into a monolog. He tended to speak more and more for posterity, his themes solidified through repetition: The American Woman (a know-nothing who will survive the male humans, and will do a better job of running the world); the fading of humor (the humiliations of the Great Depression seemed to deter writers from using humor as antidotes to life's hardships, as World War I had not); the misuses of grammar ("His finicky concern for grammar," says Alistair Cooke, "was that it was the X ray for style. He had a surgical tenderness toward syntax that wasn't simply fuss; he knew what went into making the organism of language"); animals' superiority over people; the wrongness of government inquiry into the lives of artists and writers; the stories of his own ascendancy into the loftier ranks of writing and cartooning ("He was vain," says Cooke, "but in a most agreeable way. When a bright boy is handicapped, he has to know more than other people").

After the Thurbers spent a few weeks at Hot Springs in November 1949, they returned to New York, before going on to Connecticut for the Christmas season. At the Algonquin, Thurber was, of course, interviewed on the eve of his fifty-fifth birthday. He never let any interviewer down, saying: "Man will not get anywhere until he realizes, in all humility, that he is just another of God's creatures, less kindly than Dog, possessed of less dignity than Swan."

63

That Time for Flags

I bought an American flag, five feet by three, and a white flagpole,
eighteen feet high, surmounted by a bright golden ball, and now I am
trying to figure out why. The incongruity of buying a flag and a flagpole
in the middle of December as a Christmas present for my wife has
begun to disturb me. . . . I had bought, for the yard of my home, a
flagstaff designed and intended for the grounds of an institution. Nothing smaller than a boys' school with an enrollment of four hundred
would think of ordering a pole of that heroic height.

—from "There's a Time for Flags"

When Christmas shopping in a store filled with fragile objects the year before, Thurber had overheard a clerk say, "Sweet God, here's that man again!"
Annin's, the flag store, he reasoned, would neither be jammed with Christmas shoppers nor filled with delicate items poised to humiliate a blind man.
Once at Annin's he found himself buying a flag and pole. Helen, at a loss as
to what to do with the gift, which came in several six-foot sections, had it put
in the attic of the West Cornwall house. When she sold the house and moved
to Weston, Connecticut, the flag and pole were stored in the basement of the
new home.

"My kids and I found it, still in its original packaging, after Helen's death,"
Rosemary Thurber writes. "We brought it back to South Haven, Michigan,
and the next 4th of July with great ceremony and a reading of 'There's a Time
for Flags' by various members of the family we planted the pole and raised the

flag. We fly it on special family weekends. Of course, there are only forty-eight stars on the flag. So far the FBI hasn't found out and we take turns deciding which two states we are *not* recognizing on any given weekend. I don't know who helped my father shop for the flag, but Jap Gude used to help with some of his shopping adventures."

Thurber and Helen were among those who, at times, found amusing the Whites' dependable flow of medical complaints, but 1950 yields a crop of letters by Thurber listing an astounding variety of his and Helen's own domestic afflictions. There were personal losses as well. Helen had no sooner brought her mother home from the hospital than she died in January, of heart failure.

The Thurbers' Cadillac was temporarily in New York, and Rose Algrant drove them to Pittsfield that month in a baby Austin without heat, to pick up Rosemary for a dental examination. Helen complains that they nearly froze. Rosie was found to have twenty-six cavities, requiring her to make a trip to New York from Skidmore every Saturday for several weeks. By February, Thurber had contracted a throat infection, and he also had an abscessed tooth taken out. Helen entered the hospital for the removal of an ovarian cyst. Thurber cut his cornea with the flick of a napkin, and made four trips to the Institute of Ophthalmology in Manhattan to have it treated. His thyroid condition, though slightly improved, was still bothersome and would get worse.

Their hired hand in Cornwall caught a chest cold that led to a blood clot in his kidney. Anna, his wife, collapsed and was rushed to the hospital with high blood pressure and hypertension, requiring complete rest for six months and the recruiting of new servants by Helen, all of which added to her presurgical anxieties. "I was pretty shattered," she writes, "& need some liver shots for anemia." The death of Mrs. Wismer was followed that summer by those of Carl Van Doren (Mark's brother, and a Cornwall neighbor), Thurber's old friend Dick Connell, and his old *New Yorker* colleague Morris Markey, whose death from a gunshot at his Virginia home, his widow believed, was a suicide made to look like an accident for insurance reasons.

Frank Sullivan had informed them in February that Gertrude Sayre, Joel's wife, had been in the hospital, was still confined to bed, gray and thin, and having "a tough time." Elliott Nugent "cracked up" again—two years after the last attack. "This high manic state usually lasts four months," Helen writes the Thurbers in Columbus, "then 2 months of deep depression, then about 17 or 18 months of complete normality. We're all very upset about it, and glad we're getting away, for he is a terrible problem, calls us all the time, usually in the middle of the night, and is likely to descend on us. We have decided to sail for Bermuda March 3." The Korean conflict was about to erupt, and Helen felt that it "may be our last Bermuda trip for a while, if war should come."

In Bermuda, Helen came down with a case of hives. In July, Robert wrote that Mame had herpes, and had also fallen down and was in bed, but "almost back to normal"; vitamins were helping cure the herpes. In September, Robert wrote them of the death of Althea's mother in Columbus. In November, Thurber asks Robert to postpone Mame's eighty-fifth birthday party that year, "since we are all getting older and winter trips are more risky, especially with Helen's sinus trouble and my tendency toward pneumonia. . . . We are both much better, but [Helen] is regaining her sense of taste slowly."

In his thirteen weeks in Bermuda, Thurber wrote *The 13 Clocks*—"a clock a week," Thurber noted. The book's inscription was "To Jap and Helen Gude who have broken more than one spell cast upon the author by a witch or wizard, this book is warmly dedicated."

For two decades, Gude, pleasant, diplomatic, and loyal, had handled Thurber's literary property rights for radio, TV, stage, and film adaptation with effective low-key professionalism. Over the years, he had become important to Thurber as a dependable and stalwart friend, upon whom Thurber could always call in an emotional crisis. He remained so until Thurber's death— one of the few, along with Peter De Vries, who did.

The 13 Clocks, Thurber says in the foreword, is an example of "escapism and self-indulgence." The fun he had in writing it is evident throughout. He is at home in such a fantasyland, assembling in his unique way all the elements of the classic children's fairy tale, including an evil duke, who sets sadistic tasks for the prince as the price of the hand of the princess. With his facile talent for recycling material, Thurber names several of his characters after code words he learned as a State Department clerk: the Golux, the Todal, Hagga. In June, visiting the Ted Gardiners in Columbus, he composed "looking glass limericks," "because they were backwards, sort of," explains Gardiner. "He thought them up one morning on our terrace, to amuse our two young daughters, using the names of our two cocker spaniels, Polly and Molly. I'm not sure Jim had been to bed; he liked to sit up, drink, and talk. My wife and I loved him but agreed it was good that he didn't get to Columbus more often than he did; he'd have killed us all off in short order." The looking-glass limericks:

> There once was a girl named Molly
> Who spoke in a glot that was poly;

She had cues that were curly and gigs that were whirly
And occasionally pops that were lolly.

There was a de-hoy that was hobble,
Who cast only stones that were cobble;
He had laps that were dew, liked gaws that were gew,
and ate only d'hote that was table.

In *The 13 Clocks*, the prince's task, to obtain for the duke thousands of jewels within hours, can be achieved only if Hagga can be made to cry, for her tears, whether from sadness or laughter, turn to precious stones. But she can no longer weep. The Golux does his best to make her laugh, reciting Thurber's rewritten limericks from the Gardiner visit:

A dehoy who was terribly hobble,
Cast only stones that were cobble
And bats that were ding, from a shot that was sling,
But never hit inks that were bobble.

There was an old coddle so molly,
He talked in a glut that was poly,
His gaws were so gew that his laps became dew,
And he ate only pops that were lolly.

The Gardiner girls were delighted to find their pets' names in a Thurber book, and in even better limericks, but saddened that although the lines made Hagga laugh, her tears turned to unacceptable semiprecious stones and rhinestones.

Thurber may have begun by giving himself the role of the evil duke—who was two inches taller and ten years younger: "One eye wore a velvet patch. . . . He had lost one eye when he was twelve." But he is more likely the Golux, who provides most of the humor. "Half the places I have been to, never were," the Golux tells the prince. "I make things up. Half the things I say are there cannot be found." It is the Golux who finally makes Hagga laugh and who helps the prince and princess outwit the wicked Duke. The evil duke is left to sound like Harold Ross, grumbling, "Nobody ever tells me anything." Again, the gentle Thurber character proves to be the hero of consequence in his fairy stories.

The book's lovely closing passage has been used in wedding ceremonies. The Golux tells the two lovers:

"Keep warm. . . . Ride close together. Remember laughter. You'll need it even in the blessed isles of Ever After." . . . The two white horses snorted snowy mist in the cool green glade that led down to the harbor. A fair wind stood for Yarrow and, looking far to sea, the Princess Saralinda thought she saw, as people often think they see, on clear and windless days, the distant shining shores of Ever After.

If there is a Thurber moral, it is the importance of laughter in a world of peril and skullduggery.

In May, Thurber sent the manuscript to Andy White for his comments. White replied that he found confusing the similarity of names (Mark, Mock, Hark), the lack of paragraphing to indicate that a different character has begun talking, and sacrificing "the simple fluency of tale telling in order to add another ounce of fantasy or fun." Furthermore, Princess Saralinda says or does little "that convinces the reader that she is as hot as you say she is." White also found Thurber's foreword a bit defensive, "as though you were prematurely sore because the wrong people were reading your book or the right people weren't." Explaining what a book is or isn't, added White, was "to my mind a questionable tactic, and I think you are just sticking out your zatch, and many a tosspan and strutfart will run you through."

Besides Helen, who was often overruled, only White could sit in judgment on his work and second-guess him with impunity. In response to White's comments, Thurber removed Mark and Mock from the story, paragraphed each individual's remarks, and Princess Saralinda now takes an admirable initiative in getting the thirteen clocks started, necessary for the freeing of herself and the prince. The foreword, greatly reduced, apologizes to the publisher and the book's illustrator, Marc Simont, for the changes Thurber kept making, even in the galley proofs.

The book's first printing was of nearly thirty thousand copies, followed by reprints and reissuances that leave it available in bookstores today. In December 1953, an hour-long television dramatization of *The 13 Clocks* was presented, with music by Mark Bucci. Its high-powered cast included Basil Rathbone as the villainous duke ("We all have flaws, and mine is being wicked"), Roberta Peters as Princess Saralinda, John Raitt as the prince, and Sir Cedric Hardwicke as the Golux, whose magical powers derive from being "a son of a witch."

On June 12, 1950, Kenyon College, in Gambier, Ohio, awarded Thurber an honorary doctorate of letters at its graduation ceremonies. With *The 13 Clocks* almost finished, Thurber and Helen had returned from Bermuda, spent the night at the Algonquin and taken the train to Columbus. After a visit with the family at the Southern Hotel, Robert drove them to Gambier in the aging Ford Thurber had subsidized. Helen's letter of comic exaggerations to the Williamses about the event could almost have been written by Thurber:

> Well, it was worse than I thought it would be. In the first place the ceremonies began at six A.M. because old President Whitney (1888–1912) always slept from eight in the morning until noon. We had to get up in the dark and Jamie hadn't got to sleep till two A.M. because of a bee in the room. . . . There was a ceremony called the Vine Walk, a serpentine procession covering a mile and a half and including a trip to the bell tower, six flights up, where each honoree rang the bell. You can imagine the state he was in when they reached the platform. Then came the citation with everybody standing and he was credited with "The Scene in the Bedroom," "Junior Miss," "The E.B. White Deer," "Many Moods," and "The Great Quiver." He was about to sit down when the president announced that there would be the usual ten minutes standing silence in honor of the late Dr. Whitney. During this each candidate had to hold a full champagne glass. Jamie had to use both hands and a gust of wind blew his gown out in back, so that he looked like a 1907 sports roadster about to take off.

Among others honored by Kenyon was Senator Paul Douglas of Illinois, and the commencement speaker, Thomas S. Matthews, the managing editor of *Time*. Matthews was a Thurber fan, and at the supper for the honorees the evening before the ceremonies and at the next day's luncheon, he found Thurber to be as interesting and entertaining in person as on the printed page. He decided that Thurber deserved the *Time* cover-story treatment. He asked White, John McNulty, and Alva Johnston, in turn, to write the article. The first two declined; Johnston was otherwise engaged. It was assigned to a *Time* writer whose draft, Matthews thought, missed by a mile. He showed it to the Thurbers, who agreed. With the Korean War now claiming *Time*'s pages and covers, the article was postponed. In August, Matthews met the Thurbers and Joel Sayre over drinks at the Algonquin. Thurber, in all seriousness, offered to write the article himself—in the third person, in the style of his preface to *The Thurber Carnival*. Matthews got off that hook by telling Thurber he wanted the piece to be a favorable one—a masterstroke of diplomacy. Thurber's offer to do a self-portrait for the cover—his last drawing to be published—was accepted.

Sayre, who had just quit a job writing for television, agreed to do the article. Like White, McNulty, and Gibbs, Sayre had Thurber's full confidence as a writer, though he ran into all the problems one has in writing about a close friend. "It is not easy to get you down on paper," he wrote Thurber that fall, "without kicking you in the crotch." Though Sayre included Gibbs's contention that Thurber was the nicest guy in the world until the cocktail hour, Matthews's intention to celebrate Thurber as America's foremost humorist, worthy of wider recognition, was wholly fulfilled. (Sayre was invited by Time, Inc., to stay on, as a *Life* writer.)

Matthews and the Thurbers remained friends, getting together at Matthews's summer place in Newport, Rhode Island, and in England, after Matthews quit *Time* in 1953 to write books there. Thurber's fondness for Matthews was not born of any slavish appreciation for the international publicity *Time* had provided him; Matthews was a literary man, an Oxford graduate who had been an editor on the *New Republic*. He had nurtured quality writers like James Agee at *Time* and had rid the magazine of its irritating backward sentences and snide compound adjectives, a journalistic cleansing that would greatly account for much of the admiration a grammatical purist like Thurber held for him.

Tom Bevans, production manager at Simon & Schuster, acting on an informed theory, had hopefully provided Thurber with white pastel crayons and dead black paper, which Thurber set up on an easel in his sunporch in Cornwall. It had been three years since he had drawn professionally, and for a short time he believed that he could see through the white mist sufficiently to make use of the new materials. But he took warnings from the physical and mental toll that the self-portrait had exacted, and soon announced an end to his career as a professional artist.

Wolcott Gibbs's play, *Season in the Sun*, was produced successfully in 1950. Its plot is, coincidentally, somewhat similar to the one Thurber proposed to Nugent the year before: a writer of short pieces for a sophisticated metropolitan weekly magazine wishes to quit and write a novel. The editor (Ross) visits the writer on Fire Island (where Gibbs had a summer home), and tries to lure him back to the magazine. Thurber, as usual, was at his most generous in such a circumstance involving a friend; he heralded the play as smashingly funny, was enthusiastic about its commercial success, and sent a comic letter of advice to Gibbs on how to behave during rehearsal and opening night, a letter that Gibbs quoted liberally from in a *Herald Tribune* feature on the play. Privately, Thurber felt that Anthony Ross, the actor playing Ross, did not do as good an imitation of the editor as Thurber could, and he told a visitor so. "You would have understood how funny he was if you could have seen him, Jamie," Helen told her husband, in reply. The visitor was horrified by the apparent put-down, but Thurber took it in stride.

That year, T. S. Eliot's verse play, "The Cocktail Party," also met with success on Broadway, and its meaning became the subject of lively discussion among theatergoers. Eliot had said that the play meant whatever its audiences thought it meant, and Thurber exercised his sure grasp of confusion to transform Eliot's comment into his *"What* Cocktail Party?", a cacophony of baffled opinion. Eliot, who in 1933 had been one of the first powerful voices to point out a significant seriousness in Thurber's humor, was delighted by the piece and sent Thurber a newspaper item about an escaped chimpanzee, explaining, "This struck me at once as a Thurber item, and goes to prove that London, as well as New York . . . and Columbus, is Thurber Land. And in what other metropolis would a chimpanzee, after biting Mrs. Felicity Chilcott and Mr. Arthur Westcott, surrender quietly to a police officer?" It began a lighthearted correspondence between the two men, leading to Eliot's writing that he would be in New York in December, "and if you by any fortunate chance should be there during that period, I hope that we may meet at last."

They did. It was another Mitty dream realized for Thurber—and, if we can take Eliot's appreciation of Thurber at his word, for Eliot, too.

The Korean War led Thurber to revive the fictitious Captain Blandish, for the Williams's benefit. Thurber had blamed the inept, mythical Blandish for all the military blunders of World War II, including the mistaken bombing of a Swiss village by the Americans. In the Korean conflict, Blandish's application for major is turned down because of his frequent "major" mistakes, Thurber tells the Williamses. Blandish returns from Africa with his squadron of planes, each filled to the wings with flowers. The C.O. asks, "Where's the uranium?" Blandish: "I thought you said geraniums." In another letter, Thurber continues the saga of Blandish:

> You will remember the awful dawn when he shot the bugler because he thought his sergeant had said, "The fellow was a burglar." . . . In August . . . he was ordered to proceed to Pakistan with a view to "discreetly ascertaining the situation there over a period of six weeks." He was then to report back in person. He did so, of course, and reported that everything in Parkerstown was about what you might imagine it to be in any other place of the same size in New Jersey. He said he had met a lovely couple named Mitchell, that the food in all the hotels was execrable, that he had spent several pleasant evenings with a Miss Honeycutt, but that on the whole he would have enjoyed himself much more at an hotel in New York City. As the result of his report, a lieutenant-colonel named Winterhorn suffered a severe heart attack.

Thurber's growing guest appearances on radio now extended to television. He was often on Faye Emerson's interview show—she found everything Thurber said screamingly funny. During the day, at home, he wrote on a card table, a ream of yellow copy paper stacked at one side, with dozens of pencils. Afternoons were spent working with his secretary, after which he took a two-hour nap. During dinner, he often listened to news on the cabinet Magnavox. (Radio commentator Elmer Davis, one of the few broadcasters allowed to stand up to Senator McCarthy without losing his job, became and remained Thurber's idol.) In the evening, Helen usually read to him, and both listened to radio, and to TV, especially Westerns. Thurber could follow the programs, as at the theater, with small cues from Helen. Except for musical comedies, Thurber claimed to understand about 90 percent of whatever Broadway plays they went to, with the help of her whispered fill-ins.

Pieces of what would be *The Thurber Album* had begun flowing through *New Yorker* issues, under the title "Photograph Album," from the end of 1950 into May 1952, a month after the book itself was published by Simon & Schuster. The *Album* had been inspired by Thurber's brooding interest in his origins, and the need he felt to remind his reading public that their country, caught up as it was in a paranoid fear of Communism, had once known a past of tranquillity and trust that was worth getting back to. His search for material to reconstruct that ideal heritage was only partly successful. Things had never been that good. Several of the people he retrieved as models for the memoir, he had never known well. The family's resistance to Thurber's descriptions of them finally turned the project sour. Thurber was seldom malicious in print, but *The Thurber Album* remains an elegant mixed bag of affection and disguised hostility, of hard-won truths and mild self-deceptions.

Sayre's *Time* article on Thurber had pointed out that though Thurber had been honored by Kenyon college, his alma mater had ignored him. There were reasons: some of the school's trustees and administration were still resentful of *The Male Animal*, which had made fun of "Mid-Western University"; there lingered an academic prejudice against humorists being so honored; and Thurber's coercion of the administration over the *Scarlet Fever* episode hadn't been forgotten or forgiven. Thurber's published protests against the government's loyalty investigations also caused uneasiness among the university's conservative community. (Thurber's political statements made Robert uneasy, too; he explained to a writer that "Communists were infiltrating government on every hand.")

By 1949, the fear of Soviet Communism had seriously infected the nation's politics. The Marxist takeover of China, the Russians' sudden nuclear capability, every frustration of United States foreign policy, were all, finally, suspected as the work of treasonable Americans—in government, the military, the media, and the arts. In 1950, Senator Joseph McCarthy, the chairman of the Senate Subcommittee on Government Operations, saw Communist-baiting as his chance to make political hay. Armed with subpoena powers, a Senate immunity that left his victims with no legal recourse, and a propensity for sensational headlines, he superseded Martin Dies as the primary congressional terrorist, giving the era its notorious and enduring name.

Thurber had been apolitical until after World War II; he had jeered at the leftists and at any notion that a writer must conform to the mandates of ideology. He had also allowed his name to be used on letterheads of a couple of organizations in which, he later learned, there may have been Communist influence. But now, his right to say what he wanted was threatened. His anger at the broadcast, film, and publishing industries for caving in to those who urged the blacklisting of actors, writers, and producers was one he never got over.

In that age of suspicion, a class of "experts" on "un-Americanism" acquired an unconscionable power. Film and television companies turned to them for advice on whom it was "safe" to employ and what movies and programs were "safe" to produce. One such self-appointed guardian of the nation was Vincent Hartnett, who edited *Red Channels*, a publication that targeted citizens Hartnett believed to be subversive. When asked by the American Broadcasting Company, Hartnett replied that there would be "a serious risk" in featuring the work of James Thurber. "He had a front record during the late Thirties and was involved in one front in 1947," Hartnett informed ABC. "Many will defend him as merely a militant libertarian. But it is also a fact that his works have been in great favor in Communist Circles."

The alarming factor in McCarthyism was not the self-destructive senator himself but the anemic faith in decency and constitutional behavior he exposed in the leaders of both the private and public sector—including President Eisenhower, who emerged as indecisive and spineless in the face of the McCarthy threat. As the columnist Murray Kempton pointed out, regarding Hartnett's charge against Thurber: "It is easy to imagine the condescending smiles with which the ABC executives read [Hartnett's] report, after which, of course, they went slow on using Thurber. Frank Stanton and Robert Kintner, of course, were always certain that they were Vincent Hartnett's moral superiors. I am not quite so sure. I have covered too many people too long to be capable of calibrations quite so delicate." (The Freedom of Information Act has led to the discovery that Thurber was under FBI surveillance for nearly twenty years, starting in 1939, his file running to a hundred and five pages. This wouldn't have surprised Thurber.)

Though White was allowed to protest McCarthy's tactics in his controlled and literate manner in Comment, the *New Yorker's* general position on Mc-Carthyism seemed largely one of appalled paralysis. A fiery Comment by White, taking McCarthy to task for hounding the press, was set in type and then withdrawn. A few amusing reminiscences were run in the back of the book, by Richard Rovere and others, that indirectly showed McCarthy to be a dishonest and ludicrous knave, but Thurber is right in saying that Ross discouraged such material. Ross wanted only a magazine of entertainment and factual interest, without polemics.

After Ross's death, with the Senate inquisition still raging, William Shawn continued to keep the magazine's profile a low one politically. McCarthy was in the habit of hailing before his committee writers and editors who opposed him, publicizing youthful associations and statements long since renounced by them. These humiliating punishments on national TV, radio, and in newsreels could not have been lost upon Shawn, who was terrorized by the thought of ever occupying a public spotlight of any kind. The magazine's timidity during the five years of rampant McCarthyism was one reason Thurber came to feel alienated from it.

In 1950, a craven Truman administration fired three distinguished State Department officials who had been charged by McCarthy with being Communist sympathizers. All were officially cleared of the charges, but their careers, reputations, and prospects of livelihood were ruinously compromised. The incident moved Thurber to write "Look Out for the Thing," which appeared in the *Bermudian* in October 1950. It is Thurber's finest delineation of the neurosis and terror that then gripped America. As a childish gag, someone had put up a sign on a woodland road near his Cornwall home: "Look Out for the Thing." Thurber writes that his poodle is aware of the Thing, once having fled from the sight of a boy who "had become magnified in capricious vision to the size, say, of Senator Joseph R. McCarthy." The piece continues:

> Yes, Virginia, there is a Thing. . . . It speaks in many tongues and sleeps in many minds. It invades the world and mind of Man, inhabits headlines, feeds on limelight, and attacks its prey in the dark. . . . The Thing has learned to nourish itself on suspicions, guesses, and old accusations. . . .
>
> The Thing has great power and vast ingenuity, for it can make guilt out of many things . . . association, accusation, appearance, aspect, attitude, and even ability. . . . The Thing can blacken a man at a distance of 10,000 miles, by using one or another of its many stings: the

thundering charge, the sweeping generalization, the bold assumption, the mysterious record, the secret testimony, the overheard insinuation, the patriotic gesture, the enormous lie, the fearful warning. . . .

The Thing's most recent brilliant achievement . . . was to make Man lose his faith in the practice and precept of innocence by exoneration. Now a man may be considered guilty even after he has been proven innocent. . . .

Do not attempt to take the Thing single-handed. It is armed and dangerous, and, what is worse, it has a lot of friends.

In the thirties, he had been furious with the literary Communists for their attacks on the *New Yorker,* but, as Malcolm Cowley points out, he was now standing up for freedom of speech when the ex-Communists weren't. "He hadn't changed, but society had," says Cowley. The McCarthy years made Thurber seem almost radical, he adds. American Legion posts were now opposing presentations of *The Male Animal.*

"Thurber was a hell of a man in more ways than just being a humorist," says Thurber's *New Yorker* colleague Richard O. Boyer. "He was unfailingly sympathetic to the underdog and for free speech. He continued to speak out after a lot of liberals fell silent." After Boyer, a former Communist, was dragged before McCarthy, shouting defiance at the senator during the hearing, he was given no more *New Yorker* assignments, and his drawing-account arrangement with the magazine was terminated. (He was writing his political protests on *New Yorker* stationery; Katharine White affirms).

Meanwhile the *Time* cover story on Thurber left dangling the question of why an alumnus of international standing had not been offered a degree by his alma mater. After Williams College made him an honorary Doctor of Letters in June 1951, O.S.U.'s faculty council recommended that Thurber be awarded one—at the December graduation ceremonies, rather than at the more widely publicized June commencement. It appears to have been a last-minute decision, following debate, for it was on November 28, only three weeks before the ceremony, that President Howard Bevis wrote Thurber that "pursuant to the recommendation of our Committee on Honorary Degrees, concurred in by our Faculty Council, the Board of Trustees of this University awarded you the degree of Doctor of Letters."

But word had reached Thurber that a 1948 ban on "controversial" speakers and meetings on the O.S.U. campus, though lifted in September 1950, had been reimposed a year later, just weeks before his degree had been awarded. Department heads routinely invited about two thousand speakers a year to address their students. One such invitation had gone to Professor

Harold Rugg, of Columbia University Teachers College. Dr. Rugg was a dignified old gentleman, a spirited lecturer, and a good writer who related education to social conditions. He had a sense of humor, wrote about the arts, and had been Massachusetts assistant commissioner of education. "He was cultivated, brilliant, and an important and attractive figure to us at Teachers College," says Joseph Deitch, of that institution. "He was soft-spoken, looked like Charles Ruggles and was full of lively ideas. He headed our social and philosophical Department of Education."

After Rugg delivered the annual Boyd H. Bode lectures at O.S.U.'s graduate school in July 1951, editorials in both the *Columbus Dispatch* and the *Ohio State Journal* protested, saying Rugg's books had been discredited as socialistic. Actually, Rugg's books had been critical of laissez-faire capitalism and American business in the 1920s, and espoused a "non-violent, social-democratic point of view in the 1930s," says Deitch. Rugg had supported Henry Wallace's Progressive ticket in the 1948 election, another cause for concern at O.S.U.

The editorials brought on a storm of angry letters protesting Rugg's appearance. Governor Frank Lausche asked the O.S.U. trustees to look into the matter. They ordered the 1948 ban reimposed, with the university president to screen all speakers, and denounced Rugg as a "doctrinaire propagandist rather than an educator."

The next month, a hundred and fifty members of O.S.U.'s College of Education asked that the order be rescinded. The trustees refused. President Bevis concurred, writing that "we will permit no one to speak who is known to be disloyal to our government." To Thurber's lasting credit, as much as he wanted the degree—and he agonized over his decision—he declined the offer on principle, writing Bevis:

> It is with extreme regret, and after serious consideration, that I find myself unable to accept at this time Ohio State University's offer. . . . I have faith that Ohio State will restore freedom of speech and freedom of research, but until it does I do not want to seem to approve of its recent action. The acceptance of an honorary degree right now would certainly be construed as such approval, or as indifference to the situation.

Andy White had talked him out of a letter ten times as long. Minutes of a December meeting of the trustees, following Thurber's rejection of the degree, are missing from the university records, according to Dr. James Pollard, the university's historian, but the ban was "modified" that same month, making "the fitness of speakers" again to be determined by the faculty. But, in effect, the ban remained, for, if in doubt, a faculty member was told to get advice from colleagues, from his department chairman, from the college dean and, if necessary, from the president, "who shall have final authority." Few dared to make "fitness of speaker" decisions on their own.

The week that Thurber declined the honorary degree, the *New Yorker* came out with his "Lengths and Shadows," about Joseph Denney, the late dean of O.S.U.'s College of Arts. In his portrait of Denney, Thurber works in his sermon on academic freedom. Thurber's personal knowledge of Denney had been almost entirely from attending the Shakespeare course Denney taught. Fortunately for Thurber, the professor lent himself to anecdotes, given him by a few who had known Denney well. From a tendency to imbibe too much, it is said, Denney once ran out of blackboard space in class and continued to chalk words on the adjacent wall. He was as absentminded as anyone of concentrated mind, and one morning after he had departed for class his wife found his trousers still hung over the back of a chair. Not realizing that her husband had purchased a new pair the day before, she ran to his classroom, clutching the pants and fearing the worst. (Thurber didn't use the anecdote.)

He did draw upon Denney's speech to the American Association of University Professors, thirty years before, in which he warned that their potential enemies were state legislatures, ecclesiastical bodies, and the influence of college trustees. Hence, Thurber reasoned, Denney would have led the resistance to censorship by O.S.U.'s trustees of 1951, who were, he writes, "aggressively patriotic gentlemen always ready and eager to save America from the perils of academic freedom."

Thurber, for all purposes, was Tommy Turner of *The Male Animal*, taking his controversial stand against the conservatism of "Mid-Western University" trustees. *Dispatch* editor George Smallsreed, who had been helping with Thurber's Columbus research for the *Album*, held the popular local position: "Out of the situation will come a much finer understanding of the responsibilities and purposes of the University," he writes Thurber. "If some innocent people got hurt, it is regretable [sic]. There is much to be said meritoriously about academic freedom. But at least as much ought to be said about the intellectual crises that are committed in the name of academic freedom." And when, in a "George, old boy" letter to Smallsreed, Thurber denounced the history and politics of the Wolfe family, the reactionary owners of the *Dispatch*, Smallsreed exploded with a heated defense of his employers, ending with a hot-tempered "old boy, old boy, old boy to you, too!"

Thurber changed the subject back to the *Album* research, but accidentally got his revenge two years later when he was awarded the Ohioana Sesquicentennial Medal from the Ohioana Library Association. Unable to make the trip to Columbus, he persuaded Smallsreed to deliver the remarks of acceptance. Smallsreed, told only that the subject was Thurber on humor, found himself speaking to five hundred people in defense of an unconditional right to free speech he didn't really believe in. It was a Thurber sermon, rather than entertainment. The life and health of a nation need humor, Thurber writes, but humor in America is in danger, for it "sickens in the weather of intimidation and suppression, and such a sickness could infect a whole nation." He quotes White's definition of humorous writing, which, "like poetical writing, has an extra content. It plays, like an active child, close to the big hot fire which is Truth."

Six years later, a different O.S.U. administration, remembering Thurber's *Album* eulogy to Denney, invited Thurber to deliver a lecture during the dedication of the newly constructed Denney Hall. President Novice G. Fawcett writes: "It is . . . appropriate that you, as one of [Denney's] admirers and as a distinguished alumnus of this University, participate in the dedication [and] be one of the key figures to speak . . ." The ceremony took place on April 1, 1960; Thurber, still hyperactive, though ailing, and sixty-five years old, made his last trip to Columbus. Helen delivered his remarks, forcefully and effectively:

"Faculties of American universities must withstand all pressures," Thurber quotes Denney. He invokes Shakespeare ("There was a fighting in my heart"), and adds that "the heart in which there is not fighting is as barren as the soul without conflict or the mind without anxiety or the spirit without struggle." He blessed Denney with the famous quote of Dylan Thomas: "They shall have stars at their feet and at their elbows, and death shall have no dominion, and death shall have no dominion." (Helen used the quote as a tribute of her own to Thurber in his posthumous collection, *Credos and Curios.*)

Jack Fullen, O.S.U.'s alumni secretary, who had badgered Thurber for a decade to join the alumni association, found Thurber more receptive after the Denney building's dedication. Six months before his death, Thurber wrote Smallsreed:

> I am now a friend of Jack Fullen because he became liberal-minded, beginning with his attack on Senator McCarthy in the Ohio State Monthly, but we had gone through a long fight, as you know, when the University decided to change the name of The Sun-Dial to the Scarlet Fever. . . . Professors were so scared at that time by the far Right atti-

tude of some of the trustees, that they signed their letters to me simply, "a friend." . . .

I always stuck with Jack Fullen in his courageous stand against overemphasis on football.

Fullen's stand on football at O.S.U. came to naught, but his prolonged effort to win Thurber as a contributing alumnus succeeded. Shortly before Thurber's death, the alumni office notes that "we have received in today's mail a check to cover a new member, single life membership in full, from James Thurber."

In May 1961, six months before Thurber's death, under the "modified" speaker-screening rule, President Fawcett refused to allow a meeting by Students for Liberal Action. The debate continued. The student publication from Thurber's days, the *Lantern*, protested: "We cannot understand how the appearance of even the most controversial speaker here could in any way result in the 'indoctrination' of adults who have enough intelligence and maturity to qualify for a college degree." Though Fullen believes Thurber would have accepted O.S.U.'s honorary degree after his 1960 appearance on campus, it was never offered him again. Thurber was the first in the university's history to have refused one. Thurber would have been proud of the *Lantern* editorial, and of his earlier decision. (On June 9, 1995, Thurber was posthumously awarded the Doctor of Humane Letters degree by O.S.U.)

After his death, the Ohio State University Libraries' Thurber Collection was begun, with both private and public funding, and in 1970 the board of trustees approved the establishment of "a professorship of Thurber studies." But Thurber had willed a substantial amount of his papers—mostly the research surrounding *The Years with Ross*—to Yale. For in 1953, at the height of the McCarthy epidemic, Yale had unhesitatingly awarded him the honorary Doctor of Letters degree.

64

That Country Bumpkin

This business about "sophistication" has always annoyed the hell out of some of us. If Ross and White and I are sophisticated, we don't know it. Maybe Gibbs is sophisticated. Alexander King, editor of the defunct magazine "Americana" said . . . quoting Woollcott, "Ross gets out the New Yorker with the aid of two country bumpkins." He meant White and me. I considered myself a hick until I was about thirty and could support this with many facts. I know my way around now, speak a little French, am not afraid of headwaiters . . . but surely my recent New Yorker series ["Photograph Album"] bears no traces of sophistication. E. B. White is the least sophisticated man I have ever known.

—Letter to Dale Kramer, June 14, 1951

Dale Kramer, newspaperman and biographer of Heywood Broun, was under contract to Doubleday to write a book about "major trends and personalities in wit and sophistication" during the century's second quarter, "using Ross and the magazine as a kind of story line." Ross had cooperated with Kramer on both the Broun biography and a *Harper's* article about the magazine. He talked with Kramer about his new project, thinking the *New Yorker* story was to be only a chapter of the book. When he heard that his and the magazine's names were to be used in the title, he refused Kramer further help.

Kramer, meanwhile, had interviewed more than thirty people knowledgeable about the *New Yorker* from its inception to the present. His liveliest informant was Thurber, who offered him a generous volume of anecdotes that Thurber would use himself in *The Years with Ross*. Ross left the decision to cooperate with Kramer up to his associates, but they knew what he preferred them to do. "The outlook is bad for any cooperation whatever around here," Ross wrote Kramer, "for I find everyone horrified at the idea of a book on the magazine, including, it turns out, the management, which is downright opposed."

When Ross spotted Kramer lunching with Thurber at the Algonquin, he tried to lure Thurber back to the office. But Thurber could point to something Ross had written him three years before. In 1947, Allen Churchill, preparing an article for the *American Mercury* on the *New Yorker*, had asked Ross for samples of interoffice memos that would be funny or interesting. "How do you stand about letting him have some of yours?" Ross asked in a memo to Gibbs, Thurber, and White.

> I deplore such projects . . . but don't know what to do about them, other than to be decently cooperative. This organization has been bothering everybody in New York for twenty years and I'm ashamed to do otherwise.

No such notes could be found by the three writers, but Thurber welcomed any departure from the magazine's practice of protecting its operations from the public as if they were those of the CIA. He writes Ross:

> I'm inclined to sympathize with your realization that, after all, we are always opening up other people's desks and files. I suppose we should be good sports about it. I think the whole mass of memoranda would be the making of your memoirs together, of course, with your own memos which are invariably amusing and penetrating. We have read a great many to delighted groups of cockeyed people.
>
> I can't remember any damn memo of mine at all, but I have the distinct impression that almost all of them were written in anger over real or fancied wrongs, and they have more of a fishwife's note than anything else. I have always been willing to reveal all because after twenty-five years of journalism I still hate the uninterviewable person. He is invariably a smug and cocky stuffed shirt.
>
> My chief doubt and uneasiness about a project like Churchill's is the tone that may get into it—"My God don't these boys think they're cute."

Ross had not intended that his own "notes" be shown to Churchill, nor had he been aware that Thurber had been entertaining party guests by quoting them. Thurber met with Churchill and sent him a four-page letter filled with his familiar anecdotes and opinions about Ross and the magazine. (Churchill made little use of them, the slant of his article having changed.) Ross was delighted when editorial matter got the magazine talked about, but nobody was to discuss with the media what went on in getting out the *New Yorker*. Ingersoll's 1934 *Fortune* article about the *New Yorker* had been an embarrassment and a distraction to the staff, and that was reason enough to avoid such projects.

Thurber was not the only one who saw no harm in helping a veteran newspaperman like Kramer assess the *New Yorker*'s significant role in "refocusing American humor." Frank Sullivan, Lois Long, Morris Markey, Ik Shuman, Clifton Fadiman, Fillmore Hyde, St. Clair McKelway, and Raoul Fleischmann were among those who gave him assistance. White wrote him, "I don't know anything about American humor that's fit to print," but he invited Kramer to his office. When Kramer complained to Thurber that the Whites and others were trying to "destroy" him and his book, Thurber passed Kramer's alarms on to Andy. White replied that he didn't think the *New Yorker* was trying to stop the book, "merely protesting certain things about it," and adds:

> I think Kramer was not quite forthright when he approached some of us. He wrote me a year ago and said he was writing a book on "American humor," and that naturally there would be stuff in it about the New Yorker. He asked if he could see me and I said sure. . . . When he turned up, the book had somehow acquired the title "Ross of The New Yorker." However, despite this somewhat cagey approach, I sat around for a couple of hours trying to give him what assistance I could. I also spent about a day going over his mimeographed sheets, pencilling in stuff. . . . I agree with you that The New Yorker can't expect to publish profiles, or anything else, unless it is willing to have the tables turned. I don't think Kramer has written much of a book, but that's beside the point.

White had told Kramer that "Thurber is your best source, and repeats his stories and ideas to all interviewers." But "he also warned me," says Kramer, "about Thurber as a source. Couldn't be trusted; made up things, added to the facts. Naturally I was not one to try to disprove a good story told to me by the master."

Kramer was right in suspecting efforts to discourage the book. He had been on the staff of *Yank* with Leo Hofeller during the war, but Hofeller, the *New Yorker*'s executive editor and fanatical guardian of the portals, not only snubbed him now but (it was reported to Kramer by Doubleday) tried to persuade the publisher to give up the book; whether or not this was at Ross's bidding, as Kramer believes, isn't known. Memos from Ross were shown to Kramer by Gus Lobrano, but "couldn't be found" when Kramer asked to quote from them later. Katharine White "was careful to see me several blocks from the offices," says Kramer, and, having read the manuscript, wrote him that "our strong feelings about your book were based not only on our affection to the magazine and to Ross but also to disappointment that the first really full-scale work about the New Yorker happened to be written by someone who had no ready way of sifting false legend from true history or of weighing his direct news sources unless those of us on the inside cooperated with him."

But no book that profiled a Ross not of their private and possessive perceptions would have earned the Whites' approval. When Thurber's memoirs, *The Years with Ross*, began running in the *Atlantic Monthly* in 1957, he was unquestionably writing a full-scale work about the magazine as the insider Kramer had not been—a salaried, on-the-premises employee of eight years and regular contributor for thirty. Yet the Whites approved of the series, until Thurber got into the *New Yorker*'s system of payments and Ross's personal life, when they began to regard it as a betrayal. Their complaints, that he had appointed himself a *New Yorker* spokesman without portfolio would have pertained to Kramer in 1951, as well. Thurber's focus was on the early days, for though he continued to deal professionally with the major editorial players—Ross, Shawn, Lobrano, Geraghty, and the Whites, as well as with Daise Terry, Ebba Jonsson, and Stewart Johnson, who was the head of the checking department—he knew few of the staff in 1957, and less of the magazine's operations. Though he kept casually in touch through the rumors and gossip of friends, he was never consulted on editorial matters unrelated to his work. Thus alienated, he couldn't share the staff's family sense of need for circling the wagons against any invaders of privacy—whether the need was justified or silly. It was all the more reason for advertising his earlier importance to the magazine by talking freely about the events and participants of its adolescent years. Not content as a heralded founding father of the magazine, he liked to give the impression of still being "in on things" at the office. He continued to use the magazine's stationery when answering personal mail at home or elsewhere.

Kramer's *Ross and The New Yorker* was published in the fall of 1951. Thurber's friend Lewis Gannett reviewed the book in the *Herald Tribune*, finding Kramer's facts "authentic," and Marc Connelly called the book "informative, amusing and painstakingly accurate." Frank Sullivan and Thurber not only praised it but offered jacket endorsements—which Doubleday never followed up on, complains Kramer. Sullivan wrote Kramer that it was "a hell of a good book," the job of chronicling the *New Yorker* being one "which struck me as something like untangling and codifying a hurricane." Thurber wrote Kramer, "There is a lot about Ross that I didn't know, and I think it comes out as a pretty complete picture of him and the people around him."

But the *New Yorker*'s "Briefly Noted" book column thought *Ross and The New Yorker* characterized the current staff as Thurber had worried Churchill's article might: "It makes most of the editors and contributors around the place seem as cute as performing fox terriers." Gardner Botsford, one of the fact editors, had written so sarcastic an early draft of the review that it was withdrawn and rewritten. Even so, it castigated Kramer as having "skipped over many of the people who brought [the magazine] to maturity. It is only fair to note that this is probably because Mr. Kramer got very little cooperation from members of the staff, who had no confidence in such an undertaking by an outsider."

The charge was unfair; Kramer had interviewed nearly all the principals associated with the magazine's early years, including the alumni of the Algonquin Round Table. What had been left out were many of the present-day staff, whose routine duties, set by an established magazine format, contained little of the interest that the craziness, luck, and genius of the pioneers held for a reading public. Kramer believed the new hands to be "administrators, not innovators," he explains. Though burdened by pedestrian writing, Kramer's work remains a reliable source document. That a similar fuss over Thurber's own entertaining account of Ross and the magazine would take place eight years later never occurred to Thurber, but should have.

When Thurber wrote Ross in October 1951 to say that Shawn hadn't replied to his proposal for a series on Houdini, Ross answered, in probably his last letter to Thurber that Shawn was doing two men's work and he was not to be held responsible for promptness. "He's lucky to have got through as it is, with me doing nothing at all on fact for four months and very little for six months. I used to be very helpful there (I think)."

Ross had moved to the Algonquin, largely because of a dysfunctional marriage and the wish to be near the magazine and the people who had so long helped define his life. Five days before Ross's letter to Thurber, Thurber, still not suspecting Ross's critical condition, writes Mame: "We are having dinner with Ross tonight. He is staying at the Algonquin too and seems to be getting along fine although he works too much and worries about poetry all the time. He thinks poets do not have common sense and are hard to talk to and that they make up words and have no respect for the rules of English grammar."

A month after Kramer's *Ross and The New Yorker* appeared, there was the sudden death of Ross, December 6, 1951—unforeseen by all but two or three of Ross's closest friends. Ross had suffered from duodenal ulcers since the late thirties, but few knew that he was dying from lung cancer. In near-secrecy he had been to Boston several times for treatment. Shawn and Lobrano had been managing the editorial side of the magazine for many weeks, though a harried Shawn complained that Ross, sometimes reviewing galleys and page makeup from his sickbed at his home in Stamford, and, later, from his room at the Algonquin, insisted upon last-minute changes that put publication deadlines at risk.

Ross died on the operating table at the Lahey Clinic at 6:45 P.M. Four hours later, Louis Forster, Ross's assistant, informed the Thurbers at the Algonquin that evening. Shocked, finding the news almost beyond belief, they joined others in an impromptu wake at Costello's. "Notes and Comment" was ripped out of "A" issue to make room for Ross's obituary, written with emotional difficulty by Andy White, who was at his office typewriter early the next morning, on Friday—the tenth anniversary of the attack on Pearl Harbor. A grieving Thurber was guided by an office boy from the Algonquin to the magazine's nineteenth floor where he disengaged from his escort and groped his way toward White's corner office. In the hush of the stricken premises the distraught Thurber—tears from his sightless eyes turning his narrow face into wet leather in the dim lights of the corridor, left hand sliding ahead of him along the wall—could be heard calling piteously, "Andy! Andy!" It was a moment of awfulness within awfulness.

Ross was only two years older than Thurber but as much of a father figure as Thurber would ever accept. He had admired and resented Ross, had fought and defended him, had mocked and glorified him. Throughout the shifts of love and hate, Thurber never forgot that Ross and his magazine had been the underpinning of his career. He would never feel the same toward the *New Yorker* after Ross's death. Neither would others. Thurber claimed an extraordinary personal and proprietary relationship to the magazine Ross personified, and with the founder's death the magazine was almost immediately a friendless, foreign, and unsympathetic place to him.

In his distress, angered that he would have no say in Ross's obituary, he disparaged White's imperishable words upon hearing them read, and wanted his drawing of the Thurber Dog, crouched before a tombstone, to accompany

the piece. It was mechanically impossible; the single-page Comment obituary would already crowd the type into the margins, leaving no room for a spot the size of Thurber's. White handled Thurber's disappointment in customary fashion, to gather from a letter Thurber wrote the Williamses: "White wanted to use [the drawing], but the conservative boys turned it down. White and I pledge to use it to illustrate the obituary of whichever one of us dies first. I'll write his or he will write mine." Though White survived to write Thurber's, there was no dog illustration. Nor was there one in White's *New Yorker* obituary, either. More than "the conservative boys" were against using the spot. Many shared the grief and were far from willing to have their collective feelings represented by a sad but "cute" drawing. No tombstone was involved, anyway; Ross was cremated and his ashes scattered.

For weeks the magazine seemed to drift in a leaderless vacuum. Though Ross had avoided talking to staff members in the corridors, and tried to keep out of sight, his presence had always been felt. He would pick up a telephone and startle a new Talk reporter with a query about a story in galley. Or one unexpectedly found oneself riding with him in the elevator. The elevators were the only areas of compulsory democracy within the staff's informal but standoffish hierarchy. One stood with both the lowly and the distinguished while being jolted up and down by operators who, whether physically uncoordinated or mentally unhinged, were clearly lucky to be working. During the interminable vertical rides, one might silently be handed snapshots of newborn lambs by a proud, quiet White, taken on his Maine farm. ("White is raising sheep," Thurber wrote a friend, in bafflement at the changes that continually seemed to be transforming his former colleagues.) The mania for privacy and silence kept new hires ignorant of who was who, and one wondered if other heavy hitters from the upper floors were among the passengers. Now and then, the awkward intervals of elevator entrapment yielded overheard remarks that gave lasting worth to the day. To Thurber's "It was scary enough to make your blood stand on end," White was heard to reply, "Or make your hair run cold." Ross's barked asides were always the main events:

"Hell, yes, it was a good article," he once said to John Bainbridge, "but he used all the wrong words."

Thurber wrote his personal obituary of Ross in a letter to the Williamses:

> I'm going to do a piece about Ross, but it will take time. He was the principle [sic] figure in my career and I don't know what I would have amounted to without his magazine, in which 90 percent of my stuff has appeared. He was also a great part of my life, and I realize how much I loved him and depended on him. There was no appreciation quite the same as his because it was all tied up with him and his life. What White and I did was a part of the guy, and we realize how much of our work was done with him in mind. For the first time I have become deeply aware of the chill sweeping across the cold and starry space. I felt it when Herman Miller died and I saw him only once every few years, and Ross was a part of my daily life for almost exactly a quarter of a century. It is always hard to believe that extremely vital people can die. He represented life to me the way only a few others do.

To his family he wrote, "I haven't been able to write because of many things, especially the death of Ross which has been a terrible blow to us all. I remember that Mama said about sixteen years ago that he should take care of his lungs. He didn't take care of them in time, for he was not a man to go to doctors for checkups. He suffered no pain and died under the anaesthetic."

Ross's funeral was held Monday, December 10, at Frank Campbell's funeral home in Manhattan. White, a people-watcher by nature, sat near the door to note the great and near-great of letters, theater, and the arts, who filled the chapel. Thurber and Helen arrived with De Vries and a Westport friend of the De Vrieses, Jean Stafford, who later married A. J. Liebling. It was "the first time I met [Thurber]," says Stafford, "and he created a justifiable diversion during the eulogy which, as I recall, was given (for no known reason) by the chaplain at Yale." Thurber was, indeed, outraged by the unremarkable set of words uttered by a stranger over Ross's body to a roomful of gifted writers and actors who would have known how to movingly and appropriately bless the occasion with words of their own. Though Ross and his wife had separated, but not divorced, she had the legal right to make the funeral arrangements, which included no eulogies from anyone else.

At Malcolm Cowley's suggestion, the *Reporter* magazine had asked Thurber to write a piece about F. Scott Fitzgerald, whose biography by Arthur

Mizener had renewed public interest in Fitzgerald's work. Though Thurber didn't think Fitzgerald had to be revived by Mizener or anyone else, it gave him a chance to tell of the evening he had spent with the author of *The Great Gatsby*. "I do not believe that Fitzgerald was a worse drinker than most of us," he writes Cowley. "Hemingway called Scott a rummy, O'Hara says that Eustace Tilley has no right to talk about Hemingway's drinking—obviously a crack at Gibbs and Sally Benson—as if O'Hara could not have held his own with Scott or anybody else, except Benchley and Sinclair Lewis." He spent a month on the article in Cornwall and took it with him to Bermuda in March. The *Reporter* ran "Scott in Thorns" in its April 17, 1951, issue.

While in Bermuda, he did a parody of Margaret Case Harriman's book about the Algonquin Round Table, *The Vicious Circle*. Katharine White had just purchased a similar parody from Nathaniel Benchley and, greatly upset, told Thurber she would have used his had she seen it in time. Thurber offered apologies for having upset Katharine, who was enduring a new wave of physical difficulties. "I have had that condition 'down there,' as Ohio gentlemen always refer to the region between the navel and the upper leg," he wrote Katharine. "As you know, I went to the wonderfully named Dr. Robin Hood. This is a common ailment of newspaper men and editors of magazines." He intended to revise the parody and submit it to *Harper's Bazaar*, but nothing came of it.

Thurber's thyroid difficulties may have been a form of what today is called Graves' disease, or an overactive thyroid gland that can cause a wide swing of mood and temperament. Victims can display "a tremendous spectrum of behavioral symptoms," one specialist says of the affliction. "Some are not disturbed at all; others are basket cases at the same level of illness."

Either severe hyperthyroidism, or toxic thyroid, overtook Thurber beginning in late 1951. He had been fussy and petulant before then, complaining to Mame and Robert of a life at Cornwall pestered by "dozens of college boys and girls" (friends of his popular daughter), "sightseers and autograph hunters, or interviewers and photographers, or friends out of work or sick or depressed, or publishers, agents, and advertising men," and "five hundred letters a year from friends, relatives, and strangers, many of whom want and get some kind of help."

A long stay in Bermuda in the spring of 1952 was spoiled by painful symptoms of the thyroid problem. A Bermuda doctor thought it was psychological. "I've had a neuritis headache for a month," Thurber wrote White from Bermuda, in May:

Nobody knows why. The doctor said, "Of course, you know about your own worries, problems and temperament." I told him I did in a vague kind of way; vague and voluminous. But the trouble lies somewhere between Eva Prout . . . and the fact that my French Poodle is nearly 13. I could be dead before I figured it out. I haven't had anything the doctors didn't suspect might be prostate since I was 50. And I can only guess that every symptom is a symptom of that.

But it wasn't. He had fits of near madness, raging at Williams, Helen, and visiting friends. Tense and hyperactive, he couldn't tolerate alcohol and even gave up cigarettes for a time. At a dinner party attended by a British Navy captain, Thurber referred to Winston Churchill as "a blathermouth." The captain and his wife left, says Williams, lest he hit the blind Thurber. When an Arizona reader praised the "Photograph Album" series, as finally bringing the *New Yorker* to the people, Thurber argued that the magazine intentionally and properly spurned the idea of mass circulation, wholly rejecting the compliment. He sent a former acquaintance of his father's an angry letter for telling the press that Charles Thurber had found My *Life and Hard Times* "a lot of damned nonsense."

He sent so acrimonious a letter to Jack Goodman about his handling of *The Thurber Album* that Goodman, aroused to a rage of his own, wrote Thurber that he "kissed nobody's ass." It was the kind of response Thurber actually hoped to get from those he picked on, for he needed the reassurance of reproof, and he quickly made up with Goodman. Still nervous and out of sorts, Thurber then accused Hamish Hamilton, his London publisher, of "tampering with my books," after Hamilton sent him changes they had agreed upon as appropriate for the British edition of the *Album*. "It may be that this is not a book for you, or for England," he stormed at Hamilton, "and you can get out from under if you want to." Janey Williams was the only person able to deal with him during those weeks which managed to worry and frighten so many around him. "She never let Thurber's moods and tantrums get her down," says Ronnie Williams. "She alone could get him out of his terrible fits of depression. The doctors in Bermuda were treating him with the wrong drugs—'They were way out in left field,' as Jim put it. Apparently one result of hyperthyroid is that the victim turns on his best friends. He turned on me. He'd go back to the States and his own doctors and I'd get a letter of apology, after the bad symptoms had cleared up."

"What arguments!" remembers Sara Linda Williams. "The whole house would shake."

"Ordinarily, Ronnie and Jim enjoyed their fights," says Janey, "but at dinner during his bad periods, I didn't dare serve the Jell-O; I knew it would be thrown."

"It's the only time I can remember Thurber feeling sorry for himself," says Williams. " 'Why don't all you people ask what it's like to be blind?' he'd say. 'What it feels like?' When not in that hyperthyroid grip, he rarely complained about his afflictions."

Back in the States, in October, he writes the Williamses:

I am going to see a thyroid man at Medical Center, since I have been much worse the past eight weeks. If those clowns down there had discovered my condition, as easy to detect as eight months pregnancy, I could have saved myself this burning out. Six weeks ago I was only plus 3, but the damage had been done. It may take a couple of years to get back the sense of well-being, health, and any trace of energy whatever. The prospect bores me unutterably, and it is hard to make a brave effort in this terrible world. . . . My mouth always tastes like a motorman's glove. I have to sit down to shave and I can do no writing except letters. I have been sleeping fifteen hours and getting up at noon, but in the last few days there has been a gleam of hope. I almost feel alive, can get up at ten, and now and then have a trace of appetite. For three months I had been choking everything down, including coffee. . . . I was supposed to have had another metabolism two weeks ago, but the doctor is much too busy trying to save the ancient human wrecks that overpopulate every community. I hate the medical profession with its ethics, and its ignorance, and its sulkiness. I have never known a doctor who knew anything. . . .

P.S. I used to be deeply interested in myself, but now I can't understand what I saw in me.

After some experimentation, the proper drugs were found to neutralize the toxicity. Thurber sent apologies to a number of people he had insulted, including Hamish Hamilton:

You must dismiss from your mind completely everything in connection with the Situation of a few months ago. . . . You must not expect fairness or reason from us Americans, and you must not be hurt so easily. I beg you for the third time also to remember that I was seriously ill. . . . I had lost twenty-five pounds and was probably plus 40 in metabolism. I'm taking medicine and it is somewhat better, but I'm an old shaken man who can't smoke and whose irritabilities will no doubt increase with the years.

His lethargy continued after the rages had subsided. "My thyroid rate is slowly diminishing," he wrote Robert in August, "but I still don't have much energy." To White he wrote that he couldn't tie both shoes in one continuous effort, and sometimes was too tired to brush his teeth at night. Upon receiving White's newly published *Charlotte's Web,* Thurber could only thank him with, "It starts out fine but I want to wait until my perception is back before I go on with it. I can't read or write very much and have done no casual this year, the cat one having finished last year, save for its ending. This is the longest I've gone since the 10 month nightmare in which I saw two Ann Honeycutts at once."

It wasn't until two years later, in 1954, that Thurber regained his full strength.

"The cat one" was "The Case of Dimity Ann," in which the Thurber Man compulsively keeps looping his bathrobe cord around his wife's cat to watch it free itself. (Its best time is seventeen seconds.) In the twenties, Thurber used to tie up Althea's Siamese cat in such a manner, without her knowledge:

> "The trouble was that I never told Lydia [Althea] about it, and if I tied that cat up once, I tied it up a hundred times. . . .
>
> "One day I was at the library and suddenly I stopped reading and went all the way home to tie up that damned cat. You've got to remember that the library was three miles from my house."

It was Thurber's only *New Yorker* casual in three years, though the *Album* pieces continued to run. His *Bermudian* features had become too much for him, as well; only three more appeared after the tumultuous Bermuda spring of 1952. "I wish I could promise to resume my pieces in January," he wrote Williams that fall, "but I see no hope of this for another year perhaps. After I have had some competent attention maybe the view will be brighter. Right now I'm an old torn dollar umbrella stuck in a trash bin and it is beginning to rain."

Ted Gardiner, his Columbus friend, who had been a robust drinking companion, hadn't imbibed for seven months, Thurber learned, after an automobile hit and killed his dog. Gardiner believed that it wouldn't have happened if he hadn't been drinking. He was inconsolable, and his wife took him to Europe to help him forget. "Two years ago he told me he wanted to be buried with the dog," Thurber writes his family. "It was fifteen and blind, deaf, and smelled to high heaven."

Thurber's sense of humor seemed, against all odds, intact, but his writer's block was causing Helen anxiety. "I've seen Jamie block before," she wrote Robert, "when he went blind and later when he had a nervous breakdown. He got over it and I hate to see him in one again. He's so worried about the future and so miserable."

Early in 1952, Elliott Nugent and a producer, George Schaefer, had decided to revive *The Male Animal* for a two-week run at the City Center. It was a propitious moment at which to stage the twelve-year-old comedy, for both theatergoers and critics were not only hungry for comedy but for a political message that defied Senator McCarthy's "Attila the Hun" campaign. Nugent and Thurber had originally fabricated an academic freedom dilemma for dramatic purposes, but now it could be identified with a thousand real-life instances. The play opened April 30, 1952, and audience enthusiasm moved it to the Music Box, where it ran through January 1953—a run of seventy-four more performances than it had had in 1940. Thurber and Nugent, who played Tommy again, shared 10 percent of both the receipts and profits.

Thurber was ailing in Bermuda when the play opened, but upon his return, he saw it at the Music Box and was delighted. He writes Jane Williams, who was visiting her family in upstate New York:

> Rosie [attended] a performance distinguished by a strange universal laugh from the balcony not shared by the orchestra people and puzzling to Elliott and his daughter who were on stage. . . . The balcony had spotted a mouse on stage . . . at the foot of the living room stairs. Such an unexplained laugh has an invariable effect on actors; women are sure their pants are falling off, and men are sure their pants are open. . . .
>
> A few days ago Robert Preston [as Whirling Joe Ferguson] got a nosebleed during one of his yelling scenes with Elliott, who gave him his breast pocket handkerchief, and then his pocket one. The third act that night was as bloody as the last act of Hamlet.

Thurber used the revival of *The Male Animal* to expound with renewed vigor on the Age of Suspicion. He was revolted by the withdrawal of the playwright Arthur Miller's passport, and by the question put to Miller by a member of the Un-American Activities Committee: "Do you think the artist is a special person?" In an interview with the *Times*, Thurber protested that a nation in which a congressman can seriously ask such a question "is a nation living in cultural jeopardy." He was considered reckless by some, outspoken as he was on the issue. "Blatherskites!" he is quoted in *Time*, referring to congressional "Red-probers." "The end of American comedy is in sight and the theater's gone to hell. . . . Who can write where everybody's scared? . . . I hate Communism . . . but I happen to be on one of those letterheads with Paul Robeson—and I'm not getting off . . . because I'm not letting any Congressman scare me to death." Thurber's brave voice was a sorely needed one in that period of cultural and political suppression—and cowardice.

After a performance of *The Male Animal* in 1954 at Laguna Beach, California, the *South Coast News* attacked the play for defaming "college trustees, administrators, and even realistic faculty wives," as well as big business and the teaching profession. This gave Thurber his chance for an angry article in the theater section of the *New York Herald Tribune*:

> The plan to undermine the security of the United States in three acts was entirely my own. Nugent never knew what was going on. . . . My message, or decoy, was simple enough: freedom of thought is a good idea and should be preserved. This message was approximately as subtle as hog-calling and was intended to occupy the attention of audiences while the real propaganda of the play performed its subtle deviltry in the back of their minds. My hellish over-all purpose was, of course, to destroy America's faith in realistic wives, whom I can't abide, to show that one trustee is all trustees, to ogreize big business and to rear a monument to the martyrdom of anarchists.

The critic had missed other subversive points of the play, Thurber says, including "my attack on the competence of Republican Presidents, which shows up in the line, 'Hoover can't write as well as Vanzetti.' Many people who laughed at that line later thought it over seriously and joined the party, either the Democratic, or the Communist, or the one going on at 21 after the play. I couldn't be expected to subvert everybody."

As John Hersey said of Thurber, "He is one of a few American writers who extends his responsibilities beyond literature." In a letter to Malcolm Cowley in 1952, Thurber reminds him that he was just as vehemently against the leftists of the thirties, who were for "the strangling of humor and comedy," though they had assured him that he would be allowed "a Little Red Livelihood" after the revolution:

> I have to write what I have to write, and I don't give a damn what anybody says about it. I wanted to be on the New Yorker, and I wanted

to make money, and I wanted to sell books. I am a writer like a doctor is a doctor, because I couldn't do anything else. . . . The raising of my voice now, at 57, is in defense of my livelihood rather than my profession.

That same year, the success of *The Male Animal* moved Warner Brothers to release its remake as a musical, *She's Working Her Way through College*. Its oblique, anemic dealing with academic freedom marks it as another casualty of McCarthyism, and the movie dismayed both Nugent and Thurber. They could do nothing about it, having sold the film rights a decade before.

In the Warner Brothers version, a burlesque queen (Virginia Mayo, as "Hot Garters Gertie") has written a play and enrolls at Midwest State in a playwriting course taught by "Professor Johnny Palmer," played by Ronald Reagan. The students vote to make Gertie's script a musical. Rehearsals have Mayo and Gene Nelson dancing on the professor's desk during class. When Gertie's past is discovered, the professor is told that he must expel her to keep his job. Instead, he defends the right of the burlesque queen to a college education. The evil trustee, who wants to censor the musical and kick Gertie off the campus, is quieted when Gertie reveals that he had propositioned her during her burlesque days. The names of the helpless Thurber and Nugent were dishonestly listed in the screen credits.

In April 1952, Simon & Schuster introduced *The Thurber Album*, with a printing of more than thirty thousand copies. It jumped onto the best-seller lists and was followed five months later by Hamish Hamilton's successful British publication. White acknowledged receipt of his copy ("an amazing blend of madness and affection"). "When I first saw the photographs of your private gallery of friends and relatives [in the book], most of whom from long acquaintanceship had achieved a sort of mythical quality, I got the same sort of jolt that I would get if someone suddenly produced a studio picture of Alice [in Wonderland] showing her at the time of her graduation from high school." Both he and Katharine were under the weather: "I'm expecting redwinged blackbirds to look me over, any day now, for possible nesting sites."

Told by a professor translating Thurber's work into French that his books read even better in that language, Thurber replied that he could understand that. "They tend to lose something in the original," he said. His fondness for wordplay and mimicry was ever more evident, for he was compelled to note the world by its sounds. In his "Speak that I may see thee" mode, he believed that he could guess the ages and domestic situations of people he listened to. He dwelled on, and toyed with, the words others spoke. He tells, apocryphally, of taking his leave from a family named Beebee, whose baby was called "Boo Boo," with "Bye, bye, Baby Boo Boo Beebee."

The Male Animal was grossing only ten thousand dollars a week during the summer slump, but picked up that fall. He wrote lengthy letters to White about the Korean War; White's magnificent Comment, in support of that cruel struggle, which would largely determine whether the United Nations lived or died, uplifted many a discouraged heart of that period.

The Nugents stayed overnight with the Thurbers in Cornwall on a Monday, the one day a week that *The Male Animal* was closed. Thurber and Nugent had one of their usual arguments. "The glass I threw left the plaster and lath showing between the doorjamb and the Dufy," Thurber writes the Williamses. "Norma [Nugent] was sitting eight feet away and got all the ice in her lap. We had a fine time, though."

His correspondence with the Whites was largely a reciprocal set of medical bulletins, but in early 1952 Andy wrote Thurber a lively account of a party he and Katharine had given in their New York apartment by way of acknowledging Shawn's ascendancy to editor-in-chief. A hundred and thirty-one people showed up, White writes. Peter Arno was followed at the piano by Shawn, "who is hot and who performs with the same spirit of dedication as when editing a five-part profile." Maeve Brennan, a staff writer, and Anthony West were present. West, a critic on the magazine, was the illegitimate son of Rebecca West and H. G. Wells. There was a row between Brennan and West; "the word 'bastard' got in there somewhere," says White, though he didn't hear it, for he spent most of the time in the kitchen "praying for the morning to come." The cartoonist Gluyas Williams took one drink, "and all the blood left his head and he had to be helped up to the men's coatroom, and then back to the Harvard Club."

Thurber avoided the *New Yorker*. He had always gone to see Ross after returning from Bermuda, and now he feared the sense of loss he would experience at the office. "Ross's appreciation of my writing was the one I wanted most," he writes the Williamses. "Writing for it had become a habit. I have no desire to write for the new bunch, although they are all right and I will finally."

But he was soon lamenting in interviews and on radio and TV the lack of humor appearing in the *New Yorker*, and its endless pages of the childhood reminiscences of women writers who seemed unable to get through them without repeating the phrase "it was as if." He told Kramer that the theme of Kramer's book on Ross and the *New Yorker* should have been the effect of the twenties on humorists, and pointed out that no new ones had turned up since

1930, when Ogden Nash and S. J. Perelman began writing for the *New Yorker*. Ross had been aware of the decline of humor during the McCarthy period, Thurber says in *The Years with Ross*, when he "kept urging White and Perelman and Sullivan and Gibbs and me to write something funny."

Thurber was becoming an example of his own theories; he was no longer writing the spirited humor he once did. His dwindling flow of pieces for the *New Yorker* was of gamesmanship with words, or sermons and warnings of the fearfulness of the age, disguised as fairy tales and fables, or sentimental reflections on a past that had served him so well in his earlier successes.

He had a fifth of his life span left, he told Harvey Breit in 1952, at age fifty-seven. "I expect to reach seventy-five, since the care I take of my magnificent body is well known, and my one-eighth vision happily obscures the sad and ungainly sights, leaving only the vivid and the radiant, some of whom are my friends and neighbors. My pleasures are clean and simple. I like to sit around at night holding untenable positions against logical and expert assault, [and] listening to ball games on the radio. . . . Just like you, I expect to be blown up but hope that I won't be."

65

That Master of All the Arts of Comedy

Creator of a whole gallery of real but incredible people, and a world of almost human animals, your generosity of spirit, independence of thought, and sense of the incongruous have combined to make you master of all the arts of comedy; champion of the wisely absent mind and the secret life, you have taught us to laugh at ourselves amid the predicaments and frustrations of our time. For this delight and comfort, Yale confers upon you the degree of Doctor of Letters.

—President A. Whitney Griswold, the Thurber Citation at Yale's
June 8, 1953, Commencement

He proudly wrote his Cornwall neighbors, the Kenneth MacLeans, "By the time you get this I will have been hooded. . . . I don't know who the other candidates are since I'm not supposed to know. There are usually an elderly priest, a liberal banker, a patriotic merchant with $13,000,000, and a politically safe writer. You can't tap a writer until he's sixty and no longer able to drink. . . . It's wonderful to have a blind writer who can no longer ogle the prettier wives at the teas and dinners. They don't know, however, that I can cross a dimly lighted room blindfolded and touch the prettiest bosom in the room with my index finger, nine times out of ten."

Thurber was spared the procession, and guided to the podium to receive his degree. "I could have made it easily," he wrote Jack Goodman, "since this is my last good year. Colleges wait to give a man a degree until he can no longer drink and carouse and his eyes, legs, and prostate have begun to go." He got a greater ovation than Senator William Fulbright, Helen said, and was proud to meet two other honorees, Dean Acheson, the former secretary of state, maligned by McCarthy, and Senator Prescott Bush, a Columbus native and father of the future president. "Hi, Pres," Thurber greeted him.

Ever eager to show off for Janey Williams, he had written her and Ronnie about the Yale honor: "Andy White was hooded at Yale four years ago and I have been jealous ever since because he is shorter and younger than I am. When I'm hooded I look like a great gaunt monk, but he looks like a woods creature on holiday."

He and Helen were planning to attend the Ohioana Award ceremonies in Columbus that October when "fresh hell" erupted. While reading the galley proofs of Thurber's 1953 book, *Thurber Country*, on August 20, Helen, who had had weak vision since childhood, complained of a crescent-shaped shadow in her left eye. Two days later, when there was no improvement, she and Thurber were driven from Cornwall to the Institute of Ophthalmology at the Columbia Presbyterian Medical Center, where Thurber took a room connected to Helen's. To Thurber's fright and dismay, his old eye surgeon, Dr. Gordon Bruce, who had not been well, was with his wife and son on "an extended rest," hunting and fishing in Colorado and "unavailable." Thurber panicked. Helen was his visual connection to the world, his nurse, editor, sartorial guide, business agent and partner, social secretary, sorter and adviser regarding the hundreds of letters he received, home manager and confidante, and the most reliable decipherer of his pencil scrawls. All of those responsibilities required her vision.

Thurber called Joel Sayre, John O'Reilly of the *Herald Tribune*, and Meyer Berger of the *Times*; all three were out of the office. He then phoned the Associated Press and got a New York bureau deskman, George Quist. A semihysterical Thurber asked him to help locate Bruce. Though Thurber said later that he was chagrined when his dilemma became an international news story, as a former journalist he could hardly have been surprised at the development. "The first thing I saw was the story," says Quist. "Thurber is, of course, Thurber, and his wife had been his seeing eye for years. . . . It was good human interest . . . so I put a rewrite man on to get the details from Thurber."

The story moved quickly over the local and regional wires. An hour and a half later, the AP Denver bureau reported that Bruce had been found at a Colorado ranch. He was, the reporter said, "plumb exasperated," and asked the AP to pass on his recommendation of a New York doctor and not to bother him again. Quist called Thurber, who still wished to talk to Bruce, but there was a telephone strike in Colorado. A city deskman at the *Tribune* arranged with an AT&T executive to put Thurber's call through. By then, three days had passed; Bruce was now suffering from bronchitis at the Brown Palace Hotel in Denver, but his wife assured Thurber that Dr. Graham Clark at Presbyterian, whom Bruce had recommended, was the best available surgeon for a detached retina, which was what Helen had suffered. "The first operation was a failure," says Helen, "as I discovered for myself days before Dr. Bruce got back and told me. The second operation, one day after he got back, was a success. I was in the hospital six weeks and could see to read again—with special lenses—about two months after that." The retina was intact, but a superior muscle had to be cut twice, which left Helen with a degree of double vision for nearly a year.

Embarrassed by the publicity, Thurber tried to explain to a reporter at the hospital that his near hysteria was from prospects of a life without Helen. "I can get around this room all right," he said, "but I don't know what clothes to put on. I've been described as well-tailored, but until Helen took me in hand, somebody observed that I looked as though I had been dressed by the American Can Company."

After Helen left the hospital, they remained at the Algonquin another two weeks for Helen's postoperative checkups. Helen immediately went to the hairdresser's. "If a bomb ever hits New York," said Thurber, "the men will be beating it out of town and the women will be running around to see if their hairdresser's shop was hit."

"Nearly a dozen men, all of them strangers to us, offered to give one of their eyes to Helen, with unbelievable courage and generosity," he told Smallsreed. "They all wanted to do it secretly and . . . for nothing. This kind of thing has increased our love and admiration of the human race. As it happens . . . the only part of the human eye that can be transplanted is the cornea."

If he only pretended surprise that the incident would make the news, he was truly amazed at its global coverage. The publicity led to guest appearances on the Jack Paar and Dave Garroway television shows, and turned Thurber into an amateur expert on eye care. He was made honorary chairman of a large New York benefit for the National Council to Combat Blindness, and became a clearinghouse for people concerned with eye ailments, who wished to know the better eye specialists in various cities. "I have to deal with a great many eye cases and people in mental states," he writes the Columbus Thurbers, "since I can often help them."

His own vision, which he now put at 6 or 7 percent—he could detect only shadows of movement—had diminished even more, he wrote Smallsreed. He gave this, as well as Helen's need to recuperate, as a reason for not attending the Ohioana Award ceremony in Columbus.

It had been a rough three-year period for Thurber. Though he rooted for Eisenhower over Taft in the 1952 Republican presidential primaries, he was completely won over by Adlai Stevenson's oratorical eloquence and the governor's firm stand against McCarthy's attacks on government employees. Eisenhower's semiliterate press conferences and public statements reinforced Thurber's belief that the political leaders of the country were not only permitting McCarthyism to terrify the nation but, along with advertising agencies, contributing to the erosion of literacy in America. "I blame it largely on politicians, who love to use big, blocky words, that mean so little and are so ugly," he said on Martha Deane's radio program. "[In] the UN discussion recently, 'finalize' and 'normalize' flower like weeds. . . . A politician would write to a girl that he was in love with, 'I regret that I cannot finalize the normalization of our relationship marriagewise because I am, as yet, unpredeceased by my wife deathwise.' "

Thurber's "office" was wherever Helen scheduled the two of them to be. As a team, they were most productive away from Cornwall, where Helen had household responsibilities and both liked to socialize, though knowing the day-after penalties to be paid. In November 1952, they were back at Hot

Springs, then in Cornwall for the Christmas season. In March, they were in Williamsburg, Virginia, for six weeks, and in July at Harborside Inn, Edgartown, on Martha's Vineyard. On February 14, 1953, in Philadelphia, Thurber gave away twenty-one-year-old Rosemary in marriage. (Andy White was among those who attended.) When in Williamsburg, Thurber began "The Sleeping Man," "a kind of satire on the private and public anxieties of the modern American male," he told Smallsreed. The Kafkaesque narrative takes the form of a dream. He was certain the critics would find influences of Joyce in it—his secretary had been reading parts of *Finnegans Wake* to him. "I never read enough Joyce to be influenced by him," he writes a reader, "but I love some of his wonderful wordage and idiomagic; I think my favorite thing of his is 'Alfred Lawn Tennison.' " Yet, like the blind Joyce, he proceeded to create a world of sounds, as wonderfully fantastic as the world he had been helped to imagine through imperfect eyesight, until even that ended.

He worked at "The Sleeping Man" off and on for twenty months, and believed he threw away two hundred thousand words while rewriting it. Once, when he thought it was finished, he had Helen begin to read it at a party. "She didn't get far," he says. "Somebody hissed and she stopped. It was me."

In 1954, he writes Cowley:

> I have spent a thousand hours on it, although it won't exceed 15,000 words when it's finished, and I've done about thirty complete rewrites, but have run into the well-known blank wall. . . . The . . . book . . . has some lines just for poets: "Ah, what a dusty answer gets the soul when hot for certain keys in this our life," and "Loneliest of these the married now are hung with gloom along the vow . . ."
>
> . . . Fastest writers I know are Sally Benson and John O'Hara. O'Hara, like me, is no good at plotting in advance, but his only revising, even of novels, is what he calls "pencil work," a minor change here and there in final rereading. . . . It makes you think that the boy is a genius. One thing is sure, a genius, by definition, doesn't have to go over and over his stuff. I remember Fitzgerald's exchange of letters with Wolfe about "takers out" and "putters in," the kind of argument that gets neither type of writer anywhere. Each of those men wrote exactly the way he looked.

He would abandon "The Sleeping Man" in the fall of 1954. In addition to the frustration of failure, he was not drinking or smoking and his new lifestyle drove his weight from a hundred and forty to nearly a hundred and eighty pounds. Helen, who had always been slender, loyally grew chubby along with him.

His preoccupation with Helen's eye problem left him unable to write for nearly six weeks in the late summer of 1953. He had only one casual published in the *New Yorker* that year—the brief slapstick account of an insufferable practical joker: "Shake Hands with Birdey Doggett."

In October 1953, Simon & Schuster published *Thurber Country*—nearly thirty-five thousand copies in the first printing—a collection of pieces dating from 1949, from the *New Yorker*, *Holiday*, *Cosmopolitan*, and the *Bermudian*. (Booksellers were told by Simon & Schuster salesmen to open the book immediately to "File and Forget.") It was dedicated to Rosemary and her new husband, Fred Sauers. The book jumped onto the best-seller lists and remained there for several weeks. But Thurber was undergoing more than the usual "Thurbs" that always followed the publication of one of his books. *The Male Animal* had closed in New York in January and was on national tour. "It could have had a long run," Helen laments to Robert, "but Nugent and Robert Preston both had Hollywood commitments. We are furious. Regular income from the play would mean that Jamie could take a rest from work or even begin another play."

When Raymond Swing, a broadcasting personality, asked him to contribute to the radio feature "This I Believe," the request found Thurber with little belief in much of anything at the moment:

> I believe that the imponderable is also the ineffable, and that something goes out of it when it is expressed in the well-known offhand conversational undiscipline of radio. . . . This [is] all very well, for those who are looking for icing or escape, but faith seems to me a sterner thing than that. I'm not so sure it's a time of affirmation, it may be only a time of self-delusion in which people want to be told that the house is not on fire, that the bombs won't go off after all, and that everything is going to be just dandy. I am also troubled by the fact that my belief changes from time to time and might even change during a brief broadcast. This would not reassure anybody. I also feel that networks have done more harm than any other businesses except advertising agencies in the recent years of suspicion and accusation and suppression. Furthermore, I'm not very good at this sort of thing and just don't seem to be able to know where to start. All the foregoing may be simply a defense that I don't understand very well myself. . . .
>
> Mrs. Thurber . . . joins me in sending you best wishes for a good life and whatever comes after that.

An Oregon reader wrote him a fan letter, praising Thurber's "facile pen," and Thurber took umbrage at that, too: "You're wrong about my 'facile pen.' I never had one and can only get things done by constant rewrite. For American male writers in their fifties there is no such thing as a facile pen, anyway. Guys who don't write for a living sometimes think it's a facile occupation, but it's as hard as a combination of liver surgery and ditch digging."

Inevitably, factual errors were made in a work of the length and scope of *The Thurber Album*. Poor blind Thurber, fastidious about his research, suffered over them and lost his temper when he could blame nobody but himself. He had Robert Ryder retiring to "Oakland Bay," rather than San Francisco Bay, and associated Ryder's son with the wrong university. "These mistakes would not have occurred if the great editor of the New Yorker had not died just before the piece was published in his magazine," a defensive Thurber wrote a reader pointing out the errors. "Everybody became stupid and careless for a while and the magazine made more mistakes in two weeks than it has in twenty-seven years. Now our vast checking department is back on an even keel. I have always thought that Gridley and his cannoneers would not have hit anything but the shore if Dewey hadn't been aboard."

And when a reader pointed out a Thurber mix-up of Evelyn Waugh books, he had to take responsibility:

> Only one other person has written me about my putting Evelyn between the wrong covers. I don't know what possessed me, to use one of my mother's favorite idioms. This wouldn't have happened if the piece had appeared in the New Yorker, but it was one of the Bermudian pieces. The New Yorker has a demon checking department and wouldn't think of writing about the Empire State Building without phoning to see if it is still there. One checker spent a whole afternoon with postal guides and atlases trying to find Weir—Bob Coates, then our book critic, had said that Faulkner actually writes about Weir and not the American South.

O.S.U. historian James Pollard told Thurber that he had misspelled his old journalism professor's name. Thurber replied testily, "I know how to spell Myers, but the New Yorker checkers found it spelled Meyers in some official Ohio State records, and changed it without telling me."

This is unlikely. The "vast checking department" was, at the time, six harried men, and though they should have caught a nonexistent "Oakland Bay," they would have been too intimidated to challenge Thurber on the names of his youth, given his vaunted memory and prickly resistance to correction. One extraordinary burden borne by the *New Yorker*'s busy checking department, in contrast to the operations of other publications, was an unfair and unrealistic reputation for infallibility, which sometimes fostered the laziness and carelessness of contributors. The mystique surrounding the department was perpetuated for years, also, by the lack of a letters-to-the-editor column publicizing the inevitable errors that crop up in any publication.

But to Thurber the magazine could do no right with its late editor missing. After Ross's death, he was almost immediately complaining to De Vries that Ross would not have allowed the "definite carelessness at the New Yorker" in running cartoon stereotypes. "I don't want to believe that Irvin is back," he says.

Rea Irvin wasn't, to the confusion of his widow, who writes that within a week after Ross's death, Shawn told Irvin "that he would never sell another picture to the New Yorker. All were returned from then on." This mystery involving the man who created the *New Yorker*'s first cover, giving birth to the magazine's Eustace Tilley trademark, its type style—named for Irvin—and more of its covers than those of any other artist, remains unsolved; his dismissal, as described by his widow, sounds totally uncharacteristic of the kindly Shawn. But even Thurber, a sentimentalist over the old days, apparently believed that Irvin had outlived his usefulness to the magazine.

Other contributors who had been favored by Ross were being discreetly dropped as well, further flavoring Thurber's sense of dislocation. Says Margaret Case Harriman:

> I never really "stopped" writing for the New Yorker. They just quit asking me after Ross died. . . . I haven't been able to sell them a thing since then. They turned down (with flowry phrases) two ideas for profiles I had and two pieces I sent them.

One bright spot in 1953 for Thurber was when his adored Janey and the Williams family visited New York in September. On their return to Bermuda, Thurber wrote them:

> You are the first people to call on us who are still all in one piece. Everybody else bumps into things or can't sit down or can't get up without help. I know very few people who can get out of bed in the morning without help and even my doctors complain of being old. I have discovered that women under fifty are a little too energetic for me,

now that I can see 60 on a clear day. This is the only thing I can see clearly on any day.

Cass Canfield, publisher of Harper & Bros., had been trying to woo Thurber back from Jack Goodman of Simon & Schuster; part of the strategy was to reprint some Harper editions of Thurber's earlier books. Each overture brought criticism from Thurber. The flap copy of Harper's reissue of *Fables for Our Time* "seems flat, uninviting, and written by somebody who didn't really get the point of the book," he tells Canfield. "Harper's used to do this kind of thing for my books until I took to writing the stuff myself. . . . There is a kind of genius in missing things so widely as this, and I respect it. The book has a kind of reputation, and it will probably survive this blurb."

Canfield even relinquished to Thurber Harper's rights to 50 percent of all payments for the use of his work by radio and television—no small subsidiary right, for Thurber's pieces were being adapted regularly to such programs. Thurber grudgingly acknowledged the gesture, but included it in a scolding letter to Canfield about former Harper contracts:

> No two are exactly alike, as if a different editor or lawyer had taken a swing at contracts each year. . . .
>
> I know you . . . think that my leaving Harpers was somehow capricious. . . . There were many points of irritation. . . . It hasn't been only Harpers, either. [Frank] Morley [of Harcourt Brace] was sternly opposed to contributing his help to "The Thurber Carnival." . . . "I don't think your pieces should be collected until you're dead," he said once. . . .
>
> I left Harcourt for good and sufficient reasons. I went there with Stanley Young who then quit and turned me over to Morley, who then quit and turned me over to Doris Schneider, who then quit and turned me over to nobody. For three months after the publication of "The Beast in Me" I heard nothing from its publishers. I have a good relationship with Simon and Schuster and can find no reason at all to leave them.

"Publishers never get anything completely right," Thurber writes a reader, "although they have checkers and mysterious people they call 'stylists.' I don't know what the hell they do. They never helped me."

At parties, Thurber seemed on his worst behavior if there were publishers present. Louise Connell remembers a dinner party she gave to which both Thurber and the then editor of G. P. Putnam were invited. "It was a disaster," she says. "Thurber got drunk and ugly and raved on and on about book publishers. It was a scene even his apologies the next day couldn't really make up for."

Jean Stafford remembers Thurber

> at a publication day supper party for me at the house of Eugene Reynal [her publisher] and Thurber ground out quite a few cigarettes on Mrs. R's priceless Aubusson. That was a fearfully funny party at which half the guests seemed to be in wheel-chairs or in neck-braces or wearing black patches over one eye and T. S. Matthews with his hearing aid led in Thurber who was by now quite blind. . . . At the end, nobody was left but the Thurbers and my husband [Oliver Jensen] and me and Mrs. R. found a left-over cane which she handed to Thurber who exploded in rage and immediately thereafter both he and Helen fell all the way downstairs followed by our host and there they lay at the foot, this three-part package, drunker than goats.

If publishers brought out the worst in him, it was partly from living with Ross's bitter notions of how publishing houses treated writers, and from Thurber's late belief that he had been taken advantage of by book publishers for two decades. In a way, he had been. Most authors, who lack the clout that success provides, are obliged to settle for the terms Thurber objected to, but Thurber's and White's first book was a best-seller and a classic. Nor would it have helped him to be represented by a literary agent rather than Helen. In those days, agents were not challenging the publishers' right to share in revenues from secondary uses of an author's property, or from overseas sales. As a best-selling author coveted by rival publishers, he finally discovered that he could have his way. That only increased his resentment of what he felt he had been deprived of. Even the gentle White, discussing a proposed reprint of *Is Sex Necessary?*, shared Thurber's wariness of publishers. "I don't trust publishers out of my sight," White writes him. "It is hard enough to trust them when they are plainly visible."

Still in his doldrums, after he and Helen lunched one day with Honeycutt, he writes Katharine White: "Helen says Honey's face has become kindly . . . and this is almost too much for me. I've always dreamed of hitting her with a heavy glass ashtray in my seventies and here she is on her way to becoming sainted."

The 1953 Christmas season appeared bleak. He had no sooner returned from Hot Springs than his gum became infected and his jaw swelled. He hadn't visited Columbus in three years, and after he had extolled Mame on

Mary Margaret McBride's radio program, she asked him when he would next visit his bedridden mother. Thurber mumbled that it would be that Christmas. Robert was certain that Thurber had been trapped into the commitment by McBride, and thought Thurber was unloving toward Mame when reporters weren't around. An ailing, lethargic Thurber would indeed like to have forgone the trip, writing Dorothy Miller that it was "an ordeal we have to go through with this Christmas."

They could stay only four days, Thurber wrote his brother. "As you know, Helen's eye still has double vision and I am a hundred years old, and travel and Columbus are quite a strain. . . . I am not advertising it around that I will be there. . . . Mary Margaret McBride asked about Mama and when I was going to see her, but I don't think many Columbus people heard this radio program."

But the news got around, and at Christmastime there was Thurber, as always, being photographed with his mother as part of the inevitable press interview. Upon his return he writes the Thurbers—with a copy to Rosemary:

> We got on the train all right in spite of the fact that no redcap showed up until after the train got in. Ted [Gardiner] loaded our seven bags on a truck and wheeled them to the gates himself. The station master, a friend of Ted's, kept saying everything would be fine, but he also kept calling me Mr. Gulick. We did get on the train only to find our space had been sold twice, the second time to a Mr. and Mrs. Gulick, who were put out of the compartment shouting and cursing. . . . The times are falling apart like dunked toast.
>
> We have to go to town Sunday to hear Elliott Nugent in a television version of "The Remarkable Case of Mr. Bruhl." His place has probably been taken by Gulick. . . .
>
> I made a list of two hundred Columbus people I used to know out there and all but six are dead or moved away or sick abed or in the funny house. I suppose God intends these six to be used as pallbearers. . . .
>
> It was wonderful to see Mama so bright and smart and looking so well and handsome.

A year ahead of time he was brooding over becoming sixty. In a guest column for Wolcott Gibbs's weekly, the *Fire Islander*, he writes: "With 60 staring me in the face, I have developed inflammation of the sentence structure and a definite hardening of the paragraphs." He notes that a friend of his generation "has been off his rocker for ten years. He thinks he is a cake of Ivory soap that won't float. Doesn't dare bathe for fear of drowning."

Suffering from age phobia since his thirties, Thurber wrote "How to be Sixty" for the *Bermudian,* six months before that birth date overtook him. The piece was never collected in book form:

> I won't actually be sixty until December, but that's the day after tomorrow by the clock of the apprehensive heart. . . .
>
> The Bible gives Man a life expectancy of seventy years, which leaves me only ten, but . . . the actuaries . . . allow the male . . . only about sixty-five years, and the female something like sixty-six and a half, but . . . we all know that the average male has a tough time getting through his fifties, whereas the female has developed a streak of immortality and seems likely to live forever. Vital statistics of any kind are of little value in the world of our times, in which Man is trapped by the duality of his nature; part of him is busy inventing miracle drugs and the other part is intent on devising destructive weapons . . .
>
> The first sign of old age I have noticed is my inability to bend over and tie my shoes. I have to sit up and cross my legs. This puts my right foot on the left side of my left foot, causing me to put my shoes on the wrong feet. A man in this unhappy state imparts a kind of sidespin to himself when he walks, resulting in a curious counter-clockwise motion which brings him back in a slow circle to where he had started.
>
> Since he is also likely to put his trousers on backwards (my wife sometimes finds me struggling to buckle my belt in the back, muttering, "These things were simpler when I was a boy"), the sidespin is aggravated. All this does not hamper me to any great extent, since I rarely go anywhere any more. . . .
>
> Another sign of age in the house-male is his inability to communicate easily with the house-female any longer. She seems either to be calling to him from the next room or shouting at him from the floor below, usually when an automobile is backfiring or the water is running from both faucets in the washbowl. . . . If he hears her at all, which is unlikely, she sounds as if she were talking about gleebs and throckets, or reciting something through a towel. This onset of inaudibility may result in a complete mental, if not legal, separation.
>
> Senility, by the way, as opposed to senescence, is characterized by a tendency to call a second wife by the first wife's name, but I don't think we need to go into that yet.

His lack of progress on "The Sleeping Man," which he was now calling "The Train on Track Six," was increasingly exasperating to him. Malcolm

Cowley, preparing his "A Natural History of the American Writer," wrote Thurber, who was in Bermuda, asking if he could use a Thurber quotation. Thurber, worried by his writer's block, and intrigued by Cowley's explorations in the psychology and sociology of writers, not only gave Cowley permission to use his quote, but expounded on the nature of his own writing. "Have you spent any time with the boys who are going through change of life or of religion or of viewpoint?" he asks Cowley. "In our neurotic world this late middle age or sunset of the writer is becoming more tangled than the female climacteric. This may be because women give up something they no longer want, whereas men feel everything slipping away." When he was stuck in his writing, he said, he got a lot of help from his dreams, which often gave him clues as to how to fix the problem.

His only New Yorker piece in 1954, "Get Thee to a Monastery," was about the displacement of the male actors in American theater by the female. (Shawn ran it as a "The Theatre" column.) Thurber was still plagued by ailments, physical and mental. During one of his breakdowns, Helen sent for Jap Gude, who, along with Janey Williams, was one of the few he could tolerate during an emotional crisis. "All our thanks for saving the old man's sanity these past three days," Helen wrote Gude. "He feels weak, but much better, no fever, and he has shaved, so looks a little less like Gabby Hayes."

Three of the "Mr. and Mrs. Monroe" stories were produced off-Broadway in March. His friend Wolcott Gibbs, the New Yorker's theater critic, was put on something of a spot, but got out of it with clever humor. For one thing, he found Three by Thurber "semi-autobiographical":

> They deal with rather dispirited actual experiences, the contrasting with vehement day dreams of a man who is conceivably the image the author has of himself in his moments of bleakest depression. Fortunately for my peace of mind, I know nothing of Mr. Thurber's private fantasies, but I have seen and been familiar with his outward presence for something like a quarter of a century, and the idea that he would be helpless in the face of any known social situation seems very humorous to me. There have been times when I thought that he dealt a little more erratically with life than most men I know but I have certainly never seen him defeated or even perceptibly disconcerted by it. . . . The essence of Thurber is such that in any real contest of personalities, everybody else would be well advised to take to the hills. None of this should be interpreted to mean that Mr. Thurber's literary conception of himself isn't a wonderful thing, for I think that it is one of the funniest in American humor. . . . Even the best of us see peculiar visions in our

mirrors. This brings me . . . reluctantly, to the fact that I don't believe the collection . . . works out very well as entertainment in the theatre.

On Martha's Vineyard that summer, the Thurbers were caught in Hurricane Carol, as he writes the Williamses:

> We were having breakfast in the main building when she struck. . . . An hour later the dining room tables were floating and the water in our . . . building was up to the mirrors of the first floor, and left sand and salt and seaweed when it receded, spoiling dresses and sports clothes, but not ours, since we were on the second floor. . . . We had a couple of rough nights in New York, one of them with a woman's name, too. In a post-midnight discussion I seemed to pull an arm off her chair and there was a lot of pushing and shoving. I know too many writers, I guess, and have paraphrased the old Cornish litany: From girl writers and ghost-writers and long-legged piece writers, and writers that go bump in the night, O Lord deliver us. The New Yorker seems to me to consist largely of young women from Harper's Bazaar, The Modern Priscilla, and Ladies' Needlework, all the vitality of the Ross days being gone, and only a lot of wind around the place, whispering people in rubber-soled shoes.

The "rough night" with a woman's name in New York centered on the Algonquin lobby, where St. Clair McKelway and his newest and fifth bride, Maeve Brennan, who had left *Harper's Bazaar* for the *New Yorker*, joined the Thurbers for late-evening drinks. Brendan Gill interprets the version of the event given him by Brennan:

"Thurber had always resented Mac for making off with Honeycutt, and he tried to embarrass both Maeve and Mac by bringing up the several predecessors to Maeve. 'Remember that wonderful girl you used to screw?' he'd say to Mac. 'What happened to her? Do you still see Honey? What went wrong with *that* marriage?' All this in front of the bride, who was by no means inexperienced, but also not amused. Thurber got around to insulting women writers, too, until Maeve, fed up, said to Thurber in her Dublin accent, 'You, you are nothing but an old ruin.' Thurber was sitting in his usual place, on the settee that was placed diagonally across a corner. Maeve was in one of the armchairs at the end of the coffee table. Thurber angrily reached out in his blindness, grabbed a leg of the chair Maeve was in and yanked it. Maeve tumbled backwards onto the floor. Mac leaped up and said he'd always wanted to hit a blind man. The bellhops looked through the glass partition at this drunken mêlée, and, mostly because they knew Thurber and McKelway better than they did Maeve, decided she was the problem. They picked her up, pinned her arms behind her and bundled her off, McKelway following. It was typical Thurber mischief."

Thurber and McKelway were estranged for more than three years, until McKelway, genuinely moved by admiration of Thurber's early chapters of *The Years with Ross*, appearing in the *Atlantic Monthly*, wrote him a flattering letter about them. Thurber, who was wondering how to approach McKelway to learn of *his* experiences with Ross and the magazine, seized the opportunity. Practiced at graceful conciliation, Thurber ended his letter with, "My sincere love to you and Maeve and apologies for any and all transgressions of mine. They were blind, unintentional, and, I think, misinterpreted. God knows I never intended to hit or hurt anyone and this confusion remains one of my great sorrows and bewilderments."

McKelway was pleased by the chance to participate in Thurber's memoirs, and replied with an eleven-page letter filled with facts and anecdotes about his tenure on the magazine. At the end, he acknowledges Thurber's apology: "Maeve says you never hit her or hurt her, it was only that you blew at her so hard she flew across the lobby. And don't have sorrows or bewilderments. They're not worth the trouble."

Reflecting on it all, four years later, McKelway said, "One was wrong to take Thurber seriously. What could you do—actually hit a blind man? He could be described in a hundred different ways. I found him childlike in wanting to be the center of attention and in his fear of women, but he was never mean when sober. He actually seemed very fond of me. When I would meet him during his last years he would hold my hand in a steely grip, like that of the Ancient Mariner. He maintained the position that everyone loved him—and long after the dust settled, and we could reflect on what he left us, maybe all of us did."

66

Those Further Fables

Little Miss Muffet sat in the bar of the Tuffet, drinking her bitters and rye. Along came the Spider, a tough character from the other side of town, and sat down beside her. "Scram, sister," he said, "before the naughty language in this dangerous dump offends them shell-like ears, and scares the cellophane off them angel wings. . . .

She threw what was left of her bitters and rye, and the ice, in the Spider's face, socked him one in the mush with the empty glass, crowned him King of Bye-Bye Land with an empty whisky bottle, buried him under two tables and a chair, and yawned and asked for the tab. . . .

"I wish you reminded me more of your mother," her father said when she got home.

"Crawl back into the nineteenth century, Pop, when women was ladies," said little Miss Muffet. She yawned, and got out a nightcap, swallowed it in two gulps, and hit the hay.

Moral: the only old-fashioned thing about the modern lass is her old-fashioned glass.

—from *Further Fables for Our Time*

Insomniacs who can see turn on the light at night and read. Thurber used the silent sleepless hours to revise in his head what he had written, to compose new material, to sift the dreams he awakened from for meaning, to lament man's tendency to self-destruction, and to ponder the female's inevitable—

and necessary—triumph in the battle against the male, while resenting her for it. Besides his doomsday prophecies, his few casuals in the mid-fifties continued to feature intoxicated men who play word games; lengthy Scrabble-like competitions would be played out in his mind and written up in the drunken dialog of his fictitious characters.

"Thurber had a finicky concern for grammar," says Alistair Cooke, "a scientific intelligence which passes over into his humor; he knew what went into making the organism of language, and it infuriated him that others were either too insensitive or indifferent to join him in protecting the rules from vulgar violation. I always thought his partiality toward the English was connected to his admiration for the language."

Thurber was working again, but at projects he wouldn't complete. ("I keep writing new acts for my play, and introducing new characters that I then forget about.") There was the unfinished fairy tale, "The Spoodle"— later changed to "The Grawk"—a terrible "something" that actually didn't exist, but was said to, by the kingdom's tyrannical leaders, whose power rested on a populace too frightened to act. McCarthy's power was in its final stages of self-defeat, but that would in no way lessen the moral imperative for Thurber, who continued his Swiftian warnings against it in his literary fantasies.

In 1955, Jack Goodman and Thurber collected Thurber's dog stories and drawings into *Thurber's Dogs*, published that October and dedicated to the first of Rosemary's children, Sara, who was born that year on March 31. The critics liked the book. Thurber was a favorite of book reviewers, and not until *The Years with Ross*, which a few critics—friends and admirers of the late editor—felt was unfair to Ross, did any of his books draw negative comments of any significance. But for once Jack Goodman's liberal first printing (35,200 copies) was too optimistic. There was no hardcover second printing of *Thurber's Dogs*. That same month, Hamish Hamilton brought out *A Thurber Garland*, a collection of Thurber drawings with a short preface; it was followed in December by the dog book.

Cass Canfield had been proposing to Thurber an anthology of his works, only to be told, time and again, that a concurrent publication of a Thurber book by Simon & Schuster would conflict. The long-suffering Canfield permitted Goodman to use Harper's Thurber Dog material without charging a fee. He did get Thurber's consent to reissue *The Middle-Aged Man on the Flying Trapeze* that year.

In 1955, before the publication of any of these books, the Thurbers sailed for Europe, Thurber writing Robert:

We are planning to spend the summer in France, which is after all only as far away nowadays as Columbus. A million Americans are going over this year, including most of our friends. . . . We don't sail until May 4th on the French liner Liberté, which lands at Le Havre. A couple of young doctors we know will meet us there with their car.

As Prohibition at home had helped make Paris a congenial haven for American expatriates of the twenties, a disgruntled Thurber found Europe a welcome sanctuary from a culture blighted by McCarthyism. He and Helen spent June in France, six weeks in England, and by mid-August they were back in Paris, where they remained through October. British reporters boarded the *Liberté* in Southampton to interview Thurber before the ship sailed on to Le Havre. Their adoration of the man at times led to near-incoherent copy. One giddy interviewer writes: "Thurber is so immensely wise and sensible that his attitude of mind is a slightly dreamlike quality that at times becomes slightly nightmarish."

Says Alistair Cooke: "Thurber was like an expatriate; he used his feelings for the English and for Bermuda to moderate his disgust with America. He was too tough-minded to be an Anglophile in any sentimental way. But both England and America tend to baby each other's humorists, and Thurber reveled in that. It takes both countries longer to find and appreciate their own. Eventually they do."

In Paris they were taken in hand by their friend John Duncan Miller, who had moved there from Washington the year before. The Thurbers "would come to us two or three times a week," says Miller, "and we would produce people who were interesting and interested in Thurber. There were American . . . and English friends of his there so that he never lacked for something to do in the evening. He liked parties that [went on] all night. He liked people with distinctive voices . . . and laughs. . . . I don't remember him having many French friends; I don't think the French were ever much admirers of Thurber or understood him much. [Thurber] liked the Crazy Horse Saloon in Paris. It didn't matter how long an evening of talk he had, he then wanted to go to this nightclub for half an hour . . . before he went home."

During their nearly six months abroad, the Thurbers met up with the Nugents, the Mark Van Dorens, Janet Flanner, Richard Watts, T. S. Matthews and Martha Gellhorn, his wife, Mollie Panter-Downes (writer of the magazine's Letter from London), A. J. Liebling, the Hamish Hamiltons, Nora Sayre, the Gudes' daughter, Liz, and Donald Ogden Stewart. In London, they had tea with T. S. Eliot. In Paris, Art Buchwald interviewed Thurber. ("We didn't get drunk together nor did we go to the Pigalle," says Buchwald. "I sat there in awe as he talked and I listened to every tale.")

In London, Thurber began work on an article for *Holiday* on the Loch Ness monster. Nora Sayre, who, like other young American girls abroad, was having trouble finding work, was glad to be hired as his researcher for the project. "He was very protective of me," she says. "Andy and Thurber had both written me in London, worried to hear that I was in Europe on my own. Whenever I dined with the Thurbers there, I ate spinach so they could write my parents that I was doing fine. Once, on my way to the Stafford Hotel, where the Thurbers were staying, an American Air Force character said to me, 'Hey, baby, how much do you cost?' I laughed about it to the Thurbers, but Jim got angry—Americans leading English women to believe they regarded them all as prostitutes. He kept bringing it up and saying he intended to use the incident in a piece. He finally did, seven years later, in 'The Other Room.'

"He dictated each afternoon to a secretary—British, of course, which caused some difficulties, given Jim's mumbled Midwest speech. He claimed that once he had dictated a headline to her, 'Frenzied polar bears attack two explorers in the Arctic,' and it came out 'Friends of Paul Rovere attack two exploiters in the attic.' "

The London press claimed him as their own. "The newspapers descended in force," Helen writes the Thurbers, "and poor Jamie was interviewed to the death. . . . I put him to bed Sunday night and am keeping him there until he has to go on television tomorrow . . . on . . . the show for which the editor of *Punch*, Malcolm Muggeridge, is m.c. . . . They will show blown-up reproductions of Thurber drawings to go with the light ad-lib banter. . . . There were long pieces in the Daily Mail, the Sunday Times, and the Sunday Observer. . . . David Astor, publisher of the Observer and son of the famous Lady Nancy Astor, M.P., called on us, all starry-eyed over meeting his literary hero."

A. J. Liebling saw a lot of the Thurbers in London. "I'd see all these Englishmen sitting around Thurber's hotel room," says Liebling, "drinking in everything he had to say. You can't break in on a blind man; he doesn't see the signals. People came and departed without his knowing who was in the room much of the time. Helen always got an ashtray under his cigarette when he was talking and drinking. He kept telling these journalists what a great newspaperman he had been, but there was never any news in Columbus, and the *New York Post* couldn't have known what use to make of his kind of talent. He was a little tin god to the English, who were years behind on

American writers, as we were on English writers. But I really liked salty old Thurber in those days."

The British literati found everything Thurber told them imperishable. Writer Paul Jennings remembers with wonder Thurber's suggestion that "Ping-Pong" spelled backwards sounds more like the game. "This is true," says Jennings: "gnip, gnop, gnip, gnop. Everything he said was true." Poe's raven, Thurber told Jennings, kept pronouncing "raven" backwards, with a slightly foreign accent, which gave Poe the idea for "Nevermore."

In Scotland, the Inverness authorities opened their Loch Ness files to Thurber, as had the *London Daily Mail*. (Thurber's theory as to why the monster was rarely seen: its first sight of a man was such a shock that it chose to remain submerged.) Another Thurber admirer, Wilfred Taylor, invited the Thurbers to Edinburgh, where he was taken to the Scottish Art Club. There, says Taylor, he was shortly "the centre of a circle. He sat there and just talked in his quiet, unemphatic Ohio drawl." The playwright Robert Kemp was there, and later sat up in his sleeping car "jotting down everything he could remember of James's flow of talk." It was reminiscent of when *Time*'s researchers interviewed Wolcott Gibbs for the cover story on Thurber. "They all think he's Jesus Christ," he told Honeycutt in amazement.

In Edinburgh, the Thurbers were introduced to the novelist and playwright Sir Compton Mackenzie, who remembers:

> We had a marvelous evening and I thought, Well, this really is the top in the way of a man. And at two o'clock his wife said, "Well, it's time to be going." . . . Said James, "I don't want to go yet, Helen. I'm enjoying talking here." But she said, "It's four o'clock." So, unwillingly, he agreed to go and found out when he got back to the hotel that it wasn't four o'clock but two o'clock and was absolutely furious. . . . The . . . next day, he said, "I was swindled out of a jolly good two hours last time . . . and it's not going to happen again!" We . . . did keep it up until about four."

The Whites visited London that summer, dismaying Mollie Panter-Downes, who was asked to help make their arrangements in London. ("They'll just take turns being sick over here," she told Liebling.) The Whites spent a fortnight in a country inn in Devon, and had dinner with twenty-three-year-old John Updike, who had been selling verse and fiction to the *New Yorker* for a year. His fellowship at Oxford's Ruskin School of Drawing and Fine Art was coming to an end, and he accepted the job of Talk reporter, which Katharine offered him with Shawn's agreement.

"The Whites couldn't take it," Helen writes the Columbus Thurbers, when Katharine and Andy left London for the country inn. If so, one reason they couldn't was Thurber, who was up to his old tricks, in this case tinged with his curious hostility toward Katharine. As Brendan Gill recounts in *Here at The New Yorker*, "Given his remarkably adaptable voice and a telephone (a device that renders blind people equal to the sighted), Thurber could make mischief to his heart's content." The Whites had no sooner checked into their London hotel when Thurber was on the phone, identifying himself, "in a clipped Oxford accent," as an English reporter and photographer, and asking for an interview. The publicity-shy White, of course, refused. Thurber, as journalist, asked if, at least, he could take their photograph for his newspaper. Andy agreed, if it ran only with a simple caption. And what kind of picture would it be? The British-accented response was, "A shot of Mrs. White leapfrogging naked over you." Thurber's inability to keep from laughing eventually gave him away. The Whites found nothing amusing about it, but Liebling thought it was hilarious. "Every time Joe started telling about the White-Thurber fiasco," Jean Stafford writes, "he was overcome and I never did get the story straight."

"Actually, Joe tried to bring the Whites and Thurbers together," says Nora Sayre. " 'These people really love one another,' he insisted to me, and he invited them to his hotel for drinks. They were friendly enough until two a.m., Joe told me, but by four a.m. they all hated one another again. Thurber was in fair physical shape by then, but the Whites weren't, and I think that made them a bit touchy. They complained of slipped disks and stomach pains."

While in England, the bashful White refused the singular honor of attending the weekly Wednesday luncheon meeting at *Punch*, at which the editors selected the political cartoon for the next issue; only two outsiders, Prince Philip and Mark Twain, had been allowed to join the editors at this historic ritual. Three years later, Thurber accepted the invitation White had refused, becoming the second American writer—and humorist —to be so recognized.

One subject the age-conscious Thurber was now resorting to, over and over, was the longevity of English writers compared with American writers. "Everybody here seems to last much longer than we do in America," he told Mackenzie—and everyone else he met in London and Paris. He wrote the Thurbers that he and Helen

have had quite a few dinner parties at the homes of various friends, and have met a great many writers. . . . Life in London and Paris is much more restful than in New York, and you begin to understand why French and English writers live longer than American. They simply take things much more easily. Also they go to bed earlier than we do at home, and drink less, and get more done.

He finally got it on paper with "The Moribundant Life, or, Grow Old along with Whom?" which ran in the *New Yorker* that October:

> The only elderly men of letters in America that I could think of offhand who were still alive were Robert Frost, Samuel Hopkins Adams, and Carl Sandburg. But I could reel off the names of thirty fellow-country-men whose literary careers and physical being came to an end in their fifties or forties, and at least half a dozen upon whom, though still alive, one form or another of writer's cramp had fallen. . . . I had recently frightened myself into a cold night sweat by running the list up to ninety-eight, including newspapermen and a few editors and publishers who had written something and died soon after.

He had been mulling over the temporal nature of life for some time, writing the John Duncan Millers earlier:

> Last year 20,000 persons were killed in falls, most of them in their own houses. Buster leaves one skate on the next to the top step and it's curtains for Daddy. Baby throws the soap out of the tub and screams for Mummy, who comes running and steps on the soap, and it's lilies for Mummy. . . . More mothers are shot by their children than fathers, since more guns are kept in the home than at the office. Three little darlings in Cornwall let Mummy have it, one of them a little girl of six who managed to blow Mummy to hell with a shotgun and, to quote a famous limerick, "They found her vagina in South Carolina, and bits of her anus in Dallas." People used to say, "She worked herself to death for that man and nobody knows what she saw in him." Now they say, "It's so nice her youngest daughter won't remember shooting her because she was only two at the time . . ."
>
> Let's all cheer up. . . . Most of the people we love are busy preparing a mansion for us au-dela.

In late October, they sailed for home on the *Liberté*. Mame Thurber's health had taken a turn for the worse. Helen, writing the Williamses from London, mentions that nurses were on twelve-hour duty at the Thurbers' current apartment in the Seneca Hotel in Columbus. On November 25, Mame, nearly ninety, suffered a stroke and was moved to University Hospital. Thurber and Helen immediately took the train to Columbus, but Robert doubts that Mame, who lingered through a semicoma for nearly a month, recognized them. It was the sort of dying everyone hopes a loved one will be spared. It came to an end on December 20, 1955. As Peter De Vries wrote, in his note of condolence to Thurber, "Certainly the death cannot be any worse than the dying." Thurber would have agreed; Mame had been bedridden, annoyed with herself, and in discomfort for four years.

Quartered at the Deshler-Wallick hotel in Columbus during the month-long deathwatch, Thurber began a new series of fables. Thirty-seven of them ran in the *New Yorker* from May 12 to October 13, 1956. Katharine White had obtained permission from Harper & Bros. to run certain illustrations from the 1940 *Fables for Our Time* with the new fables, and, beyond her official call of duty, obtained additional permission for their use in both the American and British editions of *Further Fables for Our Time*. Most of the other illustrations in the books are composites of Thurber's cartoons and spots over the years.

His 1940 fables are cheery contradictions of clichés and truisms, usually satires on the human condition. The humor of the 1956 fables often resides in Thurber's unexpected, Joycean gymnastics of language. In one, when the red squirrel ruins the illusions of the turtle, the moral asks, "O why should the shattermyth have to be a crumplehope and a dampenglee?" An "all is vanity" theme is offered by the young wolf who buys a Blitzen Bearcat and speeds about the city with "a speed-crazy young wolfess." The wolf fatally takes a corner "travelling at a rate of 175 miles an hour," while watching television and holding hands with the wolfess. Moral: "Where most of us end up there is no knowing, but the hellbent get where they are going."

Yet the fables show that even Thurber, who decried the growing shortage of humorists, was finding more to be bitter about than funny. They were, after all, composed against a gloomy background: his mother was dying; a cold war was on, in which two conflicting ideologies were backed by nuclear fission; and freedom of speech in America seemed to lack effective support. Thurber's strongest freedom-of-speech message is found in "The Trial of the Old Watchdog," who is accused of killing a lamb that had actually been done in by a fox. In the "kangaroo court," a witness says, "I didn't actually see this lamb-killer kill this lamb . . . but I almost did." The kangaroo judge says, "That's close enough." The jury of foxes recommends the dog's acquittal, so that he will remain a suspect the rest of his life. The prosecutor agrees: "Guilt by exoneration! What a wonderful way to end his usefulness." It sums up the essence of McCarthyist travesties.

Thurber's misanthropy is threaded throughout. When the man gloats to the dinosaur that it will be extinct ("for monstrosity is the behemother of extinction"), the dinosaur replies: "There are worse things than being extinct, and one of them is being you." And the moral of another fable goes: "Fools rush in where angels fear to tread, and the angels are all in Heaven but few of the fools are dead."

The fables continue the battle of the sexes—the female dominates the male, who is helpless without her and at risk with her. The tigress turns her arrogant mate into a tigerskin rug for her children. The grizzly is at a loss with household gadgets, which are one reason why men live domestic lives of "noisy desperation."

The *New Yorker* had rejected ten of the fables, and Thurber thought they had been turned down through a failure of nerve on the part of the editors. Gus Lobrano could probably have handled Thurber's intemperate charges, but Lobrano died of cancer in mid-February 1956, three months before the fables began to run. For Thurber, who had liked and respected Lobrano, it was the finale to any trusting relationship with the *New Yorker*. For some time, and despite their friendly correspondence, he had regarded Katharine as his editorial enemy. Lobrano had been his last link to a magazine that, to Thurber, less and less reflected Ross's judgments. "When he heard of Gus's death," says Jean Lobrano, "Thurber telephoned and said, 'I'm blind but couldn't I come over and try to help you?' When he was top dog and not competitive, there were none more kindly than Thurber."

Thurber wrote Malcolm Cowley another depressed appraisal of the times, partly conditioned by Lobrano's death:

> Everybody is afraid except the foolhardy, the foolish, and the crazy. . . .
> Gus Lobrano . . . who died at fifty-three, had been in the process of
> dying from nothing but fear for eight years, and it wasn't until he actu-
> ally developed a fatal liver condition that he achieved not only his old
> self . . . but a curious and indestructible tranquility of spirit. It was an
> amazing thing to watch.

William Maxwell followed Lobrano as Thurber's editor, and trouble began. Maxwell's explanation for refusing certain fables was that they were "famil-iar," a favorite word in *New Yorker* parlance of the day. Thurber writes Maxwell,

I have sharpened The Sleepless and the Sleeping, whose value is considerable since it is possibly the only truly merry fable. Most men can sleep; most women can't. My first wife used the expression, "a man's bed is his cradle," a common saying among wives. . . . The fable about the bears is important to me because all fable writers must have one or two dealings with the political temper of their times. The notion that this fable is familiar is downright idiotic. At least a third of my first fables bought by Ross were attacks on Naziism, intolerance and the like. It is also polemical, like my true favorite of all . . . The Case of the Guilty Watchdog. Let us all draw a distinction between the familiar and the recognizable. The recognizable, as I observed to White, is the living heart of comedy. The familiar is a seasonal categorization.

He sent rewritten versions of "The Bears and the Monkeys" and "The Sleepless and the Sleeping" to White, "for his possible amusement," he told Maxwell, "but not necessarily his intervention with Shawn." White, fond of any humanized nonhuman creature, admired Thurber as "the only living fable writer," and had declared his favorite to be "The Truth about Toads," one of the first of the fables to be published. In this unappetizing tale, a toad boasts that he has a precious jewel in his head. When he falls asleep, a woodpecker drills a hole in his skull, finding nothing. The moral: "Open most heads and you will find nothing shining, not even a mind." Thurber writes White:

> These two were rejected but I wanted you to see them. I can only think that Maxwell and Shawn are insomniacs married to wives who can sleep. The reason for the rejection of The Bears seems to me faintly idiotic. The New Yorker has a strange new and clouded definition of what it calls "familiar." . . . I have a beauty against the abuse of due process [the watchdog] but I'm actually scared to turn it in.

White, in support of Maxwell, replied that the two fables didn't "explode" for him as the others had, to which Thurber responded: "I was trying to make those two fables ring, because 70 per cent of the others are about death. I am the deathiest of the fable writers.

"Shawn once told me that you never read manuscripts, as if he never heard of THE NEW YORKER of you and me, or of your saving 'Menaces in May' and hence my further serious pieces. . . . This is the reason I turn to you for advice every decade or so—you also saw the flaw in 'Many Moons.' "

White had reminded Thurber that editors had a freedom to be wrong, to which Thurber replied: "There are certain things to which we cannot apply the word 'freedom' and the belief that all caprice, carelessness, ignorance, or anything else deserves the holy protection of American liberty is one of the weaknesses of our way of life. An editor has a right to his own taste, but not to a capricious or facetious disregard for another's. Free speech, to take up another phase of freedom, should not protect or defend loose talk."

Further Fables for Our Time, complete with the *New Yorker* rejects, was published October 31, 1956, with a first printing of thirty thousand copies. The Book Find Club accounted for another fifteen thousand, and the *New Yorker*'s business department had five thousand complimentary copies bound to send to advertising space buyers. S. J. Perelman let it be known that the fables contained "the finest writing of our time," but Thurber was upset to be told that one reviewer had called them "the tired writing of a tired man." That another critic had said, "He writes with the verve of a young man" didn't compensate him for the put-down.

The dedication page of *Further Fables for Our Time* reads: "To Elmer Davis, whose comprehension of people and persons has lighted our time, so that we can see where we are going, these fables are dedicated with admiration, affection and thankfulness." Thurber had been a faithful listener to Davis, whose defiant radio broadcasts against McCarthyism had somehow stayed on the air despite warnings to the ABC network from Vincent Hartnett, editor of *Red Channels*. Davis was in the hospital with an illness that would prove fatal. He was moved by Thurber's compassionate efforts to cheer him, and wrote Thurber that given his years of blindness, Thurber surely had too many of his own travails to worry about Davis's. Thurber gallantly tried to reassure him, writing:

> My own case is not anywhere near so bad as you might think, since I went blind over a period of sixteen years gradually and have learned to my astonishment that total blindness is not darkness but light. I had not known before that the totally blind live in a soft light, without shadow or figures or landscape, but light none the less. . . . According to . . . my eye man, only those who have both eyeballs removed would live in darkness. It is the annoyance . . . and not the disability or the tragedy of blindness that is the hardest to bear, the inability to read a letter that comes in when you are alone or to dial a number on the phone or look one up in the phone book. The loss of visual stimuli is not too important to a man like me who has total recall and can summon up images, familiar or imaginary, without much trouble. . . . I would like to see what life has done for the faces of the people I have always loved.

Further Fables earned Thurber five thousand dollars from the American Library Association's (ALA) Liberty and Justice Award ("for work in the field of imaginative literature that did most for the cause of liberty, justice and fair play"). Thurber declared the award his "proudest badge" and used the money to buy a new Cadillac. He was in Bermuda in the spring of 1957, when the award ceremony took place, and Jack Goodman acted as the surrogate recipient.

Thurber had already begun his public attacks on the *New Yorker*, while it continued to buy his casuals and fables. Though the magazine had celebrated its thirtieth anniversary with a low-key party at the Hotel Astor, *Newsweek*, in its February 21, 1955, issue, used the occasion for an article on the publication, quoting Thurber as saying, "Ross had a distinctive touch. What he did was usually right. . . . But now it's different. It's a synthetic magazine today."

Thurber was the principal source of colorful facts in the piece. Whether or not he is responsible for some of the article's critical analysis, it surely mirrors Thurber's beliefs at the time. *Newsweek* grants, as Thurber would, that "through the bright word and . . . eloquent cartoon *The New Yorker* has done a face-lifting job on the American sense of humor, in a remarkable literary combination of the factual and the fantastic." But it continues, "The [magazine's] humorous piece has almost disappeared. The effect on the reader of some issues these days is almost as solemn as the atmosphere inside the offices." With the exception of a few editors at the top, the article states, "the average editor, writer, or reporter knows as much about the goings-on in the place as one of a button factory's less distinguished employees. . . . As Shawn explains it: 'We work in an anonymous and invisible way.' "

Supporting Thurber's objections to the post-Ross practices of the fiction department, *Newsweek* canvassed twenty-five recent issues of the *New Yorker* and found that of forty-two casuals, eleven were of childhood reminiscences. "Twenty-five of the 42 stories dealt with problems that a psychiatrist might have handled more profitably. . . . *The New Yorker* has something like a monopoly on stories about frightened young girls, unwanted old ladies, sensitive young suburbanites, unwanted children, malevolent old ladies, ruined evenings at home, ugly situations in bars, ruined afternoons in the country, alcoholics married to nonalcoholics, gropers for happiness." It found the factual side of the book "Shawn's strong point," and the *New Yorker* "at its best as a reporting magazine."

Though Thurber's cooperation with *Newsweek* was viewed by *New Yorker* editorial people as consorting with the enemy, Thurber's outspokenness hardly presaged hardship for the magazine, whose circulation was at 385,000 and climbing. ("The New Yorker is as prosperous as the first combination bar and whorehouse in the Klondike," Thurber wrote Cass Canfield.) Brendan Gill believes that Thurber was the last man on the staff to play practical jokes during office hours, and that had ended in 1935. When *Newsweek* observed that earlier editors and contributors seemed to have had more fun than the current *New Yorker* staff, it was really saying that the magazine had followed its first generation of editors into middle age.

Less than a year after Thurber was lamenting the demise of old friends in "The Moribundant Life, or Grow Old along with Whom?", John McNulty also died. He had married again, in 1945, and with his wife, Faith, purchased a farm in Wakefield, Rhode Island, as a summer retreat. He died there of heart disease on July 31, 1956, at age sixty-one. Though McNulty and Thurber had no longer seen much of one another, they had continued a warm correspondence. "After a couple of reunion dinners broke up badly," writes Faith McNulty, "they found they both enjoyed letters and phone calls more. John still loved Jim, but was wary of drinks or dinners together. When Jim drank in later days he got quite quarrelsome."

Thurber was at his best when remembering people he had loved. Doubleday issued a collection of McNulty's works the next year, and Thurber wrote the introduction, which included parts of the lovely McNulty epitaph from the *New Yorker*: "When he told a tale of people or places, it had a color and vitality that faded in the retelling by anyone else."

In June 1956, the Thurbers saw Lerner and Loewe's *My Fair Lady*, and Thurber was entranced. "It was one of the wonderful experiences of our life," he writes the Williamses, "the finest use to which comedy and music have been put in thirty years. It took a great Irishman [Shaw] and a talented cast of English actors to bring dignity back to the American comedy stage."

His old friend Dick Maney was handling the production's publicity. "The show moved Thurber close to tears," says Maney. "I told the drama editor of the *Times* about Thurber's enthusiasm and the editor asked him to do a piece on it. He did. I think he just got fifty or sixty dollars for it, but it was a labor of love. Thurber was always good news in my profession. Everything he wrote came over clear as a bell. He'd written great publicity for me when I'd been hired to tout *The Male Animal*, and here was a more famous Thurber promoting *My Fair Lady*, getting the publicity I was being paid to get, of the kind that can't be bought.

"Thurber was talking about the show at Costello's one night and asked me to take him backstage to see Rex Harrison. We went to the Hellinger Theater after the evening performance. Kay Kendall, Harrison's bride-to-be, was in the dressing room. I was nervous; Rex is a snob who gets along with few people, and the Thurbers and I were drunk, but Rex pulled out a bottle and we had a party, Thurber upstaging Rex with those wildly exaggerated stories. I called around the next day to see if I'd been fired, but I think Thurber's *Times* puff saved me."

The "puff" read in part: "I can still be heard proclaiming on street corners that 'My Fair Lady' has restored comedy to a position of dignity in the theatre. Better writing is coming out of England, where a writer can work in mental serenity." Dialect and the challenge of language were his specialty, and Julie Andrews's phonetic success with "The rain in Spain stays mainly in the plain" seemed "the perfect tribute to perfection in comedy," with the effect not one of "immediate laughter, but a curious and instantaneous tendency of the eyes to fill."

Four years later, when seats to the show were finally becoming available on short notice, Maney was running Thurber's glowing encomium as a full-page advertisement in the *Times*.

On May 9, 1956, Helen had written Dorothy Miller from Bermuda that their stay there was doing wonders for Thurber but might be doing her in: "The Nugents were here, very gay and exhausting. I've felt only fair, but Jim is blooming—finished a new fairy tale and working on a play. He's tireless."

The new tale was *The Wonderful O*, whose freedom-of-speech message also made the children's story a parable for adults. Pirates, searching for treasure, take over an island community and order the letter "O" stricken from the language. The wicked leader hates "O" because his mother had become wedged in a porthole, and "they couldn't pull her in, so they had to push her out." The islanders determine that four words containing "O" not be lost: hope, love, valor and freedom.

Thurber hadn't expected the *New Yorker* to publish *The Wonderful O*, since it had never published a fairy story, but, Thurber being Thurber, Katharine White—though ailing, she had acceded to Shawn's request that she act as fiction editor after Lobrano's death—and Shawn thought that an attempt should be made to adapt it to the magazine's criteria. ("Thurber was always a sacred cow at the *New Yorker*," says Jean Lobrano.) Because it was known that Thurber regarded Katharine as an adversary, the manuscript of *The Wonderful O* was given to William Maxwell to edit.

"Thurber and I had had a cordial relationship for a year before that," says Maxwell. "Our differences over the fables had been gotten over. He liked to stay up all night drinking, and I'm a family man so I couldn't be that kind of friend to him. I liked Helen, and Thurber would make me laugh till the tears ran down my face. The 'O' was marvelous—operatic, sentimental—and I only cut its length and toned down the sentimentality. Katharine and Shawn found my version satisfactory, but I didn't have Thurber's confidence. A man has to put his trust in someone and, for Thurber, that was Helen. Though I'd been on the staff since 1938, he had never seen me, and though you can tell something of people from their voices, one has to look into their faces to know them.

"Usually, to get something into print, the magazine gives a bit and the writer gives a bit. The danger in the case of the *New Yorker* is monotony. But there must be a minimum agreement that the editor will go along with what the writer feels, unless the work is unsound, or eccentric, or morbid. You commit yourself instinctively to the writer's work and don't change your mind; you go to your grave thinking it was a poor manuscript, if you thought so once. There's a point at which you let go of responsibility; you're glad when the author says 'yes' to your 'no,' always because of your empathy with the writer.

"We had a painful meeting at the Algonquin. Helen had to go along with Thurber, and our rejection of their version so upset Thurber he had to go to his room to lie down. He wasn't ugly about it, but he wrote a letter saying the *New Yorker* needs editors with a feeling for humor."

It was the age-old dilemma: whose story is it, anyway?

In a note she wrote for her archives, Katharine says, "After I finished being Thurber's editor he was handed from one editor to another because he had reached complete blindness and a very difficult stage. It was Helen Thurber who couldn't stand one word of Jim Thurber's being cut or changed, and she and Maxwell had a falling out about how a very long fairy tale we could have used was to be cut—so it was never used."

Simon & Schuster published *The Wonderful O* in May 1957, following the printing of nearly thirty thousand copies with a smaller second printing four months later. Though Brendan Gill still wrongly believed that Thurber had committed the unforgivable toward him, his *New Yorker* review was a favorable one, finding a beguiling influence of Carroll and Joyce:

> A short, elegant, often extremely funny spin through Mr. Thurber's book-lined fancy, it . . . is written in a heightened prose that occasionally skips sidewise into meter and rhyme. . . . As a medium in the great seance of letters he is incomparable; he has only to utter an incantatory moan, and words levitate, phrases rap out unexpected messages, and whole sentences turn into ectoplasm. A prodigious performance, especially in so small a space.

Thurber saw the ALA award as strengthening his position in both the fables contretemps and the "O" donnybrook. On May 3, 1957, in a five-page letter from Bermuda, Thurber unloaded his bitter feelings about the *New Yorker* onto Katharine White:

> As you must know, the well-intentioned . . . affair of "The Wonderful O" left us all in a bad state. My thyroid had gone to 59 and Dr. Werner was seriously concerned and doubled my dose of Tapazole, so that by the time we arrived here I began to feel better physically and mentally. Actually, I have never felt better and shall continue to do so if I don't have to fret about *The New Yorker*. . . . I need a long holiday from the magazine and its high pressures. . . . I have been arranging matters toward this end, with the Fables doing well, "The Wonderful O" coming out this month, and "Alarms and Diversions" now in page proof and set for the Fall. The movie sale of "The Catbird Seat" and the five thousand dollars from ALA will easily make it possible for me to devote the rest of the year to the play, without any other work. My last piece for anybody this year was the story of the Loch Ness monster. . . . It was Roger Angell who, while on *Holiday*, suggested that I do ["The First Time I Saw Paris"]. . . . I have long had a hunch that Roger and I, with all deference to the rest of you, would be able to manage any future work of mine there with less stress and strain than I have been through last year.

Suggesting that "the unfortunate episode of 'The Wonderful O' " should not be further "brooded about" or discussed, Thurber proceeds to discuss it:

> I realize that its mutilation grew out of goodwill and even a loving admiration. The results, however, were little short of complete disaster. . . . Ross and Lobrano must have turned in their graves when a piece of mine was seized with affectionate, but violent, hands and underwent a series of changes in length, motivation, style and even content and purpose. . . . Shawn wanted 4500 words cut out. . . . Rightly or wrongly, the project of cutting out a third of one of my pieces for a magazine that has a piece this week running to 102 pages, was headed for catastrophe. The story was . . . cut from beginning to end, sometimes in every other sentence, but also contained a great deal of rewriting completely out of key with my style. . . . We must find a new system if I am to continue to write things for you. I cannot afford to risk my health and peace of mind with everything I submit. . . . My feel-

ings for the magazine and for all of you remain the same, but your letters clearly indicate that you are troubled by a dangerous state of affairs between us.

About two years ago the magazine began using the word "uncharacteristic" about certain pieces of mine. . . . You would like to have me return to a kind of piece and approach that I used years ago, but I cannot do that. What complicates the whole thing is that you have all become, in a curious inversion of Ross's famous byword "writer-conscious," extremely "editor-conscious." . . . You have fallen into the use of such pontifical and often stuffy phrases as "unanimity of opinion," "decision of the majority" and other such evidences of overwrought and over-burdened minds. This has been mentioned to me by a number of writers in the past six or eight months, some of whom may have been, I am afraid, alienated or estranged beyond recall. You have made of the New Yorker editorial judgment a rigid thing and you have developed a certain sense of false infallibility, so that Ross's wonderful ability to see the author's side and to ask for outside opinions has been lost. . . . We now come to my main point of concern and sorrow.

The ALA award was given to me for the Simon and Schuster book of fables and, alas, not for those *The New Yorker* printed. . . . In several letters, including one to Andy, I deplored the obvious intention of the magazine to reject quietly almost all the fables dealing with . . . national and international affairs and the larger issues and ideals of life, as against the slighter fables about husbands and wives and children. . . .

I must get this play done and possibly another one, without being subjected to the well-known Follow Up and I would appreciate it greatly if you saw to it that the editors do not bother me. I expect to return to the magazine's pages by 1958 which is just around the corner. I shall not violate my contract with The New Yorker, and do not want to get any letters from anybody on that point.

Katharine replied that she could write "an impassioned and detailed answer" to his letter, but wouldn't—and then proceeded to do so. She looked forward to when he would be in the mood to send something to the magazine; she and Andy hoped that he could develop a successful relationship with Roger, now a *New Yorker* fiction editor, for "since his childhood he has admired you and your writing." Thurber was completely wrong about the magazine's not wanting to deal with " 'national and international affairs and the larger issues and ideals of life.' " It was Shawn's wish and practice, "unlike Ross who always became slightly uneasy when such matters crept into Comment, casuals, and art. It wasn't his stuff, and he knew it." It was purest happenstance that some of the fables not used were on Communism and McCarthy. "We don't think our judgment is infallible, but I can assure you it was sincere." Thurber, furthermore, was "miles off" on the matter of editorial unanimity. "I've worked here almost 32 years, and I can't remember a period when there was less 'unanimity of opinion' than in the past year-and-a-half." If that phrase was ever in a rejection letter, it would probably have been only to "an old member of the family" like Thurber, "to whom some editor hated to say no at all" lest the writer think he was "being rejected on one man's (or woman's) whim. . . . The only way to run a lively and individual magazine is to have it, in the long run, reflect one man's final judgment. I thank God every day for Shawn's taste and judgment." Shawn, like Ross, was "a great editor" and "not just a pale reflection" of Ross.

In its nearly thirty-two years, she adds, the magazine has changed and is still changing. "I am glad . . . that we have the strength to say no even to our most valued contributors. No matter how often we may be wrong, if we ever gave that up, the magazine would be a goner."

Katharine resented Helen's role in the matter as much as she did Thurber's, believing, perhaps correctly, that Helen had more to do with rejecting Maxwell's rewrite of "The Wonderful O" than Thurber did. A woman justifiably proud of her own distinguished accomplishments, she had long resented Thurber's frequent representation of Helen as "the best editor next to Ross."

Katharine rarely got over such attacks on the magazine, for she saw them as attacks upon herself. She remained unable to heed Andy's pleas to forget about them for the sake of her health. Nearly a decade later, shortly before her death, she sent the exchange of letters with Thurber to the Bryn Mawr library, with a note to the librarian saying they "should be key letters for biographers of Thurber," reflecting as they did a Thurber who had begun "to be convinced of his own greatness." The big mistake on the magazine's part was ever to try to cut " 'The Wonderful O' which is not one of Thurber's greats. Maxwell labored long and hard over *his* cuts. Then he asked to see Helen Thurber's version, which he and Shawn found wholly unacceptable."

Katharine was enfeebled by illness and age when, assembling her "memos-for-file," to be preserved at Bryn Mawr, she states that Ross, Lobrano, or both, had "turned down" some of the fables that "Thurber scathingly named as rejections." (What else could they be called?) But both Ross and Lobrano had died before the completed fables were submitted. Her definitive summary was in another for-the-record note: "The sad truth is that James Thurber turned against the magazine that had 'made' him as a writer, and was in his late years very bitter toward it. We Whites are in a difficult position about him because we loved him dearly up to . . . the point when he began to attack all women, including me. He was fine when he was sober, to the very end."

Andy White kept a low profile in these periods of turbulence that his wife allowed to engulf her, though she always sought his opinion on such things, and would have wanted his endorsement of what she wrote to Thurber. White never sent a controversial letter to Thurber in his life; at his angriest with Thurber, he had once walked out on him at lunch—leaving a twenty-dollar bill on the table. Andy was conveniently beset by medical problems during the *Wonderful O* uproar, and, in the middle of it, when a distraught Thurber telephoned his side of things to White, Andy heard him out in discomfort and simply said, "I'm glad I'm not mixed up in it."

67

That Restless Force

This book began as a series of a few pieces for the *Atlantic Monthly*, but it soon became clear to me that the restless force named Harold Wallace Ross could not be so easily confined and contained.

—from the foreword to *The Years with Ross*

In June 1951, a nervous Dale Kramer, preparing his book *Ross and The New Yorker*, wrote Thurber of a rumor that Katharine White and Gibbs were coauthoring a history of the magazine that could compete with his. "Gibbs would be the last person to write about the New Yorker," Thurber reassured him, "except maybe Ross or White. Maybe Mrs. White and I could do it, but we won't. I have found out recently the trouble a man can get into writing about real people [*The Thurber Album*] . . . and I don't think I would try it again myself." And in another letter to Kramer, he states: "None of us is going to write about the New Yorker, I am pretty sure."

But a half year later Ross died and Thurber resolved to fashion some literary memorial to him in his own way, one centered on his perceptions of Ross and their relationship. He still thought the proper vehicle should be a play.

He felt the loss of Ross as he felt no other. They had stumbled across one another when both were in their mid-thirties, of uncertain expectations, lean on self-knowledge, and slow to grasp how they stood to help one another. Thurber's meager credentials as a writer had led Ross to try to make him an administrator; Ross's idea that he needed a foolproof system mounted against his own disheveled style of management often made him a danger to those trying to help him find a public for his magazine. Thurber might not have survived Ross's first impressions of him—others of the period, as hardworking and dedicated to the cause, were axed for irrational reasons—had Ross not noted the prompt confidence and fond interest of White in Thurber. The accidental match of a Thurber in search of himself and Ross's magazine experiment proved synergistic. It provided Thurber with fertile ground in which, to his own surprise, he was able to grow an unprecedented, multi-faceted talent, one whose influence continues today in the pages of the *New Yorker*. Good luck and recognition came to Thurber only after he became associated with Ross's weekly. His enlargement as artist and person was inter-twined with that of the magazine. Whatever the causes and effects of such a collaboration, somehow Thurber and the *New Yorker* rose coincidentally to become popular, respected, self-assured, and commercially successful institutions.

Ross and Thurber were never personally comfortable with one another; each retained a suspicious curiosity about the other. Their mutual admiration was not of the kind that drew them together companionably, nor did it make either less stubborn in their editor-writer battles. Both were nonstop talkers, partly because both were shy at heart. Each thought the other was naive, and because Thurber survived Ross, he got his version on record in *The Years with Ross*, a book that would never have been written had Ross outlived Thurber. It remains a tour de force, in which confirmable truths and even the more sentimental intentions are at times sabotaged by Thurber's impatience with the restrictions of literal fact. One of his responsibilities as a serious humorist, he believed, was to burnish the lackluster events of human existence to the sheen of good stories and apologize later for any wreckage. Thurber was nearly always magnanimous toward others in his published material; he rarely wished to make his negative feelings about someone a matter of public record. In *The Years with Ross*, for all the complaints of overlooking the roles of others, he provides most of the people he mentions with flashes of immortality, freezing them on a frame in the projector of his memory, heightening moments in their lives that would otherwise be lost in the dust of history. His version of Ross has survived the bitter criticism of the few who felt he had desecrated their own images of Ross, as well as their disapproval of his breaking the *New Yorker*'s code of silence on "inside" matters. Thirty-seven years after the publication of this entertaining book, one rereads it, with all its sins of ego, of exaggerations, of omissions, of score-settling, and comes away certain that whatever biographer tries to retrieve Ross from Thurber's famous account will wind up with most of the Thurberean characterizations of Ross intact. As Frank Sullivan said, in the immediate and sullen aftermath of *The Years with Ross*, "I thought Jim got Ross down almost exactly. All he left out was Ross's burbly cough, as if he had TB."

There are many instances in the book in which art distorts reality for lesser causes than to serve a greater truth. The gist of the complaints against the book was that Thurber had used a legendary icon, beyond the pale of mortal response, to elevate himself—that Thurber's importance to the magazine was made to seem greater, Ross's lesser. It was, after all, his opportunity to remind the newer generation of upstarts at the *New Yorker*, who were editing his copy without consulting him and sometimes rejecting his submissions, of his role in the magazine's successful development. But it stirred sibling rivalry among the contemporary contributors. "Ross was ringmaster of a three-ring show," Liebling says. "Thurber's was only one act. You get the impression that Ross spent most of his time worrying about Thurber."

But Thurber had contracted to offer only *his* years with Ross, and, as it turns out, spends pages extolling the contributions of the others. It is also true that during World War II, Ross, worried about the draining away of his talent by the military, seems to have become as considerate of Thurber as he had always been of White. As Ross wrote Thurber upon leafing through *The Thurber Carnival*, he had never fully realized the range and quality of what Thurber had published in the magazine. From 1942 on, Ross began to write Thurber directly, querying his galleys, sending him letters of gratitude for what he meant to the magazine, answering the letters of complaint himself that Thurber had sent to others on the staff, offering conciliatory explanations of office procedure, apologies for mishaps, and compliments on his current submissions. "Ross was always very protective toward Thurber," Shawn recalls.

The two saw little of one another socially. Ross dated and married pretty women but preferred men as off-hour companions—theater and film producers, actors, stage comedians, old newspaper hands, detectives, politicians (a raffish crowd, says Liebling), and successful, conservative businessmen interested in poker and cribbage. Thurber's lasting male friendships were with a select, accomplished few who shared his professional interests, saw the ironies of life, and understood that they were to stand up to him in his unreasonable moments. The bonds were usually those of correspondence, for most of the time he was self-exiled in Connecticut or remote refuges in Virginia, Bermuda, and Europe.

Thurber had lived for nearly thirty years with his unanswerable questions about Ross, whom he viewed as a friendly enemy, at various times an object of his anger, envy, fascination, amusement, puzzlement, and attraction. The dichotomous personality of Ross beguiled him during all the years in which he mimicked it successfully at parties while failing in trying to capture it as legitimate theater. After Ross's death, in hopes of distilling the record of an unfathomable individual to manageable form in a play, Thurber began dictating to a secretary pages of anecdotes about Ross, many of which he had given to writers Allen Churchill and Dale Kramer. By 1954, he was telling White that he had

> started something that looks like a series of three or more pieces on Ross. . . . I am using a lot of quotes from him since I remember thousands . . . including . . . "Thurber was at Tony's with an actress [Paula Trueman] last night" after which he put on that massive dejected look of his and asked plaintively, "Is Thurber attractive to women?" . . . I am doing glimpses of Harold Ross in a kind of Talk of the Town style. Chasing him from memory to memory, dealing with all his facets and maggots and prejudices, his perception, intuition and plain ignorance as they occur to me.

By 1955, he saw the series as a book. A London newspaper quoted him as saying so, and an ever-hopeful Cass Canfield wrote him that though "I suppose that the book will go to S & S," he hoped Thurber would give Harper's "a chance to make an offer." Thurber replied that he had "mentioned my future book on Ross to Jack Goodman several times in terms that commit me to his Company. . . . It won't make a volume longer than 30,000 words."

In Bermuda, the next year, he was back on the play, "The Welcoming Arms." He writes De Vries that the play would feature "the man of action [Ross] against the man of sensibility and thought [Thurber]." In March 1957, again in Bermuda, he continued work on the play, and, except for frequent allergy attacks, was having a good time "in the manner of the 1920s, rum, late hours, singing and carousing." When, the previous summer, Canfield had asked permission to do another Thurber anthology, Thurber thought it was too soon after *The Thurber Carnival*, but Helen, who had always been the stronger business-decision maker, differed. *Alarms and Diversions* (the second book Thurber dedicated to Helen) was scheduled for the fall of 1957 by Harper & Bros. "It is a collection of pieces and drawing since the Carnival," Thurber writes the John Millers, "with a few older ones that haven't been put in books."

Canfield, who, as editor-in-chief, had never published a Thurber book before, was soon being indoctrinated, Thurber sending him corrections on the first page proofs:

> Sorry for the extra work, but I have been called a precisionist—that is, one who likes to get things right so that the readers can find out what the story is about.

Galleys of the book, with "many, many corrections" needed, complained Helen, had been sent to the book clubs before the Thurbers received them. Canfield admitted "that there were an appalling number of errors in page proofs [but that] we feel confident that, in itself, won't have made any difference in the [Book-of-the-Month Club's] reaction." (The BOM ordered thirty-five thousand copies of *Alarms and Diversions* to offer as a dividend; Harper's own first printing was fifty thousand.)

In London, Hamish Hamilton was preparing to publish the book at the same time. That summer, after Jack Goodman died of a cerebral hemorrhage, Roger Machell, a Hamish Hamilton editor, quoted to Canfield from a letter Helen wrote Hamilton:

> [Goodman] was our main reason for being with Simon & Schuster and his death changes the picture somewhat. At the moment I am glad Harpers have the fall book for S. & S. is quite demoralized. Jamie is working on the first of three pieces about Harold Ross for the centennial issue of the *Atlantic Monthly*. They will eventually be a book—promised to Jack years ago, so S. & S. will do that one anyway.

Canfield thanked Machell. "Acting on your tip, I have written a letter to Thurber expressing the hope that in due course he will feel like coming back to Harpers." But Canfield again lost out, this time on a book whose initial sales would be greater than that of any other Thurber book.

Earlier, the *Atlantic Monthly* editor Charles Morton had heard of Thurber's plans for the Ross articles; in January 1957, Morton wrote to him with a request to let the *Atlantic* use something on the subject in its centennial issue, scheduled for that November. Thurber wouldn't say yes or no, and in May, in Bermuda, Thurber received other Morton letters, which helped him decide to give up "The Welcoming Arms" forever. He called Morton in Boston and agreed to do two or three articles on Ross. He eventually did ten, meeting his deadlines as conscientiously as any committed journalist.

He was mentally prepared for the Ross project. *Newsweek* had featured him in a cover story in February (in it he laments the growing shortage of literary humor, but ends on an upbeat, and, for once, never mentions the *New Yorker* negatively). *The Wonderful O* was on the best-seller lists, and he had just received the prestigious ALA award for *Further Fables*. But he worried over how the Whites would feel about the Ross articles; the *Album* experience had taught him the hazards of writing about someone dear to others. After Ross's death, there had been talk of a half dozen of the magazine's major veteran contributors, including White and Thurber, writing their impressions of Ross and combining them in a book. He now gingerly sounded out Andy:

> I'm writing several pieces for the Atlantic called "Ross," a project I've been working at for some years. Like you, I loved Ross and bore him great respect, and my pieces will all be mainly about Ross and me. A few other people I love keep coming into it, including you. . . .
>
> The New Yorker doesn't have to worry about this project, because it rises out of love and devotion, but the righter I get it the crazier it sounds. Nothing he did was more idiotic than his dogged attempt to make an executive editor out of me, and nothing more wonderful than the way he finally took me in for what I was.

He asks White to describe his start at the *New Yorker*. White responds in a detailed two-page letter. Katharine, meanwhile, had sent him a note of sympathy over the death of Jack Goodman, who had been perhaps the figure in publishing Thurber liked and trusted the most. He replies to both Whites, still defensive about the Ross project:

> Thanks for the kind letter about Jack, and Andy's just right notes about the old days. My first piece was mailed to Charles Morton today. He describes himself as a man who adored Ross. He and [Edward] Weeks [editor-in-chief of the *Atlantic*] had been at me for two years to do this stuff, which will probably run in four issues. Somebody should have done

it long ago. I'm glad that Alva Johnston once told me I should take it on. A hundred things happened to me and Ross together. . . .

I'll be asking for more help, probably yelling for it. Thank God the story's in the hands of somebody who loved Ross, the New Yorker, and almost everybody there.

The first pieces skillfully balanced Ross's eccentricities with his effectiveness as an editor, and underscored Thurber's emotional attachments to him. They were written in Thurber's anecdotal, conversational manner, the subject handled with wonder, respect, and friendly humor. Thurber sent the typescripts of the first two articles to the Whites, who were touched by them. "Both of these pieces moved me and made me feel sad," White writes Thurber, "which is about as good as you can get. I think you have succeeded wonderfully in recapturing his great restlessness. The more Ross is described, the more the mystery deepens. As you say, there is only one word for him, and the word is Ross."

The Thurbers returned from Bermuda on June 7, in poor physical shape from overwork on the Ross series and from too much nighttime socializing with the Williamses and others. They spent ten days in New York seeing their dentist and doctors. Work on the proofs of *Alarms and Diversions* had worsened the sight in Helen's "good" eye, and a cataract was forming on the eye that had been operated on four years before for a detached retina. Still, they were able to spend the summer and fall of 1957 in New York and Connecticut working on the Ross pieces, fashioning an unusual mixed breed of a book in the process. Even Thurber didn't know how to categorize it after seven chapters had been published, as he writes Sally Benson on April 25, 1958:

The book tells who he [Ross's famous query] and what happened and everything but why for Christ sake, and I guess is a biography, or maybe even a brief history of The New Yorker Magazine from 1925 to 1951. . . . Much of it is my own clashes and clinches and so on with him. . . . Old Total Recall, as they call me, remembers . . . a funny parody you did in a letter to Ross based on "My Life and Hard Times" which you called something like "The Night the Pan Overflowed Under the Refrigerator." . . . We all have done unprinted, or unprintable, parodies of each other, and I am doing one about the new lady writers that begins:

> I was almost sixteen before I realized that Robert was not teach-
> ing me ballet dancing, but seducing me. Robert was my mother's
> lover. . . .

For Thurber was writing about a magazine and editor he at times decided
had been ideal, while anguishing over the present magazine's fiction tendencies. Writing a Columbus artist whose illustrated casual Thurber had submitted to Roger Angell, he explains acidly:

> I did show [your work] to the editor in charge of me and discussed them
> with him, getting about as far as I get when I discuss my own work now.
> I failed to sell my last two things to the old magazine. It has turned to
> other types of writing than yours and mine. I liked the adventures of you
> and the daughters, but the New Yorker's Home Companion feels that we
> long ago exhausted such subjects as father and the gadgets and the like.
> As you know, we now go in for childhood reminiscences by women and
> a few broken down reporters, all of them running on endlessly.

Shawn knew of Thurber's bad-mouthing of the magazine but, ever considerate of a "founding father," agreed to Daise Terry's providing Thurber with
the use of an office and a *New Yorker* secretary, though his work was for
another publication. Liebling remembers once when crowded premises led
Terry to find an office for Thurber next to that of the blind Indian writer Ved
Mehta. Thurber refused to be thought of as blind, by himself or others, and
perfected the guise of having more vision than he had. Upon being introduced to Mehta, he reacted somewhat as he had when Jean Stafford's party
hostess had handed him a cane she thought he used: he turned and fled,
shouting, "My God! They've put me on the blind man's floor!" Librarian
Ebba Jonsson and Stewart Johnson of the checking department ran Thurber's
considerable number of research errands concerning the magazine's history.

The *Atlantic* ran an ad in the October 5, 1957, *New Yorker* of the upcoming Ross series. The ad startled most of the staff, who were unaware until
then of what Thurber was up to: "Now at last, Thurber writes about Ross. A
story of twenty-five years on the job at *The New Yorker*, its creator and editor,
told by the man who saw it all from the inside. At least five parts beginning
in the November *Atlantic*."

This created some mutterings. Thurber had left the *New Yorker* to freelance in 1935, less than nine years after joining it. By no means had he seen
it all from the inside, but as the subject drew him deeper and deeper into it,
he solicited information from former colleagues and companions of Ross

about the early days. Most of them were as charmed and pleased as White by the early articles, now on newsstands, and were flattered to have their experiences included. In addition to the Whites, he was given help by Stanley Walker, St. Clair McKelway, Frank Sullivan, Bernard Bergman, Ik Shuman, S. J. Perelman, Jane Grant, Charles Cooke, Charles Addams, Peter Arno, James Geraghty, Peter De Vries, Raoul Fleischmann, Stephen Botsford, Hawley Truax, Edmund Wilson, Ralph Ingersoll, Alistair Cooke, John Duncan Miller, Ogden Nash, John O'Hara, Sally Benson, Shirley Jackson, George Kaufman, Rogers Whitaker, Clifton Fadiman, Russel Crouse, Edward Newhouse, Philip Wylie, Charles Brackett, Lois Long, Nathaniel Benchley, Hobart Weekes, Nunnally Johnson, Howard Dietz, Dave Chasen, Henry Luce, and Marx brothers Gummo, Groucho, and Harpo. ("Ross was always showing casuals to Harpo Marx," says Maxwell, "and asking him if he thought they were funny.")

Before the first *Atlantic* article was published, Thurber had his title for the book: *The Years with Ross*. "The title came to me last night," he writes Morton, "while talking with my guardian angel and Helen and I think it is right. My story takes in more than mere working with Ross." White wrote Thurber from Maine in February 1958 that he had "heard plenty about your pieces on all sides—much favorable comment—and a lot of people seem to be reading the Atlantic for the first time in their lives." Katharine, though living in Maine, was editing fiction part-time for Shawn, which Thurber well knew when he sent this letter to White, indirectly continuing his argument with Katharine of two years before over *The Wonderful O*:

> Darn near a year and a half has now gone by since I had a piece in The New Yorker, and I really don't know whether I could make it or not again. . . . I think The New Yorker and I may have outlived each other. These things do happen. "Every magazine changes," said Liebling at lunch, and I might add to that, "Every writer changes too." It would be ridiculous to protest that the new editorial philosophy of editing has not had a great deal to do with dampening my ardor. . . . When Shawn monkeyed with my small obituary of McNulty by changing "darkened the day" to "darkened the world," my inviolability as a writer was shaken. [Shawn, fifteen years later, said he had decided Thurber's "day" was better.] Maxwell's tremendous sensitivity has made such temperaments as Dorothy Parker and me wary of working with him. I can't stand tears in a man and am not crazy about them in a woman. . . . Unhappily I have had proof that The New Yorker editors of today are

not felicitous collaborators or skillful rewriters, but they go right ahead and do it anyway.

Should Thurber not live to finish the book, he added, he wanted White to "supervise its final putting together. All the material is now on hand and most of it has been written. I know also that Gibbs and McKelway will be glad to help out. One Helen Thurber has the thing pretty well in mind and hand."

Wolcott Gibbs had told Thurber that if he did get Ross on paper accurately, nobody would believe him. "Gibbs had wanted to write a book on Ross," says Elinor Gibbs, "but when Thurber began his and asked Gibbs for help, he knew he'd never write it, so he sent everything he had on Ross to Thurber. They talked on the phone a lot."

Gibbs acknowledged most of Thurber's complaints about the current *New Yorker* crew, but said that the magazine "is deteriorating at almost exactly the right rate for me. I seem to be wearing very thin as a writer and the theater stuff I'm doing now would be embarrassing if it appeared in the magazine we used to know." He reminded Thurber, however, that stories of considerable length had, on a few occasions, preceded Shawn's editorship; Ross had agreed to purchase sixty thousand words of Elmer Rice's "Voyage to Puerilla." "As it got clearer and clearer that we were driving the readers crazy," says Gibbs, "we cut it first to forty thousand and finally to about ten thousand. I did the editing and the only serious mistake I made was cutting a bunch of Indians out of Part Two and then letting them show up, now totally unexplained, again in Part Four. It didn't seem to bother anybody, perhaps because nobody read it."

Gibbs's great regret was that he had failed on two or three occasions, when Ross was away, to put through his favorite cartoon—of two castaways on a raft, with three shirts flying from the makeshift mast, and one man saying, "I'm still hungry." Ross always got back in time to kill it. Gibbs was writing his theater reviews at home, because his children were grown and gone, and because the *New Yorker* receptionists, who no longer knew him, "treat me like a burglar." "All those new little faces just make me feel too damn old," he complained to Thurber.

I plan to go in at least on Mondays this winter because too many changes have been turning up in my copy in the magazine after I've Okayed the proof. I figure there are seven people who edit me in one way or another and they try to earn their money by making little lunatic last-minute changes, particularly the man in charge of superfluous punctuation. I have no objection to clarity but I don't like having jokes twisted around in order to be perfectly comprehensible to my cleaning woman. There is apparently no way to stop this kind of stuff except showing up in the flesh.

Gibbs agreed to edit Thurber's article on the Ross/Woollcott feud, which Thurber knew little about at first hand. In turn, Thurber wrote a flattering paragraph for the flap of Gibbs's about-to-be-published collection of writings, *More in Sorrow*. Gibbs, who had read with delight the first several articles on Ross, anticipated the publication of Thurber's book, which he wouldn't live to see, by writing in the foreword of his own book:

> The time I spent on *The New Yorker* (from 1927 up to now) has been covered by Mr. James Thurber in his book called *The Years with Ross* in a manner that should serve always as a model for such reminiscences. In addition to a phenomenal memory, Mr. Thurber has enormous persever-ance in research, a wit and style that have always commanded my stunned admiration, and, I should say, a romantic heart that has enabled him to think of his place of business as the most picturesque establish-ment in publishing history. This is a touching illusion, and I hesitate to correct it.

That July, Shawn sent Thurber, who was in London, a cablegram truly written more in sorrow: Oliver Wolcott Gibbs had died at his summer place on Fire Island, while looking over an advance copy of his book with Thur-ber's endorsement on the jacket.

On June 6, 1958, the Thurbers left on the *Mauretania* to spend the summer in Europe. The work on Ross was threatening to do them both in. Helen was keeping track of Thurber's voluminous Ross book-correspondence and his dictated rewrites, and reading and rereading material to him, all of which took their toll on her already weakened eyesight and often left her, at age fifty-six, feeling run-down. "We still have the book to put together," she wrote Dorothy Miller,

> with foreword, additional material, about 3 new pieces, restoration of cuts made for lack of space [in the *Atlantic*], with pieces on Ross by White, McKelway, Liebling, Coates, etc etc. I had a rousing fight with

Jim last night about over-elaboration of the book & whether that cleared the air or not i don't know. . . . He's terribly tired.

Thurber had been aware that other veteran *New Yorker* writers had a claim on his subject. Unable to envisage the final size of the book, in London he asked Liebling, though a "second-generation" contributor, to write up his impressions of Ross, perhaps some of it to be included in the book. Liebling soon told Thurber his impressions had turned into "a piece" in its own right. Thurber then asked White, Joseph Mitchell, Bob Coates, and St. Clair Mc-Kelway to contribute brief accounts of *their* years with Ross, to be run at the end of the book, along with Liebling's.

There was little respite abroad. When the Thurbers' ship had docked at Le Havre, a reporter from the *London Daily Express* boarded the ship for England and tape-recorded an interview with Thurber on the way. Everything Thurber said seemed to make the British newspapers. "We have stood up under sixty interviews and radio and television stuff and many big parties and long nights," Thurber writes the Williamses. He accepted the privilege White had refused, to be "called to the table" at *Punch*. He sat with its editor Bernard Hollowood and eleven other staff members at an oval pine table that dated to the days of William Thackeray, who, as essayist and illustrator, had joined *Punch* in much the same way that Thurber had joined the *New Yorker*. Over coffee and brandy, Thurber held forth on the threat of political jargon to the language and proudly penciled his "Th"—his cartoon signature—on the famous table, which also bore Twain's initials. (The venerable magazine finally folded in 1992.)

Though socially in demand, Thurber and Helen put in long hours on the book. Each afternoon, from two to five, he dictated to a secretary what he had composed and revised in his mind, and in addition scrawled out handwritten pages to be transcribed. Thurber enjoyed a lifetime free subscription to the *New Yorker*, and in London Helen was soon reading to him from the magazine a John Lardner review of a televised presentation of *The Male Animal*. In finding the performance a poor one, Lardner added that *The Male Animal* was "an already moribund play." ("I warned John he'd hear from Thurber," says Ann Honeycutt.) Thurber wrote Lardner a blistering letter and followed it with a sulky one to Shawn, whom he blamed for allowing the review to run:

> I have asked John Lardner to let you see my letter to him protesting against the untruth of his statement. . . . This is a simple distortion of fact, on a really monstrous scale, unworthy of *The New Yorker*'s pride in

precision. . . . It was simply the carelessness of a magazine grown too big to deal with precision any longer. . . . I'm sure that you will let Stew Johnson check the facts on the vitality and longevity of the Nugent-Thurber play, but I do not expect that any correction will be made [None was]. . . . It no longer makes much difference to me what you all say or do. I still hope, however, to write for the magazine again, or, what is harder right now, to want to write for it again.

The Thurbers went on to Paris. John Duncan Miller, while a political reporter in Chicago, had become friends with Adlai Stevenson, who, says Miller, was a great admirer of Thurber. "The Thurbers had been in Paris for a few weeks and suddenly Adlai Stevenson came into town and called me up," Miller recalls. "And I asked him to dinner and said, 'I will get the Thurbers for you.' I've never had an evening like it. There was simply the five of us . . . and the other three never spoke. Adlai and Thurber just talked all evening. It was the most brilliant conversation I've ever heard . . . so brilliant that I was hanging on every word and the next morning I couldn't remember a single word that had been said." ("We keep meeting Americans here that we would never meet in America," Thurber wrote De Vries, "such as Adlai Stevenson, with whom we spent a long and enjoyable evening. He may visit us in Cornwall, and you could run up, but don't bring Nixon with you.") "Thurber was a dependable Stevenson Democrat from the start," says Alistair Cooke. "Literary people, bored with the stresses of politics, are prejudiced in favor of politicians who use words eloquently and correctly; and creative people never stop looking for the knight on a white horse—but this hasn't much to do with the realities of politics."

Thurber had continued to send White manuscript carbons of his *Atlantic* articles on Ross before their publication. When they received "Ross and Money," about the *New Yorker*'s financial history and its payment to writers, Katharine took offense. White, who seemed only to echo loyally Katharine's objections to the articles, wrote Thurber in his usual style of friendly wit, granting him permission to use a White quote and suggesting how his account of teaching Ross to drive a car might be titled. Though both Whites had been moved to sentimental tears by the latest piece, Andy wrote, he added that "Katharine says you are all wet on your facts about the New Yorker payment system. . . . She advises you (and so do I) to check with Truax."

Thurber's misogyny, exacerbated by another thyroid flare-up, had been growing; he was given to screaming at Helen on occasion when she criticized something he was writing. ("We heard not only that Thurber had begun to

throw things at Helen," says Emily Hahn, "but was finding the range.") To be
told by Katharine that he was "all wet," whatever the subject, would have
been bad enough, but the money issue was a particularly sore point with him.
Katharine's charge of inaccuracy sent him into a tantrum of near lunacy. On
June 2, he wrote long and wild letters to both the Whites and to Hawley
Truax, lawyer, longtime friend of Ross, and the magazine's liaison between
editorial and business. To Truax he writes:

> The Whites recently saw the first draft of my piece on "Ross and
> Money" and wrote me that I was "all wet," which is not true. . . .
>   Almost every writer, from 1927 on, agrees with me . . . that New
> Yorker pay has nearly always been niggardly, that the drawing account
> arrangement has been badly managed and in itself bad for writers. Ross's
> childlike belief that The New Yorker couldn't afford decent pay has
> affected the life and work of a hundred writers, including me, and the
> record is not a pretty one. I was made to sell my first eight casuals for
> nothing. "Your $100 a week will take care of that," said Ross. . . .
> Kincaid [sic] got $50 a week as a reporter, Charles Cooke never more
> than $60. . . . Ross said all the time, "The magazine is a showcase for
> authors." In other words, we can't pay you a humane salary or word rate,
> but magazines that can will pick you up. They picked up Alva Johnston,
> and me, and dozens of others, or we went into the theater or the movies,
> or something, in order to live. . . . He traded on our loyalty to him
> and to the magazine. . . . His small town, small minded ideas of money
> are the worst blot on his record. The back pay from The Readers' Digest
> should have been divided among contributors, but it went for office
> supplies. The poor magazine that couldn't pay decent word rates until
> the war years sunk $600,000 of profits in Stage. This money was made
> possible by underpaid writers and artists. I don't believe Ross or Raoul
> really wanted to grind us down financially, but they didn't know what
> they were doing to us. . . . Ross was full of praise and no money, and
> The New Yorker's occasional refusal to advance me even $100 when I
> was down, made me turn to other places or to friends. . . . For the
> eight pieces making up "My Life and Hard Times" I got $3600. . . .
>   By 1940 I had not saved a dime, and was usually saved financially by
> advances from publishers or friends. [Ross] was at heart a generous man,
> and proved it in his erratic ways, but he should never have been allowed
> to deal with New Yorker money in any way. . . .
>   Raoul said Ross could have left an estate of more than $2,000,000 if
> he hadn't sold his stock. . . . I got $300 a piece through the Thirties.

In Truax's gentle manner, he refuted Thurber's characterization of Ross. He had worked with Ross "innumerable hours," and knew that "Ross was constantly keenly concerned that contributors be paid all that the earnings and well-being of the magazine made possible."

Thurber couldn't let the matter drop, and, in another letter to Truax, implied that he had discussed with psychiatrists the relation of money to Ross. There was "no easy line to follow about that wonderful and crazy man and his ideas about money and . . . his fluctuating generosity and tightness, which have puzzled all of us writers . . . except White," he wrote Truax. "Both Andy and Ross used to say that they didn't want to make any more money than they could live on comfortably." Ross, he continues, could be called "psychopathic" when it came "to finance in any field." He blamed this on Ross's rearing by a mother who had a "complex and phobia about prices, poverty, and so on." Mrs. Ross had refused to have a telephone in the house for three years because it cost a dollar a month, and when she visited Ross in New York, he had to tell her that her Algonquin meals cost only seventy-five cents and her room a dollar, writes Thurber. (According to Russel Crouse, Ross's mother, in order to avoid paying New York restaurant prices, "would sneak a toaster and grill" into a fine hotel room Ross had arranged for her, and do her own cooking until the management evicted her, leaving Ross's secretary to find other quarters for her.)

In Thurber's unbridled effort to counter Katharine White's criticism, he airs his financial grievances through a prism of near paranoia: "The magazine has had no editor besides me with any true understanding of psychology and psychiatry," he writes Truax. If others had, he goes on, they would know that Ross's revolt against his mother's financial strictness "consisted of his wild gambling . . . and his sudden bursts of generosity." When Ross praised Thurber in 1951 for his productivity, Thurber tells Truax, Ross had said, " 'I'm thinking of asking Truax to give you a medal.' Again, you see, the mother complex asserting itself. A medal, not money."

A month later, he sent Truax a copy of his "Ross and Money" article, along with reiterations of Ross's scrambled attitudes toward the subject. Embarrassingly, he was exposing his own state of mind more than Ross's:

> At least two good psychiatrists support the theory that a gambling compulsion, like Ross's, frequently is the outcome of a thrift complex. . . . The elaborate New Yorker system of pay was a Ross safeguard brought about by a purely psychological state of mind. . . .
>
> There was . . . a true wampum complex, in Ross, when you come upon that phrase of his about fifty dollars being a considerable amount.

This was his mother talking. His heavy gambling losses and his sudden flow of bonuses, are familiar symptoms of his situation. Most psychiatrists would contend that he really did not mind losing at gambling, but he had an unconscious urge to lose, as a rebellion against the strictures of his mother in Salt Lake City.

It doesn't take a professional psychologist to understand, either, why Ross sold his stock through Ingersoll to Luce, through an enemy to another enemy. This was a direct slash at Fleischmann, but Ross rationalized it by saying he didn't want any more money than he needed to live on, and he didn't want to be keeping financially involved in a magazine he edited. This kind of thing constantly comes from the psychiatrist's couch.

There is no record that Helen tried to prevent these strange clinical attacks on the sanity of Truax's close friend, nor that she was a cosponsor of them. Katharine White believed (probably correctly) that because Thurber had given little thought to his finances before his marriage to Helen, she assisted in his later preoccupation with them. A dozen years later, remembering Thurber's complaints that Harper & Bros. had cheated him and Andy, Katharine notes smugly, "I find it comical that Jim Thurber, who cared so much about money during the last part of his life—or rather, after his 2nd marriage—feels that Harper gypped him and that E. B. White, who never is concerned about his profits, made out so badly." Lacking an agent, Andy had had the New Yorker's attorney, Milton Greenstein, draw up his publishing contracts, which gave him all the secondary rights Thurber had been giving away. "Thurber just signed what Harper sent him without reading the book contract," says Katharine.

Her belief that Ross had "paid all he could" was refuted by several of those who had worked for Ross. Bernard Bergman, who had hired Alva Johnston from the Tribune by offering him three hundred dollars a week in the mid-thirties, explains why Johnston had to quit: the three hundred dollars was not his to keep but loaned to him under the drawing-account arrangement. He was unable to survive "because of the low rates he was paid," Bergman writes to Thurber.

We gave him $400 for each installment of the Mike Romanoff story. Imagine what the [Saturday Evening] Post would have paid him. Most reporter pieces were paid $200, Profiles around $300. . . . That came to about one cent a word on Profiles when you consider how most of them had to be redone and redone. . . . Didn't some guys write departments for $50–$75 a week or every two weeks or so? . . . I think Ross was always afraid . . . of the magazine going broke. He never had any idea of paying properly. He was, though, always concerned that you and Andy and other regulars who gave the magazine full time get well paid. . . . But freelancers, except those that wanted the New Yorker as a show window, shunned it, even in those days, and then left it as Alva did and Jack Alexander, etc.

Given editorial management's penurious ways, Thurber had fared comparatively well, and was not inclined to complain until the growing bitterness that followed his blindness. The Thurbers' medical bills were tremendous: in 1959, Thurber wrote a friend that he and Helen together had undergone fourteen operations since they were married. The *New Yorker*, during Thurber's time, did not offer its editorial employees or contributors any health insurance. Its idea of largesse, as late as the sixties, was to pay an employee a hundred dollars upon getting married and upon the birth of a child, but to provide no medical or hospital coverage. It is also true that the Thurbers' need for money was to support a rather high standard of living. "The Thurbers lived expensively," says Lewis Gannett. "They kept a couple to watch the Cornwall house while living away six months of the year."

Thurber's wordy (a tendency of those who dictate) and heated letter to the Whites of June 2, 1958, contained a few variations from that to Truax; in this exercise of self-pity, the thirty-six hundred dollars he had told Truax was all the magazine paid him for his "My Life and Hard Times" pieces was reduced to twenty-six hundred for the Whites' benefit. As to being told he was "all wet,"

I think you are a little damp yourselves about the payment setup, on which I am doing, and have done, immense and careful research. . . .

After fourteen years on the magazine I didn't get decent money until "The Male Animal" and have nothing to show for pieces and drawings that fill twenty books. . . . I once had to borrow $500 from the National City Bank with McKelway and Jap Gude going on my note. I had to borrow $2500 from Elliott Nugent, and damn near left The New Yorker for Paramount Pictures in order to live. . . . I know that Andy turned down a $3500 bonus, but he did get stock, and when Raoul gave me what was then 100 shares, it was only after Katharine insisted, for he was taking advantage of the fact that I was then not actually on the staff, although my output had never been greater. . . . Among Ross's excuses: pay a writer well and he stops writing; a man ought to have only enough to live on; I don't want to take away their incentive. . . .

I've gone though hell in writing this book, but I have had to learn to dismiss idiotic and unintentional slurs on my care and soundness and integrity. . . . This is not an invented book, and I come through it with my honor unscarred, and my head bloody but unbowed. . . . We now pay just one great reporter a salary, output or no output, Joe Mitchell. Since you two doubled up on income, you were better off than most of us. Helen has done $50,000 worth of editing for the New Yorker for nothing—well, I did insist that she get $700 for her work on the bloody shambles of "The Wonderful O," and it was paid. Lobrano saved my life by insisting on bonuses when I was down, blind, or otherwise sick, and saw to it that the goddam contract did not operate in my case. . . . If I am all wet, it is with blood and tears. . . .

I am sorry about all this, but I had to get it off my tortured soul and I do resent intensely being called naive or all wet. I am as good a reporter and researcher as anybody the magazine ever hired at $50 a week.

To Katharine, the *New Yorker*'s system of compensation had been the business of Ross and the magazine, and, besides being beyond questioning, was a somewhat uncivilized subject to bring up. When Katharine told one literary agent that she had decided to buy a short story and the agent asked if they could discuss price, Katharine was aghast. "Price!" she exclaimed. "Why, she will be paid at our usual rate!" The agent found herself humbly apologizing, saying, "I do have to ask these things, you know." To Katharine, it was reward enough for an author to have been selected by The Magazine— and for many writers it was. Katharine could also argue that as a literary magazine the *New Yorker* paid top dollar, but by the mid-fifties, through its teeming advertising pages and increasing circulation, it had become more profitable than many of the slicks. A dependable cash cow to senior members of the *New Yorker* business management, it had made millionaires of original investors in the magazine. Nor did key members of editorial on salary suffer financial hardship. Shawn, a substantial stockholder, was earning thirty thousand dollars as fact manager in 1949, Ross fifty thousand, with a twenty-five-thousand-dollar expense account, while hiring Talk reporters at forty dollars a week plus COLA (a cost-of-living adjustment based on 1933 Bureau of Labor statistics). Brendan Gill was hired in 1937 at forty dollars, and Liebling, surviving an impoverished apprenticeship, finally was put on a drawing account of ninety dollars a week. Though Ross avoided becoming a millionaire through his financial ineptitude, he didn't do badly. Despite large alimony and child-support payments, impulsive sales of stock at bargain prices, careless investments, large poker losses, the theft of seventy-one thousand dollars by his personal secretary, and a general financial indifference, at the time of his death he owned a country estate, maintained a luxuriously furnished Park Avenue apartment, and was driven about in a chauffeured limousine. Much is made of Ross wiping out the debts of contributors who had fallen far behind in what they owed the magazine under the weekly drawing-account system that was supposed to subsidize them. The reason was not always a lack of productivity on the part of the writers—though that was often the case—but the poor rates of purchase.

Katharine White was deservedly well compensated with a bountiful salary and *New Yorker* stock; so was Andy, when he was on salary. When he went off salary and onto "piece work," as he put it, he was paid at a higher rate than Thurber. With the wartime salary freeze, the magazine allocated a hundred thousand dollars in bonuses to be paid the half-dozen regular, veteran contributors, but most of it was paid in "surplus profits" taxes to the government, and each writer received thirty-five hundred dollars. Ross called it retroactive payment. Thurber said it was about time. White said, "I knew what I was doing," and gave it back. Because White was never asked to sign a "first refusal" contract, Katharine disputes Thurber's claim that he was obliged to. But he was. White enjoyed privileges Thurber didn't. White's independent nature always worried Ross, who had witnessed, in White's departure for *Harper's*, a commendable and greater loyalty of White to himself than to The Magazine. He was more the sacred cow even than Thurber, for the tone, style, and direction of the magazine's editorials were basically set by White. In addition to his commanding talent, he was Katharine White's husband and, like the legendary gorilla, was not going to be stopped from doing what he wished around the place. Receiving a copy of one of the Ross articles, White writes Thurber: "You say: 'Ross had Andy White write a farewell, etc.' . . . Ross never 'had' me write anything. . . . I never wrote anything on Ross's order, and it would be unfair to him and to me to suggest that there was any such procedure."

Like Hawley Truax, Katharine believed that Ross paid his writers all that the financial condition of the magazine permitted. "Rubbish!" she notes in her copy of Thurber's Ross book, where Thurber states that the magazine was on sound financial footing by 1928, the year after he joined, suggesting thereby that it could have shared more of the profits with its contributors and editors over the years. Not until well into the thirties, she writes, was the magazine in the black. But Thurber's facts, given him by Truax, are correct. The magazine first showed a profit in 1928, when it paid its first dividend to its stockholders. It earned a net income steadily until 1942, the one year it went into the red, when the war increased costs of paper and other printing operations for the suddenly larger issues, and before advertising rates could be adjusted. From 1945 on, gross revenues rose steadily over the next decade; in 1954, the magazine's net profit was nearly a million dollars.

As to Thurber's psychological explanation of why Ross suddenly sold all his stock to Time, Inc., in 1934: Ross was preparing to marry again and needed the money. He may also have foreseen his next divorce and remembered that, in his settlement with Jane Grant, he had had to give her much of his *New Yorker* stock and guarantee it against devaluation. As to Ross's frequent comments that a well-paid writer loses incentive to write, Katharine insisted that it was one of his regular jokes. That is unlikely. Liebling writes that Ross, plain and simply, hired people "as cheaply as possible so that they would work harder." A dozen other veterans agreed with Liebling and Thurber. Brendan Gill remembers bitterly Ross bragging that his writers couldn't afford a car, and shouldn't.

Thurber's complaints about inadequate compensation would have continued to apply under Shawn's stewardship. Shawn, who idolized Ross, carried on in the genteel tradition; money was a crass subject for a *New Yorker* editorial employee to bring up. He was genuinely startled when the magazine's principal sportswriter in the early fifties, Herbert Warren Wind, was lured to *Sports Illustrated* for a time by more money. "Gill and I threatened to unionize the writers," says the business writer John Brooks, a staff member for many years. "Rates were finally raised."

Like Ross, Shawn quit the magazine's board of directors, after eleven years, giving Ross's reason that an editor shouldn't be a director of his own magazine. (Some suspect that an SEC ruling that the salaries of the five highest-paid directors be published in the annual report had influenced Shawn as much as the Ross example.) In the early eighties, Shawn agreed to make stock-purchase plans available to all editorial employees and to artists and writers under contract. Two-thirds of the employees signed up to buy *New Yorker* stock periodically at 85 percent of the current market price; only half outside contributors did, many explaining that they couldn't afford the investment. Fortunately, Thurber wasn't alive to learn that Shawn rejected a standard corporate "incentive" plan that would have allowed stock options for "key" editorial people, which eventually made millionaires of some executives on the business side and on the board when the magazine was sold to the Newhouse conglomerate.

68

That Biographer and Historian

I don't know how many people will be speaking to me when the book comes out, but that's what I get for trying to be a biographer and historian.

—Letter to John O'Hara, March 19, 1958

"As the devil is afraid of music," Thurber writes Hawley Truax, "the *New Yorker* is afraid of publicity. The magazine that pilloried *Time-Fortune* made an unforgivable ass of itself in its behavior about the [1955] *Newsweek* profile. . . . Just because so many of our men have been self-conscious and hypersensitive, it is no excuse for our tearing people apart in our profiles and then refusing to give out facts about ourselves."

In 1950, the advertising department of the *New Yorker* made Philip Ewald the promotion man for the magazine. "My job was to help get favorable mention about the magazine in the business world," says Ewald. "I was close to a number of people at *Newsweek* and suggested they consider doing an article on the *New Yorker*, pegged to our thirtieth anniversary. I could do little to help them with the editorial side of the *New Yorker* story, given the barrier between the two departments, but we had a great financial story to tell. During the thirteen years I was there, we led every other consumer magazine in advertising. And I was on the three-man committee that rejected about three hundred thousand dollars a year in advertising that we judged not to be suitable for the magazine."

Shawn didn't cooperate, but a *Newsweek* reporter, dispatched by editor Frank Gibney, reached Thurber, Liebling, Freddie Packard, and a few others who were willing to talk to *Newsweek* but who knew little beyond the limits of hearsay and individual experience. Liebling was surprised to learn that there was a promotion man in the building, the *Newsweek* reporter told his editor. "What do you know about that!" Liebling exclaimed. Liebling did all he could to cooperate. When asked how many permanent writers the *New Yorker* had, he recklessly handed the reporter a mimeographed list of the staff's and contributors' home phone numbers and addresses, suggesting that the reporter might wish to telephone some of them. He thought it prudent not to be named as a source, however. The executive editor, Leo Hofeller, whose addiction to secrecy nearly amounted to denying that the *New Yorker* existed, tried to talk *Newsweek* out of doing the piece.

"I talked to Hofeller for about an hour," says the reporter. "He was very considerate and apologetic and told me nothing. He said he couldn't say anything about the details of the operation when I tried to pin him down on various editors' responsibilities. When I asked to talk to some of the editors, Hofeller said he couldn't intervene for me and doubted if this or that editor would want to say anything at all. He asked me not to quote him by name. Shawn phoned three times in the hour I was talking to Hofeller, obviously worried about how the interview was going. Many times Hofeller asked why we wanted to do a piece about the *New Yorker*, and said the magazine simply didn't wish one done, anywhere, any time.

"On the way out I ran into Hamilton Basso. He was nice and cordial. I asked him if he was on the staff and he said he wasn't sure, that he seemed to be half on and half off. I had the feeling that's the answer I'd get from anyone I met in the corridors there."

The article that resulted was what Joel Sayre calls "a valentine," with hardly a negative in it. There was little that was new. Circulation of the thirty-year-old magazine was nearing 400,000. Not mentioned was that the increased revenues were only meagerly reflected in payments to writers, artists, or the editorial staff. Shawn, says Gill, remained as tightfisted as Ross, whether out of loyalty to tradition or from private theory on the value of a thin carrot as inducement; only the more industrious, or those with private income, could still avoid the voluntary serfdom so many on the staff committed themselves to out of the desire to be associated with the *New Yorker*. Liebling is anonymously quoted in *Newsweek*; after seventeen years at the *New Yorker*, by working hard he could earn thirty thousand dollars a year, but he was still in debt to the magazine from time to time. Though Thurber was unnamed, his recognizable anecdotal version of the periodical's beginnings was included, as well as his observation that without Ross it had become "a synthetic magazine." Katharine White was fiercely opposed to his cooperating, but Thurber believed that Ross would have done so, given his cooperation with Allen Churchill for his 1948 piece in the *American Mercury*, and with Dale Kramer—until he realized that Kramer's book was to be about Ross, too. Shawn's avoidance of publicity could be considered paradoxical; what had brought him, as a young journalist, from Chicago to New York in the early thirties was his intention to do a history of the *New Yorker*. He had interviewed Benchley, Parker, and others before giving up the project and taking a job as a Talk reporter. Seven years after cold-shouldering *Newsweek*, he was asked about Thurber's disgust with the magazine's avoidance of the press and other Thurber criticisms. Shawn replied, courteously as always, but with a mild degree of temper rare in that gentle-mannered man:

"Thurber and I were never close. We had very few professional lunches together. We didn't have the social relation he had with De Vries. He was a *New Yorker* generation ahead of me. He was known, established, and important when I got here. Later, he worked more with Lobrano than with me. He was valuable in helping form the *New Yorker* and I felt he had the right to criticize it if he wanted to. He was one of the family, always welcome; there was always a room for him in the old homestead. It was intentional on my part not to fight with him—it wasn't oversight or indifference. Also, he was blind, and though he didn't ask quarter on those grounds, one couldn't be prevented from granting him it. Some of his anguish was difficult for him to bear, but he stuck it out against tremendous odds, and I admired that in him.

"He made much of Ross's announcement of our policy against the [*Reader's*] *Digest*'s reprinting our material. Nobody was bound by it, but Thurber was the only one who said, 'I want to, anyway.' His motive wasn't the money, or the need for a bigger showcase, I felt, but the need to defy Ross—to show his independence. White showed his in different ways.

"As long as Thurber wanted an office, he had one here, though he said publicly that he didn't. We made office space available for Thurber and the Whites whenever they wanted it. They're among the founders of the organization. That fact was never lost on me, whatever Thurber's charges. My response was to turn the other cheek. He was a family son who turned against the family but we continued to treat him as a member.

"As to the *Newsweek* piece, we don't like to talk about the *New Yorker* for publication. I see no reason why I should do anything but edit this magazine. It's inherent in our philosophy. We don't need to be looked at as if in the theater, like Maude Adams, nor do we think there's a special glamour to not being seen or heard from. White feels he should be writing; I feel I should be editing. If something happens on the magazine that's legitimate news, we'll talk to the press about it.

"Thurber couldn't understand that was the way we wanted it to be; he wanted it differently. His outspoken disapproval of us was sincere and honest, but there seemed inconsistencies in his feelings about us. He'd point out that there were fewer and fewer people writing humor, and then accuse us of deliberately not publishing more of it. In his writing and art, there the lines are very clear. But, perhaps as with most great writers, you seldom find consistent behavior or point of view."

The *New Yorker*, though standoffish, had continued to enjoy favorable press coverage. Published criticism that fact and fiction were running to tiresome lengths were occasionally countered with the explanation that those lengths were needed to maintain the standard ratio of editorial copy to the abundance of advertising—as though more and shorter pieces wouldn't accomplish the same end. In issue after issue, the full pages of editorial matter in the front of the book soon dwindled to a one-column trickle of print flanked by columns of advertising aimed at the affluent. The occasional humor was of a cerebral bent, allied with current events—no longer the first-person, personal predicaments that Ross, who doted on puzzlement, enjoyed. As Dorothy Parker said in a 1955 interview: "There are no humorists anymore except Perelman. There's no need for them. Perelman must be lonely. If we needed them we'd have them. The supply and demand principle. The new crop of would-be satirists write about topical topics." Thurber had put himself in a physician-heal-thyself conundrum: his own *New Yorker* pieces were offering an undernourished humor, and they were becoming few—none in 1957, one in 1958, five in 1959, two in 1960, and his last, "The Manic in the Moon," in 1961. They sermonized on such gloomy subjects as the oral and written misuse of the language, aging writers, the disappearance of clocks and time from the earth. His principal amusement was with wordplay. "I admired him, in his blindness, trying to keep writing," says Roger Angell, "but we may have stretched a bit in accepting some of those last pieces because of who he was."

"Gus always had a difficult time with Thurber, editing or, especially, rejecting his pieces," says Jean Lobrano, "but Gus believed that the Thurber work he turned down benefited Thurber's reputation in the long run." (Most of the few *New Yorker* rejects were published elsewhere.)

Liebling told Thurber that he found the *New Yorker*'s early reporting dull —that the Profiles were superficial reviews of successful people. "The liveliest reporting came later," he says, "from the late thirties on, when we took the hide off our subjects—Luce, Father Divine, Winchell, Woollcott, Wallace of the *Digest*." Thurber had no quarrel with that; his forte had been fiction and casuals, but he felt the hide-stripping was all the more reason for the magazine to be candid with the press.

In 1965, four years after his death, Thurber would have his case for just such public candor presented in a startling way, one he would surely have considered overkill. Using the magazine's fortieth anniversary as a springboard, the *Herald Tribune*'s two-year-old Sunday supplement, *New York*, turned loose one of its two staff writers, thirty-four-year-old Tom Wolfe, for a pit bull attack on Shawn and his magazine. Wolfe's two-part assault is in his exclamatory, expletive style of writing. It dismisses Thurber, Gibbs, White, Parker, and Liebling as "tiny giants"; Shawn as a "hierophant" engaged in preserving what had become Ross's "museum." A few of Wolfe's points had been Thurber's: that the *New Yorker* had managed to become "the most successful suburban woman's magazine in the country" (Thurber, eight years before, was calling it "The New Yorker's Home Companion"); that sentences were kept going endlessly by chains of parenthetical "which" clauses (Wolfe presents mind-boggling examples), and that the magazine was running "an incredible streak of stories about women in curious rural-bourgeois settings" recalling "their childhoods or domestic animals they have owned."

Wolfe's mockery of Shawn's self-conscious mannerisms drew letters of outrage, not only from *New Yorker* contributors, most of them accusing the *Trib* of resorting to tabloid journalism. "Maybe someday, all these offices of these giants, like Robert Benchley, James Thurber, Wolcott Gibbs . . . can be restored, like Colonial Williamsburg," Wolfe suggests sarcastically. (No such offices existed.) He grudgingly credits the *New Yorker* with introducing the Clarence Day pieces that culminated in the play *Life with Father*, but actually those first began to appear in *Harper's*. Only a few wall drawings by Thurber remained of "the original objects and curios" Wolfe believed existed in Shawn's "museum" of 1965.

It could be argued that the *New Yorker* had brought Wolfe's pummeling on itself. It had tried legally to keep the *Trib* from calling its Sunday supplement *New York*, because of the similarity of titles. Four years earlier, Roger Angell, in the magazine, had made fun of the *Trib*'s tendency to put headlines in question form. A freelance contributor's parody of both Wolfe and his fellow staff writer, Jimmy Breslin, had recently been published by the *New Yorker*. A few weeks before Wolfe's aggressive response, Lillian Ross had lampooned Wolfe's style in a Talk piece, that began: "Zonggggggggggg! Innnnnnnnnnnn!"

Wolfe, twenty-seven years later, writes:

THE NEW YORKER had recently done us the honor of mocking Jimmy [Breslin]'s work and mine. . . . So we were in a mischievous mood when it came to observing THE NEW YORKER'S 40th.

So we . . . decided that the thing to do was a profile—a form THE NEW YORKER had originated and named—of Shawn. Our immediate model was Wolcott Gibbs' famous profile of Henry Luce and parody of TIME back in 1936. . . . But . . . we realized that the parody style would be a dud. Most parodies of THE NEW YORKER fell flat . . . because a parody of something that is dull can only be funny for about one page. After that, it becomes as dull as its target. So I . . . hit upon the anti-parody, as I thought of it. I would profile Shawn in a style as far removed from THE NEW YORKER as I could imagine. . . . There was also an orthodox journalistic rationale to this piece. Shawn was one of the most prominent magazine editors in America—but next to nothing was known about him. He was so shy, he had not only built a wall between himself and reporters but also photographers. There *was* no photo file on Shawn. . . . As Malcolm Muggeridge put it later on, the world is used to megalomaniacs, but Shawn was that rarer bird, the minimomaniac.

My first step was to call Shawn. . . . I stated my business at some length to an aide, and, by and by, Shawn came to the telephone. He told me that he did not care to be interviewed for a profile and had no interest in one being written and that at THE NEW YORKER, when a subject did not want to be profiled, THE NEW YORKER did not proceed with the piece [a change of policy from the Ross days, apparently], and he thought I should observe this piece of protocol. I told him I understood his reasoning but that I would go ahead and write the story anyway. . . . Jim Bellows, the TRIB'S managing editor . . . immediately sent Shawn a copy of the first piece. . . .

Shawn went ballistic [in] the letter he wrote and had sent by courier to the TRIB'S publisher, Jock Whitney. . . . Whitney was a very dignified gentleman, a former Ambassador to the Court of St. James, and Shawn was one of the most respected men in journalism, and he was charging . . . that the piece was not only libelous but "murderous." [Whitney] brought the letter to Bellows and said, "Jim what on earth do we do about this?" . . . Bellows . . . said, "I'll show you what we do." Whereupon he picked up the telephone and called TIME and then NEWSWEEK and read them both the letter. Whitney couldn't believe what he was seeing and hearing. But he backed up Bellows when all hell broke loose.

It had to be the worst moment of Shawn's career. "It's something you thought could never happen," commented novelist William Gaddis, a former checker at the magazine. "Shawn was frantic," says staff writer John Brooks. "He kept calling Whitney but getting his wife, who would say, 'I'll tell Mr. Whitney you called.' Shawn was wrong not to meet with a professional journalist from a legitimate publication doing an article on him. He might not be able to control it, but he could influence it, and give the writer fewer excuses for inaccuracies."

The writer of a later article on Shawn and the *New Yorker* was given royal treatment by Shawn and his assistant, Mary Painter. "They walked me to the elevator after the interview," he told his editor, "and I almost felt they wished I wouldn't go." Thurber died too soon to witness the magazine's conversion, and though he would have regretted the use of literary terrorism to effect it, he could only have felt vindicated by his own lonely stand over the years—against any magazine snobbishly hiding behind some mystique of mystery, refusing to play by the rules it asked others to observe, and by which it lived.

The Williamses had informed Thurber that Janey was expecting her sixth child. She would be forty-three at its birth. Thurber, with his possessive and sentimental feelings toward her, was jealous and annoyed. The problem was, he wrote them, in December 1954, "six" sounds like "sex" in English and "sex" sounds like "cease" in French, which, he ordered them, "should be remembered."

> Having a child at 43 is considered de rigueur by the medicos, although a little rigorous on the cervix, the budget, and the aging father. He will be about sixty when his coming child is ten. If, at that time, 1965, Ronald should be taken by our Heavenly Father in the fifth set of a match with the old commander, it is unlikely that even the most worshipful and eligible male would care to take on a ready-made family of such size, and I abhor the idea of Janey toying with the notion of going into the de luxe white slave trade that glitters between New York and Buenos Aires. . . .
>
> I once read in a medical book . . . "one should not be cocksure about any contraceptive." . . .
>
> This business of every four years that Janey speaks of . . . would bring number 7 when Janey is 47, and somebody should put his foot down . . . or keep his pants buttoned, or something. . . .

I want to keep . . . one bottle [of Pol Roget] for Ronnie's alteration party. . . . Somebody has to do something before 2 A.M. of, say, December 25, 1958, after the [guests] have gone home and Ronnie is sitting alone in the living room drinking and glinting . . . in the belief that it's a lot of nonsense to drive all the way into town for what Peaches Browning once referred to in court as "one of those things." Anyway, the pharmacy would be closed. "The hell with it, we haven't run out of girls' names yet, and there's the plaguey hundredth chance nothing will happen." I will close with a few offhand suggestions: the wife can always lock the bedroom door. By the time he has broken it down, he ought to be worn out, at sixty. And by that time Lane Bryant may have put in a supply of perfectly darling chastity belts. There is always Denmark [for a sex change] . . . but I hesitate to recommend a mixed doubles game in which the wife accidentally deflowers her mate with a well-directed forehand smash. The trouble with Ronnie is not that he has two strikes on him, but I will not labor the points.

After the baby's birth, he continued to write Jane, advising her on diet, worried about her lifestyle. Janey got up at 7:00 A.M., fed the baby, and left for her clerical job having had nothing but coffee. Thurber warns her:

Rose Algrant who gets through the day on coffee and little else, looks a hundred years old and gets all kinds of rashes and other ailments, but has the natural constitutional strength you have. . . . All of us . . . abuse ourselves unbelievably. I have always thought you could cut way down on cigarettes. . . . Eating dinner around 10 P.M. is probably not good for you and may be one reason you aren't hungry in the morning. You always were a fast eater, too, so slow down a little. . . .

We intend to see that you take care of yourself when we get there, and we promise not to contribute to your delinquency by the all night drinking sessions the Thurbers are famous for. We are as self-destructive as anybody. . . . Naturally we all worry more about you than anybody because of the children, and I know that Ronnie will join us in a pledge of reasonable moderation. It isn't easy for me to give up smoking, but I usually average not more than two packs a week.

There was trouble in Paradise, two years later, during the Thurbers' last Bermuda stay, in 1957. Ronnie, who had medical problems, was trying to find a buyer for the *Bermudian*—he would undergo an operation in New York and later suffer from a stroke—and Jane was now dealing with six children. "We got a bit fed with Bermuda this time," Helen writes the John Duncan Millers, "(Ronnie gets more and more of a problem, and Janey more and more reconciled to it, though the children are still wonderful), and don't want to go back for a while." Meanwhile, the Williamses had given Thurber something new to worry about: his godchild, Dinah, at fourteen, had fallen for a young Scottish naval officer. Thurber writes Jane in alarm:

> When an old girl of mine named Ann Fordyce was engaged to a lieutenant in the American navy, his mother, the widow of an admiral, said, "Never marry a sailor my dear. Other women will see far more of him than you ever would." So Ann married a businessman who brought blondes to live in the guest room, and then a young doctor who took dope and died young. Her last husband was a drunken broker.
>
> What worries me about you and your female descendents is the warm emotional nature of all of you. You kiss first and think about it later, and anyone of you is likely to find yourself in the midst of a marriage that was anything but planned or thought out. That's the trouble with that ocean fairyland you live in, it can turn so easily into a flower-covered casket of youth and dreams. . . .
>
> In my book of fables, I use one Latin moral, which, translated into English, goes like this, "A fool and her legs are soon parted." . . . The worst age for any American girl is fifteen and sixteen, and when they are physically nineteen, they are in great danger, for they have the shape of a woman and the mentality of a six-week-old poodle puppy.

Dinah recovered from her infatuation with the Scot but was next in love with a French deep-sea diver. Thurber took on that problem of his godchild's, too:

> All this is known to psychologists as the Death Wish, a human phenomenon bound to flourish in a generation brought up on permissive education and self-expression. When [Morris Markey's daughter], aged five, overturned all the chairs in her parents' house, said they were horses, and then, to prove it, filled the parlor with horse manure she had got in the road, her mother was prevented from punishing her because her father said, "Don't interfere with her childish fantasies." That was a generation ago, before the spoiled American child began killing his parents because they refused him the car, or told him to do his homework, or merely said "Shut up." I figure that 15,000 families will be wiped out by toddlers and teenagers in the next ten years. . . .

I wrote you five years ago that the next war will be the war between adults and children. Every time a little child comes to our door I am afraid he will say, "Death or treat." . . .

Dinah, who has long been aware of my adoration of her mother, once said . . . "Mother, why didn't you marry Uncle Jim?" . . . The purely chronological answer is, "Because I didn't meet him until I was sixteen and I was married and pregnant." . . . Of course, Dinah has beheld the truly great happiness of her own parents and knows that her mother was married when, in worldly experience, she was about fourteen. But she also must know that premature marriage is about as comfortable and free as waltzing with Long John Silver. . . . After Dinah, God forbid, has been living for a year in a backstreet in Maracaibo, disenchantment would come a little late. I can see him now, the husband, chewing a broken toothpick, slapping his bare belly, burping, and boasting, "I can open more oysters in one hour than Pedro could open in a month." When everybody else is exploring outer space, this guy is trying to reach the bottom of the ocean. You cannot expect a man to be a good husband or perfect companion when he spends most of his life under water making goo-goo eyes through his goggles at enormous fish. . . .

Uncle Jim waited 39 years for the right girl, who had waited 32 years for him. She had a chance to marry an oiler and wiper, but she was too proud and sensible, and now she has a man with 23 books and an overactive thyroid.

From Paris, on October 10, 1958, he was imploring both the Williamses "to take wheat germ pills, and also glutanic acid pills, and live longer. They have kept me going through four months of the hardest work I have done [Ross] and with more parties, luncheons, and dinners than we have had in America in ten years."

The news from the States had not been good. Besides Gibbs's death, Coates's first wife, Elsa, had died. His second wife, "Boo," had arthritis, bursitis, and gall bladder trouble. Coates himself had got drunk at a party and dislocated his thumb. Gertrude Sayre had been confined with mental illness. (In 1960, she died, from an overdose of sleeping pills, intentionally taken, it is believed.) At Christmastime, Joel Sayre borrowed a thousand dollars from the Thurbers at Costello's one night, to attend his daughter's wedding in London, and said he then intended to go on to the Arctic Circle and write a "Letter from Lapland" for the *New Yorker*. (The loan repayment never materialized, leaving Helen lastingly resentful of Sayre.)

In Paris, Helen was down with virus and sinus problems, but a weary

Thurber, though feeling oppressed by the Whites' growing disapproval of the Ross articles, and the silence of old friends at the *New Yorker*, had managed to finish the last six chapters and mail them to the publisher, the Atlantic Monthly Press, an imprint of Little, Brown. "I am . . . a little depressed by the silence of almost everybody on *The New Yorker*, except those in the business department," he writes the Whites. "We have not heard from Miss Terry at all, and worry about it." Terry was aware of Katharine's dislike of the later *Atlantic* articles, of Shawn's and the staff's uneasiness over the series, and of Thurber's criticism of the magazine. "If he'd kept it to his own experiences, fine," Terry says, "but he tried to assess the *New Yorker* and has spoiled the chance of a good history of it ever being written." She was reflecting staff opinion that even then seemed a bit overboard.

With six chapters added to the ten expanded *Atlantic* articles, the projected Ross book was running long and the decision was made not to include the closing pieces by the other writers. Breaking the news to his disappointed colleagues kicked up Thurber's thyroid condition, as he writes McKelway:

> The Atlantic Press-Little Brown and several outside editorial opinions decided against including the End Papers. . . . The money . . . is to be retained by one and all, and it pleases me that it comes from a publisher. . . . My contract . . . did not include outside pieces, but my only purpose in putting them in was one of moving over and letting other men, just as important to Ross and The New Yorker, have their say about him. The argument that convinced me was this: I parade through sixteen chapters and then pack my colleagues in the back room. It did no good to point out that Edward Everett talked for two hours at Gettysburg and Lincoln for two minutes.
>
> So I am returning your piece, goddam it, in the confident hope that you can sell it somewhere.

A disappointed Liebling felt that it was only Thurber changing his mind. He was probably right; Thurber was in a position to dictate the publishing terms. "He blamed the publisher for discarding what he'd promised to use," Liebling complained. But most of them were able to place their own reminiscences of life with Ross in other publications. White had warmly acknowledged his check for his "Ross at the Wheel" letter on September 29, 1957, "the first I have ever received from you . . . and the first I have received for any piece of writing since March. I live entirely on my nerve these days." But more than a year later, writing from Paris, Thurber informs the Whites that "hardest of all to do was to take out the 'Endpapers' which sets for me a new, tremendous problem and anxiety. I am using only one in the book now, Andy's piece about Ross at the wheel."

White at once tried to return his check, over Thurber's protests, and said he didn't wish "Ross at the Wheel" to appear as a separate piece by itself. By then, the Whites had read the last of the *Atlantic* pieces, with growing discomfort, and White worried that the publisher would use his name in advertising or promoting the book if his signed piece appeared in it. "It would imply that the book had my total blessing," White writes Thurber, "which isn't quite the case. I liked the early chapters fine, but when you got to sex and money I faded out on you, as I hold different views. Haven't read your chapter on editing, but from the explosions in the sky over Forty-fourth Street lately I would imagine I'm not going to agree with that, either. . . .

"Nothing would make me happier than to love every single word of your book . . . but as of now, I love parts of it but not all of it, and I would be crazy to say anything different. Nobody knows better than I do how difficult it is to interpret a human being to others who knew him, too, and it is certainly natural that here and there you and I should diverge, when it comes to Ross and the magazine."

White's reference to "explosions over Forty-fourth Street" was to the reports from Angell and others on Thurber's recent, tempestuous reactions to being edited. White's reference was also in response to a letter Thurber had written the Whites in August, from England:

> I'm digging up the sad nostalgic story of how [Ross] used to ruin my Talk pieces by his rewrite. He loved such expressions as hotelward, and such, contrariwise, otherwhere, and such. I used to rewrite his rewrite and send it on with a faked R. . . . His writing of Talk was awful, his writing of letters wonderful. They were done by two absolutely different men. So were the generous lightener of burdens and the plain son-of-a-bitch two different men.

It was true that Ross's genius as copyeditor was in his queries, which focused on an antiseptic clarity and accuracy that scotched many a poetic sentence and flight of fancy. As the writer Edward Newhouse wrote Thurber, "On a short casual of mine . . . he came up with thirty queries. [Lobrano] and I . . . ignored twenty-eight of them, but the remaining two made the difference between a good story and a poor one." But Ross, whose letters were often filled with imaginative writing, turned wooden when writing for publication. Gill, as the Talk rewrite man, agrees with Thurber that Ross simply was not a *New Yorker* writer, who nonetheless didn't hesitate to insert extraneous and awkward phrases into Talk stories in misguided attempts to make them clearer or lighter. (Shawn excelled at both writing and editing; he often salvaged good ideas from poor writing, and made mediocre writers look like the *New Yorker* writers they would never be.)

Even when disagreeing with Thurber, White's letters to him were nearly always aglow with wit and congenial anecdotes about his farm life—a hen that was afraid of his wristwatch, for example—and about his health, and it is easy to conclude, rightly or wrongly, that his principal objections to Thurber's Ross pieces were more in support of Katharine's, whose vehement feelings about them recur in file memoranda and letters to others, and were continually nursed by her until her death. Thurber and White over the years had entertained one another with Ross stories, and Thurber seems never to have anticipated the Whites' objections to whatever he chose to write on the subject, though he had been warned in an earlier letter from Andy: "If I were you, I wouldn't crowd my luck. You've done just right, so far, in what you have included and excluded, and you have certainly given the reading public enough to chew on, about Harold Wallace Ross. . . ."

It was White's letter, five weeks later, that upset Thurber, who wrote Lewis Gannett of his suspicion that it was sufficiently "un-White" to be "unsubcommittee," the parent committee apparently being Katharine. "He says he 'faded from me' when I got to 'sex and money,'" he writes Gannett, "and says that he doesn't think he's going to like 'your chapter on editing,' because he has heard of high explosions in the sky over 44th Street recently. The assumption that I would let recent fights with current editors there influence my book on Ross angers the hell out of me."

To White, he writes:

> Some of your letter is you, and perfect, and some of it isn't you at all.
> . . . I do not lose great friendships for reasons of weather, mundane or
> mental. The great ones I hold onto are yours, Jap Gude's, Nugent's (and,
> boy, have we been through something [Nugent's mental affliction]),
> Sayre's and Ted Gardiner's. . . . I think that what friends have done
> for me and what I believe I have done for them form something one can
> take with him, when he leaves sex and money behind. I never argue
> with men about sex and money, only with women.

Thurber always thought he knew how to get the Whites' sympathetic attention and forgiveness by trotting out his own medical troubles:

I developed . . . in the past awful six months of soul-searching and continuous rewrite, my first bad hyper-thyroid kickup since 1952. At that time the same length of time and difficulty grew out of "The Thurber Album." In my recent iodine uptake test the Geiger counter showed that my thyroid "is either under-controlled or over-controlled." I have had to give up whiskey and all but a few cigarettes, and the doctor talks of "other measures." The effect of hyper-thyroid on the mind is bleak and bad. . . .

I have exploded only about pieces of mine submitted recently to The New Yorker. Roger [Angell] said about one query: "Shawn told me to go carefully on this one." It seems that the way the piece had to be set the word "Dixie" appeared at the end of one line, and the word "cups" at the end of the following line, thus giving "Dixie cups" to those readers who read from top to bottom and not from left to right. I was going to send Roger and Shawn a sentence like this: "Shortly after the laying of the cornerstone, a girl . . ." To our curious top-to-bottom readers this would come out as "laying a girl." As long as I have any Thurber spirit left, there will be explosions in the sky about such crap. I shall never become an intimidated New Yorker writer. I happen to love the magazine and to genuinely fear that The Cleaning Woman's Home Companion may be done in by such a rival as Esquire within a dozen years if we don't watch out.

No writing of Thurber's resulted in such public approval and private resentment as *The Years with Ross*, some of the bitterness the consequence of its commercial success. Its liberal first printing was followed by seven more. The Book-of-the-Month Club, which chose the book as one of a double selection for June 1959, printed a hundred and twenty-five thousand copies. Staff members were annoyed at the prominent role Thurber had assigned himself in the story of the magazine's development; many felt that they had not been given sufficient recognition—an occupational hazard that Dale Kramer and Brendan Gill also had to contend with. ("We outrage easily over here," Emily Hahn comments from her *New Yorker* office.) "As the *Atlantic* articles began to appear," says Joel Sayre, "you heard corridor comments like, 'Poor Hobie Weekes. Been here twenty-six years and Thurber hasn't mentioned him, or Poor Kip Orr.' This got back to Jim, who put everybody into the book."

Thurber rarely deprecated anybody in his published writing directly; one could not guess his wild psychoanalysis of Ross over money matters, written to Truax, from reading the book. He runs Ross's entertaining letters to him on the subject, which show Ross's sincere concern for whatever bothers

Thurber about the magazine's operations. Indeed, Thurber emerges the petulant and unreasonable one. He was too much the professional showman to highlight his prejudices onstage. Ever committed to telling the best story, he sails his narrative away from the shoals of rancor. He explains the reasons for the magazine's changes correctly—that World War II had forever churned up subjects of greater significance to readers than metropolitan human-interest features—the oddities of New York life that had intrigued Ross. He takes only a swipe or two at the current magazine, going back to his rescuing of Astrid Peters's "Shoe the Horse and Shoe the Mare" from John Chapin Mosher, the early reader of unsolicited manuscripts, who had found the story "a tedious bit about an adolescent female." Thurber: "I sometimes wonder what Mosher would say, if he were alive now, about the *New Yorker's* flux of stories by women writers dealing with the infancy, childhood, and young womanhood of females. 'We are in a velvet rut,' Ross once said . . . , and this was amended not long ago by a sardonic male writer to read, 'We are now in a tulle and taffeta rut.' " (The sardonic writer, of course, was Thurber.)

As White once remarked, "Whoever puts pen to paper writes about himself, whether he knows it or not." The Ross book was a memoir, as the title clearly implies, with most of the anecdotes drawn from Thurber's file-drawer memory. "There was more about Thurber than about Ross," runs a common complaint about the book. Anyone acquainted with Thurber's work would have expected nothing else, for his literary gaze was nearly always on himself. He was the subject of much of his more memorable writings, and to discuss the Ross years without featuring himself would be like a baseball manager not allowing DiMaggio or Roger Maris to bat. Thurber treated the subject of Ross as he had treated the subject of Columbus; what he wasn't directly connected with rarely interested him and got short shrift.

The wondrous story of Harold Ross's rise from semi-educated, itinerant journalist to editor of the most influential, sophisticated, and literary humor magazine of the period had been told by Kramer and rehashed every fifth anniversary by other publications. What had given life to these accounts were the anecdotes Thurber supplied. *The Years with Ross* is a pleasant read in which Thurber reclaimed his anecdotal material, refurbished it, and mixed it into the detailed information he obtained through hard-won research and his interviews of veteran collaborators. "It was the longest single exercise in journalism I ever performed," he said.

The work ostensibly posed a central question it was meant to answer, a question Thurber made a chapter heading: "Who Was Harold, What Was He?" The question was primarily an opening for Thurber's literary showmanship; a complete answer able to stay in place would, perhaps, spoil the fun surrounding the conundrum that is Ross. Perhaps James M. Cain, writing to Kramer in 1950, comes close: "With Ross, his love is the magazine. His invariable placing of it ahead of people is perhaps dismaying to many. Once you get that side of him, though, he ceases to be incomprehensible."

There is no disagreement among the critics that Thurber captures Ross's mannerisms perfectly. Even Katharine White, who went to her grave hating the book, writes: "Jim did give a notable picture of how Ross looked and talked—all that about his profanity was perfectly true, and I am profane to this day because of it."

But she found hostility in Thurber's exaggerated facts and stories, and Ross does come out second best to Thurber in incident after incident. In one sense, the book is his play about Ross that never got written, with Thurber one of the principal actors, at times a disguised Walter Mitty. It is, then, not surprising that there are moments when the fate of the magazine seems to tremble in delicate balance on whether Ross will learn who Thurber is in time to save the cliff-hanging undertaking. But it was Ross, Thurber repeatedly points out, who got the frail enterprise airborne and kept it climbing on its long, successful flight. He is careful to credit others, even speaking of Ross's pleasure at White's honorary degree at Yale, without mentioning his own.

The entrapments of autobiography defy self-concealment and include the difficulty of describing one's personal accomplishments without the appearance of preening. Thurber being Thurber, his more obvious extensions of fact—at times into fancy—often work to his disadvantage, for they condition the reader into suspecting even the many things that he reported accurately. "He heightens everything," says Katharine White, "and adds, even in a biography, things that are not true. It isn't, in most instances, that he deliberately tells lies; he just embroiders. . . . It worked fine in 'My Life and Hard Times,' which contains some of the funniest pieces ever written. . . . It didn't work so well when he did the same sort of thing in a life of a great editor, recently dead."

Lois Long looks on the bright side: "The book didn't tell the whole story at all," she says, "and most of us should be on our knees every night thanking God for what Thurber was nice enough to leave out."

It wasn't only office gossip that Thurber left out; he spared Ross a great deal as well—omitting the clear evidence of Ross's dislike of blacks, gays, and women journalists. When facts inconvenienced Ross, he ignored them. He pretended not to know that several of his male secretaries and aides over the years were homosexual. He refused to provide office space for such regular and talented fiction contributors as John Cheever, making room only for fact writers. He deliberately isolated staff members in disconnected suites throughout the building. ("Ross was a firm believer in decentralization as a means of preventing office politics, office gossip, and office amours," writes Richard Rovere. "He scattered writers here and there in the building—two, three, or four to a floor—so that they would not have much to do with one another.") New hires were never introduced to anyone else, as another controlling, antisocial measure of Ross's. Some left the *New Yorker*, after years there, still unable to match faces to names. A newly hired Shawn believed for some time that Rogers Whitaker was Ross. ("I don't think I'm mixed up on who is who," says Philip Hamburger, after more than fifty years on the staff, "but maybe I still have them wrong.") Edmund Wilson writes to Thurber:

> I did not really care much for Ross. The trouble was that he was no gentleman, and I didn't like his way of dealing with people. The assumptions about personal and business relations that decent people usually go on did not hold in the *New Yorker* office. . . . Ross was like an old newspaper man—though a rather neurotic one—and the atmosphere of the *New Yorker* was that of a newspaper office. One of the features of this was that nobody was ever introduced to anybody else. . . . There were not even editorial conferences to discuss what was going on and the editors' and contributors' ideas about it.

Writers didn't know if their pieces had been accepted, or when they would run, until, mysteriously, galley proofs turned up on their desks. The result was a mood of institutional indifference, sometimes lethal to aspiring writers in need of encouragement. Ross wanted it that way, along with subscribing to Hilaire Belloc's belief that "very little prose would be written if wealth were better distributed."

"If Liebling, or any other *New Yorker* writer, had written the book on Ross," says William Maxwell, "it would have had the same effect that Thurber's did. Ross had a personal relation with every writer. Anyone who did violence to his or her particular image of Ross would have earned a resentful reprimand, as Thurber did." As Frank Sullivan told Kramer, who complained of the hostility shown his book on Ross and the magazine by the *New Yorker* staff: "You are in the position of a portrait painter who has done a portrait of a man with a hundred wives, all critical, all in love with him, and all determined the portrait shall be perfect. . . . By him I don't necessarily mean Ross, but the magazine."

Though Thurber buttered up Shawn by writing that he had been Thurber's choice to succeed Ross, Thurber actually preferred Lobrano, the only editor besides Ross he would work with; it isn't known if anyone ever asked Thurber about the succession, anyway. Thurber blamed both Katharine and Shawn solely for the magazine changes Thurber abhorred.

"Actually," says Maxwell, "Shawn didn't kick over the traces, but if he couldn't sustain a quality in the magazine, he'd replace it. Humor wasn't really his thing. He eventually banned casuals from the back of the book and got rid of anecdotes in Talk. He was superb about fiction, as Ross was not, but the entertainment quality of the magazine suffered under Shawn. He preferred long, serious fact subjects to lighter fare. Shawn was such a fast reader, perhaps the pieces didn't seem long to him. But there had always been change, certainly under Ross. What may have haunted Thurber was the thought that the period was moving away from him, but no period will ever move away from White or Thurber any more than it will from Twain."

Besides the normal resistance to change that most people have, Thurber seems to have sensed—even feared—that the *New Yorker* would continue to flourish without much help from him. "He was a great man," James Geraghty, the art director, remarked in 1962, "and maybe genius and bitterness go together."

Katharine White, and Shawn, felt that Thurber had played up his importance to the magazine at the expense of Ross's, but Thurber could not have won many points with Katharine, for both were fully aware, despite their proper correspondence, that they despised one another. Why Thurber had let it come to that remains a mystery. Katharine had been a staunch support in getting Thurber started on the magazine, continued to encourage him, was his permissive editor for years, and was instrumental in obtaining *New Yorker* stock for him. Ross, intent on editing a "funny" magazine, interested first and foremost in facts, suspicious of fiction and poetry, had been forced by Katharine, as Gill points out, to publish O'Hara, Irwin Shaw, Vladimir Nabokov, Cheever, and other major writers. Perhaps Thurber's published appraisal of her worth to Ross was too skimpy, for it briefly describes her simply as "one of the pillars upon which Ross could lean in his hours of uncertainty about his own limitations. 'She knows the Bible, and literature, and foreign languages,' he told me the day I first met him, 'and she has taste.' "

Katharine resented the book's sounding "as if Thurber had been an editor for many, many years. . . . He also gives the impression that he was Managing Editor for a very much longer time than he was."

Katharine was jealously proprietary toward her own relationship with Ross —one that, as a career woman, she ranked in importance second only to that with Andy. Thurber's carefree romp through her territory, casually knocking about the things by which she defined herself, infuriated her. "I think the greatest distortion . . . was of his friendship with Ross," she writes. "He was not one of Ross's intimate friends until perhaps in the last months of Ross's life, when he was living in the Algonquin and Jim and Helen were living there too. . . . I think Jim's relationship probably was . . . a love-hate relationship. Ross amused him but [Thurber] was annoyed at any editing."

Her quarrels over even items of footnote worth seem to measure her antipathy toward Thurber the person, not just the memoirist. Does it matter that M. B. Levick referred to Alexander Woollcott as "Foolish," as Thurber remembers, or "Old Foolish," as Katharine does? She insisted that Thurber was wrong about the magazine's finances, but he was not. She believed that Thurber "exaggerates his intimacy with Gibbs . . . they were not pals." But indeed they had been, from the late twenties on, though they saw one another infrequently after Thurber left the staff and stayed in touch only through letters and phone calls.

But she raises legitimate points, too. There is no question that Thurber took mischievous license with the facts to get a laugh at the cost of Ross's image. "Why make him so ignorant!" Katharine asks on the book's margin, often with cause. "We all thought the chapter on sex and Ross was distasteful and untrue," she writes. "He wasn't as naive as Jim made him out." She is undoubtedly correct. Thurber believed an innocent Ross didn't get the significance of an Arno cartoon that pictures a man and woman on a country road at night—he carrying the rear seat of a car—telling a motorcycle cop: "We want to report a stolen car." McKelway insisted to Thurber, in vain, that Ross wouldn't have published it if he hadn't understood it. Ross played the prude, protective of the morals of the magazine and its readers. He really did classify women as morally "good" or "bad," and though Jane Grant, his first wife, said she was willing to sleep with him before they married, Ross would not. She claimed she never saw him nude—he wore a nightshirt—but he seems to have got over that. McKelway tells of finding Ross in his office complaining of pain from fresh burns on his genitals. Ross was a bachelor at the time, staying at the Ritz. "They ought to have covers [over] the goddam radiators there," he told McKelway. "I had this dame in bed and it got cold so I got up and walked over to the window to shut it. I had to lean over . . . this red-hot radiator. Feels like a second-degree burn."

Thurber did delete Ross's lecture to someone on why some women turn to lesbianism: "Women like love to go on for hours, and you know how men are —one, two, three, and they're back at the Stork Club." But Thurber continued to think, wrongly, that Ross was a puritan who never told a dirty joke. And that Ross was semiliterate; Thurber wouldn't believe that Ross had the ability to write the *New Yorker*'s prospectus, guessing—again wrongly—that

Marc Connelly wrote it, including the promise that the magazine would not be edited for "the little old lady from Dubuque." But Jane Grant witnessed Ross writing it, and Thurber could have checked the facts with Connelly.

Edmund Wilson throws light on the little old lady from Dubuque: Frank Crowninshield, the editor of *Vanity Fair*, where Wilson worked for a while, would edit out an esoteric sentence, explaining to the writer that the magazine was being published for the little old lady from Dubuque. The reference was well known among editors, and Ross wanted it stated that he was heading his magazine in a different direction from that of *Vanity Fair*.

Jane Grant believes that Ross often led Thurber on, pretending to be amazed at something Thurber was telling him. Ross often appeared uninformed because he kept asking questions of everyone. "He would pretend he hadn't read something just to tease Thurber and others," says Grant. "He knew the misconceptions people were under regarding him. Thurber felt both culturally superior and jealous of Harold at the same time. Harold *was* generally unread; he only read what was submitted to the magazine; his mind was striated with ignorance and knowledge, but if he had been anything like the boor in Thurber's book I would never have married him."

Yet, among the ambiguities of his feelings, Thurber did possess the wonder and affection for Ross expressed in his dedication of *The Thurber Carnival*. Rosemary Thurber remembers that her father's stories about Ross always made them laugh but brimmed with admiration for him. Even Katharine concedes that "Jim did put in some love and affection" for Ross in *The Years with Ross*. One can easily imagine Thurber saying about Ross what Liebling did. For all the difficulties Ross had caused Liebling, when Liebling was breaking into the *New Yorker*, he told Shawn, upon Ross's death, "If I knew he was going to die, I'd put my arm around his shoulder and say I'd always liked him. But if he recovered he'd never forgive me."

69

That Thurber Carnival

Et tu, Crosbe? Last year the AKRON BEACON-JOURNAL practically laid me to rest, reporting that I was not only blind, but "almost entirely bedridden now," and last Friday you said that I am not very active any more. . . .

I don't want to brag, but . . . three books of mine were published in the past twelve months. . . . I am halfway through the writing of a book about Harold Ross, and have four other short books in progress, and two plays. . . . In my spare time I have written a thousand letters this year, and [the introduction to] John McNulty's fine new collection. I did not write [Dick] Maney's book, though. It was done by Tallulah Bankhead. Poor Maney is not very active any more. . . .

If you frequented Tim's instead of Bleeck's, you would have firsthand proof of my activity, but I don't usually get there until after your bedtime. At Tim's I engage in such light pastimes as singing, debating, wine tasting, and chasing girls. A blind man could not catch girls if they didn't squeal, but a chased girl always squeals, and is easy to catch if you are as spry as I am. This keeps me in excellent condition for the daily grind. . . . This in spite of the fact that people keep shoving crutches under my arms and stretchers under my powerful physique. I am happy that the Board of Health has not yet complained about the body of my work and ordered it to be buried, but I suspect every knock on the door and every ring of the phone. Until they do come for me I will keep on going. Right now, though, I must get back to my strenuous inactivity.

—Letter to *Herald Tribune* columnist John Crosby,
November 20, 1957

Crosby apologized and said he had been warned by Ann Honeycutt, after his column appeared, that he would be hearing from Thurber. Thurber said he was helping those determined to hurry him out of the world by drinking embalming fluid, but, as he told Crosby, he continued irrepressibly active. He fought against being stereotyped as handicapped. "I used to think cripples became sweet," he told Lois Long, "but I seem to have become the worst S.O.B. in the world." Asked why, being blind, he moved about so recklessly, he compared himself to the horse on the Ed Wynn show, which kept bumping into things: "It wasn't that it couldn't see," Thurber explains, "it was just that it didn't give a good goddam."

He and Helen had returned from Europe on the *Liberté* in November 1958. James Gould Cozzens's *By Love Possessed* was on the best-seller list, and an exhausted Helen complained that they had been "by Ross possessed" the previous eighteen months. It wasn't over; the controversies over the articles continued, and Helen was soon working nine hours a day on the galley and page proofs. "There were scores of bad typos," Thurber says. "All publishers should be deported."

Thurber was under the weather, himself. "In November my thyroid kicked up," he writes the Williamses, "but now it's lying flat again like a horse's ears." On March 1, 1959, Helen went into Doctors Hospital to be operated on for another ovarian cyst. During the several weeks she was there, Thurber took a room on the family floor, preparing for an appearance that month on CBS's *Small World*, anchored by Edward R. Murrow. In a panic as always without Helen to guide him, Thurber telephoned Alistair Cooke.

"He was worried about Helen's eyes," says Cooke, "and the doctors couldn't assure him that Helen's cyst wasn't cancerous. I went to the hospital and brought him home. Jane and I were having Eric Hodgins, the *Fortune* editor, and his wife, for dinner. Thurber gave a marvelous performance till two a.m.; no one else got a word in. The Ross book was finished but not published, and Thurber tried out on us everything he'd written in it. He was a marvel to these people, funny and delightful, and lived up to everything they'd heard about him. The only mimic I'd seen better than Thurber was Charlie Chaplin, who could even sound and look like Marlene Dietrich.

"The weirdest thing about having Thurber in your home was taking him to the bathroom. One remembers a unique experience and I can't forget that one. I had never taken anyone but a small child to the john. Whenever he tried to conquer the geography of the apartment, he'd walk right into a mirror or something. He'd continue some story, as he was being guided into the bathroom, dropped his pants, stood in his garters, and managed more or less to hit the target, talking intently—'Alistair, goddam it, so and so once told me'—and so on. The greatest unpublishable Thurber cartoon would have been one of Thurber in just such a scene. He was completely trusting, endearing, like a great dog. At parties in Cornwall, Marc Simont would keep an eye on Thurber, who might get out of his chair for a moment. Marc would slide the chair under Thurber just as he sat down again, oblivious to near catastrophe. He had this ridiculous pride in saying that he could see the light when he lit a cigarette, and he'd light his hair and nose trying to find it.

"When I took Thurber home that night, descending in the elevator reminded him of when he was once on his way to a party in another apartment building and was jammed against the rear wall of the elevator. Being blind, he was counting the floors by the clicks, and at the fifteenth a woman snuggled up to him and whispered, 'Would you like to go to bed with me?' Thurber waited for seven more clicks to go by and then said, 'Are you pretty?'

"When I took him back to his hospital room, he didn't want me to leave; he was a bit frightened; he didn't break down, but it was almost too much for him. He took his coat off, tried to hang it in a wardrobe but it fell on the floor. He heard it fall, was embarrassed that I had witnessed it and then tried to hang it on a doorknob. It fell again, and he said, 'Goddam it! What a hell of a situation to be in. For the next week I'll go around hanging my coat on the floor.' We joked about it. He transmuted everything into humor. When I was to leave, he thanked me with extraordinary warmth; he was scared blue. I waited till he had undressed and got into bed. He was disabled, demobilized and disorganized without Helen. The day he heard that Helen didn't have cancer, he exploded in relief, and when she was discharged, they came to our apartment for dinner and to celebrate."

Small World was prerecorded on videotape, with Thurber in New York, Noel Coward in Jamaica, and Siobhan McKenna in Dublin. Thurber was keyed up before the taping. "He panicked at such a time," says Cooke. "One would suppose he loved to be on the air, but he was painfully self-conscious on television."

Few understood how shy Thurber was; through one excuse or another, he would get a surrogate for nearly every major public appearance he was to make—George Smallsreed for the Ohioana award; Jack Goodman for the ALA honor; Helen at the dedication of the Denney building at O.S.U. His extroverted behavior helped disguise his shyness, and the glass of whiskey was a necessary stage prop. Rosemary tells of long liquor-free periods in Cornwall when Thurber and Helen worked during the day and listened to the radio— later TV—in the evening. The moment a visitor arrived, or they walked into the company of others, Thurber needed to find his social courage in alcohol. Inevitably, eyewitnesses to the Thurber story usually remember him drinking.

Given his conversational dominance in a group, not many realized the insecurities that affected his behavior. White understood Thurber in many ways better than Thurber understood himself. In later years, a distressed Helen challenged the typescript of a Thurber biography that was disposing of her husband as little more than a tiresome drunk by the end of his life. "We never had drinks before or wine with dinner unless we had people in or were out to dinner. Alone, we drank almost nothing all those years. You have pictured those twenty years in Cornwall as one long drunken brawl." She appealed to White, who told her, "After six drinks he was as mad as the next guy, and usually a little madder [but] if Honey [Honeycutt] pictured Jim as an 'alcoholic egomaniac,' I think her choice of words was poor. Jim was never an alcoholic—just a bad drinker on occasion. I don't think alcohol ever preyed on Jim's mind, either before or after a bout with it. He had none of the telltale marks of an alcoholic. As for 'egomania,' the 'ego' is true enough (as it is with most of us who write); the 'mania' is a word best left to a psychiatrist, not to the nearest barfly."

Small World was telecast March 27, 1959, consisting largely of compliments exchanged between Thurber and McKenna, and various pleasantries from Coward. When Murrow asked, "Is there really any difference between country humor and city humor?" Thurber—less funny than usual, and someone a few of his friends were beginning not to recognize—replied:

> The humor that I write, or what passes as humor writing, is written in the country and published in the city. . . . Where I live, 125 miles from New York City, I have a farmhouse two miles from a small town, but I'm entirely surrounded by Mark Van Doren, [Lewis] Gannett and other lovely friends of mine who are writers, editors, painters. You can get an etching at any farmhouse now, but not a glass of milk. So, it practically is the city.

Coward: "I think that the city humor, the top American humor to my mind is the *New Yorker*, which really is the most urbane, witty type of city humor."

Thurber: "*What* humor in the *New Yorker*? I haven't found . . . very much. . . . Humor in the *New Yorker* reflects the decline of humor in America and I think there's been a general decline everywhere except in the development of what is called the humor of menace or even the humor of horror or even the humor of terror . . . a form of comedy that is new and rather desperately alarming to me. Living as we do . . . on the brink of 'was,' things are not as funny as they used to be."

The cheerful Coward didn't agree, finding the comment "discouraging." "You mustn't let it get you down," he counseled Thurber. "You really mustn't." (In his diary, Coward wrote that "Thurber was the dullest of the three, because he spoke too slowly and mostly about himself.")

There it was, Thurber's chronic disparagement of current humor, but this time taking the *New Yorker* down with him on international television. He seemed oblivious to the effects of his actions, continuing to submit ideas and casuals to the magazine, whose editors were ever more resentful of his public stands against the *New Yorker* and of an arrogance that seemed to be building into a Napoleonic complex, impossible for them to cope with. A physically related mental disablement of some kind was the last thing that his friends—and even his doctors—suspected, but his letters to Truax and the Whites, containing his irrational attacks on Ross and the magazine over writer compensation, were surely early warnings that a great deal more was involved than artistic temperament.

Bennett Cerf, on radio and in magazine articles, was urging that there be a Pulitzer Prize for humor. When lecturing at universities, he said, he was always asked who the greatest American humorists alive are. His reply: "Thurber and White are so far ahead of the pack that their closest pursuers are specks on the horizon. . . . Neither the Pulitzer Prize nor the National Book Awards jury has ever given a top prize to a recognized humorist. I suggest you take a long look . . . in the direction of James Thurber and Elwyn Brooks White." All this added to Thurber's feeling of never having been properly recognized. He went Cerf one better, suggesting that the Nobel Prize be given a humorist, leaving little doubt that he had himself in mind as the first recipient.

He was further alienating Shawn. The day Ross died, arrangements had been made for Shawn to be home when he got the news; it was feared that he would break down. He did, sobbing uncontrollably. He adored Ross, whose hand, in absentia, he felt to be still very much on the helm, and Thurber's attacks on the magazine were, to Shawn, as much against Ross as Shawn. In a letter written in the summer of 1958, Thurber accused Shawn of having forced contributors to delete references to Communism and McCarthyism. And when Shawn had granted him permission to use Ross's correspondence with Thurber in his book, Thurber wrote sneeringly to a friend, "Wasn't that brave and generous of him?" Shawn preferred the time-saving telephone to letter writing, but Thurber complains to De Vries, perhaps with some truth, that "Shawn . . . does not answer letters and I am told he has decided to make a policy of this to keep from being quoted in anybody's 'The Years with Shawn.'" He teased Shawn, in another letter, suggesting that Shawn was writing his own memoirs, to be called *The Tears with Thurber*. "Did you know that Shawn never answers any letters?" Thurber writes White. "After writing him four times I gave up. I am now told he is desperately afraid of being quoted."

The Thurber story had moved into that sad period in which, one by one, Thurber irrationally begins to turn on the people and institutions he had long drawn upon for his livelihood, companionship, and intellectual sustenance: his family, whose careless "stupidity" after his childhood accident, he now insisted, had been the sole cause of his loss of sight; O.S.U. (his remarks at the Denney dedication on the need for academic freedom were essentially a reprimand of the university for its restrictions on that freedom); Columbus ("We haven't been to Columbus since my mother died in December, 1955," he writes Dorothy Miller in 1957, "and don't want to go out again. It has become an enormous, vulgar, and dispiriting city."); Ross, over his financial compensation to Thurber; the *New Yorker* and the Whites; Helen, the handiest target of his misogyny and the constant reminder of his humiliating dependence; the Cornwall group, including Van Doren and even Rose Algrant, to whom he dedicated the last book to be published while he lived, *Lanterns & Lances*; and most of his supportive allies. The few who were spared included the absent Sayre, the patient De Vries, the geographically remote Ted Gardiner, the devoted Jap Gude, and, of course, his pride and joy, Rosemary. Henry Brandon, in a 1956 interview, was still finding proof of Thurber's "warm heart" but "angry mind." The angry mind seemed to have the upper hand more and more often. He was becoming a professional curmudgeon.

After his death, which began with a massive brain hemorrhage from the blood tumor and ended with pneumonia, it was suspected that several years earlier he had begun to suffer barely noticeable, apoplectic-type attacks; his frequent onsets of anger and high excitement may have been related to recurring arteriosclerosis, affecting the supply of blood and nourishment to the brain. His uncontrolled explosions of anger now took place when there had been no drinking. John Duncan Miller remembers that in 1952, when he was visiting Thurber in Bermuda, Thurber was going through a similar period of nervous, sudden, and unexplainable fury with everybody, including his best friends. "It was later diagnosed as something like 'an imbalance of lymphatic glands,'" Miller recalls. "When I saw Thurber in London the year he died, he was acting in the same irrational way."

Roger Angell, by now the only editor at the magazine able, or willing, to deal with Thurber, nursed him through the troublesome "The Wings of Henry James" and the eight casuals the magazine accepted during the last two years of Thurber's life. Here and there his writing still showed the incandescence of old, but it was a low glow. The last piece not of the "conversation-with-whiskey" genre, and worthy of afterthought, was a despairing fable called "The Last Clock: A Fable for the Time, Such as It Is, of Man," which appeared in the *New Yorker* of February 21, 1959. It is part of Thurber's doomsday report on the world's civilization teetering on the edge of "was," or oblivion. Time for mankind is running out, symbolized by an ogre who eats all the clocks he can find. Nobody can defend against the ogre, because such specialists as "the psychronologist, the clockonomist, and the clockosopher" explain that the problem doesn't fall within their areas of expertise. An old "inspirationalist" is brought in, but his communicative abilities have dissipated into "a jumble of mumble." "The final experience should not be mummum," he is heard to say. Civilization disappears, along with the last clock. Unlike *The Last Flower*, no struggling frail blossom is found at the end to signal the promise of redemption. A thousand years later, creatures from another planet excavate from the sand a clock, unrecognizable to them, and the document of the old inspirationalist. They read his summary of the best wisdom of our vanished civilization:

> We can make our lives sublime,
> And, departing, leave behind us,
> Mummum in the sands of time.

As Charles Holmes suggests, "What more grotesque epitaph for our civilization could be imagined than a garbled fragment of a second-rate nineteenth-century poem celebrating optimism and moral uplift?" But no point of view issuing from Thurber's restless mind can be considered final. In *Lanterns & Lances*, the book in which "The Last Clock" is published, he writes in the foreword: "We all know that, as the old adage has it, 'It is later than you think.' I touch on that theme myself, as every writer who can think must, but I also say occasionally: 'It is lighter than you think.' In this light, let's not look back in anger, or forward in fear, but around in awareness."

Roger Angell continually extended the hand of conciliation to the cranky, quarrelsome writer he had inherited from editors lacking the strength to deal with Thurber. A palindromist, as Thurber was, Angell would send him such ingenious specimens as "A slut nixes sex in Tulsa." Like the Whites, Angell had appreciated the early *Atlantic* articles on Ross, and wrote Thurber so. He even contributed to Thurber's store of anecdotes about the baffling Ross. At an Algonquin lunch with Ross in 1951, Angell had mentioned Hemingway, and Ross asked, "What about this Hemingway? He any good?" ("Spotty but pretty good in some of the spots," Angell told him.) Ross said he'd "tried to read one of his books once. That one about the First World War."

"*A Farewell to Arms?*" Angell prompted. "Yeah," Ross replied. He couldn't finish it, he said, because the man "kept leaving the war to go to bed with some girl. Well, I was *in* that war, and it wasn't like that at all." (Was he again playing the boob as a put-on for Angell's bemusement, as Jane Grant would have us believe?) Thurber inserted a slightly changed version of this Ross/Angell exchange in his book, unattributed.

Thurber didn't live to see the magazine ignore Ross's pledge that it would never run a column on lawyers, dogs, or baseball. Angell, a true Renaissance man, superb short-story writer and editor, became a premier reporter of baseball for the *New Yorker*. Wolcott Gibbs believes that Ross, a Brooklyn Dodger fan, decided against covering baseball in 1934, when he had just married his second wife, Frances Elie Clark, and took her to a game with Gibbs and Honeycutt. It was her first exposure to baseball. As luck would have it, Gibbs writes Thurber, no fewer than six foul balls landed in their box, convincing Frances that the point of the game was to kill the customers. She never attended another.

In his last awful months, Thurber could accept neither editing nor rejection of his pieces, blaming the magazine and not his dwindling powers. One yearns for a sound-minded Thurber who, until the last, would prove that magazine humor was alive and well by continuing to write it. S. J. Perelman was the last of the old guard still willing to do battle for the cause. Claiming to be writing "The Child's Life of Bennett Cerf" on his eighty-three-acre farm in Bucks County, Pennsylvania, Perelman realized television and movies were siphoning off the current generation of humorists from the print media. Of the usual six-man team of TV gag writers, he says, "they are well paid, but their work has no permanence." Asked what he considered to be the funniest thing in the world, he replied, "A middle-aged man trying to earn his living." The saddest? "The same thing." He ran out his life doing his best to illustrate it.

"Thurber's copy often came in clean and poor," says Angell. "One of his pieces we couldn't run because it said humor was dying; we didn't believe it, and we couldn't help him say it. The rejects upset him. When he was good, he was as good as he'd ever been, but his judgment as to *what* was good was faltering. He felt all the editors here had to agree before we'd buy something, but, actually, if any one of us gave a piece a favorable vote, it went straight to Shawn. I admired him for continuing to write, but he tried to bully me. He'd shout and carry on. 'Do you know who I am?' he'd yell at me over the phone. 'I sat at the Long Table at *Punch!*' Once Shawn pulled me aside in the corridor and asked me, 'Do you think Thurber is crazy?' Word of the grief he was causing us got around; my assistant, a young woman with a convent upbringing, once saw Thurber coming down the hall, flattened herself against the wall as he passed and stuck her tongue out at him. *The Years with Ross* made matters worse; he seemed to be saying, 'I saved the *New Yorker* from the bumpkin who founded it.' "

In the end, Thurber had no real friend at the *New Yorker* except De Vries, who was there only two days a week. He had never been easy to edit. Eleanor Gould Packard, a principal copyeditor for fifty years, recalls: "When I was new and innocent, working on copy, I found the word 'raunchy' in a Thurber piece, a word I'd never heard of, so I changed it to 'paunchy.' That was in 1945 or 1946, when we used such words. Weekes told me later I was almost fired. Years later, Thurber wrote in a piece that someone 'had a sense of false security.' I got up my courage and made it 'a false sense of security.' I was too timid to query him directly but was told he accepted it; I think he was embarrassed.

"My big triumph was when he wrote that 'facetiously' was the only word that had all six vowels in order. I pointed out that there was also 'abstemiously.' He had to accept it. I heard that once when I queried something of Thurber's, he asked, 'Who is this Eleanor Gould?' and was told, 'She's Freddie Packard's wife,' and he said, 'Well, they probably deserve each other.' I still tell that one."

The legend of a villainous Thurber continues to live on at the *New Yorker* today. Garrison Keillor, then a *New Yorker* contributor, in a theater appearance in Columbus, referred to Thurber as "mean-spirited." Rosemary Thurber was upset by the remark: "One thing my father never was, was mean-spirited," she says. Asked about it, Keillor writes that, "as for [Thurber's] 'mean-spiritedness,' I have only indirect knowledge, mostly from people here who felt that *The Years with Ross* was fiction and didn't credit Ross nearly enough for intelligence and taste." This nearly thirty-three years after the book was published and three decades after Thurber's death. Emily Hahn might have added to her "We outrage easily over here" that "We never forget the outrage, either."

Always glad to help sell his books, Thurber joined in publicizing *The Years with Ross*. He was still the delight of interviewers. "I always have seven or eight things started," he told Maurice Dolbier. "I say if a writer has a block, he ought to write on it." He told Rod Nordell, of the *Christian Science Monitor*, that he next planned a work on the letter "P": "The most fascinating letter of the alphabet—the letter of pixies like Peter Pan, Punch, Peg O' My Heart, and Pooh; of pathfinders and searchers like Ponce de Leon, Percival and Peary; of curious animals like the panda, penguin and poodle, ptarmigan and pterodactyl." Trivia? "I waste my time on it. . . . Everything can't be gloria mundi; a humorist can't take himself too seriously."

He appeared successfully on the Jack Paar TV program. To those asking about the life of the unsighted, he would give his standard reply: "The imagination doesn't go blind," and "I can still *hear* a pretty girl." His attitude toward his sightlessness left both friend and foe in awe. As Frank Sullivan said, upon Thurber's death:

> Blindness came upon him in early middle age. It meant a total readjustment of his life. It meant the curtailment, and finally abandonment, of the drawings which had become as great a part of his fame as his writing. The ordeal would have broken a lesser man or thrown him into despair. It did not break Thurber. It was a challenge, and he rode out to meet it, and he did battle with it, and he *won*. I have been reading the letters he wrote me over the years, half of them dictated since the loss of his sight. There is not a complaint or a hint of self-pity in any of them, nor a reference to his troubles.

He was more concerned with the troubles of the world. Frances Glennon, of *Life*, interviewed him in Cornwall in the summer of 1960. "He was still talking about McCarthy," she says, "and was much too intense on the subject of Red China. He exuded great gloom, and Helen called me the next day to ask me not to take him seriously. 'He's not as despairing a man as all that,' she said. I got the impression of how difficult it was for Thurber to live a personal life along with a creative one; that it was a burden being that fertile. He praised Ross—said he knew he had to have an editor like that, and he extolled Katharine White for the good taste she brought to the magazine, which Thurber considered to be the most important reason for its success."

He may have momentarily decided on prudence after the repercussions from his *Small World* appearance. His resentment of Katharine was somehow necessary to his fondness for White. There seems only one instance in which he expressed confidentially in writing what he felt about her. In 1958, Edmund Wilson, after having read the *Atlantic* articles, wrote Thurber:

> Are you planning to include anything about the Ross-Katharine White relationship, which I used to think was the real *New Yorker* axis? (I realize, of course, that this might be hard for you to handle.) They complemented and admired one another. Each had his respective way of scaring and impressing the other. Their relations were, I thought, quite

emotional; they seemed to go from crisis to crisis. As . . . Gibbs or somebody said, Katharine's prestige in the office was probably based on the fact that she was the member of the staff who had a *Bulfinch's Mythology* at home, and she must have inspired in Ross the same kind of deep respect as that teacher of his early days who had given him his reverence for the serial comma. I always felt that the real riddle of the *New Yorker* was whether its elegance and literary correctitude represented some genuine ideal of Ross's or were entirely the creation of Katharine and the rest of you.

Thurber replies:

The story of K.S.W. is one of my most difficult and sensitive areas, as you had figured it must be. Both of them are so touchy and so sick all the time that I have to handle them with surgeon's gloves. . . . I thought Ross completely over valued her ability in most areas, but especially as a rewrite editor. I told him so as early as 1927, but it wasn't until about five years before he died that he said to me, "She sits out there and gives me that copy desk editing." He had to find out everything for himself and it took a long time. She was valuable in the area of contacts with some writers, and certainly took the buck a thousand times in dealing with Woollcott and other problem adults Ross avoided. . . . He once said to me, "Everybody's afraid of Mrs. White." When I told her that three years ago she burst into tears. She used to cry every time the four of us got together and I said anything true about the office. She was afraid I was going to betray the whole place when I talked frankly to Frank Gibney who wrote the 1955 NEWSWEEK piece on *The New Yorker*.

His publishers sponsored a publication party at the Algonquin on June 3, 1959. Thurber had given them a list of nearly a hundred and fifty people to invite. He said he had had fifty-five copies of *The Years with Ross* sent to people on the *New Yorker* but received responses from only nine. Many of the staff followed Shawn's example of neither acknowledging receipt of the book nor crossing the street to the party, but the Algonquin could hardly accommodate all those who did turn up. Helen beside him, Thurber's hand shot out as she identified each guest, or as they announced themselves—Rea Irvin, Frank Sullivan, the Van Dorens, most of his Cornwall circle, and more than a hundred others. Earl Wilson covered the occasion for his syndicated column:

Tall and lean and gray, seeing little through his heavy glasses, [Thurber] leaned over his cigarette and his Scotch at a small table in the Algonquin Rose Room, greeting each of the great names brought up.

"It's Marc, Marc Connelly," shouted one, bending close. "Write another book."

"It's Buck," sang out playwright Russel Crouse . . .

Jim smiled, pawed through his . . . pockets for matches.

On they came. Ogden Nash, Margaret Case Harriman, Charles Addams. . . . He disclaimed the fame. "When [my daughter] was in college, her chemistry professor asked her 'Are you by any chance related to Professor Clarence Thurber of the Department of Chemistry at Dartmouth?' "

"A group of us went on to Costello's afterwards," says Margaret Case Harriman. "I sat next to Thurber, the master himself. We were full of Little, Brown's food and booze and stayed up until dawn damning publishers to hell."

The book was on the best-seller lists by June 14. Russel Crouse called it "a brilliant book. Catching Ross on paper must have been something like catching a tornado with a butterfly net. No one but Thurber and his warm detachment could have done it. It is fortunate for the history of American letters that it was he who did." Edmund Wilson wrote him, "Both as a literary portrait and a history of journalism it will certainly become a classic." Dorothy Parker, who was reviewing books for *Esquire,* said, "Only God or James Thurber could have invented Ross." A tabloid columnist found the book "as dull as *The New Yorker*—almost, that is," giving credence to Alistair Cooke's comment: "Stop by the National Press Club in Washington, and in no time at all you'll hear first-class journalists being maligned by third-class journalists."

Asked his thoughts about *The Years with Ross,* Shawn replied gravely, "That falls in an area I'm not sure I want to discuss. I'll talk it over with my colleagues, as well as how I feel about Thurber's charges that the *New Yorker* has changed." There was no follow-up. When *The Years with Ross* was published, Shawn ran a "Briefly Noted" review in a June 1959 issue of the *New Yorker:* "A memoir of Mr. Thurber's long association with the late Harold W. Ross, founder and first editor of *The New Yorker.* Since most of the book necessarily revolves about *The New Yorker,* the editors feel that for obvious reasons it does not lend itself to review in these pages." (Eight years before, Kramer's book, which revolved around nothing but the *New Yorker,* was reviewed and dismissed in those pages for not having been written by an insider.) Shawn provided Thurber with a decent burial in the obituary he wrote upon Thurber's death, and, in his long appreciation of Ross in Gill's *Here at The New Yorker*, he gives the devil his due: "In the early days, a small company of writers, artists and editors—E. B. White, James Thurber, Peter Arno and Katharine White among them—did more to make the magazine what it is than can be measured." But he could have had nobody but Thurber in mind when he goes on to say:

> Occasionally, when contemporaries of Ross talked about the old days on *The New Yorker*, one got the impression that he did very little to create it or run it—that in spite of his inadequacies, and somehow over his protest, a number of other people did what was necessary to put out the magazine each week. The implication was that Ross spent much of his time getting in the way of the talented people who worked for him.

Thurber plagued Shawn with rambling proposals for articles, including one on ghosts—he had been certain of their existence ever since "the night the ghost got in." He believed firmly in extrasensory perception and in the occult. He planned an article on that subject, too, involving Henry James's "The Turn of the Screw." He would doubtless have seen spectral evidence in Shawn's dying in 1992, at age eighty-five, on December 8, Thurber's birthday.

The favorable American reviews of his book led Thurber to suppose that he had nothing to worry about from abroad—the English had always pampered him and his work. One review, he had been told, would be written by Kenneth Tynan, who had become a *New Yorker* critic and who had met and liked Thurber in London. Thurber had written White about Tynan's new role on the magazine, swiping at the *New Yorker*—and indirectly at Katharine—on his way by: "We have both known Kenneth Tynan for several years and all I can say is that he is really going to be something. . . . Tynan is a brilliant writer, and perfect for the New Yorker, but he knows more than our editors and proof-readers, and I don't know how long he can stand their stupidity and their heckling and their changes." To Roger Angell, he had dismissed the few negative American reviews of *The Years with Ross* with the comment that "critical estimate at its best often shows up abroad." He had recently told the British journalist Henry Brandon: "My love of London and of England is inherited from somewhere. . . . I still feel a sense of 'getting home' when I get to London, to England. It is a country where you can hear bells ring."

As it happened, Tynan, Rebecca West, and J. B. Priestley all skewered *The Years with Ross* in London reviews, and Thurber's long emotional gravitation to the English seemed slated for redirection. His paranoia by then could outstrip John O'Hara's; to find any fault with him or his work was betrayal of the worst order. He took it out on Hamish Hamilton, his British publisher:

> We have been chilled by the British reception of the book and the reviews of Rebecca West, Tynan and Priestley, mindless, arrogant, and outrageous. . . . My love of England and London are cooling. I don't mind attack. I've had it here from Dawn Powell, Granville Hicks, and a few others, but 95% have been from excellent to wonderful. Maybe a truly good and honest book is bound to get a beating from imbeciles and decaying egos. . . .
>
> The bald and sick and insulting assumption of West, Tynan, and Priestley that they knew Ross and that I didn't seems infamous to me and somehow menacing. . . .
>
> I have been cheered a little by notes from . . . others, deploring especially the West attack. Ross did keep up a long correspondence with her, but it long ago began to get him down. . . . All my friends, and even strangers, are at a loss to understand Tynan's review, especially his "proof" that Ross had a sense of humor which I did not bring out. . . . People over here are cracking up, too, and the end is probably not far off.

Something comparable to an Old Girl Network—Janet Flanner, Jane Grant, Katharine, and others—made the negative review of *The Years with Ross* by Rebecca West its center of common opposition. West thanks Katharine for her warm endorsement of the review, adding that she was appalled by Thurber's "sourness of spirit," and tells Katharine, "I had some inkling of what you tell me out of your great knowledge—that the book does great injustice to others than Ross. . . . I loathe Thurber for doing this; and yet that he should have done it, with those gifts, suggests there is an underlying tragedy so that I can't even have undiluted consolation in loathing him." Jane Grant allowed that the book was funny "but exasperating when presented as a reality. Buffoonery, like beauty, may be in the eye of the beholder."

Though the Whites were complimented by several readers on the respect and affection Thurber had shown them in the book, Katharine would have none of it; it was what he had omitted about Andy, she explains fifteen years later to a biographer: "You say that 'Andy was a sacred cow' with Jim. I don't agree with that at all. . . . I think he really tends to downgrade the importance of Andy's work on the magazine and also the importance of News-breaks, which Jim called 'trivial.' "

Newsbreaks, those reprintings of errors in typesetting or grammar—usually from newspapers pressured by daily deadlines—appealed to Ross, and White enjoyed writing the taglines, which had to be snide to be funny. They also served as convenient devices for Carmine Peppe's page makeup. As Gill points out, no writer was ever asked to cut or add to fit a column; newsbreaks could always pad it out. With the emergence of computer-assisted composing, the number of such errors dwindled, and the current *New Yorker* seems in the process of phasing out newsbreaks altogether. Katharine's love for Andy would have underscored the importance of anything he did. "He finds [news-breaks] a valuable view of the whole nation and a comment on its social habits," she writes—surely as breathtaking a notion as it is endearing.

She was correct that Thurber shortchanged White with a hasty description of Andy's Notes and Comments as only "having an influence on local or even wider affairs." "This is, to me, the most outrageous part in the whole book," Katharine notes in her copy of the Ross volume. "If there ever was a false and belittling statement, this is it. [Andy] accomplished a great deal more than Jim said," she told the biographer. "*The Wild Flag* has some of Andy's best Comments on world government, and while he doesn't agree with all of them now, they have helped to change the public's view to a good extent about our responsibilities in the world." Quite so, and to this it could be added that White's Comments have lightened and changed for the better editorial writing everywhere. It's possible that a self-transfixed Thurber, busy trying to get the book out, simply hadn't given the matter much thought.

The long, warm correspondence between White and Thurber was already in jeopardy. Thurber's diatribes against Ross and the *New Yorker* had been tactless but worried efforts not to win White to his point of view but to justify his own. His repeated insistences to White of the value he put on their friendship were of an almost desperate sincerity. But whether or not because of Katharine's unhappiness with Thurber, White, who usually found any grudge too heavy a load to bear for long, began to see Thurber's letters to him as "patronizing." He believed that Thurber had undergone a personality change prior to his blindness; that his verbal attacks on Katharine had begun, for reasons he couldn't try to explain, after Thurber's marriage to Helen. "I felt he was jealous of me toward the end," White says, "very competitive." True, Thurber had begun comparing the number of honorary degrees he and White received, and White was the hands-down winner: Harvard, Yale, Colby, Dartmouth, Bowdoin, Hamilton, the universities of Vermont and Maine (nearly all the degrees modestly accepted in absentia). And in his diatribe to Hawley Truax, Thurber reminds him of all that he had done for the *New Yorker*—"even more than Andy." "It wasn't that Thurber felt his and White's writings were in competition," says James Geraghty. "White's trademark was style; Thurber's was many other things. I always thought what Thurber resented about White was White's virtuousness of character. But at the end Thurber was seeing everything through a distorted glass, so who knows?"

White could be kept upset in such matters only by what kept his wife upset, and in his old age, according to Linda H. Davis, Katharine's biographer, it wasn't Thurber about whom White groused after a martini, but Gill, who in his memoirs had described Katharine as "formidable." The adjective had reduced her to days of suffering, though Gill managed somewhere to make the point that in the long run it was good for the magazine that it applied. ("Katharine was as formidable as a yellow warbler," White wrote in a defensive and lovely testament of love for Katharine after her death.)

Katharine was never able to forgive Thurber. Three years before her death, she wrote to Helen, refusing to support her in condemning a somewhat jeering biography-in-progress of Thurber. In her letter, Katharine agrees with Andy that Thurber was not an alcoholic, "just a very bad drinker in some periods of his life, as you must know, having seen his two attacks on me late in the evening after he had had a lot of drinks. One happened on East 38th Street in that furnished rented apartment we took when called back from Maine by Ross during the second World War; and the other, when you and Jim and Andy and I happened to be in London at the same time. . . . I shall always cherish the memory of Jim's early friendship and try to forgive his later animosities to me and *The New Yorker*."

To others, she does her best to rise above her lasting anger with him. After pages of faulting him over the Ross book, fourteen years after its publication, she adds:

> Jim could be so wonderful and also such a wonderful friend, as he was to me in the 1920's when I had been struggling for seven years over a bad marriage, that I feel horrible to write down these things about his book. I also admire him for his spirit as a man going blind, and as a blind man. He was the least *blind* blind man I ever knew, and the most independent. He should be given great tribute for that. I think he will live forever in American letters both as a writer and an artist.

Columbus and the *Dispatch* would be the next important components that an ailing and chronically irritable Thurber would try to kick out of his history. In November 1959, the Thurbers traveled to Columbus, where Thurber was to receive a Headliner Award from the Press Club of Ohio. He was drawn there upon learning that the ten other award recipients included Milton Caniff, the golfer Jack Nicklaus, a retired U.S. Supreme Court justice, Eddie Rickenbacker, Bob Feller, legendary pitcher of the Cleveland Indians, the general manager of the Indians, track star Jesse Owens, and one or two titans of industry. The occasion began well enough. At dinner with the Ted Gardiners, Thurber was at his amusing best, telling of the time he found a piece of rubber in his scrambled eggs ("I'm afraid the chef has been kicking up his heels again, sir"). But at the black-tie ceremonies at the Neil House, of the eleven media reporters given "news awards," all but one of the recipients were from Columbus newspapers and a local TV station. This gave an inebriated Thurber the erroneous impression that he was only being recognized by the Columbus Press Club.

"Jim felt duped, foolish, and annoyed," says Patricia McGuckin, Gardiner's daughter and a *Dispatch* reporter. "Liquor didn't help. He visited the *Dispatch* and talked rather insultingly to the staff. In his hotel suite, with journalists sitting at his feet, a female reporter from the *Dispatch* decided to bait him and said, 'I read your book on Charlie Ross and didn't like it.' The result was a flash fire of invective against the press club and the entire staff of the *Dispatch* and its conservative editorial policy. He ended by shouting, 'The only one who can write a decent story on your newspaper is Patty McGuckin!' I'd been working for the paper for no more than a month, and felt very self-conscious around the newsroom for the next few days."

Thurber's old friend George Smallsreed, the *Dispatch* managing editor, was so angered that he vowed that not another line on Thurber would appear in his paper. This presented a problem to Virginia Hall Trannette seven weeks later, when *A Thurber Carnival*, the new musical revue, was to begin its road tryout at the Hartman Theater in Columbus. Trannette was handling publicity for the theater. Thurber was with the show as consultant and script doctor. The advance publicity stressed that Columbus could be considered the center of national theatrical and literary interest during the show's weeklong engagement. The mayor had agreed to proclaim a "James Thurber Week" in Columbus. Then Governor Mike DiSalle made it "James Thurber Week" for all of Ohio.

"All this put Smallsreed on the spot," says Trannette. "Thurber could be so charming when he wanted to be, and just awful at other times. He had gotten into that silly mess with the *Dispatch* when he was drinking and told everybody off, and we needed all the media publicity we could get. Smallsreed was still mad and said the *Dispatch* wasn't interested in the Thurber revue. Thurber wouldn't apologize. I nearly went crazy with the two of them acting like big babies. I finally blew my stack and told Smallsreed that the opening of a future Broadway play in his city, its author recognized by mayor and governor, was *news* and that he was acting like a fool. Smallsreed gave in. I then got to Thurber and told him he'd better behave himself, and that if I had to keep an eye on him, I'd even accompany him to the bathroom to prevent his damaging the press relations I'd finally mended for the moment."

This second black-tie event was a publicity success, if not a dramatic one —more work was needed on the show.

Thurber's downward spiral of the spirit had been mercifully arrested when Haila Stoddard, the revue's producer, came into his life with a proposal that certain of his writing and cartoons be strung together, complete with original music, as a stage production. Not only that, she had a coproducer, Helen Bonfils, who was happy and able to invest risk capital in Broadway productions; if they flopped, they were still splendid tax deductions. Ever since *The Male Animal*, Thurber had missed the hectic life of getting a play staged on Broadway. He had been struggling fruitlessly for years with his incompleted plays, and must have known during his moments of truth that nothing would come of them. He had envied Elliott Nugent his roles as actor and had hinted strongly that he had wanted to replace Nugent as Tommy Turner in *The Male Animal*, should Nugent have had reason to give up the part. As it would turn out, he would play himself in *A Thurber Carnival* on Broadway, for the last three months of its run.

"That meant as much to him as almost anything else that happened in his life," Helen says. It was Walter Mitty awakening from dream to reality, and discovering that they were one and the same.

"I'd loved Thurber's work for years," says Stoddard, "and, working with him, I learned to love him. One of my great personal satisfactions was to have helped give him what everyone agrees was probably the happiest year of his life."

70

That Ultimate Concern

We had lunch at the Algonquin with Dorothy Parker, Mr. & Mrs. Edmund Wilson, and their ten-year-old daughter, Helen. Then Wilson asked us . . . to his hotel for drinks at six. . . . Wilson was in bed by eight, but Helen and I went on to Tim's and had whiskey. . . .

We all decided that Ben Hecht was right, for once, when he said in his book about MacArthur that Charley thought he could act the same way in his fifties and sixties as he had in his thirties. Wilson even agreed on this, as he put away his highball and reached for another. I'm older than he is but can keep on going longer. . . . I found that whiskey keeps . . . my mind off my problems, which are mainly thoughts and feelings of what Tillich of Harvard calls "the ultimate concern." Even if death is 15 years away, it is just around the corner.

—Letter to John O'Hara, May 6, 1958

Wilson describes the reunion as resembling a gathering of Civil War veterans. "Thurber seems blinder than ever, one eye is quite gray, and his hair is completely white." It depressed Wilson to be sitting in the room "where the Round Table had once been," and to remember the time a group of them had sat there, on the same side of a long table, their backs to the wall, when Dorothy Parker described them as looking like "a road company of the Last Supper." "Some of Dorothy's stories had been lately rejected by *The New Yorker*," Wilson writes, "and some of Thurber's pieces also. They regarded *The New Yorker* in its present phase as something alien to them."

At Wilson's hotel apartment, later that day, "The Thurbers and I . . . gave *The New Yorker* a thorough hashing-over. Helen Thurber is extremely good at handling Jim—steers him by the elbow and guides his hand when he is shaking hands. He makes a point of looking at the person he is talking to, so you forget he doesn't see you; and it is as if she made a point of having her own eyes especially responsive in order to make up for his blindness."

Thurber once explained that he looked "straight at the person I'm talking to" because "it makes them feel better. Of course . . . Helen has to yell at me if they get up and go away, which they are sometimes likely to do . . . when I'm telling a real good story. You feel . . . foolish talking to an empty room. Even Helen isn't always too helpful. I got to the end of a great story . . . one day and expected at least a laugh. She'd gone into the bathroom . . . and all I got was the familiar domestic gurgle of running water."

Thurber's show-off letters to O'Hara and others reveal the very thing he hoped they would conceal—his fear of what lay ahead. "He had no intention of being the grand old man of letters," says Jean Lobrano, "but was determined to keep going till the end."

He did. *The Years with Ross* was still on the best-seller lists when Haila Stoddard persuaded him to let her string her favorites of Thurber's writing and drawing into a musical revue. Stoddard, an actress, was performing in the daytime TV serial "Secret Storm." "I'd been reading Thurber since I was ten years old," she says, "and could visualize some of his pieces on the stage." She roughed out a script, which she showed her friend Elliott Nugent, who called Thurber. Thurber invited her to read it to him and Helen in their Algonquin suite. "He said he'd turned down many others who wanted to do the same thing," says Stoddard, "but that I'd selected his own favorites, and he liked how I'd arranged them. He told me, 'I never thought until now my pieces would come off the page onto the stage. You can have the rights to them.'

"My wealthy Denver friend, Helen Bonfils, [who] had always been interested in the theater, told me she'd be my coproducer and that I could have all the money I needed. She liked to back entrepreneurial things that didn't work, for fun and tax purposes, and was upset when they made money."

It took three hundred and fifty thousand dollars to bring A *Thurber Carnival* to Broadway. "It would have had to run a year to a full house to get the money back," says Stoddard. "It ran for eight months, was never a sell-out, but, in the end, made money for the investors—including Bonfils, much to her annoyance. I selected Burgess Meredith to direct and stage it. I knew he was a friend of Thurber's and had directed Gibbs's *Season in the Sun*. I wanted someone who cared about Thurber's work as much as I. There wasn't a word in the final production that wasn't Thurber's."

The tryouts began in Columbus on January 7, 1960. Thurber told a reporter that the cast was amazed that a man could come back to his hometown without being greeted by the sheriff and men with shotguns. Thurber and Meredith spent early afternoons in a hotel room reworking the sketches, Thurber dictating to a production secretary, Elinor Wright. "Thurber had to O.K. every word," says Stoddard. "He'd complain that 'I did all these things originally before I was forty-five,' when he had had a different mindset. His rewrites were never quite as good as the originals, and he always knew it. His only new skit was of the men who got drunk in the department store while their wives shopped. He didn't get angry when his rewrites didn't work. He was a pro, but he didn't want to feel he was no longer as talented, either. Helen kept peace, made sure Thurber got enough sleep and food. They were both very happy with what was happening."

"Thurber had been falling into bad shape, physically and mentally, by the end of 1959," says Jap Gude. "The revue restored him to professional behavior. He was obsessed with rewriting, though. He'd dictate overnight changes from memory and bring them in the next afternoon, worn out, but always in time for rehearsal."

A reporter from the *Theatre* magazine describes such an instance:

> Mr. Thurber walked carefully down the aisle holding tightly to his wife's bent elbow. He smiled and sat down in the second row. . . . He handed Mr. Meredith some typewritten pages.
>
> The director took them and sat among his cast on stage.
>
> "Here are some thoughts Jim has given us for the second part of the sketch," he said.
>
> "You don't have to read it if you think it is awful," Thurber, the man who is generally conceded to be our greatest living humorist, called up timidly.
>
> "I think it's fine, fine," Mr. Meredith insisted. He began reading the revision and the cast listened intently. When he was through he called down to the author, "Why don't we run through the second part the way you wrote it originally and then you can see which you like better?"
>
> "Of course," Mr. Thurber answered. . . . The cast began the performance—acting it out this time. They went through it smoothly and it came out a smart, amusing, thoroughly professional scene. When it was finished, Thurber had the last word.
>
> "It's good, no question it's better than my second version."
>
> The cast members smiled and Burgess Meredith was obviously pleased.

"We'd ask him for two or three lines and he'd come back with two or three pages," Stoddard says. Helen agreed. "Ask him for a new line and he writes a new act," she told Earl Wilson.

On January 5, 1960, two days before the show opened in Columbus, Thurber was ushered into Mayor Ralston Westlake's office to receive the city's first citation of its kind, naming him "a distinguished native son." Photographers wanted Thurber to pose reading the citation, many not realizing he was blind. ("Blind Author Regains Sight in City Hall!" Thurber suggested as their headline.) At the state capitol, Governor Mike DiSalle, in a televised ceremony, read to Thurber his proclamation of James Thurber Week in Ohio, prompting Thurber to write a piece for the *Dispatch* on the need to care for one's eyes. "I felt the week should in some way be turned into something larger than a person's private enterprises," Thurber explained to the press.

Opening night was attended by more than sixteen hundred people, including both of Thurber's brothers. The reviews were favorable. Stoddard was skeptical. "There's too much Thurber adulation around Columbus," she said. "We'll know better what line changes and cuts to make in the other cities."

The show moved on to Detroit, Cleveland, St. Louis, Cincinnati, and Pittsburgh, and the Thurbers went with it. In press interviews, Burgess Meredith stuck to promoting the revue, pointing out its unique mechanical wonders—three huge turntables and a treadmill, while Thurber used most of the publicity opportunities to air his usual angst over the nature of mankind and its culture. He warned Charlotte Curtis, of the *Columbus Citizen-Journal,* and other journalists, of American complacency, congressional investigations, corruption of the language by politicians, the decline of comedy (the fault of the sponsors and producers of television shows), the inadequacy of the American school system, brutality on TV, Madison Avenue's belief that Americans are universally without taste, the reluctance of women to become involved in civic matters, the retrogression of American literature and art, and the replacement of comedy with farce—all this the usual agenda. Thurber would remain the professional curmudgeon and self-appointed guardian of the culture the rest of his days.

Asked about the adaptation of his stories to television, he said that he thought they were providing a relief from the crime shows and Westerns— letting "kids know that when you order a drink in a saloon you don't get shot in the stomach."

When *A Thurber Carnival* was judged to be nearly ready for Broadway, Thurber announced that "my chances of throwing ashtrays now are greatly reduced." The show opened in New York at the ANTA Theater, on February 22, 1960. A worn-out Thurber was backstage on opening night, and at its conclusion refused to acknowledge the "Author! Author!" calls from the audience, asking to be taken home instead. Thinking he was being led out the street door, he found himself onstage and forced to mumble something like, "We like you and we're glad you like us."

Though the reviews never led to a box office stampede, they were very favorable. *Newsweek* anointed *A Thurber Carnival* "the funniest show in town." Walter Kerr of the *Trib* was grateful for Thurber's "sociological report" that "takes sex—and a few other subjects—seriously." John Chapman of the *Daily News*, Alton Cook of the *World-Telegram,* and Charles Wagner of the *Mirror* all expressed their enjoyment. Brooks Atkinson of the *Times* called it "the freshest and the funniest show of the year." Even the dyspeptic John McCarten of the *New Yorker* admitted that he had enjoyed himself, leading to a late-blooming friendship with the Thurbers.

In April, Thurber and Helen took the train to Columbus, where Helen delivered Thurber's remarks at the dedication of Denney Hall. It was inevitable, she quoted him as saying, that he and Nugent would pattern the dean of English, in *The Male Animal,* "upon the length and light of Joe Denney," who had held high the torch of academic freedom. Alumni Secretary Jack Fullen gave a party for the Thurbers afterward, at which Thurber held the floor for four hours. He was adept at cutting short someone trying to edge him out of the spotlight: "You are aware, of course," he would interrupt, "that the Throckmorton Report disposed of that point definitely, quite contrary to the point you are making." Reference to nonexistent documentation usually retired the victim to the safety of silence.

From the Neil House, he dictated a description of the event to Kenneth Tynan, whose review of *The Years with Ross* he had decided to overlook:

> We are going back to New York alive tonight. It was a series of ordeals this time all in one day, a luncheon at the faculty club at which I sat on the right of President Novice Fawcett (shake hands with Wragford Novice), and then the dedication of Denney Hall, the new Arts and Science Building, named in honor of one of the truly first rate scholars, teachers and gentlemen of his time, which was my time in the university too. . . . Having been sick in bed for a month, I didn't have time to finish my speech and learn it too, so Helen . . . read it for me, in a very moving performance, the day was hers. Then came the reception and for some reason there wasn't a dry palm in the damn line of 70 women I shook hands with. My daughter tells me that all girls have moist hands nowadays on account of everything. [Rosemary, of course, had told him no such thing.]

It was the last time he would visit Columbus. He donated his speaker's honorarium to the university and that August sent Fullen a check for a lifetime membership in the O.S.U. Alumni Association. He could afford it. Though the week of June 25, for example, shows A *Thurber Carnival* grossing only $26,100 in a theater with a $49,178 weekly capacity, it was earning $4,000 a week for Thurber. Also, Peter Sellers's movie, *The Battle of the Sexes*, based on "The Catbird Seat," was released in April, its purchase having added to the Thurber coffers.

Tom Ewell, one of the original cast, was frequently threatening to quit, says Haila Stoddard. "He was convinced that Burgess Meredith would sooner or later want to play his part." Once, when Ewell's threat had to be taken seriously, Elliott Reid, a young actor who played comedy well, was asked to try out for the part. "We convened at Bonfils's apartment on the East River," he recalls. "Thurber was really gracious. I was impressed with his independence of movement. He smoked constantly, touched the ashtray, remembered where it was, and addressed the voices he heard. I was reminded that he was blind only when a person changed position in the room and Thurber continued to speak, looking at where the person had last been. 'Over here, Jim,' he'd be told.

"I read from 'The Night the Bed Fell,' and when I was leaving, Thurber called me back and said, 'I didn't think I could hear this material again and feel it come alive, but you did it for me. I think I'll make you my official reader.' As it turned out, Ewell stayed with the show, but Thurber's generosity that evening made the experience one I've never forgotten."

The illness mentioned in the Tynan letter was a throat virus contracted on the road tour. Its persistence led him to send out somewhat impatient letters refusing speaking engagements, article requests, and information to students asking about his life and work. He lectures one O.S.U. professor with arguments that could be applied to Thurber's own practices:

> I agree with E. B. White that there are too many interviews, too many extensive offhand babblings on all subjects, and far too much photography. It shocks me to realize that if I did not turn down such projects as yours I would never get anything else done. We are passing rapidly into an oral and photographic culture, in which the printed page may be lost forever, along with thought and meditation. Photographers and interviewers have driven me crazy for two years now, and I have resolutely decided not to be photographed or interviewed again.

Hardly. He had soon resumed his cooperative ways. A speech to ANTA—
on the crisis of comedy in the theater—was reprinted in the *New York Times*.
He was interviewed for a *Life* article that summer. His weight was a hundred
and eighty pounds, and many who met him for the first time, acquainted only
with his drawings, were surprised to see a tall, bushy-haired man, wearing
heavy spectacles. "I'm supposed to be bald and five feet, one," he told Frances
Glennon, "and people are always disillusioned when they see me. Everyone
thinks I should look like the man I draw. I draw the *spirit* of the man I am.
I'm a pussycat." But in an earlier *Life* article that year he was saying, "I'm not
mild and gentle. Let the meek inherit the earth—they have it coming to
them. I get up mad at something every morning and think I should. I used to
wake up at four a.m. and start sneezing, sometimes for five hours. I tried to
find out what sort of allergy I had but finally came to the conclusion that it
must be an allergy to consciousness."

He listened to Carlton Fredericks's morning radio advice on health. "He
went along with Fredericks on antifluoridation of water," Dr. Engel, the
Thurbers' dentist, says, "even though his teeth weren't good; I'd have to treat
him three times a year. I pleaded with him not to write an article on it. He
claimed to know more about diets than dentists; more about psychiatry than
psychiatrists. He was a food faddist; he drank fig juice. He was a pleasant guy
to talk to. He used to break me up with Thurberisms. I'd try to repeat them to
my wife and lay an egg every time. Only he could do it. Helen complained
about her health a great deal. Once she was going on and on to me about her
operations and pains. Thurber could hear her and stuck his head in the door
and said, 'Dr. Engel, didn't you know? She died this summer.' "

Occasionally, especially when depressed, he would telephone Jane Williams in Bermuda. He continued to gloat to her over his physical vitality
compared to that of her ailing husband. In April 1960, after the road tour and
the trip to Columbus, he was writing them both:

> Life is now three times as crowded as it was. It is not easy for a man who
> will be eighty in a little more than fourteen years. I can just hear Ronnie
> wailing, "He doesn't know anything about age. I'm fifty-three years old!"
> Well, it's all a matter of genes and diet . . . as I learn by following the
> radio programs of Dr. Carlton Fredericks. It now seems that my black
> lock [of hair] indicates that I have slowed down the aging process. You
> do this with a heavy intake of the Vitamin B complex, which stimulates
> the pituitary gland. . . . This is tricky, because it can give you the
> illusion of being as young as you were in 1936. . . .

We have been here in New York for the past month and we've got to slow down, black lock or no black lock. I am in close touch with the lunatic fringe, too, for everybody on that wide margin calls up writers and playwrights, or writes them asking for something.

He still talked of his play about Ross, *The Welcoming Arms,* and of an autobiography he intended to call *Long Time, No See.* His better puns and quips were gaining broad currency as epigrams: "One martini is just right; two is too many; three is not enough." Of Soviet officialdom: "Big oafs from little icons grow." Privately delivered was this baseball analogy, offered to De Vries: "Moral: It is better for a man to have two balls on him than two strikes."

Thurber had long since outgrown his awe of college professors and now took on all comers. When a Harvard professor of social relations asked permission to use Thurber's fables for a special class project, Thurber replied, "I cannot believe that any educational purpose would be served by taking my fables apart and rebuilding them in the way you suggest."

My old professor, Joseph Russell Taylor . . . once said: "Intellect is the conventional part of imagination." . . . I regard intellect as exploratory and analytical, but in no true sense creative. At least, it has nothing whatever to do with the creative process that produces imaginative work. My chief antipathy to your plan is aroused by your assumption that the humorous, the moralistic, and the sad are separate values. I have devoted a lifetime to trying to show that humor covers morals, just as, by definition, it is part and parcel of pathos, or sadness, if you will. Sid Perelman's favorite moral is my "Youth will be served, frequently stuffed with chestnuts." You don't have to ponder that very long to see that it combines your falsely disintegrated values. I have never written a fable that was nonsense, and I take it that you regard humor as just that. I have written four or five articles recently . . . sharply mourning and attacking the decline of humor and comedy in a nation that never had much of either. . . . I bewail the forces of thoughtlessness that would create a fragmentation of tragicomedy, for the trend shows up in the state of our theatre and of television and of the novel. Recently, a youngster of eleven, who shows evidences of a wild and mis-aimed tendency to combine intellect and creativity, took apart a fable of mine called "The Princess and the Tin Box." He objected to my invention of "aluminum silicate," for his intellect was fighting his less well developed creative sense. I told him there was also a thing called cranium penetrate, but that it is becoming rare in America. . . .

> Why not see if your students can write fables of their own, or even try
> to discover . . . whether they know what the fables I have written are
> about.

White's infrequent letters to Thurber remained friendly and humorous to
the end. When Andy received a request for permission to reissue *Is Sex
Necessary?* in Sweden, he writes Thurber: "Here's another one of those foreign countries interested in sex. In general, I'm against these projects, being
of a suspicious nature, but I'll go along if you want to. . . . My hunch is that
publishers like the title and don't care how dated the text is. But I don't want
to be a fusspot. There's nothing dated about your drawings, and they are
worth the price of the book no matter what price is put on it."

Thurber continued to torture Cass Canfield, who was still trying to win
him back to the Harper fold, Thurber writing: "I agree with you that one
publisher from now on is the best thing, and it still leaves me with a total of
four. Others keep calling up, too. . . . Planned publisherhood is not the
easiest thing in the world, as you know. It's like planned parenthood—you
can never tell what's going to happen between covers."

In the city, Costello's was now the only after-hours place Thurber liked at
the end of an evening. "He liked V-O whiskey, chopped steak and corned
beef hash," says Emil Stahl, the headwaiter. "Mrs. Thurber drank Ballantine
Scotch. When I'd serve him a drink I'd touch his hand with my little finger
to let him know it was there. Tim used to tell him he was ruining his walls by
drawing on them. If they came in by themselves, they liked others to join
them in a booth. Mrs. Thurber often seemed at a loss as to how to entertain a
blind man by herself. She'd tell me to invite over anyone at the bar I thought
would work out; Thurber would often sing, harmonizing with the college boys
and other customers. I'd always tell Helen when I didn't think certain strangers would be right to join them; sometimes she'd insist, get in a jam, and tell
me later, 'You were right, Emil.' "

"They were both powerful magnets to freeloaders," says Joel Sayre, "because nobody bought the Thurbers a drink in twenty-five years. The Algonquin, '21,' Tim's—all the checks went to Helen."

At the end of May, the Thurbers were having dinner at Maria's restaurant,
on East Fifty-second Street, with friends when a Thurber admirer, a former
magazine editor, introduced herself to Helen. She was invited to have her
dinner with them at their table, and later she invited them to her apartment,
on East Eighty-sixth Street, for drinks. Helen agreed, though Thurber had
wished to go to Costello's. When Thurber learned that Sayre and Arthur
Kober, an earlier *New Yorker* writer, also lived in the building, he asked his

hostess to invite them, too. Thurber was at his funniest, according to the hostess. The Thurbers remained when the others left, and Thurber managed to set fire to a chair while lighting his cigarette. Helen was in a bathroom at the time, and the hostess was in the kitchen. Thurber's frightened calls drew her back into the living room, and after trying to put out the fire, she phoned the Fire Department. Helen, cut off by the smoke, fled to the hall. A panicked Thurber groped his way into a closet before finding another bathroom, where he stuffed a bath mat under the door, opened the window, and put a wet handkerchief over his face. It was Memorial Day weekend, when the usual holiday false alarms slow responses. The firemen found both women in the hallway, and Helen frantically urged them to rescue her husband. A fireman eventually led Thurber to safety. The press coverage was extensive, and Thurber was horribly embarrassed. He told reporters that he hadn't panicked, because he had been through "five or six fires" with his family in Columbus. "My family's house was always quietly burning," he said.

Helen was now placing his pieces—not all of them *New Yorker* rejects—with such periodicals as *Suburbia Today, Saturday Review, Harper's Bazaar,* the *Atlantic, Holiday, Esquire, Theatre Arts,* and *Harper's.* "He had no first reading agreement with us after 1959," Shawn says. "He could have had one but said he didn't think it was fair to accept the bonus that goes with it because he planned to be too busy with *A Thurber Carnival.*" The *New Yorker* published only two Thurber casuals in 1960 and one, its last, in 1961—all of them protesting what current usage was doing to both the "American" and English languages.

A Thurber Carnival was forced to close by an actors' strike, after seventeen weeks. In August, to keep the show intact, Bonfils and Stoddard reopened it in the opera house in Central City, Colorado. The Thurbers were glad to join the cast to escape the summer heat in the East. Helen telephoned Stoddard, back in New York, to report that Eddie Mayehoff, Tom Ewell's replacement, was miscast. A truly funny man, Mayehoff had worked for Meredith in *Season in the Sun,* but it was clear, from audience reaction, that he was not the one to help reopen the show in New York on Labor Day. " 'You'd better get out here,' Helen told me," Stoddard says. "We rehearsed Eddie in his hotel room, and he was better, but on stage he was a fire horse, doing his *shtick.* Burgess stood by him so we left it to Thurber to cast the deciding vote. Thurber was stony quiet; he loved Burgess, cared for me and the project, but maybe because I was young, and a woman, he said, 'I'll have to stand by Burgess.' I said, 'Then kiss it good-bye.' "

In New York, before opening, the cast put on a special show, arranged by Jap Gude, for some television producers. "They hated it," says Stoddard.

"The TV deal fell through. Burgess saw the light. Mayehoff was out. I suggested dividing his parts between Paul Ford and John McGiver, and letting Thurber play the 'File and Forget' sketch. We didn't need a comic in that role but a humorist—an intellectual. No one fitted the bill better than Thurber. Jap Gude was very protective of him, as we talked it over one night at Ruby Foo's. 'The stress and excitement will kill him,' Jap told me. But Thurber was for it. He'd never mentioned wanting to do it before, but he'd always wanted to act. He went on in a couple of days."

Meredith wanted to know if Thurber would have the part memorized in time. "Memorized!" Thurber snorted. "I wrote the goddam thing. I have the whole play memorized." Asked if he were nervous, he replied that audiences didn't make him nervous; he made audiences nervous. As to what kind of performance he would give? "Well, damn it, I'll be as good as Marc Connelly." (Connelly, who occasionally cast himself in his own plays, responded, "Typical impertinence of a junior member of Actors Equity.")

Everybody associated with the revue was on edge when it reopened the night of September 12, 1960. Thurber, playing himself, sitting easily in a white armchair, wearing a jacket, slacks, and tie, was moved to a corner of the stage on the treadmill. Joan Anderson, the secretary (Elinor Wright, his temporary secretary in real life, would eventually play the part), asked, "Are you all right, Mr. Thurber?" "No," he replied, and the audience exploded in laughter. He received crashing applause upon entering, exiting, and at curtain call. He rarely flubbed a line during the run. Once, he "dictated" his home address as "Westport, Connecticut," rather than "West Cornwall," promptly stopped and ad-libbed: "These publishers have me so mixed up I don't even know where I live." It got one of the bigger laughs of the evening.

"The Thurbers were wonderful to everyone," says Daise Terry. " 'Anytime you want a pair of tickets,' they'd tell me. Whenever he came onstage, there were shouts and applause as at a football game. Later I was certain that all that excitement was what brought his ailment to a head."

The show never recovered its momentum after the actors' strike, but it lasted nearly three months, Thurber performing a total of eighty-eight times. "Jim wanted me to handle the publicity when it came back to town," says Dick Maney, "but I knew it was dead. Thurber kept it going longer than it would have without him." Critics re-reviewed the show, with praises for Thurber. Nugent commented: "That S.O.B. has been trying to get on the stage for forty years, to my certain knowledge."

Thurber had expected the play to run until the end of the year, writing the Williamses:

We want . . . a letter from you saying when you can come up here to see "A Thurber Carnival." We shall probably run through December 31 . . . and as I told you, we are going to make your visit a Christmas present, not only tickets to the show, but your air fare and accommodations at the hotel. Tonight I make my 46th appearance on stage and Helen and I do not intend to have you two miss seeing the play. We shall probably open in London with it in February, or a little later, with an all-English cast, except for Thurber as Thurber. Rosie and Fred came on to see the show from Illinois, and we had a fine time with them. In spite of the play and the hundreds of letters I have to answer, Helen and I are putting the final touches on my latest book, "Lanterns and Lances," which contains twenty-four pieces that I somehow managed to write between 1957, when I began the Ross book, and today, when I finished the last piece for the new book. . . . I've also made countless appearances on radio and television and have given out about eleven hundred interviews. This has left me no time at all to chase girls, my only regret. I will be 66 in December, but feel forty-three years younger . . . I am no longer called "Old Totters," but Junior, or Buster, by the older members of Equity.

"We spent five wonderful days up there," says Jane Williams. It was the last time the Williamses would see Thurber, though Helen would resume seasonal visits to Bermuda after his death.

The night the revue closed, Gude, Stoddard, the Thurbers, and the Ted Gardiners, who had come to New York just in time to see the last show, met at Ruby Foo's. "Everything bothered Jim that night," says Stoddard. "He and Helen wondered why Bonfils just couldn't keep the revue going for her tax purposes. She could have, but it would have ended the show in a humiliating way, with maybe only two hundred people in the audiences, or fewer. The gloss and glory of the revue would be sacrificed. It had been a glorious experience, but it had had its time." Says Ted Gardiner of that final performance: "It was the last time Jim was doing what he really liked."

The American Theatre Wing honored Thurber with a special Antoinette Perry ("Tony") Award, after the 1959–1960 theater season, "for his distinguished writing and its compilation in A Thurber Carnival." But with the revue shut down, Thurber underwent "real angst," he wrote Nugent. It was his deepest depression, he said, since that following his eye operations.

The British producer Donald Albery had expressed interest in staging the revue in London. "He wanted the American cast but couldn't pay for it," says Stoddard. "None of the Americans could afford to go. They had to pay income taxes in both countries, and in those days a star's salary in London was something like three hundred pounds a week, or about a hundred and fifty dollars. Albery wouldn't even pay their transportation, but said, 'Come on over anyway, and we'll find the equivalent of your actors in the auditions.' So we went over."

The Thurbers sailed January 20, 1961. "I will have to rewrite some of the sketches to make them suitable for English audiences," Thurber writes Nugent, "but this will not be hard." Earlier, Nugent had sent him a manuscript of his latest novel, *Of Cheat and Charmer*, asking Thurber's opinion. Too busy to read it, Thurber took the manuscript with him. Suspicious of Nugent's sophistication, he worried that the book would contain vulgarities of language, which he hated, as he hated crude bedroom and bathroom humor. He warns Nugent:

> I shall probably be severe about four-letter words and what publishers call "frankly sexual scenes." I belong to the unhappy, diminishing company of writers who deplores the fact that we have made love a four-letter word in this country. The decline of the drama and the novel into the lower corridors of bestiality is a sign of our depleted culture and we ought to all help to pull literature and the arts out of the muck and mire. Everybody knows about sex now and it does have, believe it or not, romantic aspects. . . . I hope I do not become the only survivor of a lost lyrical world. And let us remember what [the theater critic] Percy Hammond said, "Just because a thing happened is no reason it's true."

The day after he landed, Thurber was being quoted in the British newspapers: "No one seems to die over here. Every time they try to hold a memorial service the corpse writes in to say he's feeling fine. I'm sixty-six, going on fifty —I'm going backwards now—and I expect to live another thirty years. But in America love after forty is obscene, work after fifty is unlikely, and death before sixty is practically certain."

Meredith, Helen, Thurber, Gude, and Stoddard spent several weeks in London trying to cast the revue to Albery's satisfaction. "The casting of the play moves slowly but surely," Thurber writes Nugent on February 13, "and we have decided to cast it all English. Meredith, and Helen and I are having a summit conference with the producers tomorrow. Albery . . . is a jet-propelled producer, like the Americans, unsatisfied unless he is doing four things more than he should."

Albery began postponing meetings and not returning phone calls. One day, Meredith angrily told him, "If you don't call Thurber at once, we'll hold a press conference and tell how you treated a distinguished American author." It was obvious that because Thurber's material was so American, American actors would be needed, says Elliott Reid. "Albery insisted there were American actors over there, married to English actresses and vice versa, so saw no need to import any." As Thurber summed up the dilemma: "Here we go round the Albery bush."

Thurber sank back into a depression. Gude had returned to the States, to tend to his agency's business. Thurber wrote him prophetically: "I . . . feel that my life has ended with a permanent connection with 'A Thurber Carnival' and that the two or three books or plays I should love to write may never get done. . . . We are both worn thin, and have been very depressed. . . . What a world, what a species!"

Meredith announced that he was out of it for good, and returned to New York. Stoddard went home, too, and wrote the Thurbers what they mistakenly took to be a hostile letter. "Suddenly, after all this time," Helen writes Gude, "she addresses us as 'Mr. and Mrs. Thurber,' most coldly and as if we were to blame for the whole muddle." ("The letter simply had my lawyer's legalese in it," Stoddard explains. "It was their official notification that the revue was no longer under option.") Albery, suffering from stress and arthritis, was now saying that the show couldn't be cast until May, three months away. Helen began calling on other producers. Most were interested but busy with other projects. Thurber wrote to Jap Gude, who was waiting to handle any contract arrangement:

> For the first time in my life I have begun taking Miltown, three a day. . . . We are both pretty well worn down . . . and . . . are going to rest up for two or three weeks at an inn in the country, where my secretary will come in as she does here [at the Stafford Hotel].
>
> I cannot see that Helen and I have been at fault in this whole business. . . . We have merely been puzzled and confused and considerably harried by it all. . . . I understand most writers, some editors, and a few publishers, but I have never had the vaguest idea what anybody in the theatre is trying to say. I speak English, American, and some French, but I cannot talk Theatre or understand it. . . .
>
> There is one parallel in ancient history. When Caesar crossed the Rubicon he said, "The die is cast." When this got back to Rome, his wife said, to a reporter, "All I know is that he is shooting dice with a woman named Ruby Kahn." She didn't hear very well, anyway, and it is my opinion that she always thought Hannibal was a girl named Annabel. But then, as someone said to me at the conference, "Why do you

have a Japanese agent in New York?" "Because he is a Gude man," I replied.

Their escape to the country inn was hardly that, as Helen writes Gude: "Last night I went to sleep before 3:00 A.M. for the first time since we left home—then was awakened by Jamie losing his way to the can (very naturally, since this inn was built in 1550)." The whole trip to England, she said, "was a big buildup to a bigger let-down."

By mid-March, matters were worse than ever, and Nugent, a self-declared "hypo-manic," wasn't helping, as Thurber writes Gude:

> Elliott does nothing but try to get us on the phone here, and he began it this morning at . . . 3:30 in the morning over there. We have left instructions . . . to tell him that we are not in London and they don't know when we are coming back. If you run into him again, you can tell him that. . . . I suppose he wants us to tell him about his novel, which we have not had time to read, and he probably also wants to play in the Carnival here, and it has been indefinitely postponed, and I don't think it will ever be done here.

Nugent then cheerfully informed the Thurbers, still in hiding, that he had telephoned a mutual friend and suggested that he get in touch with them. "You may remember [him]," Nugent wrote, "from an evening we spent at a cheap pub known as Jack and Charlie's ["21"], some years ago. If he calls you, and I think he will, his intentions will be good so bear with the poor bastard and say a civil word if you find this possible in your present state of decrepitude and resigned despair."

Nugent had lost his tolerance for alcohol, he adds. He says that he is sorry that Helen's eye trouble is back, but "as for yours," he tells Thurber, "I think that complete blindness is probably what God meant to give you, so that you could see with that inner eye which operates so effectively in all fields of literature." Thurber had recently counted seventy-two people he had known on the *New Yorker* who died, and the thought that dear friends like Nugent were assuming various forms of human wreckage around him added to his despair over the failure to stage *A Thurber Carnival*.

"We are homesick for Cornwall," Helen writes the Williamses in April. "We would leave except for the Gudes' coming. I weigh 118 pounds now and feel lousy. We're both restless here. The play was reactivated for a week but is now dead again. We have nightmares about doing it without Meredith or

Haila or any Americans." She no longer trusted the producer or the proposed director ("one of those bearded young men").

While they were in England, *Lanterns & Lances* was published in the States, the last Thurber book to appear in his lifetime. Canfield had ventured a first printing of fifteen thousand copies. It was a Book Find Club selection, and the Book-of-the-Month Club printed twenty-eight thousand copies as a dividend selection. It got on the best-seller lists straightaway, following the usual shower of kudos that had always accompanied the issuance of Thurber books. His Joycean excursions and alliterations are recorded in it ("We supply wristwatches for witchwatchers watching witches Washington wishes watched"), as are his manipulated clichés ("More fun than a barrel of money"). He offers his own brand of newsbreaks, their meanings supposedly mangled by typesetters: "A stitch in time saves none"; "Don, give up the ship."

"Maybe you ought to do a modern Fowler, bringing the old boy up to date," Robert Coates wrote Thurber, after reading it. Thurber and Coates were making a feeble attempt at reconciliation. Coates had sent Thurber his latest novel, *The View from Here*, and Thurber had returned the favor with *Lanterns & Lances*. "Our generation is melting away like snow in the sun," Thurber tells Coates. "After Ham[ilton] Basso wrote 'The View from Pompey's Head,' I decided to write a novel about my return to Columbus and call it 'The View from Pompous Ass.'" This exchange of brief letters was their last.

For a sensitive writer, writing is the sternest act of self-confrontation, but Thurber had the fortitude to follow his own production schedule during the four months he spent in England. Writing, in fact, seemed to provide him with the ballast that kept him upright emotionally. Most of the seven pieces he wrote during his last year of life were done there. Hamish Hamilton, his British publisher, took Thurber to dinner at the Garrick Club. "The head-waiter was keen on Thurber," says Hamilton, "thrilled to see him. Thurber, on hearing this, did a dog for him on the back of a menu. I found him the ideal author to deal with, maybe because we made most of our contracts for his books with Harper and other houses, so they got the brunt of any Thurber temper."

William Thurber wrote that he was retiring from his city job in Columbus and wondered when Thurber would finish the Ross play, in which he had been promised a part. Thurber replied, "Dear old Bill. . . . Our play has been postponed over here until Autumn, and we are much too tired to try to finish the Ross play for the coming season. But I shall get around to it, and you can count on having some money in it."

He had planned to remain in England until the fall, working on the play and a special memoir he called "Autobiography of a Mind"—a literary sally into what he believed to be his powers of mental telepathy and total recall, ghosts, Houdini, and other aspects of the supernatural. But he and Helen were both discouraged by the elusive prospects of the *Carnival*. (It was finally produced the next year, after Thurber's death, starring Tom Ewell with an English cast, and it folded after a run of only a few days.) In response to Helen's pleas, Jap and Helen Gude, who had been traveling in France for three weeks, arrived in England to accompany the Thurbers home on the *Liberté*, which sailed from Southampton May 19. "We actually had a quite pleasant five or six days in London," says Gude. "Helen and Jamie were both glad to see us, and even though there was tension we had a good time meeting some of the Thurber friends . . . and acquainting the Thurbers with some of our own."

But Gude found that Thurber was intermittently behaving as if mentally unhinged. Increasingly paranoid, he was beginning to blame his troubles on Helen, calling her stupid, and sometimes accusing her of being insane and an alcoholic. Back in the States, Helen told Gude that Thurber would sit up most of the night talking to himself. Except to those who knew him well, he seemed rational in public—during press interviews or on the Martha Deane radio program. Though interruptive and somewhat aggressive on a David Susskind TV show, he made as much sense as the other panelists, who were discussing divorce in America. But he had lost touch with himself. It was a fatal breakdown of communication, and one that made him a serious social risk to others and a physical risk to himself, for he now no longer bothered to learn furniture location and continually banged into things with an almost suicidal attitude.

He resisted Gude's and Helen's efforts to get him to a psychiatrist—he had long disdained all social scientists, whom he accused of measuring what they couldn't define. Earlier in the year, he had dictated a long, strange letter to Ernest Hemingway, upon hearing of his depression and illnesses. Intended as an attempt to cheer up Hemingway—the two had met only once and didn't correspond—the letter has its moments. He informs Hemingway that after a medical examination he was told, "You have sugar in your urine and a murmur in your heart," and that he replied, "That's not a diagnosis; that's a song cue." He also went into his history of surgical operations for Hemingway's benefit, and confided his belief that medical men were finally accepting the existence "of seasonal phases of the body and the mind." "I believe that all of us, especially the men, are manic-depressives," he adds. Helen was able to talk him out of sending the letter.

He composed an unsettling fable, in a letter addressed "To Fred Allen in Heaven," in which a farmer, disguised as a scarecrow, is frightened by a crow, the crow thus becoming "a scarescarecrow." (His favorite of Allen's radio stories was the one about the scarecrow that so frightened the crows that they brought back some corn they had stolen two days before.)

In "Bateman Comes Home," there is the line, "He was chewing on a splinter of wood and watching the moon come up lazily out of the old cemetery in which nine of his daughters were lying, only two of whom were dead." Charles McDowell, Jr., a newspaperman, wrote Thurber asking if the line wouldn't be funnier without "only." Thurber replies from London that it would give the humor a "ball-bat impact" and "sacrifice rhythm to obtain it." "I would rather lose my right hand than take 'only' out of that line."

> I am working on a piece that will take up . . . Henley's line "one or two women, God bless them, have loved me," to show how it would have worried Harold Ross. Should it not be, "one or two women, God bless her and them, has and have loved me."?
>
> Not long ago the New Yorker objected to my leaving out the word "that" in some such sentence as, "He told her he loved her." I am now engaged on a series of 25 rules of my own for writing, called "The Theory and Practice of Criticising the Editing of New Yorker Articles." In it I say this, "I woke up this morning and decided that that "that" that worries us so much should be forgotten."

In August he wrote Jane Williams a letter crammed with advice on how to take care of one's health and on the temperate use of booze and cigarettes, and further carping at the changing nature of the republic, "founded by great men, and now peopled by empty-eyed neurotic arrested-development cases, who try to solve everything by facing nothing, who think that the way out is to cloud their personal situation and the world crisis with cigarette smoke and liquor fumes." A worried Helen secretly penned a long postscript to the letter before mailing it:

> Do not mention my P.S. but Jamie is in very bad shape, has been for some months. London was hell, but Cornwall has been worse, & he has turned against everyone up here except Rose & the Marc Simonts. Elliott told me that Jim has a persecution complex & is dangerous. The people up here won't let me stay in the house alone with him at night so Rose comes & sleeps in the back room. Every other day (usually after a terrifying night) he quiets down, doesn't drink & is kind & gentle—but

that only lasts one day. Jap Gude came up, took him to the Algonquin for a week, leaving me up here to get some rest, but Jap couldn't take it as Jamie hit the bottle at 5 every day & wouldn't go to bed. It's all so sad & my heart breaks for him, but he won't go to a doctor. Two young doctor friends of ours had a meeting with a great man from Neurological at Medical Centre all arranged, but Jim backed out. Fritzi, Jim's secretary . . . just came down & said she is getting very worried as he's now dictating a diatribe against everyone. I am an alcoholic and a schizophrenic (he says—& tells everyone). That's because, worn down from having guests he invited every night, I sent him to a couple of parties by himself. Now only 3 people in town will have him, or come here, & that makes it difficult. I shouldn't be telling you all this when you've been through so much, but I felt you ought to know in case something happens. Please write him & ignore what I've said (& a lot he's said) as he does count on it so. I'm really desperate.

"Helen called me," says Gude, "and I went up, spent the weekend with them and brought Jim back to the Algonquin. I got him to his thyroid specialist at Harkness Pavilion. The doctor told him he couldn't treat him successfully unless Jim had a hospital check-up. He wouldn't, and cursed the doctor in a rage. He had too much professional confidence to fear failure as a writer, but not much confidence in his physical state. He was afraid of what a doctor would tell him.

"In late summer, Jim called me and asked me to come get him. Helen said it would be a good thing for them both if I did. He couldn't stand to be with Helen by then. When, later, she came to the Algonquin, she got her own room."

Gude, during the tumultuous week with a desperately ill Thurber at the Algonquin, heard him on the phone to William Maxwell, calling him abusive names; the experience of *The Wonderful O* was apparently still on his mind. *New Yorker* staff veterans received unexpected calls from Thurber when he was back in Cornwall. "I think I still count for something down there," he would tell Freddie Packard. Whitaker, Gill, Ebba Jonsson, and Terry would receive friendlier calls. "What time is it, Terry?" he would ask her from within his darkened world a hundred miles away. "How are things going down there today? What's the weather like there?"

In England, when he had had no replies to his letters to Shawn, the Whites, or Angell in several weeks, he had written the *New Yorker*'s attorney, Milton Greenstein, that he was without any doubt "being shown the door":

They think that I am unreasonable and too outspoken, especially in my criticism of the magazine, inside and outside the Office, and I think that they are in the great and sad tradition of New Yorker secrecy, anonymity, and easily hurt feelings.

My old relationship really died with Ross and Lobrano, with whom I worked perfectly. . . . But the end finally came with the publication of "The Years with Ross" and with Mrs. White's incurable antipathy to that book, an antipathy that White shares completely. . . . Angell has tried to do his best about me, but there is that profound disparity of nature, viewpoint, and belief, and, moreover, he is, after all, Mrs. White's son, and she has said, on the phone, that I no longer regard myself as "a member of the family." The 34-year-old truth is that I never was a member of the family, because everything in me rebelled against our exclusivity and snobbishness and aloofness. . . . I have the ineradicable feeling that I am really not wanted any more.

Though Greenstein wrote him an inspired letter of reassurance, the truth was that because of the tragic effects of a tyrannical illness, Thurber *wasn't* wanted anymore. Jean Stafford and Liebling would see him in Costello's and "we avoided him as much as we could," writes Stafford. "I much regret that I didn't know him before when he was attractive because I know he must have been. Peter and Katinka De Vries were devoted to him."

"His old friends knew Thurber wasn't himself," says Nora Sayre. "The wounded were staggering away, not bruised, as in the old days, but hurt badly. He was roughing up people more than usual. Many of them were upset by Thurber after 1959. I saw him with the Gudes when Helen was in the hospital. I hugged him. He was drinking and didn't look well. He asked me to call him. I did, the next morning, and asked how things were. 'Terrible,' he said. 'You should know things are terrible and you shouldn't ask a question like that.' I asked why Helen was in the hospital. He said, 'Why? The same thing is wrong with her that's wrong with all of us; being alive.'

"He had come through for me in 1960 when my mother died—a probable suicide. Others avoided the subject but Jim talked about manic-depressive friends, how it comes in cycles. He helped me to think things out. I'd recently divorced and whenever Helen was getting ready to ask me about it, Jim would cut her off. He knew that usually the reason you leave a marriage is a good subject to stay away from.

"He had a horror of drying up as a writer and felt that writing was easier for women—that they didn't age as artists the way men did. 'You're lucky to be a woman and to want to be a writer,' he'd tell me when I was young. That was the Thurber we loved but who went away from us a couple of years before he died."

White, in Maine, was unaware of how seriously ill Thurber was. When Helen had flowers sent to Katharine in the hospital there, where Katharine had undergone surgery, White wrote the Thurbers with his usual good humor, and with Hemingway also on his mind: "I'm glad you're back in West Cornwall, as I don't trust England any more. Too flighty. I am glad I am in North Brooklin, but I am lonely—all alone by the telephone. And I am morose to think that when you die, and when I die, there won't be any bullfighter in Spain to kill two bulls in our honor."

Edmund Wilson was in New York in the summer of 1961, and met Helen Thurber in the Algonquin lobby; she confided to him that Thurber was ill and drinking too much. Later that day, Wilson and actor Mike Nichols were joined by the Thurbers for a drink. Thurber talked incessantly, listing all the celebrities who had visited him backstage during the run of *A Thurber Carnival*. After the Thurbers departed, Nichols asked Wilson why Thurber felt he had to brag about such matters. Wilson notes in his journal that he replied that "depressing though it might seem . . . getting older, for a writer, did not necessarily give you self-confidence so that you felt you could disregard the evidence of your importance. I told him that I sometimes got up at four o'clock in the morning to read old reviews of my books."

Thurber had complained to Wilson of having "vastations." Nichols asked Wilson about that, too, and Wilson told him that Thurber "had got the word from Leon Edel's biography of Henry James. The elder Henry James had used this word for a kind of blackout that he sometimes had and when his mind had simply gone blank, he hadn't known where he was."

On a weekend at Burgess Meredith's home in Rockland County, Thurber had "a vastation," blacking out. The assumption was that it was from drink, but it was probably one of an increasingly severe series of brain hemorrhages.

Haila Stoddard and Helen Bonfils, meanwhile, had produced Noel Coward's musical, *Sail Away*. They invited the Thurbers to its Broadway opening, on October 3, 1961. Shortly before the show, Helen was unable to find Thurber. "I'm trying to find my husband," she told Terry on the phone. But he wasn't at the *New Yorker* and never would be again. Someone brought him in time for the opening, but he left after the first act and was taken to Sardi's nearby for a drink.

"I realize now that Jim was jealous of Coward," says Stoddard. "A Thurber Carnival was over for him. Helen Bonfils and I had followed Thurber's production with Coward's. Jim missed being the center of attention. The glory was going to someone else."

The opening-night party, at Sardi's East, may have had more lasting significance than the play itself, which stumbled along for only a five-month run. Stoddard's husband, Whitfield Connor, brought Thurber to the party. Thurber appeared drunk; the occasion seemed organized to humiliate him. "Everyone in New York was there," Coward writes, "invited or uninvited, from Adlai Stevenson on." Coward's music was played incessantly, the walls were covered with reproductions of Coward's picture, and one room was entirely devoted to caricatures of him.

Coward had arrived with Marlene Dietrich, Myrna Loy, and Elaine Stritch; Stritch had starred in the show. Dietrich kissed Thurber on the cheek. "Who is it?" he asked. "Someone who loves you—Marlene Dietrich," she told him. Others made much of him. Lauren Bacall sat at his table. But Thurber sat there sullenly, denouncing Coward, whose British snobbishness, he said, had led to this show whose principal purpose was to feature American tourists as louts.

After much oratory and music, including some brief remarks by Coward, Thurber wanted to speak. He had been humiliated by British theater, which had failed to produce his show, and here was Coward, an Englishman, being honored for a play that made fun of Americans. He stood facing the orchestra, until someone turned him around in the right direction. "We have to get rid of Noel Coward!" he shouted. "We must get him off on the first boat!" He denounced the show as arrogantly anti-American, and was trying to sing "Bye, Bye, Blackbird" when Whit Connor and Helen got the microphone away from him. "I thought it was just some drunken fool," says Elaine Stritch. "I couldn't believe it when I learned it was Thurber."

After the microphone was taken away from him, Thurber staggered; he was quickly supported by others and taken to the Algonquin in a cab by Helen and Connor. In his room, he began a tirade of insults and hurtful comments to Helen, until Connor felt compelled to leave. The Thurbers went to bed, but about 6:00 A.M. Helen heard a crash. Thurber, apparently on his way to the bathroom, had collapsed. He was rushed to Doctors Hospital, where a tumor the size of a tangerine was removed from his brain.

As reported by the watchful press, he showed many signs of consciousness during the month that followed, but few to suggest that he actually recognized those who were allowed to see him—Helen, Gude, Dr. Duke Damon, Rosemary. Many others came by to visit with Helen, who had taken a room next door.

In his lifetime, Thurber had overcome nearly every difficulty thrown at him by a fate that seemed at times both whimsical and sadistic. In learning how to fit into the world, he had shown others how to enjoy themselves and their circumstances by letting them look through his prism of humor. And now, through bad luck he couldn't master this time around, he was being hurried out of that world, toward the end whose definition by Henry James he had long thought about. When he was visiting T. S. Eliot in London in 1955, Eliot pointed to the ceiling of his apartment and told Thurber, "I just found out the other day that Henry James died in the room above here." According to Eliot, James was supposed to have said as he lay dying, "The inevitable end —the distinguished thing," but Thurber refused to believe that James would consider distinguished something that happened to everybody. "I think his voice was getting low," said Thurber, "and that what he really said was 'the extinguished flame.' "

He had once described the abrupt end of someone's life in Columbus as like that of an electric clock that stops in a thunderstorm. Now he was struck down by his own form of lightning. His shield and sword—his humor—was beyond his reach this time. Pneumonia set in. A blood clot on his lung was detected, and he gasped out his life at 4:14 P.M. on November 2, 1961; his death was attributed to respiratory failure. Among Thurber's final, incoherent mumbling may have been the words "God bless, goddam"—Ross's farewell to McNulty, which Thurber had loved to repeat; but Helen says that very little of it could be understood. Rosemary agrees: "He would shout things now and then but they never made sense."

His month-long coma had been similar to that of Mame's, and those who loved him were relieved that he had been spared the ultimate humiliation of continuing life as a helpless invalid. "I am with you," Frank Sullivan wrote Katharine White, afterward, "in being thankful that Jim did not live on to be crippled in body and mind. I wonder that his restless spirit did not break out of that dark prison far sooner. . . . After I heard of his death I took up *The Thurber Carnival* and read the old favorites. I'm with Andy, I want to remember him as he was in his great days."

The *New Yorker* obituary, written in two parts by Shawn and White, ran in an issue thick with pages of colorful, cheery Christmas ads.

He had once written that he wished his ashes to be strewn on the seas between New York and Bermuda, but Helen found Robert and William angry that she had had him cremated, and didn't dare bury the ashes anywhere but in Columbus, near the remains of his family.

There was only a graveside service. "I kept it very brief," says the Reverend Karl Scheufler. "I didn't know the family well, but I'd preached at Mame's funeral, and I suppose that was why I was asked to preside at this one."

"The thing that most impressed me at that burial," says George Smallsreed, "was how Meredith, Gude, and I and others simply stared for ten seconds at that tiny urn, as if we were trying to convince ourselves that this could be all that remained of that powerful force, James Thurber."

Thurber's immortal, drooping, struggling little Last Flower is etched into the small tombstone on his grave.

"When we heard the news," says Emily Hahn, "McKelway arranged for Ann Honeycutt and me to meet him at Costello's. It was supposed to be a kind of memorial service to Thurber. McKelway wasn't allowed by his doctor to drink, so Ann and I got drunk. I told Maxwell the next day that we had talked about everything except Thurber. Maxwell said he understood; it was too soon to think about Thurber. We needed time to dispose of those final months when nobody could love Thurber, and wait for those marvelous memories of him to come around again. They have."

News of Thurber's death made the front page of the *New York Times* and was noted throughout the country and the world. It had somehow been easy for his thousands of admirers to think that he was as durable as most of the work he produced, and hard to believe that he could have finally lost the battle for his life.

Peter De Vries, his friend, constant to the end, writes:

> With Thurber gone there is something missing, like a star from the sky, though . . . the sentimentalists will have it that on the contrary there is another shining there. . . . Thurber, with his keen vision, saw through to the bone. Life is not a gift at all, but a purchase, paid for as we go, at prices that seem at times rather out of line. He paid as dearly as any man for his life and for his genius, with pains and privations, exactions of courage, and physical and moral trials that would have killed a dozen ordinary men.

Probably Thurber would have regretted not being allowed an end to life as graceful and natural as that of Medve, his beloved poodle—with dignity, and of no bother to anyone; or his own original, even humorous way, to meet "that distinguished thing," before submitting to the inevitable extinguishing of the flame.

Thurber had never allowed his probing, restless mind to settle on any single theological insurance policy covering the possibilities of the hereafter.

He remained agnostic and probably about where he was, philosophically, in 1927, when he was thirty-four years old and the best part of his life was ahead of him. It was before blindness and fame hit him—in White's words, when he was loved by everyone, but lonely—that he had written his brother Robert a long letter of sympathy over the death of Robert's dog, Muggs:

> I don't seem to see where anyone has figured it out, but sometimes it seems to me that time goes by like a flash of rain and that's all we amount to in this world. . . . There ought to be some point to it all and I live in the hopes that the adventure of death is something equal to the adventure of life. . . . It would seem strange to me if God made such a complicated world and such complicated people and he had no more to offer than blankness at the end, so I live in the curiosity and the hope and the excitement of what there may be afterwards and thus I have got myself to believe that those who pass on perhaps pass on to something as interesting, but lovelier and more happy, than this life.

Having left us a world generously stocked, and forever improved, with the best in humorous prose and drawings, his own hopes seem the very least we can wish for James Grover Thurber.

Books by James Thurber

Is Sex Necessary? or Why You Feel the Way You Do (*with E. B. White*)
The Owl in the Attic and Other Perplexities
The Seal in the Bedroom & Other Predicaments
My Life and Hard Times
The Middle-Aged Man on the Flying Trapeze
Let Your Mind Alone! and Other More or Less Inspirational Pieces
The Last Flower, a Parable in Pictures
Fables for Our Time and Famous Poems Illustrated
The Male Animal (*a play, with Elliott Nugent*)
My World—and Welcome to It
Many Moons
Men, Women and Dogs
The Great Quillow
The Thurber Carnival
The White Deer
The Beast in Me and Other Animals
The 13 Clocks
The Thurber Album
Thurber Country
Thurber's Dogs
Further Fables for Our Time
The Wonderful O
Alarms and Diversions
The Years with Ross
Lanterns & Lances
A Thurber Carnival (*a musical revue of his works*)
Credos and Curios
Thurber & Company
Selected Letters of James Thurber (*edited by Helen Thurber and Edward Weeks*)
Collecting Himself (*Michael J. Rosen, editor*)
People Have More Fun than Anybody (*edited by Michael J. Rosen*)

A Thurber Chronology

1861: Thurber's maternal grandfather, William M. Fisher, an Ohio farmer, born 1840, marries sixteen-year-old "Kate" Matheny. Thurber's mother, Mary Agnes (Mame) Fisher, born 1866. In 1870, Fisher begins prosperous wholesale produce business in Columbus.

1867: Thurber's father, Charles Leander (later Lincoln) Thurber, born in Indianapolis to Sarah Emeline Hull Thurber, who tells him his father, Leander Thurber, was thrown from a horse and killed during her pregnancy. She later marries and divorces Tunis Dangler, believed to be brother of Aunt Margery Dangler Albright of Columbus, who helped care for young Charles.

1892: Charles and Mame marry at her father's house in Columbus. Charles takes job in the office of the Ohio Secretary of State.

1893: William Fisher has house built for Charles and Mame at 251 Parsons Avenue, which they occupy in spring of 1893. William Fisher Thurber is born.

1894: James Grover Thurber is born, December 8.

1895: Charles loses job but is hired by Ohio governor Asa Bushnell, December 27.

1896: Robert Thurber is born.

1899: Thurbers move to 921 South Champion Avenue.

1900: James, five, starts first grade at Ohio Avenue Elementary School in September. Accompanies father to polling booth; McKinley elected president. Bushnell loses governorship, leaving Charles again unemployed.

1901: Charles made secretary to Ohio congressman. Thurber's first writing: a poem, "My Aunt Mrs. John T. Savage's Garden at 185 South Fifth Street, Columbus, Ohio."

1902: Charles sells Champion Avenue house in April; moves family to Washington; takes August rental in Falls Church, Va. Thurber loses eye in childhood accident there. In September, Thurbers move back to I St., Washington. Thurber remains at home that school year.

1903: Thurbers return to Columbus in June, live at boarding house, Park Hotel, and 625 Oak Street. Thurber begins third grade in September at

Sullivant School, with classmate Eva Prout, who becomes one of his romantic ideals in seventh grade. Charles, jobless, enters newspaper contests and
sells Underwood typewriters. Thurber learns to use one.

1904: Fourth-grade teacher at Sullivant notices Thurber's drawing ability.

1905: Charles gets "a brain disease," nearly dies. Thurbers move in with
Grandfather Fisher for several months. Over next five years, Thurber frequently sent to live with Aunt Margery Albright. Thurber writes first short
story, "Horse Sandusky and the Intrepid Scout."

1906: In sixth grade at Sullivant. Thurbers live at Norwich Hotel.

1907: Enters seventh grade at Douglas School. Charles unemployed for
two years.

1909: Writes eighth-grade class prophecy. Bids Eva Prout good-bye. Begins
Columbus East High School. All three Thurber boys affected by thyrotoxic
goiter. Charles hired as temporary employee, secretary to State Republican
Executive Committee, Ohio legislature and other freelance work.

1912: Charles, as secretary of the Progressive Party's State Campaign
Committee, backs Teddy Roosevelt; keeps the position through 1914 campaign. Thurbers live on South Seventeenth Street.

1913: Family rents 77 Jefferson Avenue for next four years—today preserved as national landmark and enlarged as The Thurber House. Thurber's
first published story appears in the X-Rays, quarterly of East High; elected
senior class president. Writes ode to dogs Rex and Scottie. Robert made
captain of school's baseball team. On September 17, Thurber enters Ohio
State University's College of Arts, Philosophy, and Science. Psychology professor Albert P. Weiss gives class a memory test, revealing Thurber's unusual
gift for retention. Rejected by Chi Phi fraternity.

1914: Attracted to columns of Robert O. Ryder, editor of Ohio State Journal from 1904 to 1929. Enrolls at O.S.U. for second year but fails to attend
classes.

1915: Re-enters O.S.U. for second year. Imitates Ryder with "Sidelights"
items printed in East High's X-Rays. Minnette Fritts and Elliott Nugent,
future friends, enter O.S.U. Sophomore Thurber is almost twenty-one. "The
night the ghost got in" takes place November 17.

1916: Charles Thurber made cashier of Columbus municipal court. Thurber is truant during second semester, avoiding military drill; disqualified as
student. President William Oxley Thompson reinstates him that fall, still a
sophomore, nearly twenty-two.

1917: Professor Joseph Russell Taylor introduces Thurber to Henry James,
and becomes a Thurber hero. Thurbers move from Jefferson Avenue to 56
North Grant Avenue. Thurber joins Phi Kappa Psi with Elliott Nugent's and

Jack Pierce's help. Thurber and Nugent are student reporters for the *Lantern*. May 18, Selective Service Act requires all men ages twenty-one to thirty to register for the draft. During fall term, he and Nugent are made coeditors of the *Lantern*. Thurber writes and draws for campus humor magazine, the *Sun-Dial*; Nugent introduces him to the Strollers, O.S.U. dramatic society.

1918: Thurbers move to 330 Gay Street. Thurber made editor of *Sun-Dial*; acts with Nugent in Strollers' production of Arnold Bennett's *A Question of Sex*. Aunt Margery Albright dies. Thurber leaves O.S.U. in June, still a junior, with only 87 credits out of the 120 needed for degree. Is accepted as State Department code clerk trainee; leaves for Washington June 21. Exchanges love letters with Minnette Fritts. Grandfather Fisher dies October 17. Thurber arrives in France November 13; works at American Embassy, Paris. Althea Adams, Thurber's future wife, matriculates at O.S.U.

1919: Writes letters home; sends occasional money to Robert, who is chronically ill. Charme Seeds looks up Thurber in Paris. Nugent gets O.S.U. degree. Thurber has attack of "nerves." Writes Eva Prout and Minnette. Peace Conference begins in Paris. Minnette marries at Christmas in Chicago.

1920: Prohibition goes into effect January 16. Sails for home in February, joins family at 330 Gay St. Thurber is "jumpy and moody." Robert has bought Muggs (the dog that bit people). Eva Prout and her mother visit Thurbers on a weekend in April. Thurber rents typewriter and writes Eva love letters. Becomes interested in new campus male dramatic group, the Scarlet Mask. In August, hired by *Columbus Dispatch* at twenty-five dollars a week as general reporter.

1921: Thurber helps write book and lyrics for, and directs, *Oh My, Omar!* for Scarlet Mask. Is influenced by Op-Ed pages of *New York World* and other out-of-town papers. Ted Gardiner and John McNulty become his close friends. Meets Herman Miller, O.S.U. English instructor. Meets Althea, O.S.U. coed, at Strollers' play rehearsal. She comes to sessions at a photographers' studio where young actors and writers—including Thurber—gather.

1922: Marries Althea May 20 at Episcopal Trinity Church in downtown Columbus; honeymoon in Washington, D.C., and New York; visit Nugents. *Many Moons* staged by Scarlet Mask, first play Thurber wrote alone; he is paid three hundred and fifty dollars. Acts as press agent for local concert series, in addition to *Dispatch* job. His poem "When Chic Harley Got Away" published in *Dispatch*.

1923: Wins first prize for essay on what Columbus would be like in 1951. Given Sunday *Dispatch* column, Credos and Curios; does forty-two half-pages; column canceled after December 9 issue. He and Althea visit New York in April, for more play reviewing; visit Nugents in Connecticut; meet

Nugent friend, who offers them cottage in Jay, New York. Thurber tours with *The Cat and the Riddle*, whose book he wrote.

1924: Leaves *Dispatch* after three years and nine months. Takes manuscript of *Nightingale* with him to cottage in Jay, N.Y., where he and Althea spend spring and summer. Unsuccessfully peddles *Nightingale* as musical comedy. Writes "Josephine Has Her Day"—first story he receives money for—published *Kansas City Star*, March 14, 1926; sells paragraph to Heywood Broun's column, "It Seems to Me," in *New York World*. But Thurber's freelancing a failure; back to Columbus; *Dispatch* doesn't rehire him. Works on Scarlet Mask's *Tell Me Not* (forerunner of *The Male Animal*); freelances as press agent.

1925: *Tell Me Not* produced; Althea does costume design, scenery, assists with lighting. Thurber goes on tour with show, occasionally fills in for actor. May 7, Thurbers sail to France, rent room in Normandy farmhouse. Works on novel; gives it up; takes job with Paris edition of *Chicago Tribune*. Sells pieces to *Kansas City Star*, *New York World*, *Detroit Athletic Club News*, *Herald Tribune Magazine*, and *Harper's*. In fall, Thurbers go to Nice, where Thurber coedits Riviera edition of *Chicago Tribune* at fifteen dollars a week; Althea is society editor.

1926: In June, Thurber returns to States; Althea remains to work for *Chicago Tribune*. Thurber borrows from family and sends for her. They spend summer in Gloversville, N.Y., summer home of cartoonist C. V. Dwiggins, where Thurber continues to freelance unsuccessfully. "Bye, Bye, Blackbird" is introduced, becoming Thurber's favorite song. He and Althea rent a basement apartment on Horatio Street; gets stream of rejections from the *New Yorker*. His "If the Tabloids Had Covered the Famous Sport 'Love-Death' Scandal of Hero and Leander," signed Jamie Machree, printed in Franklin P. Adams's Conning Tower column, *New York World*, September 28—Thurber claims that its acceptance (at no fee) persuaded him not to return to Columbus. Takes job at forty dollars a week on *New York Evening Post*.

1927: Makes first sale to *New Yorker*, "An American Romance"; two poems appear in magazine first. Is hired by *New Yorker* in February as "managing editor"; sells magazine thirteen additional casuals, one more poem, two Talk of the Town items. Shares office with E. B. White; White will remain his officemate for almost three years. Meets Ann Honeycutt that summer in Amawalk, N.Y. Helps Robert Coates join *New Yorker*. By September, no longer the managing editor, but copyediting and rewriting Talk. Wolcott Gibbs joins staff.

1928: While Althea is on a trip to Europe, Robert visits him at West Eleventh Street apartment. Muggs dies. Thurber visits Eva Prout and her husband, performing artists, at Flanders Hotel; the reunion inspires "Menaces in May," his first serious fiction sold to *New Yorker*. Contributes thirteen casuals, including first of Monroe series, thirteen Talk items, a poem, a profile, and "As Europe Sees Us" for *Sunset* magazine.

1929: *Is Sex Necessary?*, by White and Thurber, published by Harper & Bros. on November 7; White marries Katharine Angell six days later. Althea begins raising scotties and poodles at rented place in Silvermine, Conn. Thurber has twenty-three casuals in *New Yorker*, including "Our Own Modern English Usage" series and Monroe series; three "original" Talk stories, and a poem; three pieces in *Magazine of Business*. He and Althea separate, she stays in Silvermine, he at the Algonquin. Renews correspondence with Minnette Fritts, who is married with children in Seattle; courts Ann Honeycutt (his favorite), Paula Trueman, and Ann Fordyce. Nugent accepts movie contract in February, spends next ten years in Hollywood.

1930: Thurber lives at the Algonquin, visiting Silvermine on some weekends. Meets Helen Wismer at Honeycutt New Year's Day party. Sells twenty-six casuals, including "Our Pet Department" series (containing Thurber's first drawings in *New Yorker*), "The Remarkable Case of Mr. Bruhl," and "If Grant Had Been Drinking at Appomattox"; four original Talk stories; articles in *Harper's* and *Herald Tribune*. In July, visits White at Camp Otter, in Ontario. Silvermine lease up in June; they rent nearby house for summer; that fall, Althea moves back to city; she and Thurber share apartment though still living independently.

1931: First Thurber cartoons appear in *New Yorker*; *The Owl in the Attic and Other Perplexities* published by Harper & Bros. in February; sells *New Yorker* ten casuals (including "The Greatest Man in the World"), four Talk originals, twenty-three drawings. Thurber and Althea reunite. Connells rent their summer place at Greens Farms, Conn. to Thurbers. Althea informs him she is pregnant; they stay together, though she travels and he courts Honeycutt and other women. In late August, he buys a twenty-acre farm in Sandy Hook, Conn. Rosemary born in New York City, October 7. Paul Nash, English painter, visits States, praises Thurber's drawings, insists on meeting him.

1932: In spring, visits Sayres in Bermuda, where he meets Ronnie and Jane Williams. Produces fifty-seven drawings, twenty-seven casuals, two Reporter at Large articles, three Talk originals for *New Yorker*. With Althea and baby, visits the Morris Markeys in Florida; Thurber writes Honeycutt the while. *The Seal in the Bedroom & Other Predicaments* published by Harper in November.

1933: *My Life and Hard Times* pieces begin appearing, published as book that fall by Harper. Goes off salary and onto drawing account; lives at Algonquin, occasionally visits Sandy Hook on weekends. Only one Talk original, eighteen casuals, including "Life and Hard Times" series, fifty-two published drawings. Mame visits in July.

1934: Has fifty-seven drawings, twenty-two casuals published in *New Yorker*. In March, Althea and two-year-old Rosemary vacation in Bahamas; Althea has met Francis Comstock: files for legal separation. In Columbus, Thurber family survives fire in Gay Street apartment. Robert visits Thurber for several weeks. In April, his agent, Jap Gude, arranges for him to replace Alexander Woollcott on WABC, with a fifteen-minute broadcast on Thursday nights for several weeks. Squares off against literary left; spends an evening with F. Scott Fitzgerald. One-man show of his drawings in New York in December. Coates and Thurber drive to Columbus; sees Eva Prout for last time.

1935: In March, rests at Ellenville sanitarium from drink, work, concerns over Honeycutt, and impending divorce. Divorce final in May. After divorce, becomes engaged to Helen Wismer. Makes panicked trip to Columbus and brings McNulty to New York. Marries Helen June 25; honeymoon on Martha's Vineyard, near the Gudes; buys 1932 Ford, drives to North Brooklin to visit Whites; spends summer in Helen's parents' cottage in Colebrook, Conn. *New Yorker* moves from 25 West Forty-fifth Street to 25 West Forty-third Street. Thurbers rent apartment on lower Fifth Avenue; evening with Thomas Wolfe. *The Middle-Aged Man on the Flying Trapeze* published in November by Harper & Bros. Honeycutt marries St. Clair McKelway; marriage lasts little more than a year. Besides five tennis columns for the magazine, he does nineteen casuals, three Talk originals; sixty-three drawings, including advertisements. Quits Talk rewrite and regular office hours for first-refusal contract with the magazine. Drives to Columbus that Thanksgiving; Helen introduced to family and friends.

1936: His negative review of *Proletarian Literature in the United States* appears in March 25 *New Republic*. Produces forty published drawings, twenty-seven casuals and short stories, a Reporter at Large, eleven "Where Are They Now?" articles, four "Tennis Courts" columns, a Comment. Visits Bermuda in spring; renews friendship with Williamses; spends wild evening with Sinclair Lewis. Writes first casual for the *Bermudian*. Another summer in Connecticut, at Wismer cottage and rented house in Litchfield. Auto tour of Northeast.

1937: Eye begins to bother him. Sails for Europe in May; tours Normandy in Ford; three weeks in Paris; in London for Thurber art show; tours Britain, France, and Italy in Ford. *Let Your Mind Alone! and Other More or Less Inspira-*

tional Pieces published in September by Harper & Bros. Spends Christmas in Italy. Writes twenty-five casuals, five "Where Are They Now?" features, four tennis columns for *New Yorker*.

1938: Rents villa on French Riviera for four months; tours Southern France. Illustrates Ann Honeycutt's and James R. Kinney's *How to Raise a Dog*. Celebrates Fourth of July at John O'Hara's flat in London; meets Ross in London and Paris; sails for home September 1. Rents house in Woodbury, Conn.; visits Rosemary at Sandy Hook; drives to Columbus in October in new Ford. Produces thirty-seven published drawings; October article on E. B. White for *Saturday Review*; two "Where Are They Now?" articles, an Onward and Upward with the Arts, a Reporter at Large, and a tennis column, in *New Yorker*.

1939: Begins "Fables for Our Time" series in January; and "Famous Poems Illustrated" series in March. His most famous short story, "The Secret Life of Walter Mitty," appears in March. Visits Columbus, where Charles Thurber dies on Easter Sunday. In June, sails through Panama Canal to Los Angeles; works with Nugent on *The Male Animal*. Eye worsens. Play not completed, but Thurbers return to New York in September. War breaks out in Europe. Thurber composes *The Last Flower* at Algonquin; contributes sixty-three drawings to Margaret Ernst's *In a Word*; fifteen drawings to *Men Can Take It*, by Elizabeth Hawes; forty-four published drawings elsewhere, including one of his six *New Yorker* covers; ten casuals; an Onward and Upward with the Arts. In October, Thurbers return to Coast for tryouts of *The Male Animal*; Herman Shumlin agrees to produce it.

1940: *The Male Animal* opens at Cort Theater on January 9; a hit, giving Thurbers first substantial income. They go to Bermuda to recuperate. Medve, the thirteen-year-old poodle, dies at Sandy Hook. They fly by seaplane to New York to see Helen's ailing father in Newport, who dies two weeks after their arrival. Mame, with Robert, comes to New York for skin cancer operation; Thurber takes them to see *The Male Animal* with Althea and Rosemary, first time Mame meets her granddaughter. Whites solicit his choice of his pieces for their anthology, *A Subtreasury of American Humor*, to be published in 1941. After Rev. Wismer's death, Thurbers fly back to Bermuda; he becomes stockholder and board member of *Bermudian*. Returns to States in early June; rents house in Sharon, Conn. Undergoes preliminary iridectomy on cataract in mid-June. Ralph Ingersoll begins *PM*; Thurber writes "If You Ask Me" columns for it. Last of "Fables for Our Time" in *New Yorker*; "Footnote on the Future," his last piece for *New Yorker* (June 15) for fourteen months. Writes three pieces publicizing *The Male Animal*; begins frequent contributions to *Bermudian*—four in 1940. Publishes twenty-seven drawings.

Fables for Our Time and Famous Poems Illustrated published by Harper in September. Undergoes "the big operation," removal of cataract, October 21; in Connecticut that Christmas, Thurber's eye turns bad; is operated on again.

1941: Thurber hospitalized; Helen closes country house, rents apartment at Grosvenor Hotel; Thurber leaves hospital, under nurses' care, for Grosvenor; nervous, petulant. Works unsuccessfully on movie treatment of *My Life and Hard Times* with Joel Sayre; resumes *PM* column January 27. Fourth operation, March 21, for secondary glaucoma and iritis; fifth operation, April 18, to drain fluid pressing optic nerve and retina. Takes house for summer in Chilmark, on Martha's Vineyard; meets Mark Van Doren; at Vineyard, writes "The Whip-Poor-Will," first story in *New Yorker* in fourteen months. In September, sublets apartment on East Fifty-fourth Street; Margaret Thurlow, *New Yorker* secretary, takes his dictation each afternoon. He does twenty-one *PM* columns. "You Could Look It Up" appears in *Saturday Evening Post*. Has only three captioned drawings, seven spots in *New Yorker*. He and Honeycutt ejected from Foords sanitarium.

1942: Rents apartment on East Fifty-seventh Street. Coates persuades Thurber to switch from Harper & Bros. to Harcourt Brace, which publishes *My World—and Welcome to It* in October. Reviews of books by Fitzgerald, Steinbeck, and Aldous Huxley published. Movie, *Rise and Shine*, released, based on *My Life and Hard Times*. World premiere of film version of *The Male Animal* held in Columbus in March; the Thurber family attends with Thurber and Helen. Six *New Yorker* casuals include "A Friend to Alexander," "The Catbird Seat," and "A Good Man," which becomes first chapter of *The Thurber Album* ten years later. Rents in Cornwall, Conn.; works on play about Ross and the *New Yorker*. Resumes drawing: twenty are published including fifteen captioned cartoons.

1943: In January, rents apartment on East Fifty-seventh Street. War has depleted the *New Yorker* staff; Whites return to Manhattan to help Ross. Thurber's "The Cane in the Corridor" appears with only four other casuals (one in *Saturday Review*) that year; illustrates "Prehistoric Animals of the Middle West" for *Mademoiselle*; twenty-one published drawings—done with Zeiss Loop. *Many Moons* and *Men, Women and Dogs* published by Harcourt. *Many Moons* wins American Library Association's prize for best children's picture book of 1943. November, at Homestead, Hot Springs, Va.; in Columbus for ten days at Christmas, following Mame's operation. *Poetry* publishes Peter De Vries's critique of Thurber works in December, first serious comment of its kind.

1944: Newly married De Vrieses journey to New York, persuade Thurber to speak at fund-raiser for *Poetry* in April. He promotes De Vries to Ross, who hires him. Chicago Arts Club puts on last one-man show of Thurber drawings. *The Great Quillow* is published in October by Harcourt Brace. Visits Jane Williams in Geneva, N.Y. in September, where he contracts lobar pneumonia. November, his appendix ruptures at the Homestead, in Hot Springs. Operated on at C&O Railroad hospital, Clifton Forge, Va. Has fiftieth birthday, back at the Homestead. Eleven drawings published. Begins work on "Our New Natural History" series for the *New Yorker*. Whites withdraw from Thurbers socially, because of Thurber's rough treatment of Katharine. Hollywood studio gives him ten thousand dollars to adapt "The Catbird Seat" to film but, discouraged, he repays the money.

1945: Meets Minnette Fritts in New York in January, after twenty-five years. Twelve "Natural History" parts run from March 1945 to May of following year in *New Yorker*. *The Thurber Carnival* published February by Harper & Bros., one of his most successful books; his readership greatly widened. Buys hundred-year-old West Cornwall house on sixty acres. *The White Deer* published by Harcourt Brace in September. Returns to Hot Springs in November. That month, Robert Benchley dies. Writes preface to Mary Petty's *This Petty Pace* and Joel Sayre's *The Persian Gulf Command*. Refuses his election to National Institute of Arts and Letters because White is not a member. Works on film script of *The Secret Life of Walter Mitty* with Ken Englund.

1946: In January, goes to Columbus for delayed celebration of Mame's birthday; visits Herman Millers. Two captioned drawings, final four "Our Own Natural History" items, and seven "The Olden Time" drawings appear in *New Yorker*. Only one casual published—"What the Animals Were Up To," for *Life*. Adapting "Mitty" to screen; none of his material used. Fighting depression. Works on Henry James pastiche. Robert and Mame visit West Cornwall. Successfully protests O.S.U.'s dropping the *Sun-Dial*'s title. Writes introduction to Mary Mian's book, *My Country-in-Law*.

1947: January, last of "The Olden Time" series published in *New Yorker*. Sails to Bermuda in February. November 1 issue of *New Yorker* carries last original Thurber drawing. Summers in West Cornwall. "The Secret Life of Walter Mitty," produced by Samuel Goldwyn, with Danny Kaye, opens in August. Six casuals in *New Yorker*. Researches for *The Thurber Album*. Elliott Nugent is institutionalized with severe manic depression. Back to Hot Springs in November, afflicted by "The Thurbs." Protests congressional witch hunts. Works on soap-opera series.

1948: Visits Mame in Columbus for Mother's Day. Henry James pastiche, "The Beast in the Dingle," published September in both *Horizon* and *The Beast in Me and Other Animals* (Harcourt Brace). Recaptioned former drawings begin running in *New Yorker*. Fritzi Von Kuegelgen becomes his Cornwall secretary. Five articles on soap opera run as "Onward and Upward with the Arts"; five casuals; parody, "A Call on Mrs. Forrester."

1949: "File and Forget" published in January; eleven other casuals. Eight recaptioned drawings run. Visits Nassau in March, parties with J. P. Marquands, Dos Passos. In April, sails for Bermuda; Herman Miller dies. Rosemary graduates from Northampton School for Girls, injured in auto accident that summer but enters Skidmore College that fall. Thurber reviews Benchley collection for *New York Times Book Review*. Interviewed by Harvey Breit, draws self-portrait for article in *New York Times Magazine*. Begins "Letter from the States" in *Bermudian*.

1950: Helen's mother dies. Helen enters Doctors Hospital for surgery. Thurbers sail for Bermuda in March; writes most of *The 13 Clocks* there. Visits Columbus and receives honorary doctorate from Kenyon College in June. Rosemary enters University of Pennsylvania. Thurber is frequent guest on radio and television. Travels to Washington and Hot Springs in November. That month, *The 13 Clocks* published by Simon & Schuster. Article about Thurber by Lewis Gannett in *Harper's Bazaar*. "Photograph Album" series begins in *New Yorker* December 9. Writes twelve pieces for *Bermudian*.

1951: Seven "Album" pieces run in *New Yorker*, but only one casual; he quarrels with editors and the checking department; an ailing Ross has turned over most of the editing to Shawn and Lobrano. He writes ten "Letter from the States" columns for *Bermudian*. Thurbers in Bermuda March 20 to June 11. Joel Sayre's *Time* cover story on Thurber appears in July 9 issue, Thurber's self-portrait on cover his last original drawing to be published. Thurber receives honorary doctorate from Williams College. Announces he has stopped drawing. *Many Moons* is condensed in the *Reader's Digest,* broadcast on *Reader's Digest of the Air,* with Claude Rains as the Jester; made into a Columbia recording; produced as a play, runs for two weeks in New York; translated into several languages. Refuses honorary degree from O.S.U. to protest academic censorship. Assists Dale Kramer with his book about Harold Ross and the *New Yorker*. Ross dies in December.

1952: William Shawn named editor of the *New Yorker* in January. *The Thurber Album, A New Collection of Pieces About People* published in April by Simon & Schuster. During spring in Bermuda, his toxic-thyroid condition worsens; it is two years before doctors find the proper treatment; he can't tolerate alcohol, fights with everyone. *The Male Animal* revived on Broadway, runs through January 1953. At Homestead in Hot Springs in November; Christmas in West Cornwall.

1953: Thyroid condition continues to produce erratic behavior. In February, attends Rosemary's marriage to Frederick Sauers in Philadelphia. Visits

Williamsburg, Va., in March. Receives honorary degree from Yale and Sesqui-centennial Medal from Ohioana Library Association. Simon & Schuster publishes *Thurber Country* in October. Only one piece in *New Yorker*. Helen suffers detached retina; Thurber's efforts to locate his eye surgeon create international press attention. TV dramatization of *The 13 Clocks* in December. Spends Christmas with his family in Columbus, his first visit there since 1950.

1954: "Three by Thurber" produced off-Broadway in March. Spends May in Bermuda, August on Martha's Vineyard. "How to be Sixty" is his last *Bermudian* article; "Get *Thee* to a Monastery" is the only *New Yorker* casual. Continues work on play about Ross and *New Yorker*—never produced—and unfinished fairy tale, "The Spoodle." Scrap with Maeve Brennan in Algonquin lobby. Helen writes Jap Gude about Thurber's increasing mental aberrations.

1955: Resumes writing for *New Yorker*; seven casuals published. *Thurber's Dogs* published by Simon & Schuster in October, dedicated to Rosemary's first child, Sara Thurber Sauers, born March 31. Sails for France May 4; spends summer and fall in Europe, after seventeen-year absence. Works on Loch Ness monster article for *Holiday*. Becomes friends with A. J. Liebling. Whites visit London. Liebling unsuccessful in reuniting them with Thurber. Sails for home October 19. Mame dies in December, at age eighty-nine. During death watch in Columbus, Thurber begins *Further Fables for Our Time*.

1956: *New Yorker* buys thirty-seven of his forty-seven fables, carried through eleven issues, and one casual. Spends spring in Bermuda. Gus Lobrano, fiction editor of *New Yorker*, dies in mid-February; Katharine White returns from Maine to replace him temporarily. William Maxwell becomes Thurber's editor. Thurber talks publicly and negatively about the magazine. Feels isolated in West Cornwall; frequently calls old colleagues at *New Yorker* to chat. Is entranced by Broadway's *My Fair Lady*; praises it in *New York Times* piece. *Further Fables for Our Time* published by Simon & Schuster in October; wins the American Library Association's Liberty and Justice Award. Works on *The Wonderful O*. John McNulty dies in July; Thurber writes McNulty's obituary for the *New Yorker*.

1957: Has bitter fight with Maxwell over editing of *The Wonderful O* for *New Yorker* publication; withdraws manuscript; boycotts magazine for a year. *The Wonderful O* is published in May by Simon & Schuster; his editor there, Jack Goodman, dies. Harper & Bros. publishes Thurber collection, *Alarms and Diversions*, in November. "The Years with Ross" articles begin in the *Atlantic Monthly* the same month. Visits Bermuda for last time.

1958: Decides to make the Ross series a book; revives old relationships through voluminous letters of inquiry about Ross. Continues research in London. Is first American since Twain to be "called to the table" at *Punch*. Ross articles in the *Atlantic* gradually create dissension between Thurber, the Whites, and others who have their own images of Ross. Decides he has been financially cheated by the magazine for years. "Midnight at Tim's Place" is first *New Yorker* casual in more than two years, and a repeat spot drawing, the first since 1952, was the last Thurber drawing in the *New Yorker*. Returns from Europe in November. Holds New Year's Eve party for fifty people in West Cornwall.

1959: Helen operated on for ovarian cyst in March. Thurber appears on Edward R. Murrow's TV show, *Small World*. *The Years with Ross* published by Atlantic–Little, Brown in May, a Book-of-the-Month Club selection; biggest financial success since *The Thurber Carnival*. He is angered by negative reviews of the book in England. Relations with the *New Yorker* continue to deteriorate. The magazine publishes five of his casuals. Goes to Columbus in November to receive Headliner Award from the Press Club of Ohio.

1960: Haila Stoddard and Helen Bonfils produce *A Thurber Carnival*, a revue composed of Thurber prose and drawings. Thurber, as script doctor, makes a tryout tour of six cities, beginning with Columbus in January. In April, he attends dedication of Denney Hall at O.S.U., his last visit to Columbus; Helen reads his remarks. *A Thurber Carnival* opens at ANTA theater in New York in February, closed by actors' strike after seventeen weeks. Escapes apartment fire. Revue opens in Colorado in August. Spends the month there. After it returns to Broadway, in September, he joins the cast, playing himself, for eighty-eight performances. Two casuals in *New Yorker*. His work now appearing in other publications. Gives testimonial at Mark Van Doren's retirement banquet. Williamses visit from Bermuda to see the revue—the last time they would see Thurber.

1961: Thurber receives Tony Award for *A Thurber Carnival*; undergoes angst after the show closes. Sails for England in January in hopes of a British production of the revue. In April, Harper publishes *Lanterns & Lances*, last Thurber book to appear in his lifetime. Last *New Yorker* casual, "The Manic in the Moon," in August 19 issue. With tumor forming on his brain, Thurber's behavior is ever more erratic; verbally abuses Helen. Despairing of a British production of *A Thurber Carnival*, returns to the States with the Gudes. Attends opening night party for Noel Coward's *Sail Away*. Collapses, is taken to hospital October 4; dies November 2; cremated, ashes buried in Green Lawn Cemetery, Columbus.

1962: Published posthumously: *Credos and Curios*, by Harper & Row; *A*

Thurber Carnival, by Samuel French, Inc.; casuals and stories in *Atlantic*, *Harper's*, and *Playboy*.

1963: *Vintage Thurber*, with introduction by Helen Thurber, published by Hamish Hamilton, London.

1966: *Thurber & Company* published by Harper & Row.

1980: *Selected Letters of James Thurber*, edited by Helen Thurber and Edward Weeks, Atlantic–Little, Brown.

1989: *Collecting Himself*, previously uncollected Thurber, edited by Michael J. Rosen, Harper & Row.

1994: *People Have More Fun than Anybody*, more uncollected Thurber, edited by Michael J. Rosen, Harcourt Brace.

Biographical Update

The Principals

Helen Thurber, worried by what she thought was an inadequate will left by Thurber, and that his properties would fall out of favor after his death, told friends she was financially threatened. Actually, Thurber earned a hundred thousand dollars in net income in the last year of his life, and revenues from his works, which have continued in popularity, provided her with a comfortable income for the twenty-five years that she survived him.

Helen led an active career as a Thurber spokesperson, running "Thurber, Incorporated," helping to arrange subsidiary uses of his material, editing his letters, and assisting Thurber scholars in keeping alive his work and reputation.

She oversaw the brief run of *A Thurber Carnival* in London in 1962, and worked with Haila Stoddard Connor on another Thurber revue, *The Beast in Me*, which ran for only twenty-one performances in New York. She edited and wrote introductions for *Credos and Curios*, a collection of Thurber pieces, in 1962; *Vintage Thurber*, a British two-volume Thurber collection, in 1963; and *Selected Letters of James Thurber* (with Edward Weeks), in 1981.

Her most frequent companions were Haila Stoddard and Haila's husband, Whitfield Connor, who died in 1988. Helen's physical decline, Haila says, began with her dismayed reading of the typescript of the "authorized" biography in 1974, which, Helen believed, portrayed Thurber as little more than a mean, drunken nuisance with a dissipated talent in the last fifteen years of his life. She felt further betrayed by E. B. and Katharine White, who refused to support her protests to the book's author and publisher. Katharine wrote that she found the book "honest and accurate," if "somewhat pedestrian"; Andy listed only minor errors in the book associated with his and Katharine's quotations, and suggested that if Helen felt the book was sufficiently damaging, she should have it read by a "sharp" libel lawyer. Helen spent a thousand dollars in legal fees before realizing that court action would be costly and probably unsuccessful.

Following the book's publication in the spring of 1975, says Stoddard, Helen's physical and mental desolation deepened. She sold the West Cornwall house to the actor Sam Waterston and purchased a smaller one in Weston, Connecticut, near the Connors. Haila frequently entertained the De Vrieses and other friends of Helen's "to keep her cheered up." In the mid-eighties, Helen sank into lethargy. Her last year found her unwilling to open her mail, according to her secretary, Louise Webb, and her housekeeper. She died December 22, 1986, at age eighty-four, in the Norwalk (Connecticut) Hospital. Her cremated remains are buried in a small cemetery on Rattlesnake Road in West Cornwall, next to the grave of Rose Algrant, Thurber's favorite member of the Cornwall group.

Rosemary Thurber, at the end of 1986, succeeded Helen as literary conservator of the estate. Her principal regret is that Helen, in her worsening melancholy, had done nothing to prepare Rosemary for the task.

After raising a daughter and two sons, Rosemary divorced and earned a master's degree in social work at Washington University, in St. Louis, where she worked for several years putting art and humanities programs into senior centers and nursing homes. She did similar work after moving to South Haven, Michigan, but soon was managing a "fine craft" department at a local art gallery, which she eventually owned. After the gallery closed in 1994, Rosemary helped her daughter, Sara, launch the Thurber Art Works Division of James Thurber Literary Properties. Its product line includes clothing, china, and note cards bearing Thurber drawings. Sara has joined Rosemary in managing the Thurber estate.

Jap Gude continued to manage subsidiary rights for the literary properties of White and Thurber, through his agency, Stix & Gude. (After he gave up the agency, Helen went without an agent until Haila Stoddard introduced her to Lucy Kroll.) Upon retiring, Gude moved to Edgartown, on Martha's Vineyard, where he had summered for half a century in a house he owns there. Now in a nursing home on the Vineyard, as of this writing he is ninety-two, hard of hearing and frail of body, but with mental and speech faculties near normal. His wife, Helen, is a patient at Windemere (part of the Martha's Vineyard Hospital), suffering from a form of mental deterioration.

Elliott Nugent was in and out of mental institutions during the last years of his life, cursed by manic depression. In 1965, he published his memoirs, *Events Leading up to the Comedy*, in which he tells of his long association with Thurber. His memory gradually failed him, though once, in a nursing home, when he was watching the film version of *The Male Animal* on TV, he turned to a companion, smiled, and said, "I wrote that with a friend of mine." He died in New York, August 9, 1980, at age eighty-three, survived by his wife, Norma; his two daughters, Lee and Nancy; and eight grandchildren.

Peter De Vries continued commuting from Westport to the *New Yorker*, fine-tuning cartoons for the magazine two days a week, until 1986. He wrote twenty-six comic novels. Poor health restricted his writing to personal letters and "eulogies of deceased friends" after 1986. He and his wife, Katinka Loeser, remained in loyal touch with Helen Thurber until her death. Katinka preceded him in death in 1991; De Vries died of pneumonia at the Norwalk Hospital at age eighty-three, on September 28, 1993.

Joel Sayre left Time, Inc., in the mid-fifties to return to screenwriting in Hollywood. He then lived in London, and in 1960 became an instructor at the Annenberg School of Communications at the University of Pennsylvania in Philadelphia. He retired from teaching in 1965 and continued to write in New York and Virginia. In 1978, he moved to Taftsville, Vermont, where he died at age seventy-eight on September 9, 1979.

Ann Honeycutt, after her few months of married life with St. Clair McKelway, never married again, continuing to play the field and becoming a longtime and close companion of the advertising tycoon and author Bruce Barton, up to his death. She hosted her "Southern" versions of Thanksgiving dinners for her friends, featuring her excellent cooking, and ran a food catering service for a time.

She kept Thurber's letters to her a secret for years ("I lied to Thurber's biographers," she wrote E. B. White), and in the early 1980s sold them for twenty thousand dollars to a businessman interested in literature, who donated them to his alma mater, Cornell. For several years, she used the proceeds of the sale to winter in the Caribbean, but she later developed agoraphobia and became afraid to leave her apartment, despite the help of a psychiatrist.

Surviving friends included Joseph Mitchell and Charles Addams, the latter agreeing with her that they both had lived as long as they had because they were "too stubborn and mean to die." "Honey" died in her Manhattan apartment in 1989, age eighty-seven, chain-smoking to the last. Her funeral eulogy was delivered by Mitchell, who, along with Robert MacMillan, a *New Yorker* editor and friend, she named as her heirs.

Paula Trueman, the actress with whom Thurber was romantically involved in the early thirties, continued to act on stage and screen into the late 1970s. She died at age ninety-six, at New York Hospital, in 1993.

Columbus

Minnette Fritts and her husband, Dr. Oscar Proctor, after he obtained a medical degree at Northwestern University, left Chicago for Rochester, Minnesota, and his three-year fellowship at the Mayo Clinic, followed by a year of surgery training at the University of Minnesota. Their children, Sally and David, were born during those years. The family moved to Seattle. In the late forties, the Proctors divorced. At an O.S.U. reunion in Columbus, Minnette met a former friend and classmate, Kenneth Ewart. Several years later, after his wife's death, Ewart hired a detective to find Minnette. She married him in 1958 when she was sixty-three, and lived in Cuyahoga Falls, Ohio, where Ewart owned a factory. After his death in 1966, Minnette returned to the Seattle area where she died twenty-seven years later, on November 12, 1992, at age 97, of congestive heart failure.

Ted Gardiner died in Columbus, at age eighty-three, in 1981; depressed at the end, he had refused to eat or to take his medication. His wife, Julia, died at ninety-three in 1993. Their daughter Patricia McGuckin, a *Columbus Dispatch* reporter before working in public relations, died in October 1992, of pancreatic cancer. The surviving Gardiner daughter, Julia Hadley, lives with her husband, Hugh, in Columbus, and volunteers as a tour guide at The Thurber House.

Eva Prout married Ernest Geiger on April 30, 1924. In 1939, after they had retired from show business, they left Zanesville for Coral Gables, Florida, where they ran a music store. Eva last visited Columbus in 1966, after her husband's death. She was interviewed by Lewis Branscomb in Coral Gables in 1973, when she was seventy-eight, "attractive, genial and gracious," says Branscomb. The date and circumstances of her death elude inquiry.

Dorothy (Mrs. Herman) Reid Miller continued living at Fool's Paradise, in Worthington, Ohio, after her husband's death in 1949. She worked for *Current Events* magazine until 1952, when she sold her home and moved to Middletown, Connecticut, where she worked for the Wesleyan University Press. After retirement in 1964, she spent summers on Block Island. She now lives in Fort Myers, Florida.

George Smallsreed retired as managing editor of the *Columbus Dispatch* in 1962, and two years later, at age sixty-five, died in Phoenix, Arizona, of a heart attack.

At the *New Yorker*

Roger Angell has continued as a contributor and a fiction editor at the *New Yorker*.

Peter Arno, New Yorker cartoonist, died in February 1968, at age sixty-four, in Harrison, New York.

Bernard A. Bergman, Thurber friend and early *New Yorker* managing editor, returned to newspaper editing in New York and Philadelphia, worked in public relations, and spent his last ten years as the book editor of the *Philadelphia Bulletin*. He died at eighty-five, on April 11, 1980, at his Philadelphia apartment.

Maeve Brennan, McKelway's fifth wife, contributed entertaining copy to the Talk of the Town as the Long-Winded Lady, as well as short stories and book reviews. She declined mentally in later years and died at seventy-six, in November 1993.

James M. Cain died at eighty-five, at his home in Hyattsville, Maryland, of a heart attack, on October 27, 1977. After leaving the *New Yorker* he went on to write eighteen books, including *The Postman Always Rings Twice* and *Double Indemnity*.

Robert M. Coates, once Thurber's closest friend, died at Lenox Hill Hospital, in Manhattan, on February 8, 1973, at age seventy-five. He was the *New Yorker*'s art critic from 1937 to 1967, and the author of several novels and many short stories. His second wife, Astrid Peters, survived him.

Janet Flanner, who wrote the *New Yorker*'s "Letter from Paris," over the signature "Genêt," for approximately fifty years and entertained the Thurbers when they were in France, died of a heart attack, at age eighty-six, on November 7, 1978, in Lenox Hill Hospital.

Raoul H. Fleischmann, publisher of the *New Yorker*, died at age eighty-three, at his Fifth Avenue apartment, in 1969. His stepson, Stephen B. Botsford, president of the *New Yorker* from 1956 to 1961, died at age forty-seven, in 1967. Fleischmann's other stepson, Gardner Botsford, continues to edit the work of his wife, Janet Malcolm, for the *New Yorker*.

James M. Geraghty, New Yorker art editor, who handled Thurber's drawings for the magazine from 1939 on, retired in 1973 and died of a heart attack on January 16, 1983, at seventy-eight, at his winter home in Venice, Florida.

Brendan Gill continues to contribute his writing to the *New Yorker* and to concern himself actively with the cultural life of New York City.

June Grant, Ross's first wife, wrote a book called *Ross, The New Yorker, and Me,* which was published in 1968. She died on March 16, 1972, of cancer, in Litchfield, Connecticut, where she and her second husband, a former editor of *Fortune* magazine, ran a botanical nursery, the White Flower Farm.

Milton Greenstein, attorney for the *New Yorker,* who arranged contributors' contracts, reprint rights and permissions, read all the magazine's copy for libel, and succeeded Hawley Truax as liaison between the editorial and business departments, died August 2, 1991, at age seventy-nine, after several strokes. He was skilled at placating Thurber during Thurber's late period of paranoia regarding the *New Yorker*.

Emily Hahn, in her eighties, may still be found in her office at the *New Yorker,* "though I get around with a cane and fall down a lot," she says. In the early thirties, she dated Wolcott Gibbs frequently, Thurber occasionally.

Ralph Ingersoll, after World War II service, published more than twenty small-to-medium-size newspapers in the Northeast. He wrote nine books of fiction and nonfiction, including his memoirs, and retired from newspaper publishing in 1982. Though he also lived in West Cornwall, and though Thurber pays him high tribute in *The Years with Ross,* he and Thurber only rarely socialized after Ingersoll left the *New Yorker* in 1930. He died of complications resulting from a stroke, on March 8, 1983, in a Miami Beach hospital, at the age of eighty-four.

Rea Irvin, the first art editor of the *New Yorker* and creator of its cover trademark, the dandy known as Eustace Tilley, died on May 28, 1972, on St. Croix, at age ninety. He found Thurber's first drawing of a seal "inaccurate."

After Ross's death, Irvin's drawings were no longer accepted by the *New Yorker*. He retired to the Virgin Islands in 1966.

Eugene Kinkead, who researched Thurber's "Where Are They Now?" series, remained a staff writer and editor at the *New Yorker* through the eighties. He died on August 8, 1992, of cancer, at age eighty-six, at Phelps Memorial Hospital, in Tarrytown, New York.

A. J. Liebling outlived Thurber by only two years, dying of bronchial pneumonia on December 28, 1963, at age fifty-nine, at Mt. Sinai Hospital, in Manhattan.

Lois Long, who helped introduce Thurber to the speakeasies of the Prohibition era in the late twenties, retired from her "On and Off the Avenue" department at age seventy-one. She died two years later, in Saratoga, New York, on July 28, 1974.

St. Clair McKelway wrote for the *New Yorker* for ten years after Thurber's death. He divorced Maeve Brennan and was in poor health for several years before his death, on January 10, 1980, at the DeWitt Nursing Home in Manhattan, at age seventy-four.

Morris Markey left the *New Yorker* in the late thirties for Hollywood. Failing as a screenwriter, he returned to New York in 1938, to freelance as a magazine writer and write notes for the Texaco Radio Opera broadcasts. In 1949 he moved to Halifax, Virginia, near his childhood home, to write a novel. Cirrhosis of the liver kept him drinking "to kill the pain," which, along with despondency, is believed to have driven him to kill himself with a rifle. His death was officially listed as "from causes not determined," but his wife, Helen, believed he arranged his suicide to look like an accident for insurance purposes.

William Maxwell, who bore the brunt of the battle between Thurber and the *New Yorker* over the editing of *The Wonderful O*, has retired from the magazine to spend his full working time on his writing.

Joseph Mitchell continues to occupy an office at the *New Yorker*, writing about, among other things, the Honeycutt/Walker/Mitchell/Addams group of earlier years.

Ogden Nash, humorist poet and a three-month managing editor of the *New Yorker*, died May 19, 1971, at age sixty-eight, of pneumonia and kidney failure, at Johns Hopkins Hospital, in Baltimore.

Frederick (Freddie) A. Packard, whose checking department came under frequent fire from Thurber, died November 11, 1974, at seventy-one, at his apartment on Central Park West. He was one of the old-timers whom Thurber, when lonely, would occasionally talk to by phone from West Cornwall.

Dorothy Parker, who wrote two introductions for books of Thurber's drawings, which she admired, died on June 7, 1967, at age seventy-three, of a heart attack, in her Manhattan apartment.

William Shawn died at age eighty-five, December 8, 1992, at his Fifth Avenue apartment, "of natural causes." To his profound disappointment, he was removed as *New Yorker* editor by S. I. Newhouse, its owner, on February 13, 1987, ostensibly because of a slow-down in magazine circulation and advertising. He became a consulting editor at Farrar, Straus & Giroux, and was reading books and manuscripts until nearly the moment of his death.

He idolized Harold Ross, and though he refused to have Thurber's *The Years with Ross* reviewed by the *New Yorker*, he dealt with Brendan Gill's undisguised hostility toward Ross in Gill's *Here at The New Yorker* by writing his own warm, personal appreciation of Ross for inclusion in the book.

Jean Stafford, contributor to the *New Yorker*, friend of the De Vrieses and Katharine White, married A. J. Liebling on April 3, 1959. She died of cardiac arrest, after a long illness, at age sixty-three, on March 26, 1979, at the Burke Rehabilitation Center, in White Plains, New York. Her ashes are buried in Green River Cemetery, East Hampton, Long Island, beside the grave of her husband.

Daise E. Terry, who handled Thurber's mail and the many requests for reprints of his *New Yorker* pieces, was relieved of her office management duties shortly after Thurber's death and given a less demanding job. She became somewhat disoriented mentally, forgetfully turning up for work on holidays when the magazine was closed. She retired in 1968 and died August 20, 1973, at a nursing home in Alpine, California, at age eighty-nine.

R. Hawley Truax, friend of Ross for more than a quarter of a century and liaison between the business and editorial departments of the *New Yorker*, died of pneumonia at Lenox Hill Hospital on November 24, 1978, at age eighty-nine. After the death of Ross, he ably defended Ross against Thurber's wild attacks over the *New Yorker's* past payments to contributors.

Stanley Walker worked for the *New York American* and *New York Woman*, after leaving the *New Yorker*. In 1939, he was the editor of the *Philadelphia Evening Public Ledger*. In 1946, he returned to his sheep ranch in his home-town of Lampasas, Texas. He continued to write until 1962, when he learned he had cancer of the throat. He killed himself with a shotgun on November 25, 1962, at age sixty-four.

Rogers E. M. Whitaker, an editor who worked with Thurber in his earliest days at the *New Yorker*, contributed fifty-five years of work to the magazine. He was the railroad buff E. M. Frimbo and "The Old Curmudgeon" in Talk of the Town. He died at eighty-two of cancer, at Calvary Hospital in the Bronx, on May 11, 1981.

Edmund Wilson died June 12, 1972, at age seventy-seven, at his home in Talcottville, New York.

E. B. White died at his home in North Brooklin, Maine, on October 1, 1985, at age eighty-six, after a year of illness. He wrote taglines for news-breaks for fifty years, quitting only when arthritis crippled his fingers two years before his death. Explaining his pleasure in handling newsbreaks, he said, "It gives me the feeling of holding down a job and affords me a glimpse of newspapers all over the country."

After Katharine's death in 1977, White's last years were lonely ones. He cooperated willingly with Linda H. Davis on her biography of Katharine, though he died before its publication in 1987. He had little more than gram-matical suggestions for his biographer, Scott Elledge, whose book was pub-lished a year before White's death. He wrote Ann Honeycutt that his favorite review of the book was one that ended: " 'It is hard not to like E. B. White (now 84) and it is hard to dislike *E.B.White: A biography.*' . . . To which I have added the newsbreak line, 'You just have to keep working at it.' " He was looking forward to dying, he wrote in reply to a letter from Honeycutt, shortly before his death; "Giving it everything I've got." Until the end, he continued to enjoy a martini at cocktail time and having his writings read to him.

His son, Joel, of Blue Hill Falls, Maine, a naval architect, manages the Whites' literary estates, with his wife, Allene.

Katharine White continued, despite illnesses, as a *New Yorker* fiction editor until her retirement at the end of 1959, Shawn shipping manuscripts to her in Maine. She kept up a voluminous correspondence with writers, began writing "Onward and Upward" articles for the *New Yorker* about gardening, and helped answer her husband's mail.

She suffered a heart attack on July 20, 1977, at age eighty-four, and was rushed to the Blue Hill Memorial Hospital, where she died of congestive heart failure, with Andy, Roger and Carol Angell, and Joel and Allene White in attendance. A grieving Andy was unable to bring himself to attend the funeral service.

England

Hamish Hamilton, Thurber's British publisher, died in London, at age eighty-seven, in 1987.

Cyril Connolly, who published Thurber's Henry James pastiche in *Horizon*, died at age seventy-one in a London hospital on November 26, 1974. *Horizon* folded in 1950, two years after Thurber's pastiche appeared.

Noel Coward, whose prolific work as playwright earned Thurber's early admiration, died of a heart attack at his villa in Jamaica, the West Indies, on March 26, 1973, at age seventy-three.

A *Thurber Carnival*

Haila Stoddard Connor continues to live in Weston, Connecticut, and works with young playwrights and producers, often associated with the Westport Playhouse.

Burgess Meredith, who directed A *Thurber Carnival*, lives in Malibu, California, and is still active in movies. His memoirs, *So Far, So Good*, published in 1994, include an account of his association with Thurber. He has twice appeared at The Thurber House in Columbus to offer at literary events his fond recollections of Thurber.

Bermuda

Ronald Williams, plagued by several strokes, died in 1976, in Bermuda, at age seventy, of arteriosclerosis.

Janey Williams died at age eighty-four in Bermuda, of lung cancer, May 19, 1994—thirty-three years after Thurber lectured her on the dangers of smoking.

Dinah Jane Williams Darby, Thurber's godchild, died unexpectedly of an illness in 1986 in Bermuda, at age forty-six.

Sara Linda Williams Latham (Princess Saralinda in *The 13 Clocks*) is an executive with Trimingham's store in Bermuda.

The Bermudian is still published. When it was threatened by a hostile takeover in September 1961, two months before Thurber's death, Helen bought four hundred shares of the magazine's stock in her name, for nearly ten thousand dollars, which were successfully voted against a potential ownership that would have ousted Ronald Williams. Helen remained a member of the *Bermudian* board until Christmas 1973, when she gave her shares—by then worth only three thousand dollars—to "my god-daughter," Dinah Jane Williams Darby. Upon Dinah's death, her husband inherited her shares. Shortly thereafter, the magazine passed out of the family's hands, though Dinah's daughter is still on the staff.

The Cornwall, Connecticut, Area

Rose Algrant died in her nineties (she had always refused to give her exact age) of cancer of the pancreas, in her Cornwall home, on June 4, 1992.

Mark Van Doren retired from teaching at Columbia University in 1959. (Thurber spoke at the retirement dinner.) He died at seventy-eight, after surgery for circulatory problems, on December 10, 1972, at Charlotte Hungerford Hospital, in Torrington, Connecticut.

Marc Simont, Thurber friend and neighbor, who illustrated *The 13 Clocks* and *The Wonderful O*, continues with his art in West Cornwall.

Others

Franklin P. Adams entered the Lynwood Nursing Home in Manhattan in 1955 and died there, at seventy-eight, on March 23, 1960. A member of the Round Table and a close friend of Harold Ross, he published an item by Thurber in his famous newspaper column, The Conning Tower, in the *New*

York World. That event, Thurber says, was all that kept him from returning to Columbus in discouragement. Adams was on the panel of the radio program *Information, Please,* hosted by Clifton Fadiman, on which Thurber occasionally appeared.

Heywood Broun, liberal newspaper columnist and Round Table member, who persuaded Thurber, his drinking companion, to join a committee favoring a waiters' strike in the mid-thirties, died of pneumonia at fifty-one, at Columbia-Presbyterian Medical Center, in Manhattan, on December 18, 1939.

Cass Canfield was chairman of Harper & Bros.' executive committee at Thurber's death. (That same year, the publishing house was renamed Harper & Row.) In that capacity, he published the posthumous Thurber volumes, *Credos and Curios,* in 1962, and *Thurber & Company,* in 1966. Canfield was made "house senior editor" of Harper & Row in 1967. He went to his office regularly until September 1985, when he had a stroke. He died the next year, on March 27, at his Manhattan apartment, at age eighty-eight.

Alistair Cooke retired in 1972 as chief American correspondent of the *Manchester Guardian.* He still broadcasts his "Letter from America" over the BBC's World Service. In 1993, he retired from PBS's *Masterpiece Theatre* after twenty-two years as its host. He and his wife, Jane, continue to live in Manhattan.

Malcolm Cowley, literary critic and Thurber friend, died on March 27, 1989, at age ninety, of a heart attack, in the New Milford (Connecticut) Hospital.

Morris L. Ernst, Thurber's friend and attorney, died at age eighty-seven on May 21, 1976, at his Fifth Avenue apartment.

Margaret Case Harriman, chronicler of the Round Table and daughter of Frank Case, owner of the Algonquin, died at Columbia-Presbyterian Medical Center, at age sixty-two, on August 7, 1966. A contributor to the *New Yorker* for years, she was unable to get any of her work accepted there after Ross's death. She celebrated with Thurber the night of the party given upon the publication of *The Years with Ross.*

Richard S. Maney, press agent for *The Male Animal* and a Bleeck's habitué, died at seventy-seven on July 1, 1968, of pneumonia, at Norwalk Hospital in Connecticut.

John O'Hara died in his sleep, April 11, 1970, at his home in Princeton, New Jersey, probably of a heart attack, at age sixty-five.

Nora Sayre continues to write in Manhattan and teaches writing courses at Columbia University.

Notes

The following abbreviations are used throughout the notes:

JT	James Thurber
CT	Charles Thurber
RT	Robert Thurber
WT	William Thurber
MT	Mame Thurber
A	Althea Thurber/Comstock/Gilmore
OSU	The Ohio State University
EN	Elliott Nugent
CD	"The Columbus Dispatch"
C&C	"Credos and Curios"
TTA	"The Thurber Album"
MF	Minnette Fritts
EP	Eva Prout
HM	Herman Miller
HMS	Herman Millers
NYer	"The New Yorker Magazine"
EBW	E. B. "Andy" White
KSW	Katharine S. White
HWR	Harold Wallace Ross
WS	William Shawn
HT	Helen Thurber
RM	Rosemary Thurber
AH	Ann Honeycutt
McK	St. Clair McKelway
WG	Wolcott Gibbs
McN	John McNulty
JS	Joel Sayre
NS	Nora Sayre
EH	Emily Hahn

AL	Alice Leighner
SB	Samuel B. Baker
JG	John "Jap" Gude
TTC	"The Thurber Carnival"
LL	Lois Long
PDV	Peter De Vries
BG	Brendan Gill
HATNY	"Here at The New Yorker"
RW	Ronald Williams
JW	Jane Williams
RWS	The Williamses
TG	Ted Gardiner
ISN	"Is Sex Necessary?"
MLAHT	"My Life and Hard Times"
TYWR	"The Years with Ross"
DK	Dale Kramer
RATNY	"Ross and The New Yorker"
LBI	Lewis Branscomb interview
BB	Burton Bernstein
Ltr	Letter
HK	Harrison Kinney
MWAWTI	"My World—and Welcome To It"
ELUTTC	"Events Leading Up to the Comedy"
RA	Roger Angell
GS	George Smallsreed
WHIT	Rogers Whitaker
HS	Haila Stoddard
RTNYAM	"Ross, The New Yorker and Me"
RI	Ralph Ingersoll
TMAMOTFT	"The Middle-Aged Man on the Flying Trapeze"
LYMA	"Let Your Mind Alone"
MVD	Mark Van Doren
NY	New York

PREFACE

xvi   "I have professors": Ltr, HT to HK, 12/12/62.

xvii   "I'm glad to hear": Ltr, JT to HK, 12/18/50.

xviii   "You better hitch your belt up": Ltr to HK, undated, 1962.

xviii   "You're taking on something": Ltr to HK, 2/7/62.

INTRODUCTION

1. THOSE CLOCKS OF COLUMBUS

2. THAT THURBER ALBUM

3. THAT MAN WITH A ROSE

12   of a "knee disease": Ltr, JT to Donia and John McN, 11/21/37.
13   the cast subdued him: JS, NY TV "talk" show, WNDT, transcript undated.
13   "Draft Board Nights": NYer, 9/30/33.
13   "in 1917, the draft boards": PM, 12/1/40.

4. THAT LAVENDER WITH A DIFFERENCE

14   "the greatest ham actor": Ltr, 1/24/50.
14   "I've been acting since I": Martha Deane, WOR, 9/23/60.
14   "who knew the Bible": "Lavender with a Difference," NYer, 7/28/51.
15   "It was the closest I ever got": MT to Richard Oulahan, of Time, 1950.
15   "the livest wire": Ruth White, "James Thurber: His Life in Columbus," CD, 3/10/40.
15   One teacher suggested: SB, "Thurber: The Columbus Years," unpublished Master of Arts thesis, OSU, 1962.
15   "I always planned for a life": MT to Beverly Smith, CD Sunday Magazine, 6/1/52.
15   "one of the most beautiful girls": Clifford Fisher to AL, October 1969.
16   "Oh, Grandma, make her do something": SB, op. cit.
16   wanted to break a dozen eggs at once: Time, 7/9/51.
16   removed her shoe and stocking: SB thesis, op. cit.
16   pretended to be a little drunk: Ibid.
16   "She was a famous hand": TTA.
17   "My first wife used to invite": Fisher to AL.
17   "A couple of times when we thought": RT to HK.
20   "a mixture of wonder and": "Lavender with a Difference."
20   "When I used to visit the Thurber home": JS to HK, 1962.
20   ("It isn't often that my memory"): JT, Ohioana Award remarks, op. cit.
20   "My father had an outstanding": Ltr, RT to HK, 5/20/65.
21   "I couldn't even remember": MT to Oulihan, 1950.
22   "I've been inactive": CD, 6/1/52, op. cit.
22   "She didn't want to be a bother": RT to HK, 1965.
23   . . . I still can't erase from my: Ltr, RT to HK, 7/14/75.
23   "James was very generous": Ltr, RT to HK, 5/18/65.

5. THAT GENTLEMAN FROM INDIANA

25   "All we were told about Leander": Ltr, RT to HK, 5/15/65.

25   he was back in touch: Ltr, Charles H. Thurber, Sr., to RT, 12/24/61; 1/16/62; 10/22/62.

26   "Daguerreotype of a Lady": NYer, 4/28/51.

27   In an 1884 letter to Mame: 10/29.

27   "By then she was in rather": Ltr, RT to HK, 5/15/65.

27   I keep wondering why none of us: Ltr, 7/12/51.

28   "It was quite a blow to him": Ltr, RT to HK, 5/15/65.

29   "looks just like the charming miss": Ltr, 10/29/1884.

29   "I feel so sure that you and I": Ltr, undated.

29   My dear Mame: Ltr, 2/2/1890.

31   "Poor James Whitcomb Riley!": Ibid.

32   "Social levels were determined": Williamson to HK, 1962.

32   ("very old for those days"): MT to Oulahan, 1950.

33   "Willie put your father out": Ltr, 7/28/50.

33   "I think my Grandfather": WT to HK, Columbus, 1962.

34   Because I feel that I: *Saturday Evening Post*, 5/20/67.

34   "I don't think you know about all": Ltr, 12/26/58.

35   "I remember that Negro maid": MT to Oulahan.

35   "I wouldn't shoot anyone": JT to HK, 1948.

35   his brother cried: WT to HK, Columbus, 1962.

36   "My mother had a Christian": JT to HK.

36   Thurber remembers his father: Ltr, JT to Acosta, 12/26/58.

36   "I Went to Sullivant": NYer, 6/22/35.

36   "I don't remember why Charlie wanted": MT to Oulahan.

36   "We moved around so much": RT to HK, 1962.

36   "A couple of moves were made": Ltr, RT to HK, 11/15/69.

37   "I sincerely doubt": Ltr, RT to HK, 5/15/65.

37   "the state organizer of the Bull Moose Party": TTA, Simon & Schuster, 1952.

38   "doing occasional political": Ltr, RT to HK, 5/15/65.

38   "anyone desiring an interview": *Columbus Journal*, 4/30/28.

39   "Our beloved President is dead": "Mayor Secretary Issues Proclamation," RT scrapbooks.

39   "She evinced much interest": 8/30 news clipping, RT scrapbooks.

39   "His official position": 5/23/30, RT scrapbooks.

40   "What success has been mine": *Columbus Journal*, 4/30/28.

41   "Let me now introduce": *Reader's Digest*, Jan/1932.

41   "All the Thurbers were funny": JS to HK, 1962.

41   "In spite of [his] long": Sunday CD, 5/15/32.

41   "He was a good man": Meckstroth to AL.

42   "Uncle Charley would sit": Fisher to AL, 1969.

42   "The neighborhood kids liked": RT to HK.

42   "The Tree on the Diamond": NYer, 1/6/51.

43   "Probably I was taken to": Ltr, RT to HK, 5/18/65.

43   "He was addicted to contests": "Gentleman from Indiana."

43   "My father often had sidelines": Ltr, RT to HK, 5/20/65

44   "We felt as if we'd been caught": RT to HK, 1962.

44   "You can't really find": McK to HK, Century Association, NY, 1962.

44   "I always thought that my": Ltr, RT to HK, 5/18/65.

45   "Each respected the other's": Ltr, RT to HK, 5/15/65.

45   "My father frequently slept": Ibid.

46   "When [my father] worked": LBI of WT, 2/14-15/72, Thurber Collection, OSU.

46   I admired my father: Ltr to HK, 5/15/65.

48   "I realize how busy papa is": Ltr, JT to RT, 4/9/19.

48   "My father and Jim got along": Ltr, RT to HK, 5/20/65.

49   "He didn't confide in us much anymore": RT to HK, 1962.

50   "The Night the Bed Fell": NYer, 7/8/33.

50   "The Car We Had to Push": NYer, 7/15/33.

50   "More Alarms at Night": NYer, 8/26/33.

51   "went berserk while doing the dishes": "A Sequence of Servants," NYer, 9/9/33.

51   ("I don't think any servant"): RT to HK, 1965.

52   "Jim wasn't as close to his": Ltr, RT to HK, 5/20/65.

53   "never to bring any children": Ltr, JT to EN, 4/4/20.

54   "Teacher's Pet": NYer, 8/20/49.

56   "I know [Jim] felt pretty": Ltr, RT to HK, 5/18/65.

57   You have been so darned: *Ohio State Journal*, 1/1/32.

57   "In my opinion, it's a darn good book": *Columbus Citizen*, 2/11/30.

58   "Fern," he said to her: 1930, *Columbus Citizen*, circa 1933.

58   ("Jamie and I are both comedians"): MT to Oulahan.

58   "I remember there was some talk about": *Columbus Citizen*, circa 1933, RT scrapbooks.

58   Jim arranged for [his father]: Ltr, RT to HK, 5/20/65.

59   "he was proud of his son": Ltr, HT to BB, op. cit.

59   He was ill about 3 months: Ltr, MT to MF, 8/3/39.
59   "The Secret Life of Walter Mitty": NYer, 3/18/39.

6. THAT UNIQUE HERMIT

61   I sent the proof without: Ltr, JT to Thurbers, 12/22/50.
62   "the New Yorker will send you": Ltr, 3/20/51.
64   ("Robert once started a schoolyard"): MT to Oulahan.
66   I don't think you need have any qualms: Ltr, EBW to JT, 6/15/51,
      Letters of E. B. White, Harper & Row, 1976, Dorothy L. Guth, ed.
68   Dear Thurbers: Ltr, 6/12/51.
69   I knew you would be interested: Ltr, 6/15/51.
70   "He and I had some sharp exchanges": RT to HK, 1965.
70   "My brother Robert took a Freudian": Ltr, 6/26/51.
70   "in writing any story": Ltr, 6/19/51.
71   June and July 1951 will be: Ltr to Thurbers, 6/26/51.
71   Remember that a letter: Ltr to Thurbers, 7/2/51.
73   Mrs. Pennington, Maud, and Katherine: Ibid.
73   Well, *TIME* got the stories: Ltr to MT, 7/10/51.
74   Dear Mama, We just got your letter: Ltr to MT, 7/12/51.
75   William called up yesterday: Ltr to MT, 8/28/51.
75   "we both wanted you to stay": Ltr to MT, 9/6/51.
75   "I wrote my last letter": Ltr to Thurbers, 9/11/51.
76   "I'm glad the Yankees": Ltr to Thurbers, 9/20/51.
76   "I hated to see Cleveland": Ltr to MT, 9/28/51.
76   "Dear folks, we got back": Ltr to Thurbers, 11/9/51.
76   "I tried to call you": Ltr to Thurbers, 12/3/51.
77   " 'Gentleman from Indiana' will satisfy everybody": Ltr to
      Thurbers, 12/15/51.
77   "Jamie couldn't stand being estranged": HT to BB, *Thurber*, Dodd,
      Mead, 1975.
78   I didn't want to be rough: Ltr, 11/7/56.
79   "I can't help but think": Ltr to HK, 2/27/74.
79   "Who knows how one would have": Ltr to HK, 7/10/75.
79   "I firmly believe most people will": Ltr to HK, 2/27/74.
79   "I am going to write about imaginary": Ltr, 4/25/52.

7. THAT SECRET LIFE OF JAMES THURBER

81   Thurber never missed: Blanch C. Roberts to Ruth White, CD, 3/10/40.

81   "We had a terrible time getting": MT to Oulahan, 1950.

82   ("Great God Almighty"): "Lavender with a Difference," TTA.

82   John is wrong: Ltr to Smallsreed, 3/1/54.

83   But the "baccy ball" incident: Earl Fisher to AL, 10/69.

83   "due to my temper flare-ups": Ltr, RT to HK, 5/18/65.

83   "Oh, they were a lively group": MT to Oulahan, 1950.

84   "If people are curious": WT to HK, Columbus, 1962.

84   "But Thurber would have been a": Maxwell to HK, Yorktown Heights, NY, 1962.

84   "We were taking turns": JT to HK, 1948.

84   In 1927, on a business trip: WT to HK.

84   "Here's my son, Bill": LBI, WT, 2/14–15/72.

84   "I could put it down": Ibid.

85   "we all want to be something we're not": Ibid.

85   ("For God's sake, Bessie"): Ltr, JT to John and Donia McN, 11/21/37.

85   "William has no job": Ltr, undated, JT to AH, quoting Ltr, also undated, MT to JT, circa 1933–34.

87   "We were all three great mimics": WT, LBI, op. cit.

88   "But somehow it didn't work": WT to Oulahan, 1950.

88   "I told them I was James Thurber's cousin": WT to HK.

89   "Rex had markings on him": WT, unpublished article about Rex, Thurber Collection, OSU.

90   William mailed the article: Ltr, *Reader's Digest* to WT, courtesy of RD editor Frances Craighead.

90   "My oldest brother was supposed to be": "James Thurber in Conversation with Alistair Cooke," *Atlantic*, 8/56.

92   "You think of more remarkable things": Ltr, JT to WT, circa 1940.

92   "I told him to buy the seats": Ltr, 3/21/53.

92   William knew a brief moment: *Columbus Citizen*, 7/31/58.

93   It would . . . turn "Bill": Ltr, JT to RT, circa 1956.

93   "We had a memory game about": Ltr, circa 1960.

93   "My brother has a business": Ltr, RT to HK, 10/2/62.

94   "It's for life": Ltr, JT to WT, 1929.

94   "Although I write my brother": Ltr, RT to HK, 11/15/69.

8. THAT DAGUERREOTYPE OF A LADY

95   "Please go home, Jim": Croswell Bowen to HK, 1949.

96   "with that awful old woman": AH to HK.

96   "somber and tragic": Ltr, KSW to Cooke, 2/2/76.

97   "You are dealing with an": Ltr, KSW to HK, 3/23/73.

97   "Thurber did not even live at": Robert E. Morsberger, *James Thurber*, Twayne Publishers, Inc., 1964.

97   Jim wasn't put out to board: Ltr, RT to HK, 5/18/65.

98   A young cousin remembers: Thelma Roseboom, *Of Thurber & Columbustown*, by Rosemary Joyce, The Thurber House.

99   "a truly remarkable": Ltr, WT to Ronald Staub, 8/5/66.

99   Cousin Earl Fisher says: To Alice Leighner, 1969.

99   having read the reviews of a book: *Thurber*, op. cit.

99   Evidently Helen believed all: Ltr, RT to HK, 7/7/75.

100   William Maxwell believes that some of: Maxwell to HK, 1962.

100   TTC: Harper & Bros., 1945.

101   "Doc Marlowe": NYer, 11/2/35.

101   William remembers that when Thurber was: LBI, op. cit.

101   "The Figgerin' of Aunt Wilma": NYer, 6/10/50.

102   "A Portrait of Aunt Ida": NYer, 10/10/34.

9. THAT SULLIVANT SCHOOL

105   last piece he wrote: "Thurber Looks Back," CD, 10/1/61.

105   "We find that the three-story Sullivant building": Article in typescript by Myron T. Seifert, 1961.

106   Carlos Shedd: Ibid.

106   Robert agrees that Sullivant was tough: RT to HK.

106   Stewart writes that he first remembers: Donald Ogden Stewart, "Death of a Unicorn," *New Statesman*, 11/10/61.

107   "I think James is deaf": Ruth White, "James Thurber: His Life in Columbus," CD, 3/10 and 3/17/40; also, letter to *Life*, 4/22/40.

107   "Jamie was very shy": MT to Oulahan,

107   Sayre thinks it is a probability: JS to HK, 1962.

108   Margaret McElvaine his eighth-grade teacher: "Thurber," SB, *Ohio State University Monthly*, 12/61.

109   "Mr. Pendly and the Poindexter": NYer, 2/27/32.

109 "What shall we write about?" Wendell Postle, *Of Thurber & Columbustown*, op cit.; SB, MA thesis.

110 "Sex Ex Machina": NYer, 3/13/37.

110 "Given Thurber's ability": RW to HK, 1974, Bermuda.

10. THAT CONTAINER FOR THE THING CONTAINED

111 "the teacher who first got": Ltr, HT to HK, 10/9/62.

112 It is hard for me to believe: "Here Lies Miss Groby," NYer, 3/21/42.

112 "it got on my nerves": Ltr, JT to Daisy Hare, 4/22/59.

113 "affectionately and clearly": CD, 8/1/55.

113 "Only low grade I got": "Items for the Record," memo to *Time*, 1950.

113 "Midnight at Tim's Place": NYer, 11/29/58.

114 "I keep in touch with many": Patricia McGuckin, DC, 4/17/59.

114 *Lanterns & Lances*: Harper & Bros., 1961.

114 William and Robert used to "pester": Ltr, McCombs to Charles Holmes, 7/14/66.

114 I was nine and a half years old: JS, "Remembering Thurber," *Washington Post* Sunday Book World, 10/22/92.

115 "He was always reading": RT to HK, 1965.

115 "In the tranquil period": "THIX," NYer, 4/26/47.

118 Thurber enjoyed English, languages: Ltr, RT to Charles Holmes, 7/30/66.

118 "Ed Morris was the only one close friend": Ibid.

119 ("We only lost one game"): RT to HK.

119 The hush that fell: C&C, CD, 11/25/23.

11. THAT DAY THE DAM BROKE

121 number of local events: *History of the City of Columbus, Ohio*, Osman Castle Hooper, the Memorial Publishing Co., 1921.

121 thought by some music critics: TG to HK.

123 "Jim and his close friend": Ltr, RT to HK, 10/3/71.

123 "I lived in the same part of town": JS, TV panel discussion of *MLAHT*, WNDT, op. cit.

123 Ben Williamson . . . remembers taking refuge: Williamson to HK, 1962, NY.

125 "Jim is right": Smallsreed to HK, 1962.

125   Smallsreed confirms: Ltr, Smallsreed to JT, 5/18/51.

125   "The last I saw of Kuehner": Ibid.

126   James Thurber's Columbus and mine: Stewart, BBC broadcast, 12/2/61, op. cit.

126   Battle of the Bulge: Item sent JT by J. Park, 8/5/47.

12. THOSE UNIVERSITY DAYS

129   "there was evidently something wrong": EN, ELUTTC, Trident Press, 1965.

129   a "wet smack": SB thesis, op. cit.

130   "Why should I spend my afternoons": RT to HK.

131   "The Notebooks of James Thurber": NYer, 2/5/49.

132   In 1906, at age eleven: SB, *OSU Monthly*, 12/61.

133   "he did little else but sit reading": JS, *Time*, 7/9/51.

133   "None of us suspected": Ltr, RT to HK, 11/15/69.

133   "a bit of a hermit and a loner": EN, ELUTTC.

133   "He had no illness then": Ltr, RT to HK, 11/15/69.

134   "I was a great reader": Ltr, JT to Sarah Whitaker, "James Thurber on the Perplexities of Educating a Daughter," *Chicago Tribune Magazine*, 5/2/63.

13. THAT MAN FROM FRANKLIN AVENUE

137   "Franklin Avenue, U. S. A.": NYer, 5/3/52.

138   "Women are taking over the": Detroit *Times*, 1/13/60.

14. THAT NIGHT THE GHOST GOT IN

140   "It was the only time the boys": MT to Oulahan.

140   "It's true that my father and I": RT to HK, 1965.

140   "I deliberately changed the address": Ltr, JT to Bill Arter, "Thurber's Ghost House," CD Magazine, 4/2/67.

140   "She could convince the boys": Fisher to AL, Columbus, 10/69. (It may also have been Evangeline Adams, popular astrologist, whom Mame had to her house once when JT was visiting.)

141   "Mrs. Phelps": NYer, 12/12/36.

        "I'm certain it was Mame": Fisher to AL.

141   "The only time he got angry with me": MVD to HK, Falls Village, Cornwall, Ct., 1962.

142   Reich would hear footsteps: *The Thurber House Organ*, autumn 1988.

143   "No ghosts": Arter: *Columbus Vignettes II*, printed by Nida-Eckstein Printing, Inc., Columbus, Ohio, 1967.

143   he had heard footsteps creaking up and down: *The Thurber House Organ*, op. cit.

143   "as I stepped out of a car": Ibid.

15. THAT DEAR OLD CONFRÈRE, NUGEY

144   "They published suggested answers": Ltr, RT to HK, 11/15/69.

145   "Without Nugent," says Joel Sayre: To HK, 1962.

146   "merely intended to help the students learn": ELUTTC.

146   wandering "about the campus": EN, "Notes on James Thurber, the Man, or Men," NY *Times*, 3/3/40.

147   Thurber worked with the Ohio: Ltr, RT to HK, 11/15/69.

147   "W. O. T. reinstated me": Ltr, JT to James Pollard, 6/2/60.

148   "His typewriter was next to mine": MF, LBI, Seattle, 6/25/73.

149   "ability, wit and charm": EN, "Brother James Thurber," *Buckeye Phi Psi*, April 1962.

149   "It took a year to get Thurber": Damon to HK, 1962.

150   "Only Jack Pierce, besides": Williamson to HK, 1962.

150   "cheerfully submited to the semicomic tortures": ELUTTC.

151   "I've listened to this ghastly": TG to HK, 1962.

151   "With one exception, the members": *Chicago Tribune* magazine, 5/2/63.

151   Wendell Postle remembers: *Of Thurber & Columbustown*, op. cit.

152   "Don't never pinch": Ltr, McCombs to Charles Holmes, 7/14/66.

152   I suppose you have seen the Sayre piece: Ltr, 7/10/51.

152   "Nugent was a sort of Svengali": McCombs to Holmes, op. cit.

152   Thurber "was naturally a good actor": ELUTTC.

153   "Which one?": James A. Geraghty to HK, 1962.

16. THAT MAN WITH A PIPE

154   "Famous Poems Illustrated": NYer, intermittent, 3/4/39 to 10/28/39.

156   "The professor . . . who influenced": Ltr, 10/31/56.

156   "Jim Thurber came to our house": Taylor to AL, 1969.

157   "Thurber was very nervous": Pollard, LBI, 10/26/71.

157 "I showed them around": Ltr, JT to Mrs. C. H. Schwenke, 11/8/50.

158 ("I could hear Joe Taylor turning in his grave"): Ibid.

158 "was the most popular professor": Wilson, NY *Post*, 3/8/44.

158 "I have now decided to devote": Ltr, JT to Dorothy Miller, circa 1950.

159 "BΘII": NYer, 12/1/51.

159 "I entered [Graves's] short-story course": TTA.

160 "I was astounded to discover": Ltr to EN, 1951.

161 Some people, including a lot of Betas: Ltr, JT to Mrs. Schuyler Fisher, 1/5/53.

162 "Boy, cant [sic] you see the lil": Ltr, JT to EN, 10/15/18.

17. THOSE EDITORIAL DAYS

162 My memories of my editorial days: Ltr, 11/24/50.

163 "I saw a lot of Jim Thurber that year": EN, ELUTTC.

163 "Thurber did so much to help us": Carson Blair to HK, 1965, Detroit.

164 "I failed . . . to become Phi Beta": Ltr to Sarah Whitaker, op. cit.

166 All the artists who had drawn: Ltr, JT to Michael Zeamer, 1/5/46.

166 "Then, as now": Ltr, JT to Edward Spencer, 11/11/50.

167 "I did pictures for the Sun-Dial": Ltr, circa 1936.

167 "I was lucky enough to": Ltr, JT to Spencer, op. cit.

168 "All through school I kept them as": LBI, op. cit.

169 "Most of the male students": "Foreword," *Credos and Curios*, Harper & Row, 1962.

169 "We often teamed up": ELUTTC.

170 I first drove our first car: Ltr, RT to HK, 5/15/65.

170 The Reo "was unusual": "The Car We Had to Push," NYer, 7/15/33.

170 "But it was your idea": SB, "Thurber," op. cit.

171 "One of the big events at Ohio State": ELUTTC.

171 ("I've always been allergic"): NY *Daily Mirror*, RT scrapbooks.

18. THOSE DRAFT BOARD NIGHTS

173 "I always halted promptly": Thurber, *The Fire Islander*, June 1954.

173 "It was a ghastly time": LBI, op. cit.

173 "Thurber tried to sign up:" Williamson to HK, 1962.

173 I had to take off: "Draft Board Nights," NYer, 9/30/33.

174   Among the cripples who were constantly: PM, 10/1/40.

176   "that Columbus backed them": Hooper, op. cit.

176   "I saw Jim frequently": LBI, op. cit.

176   "Along about 1920, I read Scott Fitzgerald's": ELUTTC.

177   "The only girl he ever talked": RT to HK, 1965.

177   a dream of a brunette, just my type: Ltr, 6/28/18.

178   "Imagine my sentiments": Ibid.

182   "Given Thurber's family years": EH to HK.

182   "Please answer soonly": Ltr, 7/16/18.

183   about two to my one: Ltr, JT to EN, 8/25/18.

183   Minnette couldn't have held: Ibid.

185   "All the men I was dating": Benson to HK, 1949.

185   "I used to get eye-aches": Williamson to HK, 1962.

185   But Thurber was remembered by: Stephen Vincent and Rosemary
      Benet, "Thurber: As Unmistakable as a Kangaroo," NY *Herald Trib-
      une Book Review*, 12/29/40.

186   "the mere curve of a girl's cheek": Ltr, 9/15/18.

186   "with certain, sensible reservations": Ibid.

188   "All one sees here is nurses": Ltr, 10/15/18.

188   "I have not heard from M.": Ibid.

188   "Nugent advised Jim never to count on me": LBI, op. cit.

189   "The night before my Sally was born": Ibid.

189   she had "unexpectedly married": Ibid.

19. THAT FIRST TIME HE SAW PARIS

190   "The First Time I Saw Paris," *Holiday*, 4/57.

191   "Exhibit X": NYer, 3/6/48.

192   "After six or eight revisions": C&C, Sunday CD, 5/27/23.

194   "I thought one thing that": Ben Williamson to HK, 1962.

194   Thurber wrote in early 1919 to Nugent: Ltr, 4/4/20.

195   "He was a man of the world": Blair to HK, 1962.

196   "From Franklin County to Paris": JS to HK, 1962.

196   Charme wrote of him: "Jim Thurber," *Ohio State University
      Monthly*, 4/30.

196   "smart, cute, irregular, rakish blue Toque": Ltr, JT to EN, 6/11/19.

196   "clear, sweet beautiful eyes": Ltr, JT to EN, 3/20/19.

197   before "they acquire the European attitude": Ltr, JT to RT, 3/29/19.

197   "Often I decide to go home": Ltr, 4/9/19.

197   "I understand you are about to have six or": Ltr, 3/18/19.

198   Your very clever dialogue of the O. M.: Ltr, 5/31/19.
198   Thurber praised Nugent: Ltr, JT to EN, 9/24/19.
199   "the most destructive thing imaginable": Ibid.
199   "putting down sequences of words": Ltr, 6/11/19.
199   "The chimes are always chiming": Ltr, 9/24/19.
200   "I'd been receiving beautiful letters": Eva Prout Geiger, LBI, 3/9–11/73, Coral Gables, Florida.
201   I hadn't been here long: Ltr, JT to EN, 4/4/20.
202   "I am still a bit unsettled": Ltr, 3/25/20.
202   "I have no regrets, fortunately": Ltr, 4/4/20.
202   "The Other Room": *Harper's*, 7/62.
203   He reached New York: "The First Time I Saw Paris", op. cit.

20. THAT SWEETHEART WRAITH

205   Your . . . letter shows . . . you believe I am in: Ltr, 3/25/20.
205   "Dating" a married woman: Ibid.
205   "Jim sat right across the aisle": Prout, LBI, op. cit.
206   "I told her good-bye": Ltr, JT to EN, 3/25/20.
206   "Louella Parsons was the head": LBI, op. cit.
206   "the finest letter she wrote": Ltr, JT to EN, 3/25/20.
207   "Eve and I had but a very few": Ltr, JT to EN, 4/4/20.
207   "Her nerves seem to be mated with mine": Ibid.
208   "I ask so long in advance": Ltr, JT to EP, 4/6/20.
208   *The guinea pig's a funny hoggy*: Ltr, JT to EP, 4/22/20.
209   "Eve, the hope of you": Ltr, undated, probably 4/20.
210   "You must ask Freud or Bergson": Ltr, 5/4/20.
210   If you love and marry "another": Ibid.
211   "The Only Woman in the Whole World": Ltr, 5/9/20.
212   "I am not . . . disappointed": Ltr, JT to EP, 5/18/20.
212   So my letter was sarcastic: Ltr, JT to EP, undated, probably 5/20.
213   "You must understand the single-track": Ltr, 6/23/20.
214   "I had Minnette home for": Ltr, undated, probably 5/20.
214   "I am glad that Ernest was merciful": Ltr, 5/18/20.
215   "the old interest [in Eve] is a bit dimmed": Ltr, 6/9/20.
215   "I do hope Jamie will not make": Ltr, MT to MF, 9/18/29.
216   "Not at all as de profundis": Ltr, JT to EN, 8/25/20.
216   an adventure—pregnant with material: Ibid.
216   "I found out from Mamma many": Ltr, JT to RT, 9/18/53.

218   "Be sure and send me Eva's letter": Ltr, JT to RT, 12/7/46.
219   "Jim was much more romantic": LBI, op. cit.

21. THOSE MEMOIRS OF A DRUDGE

220   "The war was on": Bertha Austin, LBI, 1/undated/73, Oak Park, Illinois.
220   "a one-act piece of nonsense": Ltr, McCombs to Charles Holmes, 7/14/66.
221   "McCombs' musical play 'Taint So' . . . was": Ltr, 4/4/20.
221   "Jim told us he would": Carson Blair to HK, 1962.
222   "finally that the loss of the old left": Ltr, 6/23/20.
223   "The Civil War Phone-Number Association": NYer, 10/15/32
223   "Your summary of my crazy insanity": Ltr, 8/9/20.
223   "But I urged him to give Jim": Ltr, Finn to MF, 7/29/75.
224   ("I reminded him of a clergyman"): Smallsreed to HK, Columbus, 1962.
224   "Kuehner always called me": Ltr, Finn to MF, 7/29/75.
224   "Good shot": Ltr, Smallsreed to JT, 5/18/51.
224   "Kuehner was merely hard-boiled": Pollard to HK, 1962.
224   "When he spotted me . . . sitting at a desk": "Newspaperman—Head and Shoulders," TTA.
225   "I was on the rewrite desk": Smallsreed to HK.
225   "But didn't you find": TTA.
225   "I never saw his rough side": TTA.
225   "Jim had a desk": Smallsreed to HK.
226   There was a period when . . . Thurber: Nelson H. Budd, "Personal Reminiscences of James Thurber," *Ohio State university Monthly*, 1/62.
226   "Jim did have one advantage": Smallsreed to HK.
227   he received a letter from Smallsreed: Probably 1951.
227   "Five days after I was put on City Hall": Ltr, 1/22/21.
228   "The . . . structure burned like so much": CD, 1/13/21.
228   "floating, unemployed Negroes": JT, CD, 3/12/21.
229   My most enthusiastic, ambitious and best: Ltr, 3/19/21.
229   "So you beat me to the first sale": Ltr, undated, 3/21.
229   "best stories . . . were not the ones": Budd, op. cit.
230   ("Where do you get your ladyfingers now?"): TTA.
230   *What has become of the first movie*: JT, CD, 1/16/21.
231   "Paris, where the writer tarried": JT, CD, 1/30/21.

230 "I don't think so": "Notes of an Old Reporter," *The Bermudian*, 6/51.

230 "My shortest interview on the phone": Ibid.

232 ". . . Along comes Conrad's marvelously": CD, 2/20/21.

232 "the year the owls were so bad": "Lavender with a Difference," TTA.

233 "he knew more people in the city": "My Friend McNulty," *Credos and Curios*, Harper & Row, 1962.

233 "John and Jim were a couple of funny guys": Ltr, Donia Williamson (McNulty) Karpen to HK, 10/18/62.

233 "They also had an affinity": Ben Williamson to HK.

233 "I have had quite a melange": Ltr, 7/10/21.

234 "For all his wit": Kanode to AL, Columbus, 1962.

234 When McNulty was finally fired: Faith McNulty to HK, 1995.

235 "Harry, why am I in Athens?" Ltr, Smallsreed to HK, 9/14/62.

235 "in the early 1930s Jim was visiting": Ltr, op. cit.

235 was still getting drunk: Miller to HK, 1964.

235 Walker wrote Thurber: Ltr, 8/23/57.

236 McNulty is in fine shape: Ltr, 3/1/54.

236 "McNulty's heart condition": Ltr, 8/30/56.

236 The days didn't go by: "John McNulty," NYer, 8/4/56.

22. THAT DOG THAT BIT PEOPLE

237 "What kind of animal is he?": Ltr, JT to RT, 3/18/19.

238 "Actually, Muggs liked Jim": RT to HK, 1965, and ltr, RT to HK, 11/15/69.

238 we had a roomer, sometimes two: Ibid.

238 "Actually it wasn't a congressman": RT to HK.

238 "That weekend of the country-club": LBI, 3/9–11/73.

240 "Jim has that wrong": RT to HK, 1965.

241 "Nothing is cuter": C&C, CD, 1923.

241 "Muggs loved cars": RT to HK, 1965.

241 "Muggs had a complication of diseases": Ibid.

241 "Where we would chuck a bulldog": C&C, CD, 1923.

242 "I left him there": RT to HK, 1965.

242 "I certainly felt badly": Ltr, undated, probably March or April 1928.

242 *Harold and the Purple Crayon*: Harper & Row, 1955, (a "Harper Trophy" paperback).

243   "James used to sit and look at it": MT to Oulahan, 1950.

243   "Jim never showed any affection for Muggs": RT to HK.

243   *Thurber's Dogs*: Simon & Schuster, 1955.

244   ("Mostly mongrel"): RT to HK, 1965.

244   "An ugly thing": Fisher to AL.

244   "It was possibly the longest and certainly": "Canines in the Cellar," *Thurber's Dogs*.

244   *Somewhere beyond the brightest*: "To Scottie and Rex, a Tribute by James G. Thurber," SB, "Thurber," op. cit.

244   "In his grief over ": "An Introduction," *Thurber's Dogs*.

245   "It was . . . just when the city": "In Defense of Dogs," *Thurber's Dogs*.

245   "The Thin Red Leash": NYer, 8/13/27.

245   "I knew that Jeannie was a": "In Defense of Dogs."

245   "I know what it would": Ltr, JT to RT, undated, 1928.

246   "Jeannie had no show points": "Notes on Talking and Homing Dogs," NY *Times*, 2/8/48.

246   ". . . A female dog knows more": "And So to Medve," *Thurber's Dogs*.

247   "Jeannie . . . went around . . . wearing a martyred look": Ibid.

247   "She took to staying away for days": "Look Homeward, Jeannie," *Thurber's Dogs*.

248   "I had quite a time": "Sex Ex Machina," LYMA.

248   "Hey, get a load of this": "The Dog That Bit People," and JS to HK.

248   "So I got up on it": "And So to Medve."

248   My dog is lower: "Lo, the Gentle Bloodhound!", *Holiday*, 9/55.

249   "My indignation is still as strong": "Lo, Hear the Gentle Bloodhound," *Thurber's Dogs*.

249   "bloodhounds are too dumb": Mabel Greene, NY *Sun*, 1/18/40.

250   "Thurber had an affinity for dogs": PDV to HK, 1949.

250   She knew that the Hand: "Memorial," *Thurber's Dogs*.

251   "All but five or six of my dogs": "How to Name a Dog," *Good Housekeeping*, 10/44.

251   "My mother bought her," Ltr, RM to HK, 4/14/91.

251   "My husband had a natural": Chicago *Daily News*, 4/13/63.

23. THAT MAGIC MIRROR GIRL

252   "I want to find The Girl": Ltr, 1/22/21.

253   "He seemed like an old man": A, LBI, 8/29/73, West Cults, Scotland.

253   Althea attended Western College for Women: (O.S.U. seems not to have credited Althea with her year there; she was enrolled at OSU as a freshman.)

253   "I loved Althea": LBI, 6/25/73, Seattle.

254   "It could have been either": A, LBI, op. cit.

255   "Jim worried about boring people": Meckstroth to AL.

255   "I'll never know the right answer": Ltr, 3/25/20.

255   "whether acting or involved in": Ltr, McCombs to Charles S. Holmes, 7/14/66;

255   "In North Columbus, where the Adamses lived": McCombs to HK, 1962.

255   "Men usually go for women": Damon to HK, 1962.

256   "She was very certain of": Blair to HK, Detroit, 1962.

256   "I felt that Althea was not quite the": LBI, op. cit.

256   *Over the Garden Fence*: Johnny Jones, CD, 11/2/42.

256   "Am at work on what appears to stand": Ltr, 7/10/21.

257   "[Ralph McCombs] died nobly": Ltr, JT to Johnny Jones, CD, 1955.

257   *Indicate the exit*: CD, 10/4/21.

258   "his talented family bids fair": CD, 11/6/21.

258   "its manager spread word:" Mowrey to AL, 1969, Columbus.

258   "I had to come up with human-interest": Blair to HK.

259   "She and I are set to kick off the single": Ltr, 4/4/22.

259   Ludwig Lewisohn, whom perhaps you knew better: Ibid.

260   "Many of *my* friends were *our* friends": LBI, op. cit.

260   It was my task to worm from a heavy: Ltr, 4/4/22.

261   "Mrs. Adams was always very nice to us": RT to HK.

262   "Althea was always wonderful": Ltr, MT to MF, 8/8/39.

262   "It's a little like sleeping": TG to HK, 1962.

262   Althea and I leave here: Ltr, JT to EN, 5/18/22.

24. THOSE CREDOS AND CURIOS

263   "I first really got to know": JS, LBI, 12/75, Arlington, Va.; JS to HK, 1962.

264   "I never knew Thurber well": Typescript, 1940, Thurber Collection.

264   "I had acting in mind": "Items for the Record," op. cit.

264   a chronicling of people: Ltr, undated, 9/22.

265   His first profile: "Charles L. Schneider," Sunday CD magazine, 5/14/22.

266   *The world has moved*: "Ring Out the Old," CD, 1/19/22.

266   "as lacking in fortitude as a federal": "On the Unleashing of the Lions," Sunday CD Magazine, 3/5/22.

266   An [heir] never works: "On Society as She Is Screened," Sunday CD magazine, 3/19/22.

266   "onion sandwich parties": D. Miller to HK, 1964.

267   "Jim wrote his own titles": Smallsreed to HK.

267   "Dad Dialogs": appear in the first nine "Credos and Curios," Sunday CD magazine, 2/18/23 through 4/15/23.

268   We will say that you jaywalk: CD, 2/25/23.

269   His sleuth, Blue Ploermell: C&C, CD, 2/18/23 through 5/13/23.

271   "I never met Jim until after he left": D. Miller to HK.

271   "[It] has too much good stuff": C&C, CD, 10/28/23.

271   Thurber knew all the words: Stewart, "Death of a Unicorn," *New Statesman*, 11/10/61.

272   "You drop a feature if it isn't": Smallsreed to HK.

25. THAT DAY CHIC HARLEY GOT AWAY

274   Robert Cantwell: "Say It Isn't So, Woody," unidentified tear sheets, HK files.

274   "We went to the North-East game": CD, 11/2/21.

275   Walter Cramp's All-American football: CD, 11/27/21.

278   Too bad you cant be here to whiff: Ltr, 9/undated/22.

278   *The years of football playing reach*: CD, 10/undated/22.

279   "As much as we love": C&C, "So Shines a Good Dime in this Naughty World," Sunday CD Magazine, 10/28/23.

280   "the last and greatest": "Return of the Native," *Bermudian*, 6/50.

280   "A newspaperman I know": "Winter Thoughts," *Bermudian*, 2/51.

280   "informed by a special lunacy": Jack Fullen to HK.

280   "I always stuck with Jack Fullen": Ltr, 4/13/61.

280   "I bet even money": Ltr, JT to H. S. Warwick, 1/9/50.

281   "the first critical comment": *The Clocks of Columbus*, Atheneum, 1972.

281   "It was a very exciting time": LBI, op. cit.

282   It was me: "The Admiral on the Wheel," from LYMA, Harper & Bros., 1937.

282   The libretto of a musical comedy: Ltr, 3/1/54.

283   a comment on bullhead fishing: NY *World*, 8/14/24.

283   "Josephine Has Her Day": *Thurber's Dogs*.

284   "WELCOME HOME, JIM!" *Columbus Citizen*, 9/30/24.

284   "I still had some idea of getting a": LBI, op. cit.

285   "I saw quite a bit of the Thurbers": JS to HK.

286   "Herman recognized, as did Althea": D. Miller to HK, 1966.

286   "That's a lot of crap": HT to HK, 1962.

286   "Althea thought—and it was": HT to BB, *Thurber*.

287   "Althea forced me to give up my good": Ltr, 12/23/52.

287   "It *was* more my idea than Jim's": LBI, op. cit.

287   the family never expected James: RT to HK, 1962.

26. THAT GRANDE VILLE DE PLAISIR

288   "My Trip Abroad": *New Yorker*, 8/6/27.

289   peeled "like church bells": Ltr, undated, 1925.

289   "We had some lovely bathing": Ltr, JT to TG, 8/27/25.

290   we visited Napoleon's: Ltr, JT to the Gardiners, op. cit.

290   If he is a good traveler: "Quick, The Other Side!", *The Detroit Athletic Club News*, 11/25.

291   "Somebody must have told us": LBI, op. cit.

291   "Remembrances of Things Past": LYMA.

292   "As Thornton Wilder has said": Ltr, 6/2/60.

292   The *Tribune* "was like no other": William L. Shirer, *20th Century Journey*, Simon & Schuster, 1976.

293   "By the way, what are you": TYWR.

293   "the mecca of a large number": O. W. Riegel, unpublished memoirs.

296   Joel Sayre . . . remembers Thurber: JS to HK.

296   . . . One of my tasks: "Memoirs of a Drudge," TTC, Harper & Bros., 1945.

297   Seven years later, Thurber: "Wilson's Paris Barber Calls Him Greatest of the World-Famous," NY *World*, 9/20/25.

298   "A Sock on the Jaw": *Harper's*, 2/26.

299   It was then our custom: "Memoirs of a Drudge."

300   "It was a wonderful winter for us": LBI, op. cit.

301   A rush of people: "Wills Goes Down Fighting," *Chicago Tribune*, Riviera edition, 2/17/26, Thurber Collection.

301   A *Paris Tribune* reporter, Leo Mishkin: doctoral dissertation of Thomas Wood, Univeristy of Tulsa, cited in O. W. Riegel's memoirs.

301   "which you must never have used": Ibid.

302   "I stayed in Paris two months after Jim": LBI.

303   "I've been married four years": NS to HK.

303   I write mostly soi-disant humor: Ltr, JT to JS, quoted in "Thurber and His Humor," *Newsweek*, 2/4/57.

27. THOSE VIOLETS IN THE SNOW

305   I been in France ten years: Ltr, 5/20/26.

305   "My pieces came back so fast": TYWR.

305   Mosher, says White, discovered: Ltr, KSW to HK, 3/23/73.

306   "looking like a professor of English literature": TYWR.

306   "We saw a lot of Lillian in Paris": LBI, op. cit.

306   "We lived in a tent": Ibid.

307   "One night," says Donald: quoted by Jack Smith, Los Angeles *Times* columnist, 4/14/88.

307   I can think of no woman friend: "Footnotes on a Course of Study," LYMA.

308   "all that crazy sex stuff": L. A. *Times*, op. cit.

308   "At that time Jim seemed to loathe": JS to HK, 1962.

308   "I was about to go back": "Frankly Speaking," interview with Stephen Potter, BBC Home Service Program, 12/24/58.

309   "What are gaiety and vodka in": Ltr, *Newsweek*, op. cit.

309   "I rode subway trains, elevated trains": Joseph Mitchell, N.Y. *World-Telegram*, 12/29/34.

310   "A four-alarm fire": Robert M. Coates, "James Thurber," *Authors Guild Bulletin*, 12/61.

310   "When other reporters ": "Memoirs of a Drudge," op. cit.

310   "I found him in his room": "Notes of an Old Reporter," *Bermudian*, 6/51,

310   "The [editor] decided": Eddy Gilmore, "Blind at 67, Thurber Still Cracks the Wit," Associated Press, the *Toledo Blade*, 5/7/61.

311   "My mini-scoops on the New York *Evening*": Beverly Gay, NY *Post*, 1959

311 "Russel Crouse, Nunnally Johnson, Bruce": Ltr, 6/14/51.

311 I went up twice to her house: Ltr, 2/6/27.

312 I never knew Thurber well: Ltr, Harper, Thurber Collection.

313 "It's a nice sector": *Columbus Citizen*, 4/9/27.

313 "Thurber got lots of his good ideas": JS to HK.

313 "An American Romance": NYer, 3/5/27.

314 "I fancy a lady has": "Tidbits," NYer, 3/12/27.

314 "Some of my earliest stuff": Ltr, JT to DK, 1950.

315 "Althea did her share in those days": JS to HK.

316 But there came a time when he: NS to HK, 1991.

316 Kate and Russell Lord knew: DK, RATNY, Doubleday & Co., 1951.

316 "Andy showed Ross a clipping or two": KSW to HK, 1974.

316 "I can't remember if I first met Jim": EBW to HK.

317 "That," she replied, "is the": LBI, op. cit.

28. THOSE FIRST YEARS

322 "I live the life of a hunted animal": TYWR.

322 "Ross didn't acquire the appreciation": WHIT to HK, 1962.

323 He was an eccentric: "Introduction," *Ross*, RTNYAM, Reynal, 1968.

323 had the uneducated man's suspicion: HATNY, Random House, 1975.

324 "I was so startled, I had trouble": Gaddis to HK, 1961.

324 "In the early days, a small company of writers": HATNY.

324 "He could not only get it, he could write it": TYWR.

324 "How many fallen women to you have?" TYWR.

325 "by strictly military standards": RATNY.

325 "Harold Ross, a journalist no one had ever heard of": RTNYAM, op. cit.

325 "Hi, Anderson": TYWR.

326 "took charge of American humor": Gibbs, "Big Nemo," *More in Sorrow*, Henry Holt & Co., 1958.

327 "You know, it feels like": Margaret Case Harriman, *The Vicious Circle*, Rinehart, 1951.

327 "Dear Mary": Ibid.

327 "Ross hoped he might revive the ailing *Judge*": RTNYAM.

328 "was filled with copies of *Punch, Simplicissimus*": Ibid.

328 "I felt that Ross had not had enough": Ltr, 4/18/51.

329   "the only dishonest thing I ever did": TYWR.
329   "that those who did not know him then": RTNYAM.
329   The New Yorker starts with a declaration: NYer, 2/21/25.
331   "for there might have been a monotony of style": Ltr, Russel
       Crouse to JT, 9/4/57.
331   "Ross never understood pictures": RTNYAM.
331   Ross's search for his "magic formula": Ltr, 8/23/50.
332   If you scan the first two years: Ltr, 7/14/50.
332   I think the New Yorker was bound to: Ltr, 8/25/50.
332   for "taste, clarity, and entertainment": RTNYAM.
333   "I have an utter contempt for businessmen": Roy Hoopes, *Cain*,
       Holt, Rinehart & Winston, 1982.
333   "like killing a defenseless thing": RATNY.
336   "first heard of the existence of a magazine": TYWR.

29. THAT MANAGING EDITOR

338   "Ross had been skeptical about even": Grant to HK.
338   "the steel and the music": TYWR.
338   "Jim and I simply got thrown together": EBW to HK, 1962.
338   "I want to write": Frank Sullivan to HK, 1962.
338   "Ross always found satisfactory editors": annotations in KSW's
       copy of TYWR, 11/10/86, Bryn Mawr library.
338   "A stranger was always walking into my": WHIT to HK.
339   (Thurber declined, "being sane at the time"): TYWR.
339   "Ross seemed to demote Ingersoll once a year": WHIT to HK.
339   "But Ingersoll was no more the managing": JG to HK.
340   "But in fact . . . Ingersoll did everything": KSW to HK.
340   [Ross] sent my name in [to the Postal]: Ltr, 8/16/57.
340   "Well . . . they say people grow, don't they?": RTNYAM.
341   "Ross never knew about it": Grant to HK.
341   Ingersoll . . . was the best of all the Central: TYWR.
341   "Whenever Ross was out with": KSW, annotations, op. cit.
341   "In just five months, every senior employee": RI to HK.
342   As Claxton told Dale Kramer: RATNY.
342   "Jesus Christ! Let *me* talk!": Charles W. Morton, "A Try for The
       New Yorker," *Atlantic Monthly*, 4/63.
342   "Ross enjoyed being intellectually rough": RI, *Point of Departure*,
       Harcourt Brace & World, 1961.
343   "But without exception, he really didn't like": RI to HK.

343 a thirty-five-thousand-word article: "The New Yorker," *Fortune*, 8/34.

344 "I'll never go back": *Point of Departure*, op. cit.

344 "Why did I put up with it?": RI to HK.

345 "I found out that I was managing editor": Ltr, 10/31/56.

345 "Ross assigned a secretary to me": JT to HK.

345 "The Conscious vs. the Unconscious": LYMA, op. cit.

345 "seemed to believe that certain basic problems": *TYWR*.

346 "The confusion over partitions was really": WHIT to HK.

346 "Ann . . . I seem to have lost my shirt": RI to HK.

346 "If anything about Thurber was to grate": Ibid.

347 "We used to come in on Sunday afternoon": WHIT to HK.

348 "often became bored or infuriated": TYWR.

348 "I never thought the magazine would last": RATNY.

348 "We were badly understaffed back then": JT to HK.

348 "I was afraid of Ross": JT to Frank Gibney, op. cit.

348 "Ross came home in a rage": Grant to HK.

349 the "act of a 'sis' ": TYWR.

349 "Sam Behrman told me . . .": Ltr, Johnson to JT, 4/25/58.

349 "Ross didn't fire [him] to his": KSW annotations, op. cit.

350 "I never met the guy . . . but most of the": Ltr, 8/7/57.

350 "It's hard to remember all who came and went": WHIT to HK.

350 . . . I have done a lot of brooding about the: TYWR.

30. THOSE MIRACLE MEN

351 "You're wearing yourself down writing pieces": TYWR.

352 "Thurber is the greatest unlistener I know": TYWR.

352 "I must have done it at Thurber's request": WHIT to HK.

352 "I'm mistaken for him by some people": TYWR.

352 always afraid of Whitaker: Ltr, Shuman to JT, 8/22/58.

352 "The hell with it": TYWR.

352 Ross . . . sought only to please himself: KSW annotations.

352 "Thurber dealt with his high office": *Book of the Month Club News*, 2/45.

353 "Your husband's opinion on a practical matter": TYWR.

353 "If you write anything": Ibid.

353 "In re-reading some of the earliest [casuals]": Ibid.

353 "More Authors Cover the Snyder Trial": NYer, 5/7/27.

354 "News Of The Day: And a Little Child—": NYer, 4/2/27.

354   "Another Mother's Day": (Unlisted in JT bibliographies.)

354   "The Youngsters as Critics": NYer, 4/30/27.

355   I was [Thurber's] editor: Ltr, KSW to HK, 12/11/72.

355   "one of the pillars": TYWR.

355   "He never thought the New Yorker was going to": Ltr, KSW to JT, 8/12/57.

356   *Onward and Upward*: Harper & Row, 1987.

358   "Ross was furious that I was a woman": Scott Elledge, *E. B. White*, W. W. Norton & Co., 1984.

358   "It was never difficult to disagree with him": RTNYAM.

358   She was one of the first editors: EBW to George A. Plimpton and Frank H. Crowther, "The Art of the Essay," *Paris Review*, fall 1969.

359   "having single-handedly saved": Angell to HK, 1991.

359   Mrs. White was in part responsible: *The Outermost Dream*, Alfred A. Knopf, 1989.

359   "since he was without taste": RI, "The New Yorker," *Fortune*, 8/34.

360   Gill's book, published in 1975: HATNY.

360   "Roger told me his mother cried": BG to HK, 1989.

360   "[Ross] never wanted a literary magazine": Ltr, JT to Alistair Cooke, 8/7/57.

360   "I was the first to credit her in print": BG to HK.

361   ("She loved her job but she"): Maxwell to HK, 1962.

361   "She resented him": BG to HK.

361   "it was not easy": *The Outermost Dream*, op. cit.

361   "Dear Mrs.: You and your family": KSW annotations.

362   *Letters of E. B. White*: op. cit.

362   hanging by his legs: DK, RATNY.

362   ("I'll see you at the prescription"): Witnessed by HK.

364   ("It was my first murder"): Ltr to Alexander Woollcott; Elledge, *E. B. White: A Biography*, op. cit.

364   "gifted writers whose good sense": *E. B. White*, op. cit.

364   "I ramble terribly": Ltr, 3/26/23; Ibid.

365   "because I couldn't seem to make myself care": Ibid.

365   describes this period as his "moping years": DK, RATNY.

365   "a mail-order course in automobile": Elledge, op. cit.

365   The waitress came trotting back: DK, RATNY.

365   "The proof of humor is the": Ltr, JT to JS, 12/22/50.

366   "Are you Elwyn Brooks White?": Davis, *Onward & Upward*.

366   "I can't remember a": RI, *Point of Departure*, op. cit.

366   "those God-damned incompetent bastards": RI to HK.

366 "he was a very different fish": *Paris Review*, Fall/69.

366 "Andy was fearful of life": RI to HK.

367 I am one of the lucky: Thurber obituary, NYer, 11/11/61.

31. THAT SLIGHT BLONDE WOMAN

367 "We got on fine together": *E. B. White*, Scott Elledge; White to HK.

368 . . . Yesterday hard at work: *Letters of E. B. White*, op. cit.

368 "Charme was most helpful to us": LBI, op. cit.

368 "The work was simple": AH to HK.

369 . . . My first impression was: Ltr, undated, perhaps 1932.

373 (Ross, says Gibbs, despite Gibbs's): Ltr, WG to JT, 8/12/57.

373 "Aberrations of the creative mind had [Ross]": TYWR.

374 "As usual our bank account was overdrawn": Elinor Gibbs to HK, 1962.

374 "liberties with the language, factuality, and": *Luce and His Empire*, W. A. Swanberg, Charles Scribner's Sons, 1972.

374 "Backward ran sentences until": "Time . . . Life . . . Fortune . . . Luce," *More in Sorrow*, Henry Holt & Co., 1958.

374 "I'd put down an average of $45.6789 a week": Ltr, undated, probably 1957.

375 "generally regarded as being mean": *Luce and His Empire*, op. cit.

375 Shawn wired him: Cablegram, 8/16/58.

375 "one of the most important figures in the career": TYWR.

376 "a quivering, bright-eyed horse": "Polo in the Home," NYer, 9/17/27.

376 Mrs. Leeper, who: "The Literary Meet," NYer, 9/24/27.

376 "At breakfast the President ate a bit less": "Breakfast with the President," NYer, 11/12/27.

376 "Can you sleep?" asked the children: "A Visit from Saint Nicholas," NYer, 12/24/27.

377 "a spendthrift generation": John Updike, review of Marion Meade's *Dorothy Parker*, NYer, 4/25/88.

377 The 1920s were, for the people in [Benchley's]: *Robert Benchley*, McGraw-Hill Book Co., 1955.

378 "I was Herman's college girl": LL to HK, 1952.

381 Althea will not be home: Ltr, undated, circa 4–5/28.

382 Dear Act: I took your key back: Ltr, to Eva and Ernest Geiger, undated, probably spring, 1928.

382   Before the *New Yorker* had hired him, Thurber would later say: Ltr,
       JT to James Pollard, 6/2/60.
382   "What is that?": Ltr, JT to Henry Luce, 7/28/58.
383   "bust loose with a big scandal story": *Columbus Citizen*, 5/27/29.
383   ("Geezus, I hope they were expecting it"): TYWR.
383   "ADVICE TO AMERICAN LADIES": NYer, 6/16/28.
383   "How to Acquire Animal Crackers": NYer, 12/24/27.
384   "There remain about 10,000 [boxes]": Ltr to National Biscuit Co.
       house organ.
384   "the first Ohio State athlete to win his": ELUTTC.
384   he was, she says, "afraid of": *E. B. White*, op. cit.
384   "We were all extremely close and happy": Whites to HK.

32. THAT TALK OF THE TOWN

386   "Ross sometimes had as many as three men": TYWR.
386   "White and Thurber wrote most of the Talk": WHIT to HK.
387   " 'Talk' was just made for him": "James Thurber," *Authors Guild
       Bulletin*, 12/61.
387   "I came to the NYer in July": Ltr, RI to JT, 8/16/57.
387   "I don't know why": Ltr, JT letter to Russel Crouse, September
       1957.
387   "I did many a Talk of": Ltr, Markey to DK, circa 1950.
387   "Everybody did everything in the early days": KSW to HK.
388   "I went to Notes early": EBW to HK, 1962.
388   "I began writing Talk:" Ltr to Frank Gifford, 10/31/56.
388   ("I don't remember that Jim had any trouble"): EBW to HK.
388   I would go to a Wednesday morning: Ltr, 9/4/57.
389   "I learned a lot from E. B. White's": Ltr, JT to James Pollard,
       6/2/60.
389   I've never known, and will never know: Ltr, 3/11/74.
390   "White's final record leaves him as": BG to HK, 1989.
391   "I thought you were a genius": RATNY; ltr, WG to JT, undated,
       1957.
391   When Harold Ross lost interest in a: Ltr, 11/21/57.
391   "Are you the current punctuator?" Ltr, JT to DK, 6/18/51.
391   ("One day nearer the grave"): TYWR.
392   "Ross said to me that he": Ltr, KSW to HK, 3/23/73.
392   "kept him on in spite of": KSW annotations, op. cit.

392   "I guess Art Samuels was the most dangerous": Ltr, WG to JT, undated, probably 1957.

392   Somebody, says Mrs. White, was also: KSW annotations.

393   as a reporter in Atlanta he had occasionally: RATNY.

393   "I edited sports, fashions": Weekes to HK, 1962.

396   He put it off until Art's ship was back: TYWR.

396   while Angell "handled everything else": RI to HK.

396   the "old hen" (his expression): Ltr, KSW to JT, 8/12/57.

397   "Thurber had magnificent": *Point of Departure*, op. cit.

397   "You would rip off the Thurber dog on the": RI to HK.

397   Elsewhere, after Daise Terry reminded him: Ltr, Margaret Case Harriman to DK, 2/12/51.

397   "the dame you were wrestling with": TYWR.

398   "Someone else must have said no on": KSW annotations.

398   "One day, John Peale Bishop": Ltr, undated, circa 1957.

398   "the screwball days": A. J. Liebling to HK.

399   "In most of our high jinx": *Point of Departure*.

399   "His love life seems as mixed up as a dog's": TYWR.

399   "swarthy coloring and the hawklike": *Point of Departure*.

399   "We all liked him very much": WHIT to HK.

400   "Quick! Quick! Mr. Thurber": Ltr, KSW to JT, 8/12/57.

400   "The stories about Thurber's office behavior": *Book-of-the-Month Club News*, op. cit.

400   "Someone once told me Thurber had": EH to HK, 1966.

401   "People who try to write about:" Liebling to HK, 1962.

401   in its plain, workaday: Introduction, *This Petty Pace*, Alfred Knopf, 1945.

33. THAT MR. AND MRS. MONROE

402   "Jeannie went": Ltr, undated, probably spring, 1928.

403   "We met the Thurbers at a party": Connell to HK, 1962.

406   "I have never seen a": Ltr, Liebling to HK, 8/30/62.

407   . . . The average New Yorker writer, unfortunately: TYWR.

407   ("Too small a heart, too large"): Elledge, *E. B. White*, op. cit.

407   ("I was half in love with"): *Onward and Upward*, op. cit.

408   "It was obvious to all of us that he still": LL to HK.

408   "Jim seemed to adore Althea": RI to H.K.

408   "Three things, even as early as 1927": LBI, op. cit.

409   ("They didn't turn out"): MF (Ewart), LBI, 6/25/73.

409   I can't understand what he: Ltr, MT to MF, 9/23/29.

409   "Althea Thurber thounds": Ltr, JT to KSW, 4/24/48.

409   *Please*, I beg of you tell me: Ltr, MT to MF, 9/23/29.

410   [Jim] warned me in a letter: Ltr, MT to MF, 11/8/29.

411   ("Go ahead and call her"): AH to HK.

412   Twenty minutes before Paul arrived: Ltr, 5/4/51.

414   "was terribly afraid": *Sinclair Lewis*, McGraw-Hill, 1961.

414   "All of us are afraid to be alone": RW to HK, Bermuda.

415   "deep and lugubrious books": EBW, "Introduction," ISN, re-issue, Harper & Row, 1950.

416   ("most of them done with"): LBI, op. cit.

419   "If you know anything about": Ltr, EBW to JT, 7/27/49.

34. THAT SEAL IN THE BEDROOM

420   "Where the hell did you get the idea you could": TYWR.

420   (Katharine Angell and Ross had seen): "What Every Wife should Know" NYer, 10/12/29, from the ISN chapter "Claustrophobia, or What Every Young Wife Should Know."

420   "Actually, Ross had seen a drawing": JT to HK, 1948.

422   "a happy fellow who made enough money to live": ELUTTC.

423   "If you can't write long hand why don't": LBI, op. cit.

423   . . . After thinking it over for eight months: Ltr, JT to MF, undated, probably fall, 1929.

423   "beautiful defense of Althea": Ltr, undated, probably December 1929.

424   recklessly writing her a letter: Ltr, undated, probably January 1930.

426   "Thurber was always getting a new man hired": WHIT to HK.

426   ("They were both gods to me"): Hellman to HK, 1962.

426   "set up a system of red": KSW, TYWR annotations, op. cit.

426   "Thurber would rewrite page one of": Cooke to HK, 1962.

427   "the hot arguments": JG to HK.

427   "since his mind worked": Gibbs, *Book-of-the-Month Club News*.

428   "Thurber was especially great": Weekes to HK.

428   "It was more than a picture": Cooke to HK.

429   "Oswego marching": TYWR.

430   "Why did you make those zany remarks": RTNYAM.

430   "Ross told lots of dirty stories": McK to HK.

430   "Surviving Ross was an ordeal": Ltr, 9/17/57.

430   "Memoirs of a Banquet Speaker": NYer, 3/29/30.

431   "which is why we wanted": Chicago *Tribune*, 1/undated/30.

431   (". . . tongue in his cheek I'"): "Literary Tea [After Milling Around at Five or Six of Them]," NYer, 4/12/30.

431   "How long would that take?": "An Outline of the Byrd Report," NYer, 7/26/30.

432   "Mr. Higgins' Breakdown": NYer, 9/20/30.

432   The White House guards, several of them: "North America in Ferment," NYer, 7/27/30.

432   Thurber next needles the theater gossip columnists: "Broadway Bulletin [With all the Confusion of the Theatre Columns in the Papers]," NYer, 10/4/30.

432   "My God . . . this bird's still in bed": "So You're Going to a Hotel!", NYer, 11/1/30.

432   His first "Reporter At Large": "Cop Into College Man," NYer, 3/29/30.

432   "Thumbs Up": *Harper's*, 12/30.

433   "Business men everywhere were afraid": "On Tearing Into Business," the *Magazine of Business*, 3/29.

433   He believes nothing inspires: "The Business Outlook Is—97,000,000," the *Magazine of Business*, 5/29.

433   "the 10 or 12 distinguished": Ltr, JT to MF, undated, probably January or February 1930.

433   "Ballyhoo": *Columbus Citizen*, RT's scrapbooks.

434   "a long-legged mind which continually straddles": *Columbus Citizen*, undated, RT's scrapbooks.

434   "Who do you think you are?": OSU *Daily Lantern*, 2/25/32.

434   "Althea's lovely French poodle": Ltr, undated, op. cit.

435   The Althea situation is as complicated as ever: Ltr, JT to MF, undated, probably spring, 1930.

435   I may be married again: Ltr, JT to MF, undated, probably January or February 1930.

436   . . . She is quite famous here: Ltr, JT to MF, undated, probably spring 1930.

437   "Who are you for?": Ibid.

438   "I have always been scared,": Ltr, AH to EBW, 11/19/77.

438   One of the results of the glorious fourth: Ltr, JT to MF, undated, perhaps September 1930.

439   "there isn't any girl I consider": Ltr, JT to MF, undated; perhaps September 1930.

439   "Jim said his marriage to Althea": D. Miller to HK, 1969.

35. THAT PET DEPARTMENT

440   "Our Pet Department": NYer; the series ran intermittently between 2/22/30 to 6/7/30 and was enlarged as "The Pet Department," *The Owl in the Attic*, Harper & Bros., 1931.

442   "All the time": *Book-of-the-Month Club News*, 2/45.

442   "I don't remember just when": EBW to HK, 1962.

442   The piece on Thurber in your Nov. 6 issue: Ltr, EBW to *Washington Post*, 11/16/61.

443   Thurber says the real trouble: NY *Evening Post*, 1/30, RT's scrapbooks.

444   "Last Wednesday I broadcast": Ltr, undated, probably February 1930.

445   "the office we shared": "James Thurber": NYer, 11/11/61.

445   "Jim gave us a series of funny": the EBWs to HK, 1962.

445   "I was ten or eleven when they": Angell to HK, 1962.

446   "Nothing that has happened": Ltr, 7/31/57.

446   ("I just didn't see much of him after that"): EBW to HK.

446   ("Sooner or later . . . Jim"): Ltr, KSW to HK, 3/23/73.

447   "never suffered the imprisonment": Tynan, NYer, 1/24/77; review of Coward biography, *Remembered Laughter*, by Cole Lesley.

447   "Everybody was giving parties": JG to HK, 1962.

447   "Ann Honeycutt says sex is dirty": Terry to HK, 1962.

447   "a gala three-day holiday": Ltr, undated, probably 9/30.

448   "I'm worried about old man Thurber": Ltr, EBW to HWR, undated, probably July 1929.

448   "Thurber was having marital problems": Wright, *The Thurber House Organ*, Vol. 8, No. 2.

448   "[Thurber] takes things too": Ltr, undated, probably 7/30.

448   Jim is here: Ltr, 7/10/30, *Letters of E. B. White*, op. cit.

448   "The camp was a rugged little place": EBW to HK.

448   "In the middle of": "Suli, Suli," NYer, 5/16/36.

449   "Thurber didn't go": Ltr, 4/21/30, *Letters*, op. cit.

449   "Mrs. George I. Loon": JT, the *Otter Bee*, reproduced in the *Thurber House Organ*, op. cit.

449   "[The otter] is the only animal": Ltr, 2/24/56.

451   "[Alexander Woollcott and friends]": *More In Sorrow*, op. cit.

451   "and were so embarrassed by the trained": transcript of "Frankly Speaking," BBC broadcast, 12/24/58.

452   "Paula looked a lot like Honeycutt": EH to HK, 1969.

452   "Jim, in his better moments, reminded me": AH to HK.

453   . . . The report that goes: Ltr, JT to AH, circa 1928.

454   "It is extremely unlikely": *Book-of-the-Month Club News*, 2/45.

454   "Dick had accepted a Hollywood": Louise Connell to HK.

455   "He must have been capable of anger": Ltr, 6/51.

455   "We spent a weekend with Jim": Sylvia Godwin to HK.

457   "slender . . . with a heavy mustache": NY *Telegram*, 2/13/31.

458   "To sit down and draw": Brandon, *As We Are*, Doubleday & Co., 1961.

459   "A passing fad of the British": TYWR.

459   "Ross interviewed me in a": Donald Wharton to HK, 1962.

36. THAT APPROACHING FATHERHOOD

460   "He turned up at my apartment quite upset": AH to HK.

461   "I'm thinking of letting Nash": TYWR.

461   . . . In many ways [Ross] was a: Ltr, Nash to JT, TYWR.

461   "a young man who looked away": Roy Hoopes, *Cain*, Holt, Rinehart and Winston, 1982.

462   I admired [Thurber's] talents: Ltr, Cain to HK, 6/10/71.

462   ("You'd spend all afternoon"): TYWR.

463   If Thurber sniffed Ross: Ltr, Cain to HK, 6/20/71.

463   "Aw, Harold": *Cain*, op. cit.

463   "a compulsively neat man": Ltr, EBW to Roy Hoopes, 7/7/78.

464   On the whole, I would rather be dead: *Cain*, op. cit.

464   "Hell Only Breaks Loose Twice": NYer, 3/10/34.

464   "I never wrote him about it": Ltr, Cain to HK, 6/20/71.

465   "I was to call you": Ltr, Bergman to JT, 7/29/57.

465   ("Problem males, Ross could handle"): Weekes to HK.

465   "He had written some": Ltr, Bergman to JT, 10/4/57.

465   "I saw a sarcastic note he sent": Charles Cooke to HK.

466   "Ross tried to get . . .": Ltr, Bergman to JT, 8/5/57.

466   had warned me that Mrs.: Ltr, Bergman to JT, 9/4/57.

467   I quit because I: Ltr, Bergman to JT, 7/29/57.

467   ("He smoked cigars"): TYWR.

467   "Please don't let these gentlemen": (Typically, JT, twenty-three years later, remembered the wire as aimed at only himself and the Thurber Dog.)

467   "Rubbish": KSW, TYWR annotations.

467 "as a stupid vicious animal": Ltr, Bergman to JT, 3/1/57.

468 "easily forgotten, but he": Ltr, Walker to JT, 8/23/57.

468 "Ross had an unusual respect for": Wharton to HK, 1971.

468 "[He's] the only guy who ever told Mrs.": Ltr, 8/27/57.

468 "Can you imagine having Thurber": Kinkead to HK, 1962.

469 "We were paid space rates on whatever we came up": Ibid.

470 "In some instances, Thurber rewrote": Shawn to HK, 1962.

470 "I just estimate them": TYWR.

470 "I never thought Althea or Jim were": Ltr, 3/11/74.

471 "Grosz told me the": Ltr, Bergman to JT, 8/15/57.

471 "If Grant Had Been Drinking": NYer, 12/6/30.

471 "The Remarkable Case of Mr. Bruhl": NYer, 11/15/30.

472 "The Greatest Man in the World": NYer, 2/21/31.

472 "The Funniest Man You Ever Saw": NYer, 8/15/31.

472 it was a particularly low point in his: JG to HK, 1962.

472 "The symbolism there is pretty": JT to HK, 1948.

473 "Why Mr. Walker Went to California": NYer, 12/5/31.

473 "Subscriber's Nightmare": NYer, /1/3/31.

473 ("The Burning Deck"): NYer, 2/7/31.

473 "Cholly": NYer, 9/19/31.

473 "The Future of Element 87": NYer, 12/31/31.

474 I've been leading a mixed-up: Ltr, JT to HM, 9/22/31.

474 "We came down to New York": LBI, 8/29/73, op. cit.

475 "There was a loop of umbilical cord": Damon to HK, 1962.

475 "Jim found it very important to his ego": Ltr, 3/11/74.

475 Honeycutt affirms that she and Thurber: AH to HK.

475 "at two or three in the morning": Ltr, JG to BB, 3/undated/74.

37. THOSE DESTRUCTIVE FORCES IN LIFE

477 "Everyone knows about Thurber": Frank Sullivan, "The Private Life of James Thurber," BBC broadcast, 12/2/61.

477 "I first heard Thurber": Elinor Gibbs to HK, 1962.

477 ("It was."): HT to HK.
       "I'd just met Thurber": McK to HK.

478 ran intermittently at night: McK, "Salute to Thurber," Saturday Review, 11/25/61.

479 "How to Adjust Yourself to Your Work": NYer, 1/9/37.

479 "Thurber would call me on the phone": Whitaker to HK.

479   One evening he ran out of: SB, "Thurber," *Ohio State University Monthly*, 12/61.

479   Alan Sillitoe: "Mimic"; unidentified tear sheets, HK files.

480   "Is this Mr. Sayre?": JS to HK.

481   When he arrived at the office: Daise Terry to HK.

481   "The Advent of Mr. Moray": NYer, 4/16/32.

481   "The cruelest jokes": BG to HK.

481   "getting fooled several times": Ltr, RM to HK, 7/16/93.

481   "They were usually harmless": JS to HK.

482   "You didn't get mad at Thurber": TG to HK, 1962.

483   "Is this Gardiner 3-7503?": Patricia Gardiner McGuckin to HK, 1962.

483   "Thurber always knew": NS to HK.

483   She hated the milk: JS, Sunday *Washington Post*, op. cit.

484   "The Black Magic of Barney Haller": NYer, 8/27/32.

484   "My favorite line": NY *Evening Post*, 1/30; RT scrapbook.

484   "they are here with the reeves": "What Do You Mean It 'Was' Brillig?", NYer, 1/7/39.

485   "Destructive Forces in Life": NYer, 12/5/36.

486   As always, says Louise: To HK, 1962.

487   "Guns and Game Calls": NYer, 12/14/35.

487   "Are you the S.O.B.": McK, "Salute to Thurber," op. cit.

487   Whitaker points out the absurdity of the: To HK, 1962.

487   "And what does this float represent?": Spencer Klaw to HK, 1949.

488   (Remarkably, the radio comedy): Melvin Patrick Ely, *The Adventures of Amos 'n' Andy*, The Free Press, 1991.

488   a British talk show: "Frankly Speaking," BBC, op. cit.

488   "Back in the thirties": EBW and JT to HK, April 1949.

38. THAT ADMIRAL ON THE WHEEL

490   one of his aunts: "Recollections of the Gas Buggy," *The Thurber Carnival*, op. cit.

490   "We went up on sidewalks": MF, LBI, op. cit.

491   "Smashup": NYer, 10/5/35.

491   "The near-accident is faked": HT to HK.

491   Dinner was to be ready for me: Ltr, 8/[undated]/35.

492   "Driving meant so much to him": HT to HK.

492   Helen Thurber and I have just returned: Ltr, 8/undated/35.

493   "The Admiral on the Wheel": NYer, 2/1/36.

493   "The Character of Catastrophe": NYer, 5/28/38.

493   "a swell fellow": Ltr, JT to HMS, 10/[undated]/36.

494   "God, what a place to drive a car": Ltr, 11/21/37.

494   "We got back a little while ago": Ltr, undated, possibly summer, 1937.

494   The address I had been: JT, article in London newspaper, 1937, unidentified.

495   "That's your radio": "Recollections of the Gas Buggy."

495   "A Ride with Olympy": NYer, 4/30/38.

495   it was Thurber at the wheel: HT to HK.

496   I prefer pencil: Ltr, JT to HM, undated, possibly 1936.

498   "Jim and I would argue and argue": AH to HK.

499   James Geraghty: To HK.

499   "she hasn't been through as much": Alistair Cooke, "James Thurber," the *Atlantic Monthly*, 8/56.

500   "pick a card, any card": "Foreword," *The New Yorker Album*, Harper & Bros., 1932.

501   "Just what I feel about my": Ltr, undated, circa 1936.

502   As one climbed the new steps: Ebba Jonsson to HK, 1949.

502   "Thurber drew on the office walls": EBWs to HK.

39. THAT HIDING GENERATION

504   "Most intellectuals weren't": Gilbert Seldes to HK, Truro, MA, 1960.

504   At night I dream: Ltr, JT to AH, undated, circa 1930.

505   "Well . . . he was skilled at reversing things": AH to HK.

507   "Listen to This, Dear": *Harper's*, 1/32.

508   "The Private Life of Mr. Bidwell": NYer, 1/28/33.

508   "The Indian Sign": NYer, 2/18/33.

509   "that I am a greater writer than White": Ltr, JT to AH, undated, circa 1932.

509   *I count the raindrops*: Ltr, JT to AH, circa 1930.

510   "Helen! Thurber has lost the": Ltr, EBW to AH, 8/16/79.

510   "Carson Blair, Shooting Cop": Ltr, JT to Carson Blair, 2/24/32.

510   ("I thought for a time"): Ltr, JT to AH, circa 1932.

511   "Cabell knows that a wistful man": Ibid.

511   "You have done some superb drawings": Ltr, circa 1932.

511   ("which would kill me—which I"): Ltr, JT to AH, 2/undated/32.

512   "Honey, Honey, Bless Your Heart": *The Bermudian*, 5/52.

512   "Jim was red hot": JS to HK.

512   "I had lunch at the Algonquin today": Ltr, circa 1932.

513   "We had to go upstairs to": Ltr, HT to HK, 12/12/62.

513   "My recollection is that": Sally Benson to HK, 1949.

513   O'Hara's "arrogance": AH to HK.

514   "O'Hara was still poor": HT to HK.

514   "I knew," Gibbs said: EH to HK.

514   "Gibbs and Thurber were almost more than I could": Ibid.

514   "You're funning me, Mr. Thurber": AH to HK.

515   "We knew where we were": Ltr, JT to Frances Glennon of *Life*, 1959.

40. THAT MIDDLE-AGED MAN
ON THE FLYING TRAPEZE

516   "The Evening's at Seven": NYer, 10/22/32.

516   "No More Biographies": NYer, 3/19/32.

516   "Guessing Game": NYer, 9/24/32.

517   "Isn't Life Lovely!": NYer, 6/25/32.

517   "A Farewell to Florida": NYer, 4/30/32.

517   two Reporters at Large articles: "Blushes and Tears," NYer 9/24/32; "Georgia vs. the World," NYer, 12/31/32.

517   crosstown-bus service: "The Crosstown-Bus Situation," NYer, 5/14/32.

517   "Some Notes on the Married Life of . . .": NYer, 6/27/31.

517   "A Preface to Dogs": NYer, 1/2/32.

518   "A Farewell to Santa Claus": NYer, 12/24/32.

518   "There is no doubt in my mind": Ltr, Warfield to HK, 11/15/62.

519   "I made it the fifth grade": JT to HK, 1948.

520   "Jim," she says, "saw the potential": AH to HK.

520   "After six drinks": Ltr, EBW to HT, 3/11/74.

520   "You couldn't stay mad": quoted by Elinor Gibbs to HK.

520   "a group of us left the old": Ted Gardiner to HK, 1962.

521   "was off on some tirade": Ltr, Benchley to HK, 8/11/62.

521   "I thought we'd never": Ltr, Donia McNulty Karpen to HK, 10/18/62.

522   Benchley sometimes kept a room: AH to HK.

522   Peter Arno once took Ross: Ltr, WG to JT, undated, 1957.

522   "Polly Adler had become": Ltr, Gude to BB, 3/undated/74.

522   *A House Is Not a Home*: Rinehart & Co., Inc, 1953.

522 "my old friend Jim Thurber": Ltr, JT to WG, 9/29/52.
522 "Something to Say": TMAMOTFT; titled "Profiles: Something to Say," NYer, 7/30/32.
524 "I acted so badly": Ltr, undated, possibly 1932 or 1933.
526 "I picked up a copy": Ltr, JT to Patricia Stone, "Thurber as a Comic Artist," unpublished M.A. thesis, University of Florida., 1949.
526 "possibly the shortest and most elegant": Russell Baker, "He Knew When to Stop," NY Times, 4/12/90.
526 "Nearly every week I get": HT to HK.
526 "I find it far superior to the": Jacket copy, MLAHT.
527 One reason for both essays: HT to HK.
528 Am I right in thinking that we now get: Ltr, 7/8/58.
529 "It could be worse": Sunday CD, 1/5/41.
529 "The Threefold Problem of World . . .": NYer, 8/5/33.
529 "Tom the Young Kidnapper . . .": NYer, 6/10/33.
530 "Recollections of Henry James": NYer, 6/17/33.
530 "a remodeled farm": Columbus Journal, RT's scrapbooks.
530 "Behind the Statistics": NYer, 7/1/33.
531 "From 1927," Shawn writes: NYer, 11/11/61.
531 He sent a tart note: TYWR.

41. THAT WAR BETWEEN MEN AND WOMEN

532 "I give [W. H.] Auden credit": JT to HK, 1948.
533 In the early days of the New Yorker: "The Private Life of James Thurber," British Broadcasting Corp., 2/12/61.
534 "I saw quite a bit of": Ltr, Alec Waugh to HK, 8/1/64.
534 "He hated their goddam guts!" JS to HK.
534 a congressman replied that his wife: HT to HK.
535 "Great comics tend to be:" EH to HK, 1991.
536 "The difference," writes Thurber: "One Man in his Time," NYer, 1/20/34.
536 was "cold and gray in style": "The 'Odyssey' of Disney"; the Nation, 3/28/34.
536 "After five years under Ross, sanity": RI to HK.
536 His art grew out of: "The New Yorker," Fortune, 8/34.
538 "The editor of Fortune gets": Ltr, McK to JT, 5/25/58.
538 "Don't tell him those things": TYWR.
539 I am . . . leaving my wife: Ltr, JT to AH, circa 1932.

539 "Are these broadcasts of yours": Alton Cook, NY *World-Telegram*, 4/12/34.

539 ("Now, don't read; just tell the thing"): Ibid.

540 "It was chatty, pleasant": Ibid.

540 "This stuff is pretty": *Boston Transcript*, 4/17/34.

540 "Sh'O.K. sh'O.K.": C. Lester Walleer, Smithsonian Magazine, 1/77.

540 "popular for his": Associated Press, 8/undated/34.

541 Thurber had a genuine curiosity: Ltr, JG to BB, op. cit.

541 "I worked across the hall from Edward R.": AH to HK.

541 ("All of them gather together"): Ltr, JT to AH, undated, circa 1934.

542 the apartment had caught fire: CD, 2/2/34.

542 Most of the social gatherings: Ltr, RT to HK, 8/5/72.

545 "I met Thurber through Elliott": Connelly to HK, 1962.

545 I only met Thurber four times: Ltr, West to HK, 7/16/71.

546 "Why should I talk to you?": "Scott in Thorns," the *Reporter* magazine, 4/17/51.

546 ("I spoke to Jim's companion briefly"): AH to HK, 1986.

547 "I'd floated in from Hollywood": Elinor Gibbs to HK.

548 "Before his vision": *Book-of-the-Month Club News*, 2/45.

549 "early Butte, Montana": *Time*, 5/3/63.

549 Each player is equipped: Leslie Midgley, *How Many Words Do You Want?*, Birch Lane Press, 1989.

550 *Fanfare, the Confessions of a Press Agent*: Harper & Bros., 1957.

550 "It was a campaign of terror": Maney to HK, 1962.

551 "Maney and Thurber were hilarious": NS to HK.

551 "Thurber and I shared": Maney to HK.

552 "At '21' . . . I met . . . Ann Honeycutt': Blair to HK, 1962.

42. THAT MAN ON THE TRAIN

553 "I got the idea when my daughter was": Jt to HK, 1948.

554 "You're a millstone": NY *Daily Mirror*, 5/25/35.

554 "I thought she was being pretty nasty to Jim": RT to HK.

555 "Althea had to make the move": AH to HK.

556 "I knew him when he": Ltr, Milton Caniff to HK, 6/10/71.

556 "We were getting ready to go out": D. Miller to HK.

557 "I went down the steps": EP, LBI, 3/7 & 3/9/73.

557 "He was phoning me several": Ltr, MF to BB, 7/28/75.

557 "Eve, did Jim stop to see you?": EP, LBI, op. cit.

558   "was always a damn bore, a showoff": JS, LBI, 12/16/75.

558   "As far back as I can remember": Unpublished paper by Patricia McGuckin, 1962.

558   "Jim would come to town and we'd never know": RT to HK.

558   "He'd say that some": Ltr, Donia Karpen to HK, 10/18/62.

558   the *Columbus Citizen* reported: Earl Minderman, 3/18/35.

559   "As for staying up all night": "A Dozen Disciplines," LYMA, Harper & Bros., 1937.

560   "Thirteen Keys": NYer, 9/8/34.

560   "How to Relax While Broadcasting": NYer, 5/5/34.

560   "Are we landowners or ice dealers?": "More Ice Added to U.S. as Thousands Cheer"; NYer, 5/5/34.

560   "Has Photography Gone Too Far?": NYer, 8/11/34.

560   ("How to Tell a Fine Old Wine"): NYer, 2/24/34.

561   "Going back to places where he": "A Fairly Interesting Envelope"; NYer, 8/25/34.

561   "Pigeons on the grass, alas": "There's an Owl in my Room," NYer, 11/17/34.

562   "We just handed our book to": "Gtde," NYer, 11/24/34.

562   "Footnotes on a Course of Study": NYer, 11/7/36.

562   "Thoughts from Mr. Tierney": NYer, 2/13/32.

562   Ross asked Thurber to pretend to be: TYWR.

563   used Thurber's Valentine Gallery art show as a peg: Mitchell, NY *World-Telegram*, 12/29/34.

563   ("I thought the world of"): Ltr, Walker to JT, 8/23/57.

563   "I was surprised in later years": Mitchell to HK, 1962.

564   "Thurber was the only true genius": NY *Times*, 7/22/92.

564   "It's *still* terrible down here": Ltr, circa 1934.

565   "Though we never talked about it": AH to HK.

43. THAT GREAT HEART ANALYSIS

567   "As a person, Mac seemed everything Jim was": AH to HK.

567   "I was to edit for two days a week": McK to HK.

568   Markey angrily promised to kill: WHIT to HK.

568   "Ah, here's Mac, surrounded by beauty": McK to HK.

568   "Mac, if you keep this up": Ibid.

569   "Geezus, what now?": Ibid.

569   "You ungainly creature, you": Ibid.

569   "Jim's real trouble at the time": AH to HK.

569   "a New England robot": Ltr, WG to JT, undated, 1957.

569   "drove him even crazier": Ibid.

570   ("In many ways . . . the *New Yorker*'s debt to me"): Ibid.

570   "You ever able to call her 'Katharine'?": Ibid.

571   "giving enormous pleasure to Dotty Parker": Ibid.

571   "I never understood why I have to treat you": Ibid.

572   "What a symptomatic, tight, egocentric": Ltrs, JT to AH: undated but probably written in March and April of 1935.

575   "I always preferred the company of men to": AH to HK.

577   "Thurber always accused me of that": AH to HK.

578   ("It was a great deal of fun"): *As We Are*, op. cit.

579   "The International Spy Situation": NYer, 1/19/35.

579   "Producers Never Think Twice": NYer, 2/16/35.

584   "When I married Helen": Ltr, JT to EBW, 12/22/52, *Selected Letters of James Thurber*, Atlantic–Little, Brown, 1980.

44. THAT MENTAL CRUELTY

585   The upper classes wept into their: NY *Daily Mirror*, 5/25/35.

586   "I was convinced they both": Louise Connell to HK.

586   "The bottle didn't break": Hellman to HK.

587   "Years later, he'd be annoyed": TG to HK.

587   "anything I said negatively about Althea": RT to HK.

587   "she was rated as one of the": Ltr, JT to DK, 4/23/51.

588   "Jamie would often go to bed": HT to HK.

588   "We stayed until the latter": LBI, 1973, op. cit.

588   ("As I understand it . . . her husband digs"): TG to HK.

588   "I thought Franny Comstock was my father": RM to LBI, 11/28/72.

588   "that was our life: Cambridge during the school": LBI, op. cit.

588   "I remember stories from my": Ltr, RM to HK, 12/18/89.

589   "When I read 'The Little Girl and the' ": LBI, op. cit.

590   "I was a good deal older": RM, OSU lecture, 5/1/73.

590   If Robert resented my: RM to HK, and ltr, 12/18/89.

590   but I guess she asked when there was a need: Ibid.

590   . . . in 1947 . . . letters to the headmistress: Ltr, the *Chicago Tribune Magazine*, 5/21.

591   "My father never got over the fact": RM, OSU lecture.

591   The only Tri Delt I ever met: Ltr, JT to RM, 11/undated/47.

592   "The Godfather and His Godchild": *Further Fables for Our Time*, 1958, Simon & Schuster.

592   ("You can see why you'd wait around"): OSU lecture.

592   *The White Deer*: 1945, Harcourt Brace & Co.

593   When I first acted at Ohio State: Ltr, OSU lecture.

594   "I have found out little about marriage": Ltr, 10/undated/52.

595   The dreadful variety of tests: Ltr, JT to RM, 11/undated/52.

595   Tell Fred that the feminine: Ltr to RM, OSU lecture.

595   I woke up early: Ltr, RM lecture, op. cit.

596   . . . believes in love in the afternoon: Ibid.

597   "I never really discussed it": Ltr, RM to HK, 12/18/89.

597   "Let's give a party and have old Babe": HT to HK.

598   "put together like the insides": AH to HK.

598   "I have you to thank": AH to HK.

598   "Of course.": HT to HK.

598   "It was a good swap": JS to HK.

598   "When Helen was going with Thurber": Florence Perry to HK, 1962.

599   "Where are you, someplace in the": EP, LBI, 3/11/73.

599   "What are you waiting for?": TYWR.

600   "when my father pronounced": *Thurber*, Dodd, Mead, 1975.

600   "Helen rarely visited the magazine": Daise Terry to HK.

600   "She always went along with Jim": JS to HK.

600   "Gallant," is how Morris Ernst: Ernst to HK, 1962.

600   "a client by virtue of long friendship": JG to HK.

601   "No one was quick enough in a bar": JS to HK.

601   "Her tender, patient": "The Private Life of James Thurber," BBC documentary, broadcast 12/2/61.

45. THAT WEDDED LIFE

602   "It was embarrassing": McK to HK.

603   We had to buy a car: Ltr, undated, summer, 1935.

603   "The Departure of Emma Inch": NYer, 8/10/35.

604   "about a husband who is afraid": Ltr, op. cit.

606   "You have to walk up": Ltr, undated, winter, 1935/36.

607   "Because the show had been put out of": Weekes to HK.

607   "It isn't your house": HT to HK.

608   "I am simply not strong": PM, 10/3/40.

608   In 1953, the head of: Ltr, Oscar Cargill to JT, 1/7/53.

609   I met Thomas Wolfe only once: Ltr, 1/14/53.

609   The professor replied: Ltr, Cargill to JT, 1/31/53.

609   You will be shot: Ltr, JT to the Millers, 1935/36.

610   "A woman came in who prepared": D. to HK.

610   "A Couple of Hamburgers": NYer, 11/16/35.

611   ("You walk like a sylph, Ebba"): Jonsson to HK, 1948.

612   Helen had bought another coat: Patricia Stone to HK.

612   "too sugary and fuzzy": Ltr, undated, probably winter, 1935/36.

614   "How to Listen to a Play": NYer, 10/19/35.

614   "Mr. Thurber's manias are loose": NY *Times*, 11/24/35.

614   "may be described as": *Manchester Guardian*, 12/2/35.

614   ("Thurber preferred duck pins"): Ernst to HK.

615   Thurber brought the neuroses: "Tilley the Toiler," *Saturday Review*, 8/30/47.

615   "The atmosphere of the office was": WHIT to HK.

615   "Thurber made himself larger than life": Cooke to HK.

616   "Ross thought there was only one way": Kinkead to HK.

616   When we crossed Fifth: "Street Scene" (Talk of the Town), NYer, 12/28/35.

46. THAT LEFTIST ASSUMPTION

618   60 percent of American: Brookings Institute study.

619   "Are we important?": TYWR.

619   "irresponsible in ignoring": Scott Elledge, *E. B. White*, op. cit.

619   "has at last got out of": "Notes & Comment," 3/13/37.

619   I am no one to defend Roosevelt whole: Ltr, 3/17/37.

620   according to William Wright's biography: *Lillian Hellman*, Simon & Schuster, 1988.

620   "even during the F.D.R. madness": AH to HK.

621   "White and I have always regarded the": Ltr, 8/5/50.

621   *Total Recoil*: Kyle Crichton, Doubleday, 1960.

621   "That's enough": William Nolan, *Hammett*, Congdon & Weed, 1983.

622   It was an exciting and gratifying time: "Big Nemo," NYer, 3/18, 3/25, and 4/1/39.

623   "Notes for a Proletarian Novel": NYer, 6/9/34.

624   "a thin line of crap": Ltr, JT to DK, 8/5/50.

625   "After an Evening Spent in Reading *The Nation*": "Chronicle of a Crime"; NYer, 1/21/28.

626   great many things: Ltr, undated, probably late 1934.

628   "I'll have to get mildly cockeyed": Ltr, 1/16/35.

630   "a hell of a goddam loose word": Ltr, undated, probably March 1936.

631   Joe Freeman wrote a ten thousand word: Ltr, 8/5/50.

632   Party to which Jim Thurber referred: Ltr, 11/1/50.

632   "an impotent bourgeois . . . with nothing": Cowley, LBI, 3/27/75, Sherman, CT.

633   "What Are the Leftists Saying?": NYer, 4/10/37.

633   "How to Write a Long Autobiography": NYer, 5/15/37.

634   Anatole Broyard: NY *Times Book Review.*

634   Archibald MacLeish: TV documentary, conversation between MacLeish and MVD, undated transcript.

47. THOSE LOVELY YOUNGSTERS

636   "we ran out of tunes": "Notes in May," *Bermudian,* 5/52.

637   "get away from Helen": JG to HK.

637   "He's talking about going to": Dr. Sol Engel to HK.

637   ("If he really was in love with me"): JW to HK, 1993.

637   "You always have lighted candles": Dinah Jane Williams Darby to HK, Bermuda, 1974.

637   "Jane and I had just": RW to HK, and "From the Crow's Nest," *Bermudian,* 4/51.

639   Dear Katharine and Andy: Ltr, undated, circa 4/36.

640   "He used to wonder why he couldn't hit a": RW to HK.

640   Ada has a tennis court, on which we play: Ltr, op. cit.

641   I got the proofs: Ibid.

642   "I had a twenty-two-foot sloop": RW to HK.

642   "The Story of Sailing": *Bermudian,* 6/36.

643   "An Outline of Scientists": NYer, 9/19/36.

643   Actually, says Helen: To HK.

644   ("We are happy and calm here in"): Ltr, summer/1936.

644   . . . I'd like to do . . . a kind of Talk: Ibid.

645   "You wouldn't like it, Liebling": Liebling, "Harold Ross—The Impresario," *Nieman Reports,* 4/59.

645   "Did you know . . . that [Hobart]": Ltr, to JT, 1/undated/36.

645   Most of my better men had been slipping: Ltr, 8/14/57.

646   McKelway heard about the final: Ltr, McK to JT, 4/2/58.

646   "had been a crackerjack copy-handler": Ibid.

646   "I had been in a position": Ltr, Walker to JT, 8/14/57.

648   "the man who does not": Ltr, Hutchins to JT, 12/23/36.

648   "Thurber was rarely there when I was": McK to HK.

648   "a merciless and ruthless exposure": 7/22/40, finding of the Circuit Court of Appeals; the libel count was settled on 4/4/44, for a small amount, after six years of litigation.

649   "He was continually quitting": Ltr, McK to JT, 4/2/58.

649   "get the magazine talked about": Hobart Weekes to HK.

649   "Did you know . . . that Ross": Ltr, Walker to JT, 8/17/57.

649   Fadiman writes that his: Ltr, Fadiman to JT, 9/6/57.

650   "If you're wrong": TYWR.

650   "I used to have lunch with": Ltr, McK to JT, 4/2/58.

650   It was what became known as Ross's "don't give": Ibid.

651   ("I was . . . sick of Ik . . . taking me to lunch"): Ibid.

651   several members of the editorial board: JS, *Washington Post* Sunday book section, op. cit.

651   "Ross was drinking at the": Ltr, McK to JT, 4/2/58.

651   "There *was* talk of replacing Ross": HATNY,

651   One time K. and Andy: Ltr, McK to JT, 4/2/58.

652   Dear Raoul: Ltr, 3/19/58.

652   "I took too much of": Ltr, Fleischmann to JT, 3/28/58.

653   He was very resentful of our unsound investment: Ibid.

654   *Tonight at 8:30*: JT review, *Stage*, 12/36.

654   Dear Jim . . . I would: Ltr, Noel Coward to JT, 1/22/37.

655   "Ross came charging": Ltr, Ik Shuman to JT, 8/22/58.

48. THAT SPIDER TRAP

656   At 164th Street . . . : Ltr, JT to EBW, undated, 1936.

657   "Jim made a big hit with everyone": Sullivan to HK.

657   "It meant a lot to Jamie": HT to HK.

657   "Whenever I realize George": Ltr, undated, 1936.

657   "Goodbye, Mr. O. Charles Meyer!": NYer, 8/1/36.

658   The owner was a woman: Ltr, JT to DK, 4/23/51.

658   We have taken the most charming: Ltr, summer, 1936.

658   "will probably open my trap": Ltr, JT to EBW, fall 1936.

658   The drawing games were: LBI, 3/27/75, op. cit.

659   I had never, God bless my soul: Ltr, summer 1936.

660   "we might mention": office memo, EBW to KSW, undated.

660   Since Mr. Thurber is: Ltr, KSW to Sandburg, 5/29/36.

660   "The evening lasted to early": D. Miller to HK, 1964.

661   Look, I couldn't agree with you: Ltr, summer 1936.

662   . . . It was the last piece: Maurice Dolbier, NY *Times Magazine*, 12/4/49.

662   "Wake Up and Live, Eh?": NYer, 4/18/36.

663   *Be Glad You're Neurotic*: "Peace, It's Wonderful," *Saturday Review*, 11/21/36.

663   (*Streamline Your Mind*): "Pythagoras and the Ladder," NYer, 11/28/36.

663   (*How to Worry Successfully*): "Destructive Forces in Life" NYer, 12/5/36.

663   Mary Perin Barker: "Footnotes on a Course of Study," NYer, 11/7/36.

664   ("You can hear the"): "Food Fun for the Menfolks," NYer, 10/3/36.

664   *How to Win Friends*: "The Voice with the Smile," *Saturday Review*, 1/30/37.

664   "Miscellaneous Mentation": NYer, 5/1/37.

664   "The Case Against Women": NYer, 10/24/36.

664   A female writer "who at twenty-two is": "Miscellaneous Mentation," op. cit.

665   "Sex ex Machina": NYer, 3/13/37.

665   Eleanor Roosevelt: "My Day," NYer, 2/15/36.

665   "There is Man and there is Woman": "But Women Go On Forever," *For Men Only*, 8/37.

666   "My Memories of D. H. Lawrence": NYer, 6/27/36.

668   "Well, poor Thurber": Nelson H. Budd, *Ohio State University Monthly*, 1/62.

669   "We once had a cook": Ltr, Milton Caniff to HK 1/10/71.

670   "The corns are gittin our thrips": Ltr, summer 1936.

670   "Tempest in a Looking Glass": *Forum & Century*, 4/37.

670   I am having a show of my drawings: Ltr, summer 1936.

670   Being essentially a writer: *Art Digest*, 6/1/37.

49. THAT JOURNEY TO THE PYRENEES

673   "the little Spanish babies": Ltr, HT to BB, op. cit.

673   What we need is writers: Ltr, JT to EBW, 10/6/37.

673   . . . It is the easiest thing: Ltr, JT to EBW, 1/20/38.

673   "I, too, know what the": Ltr, EBW to JT, fall 1937.

674   . . . have for some reason: Ltr, JT to Anthony Bertram, 6/21/51.

674   "no more than a minor nervous condition: interview, May 1937, undated London newspaper.

675   "Quick to arouse": Storran Gallery art collection.

675   "I was twenty-eight": Alistair Cooke to HK, 1962.

676   . . . I have been selling: Ltr, JT to EBW, summer 1937.

677   "writes such offensive muck": Ltr, Rebecca West to JT, 12/27/37.

678   . . . enough money: Art Buchwald, column, the *Toledo Blade*, 6/9/55.

678   "I got the idea from": JT to HK, 1948.

679   I saw the David Garnett: Ltr, EBW to JT, fall 1937.

679   I am quitting partly: Ltr, EBW to KSE, 5/31/37, *Letters of E. B. White*, op. cit.

680   Dear Katharine: Ltr, JT to KSW, 7/13/37.

680   "He just sails around": Ltr, WG to EBW, 9/undated/37.

680   ". . . It's a crime": Ibid.

680   As far as I can make out: Ltr, JT to EBW, summer 1937.

681   Dear Andy: You may be: Ltr, JT to EBW, 10/6/37.

681   "The City of Light": NYer, 10/23/37.

682   "Mettez l'assiette": Nathaniel Benchley, NY *Herald Tribune*, 5/12/40.

683   "I wouldn't dwell": "Sample Intelligence Test," LYMA.

684   Thurber finds this a: "No Standing Room Only," LYMA.

685   "We loved Rome": Ltr, HT to BB, op. cit.

685   The spot shows: Ltr, JT to *New Yorker* art conference, 12/16/37.

686   "I got back from Maine": Ltr, EBW to JT, fall 1937.

686   . . . I have made an unholy mess: Ltr, EBW to JT, 1/8/38.

687   I felt I could not leave: Ltr, JT to EBW, 1/20/38.

689   "Kay loved her job": William Maxwell to HK.

689   "cover new ground, which": Ltr, EBW to HR, 9/16/38.

689   "Oh, yes, that insane": HT to HK; quoted in Thurber interviews elsewhere.

50. THAT MAN WHO KNEW TOO LITTLE

691   "pulled the blinds against": "Preface to a Life," MLAHT.

691   "The Man Who Knew Too Little": NYer, 12/4/37.

691   Thurber was mailing: Leonard Lyons, NY *Post*, RT's scrapbook.

691   "The Ordeal of Mr. Matthews": NYer, 12/6/47.

692   "Where shall we meet": TYWR.

692   "The guidebooks listed": Frederick Packard to HK.

693   "Thurber was one of our sacred cows": McK to HK.

693   "The thing to do": "Journey to the Pyrenees", MWAWTI.

693 ("An Irishman named Russell"): Ltr, JT to McN, 6/1/38.

694 "There seem to be as many": Ltr, JT to KSW, 2/23/38.

694 "they weren't really replacing": Richard Boyer to HK.

694 I'm glad McNulty has been: Ltr, JT to KSW, 1/22/38.

694 containing two or three: Ltr, JT to McN, undated, 1938.

694 I finally figured out: Ltr, JT to McN, 2/8/38.

696 ("I didn't expect them"): Ltr, JT to KSW, 1/22/38.

696 . . . Both of you like New York: Ltr, JT to KSW, 2/23/38.

696 . . . The thing that marks us: Ltr, JT to KSW, 1/15/38.

697 "You got to watch the person": Ltr, JT to KSW, 4/19/38.

697 I have long thought [Andy]: Ltr, JT to KSW, circa 1938.

698 "Ees because," he said: "Journey to the Pyrenees," MWAWTI, Harcourt Brace & World, 1942.

698 "We live in a nice flat": Ltr, JT to McN, 6/1/38.

698 "I had got my first dog": AH to HK.

699 "The flowers were red": O'Hara, Collier's, 7/8/55.

699 "an eccentric dining": Ltr, Alec Waugh to HK, 8/1/64.

699 "a figure of imposing": "That Remarkable Man, Thurber," Jack Jones, Ohio Citizen Sunday Magazine, 10/26/42.

699 [Laughton's] greatest ambition: Ltr, James K. Miller to JT, 2/28/35.

700 "Ross and McKelway had met": Mitchell to HK.

701 "Just before the War": Ltr, Liebling to HK.

701 "I'm not sure I'll live": JT to HK.

702 I wish I hadn't passed my: Ltr, JT to KSW, 4/30/38.

702 "At age sixty-five": Glenna Syse, Chicago Sun-Times, 8/15/60.

702 "Merry Birthday": Ltr, JT to Whites, 9/15/38.

703 I feel pretty far away: Ltr, JT to EBW, 9/undated/38.

703 "I'm to see Rosemary": Ltr, JT to EBW, 9/undated/38.

703 "into one of my wincing": Ltr, EBW to JT, (probably October) 1938.

704 "Talking to Jim Thurber": RT scrapbook item.

705 "It always reminds me": "Everybody is getting serious," New Republic, 5/26/58.

706 I just made a sound: Ltr, JT to HM, circa 1940.

706 I wonder if you: Ltr, JT to "Duke" Damon, 2/11/37.

51. THOSE FABLES FOR OUR TIME

708 It is nice to be back: Ltr, JT to EBW, fall 1938.

708 I was by no means satisfied: Ltr, JT to EBW, 11/undated/38.

710   *In a Word*: Alfred A. Knopf, 1939.

710   *Men Can Take It*: Random House, 1939.

711   *Tales of a Wayward Inn*: Frederick A. Stokes, 1938.

711   "the most artistic": *Herald Tribune*, 3/26/39.

712   "Everything I write I work over": *Waterbury Republican*, Sunday, 1/29/39.

712   "Thurber was a Civil War buff": McK to HK.

712   "It's the goddamdest lion fight": TYWR.

712   "Why in God's name": Ibid.

712   "into a common cornfield crow": Ibid.

712   "Dear Andy and Katharine": Ltr, undated, spring 1939.

714   "I frequently drank": Ltr, McK to JT, 4/2/58.

714   "Ross didn't put up much resistance": Kinkead to HK.

714   "Hi, Mac. Those Winchell": Ltr, McK to JT, 4/2/58.

717   "was faced with the consideration": *Newsweek*, 5/3/48.

717   "No special apology": *I Believe*, Simon & Schuster, 1939.

717   *Forum and Century*: 6/39.

717   "some goddam woman editor": JT to EBW and HK.

718   *Lord Jim*: Bantam Classic, 1981.

720   "Anodynes for Anxieties": LYMA.

721   Dear Jaime [sic]: Ltr, Benchley to JT, 2/7/45.

721   "Tim, who is a freshman": Ltr, FPA to Gus Ferber, 4/13/46.

721   Thurber began receiving letters: Ken Englund, NY *Times*, 8/10/47.

722   "Outside of a few": Englund, "The Secret Life of James Thurber," unpublished paper, Thurber Collection, OSU

722   "God bless you": TYWR.

722   "I believe we have": Ltr, JT to Goldwyn, 12/18/45.

725   "horror and struck": *Life*, 8/18/47.

725   "Did anybody get the name of that": *Time*, 8/3/47.

726   "grows almost profane": *Life*, 8/4/47.

726   "Either Mr. Thurber": *Life*, 8/18/47.

726   "that obsolete weapon": Ibid.

726   "They were many and wonderful": *Time*, 8/3/47.

727   "Jim and I corresponded": Englund, unpublished paper, op. cit.

727   "Had Walter been able": EH to HK.

52. THAT MALE ANIMAL

728   "The idea came to me": "Roaming in the Gloaming," NY *Times*, 1/7/40.

728   "It sounded good to": ELUTTC.

728   Thurber's original basic plot: Ibid.

729   "a beautiful piece of writing": Ibid.

729   "that had so damaged": Ibid.

729   Your letter found me: Ltr, JT to McN, 4/29/39.

729   "Jamie was terrible": HT to HK.

730   37 MONEY CHESTS: "The Ship's Cat," Thurber Collection.

730   I guess you better: Ltr, to Dr. Gordon Bruce, 6/9/39.

731   ("I won't be able"): ELUTTC.

731   "a genuine Thurber flavor": Ibid.

731   "a terrible age": Sarah Boynoff, Los Angeles newspaper item, 8/3/39, RT scrapbooks.

731   "Lily Pons Says": Arthur Millier, Los Angeles Times, 7/2/39.

732   a Peggy Hopkins Joyce party: HT to Jack Sher, St. Louis Post-Dispatch, 3/24/40.

732   "Will you tell me": ELUTTC.

733   I naturally asked: Ltr, JT to DK, 4/23/51.

735   I drew some (not dirty): P. Stone, MA thesis, Thurber Collection, op. cit.

735   later Helen's . . . denials: Ltrs, HT to Friedman, 10/26/61 and 11/26/61.

735   "a place like this": Friedman to HK; Ltr, Friedman to HK, 1/1/65; Cavalier, 1967.

735   "which brought back": Ltr, JT to Friedman, 7/9/59.

735   "It is the style": Diana Trilling, NY Times Book Review clipping, 1993.

735   Unstimulated, he is: "Notes on James Thurber, the Man, or Men," NY Times, 2/25/40.

736   After ten years: "The Real Man, Nugent," NY Times, 4/28/40.

737   . . . "I know I'm not a tiger": The Male Animal, Samuel French, 1941.

737   "After Mrs. Thurber had gone to bed": Ltr, JT to Michael W. Zeamer, 1/5/46.

739   "There go the most": NYer, 7/24/37.

739   "a happy miracle": Iris Barry, NY Herald Tribune, 12/3/39.

739   . . . That parable: Ltr, Ellen Glasgow to JT, 1/4/43.

739   Although he was best known: NYer, 11/11/61.

740   "my favorite Thurber book": HT inscription in copy of The Last Flower sent to HK.

741   "Nugent and I made": Ltr, JT to Russel Crouse, 9/17/57.

742 "It had been a long hot summer": ELUTTC.

743 For a writer in his middle: Ltr to Whites, 11/undated/39.

744 Elliott and I have: Ibid.

744 "I wanted the Thurbers": ELUTTC.

745 tripped over the footlights: Jack Sher, *St. Louis Post-Dispatch*, 3/24/40.

745 "I'm worried too": ELUTTC.

746 "It was heartbreaking": *World-Telegram*, 1/29/40.

746 . . . [Dick] Maney is likely: Ltr, JT to WG (undated), summer 1950.

747 Well, the great event: Ltr, Daise Terry to KSW, 1/undated/40.

749 "Well, God bless . . .": TYWR.

53. THAT ONE YEAR OF BRIGHTNESS

750 "If you need any money": Ltr, JT to HMS, 3/19/40.

750 "tall, thin, gray-haired": Frank T. Farrell, NY *World-Telegram*, 12/30/39.

750 "six foot one, with shell-rimmed glasses": *Baltimore Evening-Sun*, 1/1/40.

750 "a pleasant voice": Robert van Gelder, NY *Times Book Review*, 5/12/40.

750 Thurber would storm out: Farrell, *World-Telegram*, op. cit.

750 "Thurber has both a prodigious": "Notes on James Thurber"; NY *Times*, 2/25/40.

750 fibbed to one interviewer: Inez Robb, NY *Mirror*, 12/13/39.

750 "The silver ear trumpet": Farrell, *World-Telegram*.

750 Benchley wrote in the *Herald Tribune*: 5/12/40.

751 "Courtship through the Ages": NYer, 12/9/39.

751 "though Thurber didn't invent": "James Thurber in Conversation with Alistair Cooke," *Atlantic*, 8/56.

751 "I'll never go back": Candide, "Only Human," NY *Daily Mirror*, 1/20/40.

751 "The Man Who Hated Moonbaum": NYer, 3/16/40.

751 "Herman and I went to New York": D. Miller to HK.

752 . . . Helen and I both went: Ltr, JT to HMS 3/19/40.

752 "What Do You Mean It *Was* Brillig?": NYer, 1/7/39.

754 "as simple as tying a shoe lace": Ltr, JT to Whites, received 4/23/40.

755 I managed the week: Ibid.

758   The office, as you know . . . : Ibid.

758   . . . What I allude to laughingly: Ltr, circa spring 1940.

759   "The Story of the Bicycle": *Bermudian*, 5/40.

759   "Extinct Animals of Bermuda": *Bermudian*, 6/40.

759   Millmoss feels happier: Kenneth MacLean, the *Canadian Forum*, 12/53.

759   "Something about the creature's": "Thurber as seen by Thurber," NY *Times*, 1/28/45.

759   "Prehistoric Animals of the Middle West," *Mademoiselle*, 9/43.

760   ("I consider my years"): Ltr, Florence Butcher to HK, 8/5/64.

760   "Because it was a dangerous": Bruce to reporter, Time, Inc. library, 1954.

760   This, says Helen "cut": Ltr, HT to BB, op. cit.

760   "at least until": Ltr, HT to RWS, 7/undated/41.

761   I have not had a: Ltr, undated, late August 1940.

761   "You Could Look It Up": the *Saturday Evening Post*, 4/5/41.

762   "By God, I do, too": Ltr, HWR to JT, 10/12/49.

762   Jamie saw better for a while: Ltr, HT to RWS, late August 1940.

764   "There seemed such old-fashioned": PM, 10/15/40.

764   "has to go through a lot": PM, 9/17/40.

764   a 1926 book by Will Rogers: PM, 9/19/40.

764   long-windedness of Thomas Wolfe: PM, 12/3/40.

764   "Scattergood Baines": PM, 9/26/40.

764   He wonders why women: PM, 9/24/40.

764   Anne Morrow Lindbergh's: PM, 10/24/40.

765   Medve, the poodle: PM, 10/17/40.

765   The doctor had said: Ltr, 7/undated/41.

766   "From then on things": Ibid.

766   When I got in this morning: Ltr, Terry to KSW, 2/undated/41.

767   I . . . closed the house: Ltr, 7/undated/41.

767   Mr. Ross is back: Ltr, undated, 1941.

768   Mr. Thurber went to the hospital: Ltr, 2/12/41.

769   . . . Each operation: Ltr, HT to RWS, 7/undated/41.

770   The idea of selling: Ltr, JT to RWS, 7/undated/41.

54. THAT WHIP-POOR-WILL

771   "They performed these": NY, WNDT TV talk show, 1962, op. cit.

771   "a hundred pages to a pencil": Harvey Breit, NY *Times Magazine*, 12/4/49.

771   "the timekeeper": PM, 1/27/41.

771   the radio programs: PM, 2/3/41.

771   Wendell Willkie's English: PM, 2/27/41.

771   superiority of animals: PM, 2/24/41.

771   "Couldn't reach his throat": PM, 5/11/41.

771   "Interview with a Lemming": PM, 3/3/41.

772   eyesight of the water buffalo: PM, 3/10/41.

772   "clad only in socks": PM, 5/18/41.

772   It was a letter from a woman reader: PM, 3/17/41.

772   wished to be Hannibal: PM, 7/13/41.

773   "The Whip-Poor-Will": NYer, 8/9/41.

774   the nightmares he described: JT to HK, 1948.

774   the first story Thurber ever dictated: Ibid.

775   "a five-year nervous crack-up": Ltr, JT to Frank Gibney of News-
       week, op. cit.

774   "When I knew there wouldn't": Time, Inc., library, 1954.

775   "blindsight": NY Times, 1/15/91.

776   ("Helen, for all her gaiety"): AH to HK.

776   "several friends called us": HT to HK.

776   "Please, Jap, please": JG, the Duchess County Intelligencer, 5/91.

776   It's rather strange: Ltr, JG to BB, 3/undated/74.

776   I had just met him: The Autobiography of Mark Van Doren, Harcourt
       Brace & Co., 1958.

777   "I told him homorists": MVD to HK, 1962

779   Four weeks ago today: Ltr, 8/undated/41.

779   A great deal of modern humor: A Subtreasury of American Humor,
       Coward-McCann, Inc., 1941.

780   "I like the selections": Ltr, undated, probably September 1941.

780   I have a swell idea for a play: Ibid.

781   two book reviews: The Last Tycoon ("Taps at Assembly"), The New
       Republic, 2/9/42; The Moon Is Down ("What Price Conquest"), The
       New Republic, 3/16/42.

781   Dear Mr. Ross: Ltr, 10/20/41.

784   I just got back: Ltr, Frank Sullivan to KSW, 10/30/41.

785   "Among other things": Ltr, HT to BB, op. cit.

785   "Bruce was an advertising executive:" AH to HK.

785   We've seen neither hide nor hair: Terry to KSW, 1/undated/41.

786   "But he wouldn't go alone": AH to HK.

787   He loved to play: Ltr, Walker to HK, 8/15/62.

787   "Thurber suddenly leaped": Ltr, Benchley to HK, 8/11/62.

55. THAT CATBIRD SEAT

788 "Here Lies Miss Groby": NYer, 3/21/42.

788 "A Good Man": NYer, 5/2/42.

788 "Memoirs of a Drudge": NYer, 10/3/42.

788 "We found Jim": Louise Connell to HK.

789 "He always had an office": Weekes to HK.

789 "There was only one war": LL to HK.

789 ("It was the war"): Ltr, McK to JT, 4/2/58.

790 I address you in a state: RATNY.

791 "I don't care whether they're": Ibid.

791 "the idiots' house organ": Ltr, Walker to JT, 8/31/57.

792 "He was always trying to": Ebba Jonsson to HK, 1948.

792 "Capote gave Thurber": Ltr, HT to BB, op. cit.

792 I worked as a boy: *Thurber*, 1975, op. cit.

793 "The entire Capote story": Ltr, HT to BB, op. cit.

793 My father did not: Ltr, RM to HK, 12/1/90.

793 Katharine White also: Ltr to Charles Cooke, fall 1975.

793 "I never personally saw him": Terry to HK.

795 . . . whose death in September: Ltr, 1/28/50.

796 I loved John Mosher: Ltr, JT to KSW, 12/26/57.

796 "I had known": Ltr, HT to BB, op. cit.

796 "Years later, Jim asked me": JS to HK.

796 "Not enough is made": Cowley, LBI, 3/27/75.

797 Hemingway—well, he is one of those problems: Ibid.

797 Asked once what he would most like to see: Henry Brandon, *The New Republic*, 5/26/58.

797 "I partly guessed what to expect": RI to HK.

798 "He just didn't want": BB, *Thurber*.

798 "I should have added": Ltr, EBW to HT, 3/11/74.

799 "Dear Jim" and signed: *Time*, undated file item.

799 "that even Thurber": Elledge, *E. B. White*, op. cit.

800 Here is a copy of the petition: Ltr, JT to EBW, 3/undated/42.

800 "I don't see why we should be": CD, 3/10/42.

801 JUMPY CO-AUTHOR: CD, undated item, Thurber Collection.

802 "The Catbird Seat": NYer, 11/14/42.

802 "the weird Thurberian world": *Time*, 11/2/42.

802 "People who are morose": *Herald Tribune*, 11/1/42.

803 *Saturday Review*: 11/1/42.

803   John Chamberlain: NY *Times*, 10/31/42.
803   Helen read the Alexander: Ltr, 4/6/42.

56. THOSE MANY MOONS

805   "The name combines that of Lee Nugent": NS to HK.
805   Such good drawings: Ltr, JT to Michael W. Zeamer, 1/5/46.
806   Since I only have about one-eighth: Ibid.
806   "God, but artists are dumb!": *Newsweek*, undated clipping, 1943.
807   "On an outside backporch": "Further Thurber," MacLean, op. cit.
807   "very, very fond of women": Cowley, LBI, 3/27/75.
808   The chief dreads we had: Ltr, JT to EBWs, circa 9/41.
810   About that play: Ltr, EBW to JT, 9/1/42.
812   "Elliott [Nugent] is in": Ltr, circa 1943.
812   "But your President told me": The brussels sprout anecdote appears
        in several places in slightly different versions; e.g.: William Hickey,
        London Express Wire, *Columbus Citizen*, 6/19/55.
812   "Mr. Thurber has at last": Ltr, 12/undated/42.
813   "The Cane in the Corridor": NYer, 1/2/43.
813   He had resented Gibbs: HT to HK.
813   "If the Cornwall group": Simont to HK.
814   "It was on a tennis court": John Duncan Miller, LBI, 10/28/74.
815   Here is the letter: Ltr, 3/20/43.
816   "would be sadly incomplete": Ltr, JT to EBW, 6/9/43.
817   "and the rare appearance": Schlamm, NY *Times*, 11/21/43.
817   A full-page Bonwit Teller ad ran: NYer, 4/8/44.
817   "greying, railish six-footer": *Time*, 11/15/43.
817   "came down a flight of": *Ohio State Journal*, 12/27/43.
818   1776—and All That: NYer, April 24, 1943.
818   "I can't have three books": Ltr, 6/12/43.
818   "I got a proof of the fairy tale": Ltr, 6/9/43.
819   "There is no such thing": Malcolm Muggeridge, NY *Times*, 4/24/78.

57. THAT COMIC PRUFROCK

820   "I should know": HT to LL and HK.
820   ("How do you think Thurber got out"): Ltr, HT to BB, op. cit.
820   "Thurber was two people": Ltr, PDV to HK, 4/14/87.
821   Thomas Sugrue: *Saturday Review of Literature*, 1/2/43.
822   Dear Mr. De Vries: Ltr, JT to De Vries, 11/19/43.

822   the stage fright was real: HT to HK.

823   I shared what I think: Ltr, Caniff to HK, 6/10/71.

823   ("They never read anything I wrote"): Ben Yagoda, NY *Times Magazine*, 6/12/83.

823   "Editorial toils on that monthly": PDV, "Acutely Contemporary and Abidingly Human," *Chicago Daily News*, 4/13/63.

824   "picking his way through": Ibid.

825   . . . Thurber does not talk: *Chicago Sun*, 4/16/44.

826   "We want you and Katinka": Ltr, 4/17/44.

826   Thanks very much for your copy: Ltr, 5/5/44.

826   Mr. Thurber gave me the Comment: Ltr, 6/8/44.

827   By this time you have Ross's dazed: Ltr, 6/14/44.

828   "Hi, De Vree. Can you do the Race Track?": TYWR.

828   . . . His talent is yet to be proved: Ltr, 7/10/44.

829   "But where do you find better writing": PDV to HK.

829   "Pete's earlier novels weren't Jamie's": HT to HK.

829   "Peter De Vries does for schizophrenia": Leonore Fleischer, review of *The Cat's Pajamas*, *Life*, 1969.

829   "Pete always began by sitting down and": HT to HK.

829   Sequoia and its friends: Ltr, 9/undated/47.

830   "Autumn is the mellower season": Ltr, PDV to JT, 11/10/47.

830   Thanks for the book: Ltr, 11/25/47.

830   "The Cherboors": NYer, 8/5/44.

830   "Fairy Tales for Our Time": NYer, 9/29/45.

830   "Our New Natural History" began: NYer, 3/10/45.

831   You have a bird called a shriek: Ltr, 12/13/44.

832   "There might be a name": Ltr, HWR to JT, 12/6/44.

833   In the last seven years of his life: TYWR.

834   The whole thing was my: Ltr, PDV to HK, 5/30/89.

834   "I don't know" . . . "except": Ltr, PDV to HK, 6/15/89.

834   "His knowledge of the matter may have been": Ibid.

834   I thought you might look these: Ltr, undated, 1947.

835   I've been brooding about: Ltr to PDV, 10/16/52.

835   "Shawn seems to be": Ltr, PDV to Thurbers, 3/20/52.

836   I wonder what became of the lawyer: Ltr, 1/16/53.

837   "I started to do a novel": Ltr, 3/20/52.

837   One thing you overlooked: Ltr, JT to PDV, 3/31/52.

837   I don't know how you got to the: Ltr, 8/2/54.

837   "Officers' Mess": Ltr, JT to PDV, 8/20/54.

837   "pour new blood into": Ltr, PDV to JT, 1/7/57.

838   "You must insist that you collaborate": Ltr, 7/2/56.

838   I want to have my play make some sense: Ibid.

838   I'm glad to see the: Ltr, PDV to JT, 10/31/57.

838   There aren't any words of comfort: Ltr, 9/21/60.

839   Your words are of the kind that remind: Ltr, 9/28/60.

839   "The only time he complained": "Universal Dreamer," *Saturday Review*, 11/25/61.

58. THAT GREAT QUILLOW

840   "the man of imagination": Holmes, *The Clocks of Columbus*, op. cit.

840   Thurber is pictured: CD, 1/44, RT scrapbooks.

841   "I never could hear": RW to HK, 1974.

841   Well, here I am again: Ltr, JT to the Palmers, 9/21/44.

842   . . . The Navy doctors . . . who: Ltr, 9/30/44.

843   "Who Are You?": *Harper's*, 11/44.

843   "Some people glow inside": NYer, 7/24/43.

843   If you saw the Huxley piece: Ltr, 12/undated/44.

843   "Thurber and I are no longer the friends": EBW to HK.

844   "He was rough on women": Damon to HK.

844   "One evening he picked on": Spencer Klaw to HK, 1952.

845   "just watching him at": RM, LBI, 11/28/72.

845   "He would be suddenly angry": MVD to HK.

846   "The Notebooks of James Thurber": NYer, 2/5/49.

846   "The only woman Thurber": Ltr, Stafford to HK, 3/24/72.

846   "Jim was a dear friend": Ltr, KSW to HK, 12/11/72.

846   "He'd bring in two or three": Fanfoni to HK, 1963.

847   We wanted you to know: Ltr, undated, probably 11/44.

847   I got your note: Ltr, HWR to HT, 11/22/44.

848   I didn't break my neck: Ltr, HWR to HT, 11/30/44.

848   I had a swell time: Ltr, undated; probably 12/44.

849   "an anthology of all my books": Ltr, 6/11/44.

849   assigned a reader: Ltr, Marguerite Hoyle to Jules Englander, 12/30/49.

850   "I could have wished": Ltr, 1/15/41.

850   "The volume would be made up": Ltr, 6/4/43.

851   Dear Gene: Ltr, 6/11/43.

851   *Saturday Review*: 2/3/45.

851   *New Republic*: 4/45.

851   "Last summer, Mark Van Doren": Ltr, 3/12/45.

852 NY *Times Book Review*: 2/4/45.

852 *Herald Tribune*: 2/4/45.

852 *Time*: 2/12/45.

852 *The Constant Reader*: 2/22/45.

852 "My effect on many women": Ltr, JT to Miriam Drimmer, 11/17/45.

852 PM: 2/4/45.

854 *Book-of-the-Month Club News*: 2/45.

855 "I would be more than pleased": Ltr, 3/19/45.

855 "I have been intending to write": Ltr, 1/29/45.

855 "Looking over your latest book": Ltr, HWR to JT, 3/14/45.

856 Have you any objection to our canvassing: Ibid.

856 I am just recovering from a severe: Ltr, 2/26/46.

857 "I have been reading the": Ltr, Davis to JT, 8/19/45.

857 "one of the finest writers": Ltr, 6/23/45.

857 "I always reply promptly to girls": Ltr, United Press, 3/21/45.

857 My first child, James Thurber: Ltr, 7/6/45.

59. THAT WHITE DEER

859 "I had waited a year after hearing": Ltr, 12/9/44.

859 As bad luck would have it: Ltr, 9/26/44.

859 "I was born a Republican": Ltr, 11/7/44.

859 "I was very upset": LBI, 6/25/73.

860 Because of my difficulty: Ltr, 1/9/46.

861 I dislike hospitals so much: Ltr, JT to MF, 2/17/47.

861 I took [Minnette] in to see Andy: Ltr, 4/24/48.

862 "The last such lock I got": Ltr, JT to MF, 10/2/51.

862 *New York Times*: "Robert Benchley: In Memoriam," reprinted in *More in Sorrow*, Henry Holt & Co., 1958.

862 "It occurred to him that": Nathaniel Benchley, *Robert Benchley*, McGraw-Hill, 1955.

863 "There are millions to be made": Dorothy Herrmann, *S.J. Perelman*, G. P. Putnam's Sons, 1986.

863 "The night Ade's death": *Robert Benchley*, op. cit.

863 "Who will listen to": Frank Sullivan to HK, 1962.

863 "was very ordinary": Memo, HT to BB, op. cit.

863 "So I called Hat [one] morning": Ibid.

864 "Helen said our best alibi": JT to EBW and HK, 1949.

864 *This Petty Pace*: Alfred A. Knopf, 1945.

865   *Persian Gulf Command*: Random House, 1945.

865   "We have up the Christmas list": Ltr, 11/19/45.

865   . . . I'm sorry that that drawing: Ltr, 7/6/45.

866   Dear Richard: Ltr, HWR to Richard Rodgers, 1/29/45.

867   "He began seeing that they were done right by": TYWR.

867   "mollifying" a disturbed: KSW, TYWR annotations.

867   a five-part Profile: "The Little Magazine," NYer, 11/7 to 12/15/45.

868   "just because he struck me": Ltr, WG to JT, undated, probably August 1957.

868   "I'd have paid the *New Yorker* more": Ltr, Ik Shuman to JT, 9/undated/57.

868   "The *Digest* pays me five times more": TYWR.

868   "had made a hard rule": Ltr, Liebling to HK, 8/30/62.

869   "It was a big corporation": KSW, TYWR annotations.

869   . . . I am now completely bewildered: Ltr, HWR to JT, 3/14/45.

869   "I'm a son of a bitch": Ltr, JT to Aswell, 3/16/45.

869   I am a little terrified: Ltr, 3/19/45.

870   My new fantasy: Ltr, 12/9/44.

871   . . . It is not only a wonderful: Ltr, undated, probably 10/45.

871   "The Princess and the Tin Box": NYer, 9/29/45.

872   "at the suggestion of the publishers": Ltr, JT to Zeamer, 1/5/46.

872   ("There will be more fun"): Ltr, 11/19/43.

872   "a phase in [Thurber's]": Wilson review, NYer, 10/45.

873   "Among these younger children": Ltr, JT to Hamilton, 3/15/56.

873   "I had never before driven a blind man": JS to HK.

873   "Mame was equal to the hundred and fifty": CD, 1/14/46.

60. THAT CALL ON MRS. FORRESTER

875   . . . I never have counted on: Ltr, 1/9/46.

875   "there are far too many poetic": Ltr, 1/22/46.

876   . . . It must have been about twenty: Ltr, 1/23/46.

876   ("I may be working on it when I die"): Ltr, 3/7/46.

876   "A Call on Mrs. Forrester": NYer, 6/19/48.

876   "What the Animals Were Up To": *Life*, 1/21/46.

877   "just liked a few little": Ltr, HT to BB, op. cit.

877   I am fit again, and getting fat: Ltr, 3/7/46.

877   "At the moment the journalistic end": Ltr, 1/10/46.

878   "as an alumnus worthy of": Ltr, Fullen to JT, 1/31/46.

878   "gang of unhealthy Jews": Ibid.

878   the title itself was not: Ltr, 4/24/46.

879   "Thurber made a mountain out of": Pollard to HK, 1962.

879   "the terrible case of 'Scarlet' ": Ltr, fall 1951.

880   *My Country-in-Law*: Houghton Mifflin, 1946.

880   He was sending to Ross Talk ideas: Ltrs, 1/24 and 1/29/46.

880   "That anecdote about the boy": Ltr, 11/15/46.

880   questions for Robert: Ltrs, HWR to JT, 12/2 and 12/17/46.

881   it would be a profitable idea: Ltr, 1/29/46.

881   The fault with Talk: Ltr, HWR to JT, 11/12/46.

882   What has happened to Talk.: Ltr, JT to HWR, 11/19/46.

883   "We have been swamped": Ltr, 5/20/47.

883   "Everything you told me": Ibid.

883   . . . It is only fair to state: Ltrs, JT to Canby, 12/26 and 12/31/45.

884   "I put up E. B. White, with as great": Ltr, 1/7/46.

884   "Thurber was there working": C. Cooke to HK, 1962.

884   "This turned out to be a bad summer": Ltr, 10/21/46.

884   I feel like one of those charred carbon: Ltr, 12/4/46.

885   "When we were about to leave": Dudley Fisher to Richard Oulahan, 1950.

885   ("The Legendary Mr. Thurber"): C. Lester Walker, 7/46.

885   (*I Wish I'd Written That*): McGraw-Hill, 1946.

886   "the best juvenile book": CD, 10/11/46.

886   "We meet far too seldom": Ltr, 11/29/47.

886   "It is long since that dandy all-night": Ltr, 5/14/47.

886   I was particularly heartened: Ltr, Perelman to JT, 3/5/46.

886   I don't think you need to worry: Ltr, 5/13/47.

887   Mame "lives now in a state of": Ltr, JT to Smallsreed, 9/25/47.

887   Fitzgerald had persuaded: Undated item from *Variety*, HK files.

887   "I gather that you're an admirer": Ltr, Hersey to JT, 12/6/46.

887   made him promise to send: Ltr, Connolly to JT, 3/7/47.

887   "Bermuda, like the French Riviera": Ltr, 2/16/47.

887   "Uncle Jim brought Mother a bouquet": Dinah Jane Williams (Darby) to HK, 1974.

888   "The Waters of the Moon," NYer, 3/1/47.

888   "for sheer wizardry": Ltr, Anderson to KSW, 3/7/47.

888   "Am Not I Your Rosalind?" NYer, 11/8/47.

889   "A Call on Mrs. Forrester": NYer, 6/19/48.

890   *Vintage Thurber*: Hamish Hamilton, 1963.

890   It is we, the editorial department: TYWR.

890   "Thix": NYer, 4/26/47.

890   "Soapland": *The Beast in Me and Other Animals*, Harcourt Brace, 1948.

890   My pieces on soap opera are progressing: Ltr, 8/15/47.

891   "Well, what's the matter": Ltr, JT to the HMS, 2/25/48.

891   "I think it is astonishing" Ltr, HWR to JT, 9/8/47.

891   "If you could see": TYWR.

891   "I have heard great acclaim": Ltr, HWR to JT, 11/28/47.

891   I got a great deal of satisfaction: Ltr, 9/8/47.

892   I got that letter you sent: Ltr, undated, circa 9/47.

61. THAT BEAST IN ME

893   *The Beast in Me and Other Animals*: Harcourt Brace, 1948.

894   "as a craftsman very much": Henry Brandon, "Everybody Is Getting Serious"; *New Republic*, 5/26/58.

894   I gathered that [Roger Angell]: Ltr, 3/20/59.

895   "Shawn did the editing on this: Ltr, 10/26/59.

895   . . . We are trying to get: Ltr, 4/24/48.

896   *Times Book Review*: "Queeches, Wahwahs, Woans," 10/3/48.

896   "is such a hodge podge that practically no two reviews were": Ltr, 11/8/48.

896   "My hours were from two-thirty": Patricia Stone to HK, 1964.

898   "the analogy between dreams and wit rests on": Stone MA thesis, op. cit.

898   "Take, dears, my little sheaf": Ltr, spring 1948.

898   "He'd memorized the number of hotel steps": D. Miller to HK.

899   . . . Through the instrumentality: Ltr, HWR to JT, 8/26/48; second ltr, 8/26/48.

899   We're doubtful about the drawing: Ltr, 9/2/48.

900   I have got about seven more: JT to HWR, 10/28/48.

900   Several persons have suggested: Ibid.

900   . . . The man . . . is sitting: HWR to JT, 11/29/48.

901   The . . . revelation . . . : Ltr, JT to HWR, 11/29/48.

901   I am keeping an open mind: Ltr, JT to HWR, 12/2/48.

901   I don't know now how we: Ltr, HWR to JT, 12/7/48.

901   I keep taking a dimmer view: Ltr, JT to HWR, 12/27/48.

902   "I have just read in proof": Ltr, HWR to JT, 11/24/48.

902   "A Couple of Snapshots": NYer, 12/9/50.

902   "I am advised that *jada jada*": HWR to JT, 11/19/48.

903   "Nobody at all has got this": HWR to JT, 12/21/48.

903   "As to that phrase *Java Java*": HWR to JT, 11/29/48.

903   "seriously neurotic": ELUTTC.

903   "Nugent came to visit us": RM to HK.

903   I had dinner [at "21"]: 9/10/47.

904   "terribly drunk": Ltr, West to HK, 7/16/71.

904   "sprawled across my lap": Ltr, HT to BB, op. cit.

904   leading Ross to inform Thurber: undated, probably late December 1947.

904   I can't remember when any: Ltr, JT to HWR, 12/18/47.

904   "at last got well under way": Ltr, JT to Nugent, 7/27/48.

905   "There is a character named": Ltr, JT to HWR, 8/20/48.

905   "I haven't got time": Ltr, HWR to JT, 8/25/48.

905   "the kids put on the best": Ltr, JT to EN, 9/13/48.

905   "a constant source of": Ltr, JT to Blair, 3/23/44.

905   "Rosemary and I are both all right": JT to MT, 3/24/48.

905   "If I butchered your": Ltr, 1/8/48.

906   He lived in [an interior]": BBC's "The Private Life of James Thurber," broadcast 12/2/61.

906   . . . The husband says: "You": Henry Brandon, *As We Are*, Doubleday, 1961.

906   "Un-Americanism": Memoirs of Clark Clifford, NYer, 4/1/91; Garry Wills, "Introduction," *Scoundrel Time*, by Lillian Hellman; Little, Brown & Co., 1976.

908   "Helen read me your letter": Ltr, 12/3/47.
       "could be used as a preface": Ltr, 12/3/47.

909   I am anticipating the gruelling: Ltr, 11/24/47.

909   "I hope you escape the noose": Ltr, 11/29/47.

909   "Exhibit X": NYer, 3/6/48.

910   "as would be case if the": Ltr, 3/24/48.

910   "George Lincoln Chadwick": Ltr, 7/27/48.

910   I realize that the play: Ltr, 9/13/48.

911   "I see that I have not explained": Ltr, 10/6/48.

911   Q: How did you become: *Time*, 9/9/46.

912   "Mr Thurber stuck his head": Terry to HK.

62. THAT LETTER FROM THE STATES

913   "A Final Note on Chanda Bell": NYer, 10/15/49.

913   Wolcott Gibbs: Ltr to JT, probably fall 1949.

913   "man reaches his peak": Ltr, HWR to Sherwood, 1/18/49.

914   "The Notebooks of James Thurber": NYer, 2/5/49 ("The Case Book of James Thurber" in *Thurber Country*).

914   "I go on record": Ltr, 1/10/49.

915   "which isn't bad for us": Ltr, 1/12/49.

915   "What a Lovely Generalization!": NYer, 3/26/49.

915   A magazine that has bought: Ltr, JT to HWR, 1/17/49.

916   . . . I will say that I recognize: Ltr, 1/19/49.

916   "It was a bit awkward": Sara Dashiell to HK, 1962.

917   I was going to write Fred Allen: Ltr, JT to HWR, 3/25/49.

918   "Too long, Ross": Sullivan to HK, 1962.

918   "Letting Miss Honeycutt": Ltr, 4/5/49.

918   "At the Marquands": Ltr, 3/24/49.

918   "When I guided him": Emil to HK.

918   "Jack told me": Levy to HK.

919   "There was always some": Schwed to HK.

919   She gave up writing: Ltr, 2/25/48.

919   Do keep well: Card, HT to Thurber family, undated, probably spring 1949.

919   . . . Jamie is eating fiercely: Ltr, 4/30/49.

920   "we all have bruises": Ltr, 7/14/48.

920   It is hard to write: Ltr, 4/21/49.

920   Rosie had to crawl out: Ltr, JT to Thurbers, 8/23/49.

920   "The American Literary Scene": NYer, 7/30/49.

920   "Joyeux Noel, Mr. Durning": NYer, 7/2/49.

921   "a couple of parts of it": Ltr, 5/12/49.

921   "it might be too much": Ltr, 5/1/49.

922   ("If that book had had"): LL to HK.

922   When Thurber wrote Lobrano: 7/8/49.

922   I can understand an author's: Ltr, 7/18/49.

923   . . . I wanted to tell you: Ltr, 10/7/49.

923   "You understand as wrong": Ltr, 10/12/49.

923   He could, he claimed, remember the birthday: JT to Ed Graham, MA thesis, Dartmouth, May 1949.

924   ("I didn't charge him"): Smallsreed to HK.

924   simply wished Walden luck: Bert McCord, *Herald Tribune*, 8/26/49.
924   ("They couldn't find a thing"): Ltr, 11/29/49.
924   "I was informed that Thurber": BG to HK.
925   . . . Several persons told O'Hara": Ltr, 11/29/49.
926   As to Gill saying: Ltr, HWR to JT, 12/6/49.
926   "it was ironically": Ltr, O'Hara to JT, 3/27/58.
926   "I'm sorry you let that": Ltr, JT to O'Hara, 5/20/58.
926   "I have absolved Gibbs": Ltr, O'Hara to JT, 5/22/58.
926   "You have convinced me": Ltr, BG to HK, 7/10/91.
926   Gibbs did his best: Frank MacShane, *The Life of John O'Hara*, Dutton, 1980.
926   "but at commencement": O'Hara column, *Trenton Times-Advertiser*.
927   In his last years: Ltr, O'Hara to HK, 10/6/62.
927   You can say I said: Ltr, JT to Beverly Gary, 3/25/59.
928   It was a loving testimony: "The Incomparable Mr. Benchley," NY *Times Book Review*, 9/18/49.
929   ("His finicky concern"): Alistair Cooke to HK.
929   "Man will not get": Breit, NY *Times Magazine*, 12/4/49.

63. THAT TIME FOR FLAGS

930   "My kids and I found it": Ltr, RM to HK, 10/12/90.
931   "I was pretty shattered": Ltr, HT to Thurbers, undated, 1950.
932   "This high manic state": Ltr, HT to Thurber, op. cit.
932   "since we are all getting": Ltr, JT to RT, 11/18/50.
932   *The 13 Clocks*: Simon & Schuster, 1950.
932   "looking glass limericks": TG to HK.
934   "the simple fluency": Ltr, EBW to JT, 6/6/50.
935   Well, it was worse than I thought: Ltr, 6/12/50.
936   "It is not easy to get": Ltr, JT to RT, 12/22/50.
936   sent a comic letter of advice: *Herald Tribune*, 8/24/50.
936   he told a visitor: HK, 12/50, Thurber home, Cornwall.
937   "*What* Cocktail Party?": NYer, 4/1/50.
937   "This struck me at": Ltr, Eliot to JT, undated, 1950.
937   "and if you by any": Ltr, Eliot to JT, 11/1/50.
937   "Where's the uranium?": Ltr, JT to RWs 8/9/50.
937   . . . You will remember the awful: Ltr, JT to JW, 10/5/50.
938   "Communists were infiltrating": RT to HK.
939   "He had a front record": Murray Kempton, NY *Post*, 1950 (date unavailable).

939   under FBI surveillance: Neil Grauer, *Washington Post*, 11/6/94.

940   "Look Out for the Thing": *Bermudian*, 10/50.

941   "He hadn't changed, but": Cowley, LBI, 3/27/75.

941   "Thurber was a hell of a man": Boyer to HK, Croton-on-Hudson, NY, 1962.

941   "pursuant to the recommendation": Ltr, 11/28/51.

942   "He was cultivated": Ltr, Joseph Deitch to HK, 1963.

942   "non-violent, social-democratic": Ltr, Lawrence Cremin to HK, 1/30/63.

942   . . . It is with extreme regret: Ltr, 12/6/51.

943   "who shall have final authority": *OSU Monthly*, 6/62.

943   "Lengths and Shadows": NYer, 12/1/51.

943   He was as absent-minded as anyone: Ralph McCombs to HK.

943   "aggressively patriotic gentlemen": "Lengths and Shadows," TTA.

943   "Out of the situation": Ltr, 11/23/51.

943   "old boy, old boy": Ltr, shown HK in 1962 but missing from Smalls-reed letters donated to Thurber Collection.

944   "It is . . . appropriate": Ltr, 8/11/59.

944   I am now a friend: Ltr, 4/13/61.

945   "We cannot understand": *OSU Monthly*, 6/62.

64. THAT COUNTRY BUMPKIN

946   "major trends and personalities": Ltr, DK to HK, undated, 1949.

947   "The outlook is bad": Ltr, 10/6/50.

947   "Thurber blabs everything": TYWR.

947   "How do you stand?": Memo, 8/11/47.

947   I'm inclined to sympathize: Ltr, 8/15/47.

948   sent him a four-page letter: 9/6/47.

948   "I don't know anything": Ltr, 2/8/51.

948   Thurber passed Kramer's alarms on: Ltr, 5/15/51.

948   "merely protesting certain things": Ltr, 6/15/51.

948   "Thurber is your best source": Ltr, 11/27/50.

948   "about Thurber as a source": Ltr, DK to HK, undated, 1962.

949   "couldn't be found": DK to HK, 1962.

949   "our strong feelings" : Ltr, 6/12/51.

950   Frank Sullivan and Thurber: Ltr, DK to HK, 11/30/62.

950   "a hell of a good book": Ltr, 4/12/51.

950   "There is a lot about Ross": Ltr, 4/23/51.

950   "It makes most of the editors": DK, *The Guild Reporter*, 11/23/51.

950   "administrators, not innovators": Ltr, DK to JT, 10/27/62.

950   Shawn was doing two men's work: Ltr, 10/16/51.

950   "We are having dinner": Ltr, 10/11/51.

951   "Andy! Andy!": Mary D. Kierstead to HK.

951   disparaged White's . . . words: BG to HK.

952   "White wanted to use [the drawing]": Ltr, 12/15/51.

952   "It was scary enough": Richard Wight to HK.

953   I'm going to do a piece about Ross: Ltr, 12/15/51.

953   "I haven't been able": Ltr, 12/15/51.

953   "the first time I met": Ltr, Stafford to HK, 3/24/72.

954   "I do not believe that Fitzgerald": Ltr, 2/3/51.

954   "I have had that condition": Ltr, 5/14/51.

954   "a tremendous spectrum of": Dr. Andre Van Herle, quoted by Lawrence R. Altman, M.D., NY *Times*, 5/21/91.

954   "sightseers and autograph": Ltr to Thurbers, 8/1/51.

954   "I've had a neuritis headache": Ltr, 5/undated/52.

955   "a blathermouth": RW to HK.

955   "a lot of damned nonsense": Ltr to Charles Grant, 5/30/52.

955   "tampering with my books": Ltr to Hamilton, 4/7/52.

955   "She never let Thurber's moods": RW to HK, 1973.

955   "What arguments!": Sara Linda Williams to HK.

955   "Ordinarily, Ronnie and Jim": JW to HK.

956   . . . I am going to see a thyroid man: Ltr, 10/15/52.

956   You must dismiss from your mind: Ltr, 7/23/52.

957   "My thyroid rate is slowly": Ltr, 8/8/52.

957   "It starts out fine": Ltr, 1952.

957   "The Case of Dimity Ann": NYer, 6/7/52.

957   "I wish I could promise": Ltr, 10/15/52.

957   "Two years ago he told me": Ltr, 7/11/52.

958   "I've seen Jamie block": Ltr, undated, 1952.

958   Rosie [attended] a performance: Ltr, 7/21/52.

958   "is a nation living in": "Talk with James Thurber"; NY *Times Book Review*, 6/29/52.

959   "Blatherskites!" *Time*, 6/30/52.

959   The plan to undermine: *Herald Tribune*, 7/18/54.

959   "the strangling of humor": Ltr, 7/31/52.

960   ("an amazing blend"): Ltr, 7/13/52.

961   "The glass I threw": Ltr, 8/25/52.

961   "who is hot and who performs": Ltr, 4/6/52.

961   "Ross's appreciation of my writing": Ltr, 8/25/52.

962   "He had a fifth of his life": "Talk with James Thurber," op. cit.

65. THAT MASTER OF ALL THE ARTS OF COMEDY

963   "By the time you get this": Ltr, 6/4/53.

963   "I could have made it": Ltr, 6/11/53.

963   was proud to meet: Ltr, JT to Thurbers, 6/24/53.

963   "Andy White was hooded": Ltr, 5/21/53.

964   "The first thing I saw": Quist to *Time* reporter, Time, Inc., library.

964   "The first operation": Ltr, HT to BB, op. cit.

964   "I can get around this room": Jess Stearn, NY *Sunday News*, 8/30/53.

965   "If a bomb ever hits": *World-Telegram & Sun*, 10/31/53.

965   "Nearly a dozen men": Ltr, 9/23/53.

965   became a clearinghouse: John Ferris, NY *World-Telegram & Sun*, 9/19/54

965   "I have to deal with a great many": Ltr, 12/10/53.

965   His own vision: Ltr to Smallsreed, 9/23/53.

966   "a kind of satire on": Ltr, 9/23/53.

966   "I never read": Ltr, JT to E. Louise Mally, 1/7/54.

966   "She didn't get far": NY *World-Telegram & Sun*, 9/19/54.

966   I have spent a thousand hours: Ltr, 3/11/54.

967   "Shake Hands with Birdey Doggett": NYer, 5/9/53.

967   "It could have had a long": Ltr, HT to RT, undated, early 1954.

967   . . . I believe that the: Ltr, JT to Swing, 11/4/53.

968   "You're wrong about my 'facile' ": Ltr, JT to Albert Hermann, 6/1/53.

968   "These mistakes would not have": Ltr, JT to Harold Frasier, 12/18/52.

968   Only one other person: Ltr to Mally, op. cit.

968   "I know how to spell Myers": Ltr, 1/26/52.

969   "definite carelessness at the New": Ltr, 10/16/52.

969   "that he would never sell": Ltr, Dorothy Irvin to HK, 8/8/72.

969   I never really "stopped" writing: Ltr, Harriman to HK, 10/26/62.

969   You are the first people to call: Ltr, 10/6/53.

970   "seems flat, uninviting": Ltr to Canfield, 5/28/53.

970   No two are exactly alike": Ltr, 12/29/52.

970   "Publishers never get anything": Ltr to Mally, op. cit.

970	"It was a disaster": Connell to HK, 1962.
971	. . . at a publication day: Ltr, Stafford to HK, 3/24/72.
971	"I don't trust publishers": Ltr, 4/19/53.
971	"Helen says Honey's face": Ltr, 8/1/52.
972	"an ordeal we have to go through": Ltr, 12/16/53.
972	"As you know, Helen's eye still": Ltr, 12/10/53.
972	inevitable press interview: Norman Dohn, CD, 12/24/53; "Thurber Has His Own Brand of Humor," *Columbus Citizen*, 11/8/53.
972	We got on the train all right: Ltr, 1/5/54.
972	"With 60 staring me": "Old Newspaperman Recalls Some Troubles He's Seen," *Fire Islander*, 6/18/54.
972	"has been off his rocker": Ltr to Thurbers, 2/1/54.
973	I won't actually be sixty: *Bermudian*, 6/54.
974	"Have you spent any time": Ltr, 5/20/54.
974	"Get *Thee* to a Monastery": NYer, 8/21/54.
974	"All our thanks": Ltr, undated, probably early 1954.
974	*Three by Thurber*: "In a Glass Darkly," NYer, 3/19/55.
975	We were having breakfast: Ltr, 10/4/54.
975	"Thurber had always resented": BG to HK, 1988.
976	"My sincere love to you and Maeve": Ltr, 3/24/58.
976	"Maeve says you never hit her": Ltr, 4/2/58.
976	"One was wrong to take": McK to HK, 1962.

66. THOSE FURTHER FABLES

978	"Thurber had a finicky concern": Cooke to HK.
978	("I keep writing new acts"): JT to HK, 12/50.
979	We are planning to spend the summer: Ltr, 4/11/55.
979	"Thurber is so immensely wise": William Hickey, *London Daily Mail*, 6/19/55.
979	"would come to us two or three": Miller, LBI, 10/28/74, Thurber Collection.
979	("We didn't get drunk"): Ltr, Buchwald to HK, 12/11/91.
980	"He was very protective of me": NS to HK, 8/14/62.
980	"The Other Room": *Harper's*, 7/62.
980	"The newspapers descended": Ltr, 6/14/55.
980	"I'd see all these Englishmen": Liebling to HK, 1962.
981	"This is true . . . gnip, gnop": "James Thurber," in British *People*, 1955, by Wilfred Taylor.
981	"the centre of a circle": Ibid.

981   "They all think he's Jesus": AH to HK.

981   . . . We had a marvelous evening: Mackenzie, "The Private Life of James Thurber," BBC broadcast, 12/2/61.

981   ("They'll just take turns"): Liebling to HK.

982   "The Whites couldn't take it": Ltr, HT to Thurbers, 6/14/55.

982   "Every time Joe started": Ltr, Stafford to HK, 3/24/72.

982   "Actually, Joe tried to bring": NS to HK.

982   have had quite a few dinner parties: Ltr, 6/20/55.

983   "The Moribundant Life": NYer, 10/1/55.

983   Last year 20,000 persons were killed: Ltr, 1/7/54.

984   "Certainly the death cannot be any": Ltr, 12/20/55.

985   "When he heard of Gus's death": Lobrano to HK, 1974.

985   Everybody is afraid except: Ltr, 1956.

986   I have sharpened The Sleepless: Ltr, 3/30/56.

986   . . . These two were rejected: Ltr, 4/2/56.

986   "I was trying to make": Ltr, 4/16/56.

987   "There are certain things": Ibid.

987   "the finest writing": Ltr, Perelman to JT, 1956.

987   "the tired writing": Ltr, JT to Cowley, 1/18/57.

987   My own case is not anywhere: Ltr, 5/18/56.

988   "Ross had a distinctive touch": Newsweek, 2/21/55.

989   ("The New Yorker is as prosperous"): Ltr, 1/4/56.

989   After a couple of reunion dinners: Faith McNulty to HK.

989   McNulty epitaph: NYer, 8/4/56.

989   "It was one of the wonderful": Ltr, 6/13/56.

989   "The show moved Thurber": Maney to HK, 1962.

990   "I can still be heard": NY Times, 8/12/56.

990   full page advertisement in the Times: 3/27/60.

990   ("Thurber was always a sacred"): Lobrano to HK.

990   "Thurber and I had had a cordial": Maxwell to HK.

991   After I finished being Thurber's editor: Note, 4/8/74, Bryn Mawr Library Rare Books & Mss, KSW file.

991   A short, elegant, often extremely funny: HATNY.

993   "an impassioned and detailed": Ltr, 5/13/57.

994   "should be key letters": Note-to-file, KSW to James Tannis, director of libraries, Bryn Mawr, 4/8/74.

994   "The sad truth is that James": Ibid.

995   "I'm glad I'm not mixed up in": Ltr, JT to KSW, 5/3/57.

67. THAT RESTLESS FORCE

995 "Gibbs would be the last person": Ltr, 6/18/51.

996 "None of us is going to write": Ltr, 6/14/51.

997 "I thought Jim got Ross down": Sullivan to HK, 1962.

997 "Ross was ringmaster": Liebling to HK, 1962.

997 "Ross was always very protective": Shawn to HK, 1962.

998 started something that looks": Ltr, 6/30/54.

998 "I suppose that the book will go to S & S": Ltr, 7/11/55.

998 "mentioned my future book": Ltr, 7/21/55.

998 "the man of action [Ross]": Ltr, 7/2/56.

999 "in the manner of the 1920s": Ltr, JT to John Duncan Miller, 5/25/57.

999 "It is a collection of pieces and drawings": Ibid.

999 Sorry for the extra: Ltr, JT to Beulah Hagen, 4/20/57.

999 "many, many corrections": Ltr, HT to Hagen, 5/21/57.

999 "that there were an appalling": Ltr, 5/29/57.

999 [Goodman]was our main reason: Ltr, Machell to Canfield, 8/2/57.

999 "Acting on your tip, I have": Ltr, 8/15/57.

1000 I'm writing several pieces: Ltr, 7/26/57.

1000 Thanks for the kind letter: Ltr, 8/2/57.

1001 "Both of these pieces moved me": Ltr, undated, 1957.

1002 I did show [your work]: Ltr to Bill Arter, 11/11/57.

1002 "My God! They've put me on": Liebling to HK, 1962.

1003 ("Ross was always showing casuals"): Maxwell to HK.

1003 "The title came to me last night": Ltr, 8/6/57.

1003 Darn near a year and half: Ltr, 5/14/58.

1004 "Gibbs had wanted to write": Elinor Gibbs to HK, 1962.

1004 "is deteriorating at": Ltr to JT, undated, circa 1957.

1004 "Voyage to Puerilla": Ltr, 8/2/undated, probably 1957.

1004 "treat me like a burglar": Ibid.

1005 *More in Sorrow*: Henry Holt & Co., 1958.

1005 "We still have the book": Ltr, 5/31/58.

   "Nobody knows the trouble": *Newsweek*, 6/16/58.

1006 "We have stood up under sixty": Ltr, summer 1958.

1006 "called to the table": *Time*, 7/7/58.

1006 ("I warned John"): AH to HK.

1006 I have asked John Lardner: Ltr, 7/28/58.

1007 "The Thurbers had been in": Miller, LBI, 10/28/74.

1007 ("We keep meeting Americans"): Ltr, 10/10/58.

1007 "Thurber was a dependable Stevenson Democrat": Cooke to HK.

1007 "Katharine says you are all wet": Ltr, 5/31/58.

1007 ("We heard not only that Thurber"): Hahn to HK.

1009 worked with Ross "innumerable hours": Ltr, Truax to JT, 5/15/58.

1009 "no easy line to follow about that": Ltr, 6/24/58.

1009 "would sneak a toaster and grill": Ltr, Crouse to JT, 9/4/57.

1009 At least two good psychiatrists: Ltr to Truax, 7/2/58.

1010 "I find it comical that": KSW, note-to-file, 4/8/70, Bryn Mawr College.

1010 "because of the low rates": Undated, circa 1958.

1011 "The Thurbers lived expensively": Gannett to HK, 1962,

1012 "Price!" she exclaimed: Constance Smith to HK, 1963.

1013 "You say: 'Ross had Andy White write' ": Ltr, 4/29/58.

1013 But Thurber's facts, given: Ltr, Truax to JT, 6/15/58.

1014 it was one of his regular jokes: KSW, TYWR annotations.

1014 "as cheaply as possible": Liebling, "Harold Ross—The Impresario," op. cit.

1014 Brendan Gill remembers bitterly: BG to HK.

1014 "Gill and I threatened": Brooks to HK, 1977.

1014 rejected a standard, corporate: Gigi Mahon, *The Last Days of The New Yorker*, McGraw-Hill, 1988.

68. THAT BIOGRAPHER AND HISTORIAN

1015 "As the devil is afraid of music": Ltr, 8/25/58.

1015 "My job was to help get": Ewald to HK, 1992.

1016 "What do you know about that!": Anonymous brief to the editor, *Newsweek* library.

1016 Sayre calls "a valentine": Ltr, JT to Truax, 7/2/58.

1016 Shawn, says Gill, remained as tight-fisted: HATNY.

1017 Cooperation with Allen Churchill: "Ross of the New Yorker," *The American Mercury*, 8/48.

1017 "Thurber and I were never close": Shawn to HK.

1018 "There are no humorists": Parker, *S. J. Perelman*, Dorothy Hermann, G P. Putnam's Sons, 1986.

1018 "The Manic in the Moon": NYer, 8/19/61.

1018 "I admired him, in his blindness": Angell to HK, 1992.

1018 "Gus always had a difficult time": Jean Lobrano to HK.

1019	"tiny giants": Wolfe, "Ruler of the Walking Dead," *Herald Tribune*, 4/11–4/18/65.
1020	. . . THE NEW YORKER had recently: Ltr to HK, 6/20/91.
1021	"It's something you thought could never": Gaddis to HK.
1021	"Shawn was frantic": Brooks to HK, 1969.
1021	"They walked me to the elevator,": Research provided *Newsweek* editor, *Newsweek* library.
1021	Having a child at 43 is considered: Ltr, 12/6/54.
1022	Rose Algrant who gets through: Ltr, 3/8/57.
1022	"We got a bit fed with Bermuda this": Ltr, 8/29/57.
1023	When an old girl of mine named Ann: Ltr, 1/24/58.
1023	All this is known to psychologists: Ltr, 12/19/58.
1024	a "Letter from Lapland": Ltr, JT to O'Hara, 3/19/58.
1025	"I am . . . a little depressed": Ltr, 8/7/58.
1025	"If he'd kept it to his own experiences": Terry to HK.
1025	The Atlantic Press–Little, Brown: Ltr, 12/3/58.
1025	"He blamed the publisher": Liebling to HK.
1025	"hardest of all to do was to take out": Ltr, 10/22/58.
1026	"It would imply that the book had my": Ltr, 11/28/58.
1026	"On a short casual of mine": TYWR.
1026	Gill . . . agrees with Thurber: BG to HK.
1027	"If I were you, I wouldn't": Ltr, EBW to JT, 10/20/58.
1027	It was White's letter, five weeks later: 11/28/58.
1027	"He says he 'faded from' ": Ltr, JT to Gannett, 12/3/58.
1027	Some of your letter is you: Ltr, 12/8/58.
1028	("We outrage easily over here"): Hahn to HK.
1028	"As the *Atlantic* articles began": JS to HK.
1029	"Whoever puts pen to paper": Ltr, JT to RA, 7/2/59.
1030	"With Ross, his love is the magazine": Ltr, 11/5/50.
1030	"Jim did give a notable picture": Ltr to HK, 3/23/73.
1030	"He heightens everything": Ibid.
1030	"The book didn't tell": LL to HK.
1031	("Ross was a firm believer"): "The Magnificent Fussbudget," *Harper's*; reprinted in *Arrivals and Departures*, Macmillan, 1976.
1031	("I don't think I'm mixed up"): Hamburger to HK.
1031	I did not really care much: Ltr, 3/22/58.
1031	"If Liebling, or any other New Yorker": Maxwell to HK.
1031	"You are in the position": Ltr, 4/21/51.
1031	Though Thurber buttered up Shawn: Ltr, JT to WS, 7/28/58.
1032	"Shawn didn't kick over": Maxwell to HK.

1032   "He was a great man": Geraghty to HK.

1032   "I think the greatest distortion": Ibid.

1033   "We all thought the chapter": Ibid.

1033   she was willing to sleep with: Ltr, JT to RA, 1/20/58.

1033   "They ought to have covers": Ltr, McK to JT, 4/11/58.

1033   "Women like love": Ltr, JT to McK, 4/14/58

1034   "the little old lady": Ltr, Wilson to JT, 3/22/58.

1034   "He would pretend he hadn't": Grant to HK, 1962.

1034   Rosemary Thurber remembers: RM to HK.

1034   "Jim did put in some love": Ltr, KSW to HK, 3/23/73.

1034   "If I knew he was going to die": "Harold Ross—the Impresario," op. cit.

69. THAT THURBER CARNIVAL

1036   "I used to think": LL to HK, 1952.

1036   "In November my thyroid": Ltr, 2/3/59.

1036   "He was worried": Cooke to HK, 1962.

1037   long liquor-free periods: RM to HK.

1038   "After six drinks": Ltr, EBW to HT, 3/11/74.

1039   "Thurber was the dullest": *The Noel Coward Diaries*, edited by Graham Payne and Sheridan Morley.

1039   Thurber accused Shawn: Ltr, 7/28/58.

1039   "Shawn . . . does not answer letters": Ltr, 10/10/58.

1040   *The Tears with Thurber*: Ltr to Shawn, 5/16/59.

1040   "Did you know that Shawn": Ltr, 10/10/58.

1040   ("We haven't been to Columbus"): Ltr, 5/15/57.

1040   Thurber's "warm heart": *As We Are*, Doubleday, 1961.

1040   "It was later diagnosed": Miller, Branscomb interview, London, 10/28/74.

1041   *Lanterns & Lances*: Harper & Brothers, 1961.

1041   "A slut nixes sex": Ltr, 10/2/57.

1041   "What about this Hemingway": Ltr, 1/2/58.

1042   Ross's pledge that it would never: TYWR.

1042   As luck would have it: Ltr, undated, 1957.

1042   "The Child's Life of Bennett": Hal Boyle, Associated Press, NY *World-Telegram & Sun*, 10/23/57.

1042   "Thurber's copy came in": RA to HK.

1043   "When I was new and innocent": Gould to HK, 1993.

1043   "One thing my father never was": RM to HK.

1043   "as for [Thurber's] 'mean-spiritedness' ": Ltr, Keillor to HK, un-
        dated, 1993.

1043   "I always have seven": Dolbier, NY *Herald Tribune*, 5/31/59.

1043   "P": "The most fascinating letter": *Christian Science Monitor*, June
        1959.

1044   Jack Paar TV program: 6/2/59.

1044   Blindness came upon him: BBC broadcast, 12/61, op. cit.

1044   "He was still talking about": Glennon to HK, 1962.

1044   Are you planning to include: Ltr, 3/22/58.

1045   The story of K.S.W. is one: Ltr, 3/21/58.

1045   Thurber had given them a: Alan Williams to HK, 1962.

1045   He said he had had fifty-five: Ltr, JT to RA, 7/2/59.

1046   Tall and lean and gray: Earl Wilson, NY *Post*, 6/3/59.

1046   "A group of us went on to Costello's": Harriman to HK.

1046   "a brilliant book": Ltr, Crouse to Charles Morton, 5/4/59.

1046   "Both as a literary portrait": Ltr, JT to RA, 7/2/59.

1046   "as dull as *The New Yorker*": Ibid.

1046   "Stop by the National Press Club": Cooke to HK.

1046   "That falls in an area": Shawn to HK, 10/11/62.

1047   Shawn provided Thurber: NYer, 11/11/61.

1047   "We have both known Kenneth Tynan": Ltr, 10/10/58.

1047   "critical estimate at its best": Ltr, JT to RA, 7/2/59.

1047   "My love of London": *As We Are*, op. cit.

1047   Rebecca West . . . skewered *The Years with Ross*: London *Times*,
        7/19/59.

1048   We have been chilled: Ltr, JT to Hamilton and Roger Machell,
        7/28/59.

1048   Thurber's "sourness of spirit": Ltr, 8/7/59.

1048   "but exasperating when": Grant to HK, 9/17/62.

1048   "You say that 'Andy was a' ": Ltr, KSW to HK, 3/23/73.

1049   As Gill points out, no writer was ever asked: HATNY.

1049   "He finds [newsbreaks] a": Ltr, KSW to HK, 3/23/73.

1049   "This is, to me, the most outrageous part": Ibid.

1049   "I felt he was jealous": BB, *Thurber*, op. cit.

1050   "It wasn't that Thurber": Geraghty to HK, 10/15/62.

1050   it wasn't Thurber about whom White: Davis to HK.

1050   Gill, who in his memoirs: HATNY.

1050   ("Katharine was about as"): Ltr, EBW to AH, 4/1/84.

1050   "just a very bad drinker": Ltr, 3/11/74.

1050   Jim could be so wonderful: Ltr to HK, 3/23/73.

1051   Headliner Award account: *Columbus Citizen-Journal*, 11/16/59

1051   "Jim felt duped": McGuckin to HK, 1962.

1051   "All this put Smallsreed": Trannette to HK, 1962.

1052   "That meant as much to him": HT to HK, 1962.

1052   "I'd loved Thurber's work": Stoddard to HK, 1993.

70. THAT ULTIMATE CONCERN

1053   "Thurber seems blinder than ever": Wilson, *The Fifties*, Farrar, Straus & Giroux, 1986.

1054   "straight at the person I'm talking to": Eddy Gilmore, Associated Press, London, 1958.

1054   "He had no intention": Lobrano to HK.

1054   "I'd been reading Thurber": Stoddard to HK.

1055   "Thurber had been falling": JG to HK, 1962.

1055   the *Theatre* magazine: 2/60.

1056   "Ask him for a new line": NY *Post*, 2/22/60.

1056   "a distinguished native son": *Newsweek*, 1/13/60.

1056   ("Blind Author Regains Sight"): *Pittsburgh Sun-Telegraph*, 2/16/60.

1056   "I felt the week should": *Newsweek*, 2/1/60.

1056   "There's too much Thurber adulation": Stoddard to HK.

1057   "Author! Author!": Leonard Lyons, NY *Post*, 3/11/60.

1057   "You are aware, of course": SB, *OSU Monthly*, 12/61.

1057   . . . We are going back to New York: Ltr, 4/5/60.

1058   grossing only $26,100: *Variety*, 6/25/60.

1058   "He was convinced that": Stoddard to HK.

1058   "We convened at Bonfils's apartment": Reid to HK, 1962.

1058   I agree with E. B. White: Ltr to G. Robert Holsinger, 3/8/60.

1059   A speech to ANTA: NY *Times*, 2/21/60.

1059   "I'm supposed to be bald": "Thurber—An Old Hand at Humor with Two Hits on Hand," *Life*, 3/14/60.

1059   "He went along with Fredericks": Engel to HK, 1962.

1059   . . . Life is now three times: Ltr, 4/29/60.

1060   "Moral: It is better": Ltr, 7/2/56.

1060   "I cannot believe that": Ltr to Charles E. Bedwell, 8/25/60.

1061   "Here's another one of those foreign": Ltr, 2/8/60.

1061   "I agree with you that one publisher": Ltr, 5/2/60.

1061   "He liked V-O whiskey": Stahl to HK, 1962.

1061   "They were both powerful magnets": Sayre to HK, 1962.

1062   "My family's house was always": NY daily newspaper accounts, 5/30/60; *Newsweek*, 6/13/60; Ltr, Eileen Lange to HK, 5/9/73.

1062   "He had no first-reading": Shawn to HK, 10/11/62.

1062   " 'You'd better get out here' ": Stoddard to HK.

1063   "Memorized!": Audiotape produced by JG, "James Thurber: A Profile in Sound."

1063   "Typical impertinence": Connelly to HK.

1063   "These publishers have me so mixed up": NY *Times*, 9/22/60.

1063   "The Thurbers were wonderful": Terry to HK.

1063   "Jim wanted me to handle": Maney to HK.

1063   "That S.O.B. has been trying": *Time*, 9/20/60.

1064   . . . We want . . . a letter: Ltr, undated, fall 1960.

1064   "We spent five wonderful days": JW to HK.

1064   "Everything bothered Jim": Stoddard to HK.

1064   "It was the last time Jim": TG to HK.

1064   "real angst": Ltr, 1/3/61.

1065   "I will have to rewrite": Ltr, 1/19/61.

1065   . . . I shall probably be severe: Ltr, 1/19/61.

1065   "No one seems to die": London dispatch, *Time* library.

1065   "If you don't call Thurber": Elliott Reid to HK.

1066   "Here we go round": HT, postscript to ltr, JT to JG, 3/16/61.

1066   "I . . . feel that my life": Ltr, 2/13/61.

1066   "Suddenly, after all this": Ltr, HT to JG, undated, probably March 1961.

1066   ("The letter simply had"): Stoddard to HK.

1066   For the first time in my life: Ltr, JT to JG. 2/25/61.

1067   "Last night I went to sleep": Ltr, circa March 1961.

1067   Elliott does nothing: Ltr, 3/16/61.

1067   "You may remember [him]": Ltr, 3/23/61.

1067   "We are homesick": Ltr, 4/20/61.

1068   "Maybe you ought to do a modern Fowler": Ltr, 6/26/61.

1068   "Our generation is melting": Ltr, 7/3/61.

1068   "The headwaiter was keen": Hamilton/LBI, London, 1973.

1068   "Dear old Bill": Ltr, JT to WT, 5/10/61.

1069   "We actually had a quite": Ltr, JG to BB, March 1974.

1069   calling her stupid: JG to HK, 1962.

1069   "You have sugar in your": Ltr, JT to Hemingway (unsent), 1/11/61.

1070   "To Fred Allen": Ltr, JT to Portland Allen, 8/29/61.

1070   "Bateman Comes Home": *LYMA*.

1070   funnier without "only": Ltr, McDowell to JT, 2/9/61.

1070   "ball-bat impact": Ltr, JT to McDowell, 2/12/61.

1070   "founded by great men": Ltr, 8/26/61.

1071   "Helen called me": JG to HK.

1071   *New Yorker* staff veterans received unexpected calls: Packard, Whit-
        aker, Gill, Jonsson, Terry to HK.

1072   They think that I am unreasonable: Ltr, 4/26/61.

1072   Though Greenstein wrote him: Ltr, 5/3/61.

1072   "we avoided him as much": Ltr to HK, op. cit.

1072   "His old friends knew": NS to HK.

1073   "I'm glad you're back": Ltr, 7/8/61.

1073   "depressing though it might seem": *The Sixties*, Farrar, Straus &
        Giroux, 1993.

1073   "I'm trying to find my husband": Terry to HK.

1073   "I realize now Jim was jealous": Stoddard to HK.

1074   "Everyone in New York": *The Noel Coward Diaries*, op. cit.

1074   "Who is it?": Louis Sobol, NY *Journal-American*, 10/4/61.

1074   "We have to get rid of": Elliott Reid to HK.

1074   "I thought it was just some": Stritch to HK.

1075   "I just found out the other day": Henry Brandon, *As We Are*. Dou-
        bleday & Co., 1961.

1075   He had once described: Frances Glennon to HK.

1075   Helen says that nothing in the final: RM to HK, 1991.

1075   "I am with you": Ltr, 12/12/61.

1075   "I kept it very brief": Scheufler to AL.

1076   "The thing that impressed me": Smallsreed to HK.

1076   "When we heard the news": EH to HK.

1076   With Thurber gone there is: PDV, *Saturday Review*, 11/25/61.

1077   I don't seem to see: Ltr, circa March 1928.

Acknowledgments

Thousands of words have been written and spoken about Thurber—most of them by Thurber. But the far-ranging imagination that gained him renown as a world master of literary humor also makes many of his autobiographical references undependable as fact. Someone suggests that no one should try to write without a rock-solid sense of inadequacy, and Thurber came on the scene fully equipped. He chose to misrepresent his life at the start of his writing career because he couldn't take himself seriously, and, toward its end, because he could *only* take himself seriously. He would be tickled to know the difficulties that Thurber scholars have had in sorting his truth from invention. His best works are nearly always the product of both. A biographer can only try to get to know him through those who played, lived, worked, and corresponded with him, and then make the educated guess. Listed below are many of those people, who have my boundless thanks:

Columbus (1894–1918)

Elizabeth Acosta: the Falls Church, Va., housewife who discovered the house the Thurbers rented there in August 1902. Interview, Washington, D.C., 1963.

Samuel Baker: His Ohio State University master's thesis was the first effort to examine Thurber's days at O.S.U. Baker generously volunteered additional research on Thurber's Columbus days, refusing all but out-of-pocket compensation.

Carson Blair: classmate who worked with Thurber on O.S.U. publications. Interview, Detroit, 1962. Correspondence.

Dr. Virgil Damon: O.S.U. fraternity brother of Thurber's, and, later, the New York obstetrician who oversaw the birth of Rosemary, Thurber's daughter. Interview, Manhattan, 1962.

Earl and Clifford Fisher: Columbus cousins of Thurber. Their memories of the Thurbers' early days were ransacked on my behalf by **Alice Leighner,** native Ohioan, O.S.U. graduate, and working journalist, who, in 1969, tracked down other information about the young Thurber's environment.

John (Jack) Fullen: O.S.U. alumni secretary. Correspondence, 1962.

Donia McNulty Karpen: first wife of legendary newspaperman and *New Yorker* contributor John McNulty. Correspondence, 1962.

Newsweek's Sunday librarian, in 1962, allowed me access to the research generated by *Newsweek's* 1955 article on the *New Yorker* and its 1956 cover story on Thurber. Not certain that he should be thus helping a stranger, he requested an anonymity I continue to honor.

The Ohio State University Thurber Collection, Rare Books and Manuscripts: the mother lode of cradle-to-grave Thurber material. My visits there over the years were made fruitful by **Robert Tibbetts,** the former curator, and by his successor, **Geoffrey Smith. Elva Griffith's** help was indispensable. Much is owed to **Dr. Lewis Branscomb,** O.S.U. Professor Emeritus of Thurber Studies, for his contributions to the Thurber story through interviews with a number of the principals.

Richard Oulahan: *Time* reporter, who freely shared his and others' research notes from the 1951 cover story on Thurber, most of it never used in the article.

James Pollard: director of the O.S.U. Journalism Department and university historian. Interview, O.S.U., 1962.

Joel Sayre: writer; Thurber's lifelong friend. Interviews, Los Angeles, 1956; New York, 1957; Philadelphia, 1962.

The Thurber House: the Jefferson Avenue home of the Thurber family, 1913 to 1917. It was restored by private and institutional devotees in 1984 as a Thurber museum, bookshop, and site of a writer-in-residence program, and later expanded, with conference facilities for Thurber scholars. Executive director **Donn F. Vickers** and literary director **Michael J. Rosen** help keep the Thurber legend and spirit alive with public literary events. I thank the staff for its long and continuing support of my book's development.

Robert Thurber: interviews, Columbus, 1962 and 1965. Correspondence from 1962 to 1976.

William Thurber: interview, Columbus, 1962.

Ben Williamson: Columbus contemporary, fraternity brother, fellow code clerk of Thurber's. Interview, New York, 1962.

Columbus (1920–1925)

F. R. (Ted) Gardiner: Columbus businessman, whose nonstop friendship with Thurber began in the early 1920s. Interviews, Gardiner, his wife, **Julia,** and daughter **Patricia McGuckin,** Columbus, 1962; daughter **Julia Hadley,** telephone interview, 1994.

Ralph McCombs: high-school and college contemporary of Thurber's; collaborator on Scarlet Mask productions. Interview, Columbus, 1962.

Dorothy Miller: widow of O.S.U. instructor Herman Miller, who was Thurber's closest friend in Columbus. Interview, Block Island, 1965. Made Thurber's letters to the Millers available to me.

George Smallsreed: managing editor, the *Columbus Dispatch,* who began there with Thurber. Interview, Columbus, 1962. His correspondence with Thurber made available to me.

The *New Yorker* (1927–1935)

James M. Cain: former *New Yorker* managing editor. Correspondence, 1971.

Charles Cooke: Talk of the Town reporter through the 1930s. Interview, Washington, D.C., 1962. Correspondence.

Jane Grant: first wife of Harold Ross. Interview, Manhattan, 1962.

Emily Hahn: staff writer. Interviews, Yale University, 1972; *New Yorker,* 1991. Correspondence.

Geoffrey Hellman: staff writer. Interview, *New Yorker,* 1962.

Ralph Ingersoll: *New Yorker* managing editor, 1925–1930. Interview, New York Racquet Club, 1962. Correspondence.

Eugene Kinkead: editor and writer. Interview, *New Yorker,* 1962. Correspondence.

Lois Long: columnist for the magazine beginning in 1925. Interviews, *New Yorker,* 1952 and 1953; Algonquin Hotel, 1962 (in Rose Room session with Elliott Nugent and Helen Thurber).

St. Clair McKelway: *New Yorker* managing editor of nonfiction in mid-1930s. Interview, Century Association, New York, 1962.

Joseph Mitchell: veteran staff writer. Interviews, *New Yorker,* 1962, 1990, and 1994.

Frank Sullivan: *New Yorker* contributor. Interview, Saratoga Springs, N.Y., 1962.

Donald Wharton: former managing editor of the *New Yorker.* Interview, *Reader's Digest,* Chappaqua, N.Y., 1963.

Hobart Weekes: longtime editorial guru at the magazine. Interview, Coffee House, Manhattan, 1962.

R. E. M. Whitaker: veteran editor. Interviews, *New Yorker,* 1962.

E. B. White: interviews, *New Yorker,* 1949; Algonquin Hotel, 1962; North Brooklin, Maine, 1974. Correspondence.

Katharine Angell White: interviews, Algonquin Hotel, 1962; North Brooklin, Maine, 1974. Correspondence.

The *New Yorker* (1936–1961)

Roger Angell: senior *New Yorker* editor and contributor. Interview, *New Yorker*, 1962. Telephone interview, 1992.

Nathaniel Benchley: writer. Correspondence, 1962.

Sally Benson: *New Yorker* contributor. Interviews, *New Yorker* and Algonquin Hotel, 1949.

Peter De Vries: *New Yorker* staff contributor and cartoon editor. A dozen Thurber discussions on the premises and over luncheons, 1949 to 1954. Correspondence. And **Jan De Vries,** for her permission to reprint excerpts from her father's letters, and other Thurber-related writings.

James M. Geraghty: art editor. Interview, Cortile bar, Manhattan, 1962.

Brendan Gill: staff writer and critic. Interview, Century Association, New York, 1987. Correspondence.

E. J. Kahn, Jr.: staff writer. Interview, Truro, Mass., 1962.

A. J. Liebling: staff writer. Interview, *New Yorker*, 1962. Correspondence.

Jean (Mrs. Gustave) Lobrano: widow of *New Yorker* managing editor of fiction. Interview, Chappaqua, N.Y., 1971.

William Maxwell: *New Yorker* fiction editor. Interview, Yorktown Heights, N.Y., 1962. Telephone interview, 1994.

Faith McNulty (Martin) was helpful with the John McNulty story of later years.

John O'Hara: correspondence, 1962.

Eleanor Gould Packard: veteran *New Yorker* copyeditor. Interview, *New Yorker*, 1992.

Frederick (Freddie) A. Packard: former head of checking department. Interview, *New Yorker*, 1962.

William Shawn: former *New Yorker* editor. Interview, *New Yorker*, 1962.

Daise E. Terry: former office manager. Interview, *New Yorker*, 1962.

Stanley Walker: former *New Yorker* managing editor. Correspondence, 1962.

Dame Rebecca West: correspondence, 1971.

Linda H. Davis: biographer of Katharine White (*Onward and Upward*), a friend who unstintingly shared her research and maintained a generous moral support of this undertaking.

Other helpful staff members acquainted with the magazine's operations during the Thurber years: **Fred Keefe, Tom Gorman, Ebba Jonsson, Mary D. Rudd Kierstead, Barbara Lawrence,** and **Helen Stark.**

New York (1927–1961)

Art Buchwald: correspondence, 1992.

Milton Caniff: correspondence, 1971.

Louise (Mrs. Richard) Connell: interview, Manhattan, 1962.

Marc Connelly: interview, Manhattan, 1962.

Alistair Cooke: interview, Manhattan, 1962.

Alfred (Fritz) Dashiell, editor of the *Reader's Digest*, and wife, **Sara.** Interview, Croton-on-Hudson, N.Y., 1962.

Peggy (Mrs. Clarence) Day: interview, Truro, Mass., 1980.

Dr. Sol Engel: Thurber dentist. Interview, Manhattan, 1962.

Morris Ernst: attorney for the *New Yorker* and the Thurbers. Interviews, Manhattan, 1956 and 1962.

Stanley P. Friedman: writer. Found Thurber's "naughty" drawings at Chasen's restaurant in Hollywood. Interviews, Manhattan, Yorktown Heights, N.Y., 1964. Correspondence.

Elinor (Mrs. Wolcott) Gibbs: interview, Manhattan, 1962.

Sylvia Godwin: friend of Thurber and Althea. Interview, Manhattan, 1962.

John (Jap) Gude: Thurber's agent and close friend. Interviews, Manhattan, 1962 and 1963. And his daughter, **Elizabeth,** for reprint permissions and photographs.

Margaret Case Harriman: author of *The Vicious Circle*. Interview, Manhattan, 1962. Correspondence.

Ann Honeycutt: interviews, Manhattan, 1962, 1963, 1972, 1987, 1988, and 1989.

Dale Kramer: author of *Ross and The New Yorker*. Interviews, Manhattan, 1949 and 1950. Made available to me his correspondence associated with his book.

Phyllis Levy, editor, Simon & Schuster, interview, Manhattan, 1962.

Richard Maney: Broadway theatrical publicist. Interview, his Times Square office, 1962.

Val and **Bianca Fanfoni:** managers of Maria's restaurant. Interview, Manhattan, 1962.

Tony Randall: actor, who donated to the cause a 1958 tape recording of his backstage interview of Thurber.

Nora Sayre: writer, who knew Thurber from her childhood. Interviews, Manhattan, 1962, 1992, and 1994. Assisted with photographs, Thurber drawings. Correspondence.

Peter Schwed: editor, Simon & Schuster. Interview, Manhattan, 1956.
Emil Stahl: headwaiter, Tim Costello's. Interview, Costello's, 1962.
Peter Ustinov: Thurber acquaintance. Interview, Hotel Carlyle, Manhattan, 1963.
Alec Waugh: British writer. Correspondence, 1964.

A Thurber Carnival Theater Production

Haila Stoddard: Broadway producer. Interviews, Weston, Conn., 1991.
Patricia Stone: Thurber secretary. Interview, Manhattan, 1963.
Elliott Reid: actor. Interview, Manhattan, 1962. Correspondence.

Bermuda

Jane and Ronald Williams and daughter **Dinah Jane:** Interviews, Bermuda, 1972 and 1973. Thurber letters made available to the author.

Cornwall, Connecticut, Area

Lewis Gannett and **Mark Van Doren:** interviews, Cornwall, 1962.
Armin Landeck and **Kenneth MacLean:** correspondence, 1962.
Marc Simont: illustrator of two Thurber fairy tales. Telephone interviews, 1992 and 1994; contributed Thurber drawings and research assistance.

General

Helen Thurber, who provided me with pages of names to get in touch with, along with descriptions of their relationship to Thurber. She passed on copies of articles on Thurber, and answered a thousand questions in her acerbic but witty way. Interviewed in Cornwall, 1962; a half-dozen times at the Algonquin, 1962 and 1963; and shared with the author an all-night pub crawl, of the kind she and Thurber used to make. Correspondence, from 1962 to 1980.

Rosemary Thurber, who dutifully read a 1,915-page manuscript. Though she cringed at some of what she read about her father, she asked for no deletions. "Do what you need to do to make it truthful," she writes. "I don't need to like it." All Thurber material reproduced herein is with her gracious permission. Nothing she was able to supply for the book was withheld from me, and I remain immensely indebted to her incomparable kindnesses.

Useful correspondence was received from **Garrison Keillor,** radio personality and *New Yorker* contributor; **Charles McDowell,** newspaper columnist and TV personality; **Leslie Midgley,** one of the stalwart match game players at Bleeck's; novelist and essayist **Wilfrid Sheed;** novelist and *New Yorker* contributor **Jean Stafford; Frances Warfield,** a 1930s *New Yorker* contributor; and **Tom Wolfe,** who created a storm with an attack on the magazine in 1965.

Leo Dolenski, the affable rare manuscript librarian, made my two trips to the Bryn Mawr College Library efficient and pleasant ones.

Sally Proctor Luplow went to special efforts to provide me with the story —and photograph—of her mother, Minnette Fritts (Proctor) Ewart.

The Macdowell Colony is acknowledged gratefully for a memorable and useful time there in 1969.

My thanks to **Ramsey Marvin,** of the **Martha Kinney Cooper Ohioana Library Association,** and to the **Ohio Historical Society** for assistance rendered.

I am obliged to Cornell University's Rare and Manuscript Collection at the Carl A. Kroch Library, and the assistance of **George H. Healey** in 1970, and, in 1987, of **Donald Eddy** and **Lucy Burgess. James Tyler** was instrumental in freeing up, for the first time, Thurber's letters to Ann Honeycutt, as was **Jon A. Lindseth,** who had donated them to the library. Approval of the use of selected items from the E. B. White files was kindly granted by **Joel White.**

I offer my warm appreciation to **the Beinecke Library** at Yale University, which holds Thurber's typescripts and research from *The Years with Ross.*

And to the **New York Public Library,** which so frequently served as a home away from home through the years of this work.

William Gaddis, novelist, and stimulating friend, sacrificed his own writing time to read the Columbus section of my early manuscript.

Jay Hoster, former president of the Columbus Historical Society, volunteered to proofread my entire typescript for any inaccurate facts about his beloved Columbus, as well as for suspected grammatical impurities. He is aware of my gratitude.

Professor Scott Elledge of Cornell University, biographer of E. B. White, kindly answered a number of my questions regarding White's political positions in the 1930s.

None of the help solicited or offered in this effort frees me in any way from responsibility for what is contained herein.

Over the years I have benefited from generous people who have offered counsel, encouragement, and research—in one or two instances, typing help —for all of which I remain most thankful. They include **Joan Cash, Frances Craighead, William Ewald, William** and **E. Devin Harrison, Florence**

Kaupe, **Doris G. Kinney, Patricia Schartle Myrers, Carolyn Reil, Joanne Smyth,** and **Susan Sereni.**

Sandra Blanton, my literary agent, has patiently followed the project's progress over the past half-dozen years with persistent solicitude, assistance, and caring. No agent has had a greater claim on a property to be marketed. Or a more knowledgeable associate in that effort than **Peter Lampack.**

Patricia Strachan's enthusiasm for this project's proposal in 1992 was indispensable to its completion. Seasoned by distinguished years in book publishing, and as a *New Yorker* editor, her qualities of judgment and taste have proved to be unsurpassed, and her encouragement to this author, frequently needed, suggests a model of what a publishing relationship should be.

William Strachan, editor-in-chief and associate publisher of Henry Holt and Company, has provided the personal, top-level supervision of this book that authors usually experience only in Walter Mitty fantasies. Further good luck turned up in the person of **Sara Lippincott,** another veteran *New Yorker* editor, who did much to shepherd my manuscript to production.

Finally, a salute to the late **Ed Kuhn,** classmate, friend, and former editor-in-chief of the trade book division of McGraw-Hill, who persuaded me to get into all this thirty-four years ago.

Carnival, in *PM*, February 4, 1945; *Letters of E. B. White*, Harper & Row, edited by Dorothy L. Guth; letters in *E. B. White: A Biography*, by Scott Elledge, W. W. Norton; *Is Sex Necessary?*, 1957 edition, Harper & Row, from "Introduction" and "A Note on the Drawings in This Book"; unpublished letters and notes of Katharine S. White.

Reprinted by permission of *The New Yorker*: Excerpts from: book review of *Ross and The New Yorker*, 11/17/51; James Thurber obituary, November 11, 1961; memo by Wolcott Gibbs to James Thurber (undated), 1949; *The New Yorker* prospectus, 2/25/25; letters of Harold Ross to Peter De Vries, 6/8/44; to Helen Thurber, 11/22/44; to James Thurber, 7/10/44, 12/13/44, 1/29/45, 11/19/45, 7/6/45, 3/1/45, 3/14/45, 3/19/45, 9/10/47, (undated) 1947, 8/25/48, 8/26/48, 9/2/48, 10/21/48, 11/19/29, 11/24/48, 11/29/48, 12/7/48, 12/8/48, 12/10/48, 11/19/48, 12/21/48. © The New Yorker Magazine. All Rights Reserved.

Index